CITYGUIDE
NEW YORK

2ND EDITION

FODOR'S TRAVEL PUBLICATIONS

NEW YORK • TORONTO • LONDON • SYDNEY • AUCKLAND

WWW.FODORS.COM

A B C D

ELIZABETH

BAYONNE

St. George Station/
Ferry Terminal

2 WESTCHESTER COUNT

1

Newark
Bay

Bayonne
Bridge

Kill Van Kull
Richmond Ter.
Castleton Ave.
Clove Rd.
Prospect Ave.
Bay St.
Tompkins Ave.
Van Duzer St.
Victory Blvd.
Sand La.
Verrazano
Narrows
Bridge

Silver
Lake
Park

CLOVE LAKES
PARK

Goethals
Bridge

Forest Ave.

Richmond Ter.

Van Cortlandt
Park

Woodlawn
Cemetery

E. 233rd St.

Mosholu Pkwy.

White Plains Rd.

Gun Hill Rd.

9A

5

87

9

9A

2

South Ave.

Victory Blvd.

Bradley Ave.

Brielle Ave.

Todt Hill Rd.

Major Rd.

Staten Island Expwy.

278

Sea View Ave.

Richmond Rd.

Railway Ave.

Midland Ave.

Fr. Capodanno Blvd.

New Dorp La.

Hylan Blvd.

LATOURETTE
PARK

Richmond Hill Rd.

Richmond Rd.

Guyon Ave.

Emmet Ave.

Inwood
Hill
Park

St. Nicholas Ave.

Geo.
Wash.
Br.

Jerome Ave.

Grand Concourse

Major Deegan Expwy.

E. Fordham
Rd.

Cross Bronx

THE BRO

CROTONA
PARK

BRONX
PARK

Boston Rd.

9

87

Eastche

9A

9

6

87

95

Jerome Ave.

Grand Concourse & Blvd.

Webster Ave.

Third Ave.

Westchester Expwy.

895

STATEN ISLAND

Huguenot Ave.

Woodrow Rd.

Amboy Rd.

Hylan Blvd.

440

GREAT KILLS PARK
(GATEWAY NATIONAL
RECREATION AREA)

Hudson River

Henry Hudson Pkwy.

W. 155th St.

W. 145th St.

Broadway

87

E. 138th St.

Bruckner Blvd.

3

Arthur Kill

Arthur Kill Rd.

440

Outerbridge
Crossing

Page Ave.

Amboy Rd.

Hylan Blvd.

ATLANTIC OCEAN

7

Riverside Dr.

West End Ave.

Amsterdam Ave.

Columbus Ave.

Central Park W.

Fifth Ave.

E. 125th St.

E. 116th St.

E. 110th St.

E. 96th St.

E. 86th St.

E. 79th St.

Triborough
Bridge

8

278

Di

F.D.R. Dr.

4

9A

9

W. 72nd St.

W. 57th St.

W. 42nd St.

W. 34th St.

W. 23rd St.

E. 72nd St.

Fifth Ave.

Park Ave.

Lexington Ave.

Third Ave.

Second Ave.

First Ave.

Ave. of the Americas

Seventh Ave.

Eighth Ave.

Ninth Ave.

Tenth Ave.

E. 59th St.

E. 42nd St.

E. 34th St.

E. 23rd St.

E. 14th St.

MANHATTAN

CENTRAL
PARK

Queensboro
Bridge

Queens
Midtown
Tunnel

East River

36th

Th

McGuinness

5

NUTLEY

LYNDHURST

BERGEN

SECAUCUS

21 17

NEW JERSEY

BELLEVILLE

95

9

495

Lincoln
Tunnel

HOBOKEN

UNION
CITY

9

1

Hudson River

W. 14th St.

10

11

E. Houston St.

Delancey St.

Canal St.

E. 14th St.

Williamsburg
Bridge

Gra

Flush

M

HUDSON

KEARNY

JERSEY CITY

Holland
Tunnel

Broadway

Bowery

Manhattan Br.

12

278

Court St.

Henry St.

Columbia St.

Hoyt St.

Gowanus Expwy.

6

280

NEWARK

9

1

95

4 CITY PARK

Ellis Island

BATTERY
PARK

Statue of Liberty
(Liberty Island)

GOVERNORS
ISLAND

Brooklyn-Battery
Tunnel

Atla

4th Ave.

Gowanus Expwy.

278

ESSEX

Upper
New York Bay

7

78

Newark
International
Airport

BAYONNE

St. George Station/
Ferry Terminal

Prospect Ave.

Bay St.

Verrazano
Narrows
Bridge

UNION

ELIZABETH

1
9

95

Newark
Bay

440

Bayonne
Bridge

Kill Van Kull
Richmond Ter.

Castleton Ave.

Clove Rd.

Victory Blvd.

Van Duzer St.

Tompkins Ave.

SILVER
LAKE
PARK

CLOVE LAKES
PARK

Staten Island Expwy

278

Sand
La.

8

Goethals
Bridge

Forest Ave.

Richmond Ter.

Victory Blvd.

440

Todt Hill Rd.

Major Rd.

STREETFINDER

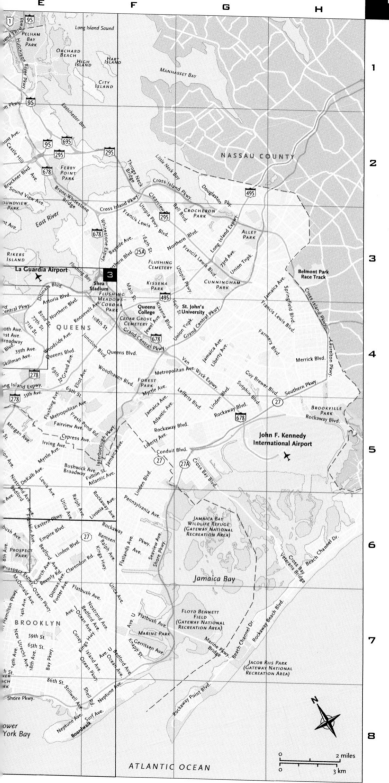

Long Island Sound

PELHAM
BAY
PARK

ORCHARD
BEACH

HIGH
ISLAND

HART
ISLAND

CITY
ISLAND

MANHASSET BAY

NASSAU COUNTY

FERRY
POINT
PARK

Throgs Neck Bridge

Bronx-Whitestone Bridge

East River

Whitestone Expwy.

Cross Island Pkwy.

Little Neck Bay

Cross Island Pkwy.

Douglaston Pkwy.

Clearview Expwy.

Bell Blvd.

CROCHERON
PARK

Francis Lewis Blvd.

164th St.

Northern Blvd.

Long Island Expwy.

73rd Ave.

ALLEY
PARK

RIKERS
ISLAND

La Guardia Airport

3

Shea
Stadium

FLUSHING
MEADOWS-
CORONA
PARK

Bayside Ave.

Northern Blvd.

FLUSHING
CEMETERY

KISSENA
PARK

Union Tpk.

CUNNINGHAM
PARK

Utopia Pkwy.

Jamaica Ave.

Springfield Blvd.

Cross Island Pkwy.

BELMONT PARK
RACE TRACK

QUEENS

Astoria Blvd.

Ditmars Blvd.

77th St.

82nd St.

Northern Blvd.

Roosevelt Ave.

108th St.

Main St.

Kissena Blvd.

Queens
College

St. John's
University

Grand Central Pkwy.

Farmers Blvd.

Francis Lewis Blvd.

Francis Lewis Blvd.

Merrick Blvd.

Laurelton Pkwy.

Woodside Ave.

Queens Blvd.

Junction Blvd.

Queens Blvd.

CEDAR GROVE
CEMETERY

Union Tpk.

Grand Central Pkwy.

Jamaica Ave.

Liberty Ave.

Guy Brewer Blvd.

39th Ave.

Skillman Ave.

69th St.

Grand Ave.

Eliot Ave.

Woodhaven Blvd.

Metropolitan Ave.

Wyck Expwy.

Van

Liberty Ave.

Southern Pkwy.

BROOKVILLE
PARK

Rockaway Blvd.

Flushing Ave.

Metropolitan Ave.

Fresh Pond Rd.

Fairview Ave.

Cypress Ave.

FOREST
PARK

Myrtle Ave.

Jamaica Ave.

Lefferts Blvd.

Linden Blvd.

Sutphin Blvd.

Rockaway Blvd.

Morgan Ave.

Myrtle Ave.

Bushwick
Broadway

Fulton St.

Atlantic Ave.

Atlantic Ave.

Rockaway Blvd.

Conduit Blvd.

John F. Kennedy
International Airport

Jackie Robinson Pkwy.

Jamaica Ave.

Irving Ave.

BROOKLYN

Nostrand DeKalb Ave.

Lewis Ave.

Ralph Ave.

Utica Ave.

Rockaway Ave.

Livonia Ave.

Linden Blvd.

Pennsylvania Ave.

Cross Bay Blvd.

JAMAICA BAY
WILDLIFE REFUGE
(GATEWAY NATIONAL
RECREATION AREA)

Cross Bay Veterans Bridge

Beach Channel Dr.

Bedford Ave.

Eastern Pkwy.

Empire Blvd.

Linden Blvd.

Kings Hwy.

Remsen
Ave.

Flatlands Ave.

Seaview Ave.

Rockaway

Pkwy.

Shore Pkwy.

Jamaica Bay

Rockaway Beach Blvd.

PROSPECT
PARK

Prospect Expwy.

Church Ave.

Beverly Rd.

Ditmas Ave.

Clarendon Rd.

Foster Ave.

Flatbush Ave.

Nostrand Ave.

Bedford Ave.

Ocean Ave.

Utica Ave.

Flatbush Ave.

Ave. U

MARINE
PARK

FLOYD BENNETT
FIELD
(GATEWAY NATIONAL
RECREATION AREA)

Beach Channel Dr.

Rockaway Beach Blvd.

Ocean Pkwy.

McDonald Ave.

Hamilton Pkwy.

59th St.

65th St.

Bay Pkwy.

Kings Hwy.

Bedford Ave.

Ocean Ave.

Coney Island Ave.

Gerritsen Ave.

Marine Pkwy.
Bridge

JACOB RIIS PARK
(GATEWAY NATIONAL
RECREATION AREA)

New Utrecht Ave.

86th St.

Stillwell Ave.

Shell Rd.

Neptune Ave.

Rockaway Point Blvd.

Shore Pkwy.

Neptune Ave.

Surf Ave.

Boardwalk

N

Lower
York Bay

ATLANTIC OCEAN

0   2 miles
0   3 km

NEW YORK OVERVIEW

A   **B**   **C**   **D**

W E S T C H E S T E R   C O U N

MOUNT
VERNON

McLean Ave.

Midland Ave.

Kimball Avenue

Hillview
Reservoir

Hillview Ave.

Wakefield Ave.

E. 242nd St.

E. 241st St.

E. 240th St.

Sandford Blvd.

YONKERS

McLean Ave.

E. 239th St.

E. 238th St.

E. 237th St.

E. 236th St.

Nereid Ave.

Pitman Ave.

Gunther Ave.

Bussing Ave.

Edenwald Ave.

Strang Ave.

E. 233rd St.

Broadway

87

WOODLAWN

E. 233rd St.

E. 233rd St.

SETON
FALLS
PARK

Baychester Ave.

9
9A

V A N   C O R T L A N D T
P A R K

Mosholu Pkwy.

WOODLAWN
CEMETERY

Jerome Ave.

Webster Ave.

White Plains Rd.

Bronx River

Bronx Blvd.

Barnes Ave.

Bronxwood Ave.

Paulding Ave.

Laconia Ave.

E. 230th St

E. 222n

H

Riverdale Ave.

Van Cortlandt
Golf
Course

E. 219th St.

E. 216th St.

Hicks St.

Kingsland

Eastchester Ro

Broadway

Van
Cortlandt
Lake

Bainbridge Ave.

Mosholu
Golf
Course

E. Gun Hill Rd.

WILLIAMSBRIDGE

E. Gun Hil

9A

MOSHOLU

Manhattan
College

Magenta St.

White Plains Rd.

Burke Ave.

Boston Road

Adee Ave.

Arnow Ave.

Allerton Ave.

Van Cortlandt Park S.

NORWOOD

Mace Ave.

Sedgwick Ave.

Mosholu Pkwy.

Waring A

Astor

5

RIVERDALE

9

87

Riverdale Ave.

Jerome
Park
Reservoir

Bailey Ave.

Goulden Ave.

W. 205th
St.

Grand Concourse & Boulevard

Bainbridge Ave.

Webster Ave.

Bronxwood Ave.

Wallace Ave.

Bronx Park E.

Bronx River Pkwy.

Bronx and Pelham Pkw.

Lydig Ave.

Neill

W. 235th St.

W. 232nd St.

KINGSBRIDGE

W. 230th St.

Broadway

Reservoir Ave.

NEW YORK
BOTANICAL
GARDEN

Lydig Ave.

Brady Ave.

Bronxdale Ave.

Rh

White Park A

Henry Hudson
Bridge

W. Kingsbridge Rd.

Major Deegan Expwy.

Martin Luther King Jr. Blvd. (University)

Jerome Ave.

Grand Ave.

Fordham
University

E. Fordham Rd.

FORDHAM

BRONX
PARK

1

INTERNATIONAL
WILDLIFE
CONSERVATION
PARK
(BRONX ZOO)

Morris Park Ave.

Van Nest

WE

INWOOD

INWOOD
HILL
PARK

Tenth Ave.

Morris Ave.

Valentine Ave.

Webster Ave.

Third Ave.

Southern Blvd.

Bronx Pk. S.

E. 179th St.

THE   BRON

FORT
TRYON
PARK

9A

9

Dyckman St.

Nagle Ave.

St. Nicholas Ave.

Broadway

Bronx
Community
College

TREMONT

E. Tremont Ave.

1

EAST TREMONT

HIGH
BRIDGE
PARK

W. Tremont Ave.

87

W. 176th St.

Crotona Pk. N.

E. 174th St.

95

CROTONA
PARK

Crotona Pk. E.

Southern Blvd.

Vyse Ave.

Sheridan Expwy.

895

Bronx River P

6

WASHINGTON
HEIGHTS

1

95

CLAREMONT
PARK

Claremont Pkwy.

Jerome Ave.

Grand Concourse & Boulevard

Walton Ave.

Morris Ave.

Webster Ave.

Teller Ave.

Third Ave.

Boston Road

Jennings St.

Freeman St.

Home St.

Watson Ave.

George
Washington
Bridge

9

95

1

HIGH
BRIDGE

Major Deegan Expwy.

High
Bridge

Sheridan Ave.

166th St.

E. 170th St.

E. 169th St.

E. 166th St.

E. 165th St.

E. 163rd St.

E. 161st St.

Tiffany St.

Kelly St.

E. 163rd St.

Bruckner Blvd.

Lafayette Ave.

Spofford Ave.

Oak Poin

RIVERSIDE
PARK

Fort Washington Ave.

St. Nicholas Ave.

Riverside Ave.

Henry Hudson Dr.

Walton Ave.

JOHN
MULLALY
PARK

Grand Concourse & Boulevard

MORRISANIA

Park Ave.

Westchester Ave.

Prospect Ave.

Kelly St.

Southern Blvd.

Garrison Ave.

Randall Ave.

278

W. 155th St.

Yankee
Stadium

E. 161st St.

E. 156th St.

E. 156th St.

MELROSE

Hudson River

W. 145th St.

Amsterdam Ave.

Broadway

9A

Frederick Douglass Blvd.

Adam Clayton Powell Jr. Blvd.

Malcolm X Blvd.
(Lenox Ave.)

Harlem River Dr.

Harlem River

87

E. 153rd St.

E. 149th St.

E. 149th St.

Third Ave.

Fifth Ave.

E. 143rd St.

MOTT HAVEN

E. 138th St.

Bruckner Blvd.

ST. MARY'S
PARK

Bruckner Expwy.

87

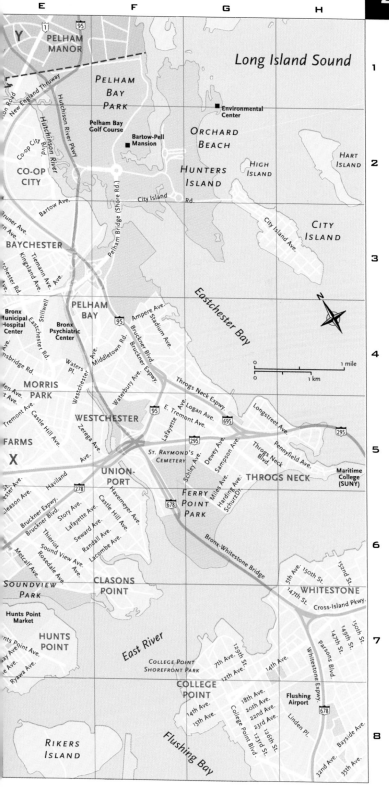

E F G H

1

PELHAM
MANOR

Long Island Sound

New England Throughway

PELHAM
BAY
PARK

Pelham Bay
Golf Course

Environmental
Center

2

Hutchinson River Pkwy

Co-op City

Hutchinson River

Bartow-Pell
Mansion

ORCHARD
BEACH

HART
ISLAND

CO-OP
CITY

Bartow Ave.

HUNTERS
ISLAND

HIGH
ISLAND

Bruner Ave.

BAYCHESTER

Tiemann Ave.

Kingsland Ave.

City Island Rd.

Pelham Bridge (Shore Rd.)

CITY
ISLAND

3

Eastchester

City Island Ave.

Bay

Eastchester Rd.

Williamsbridge Rd.

Bronx
Municipal
Hospital
Center

PELHAM
BAY

Ampere Ave.

Stadium Ave.

N

Bronx
Psychiatric
Center

Middletown Rd.

Bruckner Blvd.

Bruckner Expwy.

4

Waters
Pl.

Westchester Ave.

Waterbury Ave.

Throgs Neck Expwy.

Longstreet Ave.

0   1 mile

0   1 km

MORRIS
PARK

Tremont Ave.

Castle Hill Ave.

WESTCHESTER

Zerega Ave.

E. Tremont Ave.

Logan Ave.

Lafayette Ave.

FARMS

X

Gleason Ave.

Haviland

UNION-
PORT

St. Raymond's
Cemetery

Schley Ave.

Dewey Ave.

Sampson Ave.

Pennyfield Ave.

THROGS NECK

Throgs Neck Blvd.

Maritime
College
(SUNY)

5

Bruckner Expwy.

Havemeyer Ave.

Bruckner Blvd.

Castle Hill Ave.

Story Ave.

Lafayette Ave.

Seward Ave.

Randall Ave.

Lacombe Ave.

Miles Ave.

Harding Ave.

Schurz Ave.

FERRY
POINT
PARK

Bronx-Whitestone Bridge

6

Metcalf Ave.

Thieriot Ave.

Sound View Ave.

Rosedale Ave.

CLASONS
POINT

5th Ave.

150th St.

152nd St.

147th St.

WHITESTONE

SOUNDVIEW
PARK

149th St.

150th St.

147th St.

Cross-Island Pkwy.

Parsons Blvd.

7

Hunts Point
Market

HUNTS
POINT

East River

7th Ave.

129th St.

14th Ave.

Whitestone Expwy.

Bay Avenue Ave.

Ryawa Ave.

College Point
Shorefront Park

12th Ave.

COLLEGE
POINT

18th Ave.

20th Ave.

22nd Ave.

23rd Ave.

College Point Blvd.

126th St.

123rd St.

Flushing
Airport

Linden Pl.

32nd Ave.

Bayside Ave.

35th Ave.

8

RIKERS
ISLAND

Flushing Bay

14th Ave.

15th Ave.

THE BRONX AND NORTHERN MANHATTAN

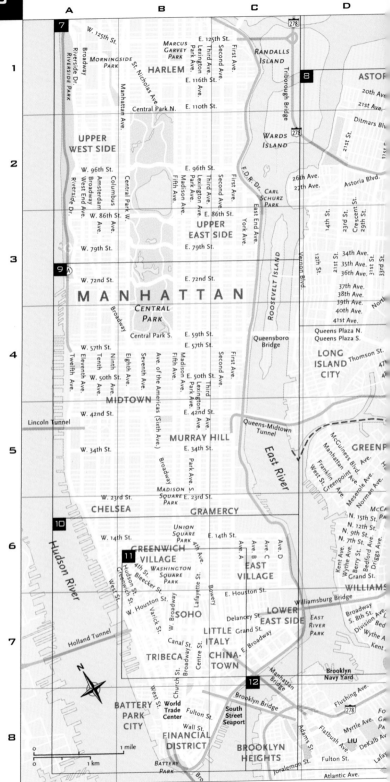

3

E F G H

La Guardia Airport

Flushing Bay

FLUSHING

1

Ditmars Blvd.
Curtis St.
Gilmore St.
23rd Ave.
100th St.
98th St.
94th St.
Astoria Blvd.

19th Ave.

Shea Stadium

FLUSHING MEADOWS–CORONA PARK

STEINWAY

Steinway St.
Grand Central Pkwy.

Grand Central Pkwy.

23rd Ave.
30th Ave.
31st Ave.
32nd Ave.
82nd St.
77th St.
71st St.

Northern Blvd.

104th St.
98th St.
Roosevelt Ave.
114th St.
111th St.

111th St.
108th St.

2

ST. MICHAEL'S CEMETERY

25th Ave.

28th Ave.
30th Ave.

31st Ave.

Broadway

CORONA

99th St.

Long Island Expwy.

QUEENS

JACKSON HEIGHTS

Elmhurst Hospital

34th Ave.
39th Ave.
37th Ave.

Elmhurst Ave.

Corona Ave.
51st Ave.
54th Ave.
56th Ave.
Junction Blvd.

Hobart St.

37th Ave.
39th Ave.
48th St.
58th St.
61st St.
64th St.

Broadway

Woodside Ave.
45th Ave.

3

Steinway St.

43rd St.
48th St.

Broadway
Queens Blvd.

WOODSIDE

Queens Blvd.

VanHorn St.

495

Queens Blvd.
Booth St.

Alderton St.

Skillman Ave.

43rd Ave.

Queens Blvd.

Greenpoint Ave.
48th St.
50th Ave.

Long Island Expwy.

51st Ave.
52nd Ave.
72nd St.
66th St.
69th St.

Grand Ave.

Caldwell Ave.
Eliot Ave.
Dry Harbor Rd.
84th St.

Woodhaven Blvd.
64th Rd.

ST. JOHN'S CEMETERY

4

495

278

MT. ZION CEMETERY

58th St.

NEW CALVARY CEMETERY

71st St.

69th St.
69th Ln.
69th St.

JUNIPER VALLEY PARK

Penelope Ave.
Furmanville Ave.

80th St.

CALVARY CEMETERY

54th Ave.

55th Ave.

Laurel Hill Blvd.

278

Maurice Ave.

Maspeth Ave.
56th Dr.

MT. OLIVET CEMETERY

Metropolitan Ave.
78th St.

Flushing Ave.

Grand Ave.

MASPETH

56th Rd.

LUTHERAN CEMETERY

RIDGEWOOD

70th Ave.
Central Ave.

MT. LEBANON CEMETERY

5

NT

Nassau St.
Lombardy St.
Porter Ave.
Maspeth Ave.

Varick Ave.

Johnson Ave.

Grand Ave.

Metropolitan Ave.
Forest Ave.
Grandview Ave.
Fresh Pond Rd.

GLENDALE

CYPRESS HILLS CEMETERY

Brooklyn-Queens Expwy.
Vandervoort Ave.
Morgan Ave.
Kingsland Ave.

LINDEN HILL CEMETERY
Fairview Ave.

Woodward Ave.
Onderdonk Ave.
Seneca Ave.
Cypress Ave.

Cypress Hills St.

278

Humboldt St.
Graham Ave.
Manhattan Ave.

Jackson Ave.
Metropolitan
Ainslie St.
Grand St.
Leonard St.
Lorimer St.
Union Ave.

Bushwick Ave.

St. Nicholas Ave.
Wycoff Ave.

Irving Ave.

Stephen St.
Decatur St.

Cypress Ave.

Interborough Pkwy.

HIGHLAND PARK

6

URG

Broadway
Harrison Ave.
Marcy Ave.
Ave.
Ave.

Flushing Ave.
Park Ave.
Marcus Garvey Ave.
Myrtle Ave.
Willoughby

Starr St.
Hart St.
Stockholm St.
Harman St.

Menahan St.
Myrtle Ave.
Linden St.

Knickerbocker Ave.
Wilson Ave.
Central Ave.
Evergreen Ave.
Bushwick Ave.
Broadway

Cooper St.

CEMETERY OF THE EVERGREENS

Highland Blvd.
Jamaica Ave.

Nostrand Ave.
Bedford Ave.

DeKalb Ave.
Lewis Ave.
Stuyvesant Ave.
Patchen Ave.
Malcolm X Blvd.

Lexington Ave.
Jefferson Ave.
Throop Ave.
Halsey St.

Saratoga Ave.
Howard Ave.
Ralph Ave.

Fulton St.
Atlantic Ave.

Pennsylvania Ave.
Georgia Ave.
Williams Ave.
Snediker Ave.

7

Pratt Institute

Franklin Ave.
Classon Ave.
Grand Ave.

Lafayette Ave.
Tompkins Ave.
Marcy Ave.

Fulton St.
Atlantic Ave.
Bergen St.
Prospect Pl.
Sterling Pl.

Bainbridge St.
Kingston Ave.
Albany Ave.
Troy Ave.
Schenectady Ave.
Utica Ave.
Rochester Ave.
Buffalo Ave.
Ralph Ave.

Howard Ave.
Sutter
Blake
Livonia Ave.

East New York Ave. Eastern Pkwy.
Rockaway Pkwy.
Saratoga Ave.
Hopkinson Ave.
Pitkin Ave.

Powell St.
Mother Gaston Blvd.
Rockaway Ave.
Riverdale Ave.
Newport St.
Lott Ave.
Hegeman Ave.

Dumont Ave.

8

Washington Ave.
Vanderbilt Ave.
Carlton Ave.

MANHATTAN AND WESTERN QUEENS

	A	B	C	D

1

LIBERTY PARK

Ellis Island

GOVERNORS ISLAND

Brooklyn-Battery Tunnel

12

Columbus St.
Henry St.
Clinton St.
Court St.
Smith St.
Hoyt St.
Bond St.
Bergen St.

President St.

CARROLL GARDENS

Conover St.
Van Brunt St.
Richards St.
Columbus St.

Gowanus Expwy.

2nd Ave.
3rd Ave.
4th Ave.

Statue of Liberty (Liberty Island)

RED HOOK

278

Ocean Ave

2

20

23rd

3

Upper New York Bay

Gowanus Expwy.

4th Ave.

36th

278

SUNSET PARK

1st Ave.
2nd Ave.
3rd Ave.
5th Ave.
6th Ave.
7th Ave.

4

Bay Ridge Ave.
72nd St.
3rd Ave.
4th Ave.
5th Ave.
6th Ave.

Gowanus Expy.

Bay Ridge Pkwy.
78th St.

BAY RIDGE

83rd St.
Ridge Blvd.
86th St.
89th St.

278

Leif Ericson Dr. (Shore Pkwy.)
Narrows Ave.
Colonial Rd.

92nd St.
Marine Ave.
Shore Rd.
4th Ave.

H

5

St. George Station/ Ferry Terminal

Richmond Ter.

NEW BRIGHTON

Bay St.

St. Paul's Ave.

STATEN ISLAND BOTANICAL GARDEN

Prospect

Jersey St.

Snug Harbor Cultural Center

Verrazano-Narrows Bridge

278

6

Castleton Ave.

STAPLETON

Forest Ave.

SILVER LAKE PARK

Howard Ave.

Victory Blvd.

Van Duzer St.

CLIFTON

Vanderbilt Ave.
Tompkins Ave.
Bay St.

ROSEBANK

Hylan Blvd.
Maryland Ave.
Fingerboard Rd.

Fort Wadsworth Naval Station

Kissell Ave.
Bard St.
Pelton Ave.

Bement Ave.
Bard St.

Clove Rd.

7

CLOVE LAKES PARK

SUNNYSIDE

Staten Island Expwy.

EMERSON HILL

Clove Rd.

Lily Pond Ave.

SOUTH BEACH

Sand La.
Linwood Ave.

Low

Slosson Ave.
Victory Blvd.
Ocean Ter.

STATEN

Fingerboard Rd.

Jerome Ave.
Lamport Blvd.

Father Capodanno Blvd.

8

278

Manor Rd.

Todt Hill Rd.
Ocean Ter.

ISLAND

St. Francis Seminary

Old Town Rd.

Richmond Rd.
Burgher Ave.
Delaware Ave.
Cromwell Ave.

Hylan Blvd.
Laconia Ave.
Quintard St.
Mason Ave.

South Beach Psychiatric Center

STREETFINDER

E   F   G   H

Prospect Pl. Underhill
ng Pl.   Ave.
ln Pl.
n St.   Flatbush Ave.
ll St.

Franklin Ave.
Eastern Pkwy.
President St.
Crown St.

Remsen Ave.

Kings Hwy.

E. 94th St.

1

Washington Ave.

Empire Blvd.
Lefferts Ave.
Maple St.
Rutland Rd.

**Brooklyn
Medical Center**

Utica Ave.

E. 55th St.

Ralph Ave.

**Brooklyn
Terminal
Market**

PARK
SLOPE

PROSPECT
PARK

6th Ave. 7th Ave. 8th Ave.

Prospect Park W.

Flatbush Ave.

Bedford Ave.

Ocean Ave.

**Kings County
Hospital**

Winthrop St.
Clarkson Ave.
Lenox Rd.
Linden Blvd.

27

Church Ave.
Snyder Ave.

**HOLY CROSS
CEMETERY**

Brooklyn Ave.
New York Ave.
Rogers Ave.

E. 52nd St.

E. 48th St.
Schenectady Ave.

E. 53rd St.

Kings Hwy.

Utica Ave.

2

Prospect Park SW.
Prospect Ave.
spect Expwy.
Prospect Ave.

Parkside Ave.

Caton Ave.
Church Ave.

Cortelyou Rd.

Ave. D
Foster Rd.

Clarendon Rd.
E. 39th St.
Albany Ave.
Farragut Rd.

E. 42nd St.

REEN-WOOD
CEMETERY

McDonald Ave.
Ocean Ave.

Albemarle
Rd.

Beverly Rd.
Coney Island Ave.
E. 8th St.
Ocean Pkwy.

Cortelyou Rd.
Dorchester Rd.
Ditmas Ave.

FLATBUSH

Flatbush Ave.

Flatlands Ave.

E. 38th St.

E. 36th St.

E. 34th St.

37th St.
39th St.
41st St.
44th St.
th St.
th St.

14th Ave.

Ave. C

Cortelyou
Rd.
Ditmas Ave.
Ave. F

18th Ave.

Foster Ave.
Glenwood Rd.
Ave. H
Ave. I
Ave. J
Ave. K
Ave. L
Ave. M
Ave. N

**Brooklyn
College**

Nostrand Ave.
Bedford Ave.
E. 27th St.
Ocean Ave.
E. 22nd St.

New York Ave.

E. 36th St.

E. 32nd St.

Burnett St.

3

B R O O K L Y N

9th Ave.
Fort Hamilton Pkwy.

**BOROUGH
PARK**

53rd St.
56th St.
59th St.
62nd St.

**WASHINGTON
CEMETERY**

Ocean Pkwy.

McDonald Ave.

E. 4th St.

Coney Island Ave.

Ave. O
Ave. P
Ave. Q
Ave. R
Ave. S
Ave. T
Ave. U
Ave. V

Kings Hwy.

Bedford Ave.

4

65th St.
Bayridge Ave.
72nd St.
Bay Ridge Pkwy.
78th St.
81st St.
83rd St.
86th St.

0th Ave.

New Utrecht Ave.

13th Ave.
14th Ave.
16th Ave.

17th Ave.
18th Ave.
19th Ave.
20th Ave.
21st Ave.
Bay Pkwy.

65th St.
W. 3rd St.
Kings Hwy.
W. 6th St.
W. 8th St.
W. 11th St.

West 5th St.
McDonald Ave.
Van Sicklen St.
E. 4th St.
E. 8th St.

Kings Hwy.

Gravesend Neck Rd.

Ocean Pkwy.

Coney Island Ave.

Ave. V
Ave. W
Ave. X
Ave. Y
Ave. Z

Ocean Ave.

5

DYKER
BEACH
PARK

ort
milton

Benson Ave.
Bath Ave.
Cropsey Ave.

Shore Pkwy.

BENSONHURST

23rd Ave.
24th Ave.
25th Ave.
26th Ave.

86th St.

Stillwell Ave.

Shell Rd.

BRIGHTON

Neptune Ave.

6

r New York Bay

Neptune Ave.

CONEY ISLAND

Boardwalk

Surf Ave.

N

7

ATLANTIC OCEAN

0   1 mile
0   1 km

8

WESTERN BROOKLYN AND NORTHEASTERN STATEN ISLAND

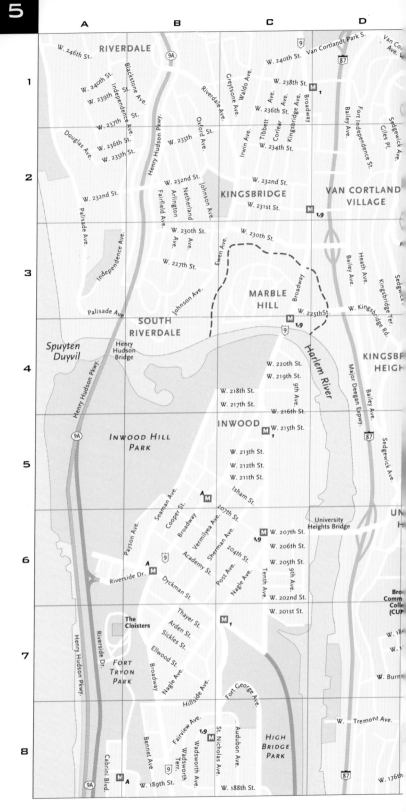

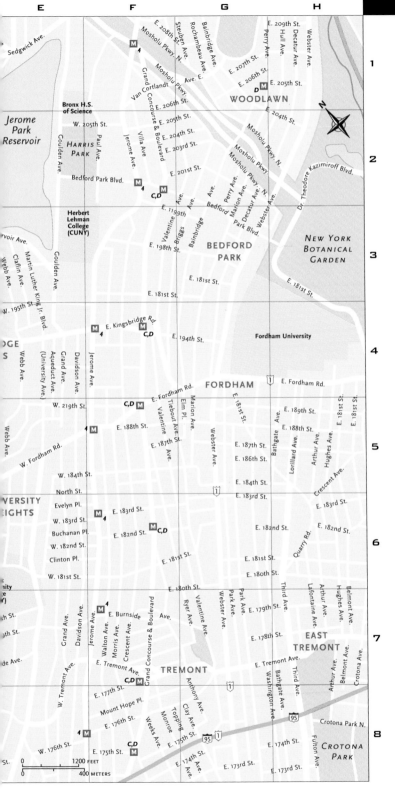

INWOOD AND THE WEST BRONX

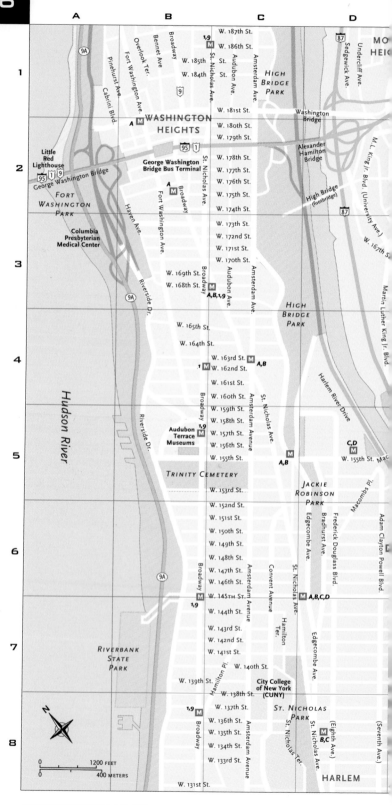

STREETFINDER

NORTHERN MANHATTAN AND THE SOUTH BRONX

A   B   C   D

1

W. 130th Ave.
W. 129th Ave.
W. 128th Ave.
W. 127th Ave.
W. 126th

Convent Ave.
St. Nicholas Ter.
St. Nicholas Ave.
Frederick Douglass Blvd.
Adam Clayton Powell Blvd. (Seventh Ave.)
Lenox Ave.

1,9 M

W. 126th St.
Martin Luther King Jr. Blvd.

A,B,C,D
M
(W. 125th St.)

La Salle St.

W. 124th St. (Eighth Ave.)

M 2,3

General Grant National Memorial (Grant's Tomb)

W. 123rd St.
W. 122nd St.
W. 121st St.

Riverside Church

Claremont Ave.
Broadway
Amsterdam Ave.
Morningside Ave.
Manhattan Ave.

W. 122nd St.

W. 120th St.

W. 120th St.

9A

St. Nicholas Ave.

W. 119th St.
W. 118th St.
W. 117th St.

2

Barnard College

MORNINGSIDE HEIGHTS

HAR

RIVERSIDE PARK

Columbia University

1,9 M

MORNINGSIDE PARK

B,C M

W. 116th St.

M 2,3

W. 115th St.

W. 114th St.
W. 113th St.
W. 112th St.
W. 111th St.

Morningside Dr.

W. 114th St.
W. 113th St.
W. 112th St.

Lenox Ave.

3

1,9 M

Cathedral Parkway

Cathedral Church of St. John the Divine

M B,C

Central Park North

M 2,3

W. 109th St.
W. 108th St.
W. 107th St.
W. 106th St. (Duke Ellington Blvd.)

Broadway
Amsterdam Ave.
Columbus Ave.
Manhattan Ave.

Frederick Douglass Circle

Harlem Mee

STRAUS PARK

W. 105th St.
W. 104th St.

B,C M

The Loch

Museu the City o

4

W. 103rd St.

M 1,9

W. 102nd St.

Frederick Douglass Houses

The Pool

W. 101st St.
W. 100th St.
W. 99th St.
W. 98th St.

Park West Village

NORTH MEADOW

EAST MEAD

W. 97th St.
W. 96th St.

96th St. Transverse

5

M 1,2,3,9

W. 95th St.
W. 94th St.
W. 93rd St.
W. 92nd St.
W. 91st St.
W. 90th St.
W. 89th St.

M B,C

JOAN OF ARC PARK

West End Ave.
Broadway
Amsterdam Ave.
Columbus Ave.
Central Park West

Jacqueline Kennedy Onassis Reservoir

9A

UPPER WEST SIDE

W. 88th St.
W. 87th St.
W. 86th St.

B,C M

6

RIVERSIDE PARK
Henry Hudson Pkwy.
Riverside Dr.

M 1,9

W. 85th St.
W. 84th St.
W. 83rd St.
W. 82nd St.

86th St. Transverse

CENTRAL PARK

M M of

East Dr.

7

E. A. Poe St.

W. 81st St.
W. 80th St.

Hayden Planetarium

B,C M

GREAT LAWN

Belvedere Lake

1,9 M

W. 79th St.

79th St. Transverse

8

W. 78th St.
W. 77th St.
W. 76th St.
W. 75th St.

American Museum of Natural History

The Lake

Wh

0   1200 FEET
0   400 METERS

STREETFINDER

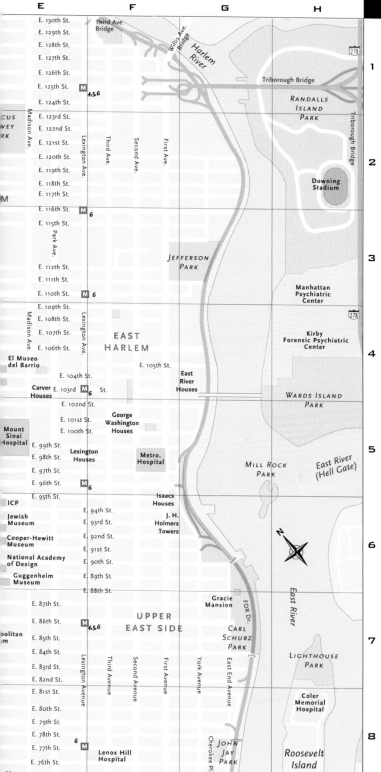

E   F   G   H

E. 130th St.
Third Ave. Bridge
E. 129th St.
E. 128th St.
Willis Ave. Bridge
E. 127th St.
Harlem River
E. 126th St.

1

E. 125th St. M 4,5,6
Triborough Bridge
E. 124th St.

RANDALLS ISLAND PARK

E. 123rd St.
CUS VEY RK
E. 122nd St.
Madison Ave.
Lexington Ave.
E. 121st St.
Third Ave.
Second Ave.
First Ave.
Triborough Bridge
E. 120th St.

2

E. 119th St.
M
E. 118th St.
E. 117th St.
Downing Stadium

E. 116th St. M 6
Park Ave.

3

E. 115th St.
JEFFERSON PARK
E. 112th St.
E. 111th St.
Manhattan Psychiatric Center
E. 110th St. M 6

E. 109th St.
Madison Ave.
Lexington Ave.
E. 108th St.
Kirby Forensic Psychiatric Center
E. 107th St.
EAST HARLEM
E. 106th St.

4

El Museo del Barrio
E. 105th St.
East River Houses
E. 104th St.
WARDS ISLAND PARK
Carver Houses
E. 103rd M 6 St.
E. 102nd St.
Mount Sinai Hospital
E. 101st St.
George Washington Houses
E. 100th St.

5

E. 99th St.
E. 98th St.
Lexington Houses
Metro. Hospital
MILL ROCK PARK
East River (Hell Gate)
E. 97th St.
E. 96th St. M 6
E. 95th St.
Isaacs Houses

ICP
E. 94th St.
J. H. Holmers Towers
Jewish Museum
E. 93rd St.

6

Cooper-Hewitt Museum
E. 92nd St.
N
National Academy of Design
E. 91st St.
E. 90th St.
Guggenheim Museum
E. 89th St.
E. 88th St.

E. 87th St.
Gracie Mansion
East River
E. 86th St. M 4,5,6
UPPER EAST SIDE
FDR Dr.
politan m
E. 85th St.
CARL SCHURZ PARK

7

E. 84th St.
E. 83rd St.
Lexington Avenue
Third Avenue
Second Avenue
First Avenue
York Avenue
East End Avenue
LIGHTHOUSE PARK
E. 82nd St.
E. 81st St.
E. 80th St.
Coler Memorial Hospital
E. 79th St.
E. 78th St.
E. 77th St. 6 M
JOHN JAY PARK

8

Lenox Hill Hospital
Cherokee Pl.
Roosevelt Island
E. 76th St.
Museum
E. 75th St.

A   B   C   D

1

Steinway Creek

N

0   1200 FEET
0   400 METERS

20th Ave.

ASTORIA

20th Rd.

21st Rd.

21st Ave.

Manhattan
Children's
Psychiatric
Center

2

21st Dr.

Ditmars Blvd.

33rd St.
35th St.
36th St.
37th St.
38th

WARDS ISLAND
PARK

M N

Triborough Bridge

Shore Blvd.

19th St.

20th St.

23rd St.

24th St.

Crescent St.

26th St.

27th St.

28th St.

29th St.

31st St.

32nd St.

33rd St.

ASTORIA
PARK

278

3

24th Ave.

Hoyt Ave. North

Astoria Blvd. N.

Astoria Park South

Hoyt Ave. South

Astoria Blvd. S.

14th Pl.

18th St.

25th Rd.

22nd St.

23rd St.

M N

26th Ave.

9th St.

26th Rd.

Astoria Blvd.

28th St.

29th St.

30th St.

Steinway St.

4

3rd St.

4th St.

8th St.

27th Ave.

12th St.

14th St.

21st St.

Newtown Ave.

27th St.

28th St.

28th Ave.

28th Ave.

Astoria Blvd.

Main Ave.

29th Ave.

30th Ave.

30th Ave.

M N

30th Ave.

Halletts
Cove

12th St.

14th St.

(Van Alst Ave.)

Crescent St.

30th Rd.

30th Dr.

31st Ave.

31st St.

32nd St.

33rd St.

34th St.

35th St.

36th St.

37th St.

38th St.

41st St.

5

31st Ave.

31st Rd.

31st Ave.

31st Dr.

Broadway

M N

Broadway

M G,R

Vernon Blvd.

33rd Rd.

33rd Ave.

29th St.

30th St.

6

RAINEY
PARK

9th St.

10th St.

11th St.

12th St.

33rd Rd.

34th Ave.

34th Ave.

42nd St.
41st St.

Steinway St.

American
Museum of the
Moving Image ■

13th St.

14th St.

35th Ave.

7

36th Ave.

M N

34th St.

35th St.

36th St.

37th St.

38th St.

37th Ave.

21st St.

22nd St.

23rd St.

24th St.

Crescent St.

27th St.

28th St.

29th St.

30th St.

31st St.

32nd St.

33rd St.

39th St.

8

38th Ave.

LONG ISLAND CITY

39th Ave.

M G,R

Vernon Blvd.

10th St.

12th St.

40th Ave.

N

M

Northern Blvd.

Honeywell St.

41st Ave.

25A

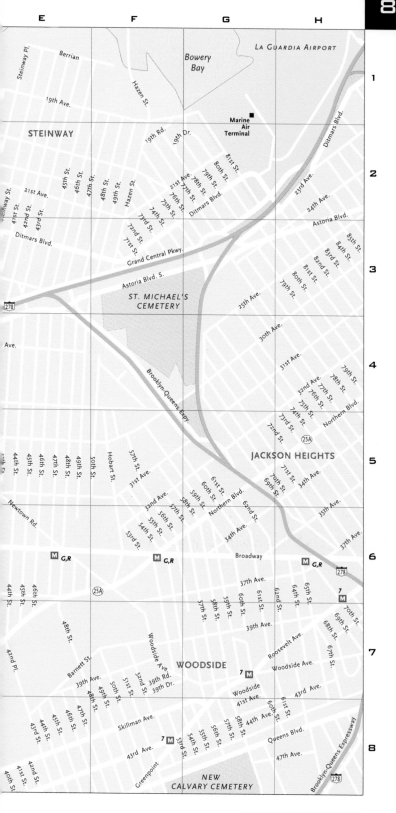

E   F   G   H

LA GUARDIA AIRPORT

Steinway Pl.
Berrian
Bowery
Bay
1
19th Ave.
Hazen St.
19th Rd.
19th Dr.
Marine
Air
Terminal
Ditmars Blvd

STEINWAY

45th St.
46th St.
47th St.
48th St.
49th St.
Hazen St.
8th St.
81st St.
21st Ave.
78th St.
77th St.
80th St.
Ditmars Blvd.
21st Ave.
24th Ave.
8th St.
83rd St.
84th St.
Astoria Blvd.

21st Ave.
41st St.
42nd St.
43rd St.
44th St.
76th St.
75th St.
74th St.
73rd St.
72nd St.
71st St.
82nd St.
81st St.
80th St.
79th St.
83rd St.
84th St.
85th St.
3
Ditmars Blvd.

Grand Central Pkwy.
25th Ave.

278
Astoria Blvd. S.

ST. MICHAEL'S
CEMETERY
30th Ave.
79th St.
4
Ave.
31st Ave.
32nd Ave.
77th St.
78th St.
76th St.
75th St.
74th St.
73rd St.
72nd St.
Northern Blvd.
25A

Brooklyn-Queens Expy.
JACKSON HEIGHTS
5
44th St.
45th St.
46th St.
47th St.
48th St.
49th St.
50th St.
Hobart St.
57th St.
31st Ave.
32nd Ave.
61st St.
60th St.
59th St.
58th St.
57th St.
56th St.
55th St.
54th St.
53rd St.
Northern Blvd.
62nd St.
71st St.
70th St.
69th St.
34th Ave.
35th Ave.
37th Ave.

Newtown Rd.
34th Ave.

M G,R
M G,R
Broadway
M G,R
278
6
44th St.
45th St.
46th St.
25A
37th Ave.
57th St.
58th St.
59th St.
60th St.
61st St.
62nd St.
65th St.
64th St.
70th St.
69th St.
68th St.
67th St.
M
7
39th Ave.
Roosevelt Ave.
42nd Pl.
48th St.
Barnett St.
39th Ave.
Woodside Ave.
32nd St.
39th Rd.
39th Dr.
WOODSIDE
7 M
Woodside Ave.
7
42nd St.
44th St.
43rd St.
46th St.
47th St.
48th St.
49th St.
50th St.
51st St.
Woodside
41st Ave.
43rd Ave.
60th St.
61st St.
Skillman Ave.
44th St.
56th St.
57th St.
Queens Blvd.
43rd Ave.
47th Ave.
40th St.
41st St.
42nd St.
43rd St.
44th St.
7 M
53rd St.
54th St.
55th St.
8
Greenpoint
NEW
CALVARY CEMETERY
Brooklyn-Queens Expressway
278

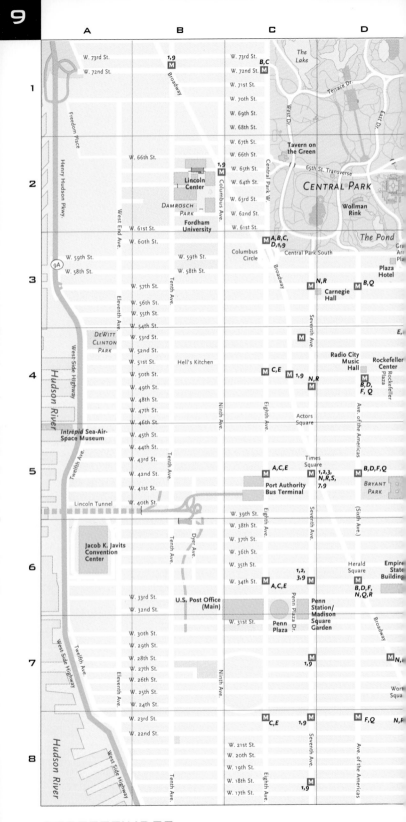

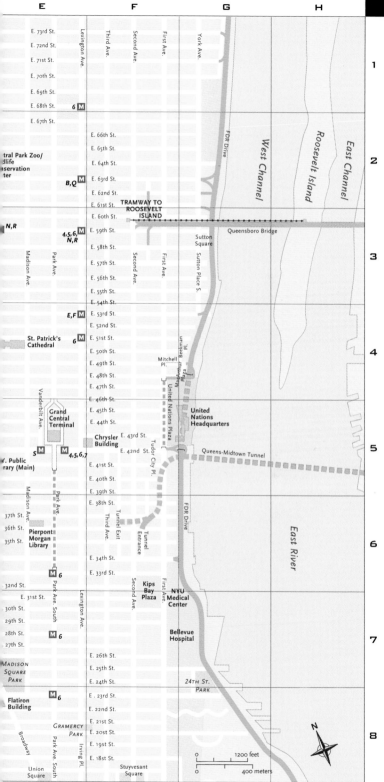

MIDTOWN MANHATTAN

10

DOWNTOWN MANHATTAN

A B C D

W. 12th St.

Greenwich Ave.

Milligan Pl.

Avenue of the Americas

W. 11th St.

W. 10th St.

W. 9th St.

Bank St.

Waverly Pl.

Patchin Pl.

W. 11th St.

W. 4th St.

Seventh Ave. S.

Fifth Ave.

1

W. 8th St.

Perry St.

Charles St.

Gay St.

Sheridan Square

1,9 Ⓜ

Waverly Pl.

MacDougal Alley

Washington Mews

MacDougal St.

Waverly Pl.

2

W. 10th St.

W. Washington Pl.

WASHINGTON SQUARE PARK

Ⓜ **A,B,C,D, E,F,Q**

West 4th St.

New York University

Christopher St.

Grove St.

Jones St.

Cornelia St.

Bleecker St.

W. 3rd St.

Commerce St.

Minetta La.

3

Greenwich St.

Bedford St.

Father Demo Sq.

Bleecker St.

Barrow St.

Morton St.

St. Luke's Pl.

Carmine St.

Downing St.

Avenue of the Americas (Sixth Ave.)

MacDougal St.

Sullivan St.

Thompson St.

La Guardia Pl.

W. Houston

4

Leroy St.

Hudson St.

Ⓜ **1,9**

Clarkson St.

Prince St.

W. Houston St.

King St.

Varick St.

Charlton St.

Ⓜ **C,E**

Spring St.

Thompson St.

West Broadway

Wooster St.

Greene St.

5

Washington St.

Vandam St.

Spring St.

Holland Tunnel Entrance

Broome St.

Dominick St.

Holland Tunnel

West St.

West Side Highway

Broome St.

Grand St.

6

1,9 Ⓜ

Ⓜ **A,C,E**

Watts St.

Hudson St.

Canal St.

Church St.

Lispenard St.

7

Desbrosses St.

Greenwich St.

Holland Tunnel Exit

Varick St.

Walker St.

Greene St.

Vestry St.

Ericsson Pl.

Laight St.

White St.

Hubert St.

Beach St.

Ⓜ **1,9**

Franklin St.

600 feet

N. Moore St.

West Broadway

Leonard St.

200 meters

Hudson River

8

Manhattan Community College

Franklin St.

Harrison St.

Staple St.

Jay St.

Worth St.

Thomas St.

N

GREENWICH VILLAGE AND SOHO

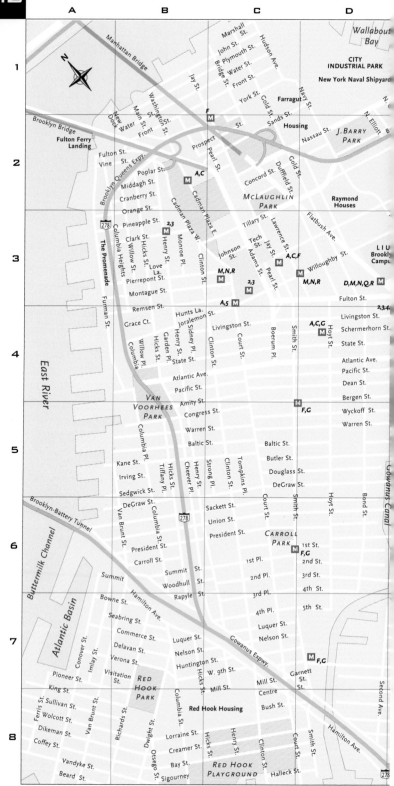

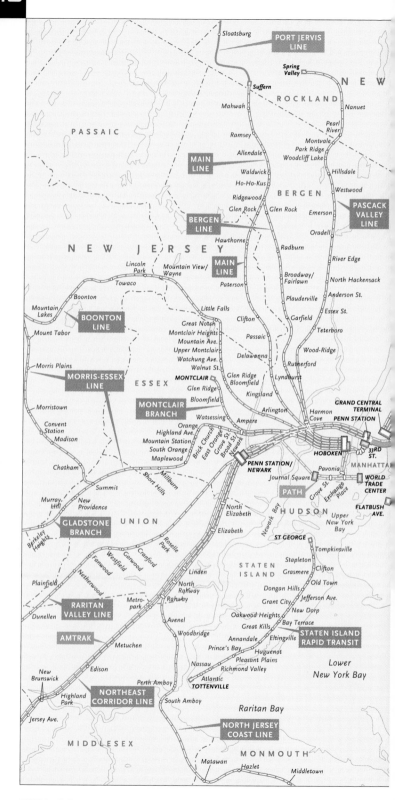

TRI-STATE COMMUTER RAIL

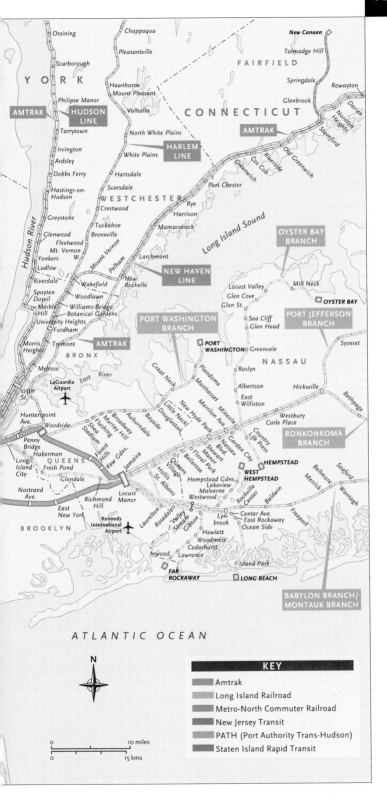

Ossining
Chappaqua
New Canaan
Pleasantville
Talmadge Hill
FAIRFIELD
Scarborough
Springdale
Rowayton
Y O R K
Hawthorne
Mount Pleasant
Glenbrook
Darien
Philipse Manor
Valhalla
Noroton
Heights
AMTRAK
HUDSON
LINE
C O N N E C T I C U T
Stamford
Tarrytown
North White Plains
AMTRAK
Old Greenwich
Irvington
White Plains
HARLEM
LINE
Riverside
Ardsley
Cos Cob
Dobbs Ferry
Hartsdale
Greenwich
Hastings-on-Hudson
Scarsdale
Port Chester
W E S T C H E S T E R
Crestwood
Rye
Greystone
Tuckahoe
Harrison
OYSTER BAY
BRANCH
Glenwood
Bronxville
Mamaroneck
Fleetwood
Mt. Vernon W.
Mount Vernon
Larchmont
Long Island Sound
Mill Neck
Yonkers
Ludlow
Pelham
NEW HAVEN
LINE
Locust Valley
Glen Cove
OYSTER BAY
Riverdale
Wakefield
New
Rochelle
Glen St.
PORT JEFFERSON
BRANCH
Spuyten
Duyvil
Woodlawn
Williams Bridge
Botanical Gardens
PORT WASHINGTON
BRANCH
Sea Cliff
Glen Head
Marble
Hill
University Heights
Fordham
PORT
WASHINGTON
Greenvale
Syosset
Morris
Heights
Tremont
AMTRAK
N A S S A U
B R O N X
Plandome
Roslyn
Melrose
East River
Great Neck
Manhasset
Albertson
East
Williston
Hicksville
Bethpage
125th
St.
LaGuardia
Airport
Little Neck
New Hyde Park
Merrion Ave.
Mineola
Country
Life Press
Westbury
Carle Place
RONKONKOMA
BRANCH
Huntspoint
Ave.
Woodside
Broadway
Auburndale
Bayside
Douglaston
Murray Hill
Flushing
Shea
Stadium
Nassau
Blvd
Garden City
Stewart
Manor
HEMPSTEAD
Penny
Bridge
Haberman
Forest
Hills
Kew Gdns.
Floral Park
Bellerose
WEST
HEMPSTEAD
Bellmore
Seaford
Long
Island
City
Fresh Pond
Q U E E N S
Jamaica
Queens
Village
Hollis
St. Albans
Hempstead Gdns.
Lakeview
Malverne
Merrick
Wantagh
Glendale
Richmond
Hill
Locust
Manor
Westwood
Rockville
Center
Baldwin
Freeport
Nostrand
Ave.
Kennedy
International
Airport
Laurelton
Rosedale
Valley
Stream
Gibson
Lyn-
brook
Center Ave.
East Rockaway
Ocean Side
East
New York
B R O O K L Y N
Hewlett
Woodmere
Cedarhurst
Lawrence
Inwood
Island Park
FAR
ROCKAWAY
LONG BEACH
BABYLON BRANCH/
MONTAUK BRANCH

A T L A N T I C   O C E A N

N

KEY
Amtrak
Long Island Railroad
Metro-North Commuter Railroad
New Jersey Transit
PATH (Port Authority Trans-Hudson)
Staten Island Rapid Transit

0   10 miles
0   15 kms

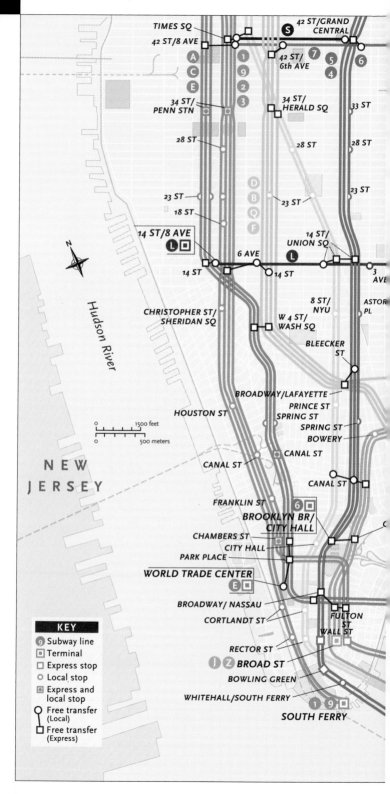

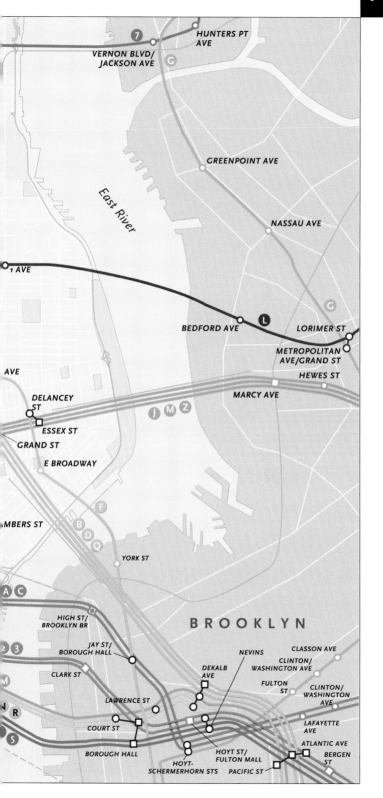

HUNTERS PT
AVE

VERNON BLVD/
JACKSON AVE

East River

GREENPOINT AVE

NASSAU AVE

1 AVE

BEDFORD AVE

LORIMER ST

METROPOLITAN
AVE/GRAND ST

HEWES ST

AVE

MARCY AVE

DELANCEY
ST

ESSEX ST

GRAND ST

E BROADWAY

MBERS ST

F

YORK ST

BROOKLYN

HIGH ST/
BROOKLYN BR

JAY ST/
BOROUGH HALL

NEVINS

CLASSON AVE

CLINTON/
WASHINGTON AVE

DEKALB
AVE

FULTON
ST

CLINTON/
WASHINGTON
AVE

CLARK ST

LAWRENCE ST

LAFAYETTE
AVE

COURT ST

ATLANTIC AVE

BOROUGH HALL

HOYT-
SCHERMERHORN STS

HOYT ST/
FULTON MALL

PACIFIC ST

BERGEN
ST

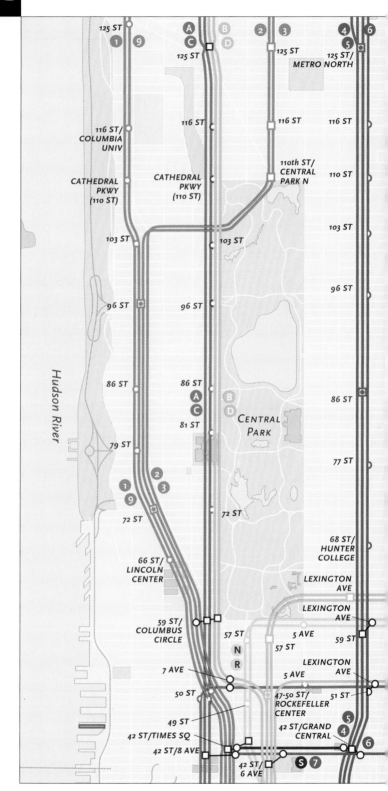

SUBWAYS

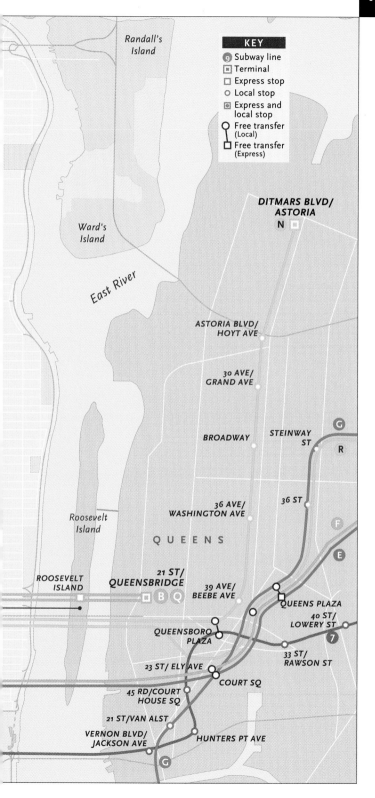

KEY
- Subway line
- Terminal
- Express stop
- Local stop
- Express and local stop
- Free transfer (Local)
- Free transfer (Express)

Randall's Island

Ward's Island

East River

DITMARS BLVD/ ASTORIA
N

ASTORIA BLVD/ HOYT AVE

30 AVE/ GRAND AVE

BROADWAY

STEINWAY ST

G

R

Roosevelt Island

36 AVE/ WASHINGTON AVE

36 ST

F

E

Q U E E N S

ROOSEVELT ISLAND

21 ST/ QUEENSBRIDGE
B Q

39 AVE/ BEEBE AVE

QUEENS PLAZA

40 ST/ LOWERY ST

QUEENSBORO PLAZA

33 ST/ RAWSON ST

7

23 ST/ ELY AVE

COURT SQ

45 RD/COURT HOUSE SQ

21 ST/VAN ALST

VERNON BLVD/ JACKSON AVE
G

HUNTERS PT AVE

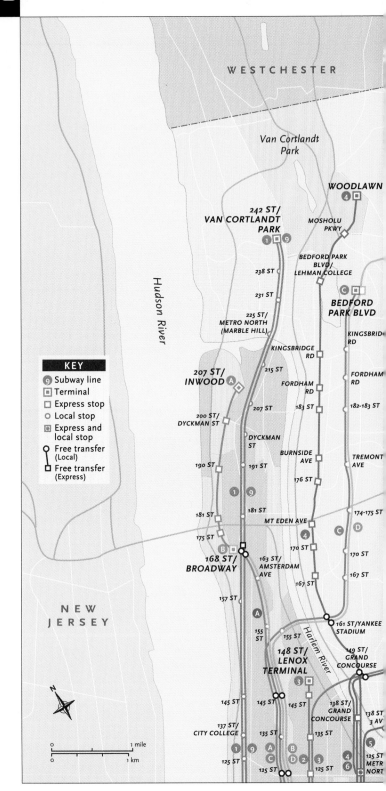

SUBWAYS

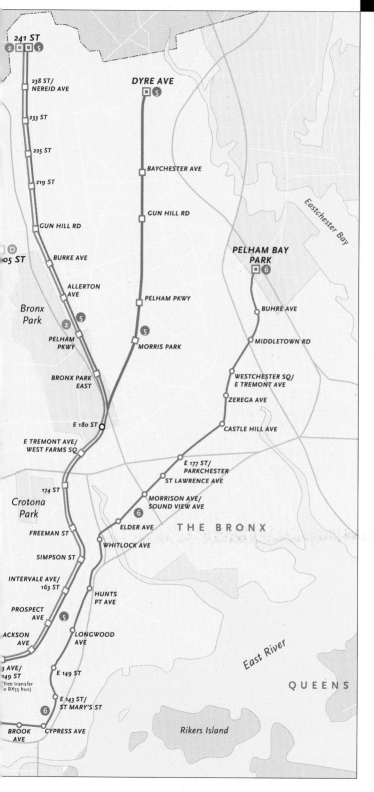

241 ST

238 ST/
NEREID AVE

233 ST

225 ST

219 ST

GUN HILL RD

BURKE AVE

ALLERTON
AVE

Bronx
Park

PELHAM
PKWY

BRONX PARK
EAST

E 180 ST

E TREMONT AVE/
WEST FARMS SQ

174 ST

Crotona
Park

FREEMAN ST

SIMPSON ST

INTERVALE AVE/
163 ST

PROSPECT
AVE

ACKSON
AVE

3 AVE/
149 ST
(free transfer
o BX55 bus)

BROOK
AVE

05 ST

DYRE AVE

BAYCHESTER AVE

GUN HILL RD

PELHAM PKWY

MORRIS PARK

PELHAM BAY
PARK

BUHRE AVE

MIDDLETOWN RD

WESTCHESTER SQ/
E TREMONT AVE

ZEREGA AVE

CASTLE HILL AVE

E 177 ST/
PARKCHESTER
ST LAWRENCE AVE

MORRISON AVE/
SOUND VIEW AVE

ELDER AVE

WHITLOCK AVE

THE BRONX

HUNTS
PT AVE

LONGWOOD
AVE

E 149 ST

E 143 ST/
ST MARY'S ST

CYPRESS AVE

Eastchester Bay

East River

QUEENS

Rikers Island

BRONX AND NORTHERN MANHATTAN

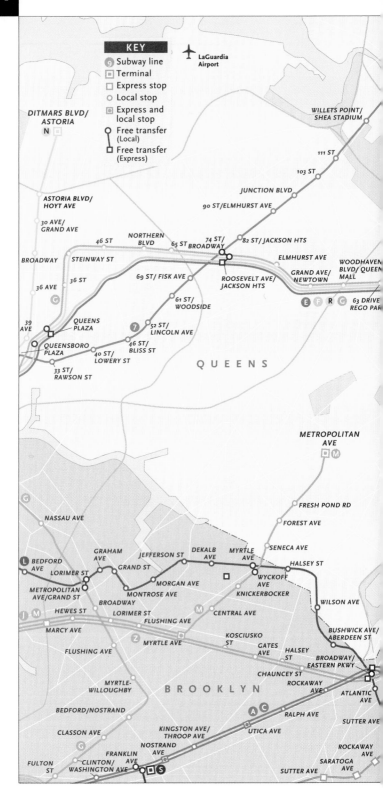

KEY

⑨ Subway line
▣ Terminal
▫ Express stop
○ Local stop
▣ Express and local stop
○ Free transfer (Local)
▫ Free transfer (Express)

✈ LaGuardia Airport

DITMARS BLVD/ ASTORIA N

WILLETS POINT/ SHEA STADIUM

111 ST

103 ST

JUNCTION BLVD

ASTORIA BLVD/ HOYT AVE

90 ST/ELMHURST AVE

30 AVE/ GRAND AVE

82 ST/JACKSON HTS

NORTHERN BLVD

65 ST

74 ST/ BROADWAY

46 ST

ELMHURST AVE

BROADWAY

STEINWAY ST

WOODHAVEN BLVD/ QUEENS MALL

GRAND AVE/ NEWTOWN

36 AVE

36 ST

69 ST/ FISK AVE

ROOSEVELT AVE/ JACKSON HTS

E F R G 63 DRIVE REGO PARK

61 ST/ WOODSIDE

39 AVE

QUEENS PLAZA

⑦

52 ST/ LINCOLN AVE

QUEENSBORO PLAZA

40 ST/ LOWERY ST

46 ST/ BLISS ST

Q U E E N S

33 ST/ RAWSON ST

METROPOLITAN AVE M

FRESH POND RD

FOREST AVE

G

NASSAU AVE

SENECA AVE

GRAHAM AVE

JEFFERSON ST

DEKALB AVE

MYRTLE AVE

HALSEY ST

L BEDFORD AVE

GRAND ST

WYCKOFF AVE

LORIMER ST

MORGAN AVE

KNICKERBOCKER

WILSON AVE

METROPOLITAN AVE/GRAND ST

MONTROSE AVE

BROADWAY

BUSHWICK AVE/ ABERDEEN ST

J M HEWES ST

LORIMER ST

M CENTRAL AVE

FLUSHING AVE

MARCY AVE

Z MYRTLE AVE

KOSCIUSKO ST

GATES AVE

HALSEY ST

BROADWAY/ EASTERN PKWY

FLUSHING AVE

CHAUNCEY ST

MYRTLE- WILLOUGHBY

ROCKAWAY AVE

ATLANTIC AVE

B R O O K L Y N

BEDFORD/NOSTRAND

A C

RALPH AVE

SUTTER AVE

CLASSON AVE

KINGSTON AVE/ THROOP AVE

UTICA AVE

ROCKAWAY AVE

G FRANKLIN AVE

NOSTRAND AVE

SARATOGA AVE

FULTON ST

CLINTON/ WASHINGTON AVE

S

SUTTER AVE

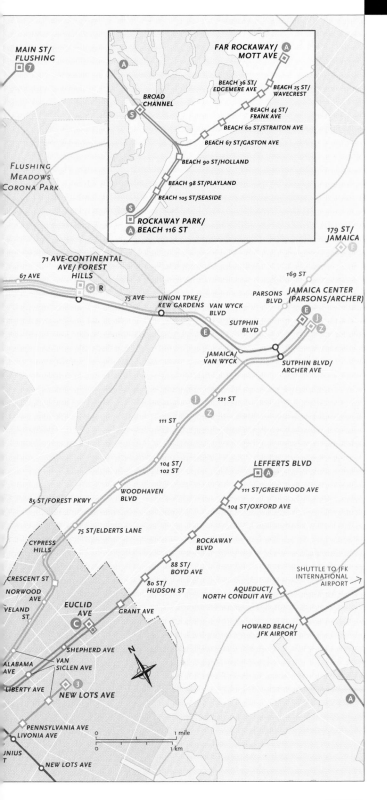

MAIN ST/
FLUSHING
7

FAR ROCKAWAY/
MOTT AVE   A

A

BEACH 36 ST/
EDGEMERE AVE   BEACH 25 ST/
WAVECREST

BROAD
CHANNEL   BEACH 44 ST/
FRANK AVE
S
BEACH 60 ST/STRAITON AVE

BEACH 67 ST/GASTON AVE

FLUSHING
MEADOWS
CORONA PARK   BEACH 90 ST/HOLLAND

BEACH 98 ST/PLAYLAND

S   BEACH 105 ST/SEASIDE

ROCKAWAY PARK/
A   BEACH 116 ST

179 ST/
JAMAICA
F

71 AVE-CONTINENTAL
AVE/ FOREST
HILLS   169 ST
67 AVE   G   R
75 AVE   UNION TPKE/   PARSONS   JAMAICA CENTER
KEW GARDENS   VAN WYCK   BLVD   (PARSONS/ARCHER)
BLVD   E
SUTPHIN   J
E   BLVD   Z

JAMAICA/
VAN WYCK   SUTPHIN BLVD/
ARCHER AVE

J   121 ST
Z
111 ST

104 ST/
102 ST   LEFFERTS BLVD
A
WOODHAVEN   111 ST/GREENWOOD AVE
85 ST/FOREST PKWY   BLVD
104 ST/OXFORD AVE

75 ST/ELDERTS LANE   ROCKAWAY
BLVD
CYPRESS
HILLS   SHUTTLE TO JFK
88 ST/   INTERNATIONAL
CRESCENT ST   80 ST/   BOYD AVE   AIRPORT
NORWOOD   HUDSON ST   AQUEDUCT/
AVE   NORTH CONDUIT AVE
VELAND   EUCLID   GRANT AVE
ST   AVE
C   HOWARD BEACH/
JFK AIRPORT
SHEPHERD AVE   N
ALABAMA   VAN
AVE   SICLEN AVE
LIBERTY AVE
NEW LOTS AVE
A
PENNSYLVANIA AVE
LIVONIA AVE
0   1 mile
NIUS
T   0   1 km
NEW LOTS AVE

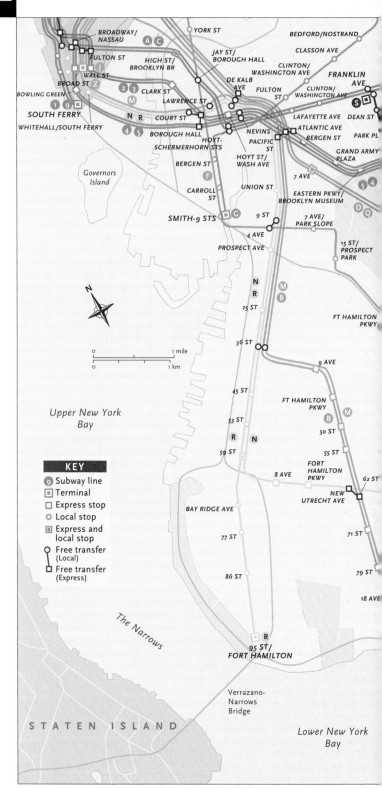

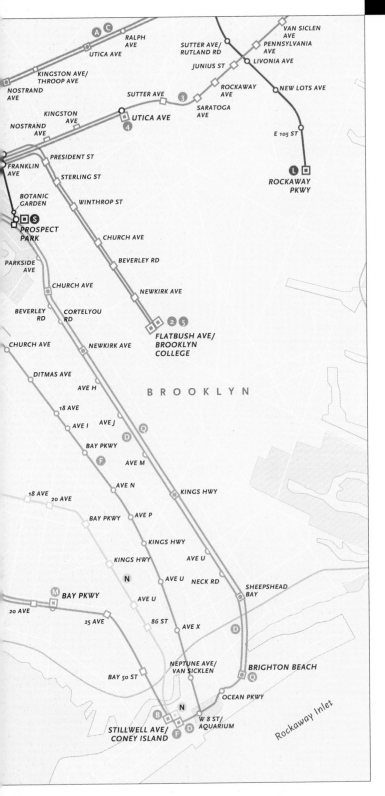

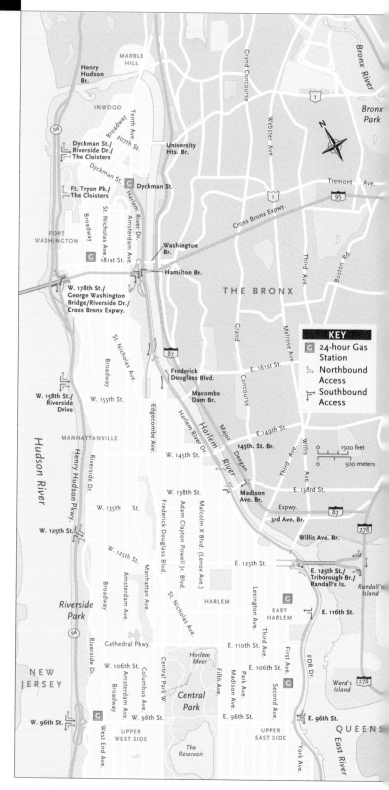

DRIVING UPTOWN: ENTRANCES & EXITS

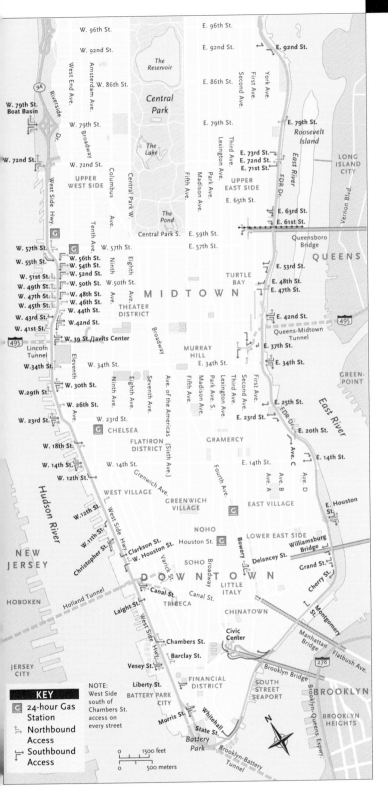

DRIVING DOWNTOWN: ENTRANCES & EXITS

KEY
- **P** Parking
- **G** Gasoline
- → One-way street
- ←→ Two-way street
- — Major thoroughfare

DRIVING

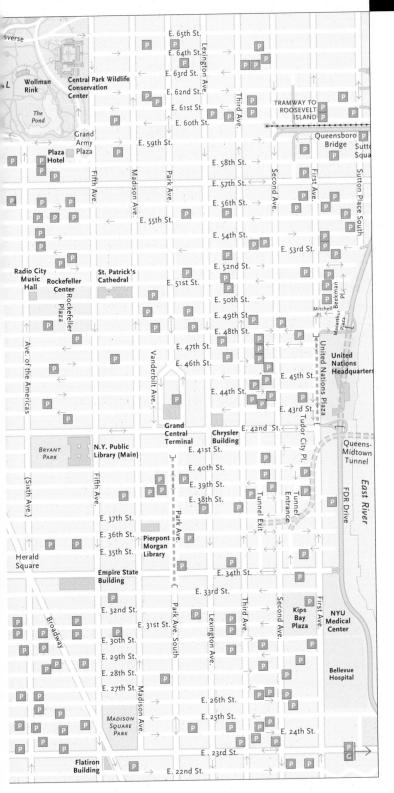

MIDTOWN MANHATTAN

KEY
— Northbound
— Southbound
— Eastbound
— Westbound
(101) Route number
20 Terminal

BUSES

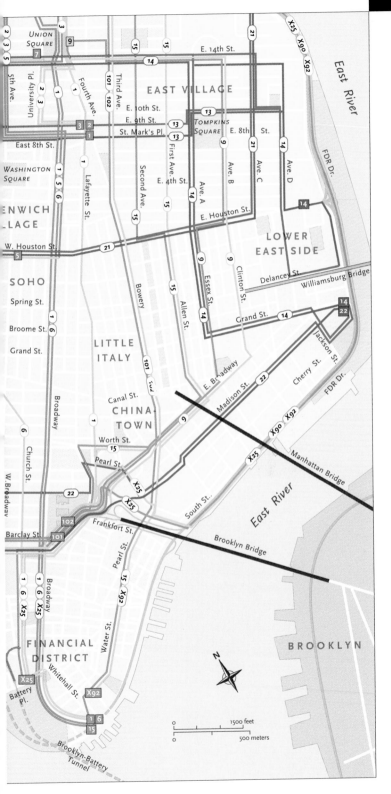

East River

FDR Dr.

E. 14th St.

Union Square

EAST VILLAGE

E. 10th St.
E. 9th St.
St. Mark's Pl.

Tompkins Square

East 8th St.

E. 8th St.

Washington Square

GREENWICH VILLAGE

W. Houston St.

E. Houston St.

LOWER EAST SIDE

University Pl.

Fourth Ave.

Third Ave.

Lafayette St.

Second Ave.

First Ave.

E. 4th St.

Ave. A

Ave. B

Ave. C

Ave. D

Delancey St.

Williamsburg Bridge

SOHO

Spring St.

Broome St.

Grand St.

LITTLE ITALY

Bowery

Allen St.

Essex St.

Clinton St.

Grand St.

Jackson St.

Cherry St.

FDR Dr.

Broadway

Church St.

W. Broadway

Canal St.

CHINATOWN

Worth St.

Pearl St.

E. Broadway

Madison St.

South St.

Frankfort St.

Barclay St.

FINANCIAL DISTRICT

Whitehall St.

Battery Pl.

Pearl St.

Water St.

Broadway

Manhattan Bridge

East River

Brooklyn Bridge

BROOKLYN

N

0   1500 feet
0   500 meters

Brooklyn-Battery Tunnel

BUSES

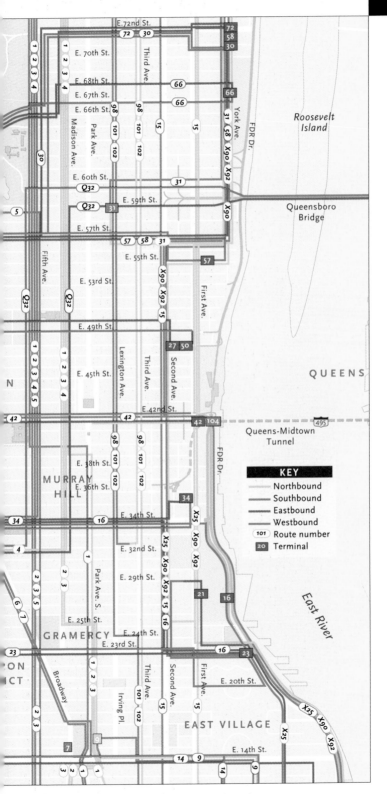

KEY

Northbound
Southbound
Eastbound
Westbound
101 Route number
20 Terminal

Roosevelt
Island

Queensboro
Bridge

QUEENS

Queens-Midtown
Tunnel

East River

MURRAY
HILL

GRAMERCY

EAST VILLAGE

MIDTOWN

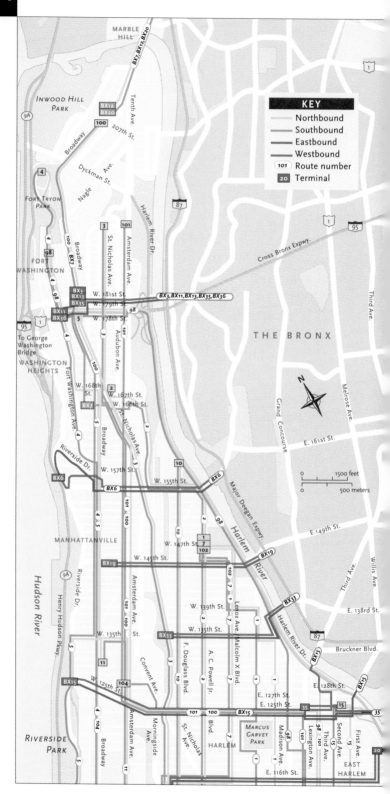

BUSES UPTOWN

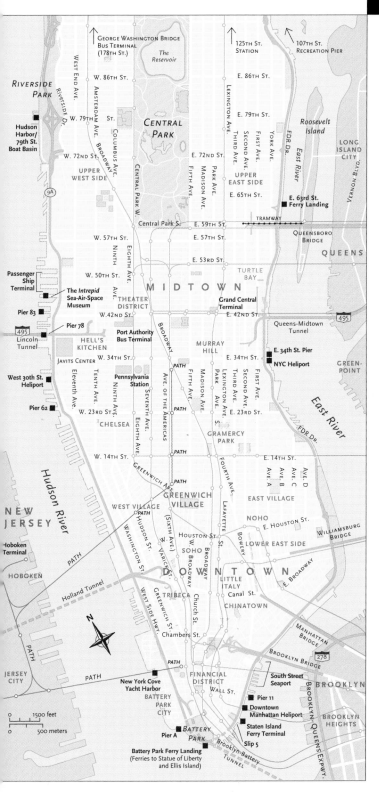

The Sourcebook
For Your City

MANY MAPS • WHERE & HOW

FIND IT ALL • NIGHT & DAY

ANTIQUES TO ZIPPERS

BARGAINS • BAUBLES • KITES

ELEGANT EDIBLES • ETHNIC EATS

STEAK HOUSES • FISH HOUSES

BISTROS • TRATTORIAS

CLASSICAL • JAZZ • CABARET

COMEDY • THEATER • DANCE

BARS • CLUBS • BLUES

COOL TOURS

HOUSECLEANING • CATERING

LOST & FOUND • THE CABLE GUY

GET A LAWYER • GET A DENTIST

GET A NEW PET • GET A VET

MUSEUMS • GALLERIES

PARKS • GARDENS • RINKS

AQUARIUMS TO ZOOS

BASEBALL TO ROCK CLIMBING

FESTIVALS • EVENTS

DAY SPAS • DAY TRIPS

HOTELS • HOT LINES

PASSPORT PIX • TRAVEL INFO

HELICOPTER TOURS

DINERS • DELIS • PIZZERIAS

BRASSERIES • CAFÉS

BOOTS • BOOKS • BUTTONS

BICYCLES • SKATES

SUITS • SHOES • HATS

RENT A TUX • RENT A COSTUME

BAKERIES • SPICE SHOPS

SOUP TO NUTS

Fodor's

CITYGUIDE
NEW YORK

FODOR'S TRAVEL PUBLICATIONS

NEW YORK • TORONTO • LONDON • SYDNEY • AUCKLAND

WWW.FODORS.COM

FODOR'S CITYGUIDE NEW YORK

EDITOR
Stephanie Adler

EDITORIAL CONTRIBUTORS
Stephen Brewer, Mitchell Davis, John Donohue, Melisse Gelula, Melissa Klurman, Christina Knight, Lynn Konstantin, Heather Lewis, Cara Maniaci, Jane Miller, Margaret Mittelbach, Jennifer Paull, Tim Reynolds, Sasha Smith, Tom Steele, Alex Tressman, Melissa Wagenberg

EDITORIAL PRODUCTION
Brian Vitunic

MAPS
David Lindroth Inc., *cartographer*; Bob Blake and Rebecca Baer, *map editors*

DESIGN
Fabrizio La Rocca, *creative director*; Allison Saltzman, *text design*; Tigist Getachew, *cover design*; Jolie Novak, *photo editor*

PRODUCTION/MANUFACTURING
Robert B. Shields

COVER PHOTOGRAPH
James Lemass

Series created by Marilyn Appleberg

COPYRIGHT

SPECIAL SALES

CONTENTS

METROPOLITAN LIFE

O n a bad day in a big city, the little things that go with living shoulder-to-shoulder with a few million people wear us all down. But the special pleasures of urban life have a way of keeping us out of the suburbs—and thankful, even, for every second of stress. The field of daffodils in the park on a fine spring day. The perfect little black dress that you find for half price. The markets—so fabulously well stocked that you can cook any recipe without resorting to mail-order catalogs. The way you can sometimes turn a corner and discover a whole new world, so foreign you can hardly believe you're less than a mile from home. The never-ending wealth of possibilities and opportunities.

If you know where to find it all, the city cannot defeat you. With knowledge comes power. That's why Fodor's has prepared this book. It will put phone numbers at your fingertips. It'll take you to new places and remind you of those you've forgotten. It's the ultimate urban companion—and, we hope, your **new best friend in the city.**

It's the **citywise shopaholic,** who always knows where to find something, no matter how obscure. We've made a concerted effort to bring hundreds of great shops to your attention, so that you'll never be at a loss, whether you need a special birthday present for a great friend or some obscure craft items to make Halloween costumes for your kids.

It's the **restaurant know-it-all,** who's full of ideas for every occasion—you know, the one who would never send you to Café de la Snub, because he knows it's always overbooked, the food is boring, and the staff is rude. We'll steer you around the corner, to a perfect little place with five tables, a fireplace, and a chef on her way up.

It's a **hip barfly buddy,** who can give you advice when you need a charming nook, not too noisy, to take a friend after work. Among the dozens of bars and nightspots in this book, you're bound to find something that fits your mood.

It's the **sagest arts maven you know,** the one who always has the scoop on what's on that's worthwhile on any given night. In these pages, you'll find dozens of concert venues and arts organizations.

It's also the **city whiz,** who knows how to get you where you're going, wherever you are.

It's the **best map guide** on the shelves, and it puts **all the city in your briefcase** or on your bookshelf.

Stick with us. We'll lay out all the options for your leisure time—and gently nudge you away from the duds—so that you can truly enjoy metropolitan living.

YOUR GUIDES

No one person can know it all. To help get you on track around the city, we've hand-picked a stellar group of local experts to share their wisdom.

Sometime between rating restaurants across the country, writing cookbooks, and producing the publications of the James Beard Foundation, **Mitchell Davis** and his colleague **Jane Miller** have acquainted themselves personally with most New York City restaurants worth knowing, in all five boroughs.

Brooklyn resident **John Donohue** has spent each of the last nine New Year's Days exploring distant corners of New York City, places like Coney Island's desolate boardwalk and Staten Island's Fresh Kills Landfill. During the rest of the year he writes for *The New Yorker,* where he's an editor of the Goings On About Town section, and on his time off he enjoys the greener portions of the five boroughs. For this edition, John covered New York's two wild sides—its outdoors and its nightlife.

Being a resident know-it-all inspired **Melisse Gelula**'s update of the CitySources chapter. Although she now lives and works in New York City, Melisse has resided in all the great North American cities: Toronto, Chicago, San Francisco, and Iowa City.

Melissa Klurman was slathered with yogurt, rubbed with hot stones, waxed, plucked, and manicured—all in the pursuit of the best beauty experiences in New York. Having suffered in the name of beauty, she consoled herself with a tour of the city's top bakeries and gourmet outlets. An editor at Fodor's, Melissa has also written for *UpClose New York, Cityguide Washington, D.C.,* and a number of Web sites.

Since attending a graduate course at Sotheby's auction house, **Lynne Konstantin**'s friends and family believe her to be a walking-talking version of the Antiques Road Show. True or not, she knows where to get the best finds in New York City.

An art historian by day, **Cara Maniaci** has an eye for detail. It came in handy for this assignment, during which she scoured the five boroughs for the best of everything from kites to coins, electronics to jewelry.

Since moving to New York more than a decade ago, **Margaret Mittelbach** has written about all aspects of the city: animal, vegetable, and mineral. On any given day you might find her examining the Art Deco interiors of midtown skyscrapers, ogling great blue herons at the Jamaica Bay Wildlife Refuge, or raising the ghost of Boss Tweed at Brooklyn's Green-Wood Cemetery. She is coauthor of *Wild New York,* an acclaimed guide to the city's wildlife, wild places, and natural history.

Shopping fanatic **Jennifer Paull,** our women's-clothing scout, has braved unkind dressing-room mirrors and slithered into embroidered silk, grubby denim, and talcum-dusted rubber in more stores than she cares to remember.

This is **Tim Reynolds**'s second trip for Fodor's through the art galleries of NYC, and his first survey of men's shopping. What did he learn? Clothing is sometimes art but art should never be printed on clothing. Also, people who sell expensive paintings are generally more friendly if you're wearing Prada.

Shopping updater **Sasha Smith,** who recently moved to Ann Arbor, Michigan to pursue an MFA in fiction, yearns for the well-stocked wine stores and book emporia of her native New York.

Arts writer and restaurant reviewer **Tom Steele** was the founding editor of *TheaterWeek, Opera Monthly,* and the *New York Native,* among other publications. His writing has appeared far and wide, and he is currently food editor for *Our Town* and *Manhattan Spirit.* He is writing a cookbook for people with small kitchens.

Food columnist and Ninth Avenue aficionado **Alex Tressman** covered restaurants in Chelsea, Hell's Kitchen, and the Theater District. Like most New Yorkers, Tressman considers the subject of restaurants and dining out supremely important and gladly brings 15 years of food and travel writing experience to our chapter.

Marilyn Appleberg, who conceived this series, is a city-lover through and through. She plots her urban forays from an archetypal Greenwich Village brownstone with two fireplaces.

It goes without saying that our contributors have chosen all establishments strictly on their own merits—no establishment has paid to be included in this book.

HOW TO USE THIS BOOK

The first thing you need to know is that everything in this book is **arranged by category and in alphabetical order within category.**

Now, before you go any farther, check out the **city maps** at the front of the book. Each map has a number, in a black box at the top of the page, and grid coordinates along the top and side margins. On the text pages, every listing in the book is keyed to one of these maps. Look for the map number in a small black box preceding each establishment name. The grid code follows in italics. For establishments with more than one location, additional map numbers and grid codes appear at the end of the listing. To locate a museum that's identified in the text as **7** *e-6*, turn to Map 7 and locate the address within the e-6 grid square. To locate restaurants nearby, simply skim the text in the restaurant chapter for listings identified as being on Map 7.

Where appropriate throughout the guide, we name the neighborhood in which each sight, restaurant, shop, or other destination is located. We also give you the nearest subway stop, plus complete opening hours and admission fees for sights; closing information for shops; credit-card, price, reservations, and closing information for restaurants; and credit-card information for nightspots.

At the end of the book, in addition to an **alphabetical index,** you'll find **directories of shops and restaurants by neighborhood.**

Chapter 7, City Sources, provides resources and essential information for residents and visitors alike—everything from vet and lawyer-referral services to entertainment hot lines.

We've worked hard to make sure that all of the information we give you is accurate at press time. Still, time brings changes, so always confirm information when it matters—especially if you're making a detour.

Feel free to drop us a line. Were the restaurants we recommended as described? Did you find a wonderful shop you'd like to share? If you have complaints, we'll look into them and revise our entries in the next edition when the facts warrant. So send us your feedback. Either e-mail us at editors@fodors.com (specifying *Fodor's CITYGUIDE New York* on the subject line), or write to the *Fodor's CITYGUIDE New York* editor at 280 Park Avenue, New York, New York 10017. We look forward to hearing from you.

Karen Cure

Karen Cure
Editorial Director

chapter 1

RESTAURANTS

New York has become the restaurant capital of the planet. No other city has New York's variety of cuisine, from ethnic and haute French to pan-Asian and New American. Downtown in particular has seen a veritable avalanche of restaurant openings, as old areas are renovated, lofts are fancifully redesigned, and discriminating diners move in. Loft locus Tribeca packs some of the city's finest restaurants. Chelsea, a fast-growing gallery center, and the Flatiron District have also become hot dining districts. SoHo continues to add venues to its stylish roster; you can find somewhere to dine in this area virtually around the clock. New eateries have begun to appear in the former meat-packing district in southwest Chelsea as restaurateurs keep coming up with new "next big things."

general information

NO SMOKING

Smoking is not allowed in most restaurants, though you may be permitted to smoke at the bar or at a table outside, if al fresco dining is available. Some restaurants have smoking/dining areas near the bar. Restaurants with fewer than 35 seats often have smoking areas, but if a nearby table requests that you refrain, refrain you must.

RESERVATIONS

It's not only common courtesy to make reservations at a restaurant—when you call you might discover that the restaurant is closed for a private party, or that the air conditioning is on the blink, or some other important consideration. Likewise, if you can't make it at your reserved time (give or take 20 minutes), or if you can't make it at all, definitely call the restaurant. Believe it or not, cumulative no-shows can seriously hurt a restaurant.

TIPPING

The rule of thumb for wait-service tips is at least 15% of the total (exclusive of tax), a figure easily calculated by doubling the amount of the 8¼% city sales tax. It's safe to say that New Yorkers tend to leave closer to 20%. Most restaurants add a service charge for large parties, so if you are dining with a group of six or more, be sure to check the bill carefully before leaving a tip.

PRICE CATEGORIES

Very Expensive ($$$$)	over $60
Expensive ($$$)	$40–$59
Moderate ($$)	$20–$39
Inexpensive ($)	under $20

*Price for a three-course dinner per person, minus drinks, service, and tax.

restaurants by cuisine

AFGHAN

9 f-3
PAMIR

A popular place for a quick, light dinner, Pamir serves dependable, budget-price, Afghan fare in an exotic setting. Locals like the large portions of succulent shish kebabs and other grilled meats and stews. *1065 1st Ave. (at 58th St.), Upper East Side, 212/644–9258. AE, D, DC, MC, V. Closed Mon. Subway: 59th St./Lexington Ave.* $

7 f-8
1437 2nd Ave. (at 75th St.), Upper East Side, 212/734–3791. Subway: 77th St. $

AMERICAN

4 7-c
AESOP'S TABLE

For Manhattanites phobic about crossing the water, this new restaurant near the ferry is a good choice for a first excursion to Staten Island. The garden has an excellent view of the skyline and the New American food is always enticing. *1233 Bay St. (at Maryland Ave.),*

Rosebank, Staten Island, 718/720–2005.
AE, D, MC, V. Closed Sun.–Mon. $$

9 *e-8*
ALVA

Alva is the ultimate neighborhood
restaurant, its cozy bar draped with reg-
ulars enjoying the perfect combination
of intimacy and excitement. But past the
bar lies a sophisticated dining room that
pays visual homage to its namesake,
Thomas Alva Edison, with dim, exposed
bulbs and black-and-white photographs.
The American bistro fare is quite deli-
cious, and it's a bargain considering the
location. For a great lunch: Dive inside
for the fabulous Cuban sandwich at the
bar. 36 E. 22nd St. (between Park Ave. S
and Broadway), Flatiron District, 212/228–
4399. AE, DC, MC, V. No lunch weekends.
Subway: 6 to 23rd St. $$

9 *e-6*
AN AMERICAN PLACE

On an unassuming Murray Hill side
street, celebrated chef Larry Forgione
wins raves for his artfully presented,
American-grown foodstuffs. The setting
is handsome and spacious, and the
wine selection (American only) is excellent. Enjoy barbecued mallard, Key West
shrimp with mustard sauce, chicken
breast sautéed with apple-cider vinegar,
three-smoked-fish terrine, or sweet-
potato ravioli. 2 Park Ave. (at 32nd St.),
Murray Hill, 212/684–2122. Reservations
essential. Jacket and tie. AE, DC, MC, V.
Closed Sun. No lunch Sat. Subway: 33rd
St.; 34th St./Herald Sq. $$$$

9 *d-3*
BEACON

Rainbow Room veteran Waldy Malouf
delves deeply into grilling at this luxurious, complex new space, filled with
loopy balconies and egalitarian see-and-
be-seen seating. House-baked breads
are perfection, and the special cocktails
will really clean your clock. Then tear
into some wood-roasted Malpeque oysters that will flood you with sumptuous
flavors. The main event is grilled meat,
fish, or game. To get in touch with your
inner Neanderthal, go for a 12- or 18-
ounce hunk of Argentinean ranch-
grazed rib-eye steak that gets precisely
the kind of grill crusting that it begs for.
Finish with one of the yowlingly tasty
soufflés. 25 W. 56th St. (between 5th and
6th Aves.), Midtown, 212/332–0500. AE,
MC, V. Subway: B, Q, N, R to 57th St. $$

10 *f-6*
BRIDGE CAFE

Nestled beneath the Brooklyn Bridge in
a wood-frame building from around
1800, this cozy and friendly former long-
shoremen's café is now a favorite with
Wall Street suits. Try soft-shell crabs in
season, grilled trout, red snapper with
vegetable risotto, and the excellent
pecan pie. 279 Water St. (at Dover St.),
Lower Manhattan, 212/227–3344. AE, DC,
MC, V. No lunch Sat. Brunch Sun. Sub-
way: Fulton St. $$

11 *d-7*
BUBBLE LOUNGE

And what a lounge it is! Quaff some
bubbly from the impressive champagne
list and find yourself flattered by the red
velvet curtains, brick walls, high ceilings,
comfortable couches, and other beautiful people. The food is secondary; have
some caviar or pâté, then go somewhere else for dinner. Reserve ahead
with a party of six or more. 228 W.
Broadway (between Franklin and White
Sts.), Tribeca, 212/421–3433. AE, DC, MC,
V. No lunch. Subway: Franklin St. $$

9 *e-8*
CANDELA

This former brick warehouse near Union
Square has been transformed into a sort
of baronial hall, with wrought-iron rail-
ings, huge, dark mirrors, lighted tapers,
and wooden booths. The menu is
broad-ranging—spicy focaccia, a three-
tier seafood platter, hummus, fried cala-
mari, chicken wontons, short ribs—the
bar is hopping, and the crowd is young.
116 E. 16th St. (between Irving Pl. and
Park Ave. S), Gramercy, 212/254–1600.
AE, MC, V. Brunch Sun. $$

11 *5e*
CANTEEN

A-list celebrities and hip downtowners
have discovered this basement space,
decorated in the color scheme of a '70s
rec-room with a chic post-modern aesthetic: think vast white walls, Tang-
orange chairs in space-age shapes, and
brown circular booths that look like
modular sofas. By contrast, the food is
traditional down-home American—macaroni and cheese, pork chops with buttermilk smashed potatoes, and lobster
and cod pan roast. Though most who
dine here dress like they can afford to
pay top dollar, prices are surprisingly

reasonable. *421 Mercer St. (at Prince St.), SoHo, 212/431–7676. AE, MC, V. Subway: Prince St. $$–$$$*

10 *e-5*

CITY HALL

You can't help but chuckle at the salad—an old-fashioned wedge of iceberg lettuce served with Russian dressing—but the real surprise will be how much you like it. She-crab soup, chilled seafood platters, Delmonico steak, broiled salmon, and grilled calf's liver are other well-executed dishes that hearken back to our city's dining past. Cub Room (*see below*) chef-owner Henry Meer has created a tasteful New York theme restaurant, complete with back-lit black and white photographs of old New York. Before you hit the dining room, with its impressive raw bar, hit the roomy and elegant bar area, where man-size drinks and delicious homemade potato chips will take the edge off the most wearying day. *131 Duane St. (between Church St. and W. Broadway), Tribeca, 212/227–7777. Reservations essential. AE, MC, V. Closed Sun. Subway: Chambers St. $$$*

11 *d-1*

CLEMENTINE

The bar in front is packed; the large, muted-gold dining room is bedecked with brown banquettes and sconces shaped like art deco portholes. The place is very much a scene, but the food is superior; chef John Schenk's cooking is bold, vigorous, and unusual. Consider squid stuffed with merguez sausage, couscous, and spicy tomato-cumin broth; fried green tomatoes with barbecued baby-back ribs; and pork loin rubbed with chiles. The terrific desserts include dark-chocolate crepes with tangerine sauce and strawberry-rhubarb pie with coconut sorbet. *1 5th Ave. (at 8th St.), Greenwich Village, 212/253–0003. AE, D, DC, MC, V. No lunch. Subway: 8th St. $$*

11 *d-4*

CUB ROOM

A constant, lively bar scene keeps this brick and wood restaurant packed. Make your way to the dining room, in back, for a quieter experience. The menu is far-reaching (sometimes a bit too far) but with some fine dishes, including tuna in a sesame-seed crust on soy-flavored Asian greens and pot roast with braised

red cabbage and spaetzle. *131 Sullivan St. (at Prince St.), SoHo, 212/677–4100. AE. No lunch Sat., Sun., or Mon. Brunch Sun. Subway: Spring St.; Prince St. $$$*

11 *d-8*

DUANE PARK CAFE

This sleek restaurant has a Japanese chef whose cooking synthesizes Italian, Japanese, Cajun, and Californian styles. Pasta is made on the premises. Try the grilled quail with homemade sausage, the roast leg of lamb with polenta, and the excellent sorbets. *157 Duane St. (between Hudson St. and W. Broadway), Tribeca, 212/732–5555. Reservations essential. AE, DC, MC, V. Closed Sun. No lunch Sat. Subway: Chambers St. $$$*

11 *h-1*

FIRST

With huge booths, low lights, professional service, and Sam DeMarco's internationally accented cuisine, First was at first too trendy (read: attitudinal) for words, but it has transcended its own hipness with aplomb. Open almost until dawn, it's truly a place to enjoy New York. Check out the creative martini selection, including one flavored with a rose-scent syrup and "tinis" (a little—or not so little—flask of top-shelf vodka tucked into an individual ice bucket and served with a miniature martini glass). Of course, you shouldn't neglect the food—try the Long Island duck marinated in soy honey, and especially the Sunday-night roast suckling pig and the deeply comforting warm chocolate pudding. *87 1st Ave. (between 5th and 6th Sts.), East Village, 212/674–3823. AE, MC, V. No lunch. Brunch Sun. Subway: 2nd Ave., Astor Pl. $$*

11 *f-3*

FIVE POINTS

There is a sophisticatedly organic feel to the decor at Five Points, which employs running water, lots of blond wood, pots of grass on the tables, and soft lighting. The American/Mediterranean menu serves up hearty dishes like seafood stew with grilled octopus, pan-roasted herb-stuffed chicken, and casserole of wood-oven baked lamb. Of note is the small wine list that emphasizes moderately priced bottles. *31 Great Jones St. (between Lafayette St. and Bowery), East Village, 212/253–5700. AE, MC, V. Closed Sun. No lunch. Subway: Bleecker St./Broadway–Lafayette St. $$*

`10` *e-1*

GOTHAM BAR & GRILL

After 15-plus years, this remains one of city's best restaurants, a testament to chef and owner Alfred Portale's many talents. The dining room is a multilevel postmodern brasserie with 17-ft ceilings, soft lighting, and cast-stone ledges that give the sense of a garden courtyard. Portale was the first to serve "architectural" food, and he still does it better than anyone else. Try the chilled seafood salad, the rack of lamb, and any of the desserts. *12 E. 12th St. (between 5th Ave. and University Pl.), Greenwich Village, 212/620–4020. Reservations essential. AE, DC, MC, V. No lunch weekends. Subway: 14th St./Union Sq. $$$$*

`9` *e-8*

GRAMERCY TAVERN

Opened by Danny (Union Square Café, *see below*) Meyer, this large and handsome restaurant encompasses three suave dining areas and a tavern room, which features a less expensive menu and a magnificent bar. Wooden beams, white walls, and country artifacts lend a rustic feel. The seasonal food, courtesy of brilliant chef Tom Colicchio, is deeply flavored and absolutely superb: exemplary tuna tartare with sea urchin and cucumber vinaigrette; lobster and artichoke salad; tender braised beef cheeks; roasted sea bass; a very fine cheese board. Desserts, care of pastry chef Claudia Fleming, are imaginatively spectacular: unforgettable coconut tapioca with passion fruit sorbet, and the best chocolate cookies you've ever tasted. *42 E. 20th St. (between Broadway and Park Ave. S), Gramercy, 212/477–0777. Reservations essential for dining room, not accepted for the less formal "tavern." AE, DC, MC, V. No lunch weekends. Subway: 6, N, R to 23rd St. $$$$*

`11` *b-3*

THE GRANGE HALL

American farm cooking is served here in a mostly minimalist setting (introduced by an Art Deco bar) in a quiet section of the West Village. Highlights are the good, hearty breakfasts, organic sandwiches, pork chops with apples, and lamb steak with rosemary. Desserts include coconut cake, pies, and cobblers. *50 Commerce St. (at Barrow St.), West Village, 212/924–5246. AE. Brunch weekends. Subway: W. 4th St./Washington Sq.; Christopher St./Sheridan Sq. $*

`10` *d-6*

THE GRILL ROOM

From its clubby, rather corporate perch (wood paneling, marble floors), this restaurant overlooks the yacht marina to New Jersey, the Statue of Liberty, and Ellis Island. Larry Forgione's old-style American cooking is superior: shrimp cocktail; smoked-salmon napoleon with caviar; meltingly tender lamb; and simple, exceptional simple fish. For dessert there is a fine cheesecake and a chocolate pudding. *2 World Financial Center, 225 Liberty St., 2nd floor, Lower Manhattan, 212/945–9400. Reservations essential. AE, DC, MC, V. Closed weekends. Subway: Cortlandt St./World Trade Center. $$$$*

`11` *c-2*

HOME

This tiny restaurant's storefront consists of secondhand books in a bay window. Inside, there is always a crowd, with some enjoying the year-round (heated) garden. Chef David Page makes good, seasonal country food: blue-cheese fondue with caramelized shallots, roast chicken with onion rings, excellent fish, and a fine chocolate pudding. *10 Cornelia St. (between Bleecker and W. 4th Sts.), West Village, 212/243–9579. No credit cards. Subway: W. 4th St./Washington Sq. $$*

`10` *d-6*

HUDSON RIVER CLUB

The Hudson River Club is one of the prettiest places to dine and imbibe in the Wall Street area. The dining rooms are posh but unpretentious, with views of the yacht marina, the Statue of Liberty, and Ellis Island. Feast on food and wine originating in the Hudson Valley. Sunday brunch is lovely. *4 World Financial Center, 250 Vesey St., 2nd floor, Lower Manhattan, 212/786–1500. Reservations essential. Jacket and tie. AE, MC, V. Brunch Sun. Subway: Cortlandt St./World Trade Center. $$$$*

`11` *d-7*

INDEPENDENT

Crowded and trendy, this bilevel bistro has a clubby, turn-of-the-20th-century feel. Downstairs there's a small bar and a row of candlelit tables (where you can smoke); upstairs, a larger dining room. The straightforward American menu includes fried calamari, pork ribs with applesauce, steak with fries, lamb stew with artichokes and thyme, and, for dessert, an excellent thin-crusted apple tart. *179 W. Broadway (between Worth and Leonard Sts.), SoHo, 212/219–2010. Reservations essential. AE, DC, MC, V. Subway: A, C, E to Canal St. $$*

10 *d-1*
INDIGO

This former carriage house in the West Village serves delicious food at budget prices. The eclectic menu includes Thai grilled-beef salad, chicken satay, roast cod with couscous, and pork loin glazed with tamarind; and there is a large, attractive zinc bar. *142 W. 10th St. (between Greenwich Ave. and Waverly Pl.), West Village, 212/691–7757. AE. No lunch. Subway: Christopher St./Sheridan Sq. $$*

9 *d-3*
JACK'S FIFTH

Tucked into one of the most deluxe locations in Manhattan, just across from the Plaza Hotel, newcomer Jack's Fifth features circular high-back booths that afford a rare degree of privacy. Chef Herb Wilson has created a contemporary American menu with some very becoming and extravagant touches. A huge wedge of hazelnut-crusted seared foie gras is served in a figgy engulfment with utterly voluptuous results. Diver sea scallops a full 2 inches in diameter are carefully seared and thoughtfully sauced in a slightly spicy red-pepper coulis. Heather Carlucci's desserts include a luscious lemon meringue parfait sided by a rich coconut sorbet and succulent guava granita. This is a kitchen—and a restaurant—singing with flavors and fresh ideas. *8 W. 58th St. (near 5th Ave.), Midtown, 212/750–7474. AE, MC, V. Subway: N, R to 5th Ave. $$*

11 *e-4*
JERRY'S

This SoHo fixture is busy from breakfast through late night. The downtown decor features zebra prints, tile floors, and red-leather banquettes; daily specials are chalked on a blackboard. The convivial bar is a good meeting place. Try the blackened tuna with orzo or the lamb paillard with fried baby artichokes. Desserts are homey and satisfying. *101 Prince St. (between Greene and Mercer Sts.), SoHo, 212/966–9464. AE, MC, V. No dinner Sun. Subway: Prince St.; Spring St.; Bleecker St.; Broadway–Lafayette St. $$*

7 *f-7*
KINGS' CARRIAGE HOUSE

A perfect spot for a rainy night, this comfortable restaurant inhabits a beautifully restored brownstone on a quiet, tree-lined street. The two dining rooms are on separate floors and have different furnishings, both including hand-painted walls and antique tables and chairs. The food is as warm and comforting as the manor-house atmosphere: roasted venison is served with homemade fruit chutney, and wild Alaskan salmon comes perfumed with native herbs. *251 E. 82nd St. (between 2nd and 3rd Aves.), Upper East Side, 212/734–5490. AE, DC, MC, V. Closed Sun. Subway: 4, 5, 6 to 86th St. $$*

11 *d-6*
LUCKY STRIKE

A late-night haunt of models and artists, this crowded bistro is adorned with faded silver mirrors with the menu and wine list scrawled on them. Try a hamburger with fries, fried calamari, roast chicken, or steak. *59 Grand St. (at Wooster St.), SoHo, 212/941–0479. AE, MC, V. Subway: A, C, E to Canal St. $$*

9 *f-4*
MARTELL GRILL

Inspired chef Neal Myers has brought the best of his signature dishes from Tatou, Ben Benson's, and Tupelo Grill to this East Sider, and kept the prices as friendly as he is. In a lively Old New York bar setting, feast on seven-onion soup engulfed by a swatch of tender puff pastry; simply the best nachos in town, featuring authentic LBJ-ranch chili; perfectly grilled hanger steak; a moist, tender hunk of cod anointed with truffle butter, all on a bed of chivey whipped potatoes; and—oh, why not?—Snickers pie for dessert. *948 1st Ave. (between 50th and 51st Sts.), Midtown, 212/207–6600. AE, MC, V. Subway: 51st St./Lexington–3rd Aves. $$*

9 *d-8*
MESA GRILL

Terrific Southwestern in New York City? Superstar chef, "grillin' and chillin' " Bobby Flay, at the peak of his form, serves up his highly stylized, delightfully spicy fare at this Flatiron District destination. The brash award-winning design offers an amusing counterpoint to the imaginative cooking. Try El Tesoro Reposado tequila in your margarita, then tuck into the intense chipotle- and hoisin-dappled duck confit blue-corn tortilla. Follow with pan-roasted rabbit loin medallions, enrobed by a pineapple–red chile vinaigrette. Wayne Harley Brachman's desserts—caramelized bananas Foster with butter-pecan ice cream is one option—are fanciful. Brunch is scrumptious. During peak hours, the restaurant can get quite loud. If you shun din, ask to be seated upstairs. *102 5th Ave. (between 15th and 16th Sts.), Flatiron District, 212/807–7400. Reservations essential. Brunch Sun. AE, MC, V. Subway: 14th St./Union Sq. $$$*

9 C-2
O'NEALS'
Featuring the most reasonably priced food near Lincoln Center, O'Neals' is also very child-friendly. The restaurant stays open every night until at least midnight (or "until the fat lady sings" at the Metropolitan Opera House just across Broadway).The menu offers something for pretty much everyone, from French onion soup or crab cakes to burgers or veal Milanese. A three-course pre-theater dinner (served from 4:30 to 8) is offered for $25.95. *49 W. 64th St. (near Broadway), Upper West Side, 212/787–4663. AE, MC, V. Subway: 66th St., Lincoln Center. $$*

9 e-4
OSCAR'S
Poised on the northeast corner of the venerable Waldorf–Astoria, Oscar's has joined in the hotel's multi-million-dollar renovation. Named for New York's most legendary maitre d', Oscar Tschirky (who invented lobster Newburg, veal Oscar, and Waldorf Salad), the gently priced menu was devised with his original cookbook as inspiration. Oscar salad is an enormous tower of stingingly fresh greens hugged by plentiful slender slices of pink grilled veal, lightly dressed with a fragrant tarragon cream. A few pudgy crab cakes and blanched asparagus ribbons complete the dish. Custardy chicken potpie is exemplary in its tawny, egg-brushed crust. Rice pudding is appropriately sumptuous. *E. 50th St. at Lexington Ave., Midtown, 212/879–4920. AE, MC, V. Subway: 51st St./Lexington–3rd Aves. $$*

11 a-1
PARIS COMMUNE
Try and score a seat by the small fireplace to experience the full effect of this neighborhood spot. Even if you're not near the fireplace the whole dining room is pleasant, with worn wood floors, ceiling fans, and gilt-framed mirrors for decor. There is a selection of basic pasta dishes, appetizers, and comfort food such as meatloaf, as well several more creative dishes such as skate with blood orange, ginger, and Champagne reduction. *411 Bleecker St. (between Bank and W. 11th Sts.), West Village, 212/929–0509. AE, MC, V. No lunch weekdays. Subway: A, C, E to 14th St.; L to 8th Ave. $$*

9 d-1
PARK VIEW AT THE BOATHOUSE
On a wide boardwalk along the northeastern rim of the lake in Central Park, the Boathouse is a glorious and restful setting for dining in benevolent weather. (In cold weather, the restaurant is taken indoors, where the atmosphere is invitingly ski-lodge-ish.) This magical refuge recently acquired one of New York's hottest young chefs, John Villa, and his cooking is *just* fancy enough for this special place. Pork tenderloin is seldom given such a robust treatment: It's hoisin-crusted, perfectly roasted, and partnered with a kafir lime and rice cake that's topped by a seared giant sea scallop. Finish with, say, a pineapple "carpaccio" with guava sherbet. Try to time your evening meal so that you can catch the sunset. As the shadows lengthen, a limpid Maxfield Parrish radiance sets in. *Central Park (enter at E. 72nd St. and bear right on Park Dr. N), Upper East Side, 212/517–2233. Reservations essential. AE, MC, V. Subway: 68th St./Hunter College. $$*

11 a-1
THE PLACE
You may think this restaurant has an odd name until you settle into the cozy dining room and make it your own. A large part of the appeal is that they treat you like it's your place. The food is in line with the atmosphere: homey, American cooking with a little bit of spice and a lot of potatoes. Such creative dishes as white gazpacho and asparagus and rock shrimp risotto are excellent. *310 W. 4th St., between Bank and W. 12th Sts., West Village, 212/924–2711. No credit cards. No lunch. Subway: Christopher St./Sheridan Sq. $$*

11 *d-4*

QUILTY'S

A sleek, off-white storefront named after the character in Nabokov's *Lolita*, Quilty's is decorated with butterflies in framed display cases and has, of all things, a New England look. The elegant American cooking has Mediterranean and Asian accents: grilled octopus, gulf shrimp and shiitake mushrooms, glazed grilled salmon with roast-beet salad, sirloin in balsamic vinegar sauce. *177 Prince St. (between Sullivan and Thompson Sts.), SoHo, 212/254–1260. AE, DC, MC, V. Brunch Sun. Subway: Spring St. $$$*

9 *b-5*

RACHEL'S AMERICAN BISTRO

Theater-goers and locals alike are charmed by Rachel's soothing space, pressed-tin ceiling, and homey decor of the old-mirrors-and-dried-flowers variety. Quarters may be a bit cramped, but service is stellar—friendly and professional—and high-quality ingredients elevate a menu of simply prepared New American dishes. Best of all you'll find it very, very light on your wallet. *608 9th Ave. (between 43rd and 44th Sts.), Hell's Kitchen, 212/957–9050. AE, MC, V. Subway: A, C, E to 42nd St. $–$$*

9 *c-3*

REDEYE GRILL

If America is about size and crowds and money and choice and abundance, then the Redeye Grill is a quintessentially American restaurant. The place is always packed, and the menu offers a little of everything, with an emphasis on seafood: lobster in salad, in potpie, and grilled; salmon cured like pastrami, smoked, and grilled; sturgeon, sable, pasta, steak, and burgers. It's no wonder the crowd is diverse. Desserts such as banana-cream pie and chocolate mousse are deliciously rendered classics. Nothing's really great, except maybe the whole idea; but nothing really disappoints, either. *890 7th Ave., at 56th St., Midtown, 212/541–9000. Reservations essential. AE, D, DC, MC, V. Subway: 57th St. $$$*

11 *f-4*

RIALTO

Rialto—with its shabby-chic dining room, pressed tin walls, simple wooden chairs, burgundy banquettes, and back garden—is almost the perfect neighborhood restaurant. The New American menu delivers interesting, but not overly exotic offerings, such as grilled tuna with Asian spiced fries, roasted garlic soup, and a superlative hamburger. The main detracting feature is the difficulty it takes to secure a table, but the wooden bar is a great place to hang out while waiting. *26 Elizabeth St. (between Houston and Prince Sts.), SoHo, 212/334–7900. AE, MC, V. Subway: 6 to Spring St. $$*

9 *d-3*

SALT

This relatively new, resplendently tasteful SoHo-esque bar and restaurant with clean, inviting lines and a very friendly staff offers state-of-the-art American cuisine with wide-ranging, often spicy, complex flavors. Chef/owner Patrick Adams makes a spectacular salmon tartare, luscious calamari rings with a soy-tamarind dipping sauce, perfect hanger steak frites, and quite lavish desserts. There's an especially good wine list, but whatever you do, don't miss the chocolate martinis! *507 Columbus Ave. (between 84th and 85th Sts.) Upper West Side, 212/875–1993. AE, MC, V. Subway: B, C to 86th St. $$*

11 *e-4*

SAVOY

Peter Hoffman's cooking has come into its own. Here it's served on two floors of an 1830s redbrick building, with working fireplaces, exposed-brick walls, and a cozy upstairs room (with bar) where you can savor a prix-fixe meal cooked by Hoffman himself Tuesday–Saturday. Try the smoked skate with capers and fries, sea scallops in Riesling sauce, or venison with black beans and swiss chard. *70 Prince St. (at Crosby St.), SoHo, 212/219–8570. Reservations required. AE, DC, MC, V. Closed Sun. No lunch Mon. Subway: Prince St.; 6 to Spring St.; Broadway–Lafayette St. $$$$*

10 *d-4*

SCREENING ROOM

There's a commercial movie theater attached to this New American restaurant with a film theme, and there are even screening rooms available to rent. The idea was to create a multi-purpose space that would celebrate independent filmmaking and fine food at the same time. The movies and food are, for all intents and purposes, separate, except for the great dinner-and-a-movie bargain for $30, and the fact that lots of employees of nearby Miramax can often be found dining or having drinks at the long and elegant bar. *54 Varick St. (between Canal and Laight St.), Tribeca, 212/334–2100. AE, D, DC, MC, V. Closed Sat. No lunch Mon. Subway: A, C, E to Canal St. $$*

.11. g-2

SIN SIN

Effortlessly sleek, copper-toned, and very up-to-the-minute, this comely new-comer with a light Irish accent offers really and truly succulent "global American" food at friendly prices. The upstairs Leopard Lounge has swank to spare. All this, combined with the fact that full dinners are served until until 4 AM, makes Sin Sin an important new East Village destination. *248 E. 5th St. (at 2nd Ave.), East Village, 212/253–2222. AE, MC, V. Subway: 2nd Ave., Astor Pl. $$*

11 e-4

SOHO KITCHEN & BAR

This cavernous SoHo wine bar boasts a 60-ft-long bar and a long run of popularity, now drawing its share of tourists as well as locals. The city's largest Cruvinet dispenses over 120 choice wines by the glass, including champagnes. Nibbles include pizzas, pasta, salads, and burgers, all available at the bar or at tables. Along for the ride? Draft beer and ales are also available. *103 Greene St. (between Prince and Spring Sts.), SoHo, 212/925–1866. Reservations not accepted. AE, DC, MC, V. Subway: Prince St. $$*

11. h-4

TORCH

All the tables at this scaled down supper club overlook a stage where excellent singers and musicians perform jazz standards on a nightly basis. Selections from the tiny raw bar will always enhance the mood, and while the food is not exceptional it is good enough, especially when the scene is so electric. *137 Ludlow St. (between Rivington and Stanton Sts.), Lower East Side, 212/228–5151. AE, DC, MC, V. No lunch. Subway: Delancey St. $$$*

11. c-7

TRIBECA GRILL

The flagship venture of the Robert DeNiro–Drew Nieporent partnership, this converted Tribeca warehouse has a consistently charged atmosphere, both at the well-spaced tables and at the

exquisite bar in the middle of the dining room. Chef Don Pintabona serves classic American grill food with creative international accents, such as lamb paillard with Israeli couscous or seared tuna with sesame noodles. The wonderful banana tart with chocolate-malt ice cream is a must. *375 Greenwich St. (at Franklin St.), Tribeca, 212/941–3900. AE, DC, MC, V. No lunch weekends. Brunch Sun. Subway: Franklin St. $$$*

9 e-8

UNION SQUARE CAFE

One of the city's very favorite restaurants, this Flatiron District phenom has three dining areas and a long, lively bar where you can also dine. Michael Romano's cooking, with California/Italian overtones, is superb. Have the black-bean soup with a shot of Austrian sherry; fried calamari with anchovy mayonnaise; marinated "filet mignon" of tuna; addictive hot garlic potato chips; smoked black-angus shell steak with mashed potatoes and frizzled leeks; and perhaps banana tart with caramel and macadamia nuts. The restaurant set a new standard for impeccable service. *21 E. 16th St. (off Union Sq. W), Flatiron District, 212/243–4020. Reservations essential. AE, DC, MC, V. No lunch Sun. Subway: 14th St./Union Sq. $$$$*

9 e-8

VERBENA

Refined and romantic, Verbena complements its large, enchanting garden with subtle and seasonal cooking by chef and owner Diane Forley. Try her foie gras with salsify, prunes, and pearl onions; homey roast chicken with celery root and wild rice; and crème brûlée scented with verbena. Desserts are especially wonderful, so save room. *54 Irving Pl. (at 17th St.), Gramercy, 212/260–5454. AE, DC, MC, V. Brunch weekends. Subway: 14th St./Union Sq. $$$*

9 c-1

VINCE & EDDIE'S

Not many restaurants in Manhattan offer a country environment, but sitting among the gingham curtains, exposed brick, and plank floor of this quiet American bistro is truly transporting. Hearty fare such as roasted chicken, veal shank, and mashed potatoes is the perfect antidote to chilly New York winters. The whole package is terrific before or after a Lincoln Center event. *70 W. 68th St.*

(between Columbus Ave. and Central Park W), Upper West Side, 212/721–0068. Reservations essential. AE, DC, MC, V. Brunch Sun. Subway: 66th St./Lincoln Center. $$

10 e-7

WALL STREET KITCHEN & BAR

Want to hang out with investment bankers? Look no further. Although there is an excellent wines-by-the-glass list—many of which can be ordered by tasting "flights"—this place often feels more like a frat party than a destination for serious oenophiles. Most don't go for dinner but there is a full menu that leans toward upscale bar food. The soaring space, formerly a bank, is divided into several smaller areas. 70 Broad St. (at Beaver St.), Lower Manhattan, 212/797–7070. AE, D, DC, MC, V. Closed weekends. Subway: Bowling Green. $$

3 c-5

WATER'S EDGE

Who would ever guess that the barren, industrial stretch of waterfront in Long Island City is home to a restaurant as lovely as the Water's Edge? The view of the twinkling Manhattan skyline across the East River at night is breathtaking, and the well executed American menu does an admirable job of trying to compete with the scenery. Service is attentive and caters to those visiting for a special occasion. A free water taxi transports guests between the restaurant and Manhattan. 44th Dr. between the East River and Vernon Blvd., Long Island City, Queens, 718/482–0033. Reservations essential. AE, DC, MC, V. Subway: 23rd St./Ely Ave. $$$

10 d-6

WILD BLUE

This tiny space on the 107th floor of the World Trade Center—it once housed Cellar in the Sky—has been transformed into a casual eatery with a straightforward steakhouse-style menu, a superb wine list, and an absolutely breathtaking view. Simple entrées such as grilled Atlantic halibut or char-broiled New York strip steak appear perfectly cooked but side dishes are disappointing. Despite occasional culinary missteps the view combined with exceptional service will guarantee a good time. 1 World Trade Center, Lower Manhattan, 212/524–7107. Reservations essential. AE, DC, MC, V. Subway: Cortlandt St., World Trade Center. $$$

10 c-1

YE WAVERLY INN

This 150-year-old Greenwich Village town house has been a restaurant since 1920, always retaining its Colonial-tavern feel. The food matches the ambience: simple and comfortable. Look for passable pot-pies, Southern fried chicken, and other traditional American dishes. In summer there's a pleasant back garden; in winter, two working fireplaces. 16 Bank St. (at Waverly Pl.), West Village, 212/929–4377. AE, DC, MC, V. Brunch weekends. Subway: Christopher St./Sheridan Sq. $

11 e-4

ZOË

Zoë is a big, very noisy, very SoHo restaurant with an open grill in the back and a long bar up front. Many dishes are wood-grilled or cooked on the rotisserie. Try the salmon tartare with mango-chile salsa, grilled tuna with wok-charred vegetables, grilled buffalo sirloin with garlic-potato cake. 90 Prince St. (between Mercer St. and Broadway), SoHo, 212/966–6722. AE, DC, MC, V. No lunch Mon. Brunch weekends. Subway: Prince St.; Spring St.; Bleecker St./Broadway–Lafayette St. $$

AMERICAN CASUAL

11 d-3

AGGIE'S

This updated luncheonette is a great place for a casual, downtown breakfast or brunch—if you can also handle the wait. Expect hearty and wholesome home cooking and great coffee. 146 W. Houston St. (at MacDougal St.), SoHo, 212/673–8994. No credit cards. Subway: Christopher St./Sheridan Sq. $

11 f-2

B-BAR

American food and lots of models are the story of the B Bar, in a former gas station with a velvet rope at the door. Opt for a simple burger or more complex fish and pasta dishes. The scene starts late. A particularly inviting and spacious outdoor dining area is available in gentle weather. 40 E. 4th St. (between Lafayette St. and Bowery), East Village, 212/475–2220. AE, MC, V. Brunch weekends. Subway: Bleecker St., Broadway–Lafayette St., Astor Pl. $$

9 *f-3*

BILLY'S

In business since 1870, this East Side institution is cherished by the Sutton Place crowd, who enjoy it as a refuge from their more serious dining locales. The old tavern serves steaks and other pub fare from a blackboard menu, and beers and stout on tap. *948 1st Ave. (between 52nd and 53rd Sts.), Midtown, 212/355–8920. Reservations not accepted. AE, DC, MC, V. Subway: 51st St./Lexington–3rd Aves. $$*

10 *e-5*

BODEGA

There's a full bar at this relaxed, diner-style (plastic banquettes and Formica tables) eatery that has become a Tribeca favorite. It's open all day and the menu doesn't change much from lunch to dinner; there's a grilled prime rib sandwich with zesty horseradish mayo, a black-bean quesadilla, fried calamari, tortilla soup, and an all-day omelet. *136 W. Broadway (between Thomas and Duane Sts.), Tribeca, 212/285–1155. AE, MC, V. Subway: Chambers St. $*

9 *c-3*

BROADWAY DINER

These diners don't offer much in ambience or cuisine, but they're good and reliable when you want a fast and inexpensive bite. The typical menu (with a few innovations thrown in) features everything from chef salads to grilled fish. Breakfast and brunch are packed on weekends, and lunch can be chaotic midweek. Service is nothing to write home about, but your coffee cup is always refilled. *1726 Broadway (at 55th St.), Midtown, 212/765–0909. Reservations not accepted. AE, DC, MC, V. Subway: 59th St./Columbus Circle. $*

9 *e-3*

590 Lexington Ave. (at 52nd St.), Midtown, 212/486–8838. Subway: 51st St./Lexington–3rd Aves.

9 *c-3*

BROOKLYN DINER USA

Though less authentic than the name would suggest—at what diner in Brooklyn would your eggs be served with crispy polenta fries instead of potatoes?—this quasi-theme restaurant delivers decent food and good value. Though the large portions of American standbys such as burgers and hot dogs

make it difficult, try to save room for one of New York's best sundaes. *212 W. 57th St. (between Broadway and 7th Ave.), Theater District, 212/581–8900. Reservations not accepted. AE, DC, MC, V. Subway: N, R to 57th St.; 1, 9, A, B, C, D to 59th St./Columbus Circle. $$*

10 *d-5*

BUBBY'S

Always the most popular neighborhood brunch spot, these days crowds from all over the city line up on weekends, clamoring for coffee and fresh squeezed juice. The dining room is homey and comfortable with attractive furnishings and plate-glass windows. Brunch favorites include grits, homemade granola, or entrées like sour cream pancakes and smoked trout with scrambled eggs. Eclectic comfort food such as macaroni and cheese, fusilli with wild mushrooms, or shepherd's pie make up the lunch and dinner menus. All of the homemade pies rock. But even though the restaurant expanded recently, you'll still usually suffer an interminable wait. *120 Hudson St. (at N. Moore St.), Tribeca, 212/219–0666. AE, DC, MC, V. Brunch weekends. Subway: Franklin St. $$*

9 *c-8*

CAFETERIA

"Highly stylized" and "hopelessly hip" may well describe both the decor and clientele here; the food, however, is anything but. Stellar breakfasts—silver dollar pancakes with berries and whipped cream, ham steak with cheese grits and red-eye gravy—are served all day, and excellent lunch and dinner entrées tend toward the homey with such flourishes as rosemary-roasted apples served with the smoked pork chops and spicy fried oysters topping Caesar salad. Don't expect to find any ladies in hair nets at this cafeteria; service is of the restaurant variety, with just a touch more attitude than usual. *119 7th Ave. (at 17th St.), Chelsea, 212/414–1717. Reservations essential. AE, DC, MC, V. Subway: A, C, E to 14th St.; L to 8th Ave.; 1, 9 to 18th St. $–$$*

9 *b-7*

CHELSEA COMMONS

The small garden patio in back is a real find in good weather; it might even elevate the burger-and-beer dining to a romantic experience. Inside can be described as a neighborhood pub, and you won't be quite as charmed if you have to eat at one of the rickety tables here. Still, the competently prepared menu of standbys like nachos, fish-and-chips, and pork chops is better than you might expect; the staff and crowd are super friendly; and there's a decent jukebox. *242 10th Ave. (at 24th St.), Chelsea, 212/929–9424. AE, D, DC, MC, V. Subway: C, E to 23rd St.* $

10 *c-1*

CORNER BISTRO

You won't understand why you've come to eat at this dark, neighborhood bar until you taste a Bistro Burger. With or without bacon and cheese, the burger's juices drip down your chin and the flavor can't be beat. The thin-cut fries aren't bad, either. That everything is served on paper plates is almost endearing. Why it's called a bistro you'll probably never know. *331 W. 4th St. (at Jane St.), West Village, 212/242–9502. No*

BAR DINING

Dining at the bar of a restaurant has a strong appeal for many. It's often less expensive, more on-the-go, and sometimes features entirely different dishes that are more maneuverable for those perched on a stool.

Alva (American)
  The scrumptious Cuban sandwich is served only at the bar.

Bolivar (Latin)
  Several of the superb dishes here seemed designed for bar consumption.

Gramercy Tavern (American)
  The tavern menu is completely different from the dining room's, benevolently priced and less formal.

Gotham Bar & Grill (American)
  Many diners prefer the beautiful bar here: It's much more expedient.

Lobster Club (Contemporary)
  The perfect place to devour the sumptuous lobster club sandwich is at the bar.

Tabla (Indian)
  The Indian/American "bread bar" menu is utterly delightful.

Union Square Café (American)
  This highly beloved restaurant is famous in part for its superb bar menu.

---

credit cards. Subway: A, C, E to 14th St.; L to 8th Ave. $

12 *g-7*

DIZZY'S

The soi-disant "finer diner," Dizzy's is hands-down the top neighborhood joint for a casual meal in the Slope. The food is more than a step above diner grub—salads are generous; seasoned fries crispy; and sandwiches on delectable thick-sliced bread. If you're not up for a full prix-fixe brunch on weekend mornings (and you're ready to forego the pre-brunch muffin basket), grab a stool at the counter, where you can order off the well-priced breakfast and lunch menus. Whatever you do, come early. *511 9th St. (at 8th Ave.), Park Slope, Brooklyn, 718/499–1966. No credit cards. Brunch weekends. Subway: F to 7th Ave.* $

7 *b-7*

EJ'S LUNCHEONETTE

The decor invokes the 1950s, when cherry pie and egg creams were the thing, and it somehow persuades crowds to forget their current dietary habits and order enormous omelets or waffles slathered with butter and layered with pecans. The menu has a large selection of retro diner items, from root beer on tap to Salisbury steak and macaroni-and-cheese; but there are some concessions to post-1960 cuisine, such as the balsamic vinaigrette that dresses the Cobb salad or the grilled vegetable sandwich on seven-grain bread. Steer clear of weekend brunch hours unless you can get there by 10 AM or don't mind waiting at least 45 minutes. *447 Amsterdam Ave. (between 81st and 82nd Sts.), Upper West Side, 212/873–3444. Reservations not accepted. No credit cards. Breakfast daily. Subway: 1, 9 to 86th St.* $

9 *e-1*

1271 3rd Ave. (at 73rd St.), Upper East Side, 212/472–0600. Subway: 77th St.

11 *d-1*

432 6th Ave. (between 9th and 10th Sts.), Greenwich Village, 212/473–5555. Subway: W. 4th St./Washington Sq.

9 *b-8*

EMPIRE DINER

This 24-hour Art Deco diner is a magnet for après-club late-night snacks. Ever stylish, it was here long before Chelsea became trendy. The menu is pricey for diner fare, but the food is generally good. There's live piano music all week, and you can sit outdoors in summer, albeit overlooking somewhat grubby Tenth Avenue. *210 10th Ave. (at 22nd St.), Chelsea, 212/243–2736. Reservations not accepted. AE, MC, V. Subway: C, E to 23rd St. $*

11 *e-5*
FANELLI
Housed in a building that was erected in 1857, when the area was more known for upscale brothels than European designer boutiques, it is one of the oldest bar-restaurants in the city, and a refreshing change from the mostly pretentious SoHo environs. The menu is fine and serviceable, with sandwiches, omelets, and pasta dishes at reasonable prices. And the gorgeously timeworn original bar serves good draft beer to the clamoring customers who are sick of shopping for overpriced clothes. *94 Prince St. (at Mercer St.), SoHo, 212/226–9412. AE, MC, V. Subway: Prince St. $*

11 *f-2*
GREAT JONES CAFE
Pop into this crowded, down-home Bowery spot for flavorful burgers, chili, red- or bluefish fillets, and the house drink—a jalapeño martini. To top it all off, the jukebox still works. The noise is deafening, but the crowd doesn't seem to mind. *54 Great Jones St. (between Bowery and Lafayette St.), East Village, 212/674–9304. No credit cards. Subway: 8th St.; Astor Pl. $*

9 *b-1*
IT'S A WRAP
Though some strongly feel that the "wrap" sandwich craze has fully run its course, sandwich emporiums are popping up across the country. It's a Wrap is one of the few places (along with the burgeoning Cosí chain) where they actually make their own bread. As opposed to the many wraps about town that resemble glorified burritos, these resemble an Indian naan: chewy flatbread is wrapped around new and classic hot and cold fillings, including curried lentils, turkey and bacon, and roasted lamb. A fresh juice bar and homey desserts such as Rice Krispie marshmallow treats complete the satisfying experience. *2012 Broadway (between 68th and 69th Sts.), Upper West Side, 212/362–7922. Reservations not accepted. No credit cards. Subway: 66th St./Lincoln Center. $*

7 *f-8*
J. G. MELON
J. G. Melon's bar burger has long been called the best on the Upper East Side. Locals love to hang out and sample the large beer selection while digging into a no-frills burger and a bowl of waffle-cut fries. Red-and-white check tablecloths and sports on the TV complete the aesthetic. *1291 3rd Ave. (at 74th St.), Upper East Side, 212/744–0585. Brunch Sun. Subway: 77th St. $*

12 *d-3*
JUNIOR'S
This famous restaurant is most known for its New York–style cheesecake, but the huge menu also has the Jewish specialties that originally made the restaurant famous—corned beef, pastrami, chopped liver, and other sandwiches served on fresh-baked club rye—as well as some soul food offerings and complete dinners. The rugelach aren't bad either. Sure you can find better food and better service, but some kind of irreplaceable nostalgia makes a meal at Junior's a worthwhile experience. *386 Flatbush Ave. ext. (at DeKalb Ave.), Downtown Brooklyn, 718/852–5257. AE, DC, MC, V. Subway: DeKalb Ave. $*

10 *d-6*
KITCHENETTE
Small and comfortable, this popular downtown hangout serves comfort food to match the atmosphere. Weekend brunch is particularly popular, with oversize stacks of pancakes, French toast, good coffee, and other necessities. Don't miss the well-priced dinner specials, like meatloaf and roasted chicken. Although the no-frills decor and slow service are too much for some diners to take, for others they just add to the experience. *80 W. Broadway (at Warren St.), Tribeca, 212/267–6740. AE. Brunch weekends. Subway: Chambers St. $*

9 *b-6*
MARKET CAFÉ
It's hard to say enough about the superb American bistro-style food that the Market Café seems to offer up effortlessly. Salads, simple entrées, and home-style baked desserts are prepared with finesse and fabulously fresh ingredients, and the burger is a contender for best in New York. Add to that a charmingly retro decor and friendly staff and you'd have a winner anywhere, but it's

particularly appreciated in the wasteland near the Javits Convention Center. *496 9th Ave. (between 37th and 38th Sts.), Hell's Kitchen, 212/967–3892. Reservations essential. AE, D, DC, MC, V. Subway: A, C, E to 42nd St. $–$$*

---

7 *b-8*

MISS ELLE'S HOMESICK BAR AND GRILL

Even more comfortable than home, this tumbling space that ends in a huge greenhouse room offers up huge portions of comfort food that will indeed make you pleasantly homesick. Don't miss the spectacular pork chops and succulent chicken breast *Française*. And leave plenty of room for the supple banana cream pie. An especially luscious Sunday brunch is served here. *226 W. 79th St. (between Amsterdam Ave. and Broadway), Upper West Side, 212/595–4350. AE, MC, V. Subway: 79th St. $*

---

9 *d-3*

OAK ROOM AND BAR

This traditional wood-paneled restaurant and bar in the famed Plaza is still one of the classiest spots in town for a drink. Order light fare from the bar menu, or sit inside the restaurant for some heartier American food. If you aren't wearing a jacket and tie, you can order from the Oak Room menu and be served in the bar. *Plaza Hotel, 768 5th Ave. (at 59th St.), Midtown, 212/546–5330. AE, DC, MC, V. Subway: 5th Ave./60th St. $$*

---

9 *f-3*

P. J. CLARKE'S

P. J. Clarke's is the classic Old New York saloon. At lunch and happy hour, Midtown men pack the extremely popular front room for a beer, a burger, or both. If you're more interested in eating than socializing, elbow your way to the dark and atmospheric dining room in the back. Best bites include the burgers, home fries, chili, cold poached salmon, and spinach salad. *915 3rd Ave. (at 55th St.), Midtown, 212/759–1650. AE, DC, MC, V. Open until 4 AM. Subway: 59th St./Lexington Ave. $*

---

9 *e-8*

PETE'S TAVERN

O. Henry, who lived across the street, penned "The Gift of the Magi" in this 1864 tavern. The original bar is quite popular, as is the sunny sidewalk café in summer. The menu mixes old-fashioned Italian food with hefty burgers and Reubens. *129 E. 18th St. (at Irving Pl.), Gramercy, 212/473–7676. AE, DC, MC, V. Subway: 14th St./Union Sq. $*

---

7 *b-7*

POPOVER CAFÉ

The weekend lines outside this Upper West Side brunch spot remind you that the local demand for comfort food far exceeds the supply. Wonderful omelets, cheese grits, creative pancakes, and, of course, warm popovers with strawberry butter attract families and friends toting the Sunday *Times*. More lunchlike options are sandwiches, hearty burgers, and tasty salads. *551 Amsterdam Ave. (at 87th St.), Upper West Side, 212/595–8555. Reservations not accepted. AE, MC, V. Subway: 1, 9 to 86th St. $*

---

9 *b-3*

ROUTE 66 CAFÉ

If you still think "glorified diner" is a pejorative, give Route 66 a try. True, the decor gives only a half-hearted nod to the restaurant's eponymous roadway, and service could be better, but with comfortable seating and reasonable prices the complaints are few. The real draw is a menu of huge and well-prepared salads, burgers, pastas, and sandwiches; the juice bar is a plus if you prefer a vitamin-induced boost to a caffeine buzz. Neighborhood residents find take-out a palatable option when waits (particularly at brunch) are long. *858 9th Ave. (between 55th and 56th Sts.), Hell's Kitchen, 212/977–7600. AE, D, DC, MC, V. Brunch weekends. Reservations not accepted. Subway: 59th St./Columbus Circle. $*

---

7 *e-6*

SARABETH'S

Sarabeth's is still considered *the* place for brunch on the East Side, so the wait can be torture. But if you get there early, you'll enjoy an elegant country breakfast à la Martha Stewart. Omelets, homemade muffins, potato and cheese blintzes, pancakes with fresh fruit, pumpkin waffles, and other tempting home-style entrées are served all day, every day. Wonderful marmalades, Linzer tortes, and shortbreads are available for takeout. *1295 Madison Ave. (between 92nd and 93rd Sts.), Upper East Side, 212/410–7335. AE, DC, MC, V. Breakfast daily. Subway: 6 to 96th St. $*

7 *e-8*

Whitney Museum of American Art, 945 Madison Ave. (at 75th St.), Upper East Side, 212/570–3670. Closed Mon. Subway: 77th St.

7 *b-7*

423 Amsterdam Ave. (between 80th and 81st Sts.), Upper West Side, 212/496–6280. Subway: 79th St.

9 *f-2*

SERENDIPITY 3

For over 35 years this combo ice cream parlor/gift shop has been an inviting spot for lunch, brunch, and late-night snacks. Standing favorites on the child-friendly menu include a wide range of burgers, foot-long hot dogs (with or without chili), French toast, omelets, ice cream, and Serendipity's signature dish, frozen hot chocolate. Lines can be long, but you can divert yourself during the wait by playing with the tchotchkes and novelties for sale. Decor falls into the "whimsical" category, with antiques, flashes of pink, Tiffany lamps, and a general sense of bells and whistles. 225 E. 60th St. (between 2nd and 3rd Aves.), 212/838–3531. AE, DC, MC, V. BYOB. Brunch Sun. Subway: 59th St./Lexington Ave. $

9 *b-6*

SKYLIGHT DINER

Its art deco–style decor may not be authentic, and its location at the grimy west end of 34th Street is anything but scenic. Still, it's hard to beat this clean, exceptionally friendly diner for quick, quality eats in the Penn Station area. All the classics—big salads, decent burgers, and every sandwich and omelet combination imaginable—are served round-the-clock by a charming, chatty waitstaff. 402 W. 34th St. (between 9th and 10th Aves.), Garment District, 212/244–0395. AE, D, DC, MC, V. Subway: 34th St./Penn Station. $

11 *f-3*

TEMPLE BAR

One of downtown's coolest bars, Temple Bar has lost its trendiness but not its style—which means you can almost always find a seat, and you can hear yourself think. The vodka menu is unmatched; the martinis are gigantic and delicious; and the food is pretty good, too. Try the gourmet pizzas and oysters. 332 Lafayette St. (between Houston and Bleecker Sts.), Greenwich Village,

212/925–4242. Subway: Bleeker St./ Broadway–Lafayette St. $$

11 *d-4*

TENNESSEE MOUNTAIN

Feel like ditching the city? This popular SoHo spot could be anywhere in the United States. Fill up on meaty beef and babyback ribs; fried onion loaf; corn bread; and meat or vegetarian chili. If you still have room, chase it all with a piece of apple-walnut or pecan pie. There's also a new Theater District outpost. 143 Spring St. (at Wooster St.), SoHo, 212/431–3993. AE, MC, V. Subway: Spring St. $$

9 *d-5*

121 W. 45th St. (between Broadway and 6th Ave.), Theater District, 212/956–0127. B, D, F, Q to 47–50 Sts./Rockefeller Ctr.

9 *e-2*

VIAND

This tiny New York coffee shop is famous for its turkey, roasted right before your eyes and carved steaming-hot to order. Have it in sandwiches, chef salads, or with gravy and cranberry sauce. The service is fast, but space is scarce, so expect a wait. Why not enjoy a bit of the killer rice pudding until a table is free? There's also a full diner menu. 673 Madison Ave. (at 61st St.), Upper East Side, 212/751–6622. Reservations not accepted. No credit cards. Subway: 59th St./Lexington Ave. $

10 *d-5*

WALKER'S

When all you want is a great burger and a pint of cold beer but you crave atmosphere and service that is a notch above Corner Bistro (above), head to Walker's. The restaurant is located down the block from a police precinct stable, where the NYPD's horses are housed, and the spot maintains an unconscious raffishness that suggests the city's colorful past. There are other choices for non burger-eating diners, and the occasional live jazz performance. 16 N. Moore St. (at Varick St.), Tribeca, 212/941–0142. AE, DC, MC, V. Subway: A, C, E to Canal St. $

11 *a-1*

WHITE HORSE TAVERN

Dylan Thomas drank himself to death here and many other literary figures managed to tie one on at the scarred wood bar. These days moms dine on hefty burgers with their little ones at the outdoor picnic tables by day and neighborhood dwellers interested in cold beer and mingling congregate by night. *567 Hudson St. (at W. 11th St.), West Village, 212/989–3956. No credit cards. Subway: A, C, E to 14th St.; L to 8th Ave. $*

ARGENTINE

`9` *b-5*

CHIMICHURRI GRILL

Argentine beef—leaner and grassier than its American counterpart—has only recently become available in this country, and this elegant little restaurant is an excellent place to give it a try. Don't, however, overlook a host of other lovingly prepared dishes such as chorizo and morcilla sausages, flaky empanadas, and Italian-style pastas. Argentine red wines—an exceptional value—are offered in addition to a full bar. *606 9th Ave. (between 43rd and 44th Sts.), Hell's Kitchen, 212/586–8655. Reservations essential. AE, DC, MC, V. Closed Mon. No lunch Sun. Subway: A, C, E to 42nd St. $$*

BARBECUE

`11` *b-3*

BROTHERS BBQ

Dig in to the hearty and satisfying food at this spacious downtown barbecue haven. Ribs, chicken, brisket, and Cajun shrimp come in giant portions, with such appropriate and delicious sides as greens, cornbread, coleslaw, and potato salad. Desserts are simple and rich. The decor is Midwestern kitsch; think traffic lights and memorabilia. *225 Varick St. (between Houston and Clarkson Sts.), SoHo, 212/727–2775. Subway: Houston St. $$*

`10` *b-1*

HOG PIT

At least you can say you went straight to the source. This meatpacking-district barbecue joint and restaurant serves large portions of American food—everything from barbecued ribs and chicken to good ol' home cookin', like meatloaf, mac and cheese, and collard greens. All of the traditional slaws and sides are there, too. Though there is better barbecue to be had, the Hog Pit saves you the trip to Kansas City or Memphis. *22 9th Ave. (at 13th St.), West Village, 212/604–0092. AE, MC, V. No lunch. $*

`9` *d-5*

VIRGIL'S REAL BBQ

When you're stuck for a pre-theater meal, remember that there's almost always a free table at this immense barbecue joint—one of the best in the city—where the portions are large, the service is friendly, and the atmosphere is noisy and fun (if a bit touristy). Highlights are the barbecued shrimp, chicken, beef, pork ribs, and pulled-pork sandwiches. Sides of cornbread, coleslaw, potato salad, baked beans, and other summertime favorites make dinner here feel like a country picnic. *152 W. 44th St. (between Broadway and 6th Ave.), Theater District, 212/921–9494. AE, DC, MC, V. Subway: 42nd St./Times Sq. $$*

BELGIAN

`11` *f-2*

BELGO

This high-concept Belgian theme restaurant from England has made an impression on design-conscious New Yorkers. From the street Belgo looks like a spaceship launch pad, and the interior design is only slightly less stark. Despite the illusion of spaciousness, eating and lounging areas are actually very cramped. Waiters all in black—and in monks' robes, no less—buzz around the bilevel dining rooms (separated by long ramps) offering an impressive array of imported beers and standard Belgian fare (*moules frites*, waterzooi) that only aspires to be fresh and flavorful. The noise is deafening. *415 Lafayette St. (between Astor Pl. and 4th St.), Greenwich Village, 212/253-2828. Subway: Astor Pl. $$*

`10` *c-1*

CAFÉ DE BRUXELLES

Bruxelles serves the hearty cuisine of Belgium in a handsome European setting. Classics like waterzooi de poulet, *carbonnade flamanade* (classic Belgian beef stew with beer, onions, and bacon), *boudin blanc* (sausage usually made with pork and chicken) are complemented by cones of crisp Belgian frites and an extensive (and pricey) list of imported beers. *118 Greenwich Ave. (at 13th St.), West Village, 212/206–1830. AE, MC, V. Subway: A, C, E to 14th St.; L to 8th Ave. $$*

10 b-1

MARKT

This huge Belgian restaurant, situated on the edge of the meatpacking district, feels like a typical European brasserie with its wood tables, globe light fixtures, and a long bar. As expected the kitchen turns out a variety of moules frites—mussels can be dry but the fries are right on—as well as more obscure Belgian dishes such as *stoemp* (mashed potatoes) and *carbonnade* (beef stew). A good selection of Belgian beers is available to wash it all down. *401 W. 14th St. (at 9th Ave.), West Village, 212/727-3314. Reservations recommended. AE, MC, V. Subway: A, C, E to 14th St., L to 8th Ave. $$*

11 b-3

PETIT ABEILLE

It's hard to find home-style European food prepared this well, especially at these prices. In the space where Marnie's Noodle Shop used to be, this tiny Belgian café on Hudson Street serves delicious *soupe aux moules* (mussel soup); hearty entrées; and, of course, crisp and tasty French fries. The brunch, featuring omelets and fresh Belgian waffles, is also good. The original store, on 18th Street, serves lunch only—and how. *466 Hudson St. (between Barrow and Grove Sts.), West Village, 212/741-6479. AE, MC, V. Brunch weekends. Subway: Christopher St./Sheridan Sq. $*

10 c-1

400 W. 14th St. (at 9th Ave.), West Village, 212/727-1505. Subway: A, C, E to 14th St.; L to 8th Ave.

9 c-8

107 W. 18th St. (between 6th and 7th Aves.), Chelsea, 212/604-9350. No dinner. Subway: 1, 2, 3, 9 to 14th St.

BRAZILIAN

9 c-4

CHURRASCARIA PLATAFORMA

This New York outpost of a São Paolo favorite so perfectly captures the feeling of a Brazilian barbecue restaurant that you'll be surprised to emerge back into Manhattan. While the jazz trio plays Jobim classics, an endless parade of waiters with giant skewers of grilled meats whizzes by. Chicken, turkey, salmon, lamb, prime rib, top sirloin, and other carnivore favorites, each marinated in different seasonings, are deposited on your plate in succession until you say "when" by turning your green chip over to red. You're supposed to begin with the equally impressive salad bar, but be careful not to fill up. The restaurant can easily accommodate large groups. (Though it seems odd for such a good-time place, management claims that shorts, sandals, and tank tops are verboten after 5 PM.) *316 W. 49th St. (between 8th and 9th Aves.), Theater District, 212/245-0505. AE, D, DC, MC, V. Subway: C, E to 50th St. $$*

9 e-8

COFFEE SHOP

True, this trendy Brazilian eatery has an unlikely name, but those velvet ropes tell you that it attracts a mighty stylish crowd. One wonders how all those beautiful people can sit at the sidewalk tables all day long, and how any place can stay so busy until dawn. For all the attitude, the *feijoada* (a platter of thinly sliced meats accompanied by rice, black beans, vegetables) isn't bad, but don't expect any sparks from the kitchen. It's not about food. *29 Union Square W (at 16th St.), Flatiron District, 212/243-7969. AE, MC, V. Subway: 14th St./Union Sq. $*

3 g-2

GREEN FIELD CHURRASCARIA

This cavernous restaurant is one of your better bets if you want a traditional all-you-can-eat Brazilian churrascaria. The place bustles with energy as the large waitstaff marches around the restaurant, which is easily the size of an airline hangar, proudly bearing cuts of tender meat on skewers. Before the beef, however, there is a salad bar that appears to go on forever. The place is a fantastic bargain for big eaters. *108-01 Northern Blvd. (at 108th St.), Corona, Queens, 718/672-5202. AE, MC, V. Subway: 103rd St./Corona Plaza. $$*

9 b-4

RICE 'N' BEANS

"Sublime" is the only way to describe what the cooks at this Brazilian storefront do with the lowly legume. Order the eponymous dish by itself (you won't go hungry), or eat it with any of the excellent fish, chicken, or meat entrées. The restaurant's about as big as a pillbox, so consider take-out unless you want to jam yourself in and become buddies with folks at the next table. *744 9th Ave. (between 50th and 51st Sts.), Hell's Kitchen, 212/265–4444. Reservations not accepted. D, MC, V. Subway: C, E to 50th St. $*

11 *c-3*

120 W. 3rd St. (between MacDougal St. and 6th Ave.), Greenwich Village, 212/375–1800. Subway: W. 4th St. /Washington Sq.

11 *f-1*

RIODIZIO

The *rodizio*, an all-you-can-eat rotisserie meal for $27.95, is one reason why this place has been packed since it opened. The restaurant occupies a vast loft space a few doors down from the Public Theater and is huge and noisy, with an enormous bar flanked by an attractive display of seafood. Forget Brazilian samba: your meal is accompanied by thundering disco. *Caipirinhas*, made with lime, sugar, and *cachaça* (a Brazilian liqueur made from sugar cane), are served by the pitcher. The grilled meats and fish are first-rate, and come with a huge house salad, black beans, collard greens, brown rice, polenta, and fried plantains. Be very hungry. *417 Lafayette St. (near Astor Pl.), Greenwich Village, 212/529–1313. AE, MC, V. Brunch weekends. Subway: Astor Pl. $$*

CAFÉS

9 *c-3*

CAFE EUROPA

Whether you need a place to refuel after shopping or are meeting an old friend to catch up, this Midtown café is like an oasis in the rendezvous desert—and it has two locations to boot. Simple salads, good sandwiches, a large selection of desserts, and good coffee make it the perfect pit stop. *205 W. 57th St. Midtown, 212/977–4030. Reservations not accepted. AE, D, DC, MC, V. Subway: 57th St. $*

9 *d-4*

1177 6th Ave. (at 46th St.), Theater District, 212/575–7272. Subway: 47th–50th Sts./Rockefeller Ctr.

11 *d-3*

CAFFÉ DANTE

Frothy cappuccino, bracing espresso, teas, pastries, salads, and little sandwiches make up one of the Village's more inviting Italian cafés. Dante is a throwback to a time before Starbucks, when Mediterranean cooking meant lying in the sun. *79 MacDougal St. (between Bleecker and Houston Sts.), Greenwich Village, 212/982–5275. No credit cards. Subway: Houston St.; W. 4th St./Washington Sq. $*

11 *b-2*

CAFFE VIVALDI

Just off the chaotic runway that is Bleecker Street in these parts, Caffe Vivaldi quietly serves coffees, teas, biscotti, and desserts amid dark wood, old-fashioned sketches and prints, and often a good deal of smoke. In winter, wait for a table near the fireplace; it's worth it. *32 Jones St. (between Bleecker and W. 4th Sts.), 212/929–9384. Reservations not accepted. No credit cards. Subway: W. 4th St./Washington Sq. $*

10 *f-5*

CHINATOWN ICE CREAM FACTORY

Though this ice-cream shop is not a restaurant by any means it is the perfect stop on your way home from eating in Chinatown. The green tea is light and fragrant, with just a hint of tea flavor, while red bean is more pronounced. There are of course such old standbys as chocolate and vanilla, but those with more adventurous palates should try the knockout lychee sorbet. *65 Bayard St. (between Mott and Elizabeth Sts.), Chinatown, 212/608–4170. No credit cards. Subway: 6, N, R to Canal St. $*

7 *c-7*

COLUMBUS BAKERY

The open, self-service concept of these stylish bakeries adds to their pleasantly frenetic energy. Make your selection from a counter overflowing with baked goods—quiches, tarts, cakes, pastries, muffins—and very light lunch fare. Though a few things, the breads in particular, look better than they taste, the comfortable chairs, casual service, and neighborhood atmosphere make these places very popular for a quick bite. *474 Columbus Ave. (at 83rd St.), Upper West Side, 212/724–6880. Reservations not accepted. AE, D, MC, V. Subway: 79th St. $*

9 *f-3*

957 1st Ave. (between 52nd and 53rd Sts.), Midtown, 212/421–0334. Subway: 51st St./Lexington–3rd Aves.

11 *b-3*

CONES

To call the homemade, creamy, rich frozen desserts served at this Greenwich Village shop "ice cream" doesn't do them justice. "Gelato" comes closer, but the stuff at Cones is nothing like what you might find at the bad Italian cafés in the neighborhood. This more closely resembles the best gelato in Italy—or would you believe, Argentina, whence the brothers who own Cones originate. To pick a favorite is impossible. The nut-based flavors are intense; the fruits taste just picked. You can try them all before you order, or order a couple of large cups (three flavors each) and share. *272 Bleecker St. (between 6th and 7th Aves.), West Village, 212/414–1795. No credit cards. Closed in winter. Subway: W. 4th St./Washington Sq. $*

7 *b-7*

EDGAR'S CAFÉ

The bright, almost surreal interior of this European-style café is a tribute to its namesake, Edgar Allan Poe. People talk for hours here over light salads, sandwiches, and most of all, appealing desserts. A full selection of coffees and teas and pleasant service make this the perfect place to grab a bite and some quality time after a movie—but everyone on the West Side knows it, so you may have to wait for a table. It's worth noting that the place is open 365 days a year. *255 W. 84th St. (between Broadway and West End Ave.), Upper West Side, 212/496–6126. Reservations not accepted. No credit cards. Subway: 1, 9 to 86th St. $*

11 *f-5*

FERRARA

This famous, lively, very bright café claims to be America's oldest pasticceria, and the honor draws crowds (of tourists) that spill out onto Little Italy's streets in summer. If you can hold out for a seat, you'll enjoy espresso, cappuccino, pastry, and gelati the way they were meant to be. You can also take home boxes of Ferrara's delicious *torrone* candy. *195 Grand St. (between Mulberry and Mott Sts.), Little Italy, 212/226–6150. Reservations not accepted. No credit cards. Subway: Grand St.; Spring St.; Canal St. $*

7 *b-3*

HUNGARIAN PASTRY SHOP

Cramped, cozy, and timeless, if tired, this Columbia University hangout serves good poppy-seed pastries, Linzer torte, and cappuccino. You can sit for hours with a newspaper or book and nobody will bother you. *1030 Amsterdam Ave. (between 110th and 111th Sts.), Morningside Heights, 212/866–4230. Reservations not accepted. No credit cards. Subway: 110th St./Cathedral Pkwy. $*

9 *b-8*

LE GAMIN

Scuffed wood floors, rickety tables, and indifferent service—just like Paris, but without as much cigarette smoke. Still, these cafés have charm to spare, and the huge bowls of steaming café au lait and selection of authentic crepes and baguette sandwiches make them perfect places in which to grab a quick morning bite or while away an afternoon. If you go for brunch, expect to wait for a table (and wait and wait). *183 9th Ave. (at 21st St.), Chelsea, 212/243–8864. Reservations not accepted. No credit cards. Subway: C, E to 23rd St. $*

11 *c-4*

50 MacDougal St. (between Prince and Houston Sts.), Greenwich Village, 212/254–4678. Subway: C, E to Spring St.

11 *a-1*

MAGNOLIA BAKERY

If you grew up in a small town during the 1950s, Magnolia Bakery will feel like home. If you didn't, one bite of the golden cupcake with chocolate buttercream frosting and sprinkles will make you wish that you had. Although all of the homey baked goods in this small storefront are authentic—the banana pudding is made with Nilla wafers and the hummingbird cake is so dense one slice can feed two—they aren't all equally good. The golden cupcakes are wonderful (the chocolate ones are a little dry), as are most of the bundt and layer cakes, which are served in very generous portions. The apple pie filling tastes canned and the rice pudding has a slight fake flavor. But there's no denying the nostalgia everything in this place evokes. *401 Bleecker St. (at W. 11th St.), West Village, 212/462–2572. No credit cards. Subway: A, C, E to 14th St.; L to 8th Ave. $*

11 *d-6*

PALACINKA

Palacinka is the word for crepe in Hungarian and this little café, decorated with a pleasing mix-and-match of vintage objects, tin ceilings, small metal tables, and folding chairs, delivers just that. On the savory side crepes are filled with ingredients such as roasted tarragon chicken, goat cheese, and roasted peppers, or ham, Gruyère, and egg, and each comes with a pile of lightly dressed greens. The sweet crepes range from the classic butter and sugar to a rich concoction of chestnut cream and crème fraîche. There are also a couple of sandwiches and salads. Throw in a huge cup of the frothy hot chocolate and Palacinka will surely become your new favorite SoHo café. *28 Grand St. (between 6th Ave. and Thompson St.), 212/625–0362. No credit cards. Subway: A, C, E to Canal St. $*

10 *f-1*
VENIERO'S
A bakery and café since 1894, the venerable and obviously beloved Veniero's continues to pack 'em in, and with good reason. They come from all over town for espresso, cappuccino, and scrumptious traditional Italian pastry, as well as fresh fruit ices in summer. Hope that sfogliatelle is still warm when you arrive—it often is. *342 E. 11th St. (between 1st and 2nd Aves.), East Village, 212/674–4415. AE, DC, MC, V. Subway: 14th St./Union Sq.; L to 1st Ave. $*

CARIBBEAN

10 *f-1*
BAMBOU
Noël Coward would be quite at home in this attractive and elegant restaurant, which rather resembles a grand old mansion in Jamaica. Fairly searing "jerk" pork and chicken—marinated in chiles and spices and smoke-grilled over pimento (allspice) wood fires—are accompanied by bouillabaisse, braised oxtail, and coconut crème brûlée. *243 E. 14th St. (between 2nd and 3rd Aves.), East Village, 212/505–1180. Reservations essential. AE, MC, V. Closed Sun. No lunch. Subway: 14th St./Union Sq. $$*

10 *d-1*
NEGRIL
Spicy fare and cold drinks to wash it down are the hallmarks of Jamaican restaurants, and Negril happily excels at both. The jerked dishes (chicken, beef, pork, or fish) are excellent, as are the potent blender drinks (stick to a bottle of Red Stripe if you're a lightweight). Be

sure to make reservations or expect a wait, particularly on weekends. *362 W. 23rd St. (between 8th and 9th Aves.), Chelsea, 212/807–6411. AE, DC, MC, V. Subway: C, E, 1, 9 to 23rd St. $*

CHINESE

9 *f-3*
BEIJING DUCK HOUSE
This is the place for those who can't anticipate a craving for Peking duck 24 hours in advance: 20 minutes after you order, a whole duck, perfectly crisp, is carved at your table and presented with all the trimmings (pancakes, scallions, cucumbers, and hoisin sauce). If you're really hungry, start with the duck soup. Don't let the uptown address fool you; the spirit is Chinatown-informal. *236 E. 53rd St., Midtown, 212/759–8260. AE, DC, MC, V. Subway: 51st St./Lexington–3rd Aves. $$*

9 *f-4*
CHIN CHIN
Jimmy Chin's large and casual but extremely stylish restaurant features imaginatively prepared nouvelle-Chinese offerings, including shredded duck salad, vegetable-duck pie, grilled baby quail, steamed or crispy whole bass, and veal medallions with spicy pepper sauce. The atmosphere, like the food, is swanky and contemporary. *216 E. 49th St., Midtown, 212/888–4555. Reservations essential. AE, DC, MC, V. No lunch weekends. Subway: 51st St./Lexington–3rd Aves. $$$*

9 *f-2*
CHINA FUN
All baking and barbecuing are done on the bright, clean premises with the very freshest ingredients at these popular restaurants. The highly reasonable menu is overflowing with Cantonese, Szechuan, and Hunan classics, but the elegant and resourceful Dorothea Wu and her chefs also have Chinese fun with a variety of special entrées and an ample and celebrated selection of dim sum. *1239 2nd Ave. (at 65th St.), Upper East Side, 212/752–0810. MC, V. Subway: 68th St./Hunter College. $*

9 *c-1*
246 Columbus Ave. (at 72nd St.), Upper West Side, 212/580–1516. Subway: B, C to 72nd St.

9 *c-4*

1653 Broadway (at 51st St.), Theater District, 212/333–2622. Subway: 49th St.

10 *f-5*

JING FONG

This glitzy, multi-level Chinese-food palace—known for its dim sum, the traditional meal served Sunday morning, comprised of an astonishing array of small dishes and dumplings— is the closest you'll come to Hong Kong in Chinatown. Go early to avoid interminable waits—and to get first pick of such delicacies as fresh, sweetened bean curd served from a barrel; deep-fried shrimp with their heads and their shells; and fresh clams in black-bean sauce. Shrill-voiced servers push food trolleys around the dining room, calling out the name of each item in Cantonese. Whether or not you understand exactly what they're saying, you can count on finding delicious *har gow* (steamed shrimp dumplings), *shu mai* (steamed pork dumplings), *chow fun* (wide rice noodles with dried shrimp), turnip cake, sesame balls, and custard tarts among the offerings. Perhaps there are better places for dim sum in Chinatown, and certainly in Flushing, but none as lively and fun as Jing Fong. *20 Elizabeth St. (between Bayard and Canal Sts.), Chinatown, 212/964–5256. AE, MC, V. Subway: 6, N, R to Canal St. $*

11 *g-7*

JOE'S SHANGHAI

This Chinatown outpost of the famous Flushing restaurant is every bit as good as the original and a little busier; be prepared to wait. Shanghai cuisine is richer than other Chinese food, so come hungry. For starters, don't miss the steamed soup dumplings (pork or pork with crab) or the turnip shortcakes. Traditional, delicious, and very rich main dishes include lion's head (actually pork meatballs), braised pork shoulder, and homemade Shanghai noodles. The braised bean curd on spinach and eggplant in garlic sauce is also superb. Just stay away from the whole fish. And what's "vegetarian duck"? *9 Pell St. (between Mott St. and Bowery), Chinatown, 212/223–8888. No credit cards. Reservations not accepted. Subway: 6, N, R, J, M, Z to Canal St. $*

10 *f-5*

LIN'S DUMPLING HOUSE

If pork and leek, crabmeat, or scallop and pork dumplings sound good, head to Dumpling House. Most of the dumplings—about 10 varieties, not to be confused with the soup-filled Shanghai-style dumplings popular all over Chinatown—are available fried, steamed, or boiled and all are equally delicious. There is also a full menu of tasty Chinese favorites and more exotic dishes such as pig's ears and cherry clam and ginger soup. *25 Pell St. (between Mott St. and Bowery), Chinatown, 212/577–2777. No credit cards. Subway: 6, N, R to Canal St. $*

11 *g-7*

MANDARIN COURT

Though not as impressive in setting or scope as Chinatown's huge dim sum emporia, this small restaurant has a terrific selection of dumplings and other dimsum favorites. Because the carts have less surface area to cover, the food is often fresher and hotter, too. *61 Mott St. (between Canal and Bayard Sts.), Chinatown, 212/608–3838. AE, MC, V. Subway: 6. N, R, J, M, Z to Canal St. $*

9 *f-3*

MR. CHOW

As you pass through the Lalique doors, you realize that this restaurant is as much about sleek setting and hip crowd as it is about food—here, Chinese with a touch of French and California thrown into the wok. Overlook the frenetic ambience to enjoy the crispy spinach, gambler's duck, drunken fish, and Grand Marnier shrimp. *324 E. 57th St. (between 1st and 2nd Aves.), Midtown, 212/751–9030. Reservations essential. AE, DC, MC, V. No lunch. Subway: 59th St./Lexington Ave. $$$*

11 *g-7*

NY NOODLE TOWN

Open until 3 AM, this humble restaurant has some of the best Chinese food in Chinatown. Order the shrimp-dumpling soup, barbecued duck with flowering chives, and salt-baked soft-shell crab (in season). Barbecued pork and the other items hanging in the window are also delicious. Oddly enough, the noodles aren't the greatest. *28 Bowery (at Bayard St.), Chinatown, 212/349–0923. No credit cards. Subway: 6, N, R, J, M, Z to Canal St. $*

7 *f-8*

PIG HEAVEN

The delicious and authentic food is served in a recently renovated, handsome setting. While pork is the menu's mainstay, there are plenty of other options for those who'd rather pass on porcine heaven. Don't miss the dumplings—they're all winners, fried, steamed, or boiled. Prices are higher than in Chinatown, but still quite reasonable. *1540 2nd Ave. (at 80th St.), Upper East Side, 212/744–4333. AE, DC, V. Subway: 77th St. $$*

3 *g-3*

PINGS

Manhattan's upscale Chinese restaurants may look fancier than this Elmhurst, Queens, establishment, but none of them serves more sophisticated food. From extravagant Cantonese specialties such as shark-fin soup and braised, dried abalone, to more familiar dishes such as roasted duck and fried rice, the cooking of chef-owner Ping draws raves. Ping's other specialties include giant lobsters, served steamed with braised noodles; stir-fried pea shoots; and sweet dim sum. To ensure an other-worldly experience, gather a large group, call ahead to set up a banquet and be prepared to spend a lot of money on the Chinese meal of your life. Otherwise, of course, you can always just order off the menu. *8302 Queens Blvd., Elmhurst, Queens, 718/396–1238. AE. Subway: Grand Ave. $$*

9 *e-3*

SHUN LEE PALACE

Shun Lee offers impeccably prepared Hunan and Szechuan dishes in two of the city's truly plush Chinese settings. There's a low-calorie menu for dieters, but the temptations of the regular menu are pretty irresistible—hot-and-sour cabbage, lobster Szechuan, beggar's chicken, crispy whole sea bass, shrimp puffs, spicy Hunan duckling with a smoky flavor. Occasional guest chefs from Hong Kong augment the regular menu. The Lincoln Center location is convenient for pre-concert meals, and the less formal café there is quicker and more reasonably priced. But now there's also a $19.99 prix-fixe lunch at the Palace. *155 E. 55th St. (between Lexington and 3rd Aves.), Midtown, 212/371–8844. Reservations essential. AE, DC, MC, V. Subway: 59th St./Lexington Ave.$$*

9 *c-2*

43 W. 65th St., Upper West Side, 212/595–8895. Subway: 66th St./Lincoln Center.

10 *f-4*

SWEET-N-TART

This tiny Chinatown "diner" is packed until the wee hours with a young, trendy Asian crowd. The food is inexpensive and superb. Highlights include fried rice with Chinese sausage in bamboo, yam noodle soup with assorted dumplings, and ginger and scallion lo mein. An array of special hot and cold drinks (called "teas") should not be missed. The mango shakes with tapioca pearls or black sago balls and the hot almond tea are among the best. *76 Mott St. (at Canal St.), Chinatown, 212/334–8008. No credit cards. Subway: 6, N, R to Canal St. $*

11 *g-7*

TAI HONG LAU

First-rate seafood, dim sum, and Peking duck in an upmarket setting make Tai Hong Lau one of Chinatown's best restaurants. The flip side: it has some of Chinatown's rudest waiters. *70 Mott St. (between Bayard and Canal Sts.), Chinatown, 212/219–1431. AE. Subway: Canal St.; Grand St. $*

10 *f-4*

YUMEE NOODLE

Situated off a hidden Chinatown alleyway, this excellent Cantonese noodle shop is worth hunting down. One of the restaurant's specialties—despite the place's name—is a rice casserole baked with any number of toppings, among which might be pork, chicken, and a variety of exotica. To eat it, you stir in some soy sauce and the crunchy crust that forms on the bottom incorporates into the dish giving it an interesting texture. Noodle dishes are also very good. The only disappointments are the barbecued items hanging in the window, which are better prepared elsewhere. *48 Bowery (between Canal and Bayard Sts.), Chinatown, 212/374–1327. No credit cards. Subway: 6, N, R to Canal St. $*

CONTEMPORARY

11 d-1
ALAIA

South Park jokes aside, lots of good things come with being a Baldwin. Among the latest of the brothers' undertakings is Stephen and Billy's Alaia, a trendy restaurant in the former Mirezi space. Those who remember Mirezi will find the interior somewhat changed, and no trace of the former establishment's Asian influence. What is left is a comfortable, contemporary restaurant that serves Mediterranean-influenced food. Still, what brings most diners to Alaia is the hope of sighting a member of one of New York's favorite families or one of the Baldwins' many, many friends. *59 5th Ave. (between 12th and 13th Sts.), Greenwich Village, 212/242–9709. Reservations essential. AE, DC, MC, V. Subway: 14th St./Union Sq. $$$*

10 e-8
AMERICAN PARK AT THE BATTERY

This is waterside dining at its finest. In up-and-coming Battery Park, this airy dining room is distinguished by an incredible view of the Statue of Liberty and Ellis Island. True to the spirit of New York the menu is more or less American with flavors borrowed from many far-flung cuisines. An outdoor café right on the water is set up as a casual grill in summer months. Also outside is an ingenious table (for groups of 10–12) with a hollowed out pool in the middle, where family-style dinner floats in wooden dishes. *Battery Park at State St., Lower Manhattan, 212/809–5508. AE, MC, V. Reservations essential. No lunch Sat. Subway: South Ferry. $$$*

9 e-2
AUREOLE

It's virtually unanimous: Some of the city's best food is served in the elegant, duplex dining room of this flower-bedecked town house. Chef Charles Palmer prepares an exquisite array of dishes with the freshest seasonal ingredients, and New Yorkers consistently vote him one of the city's best chefs. The presentations are as startling as the prices, but there's also a reasonably priced prix-fixe dinner. Decorated with caramel curlicues and tuile triangles, the desserts are utterly otherworldly. *34 E. 61 St. (between Madison and Park Aves.), Upper East Side, 212/319–1660. Reserva-tions essential. AE, MC, V. Closed Sun. Subway: 5th Ave. $$$$*

11 h-4
BABY JUPITER

For at least a decade, the once seedy Lower East Side has been on the brink of blossoming into a major food and drink destination; buds like Baby Jupiter have led the way. The menu brings together Cajun and Asian influences, with such results as honey-barbecued salmon with basil risotto and a nori salad. In the lounge you can often catch live music and comedy acts. *170 Orchard St. (at Stanton St.), Lower East Side, 212/982–2229. MC, V. No lunch. Subway: F to 2nd Ave. $*

9 d-5
BRYANT PARK GRILL

It's hard to believe that this immense and stylish restaurant looks out onto the same Bryant Park that used to shelter the city's drug dealers and homeless. But once the nearby fashion and publishing industries turned the park into a scoping ground, it seemed only fitting that a decent restaurant follow them. Both the food and the service are competent, and portions are huge. The more relaxed outdoor café, on the restaurant's roof (open mid-April–mid-October), is idyllic on cool summer nights. *25 W. 40th St. (between 5th and 6th Aves.), Garment District, 212/840–6500. Reservations essential for dining room. AE, D, DC, MC, V. Subway: 42nd St. $$*

9 d-3
CHINA GRILL

Although the atmosphere is corporate—suits and cell phones abound—the food at this very noisy Midtown power-lunch spot is satisfying and delicious. Asian-inspired appetizers such as roasted beet dumplings, crunchy calamari salad, and cured salmon rolls are large enough to share, as are most of the entrées. Try the wasabi-crusted cod on mashed potatoes, the Szechuan spiced beef, or the black pasta with shrimp. Service is friendly, if reserved. *52 W. 53rd St., Midtown, 212/333–7788. Reservations essential. AE, DC, MC, V. Subway: 5th Ave./53rd St. $$$*

10 g-2
COUP

This sleek, beautifully lit, curvaceous, split-level space features two lovely outdoor deck areas. Chef Kevin Roth has cooked all over America, and that quickly becomes obvious. His seasonal menus nudge flavors together because they inevitably fall in love. Steak and blue cheese quesadilla with a sour-cherry chutney will leave you panting. Daring hemp and poppy seed–crusted tuna loin takes you on a neo-Polynesian ride, with very deep, fruity flavors. Grilled filet mignon bestows considerable dignity upon its bed of summer beans and fingerling potatoes. The chef's sweet tooth, which bares itself often during the meal, comes into its own at dessert. Pineapple upside-down cake is a special labor of love. Small wonder this new Coup is so popular. *509 E. 6th St. (between Aves. A and B), East Village, 212/979–2815. Reservations recommended. AE, MC, V. No lunch. Brunch Sun. Subway: Astor Pl., 2nd Ave. $$*

11 a-1
EQ

When the economy's healthy, some restaurants fill a niche by taking care of excess disposable income. EQ is one of them. At half the price this would be a charming Greenwich Village establishment with very decent food. But at the going rate, diners are left to wonder what they are paying for. It certainly isn't the setting, which seems makeshift at best, or the size of the portions. The food is good, but not that good, and the service tends toward pretentious. Regardless, the restaurant fills each night with, as one might expect, people who look like they don't know what to do with their annual bonuses. *267 W. 4th St. (at Perry St.), West Village, 212/414–1961. AE, MC, V. Closed Sun. No lunch. Subway: Christopher St./Sheridan Sq. $$$*

7 f-7
ÉTATS-UNIS

As the name implies, this is American cooking from a French perspective, a refreshing twist from the New American trend of rushing toward foreign ingredients at the expense of our native bounty. The results are wonderful: Corn soufflé sits on wild greens dressed in a raspberry vinaigrette; Colorado beef is coated with peppercorns, simply seared, and served with a potato galette, or whatever potato the chef is in the mood to make that day. The small, cheerful room and exposed kitchen make you feel like you're in the chef's home, and the clientele is so regular that it sometimes seems as if only the restaurant's

"family" is allowed in. If you're lucky enough to get a reservation, take it and run. *242 E. 81st St. (between 2nd and 3rd Aves.), Upper East Side, 212/517–8826. Reservations essential. AE, MC, V. Closed Sun. No lunch. Subway: 77th St. $$*

9 d-3
JUDSON GRILL

With the soaring feel of the dining room on a luxury ocean liner, this Midtowner has become a favorite meeting place for New York's power brokers. Chef Bill Telepan's seasonal menus feature contemporary American dishes. All bear his distinctive intonations—from delicate pinkytoe crab in a martini glass with a dollop of sevruga caviar to duck breast with wild-rice-bread pudding and cherry compote. The impressive wine list with hard-to-find American labels and vintages, and Ann-Michele Andrews's great desserts, including the restaurant's signature Jack Daniels chocolate ice cream soda, perfectly partner Telepan's playful scope. The restaurant just feels very important, and so will you while you're there. *152 W. 52nd St. (between 6th and 7th Aves.), Midtown, 212/582–5252. Reservations essential. AE, DC, MC, V. Closed Sun. Subway: 49th St.; 50th St. $$$*

7 f-8
LENOX ROOM

This is where Upper East Siders come when they don't want the fuss and formality of Daniel or Le Cirque 2000. Dashing co-owner and host Tony Fortuna oversees the kitchen here, and the menu is contemporary American with a decidedly French accent. There's a fantastically luxurious raw bar with shellfish displayed on dozens of pounds of crushed ice, and a bold array of flavors among the entrées. Try the sumptuous venison or quail preparations and the caramelized banana parfait or the cheek-puckering double-lemon tart. The bar features very comfortable seating and selection of $6 tasting plates help make the restaurant a neighborhood hangout. *1278 3rd Ave. (between 73rd and 74th Sts.), Upper East Side, 212/772–0404. AE, D, DC, MC, V. Subway: 77th St. $$*

9 e-3
LITTLE DOVE

With a legacy of one of the most beloved restaurants in Manhattan's dining history—Sign of the Dove—this delightfully diminutive (seating just 50), almost erotic Little Dove recently took wing. The softly lit room really feels like a boudoir, complete with crushed Moroccan velvet curtains and slip covers. The menu fits the space: eight appetizers and seven entrées. A supple sea bass carpaccio shimmers with basil chiffonade in a gentle lime and olive oil broth. The ultimate comfort food: State-of-the-art risotto stirred with plenty of chopped chanterelle mushrooms and truffle shavings stays piping hot, thanks to a molten cheese fonduta at its center. End with a baby grilled pumpkin stuffed with a rich cheesecake filling and surrounded by a raisin and dried cherry compote. This is a very special, hopelessly romantic place. *200 E. 60th St. (at 3rd Ave.), 2nd floor, Upper East Side, 212/ 861–8080. AE, MC, V. Subway: 59th St./Lexington Ave. $$*

7 *e-8*

LOBSTER CLUB

Everyone loves comfort food, and this is where the Park Avenue crowd goes to get it. Chef Anne Rosenzweig reinterprets the comfort foods of yore to give them a modern spin. Over red-check tablecloths, wealthy locals savor meatloaf with mashed sweet potatoes, fried rock shrimp served in a paper cone, and buttery roast chicken served with Provençal fries. The signature dish is the restaurant's namesake—a lobster club sandwich of Dagwood proportions. The location, in a brownstone on a tree-lined side street near the Metropolitan Museum of Art, adds to the homey atmosphere. Make a reservation or prepare for a long wait. *24 E. 80th St. (between 5th and Madison Aves.), Upper East Side, 212/ 249–6500. Reservations essential. AE, D, DC, MC, V. Subway: 77th St. $$*

11 *e-5*

MERCER KITCHEN

The scene here, in the basement of the Mercer Hotel, may be hipper-than-thou, but diners looking for more than a scene are coming for the food. Jean-Georges Vongerichten has created a sleek, industrial space that's oddly comfortable, and interestingly organized his menu according to where in the kitchen each dish originates. Dinner offerings might include black sea-bass carpaccio with lime juice, coriander, and mint (from the raw bar); figs with prosciutto, aged balsamic vinegar, and rosemary flatbread (from the pantry); Alsatian tarte flambée with fromage blanc, onions, and bacon (from the pizza oven); roasted lobster with tagliatelle and red-wine sauce (from the rotisserie); or lamb steak with tomato-orange marmalade (from the grill). *The Mercer Hotel, 99 Prince St. (at Mercer St.), SoHo, 212/966–5454. Reservations essential. AE, DC, MC, V. Brunch Sun. No dinner Sun. Subway: Prince St. $$$*

11 *f-6*

O'NEILS GRAND STREET

Supposedly, under this bar, there remains a fragment of a tunnel that once allowed New York City police chief Theodore Roosevelt to sneak away from the police station across the street for a drink. The exquisitely paneled room, off the beaten path, is a calm oasis on the edge of Chinatown and far away from the commotion of SoHo. The dark, sexy lounge is a great place for a cocktail and a light nibble, or you can have a real meal of good New American fare at one of the tables up front. *174 Grand St. (between Centre and Mulberry Sts.), SoHo, 212/941–9119. AE, DC, MC, V. Closed Sun. Subway: 6, N, R to Canal St. $$*

9 *d-3*

OSTERIA DEL CIRCO

Opened by the three sons of Le Cirque owner Sirio Maccioni, this contemporary Italian eatery comes alive with circus-tent decorations and dancing sculptures. The line of celebrities waiting for tables creates a frenzied atmosphere. Traditional Tuscan specialties such as a 30-vegetable soup and salt cod *alla livornese* go up against contemporary favorites such as tuna carpaccio and lobster salad. Pizzas, pastas, and rotisserie items (particularly the duck) are excellent. Save room for dessert: the *bomboloncini*—little Italian donuts filled with chocolate, vanilla, and raspberry— have been voted the best in the city, and the other sweets are pretty spectacular, too. The reasonably priced list of Italian wines is also worth checking out. *120 W. 55th St. (between 6th and 7th Aves.), Midtown, 212/265–3636. AE, DC, MC, V. Subway: 57th St. $$$*

9 *c-4*

PALLADIN

A classy Adam Tihany–designed space, a terrific location in the ultra-hip Time Hotel, and superstar Jean-Louis Palladin overseeing the kitchen made this one of the most auspicious restaurant openings in years. Still, despite flashes of brilliance, so far this newcomer has failed to live up to expectations. Only a few of the offerings—a delicate octopus ceviche served in a parfait glass, and a rich herbed capon over a red-wine reduction—seem indicative of Jean-Louis's innovative, artistic approach. Rumor has it that Jean-Louis will be spending more time on the premises, so perhaps this underachiever will begin to live up to its potential. *222 W. 49th St. (between Broadway and 8th Ave.), Theater District, 212/320–2929. Reservations essential. AE, DC, MC, V. Closed Sun. Breakfast daily. No lunch Sat. Subway: 50th St. $$$$*

A BREATH OF FRESH AIR

New York may be an asphalt jungle, but there are eateries for every budget that offer a breath of real, unconditioned air on a hot summer night.

Bryant Park Grill (Contemporary)
In the summer, this place heaves a collective sigh when the after-work crowds loosen their ties.

Danal (Tea)
If you missed the train to the Hamptons, get a little country in this homey café's garden.

Chelsea Commons (American Casual)
A friendly neighborhood bar with a brick-lined oasis in back; the lovely setting elevates the typical pub grub.

Le Jardin Bistro (French)
The garden is as ethereal as the food is hearty. You'll never want to leave.

Park View at the Boathouse (American)
On the lake in Central Park, this place was for years a drinks-only destination. Finally, a new chef has created a menu worthy of the view.

Provence (French)
The SPF-conscious are well protected in this bistro's small, tented garden.

---

10 *e-1*

POP

One of the only restaurants on Fourth Avenue, Pop is the *very* last word in trendy overnight sensations that are clearly here to stay. The sleek, sexy decor immediately enrobes you and makes you feel comfortably puissant. Every aspect of your meal's presentation is carefully and uniquely conceived, from the space-age flatware to the loose-leaf menu, which includes a bang-up wine list. And chef Brian Young's brilliant French/contemporary American is always ready to tantalize. Begin with his signature shaved clam tartare with ginger, chive, and pepper oil, and clams on the half-shell will never seem right again. Rack of lamb is unusually juicy and tender, and salmon au poivre is a flank of heaven. Desserts are resplendently delicious. The later it gets, the more of a boisterous—but always poised—party Pop becomes. *127 4th Ave. (between 12th and 13th Sts.), Greenwich Village, 212/767–1800. AE, MC, V. No lunch. Subway: 14th St./Union Sq. $$$*

9 *b-8*

THE RED CAT

Fairly spacious quarters, a happening bar scene (stop by for a bowl of fresh radishes that you dip into a small bowl, or "cellar" of sea salt), and bright, original decor gave the Red Cat a running start. But it's the seasonally sensitive, carefully prepared menu that has earned this restaurant its reputation. Offerings change regularly, but recent standouts have included foie gras with caramelized nectarines and an arctic char with wild mushrooms and truffle vinaigrette. *227 10th Ave. (between 23rd and 24th Sts.), Chelsea, 212/242–1122. Reservations essential. AE, DC, MC, V. No lunch. Subway: C, E to 23rd St. $$*

9 *d-8*

THE TONIC

A 19th-century mahogany bar; an airy, tile-floor dining room; and huge bouquets of flowers make this ambitious newcomer one of Chelsea's classiest restaurants. The New American menu takes some chances that you'll either love or hate, like citrusy tuna tartare paired with seaweed salad and mango coulis, and saddle of lamb wrapped in eggplant and served with a zucchini-basil sauce. Prices are steep, but partly justified by the quality of the ingredients. *108–110 W. 18th St. (between 6th and 7th Aves.), Chelsea, 212/929–9755. Reservations essential. AE, DC, MC, V. Brunch weekends. Subway: 1, 9 to 18th St. $$$*

9 *e-7*
27 STANDARD
With its low lights and gloriously high ceilings, 27 Standard brings terrific food and live jazz together like nowhere else on earth. Full performances are in the jazz club downstairs; the restaurant recently found its perfect new chef in Matthew Lake, who composes flavor upon flavor with results as intense and memorable as great jazz itself. Buttery seared foie gras is courted by a luscious shallot-berry compote. Buttermilk-fried oysters get a lime drizzle and a sultry roasted corn-green chile relish. Rare tuna, so often bland, here receives a complex studding of pine nuts, grilled shiitake mushrooms, and ruddy peppers. *116 E. 27th St. (between Lexington and Park Aves.), Murray Hill, 212/576–2232. AE, MC, V. Subway: 6 to 28th St.$$*

11 *f-5*
VELVET RESTAURANT AND LOUNGE
The blood red walls may be oddly bordello-esque, but the well-made cocktails, lounge scene, and eclectic menu will bring you right back to a New York vibe. The food, which takes cues from all over the globe, is uniformly good—salmon tartare is fresh and zesty, *sambal oelek–*rubbed pork loin is spicy and exotic. (Sambal oelek is a spicy Thai condiment made from hot peppers.) After dinner you can relax to music (some nights live) in the upstairs lounge. *223 Mulberry St. (between Prince and Spring Sts.), SoHo, 212/965–0439. AE, D, MC, V. No lunch. Subway: Spring St. $$*

9 *e-3*
VONG
The second of Jean-Georges Vongerichten's four New York restaurants (*see* Jo Jo and Jean-Georges, *below,* and Mercer Kitchen *above*), Vong gives life to the chef's love of Asian cuisine. Here he fuses French and Thai, and brings even peanut sauce to new heights. Presentation is emphasized: Spectacular food is showcased in dazzling dishes of varying size, color, and shape. The Thai decor is exotic and rich, with a thoroughly contemporary flair. While some complain about the prices, others say don't sweat it—this is Jean-Georges Vongerichten, and you're in for the meal of your life. *200 E. 54th St., Midtown, 212/486–9592. AE, DC, MC, V. No lunch weekends. Subway: 51st St./Lexington–3rd Aves. $$$*

9 *e-1*
WILLOW
The charm of this elegant turn-of-the-20th-century townhouse adds to the food's charisma, which is standard New American: goat cheese, wild greens, duck. The menu is not groundbreaking, but the chef executes it well, and if you factor in the soft lighting and view of the tree-lined street through the leaded-glass windows, you end up with a worthwhile experience. The downstairs room has a simpler menu of lighter meals, and on sunny days lunch is served on lovely sidewalk tables. *1022 Lexington Ave. (at 73rd St.), Upper East Side, 212/717–0703. Reservations essential for dinner. AE, DC, MC, V. Subway: 68th St./Hunter College. $$*

CONTINENTAL

7 *c-1*
CAFÉ DES ARTISTES
The beautiful, nostalgic ambience; the imaginative kitchen that produces such poised Continental specialties; and the famous, sweetly lascivious murals by Howard Chandler Christy—all fully restored after a fire in late 1997—make this West Side classic a favorite for romance. For intimacy in the evening, request one of the nooks surrounding the bar in the rear. Don't miss the foie gras floating on poached pears and peaches, and the steak tartare (which is actually lightly seared and cleverly studded with pine nuts) is justifiably famous. The parlor, adjacent to the main dining room, is easier on the wallet, just as charming, and far more accessible; reservations aren't even necessary. *1 W. 67th St. (on Central Park W), Upper West Side, 212/877–3500. Reservations essential. AE, DC, MC, V. Subway: 66th St./Lincoln Center. $$$*

9 *e-7*
ELEVEN MADISON PARK
New York's most beloved restaurateur, Danny Meyer, whose Union Square Café and Gramercy Tavern top many a favorite

restaurant list, recently opened Eleven Madison Park and Tabla (*see below*) in a spectacular Art Deco space right on Madison Park. The menu is an homage to the Continental cuisine that was served in this once-highly-fashionable neighborhood's restaurants around the turn of the 20th century. An appropriately French wine list boasts some great bottles and years. Kerry Heffernan's menu has a few historic startlers, such as beef shank–foie gras–veal feet terrine, but the seafood is exemplary. Save room for a plate of special lemon desserts. *11 Madison Ave. (at 24th St.), Murray Hill, 212/ 889–0905. Reservations essential. No lunch Sun. AE, MC, V. Subway: 6 to 23rd St. $$$*

9 *e-3*

FOUR SEASONS

Courtesy of Mies van der Rohe, this large, spectacularly beautiful, modern restaurant is one of the most famous dining destinations in New York, and the city's only restaurant with landmark status. The Grill Room has long been favored for power lunches by publishing, fashion, and financial movers and shakers. The more lavish and romantic Pool Room, centered around an illuminated marble pool, is popular for the prix-fixe pre-theater dinner, as well as post-theater meals. As the name implies, master chef Hitsch Albin's Continental menu changes with the seasons. *99 E. 52nd St. (between Lexington and Park Aves.), Midtown, 212/754–9494. Reservations essential. AE, DC, MC, V. No lunch weekends. Subway: 51st St./Lexington–3rd Aves. $$$$*

11 *b-2*

ONE IF BY LAND, TWO IF BY SEA

If only the food were as appealing as the setting: a roaring fire, fresh flowers, shimmering candlelight, and a live pianist, all in Aaron Burr's former carriage house. The continental entrées, such as beef Wellington and rack of lamb, are nothing more than edible, but the restaurant persists as a favorite spot for intimate dinners. *17 Barrow St. (between W. 4th St. and 7th Ave. S), West Village, 212/228–0822. AE, DC, MC, V. No lunch. Subway: Christopher St./Sheridan Sq. $$$*

9 *e-7*

SONIA ROSE

Many New Yorkers revere the cozy Sonia Rose as a romantic destination, and it's true that the restaurant's provincial atmosphere at its new location offers a change of pace. The three-course prix-fixe menu (with some supplements) is quite reasonable, but something about the French-eclectic food falls a little short—perhaps it's the fact that the entrées seem virtually interchangeable, with similar sauces and the same side dishes. Still, you'll certainly have a quiet, pleasant evening. *150 E. 34th St., (between Lexington and 3rd Aves.) Murray Hill, 212/545–1777. Reservations essential. AE, MC, V. Subway: 6 to 28th St. $$*

9 *c-1*

TAVERN ON THE GREEN

This, the most profitable restaurant in America, is the place New Yorkers pretend to shun—and can't wait for family or friends to visit so they can take them there. With 27,000 square ft, six dining rooms, and glorious Central Park surrounding it, the eatery offers a cavalcade of larger-than-life renditions of American Popular Standards, with a totally overwhelming wine list of over 800 selections. Perfect Caesar salad, user-friendly spice-rubbed barbecued ribs, and magnificent roast prime rib, dry-aged to collapsing tenderness, and served (if you like) on the bone for maximum flavor. Yorkshire pudding? Of course. Note that the Tavern no longer has a dress code. *Central Park W at 67th St., Upper West Side, 212/873–3200. AE, D, DC, MC, V. Subway: 66th St./Lincoln Center; B, C to 72nd St. $$$*

9 *d-3*

21 CLUB

Triple-parked limos mark this clubby establishment in a renewed but unchanged turn-of-the-20th-century setting. The noisy and celebrated downstairs bar is where the power folks lunch and sup; the upstairs is quieter, and less interesting. Accomplished new chef Erik Blauberg has changed the menu substantially with his light touch and contemporary bent, but you can still order the famous oversize (and pricey) "21" burger or the steak tartare. The wine list is impressive, and if you're someone special (say, Gerald Ford) you can even lay away some special vintages for your next visit. Ask for a tour of the fascinating wine cellar in any case. For a rare treat, splurge on the private dining room near the wine cellar; this special enclave is one of the most beautiful in the city. *21 W. 52nd St. (between 5th and 6th Aves.), Midtown, 212/582–7200.*

Reservations essential. AE, DC, MC. Closed weekends in summer. Subway: 5th Ave./53rd St. $$$$

10 d-6

WINDOWS ON THE WORLD

A quarter of a mile in the sky, Windows is quite simply one of the world's most spectacular restaurants. Reopened in 1996 with an exciting new chef, Michael Lomonaco (of 21 Club and TV Food Network fame), the restaurant features contemporary Continental food, decent service, and an exceptional and unexpectedly affordable wine list. Cocktails and hors d'oeuvres (à la carte) are served every day after 3 PM, piano music begins at 4, and it's all backed by one of the world's most exciting views. Reserve far in advance and pray for a clear night. *1 World Trade Center, 107th floor, Lower Manhattan, 212/938–1111. Reservations essential. Jacket and tie, no denim. AE, DC, MC, V. Subway: Cortlandt St./World Trade Center. $$$*

CUBAN

11 b-3

LITTLE HAVANA

This tiny Cuban restaurant couldn't be any cuter. The kitchen, with its light touch and organic ingredients, makes a departure from most of New York's other Cuban eateries. The result is food that's bright and flavorful—from the standard *arroz con pollo* (rice and chicken) to the tamales with or without meat to the traditional *ropa vieja* (braised shredded beef). Prices are moderate and the restaurant is a perfect backup-plan when others on the block are packed. *30 Cornelia St. (between Bleecker and W. 4th Sts.), West Village, 212/255–2212. AE, DC, MC, V. Closed Mon. Subway: W. 4th St./Washington Sq. $*

9 c-3

VICTOR'S CAFE 52

Victor was the pioneer purveyor of upscale Cuban cuisine and atmosphere in his longtime café on Columbus Avenue. He's now been firmly ensconced in the Theater District for years, serving hearty paella, ropa vieja, grilled pork chops, black bean soup, fried bananas, and strong Cuban coffee, among other delicacies. Nightly entertainment adds to the fun. *236 W. 52nd St. (Broadway and 8th Ave.), Theater Dis-*

trict, 212/586–7714. AE, DC, MC, V. Closed Sun. Subway: 50th St. $$

DELICATESSENS

9 c-3

CARNEGIE DELICATESSEN

With ridiculously huge portions, this famous deli draws chaotic crowds of locals and tourists. The good, Jewish-style dishes are certainly not kosher, but they're about as authentic as New York Jewish cuisine gets. The deliciously fatty pastrami and succulent dry corned beef are made on the premises, and they're piled higher on rye than any sandwich you've ever seen. Don't miss the borscht with about a pint of sour cream in and on it, or the creamy cheesecake. Be prepared to sit with strangers at the long tables, to get barked at by waiters, and to take home the leftovers. *854 7th Ave. (at 55th St.), Midtown, 212/757–2245. No credit cards. Subway: 7th Ave.; N, R to 57th St. $$*

9 e-2

KAPLAN'S AT THE DELMONICO

This informal spot for hearty, Jewish-deli food is convenient to 57th Street shopping. The corned-beef and pastrami sandwiches are the way to go, but the menu offers a full range of options. *59 E. 59th St. (between Madison and Park Aves.), Midtown, 212/755–5959. AE, DC, MC, V. Subway: 5th Ave./60th St. $*

10 g-3

KATZ'S DELICATESSEN

A Lower East Side institution, Katz's has terrific hot dogs, inexpensive pastrami, and the best hand-cut, corned-beef sandwiches in town (not kosher). On Sunday it's particularly unbeatable for local color and informality, especially on the part of the waiters; but if you're not in the mood, self-service is always an option. *205 E. Houston St. (at Ludlow St.), Lower East Side, 212/254–2246. No credit cards. Subway: 2nd Ave. $*

10 f-1

SECOND AVENUE KOSHER DELICATESSEN

Bar none, this is hands-down the best kosher deli in the city. Though some of the rough-and-tumble charm was renovated out of the hectic setting, delicious hot Jewish meals still vie aggressively with traditional deli delights for diners' affections (and arteries). A good lunch bet is matzo-ball soup and half a sandwich (the pastrami is to die for); for dinner on cold winter nights, try *cholent* (Jewish cassoulet) or chicken in the pot. You can always take the stuff out, or have your next event catered—think beautiful platters, and chopped liver in the shape of a heart. *156 2nd Ave. (at 10th St.), East Village, 212/677–0606. Reservations not accepted. AE, DC, MC, V. Subway: Astor Pl.; 2nd Ave. $*

EASTERN EUROPEAN

7 *e-6*
ANDRUSHA

Among Andrusha's many charms is its owner, Liana Fingesten, who devises and daily prepares the "eclectic European cuisine"—meaning pretty much the best of high-end Czech and Russian cooking, prepared with conspicuously fresh ingredients. Share the assortment of appetizers, including salmon-roe-stuffed new potato, cognac-infused chicken liver pâté with madeira jelly, roasted beet salad, smoked salmon, and eggplant tartare. Follow with *pelmeni*—little dumpling pouches of savory ground beef, spiced to the nines. Duck is aggressively roasted to leave the skin crackling and the meat extremely rich. Finish with beautiful blueberry blinis. *1370 Lexington Ave. (between 90th and 91st Sts.), Upper East Side, 212/369–9374. AE, V. Subway: 4, 5, 6 to 86th St. $$*

7 *b-7*
BARNEY GREENGRASS

Self-proclaimed "sturgeon king" Barney Greengrass is tops for breakfast and brunch. If you don't like to wake up to orange juice, how about a cold glass of borscht? Order a large platter of smoked salmon and, of course, sturgeon; or try the scrambled eggs with onions and smoked sturgeon. Fresh bagels, bialys, and cream cheese round out the meal. If you still have room, try an individual chocolate babka for dessert. Only complete parties will be seated. *541 Amsterdam Ave. (between 86th and 87th Sts.), Upper West Side, 212/724–4707. Reservations not accepted. No credit cards. Subway: 1, 9 to 86th St. $*

10 *f-3*
SAMMY'S ROUMANIAN

Eating at Sammy's is like attending a bar mitzvah in the Catskills. Rumored to be a favorite hangout of cardiologists, Sammy's serves up Romanian tenderloin steak "with or without garlic," potatoes with gribenes, veal chops, stuffed cabbage, egg creams, and other specialties, all clogging their way to your heart. The pitchers of *schmaltz* (chicken fat), bottles of seltzer, and bowls of pickles on the table add a certain charm. *157 Chrystie St. (between Delancey and Rivington Sts.), Lower East Side, 212/673–0330. AE, DC. Subway: Grand St. $$*

11 *g-1*
VESELKA

A better bowl of borscht you will not find; it's served here with slices of delicious homemade egg bread. The pierogis—filled with cheese, mushroom and sauerkraut, or potato—and blintzes aren't bad, either. Renovated in 1996, this 24-hour, perpetually popular coffee shop may be the last place in New York where communist intellectuals congregate freely. *144 2nd Ave. (at 9th St.), East Village, 212/228–9682. Reservations not accepted. AE, MC, V. Subway: Astor Pl. $*

ECLECTIC

9 *d-3*
ATLAS

With a glorious view of Central Park right out the glass north wall of the restaurant, this prime location also features prime, conspicuously versatile cooking from Thomas Beres: astonishing chicken liver croquettes with the crunch and spice of a great samosa; pristine sashimi of house-smoked salmon; roast prime rib of lamb glazed with lavender; unforgettable garlic butter French fries. Wildly inventive desserts (by Richard Gaetano) follow, such as "Gone Bananas," which features a chocolate Curious George fooling around with a curvaceous lengthwise banana chip, all set on a pudding parfait. All in all, this is a very special new place. *40 Central Park S (between 5th and 6th Aves.), Midtown, 212/759–9191, AE, MC, V. Subway: N, R to 5th Ave. $$$*

10 *d-3*

BLUE RIBBON

The line spills onto the street outside this cheerful storefront, which serves until 4 AM. (Tip: It's a popular late-night haunt for chefs.) There's a raw bar; a pupu platter; a shrimp Provençal; and a heavenly, dark mousselike chocolate cake. The place is noisy, and waits can be long, but the food is worth it. *97 Sullivan St. (between Spring and Prince Sts.), SoHo, 212/274–0404. AE, D, DC, MC, V. Closed Mon. No lunch. Subway: Spring St.; Prince St. $$*

9 *c-8*

BRIGHT FOOD SHOP

Asia and the American Southwest meet at this former coffee shop. The atmosphere is lunch counter, but the food is mega-fusion ("moo shu mex vegetable handrolls with chipotle-peanut sauce") and great. Flavors are bold and the portions are filling. Take-out is available next door at Kitchen Market. *216 8th Ave. (between 21st and 22nd Sts.), Chelsea, 212/243–4433. No credit cards. Subway: C, E to 23rd St. $$*

9 *f-4*

DELEGATES' DINING ROOM

Whether or not you're visiting the U.N., this is a fine place to lunch on Midtown's east end. The buffet food is good (representing the diverse origins of those who dine here), the setting civilized, and the view of the East River lovely. At neighboring tables are ambassadors and attachés. *United Nations, Conference Bldg., 1st Ave. at 46th St. (visitors' entrance), 4th floor, Midtown, 212/963–7625. Reservations essential. AE, DC, MC, V. Photo ID required. No dinner. Closed weekends. Subway: 42nd St./Grand Central. $*

10 *e-1*

GALAXY GLOBAL EATERY

And now for something completely different: Mind-of-her-own chef Deb Stanton has devised a fascinating, mostly salubrious, breakfast-lunch-and-dinner menu that offers generous portions and tops out at just $9.95. It may take you a while to get oriented in the intergalactic diner-on-Mars atmosphere, with its ultramarine glittering ceiling and cozy booths. Note that hemp (in various incarnations) is used in many of the dishes—even in Granny Smith's hemp-crusted apple pie. Standouts are "Thai'd pizza," actually a handroll tied with scallions and stuffed with turkey bacon, mozzarella cheese, grilled chicken, and peanut sauce; and pequillo peppers stuffed with prunes, hempnut, asparagus, spinach, fennel, and couscous. In addition to being a decidedly offbeat place to bring a date, it's also great for restless, fussy children. *15 Irving Pl. (at 15th St.), Gramercy, 212/777–3631. MC, V. Subway: 14th St./Union Sq. $*

9 *b-8*

LOT 61

This far-west Chelsea nightspot has about all you could want in a club—a dramatic space with some very interesting art, an exceptionally au courant crowd, and excellent (if pricey) drinks—and a dinner reservation is a tried-and-true way to avoid a wait behind velvet ropes. The eclectic menu is stronger on appetizers (baby lamb chops and the Asian-influenced crab salad are good choices) than it is on entrées, the latter being over-wrought and over-styled, so grazing is the way to go. *550 W. 21st St. (between 10th and 11th Aves.), Chelsea, 212/243–6555. Reservations essential. AE, D, MC, V. Closed Sun. No lunch. Subway: C, E to 23rd St. $$*

10 *e-7*

MANGIA

One of the first gourmet fast food eateries to grace the Wall Street area, Mangia still holds a special place in many a trader's heart. The salads are fresh and flavorful, the overstuffed sandwiches come on a variety of breads, and the baked goods are out of this world. Best of all, you can get in and out in a matter of minutes without needing to cash in a bond. *40 Wall St. (between Broad and William Sts.), Lower Manhattan, 212/425–4040. AE, D, DC, MC, V. No dinner. Closed Sun. Subway: Wall St. $$*

9 *e-4*

16 E. 48th St. (between 5th and Madison Aves.), Midtown, 212/754–7600. Closed weekends. Subway: 51st St./Lexington–3rd Aves.

9 *d-3*

50 W. 57th St. (between 5th and 6th Aves.), Midtown, 212/582–5882. Subway: N, R to 57th St.

11 e-4

MATCH DOWNTOWN

A popular place for a drink both early and late at night, this lofty, bilevel restaurant is outfitted with booths, industrial beams, and wood paneling. The food is utterly multicultural—dim sum, sushi, Southwestern, and French—and there's an oyster bar for good measure. 60 Mercer St. (between Houston and Prince Sts.), SoHo, 212/343–0830. AE, DC, MC, V. Brunch weekends. Subway: Prince St.; Bleecker St./Broadway–Lafayette St. $$

9 e-2

MATCH UPTOWN

What do you call a restaurant that serves sushi, pasta, and spit-roasted baby chicken on one menu? It doesn't really matter, because people aren't here for the food; they're here for each other. The bar/lounge area is as big as the dining room, and its din travels throughout the restaurant. Still, the decor is beautiful; a sort of Asia–meets–Park Avenue library, accented by dramatic flower arrangements. Some call the food "fussy" and find the portions too tiny, but if you stick to the seared peppered tuna, pan-roasted salmon, and chocolate-banana torte, you won't go wrong. 33 E. 60th St. (between Madison and Park Aves.), Midtown, 212/906–9173. Reservations essential. AE, DC, MC, V. No lunch weekends. Subway: 59th St./Lexington Ave. $$$

7 b-7

MERCHANTS NY

This small chain of large "multi-area restaurants" features a thriving bar, various cozy candlelit dining areas, and a virtual living room that puts most "lounges" around town to shame. The attentive, carefully trained staff will bring you state-of-the-art renditions of beloved clichés such as tuna tartare or steak au poivre, or unusual creations such as masala-rubbed salmon fillet with cucumber-yogurt sauce or grilled trout stuffed with leeks, tomato, garlicky asparagus, and pine-nut sofrito. The bar is extraordinarily well stocked; there are even 18 very different martinis available. 521 Columbus Ave. (at 85th St.), Upper West Side, 212/721–3689. AE, MC, V. Subway: 1, 9 to 86th St. $$

9 f-2

1125 1st Ave. (at 62nd St.), Upper East Side, 212/832–1551. Subway: 59th St./Lexington Ave.

9 c-8

112 7th Ave. (at 17th St.), Chelsea, 212/366–7267. Subway: 18th St.

9 b-5

REVOLUTION

This is one of the better meet-for-a-drink spots along the Ninth Avenue strip and, if drinks turn into dinner, the dining room in back offers some passable eclectic fare. Forgo the overwrought and pretentious pastas such as farfalle with grilled chicken and caramelized cauliflower in Armagnac sauce in favor of such simpler dishes as the boneless roasted chicken with smashed sweet potatoes or the buffalo burger. 611 9th Ave. (between 43rd and 44th Sts.), Hell's Kitchen, 212/489–8451. AE, D, DC, MC, V. No lunch. Subway: A, C, E to 42nd St. $$

11 f-5

RICE

First you'll choose from among different types of the signature grain—basmati, brown, Thai black, or Bhutanese red. Then you can add a savory topping such as Jamaican jerk chicken wings, warm lentil stew, or Indian chicken curry. Next thing you know you're eating a strangely exotic yet surprisingly comforting meal at this tiny dark storefront with a brick wall and tiny tables. Prices are gentle; the portions tend to be a little small but the rice is filling. 227 Mott St. (between Prince and Spring Sts.), SoHo, 212/226–5757. No credit cards. Subway: 6 to Spring St. $

11 b-3

SHOPSIN'S GENERAL STORE

If owner Kenny Shopsin doesn't like your attitude, thinks you might be a corporate exec, or is just having a bad day, he will not hesitate to curse at you and throw you out onto the street. So watch your step or you'll miss an eclectic selection of more than 200 (really!) soups and hundreds of entrées. The best meal, though, is breakfast, which is served only on weekdays because the weekends are too busy. (And during the week the place is open only till 7 PM.) The coffee is good, but you have to get it yourself (the milk is in the fridge). If you don't like it, you know what you can do. 63 Bedford

St. (at Morton St.), West Village, 212/924–5160. DC, MC, V. Closed weekends. Subway: Christopher St./Sheridan Sq. $

9 f-2

TOMASHI

In line with the recent (and usually disastrous) trend that combines Chinese and Japanese cuisine under one roof, Tomashi surpasses them all by adding mainland Chinese cuisine to standard Szechuan and excitingly fresh Japanese. The prodigious sushi bar does everything from sashimi to "tiger eye" (a sliced handroll of fluted squid, salmon, and seaweed). Don't miss the clam and bean-curd soup, the spicy sliced pork appetizer that brings back pork the way it used to taste, and the shockingly good sliced beef with peppercorns. 1367 1st Ave. (between 73rd and 74th Sts.), Upper East Side, 212/535–8726. AE, MC, V. Subway: 77th St. $$

9 e-7

UNION PACIFIC

One of Manhattan's most beautiful and important new restaurants, Union Pacific begins with a waterfall at the entryway and gets even more soothing inside. Rocco DiSpirito's feverishly delicious fusion cooking is breathtakingly delicious. Start with definitive, deep crimson bluefin tuna tartare and move on to blue crab with chanterelles and leeks, then try strawberry charlotte with pistachio ice cream. There's a superlative wine list that aims to partner the extraordinary cuisine. 111 E. 22nd St. (between Lexington Ave. and Park Ave. S), Gramercy. 212/995–8500. Reservations essential. AE, MC, V. Subway: 4, 5, 6 to 23rd St. $$$$

ETHIOPIAN

11 f-4

GHENET

African-inspired art adorns the walls at this welcoming Ethiopian restaurant where the food is authentic, spicy, and delicious. No utensils are offered and none are needed—a never-ending supply of spongy injera bread is used to scoop up the flavorful food. In addition to tasty poultry and meat dishes, there is a good selection of vegetarian dishes such as rich and fragrant collard greens with Ethiopian spices, and a dish of spicy potatoes with cabbage and carrots

in an onion sauce. The menu suggests wine pairings for each dish. 284 Mulberry St. (between Houston and Prince Sts.), SoHo, 212/343–1888. AE, MC, V. Closed Mon. Subway: 6 to Spring St. $

9 b-4

MESKEREM

Be prepared to eat with your hands at this authentic, no-frills Ethiopian joint. The best dishes come unceremoniously blobbed on huge pieces of injera, a soft, yeasty, lightly tangy flat bread traditionally used as both plate and utensil. Expect deeply spiced, currylike stews; the lamb selections are excellent, as is the vegetarian combination. 468 W. 47th St. (between 9th and 10th Aves.), Hell's Kitchen, 212/664–0520. D, MC, V. Subway: C, E to 50th St. $

FRENCH

11 c-5

ALISON ON DOMINICK STREET

This understated restaurant is worth the trek; wonderful country-French food is served in a romantic, candlelit setting. Try the ragout of mussels, braised lamb shank, or sautéed sea bass in a tarragon-flavor broth; then go for the chocolate-hazelnut ice cream or crème brûlée. 38 Dominick St. (between Varick and Hudson Sts.), West Village, 212/727–1188. Reservations essential. AE, MC, V. Subway: 1, 9, A, C, E to Canal St. $$$$

11 f-3

ASTOR RESTAURANT AND LOUNGE

A roomy, handsomely lit, up-to-the-moment bistro with deep cranberry leather banquettes and booths makes a commodious showcase for Scott Snyder's scintillating dishes, all gently priced. Particularly succulent calamari—fried tentacles, grilled body, roasted eggplant and pepper compote—make the perfect opening. Seared tuna steaks are staked on a smashed potato wedge in a lemony broth threaded with escarole. And the tangy lemon tart will leave you panting. Downstairs is a state-of-the-art lounge where some very attractive people hang out. 316 Bowery (at Bleecker St.), East Village, 212/253–8644. AE, MC, V. Subway: Bleecker St./Broadway–Lafayette St. $$

11 *e-5*

BALTHAZAR

Balthazar is a serious scene and difficult to get into. (Just getting them on the phone becomes a crusade.) Keith McNally's recreation of a French brasserie with an adjacent bakery is a smash hit—crowded and noisy, but invigorating. The decor—fin-de-siècle mirrors, tile floor, banquettes—makes the place look a hundred years old. And lo, the food is good: try the *plateau de fruits de mer* (raw-bar platter), creamy country rillettes of rabbit with marinated mushrooms, warm goat-cheese tart with caramelized onions, duck shepherd's pie, or seared salmon with porcini and polenta. For dessert, there is a wonderful lemon mille-feuille with sorbet and a fine crème brûlée. *80 Spring St. (between Broadway and Crosby St.), SoHo, 212/965–1414. Reservations essential. AE, MC, V. Subway: Spring St.; Prince St. $$$*

10 *d-1*

BAR SIX

The bar is always packed at this noisy hot spot, which comes complete with a chic and aloof waitstaff and matching clientele. Once you get past the bar, you'll find yourself in an attractively pared-down bistro with decent, inexpensive French-Moroccan dishes such as lamb couscous with preserved lemon. Be prepared for noise at night, when the music pounds and the crowd is in high spirits. *502 6th Ave. (between 12th and 13th Sts.), Greenwich Village, 212/691–1363. AE, MC, V. Subway: F to 14th St.; L to 6th Ave. $*

10 *e-7*

BAYARD'S

The site of this landmark building has been a center of city life since New York's days as a Dutch colony. The current structure was built in 1837 and in 1914 became the India House, a club for businessmen who specialized in foreign trade. It became a restaurant in 1998, and the interior was painstakingly restored and many original details, including major nautical artwork and artifacts, were uncovered, and contribute to the beautiful setting. The menu, crafted by chef Luc Dendieval, offers such formal French dishes as *cassolette* (a small casserolelike pan) of sweetbreads, *côte de boeuf sauce Choron* (beef served with a tomato-béarnaise sauce), and salmon in a soft leek crust.

India House, 1 Hanover Sq., Lower Manhattan, 212/514–9454. AE, DC, MC, V. Reservations essential. Closed Sun. No lunch Sat. Subway: $$$

11 *f-4*

BISTRO MARGOT

Inexpensive French home cooking is served here in rather cramped but friendly surroundings. The menu sticks to basic bistro fare—good paté, steak frites, and the like. *26 Prince St. (between Elizabeth and Mott Sts.), SoHo, 212/274–1027. Subway: Prince St.; Bleecker St./Broadway–Lafayette St. $*

11 *c-4*

BLUE RIBBON BAKERY

Sometimes things unforetold change destiny, and such was the case with the Blue Ribbon Bakery. During its renovation in 1997, the Bromberg brothers, of Blue Ribbon (*see* Eclectic, *above*) and Blue Ribbon Sushi (*see* Japanese, *below*), came upon a century-old Italian-tile coal-burning oven. The pair were so enamored of their discovery that they let it dictate the destiny of the restaurant. There are hefty sandwiches on homemade bread (from the oven of course), lots of baked goods, and entrées that include trout and Cornish game hen (also from the oven). There are also small plates of charcuterie, pâté, and tapas style dishes. The basement dining room is dark and intimate, with a private area for parties of 8–10 that also affords a view of the oven. Upstairs is a Parisian style café, perfect for lingering over a glass of good wine and conversation. *33 Downing St. (at Bedford St.), West Village, 212/337–0404. Reservations not accepted. AE, DC, MC, V. Closed Mon. Subway: Houston St. $$*

11 *d-8*

BOULEY BAKERY

Who wouldn't want to try a sandwich by the chef once considered the best in this city of great chefs? Walk into the bakery side of this unusual "café" and order away. On the other side, you can sit at one of the 12 coveted elegant tables and enjoy the master in his true form. Tableside bread service—at least 12 varieties are always offered—starts the parade of interesting dishes, most good, some great. But despite the casual-sounding name, you'll pay formal prices in the dining room. *120 W. Broadway (between Duane and Reade Sts.), Tribeca, 212/964–*

2525. *Reservations essential. AE, MC, V.
Subway: Chambers St. $$$$*

9 *f-3*
BOUTERIN

The honeyed glow inside Bouterin spills
across the fresh flowers and auberge
bric-a-brac. Chef/owner Antoine
Bouterin is obsessed with elongating
the flavors of every ingredient in his
Provençale cooking. A bay scallop gratin
with elbow macaroni is deeply comforting, and the onion tart with anchovies
and olives is moan-inducing. The seven-
hour simmer given the luxurious lamb
stew renders the meat spoon-tender.
And the "Floating Island" features twin
meringues floating on a pond of perfectly smooth crème Anglaise. *420 E.
59th St. (between 1st and York Aves.),
Midtown, 212/758–0323. Reservations
essential. AE, MC, V. Subway: 59th
St./Lexington Ave. $$*

9 *f-4*
BOX TREE

This Art Nouveau town house not only
serves classic French food, but has
charming rooms upstairs for those
interested in spending the night. If
that's not romantic, what is? Attentive
service and a fireplace help kindle those
amorous sparks, and the caviar with bli-
nis and chilled vodka catalyze matters
even further. It's small and very pricey,
but no one ever said love was cheap.
*242 E. 49th St. (between 2nd and 3rd
Aves.), Midtown, 212/758–8320. Reserva-
tions essential. AE, MC, V. No lunch
weekends. Subway: 51st St./Lexington–3rd
Aves. $$$$*

9 *b-1*
CAFÉ LUXEMBOURG

Reminiscent of 1930s Paris, the Art
Deco Luxembourg continues to be one
of the most popular late-night see-and-
be-seen spots in town, with plenty of
stargazing opportunities and highly flat-
tering lighting. Best of all, you can also
have a wonderful meal. The menu
ranges from simple brasserie fare—
steak and pommes frites—to imagina-
tive seasonal creations. Additional
tables have been added, but the restau-
rant still gets so crowded that you'll
have to wait a bit even if you have a
reservation. *200 W. 70th St. (between
Amsterdam and West End Aves.), Upper
West Side, 212/873–7411. AE, MC, V. Sub-
way: 1, 2, 3, 9 to 72nd St. $$$*

11 *b-2*
CAFÉ MILOU

The main draw at this clubby French
bistro is its hours—the place stays open
24 hours a day. The basic French food is
good and simple. The *croque monsieur*
(a French-style grilled ham-and-cheese
sandwich) is superlative, and the crispy
frites will satisfy any late night hunger
pang. Steamed mussels served in a
cast-iron skillet are both novel and satisfying. *92 7th Ave. S (between Bleecker and
Grove Sts.), West Village, 212/414–9824.
AE, V, MC. Subway: Christopher
St./Sheridan Sq. $$*

9 *d-5*
CAFÉ UN DEUX TROIS

This large, convivial Parisian brasserie–
style eatery is perfect for pre-theater din-
ner. Leftover Corinthian columns, Cray-
olas for doodling on the paper
tablecloths, and a menu offering moder-
ately priced basic-and-better French fare
attract a diverse and noisy crowd. Ser-
vice can be dicey (take this into account
if you're trying to make curtain time),
but you'll still leave happy. *123 W. 44th
St. (between Broadway and 6th Ave.),
Theater District, 212/354–4148. AE, DC,
MC, V. Subway: 42nd St./Times Sq. $$*

10 *c-4*
CAPSOUTO FRÈRES

The biggest problem with dining at Cap-
souto Frères is finding the obscure
Tribeca street corner where it is located.
Once inside, however, the romantic interior, a unique take on timeless country
French in a converted warehouse space,
will put you at ease. The traditional
French food is good but sighs of ecstasy
are to be reserved for the excellent soufflé at the meal's end. *451 Washington St.
(at Watts St.), Tribeca, 212/966–4900.
Reservations essential. AE, DC, MC, V. No
lunch. Subway: 1, 9 to Canal St. $$$*

11 *c-7*
CHANTERELLE

In Tribeca's historic Mercantile
Exchange Building, chef David Waltuck
serves sublime nouvelle French cuisine
in a light, pretty dining room where the
service, under the direction of Karen
Waltuck, makes everyone feel like a priv-
ileged guest. Make tracks for chef Wal-
tuck's signature seafood sausage, rack
of lamb, Arctic char, and excellent
desserts, and dip into the well-chosen
cheese board. The prix-fixe menu, which

changes weekly, is expensive but worth it. *2 Harrison St. (at Hudson St.), Tribeca, 212/966–6960. Reservations essential. AE, MC, V. Closed Sun.–Mon. Subway: Franklin St. $$$$*

9 *c-7*

CHELSEA BISTRO AND BAR

One of New York's best neighborhood restaurants, this comfortable bistro with booths and polished mirrors serves high-tone, well-seasoned French food, redolent of fresh herbs and country flavors. Don't miss the foie-gras ravioli. A fireplace and enclosed garden terrace are bonuses. *358 W. 23rd St. (between 8th and 9th Aves.), Chelsea, 212/727–2026. AE, MC, V. No lunch. Subway: C, E to 23rd St. $$$*

7 *e-2*

DANIEL

The chef and owner of this four-star establishment, Daniel Boulud, first made a name for himself at Le Cirque. Now that he's in his own kitchen, critics and diners lunge en masse to his creations, and reservations can be very tough to obtain. The somewhat eccentric dining room is intended to resemble a Venetian palace. The entire staff is surprisingly attentive and friendly, the crowd is eclectic, and the food is some of the best in New York. Classic French dishes share the menu with updated versions of more rustic cuisine. Some of the more popular dishes include roasted squab with foie gras, lobster with wood sorrel in mushroom broth, an astonishing oxtail terrine, and black sea bass wrapped in crisp potatoes. *60 E. 65th St. (between Madison and Park Aves.), Upper East Side, 212/288–0033. Reservations essential. AE, D, MC, V. Subway: 68th St./Hunter College. $$$$*

7 *e-7*

DEMARCHELIER

Both the food and decor of this neighborhood bistro are trés French. The menu holds no surprises: steak-frites, salmon with beurre blanc, sole meunière, and onion soup. Unfortunately, the service is also authentic. The classic apple tart is a great ending for your meal. *50 E. 86th St. (between 5th and Madison Aves.), Upper East Side, 212/249–6300. AE, MC, V. Subway: 4, 5, 6 to 86th St. $$*

11 *d-5*

FELIX

A lively, neighborhood French bistro with doors that open onto the street in warm weather, this corner restaurant attracts lively, young Europeans, shoppers, and gallery-goers. The food is classic: onion tart, steak-frites, and seven-hour braised leg of lamb. *340 W. Broadway (at Grand St.), SoHo, 212/431–0021. AE. Subway: Canal St. $$*

10 *b-1*

FLORENT

This gritty storefront in the meatpacking district has become a wee-hours mecca for breakfast and for the crowd—a stylish but egalitarian mixture of up- and downtowners. The reasonably priced dishes include wonderful French onion soup, couscous, sweetbreads, mussels in white-wine broth, duck mousse, and *boudin noir* (blood sausage). Sit at the counter (think diner) or proper tables (think bistro). *69 Gansevoort St. (between Washington and Greenwich Sts.), West Village, 212/989–5779. No credit cards. Open 24 hours. Subway: A, C, E to 14th St.; L to 8th Ave. $$*

11 *d-4*

FRONTIÈRE

Frontière is a pretty, romantic little spot with exposed-brick walls, candles, and a lovely old zinc bar. Try the grilled wild-mushroom salad with warm potatoes, the côte de boeuf for two, or the sautéed salmon with grilled spinach, fried potatoes, and béarnaise sauce. *199 Prince St. (between MacDougal and Sullivan Sts.), SoHo, 212/387–0898. AE, DC, MC, V. Subway: Spring St. $$$*

11 *d-4*

JEAN CLAUDE

This noisy, crowded, friendly bistro feels strikingly like Paris. The food is highly refined, and the menu changes daily. The fish, leg of lamb with roast-garlic mashed potatoes, and crème brûlée are all excellent. *137 Sullivan St. (between Houston and Prince Sts.), SoHo, 212/475–9232. No credit cards. No lunch. Subway: Spring St. $$*

9 *c-2*

JEAN GEORGES

Rarely does a restaurant open to such ecstatic acclaim. Jean-Georges Vongerichten (of Vong [see above] and Jo Jo [see below] fame) is back in his haute-French mode. Adam Tihany's decor is elegantly minimalist, allowing Central Park to encroach voluptuously. The food is formal French. Highlights on one seasonal spring menu include asparagus spears with morel sauce, skate with brown butter, and sweetbreads with demi-glace. Summer brings lemony young garlic soup with a floating stack of fresh herbs and user-friendly frog's legs on the side. And pastry chef Eric Hubert practically reinvents dessert. A crème brûlée sampler—five varieties, including green tea and licorice—is other-worldly. The emphasis is on tableside service, not for show but for pampering. For a less expensive, less formal experience you can also try the Mistral Terrace (al fresco) or the Nougatine Room (open for breakfast), each with a different, lighter menu. *Trump International Hotel and Tower, 1 Central Park W (at 59th St.), Midtown, 212/299–3900. Jacket and tie required. Reservations essential. AE, DC, MC, V. Subway: 59th St./Columbus Circle. $$$$*

9 *e-1*

JO JO

The space is somewhat cramped in this Upper East Side brownstone, but once you're seated, you won't care: This is some of the very finest cooking in town. Jean-Georges Vongerichten's flagship still draws quite a crowd after more than five years of consistently inventive and delicious—and salubrious—food, based in his Alsatian roots but influenced by his love for Asian cuisine, all sorts of herbs, and straight-ahead flavors. To experience his profound understanding of vegetables, try the signature 27 vegetables simmered in their own juices and dribbled with chive oil. Follow with heavenly steamed black bass with a confit of carrots, or roasted lamb loin with artichokes and fava beans. For dessert: the world-famous Valrhona fallen chocolate cake, imitated everywhere, but never equaled. Try for a table upstairs; downstairs can get fairly noisy. *160 E. 64th St. (between Lexington and 3rd Aves.), Upper East Side, 212/223–5656. Reservations essential. AE, D, DC, MC, V. Closed Sun. No lunch Sat. Subway: 59th St./Lexington Ave. $$$*

9 *f-2*

L'ABSINTHE

If you're craving a true Paris fix, look no further. Highly stylized, the dining room is lined with giant gleaming mirrors and filled with a steady golden light. Chef and co-owner Jean-Michel Bergougnoux's dishes are as carefully composed as a classic elegy. Start with champagne and sautéed foie gras, or stay down to earth with snail fricassée with a Parmesan tuille and a deep-fried slice of prosciutto. Follow with mushroom-crusted lamb rack chop or "L'Absinthe surf and turf"—a perfectly roasted lobster tail and a rich slab of grilled hanger steak. Desserts are not to be missed: the ubiquitous "molten" chocolate cake gets its due here. *227 E. 67th St. (between 2nd and 3rd Aves.), Upper East Side, 212/794–4950. AE, MC, V. Subway: 68th St./Hunter College. $$$*

4 *b-12*

LA BOUILLABAISSE

Since the opening of this Brooklyn bistro more than a decade back, the subway is enough to transport New Yorkers to what feels like a restaurant on a quiet street in Paris. The menu is presented on a blackboard, brought to your table for inspection. The food is unpretentiously excellent. You'll always find satisfaction in the signature stew with lots of fish and a rich, flavorful broth. If you like sweetbreads, here's where to have them. A huge portion is crisply fried in butter and served with mashed potatoes and braised red cabbage. Other offerings change seasonally. The staff is always friendly, if sometimes so busy it's hard to get their attention. *145 Atlantic Ave. (between Clinton and Henry Sts.), Brooklyn Heights, 718/522–8275. No credit cards. No lunch weekends. Subway: N, R, 2, 3 to Court St. $$*

9 *d-3*

LA CARAVELLE

La Caravelle has been one New York's most fashionable classic-French restaurants for over 30 years. The food has gone up and down during that time, but under chef Cyril Renaud's utterly delicious tenure, the restaurant is now riding the crest of its wave. Nobody does the classics—quenelles, foie gras, terrines—better. Service is heavy on the tableside show, but the effect is charming in this amiable setting. *33 W. 55th St. (between 5th and 6th Aves.), Midtown, 212/586–4252. Reservations essential. AE, DC, MC, V. Closed Sun. and holidays. Subway: 5th Ave./53rd St. $$$$*

9 *e-3*

LA CÔTE BASQUE

Although this institution had to relocate down the street in 1995, not much has changed (least of all those spectacular murals), and in fact some feel that the move jogged the institution out of a long lull. Pushing 40, the restaurant still prepares classic French cuisine precisely as it was meant to be. Chef Jean-Jacques Rachou's oak-smoked salmon, cassoulet, and Dover sole are among the best choices, each skillfully plated tableside by dexterous waiters, who have been known to toss attitude around with the entrées. Prices are high, but portions are large. *60 E. 55th St. (between 5th and 6th Aves.), Midtown, 212/688–6525. Reservations essential. AE, DC, MC, V. Closed Sun. Subway: 5th Ave./53rd St. $$$$*

7 *f-7*

LA FOURCHETTE

This extremely poised new showcase for the considerable talents of young chef Marc Murphy is absolutely impeccable. Set in one of the tallest buildings on the Upper East Side, the bilevel dining room is awash in enticing aromas. There is a lovely atrium in back, and a festively appointed private outdoor patio. There is a superb, mostly French wine list offering 180 bottles. Tuck into foie gras terrine with sweet onion compote; fresh fettuccine with all-the-rage cod cheeks and tomato confit; and ruby-rare squab breast wrapped in Swiss chard leaves, braised, and broiled. Finish with unabashed 10-yolks-to-the-quart-of-cream crème brûlée, and you won't forget La Fourchette any time soon. *1608 1st Ave. (at E. 84th St.), Upper East Side, 212/249–5924. AE, MC, V. Subway: 4, 5, 6 to 86th St. $$$*

9 *e-1*

LA GOULUE

This highly evocative, Art Nouveau Parisian setting serves traditional brasserie food and happens to be more comfortable than most of its Madison Avenue French neighbors—hence the usual presence of celebrities. True to the neighborhood (and to Paris itself), sidewalk seating is available for optimal people-watching. *28 E. 70th St. (off Madison Ave.), Upper East Side, 212/988–8169. AE, DC, MC, V. Closed Sun. Subway: 68th St./Hunter College. $$$*

9 *e-3*

LA GRENOUILLE

La Grenouille is the grand dame of New York's haute-French cuisine, complete with a lush floral arrangements, a deeply romantic setting, and absolutely impeccable service. Enjoy beautifully prepared and perfectly served food (quenelles are particularly tender and fine) among New York's power elite and other crowned heads—if you can afford the prix-fixe. *3 E. 52nd St. (between 5th and Madison Aves.), Midtown, 212/752–1495. Reservations essential. AE, DC, MC, V. Closed Aug., and Sun.–Mon. Subway: 5th Ave./53rd St. $$$$*

9 *d-4*

LE BERNARDIN

GQ recently touted this beautiful and spacious French restaurant as the best in the country; the magazine's not alone in this assessment. The emphasis is on seafood, and in chef Eric Ripert's hands, marine life becomes manna. Frothy "lobster cappuccino" bisque, Spanish mackerel tartare—anything is possible. The service is doting; the wine list extensive; and, for a new taste sensation, the sommelier will recommend some light-bodied reds that go well with creatures of the sea. The bill can be a shock, but what price the food of the gods? *Equitable Bldg., 155 W. 51st St. (between 6th and 7th Aves.), Midtown, 212/489–1515. Reservations essential. Closed Sun. No lunch weekends. Subway: 49th St.; 47th–50th Sts./Rockefeller Center. $$$$*

9 *e-2*

LE BILBOQUET

A small, informal, yet fashionable destination, Le Bilboquet is a good place for an alfresco lunch in season, with sidewalk seating and wonderful salads. Evenings inside are filled with very attractive people and joie de vivre—i.e., a lot of ambient noise. *25 E. 63rd St. (between Madison and Park Aves.), Upper East Side, 212/751–3036. Reservations essential. AE. No dinner Sun. Subway: 59th St./Lexington Ave. $$*

9 *e-4*

LE CIRQUE 2000

Gone are the low ceilings and monkey sconces: picture a spaceship landing in an Italian piazza. From the roller-coaster curves of the futuristic bar to the soaring, gilded, turn-of-the-20th-century ceilings, Adam Tihany's loopy design for

Sirio Maccioni's new dining room of the rich and famous is certainly a study in contrasts. No surprises emerge from the multimillion-dollar kitchen; just straightforward, modern, state-of-the-art French cooking. Service can be doting or nonexistent, depending on your stature. Love it or hate it, this is a restaurant that must be experienced to be believed. Order the crème brûlée for dessert and you'll leave happy. *New York Palace Hotel, 455 Madison Ave. (between 50th and 51st Sts.), Midtown, 212/303–7788. Reservations essential. AE, DC, MC, V. Subway: E, F to 5th Ave./53rd St.; 51st St./Lexington–3rd Aves. $$$$*

10 *b-1*

LE GANS

Picking up on two trends—New Yorkers' renewed fascination with bistros and the development of the meatpacking district—Le Gans opened in 1998 and immediately attracted a fashionable crowd. The long, narrow restaurant is tastefully decorated. Simple, classic food such as goose terrine with fresh brioche and pan-fried soft-shell crab are well prepared, if a tad expensive, but stay away from the salt-baked fish. Reservations are recommended. *46 Gansevoort St. (at Greenwich St.), West Village, 212/675–5224. AE, DC, MC, V. No lunch. Subway: A, C, E to 14th St., L to 8th Ave. $$*

11 *b-3*

LE GIGOT

This adorable French bistro—on a block-long strip filled with great eateries—sets the mood with wood floors, mirror walls, dim sconces, and tables that are all but on top of one another. The menu sticks fairly close to bistro classics (bouillabaisse, steak frites, duck confit) and won't offer any culinary epiphanies. But the food is distinguished by the fact that it's lovingly prepared and always tasty. *18 Cornelia St. (between Bleecker and W. 4th Sts.), West Village, 212/627–3737. AE. No lunch. Subway: W. 4th St./Washington Sq. $$*

11 *f-5*

LE JARDIN BISTRO

On a forgotten block just east of SoHo, Le Jardin Bistro feels like a country French restaurant that's been around forever. The food too is classic country French cooking—bouillabaisse, cassoulet, and the like—that speaks for itself without creative enhancements. The charming handwritten menu, bucolic back garden, pretty lace curtains, and the worn wood floors and tables create a cohesive and transporting dining environment. The service is warm and attentive, especially considering the reasonable menu and wine list. *25 Cleveland Pl. (between Kenmare and Spring Sts.), SoHo, 212/343–9599. Reservations essential. AE, DC, MC, V. Subway: 6 to Spring St. $$*

9 *e-7*

LES HALLES

This très Parisian butcher shop and bistro is casual and cacophonous, with a charming, fin-de-siècle decor. As the shadows lengthen, eager diners pack in like sardines—with very good reason—for the *frisée aux lardons* (frisée salad with bacon) with Roquefort; rich and ruddy rillettes; authentic cassoulet; boudin noir with apples; terrific steak frites (more than a few maintain that the fries are the best in town); supple steak tartare made tableside; and the interesting, affordable wine list. *411 Park Ave. S (between 28th and 29th St.), Murray Hill, 212/679–4111. Reservations essential. AE, DC, MC, V. Subway: 33rd St. $$*

9 *e-3*

LESPINASSE

Only a few years old, this over-the-top formal restaurant has helped revive fine dining in New York and hotel dining everywhere. Chef Christian Delouvrier creates food that wallops you with flavor and offers an interesting contrast to the soothing decor and quietly rich ambience. The impeccable wait staff takes care of your every need while you concentrate on the chef's otherworldly creations. If you're lucky, these will include ragout of squab, braised salmon with crispy artichokes, or chocolate-banana soufflé. The large wine selection is made more approachable by an aim-to-please sommelier. *St. Regis Hotel, 2 E. 55th St. (between 5th and Madison Aves.), Midtown, 212/339–6719. Reservations essential. Closed Sun. Breakfast daily. Subway: 5th Ave./53rd St. $$$$*

9 *e-8*

L'EXPRESS

This wildly popular Flatiron District bistro is open 24 hours, and the later you visit, the better the experience you'll have. During peak hours, the place is often so mobbed that it doesn't exactly earn its name. The menu is more wide-ranging than that at most bistros in town, stretching to include such specialty items as blood sausage, roasted pig's foot, and pike quenelles. Seafood-of-the-day is usually splendid. *249 Park Ave. S (at 20th St.), Flatiron District, 212/254–5858. AE, MC, V. Subway: 6, N, R to 23rd St. $$*

10 *c-1*

LE ZOO

This somewhat cramped yet cozy bistro serves reasonably priced French items that often sound better than they taste. The seasonal, creamless turnip soup is smooth and satisfying, and the chicken breast with chanterelles is flavorful. The adorable French hosts are gracious and attentive, which can make up for the fact that you must climb over a radiator to get to your table. *114 W. 11th St. (at Greenwich St.), West Village, 212/620–0393. Reservations not accepted. AE, MC, V. No lunch. Subway: Christopher St./Sheridan Sq. $$*

10 *f-3*

LUCIEN

This first-class bistro, pulled together by a master restaurateur, in a neighbor-

---

---

hood fairly wailing for one, features state-of-the-art bistro fare, from exemplary, squeaky-clean mussels to plump, tender steak frites to a bulging wedge of tarte Tatin with cinnamon ice cream. Prices are low enough to keep the place perpetually jammed until 2 AM, but don't let that dissuade you: Sink in and you'll be smiling in no time. *14 1st Ave. (between 1st and 2nd Sts.), East Village, 212/260–6481. AE, MC, V. Subway: 2nd Ave. $*

9 *f-4*

LUTÈCE

It's hard to believe a company known in New York for its garish theme restaurants purchased this restaurant from fabled French chef André Soltner—but they've installed the inspired Eberhard Mueller in the kitchen, and he's turning out very fine, somewhat lighter contemporary-French fare, with a few Alsatian classics held over from the Soltner days. The room has been nicely updated, but the staff still won't smile. *249 E. 50th St. (between 2nd and 3rd Aves.), Midtown, 212/752–2225. Reservations essential. AE, DC, MC. Closed Sun. Subway: 51st St./Lexington–3rd Aves. $$$$*

11 *d-7*

MONTRACHET

One of the first restaurants to open in Tribeca, Drew Nieporent's Montrachet remains a fine choice for fine, imaginative French nouvelle cuisine in a spare, high-ceiling contemporary setting. The prix-fixe menu includes inventive fish choices, such as house lobster salad with asparagus and passion fruit vinaigrette, and truffle-crusted salmon, as well as elegant desserts. Spend some time perusing the award-winning wine list. *239 W. Broadway (between Walker and White Sts.), Tribeca, 212/219–2777. AE. Reservations essential. No lunch Mon.–Thurs. and Sat. Closed Sun. Subway: Canal St. $$$*

11 *d-8*

ODEON

This large, '30s-style cafeteria is one of Tribeca's original late-night in spots. The French-bistro food is not terribly ambitious, but it always manages to please. The softly lit, low-frills ambience is timeless, as is the intriguing cast of characters, especially in the wee hours. *145 W. Broadway (at Thomas St.), Tribeca, 212/233–0507. AE, DC, MC, V.*

No lunch weekends. Brunch Sun. Subway: Chambers St. $$

10 b-1
PASTIS

A spinoff of Balthazar (*above*), Pastis offers twice the ambiance and half the hassle of the original. A no-reservations policy assures you'll get a seat, though you'll have to wait for it, and the menu offers the simple dishes that are best at Balthazar—steak frites, leeks vinaigrette, salmon in a herbal sauce, and of course the excellent crusty bread—at slightly lower prices. The casual atmosphere, with everything from French accordion music to the Rolling Stones emanating from the sound system, makes it perfect for any occasion. *9 9th Ave. (at Little W. 12th St.), Chelsea, 212/929–4844. Reservations not accepted. AE, DC, MC, V. Subway: A, C, E to 14th St.; L to 8th Ave.* $$–$$$

12 c-5
PATOIS

Alan Harding's tiny bistro has become the perfect neighborhood spot, thanks to its cool, relaxed atmosphere and delicious, reasonably priced fare. Standouts are the goat cheese and roasted tomato charlotte, grilled salmon with red pepper sauce, and prime rib with fries and red-wine sauce. There's even a tented garden out back that has a cozy, cabin-like feel, and patrons must pass though the crowded kitchen to get to it. *255 Smith St. (between Douglass and Degraw Sts.), Carroll Gardens, Brooklyn, 718/855–1535. AE. No lunch. Subway: Carroll St.* $

9 e-4
PEACOCK ALLEY

Set like a sumptuous emerald in the gallant Waldorf–Astoria is one of the city's finest restaurants, showcasing the passionate inspirations of chef Laurent Gras. The extravagantly elegant dining room comes with its own special hush. Menus are strictly seasonal, and organized thematically. In a unique departure—a quiet revolution in high dining—portions are sized between an appetizer and an entrée, and priced to encourage you to order at least three (one course: $22, two: $40, three: $54, four: $67). Hopefully, the incredible Venetian pasta will be on the menu when you visit: Foie gras is poached in a black truffle emulsion, tucked into a large pasta tube, and floated on mascarpone/Parmesan sauce.

It's doubtful that you'll find anything less than superb, but pay particular attention to whatever game and seafood are featured. And desserts are as insanely good as everything else, so try to save room. It's expensive, but worth every cent. *301 Park Ave. (at 50th St.), Midtown, 212/872–4895. AE, MC, V. Reservations essential. Subway: 51st St./Lexington–3rd Aves.* $$$$

9 d-3
PETROSSIAN

Amid lush Belle Epoque decor, deeply elegant caviar service awaits you at this posh Parisian palace. The $75 tasting of Beluga, Osetra, and Sevruga caviars arrives in a beautiful, three-side Christofle holder; the gold-plate paddle pushes the experience right over the top. An icy glass of champagne or premium vodka makes this the perfect pretheater stop (or, more appropriately, pre-opera, with Lincoln Center so nearby). There are also bargain prix-fixe lunch and dinner menus available. *182 W. 58th St. (at 7th Ave.), Midtown, 212/245–2214. AE, MC, V. No lunch Sun. Subway: 57th St.* $$$

9 c-2
PICHOLINE

Picholine *is* the French countryside. Chef/owner Terrance Brennan's Mediterranean state of mind is announced with the bowl of olives (*picholines*) brought to your table with a basket of fresh-baked bread, and dominates the entire enticing menu. Delicate pastas, perfectly cooked whole fish, hearty game dishes . . . everything is delicious. Don't miss the cheese course; the restaurant actually has a cave in which they ripen the finest selection of cheeses in the city—some even say the best outside of France. The award-winning, friendly wine-and-cheese steward will guide you to the best choices. *35 W. 64th St. (between Broadway and Central Park W), Upper West Side, 212/724–8585. Reservations essential. AE, D, DC, MC, V. Subway: 66th St./Lincoln Center.* $$$

11 d-4
PROVENCE

This rustic SoHo bistro wins high marks for its authentic Provençal food, moderate prices, and romantic little tented garden, complete with flower-encircled stone fountain. Try the bourride, a garlicky Mediterranean fish stew; steak-frites; braised rabbit; and bouillabaisse.

The Provençal wines are well-priced. *38 MacDougal St. (between Prince and Houston Sts.), SoHo, 212/475–7500. AE. Subway: C, E to Prince St. $$$*

7 *f-8*

QUATORZE BIS

Uptowners once trekked downtown for this off-the-beaten-track charmer. The downtown location is long closed, but its uptown outpost remains packed. The reasonably priced, reliable bourgeois-French fare; the compatible wine list; and the casual, authentic bistro setting combine to bring you pretty close to Paris. Have the steak frites. *323 E. 79th St., Upper East Side, 212/535–1414. Reservations essential. AE, MC, V. Subway: 77th St. $$*

11 *d-4*

RAOUL'S

Raoul's is a permanent fixture in an ever-changing neighborhood. Brave the dark, noisy, and smoky bar; the equally dark front room; and the bustle of the kitchen to get to the somewhat more serene dining room. Stick to the basics—veal chop, the roasted chicken, seared tuna—and enjoy a fine meal. *180 Prince St. (near Sullivan St.), 212/966–3518. Reservations essential. AE, MC, V. No lunch. Subway: C, E to Spring St. $$$*

11 *c-4*

RESTAURANT BOUGHALEM

If only all the small French restaurants lining Greenwich Village streets had food as good as at this neighborhood destination. Ex-Bouley chef James Rafferty prepares a seasonal menu that might include appetizers of roasted cod cakes or potato and cheese dumplings with an herbed mayonnaise, and entrées of a succulent sea bass accompanied by a sautée of broccoli rabe or an impressive grilled chicken. Tall and handsome, Monsieur Boughalem is a most gracious host and will probably greet you warmly at the door, a good thing because he will inevitably tell you to wait on the street for a table as the restaurant doesn't take reservations, and the bar is usually full. *14 Bedford St. (between Downing and Houston Sts.), 212/414–4764. No credit cards. No lunch. Subway: Houston St. $$*

11 *d-5*

SOHO STEAK

The manly name belies the fact that SoHo Steak is really a French bistro that happens to serve wonderful food, mostly meat, at reasonable prices. Tables are close together—really close—but the fashionable crowd is usually happy, no doubt because of the excellent filet mignon, or the like, on the table in front of them. Other delicious dishes include braised oxtail raviolo and double-cut pork chops from the wood-burning oven. There are a couple of concessions for non-carnivores, as well as a pleasant Sunday brunch. *90 Thompson St. (between Prince and Spring Sts.), SoHo, 212/226–0602. No credit cards. No lunch. Brunch weekends. Subway: A, C, E to Canal St. $$*

9 *f-2*

STEAK AU POIVRE

Newly transformed and expanded, this popular restaurant now features chef David Ruggerio cooking French with all the passion of an Italian in Paris: ardent, radiant, and totally accessible. The season-driven, reasonably priced menu always features an appropriate foie gras preparation that you'll need to try. Squab with frisée and poached sour cherries with hollandaise sauce and white truffle oil is particularly fine. For the eponymous beef, you may choose shell, skirt, or filet mignon, and, if you wish, forego the pepper for béarnaise or bordelaise. Frites are mighty fine, but lunge for the creamed spinach with onion rings. Ruggerio does all the desserts himself, too, and they are not to be missed. Dive for a luscious blueberry financier if it's available. *1160 1st Ave. (between 63rd and 64th Sts.), Upper East Side, 212/758–3518. AE, MC, V. No lunch. Subway: 68th St./Hunter College. $$*

11 *a-1*

TARTINE

Tartine is French for something, anything, spread on bread. (The verb *tartiner* is used for the act of spreading something on bread). Language class aside, Tartine is also the name of this tiny restaurant in west Greenwich Village, where the neighborhood gathers at breakfast for café au lait and croissants, at lunch for things spread on baguettes, and at dinner for simple French food such as quiches and salads, at very reasonable prices. Due to the diminutive size, there is often a wait. *253 W. 11th St. (at W. 4th St.), West Village, 212/229–2611. No credit cards. Brunch weekends. Subway: A, C, E to 14th St.; L to 8th Ave. $$*

7 *e-8*

TROIS JEAN

Most consider this the best French bistro in the neighborhood. The two brownstone floors seat about 90, and the place is usually packed with intensely devoted locals, who come back again and again for the roasted slab of foie gras on peppery Le Puy lentils, the glazed-earthenware-potted cassoulet (widely regarded as the most succulent in Manhattan), the bitter chocolate fondant, and the made-to-order warm apple tart. Reasonable prix-fixe menus are available. *154 E. 79th St. (between Lexington and 3rd Aves.), Upper East Side, 212/988–4858. Reservations essential. AE, DC, MC, V. Closed Sun. in July and Aug. Subway: 77th St. $$$*

GREEK

10 *f-1*

BRIAM

Authentic home-style Greek cooking, including inventive specialties that incorporate goat and octopus, is served in a devoutly Mediterranean setting at friendly prices. The salads and whole grilled fish are tops; you'll be surprised not to find a beach out in back. Nine different ouzos are offered. Any one of them will really clean your clock. *322 E. 14th St. (between 1st and 2nd Aves.), East Village, 212/253–6360. AE, DC, MC, V. Closed Mon. Subway: 14th St./Union Sq.; L to 1st Ave. $*

3 *e-3*

CHRISTO'S HASAPO-TAVERNA

Unlike most of the other tavernas that dot the streets of Astoria the menu at Christo's focuses as much on excellent steak as it does on more traditional Greek specialties. The atmosphere is congenial and fun and the staff is always welcoming. When you factor in the low prices for the high quality, you can't go wrong. *41–08 23rd Ave. (at 41st St.), Astoria, Queens, 718/726–5195. AE, MC, V. Closed Mon. July–Aug. Subway: N to Astoria/Ditmars Blvd. $$*

3 *d-2*

ELIAS CORNER

Astoria is full of Greek restaurants, but this is the one with an hour wait to get in. The grilled fish has been touted by everyone from the former restaurant

critic of the *New York Times* to the city's best French chefs. Whole fish are grilled over an open fire and drizzled with extra-virgin olive oil and fresh herbs. Unfortunately, nothing else on the menu—not the traditional Greek salads or side dishes—compares to the quality and freshness of the fish. But that doesn't make the wait for a table any shorter. *24–02 31st St. (at 24th Ave.), Astoria, Queens, 718/932–1510. No credit cards. No lunch. Subway: Astoria/Ditmars Blvd. $$*

9 *d-3*

ESTIATORIO MILOS

The soaring 26-ft ceilings; stretched white scrims; and stark, neoclassical decor of this new Greek seafood restaurant at once evoke Santorini, the Acropolis, a Fellini movie, and a chic Manhattan club. The whole fish (on display on a mountain of crushed ice, near the open kitchen) are so fresh, you can almost smell the Mediterranean. The special appetizer of paper-thin slices of eggplant and zucchini, fried with saganaki cheese and served with a *tzatziki* (a yogurt and cucumber dip) dipping sauce, set the tone for the light, flavorful fare to come. An authentic Greek salad (no lettuce) comes garnished with creamy, goat's milk feta cheese and plump kalamata olives. Gently grilled fish with a light lick of olive oil and a squirt of lemon is the climax. And believe it or not, the thickened goat's milk yogurt drizzled with dark wild honey is one of the best desserts in town. *125 W. 55th St. (between 6th and 7th Aves.), Midtown, 212/245–7400. AE, DC, MC, V. Subway: 57th St. $$$*

8 *d-6*

KARYITIS

The owners of this taverna try a little harder to cultivate atmosphere than many of the others in Astoria; there's even live piano music nightly. The fare is simple and good: grilled fish, salads, lamb, and authentic desserts. *35–03 Broadway (between 35th and 36th Sts.), Astoria, Queens, 718/204–0666. AE, MC, V. Subway: N to Broadway. $$*

9 *d-3*

MOLYVOS

It's almost impossible to find Greek food this good in Greece, let alone

43

Manhattan. In this gorgeously appointed, spacious restaurant, executive chef Jim Botsacos starts you off with perfect prepared *mezes* (little bites such as voluptuous caviar mousse; sweet roasted beets with marinated giant beans; stingingly delicious grilled marinated sardines). Follow with the best grilled baby octopus on the continent; and achingly delicious entrées such as flavorful rabbit stew with red wine and piquant pearl onions, and various daily whole fish, simply grilled and dappled with a bit of olive oil and lemon (filleted, if you wish). Desserts follow the straight-ahead luscious simplicity: honey-drenched buttermilk yogurt with crushed walnuts, and custard in phyllo will curl your toes. There are 10 ouzos to choose from, and a fascinating selection of Greek wines. *871 7th Ave. (between 55th and 56th Sts.), Midtown, 212/582–7500. AE, D, DC, MC, V. Subway: 57th St. $$$*

9 *d-8*

PERIYALI

Just about the only thing unusual about the menu at this upscale Greek taverna is that everything tastes so good. Delicate and smoky grilled octopus, whole grilled fish, lamb on skewers, and other Greek specialties join more contemporary dishes such as salmon in phyllo on the menu. Don't leave without sampling the homemade baklava. *35 W. 20th St. (between 5th and 6th Aves.), Flatiron District, 212/463–7890. Reservations essential. AE, MC, V. No lunch weekends. Subway: F, N, R to 23rd St. $$*

3 *d-3*

UNCLE GEORGES

This giant 24-hour Greek restaurant would fit nicely into the commotion of Athens' plaka. The satisfying food— grilled meats and seafood, tangy tzatziki, smoky *taramasalata* (carp roe and olive oil spread), and stick-to-your-ribs moussaka—is served in large portions. Despite the 200-plus seats, there is almost always a wait, but the service is friendly and efficient. Strong coffee and buttery baklava are a must. *33–19 Broadway (at 34th St.), Astoria, Queens, 718/626–0593. No credit cards. Subway: N to Broadway. $*

HUNGARIAN

7 *f-7*

MOCCA HUNGARIAN

Locals depend on this Old World outpost for extremely hearty and inexpensive Hungarian fare. The goulash and stuffed cabbage may not be gourmet, but they're comforting, filling, and reliably delicious. *1588 2nd Ave. (between 82nd and 83rd Sts.), Upper East Side, 212/734–6470. No credit cards. Subway: 4, 5, 6 to 86th St. $*

INDIAN

New York's best-known destination for Indian food is Sixth Street between First and Second avenues (map 11/g-1). This short strip packs about 20 Indian restaurants, many festively lit year-round with variously colored Christmas lights. Affectionate (and some not-so-affectionate) rumors circulate about the provenance of the food here; some say that all of these storefronts get their meals from the same giant kitchen under the street. It's not haute, but it's tasty, filling, and incredibly cheap, with many entrées under $10; Mitali and Passage to India are particularly good bets. Somewhat more expensive and, many feel, the best of the lot is Haveli, located just around the corner on Second Avenue just south of Sixth Street. Venture beyond Sixth Street for the city's most inspiring Indian cuisine, most of it still reasonably priced. Further uptown, along an aromatic stretch of Lexington Avenue in the mid-20s (sometimes called "Curry Hill" instead of Murray), may be found several adroit Indian restaurants. Especially good is Pongal.

11 *d-4*

BALUCHI'S

Lavishly decorated with Indian artifacts, these inexpensive restaurants offer reliable tandoori food (curries and tasty breads), plenty of spiciness, and good service. *193 Spring St. (between Sullivan and Thompson Sts.), SoHo, 212/226–2828. AE, DC, MC, V. Subway: Spring St. $*

7 *f-7*

1565 2nd Ave. (between 81st and 82nd Sts.), Upper East Side, 212/288–4810. Subway: 4, 5, 6 to 86th St.

.11. c-2

361 6th Ave. (between W. 4th St. and Washington Pl.), Greenwich Village, 212/929–2441. Subway: W. 4th St./Washington Sq.

9 d-3

BOMBAY PALACE

Some insist that this handsomely decorated Midtown restaurant offers some of the best Northern Indian cuisine in town. The tandoori dishes, curries, unusually delicious breads, and other traditional specialties are not cheap, but they are very skillfully prepared. The reasonably priced and fabulously popular lunch buffet offers a wide variety and frequently attracts more than a few familiar faces from nearby network headquarters. 30 W. 52nd St. (between 5th and 6th Aves.), Midtown, 212/541–7777. AE, MC, V. Subway: 5th Ave./53rd St. $$

11 e-11

CAFE SPICE

It's not quite clear what kind of audience Cafe Spice is looking to attract. The food isn't good enough to attract Indian gourmets nor interesting enough to entice less adventurous eaters. Perhaps NYU students afraid to take their parents to Sixth Street make up the bulk of the clientele. Still, if you order well, you can get a decent meal here. The appetizer assortment and the tandoori items are safe bets. 72 University Pl. (between 10th and 11th Sts.), Greenwich Village, 212/253–6999. AE, MC, V. Subway: 14th St./Union Sq. $

9 f-3

DAWAT

When Dawat opened in 1986, the menu (overseen by actress–food writer Madhur Jaffrey) and the elegant setting made it New York's reigning *rani* of Indian eateries, and it's been justifiably popular ever since. While some claim the Indian restaurant scene has finally caught up with it, loyalists insist that Dawat still serves the most imaginative and best-executed Indian cuisine in town. Certainly, the marinated, tandoori-grilled-and-braised whole leg of lamb is extraordinarily tender and delicious. The usual roasted breads are unusually toothsome, too. The well-priced lunch makes it a terrific Midtown choice. 210 E. 58th St. (between 2nd and 3rd Aves.),

Upper East Side, 212/355–7555. Reservations essential. AE, MC, V. No lunch Sun. Subway: 59th St. $$

3 f-3

JACKSON DINER

Neighborhood folk and Manhattanites flock to Jackson Diner. It recently relocated to a bigger space—complete with a spice-color design scheme—but continues to serve cheap, spicy, authentic Indian fare in huge portions. Despite its popularity, there is a vocal contingent who will tell you the place is overrated. 37–47 74th St. (between Roosevelt and 37th Aves.), Jackson Heights, Queens, 718/672–1232. No credit cards. Subway: Jackson Heights/Roosevelt Ave. $

9 d-3

NIRVANA

Nirvana's claim to fame is its extremely romantic setting, overlooking Central Park. The view is more memorable than the food—quite decent Indo-Bengali cuisine, and some spectacular *poori* (fluffy, delicately fried bread)—but the feeling of being in another world makes the experience heady and pleasant. As if the view weren't enough, dinner is usually accompanied by live sitar music. 30 Central Park S (between 5th and 6th Aves.), 15th floor, Midtown, 212/486–5700. Reservations essential. AE, DC, MC, V. Subway: 57th St. $$

9 e-7

PONGAL

Don't let the fact that it's vegetarian and kosher distract you. From the papadams and green-mango relish that arrive when you sit down, to the spicy chopped *kachumar* salad (of minced cucumbers, onions, and tomatoes), to the light and fragrant curries, giant paper-thin *dosai* (a crepe-like pancake made of rice flour and filled with potatoes, onions, and spices), and other specialties from southern India, the food at this quaint restaurant is nothing short of remarkable. Order the Mysore Special or the Gujarati Thali (on the back of the menu) to sample several dishes at one sitting. 110 Lexington Ave. (between 27th and 28th Sts.), Murray Hill, 212/696–9458. AE, MC, V. Subway: 6 to 28th St. $

9 *e-7*

TABLA

Floyd Cardoz's exciting and vivid cooking is best characterized as American ingredients with Indian spices and techniques. Thus, in a soaring mosaic-filled setting, you'll encounter such dishes as foie gras with black-pepper–anise–pear compote, crab cakes jolted with Goan spices, and sweet-potato cheesecake with a cumin-cornmeal crust. It's pricey, so you might want to dine at the "bread bar," where exotic naan is served with cumin-chili-cheddar fondue, among other condiments. This is the latest and most exotic jewel in restaurateur Danny Meyer's well-deserved crown. *11 Madison Ave. (at 25th St.), Murray Hill, 212/889–0667. AE, MC, V. Subway: N, R, 6 to 23rd St. $$$*

IRISH

9 *c-6*

TIR NA NÓG

One of the best bets close to Madison Square Garden (it's directly across Eighth Avenue), this upscale pub-cum-restaurant with imported antiques, stained glass, and friendly service could make even Rangers fans behave. The chef puts out decent Celtic-American dishes such as roasted portobello mushrooms with polenta and field greens and braised red snapper with spaghetti squash in a fennel broth, but it's his updated takes on traditional Irish fare—such as oak-roasted salmon and the city's best shepherd's pie—that deserve accolades. There's live music Friday and Saturday nights. *5 Penn Plaza (8th Ave. between 33rd and 34th Sts.), Garment District, 212/630–0249. AE, DC, MC, V. Subway: 34th St./Penn Station. $$*

ITALIAN

12 *f-6*

AL DI LA TRATTORIA

The appealingly worn long wooden tables at this neighborhood trattoria make for an almost communal dining experience. The decor is homey and inviting, with lace curtains and rustic wood tables and chairs. There's always a mass of patient people milling on the sidewalk who know the wait will be rewarded with plates of homemade pasta, and well executed entrées such as steak tagliata. *248 Carroll St. (on 5th Ave.), Park Slope, Brooklyn, 718/783–4565. MC, V. Reservations not accepted. Closed Tues. No lunch. Subway: Atlantic Ave., Pacific St. $$*

11 *d-7*

ARQUA

This sparse restaurant is lauded for its excellent *cucina nuova*. Pastas are heavenly—the gnocchi are light (!), the daily risotto rich. Other good bets are fish soup, calves' liver with onions and polenta, and grilled chicken. For dessert, the standard ricotta cheesecake and tiramisu are best. *281 Church St. (at White St.), Tribeca, 212/334–1888. AE. Subway: Franklin St. $$$*

11 *c-2*

BABBO

This elegant Italian is the baby of TV personality Mario Batali (also of Pò, *below*) and restaurateur Joseph Bastianich (of Becco, *below*, and Frico Bar). As soon as it opened, Babbo (a contraction of the owners' names and the Italian word for "daddy") had become one of the hottest tickets in town. This is Italian food as it was meant to be: The finest ingredients are combined with impeccable technique and a passion for adventure. A five-course pasta tasting menu is ethereal, as is the tender roast suckling pig. The place is particularly popular with fans of organ meats, who appreciate the delicious lamb's tongue salad, the calves' brain ravioli, and the warm head cheese (yes, really). The only challenge is getting a reservation. *110 Waverly Pl. (between MacDougal St. and 6th Ave.), Greenwich Village, 212/777–0303. Reservations essential. AE, MC, V. No lunch. Subway: W. 4th St./Washington Sq. $$$*

11 *c-3*

BAR PITTI

Here's a friendly Tuscan restaurant with excellent, inexpensive food, an attractive clientele, and outdoor tables in summer. Try the bruschetta; the white-bean salad with tuna, red onions, and olive oil; the *panzanella* (bread salad with roast peppers); and the chicken Milanese with arugula. Pastas change daily. *268 6th Ave. (between Bleecker and Houston Sts.), Greenwich Village, 212/982–3300. No credit cards. Subway: W. 4th St./Washington Sq. $$*

9 c-4

BARBETTA

This century-old Italian serves traditional Piemontese specialties in four sumptuously appointed town houses. The innovative food is wedded to tradition, and is bound to please—rich *fonduta* (fondue) in a "bird's nest" with quail eggs, truffles, and braised beef with polenta, and other regional classics. But in late spring and summer, the real draw is the luxurious outdoor garden, an oasis in the Theater District. In off months, when white Alba truffles are in season (mid-Oct.– Dec.), this is a particularly good place to splurge. Service is madness pre- and post-theater, but indulgent during the show. *321 W. 46th St. (between 8th and 9th Aves.), Theater District, 212/246–9171. AE, DC, MC, V. Closed Sun. Subway: A, C, E to 42nd St. $$$*

9 c-4

BECCO

Though the name is Italian for "little beak," you'll need more than a bird's appetite to enjoy this busy trattoria. À la carte selections are available, but go for the prix-fixe menu. You'll be presented with an array of antipasti as soon as you sit down, including fried and/or grilled vegetables, white-bean spread, and fresh breads. Waiters roam the room with pans of pasta for you to sample, such as fresh pappardelle with duck ragu, orechiette with broccoli rabe, fresh gnocchi with tomato sauce—the selection changes daily. If you still have room, you can upgrade to an entrée; osso buco, rabbit stew, roasted lamb, suckling pig, and a selection of fish are usually on the list. Still hungry? The bread pudding is fantastic. Wines are all priced at $18 per bottle. The experience is fast, friendly, fun, and delicious. *355 W. 46th St. (between 8th and 9th Aves.), Theater District, 212/397–7597. Reservations essential. AE, D, DC, MC, V. Subway: A, C, E to 42nd St. $$*

11 f-6

BENITO II

As is true at most of the restaurants in this rapidly shrinking pocket of Italian pride, there isn't much here in the way of authentic cuisine or charming atmosphere. But unlike others in the neighborhood (including the separately owned Benito I across the street), Benito II doesn't aspire to anything more than fresh tomato sauce, perfectly al dente pasta, lots of garlic, and cheap prices. All of which it delivers admirably well. *163 Mulberry St. (between Broome and Grand Sts.), Little Italy, 212/226–9012. No credit cards. Subway: 6 to Spring St. $*

9 e-3

BICE

This extremely successful Italian bistro was imported from Milan, where the original Bice was founded in 1926. Needless to say, the New York cousin attracts what might be called a Roman crowd— beautiful and fashion-forward. Regulars flock for the heavenly but high-priced Milanese pasta, risotto, grilled dishes, and game (in season). The service can be pretentious to the point of offense. *7 E. 54th St. (between 5th and Madison Aves.), 212/688–1999. Reservations essential. AE. Subway: E, F to 5th Ave. $$$$*

9 c-7

BIRICCHINO

The location on a grimy street in the no-man's land between Madison Square Garden and Chelsea may seem less than auspicious, and the marble-and-vinyl decor is a bit tacky, but this is the place to go for fresh, homemade Italian sausage. Five varieties are offered daily, the likes of which—chicken with mushroom, veal with sundried tomato, and classic sweet pork—are guaranteed to warm the hearts of sausage fans. A solid menu of Italian pastas and other classics is also on offer. *260 W. 29th St. (at 8th Ave.), Garment District, 212/695–6690. AE, D, DC, MC, V. Closed Sun. No lunch Sat. Subway: 1, 9 to 28th St. $$*

9 b-7

BOTTINO

Despite some convincing evidence to the contrary, chic people dressed in black like good food too. They get it alla italiana at this smartly designed west Chelsea restaurant, where a table can be as hard to come by as at Balthazar. The menu is straightforward—ripe Anjou pears with Tuscan pecorino to start, homemade leek tortelloni, grilled salmon, roasted chicken, lamb or steak to follow. In summer, a garagelike glass door opens to a beautiful, secluded garden. Service can be slow. *246 10th Ave. (between 24th and 25th Sts.), Chelsea, 212/206–6766. Reservations essential. AE, MC, V. No lunch Sat.–Mon. Subway: C, E to 23rd St. $$$*

7 *g-8*

BRUNELLI

Effulgent owner Russ Brunelli transmits the kind of delightful energy that perhaps only Italian-American restaurateurs can conduct. The seven glittering chandeliers might make the place look unaffordable, but most entrées are under $20. If you're in no hurry, begin with an absolutely gigantic stuffed artichoke, with buttery breadcrumbed petals that will keep you and yours busy for about a half-hour. The *spiedino* is not to be missed: an egg-battered fried mozzarella sandwich that's dappled with a lusty tomato/anchovy gravy. Then tuck into a huge veal chop, butterflied and pounded to 19" x 12", then breaded and fried and covered with diced fresh tomatoes, basil, and red onions—a kind of veal bruschetta. *1409 York Ave. (at 75th St.), Upper East Side, 212/744–8899. AE, MC, V. Subway: 77th St. $$*

10 *e-1*

BUSSOLA BAR AND GRILL

Bussola serves Roman and Sicilian cooking in a cheerful, relaxed setting. The swordfish carpaccio and homemade squid-ink pasta are quite wonderful; salads are generous and fresh; and desserts are outstanding. Favorite sweets are the ricotta gelato with preserved orange peel, hazelnut ice cream, and creamy tiramisu dusted with chocolate powder. *65 4th Ave. (near 10th St.), Greenwich Village, 212/254–1940. AE, MC, V. Closed Sun. Subway: Astor Pl.; 14th St./Union Sq. $$*

9 *e-8*

CAMPAGNA

This handsome, country-style trattoria serves earthy Italian food expertly prepared by chef/owner Mark Strausman, who just published an endearing cookbook. Try the antipasti (on gleaming display as you enter), gnocchi with wild mushrooms and truffle oil, toothsome pastas, and rib-eye steak with mashed potatoes. Everything is absolutely first-class. *24 E. 21st St. (between Broadway and Park Ave.), Gramercy, 212/460–0900. AE, DC, MC, V. No lunch weekends. Subway: 6, N, R to 23rd St. $$$*

7 *b-6*

CARMINE'S

The portions are huge and the wait is long at these family-style Italian trattorias. Everything, from the spaghetti with red sauce to the fancier veal dishes, satisfies, and sharing huge, family-size portions is de rigeur. Chicken contadina (with sausage and peppers) is especially recommended. The kitchen has a heavy hand with garlic, so don't plan to kiss anyone after dinner. The atmosphere is bustling and loud. *2450 Broadway (between 90th and 91st Sts.), Upper West Side, 212/362–2200. Reservations not accepted. AE, MC, V. Subway: 1, 2, 3, 9 to 96th St. $$*

9 *c-5*

200 W. 44th St. (between 7th and 8th Aves.), Theater District, 212/221–3800. Subway: 42nd St./Times Sq.

11 *c-3*

CENT'ANNI

This small, crowded, casual West Village trattoria serves simple and very good Florentine food. Try the wonderful seafood salad, grilled veal chop, or pasta, and finish with the zabaglione. *50 Carmine St. (between Bedford and Bleecker Sts.), West Village, 212/989–9494. AE, MC, V. No lunch weekends. Subway: W. 4th St./Washington Sq. $$*

7 *e-8*

COCO PAZZO

Another hit from restaurateur Pino Luongo, this lively, unpretentious, East Side Italian place is a good stop for truly excellent, robust, regional-Italian specialties. The well-dressed local crowd (often joined by celebrities) enjoys a nightly array of hot and cold antipasti, as well as risotto, rigatoni with sausage and peas, and a wide array of game choices. The daily specials are always interesting. *23 E. 74th St. (between 5th and Madison Aves.), Upper East Side, 212/794–0205. Reservations essential. AE, MC, V. Subway: 77th St. $$$*

9 *c-8*

COLA'S

With cheerful and tasteful decor, earnest servers, and astoundingly low prices for delicious Italian fare, what's not to like? The answer is a tiny space far exceeded by its eager clientele, decibel levels that approach ear-splitting, and the occasional botched order. Still, with every pasta under $10 and dishes such as veal scallopine, monkfish, and Tuscan veal stew only a few bucks more, the worst you can give it is a conditional thumbs up. *148 8th Ave. (between 17th and 18th Sts.), Chelsea, 212/633–8020. Reservations* *not accepted. MC, V. No lunch. Subway: A, C, E to 14th St.; 1, 9 to 18th St. $*

12 e-5
CUCINA

Michael Ayoub has created a Brooklyn haven with this casual trattoria, where the portions are large, the flavors robust, and the prices right. It's hard to get a table in this giant space. Choose from the temptations on the antipasti table, ask for a half-order of pasta, and enjoy the generous entrées, such as succulent osso buco. *256 5th Ave. (between Carroll St. and Garfield Pl.), Park Slope, Brooklyn, 718/230–0711. Reservations essential. AE, MC, V. Subway: N, R to Union St. $$*

11 g-2
CUCINA DI PESCE

Hearty portions of inexpensive, Italian fish specialties, served with heaping mounds of pasta, draw somewhat better-dressed patrons than you might expect. Dip into the mound of free mussels at the crowded bar. *87 E. 4th St. (between 2nd and 3rd Aves.), East Village, 212/260–6800. Reservations not accepted. No credit cards. Subway: 2nd Ave.; Astor Pl. $*

11 b-2
CUCINA STAGIONALE

Despite the name, nothing changes with the seasons at this inexpensive and good Italian eatery. The menu includes myriad pastas and other starters—fusilli with sundried tomato, Gorgonzola, and caper sauce is among the best— and equally numerous entrées, including veal and salmon, each ample, tasty, and well prepared. The free antipasto is a welcome touch. *275 Bleecker St. (between 6th and 7th Aves.), West Village, 212/924–2707. Reservations not accepted. No credit cards. BYOB. Subway: W. 4th St./Washington Sq. $*

11 c-4
DA SILVANO

Even with a reservation you might find yourself waiting up to an hour for your table at this popular trattoria, which spills onto the Avenue of the Americas but still can't keep up with demand. A more thoroughly Italian experience would be hard to imagine, right down to the friendly if ineffective service and the hit-or-miss menu, which hits high notes on some dishes (the antipasti offer the best odds for success) and falls flat on others (oddly, the pastas). Whole grilled fish and braised meats are usually well prepared. Lobster has a tendency to be overcooked. *260 6th Ave. (between Houston and Bleecker Sts.), Greenwich Village, 212/982–2343. Reservations essential. AE, MC, V. Closed 3 wks in Aug. Subway: W. 4th St./Washington Sq. $$$*

5 h-5
DOMINICK'S

Arthur Avenue in the Bronx has long been considered a more authentic Little Italy than the touristy strip in Manhattan. One of the best and most popular restaurants on the avenue is Dominick's, where tough waiters preside over communal tables in a room that is more or less devoid of ambience. The food is good Southern Italian, with lots of red sauce and mozzarella. *2335 Arthur Ave. (at 187th St.), Arthur Avenue, Bronx, 718/733–2807. No credit cards. $$*

11 e-5
DOWNTOWN

Downtown attracts the same decadent crowd you see of an evening at Harry's Bar in Venice (and at Harry Cipriani's uptown—*see below*), knocking back Bellinis at the bar. The stylish food is expensive but good: *vitello tonnato* (cold roasted veal in a sauce of puréed tuna and anchovies), crisp fried calamari with a vivid tomato sauce, ravioli stuffed with veal, grouper *alla carlina* with caper sauce. Desserts are ample, and include lemon and vanilla-cream cakes suffused with frosting and meringue. *376 W. Broadway (near Broome St.), SoHo, 212/343–0999. Reservations essential. AE, DC, MC, V. Subway: Canal St. $$$*

7 f-7
ELIO'S

Woody Allen had a window table here for years, and many less-famous locals have become regulars as well. The star-studded crowd and the chef's admirable Northern Italian fare have kept Elio's extremely popular. The handsome, wood-paneled setting is lively and noisy; expect a wait, even with a reservation. The veal Milanese and the basket of fried zucchini are menu favorites. *1621 2nd Ave. (between 84th and 85th Sts.), Upper East Side, 212/772–2242. AE, MC, V. No lunch. Subway: 4, 5, 6 to 86th St. $$$*

7 f-7
ERMINIA

This family-run restaurant is one of the best-kept secrets on the Upper East Side. Candlelit, cozy (40 seats), and inviting, it's a great place for special occasions. Go for entrées grilled over a Tuscan-style wood fire, tasty pastas, and bruschetta and crostini (toasted bread drenched with olive oil and garlic), or just go because it's one of those intimate, beautiful eateries that you normally find only on small, winding streets in the Village. *250 E. 83rd St., between 2nd and 3rd Aves., Upper East Side, 212/879–4284. Reservations essential. AE. Closed Sun. Subway: 83rd St. $$$*

9 f-3
FELIDIA

New York's—and public television's—mother of Italian cuisine, Lidia Bastianich, creates a menu of wonderfully original Northern Italian creations for this handsome restaurant. Downstairs, where the exposed brick and wood create a sophisticated warmth, is perfect for dinner, while the painted walls and skylight upstairs make for a cheerful lunch. Don't miss the tasty antipasti, homemade pastas with seasonal ingredients, and rustic regional specialties. An exceptional Italian-wine selection puts the finishing touch on a great meal. *243 E. 58th St. (between 2nd and 3rd Aves.), Upper East Side, 212/758–1479. Reservations essential. AE, DC, MC, V. Closed Sun. No lunch Sat. Subway: 59th St./Lexington Ave. $$$$*

9 d-7
FOLLONICO

If the dining room had windows overlooking rolling vineyards—or any windows at all, for that matter—Follonico might just be the most effectively Tuscan dining room in the city. Chef Alan Tardi serves contemporary Italian cuisine, much of it prepared in the wood-fired oven visible from the dining room; the menu is heavy on game (in season) and light in texture. Pastas, such as the giant open-mushroom raviolo, are all interesting and tasty; the fiorentina steak for two tastes unusually beefy and is cooked just right; and the crisp *grissini* (bread sticks) on the table are addictive. *6 W. 24th St. (between 5th and 6th Aves.), Flatiron District, 212/691–6359. Reservations essential. AE, MC, V. Subway: F, N, R to 23rd St. $$$*

10 d-6
GEMELLI

Tony May, the unofficial ambassador of Italian cuisine who pleased uptown palates for years at San Domenico, has brought his authentic fare to the World Trade Center with Gemelli. The name is Italian for "twins," but it also denotes the restaurant's signature pasta shape, a satisfying, double-rolled noodle served alla gricia with onion, pancetta, and pecorino cheese. The food is rustic and very Italian—cured beef with goat cheese, sea bass in clam broth, roasted lamb chops with grilled vegetables—and the kitchen has a generous hand with herbs and extra-virgin olive oil. Beware of the absurd $3 surcharge for sharing pasta dishes. *4 World Trade Ctr. (between Church and Day Sts.), Lower Manhattan, 212/488–2100. AE, DC, MC, V. No lunch weekends. Subway: World Trade Ctr. $$*

7 b-6
GENNARO

The terrific Italian food at this tiny restaurant attracts crowds to an otherwise nearly cuisine-free neighborhood. Both the appetizers, such as *ribollita* (a hearty Tuscan soup), grilled scallops on white beans, and beef carpaccio, and the classic homemade pastas, such as potato gnocchi with fresh tomato sauce and orecchiette with broccoli and provole, have plenty of allure; and such entrées as tender osso buco and garlic-perfumed roasted Cornish hen add to the draw. Perhaps the best reason for the schlep, however, is the price. All of this means that lots of people wait endlessly for one of the 14 tables. Call before you go, not for a reservation, but to be sure they're open—otherwise, you might arrive to find a handwritten sign saying something like, "Sorry, Gennaro is tired and has stayed home today." *665 Amsterdam Ave. (between 92nd and 93rd Sts.), Upper West Side, 212/665–5348. Reservations not accepted. No credit cards. Subway: 1, 2, 3, 9 to 96th St. $$*

11 d-3
GRAND TICINO

Fans of *Moonstruck* will recognize this quaint restaurant from the film. A Village institution, the place has served many a good pasta, and other simple Italian favorites, to the various artistic types that populated the neighborhood in bygone years. *228 Thompson St. (between*

W. 3rd and Bleecker Sts.), Greenwich Village, 212/777–5922, Reservations essential. AE, DC, MC, V. Closed Sun. Subway: W. 4th St./Washington Sq. $$

9 e-2

HARRY CIPRIANI

An elegant, well-heeled, international set, including some major celebrities, veritably floats through the revolving door, missing nary a beat before grasping a Bellini. As always, Cipriani serves wonderful Northern Italian food to a sophisticated crowd in a sophisticated setting. The atmosphere will make you homesick for Venice, but the bill will make you think, "Maybe next year." Hotel Sherry-Netherland, 781 5th Ave. (at 59th St.), Midtown, 212/753–5566. Reservations essential. AE, DC, MC, V. Subway: N, R to 5th Ave. $$$$

9 e-7

I TRULLI

One of the most authentic Italian dining experiences in New York, this charming, casual restaurant (with a beautiful garden in season and a crackling fireplace the rest of the year) is comfortable and welcoming. The warm crusty bread is served with a sinfully good ricotta-and-roasted-garlic spread, and it's all uphill from there. The pastas are all interesting, the entrées flavorful, and the desserts baked fresh each day. Even the service is enchanting. 122 E. 27th St. (between Lexington and Park Ave. S), Murray Hill, 212/481–7372. Reservations essential. AE, MC, V. Subway: 6 to 28th St. $$$

10 e-1

IL CANTINORI

Il Cantinori is a highly venerated Village Italian restaurant known for lovely, uncomplicated Tuscan specialties served in two subtly charming, rustic dining rooms. The front room spills out onto the street in kind weather. The wonderful and unusual daily specials, cold antipasti, velvet pasta, and grilled meats and vegetables come with wonderfully high prices. Watch for celebrities. 32 E. 10th St. (between Broadway and University Pl.), Greenwich Village, 212/673–6044. Reservations essential. AE, MC, V. Subway: 8th St.; Astor Pl. $$$

11 d-2

IL MULINO

Some consider this the best Italian restaurant in the city, but cognoscenti of Italian food consider it the biggest farce. Glorified Little Italy specialties command prices in the stratosphere—be prepared to pay upwards of $50 for one of the many enticing-sounding specials recited tableside. Do yourself and your wallet a favor, and skip that two-month waiting list altogether. 86 W. 3rd St. (near Sullivan St.), Greenwich Village, 212/673–3783. Reservations essential. AE. Subway: W. 4th St./Washington Sq. $$$$

9 e-2

IL TOSCANACCIO

This beautifully rustic Midtown eatery is another from Pino Luongo (see Coco Pazzo, above, and Le Madri, below), who seems to lead New York's pack in successful Italian restaurants. This one focuses on Tuscany's home cooking (the restaurant's name refers playfully to those "naughty" Tuscans), and its crowd runs the gamut from glamorous models to corporate lawyers. Regulars love the antipasto, which changes according to the chef's many whims; the lamb stew, served in a fresh-baked bread bowl; and seasonal pastas. The atmosphere is high-class but casual, so don't be surprised if the table next to you leans over and asks what smells so good. 7 E. 59th St. (between 5th and Madison Aves.), Midtown, 212/935–3535. Reservations essential. AE, DC, MC, V. No lunch weekends. Subway: 59th St./Lexington Ave. $$$

11 c-4

'INO

This 20-seat storefront wine-bar takes its name from the Italian panino (a sandwich pressed in a toaster), one of three items on the menu. These aren't just any sandwiches, though; they're on homemade bread and filled with such fresh ingredients as portobello mushrooms, homemade mozzarella, prosciutto, and the like. The other two menu items are bread-related as well: bruschetta and tramezzini (on thick slices of crustless white bread). An admirable and reasonable selection of wines, mostly Italian, is served from the six-stool bar by the glass, half-carafe, and bottle. Keep this place in mind next time you catch a screening at Film Forum. 21 Bedford St. (at Downing St.), West Village, 212/989–5769. Reservations not accepted. No credit cards. Subway: W. 4th St./Washington Sq. $

10 *d-1*

LA NONNA

Old-style Italian food is served in a West Village brownstone with a garden. The large dining room has exposed-brick walls and—Eureka!—well-spaced tables. Try the linguine with lobster, roast pork loin in chianti-and-sage sauce, or veal Milanese topped with tomatoes and arugula. *133 W. 13th St. (between 6th and 7th Aves.), West Village, 212/741–3663. AE, D, DC, MC, V. Closed Sun. No lunch. Subway: 1, 2, 3, 9 to 14th St. $$$*

9 *d-8*

LE MADRI

This spacious, high-ceiling hot spot has died down somewhat since neighboring Barneys closed, but the menu still offers consistently fine and imaginative Tuscan-style cooking. The great pizzas come from a central, wood-burning oven. Pan-roasted salmon rests comfortably on a low turret of creamy mashed potatoes, surrounded by caramelized pearl onions and partnered with plum chutney. Desserts include a nougat-flavor *panna cotta* ("cooked cream," a silky egg custard) with just the right silky squirm. The outdoor patio is lovely in season. *168 W. 18th St. (at 7th Ave.), Chelsea, 212/727–8022. Reservations essential. AE, MC, V. Subway: F to 14th St. $$$*

11 *d-4*

LUPA

Mario Batali and Joseph Bastianich, the team behind the sensational Babbo (*above*), have produced this more casual, more moderately priced offspring just a couple of blocks away. Like the setting, the food is more casual than at Babbo, but fresh pasta dishes such as pappardelle with rabbit ragù, and hearty entrées such as braised oxtail are every bit as satisfying, if on the small side. The front room of the restaurant is seated on a first come, first served basis, and reservations are taken for the back. *170 Thompson St. (between Bleecker and Houston Sts.), Greenwich Village, 212/982–5089. AE, DC, MC, V. Closed Sun. Subway: W. 4th St./Washington Sq. $$*

10 *c-2*

MALATESTA TRATTORIA

Italian is the favored language at this small trattoria where the food is fresh and flavorful, the atmosphere congenial (even if you only speak English). A specialty is the *piadina*—an Italian tortilla—that comes with one of several fillings, among which might be fresh arugula and Parmesan or sautéed spinach. Pastas are well cooked and seasoned with flair, and entrées, particularly the lamb chops, are satisfying. The portions are ample and an inexpensive wine complements the food. If uptown Italian eateries are too expensive, and Little Italy too red-saucy, Malatesta is a perfect middle ground. *649 Washington St. (at Christopher St.), West Village, 212/741–1207. No credit cards. No lunch weekdays. Subway: Christopher St./Sheridan Sq. $$*

3 *d-4*

MANDUCATI'S

A notch above the many casual, family-style spots in the neighborhood, Manducati's complements its red sauce and good homemade pasta and a well-chosen wine list. It may be off the beaten path, but regulars find the homey conviviality, especially among the New York–accented waitresses, appealing. On weekends two dining rooms and the bar area fill to the max. *13–27 Jackson Ave. (at 47th Ave.), Long Island City, Queens, 718/729–4602. AE, DC, MC, V. Subway: 7 to Vernon Blvd./Jackson Ave. $$*

7 *f-8*

MEZZALUNA

This bustling trattoria drew the in-crowd in the '80s. The crowd may be less chic today, but the food is just as good. As the name suggests, the decor is celestial, with a cloud-painted ceiling sprinkled with eponymous half-moons. Alas, the seating is not so airy; diners sit shoulder-to-shoulder and listen to ear-blasting music. The limited menu includes beef carpaccio with a choice of fixings, main pasta courses that change daily, vegetable and herb designer pizzas from wood-burning ovens, and cheese, fruit, or sorbet for dessert. *1295 3rd Ave. (between 74th and 75th Sts.), Upper East Side, 212/535–9600. Reservations not accepted. AE. Subway: 68th St. $$*

11 *d-4*

MEZZOGIORNO

From the owners of the miniscule Mezzaluna comes another trendy, very Italian trattoria, this one with a bit more breathing room. Count on an excellent array of carpaccios, thin-crust brick-oven pizzas (at lunchtime and late at night), pastas, salads, and a great tiramisu for dessert. You can also dine at the long, marble-top bar. *195 Spring St. (at Sullivan St.), SoHo, 212/334–2112. AE. $$*

12 *b-2*
NOODLE PUDDING
If you eat one meal in Brooklyn Heights, eat it here. The food is Italian, not Jewish: The name is a loose translation of the owner's last name, Migliaccio, which he shares with a Neapolitan dessert. Surprisingly, pasta is not the kitchen's strong point (save for the lasagna, which changes daily). Opt instead for fish, usually generously portioned, lightly grilled, and served with a dressing of extra-virgin olive oil and a bed of fresh steamed vegetables. Braised osso buco, roasted chicken, and baked rabbit are good alternatives to the fish, and to start, try an appetizer of carpaccio, fried calamari, or mussels in spicy tomato sauce. *38 Henry St. (between Cranberry and Middagh Sts.), Brooklyn Heights, 718/625–3737. Reservations not accepted. No credit cards. Closed Mon. No lunch. Subway: 2, 3 to Clark St. $$*

9 *e-8*
NOVITÁ
Innovative Italian cooking in a minimalist setting sums up this comfortable, largely yellow Flatiron District haunt, lit with Murano glass sconces. It's a favorite with Elite models, who can be seen tucking into red snapper, handmade pasta, and roasted breast of duck with Barolo sauce, pine nuts, and pomegranate seeds. Have the warm chocolate tart for dessert. *102 E. 22nd St. (at Park Ave. S), Gramercy, 212/677–2222. AE, DC, MC, V. No lunch weekends. Subway: 6 to 23rd St. $$$*

9 *c-4*
ORSO
This casual northern-Italian trattoria on Restaurant Row garners raves for pre- and post-theater pastas, thin-crust pizzas, and tasty grilled entrées. The open kitchen adds to the convivial atmosphere. After the curtain falls, Broadway's show-biz crowd fills the bar and the vaulted, whitewashed, skylit back room. *322 W. 46th St. (between 8th and 9th Aves.), Theater District, 212/489–7212. Reservations essential. MC, V. Subway: A, C, E to 42nd St. $$*

9 *d-4*
PALIO
Wrapped by a striking four-wall mural of the Siena Palio by Sandro Chia, the circular bar at this posh Italian restaurant is an excellent stop for drinks, and you can grab a bite here if you wish. But if you must *dine,* take the elevator to the second-floor dining room, where worn leather banquettes and wood-grained walls make you feel like you're sitting in a boardroom. Though exorbitantly priced, the food is quite wonderful. Homemade pastas, perfect risottos, seafood, meat, and game dishes recall fine restaurants in northern Italy—and are priced to match. *Equitable Center, 151 W. 51st St. (between 6th and 7th Aves.), Midtown, 212/245–4850. Jacket required (dining room only). Reservations essential. AE, DC, MC, V. Subway: 49th St.; 47th–50th Sts./Rockefeller Center. $$$$*

7 *e-7*
PARIOLI ROMANISSIMO
Housed in a turn-of-the-20th-century brownstone, this long-standing, luxurious restaurant serves good Northern-Italian dishes to a rich and famous clientele. Regulars love the veal and pasta dishes, which some say are unequaled in the city, and the doting, formal service. *24 E. 81st St. (between 5th and Madison Aves.), Upper East Side, 212/288–2391. Reservations essential. AE, DC, MC, V. Closed Sun. and Mon. Subway: 4, 5, 6 to 86th St. $$$$*

9 *c-3*
PATSY'S
Founded in 1944, Patsy's has remained strictly in the Scognamillo family, employing only three chefs: grandfather "Patsy", then his son Joe, and, for the last 15 years, his grandson Sal, whose ways with tried-and-true Neopolitan fare with complex flavors and uncompromisingly fresh ingredients are truly inspired. Begin with superb *spiedino*—slabs of fresh mozzarella, breadcrumbed, deep fried, and sauced with anchovy butter—and you'll never want "fried mozzarella sticks" again. Linguine with fresh clams and just a touch of tomato is relentlessly delicious. Calamari are stuffed to bursting with chopped shrimp, crab, lobster, breadcrumbs, and toasted pine nuts. There are "Patsy's" restaurants all over Manhattan—accept no substitutes. It's West 56th Street, or bust. *236 W. 56th St. (between Broadway and 8th*

Ave.), Midtown, 212/247–3491. AE, DC, MC, V. Subway: 57th St; 59th St./Columbus Circle. $$

11 *a-2*

PEPE VERDE

This West Village outpost of the tiny Pepe Rosso SoHo storefront serves a similar array of made-to-order pastas and simple Italian food. We're not talking spaghetti and meatballs, but authentic dishes including pesto, gnocchi, fresh tomato sauce, homemade focaccia, sandwiches, and salads. Though the kitchen here has less finesse than its downtown counterpart, this one still offers a satisfying meal at very reasonable prices, and there are about three times as many seats. *59 Hudson St. (between Perry and W. 11th Sts.), West Village, 212/255–2211. No credit cards. Subway: A, C, E to 14th St.; L to 8th Ave. $*

11 *c-1*

PIADINA

A rustic wooden sign hangs outside this intimate, candlelit restaurant that attracts a regular following who love the simple food, gentle prices, and romantic atmosphere. The appealing, narrow space is bordered on one side by a brick wall and on the other by a stucco wall with wooden beams, both of which are adorned with Italian textile prints. The menu highlights *piadina*—a specialty from the Romagna region of northern Italy—which is unleavened bread baked in a coal oven coated with cheese and other toppings, as well as pasta and other entrées. *57 W. 10th St. (between 5th and 6th Aves.), Greenwich Village, 212/460–8017. No credit cards. No lunch. Subway: W. 4th St./Washington Sq. $$*

10 *c-1*

PICCOLO ANGOLO

Don't ask for directions to this popular Italian eatery; few people know that Hudson Street continues past Eighth Avenue. Instead, just follow your nose—you'll smell the garlic sautéeing in olive oil a block away—and look for the hungry crowd milling about on the sidewalk while waiting for a table. Be prepared for the rapid-fire recitation of specials when you sit down. The pastas are all fresh, the classic Italian entrées are generous and well seasoned—the veal is particularly good—and the service is friendly, efficient, and very Italian. *621 Hudson St. (at Jane St.), West Village, 212/229–9177.*

D, MC, V. No lunch. Subway: A, C, E to 14th St., L to 8th Ave. $$

9 *b-4*

PIETRASANTA

This Ninth Avenue veteran couldn't be more appreciated by neighborhood residents and theater-goers. The light, open space and attentive staff both hold up well even during the pre-curtain rush, and a few street-side tables outside are appreciated in summer. A basket of warm bread with a sundried-tomato caponata is a nice welcome, as are the reasonably priced wine list and solid menu of fresh, simple, perfectly cooked Italian standards. Desserts are inventive and worth the splurge—just try to resist the coconut panna cotta or white-chocolate cheesecake with mascarpone and berries. *683 9th Ave. (at 47th St.), Hell's Kitchen, 212/265–9471. AE, MC, V. Brunch weekends. Subway: C, E to 50th St. $$*

11 *b-3*

PÒ

This tiny neighborhood restaurant is where the phenomenon of Mario Batali—chef/co-owner of Babbo (*above*), television star, and cookbook author—began. (It's also what started the transformation of Cornelia Street into another Restaurant Row.) One of Batali's signature dishes is white-bean ravioli with a brown butter and sage sauce. Osso buco, perfumed with orange, is also great. Batali's inventive Italian cooking still draws raves, but the limited number of seats makes it as hard to get a reservation for dinner here as it is for a meal at Babbo. Go instead for lunch during the week, when the neighborhood quiets down, and you'll have a better chance at success. *31 Cornelia St. (between Bleecker and W. 4th Sts.), West Village, 212/645–2189. AE, MC, V. Reservations essential. No lunch Mon.–Tues. Subway: W. 4th St./Washington Sq. $$*

11 *f-7*

PUGLIA

This festive Little Italy original (since 1919) now has an attached lounge, where Sinatra/Rat Pack cover acts, who spill over into the dining room, perform nightly. The tables are set up cafeteria-style, with long communal tables, but the waitstaff is pleasant and efficient. There's lots to eat: steak contadina (grilled country-style), stuffed veal chop, tortellini alfredo, and spaghetti bolognese, all best washed down with cheap red wine or a pitcher of beer. *189 Hester St. (between Mott and Mulberry Sts.), Little Italy, 212/966–6006. AE, DC, MC, V. Subway: 6 to Spring St. $*

12 *c-4*

QUEEN

Some people consider Queen one of the best Italian restaurants in New York City—not just Brooklyn. That's saying a lot, but it is a good place to fill up on good Italian food. The antipasti change seasonally, the pastas are made to order, and the entrées are large enough to feed two (especially if you order a pasta to start). The restaurant is always packed with a neighborhood crowd. *84 Court St. (between Livingston and Schermerhorn Sts.), Brooklyn Heights, 718/596–5955. AE, MC, V. No lunch weekends. Subway: Borough Hall. $$*

9 *d-3*

REMI

The elegant, two-story dining room, dominated by a spectacular mural of Venice and boldly striped banquettes, makes dining on tuna ravioli in ginger sauce, carpaccio, risottos, and wonderful vegetable antipasto even more pleasant. The bar serves far and away the best Bellinis in town. Remi-to-Go, in a glass-enclosed passageway next to the restaurant, serves breakfast and light lunch. *145 W. 53rd St. (between 6th and 7th Aves.), Theater District, 212/581–4242. Reservations essential. AE, D, DC, MC, V. Subway: 5th Ave./53rd St. $$$*

9 *d-8*

RISTORANTE DA UMBERTO

The lacquered red exterior may be a bit of a shock, but inside everything is calm and conservative—including the predominately older, uptown clientele. The draw is excellent Tuscan food and a terrific wine list heavy on high-end selections. Service is gracious and accommodating. *107 W. 17th St. (between 6th and 7th Aves.), Chelsea, 212/989–0303. Reservations essential. AE. Closed Sun. No lunch Sat. Subway: 1, 9 to 18th St. $$$*

11 *d-8*

ROSEMARIE'S

This cozy and comfortable neighborhood trattoria is frequented by artists and Wall Street execs. Good bets are

pasta (pappardelle with porcini, tomato, and cream; gnocchi with shrimp), seared tuna with couscous, and osso buco, followed by tiramisu for dessert. *145 Duane St. (between W. Broadway and Church St.), Tribeca, 212/285–2610. AE, MC, V. Closed Sun. Subway: Chambers St. $$$*

9 *d-3*

SAN DOMENICO NY

Possibly New York's most ambitious Italian restaurant, San Domenico serves beautifully presented traditional and innovative Italian cuisine in uncompromisingly luxurious surroundings. Chef Odette Fada is known for her homemade pastas, and she has lightened the menu from days of yore, but the signature ravioli (with ricotta, soft egg yolk, butter, Parmesan, and white truffles) is still available. Game is also a specialty in season. Prices are very high. *240 Central Park S, Midtown, 212/265–5959. Reservations essential. AE, DC, MC, V. Subway: 59th St./Columbus Circle. $$$$*

9 *e-7*

SCOPA

If you've spent any time crawling around Italy in search of—and finding—great food, many of chef Vincent Scotto's preparations will be thrillingly familiar, but all bear his mark. The menu changes constantly, and Vincent is justifiably famous for his revelatory grilled pizzas, with their scorched grill marks and paper-thin, yet chewy crusts. Lunge if grilled sweet onion rings with parmigiano-reggiano are on the menu, and have them drizzled with Modena balsamic. Scotto's risottos and pasta preparations are almost as famous as his pizzas, and his seafood is always exemplary. In a neighborhood exploding with important new restaurants, Scopa places high among the best Italian restaurants in New York. *26 E. 28th St. (near Madison Ave.), Murray Hill, 212/686–8787. AE, MC, V. Subway: 6 to 28th St. $$*

9 *b-8*

SIENA

This modern trattoria with soothing, sophisticated decor offers a well-edited menu of great Tuscan fare. The emphasis is on such earthy dishes as *ribollita* (Tuscan bread soup), crispy oven-roasted whole red snapper flavored with rosemary and olive oil, and papardelle pasta with rabbit and wild mushrooms. The predominantly Italian wine list offers a great selection of inexpensive Chiantis. Siena closes some Sundays during the summer. *200 9th Ave. (between 22nd and 23rd Sts.), Chelsea, 212/633–8033. AE. No lunch. Subway: C, E to 23rd St. $$*

11 *b-1*

TANTI BACI CAFFÉ

Of all the inexpensive Italian restaurants in and around Greenwich Village, this is the one that conjures warm feelings from just about everyone who's been there. Perhaps it's because of the rathskeller location that makes you feel like a real native for having found it (though the recent opening of Tanti Baci Flower Room on Seventh Avenue South now allows you a choice of atmosphere), or the friendly neighborhood crowd inside. It may even be the food, which although not outstanding, is fresh, well prepared, satisfying, and very inexpensive. You can mix and match pasta shapes and sauces, or opt for the classic Italian entrées, salads, and desserts. Service is friendly if a bit sporadic. *163 W. 10th St. (between 7th Ave. S and Waverly Pl.), West Village, 212/647–9651. MC, V. No lunch. Subway: Christopher St./Sheridan Sq. $$*

9 *c-3*

TRATTORIA DELL'ARTE

The amusing decor—oversize proboscises and other body parts—and the lively, upbeat attitude of this casual and intensely popular trattoria make it a best bite pre- or post–Carnegie Hall. Portions, like the noses on the wall, are huge. Antipasto platters for two; thin-crust pizzas; pastas (available in half portions); grilled meats and fish; and other Italian fare are all well prepared. *900 7th Ave. (at 57th St.), Midtown, 212/245–9800. AE, MC, V. Reservations essential. Subway: 57th St. $$*

10 *e-8*

VIVOLO

This place serves simple, old-fashioned Italian food in a handsome, century-old brownstone with two working fireplaces. You have your choice of atmosphere—dark and clubby downstairs; high, frescoed ceilings upstairs—but either scene is romantic. The friendly service and well-priced early-bird dinner keep the locals coming. *140 E. 74th St. (between Lexington and Park Aves.), Upper East Side, 212/737–3533. AE, DC, MC, V. Closed Sun. No lunch Sat. Subway: 68th St./Hunter College. $$*

JAPANESE

11 *d-4*

BLUE RIBBON SUSHI

Blue Ribbon Sushi serves excellent fresh sushi and sashimi—with creative twists such as filet-mignon sushi and a delicious lobster hand roll—as well as a decent selection of sake. The waitstaff is efficient, and the decor is stylish Japanese. Be prepared to wait for a table. *119 Sullivan St. (between Spring and Prince Sts.), SoHo, 212/343–0404. Reservations not accepted. AE, MC, V. Closed Mon. No lunch. Subway: Spring St.; Prince St. $$*

11 *e-3*

BOND ST

The ultra-stylish setting—sheer curtains, lots of black—complements the achingly trendy crowd that dines here. The food is very good, despite the fact that most of the clientele look like they never eat. If you go for the well prepared sushi, you'll find rare treats—four types of yellowtail, jumbo sweet shrimp, unusual caviar—among the offerings. But the kitchen does an admirable job of preparing interesting alternatives to raw fish, too, such as broiled Chilean sea bass marinated in hearty red miso, rack of lamb with Asian pear and shiso sauce, or hot soba soup with duck and scallion. It will be hard to pick your server out from the beautiful masses, but they don't really seem like they want to be there anyway. *6 Bond St. (between Broadway and Lafayette St.), Greenwich Village, 212/777–2500. Reservations essential. AE, MC, V. Closed Sun. No lunch. Subway: Bleecker St./Broadway–Lafayette St. $$$*

11 *f-1*

HASAKI

Wonderfully fresh and exquisitely presented sushi is your reward for waiting eons for a table. Don't be deterred; the results are worth it, especially if you give the sushi chef the green light to surprise you. *210 E. 9th St. (between 2nd and 3rd Aves.), East Village, 212/473–3327. Reservations not accepted. AE, MC, V. No lunch. Subway: Astor Pl. $$*

9 *e-4*

HATSUHANA

While higher marks go to the original (48th St.) for atmosphere and consistency, true sushi connoisseurs know that both of these pricey bars are among the very best in town—that's why they wait so long. The teriyaki isn't bad, either, especially with one of the menu's several Japanese beers. *17 E. 48th St. (between 5th and Madison Aves.), Midtown, 212/355–3345. Reservations not accepted. AE, DC, MC, V. No lunch Sun. Subway: 51st St./Lexington–3rd Aves. $$*

9 *e-4*

237 Park Ave. (at 46th St.), Midtown, 212/661–3400. Subway: 42nd St./Grand Central.

11 *e-4*

HONMURA AN

Honmura An is the best place in town for authentic Japanese noodle dishes (which, traditionally, must be slurped). The restaurant makes its own soba noodles daily; you can watch a chef at work in a glassed-in room at the back. Try the seasonal tasting menu and the giant prawn tempura. The dining room, on the second floor of a SoHo warehouse, is spacious and comfortable. *170 Mercer St. (between Prince and Houston Sts.), 212/334–5253. Reservations essential. AE, DC, MC, V. Closed Mon. No lunch Sun. or Tues. Subway: Prince St.; Spring St.; Bleecker St./Broadway–Lafayette St. $$$*

9 *e-4*

INAGIKU

Inagiku's diners are a healthy mix of European tourists and guests of the Waldorf-Astoria, where the restaurant is housed, but there is always a marked Japanese presence as well—an important indication of quality in any Manhattan Japanese restaurant. The beautiful, idiomatic space is highly dignified, yet relaxing. Start with special sake from the large list, and chef Harou Ohbu's "Sashimi Extravaganza," prepared for two to four diners. Wasabi root is grated for you at the table. Then choose from 23 classic little dishes. Don't miss *unagi hakata*, a pair of Napoleonic stacks of barbecued eel with enoki and shiitake mushrooms, or the butterflied lobster tail tempura. *111 E. 49th St. (between Lexington and Park Aves.), Midtown, 212/355–0440. AE, MC, V. Subway: 51st St./Lexington–3rd Aves. $$$*

10 *e-1*

JAPONICA

This restaurant is always so busy that you can be sure the sushi is fresh. The sizable menu—which includes sushi, sashimi, tempura, and teriyaki—has something to delight every Japanese-food lover. If you can't decide, economical combo plates offer a taste of several different dishes. Be prepared to wait during peak hours. *90 University Pl. (at 11th St.), Greenwich Village, 212/243–7752. Reservations not accepted. AE. Subway: 14th St./Union Sq. $*

10 *d-5*

NEXT DOOR NOBU

Drew Nieporent, the owner of Nobu *(below)*, has finally heeded the cries of distraught would-be customers who were perpetually unable to secure a reservation at his famed restaurant. Next Door Nobu is strictly first-come, first-served, which means painfully long waits, but non-VIPs are thrilled to have the opportunity to sample Nobu Matsuhisa's unique style of Japanese cooking. The menu focuses more on sushi and raw-bar offerings, and is slightly less expensive than the one next door. The décor is fancifully Japanese and

STARGAZING

If you keep track of your run-ins, here are some places to up the ante:

Pastis (French)
You'll be in good company if you can get in, but try not to sprain your neck.

First (American)
Service in the wee hours means that you can watch the stars and see the sun come up.

Indochine (Vietnamese)
If you're a model—or just look like one—or will even settle for watching one, you'll find a glamorous backdrop here.

Nobu (Japanese)
Probably the most imaginative Japanese food in America—with a crowd to match.

Pravda (Russian)
Great appetizers, 65 kinds of vodkas, a fun scene—hey, maybe someone's watching you.

includes a wall papered with nori. *105 Hudson St. (between Franklin and N. Moore Sts.), Tribeca, 212/334–4445. AE, DC, MC, V. Reservations not accepted. No lunch weekends. Subway: 1, 9 to Franklin St.* $$$

11 *c-7*

NOBU

Nobu is one of New York's most exciting restaurants, and getting a reservation here can be a frustrating experience. But the food is sensational, reflecting chef Nobu Matsuhisa's time in Latin America—think "unusual use of chiles." Try the glazed black cod, the yellow-tail sashimi, squid ceviche, or the tartare of *toro* (tuna belly), and tuna salad with ponzu sauce. Best of all, put yourself in the hands of the chef—but be prepared to pay. If you can't get a reservation, go anyway and you will probably be seated at the sushi bar, which is a show in itself. You can also try Next Door Nobu (*above*), with its egalitarian no-reservations policy. *105 Hudson St. (at Franklin St.), Tribeca, 212/219–0500. Reservations essential. AE, DC, MC, V. No lunch weekends. Subway: Franklin St.* $$$$

10 *e-5*

OBECA LI

The Asian high-tech décor, with lots of streamlined wood accents, makes this a popular spot for arty Tribeca scenesters. There's a huge staircase at the front of the bilevel restaurant and the space is divided into several smaller rooms, each with a slightly different vibe. (Perhaps the layout confuses the waitstaff, who seem perpetually absent.) Tasting plates, a kind of Japanese tapas, make up half the menu. Here you'll find such dishes as shrimp and enoki mushrooms with clam sauce, "shabu shabu" sirloin, and seared scallops with watercress and hijiki seaweed. The rest of the menu is sushi and entrées with minimal Asian influences, such as chicken paillard on a bed of shiitake risotto. *62 Thomas St. (between Church St. and W. Broadway), Tribeca, 212/393–9887. AE, MC, V. Subway: Chambers St.* $$$

10 *f-1*

SHARAKU

The first (and certainly the largest) East Village Japanese restaurant to ride the 1980s sushi craze, Sharaku gets every-

thing right, and at comparatively friendly prices. The place is therefore often very crowded, with a strong Japanese presence (always a good sign). The sushi bar is prodigious and its chefs are deeply focused; the chirashi is a favorite. *8 Stuyvesant Pl. (near 3rd Ave.), East Village, 212/598–0402. AE, MC, V. Subway: Astor Place.* $$

11 *b-2*

TAKA

Two things distinguish Taka from the many other small, cozy Japanese restaurants around the city: The sushi chef is a woman; and all of the beautiful ceramic dishes, in organic shapes and colors, are custom-made for the restaurant by her. Furthermore, the fish is always fresh and several creative rolls add flair to the meal. *61 Grove St. (between Bleecker St. and 7th Ave. S), West Village, 212/242–3699. AE, MC, V. Subway: Christopher St./Sheridan Sq.* $$

11 *h-1*

TAKAHACHI

The best sushi bargain in town, this no-frills East Villager is always packed with a young crowd, hungry for swimmingly fresh slabs of yellowtail, tuna, and salmon. Don't expect anything unusual, and don't demand too much of the frenzied waitstaff; just pray they're not out of sea urchin. Prepare for a wait. *85 Ave. A (between 5th and 6th Sts.), East Village, 212/505–6524. No lunch. AE, MC, V. Subway: Astor Place.* $

11 *d-4*

TOMOE SUSHI

Few restaurants have as loyal a following as this small sushi place in the West Village. A line begins to form a full hour before the doors open at 5 in the evening and it doesn't subside until they close five or so hours later. What people wait upwards of an hour for is fresh, generously portioned sushi at reasonable prices, and other well prepared Japanese food. There are no fireworks, but the food never disappoints. And many a new friendship has been made waiting on line or while sitting at the tightly packed tables. *172 Thompson St. (between Bleecker and Houston Sts.), West Village, 212/777–9346. AE. Reservations not accepted. Closed Tues. Subway: 1, 9 to Houston St.* $$

9 *e-8*

YAMA

Yama is the place to take anyone who insists that sushi isn't filling. These huge slabs of sushi and sashimi literally fall off the plate. Moreover, the fish is always extremely fresh, tender, and delicious. The drawbacks are the inevitable wait outdoors and the nonexistent decor. The original store, on 17th Street, is the one to hit; the new Houston Street outpost doesn't measure up. *122 E. 17th St. (at Irving Pl.), Gramercy, 212/475-0969. Reservations not accepted. AE, MC, V. Closed Sun. No lunch Sat. Subway: 14th St./Union Sq. $$*

11 *d-3*

92 W. Houston St. (between LaGuardia Pl. and Thompson Sts.), Greenwich Village, 212/674-0935. Subway: Bleecker St./Broadway-Lafayette St.

10 *d-3*

38-40 Carmine St. (between Bedford and Bleecker Sts.), West Village, 212/989-9330. Subway: Christopher St./Sheridan Sq.

10 *d-5*

ZUTTO

Long before Nobu arrived to define Tribeca sushi, neighborhood residents were content to eat reasonably priced raw fish with minimal fanfare at Zutto. Offerings are always fresh and seasonal delicacies often add to the menu. While the restaurant has never been destined to win any design awards the spare room is serene and pleasing. *77 Hudson St. (between Harrison and Jay Sts.), Tribeca, 212/233-3287. Subway: Franklin St. $$*

KOREAN

11 *f-5*

CLAY

Hip downtowners flock to this sleek, diminutive restaurant for tasty Korean food at reasonable prices. Scallion and seafood pancakes (*pa-jeon*) are delectable and the traditional *bibimbop* (a rice bowl with vegetables and ground meat) is satisfying. The traditional accompaniment, *soju*, a Korean sweet-potato vodka, slides down easily and—along with the pulsing music—will prime you for a night on the town at the other chic haunts in the neighborhood. *202 Mott St. (between Kenmare and Spring Sts.), SoHo, 212/625-1105. AE, MC, V. Subway: Spring St. $*

11 *h-1*

DOK SUNI

This tiny storefront has a small, dark dining room with exposed bricks and just a dozen tables, piped-in rock music, and pleasant service. It serves home-style Korean cooking—fresh, simple, and, of course, spicy, but never greasy or heavy. The kimchi and spicy broiled pork ribs are great. *119 1st Ave. (between 7th and 8th Sts.), East Village, 212/477-9506. Reservations not accepted. No credit cards. No lunch. Subway: Astor Pl.; 2nd Ave. $*

9 *e-6*

HANGAWI

Everything but the kimchi is bound to baffle the uninitiated in this serene dining room, where you sit shoeless at a sunken table under dark-wood beams. Hangawi specializes in vegetarian Korean mountain cooking, whatever that is; the only way to start is to order a prix-fixe "Emperor's Meal," which translates loosely into a parade of exotic vegetable dishes that are at worst interesting and at best delicious. There are no fewer than 10 courses, several of which you may have to assemble yourself; and by the time you hit the last one your table will be covered with about 20 little bowls of unidentifiable but delicious things. If only the waitstaff could translate the names of the rare wild herbs into English . . . . Try one of the many teas—date and citrus are wonderful—and the milky-white Korean sake. *12 E. 32nd St., Garment District, 212/213-0077. AE, MC, V. Reservations essential. Subway: 34th St./Herald Sq.; 33rd St. $$*

11 *d-3*

JUNNO'S

Master mixologist Junno Lee has created an innovative selection of specialty cocktails—the soju lemonade, made with Korean sweet-potato vodka, is exceptional—at his spare bar/restaurant. Food is sometimes an afterthought with such a lively bar scene, but a couple of dishes are worth sampling, such as the grilled squid with miso, beef shortribs, and wakame seaweed salad. *64 Downing St. (between Bedford and Varick Sts.), West Village, 212/627-7995. AE, MC, V. Subway: Houston St. $-$$*

1 *f-3*

KUM GANG SAN

This 24-hour Korean eatery is almost the size of the Seoul airport and comes complete with a waterfall. There are tables as far as the eye can see, and as soon as you've grabbed one, one of the countless bowls of delicious kimchi (often spicy pickled vegetables and dried fish) will materialize. The highlight is excellent Korean barbecue, especially the beef shortribs, but there is also a full menu to choose from. *138–28 Northern Blvd. (at Union St.), Flushing, Queens, 718/461–0909. AE, MC, V. Subway: Main St.–Flushing.* $

9 *d-6*

NEW YORK KOM TANG SOOT BUL HOUSE

Korean "Seoul" food at its best is served at this lively restaurant on the 32nd Street strip. For the barbecue experience, cook thin slices of beef (*bul go gui*) or other marinated meats over red-hot coals, top with chilies and raw garlic, and wrap in lettuce. The large second-flour dining room is the more festive of the two, with communal tables situated around tabletop barbecues. The waitstaff speaks little English so be prepared for a lot of gesturing. *32 W. 32nd St. (between 5th and 6th Aves.), Garment District, 212/947–8482. AE, MC, V. Subway: 34th St./Herald Sq.* $

KOSHER

9 *d-5*

LE MARAIS

The Jewish younger sister of Les Halles, Le Marais offers the best kosher steaks in town, but also fine smoked fish, duck rillettes, French fries, and creamless desserts. Obviously well-trusted, the restaurant can be jammed during peak hours. *150 W. 46th St. (between 6th and 7th Aves.), Midtown, 212/727–8022. AE, MC, V. Subway: B, D, F, Q to 47–50th Sts./Rockefeller Center.* $$

10 *g-3*

RATNER'S DAIRY RESTAURANT

This famous kosher-dairy Jewish restaurant offers an extensive range of well-prepared dishes–vegetable goulash, assorted soups, matzo brie, stuffed cabbage, blintzes, mushroom cutlets, and baked stuffed fish. The waiters are straight from Central Casting, and the chef has a traditional heavy hand with the salt. Sundays are hectic. Oddly enough, the back room was recently turned into a tragically hip cocktail lounge with a similar menu and an extensive martini selection; needless to say, it attracts a different sort of Lower East Side crowd. *138 Delancey St. (between Norfolk and Suffolk Sts.), Lower East Side, 212/677–5588. AE, MC, V. Subway: Delancey St.* $

LATIN

9 *c-3*

BISTRO LATINO

As you climb the narrow, worn staircase to this hidden, second-floor restaurant, you may wonder what you're getting yourself into; after all, you're not that far from Times Square. Rest assured: Behind the door is a fun-filled evening of cool rhythms and hot food. Enjoy succulent seafood, ceviche, and paella as you tango and samba the night away; chef Rafael Palomino's contemporary interpretations of South American classics will dance on your tongue. It's part kitsch, part Havana, and all very enjoyable. *1711 Broadway (at 54th St.), Midtown, 212/956–1000. AE, D, DC, MC, V. Closed Mon. in Aug. Subway: 57th St.* $$

9 *f-3*

BOLIVAR

Happily filling the exalted Arizona 206's space, Bolivar is a perfect fit. The bar at the entryway remains impressive, yet intimate. The graceful, cavelike space features impeccably clean lines and gorgeous lighting. The staff is very attractive, seriously in love with the food served, and happy to be there. Executive chef Andy D'Amico and his chef de cuisine Larry Kolar helm the kitchen and grill with substantial flair and assurance. Many feel that the lobster chowder is the best chowder served in the city. Chunks of tail meat commingle in a creamy broth with cubes of skin-on russets, corn, peas, and rice, and a perfectly poached egg rests at one corner of the generous bowl. Ceviches are all made with sushi-grade seafood. But the main event is the food grilled on the gigantic parilla. Argentinean ribeye, whole fish, and leg of lamb are standouts. Prices are remarkably friendly as well. *206 E. 60th St., between 2nd and 3rd Aves., Upper East Side, 212/838–0440. AE, MC, V. Subway: 59th St./Lexington Ave.* $$

11 f-4

CAFÉ HABANA

When the surrounding neighborhood was still bohemian and offbeat, this space was a fun local diner. The current owners, who also own Rialto down the block, wanting to preserve the feel of the place, opened this Cuban/Mexican-theme restaurant. Excellent Latin diner fare such as Cuban sandwiches, rice and beans, and *camarones al ajillo* (shrimp in garlic sauce) are all provided at budget prices. And, true to the owners' vision, the cheery space, with blue booths and pale green Formica tables, is usually filled with artist types eating late breakfasts and tapping their feet to festive Latin beats. *17 Prince St. (at Elizabeth St.), Lower East Side, 212/625–2001. AE, DC, MC, V. Subway: 6 to Spring St. $*

11 c-1

L RAY

This bilevel restaurant in the heart of Greenwich Village buzzes with a young crowd, excited by the Latin fusion menu spiced up with plenty of Cajun accents. The extensive menu has everything from popcorn shrimp to pork chop *mojo* (a citrus sauce) to simple grilled fish served with a choice of fresh salsas. The chef draws his inspiration from that soulful cuisine. Though noisy and a little cramped, the high energy level contributes to the festive atmosphere. *64 W. 10th St. (between 5th and 6th Aves.), Greenwich Village, 212/505–7777. MC, V. Subway: W. 4th St./Washington Sq. $$*

9 e-8

PATRIA

This festive, loopy Flatiron District hot spot serves up creative and scrumptious *nuevo latino* fare to arouse even the most jaded palate. Sip a *mojito* while you play with a mortar of butter, cream cheese, and roasted garlic to spread on your warm olive bread. New chef Andrew DiCataldo has devised a most unusual menu. Tuna ceviche, limey and suffused with flavor, is served in a split coconut nested in crushed ice. A "suckling pig combo" features two graceful bone-on rib chops that amount to luxury finger-food, and a leg that's been rubbed in deep, dark spices and watchfully braised. Pastry chef Gilles Delaloy is having the time of his life, pulling together such desserts as pineapple-coconut "ceviche," for which the flesh of those two tropical staples is seasoned with

cilantro oil and coconut milk, and served with a piña colada granita. Be aware that the zing of these flavors is quite addictive, and that zing costs a hell of a lot more than rice and beans, especially via the new prix-fixe menu. Still, you won't find this fare anywhere else. *250 Park Ave. S (at 20th St.), Gramercy, 212/777–6211. Reservations essential. AE, MC, V. Subway: N, R, 6 to 23rd St. $$$*

10 d-3

VANDAM

Some folks just know how to attract a crowd. In the case of Frederick Lesort (of Le Bilboquet, *above*, and The Lemon), that crowd is beautiful, stylish, and into good food. At Vandam, the latest entry in the trendy bistro scene, chef Fernando Trocca's Latin-inspired food ranges from tapas to Argentinean beef, and the servers are as attractive as the diners. The lively bar scene kicks in just after work and carries on into the evening. *150 Varick St. (at Vandam St.), SoHo, 212/352–9090. AE, MC, V. No lunch. Subway: Houston St. $$*

MALAYSIAN

11 g-5

NYONYA

Filled with Malaysians, which inspires confidence, this noisy and often hectic restaurant serves good food at very low prices. Try the Oriental sesame rolls or a whole deep-fried fish. *194 Grand St. (at Mott St.), Little Italy/Chinatown, 212/343–8899. No credit cards. Subway: Grand St.; Spring St.; Bowery. $*

1 f-3

PENANG

There are now three Manhattan outposts of this fabulous Flushing restaurant; would that the food at any of them were as good as the original. For an authentic Malaysian experience, make the trip to Queens. Don't miss the coconut shrimp, or the pull-apart roti appetizer with a fragrant chicken-curry dipping sauce. The whole fish and homemade Malaysian noodles are also good. The Manhattan stores, alas, are merely cheap places to eat with 1960s Vistavision Tiki-Hut décor and merely okay food. *38-04 Prince St., Flushing, Queens, 718/321–2078. Reservations not accepted. AE, MC, V. Subway: 7 to Main St./Flushing. $*

7 *f-7*

1596 2nd Ave. (at 83rd St.), Upper East Side, 212/585–3838. Subway: 4, 5, 6 to 86th St.

11 *e-5*

109 Spring St. (between Greene and Mercer Sts.), SoHo, 212/274–8883. Subway: Spring St.

9 *b-1*

240 Columbus Ave. (at 71st St.), Upper West Side, 212/769–3988. Subway: B, C to 72nd St.

MEDITERRANEAN

9 *f-2*

EAST RIVER CAFÉ

Gleaming French doors run along the front and north side of the restaurant; inside are vintage Hollywood studio portraits, Persian rugs, and gentle live light jazz piano. Sweet young clams are steamed with Venetian abandon in garlicky white wine. Desserts are scrumptious, especially layered chocolate buttercream and white chocolate mousse cake. Note that the restaurant offers "midnight supper" Thursday through Saturday until 3 AM. 1111 1st Ave. (at E. 61st St.), Upper East Side, 212/980–3144. AE, MC, V. Subway: 59th St./Lexington Ave. $$

11 *f-3*

IL BUCO

Il Buco is an antiques shop by day, a Mediterranean restaurant by night. The dark, candlelit rooms looks like the setting for a film scene of bohemian Village life in the '50s. The menu consists of tapas, including vigorously seasoned baby eel and octopus; gutsy and very good saffron rice cakes (arancini); and grilled sea scallops with capers and olives. 47 Bond St. (between Lafayette St. and Bowery), East Village, 212/533–1932. Reservations essential. AE. No lunch. Closed Mon. Subway: Bleecker St./Broadway–Lafayette St. $$

9 *f-2*

MATTHEW'S

The enduring flagship of young dynamo chef Matthew Kenney is in especially splendid form. Rightfully compared in appearance with the set designs of Casablanca, this place will make you feel as if you've stepped into a daguerrotype. Tuna tartare virtually rejuvenates this

cliché with a spicy green olive tapenade. Roasted panko-crusted cod with manila clams, roasted tomatoes, and saffron-tinged Yukon gold potatoes is even better than it sounds. In season, there are tender venison medallions set about with champagne grapes. A phyllo cup holding basmati rice pudding is delightful. 1030 3rd Ave. (at E. 61st St.), Upper East Side, 212/838–4343. AE, MC, V. Subway: 59th St./Lexington Ave. $$

9 *e-8*

METRONOME

In a soaring, 12,000-square-ft space festooned with deliberately schizoid Deco/Art Nouveau/Bauhaus touches, you'll find reasonably priced fare, from voluptuous crab cakes and supple beef carpaccio to straight-ahead prime rack of lamb and hale salmon crusted with crushed fennel and coriander seeds. Banana challah bread pudding is warm and lovely in its streaky milk chocolate gravy. There's jazzy live music and dancing Thursday–Saturday evenings. 915 Broadway (at 21st St.), Flatiron District, 212/505–7400. AE, MC, V. Subway: N, R, 6 to 23rd St. $$

11 *c-8*

SPARTINA

Chef and owner Stephen Kalt has created a relaxed haven in ultrachic Tribeca with this comfortable, unpretentious Mediterranean restaurant; it feels like it's been here forever. The tasty food makes up for the occasionally too-casual service. Try the delicious pizzas, lamb shank Catalan, or black linguini with stewed calamari and chorizo. 355 Greenwich St. (at Harrison St.), Tribeca, 212/274–9310. AE, MC, V. Subway: Franklin St. $$

7 *b-8*

SPAZZIA

Following the smooth success of their Spartina (see above), co-owners Cindy Smith and chef Stephen Kalt shot uptown to open Spazzia, a graceful space that formerly housed the far less ambitious Museum (of Natural History) Café. The chef has imported his spectacular grilled pizza from downtown, and it's feathery enough for two to split as an appetizer. Especially fine is a frequent special: smoked salmon draped across fontina cheese, all studded with ruby salmon roe. However, you mustn't miss grilled squid on a glistening mound of squid-ink black rice that engulfs you like the warmest reaches of the Mediterranean. Pepper-crusted tuna is spicy, and whole huge grilled shrimp on linguine with a confetti of corn and cockles are especially robust. *366 Columbus Ave. (at 77th St), Upper West Side, 212/799–0150. AE, MC, V. Subway: B, C to 72nd St. $$*

MEXICAN

7 b-8
CITRUS BAR & GRILL

This big, loopy party of a place serves some of the best margaritas in town. Chile peppers—cascabel, ancho, pasilla, and poblano—are all over the menu, but the heat can be turned down to order. Chicken sausage and habanero jack flautas on a honeyed triple-sec roasted corn sauce are addictively delicious. So is marinated and grilled skirt steak in a sweet cascabel-coffee-nutmeg barbecue sauce with fried ribbon onion rings and cheddar mashed potatoes. Squeeze, the hopping downstairs lounge, completes the party. *320 Amsterdam Ave. (between 75th and 76th Sts.), Upper West Side, 212/595–0500. AE, MC, V. Subway: 1, 2, 3, 9 to 72nd St. $$*

11 h-4
EL SOMBRERO

They'll even give you margaritas-to-go at this almost-seedy diner-style Mexican café, which is nicknamed "the hat" after the huge neon sign out front. The food is of the too cheesy, taco-enchilada brand of Mexican cuisine, but it is filling enough to take the edge off the tequila (margaritas come in pitchers, too). Expect a fun, noisy crowd, loud Latin music, and a potential hangover. *108 Stanton St. (at Ludlow St.), Lower East Side, 212/254–4188. No credit cards. Subway: 2nd Ave. $*

10 d-5
EL TEDDY'S

A Statue of Liberty crown graces the roof of this Tribeca fixture, and the awning resembles a faux Gaudì sculpture. Inside, the funky décor includes mosaics, lit dioramas, and lots of color. The active bar provides potent margaritas, served on the rocks or straight up, and a watchable crowd. Once you make your way to one of the oversize booths should food happen to arrive—the service is maddeningly slow—you'll be treated to upscale Mexican concoctions

made with the freshest ingredients. Skip dessert and just order a cup of the strong coffee: It comes with dishes of natural sugar crystals and Mexican chocolate shavings. *219 W. Broadway (between Franklin and White Sts.), Tribeca, 212/941–7070. AE, MC, V. No lunch weekends. Subway: Franklin St. $$*

7 b-6
GABRIELA'S

It's not the quietest place, and the service isn't always speedy, but you probably won't find better value at any other Mexican restaurant in Manhattan. The flavors are authentic, the corn tacos are fresh, and the *posole* may be the most satisfying soup you've ever tried. The roasted chicken and pork are pretty good, too. Expect an extended wait for a table during peak hours; defuse the waiting experience with a margarita or sangria. *685 Amsterdam Ave. (at 93rd St.), Upper West Side, 212/961–0574. AE, MC, V. Subway: 1, 2, 3, 9 to 96th St. $*

7 a-5
MAMA MEXICO

Two brothers, taught to cook by their Mama in a small Mexican village, braved the trip north and brought along a sunny friendliness and some of the best authentic Mexican cooking around. Terrific guacamole, made tableside, can be nice and spicy (for a change). Perfect grilled squid, jumbo grilled lamb rack chops in a ruddy gravy, zippy chicken mole, and *real* beef tacos. Even the rice and beans are quite thoughtfully prepared. Befriend brother Juan (an easy task) and he'll let you sample house-infused pineapple tequila. There's also terrific live mariachi music on Friday night. *2672 Broadway (between 101st and 102nd Sts.) Upper West Side, 212/ 864–2323. AE, MC, V. Subway: 1, 9 to 103rd St. $$*

9 f-2
MAYA

Executive chef Richard Sandoval has created spectacular and benevolently priced dishes that are precisely the way you always hoped Mexican food would taste. Small wonder Maya is always jammed. Margaritas are downright sinewy. Chiles rellenos (stuffed with shrimp and manchego cheese) are ridiculously delicious. Guacamole is spicy on request, so request. Butterflied, lime-marinated, and grilled beef tenderloin, plated with a cheese enchilada dap-

pled with mole sauce, is remarkably flavorful. And buttery crepes folded into
purses and sauced with a warm goat
milk reduction on a plate studded with
roasted pecans may reduce you to tears.
*1191 1st Ave. (between 64th and 65th
Sts.), Upper East Side, 212/585–1818.
Reservations essential. AE, MC, V. Sub-
way: 68th St./Hunter College. $$*

11 *a-2*

MEXICANA MAMA

Bring your own six-pack of Dos Equis—
a friendly waitress will bring the limes—
to this adorable storefront where the
food is cheap and traditional. Then get
ready to chow down on three kinds of
salsa, quesadillas, enchiladas, chicken
mole, and the tour-de-force: chile rel-
leno. *525 Hudson St. (between Charles
and W. 10th Sts.), West Village, 212/924–
4119. No credit cards. No lunch Sun. Sub-
way: A, C, E to 14th St.; L to 8th Ave. $*

10 *c-1*

MI COCINA

Authentic regional Mexican cooking (no
spicy baby-food pap here) is served here
in cramped but convivial surroundings.
Try the tamales steamed in Swiss chard;
empanadas with beef, raisins, and
olives; or shrimp in adobo sauce. *57 Jane
St. (at Hudson St.), West Village, 212/627–
8273. AE, DC, MC, V. No lunch. Brunch
Sun. Subway: A, C, E to 14th St.; L to 8th
Ave.; Christopher St./Sheridan Sq. $$*

9 *f-3*

ROSA MEXICANO

Many hold this festively elegant Mexican
restaurant in high esteem, and not only
for its wonderful guacamole (made to
your specifications tableside) and signature pomegranate margaritas. The menu
and the kitchen, all under the fastidious
supervision of Josefina Howard, feature
mildly spiced regional dishes—not Tex-
or Cal-Mex. Try the flaming fajitas, or the
lamb shank steamed in a parchment
pouch with three chilis, or beef tenderloin with a wild mushroom tequila
sauce. *1063 1st Ave. (at 58th St.), Upper
East Side, 212/753–7407. AE, DC, MC, V.
Subway: 59th St./Lexington Ave. $$$*

9 *f-4*

ZARELA

Zarela's is one of the more popular
spots for "gourmet" Mexican.
Renowned Mexican chef Zarela Mar-
tinez showcases her zesty, authentic
home cooking in an even zestier envi-
ronment. If you'd rather skip the fiesta
atmosphere, opt for the somewhat qui-
eter dining area upstairs, but anywhere
you sit, it's a great party. But don't miss
the poblano chile relleno, the roasted
marinated pork tenderloin, and plenty of
the loopiest margaritas in town. *953 2nd
Ave. (between 50th and 51st Sts.), Mid-
town, 212/644–6740. Reservations essen-
tial. AE, DC, MC, V. No lunch weekends.
Subway: 51st St./Lexington–3rd Aves. $$*

MIDDLE EASTERN

9 *b-4*

AZURI CAFÉ

This tiny kosher storefront serves up the
best falafel in the city—and, according
to winsome ex-pats, the best outside
Israel. Chicken and beef kebabs are also
excellent and come with the same outstanding salads and condiments as the
falafel. Service can cool, but compliment
the food and it'll warm up. There's no
décor but for three rickety tables, so
consider take-out. *465 W. 51st St.
(between 9th and 10th Aves.), Hell's
Kitchen, 212/262–2920. Reservations not
accepted. Breakfast daily. No credit cards.
Subway: 50th St. $*

11 *d-7*

LAYLA

Layla looks like a Middle East nightspot,
with Moroccan tiles and dioramas of
belly dancers and pashas (a real-life
belly dancer appears once nightly).
North African cooking is reinterpreted
here, with great success. Try the *meze*
(appetizers), including feathery *borek*
(phyllo dough filled with sharp feta
cheese), fresh sardines, octopus salad,
and dips served with pita. The lamb
kebabs glazed with pomegranate and
the pigeon in vine leaves are also worthwhile. *211 W. Broadway (at Franklin St.),
Tribeca, 212/431–0700. AE, DC, MC, V.
No lunch. Subway: Franklin St. $$$*

11 *a-3*

MOUSTACHE

You won't be able to contain yourself
when you're presented with a pita—a
piping hot pillow of dough straight from
the oven—and a selection of delicious
salads waiting to be scooped up. This is
only part of the reason that crowds wait
patiently outside Moustache for one of
the 10 copper-top tables. The pitas are

followed by delicious entrées, including leg of lamb or merguez sausage sandwiches or, if you're particularly hungry, the *ouzi*, a large phyllo package stuffed with chicken and fragrant rice. The falafel is bland and overcooked but nothing else on the menu disappoints. Although the service can be slow—it takes time to roll out those pita to order—it is always friendly. For quickest seating, plan to eat at off times. *90 Bedford St. (between Barrow and Grove Sts.), West Village, 212/229–2220. No credit cards. Subway: Christopher St./Sheridan Sq. $*

11 *h-1*

265 E. 10th St. (between 1st Ave. and Ave. A), East Village, 212/228–2022. No credit cards. Subway: Astor Pl.

PAN-ASIAN

7 *f-8*
ORIENTA
It feels like a SoHo bistro, but this small crowd-pleaser is definitely Uptown, and definitely not a bistro. The kitchen turns out creative and well-presented Thai-Vietnamese cooking for a beautiful crowd that actually comes to eat. Amber lighting and large windows along the street soften the cramped quarters. *205 E. 75th St. (between 2nd and 3rd Aves.), Upper East Side, 212/517–7509. Reservations essential. AE, DC, MC, V. No lunch. Subway: 77th St. $$*

11 *h-1*
O.G. (ORIENTAL GRILL)
The decor is minimal: Japanese light fixtures on peach walls (so far as we could tell in the dim lighting), dark-blue banquettes, brown-paper tablecloths, and votive candles. The clever combinations of oriental techniques and ingredients—Japanese, Thai, Chinese, and Indonesian—mean that each dish is well-conceived, not forced or bizarre (despite what you might think about banana wontons flambé). *507 E. 6th St. (between Aves. A and B), East Village, 212/477–4649. MC, V. No lunch. Subway: 2nd Ave. $*

7 *c-7*
RAIN
Rain feels like a post-college party on weekend nights, but the food at this contemporary Pan-Asian restaurant is skillfully prepared and delicious. The menu reads like the greatest hits of Thai, Viet-namese, and Malaysian cooking. Appetizers of green-papaya salad and summer rolls wrapped in rice paper are cool and refreshing. The coconut chicken soup tastes like the real McCoy. For the main course, try the stir-fried beef in peanut sauce or the Chinese eggplant in bean sauce. Nothing disappoints, though some dishes are more authentic than others. Wash it all down with one of many Asian beers. *100 W. 82nd St. (between Amsterdam and Columbus Aves.), Upper West Side, 212/501–0776. AE, DC, MC, V. Subway: 79th St. $$*

9 *e-8*
REPUBLIC
Republic is noisy, crowded, and doesn't take reservations unless you're having a good-size party. But it's fun, with a sleek, spare, neo-warehouse design and long, polished, blond-wood tables for communal seating. (Sit at the bar if you're shy.) This is essentially a sophisticated noodle house. Try curried chicken on skewers; spicy seafood salad; noodle dishes, including curried duck in chicken broth with taro chips; shrimp wontons in chicken broth; and pad thai. For dessert, the coconut ice cream is conspicuously divine. *37 Union Sq. W (between 16th and 17th Sts.), Flatiron District, 212/627–7172. AE, DC, MC, V. Subway: 14th St./Union Sq. $*

7 *b-7*

2290 Broadway (between 82nd and 83rd Sts.), Upper West Side, 212/579–5959. Subway: 79th St.

PIZZA

11 *d-3*
ARTURO'S PIZZERIA
Serving what many consider the best coal-oven pizza in town, Arturo's is a popular choice for those who can't get into Lombardi's. Live music starts nightly at 6 PM, and the setting is fun and timeless, if somewhat decrepit. *106 Houston St. (at Thompson St.), Greenwich Village, 212/677–3820. AE, MC, V. No lunch. Subway: Houston St.; Broadway–Lafayette St. $*

12 *b-2*
GRIMALDI'S
Frank Sinatra made frequent pilgrimages to this red-check tableclothed classic (formerly known as Patsy's) where great (some say the best) New York-

style pizza reigns supreme. The walls are covered with autographed black- and white-photos, and Frank Sinatra's silky voice emanates from the jukebox. Patsy usually sits at the table in the far right corner, making sure everyone is happy with the pies coming out of the coal-fired oven. Any combination of toppings is available, but be careful because the price adds up quickly. You can get salads and pastas with red sauce, but why bother when the pizza is so good. *19 Old Fulton St. (between Front and Water Sts.), Brooklyn Heights, 718/858–4300. Reservations not accepted. No credit cards. Subway: High St./Brooklyn Bridge. $*

11 *c-3*

JOE'S PIZZA

If all you want is a slice of thin, crisp New York pizza at its best, drop into Joe's. A sprinkling of hot pepper flakes, garlic powder, oregano, and Parmesan cheese will make you think you've died and gone to heaven. Find a place to indulge; there's no seating here. *7 Carmine St. (at Bleecker St.), West Village, 212/255–3946. No reservations. No credit cards. Subway: W. 4th St./Washington Sq. $*

11 *c-2*

JOHN'S PIZZERIA

As far as purists are concerned, this longtime Village pizzeria serves the city's only real pizza, baked in stone-floor ovens—thin-crusted, garlicky, and topped with fresh ingredients. Devour your pie (you can't order by the slice) on old-fashioned, red-check tablecloths, below celebrity photos, and painted murals of Italy. The Village original serves beer and wine, and some of the spin-off locations have full bars. The other branches are all splendid, but there's something about the original that keeps the lines long during peak hours. *278 Bleecker St. (between 6th and 7th Aves.), West Village, 212/243–1680. Reservations not accepted. No credit cards. Subway: W. 4th St./Washington Sq. $*

9 *c-2*

48 W. 65th St. (between Central Park W and Columbus Ave.), Upper West Side, 212/721–7001. Subway: 66th St./Lincoln Ctr.

9 *c-5*

260 W. 44th St. (between Broadway and 8th Ave.), District, 212/391–7560. Subway: 42nd St./Times Sq.

9 *f-2*

408 E. 64th St. (between 1st and York Aves.), Upper East Side, 212/935–2895. Subway: 68th St./Hunter College.

9 *e-8*

LA PIZZA FRESCA

Count on this find opposite the glitzy Gramercy Tavern for powerfully flavored pastas and risottos, huge arugula salads sparkling in a dressing of good olive oil and fresh lemon juice, and pizzas whose thin, crisp crusts are blistered and savory from the wood fire in the beehive brick oven at the back of the room. With the wood fire casting its glow on the rear tables and the sponged ochre walls, warm and mellow are the operative words here; La Pizza Fresca is particularly soothing at the end of a long day, or after a movie at the Loews 19th Street Theatre. Moreover, the prices are noticeably reasonable, even if the mostly young waitstaff often needs a gentle nudge. *31 E. 20th St., Flatiron District, 212/598–0141. AE, DC, MC, V. No lunch Sun. Subway: 6, N, R to 23rd St. $$*

11 *f-5*

LOMBARDI'S

One of New York's original pizza-making families, the Lombardis have become synonymous with delicious coal-oven pizza. The secret is in the crust, which, according to finicky pizza lovers, has more flavor here than anywhere else. The best salad in any pizza joint and a comfortable, casual atmosphere make the experience a must. *32 Spring St. (between Mott and Mulberry Sts.), Little Italy, 212/941–7994. No reservations. No credit cards. Subway: 6 to Spring St.; Broadway–Lafayette St. $*

7 *f-2*

PATSY'S PIZZA

A contender for the best slice in the city, this no-frills pizza joint—the first to bear the Patsy's name—recently added a dining room so you can sit down. That's about all that has changed in almost a century, except for the neighborhood around it. (You'll notice lots of other Patsy's locations around town, but this is by far the best.) *2287–91 1st Ave. (between 117th and 118th Sts.), Harlem, 212/534–9783. No credit cards. Subway: 6 to 116th St. $*

9 *e-2*

SERAFINA FABULOUS GRILL

It's easy to see why this enormous place is consistently thronged, usually by the cellular phone crowd that works in the neighborhood: Serafina's brilliant, indefatigable young chef Giorgio Rocchi and his vast wood-burning oven turn out consistently spectacular fare at reasonable prices. Service is extraordinarily focused; the wine list is exemplary. Not to be missed: lobster carpaccio, risotto "Veuve Clicquot" with black truffles, filet mignon from corn-fed Colorado bovines, and luscious salt-baked branzino. Desserts follow suit: grilled apple torte; supple coconut flan; and (for once) light, fluffy, dignified tiramisu. *29 E. 61st St. (between Park and Madison Aves.), Upper East Side, 212/734–2676. AE, MC, V. Subway: 59th St./Lexington Ave. $$*

10 *e-2*

393–399 Lafayette St. (at E. 4th St.), East Village, 212/995–9595. Subway: Bleecker St./Broadway–Lafayette St.

7 *e-8*

SERAFINA FABULOUS PIZZA

There is a full menu at this sparkling Italian oasis, but the thin-crust, crispy, and intensely flavorful brick-oven pizza is simply not to be missed. You'll want to begin with lobster "carpaccio"—thin slices of lobster with a chiffonade of arugula, chopped corn, and hearts of palm. And finish with supple panna cotta. The restaurant occupies the top two floors of a Madison Avenue building, but in summer the ceiling on the top floor retracts to form a lovely terrace, and downstairs, windows are flung open to what you'll swear are Mediterranean breezes. The hand-painted walls and terra-cotta floors add to the Italian look, as do the Italian accents, which start to fill the restaurant at about 9 PM. *1022 Madison Ave. (at 79th St.), Upper East Side, 212/734–2676. No reservations accepted. AE, DC, MC, V. Subway: 77th St. $*

POLISH

3 *d-6*

KASHA'S

From the street you might mistake this little, almost dingy restaurant for an ordinary diner. But the made-to-order Polish food sets Kasha's apart. Frequented by an arty Williamsburg crowd (often seen eating breakfast at 4 in the afternoon), the restaurant specializes in Eastern European brunch foods such as blintzes, apple pancakes, and latkes, each fried in butter to order. The cabbage rolls are of the salt-and-pepper variety (as opposed to the tomato-based sweet and sour kind), but they will satisfy your craving for any Polish home cooking. Even the coffee is delicious. *146 Bedford Ave. (at N. 9th St.), Williamsburg, Brooklyn, 718/387–8780. AE, MC, V. Subway: Bedford Ave. $*

3 *d-6*

LOMZYNIANKA

Don't worry, few non-Poles have a clue as to how to pronounce the name of this Polish café, but luckily the menu is translated into English. Your order will depend on your taste for adventure—there's everything from rich borscht, flavorful kielbasa, and hearty goulash to earthy tripe and tongues in horseradish sauce, and of course, pierogies. Prices are so low you will think they are written in *zlote*. *646 Manhattan Ave. (at Nassau St.), Greenpoint, Brooklyn, 718/389–9439. No credit cards. Subway: Greenpoint Ave. $*

PORTUGUESE

7 *b-7*

LUZIA'S

Though recently expanded, this neighborhood restaurant has maintained its mom-and-pop charm. Classic dishes such as *caldo verde* (potato and kale soup) and *bacalhau* (salt cod with potatoes and eggs) mingle well with Luzia's other home cooking, such as white-bean salad and peppery chicken legs. Don't miss the flan for dessert. *429 Amsterdam Ave. (between 80th and 81st Sts.), Upper West Side, 212/595–2000. Reservations not accepted. AE, DC, MC, V. Subway: 1, 9 to 86th St. $$*

RUSSIAN

9 *e-3*

CAVIAR RUSSE

This chandeliered Russian jewel box is tucked upstairs in a Midtown lair. Under a robin's-egg blue ceiling lurk opulent Georgian murals, green velvet banquettes, and wall-to-wall luxury. Splurge on the prix-fixe $75 seven-course tasting menu, and start with a tasting of the house caviars to appreciate fully the voluptuous fruits of the sturgeon's labors. Feast on butterflied jumbo shrimp hugging crabmeat and young crayfish accented by fresh horseradish, all dappled with Sevruga caviar. The cheese course is exemplary. Here's a special-occasion restaurant that will overjoy you. *538 Madison Ave. (between 54th and 55th Sts.), Midtown, 212/980–5908. AE, MC, V. Subway: 59th St./Lexington Ave. $$$$*

9 *c-4*
FIREBIRD
Prerevolutionary indulgence is the name of the game at this lush dining spot on Restaurant Row, where all of the classics—blini, smoked salmon, caviar, borscht, champagne, frozen vodka—are in fine form. Of the myriad *zakuski* (appetizers), the walnut and chicken *satsivi* (a shredded specialty of Georgia) is particularly good. Other appetizers include baked noodles with poppy seeds, and lamb dumplings with minted sour cream. The entrées run the gamut from a light grilled sturgeon with mustard sauce to a hefty portion of roast goose. Desserts are something of a disappointment, and the service is spotty, but you can't help being pleased, as you sit among the ornate antiques, with the general authenticity. The Firebird Café next door offers the same menu and cabaret entertainment nightly. *365 W. 46th St. (between 8th and 9th Aves.), Theater District, 212/586–0244. AE, D, DC, MC, V. Subway: A, C, E to 42nd St. $$$*

11 *f-4*
PRAVDA
Another lively creation of Keith (Balthazar) McNally (*see above*), Pravda serves 65 different vodkas along with blinis and caviar, French fries wrapped in Russian newspaper, and *zakuski* (appetizers) such as *pirozki* (dumplings) with spinach and cheese or a smoked-fish platter. Popular entrées include chicken Kiev and beef stroganoff. The scene is fun, with some of the most beautiful people in town. *281 Lafayette St. (between Houston and Prince Sts.), SoHo, 212/226–4696. Reservations essential. AE, MC, V. No lunch. Subway: Bleecker St./Broadway–Lafayette St.; Prince St. $$*

4 *h-5*
RASPUTIN
Visit this cavernous Russian nightclub-restaurant late on a weekend and you'll wake up the next morning transformed. This will be due partly to your throbbing headache (from copious vodka consumption) and partly to your hazy memory of the wild floorshow, one that rivals almost anything in Vegas. Food is pretty much beside the point, but keeps on coming throughout the evening—sample everything and maybe some of the traditional Russian dishes will surprise you. *2670 Coney Island Ave. (at Ave. X), Brighton Beach, Brooklyn, 718/332–8111. AE, MC, V. No lunch. Subway: Ave. X. $$$*

9 *d-3*
THE RUSSIAN TEA ROOM
In the annals of see-and-be-seen theatrical Power Dining, the RTR held a unique position from the moment it opened in 1927. But New Yorkers and veteran tourists were devastated when RTR was shuttered in 1995. Impresario Warner LeRoy, who resuscitated Tavern on the Green, rebuilt RTR from the ground up, creating four all-new floors and adding 500 seats. That throbbing red ground floor is back, and so is a tunic-clad waitstaff, and the other three floors are absolutely breathtaking. Begin, of course, with vodka: There are dozens, more than a few house-infused. Next up: blini with caviar, annointed with melted butter and crème fraîche and rolled into flutes at your table. On a good night, chicken Kiev is the best you'll ever find, stuffed with herbed butter, breaded, and deep fried just until the tender juiciness peaks. Fromage *kissel* (a fluffy cheesecakelike tart) makes a delicious finale. The return of one of the most beloved restaurants in the history of New York City is simply not to be missed. *150 W. 57th St. (east of Carnegie Hall), Midtown, 212/972–2111. AE, MC, V. Subway: 57th St. $$$*

SCANDINAVIAN

9 *d-3*
AQUAVIT
This handsome two-level townhouse (formerly owned by Nelson Rockefeller) is the perfect setting for the elegant food of wunderkind Swedish chef Marcus Samuelsson. The more formal dining room, downstairs, offers an array of

Swedish specialties (including smoked fish and herring) and some innovative seafood and meat dishes. The soaring atrium and soothing waterfall make the evening relaxing and memorable. Upstairs, the more casual and less expensive bar and café offer lighter fare: Danish open sandwiches, Swedish meatballs, smorgasbord plates, and a variety of aquavits. This restaurant has been called the finest Scandinavian restaurant in the country, though admittedly the competition is not stiff. *13 W. 54th St. (between 5th and 6th Aves.), Midtown, 212/307–7311. Reservations essential. AE, MC, V. Closed Sun. Subway: 5th Ave./53rd St.* $$$

9 *d-3*

CHRISTER'S

A native Swede, chef Christer Larsson has a flair for seafood, particularly the cold-water fish of his homeland. In the urban-lodge setting of his dining room—think Ralph Lauren meets Pee Wee's Playhouse—salmon cookery is elevated to an art form, and herring becomes a noble fish. Whether marinated with lime and ginger or simply cured with sugar and salt to make gravlax, the salmon never bores. Other fish are prepared with equal skill; the dill pancakes with smoked arctic char have become a signature. Here, Swedish specialties such as *fricadelles* (veal meatballs served on mashed potatoes) have nothing in common with the sickeningly sweet hors d'oeuvres popular in the 1960s. For dessert, try the *pavlova*, an airy meringue confection that sends you floating out the door. *145 W. 55th St., Midtown, 212/974–7224. AE, DC, MC, V. Closed Sun. Subway: 57th St.* $$$

SEAFOOD

11 *c-3*

AQUAGRILL

This cheerful, yellow-and-blue, candlelit fish restaurant is casual and laid-back. It has a first-rate oyster bar and terrific fish dishes, with interesting combinations such as sautéed mussels and snails with potato hash and fried leeks, or grilled salmon in a lovely falafel crust with lemon-coriander vinaigrette. *210 Spring St. (at 6th Ave.), SoHo, 212/274–0505. Reservations essential. AE, MC, V. Closed Mon. Subway: Spring St.* $$–$$$

9 *e-8*

BLUE WATER GRILL

Into a former bank with marble floors comes this bustling fish restaurant with a terrific oyster bar and first-rate seafood of all fins and stripes. Try the crab cakes, shrimp wonton, or blackened swordfish with salsa, and for dessert, the strawberry shortcake. Sunday brunch is accompanied by live jazz. *31 Union Sq. W (between 16th and 17th Sts.), Flatiron District, 212/675–9500. AE, MC, V. Subway: 14th St./Union Sq.* $$

9 *c-8*

CHELSEA LOBSTER COMPANY

If you can't make it to Montauk, forgive the cavernous, rigidly geometric space here and focus instead on the inventive seafood menu. There are a great bread basket (the corn sticks are tops), a reliable raw bar, a good selection of chowders, and deftly prepared entrées. If you have the appetite, lobsters in the 2-pound range (steamed, baked, or stuffed with crabmeat) are a relative bargain. This is also one of the few places in the city you can order a lobster roll. *156 7th Ave. (between 19th and 20th Sts.), Chelsea, 212/243–5732. Reservations essential. AE, D, DC, MC, V. Brunch weekends. Subway: C, E to 23rd St.; 1, 9 to 18th St.* $$–$$$

7 *b-6*

DOCK'S OYSTER BAR & SEAFOOD GRILL

Both of these friendly restaurants offer fresh, no-nonsense seafood in a stylish, casual, black-and-white setting. Best bites include fried oysters, fried clams, steamed lobsters, and crunchy cole slaw. Try to save room for the great desserts. *2427 Broadway (between 89th and 90th St.), Upper West Side, 212/724–5588. AE, D, DC, MC, V. Subway: B, C to 86th St.* $$

9 *f-5*

633 3rd Ave. (at 40th St.), Midtown, 212/986–8080. Subway: 42nd St./Grand Central.

9 *d-3*

FISH

Obviously, you'd come here for seafood; the proud menu offers only two non-seafood entrées. Deep-fried oysters with a ginger-wasabi mayonnaise give a good slug of briny flavor with an Asian kick. Searing calamari *fra diavolo* belongs on its red pepper linguine, and grilled honey-mustard salmon with arugula, endive, and raspberry vinaigrette is a fine tangle of flavors. The décor is nothing fancy, but the price is right for this Columbia University–area favorite. *2799 Broadway (at 108th St.), Upper West Side, 212/864–5000. Subway: Cathedral Parkway (110th St.).* $

9 *d-4*

LE BERNARDIN
See French, *above.*

2 *h-3*

LOBSTER BOX
As you might expect, lobster is the specialty at this City Island mainstay. Try it steamed, with pasta, stuffed, or one of about a dozen other ways. You can also opt for other varieties of fresh seafood and fish. The restaurant overlooks a working harbor, with the lazy passage of boats as a pleasant backdrop. *34 City Island Ave. (between Rochelle and Belden Sts.), City Island, Bronx, 718/885–1952. AE, D, DC, MC, V. Closed Nov.–Mar.* $$

9 *d-3*

MANHATTAN OCEAN CLUB
Some of the finest seafood in town, and the friendly service and contemporary atmosphere keep the lovely dining room filled. Among the myriad dishes, the simplest are best: crab cakes, swordfish en brochette, and blackened redfish, for instance. The wine list is substantial. Don't expect to be out quickly; although congenial, the staff will keep you waiting. *57 W. 58th St. (between 5th and 6th Aves.), Midtown, 212/371–7777. AE, DC, MC, V. Subway: 57th St.* $$$

9 *e-3*

OCEANA
Chef and sorcerer Rick Moonen has created the ultimate fish restaurant, right down to the décor, which virtually transports you to a luxury ocean liner. The service is smooth and doting, the wine list is superb (and 45 pages long!), and the 100% seafood menu is nothing short of spectacular, from magical crab cakes to *the* definitive bouillabaisse or "everything"-crusted tuna medallions or the monkfish of your dreams. Desserts—hardly an afterthought—are unusually whimsical and utterly delightful. With a prix-fixe $65 three-course dinner, it's pricey, but those who take the plunge come out knowing that it was worth every penny. *55 E. 54th St. (between Madison and Park Aves.), Midtown, 212/759–5941. Reservations essential. AE, MC, V. Closed Sun. Subway: 5th Ave./53rd St.* $$$$

9 *e-5*

OYSTER BAR & RESTAURANT
After a serious fire early in 1998, reconstruction, restoration, and a new chef have breathed considerable aquatic life into a spot frequented mainly by commuters and tourists. This Grand Central Station landmark, opened in 1915, claims it serves the most seafood in the world, and it probably does. Go for the wide selection of fresh oysters (flown in daily), six versions of clam chowder, oyster po' boys, and grilled fresh fish. Wines and desserts are equally various. You can sit at the old-fashioned lunch counter or in the dining room proper, although the beautiful tiled curvaceous ceiling of the latter results in a lot of clatter. *Grand Central Terminal, Lower level, 42nd St. at Park Ave., Midtown, 212/490–6650. AE, DC, MC, V. Closed weekends. Subway: 42nd St./Grand Central.* $$

11 *b-3*

PEARL OYSTER BAR
This friendly New England oyster bar run by Mary Redding and Rebecca Charles is one of the most enjoyable places to go for a casual meal. The place has recently expanded—before it was just a counter—affording more spots for regulars who love the Maine-style lobster roll, fried oyster po' boy, chowder, steamers in a bucket, and bouillabaisse. A nice selection of wines by the glass complements the food, which might be served by one of the chefs if the waitress is too busy. *18 Cornelia St. (between Bleecker and W. 4th Sts.), West Village, 212/691–8211. MC, V. Closed Sun. Subway: W. 4th St./Washington Sq.* $$

9 *d-4*

SEA GRILL
This elegant Rockefeller Center restaurant was designed to draw the sophisticated New Yorker as well as the tourist. The view of the skating rink ensures the happiness of the latter, and chef Ed Brown's cooking steadily enthralls the locals. Although many lay similar claims, Brown's Maryland crab cakes may well be the best in the city. The other seafood options, some classic,

some contemporary, are pretty great as well. The wine list is excellent. Complimentary parking is available at the Rockefeller Center Garage from Monday to Saturday after 5:30 PM. *19 W. 49th St. (between 5th and 6th Aves.), Midtown, 212/332–7610. Reservations essential. AE, DC, MC, V. Closed Sun. Subway: 47th–50th Sts./Rockefeller Center. $$$*

9 f-1
TRATA

Breezy as the northern Mediterranean, Trata has been jammed since the very moment it (recently) opened, so needful is this neighborhood of moderately priced, pristinely prepared Greco seafood. The casual dining room features a handsome spread of dozens of whole fish (including some rarities such as sargos and loup de mer) arranged on crushed ice, which are grilled to order. Startlingly delicious charcoal-grilled octopus makes the perfect opener, and honey-drizzled thickened goat's milk yogurt makes the perfect finish. *1331 2nd Ave. (between 70th and 71st Sts.), Upper East Side, 212/535–3800. AE, MC, V. Subway: 68th St./Hunter College. $$*

SOUL

6 d-6
CHARLES' SOUTHERN STYLE KITCHEN

Charles serves some of the best soul food in Harlem. Ribs, oxtails, black-eyed peas, okra, macaroni and cheese, collard greens, and candied yams are all here. But the excellent fried chicken is the specialty, and if you stand by the takeout counter you can watch Charlie dip pieces of chicken in his peppery batter and fry it to a crispy golden brown in a giant cast iron skillet. The only occasional disappointment comes when Charlie decides to take the day off and the kitchen is closed. *2841 Frederick Douglass Blvd. (between 151st and 152nd Sts.), Harlem, 212/926–4313. No credit cards. No lunch Mon. Subway: C, D to 155th St. $*

6 c-6
COPELAND'S

Though Sylvia's gets all the publicity, many insider's believe this is the only place in Harlem for authentic soul food. From fried chicken to smothered pork chops to ribs, Copeland's has everything your heart desires (especially choles-

terol). Put on your best hat for the Sunday Gospel Brunch and dig in. *547 W. 145th St., Harlem, 212/234–2357. AE, MC, V. Closed Mon. Subway: 145th St. $$*

9 b-5
SOUL CAFÉ

This comfortable, spacious dining room—albeit with a sense of circa-1970 "luxe"—serves some of best and most upscale soul food in the city. The grilled lamb ribs with mint-julep barbecue sauce are a revelation to rib lovers, and equally laudatory are Caribbean-influenced dishes such as coconut shrimp and jerked duck breast. Fans of traditional soul sides—candied yams, macaroni-and-cheese, collard greens—will be in heaven. Live jazz, funk, or R&B is featured most weekend nights on a small stage near the hopping bar; check what's on offer and request a quiet table if it's not your cup of tea. *444 W. 42nd St. (between 9th and 10th Aves.), Hell's Kitchen, 212/244–7685. Reservations essential. AE, D, MC, V. No lunch. Brunch Sun. Subway: A, C, E to 42nd St. $$–$$$*

7 d-1
SYLVIA'S

Sylvia Woods is known as the Queen of Soul Food, and her restaurant has been a Harlem institution for more than 30 years. Though there are probably better cooks, you shouldn't hesitate to head uptown for some of Sylvia's down-home Southern specialties, including her braised ribs, fried or smothered chicken with black-eyed peas, collard greens, yams, sweet-potato pie, and fresh-baked corn bread. Sunday brunch is served to the showiest ladies' hats in town, with the inspirational tunes of local gospel singers and two jukeboxes adding to the indelible '50s flavor. *328 Lenox Ave. (at 126th St.), Harlem, 212/996–0660. Reservations not accepted. No credit cards. Subway: A, B, C, D to 125th St. $*

SOUTHERN

11 e-2
ACME BAR & GRILL

This funky roadhouse setting is festooned with dozens of bottles of different hot sauces on ledges that run throughout the space. The home-style food is well priced and tasty, usually heavy and sometimes tongue-searing. Southern specialties include steamed oysters, fried shrimp, blackened trout, oyster po' boys, grilled pork chops, catfish sandwiches, and sides of corn fritters, hush puppies, and black-eyed peas. *9 Great Jones St. (between Broadway and Lafayette St.), East Village, 212/420–1934. D, DC, MC, V. Reservations not accepted. Subway: Astor Pl. $*

9 *C-4*

B. SMITH'S

Run by the model-turned-restaurateur-and-author (and all-around celeb) B. Smith, this stylish spot has great people-watching and an intriguing menu of very good contemporary Southern and global-eclectic fare. Smith moved to more spacious quarters in late 1999, but you should still make a reservation for pre-theater dining, although you'll usually get a table at other times without much problem. *320 W. 46th St. (between 8th and 9th Aves.), Theater District, 212/315–1100. Brunch Sun. AE, D, DC, MC, V. Subway: 50th St. $$*

SOUTHWESTERN

9 *f-2*

TAPIKA

The award-winning design of this urban Southwestern is as fanciful as chef David Walzog's innovative cooking. This food is not for the timid. Chiles pop up everywhere, dried, ground, and dusted on the fried cornmeal strips and whipped into

the Caesar-salad dressing. Other temptations include tequila-cured salmon and vegetable-stuffed chiles rellenos with smoked tomato salsa. Steak, pork, and other meats are grilled to perfection and come adorned with an exciting array of sides. *950 8th Ave. (at 56th St.), Midtown, 212/397–3737. AE, DC, MC, V. Subway: 59th St./Columbus Circle. $$$*

SPANISH

9 *e-8*

BOLO

The burgeoning fame of chef/co-owner Bobby Flay has drawn major attention to this popular Flatiron District restaurant with a palpable Spanish accent. The extremely vivid food— pequillo peppers stuffed with salmon tartare, seared duck breast with soft mascarpone polenta, shellfish and chicken paella—is succulent. The menu is continually evolving, the decor is quirky and pretty, and the crowd is, well, there. Don't pass up the luscious sangria, then move on to one of the spicy, full-bodied Riojas. *23 E. 22nd St. (between Broadway and Park Ave. S), Flatiron District, 212/228–2200. AE, MC, V. Subway: 6, N, R to 23rd St. $$$*

10 *C-1*

EL CID

An extensive list of standards—garlic shrimp, imported sausages and cheeses, marinated mussels—plus such seasonal specialties as baby eels or wild mushrooms, made El Cid popular long before tapas bars were trendy. It's pretty authentically Spanish in ways both good and bad: Cramped tables, minimal decor, and noise are the down side, while low prices, knowledgeable waiters, and simple, tasty food compensate. There's a wine list with some good Spanish vintages, but the potent house sangria is the drink of choice. *322 W. 15th St. (between 8th and 9th Aves.), Chelsea, 212/929–9332. Reservations essential. AE, DC. Closed Mon. No lunch. Subway: A, C, E to 14th St.; L to 8th Ave. $$*

10 *C-1*

EL FARO

Redolent with garlic, this small, extremely popular West Villager has been serving hearty portions of pungent Spanish food for over 30 years. The decor is appealingly kitschy. Be prepared to wait. *823 Greenwich St. (at Horatio*

FIRESIDE ROMANCE

The only thing harder to find in New York than romance itself is a working fireplace. If you've found the first, here's where they throw a log on:

Savoy (American)
   This charming and elegant nook on the edge of SoHo keeps three fires burning for you.

Verbena (American)
   The flickering light is the ornamentation for this zenlike room.

Vivolo (Italian)
   In a late-1800s brownstone, fireplaces warm both the dimly-lit downstairs and the frescoed upstairs.

Ye Waverly Inn (American)
   Ye olde quaintest tavern in the city, in the West Village.

St.), West Village, 212/929–8210. Reservations not accepted. AE, DC, MC, V. Subway: A, C, E to 14th St.; L to 8th Ave. $$

9 d-8

FRANCISCO'S CENTRO VASCO

Crowds of eager diners (many of the bridge-and-tunnel variety) descend nightly on this noisy, dumpy Spanish old-timer in search of bargain-priced lobsters and paella. The sangria flows pretty freely, and only a cynic wouldn't get caught up in the convivial atmosphere. Reservations are accepted only for parties of six or more, but long waits are unusual. 159 W. 23rd St. (between 6th and 7th Aves.), Chelsea, 212/645–6224. AE, DC, MC, V. No lunch weekends. Subway: C, E, 1, 9 to 23rd St. $$

9 f-4

MARICHU

Marichu's chef is a former diplomat who must have realized how parched the U.N. area is for interesting restaurants. This enchanting restaurant turns out delicious Basque cooking—particularly seafood—with a contemporary presentation. The satisfying combination has hooked those in the U.N. area, and the cheery atmosphere and back garden are helping this relative newcomer gain a wider audience. 342 E. 46th St. (between 1st and 2nd Aves.), Midtown, 212/370–1866. Reservations essential. AE, MC, V. Closed Sun. Subway: 42nd St./Grand Central. $$

10 b-1

RIO MAR

It's doubtful a restaurant like this ever existed in Spain, but at one time this was all that Americans wanting Spanish food could hope for. The upstairs dining room is "Spanish" in an old-time sort of way, but the staff is genuinely glad to see you. The quasi-traditional food—garlicky tapas, paella, chicken and rice, seafood stews—is served in large portions, and low prices keep the place packed. 7 9th Ave. (at Little W. 12th St.), West Village, 212/242–1623. AE. Subway: A, C, E to 14th St.; L to 8th Ave. $$

11 f-3

SALA

This intensely popular, idiomatic newcomer offers some of the most dazzling Spanish cooking this side of Barcelona. The dining room is a highly theatrical indoor Spanish courtyard complete with faux backlit casement windows. The menu changes daily, but usually there are croquetes that redefine croquettes—more like deep-fried breaded pouches of thick savory pudding. The fried chunks of potato, rubbed with hot-and-sweet paprika and dribbled with thick béchamel sauce are the stuff of dreams. Steaks and chops are superbly turned out. Be prepared for quite a party. 344 Bowery (near Great Jones St), East Village, 212/979–6606. AE, MC, V. Subway: Bleecker St./Broadway–Lafayette St. $$

9 f-3

SOLERA

Authentic Spanish cooking is presented with heart and soul in this delightful little Midtown eatery. The food is seriously good (some argue it's the best Spanish in town), and the following is accordingly fierce and loyal, despite the above-average prices for this light, Mediterranean fare. The service is unusually focused, too. 216 E. 53rd St. (between 2nd and 3rd Aves.), Midtown, 212/644–1166. AE, MC, V. Closed Sun. Subway: 51st St./Lexington–3rd Aves. $$

STEAK

9 d-4

BEN BENSON'S

Like its founder and owner, Ben Benson's is unique. Some restaurants are described as masculine; BB's is downright butch. Everywhere you look there is a hunting lodge adornment to set the carnivore in you yowling. Plenty of celebs are attracted to the place, and it's usually packed to the gills, but a well choreographed staff maneuvers through the crowds with breathtaking ease. Everything served here is absolutely top-of-the-line, from great breads to dry-aged, prime steaks procured from the best suppliers in the Northeast. All meats are flash-broiled in an 800-degree oven, and the sting of the grill is sustained in every succulent mouthful. 123 W. 52nd St. (between 6th and 7th Aves.), Midtown, 212/581–8888. AE, MC, V. Subway: 47–50th Sts./Rockefeller Center. $$$

9 *e-4*

BULL & BEAR

This is the place to feel utterly pampered by agreeably old-fashioned service, by luxurious comfort food prepared with confidence and flair, and by a sommelier totally adroit at matching food with wine from around the world. Ensconced in all the gleam and glitter of the restored Waldorf-Astoria, this deeply masculine, clubby, walnut-paneled room has never looked more impressive. Start with dense crab cakes stepped up with a cayenne-spiked corn relish and a bowl of B&B's famous black bean soup. Then tuck into a 2-inch-tall slab of dry-aged Black Angus prime rib partnered by (of course) crisp/tender Yorkshire pudding. A free-form key lime tart makes the perfect finish. You'll leave feeling very important, indeed. *570 Lexington Ave. (at 49th St.), Midtown. 212/872–4900. AE, DC, MC, V. Subway: 51st St./Lexington–3rd Aves. $$$*

9 *b-5*

CHIMICHURRI GRILL

See Argentine, *above.*

7 *f-6*

DAN MAXWELL'S

If you're in the mood for a big New York steak but not big New York prices, this is the place for you. Rib, skirt, and strip steaks (or salmon and chicken, for the faint of heart) are served with your choice of potatoes and a salad for under $20 a person. Some say the fried onions are "the best ever." As in every steak house, gooey desserts are in order; the triple chocolate-mousse cake is a favorite. The atmosphere is neighborhoody, the service friendly and efficient. *1708 2nd Ave. (between 88th and 89th Sts.), Upper East Side, 212/426–7688. AE, D, DC, MC, V. Subway: 4, 5, 6 to 86th St. $*

9 *b-8*

FRANK'S

This old Italian steak house opened in 1912 in the Gansevoort meatpacking district. Despite having moved from its original store, a block north, in the mid-1990s due to fire, the place still has plenty of character. Count on good steaks, surf 'n' turf, double-thick lamb chops, and giant salads. The cheesecake is terrific. *85 10th Ave. (at 15th St.), Chelsea, 212/243–1349. Reservations essential. AE, DC, MC, V. Closed Sun. Subway: A, C, E to 14th St.; L to 8th Ave. $$$*

9 *c-4*

GALLAGHER'S STEAK HOUSE

The most casual of the New York steak houses, with checkered tablecloths and photos of sports greats on the walls, Gallagher's has no pretensions—through the window from the street you can even peer into the dry-aging room where slabs of meat ripen to perfection. You won't be disappointed with the aged sirloin steaks, oversize lobsters, or any of the fabulous potato dishes. *228 W. 52nd (between Broadway and 8th Ave.), Theater District, 212/245–5336. AE, D, DC, MC, V. Subway: 50th St. $$$*

12 *f-6*

MIKE & TONY'S

This neighborhood steak house is owned by chef Michael Ayoub, whose popular Cucina (*above*) is just down the street. The atmosphere is congenial. Notice the unusual light fixtures, made by Ayoub, who seems to be as good at glass-blowing as he is at cooking. The steaks, made from prime aged beef, are perfectly cooked. The seafood is fresh, and the sides are all delicious. What more could you want? (Besides maybe an outpost in Manhattan.) *239 5th Ave. (at Carroll St.), Park Slope, Brooklyn, 718/857–2800. MC, V. No lunch. Subway: Union St. $$$*

10 *c-1*

OLD HOMESTEAD RESTAURANT

Open since 1868—which may be when they last redecorated—this is New York's oldest steak house, appropriately located in the meatpacking district. In addition to the steaks— including a Japanese Kobe steak at $125 a serving (reserve it a few days in advance)—the menu offers generous portions of shrimp, lobster, and prime rib. *56 9th Ave. (between 14th and 15th Sts.), Chelsea, 212/242–9040. AE, DC, MC, V. Subway: A, C, E to 14th St.; L to 8th Ave. $$$*

9 *f-4*

PALM RESTAURANT

Sawdusted floors and caricatures on the walls create the nostalgic backdrop for this very noisy, upbeat, and masculine steak and lobster house. Once considered the best by many, the Palm has paled some with time and the demands of managing its worldwide empire, but its history of famous and powerful famous clients (painted on the walls) still adds flavor to the high-quality steaks and enormous lobsters. Watch the bill add up—cottage fries, onion rings, and vegetables are all à la carte. If the restaurant is too crowded, go across the street to Palm Too. *837 2nd Ave. (between 44th and 45th Sts.), Midtown, 212/687–2953. Reservations essential. AE, DC, MC, V. No lunch weekends. Subway: 42nd St./Grand Central. $$$$*

1 *e-5*
PETER LUGER'S
No one really disputes the idea that this is the best steak you will ever eat. The setting is German beer hall—harsh lights, bare wood tables—rather than gentlemen's steak house, and you'll never see a menu; the friendly waiters know that all you want is shrimp cocktail, tomato-and-onion salad, home fries, creamed spinach, French fries, and a big, beautiful, dry-aged, perfectly cooked porterhouse steak big enough to feed everyone in your party. Save the steak sauce for the fresh onion rolls. If you have room left over, order the pecan pie or the cheesecake—both of which, in case you haven't had enough fat, come with a big bowl of *schlag* (whipped cream). If you arrive in a taxi, the restaurant's own car service will take you home. *178 Broadway (at Driggs Ave.), Williamsburg, Brooklyn, 718/387–7400. Reservations essential. No credit cards. Subway: J, M, Z to Marcy Ave. $$$*

9 *c-5*
PIETRO'S
Regulars still flock to this 50-year-old Italian steak house, now in relatively new quarters. Pietro's serves Italian veal, chicken, and pasta dishes, as well as an exemplary Caesar salad, but it's basically known for its porterhouse, served with delicious shoestring, Lyonnaise, or au gratin potatoes. The friendly staff is happy to modify almost anything on the menu to suit your tastes. *232 E. 43rd St. (between 2nd and 3rd Aves.), Midtown, 212/682–9760. Reservations essential. AE, DC, MC, V. Closed Sun. Closed Sat. in summer. No lunch Sat. Subway: 42nd St./Grand Central. $$$$*

9 *f-4*
SMITH & WOLLENSKY
Women beware: This is where Midtown business*men* enjoy steak. The clubby atmosphere and extensive wine list speak to a certain clientele that sometimes makes it difficult for women to get the best service. But the beautiful steak is well prepared, portions are generous, and the side dishes are good. Limited non–red-meat selections are available, but you're better off eating elsewhere if you're looking for a light meal. Next door to the dining room is Wollensky's Grill, a bit cheaper. *201 E. 49th St. (at 3rd Ave.), Midtown, 212/753–1530. Reservations essential. AE, DC, MC, V. No lunch weekends in dining room. Subway: 51st St./Lexington–3rd Aves. $$$–$$$$*

9 *f-4*
SPARK'S STEAK HOUSE
If you're yearning for a macho atmosphere, head right over to this informal, clubby restaurant, well known for very fine steaks and lobsters that require a superhuman appetite. The double lamb chops also draw raves. An excellent wine list has earned the restaurant several awards. *210 E. 46th St. (between 2nd and 3rd Aves.), Midtown, 212/687–4855. Reservations essential. AE, DC, MC, V. Closed Sun. No lunch Sat. Subway: 42nd St./Grand Central. $$$*

SWISS

11 *f-1*
ROETTELLE A. G.
Here's a charming find in (but not of) the East Village for a simple, inexpensive, satisfying Euromeal. German, Swiss, Italian, and French cooking are all represented nightly on the changing menu. Try the classic Swiss fondue; the smoked, mustard-infused pork chop with spaetzle and red cabbage; the sautéed chicken breast with sun-dried tomatoes and hazelnuts; or the veal in mushroom cream sauce with wonderful Swiss-style *rösti* (potato pancakes). Try to get a seat in the trellised garden. *126 E. 7th St. (between 1st Ave. and Ave. A), East Village, 212/674–4140. MC, V. Closed Sun. Brunch Sat. Subway: 8th St.; Astor Pl. $$*

TEA

10 *e-1*
DANAL
Whether you're sitting on the sofa; at one of the country tables; or, in fine weather, in the rear garden, this popular, first-rate French bistro feels like an

enchanted lakeside cottage. American brunch is lovely (and intensely popular) as well. *90 E. 10th St. (between 3rd and 4th Aves.), East Village, 212/982–6930. Reservations essential. AE, MC, V. Subway: 8th St.; Astor Pl. $$*

10 *c-1*

TEA & SYMPATHY

This authentic little English tearoom looks rather like your quirky old aunt's apartment. When it isn't teatime, the food is traditional, hearty British fare. No one argues with the tea, but the long wait, cramped space, and worn decor leave some wanting. *108 Greenwich Ave. (between 12th and 13th Sts.), West Village, 212/807–8329. Reservations not accepted. AE, MC, V. Subway: A, C, E to 14th St.; L to 8th Ave. $*

9 *b-8*

WILD LILY TEA ROOM

A gem worthy of its place among the Chelsea galleries, this very special tearoom is a world away from the stresses of city life. The tiny goldfish pond, set into the floor and perfect in every detail, is guaranteed to cure whatever ails you. Food (finger sandwiches, scones, and delicate Asian specialties) is served on lovely china, and teas are described on the menu with such eloquence you might mistake the list for a book of poetry. *511 W. 22nd St. (between 10th and 11th Aves.), Chelsea, 212/691–2258. Reservations essential. AE, DC, MC, V. Closed Mon. Brunch Sun. Subway: C, E to 23rd St. $–$$*

TEX/MEX

10 *c-1*

BENNY'S BURRITOS

For cheap and cheerful Tex/Mex on either end of the Village, head over to cramped and rowdy Benny's, ever popular with the budget crowd. Lava lights, Formica, and a jukebox with period tunes form a retro backdrop for the humongous, foot-long, overstuffed burritos and zippy margaritas. Beware: finish the whole thing and you'll suffer. *113 Greenwich St. (at Jane St.), West Village, 212/633–9210. No reservations. No credit cards. Subway: A, C, E to 14th St.; L to 8th Ave. $*

11 *h-1*

93 Ave. A (at 6th St.), East Village, 212/254–2054. Subway: 2nd Ave.

9 *c-8*

ROCKING HORSE CAFÉ

Here you'll find good, fairly authentic Tex-Mex fare that's a step above the usual south-of-the-border slop. Preparation can sometimes suffer under the weight of the crowds here—seafood can be overcooked, beans can be gluey, and anything can be over- or under-seasoned—but after a few of the justly celebrated margaritas it's unlikely you'll care. *182 8th Ave. (between 19th and 20th Sts.), Chelsea, 212/463–9511. AE, MC, V. Brunch weekends. Subway: 1, 9 to 18th St. $$*

THAI

3 *d-5*

AMARIN CAFE

On the border of Greenpoint and Williamsburg in Brooklyn, this casual restaurant serves some of the freshest, most fragrant Thai food in town. Everything is spicy, not just the fiery red Penang curries. Lemongrass, coconut, and chicken soup; stir-fried chicken with basil and hot peppers; pad thai; and other traditional dishes are skillfully prepared. The service is extremely attentive and friendly. If one of your dishes is hotter than your palate can handle, the staff will gladly make it for you again with less spice. *617 Manhattan Ave. (between Driggs and Nassau Aves.), Greenpoint, Brooklyn, 718/349–2788. No credit cards. Subway: L to Lorimer St. $*

7 *f-8*

BANGKOK HOUSE

The atmosphere is stark and somewhat dreary, but the restaurant is highly rated for authentic Thai fare, much of which maintains the appropriate sizzle. Try the "jungle curry," the pork in green curry, or the barbecued chicken (*gai yang*). Wash it down with something from the nice selection of Thai beers. *1485 1st Ave. (at 77th St.), Upper East Side, 212/249–5700. AE, DC, MC, V. No lunch. $*

3 *5-3*

JAI-YA THAI

There's not much in terms of decor to recommend Jai-Ya-Thai. What there is, however is boldly spiced, flavorful Thai food—such as curries, pad thai, and satays—that proves to be strangely addictive. There is a Manhattan branch, but true fans find the original Queens location more authentic. *81–11 Broadway (between 81st and 82nd Sts.), Elmhurst, Queens, 718/651–1330. AE, DC, MC, V. Subway: Elmhurst Ave. $*

9 *b-8*
JAMES
Well-prepared, non-traditional Thai dishes—such as mussels in a lemon-grass-tomato broth served with curry-spiced fries and skirt steak au poivre in a lemon-chili sauce—make this 12-table newcomer popular with the Chelsea gallery crowd. The sticky rice is heavenly, as is the fragrant, spicy baby eggplant in a sweet-and-sour sauce. Desserts are just as successful, with ginger crème brûlée and cranberry-orange sorbet standouts. Reservations are accepted only for parties of six or more. *205 10th Ave. (between 22nd and 23rd Sts.), Chelsea, 212/741–7925. AE. Closed Sun. Subway: C, E to 23rd St. $–$$*

11 *d-5*
KIN KHAO
The inevitable wait for a table is made exponentially more exciting if you order a ginger kamikaze made with the restaurant's exceptional house-made ginger vodka. The slightly above-average food—the sticky rice and whole fish are delicious—doesn't suffice to explain the enormous popularity of this restaurant. It could be the chic decor, beautiful servers, or maybe just the liveliness of the very downtown scene. *171 Spring St. (between Thompson St. and W. Broadway), SoHo, 212/966–3939. AE, MC, V. No lunch. Subway: C, E to Spring St. $$*

3 *d-6*
PLAN EAT THAILAND
This once tiny storefront restaurant in a Polish section of Williamsburg has tripled in size and added a sushi and sake bar. It still serves a delicious selection of Thai street food, somewhat toned down for the American audience. Still, the flavors are fresh and fragrant. Try the noodle dishes, the green-papaya salad, and the satay. And why not order a couple of sushi rolls while you're at it? *141 N. 7th St. (between Bedford Ave. and Berry St.), Williamsburg, Brooklyn, 718/599–5758. Reservations not accepted. No credit cards. Subway: Bedford Ave. $*

9 *c-4*
PONGSRI THAI
You'll dine well on spicy Thai specialties both uptown, in the spacious Theater District quarters, or downtown, in the more spartan Chinatown shop. The coconut chicken soup, rich duck curry, and sticky rice are among the highlights. Be prepared to pay more for the same dishes uptown. *244 W. 48th St. (between Broadway and 8th Ave.), Theater District, 212/582–3392. AE, DC, MC, V. Subway: 50th St. $*

11 *f-7*
106 Bayard St. (at Baxter St.), Chinatown, 212/349–3132. Subway: 6 to Canal St.

9 *c-8*
ROYAL SIAM
Royal Siam is one of the best restaurants in trendy Chelsea, where the restaurant scene hasn't quite caught up to everything else. Classic Thai dishes, such as pad thai and shrimp in red curry, are well executed, and the service is friendly. The decor recalls suburban Chinese restaurants, complete with lacquered furniture and polyester tablecloths. *240 8th Ave. (between 22nd and 23rd Sts.), Chelsea, 212/741–1732. Reservations not accepted. AE, MC, V. Subway: C, E to 23rd St. $*

TURKISH

9 *f-3*
DENIZ A LA TURK
Deniz fills a surprising gap in this city's array of cuisines with flourish, refinement, and acres of flavor. Thanks to new owner Adem Desdemir's devotion to Turkish traditions, the restaurant turns out dishes that deeply trust their main ingredients. Many of the dishes will rekindle unexpected memories of the days when straight-ahead cooking and great ingredients were practically common. Succulent pan-fried flutes of filo dough stuffed with lemony spinach and feta cheese arrive piping hot. But it is fish for which Deniz is best known (Deniz means "ocean" in Turkish). Charcoal-grilled whole striped bass is feather-tender, pure, and fresh, filetted tableside and given little more than a squeeze of lemon. The desserts are luscious, as well. *400 E. 57th St. (between 1st Ave. and Sutton Pl.), Midtown, 212/486–2255. AE, MC, V. Subway: 59th St./Lexington Ave. $$*

9 e-7

TURKISH KITCHEN

The food at this comfortable restaurant is rather like Middle Eastern cooking, only more sophisticated. The traditional salads, such as hummus and babaghanoush, are good starters, as are the fried cheese and chicken livers with parsley and lemon. For dinner itself, try whatever lamb preparation is available or the dumplings in yogurt sauce. *386 3rd Ave. (between 27th and 28th Sts.), Murray Hill, 212/679–1810, AE, MC, V. Subway: 6 to 28th St.* $

VEGETARIAN & MACROBIOTIC FOOD

9 e-6

HANGAWI
See Korean, *above.*

7 b-8

JOSIE'S

Can you imagine a health-food theme restaurant? Josie's comes pretty close. The food is fresh, much of it is organically grown or raised, and the emphasis is on light, healthy fare. Many of the dishes are vegetarian, and some are dairy-free; not surprisingly, tofu, tempeh, fish, and seafood feature prominently. It's always busy, and the service is always friendly. *300 Amsterdam Ave. (at 74th St.), Upper West Side, 212/769–1212. AE, MC, V. No lunch. Subway: 1, 2, 3, 9 to 72nd St.* $$

11 f-5

SPRING STREET NATURAL RESTAURANT

This natural eatery spotlights fresh fish, fowl, and seafood while barring chemicals, preservatives, and red meat. Specialties include vegetarian lasagna, sautéed chicken breast with shiitake mushrooms, baked fillet of bluefish, and garlic chicken marinated in raspberry vinegar; but alas, most sound better than they taste. *62 Spring St. (at Lafayette St.), SoHo, 212/966–0290. Reservations not accepted. AE, DC, MC, V. Subway: 6 to Spring St.; Broadway–Lafayette St.* $

7 b-8

ZEN PALATE

Something like a cross between a Buddhist temple and a coffee bar, this Pan-Asian minichain with a takeout option offers a quick, healthy, vegetarian alternative to the ubiquitous salad bar. To a base of noodles or rice you can add toppings of vegetables, sauces, broths, and other condiments. Dumplings and stir-fries are also available. Though the flavors tend more toward Zen than toward other Asian palates, you always feel good about yourself when you finish a meal here. *2170 Broadway (between 76th and 77th Sts.), Upper West Side, 212/501–7768. AE, DC, MC, V. Subway: 79th St.* $

9 c-4

663 9th Ave. (at 46th St.), Hell's Kitchen, 212/582–1669. Subway: A, C, E to 42nd St.

9 c-4

34 Union Sq. E (at 16th St.), Flatiron District, 212/614–9291. Subway: 14th St./Union Sq.

VIETNAMESE

11 g-7

BO KY

Enjoy a terrific lunch for under $5 at this unpretentious (read: down-and-dirty) soup shop. The rich, spicy, chicken-coconut curry soup with eggplant, potatoes, and egg noodles is absolutely delicious, as is the unfortunately named beef-belly soup with noodles. The other soups are good, too, but you're best off staying away from the barbecued items. To cut the richness, order "vegetable," which inevitably turns out to be Chinese broccoli in oyster sauce. *80 Bayard St. (between Mott and Mulberry Sts.), Chinatown, 212/406–2292. Reservations not accepted. No credit cards. Subway: 6, N, R, J, M, Z to Canal St.* $

11 d-3

CAN

The sleek dining room has a skylight in the back, red carpeting, red chairs, and white tablecloths. The French/Vietnamese food is straightforward and consistent. Try the summer rolls, skewers of grilled chicken and beef with peanut-coconut sauce, and whole sea bass fried in a wok. The crème brûlée is first-rate. *482 W. Broadway (at Houston St.), SoHo, 212/533–6333. AE, DC, MC, V. Subway: Bleecker St./Broadway–Lafayette St.* $$

11 f-2

INDOCHINE

Trendy Vietnamese/Cambodian cuisine is served in a clamorous, Hollywood-glam setting, where it seems as if you need a cell phone to get your waiter's attention. You can dine well just by sharing a bunch of appetizers, such as Vietnamese ravioli, stuffed boneless chicken wings, frogs' legs in coconut milk, and scampi *beignet* (fritter). Watch out though—the tab can add up quickly. Sit up front if you want some peace and quiet—and if you want to keep tabs on who's coming and going. *430 Lafayette St. (between Astor Pl. and E. 4th St.), East Village, 212/505–5111. AE, DC, MC, V. Subway: Astor Pl. $$*

11 f-4

MEKONG

This dimly lighted Vietnamese place has paper tablecloths, candles, bamboo curtains, and pictures of a Mekong sunset. The cooking is light with clear flavors, and seasoned with fresh mint. Try the sizzling shrimp, barbecued beef in shiso leaves, summer rolls, and curries. *44 Prince St. (near Mulberry St.), SoHo, 212/343–8169. AE, MC, V. Subway: Bleecker St./Broadway–Lafayette St.; Prince St. $*

7 f-7

MISS SAIGON

Whatever it lacks in atmosphere, this small but popular restaurant makes up for in tasty Vietnamese cooking. Locals line up out the door to taste the grilled shrimp paste, green papaya and beef salad, and lemongrass pork with garlic and sesame seeds. The moderate prices contribute to the popularity; if you can, try the place at lunchtime, when it's less hectic and even cheaper. *1425 3rd Ave. (between 80th and 81st Sts.), Upper East Side, 212/988–8828. Reservations not accepted. AE, DC, MC, V. Subway: 4, 5, 6 to 86th St. $*

7 b-7

MONSOON

Among the first restaurants to take authentic Vietnamese food outside Chinatown, Monsoon offers a fast, cheap alternative to Chinese food from its two Upper West Side locations. The menu hides no surprises. The classic rice-paper–wrapped summer rolls and shrimp-wrapped sugarcane are reliable starters; classic beef soups and noodle dishes satisfy; and a crispy, sweet version of Vietnamese barbecued pork chops, sliced extra thin, is delicious. Be prepared to wait. *435 Amsterdam Ave. (at 81st St.), Upper West Side, 212/580–8686. Reservations not accepted. AE, DC, MC, V. Subway: 79th St. $*

7 b-3

2850 Broadway (at 110th St.), Upper West Side, 212/655–2700. Subway: 110th St./Cathedral Pkwy.

10 f-5

NHA TRANG

Negotiating a Vietnamese menu can be challenging for novices. At Nha Trang, one of Chinatown's most popular Vietnamese eateries, a good meal can be had by following these simple rules: Start with a large, steaming bowl of spicy sweet and sour seafood soup (a "small" will feed three or four) and an order of shrimp grilled on sugarcane; and follow up with the paper-thin pork chops grilled crispy and the deep-fried squid served on a bed of shredded lettuce with a tangy dipping sauce. If you decide to explore the menu on your own, ask the waiter for suggestions—the staff is glad to show you the ropes. *87 Baxter St. (between Bayard and Canal Sts.), Chinatown, 212/233–5948. No credit cards. Subway: 6, N, R to Canal St. $*

11 g-7

VIET-NAM

It's hard to find, but this cheap, grungy Chinatown dive is the real thing, serving authentic and tasty Vietnamese dishes. Try anything in the pungent black-bean sauce; the green-papaya and beef-jerky salad; and the beef cubes with watercress, exceptional when dipped in tangy lemon-pepper sauce. Go with an adventurous palette, and don't be put off by the cafeteria atmosphere. *11–13 Doyers St. (between Bowery and Pell St.), Chinatown, 212/693–0725. Reservations not accepted. AE. Subway: Canal St. $*

chapter 2

SHOPPING

New Yorkers have discriminating tastes, and they know how to use them; spread these across a complete range of incomes and, of course, zillions of people, and you've got a nearly exhaustive stock of merchandise. Glance through this chapter and you're bound to notice how many stores you've never even seen—or how many you've whizzed past without noticing. Or, more to the point, for native and visitor alike, New York can be a mighty exciting place to shop. Be aware, though that what this city specializes in is a carefully tailored selection of goods (you might be stumped if you're searching for a new set of poolside furniture)—making it, in the end, a city whose merchants cater to its population, and a rather remarkable population at that.

Not that shopping in New York is necessarily a breeze. For one thing, you generally have to walk or take a subway or taxi from store to store; you can't just throw your purchases in the back seat of a car. We've all experienced that pang of sympathy when some poor soul who's just bought a new TV steps onto a crowded subway. Local service can also try your patience; not for New York is the warm-hearted entrepreneur who slowly wraps your items in decorative tissue paper and tells you she hopes you're delighted with your purchase. Then again, New York is nothing if not inconsistent, so don't be surprised if you come upon the friendliest service you've ever encountered. And whatever happens during your shopping expedition, you'll probably have an experience that is, if nothing else, memorable.

major destinations

DEPARTMENT STORES

Most department stores and, increasingly, designer boutiques offer the services of personal shoppers. You'll have to schedule an appointment a few days in advance, but for the price of spontaneity, you get a store-specific guru. The consultant will either walk with you through the store or, if you describe your size, budget, and taste, run off and make the appropriate selections so you can hit the dressing room ASAP. There is no obligation to buy, and the service is free.

9 e-2

BARNEYS NEW YORK
Having survived financial ups and downs that forced the closing of its landmark Chelsea store, Barneys manages to keep its cutting edge. Having begun life in the men's-suit business, Barneys is still known for its classically tailored and made-to-measure items (for the man's-eye view, see Contemporary in Men's Clothing, below). The women's floors have an amazing range of high-end designers, from the minimalism of Jil Sander to the blue-blood class of Hermès to the extravagance of Christian Lacroix. Barneys also continues to champion the up-and-coming, such as Olivier Theyskens and Martin Margiela. Women's shoes are thick with labels as well (Prada, Dries van Noten), with scads of Manolo Blahniks. The Chelsea Passage level has a small selection of children's clothes plus all of those objets that aren't exactly fashion but still look fabulous: Philippe Starck kitchenware, stationery, vases, crystal, china, beaded cocktail napkins. If the prices and the attitude leave you winded, you can still find something that invokes extravagance: spring for a pair of caviar spoons. The latest revamp is the addition of a second Co-op floor, where designs are more street-stylish and prices are lower. You might hear some squabbling, but it most likely isn't a pair of women fighting over the Katayone Adeli or Built by Wendy racks. Rather, it's the caged birds which hang between the floors. At press time, Barneys planned to turn its warehouse (255 W. 17th Street, site of the famous sales) into an entire Co-op store by spring 2000. 660 Madison Ave. (at 61st St.), Upper East Side, 212/826–8900, Subway: 59th St./Lexington Ave.

10 d-7

World Financial Center, 225 Liberty St. (near West St.), Lower Manhattan, 212/945–1600. Subway: World Trade Ctr.

9 *d-3*

BERGDORF GOODMAN

With a men's and a women's store facing each other across 5th Avenue, Bergdorf Goodman dominates a solid block of good taste. The atmosphere in both is understated and unmistakably wealthy; the younger clothing lines are best suited to teens with a trust fund. But while the building itself whispers "old money," the selections are far from old-fashioned. Shoe mavens could be rendered delirious by the couture heels: Manolo Blahnik, Christian Louboutin, Jimmy Choo, and Emma Hope's "regalia for feet." Upstairs, many designer labels hold court in separate alcoves: John Galliano, Balenciaga, Valentino, Chanel, and their four-digit brethren. (With all of these niches, you need a good sense of direction to get back to the escalators.) The choice of relatively casual clothing is happily original, too; such familiar brands as Donna Karan are joined by Claude Pierlot, Philosophy di Alberta Ferretti, and the raucous colors of Voyage. If you pass an abandoned-looking clothes rack on any of the floors, go ahead and riffle—these are normally reduced-price goods. The beauty salon has managed to one-up its competitors by operating in the Goodman family's former penthouse apartment. The home department has roomsful of especially wonderful linens, tableware, and gifts. For Bergdorf Goodman Men, *see* Clothing for Men–Classic, *below. 754 5th Ave. (at 57th St.), Midtown, 212/753–7300. Subway: E, F, N, R to 5th Ave.*

9 *e-3*

BLOOMINGDALE'S

To tourists, Bloomie's is as New York as yellow cabs. To New Yorkers, Bloomie's is a good place to go for a sale on, say, hosiery or bedding. Everyone comes here at some point. The ground floor includes a portion of the menswear collection, mainly ties and shirts for the frantic 11th-hour shopper, and the maze-like cosmetics area, whose mirrors and shiny black walls can be completely discombobulating. (Enter on 3rd Avenue instead of Lexington Avenue to avoid this experience.) Big-gun designers such as Calvin Klein, Donna Karan, and Ralph Lauren seem to be everywhere. Their names pop up on casual clothes, dressy suits, and underwear, petites and plus sizes, not to mention in the home sec-

tion. But buyers also reach out to the more avant-garde (Helmut Lang, Alexander McQueen) and upwardly mobile (Theory, Daryl K.). As for atmosphere, Bloomie's definitely subscribes to the right-between-the-eyes school of marketing. If you brave the clothing sales, prepare for a scrimmagelike experience amid messy piles and racks of merch. *1000 3rd Ave. (at 59th St.), Midtown, 212/705–2000. Subway: 59th St./Lexington Ave.*

9 *e-5*

LORD & TAYLOR

Once inside this 5th Avenue veteran, you might think the ground floor goes on forever. A trick of mirrors reflecting the arched white ceiling, this impression of cosmetic-department infinity is the store's most overwhelming aspect. (Make an immediate right from the entrance to get to the up escalator.) For the most part, L&T is a decidedly ladylike experience, with some floors decorated in powder-pink and white. Clothes lean heavily toward conservative American designers throughout; think St. John and Liz Claiborne for women, Nautica and Perry Ellis for men, Ralph Lauren everywhere. *424 5th Ave. (at 38th St.), Garment District, 212/391–3344. Subway: 34th St./Herald Sq.*

9 *d-6*

MACY'S

If you don't know the floor plan by heart (many do), Macy's requires the patience of a saint, or a stiff drink. With nine floors (not including the famous Cellar marketplace) and too few signs directing you to either the Broadway building or the 7th Avenue building, you can easily find yourself among the baby booties when you're looking for luggage. Macy's has tons of almost everything, from sports gear to pianos. Major labels such as DKNY, Polo, Tommy Hilfiger, and Calvin Klein show up on floor after floor, from men's and women's jeans to suits. Dig a little deeper and you'll find some lesser-known streetwear labels such as Phatfarm and Diesel. What Macy's doesn't have is couture—it skips from "better sportswear" to a limited selection of tuxedos, lower-end formal dresses (think Jessica McClintock), dressy topcoats, and furs. Service can be amiably casual or surly, but is reliably slapdash. The list of amenities is impressive; there's even a post office. At press time, the store was still renovating in places. *155 W. 34th St. (Herald Sq.), Garment District, 212/695–4400. Subway: 34th St./Herald Sq.*

9 e-4
SAKS FIFTH AVENUE
For his-and-hers takes on Saks, *see* Clothing for Women–Contemporary and Clothing for Men—Classic, *below.*

9 d-6
STERN'S
The linchpin of the Manhattan Mall (*see* Malls, *below*), Stern's is a very manageable department store. Compared to Manhattan's other mega-emporia, selections here are smaller and more moderately priced. Men's and women's clothes tend to be casual, though there are a few nice suits lying around. Housewares, linen, appliances, and electronics are equally relaxed and reasonably priced. *899 6th Ave. (at 33rd St.), Garment District, 212/244–6060. Subway: 34th St./Herald Sq.*

9 e-3
TAKASHIMAYA
As Takashimaya sees it, New York is the logical intermediary between Paris and Tokyo. The mingling aesthetics have resulted in a space of impeccable design, and the store has accomplished the unthinkable by creating a perpetually calm atmosphere. The home collection is the most renowned, featuring such finery as delicate tablewares, lacquered chopsticks and silverware, and throw pillows covered in patchworks of patterned silks ($75–$365). Some pieces are antique, such as the bamboo baskets or Japanese chests. Clothing for both men and women is limited to what Takashimaya calls "details." For men this means shirts, ties, watches, and the odd coat. For women, the "cause for indulgence" could be seed-pearl jewelry, hair ornaments, or silk scarves and purses. Head up to the 5th floor (loungewear, bedding, baby clothes) for silk robes, Japanese-style velvet thongs, and pale linens that will have you rethinking your bedroom. The ground-floor cosmetics section (don't worry, no one wields a spritzer here) has some rare product lines, including soaps and scents by Santa Maria Novella of Florence. The beautiful gardening section, visible through the storefront windows, has glazed pots ($10–$35), gardening

tools, and rather fascinating plants. Descend to the basement for beautiful teapots, loose teas, and perhaps a bento box lunch. *693 5th Ave. (between 54th and 55th Sts.), Midtown, 212/350–0100. Subway: 5th Ave./53rd St.*

MALLS

A Manhattan mall is nearly an oxymoron, but there are a few, not as intriguing as the prime shopping neighborhoods but easier on the legs.

9 d-6
HERALD CENTER
This budget-oriented retail center was hard to get off the ground, but it's braving the traffic well. The main draws are the giant Toys 'R' Us and Kids 'R' Us stores, as well as branches of Daffy's and Payless Shoes. *1 Herald Sq. (at W. 34th St.), Garment District, 212/634–3883. Subway: 34th St./Herald Sq.*

9 d-6
MANHATTAN MALL
Like any mall worth its salt, this complex has a skylit atrium, a huge food court, and lots of neon. Stern's anchors the usual bevy of chain and novelty stores—the goofy-tie shop, the candle store, the baseball-cap cart. On the whole, merchandise is low on the price scale; clothing stores include Aéropostale, Express, and Bolton's. There are also branches of Ann Taylor and Nine West, though, amazingly, there's no Gap . . . yet. *6th Ave. at 33rd St., Garment District, 212/465–0500. Subway: 34th St./Herald Sq.*

11 f-7
SOUTH STREET SEAPORT MARKETPLACE, PIER 17
In this outdoor mall reminiscent of Boston's Quincy Market, you'll find three clusters of stores: one on a pedestrians-only extension to Fulton Street; one in the Fulton Market building, the original home of NYC's fish market; and one at Pier 17. Squint at the old buildings and you can still make out a few painted signs from the old fish merchants. Many of the stores along the cobble streets are outlets of chains, such as Ann Taylor, Victoria's Secret, and Liz Claiborne; Manhattan's first J. Crew store is in one of the Seaport's historic waterfront hotel buildings. Pier 17 is also dominated by such retail giants as The Gap, but there are a few unusual

boutiques, such as Mariposa, which sells brilliantly colored butterflies encased in Lucite. *Fulton and Water Sts., Lower Manhattan, 212/732–7678. Subway: Fulton St.*

9 *e-3*
TRUMP TOWER
The soaring marble atrium, with its wall of water and bronze tones at every turn, makes this place unmistakably Trump. Finding a knockout gem here is no trouble; Cartier, Harry Winston, and Asprey all have branches on site. The glamour quotient is further upped by such vendors as Salvatore Ferragamo and Caviar Direct. Since the sprawling Abercrombie & Fitch decamped in 1997, the most youth-accessible place is probably the Tower Records outpost in the basement. *725 5th Ave. (at 56th St.), Midtown, 212/832–2000. Closed Sun. Subway: E, F to 5th Ave.*

specialist shops

ANTIQUES

Nearly every neighborhood in New York has its own array of antiques stores, but there are some well-known pockets. These include SoHo (especially Lafayette St. south of Houston St.); 9th–13th streets between Broadway and 2nd Avenue; and Madison and Lexington avenues from 72nd to 86th streets.

New York also has several flea markets, antiques centers, and seasonal antique shows. The Manhattan Art & Antiques Center (1050 2nd Ave., between 52nd and 53rd Sts.) is a Midtown classic. The 26th Street Flea Market (6th Ave. from 24th to 27th Sts.) is open for mass consumption on weekends, and its organizer, the Annex Antiques Fair & Flea Market, also maintains an indoor venue on 25th Street between 6th and 7th avenues.

Call Stella Management (212/255–0020) for information on the Triple Pier Expo, and Gramercy Park Antiques shows; call Sanford Smith Associates (212/777–5218) for information on the Fall Antiques and the Modernism shows. Anna and Brian Haughton Art and Antique Fairs (212/642–8572) organizes

the International Fine Art & Antique Dealers show; Wendy Management (914/698–3442) handles the New York Armory Antiques shows. Metropolitan Art and Antiques (212/463–0200) also produces several shows a year. For a full review of the Armory show, see Events–January in Chapter 4.

auction houses

9 *e-2*
CHRISTIE'S AND CHRISTIE'S EAST
New York's branches of the famed London house hold auctions of fine art, furnishings, tapestries, books, and manuscripts and appraise art at no charge. "Low-end" antiques and collectibles are often up for grabs. *20 Rockefeller Plaza (49th St. between 5th and 6th Ave.), Midtown, 212/636–2000, subway 47th–50th St./Rockefeller Ctr.*

9 *f-2*
219 E. 67th St. (between 3rd and 2nd Aves.), Upper East Side, 212/606–0400; information on current sales, 212/452–4100; information on lectures and courses, 212/355–1501. Subway 68th St./Hunter College.

9 *e-7*
HARMER
Harmer specializes in stamps: They auction, appraise, and arrange private treaties. *3 E. 28th St. (between 5th and Madison Aves.), Murray Hill, 212/532–3700. Subway: 6 to 28th St.*

7 *f-8*
PHILLIPS AUCTIONEERS
Founded in London in 1796, Phillips still holds fine art and estate sales. Items are displayed three or four days before the auction. Watch the paper for Phillips' ads. *406 E. 79th St.(between 1st and York Aves.), Upper East Side, 212/570–4830. Subway: 77th St.*

9 *g-1*
SOTHEBY'S
Appraiser and auctioneer since 1744, the world-famous Sotheby's sells paintings, jewelry, furniture, silver, books, porcelain, Orientalia, rugs, and more. The house is exciting to visit even if you won't be buying. Sotheby's Arcade, a sort of junior Sotheby's, sells more affordable pieces.

1334 York Ave. (at 72nd St.), 212/606–
7000 (call this number for the education
department and Sotheby's Arcade) or 212/
606–7909 (24-hr auction and exhibition
line). Subway: 77th St.

9 e-7

TEPPER GALLERIES

Large and lively, Tepper is popular with
collectors for its fine furniture, paintings, rugs, accessories, and jewelry. Auctions are every other Saturday; viewing
is on Thursday and Friday. 110 E. 25th
St., Gramercy, 212/677–5300. Subway: 6
to 23rd St.

7 e-7

WILLIAM DOYLE GALLERIES

Estates are the specialty here, particularly 18th- and 20th-century decorative
and fine arts including furniture, paintings, rugs, and accessories. Auctions
are usually held every other Wednesday,
sometimes weekly; viewing runs from
Saturday through Tuesday. The tag sale
next door can yield bargains. 175 E. 87th
St. (between Lexington and 3rd Aves.),
Upper East Side, 212/427–2730. Subway:
4, 5, 6 to 86th St.

antiques centers and flea markets

Even among bargain-savvy Manhattanites, flea markets are a bastion of affordable goods.

9 d-7

ANNEX ANTIQUES FAIR & FLEA MARKET

Year-round, in nearly every kind of
weather, the Annex draws the curious. A
serious dealers' market with quality
antiques and collectibles, the market is
particularly strong on silver, jewelry, vintage clothing, glass, Americana, Victori-
ana, and ephemera, but there's much
more. The stock varies from week to
week, as most of the dealers are itiner-
ant; they go where the action is. One
block south of the Annex is a more
chaotic lot with a preponderance of
junk; it's also worth a look for good vintage clothing and the occasional quilt.
On Sunday, yet more dealers set up
shop in a garage on 25th Street between
6th and 7th avenues. Parking for all
Annex events is free. 6th Ave. and 26th
St., Chelsea, 212/243–5343. Admission.
Subway: F to 23rd St.

9 d-7

CHELSEA ANTIQUES BUILDING

For antiques shopping in a conveniently
mall-like setting, hit these 12 floors of
antiques and collectibles any day of the
week. 110 W. 25th St., Chelsea, 212/929–
0909. Subway: F, 1, 9 to 23rd St.

9 f-1

GREENFLEA'S MARKET AT P.S. 183

With both indoor and outdoor venues,
this Saturday market is a friendly place
to scout good-quality antiques and collectibles, including jewelry and linens.
New goods and fresh produce round
out the shopping experience. P.S. 183
(1st Ave. and 67th St.), Upper East Side,
212/721–0900. Subway: 68th St./Hunter
College.

7 b-8

GREENFLEA'S MARKET ON COLUMBUS

Greenflea's now rivals 26th Street as the
Sunday flea market, though it's dark the
rest of the week. Two hundred vendors
offer antiques, collectibles, old clothes,
jewelry, and new merchandise in both
indoor and outdoor venues. Columbus
Ave. and 76th St., Upper West Side, 212/
721–0900. Subway: 79th St.

9 f-3

MANHATTAN ART & ANTIQUE CENTER

This is a class act. Under one roof, more
than 100 shops and galleries sell a great
selection of antiques and fine-art objects
from around the world. Prices range
impressively from $10 to $300,000. 1050
2nd Ave. (near 56th St.), Midtown, 212/
355–4400. Subway: 59th St./Lexington Ave.

11 e-2

TOWER FLEA MARKET

These mainly young and earnest artisans and designers sell T-shirts, clothes,
jewelry, hats, and other adornments
every weekend. Broadway and 4th St.,
Greenwich Village, no phone. Subway: 8th
St.; Astor Pl.

collectibles

9 e-2

A LA VIEILLE RUSSIE

This exquisite collection of Russian art
and antiques includes clocks and art

objects—especially icons, Fabergé, silver and porcelain, antique jewelry, and snuff boxes. *781 5th Ave. (at 59th St.), Midtown, 212/752–1727. Subway: N, R to 5th Ave.*

11 *e-4*

BACK PAGES

Back Pages is a center for antique amusement and slot machines, Wurlitzer jukeboxes, Coca-Cola vending machines, player pianos, and other large items. They also restore. Appointments are advised. *125 Greene St. (near Prince St.), SoHo, 212/460–5998. Subway: Prince St.*

7 *e-7*

BERNARD & S. DEAN LEVY, INC.

This lovely town-house gallery has top-quality late-17th- to early-19th-century American antiques, furniture, silver, paintings, and decorative wares. *24 E. 84th St., Upper East Side, 212/628–7088. Subway: 4, 5, 6 to 86th St.*

11 *d-4*

BERTHA BLACK

A tiny SoHo shop with antique American painted furniture, folk art, and country dining accessories, Bertha Black also carries an extensive collection of Mexican retablos and santos, 1820–1900. *80 Thompson St. (near Spring St.), 212/966–7116. Closed Mon.–Tues. Subway: C, E to Spring St.*

9 *f-2*

CHICK DARROW'S FUN ANTIQUES

For the Peter Pan in your family, hit Chick Darrow's, with antique toys of every description: autographs, wind-ups, mechanical banks, carousel animals, toy soldiers, animation art, arcade machines. Prices range widely, from $2 to $5,000. *1101 1st Ave. between 60th and 61st Sts., Upper East Side, 212/838–0730. Closed Sun.–Mon. except by appt. Subway: 59th St./Lexington Ave.*

10 *f-1*

COBBLESTONES

The best word for this stuff is stuff—a lot of fun old stuff. Kitchen utensils, costume jewelry, books, glassware, sunglasses, hats, cigarette cases, evening bags . . . you never know what you'll find. *314 E. 9th St., Greenwich Village,* 212/673–5372. Closed Mon. Subway: 8th St.; Astor Pl.*

10 *e-1*

DULLESVILLE

Jewelry, pottery, and decorative objects from 1900 through the 1960s—including one of the largest collections of Bakelite in the country—are joined by a good deal of ware by Russell Wright. *143 E. 13th St., Greenwich Village, 212/505–2505. Subway: 14th St./Union Sq.*

11 *d-5*

ECLECTIQUES

This aptly named shop carries an interesting mix: Art Deco, Art Nouveau, 1920s Mica lamps, Mission furniture, 20th-century oils and illustrations, paisley shawls, and vintage Vuitton luggage. *55 Wooster St. (at Broome St.), SoHo, 212/966–0650. Subway: Canal St.*

9 *f-2*

ELIZABETH STREET CO.

Still named for the street in SoHo where its former owners, Urban Archaeology, had a location, this eclectic boutique of garden statuary, fireplace surrounds, and French and English decorative objects is now a little bit of SoHo on the Upper East Side. *1176 2nd Ave. (at 62nd St.), 212/644–6969. Subway: 59th St./Lexington Ave.*

7 *e-7*

HUBERT DES FORGES

Forges can be counted on for lovely French and English antiques and decorative accessories. *1193 Lexington Ave. (near 81st St.), Upper East Side, 212/744–1857. Closed weekends. Subway: 77th St.*

9 *f-8*

IRVING BARBER SHOP ANTIQUES

These cramped quarters overflow with glassware, costume jewelry, beaded evening bags, prints, and sometimes antique linens, quilts, and vintage cloths. Browse—gingerly. *210 E. 21st St. (between 3rd and 2nd Aves.), Gramercy, no phone. Closed weekends. Subway: 6 to 23rd St.*

7 *f-8*

JANA STARR ANTIQUES

Focusing on the period 1900–1930, Starr is jam-packed with wedding dresses from the turn of the 20th century to the 1950s, but also manages to stuff into its tight quarters beautiful embroidered table and bed linens, jewelry, hats, gloves, dressing-table items, bags, antique laces and textiles, walking sticks, all obviously gathered with care. She also rents period props. *236 E. 80th St. (between 3rd and 2nd Aves.), Upper East Side, 212/861–8256. Closed Sun. Subway: 77th St.*

9 *f-1*

JEAN HOFFMAN ANTIQUES
The other half of what was formerly Jana Starr–Jean Hoffman Antiques, Hoffman also has an eye for wedding accessories, from the turn of the century to the present: pocketbooks, fans, gloves linens, and gift items. *207 E. 66th St., (between 3rd and 2nd Aves.), Upper East Side, 212/535–6930. Closed Sun.–Mon. Subway: 68th St./Hunter College.*

10 *c-1*

LE FANION
Feel like Provence? Peruse French country antiques, contemporary ceramics, and crystal chandeliers in a shop with a deliciously country atmosphere. *299 W. 4th St. (at Bank St.), West Village, 212/463–8760. Closed Sun. Subway: Christopher St./Sheridan Sq.*

7 *e-8*

LEO KAPLAN LTD.
Leo Kaplan has an extensive selection of French and American modern paperweights; 18th-century English pottery and porcelains; Russian enamels; English and French cameo glass of the Art Nouveau period; and contemporary studio glass. *967 Madison Ave. (near 75th St.), Upper East Side, 212/249–6766. Subway: 77th St.*

9 *f-3*

LILLIAN NASSAU LTD.
This is the place for Art Nouveau and Art Deco pieces, especially Tiffany glass and rare art glass as well as furniture and sculpture. *220 E. 57th St. (between 2nd and 3rd Aves.), Midtown, 212/759–6062. Subway: 59th St./Lexington Ave.*

7 *e-8*

LINDA HORN ANTIQUES
Linda has quite an eye for the unusual. Check out her opulent treasures from the 18th and 19th centuries in a setting to match. *1015 Madison Ave. (near 78th St.), Upper East Side, 212/772–1122. Subway: 77th St.*

11 *d-4*

MOOD INDIGO
The 1930s and '40s get their due in this inviting shop full of Russell Wright, Fiesta, and Harlequin ware; Art Deco chrome accessories; and a wonderful selection of Bakelite jewelry. *181 Prince St. (near Thompson St.), SoHo, 212/254–1176. Closed Mon. Subway: Prince St.*

7 *b-8*

MORE & MORE ANTIQUES
Steve Mohr has one of the best eyes in the business, and his wonderful shops are brimming over with late-19th- to early-20th-century French and English decorative antiques, with a bent toward the Victorian. Offerings include paisleys, wonderful hand-painted china, beadwork, bamboo furnishings, rugs, screens, and an eclectic selection of jewelry, from 1840 to 1940. *360 Amsterdam Ave. (at 78th St.), Upper West Side, 212/580–8404. Subway: 79th St.*

9 *e-2*

MORIAH
Antique Judaica, prints, engravings, and curios make up this unique mix. *699 Madison Ave. (near 62nd St.), Upper East Side, 212/751–7090. Closed weekends. Subway: 59th St./Lexington Ave.*

9 *f-2*

OLD VERSAILLES, INC.
The specialty here is, bien sûr, French and Continental antiques and furniture. *315 E. 62nd St. (between 2nd and 1st Aves.), 3rd floor, Upper East Side, 212/421–3663. Closed weekends. Subway: 59th St./Lexington Ave.*

7 *e-8*

PRICE GLOVER INC.
English pewter, pottery, and brass, circa 1690–1820, are joined by early-19th-century English brass light fixtures, and Chinese furniture, 1600–1700. *59 E. 79th St. (near Madison Ave.), 3rd floor, Upper East Side, 212/772–1740. Closed weekends. Subway: 77th St.*

9 *e-1*

PRIMAVERA GALLERY
These decorative arts include paintings, furniture, glass, and jewelry from the turn of the 20th century to the 1950s. *808 Madison Ave. (near 68th St.), Upper East Side, 212/288–1569. Subway: 68th St./Hunter College.*

11 *e-4*

SARAJO

Sarajo's large and impressive selection of textiles, antique furniture, and objects comes from Central Asia, Africa, the Far East, and Central and South America. *130 Greene St. (between Prince and Houston Sts.), SoHo, 212/966–6156. Subway: Prince St.*

7 *e-7*

TROUVAILLE FRANÇAISE

Muriel Clark collects and purveys treasures from France and Belgium with loving care: antique bed and table linens, laces, curtains, christening gowns, and much more. *Upper East Side, 212/737–6015. Open by appt. only. Subway: 4, 5, 6 to 86th St.*

9 *d-7*

WAVES

Vintage radios, wind-up phonographs, old telephones, and neon clocks are sold, repaired, and rented; other communications memorabilia include old advertisements and 78-rpm records. *110 W. 25th St. (between 6th and 7th Aves.), 10th floor, Chelsea, 212/989–9284. Subway: B, F, Q, 1, 9 to 23rd St.*

furniture

11 *c-4*

CARPE DIEM ANTIQUES

This excellent cache of '50s and '60s furniture includes a particularly notable collection of lamps. *187 6th Ave. (between Spring and Prince Sts.), SoHo, 212/337–0018. Closed Mon. Subway: C, E to Spring St.*

11 *d-3*

COBWEB

Cobweb has a good selection of ethnic antique furniture and accessories from Europe and the Middle East. *116 W. Houston St. (at Sullivan St.), West Village, 212/505–1558. Subway: Houston St.*

11 *d-4*

EILEEN LANE ANTIQUES

Spacious quarters show off a lovely and well-priced selection of Swedish and Viennese Biedermeier and Art Deco furniture, as well as period art glass and alabaster lighting. *150 Thompson St. (between Prince and Houston Sts.), SoHo, 212/475–2988. Subway: C, E to Spring St.*

9 *f-1*

EVERGREEN ANTIQUES

Some of this rustic, 18th- and 19th-century Scandinavian pine furniture has its original hand-painted finishing. Accents include rag rugs, pottery, and wooden boxes. *1249 3rd Ave. (at 72nd St.), Upper East Side, 212/744–5664. Subway: 68th St./Hunter College.*

7 *e-8*

FLORIAN PAPP

Since 1900, Papp has been a source for antiques from the William and Mary, Sheraton, and other periods of fine English and European furniture, and the store now carries Victorian items as well. *962 Madison Ave. (near 76th St.), Upper East Side, 212/288–6770. Subway: 77th St.*

11 *e-4*

GALLERY 532

Original furniture and ceramic pieces will delight the Arts & Crafts lover. *142 Duane St. (between Church St. and W. Broadway), Tribeca, 212/219–1327. Subway: Chambers St.*

11 *f-3*

GUÉRIDON

The name means "side table" in French, and the store boasts a wide array of these and other funky modern pieces at a range of prices to suit almost any budget. The owners are highly knowledgeable and equally charming. *359 Lafayette St. (between Bond and Bleecker Sts.), 212/677–7740. Subway: Bleecker St.; Broadway–Lafayette St.*

10 *e-1*

HOWARD KAPLAN ANTIQUES

An early purveyor of the Rustic French look, Howard Kaplan now carries a broader range of French (including country) and 19th-century English furnishings and a luscious group of decorative accessories, all in a beautiful shop. *827 Broadway (near 12th St.), Greenwich Village, 212/674–1000. Closed weekends. Subway: 14th St./Union Sq.*

11 *e-4*

INTÉRIEURS

Alas, this truly choice contemporary furniture, along with lighting, tabletop items, and other accessories from France, comes with equally choice prices. Be prepared to drool, and bring the platinum card. *114 Wooster St. (between Spring and Prince Sts.), SoHo, 212/343–0800. Subway: 6 to Spring St.*

9 *e-3*

ISRAEL SACK INC.

A patriarch of still-existing antique-furniture galleries, Israel Sack was begun almost 100 years ago, and the tradition of showing some of the finest 17th-, 18th-, and early 19th-century American furniture is continued by Sack's octegenarian sons Albert, Harold, and Robert. Prices range from $3,000 to $3 million and beyond. *730 5th Ave. (between 56th and 57th Sts.), Suite 605, Midtown, 212/399–6562. Subway: B, Q to 57th St.*

7 *e-8*

LEIGH KENO AMERICAN ANTIQUES

The patriarch of the "new generation," Keno is one half of the wunderkind twins who began collecting while still in short pants (brother Leslie is a specialist at Sotheby's). Included among the finds are an emphasis on 18th-century American furniture and paintings. *980 Madison Ave. (at 76th St.), Upper East Side, 212/734–2381. Subway: 77th St.*

11 *f-4*

LOST CITY ARTS

Architectural antiques and Americana join advertising icons and Art Deco. *275 Lafayette St. (between Prince and Houston Sts.), SoHo, 212/941–8025. Subway: Broadway–Lafayette St.; Prince St.*

9 *f-3*

NEWEL ART GALLERIES

It takes six stories to house this supreme collection of antique furnishings from the Renaissance to Art Deco, with an emphasis on the unusual and whimsical. They cater to those in the trade, stylists scouting props, and those who know exactly what they want. *425 E. 53rd St. (near 1st Ave.), Midtown, 212/758–1970. Closed weekends. Subway: 51st St./Lexington–3rd Aves.*

11 *a-1*

PIERRE DEUX ANTIQUES

Pierre Deux specializes in exquisite 18th- and 19th-century country French furniture and accessories. *367 Bleecker St. (at Charles St.), West Village, 212/243–7740. Subway: Christopher St./Sheridan Sq.*

10 *e-1*

RETRO MODERN STUDIO

The collection centers on European and American designer Art Deco furniture, lighting, and fine-art objects. *58 E. 11th St. (between Broadway and University Pl.), 2nd floor, Greenwich Village, 212/674–0530. Closed Sun. Subway: 8th St.; Astor Pl.*

10 *c-2*

THE RURAL COLLECTION

You can go home again: finds from the farm, old cupboards, and weather-worn painted furniture from the Midwest are priced very reasonably here. *117 Perry St. (between Greenwich and Hudson Sts.), West Village, 212/645–4488. Subway: Christopher St./Sheridan Sq.*

11 *e-3*

SECONDHAND ROSE

The focus here is 20th-century American decorative arts: Donald Desky, Gilbert Rohde, R. T. Frankl, Paul Evans, Charles Eames. Also on hand are antique wallpaper and fabrics. A splendid collection, if it's your cup of tea. *138 Duane St. (between Church and W. Broadway), Tribeca, 212/393–9002. Subway: Chambers St.*

7 *f-8*

TREILLAGE

Owned by Bunny Williams and John Rosselli, Treillage has made its name with furniture and accessories for the garden, but it now features an interesting selection of tableware and lighting as well. *418 E. 75th St. (between 1st and York Aves.), Upper East Side, 212/535–2288. Subway: 77th St.*

11 *d-7*

WYETH

Come here for steel furniture and other stylish Americana. *151 Franklin St. (between Hudson and Varick Sts.), West Village, 212/925–5278. Subway: Franklin St.*

quilts

Most antiques stores have a few quilts in stock, but these shops have built collections of outstanding quality, originality, and quantity.

9 *e-3*

GAZEBO

A must for the hearth-and-home enthusiast, this Midtown shop features American quilts mainly from the 1920s and '30s, and new ones in traditional patterns. They're happy to take custom orders. Vintage wicker furnishings and accessories, old and new baskets, silk flowers, and other accessories round out the beautiful displays. *114 E. 57th St. (between Park and Lexington Aves.), Midtown, 212/832–7077. Subway: 59th St./Lexington Ave.*

10 *b-1*

KELTER-MALCE ANTIQUES

Kelter and Malce have a very large, very fine collection of antique American quilts along with folk art, rag rugs, antique Native American textiles, and pottery. *74 Jane St. (near Washington St.), West Village, 212/989–6760. Open by appt. only. Subway: A, C, E to 14th St.*

9 *f-3*

LAURA FISHER

Fisher has an exciting collection of pieced and appliquéd quilts, circa 1830–1930, including Amish and crib quilts. The wares extend to paisley shawls, woven coverlets, Marseilles bedspreads, hooked and Native American rugs, needlework, and decorative Victorian accessories. *Manhattan Art & Antiques Center, 1050 2nd Ave. (at 55th St.), Midtown, 212/838–2596. Closed Sun. Subway: 59th St./Lexington Ave.*

11 *a-1*

SUSAN PARRISH ANTIQUES

Knowledgeable and caring, Susan Parrish has a lovely selection of pretty quilts, original 18th- and 19th-century painted American country furniture, and Native American weavings. *390 Bleecker St. (near Perry St.), West Village, 212/645–5020. Closed Sun. Subway: Christopher St./Sheridan Sq.*

7 *g-8*

WOODARD & GREENSTEIN AMERICAN ANTIQUES

A known and respected source for American quilts from the 1850s on, Woodard & Greenstein also carry hooked rugs, samplers, game boards, baskets, and much more—mint Americana. *506 E. 74th St. (near York Ave.), 5th floor, Upper East Side, 212/988–2906. Subway: 77th St.*

ART SUPPLIES

9 *d-4*

ARTHUR BROWN & BROS., INC.

Long established, this superior art- and drafting-supply store has a fantastic pen department. *2 W. 46th St. (between 5th and 6th Aves.), Midtown, 212/575–5555. Subway: B, D, F, Q to 42nd St.*

11 *e-4*

KATE'S PAPERIE

See Stationery & Office Supplies, *below.*

9 *c-3*

LEE'S ART SHOP

Right across the street from the Art Students' League, Lee's caters to both professional and amateur artists. The large inventory includes stationery, pens, gifts, paint and brushes, and architectural and drafting supplies, and they're happy to frame your masterpiece once you're finished. *220 W. 57th St. (between 7th Ave. and Broadway), Midtown, 212/247–0110. Subway: N, R to 57th St.; 59th St./Columbus Circle.*

10 *e-1*

NEW YORK CENTRAL

Serving New York's artists for over 80 years, New York Central has the finest of everything: handmade papers, parchment, 3,000 different pastels, 200 different canvases, and much more, all for 20%–40% less than elsewhere. They specialize in finding the "impossible." *62 3rd Ave. (near 11th St.), East Village, 212/473–7705. Subway: 3rd Ave.; Astor Pl.*

11 *e-6*

PEARL

With nine floors of art supplies, Pearl is the world's largest art, craft, and graphics discount center—no mean feat. It's a wonderful source for this stuff, as well as house and industrial paints at 20%–50% off. *308 Canal St. (between Church St. and Broadway), SoHo, 212/431–7932. Subway: Canal St.*

9 *f-8*

207 E. 23rd St. (between 3rd and 2nd Aves.), 212/592–2179. Subway: 6 to 23rd St.

9 *d-8*

SAM FLAX, INC.

Sam Flax adds school and office supplies to its admirably complete selection of art materials. *12 W. 20th St. (between*

5th and 6th Aves.), Chelsea, 212/620–3038. Subway: F to 23rd St.

9 *e-3*

425 Park Ave. (at 55th St.), Midtown, 212/620–3060. Subway: 59th St./Lexington Ave.

10 *e-1*

UTRECHT ART AND DRAFTING SUPPLIES

Utrecht makes its own huge stock of paint, art, and drafting supplies right down the road in Brooklyn. Prices are reasonable, and quality is high. Other manufacturers' supplies are discounted as well. *111 4th Ave. (at 11th St.), East Village, 212/777–5353. Subway: 8th St./Astor Pl.*

9 *e-6*

215 Lexington Ave. (at 33rd St.), Murray Hill, 212/683–8822. Subway: 33rd St.

BASKETS

10 *c-1*

CHELSEA MARKET BASKETS

From tiny table-top sizes to giant woven picnic hampers, this shop has a wide selection of well-crafted baskets. Gift baskets filled with a selection of Chelsea Market goodies are also available. *75 9th Ave. (between 15th and 16th Sts.), Chelsea, 888/727–7887. Subway: A, C, E to 14th St.*

BEAUTY

beauty services

New York is a city with something for everyone, and beauty services are no exception. With enough time, and money, experts will slough your skin with sugar, wrap you in seaweed, submerge you in mud, encase you in wax, rub you with stones—and basically find a way to pamper you with any material they can get their hands on. The results are usually heavenly, but be warned—if it sounds too good to be true, it probably is.

9 *e-3*

AVON CENTRE

This is not your mother's Avon. Gone are the days of apricot lipstick and door-to-door sales. In their place is this slick spa that sports a waiting room as large

as a hotel lobby and top-notch treatment rooms. Massages are delightful, facials are first class, and eyebrow guru Eliza is the best in the city—as you'll begin to discover when you try to get an appointment. Brad Johns, the king of blonde, is slated to take over the hair salon. *Trump Tower, 725 5th Ave. (at 57th St.), 5th floor, Midtown, 212/310–6305. Subway: N, R to 5th Ave.*

9 *e-4*

AWAY SPA

Your reward for traversing the frenetic lobby of the W Hotel is the quiet and elegant atmosphere of this New Age-style spa. Come with an open mind and try such unique treatments as color hydrotherapy, aura imaging, and the Javanese Lulur—a Far East treatment where you'll be massaged with rice, turmeric, and yogurt and leave feeling sensuously smooth. There's also a full menu of more traditional skin and body treatments. *W Hotel, 541 Lexington Ave. (at 49th St.), Midtown, 212/407–2970. Subway: 51st St./Lexington–3rd Aves.*

11 *e-4*

BLISS SPA

Possibly the first spa that's as trendy as a nightclub—wasn't that Uma?—Bliss is so popular it can often take months to get an appointment here. What awaits when you finally make it in? Wine and cheese in the lounge area, oxygen facials, dreamy pedicures, and first-rate massage. *568 Broadway (at Prince St.), 212/219–8970. Subway: Broadway–Lafayette St.; Prince St.*

9 *e-3*

19 E. 57th St. (between 5th and Madison Aves.), 3rd floor, Midtown, 212/219–9870. Subway: 57th St.

9 *d-3*

CHRISTINA & CARMEN

This Romanian mother-and-daughter team uses traditional techniques in their deep pore-cleansing facials, body-sloughing with paraffin, and stress-relieving shiatsu massage. *128 Central Park S (between 6th and 7th Aves.), Midtown, 212/757–5811. Subway: B, Q, N, R to 57th St.*

9 *e-3*

CHRISTINE VALMY

Renowned skin-care expert Christine Valmy helped American women discover skin care. Using Swiss fresh-cell therapy, she gives both men and women two-hour facials and offers post–plastic surgery care, makeup, and foot massage. A special pretheater package includes facial, manicure, shampoo, and blow-dry. Weekdays you can opt for a lower-price facial by a supervised student at the Valmy School for Aestheticians (212/581–1520 for appt.). *767 5th Ave. (at 58th St.), Midtown, 212/752–0303. Subway: N, R to 5th Ave.*

9 *d-3*

101 W. 57th St. (between 6th and 7th Aves.), Midtown, 212/581–9488. Subway: B, Q to 57th St.

9 *d-3*

DIANE YOUNG

Come here for holistic skin care in a beautiful setting. Young offers facials, treatments, herbal aromatherapy, expert nutritional advice, makeup lessons, manicures, pedicures, Swedish massage, waxing, and electrolysis (with disposable needles). *38 E. 57th St., Midtown (near Madison Ave.), 212/753–1200. Subway: N, R to 5th Ave.*

9 *d-3*

DORIT BAXTER

Facials, body scrubs and treatments, and a full-service salon are wrapped up in a convenient Midtown location. *47 W. 57th. St. (between 5th and 6th Ave.), Midtown, 212/371–4542. Subway: B, Q to 57th St.*

9 *e-1*

ELENA POCIU

Romanian-born Pociu runs a full-service skin-care salon, specializing in facials. Her masks are made on the premises. *23 E. 67th St. (near Madison Ave.), Upper East Side, 212/717–5543. Subway: 68th St./Hunter College.*

9 *e-3*

ELIZABETH ARDEN/ THE SALON

Just knock on the red door for head-to-toenail pampering in this Midtown mini-ispa. Expert facials and free makeup applications are among the many highlights. Treat yourself or a loved one to a Miracle Morning or a Main Chance Day: You get a spell in the sauna followed by massage, haircut and styling, facial, manicure and pedicure, eyebrow shaping, and makeup. *691 5th Ave. (near 54th St.), 212/486–7900. Subway: E, F to 5th Ave.*

11 *d-4*

ERBE

A favorite with SoHo denizens, Erbe offers both facials and massages as well as an amazing line of Italian herb- and flower-based skin products. *196 Prince St. (near MacDougal St.), SoHo, 212/966–1445. Subway: Prince St.*

9 *f-3*

ESTEE LAUDER

Reward yourself after a hard day of shopping at this spa nestled in the heart of Bloomingdale's. Facials are a specialty here, and are an exceptionally good value for the level of expertise and amount of attention involved. Other top choices include a jet-lag treatment, sunless tanning, massage, and pedicure. *1000 3rd Ave. (at 59th St.), 212/705–2318. Subway: 59th St./Lexington Ave.*

9 *e-3*

FREDERIC FEKKAI BEAUTÉ DE PROVENCE

The top floors of celebrity stylist Fekkai's Provençal-style townhouse serve as a home to upscale body and facial services ranging from European facials to sunless tanning treatments. *15 E. 57th St. (near Madison Ave.), Midtown, 212/753–9500. Subway: E, F, N, R to 5th Ave.*

9 *e-3*

GEORGETTE KLINGER SKIN CARE

Klinger's famously expert skin treatments include surface peeling, deep-pore cleansing, and scalp care for both women and men. Take advantage of the new full-day, full-body "Intensive Curriculum," also for both sexes. The only drawback is a hard sell of the product line. *501 Madison Ave. (near 52nd St.), Midtown, 212/838–3200. Subway: 51st St./Lexington–3rd Aves.*

7 *e-8*

978 Madison Ave. (near 77th St.), Upper East Side, 212/744–6900. Subway: 77th St.

9 *e-3*

JANET SARTIN

Come in for a consultation and get a product-and-treatment prescription from a world-famous skin expert— Sartin herself charges $400 for a 90-

minute pore-cleansing facial. The staff is well trained, and the clientele is high on the social registry. *480 Park Ave. (near 58th St.), Midtown, 212/751–5858. Subway: 59th St./Lexington Ave.*

9 e-3
LIA SCHORR SKIN CARE
Every client's skin is analyzed prior to treatment, resulting in sensible care, especially for sensitive and acne-plagued skin. The restorative Day of Beauty includes a facial, body massage, manicure, pedicure, makeup, and snack. Men are welcome, too. *686 Lexington Ave. (near 57th St.), Midtown, 212/486–9670. Subway: 59th St./Lexington Ave.*

9 f-3
MARIO BADESCU SKIN CARE
Sadly, Mario is gone, but his expert analyses and natural-formula skin products for women and men still have a loyal following. Other options include manicures, pedicures, massage, waxing, and electrolysis. *320 E. 52nd St. (between 2nd and 3rd Aves.), Midtown, 212/758–*

TWINKLE TOES

In a city where we often walk for miles on hard concrete just to get the subway, it's important to give you toes a little TLC. Treat your feet at one of the specialty pedicurists below (see Day Spas in Chapter 3 for addresses):

Avon
The peppermint massage cream here will make your toes tingle.

Bliss
Your tootsies are soaked in hot paraffin wax for 90 minutes and come out feeling like a baby's bottom.

Four Seasons
In a luxurious private room, an ace pedicurist massages and scrubs until feet are party perfect.

J. Sisters
Brazilian style pedicures—a messy, slap-on polish job which is then meticulously cleaned up—can take as much as 1½ hours.

Warren-Tricomi
A Moroccan souk acts as an oasis for your feet.

1065. Subway: 51st St./Lexington–3rd Aves.

11 d-7
MILLEFLEURS
Patterned after an Egyptian temple, Millefleurs offers herbal wraps, scrubs, massages, facials, reflexology, acupuncture, and even colonics in an incredible setting complete with waterfalls. *6 Varick St. (at Franklin St.), Tribeca, 212/966–3656. Subway: Franklin St.*

9 a-7
ORIGINS FEEL-GOOD SPA
Reward yourself after a hard Chelsea Piers workout at this somewhat cramped spa where massage, reflexology, facials, acupressure, and body treatments are administered using the popular line of Origins products. *The Sports Center, Pier 60, Chelsea Piers (12th Ave. and 23rd St.), Chelsea, 212/336–6780. Subway: C, E to 23rd St.*

9 d-3
PENINSULA SPA
Tucked in the Peninsula Hotel, this truly deluxe facility provides all the expected treatments plus a full gym, a salon, and an incredible outdoor pool by which to take in the equally incredible view. Facials here are some of the best in the city. *700 5th Ave. (at 55th St.), 21st floor, Midtown, 212/903–3910. Subway: N, R to 5th Ave.*

9 e-2
PETER COPPOLA SALON
A solid hour of old-fashioned pampering, using hypo-allergenic Italian products, cleans your skin without the usual squeezing. *746 Madison Ave. (between 64th and 65th Sts.), Upper East Side, 212/988–9404. Subway: 68th St./Hunter College.*

11 e-5
SOHO SANCTUARY
An oasis of tranquillity in a hectic city, this women-only spa combines traditional facials and massages with New Age music, meditation, and yoga to such a positive effect that you'll feel light-years away from the tension that sent you there. The super-spacious locker area includes a soothing eucalyptus steam room. *119 Mercer St. (between Prince and Spring Sts.), SoHo, 212/334–5550. Subway: Prince St.*

11 c-7

ULA SKIN CARE SALON

In a discreet Tribeca location, Ula offers nine different facials and seven different body treatments plus waxing, electrolysis, manicures, and pedicures in a highly relaxing setting. *22 Harrison St. (between Hudson and Greenwich Sts.), 212/343–2376. Subway: Franklin St.*

11 c-3

YANA HERBAL BEAUTY SALON

Fans of Yana's have raved about her relaxing herbal facials for years. A little-known fact is that Yana also waxes, using the ancient Middle Eastern technique that involves sugar instead of wax. *270 6th Ave. (between Houston and Bleecker Sts.), West Village, 212/254– 6200. Subway: W. 4th St./Washington Sq.*

fragrances & skin products

All major department stores have a full line of fragrances for both men and women on their main floor, often with live representatives ready and eager to spray you. Be warned that counterfeit fragrances, packaged to look like the real thing, are showing up all over town; to avoid getting fooled, buy in reputable shops.

9 c-8

ALCONE

Although primarily a supplier of theatrical makeup, Alcone has become popular with models, actresses, and makeup artists, who come for brands not found in other stores. *235 W. 19th St. (between 7th and 8th Aves.), Chelsea, 212/633–0551. Subway: C, E to 23rd St.*

11 c-4

AVEDA

Aveda offers European hair and skin-care products, makeup, bath preparations, and home fragrance, all made with natural ingredients. Tired of shopping? The Spring Street and West Broadway stores also offer massages and facials. *233 Spring St. (between 6th Ave. and Varick St.), West Village, 212/807– 1492. Subway: C, E to Spring St.*

11 d-4

456 W. Broadway (between Prince and Houston Sts.), SoHo, 212/473–0280. Subway: Broadway–Lafayette St.

9 d-8

140 5th Ave. (at 19th St.), Flatiron District, 212/645–4797. Subway: N, R to 23rd St.

9 e-3

509 Madison Ave. (between 52nd and 53rd Sts.), Midtown, 212/832–2146. Subway: E, F to 5th Ave.

11 e-1

THE BODY SHOP

This hugely successful toiletry chain has cheery shops citywide. The fragrant, all-natural products come in recyclable packaging, do not pollute the water, and have not been tested on animals—and in addition to saving the earth, they cleanse, polish, and protect the skin and hair. For a full list of locations call 800/ 541–2535. *747 Broadway (near Astor Pl.), East Village, 212/979–2944. Subway: 8th St.; Astor Pl.*

9 d-6

Manhattan Mall, 901 6th Ave. (at 33rd St.), Garment District, 212/268–7424. Subway: 34th St./Herald Sq.

9 e-2

773 Lexington Ave. (at 61st St.), Upper East Side, 212/755–7851. Subway: 59th St./Lexington Ave.

7 b-8

2159 Broadway (at 76th St.), Upper West Side, 212/721–2947. Subway: 79th St.

9 e-2

BOYD CHEMISTS

Boyd sells a dazzling array of European makeup and treatment products in addition to their own line, and now also has a salon facility for haircuts, facials, and waxing. Experts-in-residence give beauty advice, makeup demonstrations, lessons, and encouragement to further ensure this is a mecca for beautiful people and wannabes alike. Oh, and they still fill prescriptions. *655 Madison Ave. (near 60th St.), Upper East Side, 212/838– 6558. Subway: 59th St./Lexington Ave.*

9 e-2

CAMBRIDGE CHEMISTS

The fine British toiletries here include Floris of London, Penhaligons, Cyclax, Innoxa, Sabona of London, and Simpson (shave brushes), and extend to French, Swiss, and German items. *21 E. 65th St. (near Madison Ave.), Upper East Side, 212/734–5678. Subway: 68th St./Hunter College.*

9 *e-4*

CASWELL-MASSEY CO.

In business since 1752, Caswell-Massey is the oldest apothecary in the United States. (The original store was in Newport, Rhode Island.) The cologne specially blended for George and Martha Washington and Lafayette, the cold cream made for Sarah Bernhardt, and the world's largest collection of imported soaps—including pure Castile by the pound—are all for sale in this pretty and fragrant shop. Also on offer: one-of-a-kind silver jars and wood and faux-ivory brushes. *518 Lexington Ave. (at 48th St.), Midtown, 212/755–2254. Subway: 42nd St./Grand Central.*

10 *d-6*

World Financial Center, Battery Park City (West and Liberty Sts.), Lower Manhattan, 212/945–2630. Subway: World Trade Ctr.

10 *d-1*

C. O. BIGELOW CHEMISTS

A pharmacy the way pharmacies used to be, Bigelow's has been in the same place since 1838, but its stock has changed with the times. Besides the usual items, the store has a huge selection of homeopathic remedies, various cosmetics (especially European), a nice array of toiletries, and makeup accessories. *414 6th Ave. (between 9th and 10th Sts.), Greenwich Village, 212/533–2700. Subway: W. 4th St./Washington Sq.*

9 *e-4*

COSMAIR BEAUTY RESPONSE CENTER

Anyone willing to test new fragrances and cosmetics from well-known manufacturers can get free products here. Make an appointment, fill out a profile, and, if accepted, go home to evaluate the products and come back to report the results. Guinea pigs receive a gift after each visit. *575 5th Ave. (at 47th St.), 8th floor, Midtown, 212/984–4164. Subway: B, D, F, Q to 42nd St.; E, F to 5th Ave.*

9 *f-3*

COSMETIC SHOW

This shop is a true find—if you can find it, as there are no obvious signs. Go to the building entrance, but don't go inside; look left and you'll see some doors, one with a sign reading "Cosmetics." Voilà! Inside, bargains abound on name-brand products. *919 3rd Ave. (at 56th St.), Midtown, 212/750–8418. Subway: 59th St./Lexington Ave.*

9 *d-5*

COSMETICS PLUS

Cosmetics Plus has one of the largest selections of cosmetics and fragrances in the city, all at discounted prices. *518 5th Ave. (near 43rd St.), Midtown, 212/221–6560. Subway: B, D, F, Q to 42nd St.*

9 *d-7*

275 7th Ave. (at 26th St.), Chelsea, 212/727–0705. Subway: 1, 9, C, E to 23rd St.

9 *e-3*

515 Madison Ave. (near 53rd St.,), Midtown, 212/644–1911. Subway: 51st St./Lexington–3rd Aves.

9 *d-3*

666 5th Ave. (between 52nd and 53rd Sts.), Midtown, 212/757–2895. Subway: E, F to 5th Ave.; and other locations.

9 *d-4*

CRABTREE & EVELYN

England's famed all-natural toiletries and comestibles are beautifully packed and presented for a touch of luxury. Gift baskets can be made to order. *Rockefeller Center Promenade (620 5th Ave., between 49th and 50th Sts.), Midtown, 212/581–5022. Subway: 47th–50th Sts./Rockefeller Ctr.*

9 *e-3*

520 Madison Ave. (at 53rd St.), Midtown, 212/758–6419. Subway: E, F to 5th Ave.

10 *e-6*

151 World Trade Center (Church and Vesey Sts.), concourse level, Lower Manhattan, 212/432–7134. Subway: World Trade Ctr.

7 *e-6*

1310 Madison Ave. (at 93rd St.), Upper East Side, 212/289–3923. Subway: 4, 5, 6 to 96th St.

11 *e-3*

CREED

Now is your opportunity to live like royalty. Simply stop by this 240-year-old British import and purchase one of the custom fragrances the perfume house has created for nobles ranging from George III to Queen Victoria. In addition, there are literally hundreds of other scents to choose from. *9 Bond St. (between Broadway and Lafayette St.), NoHo, 212/228–1940. Subway: Bleecker St.*

9 *c-1*

FACE STOCKHOLM

A household name in Sweden, Face offers fabulous makeup in seasonally changing palettes. Trendy lipstick and nail-polish shades are especially popular. *224 Columbus Ave. (at 71st. St.), 212/769–1420. Subway: 72nd St.*

11 *e-4*

110 Prince St. (at Greene St.), SoHo, 212/334–3900. Subway: Prince St.

9 *d-7*

FIFTH AVENUE PERFUMES, INC.

Make the trip for discounted prices—in the 50% range!—on popular fragrances normally found in high-end stores. *246 5th Ave. (at 28th St.), Murray Hill, 212/213–9321. Subway: N, R to 28th St.*

7 *e-7*

FRESH

A buffet of quirky bath and body products, from craveable chocolate-milk soap to a more diet-conscious sounding soy lotion. *1061 Madison Ave. (at 82nd St.), Upper East Side, 212/396–0344. Subway: 4, 5, 6 to 86th St.*

11 *d-5*

57 Spring St. (between Lafayette and Mulberry Sts.), Nolita, 212/925–0099. Subway: 6 to Spring St.

9 *e-2*

IL MAKIAGE

An Upper East Side trendsetter, Il Makiage has more than 200 eye and cheek colors and updates them seasonally. Makeover programs range from an elementary eye primer to a full makeup consultation and are really quite special. *107 E. 60th St. (between Park and Lexington Aves.), Upper East Side, 212/371–3992. Closed Sat. Subway: 59th St./Lexington Ave.*

9 *e-8*

JAY'S PERFUME BAR

This stretch of 17th Street has several small, no-frills, down-and-dirty discount fragrance shops. Don't expect great service, but do expect great deals. *14 E. 17th St. (between 5th Ave. and Union Sq. W), Flatiron District, 212/243–7743. Subway: N, R to 23rd St.; F to 14th St.*

10 *f-1*

KIEHL'S PHARMACY

Since 1851 this fascinating pharmacy, now a New York institution, has carried a large selection of pure essences, perfumes, homeopathic remedies, and cosmetics, and all-natural ingredients for remedies to cure whatever ails you. The store makes all of its own products on the premises, including the "Age Deterrent" cream. Alas, they no longer carry leeches, but they do stock more than 300 different treatments for hair, body, skin, and nails. The staff is both knowledgeable and helpful and distributes handfuls of samples. *109 3rd Ave. (near 13th St.), East Village, 212/677–3171 or 212/475–3698. Subway: 3rd Ave.*

7 *e-8*

LAURA GELLER MAKEUP STUDIOS

A former makeup artist on Broadway, Geller will make you up, give you a makeup lesson, sell you her own products, and make up your wedding party when the time comes. *1044 Lexington Ave. (at 74th St.), Upper East Side, 212/570–5477. Subway: 77th St.*

9 *e-4*

L'OCCITANE

Stepping into one of these boutiques is like crossing the threshold into Provence. Lovely soaps, shampoos, and body creams are scented with lavender, thyme, and a host of other herbs. Beautiful packaging make items from here especially well-received gifts. *510 Madison Ave. (at 48th St.), Midtown, 212/826–5020. Subway: E to 5th Ave.*

11 *d-5*

146 Spring St. (at Wooster St.), SoHo, 212/343–0109. Subway: 6 to Spring St.

9 *b-2*

198 Columbus Ave. (near 69th St.), Upper West Side, 212/362–5146. Subway: 66th St./Lincoln Ctr.

11 *c-1*

M.A.C

M.A.C., Make-Up Art Cosmetics, was created by makeup artist Frank Toskan in 1984. The popular products are vitamin-enriched, contain no mineral oil or fragrance, are not tested on animals, are extraordinarily long-lasting, and come in a variety of textures as well as tints—

and the store recycles the containers (six empties and you get a free lipstick). It's geared toward makeup professionals, but clients include Cher, Madonna, Gloria Estefan, and Paula Abdul. *14 Christopher St. (near 6th Ave.), West Village, 212/243–4150. Subway: Christopher St./Sheridan Sq.*

11 *d-4*

113 Spring St. (near Wooster St.), SoHo, 212/334–4641. Subway: C, E to Spring St. Closed Mon.

11 *d-4*

MAKE-UP FOREVER

Hip and happening makeup keeps downtowners happy—even if they now live uptown. *409 W. Broadway (between Spring and Prince Sts.), SoHo, 212/941–9337. Subway: C, E to Spring St.*

9 *e-3*

Michel Beauty Salon, Trump Tower (725 5th Ave., at 56th St.) Midtown, 212/757–5175. Subway: E, F to 5th Ave.

9 *d-8*

THE MAKEUP SHOP

Led by makeup artist Tobi Britton, The Makeup Shop offers makeovers, makeup lessons, eyebrow shaping, and a whole line of products. *131 W. 21st St. (between 6th and 7th Aves.), Chelsea, 212/807–0447. Subway: F, 1, 9 to 23rd St.*

9 *e-3*

MARY QUANT

A legend in London for her daring makeup colors made famous during the swinging 60s, the still funky, but somewhat subdued, queen of mod has recently opened this, her first retail outlet in the States. There are rainbows of colors for eyes, lips, cheeks, and nails: try a fuchsia eye shadow, one of 120 shades available. *520 Madison Ave. (between 55th and 56th Sts.), Midtown, 212/980–7577. Subway: N, R to 5th Ave.*

11 *d-4*

ORIGINS

This user-friendly SoHo store features exclusively Origins products: soaps, oils for massage and bath, lotions, aromatherapy, skin treatments, and related accessories. *402 W. Broadway (at Spring St.), SoHo, 212/219–9764. Subway: C, E to Spring St.*

11 *d-1*

PATRICIA FIELD

These are the raw materials for the downtown avant-garde look—nonsmudge matte liners, matte lipsticks and lip pencils, lip paint from Japan. Even your mother won't recognize you. Note: The SoHo store is called Hotel Venus, but it's still the funky Pat Field that you know and love. *10 E. 8th St. (near 5th Ave.), East Village, 212/254–1699. Subway: 8th St., Astor Pl.*

11 *d-5*

382 W. Broadway (between Broome and Spring Sts.), SoHo, 212/966–4066. Subway: C, E to Spring St.

11 *e-1*

PERFUMANIA

The nationwide chain stocks hundreds of fragrances, from high-end designer scents to the more obscure. They promise an average discount of 70%. *755 Broadway (at 8th St.), Greenwich Village, 212/979–7674. Subway: 8th St.*

9 *d-6*

20 W. 34th St. (between 5th and 6th Aves.), Garment District, 212/736–0414. Subway: 34th St./Herald Sq.

9 *e-2*

782 Lexington Ave. (between 60th and 61st Sts.), Upper East Side, 212/750–2810. Subway: 59th St./Lexington Ave.

7 *b-7*

2321 Broadway (at 84th St.), Upper West Side, 212/595–8778, Subway: 1, 9 to 86th St.; other locations.

11 *e-2*

RICKY'S

A wall of brushes, rainbows of hair color, plastic containers from mini to maxi, a house makeup line—Mattesse—that bears a striking resemblance to M.A.C. and Bobbie Brown, and incredibly low prices make these stores a must stop for beauty mavens in the know. *718 Broadway (at Washington Pl.), West Village, 212/979–5232. Subway: 8th St.*

9 *c-3*

988 8th Ave. (at 58th St.), Midtown West, 212/957–8343. Subway: 59th St./Columbus Circle.

11 *e-1*

44 E. 8th St. (at Greene St.), West Village, 212/254–5247. Subway: 8th St.

`10` *d-1*

466 6th Ave. (between 11th and 12th Sts), West Village, 212/924–3401. Subway: F, L, Q to 14th St.

`11` *e-5*

590 Broadway (between Houston and Prince Sts.), SoHo, 212/226–5552. Subway: Prince St.

`11` *e-5*

SEPHORA

You'll feel like a kid in a candy store at this French import beauty emporium; the front has the dazzling jewel tone signature line of bath products, candles, and aromatherapy oils. In back, hip homespun makeup lines and scrumptious beauty imports from around the globe. Along the walls is an exhaustive collection of perfumes in alphabetical order. Dig in! *555 Broadway (between Prince and Spring Sts.), SoHo, 212/625–1309. Subway: Prince St.*

`9` *e-4*

636 5th Ave. (between 50th and 51st Sts.), Midtown, 212/245–1633. Subway: 47th–50th St./Rockefeller Ctr.

`10` *d-6*

204 World Trade Center Mall (in World Trade Center), Tribeca, 212/432–1311. Subway: Cortlandt St.; World Trade Ctr.

`11` *d-5*

SHU UEMURA

On of the most popular Asian beauty lines, the store carries a nice selection of skin care products and makeup. Light simulators let you test how your color choices will look in office light or daylight. *121 Greene St. (between Prince and Houston Sts.), SoHo, 212/979–5500. Subway: Prince St.*

`9` *e-2*

TRISH MCEVOY

While you can buy the luxe makeup line bearing her name at top department stores, this is the only spot where intense one on one lessons with the master, or one of her personally trained staff, are available. Prices with McEvoy are incredibly steep, but the other makeup artists here are quite skilled as well. The price of a lesson ($200 and up) includes all makeup used on you; applications for special events are also available. *800A 5th Ave. (near 61st St.), Upper East Side, 212/758–7790. Subway: N, R to 5th Ave.*

hair care

New Yorkers know that hair is an important accessory, and that it can cost a fortune in upkeep. What many don't know is that almost every high-end salon has a training night at least once a month, when haircuts and color are either greatly discounted or free. The catch is that a student cuts your hair, but the proceedings are highly supervised, and you never know who that student will be in three years.

Note that many salons are closed on Monday.

`9` *d-3*

ANGELA COSMAI

Cosmai is the premier colorist in the city, dying the locks of socialites and starlets alike in her low-key salon in a Midtown brownstone. Using only plant-based dyes, Cosmai and her staff not only create completely natural and healthy looking color, but also fix a plethora of unfortunate coloring jobs. Other services available include precision haircuts and expert blowouts. All of this expertise does not come cheap, but training nights here are especially good. *16 W. 55th St. (between 5th and 6th*

RUGGED GOOD LOOKS

Men are starting to get equal time at salons and spas throughout the city. Below are a few that go out of their way to make the boys feel at home (see Day Spas in Chapter 3 for addresses):

Avon
> *Great massages and a men's locker room with super-intense multi-head showers.*

Bliss
> *The macho locker rooms here come complete with beer and copies of Sport's Illustrated and the Robb Report.*

Origins
> *A full gym is adjacent to the Spa's locker room so you can combine a workout with some manly primping.*

Peninsula Spa
> *Making great pains to soothe their male clientele, the Spa introduced a men's facial which concentrates on such guy problems as razor burn and ingrown hairs.*

Aves.), 2nd floor, Midtown, 212/541–5820. Subway: B, Q to 57th St.

11 e-1
ASTOR PLACE BARBER STYLIST
Success story: A family-owned 1940s barbershop finds new life as the in place to have your tresses trimmed—if you're young or adventuresome. Choose from the Guido, Detroit, Little Tony, Punk, Mohawk, James Dean, Fort Dix, Sparkle Cut, What-the-Hell, Spike, Spina di Pesce . . . . It's cheap and fun, but you may have to wait up to two hours on weekends. The street scene is interesting in itself. They still give shaves, and now have an annex for perms, manicures, pedicures, facials, and all the rest. 2 Astor Pl. (near Broadway), Greenwich Village, 212/475–9854 or 212/475–9790. Subway: Astor Pl.

9 e-3
FREDERIC FEKKAI BEAUTÉ DE PROVENCE
A fashion-world darling, Fekkai now reigns in his own wonderful salon in the Chanel building, creating elegant, feminine looks in quiet private rooms. Clients include Cindy Crawford, Sigourney Weaver, and Kelly McGillis. 15 E. 57th St. (near Madison Ave.), Midtown, 212/753–9500. Subway: N, R to 5th Ave.

9 d-3
GARREN NEW YORK AT HENRI BENDEL
A fashion-world favorite—he made over Lisa Marie Presley for her Vogue cover shoot—Garren recently opened a full-service salon at Henri Bendel. 712 5th Ave. (at 56th St.), Midtown, 212/841–9400. Subway: N, R to 5th Ave.

9 b-1
GEMAYEL SALON
Gemayel is the Upper West Side choice for fun, trendy cuts at reasonable prices. 2030 Broadway (at 70th St.), Upper West Side, 212/787–5555. Subway: 1, 2, 3, 9 to 72nd St.

9 b-1
HAROLD MELVIN BEAUTY SALON
Specializing in African-American hair, Melvin has built quite a reputation among celebrities, and has done hair for magazine shoots and movie sets. 137 W. 72nd St. (between Broadway and Colum-

bus Ave.), Upper West Side, 212/724–7700. Subway: 1, 2, 3, 9 to 72nd St.

9 e-7
JEAN LOUIS DAVID
Drop in here for the streamlined, quick-service approach. Designer cuts, styles, perms, and colors take less than an hour and are very reasonably priced. They don't make appointments, but you can wait for your favorite stylist if you want an ongoing relationship. 303 Park Ave. S (at 23rd St.), Gramercy, 212/260–3920. Subway: 6 to 23rd St.

9 e-4
367 Madison Ave. (at 46th St.), Midtown, 212/808–9117. Subway: 42nd St./Grand Central.

9 d-4
1180 6th Ave. (at 46th St.), Midtown, 212/944–7389. Subway: 47th–50th Sts./Rockefeller Ctr.

9 b-1
2113 Broadway (73rd St.), Upper West Side, 212/873–1850. Subway: 1, 2, 3, 9 to 72nd St.; other locations.

10 e-7
JOHN ALLAN'S
A respite for busy Wall Streeters, John Allan is a full-service salon for men only. Between haircuts and manicures, you can mess around with the pool table, drum set, and requisite humidor. 95 Trinity Pl. (at Thames St.), Lower Manhattan, 212/406–3000. Subway: Wall St.

9 d-3
JOHN BARRETT
Ensconced in the penthouse suite at Bergdorf Goodman, Barrett and his staff excel at precision cuts. Barrett makes a point of working on the floor, something other celebrity stylists do very little of—however, a meeting with the master needs to be booked at least a month in advance. 754 5th Ave. (at 58th St.), Midtown, 212/872–2700. Subway: N, R to 5th Ave.

11 d-4
JOHN DELARIA
This busy SoHo salon has three floors of stylists trained in every look from classic to au moment. Walk-ins are usually accommodated, and prices are reasonable. 433 W. Broadway (between Prince and Spring Sts.), SoHo, 212/925–4461. Subway: C, E to Spring St.

11 *d-6*

JOHN MASTERS ORGANIC HAIRCARE

Masters and his colleagues specialize in color, using only plant- and vegetable-based dyes at this shoe-box downtown salon. *79 Sullivan St. (near Canal St.), SoHo, 212/343–9590. Subway: A, C, E to Canal St.*

9 *d-3*

LINDA TAM SALON

Chosen for "Best Hair Coloring" by New York Press, Linda Tam is not cheap, but followers swear to a no-nonsense color job that won't fade after a few washes. *680 5th Ave. (between 53rd and 54th Sts.), Midtown, 212/757–2555. Subway: E, F to 5th Ave.*

9 *e-1*

LOUIS LICARI COLOR GROUP

For blended tone-on-tone coloring and a beautifully healthy, natural look, he's the tops—just ask Christie Brinkley, Ellen Barkin, or Jessica Lange. Ask also about training nights, for huge discounts on cut or color. Come in for a free consultation weekdays 9–5. *797 Madison Ave. (near 67th St.), Upper East Side, 212/517–8084. Subway: 68th St./Hunter College.*

9 *c-8*

MARIO NICO

Velvet settees, marble floors, and gold mirrors help lend an air of elegance to this small salon in Chelsea. Nico himself is a lot like the clientele, fashionable and hip but without an attitude. Prices are quite reasonable considering the surroundings and the level of expertise. *266 W. 22nd St. (between 8th and 9th Aves.), Chelsea, 212/727–8464. Subway: C, E to 23rd St.*

9 *e-2*

MARSHALL KIM

Kim is a favorite neighborhood barber with Upper East Siders. *788 Lexington Ave. (at 61st St.), Upper East Side, 212/486–2453. Subway: 59th St./Lexington Ave.*

9 *e-3*

ORIBE SALON LTD.

Now firmly ensconced behind Elizabeth Arden's red door, Oribe is booked months in advance. He's usually at photo shoots—you know, tending the models' tresses. This is the trendiest

salon in town for individual, feminine-sexy looks like those of Kelly Klein, Darryl Hannah, and Linda Evangelista. *691 5th Ave. (at 54th St.), Midtown, 212/319–3910. Subway: E, F to 5th Ave.*

11 *a-1*

PERRY WEST

There's always a wait—but a fun one—for chatty and fun owner Bentley Rand, formerly of Bumble & Bumble, who gives cuts and colors in a cozy West Village setting. *55 Greenwich Ave. (at Perry St.; enter on Perry), West Village, 212/463–0387. Subway: Christopher St./Sheridan Sq.*

9 *e-3*

PIERRE MICHEL COIFFEUR

A longtime specialist in the treatment and styling of long hair, Pierre Michel is also a full-service beauty salon for both men and women. *Trump Tower (725 5th Ave., at 56th St.), Midtown, 212/593–1460. Subway: N, R to 5th Ave.*

9 *d-3*

Plaza Hotel, 5th Ave. and 59th St., Midtown, 212/593–7930. Subway: N, R to 5th Ave.

11 *a-1*

ROBERT KREE

This light, airy, open West Village salon gives great cuts that turn first-time clients into loyal devotees. It looks trendy, but there's no attitude. *375 Bleecker St. (between Charles and Perry Sts.), West Village, 212/989–9547. Subway: Christopher St./Sheridan Sq.*

11 *c-4*

SPACE

The space makes the experience at this SoHo salon. The high ceilings and enormous windows fill the place with light, creating a serenity that's pervasive. Whether you've come for a simple cut, expert color, or a Brazilian bikini wax—for which beautician Ceia Creme is well known—you'll leave feeling pampered. *155 6th Ave. (at Spring St.), SoHo, 212/647–8588. Subway: C, E to Spring St.*

9 *c-8*

SUITE 303

Everything about this salon says cool—from its location in the notorious Chelsea Hotel, to its unmarked door, to its hip clientele of downtown rockers and models. Any of the stylists can give you a great cut, but only April can sculpt your eyebrows to perfection. *Chelsea Hotel, Room 303, 222 W. 23rd St. (between 7th and 8th Aves.), Chelsea, 212/ 633–1011. Subway: 1, 9 or C, E to 23rd St.*

9 *e-2*

VIDAL SASSOON

The man who liberated hair now has 32 stylists and a helpful staff, providing cuts, color, and perms for both men and women. *767 5th Ave. (at 59th St.), Midtown, 212/535–9200. Subway: N, R to 5th Ave.*

10 *d-1*

90 5th Ave. (at 15th St.), Flatiron District, 212/229–2200. Subway: 14th St./Union Sq.

9 *d-3*

WARREN TRICOMI

Downtown style comes uptown in this fanciful full-service salon, with a regular clientele including many celebs who trust the flying blades of Edward "Scissorhands" Tricomi. *16 W. 57th St. (between 5th and 6th Aves.), Midtown, 212/262–8899. Subway: N, R to 5th Ave.*

BICYCLES

9 *c-7*

DIFFERENT SPOKES

A fireman and a tie salesperson teamed up with one of New York's best bike mechanics to open this crackerjack shop. Ask any bike messenger about the quality of the repairs. You get all the best brands, great service, and generous opening hours. *240 7th Ave. (at 24th St.), Chelsea, 212/727–7278. Subway: 1, 9 to 23rd St.*

10 *h-4*

FRANK'S BIKE SHOP

Frank sells and repairs. The stock includes Schwinn, GT, Giant, Ross, Bianchi, Mongoose, Raleigh, and Diamond. *533 Grand St. (near Lewis St.), Lower East Side, 212/533–6332. Subway: Grand St.; Delancey St.*

10 *f-1*

METRO BICYCLE STORES

Metro sells a complete line of performance parts, accessories, and clothing for racing, touring, and road, mountain, and city biking. They also rent bikes and do expert repairs. *332 E. 14th St., East Village, 212/228–4344. Subway: 1st Ave.*

9 *c-4*

360 W. 47th St., Theater District, 212/581– 4500. Subway: N, R to 49th St.

7 *e-6*

1311 Lexington Ave. (at 88th St.), Upper East Side, 212/427–4450. Subway: 4, 5, 6 to 86th St.

7 *b-5*

231 W. 96th St. (at Broadway), Upper West Side, 212/663–7531. Subway: 1, 2, 3, 9 to 96th St.; other locations.

BOOKS

general

11 *c-1*

BARNES & NOBLE, INC.

Long a downtown institution, Barnes & Noble has lately sprouted superstores all over the city. Some branches have specialties; the store that started it all, on lower 5th Avenue, has an excellent selection of textbooks, and the Lincoln Square branch keeps its eye on the performing arts. The stores bring in big names and talented younger writers for regularly scheduled readings. *105 5th Ave. (at 18th St.), Flatiron District, 212/ 807–0099. Subway: 14th St./Union Sq.*

9 *d-8*

675 6th Ave. (at 22nd St.), Chelsea, 212/ 727–1227. Subway: 1, 9 to 23rd St.

9 *f-3*

Citicorp Center (3rd Ave. and 54 St.), Midtown, 212/750–8033. Subway: 51st St./Lexington–3rd Aves.

11 *e-8*

4 Astor Pl. (between Broadway and Lafayette St.), Greenwich Village, 212/ 420–1322. Subway: Astor Pl.

9 *b-2*

1972 Broadway (at 66th St.), Upper West Side, 212/595–6859. Subway: 66th St./Lincoln Ctr.; and other locations.

9 *e-3*

BORDERS BOOKS & MUSIC

What was once a cozy Ann Arbor independent is now very much a part of the New York landscape. The World Trade Center store is a hive of activity downtown, and the newer branch on Park Avenue adds some literary interest to an otherwise quiet stretch. The selections are vast and dense, the chain's resources excellent. As long as you've got stamina, it's hard to beat Borders for a healthy mixture of quantity and quality. *461 Park Ave. (at 57th St.), Midtown, 212/980–6785. Subway: 59th St./Lexington Ave.*

10 *d-6*

5 World Trade Center (Church and Vesey Sts.), Lower Manhattan, 212/839–8049. Subway: Cortlandt St./World Trade Ctr.

9 *c-3*

COLISEUM BOOKS, INC.

Large, well-located, well-stocked, and well-run, Coliseum is great for current paperbacks, hardcovers, reference books, and a good variety of remainders. *1771 Broadway (at 57th St.), Midtown, 212/757–8381. Subway: 59th St./Columbus Circle.*

7 *e-6*

THE CORNER BOOKSTORE

This welcoming Carnegie Hill shop specializes in literature, art, architecture, and children's books. They'll fill special orders in one day, search for out-of-print titles, and gift-wrap your choices for free. An Upper East Side perk: house accounts, even for children. *1313 Madison Ave. (at 93rd St.), Upper East Side, 212/831–3554. Subway: 6 to 96th St.*

9 *d-4*

GOTHAM BOOK MART AND GALLERY

Once a literary mecca, the Gotham Book Mart endures. It's particularly strong in theater, general literature (especially fiction and classics), 20th-century first editions, film, and philosophy, and has the city's largest selection of poetry. For those with arcane requirements, the store gets a whopping 250 literary and small-press magazines. *41 W. 47th St., Midtown, 212/719–4448. Subway: 47th–50th Sts./Rockefeller Ctr.*

9 *e-1*

LENOX HILL BOOKSTORE

Among the many strengths of this shop is the fabulous fiction section. They often have signed editions of hot new hardbacks. *1018 Lexington Ave. (between 72nd and 73rd Sts.), Upper East Side, 212/472–7170. Subway: 6 to 77th St.*

9 *d-4*

MCGRAW-HILL BOOKSTORE

This shop specializes in business, engineering, and computer science titles

from various publishers. It's located two levels below ground in a subterranean arcade; easiest access is from the lobby of 1221 6th Avenue. *1221 6th Ave. (between 48th and 49th St.), Midtown, 212/512–3456. Subway: 47th St./Rockefeller Ctr.*

9 *d-3*

RIZZOLI

Rizzoli is famously strong in art, architecture, photography, and university-press titles, but people of letters can also pick up Italian books, translations, foreign magazines and newspapers, and classical recordings. *31 W. 57th St. (Sohmer Bldg., between 5th and 6th Aves.), Midtown, 212/759–2424. Subway: B, Q to 57th St., N, R to 5th Ave.*

11 *d-4*

454 W. Broadway (near Prince St.), SoHo, 212/674–1616. Subway: C, E to Spring St.

10 *d-6*

3 World Financial Center, Battery Park City (at Vesey St.), Lower Manhattan, 212/385–1400. Subway: World Trade Ctr.

10 *f-1*

ST. MARK'S BOOKSHOP

One of the hippest bookstores in the city, St. Mark's focuses on the humanities of the moment, including literature, poetry, drama, criticism, women's studies, contemporary theory, foreign titles, and small-press offerings. Spoken-word records and tapes are also on hand. *31 3rd Ave. (at 9th St.), East Village, 212/260–7853. Subway: Astor Pl.*

11 *e-1*

SHAKESPEARE & COMPANY

They have a good selection of fiction, poetry, philosophy and general nonfiction titles, but the staff has a little too much attitude. *716 Broadway (at Washington Pl.), Greenwich Village, 212/529–1330. Subway: 8th St.*

9 *e-1*

939 Lexington Ave. (between 68th and 69th Sts.), Upper East Side, 212/570–0201. Subway: 68th St./Hunter College.

9 *8-f*

137 E. 23rd St. (between Lexington and 3rd Aves.), Gramercy, 212/220–5199. Subway: 6 to 23rd St.

10 *8-e*

1 Whitehall St. (between Bridge and Stone Sts.), Lower Manhattan, 212/742–7025. Subway: Bowling Green.

10 *e-1*

THE STRAND

America's largest secondhand bookstore has 8 mi of books (that's 2 million titles)—in appropriately dusty quarters in its main Greenwich Village store. Head downstairs for review copies of new books at 50% off. History, art, and Americana are particular strengths, both new and used. Warning: You'll spend more time and money than you intended. *828 Broadway (at 12th St.), Greenwich Village, 212/473–1452. Subway: 14th St./Union Sq.*

10 *f-7*

95 Fulton St. (between William and Gold Sts.), Lower Manhattan, 212/732–6070. Subway: 2, 3 to Fulton St.

10 *d-1*

THREE LIVES & CO.

Three women own this lovely bookshop, named for the Gertrude Stein work and dedicated to literature. Salon readings by noted authors are a special feature. *154 W. 10th St. (between 6th and 7th Aves.), West Village, 212/741–2069. Subway: Christopher St./Sheridan Sq.*

11 *f-2*

TOWER BOOKS

Tower is a good downtown browsing spot (the store stays open until midnight) and holds the usual author readings, signings, and special events. The discount scheme is very competitive. *383 Lafayette St. (at 4th St.), Greenwich Village, 212/228–5100. Subway: 8th St.*

antiquarian

9 *d-8*

ACADEMY BOOK STORE

This shop specializes in art, literature, history, photography, the social sciences, and out-of-print books. *10 W. 18th St. (between 5th and 6th Aves.), 212/242–4848. Subway: F to 14th St.*

7 *b-7*

GRYPHON BOOKSHOP

This general-interest used bookstore has a large selection of soft- and hardcover titles on the arts and humanities, as well as a small but impressive cookbook collection. *2246 Broadway (between 80th and 81st Sts.), Upper West Side, 212/362–0706. Subway: 79th St.*

9 *d-3*

J.N. BARTFIELD

Bartfield has one of the most impressive collections of leather-bound books, rare books, and first editions in the city, and will appraise collections. *30 W. 57th St. (between 5th and 6th Aves.), 3rd floor, Midtown, 212/245–8890. Subway: B, Q to 57th St.; N, R to 5th Ave.*

9 *d-8*

LARRY LAWRENCE RARE SPORTS

Larry specializes in rare sports books and ephemera. He no longer has an office but will make house calls to show you his wares. *212/362–8593. Open by appt. only.*

9 *d-7*

OLD PAPER ARCHIVE

It's as quaint as it sounds, and carries antique prints, children's books, movie posters, and antique prints on the performing arts. *122 W. 25th St. (between 6th and 7th Aves.), Chelsea, 212/645–3983. Subway: F, 1, 9 to 23rd St.*

special interest

9 *b-1*

APPLAUSE THEATER AND CINEMA BOOKS

Applause concentrates on film and theater books and also carries a small selection of audio and video tapes. *211 W. 71st St. (between Broadway and West End Ave.), Upper West Side, 212/496–7511. Subway: 1, 2, 3, 9 to 72nd St.*

10 *c-1*

BIOGRAPHY BOOKSHOP

True to its name, this appealing West Village shop specializes in biographies, diaries, and autobiographies as well as select fiction. *400 Bleecker St. (at 11th St.), West Village, 212/807–8655. Subway: Christopher St./Sheridan Sq.*

7 *b-6*

BLACK BOOKS PLUS

African-American history, art, literature, and general studies prevail. *702 Amsterdam Ave. (at 94th St.), Upper West Side, 212/362–7229. Subway: 1, 2, 3, 9 to 96th St.*

9 d-8

BOOKS OF WONDER

This is the largest collection of new, used, and out-of-print children's books in the city. The selection of 19th- and early-20th-century picture books and the knowledgeable staff are added draws. *16 W. 18th St. (between 5th and 6th Aves.), Chelsea, 212/989–3270. Subway: F to 14th St.*

9 d-7

CENTER FOR BOOK ARTS

It's kind of meta: Here are books on the book arts, including binding and printing, and classes teaching the techniques. *28 W. 27th St. (between Broadway and 6th Ave.), 3rd floor, 212/460–9768. Subway: N, R, 1, 9 to 28th St.*

10 e-1

CHESS BOOKS

Yes, it's an entire store full of new and used books on chess, as well as chess-playing equipment. The store also offers weekly children's classes and lectures for adults. *80 E. 11th St. (at Broadway), Suite 334, Greenwich Village, 212/533–6381. Subway: 8th St.; Astor Pl.*

9 b-1

CIVILIZED TRAVELLER

Everything you might need for a civilized trip, beginning with videos, maps, and guidebooks and moving on to irons, coffeemakers, security devices, converters, binoculars, games, and specialty luggage. *2003 Broadway (at 68th St.), Upper West Side, 212/875–0306. Subway: 66th St./Lincoln Ctr.*

9 e-2

864 Lexington Ave. (at 65th St.), Upper East Side, 212/288–9190. Subway: 68th St./Hunter College; and other locations.

9 e-6

COMPLEAT STRATEGIST

The stock covers military and war games, science fiction, and fantasy. *11 E. 33rd St. (between 5th and Madison Aves.), Midtown, 212/685–3880. Subway: 33rd St.*

9 e-6

THE COMPLETE TRAVELLER BOOKSTORE

This attractive Murray Hill shop is devoted to travel. In the first room, pick up guidebooks, maps, and dictionaries for the destination of your choice; in the second, browse hungrily among the used and rare travel books, including well-loved, yellowing travelogues and original WPA guides. New travel literature, posters, and art books round out the mix. It's worth a trip. *199 Madison Ave. (at 35th St.), Murray Hill, 212/685–9007. Subway: 33rd St.*

9 d-8

A DIFFERENT LIGHT BOOKSTORE

These books were written by and for gays and lesbians, covering everything from gay and lesbian studies and the social sciences to erotica and travel. *151 W. 19th St. (between 6th and 7th Aves.), Chelsea, 212/989–4850. Subway: 18th St.*

9 d-4

DRAMA BOOK SHOP

The Drama Book Shop is well known for its extensive and well-organized selection of theater (especially criticism), film, and TV titles and published plays. You can also hunt down vocal scores and selections from Broadway musicals. *723 7th Ave. (near 48th St.), 2nd floor, Theater District, 212/944–0595. Subway: N, R to 49th St.*

10 d-1

EAST-WEST BOOKS

True to its name, this spiritual book store carries titles on Buddhism, Christianity, and pretty much everything in between. *78 5th Ave. (near 14th St.), Flatiron District, 212/243–5994. Subway: F to 14th St.*

9 c-7

FASHION INSTITUTE OF TECHNOLOGY BOOKSTORE

The bookstore of the prestigious fashion college covers all aspects of the industry, including design and marketing. *227 W. 27th St. (between 7th and 8th Aves.), A-Building lobby. Garment District, 212/217–7717. Subway: 1, 9 to 28th St.*

9 d-3

HACKERS ART BOOKS

This large specialty shop has old, new, and rare titles on art, architecture, and crafts, and reprints of important art books. *45 W. 57th St. (between 5th and 6th Aves.), 5th floor, Midtown, 212/688–7600. Subway: B, Q to 57th St.*

7 *e-6*

JEWISH MUSEUM BOOKSHOP

Selections cover all aspects of Jewish history and culture. *1109 5th Ave. (at 92nd St.), Upper East Side, 212/423–3211. Closed Sat. Subway: 6 to 96th St.*

9 *d-4*

KINOKUNIYA BOOKSTORE

Kinokuniya is one of the largest book-store chains in Japan. These two floors of books in Japanese cover every topic imaginable; you'll also find books about Japan in English. *10 W. 49th St. (between 5th and 6th Aves.), Midtown, 212/765–1461. Subway: 47th–50th Sts./Rockefeller Ctr.*

7 *e-6*

KITCHEN ARTS & LETTERS

For the cook in your life, Kitchen Arts & Letters has books from all over on food, cooking, and wine; food ephemera; orig-inal art and photography of food; and stationery items with a culinary theme. *1435 Lexington Ave. (near 93rd St.), Upper East Side, 212/876–5550. Closed Sun. Sub-way: 6 to 96th St.*

7 *b-3*

LABYRINTH BOOKS

This relative newcomer to New York's dwindling roster of independent book-shops (the store opened in 1997) carries academic titles, many from university presses, as well as scholarly remainders and fiction. *536 W. 112th St. (near Amsterdam Ave.), Morningside Heights, 212/865–1588. Subway: 110th St./Cathe-dral Pkwy.*

10 *d-1*

LECTORUM

This store specializes in Latin American fiction, nonfiction and magazines, all in the original Spanish. *137 W. 14th St. (between 6th and 7th Aves.), Chelsea, 212/741–0220. Subway: 1,2,3,9 to 14th St.*

9 *d-4*

LIBRAIRIE DE FRANCE

An excellent source for French and Spanish books, this shop stocks new releases, dictionaries, cookbooks, mys-teries, history and social science titles, as well as literary fiction. *6105 5th Ave. (in the Rockefeller Center Promenade), Midtown, 212/581–8810. Subway: 47th–50th Sts./Rockefeller Ctr.*

7 *e-6*

THE MILITARY BOOKMAN

Sure enough, the selection focuses on military, naval, and aviation history, including out-of-print and rare books. *29 E. 93rd St. (between 5th and Madison Aves.), Upper East Side, 212/348–1280. Closed Sun.–Mon. Subway: 4, 5, 6 to 96th St.*

9 *d-7*

MILLER'S

Miller's has been a leading source of equestrian books, riding apparel and saddles for 75 years. *117 E. 24th St. (between Park and Lexington Aves.), Gramercy, 212/673–1400. Subway: 6 to 23rd St.*

9 *f-2*

MURDER INK

If you can't get enough of mystery and suspense novels, Murder Ink has them new, used, and out-of-print. *2486 Broad-way (between 92nd and 93rd Sts.), Upper West Side, 212/362–8905. Subway: 1, 2, 3, 9 to 96th St.*

9 *d-3*

MYSTERIOUS BOOKSHOP

New, used, and out-of-print murder, mystery, and mayhem are the selling points; the staff will also search for rare books. Mystery paraphernalia adds a graphic touch. *129 W. 56th St. (between 6th and 7th Aves.), Midtown, 212/765–0900. Closed Sun. Subway: B, Q, N, R to 57th St.*

9 *e-5*

NEW YORK ASTROLOGY CENTER

A complete line of astrology books is supplemented by titles on acupuncture and the healing arts. *370 Lexington Ave. (at 41st St.), Suite 416, Midtown, 212/949–7211. Subway: 42nd St./Grand Cen-tral.*

11 *e-5*

NEW YORK OPEN CENTER BOOKSHOP

The selection here includes holistic medicine, Eastern studies, health and nutrition, and meditation. *83 Spring St. (between Broadway and Crosby Sts.), SoHo, 212/219–2527. Subway: 6 to Spring St.*

`11` a-2

OSCAR WILDE MEMORIAL BOOKSHOP

Specializing in gay and lesbian titles, this shop also sells stationery, cards, records, films, T-shirts, and jewelry. *15 Christopher St. (between 6th and 7th Aves.), West Village, 212/255–8097. Subway: Christopher St./Sheridan Sq.*

`10` d-1

PARTNERS & CRIME MYSTERY BOOKSELLERS

For the serious aficionado, this downtown shop has new, used, and antique books on crime, mystery, espionage, and the like. *44 Greenwich Ave. (between 6th and 7th Aves.), West Village, 212/243–0440. Subway: F, 1, 2, 3, 9 to 14th St.*

`10` e-3

PERIMETER BOOKS ON ARCHITECTURE

Perimeter's collection focuses on architecture and design. *21 Cleveland Pl. (near Spring St.), SoHo, 212/334–6559. Subway: 6 to Spring St.*

`11` e-4

A PHOTOGRAPHER'S PLACE

This may be the city's best selection of photography books, both new and used. *133 Mercer St. (between Prince and Spring Sts.), SoHo, 212/431–9358. Subway: Prince St.; 6 to Spring St.*

`11` d-3

SCIENCE FICTION SHOP

True to its name, this store carries science fiction, horror, and fantasy titles, including rare and used books. *214 Sullivan St. (between Bleecker and W. 3rd Sts.) Greenwich Village, 212/473–3010. Subway: W. 4th St./Washington Sq.*

`10` e-7

TRINITY BOOKSTORE

Come here for a curious combination of financial and religious books. *74 Trinity Pl. (near Rector St.), Lower Manhattan, 212/349–0376. Closed weekends. Subway: Rector St.*

`9` e-4

URBAN CENTER BOOKS

Run by the Municipal Art Society, Urban Books specializes in architecture, urban design and planning, and historic preservation. *457 Madison Ave. (near 51st St.), Midtown, 212/935–3595. Closed Sun. Subway: 51st St./Lexington–3rd Aves.*

BUTTONS

Most button and notions shops are in the West 30s between 5th and 6th avenues, and on 6th Avenue between 34th and 39th streets.

`9` c-5

GORDON BUTTON CO.

Think about it: Ten million buttons and buckles in 5,000 varieties, from classic to novelty, from 10¢ to $2 each—and lo, service with a smile. *222 W. 38th St. (between 7th and 8th Aves.), Garment District, 212/921–1684. Closed weekends. Subway: 34th St./Herald Sq.*

`9` e-2

TENDER BUTTONS

This special shop displays every kind of button imaginable, including sets of old and rare buttons and antique buckles and cufflinks. Prices range from 25¢ to $3,500. *143 E. 62nd St. (between Lexington and 3rd Aves.), Upper East Side, 212/758–7004. Closed Sun. Subway: 59th St./Lexington Ave.*

CANDLES

Candles have become so popular that almost every gift, home-furnishings, or department store has a selection. These stores sell candles exclusively.

`11` d-5

ANGELIC

Votives in a rainbow of colors are arrayed like the offerings in a candy shop in this tiny

SoHo storefront. *160 Spring St. (at W. Broadway), SoHo, 212/334–3039. Subway: Spring St.*

`11` b-2

CANDLE SHOP

It's the best, with candles in every color, shape, and size for every occasion, and holders in which to plunk them. *118 Christopher St. (near Bleecker St.), West Village, 212/989–0148. Subway: Christopher St./Sheridan Sq.*

9 *d-8*

CANDLESHTICK

If you can picture it, they carry it. Feast your nose on the scented candles, and your eyes on the candlesticks and decorative votives. *181 7th Ave. (between 20th and 21st Sts.), Chelsea, 212/924–5444. Subway: 1, 9 to 23rd St.*

7 *b-6*

2444 Broadway (between 90th and 91st Sts.), Upper West Side, 212/787–5444. Subway: 1, 2, 3, 9 to 93rd St.

10 *f-1*

ENCHANTMENTS, INC.

This is the best selection of specifically inexpensive candles downtown, from votives to tapers to columns to those already poured into a jar. *341 E. 9th St. (between 2nd and 1st Aves.), East Village, 212/228–4394. Subway: 8th St./Astor Pl.*

11 *d-6*

LEMON GRASS

In addition to delightfully scented candles in sizes from tiny votive to giant four-wick table centerpieces, the store also sells whimsical soaps. *367 W. Broadway (at Broome St.), SoHo, 212/343–0900. Subway: 6 to Spring St.*

CLOTHING FOR WOMEN/GENERAL

conservative

9 *e-2*

AQUASCUTUM OF LONDON

The funny name derives from the Latin for "water shield," and that's what this very British firm does best. A lined raincoat—trench-style, of course—can run over $600. But there is bait beyond the trench coat, such as the quilted silk or microfiber short jackets or the "Voyager," a microfiber raincoat that compactly self-zips into a pouch. (Far better than packing a collapsible umbrella.) Country-home-appropriate clothes go the proper route of long pleated skirts, traditional blazers, and knitwear. Triple-digit price tags are the norm. *714 Madison Ave. (between 63rd and 64th Sts.), Upper East Side, 212/753–8305. Subway: 59th St./Lexington Ave.*

9 *e-5*

BROOKS BROTHERS

The women's clothes in this menswear bastion are often variations on old-boy standards. Women can snag cotton polos (about $35), loafers, and men's-style, French-cuff dress shirts (about $60), plus such demure separates as pleated skirts and silk or merino wool twinsets. The Madison Avenue branch has a larger selection; the Fifth Avenue store beckons the younger set with glass and chrome instead of dark wood and thick carpeting. *346 Madison Ave. (at 44th St.), Midtown, 212/682–8800. Subway: 42nd St./Grand Central.*

10 *e-6*

1 Church St. (Liberty Plaza), Lower Manhattan, 212/267–2400. Subway: World Trade Ctr.

9 *e-4*

666 Fifth Ave. (at 53rd St.), Midtown, 212/261–9440. Subway: 47th–50th St./Rockefeller Ctr.

9 *e-3*

BURBERRY

With a sports-mad house designer, Burberry's functional aspects are still going strong—with a rising temperature. Motorcycle influences speed up the jackets and pants; trench coats come in gunmetal gray. The trademark oversize plaid still comes in familiar forms, too, making up pleated kilts (about $200) and lining trench coats (over $1,000). *9 E. 57th St. (between 5th and Madison Aves.), Midtown, 212/371–5010. Subway: E, F, N, R to 5th Ave.*

9 *d-3*

ESCADA

Everything in this store appears to have a high-gloss polish, from the gold-tone railings to the buttons and sequins to the bright colors on the racks (royal purple, taxicab yellow). Suits are nicely shaped, and skirts are normally just above the knee; even the few denim items look tailored. *7 E. 57th St. (between 5th and Madison Aves.), Midtown, 212/755–2200. Subway: E, F, N, R to 5th Ave.*

7 *c-8*

LAURA ASHLEY

The Upper West Side shop is the last New York bastion of this squeaky-clean clothier. Downstairs are the mother-and-child lines and home furnishings; upstairs is a small selection of casual clothes, often in—yes—floral patterns. But this isn't a merciless flood of old-fashioned cabbage roses; there are pin-dot blouses, long madras or striped dresses, and versatile pastel separates. Still, a straw hat would go well with almost anything except the nightgowns. *398 Columbus Ave. (at 79th St.), Upper West Side, 212/496–5110. Subway: 79th St.*

7 *e-8*
NORIKO MAEDA
This ultrafeminine store—perfumed air, silver tea service—is the designer's only post outside Japan. Some suits seem to be nodding to Audrey Hepburn, with their three-quarter-length sleeves and matching purses. Most start around $1,000 and can go up to more than double that. *985 Madison Ave. (between 76th and 77th Sts.), Upper East Side, 212/717–0330. Subway: 77th St.*

9 *e-3*
ST. JOHN
Owing more than a little to Chanel, this designer's suits are often two-tone with quarter-size gold buttons; others have a whiff of the nautical about them. Classic look notwithstanding, most fabrics have a certain percentage of rayon. *665 5th Ave. (at 53rd St.), Midtown, 212/755–5252. Subway: E, F to 5th Ave.*

contemporary

11 *f-4*
A DÉTACHER
"To be detached," they call themselves, but it's easy to fall for these spare, knowing designs. Dresses, skirts, and tops are tweaked with off-kilter gathers, pleats, and seams; most cost the same as a good pair of shoes. *262 Mott St. (between Prince and Houston Sts.), Nolita, 212/625–3380. Subway: Bleecker St. or Broadway/Lafayette.*

10 *f-7*
ABERCROMBIE & FITCH
Wholesome and urbanely rugged (lots of plaid, woolly sweaters, flannel shirts), this chain tweaks its apple-pie image by finding excuses to show nude young men in its print ads. It also has the audacity to make a point of not producing any all-black clothes. *110 Water St. (at Fulton St.), Lower Manhattan, 212/809–9000. Subway: Fulton St.*

11 *e-4*
AGNÈS B.
These stores feel more authentically French than a squashed beret. The French adoration for the "7th art," i.e., the movies, is indulged with posters (Godard, not Spielberg) and the occasional T-shirt proclaiming "j'aime le cinéma." The separates are low-key but flatteringly cut; seasonal staples are, naturally, in black and white. With its small but choice range of shoes, filmy scarves, and even makeup, this line could outfit you completely, without making you a cookie cutter. Just remember not to pronounce the "g" when you tell people where you got those trim pants. *116 Prince St. (between Greene and Wooster Sts.), SoHo, 212/925–4649. Subway: Prince St.*

7 *e-7*
1063 Madison Ave. (between 80th and 81st Sts.), Upper East Side, 212/570–9333. Subway: 77th St.

9 *d-8*
13 E. 16th St. (between Union Sq. and 5th Ave.), Chelsea, 212/741–2585. Subway: F to 14th St.

7 *e-8*
ALICIA MUGETTI
This store gives new meaning to the concept of the flowered silk dress. The softly hued silk, often crinkled, is embroidered or exquisitely hand-painted. Many of the gauzy items need to be layered. *999 Madison Ave. (between 77th and 78th Sts.), Upper East Side, 212/794–6186. Subway: 77th St.*

11 *d-4*
186 Prince St. (at Sullivan St.), SoHo, 212/226–5064. Subway: Prince St.

9 *e-2*
ANN TAYLOR
Like a good hardware store, Ann Taylor has nearly everything on hand for a quick fix-it. You can put together a very presentable boardroom outfit in no time, from crisp white blouse to hose; all you need to bring from home are your skivvies. A tidy skirt suit runs about $400; put it together with an embroidered shell or merino wool sweater and you're set. Many items are dosed with rayon, but those that aren't are still reasonably priced, like the silk blouses for under $100. The Madison Avenue location is the biggest; four stories tall, it's got an entire floor for petites. The Loft

store (150 E. 42 St., at Lexington Ave., tel. 212/883–8766; 1492 3rd Ave., at 84th St., tel. 212/472–7281; 1155 3rd Ave., at 68th St., tel. 212/772–9952) carries only the more casual lines. *645 Madison Ave. (at 60th St.), Upper East Side, 212/832–2010. Subway: 59th St./Lexington Ave.*

9 *b-1*

2015–2017 Broadway (at 69th St.), Upper West Side, 212/873–7344. Subway: 72nd St.

9 *e-4*

850 3rd Ave. (at 52nd St.), Midtown, 212/308–5333. Subway: 51st St./Lexington–3rd Aves.; other locations.

11 *e-4*

ANNA SUI

Anna Sui is not a designer opposed to rhinestones. Her purple-and-black SoHo boutique is bedecked with neon posters of alternative bands (Hole, the Beastie Boys) to match the rock-star clothes. Fringe, glitter, and suede make regular appearances; dresses, often with swirly takes on 70s themes, ring up to a couple hundred. If you're not up to this, try the tongue-in-cheek silk-screened T-shirts, some with rock-poster takeoffs, one with an image of James Iha of the Smashing Pumpkins. *113 Greene St. (between Spring and Prince Sts.), SoHo, 212/941–8406. Subway: Prince St.*

11 *d-5*

ANNE FONTAINE

A Parisian staple now making its way onto the East Coast, Anne Fontaine is the antidote to men's-style white shirts. Snowy rows play with the classic button-down, giving it laced cuffs, oversized mother-of-pearl buttons, white-on-white embroidery, or a gathered neckline. Most are in the $150–$200 range, and there are a few styles in black. *93 Greene St. (between Prince and Spring Sts.), SoHo, 212/343–3154. Subway: Prince St.*

9 *e-2*

791 Madison Ave. at 67th St., 212/639–9651.

11 *e-1*

ANTIQUE BOUTIQUE

Shifting its focus from vintage to decidedly modern, this place almost belies its name. Browse innovative designs from the futuristic to the funkily deconstructed; labels are both local and international. But head to the back and you can still find carefully chosen vintage pieces (helpfully labeled as such) ranging

from Lee western-style shirts to silver-spangled disco tops. Plus, they showcase collector-quality denim from Levi's to Sergio Valente (again, they're ahead of the curve). *712 Broadway (between Astor Pl. and E. 4th St.), Greenwich Village, 212/995–5577. Subway: Astor Pl.*

11 *d-5*

ANTHROPOLOGIE

You won't be surprised to hear that this store is a corporate sibling of Urban Outfitters. It lures those who have outgrown patchouli oil and butterfly chairs with the same basic layout: not-too-serious housewares, not-too-fancy clothes. Trends are mellower here than at Urban; a crinkly silk or batik-print skirt could be paired with a crochet cardigan, for instance. Prices are moderate if not college-student-cheap: about $80 for an embroidered shirt or a parachute-fabric skirt. *375 W. Broadway (between Broome and Spring Sts.), SoHo, 212/343–7070. Subway: 6 to Spring St.*

10 *e-1*

85 5th Ave., at 16th St., Flatiron District, 212/627–5885. Subway: 14th St./Union Sq.

11 *e-4*

A.P.C.

This place is for dressed-down starlets on a first-name basis with Sophia Coppola. Make your way across the rough-hewn, slightly warped floorboards to the hanging racks of ultracool French simplicity: straight-leg pants (starting around $110), cotton poplin shirts, indigo jeans, khakis, and the like. Most are in neutral, solid colors, but there are occasional outbursts—orange or eggplant cotton velvet, for instance. *131 Mercer St. (between Prince and Spring Sts.), SoHo, 212/966–0069. Subway: Prince St.*

11 *e-4*

ARMANI EXCHANGE

This "casual essentials" fiefdom of the Armani empire provides the requisite blond-wood, high-ceiling environment. The beige, black, and denim staples are occasionally punctuated with an interesting green or blue. Those anxious to donate free chest advertising will find plenty of A/X-logo T-shirts and sweaters. *568 Broadway (at Prince St.), SoHo, 212/431–6000. Subway: Prince St.*

9 *e-4*

645 5th Ave. (at 51st St.), Midtown, 212/980–3037. Subway: 47th–50th St./Rockefeller Ctr. or 51st St./Lexington–3rd Aves.

11 *d-5*
BAGUTTA
The labels sound like Barneys: John Galliano, Alexander McQueen, Ann Demeulemeester, Chloé. But you won't have to rack-rake so strenuously in this SoHo space; they've winnowed out choice bits for you, like a mink-tipped Dolce & Gabbana jacket or svelte knits and suits by Narcisco Rodriguez. *402 W. Broadway (between Spring and Broome Sts.), SoHo, 212/925–5216. Subway: 6 to Spring St.*

9 *e-4*
BANANA REPUBLIC
England and France may have balked, but Banana Republic has fully embraced the Euro. The rhino T-shirts are fully extinct; look instead for slim black suits, leather coats, and filmy neck scarves. As the most sophisticated sector of the Gap enterprise, Banana Republic gets to dabble in black-and-white photos and curvy cologne bottles. Technofibers may come and go, but you can depend on lightweight wool trousers (about $130), velvet tops (polyester), and little-boy tees for $20. The khaki selection is blessedly less complicated than the Gap's; the fabric has a tad more heft, as does the price tag. If this keeps up, the store may have to change its name to something in a romance language. *626 5th Ave. (at 50th St.), Midtown, 212/974–2350; Menswear only: 655 5th Ave. (at 52nd St.), Midtown, 212/644–6678. Subway: E, F to 5th Ave.*

7 *e-7*
1136 Madison Ave. (between 84th and 85th Sts.), Upper East Side, 212/570–2465. Subway: 4, 5, 6 to 86th St.

9 *e-3*
130 E. 59th St. (at Lexington Ave.), Midtown, 212/751–5570. Subway: 59th St./Lexington Ave.

11 *e-5*
Women's only: 552 Broadway (between Prince and Spring Sts.), SoHo, 212/925–0308. Subway: Broadway/Lafayette; and other locations.

11 *d-5*
BARBARA BUI
Thanks to this Parisian designer we can inch closer to that mythically cool, aloof, City of Light elegance—at least from the outside. Long, lean silhouettes are achieved with stretchy wool pants and close-fitting jackets. Textures are also appealing; a cowl-neck top with a built-in waist pack is done in downy fleece, while a jacket could be made of silk bonded with resin. For the ultimate hands-off trip, choose one of the shirts vacuum-packed in plastic. *115 Wooster St. (between Prince and Spring Sts.), SoHo, 212/625–1938. Subway: Prince St. or C, E to Spring St.*

9 *e-2*
BCBG
This French acronym for "bon chic bon genre" is almost the equivalent of WASP—but there's nary an oxford shirt in sight. BCBG was one of the first "casual" designers to crash the couture-show circuit with catwalks of its own. Besides carrying many New York standbys (black technofiber pants, cashmere sweaters, slip dresses, all generally in the $150–$250 range), it throws in some fun pieces, such as an embroidered or beaded skirt or a shearling wrap. A smaller offshoot at 744 Madison (tel. 212/794–7124) focuses on the higher-end items. *770 Madison Ave. (at 66th St.), Upper East Side, 212/717–4225. Subway: 68th St./Hunter College.*

11 *d-4*
BETSEY JOHNSON
A branch may have opened in swanky SoHo, but these stores retain their sense of humor. Most still have their signature hot-pink interiors, but the downtown boutique is a sunny yellow splashed with crimson flowers, with a boudoir-y lounging room in back. Most designs get a sexy twist; schoolgirl plaid becomes a bustier, flowered dresses get lingerie straps and a clingy cut. *138 Wooster St. (between Prince and Houston Sts.), SoHo, 212/995–5048. Subway: Prince St.; Broadway/Lafayette.*

9 *c-1*
248 Columbus Ave. (between 71st and 72nd Sts.), Upper West Side, 212/362–3364. Subway: 72nd St.

9 *f-2*
251 E. 60th St. (between 2nd and 3rd Aves.), Upper East Side, 212/319–7699. Subway: 59th St./Lexington Ave.

7 *e-7*
1060 Madison Ave. (between 80th and 81st Sts.), Upper East Side, 212/734–1257. Subway: 77th St.

10 g-2
BLUE

Blue is a godsend for those whose budget doesn't quite equal their taste: it has simple and classy cocktail dresses, more-formal styles, and even bridal gowns. You can have anything made to order—all this without a stuffy attitude or a hefty price tag. *125 St. Mark's Pl. (between 1st Ave. and Ave. A), East Village, 212/228–7744. Subway: Astor Pl.*

11 f-3
BOND 07

The awesomely offbeat clothes—wacky shirts by Custo, Fake cashmere sweaters—can make most people happy. But the store comes into its own with its tantalizing, out-of-the-ordinary accessories: purses by Louison and Patch, quirky hats, glamour sunglasses, playful shoes. Stock is often limited, so don't hesitate over your purchases. *7 Bond St. (between Lafayette St. and Broadway), Greenwich Village, 212/677–8487. Subway: Astor Pl.*

11 f-4
CALYPSO

Born on St. Barthélemy, Calypso has found a cozy niche in Nolita and is starting to move uptown. Snug cashmere sweaters; fringed, embroidered shawls; and long, full, raw silk skirts come in equatorial colors: orchid, deep pink, peacock blue. Sequined bikinis and delicate slip dresses beg you to take them back to the Caribbean. *280 Mott St. (between Prince and Houston Sts.), East Village/Little Italy, 212/965–0990. Subway: Bleecker St.*

11 e-6

424 Broome St. (between Crosby and Lafayette Sts.), Chinatown, 212/274–0449. Subway: Spring St.

7 e-8

935 Madison Ave. (between 74th and 75th Sts.), Upper East Side, 212/535–4100. Subway: 77th St.

11 d-6
CATHERINE

Catherine's first major style impact was its magnification of the cowboy hat trend—they suddenly had people wearing them in purple or dalmation. Now things such as buttercup yellow leather shorts, hot pink frilled skirts, retro embroidered flowers, and fringed tops continue to dollop insouciance on the fashion landscape. *468 Broome St. (at Greene St.), SoHo, 212/925–6765. Subway: Spring St.*

9 d-8
CLUB MONACO

Club Monaco gear won't break your wallet or make your mother cringe. Clothes circle around neutrals with a few accent colors, making things easier for the matching-impaired. The styles pick up just enough trends to be interesting, and can still work for the office or dinner out. Weigh your choices, though: $50 for a straight twill skirt sounds good, but $40 for a rayon or tricot cotton tank is a bit much. *160 5th Ave. (between 20th and 21st Sts.), Chelsea, 212/352–0936. Subway: F to 23rd St.*

9 f-2

1111 3rd Ave. (at 65th St.), Upper East Side, 212/355–2949. Subway: 68th St./Hunter College.

7 b-7

2376 Broadway (at 87th St.), Upper West Side, 212/579–2587. Subway: 1, 9 to 86th St.

11 e-5

520 Broadway (at Spring St.), SoHo, 212/941–1511. Subway: 6 to Spring St.

11 e-4
COSTUME NATIONAL

A glowing white display case separates the men's and women's racks here—a rare streak of light in an otherwise murky store. Black rules the vampy night-crawler selection, with a few things such as a pea-green python jacket or dark purple leather standing out against inky knit dresses, faux fur, and low-slung pants. *108 Wooster St. (between Spring and Prince Sts.), SoHo, 212/431–1530. Subway: C, E to Spring St.*

9 f-2
CP SHADES

This company projects a "natural fibers" image, and in a way it lives up to it—if you consider chemically processed wood pulp (a.k.a. rayon) natural. Linen and cotton crop up on the labels too, though, and the stock turnover is brisk. Styles tend to be loose and drapey, colors subdued. *1119 3rd Ave. (between 65th and 66th Sts.), Upper East Side, 212/759–5710. Subway: 68th St./Hunter College.*

11 *d-4*

154 Spring St. (between Wooster St. and W. Broadway), SoHo, 212/226–4434. Subway: Spring St.

9 *c-1*

300 Columbus Ave. (at 74th St.), Upper West Side, 212/724–9474. Subway: B, C to 72nd St.

11 *d-4*

CYNTHIA ROWLEY

This is not Fran Liebowitz territory. Cynthia Rowley's shop is lined with simply cut dresses, both short and long, often in silk, eyelet lace, or mildly retro printed cotton. There are pants, too, but you're more likely to find cigarette or capri cuts than classic trousers. Colors are cheerful—buttercup yellow, bottle green, candy pink. Even the dressing rooms are upbeat; step inside, and the curtain is covered with "you're so pretty" exclamations. Prices generally fall in the $150–$250 range. 112 Wooster St. (between Prince and Spring Sts.), SoHo, 212/334–1144. Subway: Prince St.

11 *d-4*

D&G

Glamourpusses Dolce & Gabbana spin ideas for their "Young Collection" off their couture lines. Leopard prints, lingerie straps, crochet, and black are as present here as at the designer store, but with less detail and a lower (if not exactly low) price tag. 434 W. Broadway (between Spring and Prince Sts.), SoHo, 212/965–8000. Subway: C, E to Spring St.

9 *e-3*

DANA BUCHMAN

These dressy separates can often be worn for years without looking dated or staid. Try a ruby silk suit or a square-neck sweater and notice the thoughtful tailoring touches, such as a bra-strap securer in a tank-style shell. Stylized floral or batik designs show up often on long dresses or wrap skirts. A good stock of petites is in back. 65 E. 57th St. (between Park and Madison Aves.), Midtown, 212/319–3257. Subway: 59th St. or N, R to 5th Ave.

11 *f-1*

DARYL K

This designer's goal is to make your sit-down look good in a pair of jeans. This may well happen if you have the hips of a 12-year-old boy. The signature jeans

(over $100) tend to have a short rise and skinny legs; try the slacks if you need something higher-waisted. (Grab the jacket too and you've got a very downtown suit.) For something cheaper, such as a kangaroo-pocket sweatshirt or graffiti-print Ts, look for the K-189 label. 208 E. 6th St. (between 2nd and 3rd Aves.), East Village, 212/475–1255. Subway: Astor Pl.

11 *f-3*

21 Bond St. (between Lafayette St. and Bowery), East Village, 212/777–0713. Subway: Bleecker St., 2nd Ave.

9 *e-2*

DIESEL

With the washing machine–like windows and an in-house DJ, the Lexington Avenue superstore pitches to the hip. The SoHo space may be much smaller, but it carries a good cross-section of the street style lines. At $100 or more, the jeans may give you pause, but at least they give you plenty of options, with men's, women's, and unisex fits of varying degrees of bagginess, flare, and denim darkness. More intriguing are the new fabrics, such as "TK1 irony" with metallic fibers or "sunfit," which absorbs UV rays and deflects heat. 770 Lexington Ave. (at 60th St.), Upper East Side, 212/308–0055. Subway: 59th St./Lexington Ave.

11 *d-5*

416 W. Broadway (between Prince and Spring Sts.), SoHo, 212/343–3863. Subway: C, E to Spring St.

9 *e-3*

DKNY

Donna Karan's hotly anticipated hometown flagship store finally opened in time to lure the fall 1999 shoppers. As a breathlessly hip lifestyle store, it's been likened to a three-ring circus. Indeed, what with all the shiny décor happening on the ground floor, it can be hard to concentrate; the eye skips from designer chairs to motorcycles to healing incense. Upstairs you can circulate among the various women's lines with fewer distractions. Sprinkled among the DKNY labels you'll find individual vintage pieces; for instance, a lace dress or 1930s sequined bolero jacket could hang among the crisp white shirts or black cashmere sweaters. This approach hits the nail on the head—it answers the ultimate fashion-plate demand by providing both designer "essentials" and unique items that no one else has. The clothing and furniture/home accessories/whatever stock changes rapidly, catering to those who are constantly on the fashion make. Will this fast-paced, constant-diversion strategy succeed? Stay tuned. *655 Madison Ave. (at 60th St.), Upper East Side, 212/223–3569. Subway: 59th St./Lexington Ave.*

11 *f-2*
DOLLHOUSE

For trendy, low-priced sportswear, these are good pickings—especially if you've made stretch viscose your friend. Flood pants and capris for under $50, short dresses for under $75, sparkly tube tops, and little-girl blouses make for light-hearted impulse buys. *400 Lafayette St. (at E. 4th St.), Greenwich Village, 212/ 539–1800. Subway: Astor Pl.*

11 *d-4*
DOSA

This store's modest size actually works for it, and it's in keeping with the serene, Eastern-influenced designs. Flourishes are kept to a minimum, but not a bare minimum—a pair of silk pants could gather into a drawstring, or a silk blouse could be made up in iridescent green/gold. *107 Thompson St. (at Spring St.), SoHo, 212/431–1733. Subway: C, E to Spring St.*

11 *d-5*
EILEEN FISHER

Cinched waists will never happen at Eileen Fisher. Her comfortably fluid dresses and skirts are lifesavers during a New York summer. *395 W. Broadway (between Broome and Spring Sts.), SoHo, 212/431–4567. Subway: Spring St.*

9 *e-3*
521 Madison Ave. (at 53rd St.), Midtown, 212/759–9888. Subway: E, F to 5th Ave.

7 *e-8*
1039 Madison Ave. (at 79th St.), Upper East Side, 212/879–7799. Subway: 77th St.

7 *c-8*
341 Columbus Ave. (at 76th St.), Upper West Side, 212/362–3000. Subway: 72nd St.

9 *e-8*
103 5th Ave. (at 17th St.), Chelsea, 212/ 924–4777. Subway: F to 14th St., N, R to 23rd St.

9 *e-2*
EMILIO PUCCI

Yes, it's the original. Ring the bell, walk up the pink-carpet stairs, and you'll find yourself surrounded by the timelessly psychedelic swirls of Pucci's dresses, scarves, blouses, even bikinis. The color palette is often a late-'60s time capsule: pink-and-purple combinations, or yellow-and-almost-avocado. *24 E. 64th St. (between Madison and 5th Aves.), Upper East Side, 212/752–4777. Subway: 68th St./Hunter College.*

9 *e-3*
EMPORIO ARMANI

It's funny how after half an hour here, you start thinking of white as a dazzling color. Somber tones dominate just about every season's palette, but think of it this way: dark colors hide spots, so they'll make great traveling clothes. Armani's way with a suit jacket is still obvious in this midrange label; the soft shoulders and plush fabrics are hard to resist, though you'll pay for the privilege of giving in. Fittingly discreet handbags, shoes, and accessories are also available. *601 Madison Ave. (between 57th and 58th Sts.), Midtown, 212/317–0800. Subway: 59th St./Lexington Ave.*

9 *d-8*
110 5th Ave. (at 16th St.), Chelsea, 212/ 727–3240. Subway: F to 14th St.

7 *e-8*
EN SOIE

Come here when you need an immediate pick-me-up. The playfulness of the interior (colorful bibelots everywhere; small, fanciful antlered heads in the dressing rooms) belies a very serious raison d'être: exquisite silk. There are blouses, scarves, even bolts of it, all beautifully textured; the original Swiss house that provided fabric to Dior. A silk taffeta blouse can run about $240, a long, full, raw silk skirt about $340. *988 Madison Ave. (at 77th St.), Upper East Side, 212/717–7958. Subway: 77th St.*

9 *e-2*
ETRO

The sartorial Italians have scored another hit with these softly exotic designs. The trademark paisley curls around scarves, evening trousers, and swimsuits; blouses and dresses are soaked with rich colors (deep blue, plum, russet). Even traditional button-downs are tweaked—perhaps striped with vertical wavy lines or layered three-deep. *720 Madison Ave. (between 63rd and 64th Sts.), Upper East Side, 212/317-9096. Subway: 68th St./Hunter College.*

9 *d-4*

FRENCH CONNECTION

A mix of lightning-speed runway steals and wardrobe staples in vivid hues, the (British) French Connection is at best a quick fix. Most choices are reasonably priced, at about $50 for a boxy, wool V-neck sweater, roughly $100 for flat-front pants; a long linen sundress; or a beaded, fine-spun wool cardigan. However, something is generally left to be desired—a little too sheer here, a little too tight there. There are plenty of Ts, often with a dash of Lycra, though you may have to put up with a variant of their wink-wink "fcuk" logo. *1270 6th Ave. (at 51st St.), Midtown, 212/262-6623. Subway: 47th-50th St./Rockefeller Ctr.*

11 *e-2*

700 Broadway (at E. 4th St.), Greenwich Village, 212/473-4486. Subway: 8th St.

11 *d-4*

435 W. Broadway (at Prince St.), SoHo, 212/219-1197. Subway: Prince St.

7 *c-8*

304 Columbus Ave. (between 74th and 75th Sts.), Upper West Side, 212/496-1470. Subway: 72nd St.

9 *e-3*

GAP

It's hard to go six blocks without running into one of these look-alike student-wardrobe chains. With stacks of chinos, cotton Ts and tanks plain and ribbed, button-downs, and straightforward sweaters, it's easy to outfit as Everykid. Finding the right pair of khakis (about $40) or jeans (boy fit to boot cut, sandblasted to indigo, roughly $30–$50) can translate into 45 minutes in the dressing room, but with patience you can emerge victorious. For extra gratification, look for the three magic numbers: the $9.99, $19.99, and $29.99 sale price tags. Larger stores have pajamas, underwear, sweats, toiletries, and perfume—bonus point for the cool cube bottle design. The multistory midtown Fifth Avenue store even has Gap browser stations. *680 Fifth Ave. (at 54th St.), Midtown, 212/977-7023. Subway: 47th-50th St./Rockefeller Ctr.*

9 *d-6*

60 W. 34th St. (Herald Sq.), Garment District, 212/643-8960. Subway: 34th St./Herald Sq.

9 *f-3*

734 Lexington Ave. (at 59th St.), Midtown, 212/751-1543. Subway: 59th St./Lexington Ave.

9 *f-2*

1131–1149 3rd Ave. (between 66th and 67th Sts.), Upper East Side, 212/472-5559. Subway: 68th St./Hunter College; and other locations.

11 *e-5*

GUESS?

Long after contributing to the early designer-jean deluge, Guess? continues to revel in ring-spun denim. Sort through everything from Daisy Duke short-shorts (about $40) and indigo narrow-legs to relaxed-fit jeans ($60–$70-ish) and baggy overalls (about $80). Besides the natural counterparts (white shirts, black leather jackets, shades), there's also plenty of cleavage-hugging spandex (tanks, stretchy button-downs, bikinis). *537 Broadway (between Prince and Spring Sts.), SoHo, 212/226-9545. Subway: Prince St.*

11 *d-5*

HELMUT LANG

A fashionista favorite, this Austrian designer's boutique embodies his detached aesthetic. Freestanding walls segment the stark space. On the racks, stern tailoring is sometimes relieved by soft fabrics (gauze, sheer silk, suede), utilitarian touches (holster bags), or unsettling details (pants with tufted silk at the waistband, extended sleeves). A few colors occasionally break the overriding cream-black-white scheme. But the coolness does not come cheap—trousers run about $500, denim around $300. *80 Greene St. (between Spring and Broome Sts.), SoHo, 212/925-7214. Subway: Spring St.*

9 *e-3*

HENRI BENDEL

Lately, Bendel's has been straddling varied tastes. Younger, trendier lines such as Catherine and Rebecca Danenberg migrate here from downtown, and there are plenty of fun-but-glam accessories to match. Bendel's own clothes are nicely understated, especially their sweaters. On the upper floors you'll find more established designers, such as Michael Kors and Jean-Paul Gaultier. The first-floor cosmetics selection eschews the familiar (no Lancôme, Chanel, or Clinique) for such favorite newcomers as Laura Mercier and Lorac; M.A.C perches in the Gilded Cage. Alas, there's no shoe department, but there is a serene and modern tea room on the second floor; try to get a table by the Lalique windows. *712 5th Ave. (at 56th St.), Midtown, 212/247–1100. Subway: E, F to 5th Ave.*

11 *f-4*
HENRY LEHR
After decamping from Madison, Henry Lehr settled his denim reputation downtown. Fine-wale corduroy jackets from Katayone Adeli, Fake cashmere sweaters, and embroidered jeans make good, if not inexpensive, casualwear. Another storefront up the street (268 Elizabeth St.) provides the necessary T-shirts—low-cut James Perse for about $50, retro designs from Jet—plus an accessory or two, such as decorated clogs. *232 Elizabeth St. (between Houston and Prince Sts.), Nolita, 212/274–9921. Subway: Bleecker St.*

9 *e-2*
ICEBERG
This store scratches the dressy-but-not-formal itch with its dresses and separates. Look for uncommon fabrics, such as a watered taffeta coat or laser-pierced leather pants. *772 Madison Ave. (at 66th St.), Upper East Side, 212/249–5412. Subway: 77th St.*

7 *e-8*
INTERMIX
The uptown store made quite an inroad on the Upper East Side: it imported a horde of young, downtown designers. It feels like half of SoHo and Nolita are here: Kate Spade bags and Sigerson Morrison shoes, Helmut Lang jeans, dresses from Tracy Feith and Catherine. *1003 Madison Ave. (between 77th and 78th Sts.), Upper East Side, 212/249–7858. Subway: 77th St.*

9 *e-8*
125 Fifth Ave. (between 19th and 20th Sts.), Chelsea, 212/533–9720. Subway: N, R to 23rd St.

7 *e-8*
ISSEY MIYAKE
Miyake is to polyester what Fortuny was to silk. The bare bones of this shop focus all attention on the uncommon clothes, whose ultratight pleats either cling to the body or form geometric shapes. *992 Madison Ave. (at 77th St.), Upper East Side, 212/439–7822. Subway: 77th St.*

9 *e-8*
J. CREW
Ever the purveyors of rugged East Coast chic, these stores sell everything from the ubiquitous roll-neck sweaters, car coats, and flannels to prettily embroidered sweaters, gabardine suits, and silk button-downs. While they don't carry everything that's in the catalogs you've been getting every three weeks, they do have sales quite often, and after all, there's nothing like instant gratification. *91 5th Ave. (at 17th St.), Chelsea, 212/255–4848. Subway: F to 14th St.; N, R to 23rd St.*

11 *e-4*
99 Prince St. (between Mercer and Greene Sts.), SoHo, 212/966–2739. Subway: Prince St.

9 *d-4*
30 Rockefeller Plaza, Midtown, 212/765–4227. Subway: 47th–50th St./Rockefeller Ctr.

10 *f-7*
203 Front St. (South Street Seaport), Lower Manhattan, 212/385–3500. Subway: Fulton St.

9 *e-5*
J. PETERMAN
You no longer have to use your imagination on the catalog's illustrations—this purveyor of romanticized clothing and doodads has pulled into Grand Central Station. Slink into a Casablanca trench-coat, a Harlowesque silk gown, or a Hepburnian pair of leggy pants. However, you'll have to go back to the catalogs for the Bulwer-Lyttonesque descriptions. *107 E. 42nd St. (between Park and Lexington Aves.), Midtown, 212/370–0855. Subway: 42nd St./Grand Central.*

11 *f-4*
JADE
Toothsome silks with an Asian bent fill the racks: iridescent blouses; frogged, raw silk mandarin dresses (about $125);

even flowered silk purses (roughly $80). *280 Mulberry St. (between Prince and Houston Sts.), Nolita, 212/925–6544. Subway: Broadway/Lafayette.*

10 *b-1*

JEFFREY

On a trip to Jeffrey you could easily run into one of those particularly New York contrasts—in this case, a limo or two pulled up in front of hardbitten delivery trucks. Once inside and up a few stairs you'll be looking at the stuff of a shoe hound's dreams: displays of shoes march straight down the center of the store. They can slake virtually any shoe-thirst, whether it's for velvet slippers, woven slides, spindly heels by Louboutin and Blahnik, or understated flats by Ferragamo or Jil Sander. And, God bless them, they carry a wide range of sizes. The clothing selection is carefully pruned, with tight selections from big guns like Gucci, Helmut Lang, and Josephus Thimister. Keep looking and you'll find some interesting, less-exposed items, like Courrèges shifts or Samsonite shirts. The cosmetics and handbags selections are limited but choice (think Nars and Celine, respectively). *449 W. 14th St. (between Washington St. and 10th Ave.), West Village, 212/206–1272. Subway: A, C, E to 14th St.; L to 8th Ave.*

11 *d-5*

JILL STUART

Now safely ensconced as a young-fashionable favorite, Jill Stuart continues to turn out girlish frocks. Fresh, gauzy, flower-print shells and dresses appear each spring. Standards get the femme treatment, too; blouses could be double-dosed with ruffles, at both cuff and hem, while a beige skirt could have a shocking-pink panel at the bottom. The racks are organized by color, and most items come in a variety of colors, so if you don't like the green or blue, just head over to another section. Price-wise, these clothes are meant for ladies with high credit limits. *100 Greene St. (between Prince and Spring Sts.), SoHo, 212/343–2300. Subway: Prince St.*

9 *e-1*

JOSEPH

Some people call this place "the pants store," and that's not far from the truth. Pants practically dominate the window displays and sprawl their skinny legs on the walls. Virtually everything, be it

denim, cotton, or linen, has a certain amount of stretch, and there are a few unconventional fabrics (such as the shiny, ultra-lightweight "mirror" fabric made of plastic with metal fibers). The 804 Madison Avenue store has tops, too—jackets and shirts with trim lines to match. *804 Madison Ave. (at 68th St.), Upper East Side, 212/570–0077. Subway: 68th St./Hunter College*

9 *e-1*

796 Madison Ave. (at 67th St.), Upper East Side, 212/327–1773. Subway: 68th St./Hunter College.

11 *e-4*

115 Greene St. (between Prince and Spring Sts.), SoHo, 212/343–7071. Subway: Spring St.

9 *e-1*

KENZO BOUTIQUE

You don't have to wait for spring to find flowery clothes at Kenzo. The cheerful colors of the knits and blouses run year-round; suits are usually a bit more subdued. *805 Madison Ave. (between 67th and 68th Sts.), Upper East Side, 212/717–0101. Subway: 68th St./Hunter College.*

11 *d-5*

KIRNA ZABÊTE

Cheerfully dubbing itself "the shangri-la of shopping," Kirna Zabête proves you can grin and still be cutting-edge. While the overall feel is lighthearted (friendly salespeople, candy bins, and purple floors), the selection is seriously high-caliber. Scan the signs above the racks and you'll see a roster of hard-to-find designers: Clements Ribeiro, Josephus Thimister, Olivier Theyskens, Paul Smith. Accessories can be cunning (Lulu Guinness and Anya Hindmarch handbags) or startling (horsehair earrings or horned headbands). Head downstairs and the fun continues with Wink cordouroys, Passion Bait lingerie, and Burberry dog coats. You might even be tempted to show your true colors with an e.vil tee emblazoned "little miss golddigger." Big plus in the dressing rooms: three-way mirrors so you can see the back of that Balenciaga. *96 Greene St. (between Prince and Spring Sts.), SoHo, 212/941–9656. Subway: Prince St.*

11 *f-4*

LABEL

The clothes here have subversion in their seams—whether the designer's ping up edgy Ts or street-smart tops, skirts, and dresses with drawstrings, zippers, or Velcro tabs. Riot grrrls will have a field day. *265 Lafayette St. (between Prince and Spring Sts.), East Village, 212/966–7736. Subway: Prince St.; 6 to Spring St.*

11 *f5*
LANGUAGE

One of the groundbreaking lifestyle stores, Language will quickly convince you that outstanding design is a sort of universal tongue. The conversations around you may be in Japanese or Spanish, but everyone here seems to Get It. The clothing selection is supplemented with ultrastylish nonwearables: Campana chairs and Chinese antiques, Comme des Garçons perfume and the latest edition of *Visionaire*. Yank your attention back to the racks for Chloé separates, touch-me cashmeres by John Bartlett and Language's own line, Earl Jeans leather, and the extensive pashmina selection. *238 Mulberry St. (between Prince and Spring Sts.), Nolita, 212/431–5566. Subway: 6 to Spring St.*

11 *e-3*
LE CHÂTEAU

An excellent place for an unabashed knockoff, or something to wear below 14th Street. They cadge quite well and keep an eye on trends. It's hardly verisimilitude, and prices are low; as an extra nudge, there's some tulle and marabou around the edges. Also look for deals such as a pair of cotton tank tops for $12. *611 Broadway (at Houston St.), Greenwich Village, 212/260–0882. Subway: Broadway–Lafayette St.*

9 *d-6*
34 W. 34th St. (between 5th and 6th Aves.), Garment District, 212/967–0025. Subway: 34th St./Herald Sq.

9 *e-1*
LES COPAINS

The day and evening wear here is so high-quality it's practically Old World. Trouser pockets are perfectly placed, wool is blended with cashmere or silk so it's not itchy—the attentive details add up. (As will the bill; one outfit can break $1,000.) Bear in mind that the cuts run a bit small. For something more casual, seek out the Trend Les Copains line. *807 Madison Ave. (between 67th and 68th Sts.), Upper East Side, 212/327–3014. Subway: 68th St./Hunter College.*

9 *e-3*
LEVI'S

Custom tailoring's not just for suits anymore. At these two stores, you can actually have a pair of jeans tailored with just the right length, width, fly, and slouch; they cost only $15 more than a regular pair and take three weeks to produce. You can even have them shipped to your door. If you'd just like to grab a pair off the stacks, you can choose from flares, slim fit, relaxed fit, and of course, the classic, button-fly 501s (deep blue or broken in). *3 E. 57th St. (just off 5th Ave.), Midtown, 212/838–2188. Subway: E, F, N, R to 5th Ave.*

9 *e-3*
750 Lexington Ave. (at 59th St.), Upper East Side, 212/826–5957. Subway: 59th St./Lexington Ave.

9 *e-2*
LUCA LUCA

A welcome relief from the black-and-beige blahs. Instead of serving as the be-all and end-all, black is used to offset appealing colors, from soft lavender to kelly green. *690 Madison Ave. (at 62nd St.), Upper East Side, 212/755–2444. Subway: 59th St./Lexington Ave.*

7 *e-8*
1011 Madison Ave. (at 78th St.), Upper East Side, 212/288–9285. Subway: 77th St.

9 *e-1*
MALO

The plush cashmere here often appears in an extra-comfortable guise: drawstring pants, tunic-style tops, roomy cardigans. The palette is generally soft: oatmeal, slate gray, dark marine blue. *814 Madison Ave. (at 68th St.), Upper East Side, 212/396–4721. Subway: 68th St./Hunter College.*

11 *d-5*

125 Wooster St. (between Prince and Spring Sts.), SoHo, 212/941–7444. Subway: Prince St.

11 *e-4*

MARC JACOBS

Ah, another bare-bones boutique, this one with men's and women's wear in two separate straight lines. It's hard not to warm to the fabrics, though: divine silk, cashmere, soft wool. Instead of fashion histrionics, you'll find a few quiet quirks, such as an oversized scallop or restrained ruching. To anyone plugged in to fashion, the details are an instant ID. 163 Mercer St. (between Prince and Houston Sts.), SoHo, 212/343–1490. Subway: Prince St.

9 *e-1*

MAXMARA

One of the best "bridge" designers, MaxMara tends to show monochromatic suits enlivened with texture, such as a nubbly tweed or draped wool crepe. Most pieces are in neutrals, but a flash of lipstick-red or primary yellow isn't out of the question. 813 Madison Ave. (at 68th St.), Upper East Side, 212/879–6100. Subway: 68th St./Hunter College.

7 *e-8*

MISSONI

This boutique is almost entirely devoted to knits—the distinctive, multicolor stripes zigzag through mohair, rayon, and wool in scarves, sweaters, long sparkly dresses, even bikinis. The colors can be toned down (gold, beige, and bone) or eye-popping (sharp green, deep purple, and blue). 1009 Madison Ave. (at 78th St.), Upper East Side, 212/517–9339. Subway: 77th St.

9 *e-1*

MÉNAGE À TROIS

Look up at this store's second-story window to catch a glimpse of some very feminine trappings, such as bias-cut skirts or airy ruffled sleeves. In some cases you can custom mix-and-match a particular fabric and dress pattern. 799 Madison Ave. (between 67th and 68th Sts.), Upper East Side, 212/396–2514. Subway: 68th St./Hunter College.

11 *e-4*

MIU MIU

New Yorkers' insatiable hunger for Miuccia Prada's designs won the city the first Miu Miu boutique in North America. Prada trends, such as utility bags and streamlined sport shoes, are put through a funk filter. And corresponding to the shop's younger audience, the prices are relatively lower. The colors can be hard to wear, but there's always black—and a quick stock turnover. 100 Prince St. (between Mercer and Greene Sts.), SoHo, 212/334–5156. Subway: Prince St.

9 *e-2*

MORGANE LE FAY

The strongest influences here are not from this century or even from the last: there are lacings, rows of small mother-of-pearl buttons, and layers of chiffon over silk or wool. Many pieces are in soft grays, ivory, or black, but you can also move into something like wine red or slate blue. The echoing Wooster Street space has a rich selection of the billowing bridal and ball gowns. 746 Madison Ave. (between 64th and 65th Sts.), Upper East Side, 212/879–9700. Subway: 68th St./Hunter College.

11 *d-5*

67 Wooster St. (between Spring and Broome Sts.), SoHo, 212/219–7672. Subway: C, E to Spring St.

11 *d-4*

152 Spring St. (between Wooster St. and W. Broadway), SoHo, 212/925–0144. Subway: C, E to Spring St.

9 *e-3*

NICOLE FARHI

British import Farhi often hits just the right balance of soft-spoken desirability. The store's cool demeanor doesn't slip into sterility; likewise, the sophisticated clothes are warmed up with an inviting texture or flattering cut. A basic jacket or skirt could be done in fuzzy black alpaca; a tweedy blue-black wool makes a fantastic three-quarter-length coat. There are some hard-to-wear colors (orange, a sallow yellow), but plenty of black and neutrals to fall back on. Downstairs are her "lifestyle" choices: glassware and dishes, a few antiques. There's also a restaurant, should you feel peckish. 10 E. 60th St. (between Madison and 5th Aves.), Upper East Side, 212/223–8811. Subway: N, R to 5th Ave.

11 *d-4*

NICOLE MILLER

Instant recognition of a Miller design is almost guaranteed. The designer made her name with funny, themed silk prints. On the flip side of the coin are some simple dresses in solids. *134 Prince St. (between Wooster St. and W. Broadway), SoHo, 212/343–1362. Subway: Prince St.*

9 *e-2*

780 Madison Ave. (between 66th and 67th Sts.), Upper East Side, 212/288–9779. Subway: 68th St./Hunter College.

9 *d-8*

OLD NAVY

Cotton is king here—and cheap. Judging from the big, black supermarket shopping carts, they assume you'll be buying in bulk. Old Navy's own fashion timeline puts them somewhere between the '40s and '50s, but there's scant evidence of this beyond the retro (though multiculturally correct) edge to the mannequins and advertising. Instead, clothes are functional, casual, and vaguely trendy—capri and cargo pants have rack space alongside the Ts. Here's a sampling of what $30 will get you: a fleece vest, a pair of jeans (some under $25!), a couple of thermal shirts or tanks, an Old Navy disco-mix CD, or half a dozen tubes of body glitter. Be sure to scope out the clearance racks— when was the last time you saw a $3.99 price tag in a clothing store? Shoes, unfortunately, are generally unexciting. *610 6th Ave. (at 18th St.), Chelsea, 212/645–0663. Subway: F to 14th St.*

11 *e-5*

503–511 Broadway (between Spring and Broome Sts.), SoHo, 212/226–0865. Subway: 6 to Spring St.

9 *d-6*

150 W. 34th St. (at Broadway), Garment District, 212/594–0049. Subway: 34th St./Herald Sq.

7

300 W. 125th St. (between 8th and St. Nicholas Aves.), Harlem, 212/531–1544. Subway: A, B, C, D to 125th St.

11 *d-1*

PATRICIA FIELD/ HOTEL VENUS

A club kid's answer to the invading SoHo boutiques, these two stores are indefatigable. (Patty Field's is on East 8th, Hotel Venus on West Broadway.)

They're crammed with kitsch accessories, feather boas, rhinestones, drag-queen makeup, and skin-tight anything. The clothes aren't as cheap as you might wish; the best or craziest stuff (fuschia and gold capris, disco mesh halters, polyurethane five-pocket pants) always seems to be way over $50. The T-shirts are lower-priced; many proudly announce up-yours things like "Rude" or "F*ck me I'm famous." The beauty salon (212/598–0395) turns out some awesome dye jobs; leopard-spot is popular. *10 E. 8th St. (between 5th Ave. and University Pl.), Greenwich Village, 212/254–1699. Subway: 8th St.; Astor Pl.*

11 *d-5*

382 W. Broadway (between Spring and Broome Sts.), SoHo, 212/966–4066. Subway: C, E to Spring St.

11 *d-4*

PHILOSOPHY DI ALBERTA FERRETTI

The "you are you" philosophy espoused here happily leads to interesting contrasts: perfectly executed inverted pleats and rough, exposed seams; precise lines of caviar beads and free-form drizzles of rubber; unassuming earth tones and bright hibiscus pink. They normally put out just one example of each piece, so go ahead and ask for other sizes. *452 W. Broadway (between Prince and Houston Sts.), SoHo, 212/460–5500. Subway: Broadway/Lafayette.*

11 *d-5*

PLEATS PLEASE

Even looking in the window of this shop is a high-tech tease—the glass becomes transparent or opaque depending on your angle. Here Here the house of Issey Miyake (*see above*) renders less cerebral variants on the tightly pleated polyester theme. Hues are punchier, with solid colors joined by speckles, color blocks, or graphics, and the designs generally stick to simple long skirts and dresses, tunics, and blouses. Sizing (3, 4, or 5) is based primarily on length, as the pleating will expand to fit your width. Price tags dangle at the several-hundred mark. *128 Wooster St. (at Prince St.), SoHo, 212/226–3600. Subway: Prince St.*

9 *e-1*

POLO/RALPH LAUREN

Lauren's flagship store, ensconced in a grand, beautifully renovated turn-of-the-

20th-century town house, is one of New York's most distinctive shopping experiences. The atmosphere is scrupulously groomed; portraits are clustered over carpeted stairs, polished display cases gleam. The women's clothes run from casual madras shorts and cashmere cable-knits (perfect for the Easthampton bungalow) to glimmering, silk evening gowns (perfect for the Academy Awards). Across the street is another Ralph Lauren boutique, this one modern and glossy, with chiseled, tough-jawed mannequins in the windows. It focuses on casual clothes, sports gear, and vintage pieces Europeans love to snatch up: old denim, motorcycle boots, worn college T-shirts. The latest branch, in SoHo, has an outdoorsy feel (canoes on the ceiling, that sort of thing). The decor may be rough-hewn but the selection isn't—besides the Sport lines and casual clothes, you can weigh a suede skirt, ebony evening separates, or palazzo pants better suited for Bermuda than Maine. *867 Madison Ave. (at 72nd St.), Upper East Side, 212/606–2100; 888 Madison Ave. (at 72nd St.), Upper East Side, 212/434–8000. Subway: 68th St./Hunter College.*

11 *d-5*

379 W. Broadway (between Spring and Broome Sts.), SoHo, 212/625–1660. Subway: C, E to Spring St.

11 *e-5*

QUIKSILVER

The SoCal term "Roxy girls," a.k.a. surfer girls, comes from the women's line of this long-established surf outfitter. Boardshorts (quite a bit shorter than boys') and bikinis should get you thinking of sand between your toes. Sizing runs on odd numbers, and the cuts are often on the small side, so go up one from your usual size—for instance, if you're normally an 8, get a 9. Load up, then head to the dressing rooms, in the back past the giant hip-wiggling Hawaiian girls. You can also bag such gear as flip-flops, Hawaiian-print backpacks, and Sex Wax. *109–111 Spring St. (between Mercer and Greene Sts.), SoHo, 212/334–4500. Subway: Prince St.*

9 *e-4*

SAKS FIFTH AVENUE

The line of flags along Saks' façade is enough to rally the most exhausted shopper. It's a great place for a clotheshorse mother–daughter shopping trip. Not only are there plenty of designers to please both the 20s and 50s sets, but the atmosphere is generally calm, not nerve-fraying. (And, as it's a fashion-only department store, there are no linens or Lladró figurines to get in the way.) The women's designer sections form a phalanx of international labels (Thierry Mugler, Sonia Rykiel, Moschino, Dolce & Gabbana) as well as American standards (Calvin Klein, Donna Karan, Ralph Lauren). Many of these designers pop up again in funkier incarnations (D&G, DKNY) along with such newcomers as Collette Dinnigan. And all ages can slip into such a hip-again number as a Diane von Furstenberg wrap dress. As for women's shoes, Saks has one of the biggest selections of Ferragamos outside, well, Ferragamo. *611 5th Ave. (at 50th St.), Midtown, 212/753–4000. Subway: E, F to 5th Ave.*

9 *e-1*

SCOOP

With its excellent sampling of young, pricey designers, this store injected a bit of SoHo into the Upper East Side. The labels are a strong cross-section of chipper haute funk, but racks are arranged by color rather than designer. Scoop up (sorry, couldn't help it) TSE and Cashmere Studio shells, skinny Chaiken & Capone or Theory pants, a Tocca dress or two, plus a few accessories, and you're ready to take on the weekly-manicure set. The Third Avenue store has two annexes: "Street", with more casual threads, and "What's the Scoop?" for accessories. A beach-oriented branch cropped up in East Hampton. *1275 3rd Ave. (between 73rd and 74th Sts.), Upper East Side, 212/535–5577. Subway: 6 to 77th St.*

11 *e-5*

532 Broadway (between Prince and Spring Sts.), SoHo, 212/925–2886. Subway: N, R to Prince St. or 6 to Spring St.

7 *e-7*

SEARLE

Searle is an exclusively East Side phenomenon. The knits are covetable—there's lots of chenille—but most outstanding are the coats. Wool, leather, shearling, pea coats, reversible coats . . . to get your foot in the door, go to a trunk show at the 605 Madison Avenue branch. Summer brings tempting separates, including fitted T-shirts with necklines to flatter every *poitrine*. *605 Madison Ave. (at 58th St.), Midtown,*

212/753–9021. Subway: 59th St./Lexington Ave.

9 *e-2*

1051 3rd Ave. (at 62nd St.), Upper East Side, 212/838–5990. Subway: 59th St./Lexington Ave.

-9- *e-1*

860 Madison Ave. (at 70th St.), Upper East Side, 212/772–2225. Subway: 68th St./Hunter College.

7 *e-8*

1035 Madison Ave. (at 79th St.), Upper East Side, 212/717–4022. Subway: 77th St.

7 *e-8*

1124 Madison Ave. (at 84th St.), Upper East Side, 212/988–7318. Subway: 4, 5, 6 to 86th St.

11 *f-3*

SPOOLY D'S

The common denominator among these new and vintage pieces is their downtown hipness. Straight-cut pants by Katayone Adeli, separates (such as oxford-cloth skirts) by Wink, and dark Earl jeans join vintage piqué shifts and cocktail dresses. It's just a skip away from the going-uptown Bleecker Street subway stop. *51 Bleecker St. (at Lafayette St.), East Village, 212/598–4415. Subway: Bleecker St.*

11 *d-5*

STEVEN ALAN

Clothes are often coy but not necessarily cheap in these cramped quarters. Short-in-the-tooth designers include Milk Fed, Built by Wendy, and p.a.k; there are also more established (but still funky) secondary lines such as downtown denim diva Daryl K's K-189 and Martin Margiela's 6. The clothes on display tend to be in small sizes; you may have to ask them to bring out anything larger than a 6. Dodge the three-digit prices by heading to the outlet store at 330 East 11th Street (212/982–2881). *60 Wooster St. (at Broome St.), SoHo, 212/334–6354. Subway: Spring St.*

11 *h-4*

TG 170

Among the boutiques that are pushing east beyond Nolita, this is one of the best. Flip through downtown separates such as wool tanks with leather edging or paisley silk skirts, then look above and below the racks for street-y addi-

tions such as Freitag messenger bags, which are made from tarps. *170 Ludlow St. (between Stanton and Houston Sts.), Lower East Side, 212/995–8660. Subway: 2nd Ave.*

11 *e-4*

TOCCA

Feeling girly? Float down to Tocca for a liberal helping of slip dresses, eyelet cotton, embroidered flowers, and dangling beaded necklaces. The dressing rooms styled as peaked tents are cool, and the slightly retro aspect makes the merchandise hip . . . but the couple-hundred-dollar price tags require a grown-up budget. *161 Mercer St. (between Houston and Prince Sts.), SoHo, 212/343–3912. Subway: Prince St.*

11 *f-5*

TRACY FEITH

These clothes practically radiate "steamy tropical island." Tissue-thin, intensely colored silk is whipped into curvy, spaghetti-strap dresses and wrap skirts. Fuschia, purple, apple green, cerulean blue in paisleys and florals—it all looks best with a tan and will pack to nothing in your suitcase. Most are in the $175–$300 range. Sizing runs as petite, 1, 2, and 3, so you may have to try on a few things to find the right fit. *209 Mulberry St. (between Spring and Kenmare Sts.), Nolita, 212/334–3097. Subway: 6 to Spring St.*

11 *g-1*

TRASH AND VAUDEVILLE

True to its St. Mark's form, Trash and Vaudeville is a good source of club wear. The racks can outfit rockabillies, punks, and goths; Lou Reed reportedly trolls for tight jeans here. Slouch your way among black spiderweb dresses, python print pants, and shirts printed with drag queens. There's plenty under $100. *4 St. Mark's Pl. (near 2nd Ave.), East Village, 212/982–3590. Subway: Astor Pl.*

9 *e-1*

TSE CASHMERE

Good-girl cardigans aren't the only things on TSE's mind; recent collections have shown zip-front "sweatshirts" with fur-trim hoods, shift dresses with panels of silk satin, trousers, and overcoats, all in impossibly soft cashmere. There are also forays outside the realm of cashmere—stretch wool pants, silk separates, even a little angora. But don't move too fast past the sweater basics (round neck, V-neck, turtleneck), whose soft colors and stitching make them endlessly desirable—even at multi-hundreds a pop. A spinoff branch, TSE Surface (226 Elizabeth St., 212/343–7033), uses a bright, juiced-up color palette for its lower-priced designs. *827 Madison Ave. (at 69th St.), Upper East Side, 212/472–7790. Subway: 68th St./Hunter College.*

9 *e-4*

UNITED COLORS OF BENETTON

For the most atmospheric Benetton experience, head to the flagship in the Beaux Arts Scribner building at 5th Avenue and 48th Street. Despite the building's pedigree, the clothes aren't too serious: pastel tricot knits; candy-color, stretchy separates; some neutral-color base pieces. It's still a good place to find sweaters in a wide range of colors. Drop in on one of the readings the store hosts in the espresso bar—not the 92nd St. Y, but they do call in some big shots. This reference to the building's literary history may have you waxing nostalgic for the building's original tenant, the retail store of the august Scribner publishing house, or seething at Benetton's condescension. *597 5th Ave. (between 48th and 49th Sts.), Midtown, 212/593–0290. Subway: E, F to 5th Ave.*

9 *f-2*

805 Lexington Ave. (at 62nd St.), Upper East Side, 212/752–5283. Subway: 59th St./Lexington Ave.

11 *e-1*

749 Broadway (at 8th St.), Greenwich Village, 212/533–0230. Subway: 8th St.; and other locations.

11 *e-3*

URBAN OUTFITTERS

This chain rides trends hard and long. Street fashions are quickly snatched up and thrown into dozens of combinations, such as the drawstring/cargo and sari fabric/Indian gauze fads. These duds aren't meant to last forever, but then again you can put together an outfit for under $75. They've also got silly accessories, cheap, semi-disposable housewares (candles, throw pillows, butterfly chairs, beanbags), cards, and toys (MadLibs, anyone?). *628 Broadway (between Houston and Bleecker Sts.), Greenwich Village, 212/475–0009. Subway: Bleecker St./Broadway–Lafayette St.*

11 *c-1*

374 6th Ave. (at Waverly Pl.), West Village, 212/677–9350. Subway: W. 4th St./ Washington Sq.

9 *e-3*

127 E. 59th St. (between Lexington and Park Aves.), Midtown, 212/688–1200. Subway: 59th St./Lexington Ave.

11 *g-1*

162 2nd Ave. (between 10th and 11th Sts.), East Village, 212/375–1277. Subway: Astor Pl.

11 *d-3*

VERONICA BOND

An unexpected bolt of quality just north of Houston. The dimpled Veronica (sweeter than Archie's) creates some mighty enticing clothes: deep-V tops, tummy-baring gowns, svelte coats. Prices are very reasonable considering the workmanship. One thing to keep in mind: Veronica doesn't open until 2. *171 Sullivan St. (between Houston and Bleecker Sts.), West Village, 212/254–5676. Subway: W. 4th St./Washington Sq.*

11 *e-4*

VIVIENNE TAM

Embroidered flowers and koi fish aren't just for Chinatown anymore. Tam's designs are often a cultural grab bag— Mao Zedong's face shows up in the darndest places. Fabrics sometimes wander from the beaten path; many shirts are made of sheer nylon mesh, printed with deep colors or perhaps sequined with sprays of flowers. Cotton jackets and pants could be coated with polyurethane, and a line of shifts, pants, and zip-front jackets was made from olefin, the treated paper used for FedEx envelopes. *99 Greene St. (between Prince and Spring Sts.), SoHo, 212/966–2398. Subway: Prince St.*

11 *f-4*

WANG

One of the rash of Mott Street boutiques, Wang shows a keen eye for detail. Edged and contrast-stitched pockets show up in unexpected places, or a small line of ruffle suddenly flirts with your shoulder or skirt hem. Best of all, prices are relatively low—$170 for a nonubiquitous black dress. *219 Mott St. (between Prince and Spring Sts.), SoHo/Nolita, 212/941–6134. Subway: Broadway–Lafayette St.*

11 f-5

X-LARGE

Despite the name, the clothes here won't swim on you—check the tags and you'll see that they're relatively "mini." Most items, from uniform-style shirts and hooded sweatshirts to stretch twill skirts or zip-front jackets, are under $100. At these prices, you'll still have some money left over for the CBGBs cover. *267 Lafayette St. (at Prince St.), SoHo, 212/334–4480. Subway: Bleecker St. or Prince St.*

11 e-6

YELLOW RAT BASTARD

If you need a dose of aggressive streetwear, you've arrived. Ultra-baggy jeans by Fubu and Diesel, tough-girl pants and shorts by Buggirl (about $60), smart-ass T-shirts by Porn Star and Fuct (roughly $30)—just make sure you've got the right attitude to wear them. *478 Broadway (between Broome and Grand Sts.), SoHo, 212/219–8569. Subway: N, R to Canal St.*

11 e-4

ZARA

Emphasizing their international status, Zara lists over a dozen countries' currencies on each price tag. But what this store boils down to is a stash of low-price, solid-color basics, from miniskirts to sweater sets. You can even get a pinstripe suit for under $200 if you don't mind 100% polyester. *580 Broadway (between Houston and Prince Sts.), SoHo, 212/343–1725. Subway: Broadway/Lafayette.*

9 e-3

750 Lexington Ave. (between 58th and 59th Sts.), Upper East Side, 212/754–1120. Subway: 59th St./Lexington Ave.

9 d-8

101 5th Ave. (between 17th and 18th Sts.), 212/741–0555. Subway: N, R to 23rd St.

designer

9 e-2

CALVIN KLEIN

This pared-down store is no catch-all CK emporium; it skims the cream of the designer's collections. And while the ad campaigns might sometimes cause a ruckus, most designs are highly understated. Unadorned suits, overcoats, dresses, and blouses stream by in a wash of cream, beige, olive, and of course, black. (For the color-starved, there are occasional punctuation pieces in, say, aqua or chartreuse.) Upstairs on the mezzanine are the bathing suits, lingerie, and evening wear—though more than one customer has been overheard mistaking the long, thin-strap silk dresses for nightgowns. The neighboring evening accessories should have been a tip-off; the tiny, boxlike purses are hopelessly refined. If the shoes and handbags here are too steep for you, there's recourse in a more casual, shoes-and-bags-only CK SoHo boutique (133 Prince St.). *654 Madison Ave. (at 60th St.), Upper East Side, 212/292–9000. Subway: 59th St./Lexington Ave.*

9 e-2

CERRUTI

The precise tailoring that made Cerruti's name in men's suits is equally in evidence in the women's line—but that's not to say it runs to masculine styles. Besides pieces like classic, single-pleat trousers, look for softly structured knits and long, simply cut dresses. *789 Madison Ave. (at 67th St.), Upper East Side, 212/327–2222. Subway: 68th St.*

9 e-3

CHANEL

This slim, gray building is a true Chanel temple, where even the doorknobs (modeled after the bottle stoppers on No. 5 perfume) pay homage. The interior shines with black lacquer and mirrors, and a grand double staircase leads you upstairs. House designer Karl Lagerfeld concocts a successful mix of classic Chanel design elements and modern forms. The cap-toe shoe, the exquisite tweed suits, the signature camellia and interlocking "C"s continue to be subtly reinvented; they're joined by such pieces as the ergonomic "millennium bag." The second story is lent extra glitter with the jewelry boutique; higher up roosts Frédéric Fekkai's five-story beauty salon. *15 E. 57th St. (between 5th and Madison Aves.), Midtown, 212/355–5050. Subway: E, F, N, R to 5th Ave.*

9 e-1

CHLOÉ

With Stella McCartney in the driver's seat, this redoubtable Parisian fashion house has had quite a makeover. Feminine styles, such as draped necklines or spaghetti-strap tops, are joined by the frankly sexy (corset-laced bustiers) and slyly kitschy (aviator sunglasses with a small crystal heart, 70s-ish airbrushed shirts). Likewise, the palette ranges from ladylike soft lavender and blue to hot pink and vavoom red. *850 Madison Ave. (at 70th St.), Upper East Side, 212/ 717–8220. Subway: 68th St.*

9 *e-3*

CHRISTIAN DIOR

Having scored the boutique space in the gorgeous new LVMH building, Dior shifts into even higher gear. The interior's classic dove gray has made way for pearly and chill-silver tones. Accessories (including the Lady Dior handbag with the signature oversized beads on the handle), cosmetics, and shoes are on the ground floor; waft upstairs to reach the clothes. House designer John Galliano's wild streak makes itself known with exaggerated necklaces, deep shawl collars, and other flourishes. Whether the outfit is sedate or over-the-top, the tailoring is utterly perfect. *19 E. 57th St. (between 5th and Madison Aves.), Midtown, 212/931–2950. Subway: E, F to 5th Ave.*

9 *b-8*

COMME DES GARÇONS

This house is often years ahead of the others, both in terms of its clothes and its retail concept. After pioneering the minimalist store look in SoHo, it moved to its current space in far west Chelsea in 1998, where many cutting-edge galleries have gathered. The store itself is mesmerizing; you walk in through a steel tunnel, then land in a gleaming, white space carved up by curving walls strongly reminiscent of Richard Serra's Torqued Ellipses sculptures. Rei Kawakubo's designs keep pace with this groundbreaking approach. Dresses are sculptural and complex—you may need to ask how they're meant to be put on. A definite statement. *520 W. 22nd St. (between 10th and 11th Aves.), Chelsea, 212/604–9200. Subway: C, E to 23rd St.*

9 *e-1*

DOLCE & GABBANA

Somewhere among the buzzing synapses of Domenico Dolce and Stefano Gabbana, Sicilian widows became founts of sex appeal—and the resulting combination of bosomy black and movie-star flair is intoxicating. Sweep

upstairs to try on sheer leopard prints, corset-influenced slinky black dresses, bead-encrusted bustiers, and devastating mules. The store itself keeps the number of baroque-Italian references down, but the dressing rooms are swathed in lush ruby velvet, and there's a lovely little terrace. *825 Madison Ave. (between 68th and 69th Sts.), Upper East Side, 212/249–4100. Subway: 68th St./Hunter College.*

9 *e-1*

EMANUEL UNGARO

This store isn't nearly as serious as you might think. Granted, the heavily beaded evening jackets haven't changed a bit, but the suits have wonderfully textured fabrics, rich colors, and the occasional surprise, such as color-tipped Mongolian lamb trim. *792 Madison Ave. (at 67th St.), Upper East Side, 212/249– 4090. Subway: 68th St./Hunter College.*

9 *e-2*

GEOFFREY BEENE

This small boutique, tucked near the entrance to the Sherry-Netherland hotel, may not pack the floor space of the Madison Avenue flagships, but it's got an enviable stable of curvaceous evening dresses. The day wear is no slouch, either. *783 5th Ave. (between 59th and 60th Sts.), Midtown, 212/935–0470. Subway: N, R to 5th Ave.*

9 *e-1*

GIANFRANCO FERRE

A shiny, steely decor is Ferre's backdrop for extravagant women's prêt-à-porter. There's a bit of old Hollywood in the giant collars, the oversize buttons, and the sometimes revealing ensembles. *845 Madison Ave. (at 70th St.), Upper East Side, 212/717–5430. Subway: 68th St./Hunter College.*

9 *e-4*

GIANNI VERSACE

With his trademark blend of deference and rebelliousness, Versace restored this turn-of-the-20th-century 5th Avenue building, inlaid his Medusa-head logo on the sidewalk out front, and limned the interior with neon lights. The five floors encompass all of Versace's designs, from housewares to $150 jeans to couture. It's possible to find something relatively sedate, such as a mid-length black coat, but with Donatella at the helm there's always something daring with revealing slits, metal mesh, fur trim, or brash color. The Madison Avenue branch hones in on the higher-end clothes and accessories. *647 5th Ave. (between 51st and 52nd Sts.), Midtown, 212/317–0224. Subway: E, F to 5th Ave.*

9 *e-1*

815 Madison Ave. (between 68th and 69th Sts.), Upper East Side, 212/744–6868. Subway: 68th St./Hunter College.

9 *e-2*

GIORGIO ARMANI

Armani managed to top them all with his molto minimalist flagship store. Yet it's far from hard-edged; the muted tones and inviting fabrics make you want to whisper. The clothes are reverentially displayed, from the Black Label couture (up to five figures) to the shoes and sportswear. Who else could make a svelte ski jacket? *760 Madison Ave. (between 65th and 66th Sts.), Upper East Side, 212/988–9191. Subway: 68th St./Hunter College.*

7 *e-8*

GIVENCHY

Givenchy has managed to keep this boutique intimate. No towering structure, no espresso bar . . . instead the clothes are sometimes guarded by sleek white dog figures (and can look a little crowded on the rack). There are ladies-who-lunch suits with strong shoulders and nipped-in waists, some beautiful purses and accessories, and formal gowns in the back. *954 Madison Ave. (at 74th St.), Upper East Side, 212/772–1040. Subway: 77th St.*

9 *e-3*

GUCCI

Tom Ford's design revamp has made Gucci one of the most gawked-at stores in the city. Sexy, decadent-rocker clothes have transformed Gucci's name from stale to edgy. Along with the outré (lace pants, tight leather, Cher-esque floral prints) are some perfectly wearable suits and dresses, plus the oft-copied shoes and accessories. At press time the original store at 5th Avenue and 54th Street was shrouded in construction work; keep an eye out for its reopening in 2000. *10 W. 57th St. (at 5th Ave.), Midtown, 212/826–2600. Subway: N, R to 57th St.*

9 *e-3*

HERMÈS

Hermès goes far beyond scarves and handbags. Upstairs are flawless, quietly tasteful clothes, from decoratively stitched gloves to single-pleat wool pants and silk blouses. Many pieces cost around $1,000; after those prices, the crimson riding jacket at about $850 may sound feasible. At press time, a new location was shrouded in the signature orange on the northeast corner of Madison Avenue at 62nd Street. *See also* Handbags, *below. 11 E. 57th St. (between Madison and 5th Aves.), Midtown, 212/751–3181. Subway: N, R to 5th Ave.*

9 *e-2*

KRIZIA

Look through the pieces and you'll notice a certain animal figure cropping up—a jaguar, or perhaps an eagle. This is the "protector" of that particular collection, something that began as a whim and is now a Krizia signature. This is a good place to go suit shopping; the jackets are often more interesting than the standards. *769 Madison Ave. (at 66th St.), Upper East Side, 212/879–1211. Subway: 68th St./Hunter College.*

11 *d-5*

LOUIS VUITTON

As though designer Marc Jacobs didn't have his hands full with his own label (*see above*), he's lavishing talent on the relatively new Vuitton clothing line. The signature check and monogram make just-enough appearances, such as on sling-back pumps or belted raincoats. Understated luxe infuses both the extravagant (buttery suede pants) and the practical (water-resistant ponchos). Of course, all this comes at prices that could choke a horse. *116 Greene St. (between Prince and Spring Sts.), SoHo, 212/274–9090. Subway: Prince St.*

9 *e-1*

MOSCHINO

Moschino's flagship is crazy, silly, and a helluva lot of fun. Once drawn in by the tongue-in-cheek window displays, you'll be adrift in smiley faces, bright mosaic floors, and murals trumpeting maxims such as "It's Better to Dress As You Wish Than As You Should!" The women's Cheap and Chic line is on the ground floor (more teasing sayings on the T-shirts); women's couture is up the curving staircase, with its question-mark shaped bars. Don't worry: things don't get serious even when the price tags hit four figures—chairs in the couture area are upholstered with red-check table-cloth fabric, and there's a sculpted bowl of spaghetti on a table. Make sure you visit the "Toy-lette," which has walls of Lego and a Monopoly-board mirror. *803 Madison Ave. (between 67th and 68th Sts.), Upper East Side, 212/639–9600. Subway: 68th St./Hunter College.*

9 *d-3*

OMO NORMA KAMALI

One thing this store doesn't have to worry about is being run-of-the-mill. The dun interior, with its blocky, disjointed stairways and mysterious corners, looks like a cross between an army bunker and a set from the *Star Wars* trilogy. Against this grim background, the gleaming satin of a skirt or the shirring of a white bathing suit may be some-thing of a shock. Kamali is unfailingly creative, dreaming up everything from parachute-ready outfits to gathered vel-vet tops, puffy coats to fringe-covered pants. Downstairs are low-key casual clothes, often in fleece or cotton knits. *11 W. 56th St. (between 5th and 6th Aves.), Midtown, 212/957–9797. Subway: E, F to 5th Ave.*

9 *e-1*

PRADA

It's a dream come true for the status-hawks: Prada is going like gangbusters, doing double time both uptown and down. Within the Madison Avenue store's pale-green walls (they call the color "verdolino"; keep this in mind if you think you're getting land-bound mal de mer) is one of the biggest Prada selections outside Milan. The women's collections include pale gossamer dresses, occasional flashes of brightly colored trim, and stark black technofab-ric suits. Naturally, you'll also find plenty of the items that fueled the frenzy: sleek black nylon bags and thick-sole shoes. The small 57th Street boutique stocks only the coveted shoes. Hit the Wooster Street store for the sport lines—ski jack-ets, tennis whites (and blacks), sailing gear. At press time, a second SoHo loca-tion was in the works on the northwest corner of Prince Street and Broadway. *841 Madison Ave. (at 70th St.), Upper East Side, 212/327–4200. Subway: 68th St./Hunter College*

9 *e-3*

724 5th Ave. (between 57th and 56th Sts.), Midtown, 212/664–0010. Subway: N, R to 5th Ave.

11 *d-5*

116 Wooster St. (between Prince and Spring Sts.), SoHo, 212/925–2221. Sub-way: C, E to Spring St.

9 *e-3*

45 E. 57th St. (between Madison and Park Aves.), Midtown, 212/308–2332. Subway: E, F, N, R to 5th Ave.

9 *e-1*

SONIA RYKIEL BOUTIQUE

Malcolm McLaren once wrote a song called "Who the Hell Is Sonia Rykiel?" Now that Rykiel has a boutique on Madison, there's no excuse for asking the question. The grande dame of French knitwear creates lovely sweaters, sometimes sprinkled with rhinestones, sometimes sailor-striped. *849 Madison Ave. (between 70th and 71st Sts.), Upper East Side, 212/396–3060. Subway: 68th St./Hunter College.*

9 *e-1*

VALENTINO

Fabric snobs will be in seventh heaven: you can drape yourself with camel hair, satin, suede, cashmere/silk, and cash-mere/angora blends—and let's not for-get the pure silk linings. The designs serenely possess true cinematic glam-our, with elegant silhouettes and strik-ing (but not overpowering) details. Coats often have fur collars or trim; dresses and suits are enhanced with just enough embroidery, cutwork, bead-ing, or braid. The store is serene, with smooth marble, the occasional well-placed orchid, and a courtyard garden. *747 Madison Ave. (between 68th and 69th Sts.), Upper East Side, 212/772–6969. Subway: 68th St./Hunter College.*

7 *e-8*

VERA WANG

Justly famous for her bridal gowns, Wang also has a stunning selection of made-to-order evening wear. Choosing one of these gowns is an event in itself, and happens by appointment only, so call a few days in advance. Turn to the shimmering footwear collection once you've found your showstopper; the shoes are dyed to match. *991 Madison Ave. (at 77th St.), Upper East Side, 212/628–3400. Subway: 77th St.*

11 *d-5*

VIVIENNE WESTWOOD

A good shock goes a long way, as this British designer can attest. Long a bastion for outrageous design, Westwood gives us the bustiers and towering, fetishy platform shoes that rocked runways years ago. The audacious spirit is still fresh, running from trashed denim in the Anglomania line to giant buttons and vibrant colors for the suits. Cuts run small, so take the next size up to the fitting room—and even then you may find yourself holding your breath. *71 Greene St. (between Spring and Broome Sts.), SoHo, 212/334–5200. Subway: Spring St.*

11 *e-5*

YOHJI YAMAMOTO

These designs aren't always as severe as they seem. Fabric is folded, pleated, gathered, and slashed; sleeves can erupt into ruffles while a strict pinstripe jacket could be detailed with rough, unbleached linen. As though not to compete with the structures, the palette generally circles around black, white, and beige. *103 Grand St. (at Mercer St.), SoHo, 212/966–9066. Subway: N, R to Canal St.*

9 *e-1*

YVES SAINT LAURENT

Seemingly frozen in their black, purple, and orange moment, the clothes here are eternally theatrical. Heavy velvets appear in the women's section year-round. *855 Madison Ave. (at 71st St.), Upper East Side, 212/988–3821. Subway: 68th St./Hunter College.*

discount & off-price

Though discount designer clothes can now be found all over town, the traditional bargain-hunting area is the Lower East Side. Orchard Street has the highest concentration of shops, with everything between chic and schlock. Sunday is a hectic but very New York experience, not to be missed; Orchard Street itself becomes a pedestrian mall. If you can, leave your car at home.

10 *e-6*

CENTURY 21

Century 21 still claims to be "New York's best-kept secret" despite numerous breathlessly enthusiastic articles exposing it. True, it's a bit out of the way (down in the financial district), but don't let that stop you. The women's sections are consistently rich with steals; discounts generally start at a third off and often go much lower. Signs over the clothing racks tip you off to the various designers. Whether you're looking for something conservative or outré, you'll find something to fit the bill, such as gray flannel Burberry trousers (about $90), checked Prada pants (about $190), or a Versace jacket ($600, down from $1,575). The shoes and lingerie sections keep pace, with such bargains as Calvin Klein slingbacks for $100 and La Perla bras for just under $50. The crowds can induce heart palpitations in the uninitiated. *22 Cortlandt St. (at Trinity Pl.), Lower Manhattan, 212/227–9092. Subway: Cortlandt St./World Trade Ctr.*

9 *d-6*

DAFFY'S

The Daffy's experience can fluctuate, from depressing racks of lurid polyester (Herald Ctr.) to well-tended cruise wear (57th St.). You may have to wander through racks of undesirables to hit upon something, but you'll know it when you do: Cynthia Rowley dresses at one-third the list price, Calvin Klein underwear at half, or maybe a coup from a store closing. The European designers section has lots of mysterious "Made in Italy" labels, but you could turn up an Armani blazer for under $350. Be sure to inspect the more delicate items, as they can be manhandled beyond repair. *1311 Broadway (at 34th St.), Garment District, 212/736–4477. Subway: 34th St./Herald Sq.*

9 *e-8*

111 5th Ave. (at 18th St.), Flatiron District, 212/529–4477. Subway: F to 14th St., N, R to 23rd St.

9 *e-5*

335 Madison Ave. (at 44th St.), Midtown, 212/557–4422. Subway: 42nd St./Grand Central.

9 *e-3*

135 E. 57th St. (between Lexington and Park Aves.), Midtown, 212/376–4477. Subway: 59th St./Lexington Ave.

9 *c-8*

LOEHMANN'S

Loehmann's rep as one of the city's best designer discounters took a few knocks after it opened stores across the country. Happily, you can still dredge up a great bargain or two here in its hometown; stock quality varies, but it's replenished quickly. Expansive selections of sportswear, suits, and coats are diluted with racks of unrecognizable labels, but you can nab something such as a BCBG cardigan or Polo twill pants. The highest fashion concentration is in the upstairs Back Room, where the clothes are 30%–65% off. Three familiar names show up a lot: Donna Karan, Calvin Klein, and Ralph Lauren. Rake through the separates and you could find a stunning deal such as a Donna Karan lambskin jacket for $450, down from $1,795. *101 7th Ave. (at 16th St.), Chelsea, 212/352–0856. Subway: 1, 2, 3, 9 to 14th St.*

9 *e-3*

SYMS

Syms' educated consumers have enabled the store to snag a Park Avenue address. Skip the dubious racks of shorts sets and head to the humble, hand-lettered signs marked "couture," where the range of designers is far from shabby: Gianfranco Ferre, Krizia, Dolce & Gabbana, Gianni Versace. Granted, the wares may be a collection or two old, but if you pick classic styles, the look won't tell. Prices are normally slashed about 50%; gauge about $160 for Calvin Klein black wool trousers. More stunning deals are not uncommon, however, like a $920 Donna Karan winter-white wool/cashmere skirt for $119. Predated automatic markdown tickets on some clothes chart the prices' precipitous plunge. The shoe selection may require a little more weeding, but finds such as moc-croc Ralph Lauren flats for under $100 are standard. *400 Park Ave. (at 54th St.), Midtown, 212/317–8200. Subway: 51st St./Lexington–3rd Aves.*

10 *e-7*

42 Trinity Pl. (at Rector St.), Lower Manhattan, 212/797–1199. Subway: Rector St.

plus sizes

Among the department-store selections, Macy's has one of the most extensive large-size collections, called Macy Woman. Saks' Salon Z has some great designer lines, such as Dana Buchman, plus a special intimate-apparel area.

9 *e-2*

ASHANTI LARGER SIZES

These unique styles in large sizes (14–30) are often made of handwoven and hand-dyed fabrics. *872 Lexington Ave. (between 65th and 66th Sts.), Upper East Side, 212/535–0740. Subway: 68th St./Hunter College.*

7 *b-7*

DAPHNE

There's an ethnic twist to most of the clothes here—batik-style prints, chunky jewelry—and often flattering cuts such as bias-cut skirts and tapered pants. *467 Amsterdam Ave. (between 82nd and 83rd Sts.), Upper West Side, 212/877–5073. Subway: 79th St.*

7 *c-1*

LANE BRYANT

One of the spearheading mass-marketers for larger sizes (going back to 1916!), Lane Bryant carries both casual and moderately dressy lines in sizes 14–28. *222–224 W. 125th St. (between 7th and 8th Aves.), Harlem, 212/678–0546. Subway: 2, 3, A, B, C, D to 125th St.*

9 *e-2*

MARINA RINALDI

For stylish dressing, this place is a gold mine. Weekend wear, business suits, evening clothes, accessories—all pick the right current looks, from tunic cuts to tie-back dresses. Sizing is Italian; just ask the staff for a translation. *800 Madison Ave. (between 67th and 68th Sts.), Upper East Side, 212/734–4333. Subway: 68th St.*

resale

7 *e-7*

ENCORE

It may not look like much from the outside, but once inside great finds will jump out at you. A 15-minute run-through could turn up a Philip Treacy hat for under $100, a Gucci silk blouse or Bottega Veneta flats for under $150, or TSE and Malo cashmeres for under $300. Since the stock reflects the original owners' closets, there are plenty of black dresses and suits. *1132 Madison Ave. (between 84th and 85th Sts.), 2nd floor, Upper East Side, 212/879–2850. Subway: 4, 5, 6 to 86th St.*

11 *f-4*

INA

This pair of resale shops focuses on designer separates rather than full-blown, four-figure suits. This makes it easier to add an Alexander McQueen embroidered skirt (about $220) or Miu Miu pants (around $200) to your closet. Rifle through the choice shoes and you just may stumble upon Manolo Blahniks for under $300 or Stephane Kélian sandals. *21 Prince St. (between Mott and Elizabeth Sts.), SoHo/Little Italy, 212/334–9048. Subway: Prince St.*

11 *d-4*

101 Thompson St. (between Prince and Spring Sts.), SoHo, 212/941–4757. Subway: C, E to Spring St.

11 *h-5*

KLEIN'S OF MONTICELLO

One of Orchard Street's more genteel shopping experiences, Klein's regularly provides deals on relatively conservative, dressy clothes like Malo cashmeres, Les Copains suits, and Max Mara coats. *105 Orchard St. (at Delancey St.), Lower East Side, 212/966–1453. Subway: Delancey St.*

7 *e-8*

MICHAEL'S

A small black sign at the cash register reminds you, "The treasure you see today may not be here tomorrow." The women who shop here take this to heart: there's an air of unusual seriousness to the browsing. There are special areas for Chanel/Hermès and Dolce & Gabbana (classic Chanel suits go for a cool $1,000), plus rich racks of separates. Brides can make an appointment to see the gown selection; all are no more than two years old. *1041 Madison Ave. (at 79th St.), Upper East Side, 212/737–7273. Subway: 77th St.*

9 *d-8*

OUT OF OUR CLOSET

Small and select, this store maintains a reliably chic stock, with finds like a $390 Prada shift dress previously owned by Cameron Diaz and a $375 Helmut Lang cadet suit with the tags still on. They're not total label snobs, though—you could find a particularly cool Banana Republic shirt within arm's reach of a Hermès or Armani blouse. *136 W. 18th St. (between 6th and 7th Aves.), Chelsea, 212/633–6965. Subway: 1, 9 to 18th St.*

vintage

Most vintage-clothing shops have a final-sale policy, so purchase carefully

and wisely. East 7th Street is a good place to start.

11 *e-5*

ALICE UNDERGROUND

Having shuffled locations over the past few years, Alice finds its latest store the brightest and least crowded. (Being above ground will do that to you.) While the thrift-store standards—letter jackets, leather coats—have a decent amount of rack space, they don't overwhelm the cashmere sweaters ($45–$85), filmy nightgowns, suede miniskirts ($40-ish), and well-preserved beaded tops. Some things are really used, not vintage (Tommy Hilfiger). Linens and lots of crocheted doilies are in the back room. Scout around for the store's own label on bowling shirts with atmospheric slogans such as "Laverne's Cocktail Lounge." *481 Broadway (between Broome and Grand Sts.), 212/431–9067. Subway: 6 to Spring St.; N, R to Canal St.*

11 *e-1*

ANTIQUE BOUTIQUE

See Contemporary, *above.*

11 *e-5*

CANAL JEAN COMPANY

One of downtown's best pawing-around spots, this sprawling space caters to at least half-a-dozen clothing personalities. In five minutes, you can lay hands on rubber fetish wear, sarong skirts ($15–$20), vintage housedresses, punky plaid pants (about $75), and wildly printed Todd Oldham jeans (roughly half that). Climb to the mezzanine for underwear, including Calvin Klein and Ralph Lauren (damn, the bras are still $30). The upper floor is loaded with Levi's. Down in the basement are more vintage racks with a huge coat selection and Army-Navy surplus. *504 Broadway (between Spring and Broome Sts.), SoHo, 212/226–1130. Subway: 6 to Spring St.; N, R to Canal St.*

10 *e-1*

CHEAP JACK'S

The ordinary size of this store's entrance belies the huge amount of clothes-jammed space upstairs, downstairs, and in between. Push through the racks and you'll brush against everything from shagadelic blue velvet blazers to Chinese silk jackets, stiff lederhosen to slippery soccer shirts. However, Jack isn't as cheap as you'd like him to be—over $50 for corduroy bell-bottoms, more than a couple of hundred for most of the coats, be they faux leopard or military wool. *841 Broadway (between 13th and 14th Sts.), Flatiron District, 212/777–9564. Subway: 14th St./Union Sq.*

11 *d-5*

THE 1909 COMPANY

These classy two-piece suits and cashmere sweaters look like they once belonged to a dame d'un certain âge. The scarves, gloves, and crocheted or beaded bags are appropriately dainty. *63 Thompson St. (between Spring and Broome Sts.), SoHo, 212/343–1658. Subway: A, C, E to Canal St.*

11 *h-1*

RESURRECTION

A fabulous source for 60s fashion, these stores are regularly picked over by celebrities and the stylists who dress them. Check the windows for Jean Muir, swirls of Pucci (around $150 and up), and the strict lines of Courrèges (can be well over $400). There are also more humble choices, such as sport coats, jeans, and fatigues. The shoe selection is generally far superior to that in most vintage shops, ranging from blunt-nose pumps to knee-high boots. *123 E. 7th St. (between 1st Ave. and Ave. A), East Village, 212/228–0063. Subway: Astor Pl.; 2nd Ave.*

11 *f-5*

217 Mott St. (between Prince and Spring Sts.), Nolita, 212/625–1374. Subway: Spring St.

10 *e-2*

SCREAMING MIMI'S

Vintage here doesn't go too far back—mostly to the '60s and '70s—but the finds (dashikis, 1960s sundresses in the $50 range, flares) repeatedly end up in fashion spreads. The stock is in consistently great condition, from the polyester shirts to the kooky shoes up front. Hike the stairs to the narrow loft and you might find some Playboy bunny picks or Mai Tai glasses among the housewares. Definitely worth repeat visits. *382 Lafayette St. (at E. 4th St.), East Village, 212/677–6464. Subway: Astor Pl.; Broadway–Lafayette St.*

11 *d-3*

THE STELLA DALLAS LOOK

Barbara Stanwyck would be perfectly happy here. Specializing in '40s clothes, this Village boutique has some swell dresses, generally of high quality. *218 Thompson St. (between W. 3rd and Bleecker Sts.), West Village, 212/674–0447. Subway: W. 4th St./Washington Sq.*

11 *g-1*

TOKIO 7

Japanese Kewpie dolls beckon from the display windows; inside are crowded racks of clothes a few seasons old. Most choices are downtown get-around favorites (Tocca, agnès b., or A.P.C separates for under $100), with a few couture names mixed in Scout around for the under-$10 bin. *64 E. 7th St. (between 1st and 2nd Aves.), East Village, 212/353–8443. Subway: 1st Ave.; Astor Pl.*

11 *d-5*

WHAT GOES AROUND COMES AROUND

This is no fly-by-night operation; What Goes Around Comes Around is known for its collectible denim and high-quality pickings. They're quick to jump on trends, such as Lily Pulitzer skirts (about $85) and Pucci shirts ($350–$375), and sometimes, as in the case of 70s concert T-shirts, they catch them good and early. *351 W. Broadway (between Broome and Grand Sts.), SoHo, 212/343–9303. Subway: N, R to Canal St.*

CLOTHING FOR WOMEN/SPECIALTY

furs

New York's wholesale, and to some extent retail, fur district is centered around 7th Avenue and 30th Street. On weekdays the area bustles with activity as merchandise is carted or carried through the streets; on weekends many places are closed, or open by appointment only. Besides the individual storefronts, there are a few tall buildings filled with furriers; if you're curious, just go in and look at the directory. Remember that some furriers close for part of August. Several department stores, such as Bloomingdale's, have fur salons as well.

9 *e-3*

FENDI

Animal products (fur and leather) being the Fendi backbone, you'll find extremely high quality, and prices, in their second-floor salon. Fendi specializes in furs other than the serviceable mink: sable, chinchilla, lynx. Styles are extravagant, even in mink; you'll find oversize collars, interesting piecing, and out-there styles like fox and goat tufts or dyed baby-blue and brown ponyskin. *See also Handbags, below. 720 5th Ave. (at 56th St.), Midtown, 212/767–0100. Subway: E, F to 5th Ave.*

9 *d-7*
FURS BY DIMITRIOS
The salespeople here are more than happy to help out a fur novice. Coat designs are straightforward, and the company believes staunchly in American mink. Dimitrios is one of the few storefronts in the 30th Street area that's open on Saturday. *130 W. 30th St. (between 6th and 7th Aves.), Garment District, 212/695–8469. Subway: 34th St./Penn Station; 1, 9 to 28th St.*

9 *e-2*
J. MENDEL
This Parisian firm has impeccable, weak-in-the-knees coats. They're often in mink, or in thick cashmere with fur trim, and you can easily find a slim style that's not overwhelming. Besides the beautiful, long, classic shapes, there are lighter takes like zip-front or poncho styles. *723 Madison Ave. (between 63rd and 64th Sts.), Upper East Side, 212/832–5830. Subway: 59th St./Lexington Ave.*

9 *d-7*
150 WEST 30TH STREET
This towering building is heavy with furriers, including the traditional craftsman Ben Kahn (212/279–0633) and George Mamoukakis Furs (212/564–2976), which carries mainly mink. *150 W. 30th St. (between 6th and 7th Aves.), Garment District. Subway: 34th St./Penn Station; 1, 9 to 28th St.*

9 *e-3*
REVILLON
Another Parisian firm, Revillon is luxurious without being old-fashioned. Besides the dignified minks and foxes, there are short, zippered jackets and brightly dyed fur accessories (scarves, purses in Mongolian lamb). For something less conspicuous, there are fur-lined coats in wool, silk, or water-resistant microfiber. *717 5th Ave. (at 56th St.), Midtown, 212/317–0039. Subway: E, F to 5th Ave.*

9 *d-3*
RITZ THRIFT SHOP
This is an excellent place to try for a "gently worn" fur. You can get a basic mink for around $700, though prices go up to about $5,000 (with a few $10,000-plus beauties thrown in). Everything is cleaned and glazed, and your purchase comes with free alterations and free storage. *107 W. 57th St. (between 6th and 7th Aves.), Midtown, 212/265–4559. Subway: 57th St.*

9 *d-7*
345 7TH AVENUE
With 25 floors filled predominantly with furriers, you can hardly go wrong. David and Daniel Antonovich are here (212/244–3161 or 212/244–0666), and there are plenty of other glamorous names, like Furs by Frederick Gelb (212/239–8787), which is a good place to go for sable. *345 7th Ave. (between 29th and 30th Sts.), Garment District. Subway: 1, 9 to 28th St.; 34th St./Penn Station.*

gloves

9 *e-6*
LACRASIA
The practice of wearing gloves for fashion or propriety instead of just warmth may be history, but LaCrasia is a wonderful holdout. Do your hands a favor and have them fitted for a custom pair. LaCrasia's work goes far beyond the short, everyday variety—for a heady draft of elegance, try the elbow-length or long gloves. Diehards can make an appointment to see the Glove Museum. For a lighthearted pair, nip into the Grand Central Station branch. *304 5th Ave. (between 32nd and 31st Sts.), Garment District, 212/594–2223. Subway: 33rd St.*

9 *e-5*
Grand Central Station, Midtown, 212/370–0310. Subway: 42nd St./Grand Central.

handbags

New York's department stores have large selections of handbags in all price ranges. Chain stores such as Banana Republic can be good resources for decent knockoffs. For something even cheaper (because you can bargain down to $20), hit Canal Street. You may even be able to watch them stapling on your Prada logo. *See Leather Goods & Luggage, below.*

9 e-1

ALAIN MIKLI OPTIQUE

Granted, this is an eyewear store; but alongside those funky frames are some killer handbags and totes—pearlized plastic on the outside, leather on the inside. In fact, the bags are made of the same material as some of the frames, so obsessive accessory-matchers can let loose. *880 Madison Ave. (between 71st and 72nd Sts.), Upper East Side, 212/472–6085. Subway: 68th St./Hunter College.*

11 f-5

AMY CHAN

The signature look here stems from the acetate chips covering the soft bags. Sturdy heat bonding means they'll wear better than sewn or glued decorations, and they give the surface a modern shimmer. Discreet black and brown models are joined by those in fire-engine red and disco iridescent silver. Most start just around $125; also scout around for such finds as painted canvas parasols ($60). *247 Mulberry St. (between Prince and Spring Sts.), Nolita, 212/966–3417. Subway: 6 to Spring St.*

9 e-3

ANYA HINDMARCH

If you're ever to empty your wallet while buying a new one, this may be the place to do it. Your eye might catch one of the tiny coin purses or a satin bag with a funny silkscreened photo on the front. The next thing you know, you're reeled in by the beaded strap of an evening bag or a leather passport holder decorated to look like an envelope. *29 E. 60th St. (at Madison Ave.), Midtown, 212/750–3974. Subway: N, R to 5th Ave.*

9 e-2

ARTBAG

Besides selling new bags, this store is essential for those who can't part with their old ones: they arrange expert, albeit expensive, handbag repairs, plus custom jobs, alterations, and reconditioning. While they inspect your scruffy tote, check out the gleaming wares, some in alligator or ostrich. *735 Madison Ave. (at 64th St.), Upper East Side, 212/744–2720. Subway: 68th St./Hunter College.*

11 f-4

BLUE BAG

Like Calypso (*see* Clothing, *above*), this is a St. Barth's import, giving us parched New Yorkers another swig of color and fun. Bags run from plain-and-simple (woven straw) to medium-well (patterned silk, painted fabric) to State-ment (dripping with fringe). *266 Eliza-beth St. (between Prince and Houston Sts.), Nolita, 212/966–8566. Subway: Bleecker St.*

9 e-2

COACH

See Leather Goods & Luggage, *below.*

9 e-3

FENDI

The baguette bag put Fendi firmly back onto society ladies' must-have lists. Besides the traditional cocoa-color dou-ble-Fs, you'll find suede and beading, mother-of-pearl detailing and sequins. *See also* Furs, *above. 720 5th Ave. (at 56th St.), Midtown, 212/767–0100. Subway: E, F to 5th Ave.*

11 h-4

FINE & KLEIN

One of the best Lower East Side dis-count anythings, Fine & Klein sells chichi day and evening bags at great dis-counts. If you have your heart set on something in particular, come with a picture and style number; often they can track it down or order it. Sunday is a feeding frenzy, so try to come on a week-day. *Closed Sat. 119 Orchard St. (between Delancey and Rivington Sts.), Lower East Side, 212/674–6720. Subway: Delancey St.*

9 c-1

FURLA

This Italian firm specializes in smooth, classic shapes—but not too classic. A rectangular bag could have an extended line; flower-shape cutouts could lighten a square purse. Accessories include some adorable coin purses shaped like fruit. *159A Columbus Ave. (at 67th St.), Upper West Side, 212/874–6119. Subway: 66th St./Lincoln Ctr.*

9 e-2

727 Madison Ave. (between 63rd and 64th Sts.), Upper East Side, 212/755–8986. Subway: 59th St./Lexington Ave.

11 d-5

430 W. Broadway (between Prince and Spring Sts.), SoHo, 212/343–0048. Sub-way: C, E to Spring St.

9 *e-3*
HERMÈS
Once a saddler, always a saddler. After well over a century, Hermès still has beautiful saddles and bridles (upstairs), as well as the famous scarves (about $275) and trim "Kelly" bags designed for Grace herself. At press time, they were on the move to Madison Avenue at 62nd Street. *11 E. 57th St. (between 5th and Madison Aves.), Midtown, 212/751–3181. Subway: E, F to 5th Ave.*

11 *f-4*
JAMIN PUECH
With an amazing color sensibility and a fin-de-siècle taste for richesse, this design team pulls off luxury without stuffiness, hipness without trendiness. Small sequined rounds glow in plum or chartreuse, patchworks are pieced of ponyskin or tweed, and if you haven't had enough, you can wrap something feathery around your neck. *252 Mott St. (between Prince and Houston Sts.), Nolita, 212/334–9730. Subway: Broadway/Lafayette or 6 to Spring St.*

7 *e-8*
JUDITH LEIBER
These small, sparkling cases are meant to be cradled in the palm rather than slung over the shoulder. The bejeweled shapes include fruit, animals, and even seashells—beautiful, certainly, but you may have to ask your escort to carry your wallet. *987 Madison Ave. (between 76th and 77th Sts.), Upper East Side, 212/327–4003. Subway: 77th St.*

11 *e-5*
KATE SPADE
There's little leather here, and no attitude from either the stock or the salespeople. Instead, you'll find the original satin-finish microfiber handbags and totes (even one for gardening) that are copied high and low, plus pared-down designs in various textiles—candy-stripe silk, straw, canvas and grosgrain ribbon. You could also come away with scarves, a blouse, or some wonderfully simple pajamas. The clothes and accessories, though, are in exclusively short supply. Of course, "simple" doesn't mean "cheap." *454 Broome St. (at Mercer St.), 212/274–1991. Subway: C, E to Spring St.*

9 *e-2*
LONGCHAMP
Long a Parisian favorite, Longchamp introduced its own boutique here in fall 1999. Most bags are in leather, from high gloss to matte finishes. Styles are modern without being trendy; they range from slim shoulder bags to polished backpacks, plus accessories such as wallets, cell-phone holders, and belts. *713 Madison Ave. (at 63rd St.), Upper East Side, 212/223–1500. Subway: 59th St./Lexington Ave.*

9 *e-3*
LOUIS VUITTON
Vuitton's famous monogram adorns everything from wallets and yen holders to backpacks and dog carriers, and in the past few collections there's been a new, quick-paced energy. Besides the brown-on-brown LVs, there's the Epi leather line, with a striated texture and fun colors (blue, rain-slicker yellow), the reintroduced brown checkerboard "Damier" canvas, and the "Monogram Vernis," which plugs the magic letters into shiny dyed leather (powder blue, lime green). Shapes are racing ahead too, from small-scale oblong clutches to square holdalls. *49 E. 57th St. (between Park and Madison Aves.), Midtown, 212/371–6111. Subway: E, F to 5th Ave.*

11 *d-5*
116 Greene St. (between Prince and Spring Sts.), SoHo, 212/274–9090. Subway: Prince St.

9 *e-3*
TOD'S
See Shoes & Boots, *below.*

hats
Handmade hats can be expensive accessories (we're talking the same price arena as Hermès scarves), but the attention they draw can be well worth it. For the caviar of the hat world, otherwise known as designer Philip Treacy, head to Bergdorf's—or London.

11 *d-4*
THE HAT SHOP
Hats climb the walls, inviting a try-on (as do the friendly salespeople). Traditional shapes are often tweaked; a brimmed straw hat, for instance, could be hooked with fishing flies or corset-laced with ribbon. The cocktail hats are

tiny, Dr. Seuss—like things with a precarious plume or two. Everything can be made to order at no extra charge. *120 Thompson St. (between Prince and Spring Sts.), SoHo, 212/219—1445. Subway: Prince St.*

11 *f-4*
KELLY CHRISTY
Woven berets, sun hats with a rose hidden under the wide brim, fall felts, and other confections can be made to order; you can even custom-pick the colors. Prices start around $200. *235 Elizabeth St. (between Houston and Prince Sts.), SoHo/Little Italy, 212/965—0686. Subway: Broadway—Lafayette St.*

lingerie & nightwear
For sheer volume and selection, department stores are dependable standbys. Macy's has a massive selection, and Bloomingdale's still makes those days-of-the-week underpants. In most small boutiques the focus is on fancier, pricier, more decorative lingerie.

9 *e-1*
BRA SMYTH
This dedicated shop really knows its inventory; it's even got a bra hot line (800/BR—9466). Lacy, expensive European imports predominate—Aubade, Chantelle, even Lise Charmel's authentic Chantilly lace. Look for Hanro and Donna Karan for plainer, cheaper goods. They've also got a great selection of minimizers, uplift bras, and seamless underwear. And they'll do alterations not only on their stock but on your own. *905 Madison Ave. (between 72nd and 73rd Sts.), Upper East Side, 212/772—9400. Subway: 77th St.*

9 *e-2*
FOGAL
Fogal carries Swiss-made pantyhose, stockings, and bodysuits in more than 100 colors. And then there's "festivale," a sheer stocking with a tuxedo stripe of crystals up the side. *680 Madison Ave. (between 61st and 62nd Sts.), Upper East Side, 212/759—9782. Subway: 59th St./Lexington Ave.*

9 *e-3*
510 Madison Ave. (at 53rd St.), Midtown, 212/355—3254. Subway: E, F to 5th Ave.

11 *d-4*
JOOVAY
This store is so petite that it literally has underwear up to the ceiling. One wall climbs with underpinnings: Rigby & Peller, with Queen Elizabeth II's seal of approval (and a royal price tag), La Perla, Mystère, Josie by Natori (bras about $25), and Oroblu hosiery. The other is hung with nightgowns, PJs, and robes; look for the silk gowns with a textured, almost seersucker, finish or contrast-color lace. *436 W. Broadway (between Prince and Spring Sts.), SoHo, 212/431—6386. Subway: Prince St.; 6 to Spring St.*

9 *e-1*
LA PERLA
Unabashedly gorgeous underpinnings hit the seduction buttons with lashings of creamy lace, embroidery, and unadorned silk. The tricky part for the uninitiated is the Italian sizing—bras do not have cup sizes but are sized 1, 2, and so on. Check the labels for translated measurements; the cups are approximately B to C. (If you're still not sure, the staff will be happy to help fit you.) *777 Madison Ave. (between 66th and 67th Sts.), Upper East Side, 212/570—0050. Subway: 68th St./Hunter College.*

10 *e-1*
LA PETITE COQUETTE
The autographed photos on the walls have extra cachet here; one thank-you came from Frederique, longtime Victoria's Secret model. (If she's spent that much time in just her underwear, she must know whereof she speaks.) The silky stuff is on the ground level—some Aubade (about $150 for a stunning bustier), Le Mystère, and La Petite Coquette's own rainbow selection of silk slips, camisoles, and nightgowns (around $70 for a full slip). Downstairs are cotton nightgowns and a few children's items. *51 University Pl. (between 9th and 10th Sts.), Greenwich Village, 212/473—2478. Subway: 8th St.*

11 *d-5*
LE CORSET
Sashaying beyond the norm, this boutique is made for indulgences. You could find something such as handmade silk-and-lace bra and underwear sets, white cotton PJs stitched with pale green "zzz"s, even a few dusty-pink vintage girdles. And of course there's the

store's namesake, from vampy black to lacy white. *80 Thompson St. (between Spring and Broome Sts.), SoHo, 212/334–4936. Subway: C, E to Spring St.*

9 *e-3*
WOLFORD
Hosiery here runs about $25 and up, but if you invest in "Individual 10," a sheer stocking with a high percentage of Lycra, you stand a good chance of wearing it several times. Short- and long-sleeved bodysuits cost roughly double the price of hosiery; the bathing suits have the same seamless fit. And then there's StarckNaked, a multifunctional set of Lycra tubes designed by Philippe Starck, which you can turn into a tank dress, miniskirt, etc. *619 Madison Ave. (between 58th and 59th Sts.), Midtown, 212/688–4850. Subway: 59th St./Lexington Ave.*

7 *e-8*
996 Madison Ave. (between 78th and 77th Sts.), Upper East Side, 212/327–1000. Subway: 77th St.

maternity wear
All of New York's department stores have maternity departments, but only Bloomingdale's and some specialty boutiques carry Belly Basics, a boxed set of supremely comfortable, stretchy clothes like leggings and tunics. The combination of nonelastic waistbands and flattering fabrics and styles made these mix-and-match kits quick sellouts.

9 *e-1*
LIZ LANGE
Ms. Lange is of the "don't lose your fashion edge just because you're expecting" school. The slim pants, twinsets, and strappy dresses are pared-down but high-quality, and they don't shy away from sex appeal. By using stretch fabrics (everything from cashmere to denim) and elastic waistbands, she's eliminated the need for maternity panels. Many of the separates can be mix-and-matched; the ability to make several outfits out of a few pieces is especially welcome, since the styles don't come cheap. *958 Madison Ave. (between 75th and 76th Sts.), Upper East Side, 212/879–2191 or 888/616–5777. Subway: 77th St.*

9 *f-2*
MIMI MATERNITÉ
The approach here is not just ribbons and bows—when leggings and an oversize oxford shirt won't pass muster, they come through with business suits and dress-up knits. Current trends find their way in too, such as the capri pants with a stretchy front panel or a raw-silk evening suit. *1021 3rd Ave. (between 60th and 61st Sts.), Upper East Side, 212/832–2667. Subway: 59th St./Lexington Ave.*

9 *b-1*
2005 Broadway (at 69th St.), Upper West Side, 212/721–1999. Subway: 66th St./Lincoln Ctr.

7 *e-7*
1125 Madison Ave. (at 84th St.), Upper East Side, 212/737–3784. Subway: 4, 5, 6 to 86th St.

10 *d-6*
2 World Financial Center (near Liberty St.), Lower Manhattan, 212/945–6424. Subway: World Trade Ctr.

9 *f-1*
MOM'S NIGHT OUT
This second-floor boutique fills a small but crucial niche: it specializes in maternity evening wear and cocktail-dress rentals. Renters can choose from over 300 styles and colors; a three- to four-day rental can run anywhere from $95 to $220. If you're thinking of investing in four-months-at-a-time evening wear, you can browse through the styles, create a design, and have an outfit custom-made. There's also a small ready-to-wear selection. Call ahead; you may need to make an appointment. *147 E. 72nd St. (between Lexington and 3rd Aves.), Upper East Side, 212/744–6667. Subway: 68th St./Hunter College.*

7 *e-7*
MOTHERHOOD MATERNITY
A less-expensive chain, these stores concentrate on casual items such as denim overalls or jumpers and T-shirts. *1449 3rd Ave. (at 82nd St.), Upper East Side, 212/734–5984. Subway: 4, 5, 6 to 86th St.*

9 *d-8*
641 6th Ave. (at 20th St.), Chelsea, 212/741–3488. Subway: F to 23rd St.

9 *d-6*
Manhattan Mall (see Malls, above), 212/564–8170. Subway: 34th St./Herald Sq.

9 *e-3*

PEA IN THE POD

Though the name is lighthearted, the clothing is in all seriousness: comfortable and well-made casual and career clothes, even bathing suits. *625 Madison Ave. (between 58th and 59th Sts.), Midtown, 212/826–6468. Subway: 59th St./Lexington Ave.*

shoes & boots

The crowded stretch of 8th Street between 5th and 6th Avenues is commonly known as Shoe Street. And so it is—especially for those who have yet to hit the corporate hamster wheel. The stores lining this block specialize in mean-looking boots, outrageous platforms, and skateboard-worthy sneakers.

9 *e-1*

ANDREA CARRANO

This store has a laser-specific, perfectly fulfilled purpose: round-toe, low-vamp ballerina flats in every color imaginable, from simple black suede to half a dozen blues to metallic bronze. *955 Madison Ave. (at 70th St.), Upper East Side, 212/772–3144. Subway: 68th St./Hunter College.*

9 *e-3*

BALLY OF SWITZERLAND

The classic, cap-toe pumps are still here, but designs are branching out into such things as sport shoes and suede pumps with saucily-curved heels. *628 Madison Ave. (at 59th St.), Midtown, 212/751–9082. Subway: 59th St./Lexington Ave.*

9 *e-3*

BELGIAN SHOES

If you'd like a real touch of Henri Bendel, you'll visit this modest store instead of the namesake emporium on 5th Avenue. Bendel sold the big store decades ago, then kept his hand in with these soft-sole, loaferlike flats. (The tiny-bow-on-the-vamp style is originally his.) The premise might be casual, but the materials (raspberry velvet, black suede) and the price tag (a few hundred) certainly aren't. Don't wait too late in the day to visit; it closes a little earlier than most boutiques. *110 E. 55th St. (between Park and Lexington Aves.), Midtown, 212/755–7372. Subway: E, F to 5th Ave.*

9 *e-2*

BOTTEGA VENETA

Many of these shoes would look right on Rita Hayworth—satin shoes sprinkled with rock crystals or done in the company's signature weave. But there's an increasingly modern edge, with stiletto boots and wedges. If it's flats you need, slide into a pair of leopard loafers. The cost of such sophistication is in the multi-hundreds, but the twice-a-year sales are phenomenal. *635 Madison Ave. (between 59th and 60th Sts.), Midtown, 212/371–5511. Subway: 59th St./Lexington Ave.*

9 *e-1*

CHARLES JOURDAN

Many of these pairs are distinctly flirty: suede and patent leather T-straps, faux-snakeskin, open-toe heels, a few rhinestones here and there. "Bis" on the label means more casual/less expensive. *777 Madison Ave. (between 66th and 67th Sts.), Upper East Side, 212/486–2350. Subway: 68th St./Hunter College.*

9 *e-1*

CHRISTIAN LOUBOUTIN

This French import could give Manolo a run for his money. If you find yourself among a flock of gilded ladies, look for the flash of a crimson sole—it's Louboutin's signature. The niches in his boutique hold everything from pointed silk mules to low-vamped, strappy, sky-high heels, all perfectly balanced. Look for whimsical fillips, like a mosaiced heel. Prices are mostly $400-ish. *941 Madison Ave. (between 75th and 74th Sts.), Upper East Side, 212/396–1884. Subway: 77th St.*

11 *d-4*

CHUCKIES

Don't let the name fool you; this is no kiddie outlet. Chuckies has a dashing selection of designer shoes—lots of Dolce & Gabbana (at the 3rd Avenue store), some Sonia Rykiel and Jimmy Choo, and Chuckies' own line of cool pumps and boots. *399 W. Broadway (between Spring and Broome Sts.), 212/343–1717. Subway: Prince St.*

9 *f-2*

1073 3rd Ave. (between 63rd and 64th Sts.), Upper East Side, 212/593–9898. Subway: 59th St./Lexington Ave.

9 e-2

COLE-HAAN

Cole-Haan's woven, moccasin, and loafer styles go through endless permutations and combinations. The shelves are filled with versatile brown or black—not adventurous, but very well made. Moccasins average around $165. *667 Madison Ave. (at 61st St.), Upper East Side, 212/421–8440. Subway: 59th St./Lexington Ave.*

9 e-4

620 5th Ave. (at 50th St.), Midtown, 212/765–9747. Subway: E, F to 5th Ave.

9 e-4

JIMMY CHOO

Starlet shoes from tip to heel, these resemble their patrons: they're slender and expensive. Styles range from pointy-toe stilettos to svelte slides, patent leather to denim. Prices start around $300. *645 Fifth Ave. (at 51st St.), Midtown, 212/593–0800. Subway: 47th–50th Sts./Rockefeller Ctr.*

9 e-1

JOAN & DAVID

Stylish but never trendy, Joan & David always manage to produce a perfect brown wing tip for fall and a lovely, strappy sandal for summer. They also make some graceful clothes and substantial pendant necklaces. *816 Madison Ave. (at 68th St.), Upper East Side, 212/772–3970. Subway: 68th St./Hunter College.*

9 e-8

104 5th Ave. (at 16th St.), Chelsea, 212/627–1780. Subway: F to 14th St.

11 e-4

JOHN FLUEVOG SHOES

Inventor of the Angelic sole (protects against most earthly liquids "and Satan"), Fluevog carries big, thick shoes and boots. These are no Doc Martens knockoffs, though—the liberal use of platforms, curvaceous heels, and extremely pointy toes on the various styles ensures the difference from the yellow-stitched standard. There's a Cuisinartlike blend of influences, with geisha, wing tip, cowboy, Space Age, and roller derby ideas all jumping in. *104 Prince St. (between Mercer and Greene Sts.), SoHo, 212/431–4484. Subway: Prince St.*

11 e-4

KENNETH COLE

Posters on the walls trumpet clever, liberal sayings ("Shoes shouldn't stay in the closet either") to match the clever, liberal shoes. They're also delving further into accessories and clothing, much in leather, all of it aiming for hipness. *597 Broadway (between Houston and Prince Sts.), SoHo, 212/965–0283. Subway: Broadway–Lafayette St.*

7 b-8

353 Columbus Ave. (between 76th and 77th Sts.), Upper West Side, 212/873–2061. Subway: 79th St.

9 e-8

95 5th Ave. (at 17th St.), Chelsea, 212/675–2550. Subway: F to 14th St.; N, R to 23rd St.

11 d-1

KINWAY INDUSTRIES LTD.

Nothing dainty here (including the decor)—it's crammed with well-priced Converse, Airwalk, and Simple sneakers plus Sketchers, Doc Martens, and Frye boots. *5 W. 8th St. (between 5th and 6th Aves.), Greenwich Village, 212/777–3848. Subway: 8th St.; W. 4th St./Washington Sq.*

11 d-1

LUICHINY

This little store holds the title of Biggest Shoes on West 8th Street. With platforms and towering heels, most of the stock defies anything under 6 inches tall. Relatively sedate styles include stacked sandals or slides with inflatable uppers—and then there are the unmissable knee-high, platform, glitter boots. *21 W. 8th St. (between 5th and 6th Aves.), Greenwich Village, 212/477–3445. Subway: 8th St.; W. 4th St./Washington Sq.*

9 d-4

MANOLO BLAHNIK

Blahnik's spindly-heel, pointy-toe shoes are the last word in luxury. Society dames swear by them, Hollywood types teeter in them, and Tori Amos loves them—all with good reason. The vamps are the shoe equivalent of a well-cut low neckline, making the foot a sensual thing indeed. A simple satin evening pump is roughly $400; prices can skyrocket to over $2,000. *31 W. 54th St. (between 5th and 6th Aves.), Midtown, 212/582–3007. Subway: E, F to 5th Ave.*

9 *e-2*

MARAOLO

Midtown Manhattan is crawling with Maraolo-shod cubicle farmers. This is the place to go for a shiny moc-croc or trim pump. The West 72nd Street location is a factory outlet, with shoes priced between $19 and $99. *782 Lexington Ave. (at 61st St.), Upper East Side, 212/832–8182. Subway: 59th St./Lexington Ave.*

9 *b-1*

131 W. 72nd St. (between Columbus Ave. and Broadway), Upper West Side, 212/787–6550. Subway: 72nd St.

9 *e-3*

551 Madison Ave. (at 55th St.), Midtown, 212/308–8794. Subway: E, F to 5th Ave.; and other locations.

10 *e-1*

99x

These Brits have an enviably encyclopedic selection of Doc Martens and creepers. *84 E. 10th St. (between 3rd and 4th Aves.), East Village, 212/460–8599. Subway: Astor Pl.*

9 *e-8*

OTTO TOOTSI PLOHOUND

An essential part of many downtown closets, these shoes are often chunky-soled and somewhat heftily priced. Most shoes, including the store's own label, are made in Italy—you'll regularly find Costume National, Miu Miu, Michel Perry, and a few designer numbers by Anna Sui or Vivienne Westwood. During sales, you can get some good stompers for about $90. *137 5th Ave. (between 20th and 21st Sts.), Chelsea, 212/460–8650. Subway: F to 23rd St.*

9 *e-3*

38 E. 57th St. (between Park and Madison Aves.), Midtown, 212/231–3199. Subway: 59th St./Lexington Ave. or N, R to 5th Ave.

11 *d-4*

413 W. Broadway (between Prince and Spring Sts.), SoHo, 212/925–8931. Subway: C, E to Spring St.

9 *e-1*

PETER FOX

It's hard to pin down the lavish, offbeat look of these shoes—retro lines such as

Louis heels are mixed with modern round toes or low platforms. The vintage romanticism has led them onto Broadway and the silver screen; Kate Winslet wore a pair in *Titantic*. There's a particularly substantial selection of bridal shoes; prepare for lots of lustrous satin and bows. *806 Madison Ave. (at 68th St.), Upper East Side, 212/744–8340. Subway: 68th St./Hunter College.*

11 *d-4*

105 Thompson St. (between Prince and Spring Sts.), SoHo, 212/431–7426. Subway: C, E to Spring St.

11 *d-1*

PETIT PETON

You can turn up some funky finds here, even by West 8th Street's standards; strappy heels by Claudio Merazzi, for instance, come plumed with feathers. *27 W. 8th St., Greenwich Village, 212/677–3730. Subway: 8th St.; W. 4th St./Washington Sq.*

9 *e-2*

ROBERT CLERGERIE

These classy French shoes make their own fun: a pair of flats could have turned-up toes, an oxford could have its lacings shifted to the side. The various styles of high-vamped, dark-fabric-covered shoes work well with pants suits. Most pairs run in the hundreds of dollars. *681 Madison Ave. (between 61st and 62nd Sts.), Upper East Side, 212/207–8600. Subway: 59th St./Lexington Ave.*

9 *e-4*

SALVATORE FERRAGAMO

Giant photos of happy customer Audrey Hepburn beam down on the gorgeous goods. These shoes know how to flatter a woman's foot—molded insteps, heels just the right height. Traditional styles, such as the square bow on the vamp, are still holding their own, though you can also find updated loafers and teasing sandals. *661 5th Ave. (between 52nd and 53rd Sts.), Midtown, 212/759–3822. Subway: E, F to 5th Ave.*

9 *e-1*

SERGIO ROSSI

These beaded stilettos and thin patent leather straps are sure to draw attention to your pedicure. More substantial shoes could include pointy crocodile pumps or ponyskin loafers. *835 Madison Ave. (between 69th and 70th Sts.), Upper East Side, 212/396–4814. Subway: 77th St.*

9 *e-5*

SELBY FIFTH AVENUE

You'll never have to worry about pinched toes with this selection, which includes Easy Spirit, Mephisto, Nickels, and Clarks. Selby's own line is both cheaper and sleeker. *417 5th Ave. (at 38th St.), Garment District, 212/328–1020. Subway: B, D, F, Q to 42nd St.*

9 *e-2*

1055 3rd Ave. (between 62nd and 63rd Sts.), Upper East Side, 212/328–1001. Subway: 59th St./Lexington Ave.

11 *d-1*

SEVEN BOUTIQUE LTD.

Cowboy boots and (almost) nothing but—they come in ostrich, snakeskin, ponyskin, lizard, and over a dozen colors. *19 W. 8th St. (between 5th and 6th Aves.), Greenwich Village, 212/533–5909. Subway: 8th St.; W. 4th St./Washington Sq.*

11 *f-4*

SIGERSON MORRISON

Shoe boxes line the walls of this tiny boutique; peer down and you'll find delicate leather shoes at your feet. Pay close attention to the details, such as small buckles or interesting hues (pale dove gray, bronzey brown). While some styles are whittled into narrow toes, you can generally find rounded slippers as well. Prices generally hover around $250. *242 Mott St. (between Houston and Prince Sts.), SoHo/Little Italy, 212/219–3893. Subway: Broadway–Lafayette St.*

11 *d-4*

STEPHANE KÉLIAN

Kélian's woven beauties are a Eurohound's favorite; they do wonders to an all-black outfit. Sometimes the woven or strappy leather uppers are laced with a hard-to-match but too-chic color, such an ochre or burnt orange. They've also dabbled in thick soles, wedges, and pencil-thin heels. For perfect coordination, peruse the handbag selection. *158 Mercer St. (between Houston and Prince Sts.), SoHo, 212/925–3077. Subway: Broadway–Lafayette.*

9 *e-2*

717 Madison Ave. (between 63rd and 64th Sts.), Upper East Side, 212/980–1919. Subway: 68th St./Hunter College.

9 *e-3*

STUART WEITZMAN

Never let it be said that these guys don't love their shoes—cards, napkins, and other shoe-oriented accessories peek from the corners. And the selection is happily wide-ranging, in terms of both style and size: rubber-sole loafers; knee-high nappa boots; peau de soie evening pumps; from C to AAA in width and sized from 4–12. *625 Madison Ave. (between 58th and 59th Sts.), Midtown, 212/750–2555. Subway: 59th St./Lexington Ave.*

9 *e-3*

TOD'S

The Eurofave driving shoe has upped its American profile with new boutiques in major cities. The various loafer styles come in sedate black and brown or something eye-catching such as red crocodile; if you can't find exactly what you want, head to the custom area in back. The workmanship is excellent, and you'll pay several hundreds for it. If you've got any spare hundreds left over, browse through the bags, from untreated leather handbags to the signature studded "8" bag in dyed ponyskin. *650 Madison Ave., (at 60th St.), Midtown, 212/644–5945. Subway: 59th St./Lexington Ave.*

9 *e-2*

UNISA

This is a fantastic place to get a lower-priced take on a trend. Thick-sole slides or wedges are under $50, while grown-up pumps and loafers are just under $60. *701 Madison Ave. (at 62nd St.), Upper East Side, 212/753–7474. Subway: 59th St./Lexington Ave.*

9 *e-1*

VARDA

These handmade Italian shoes are worth every penny. The exclusive designs often have softly rounded or open toes, T-straps or ankle straps, and not-too-spindly 2- or 3-inch heels. You can have most styles in any color you want—as long as it's black. *786 Madison Ave. (between 66th and 67th Sts.), Upper East Side, 212/472–7552. Subway: 68th St./Hunter College.*

11 d-4

149 Spring St. (between W. Broadway and Wooster St.), SoHo, 212/941–4990. Subway: Spring St.

9 e-2

VIA SPIGA

The first U.S. branch of this Italian shoemaker has wooed the city with just what it likes—mostly black shoes and low boots, many in buffed-to-a-shine calfskin or soft-as-butter suede. 765 Madison Ave. (between 65th and 66th Sts.), Upper East Side, 212/988–4877. Subway: 68th St./Hunter College.

9 e-2

WALTER STEIGER

Following trends from a discreet distance, Walter Steiger makes lovely pumps (about $300), some in textured leather or fabric—wool flannel, for instance. There's also quite a range of golf shoes—those white leathers and cleats come spiked in candy colors. 739 Madison Ave. (between 65th and 66th Sts.), Upper East Side, 212/570–1212. Subway: 68th St./Hunter College.

9 e-3

417 Park Ave. (at 55th St.), Midtown, 212/826–7171. Subway: Lexington Ave.

swimsuits

Most department stores have year-round swim- and cruisewear departments. If you need a workhorse suit, try a sporting-goods store (see Sporting Goods & Clothing, below).

11 e-5

KEIKO

Tug no more on the back end of your bathing suit—here you can have it customized to fit. Keiko herself once worked for Warner Bros., which may have something to do with the kapow! primary-color palette. Styles range from string bikinis to boy-cut tanks to tankinis. 62 Greene St. (between Spring and Broome Sts.), SoHo, 212/226–6051. Subway: 6 to Spring St.

7 e-8

WATER WEAR

No matter what time of year your cruise departs, Water Wear is waiting with a full selection of swimsuits. You may have to duck some garish getups, but there's almost always something accept-able. Big bonus: Bikini tops and bottoms can be bought separately. 1349 3rd Ave. (at 77th St.), Upper East Side, 212/570–6606. Subway: 77th St.

CLOTHING FOR MEN/GENERAL

classic

ALFRED DUNHILL TAILORS OF LONDON

See Custom, below.

9 e-2

AQUASCUTUM OF LONDON

This is the New York home of an English clothing firm famed for its trench coats and luxurious tailoring. Highlights are cashmere sweaters, tweed coats, and snappy London pinstripes that would make a Lloyds adjuster weep with pleasure. 714 Madison Ave. (between 63rd and 64th Sts.), Upper East Side, 212/753–8305. Subway: 59th St./Lexington Ave.

9 d-8

BANANA REPUBLIC

BR's come a long way since first opening as a dorky pseudo-safari outfitter in the mid-80s. Since reinventing themselves as purveyors of casual urban chic, they've been on an unending quest to make cotton sexy. In that spirit, and one of remaining vaguely trendy, nearly everything these days is ribbed, fitted, and v-necked. They still retain a lovely selection of classic dress shirts, underwear, khakis, and semi-dressy shoes. 655 5th Ave. (at 52nd St.), Midtown, 212/644–6678. Subway: E, F to 5th Ave.

9 e-4

89 5th Ave. (at 18th St.), Flatiron District, 212/366–4630. Subway: F to 14th St., N, R to 23rd St.

7 e-7

1136 Madison Ave. (at 84th St.), Upper East Side, 212/570–2465. Subway: 4, 5, 6 to 86th St.; and other locations.

9 d-3

BERGDORF GOODMAN MEN

Once revolutionary—a throwback to the refined era of clubby gentleman's haberdashery with curveballs such as Prada, Dolce & Gabbana, and Gaultier tossed in—this spectacular emporium across the street from the Plaza Hotel has lately retrenched, aiming to garner "serious" dressers and leave the friskier stuff (Gucci thongs, Matsuda sarongs) to the boutiques stretching north on Madison Avenue. Featured are Romeo Gigli, Giorgio Armani, and Gucci as well as perhaps the best shoe selection in Manhattan, with To Boot and J.P. Tod anchoring the high end. Pampering for the affluent executive includes custom tailoring, a concierge, a café, a penthouse hair salon, the use of cellular phones, and a putting green. *745 5th Ave. (at 58th St.), Midtown, 212/753–7300. Closed Sun. Subway: N, R to 5th Ave.*

9 *e-3*

BIJAN

If you have extravagant taste and a bankroll to match—oh, and an appointment—this haute haberdasher from Rodeo Drive offers, among other frills, shirts that start at $240 and ties at $110(!). *699 5th Ave. (between 54th and 55th Sts.), Midtown, 212/758–7500. Closed Sun. Subway: E, F to 5th Ave.*

9 *e-4*

BRIONI

Elegant Italian men's clothing, featuring sumptuous fabrics and classic European styling and cut, sells for appropriately high prices at this luxurious, inviting boutique. Suits can be made to measure. *55 E. 52nd St. (between Madison and Park Aves.), Midtown, 212/355–1940. Subway: E, F to 5th Ave.*

9 *d-6*

BROOKS BROTHERS

Since 1818 they've stood above and beyond fashion as the makers of the finest classic suit money can buy. But these days that isn't enough. With so many imitators nipping at their heels and their profits, Brooks Brothers sullied their dignified, discreet image in the early '90s by coming up with some bizarre Euro designs in an attempt to update and hold their market share. When it didn't work they scaled back to what they always did best, gray-wool sack suits, navy blazers, seersucker, repp ties, formal wear, and of course the original, glorious, 5-trillion thread count cotton dress shirt, tailored to perfection. The difference now is that they house it all in a huge, glitzy new storefront on Fifth Avenue and have hired a new model (in his 20s) for their advertising: a kinder, gentler WASP. *666 5th Ave. (at 52nd St.), Midtown, 212/261–9440. Subway: 5th Ave./53rd St.*

9 *d-5*

346 Madison Ave. (at 44th St.), Midtown, 212/682–8800. Subway: 42nd St./Grand Central.

10 *e-6*

1 Church St. (Liberty Plaza), Lower Manhattan, 212/267–2400. Subway: World Trade Ctr.

9 *b-8*

CAMOUFLAGE

These Chelsea specialty shops feature classic, American-made menswear with an upbeat, imaginative feel, plus more-casual threads at No. 139. Don't miss the elaborate selection of ties. *139–141 8th Ave. (at 17th St.), Chelsea, 212/741–9118 or 212/691–1750. Subway: A, C, E to 14th St.; L to 8th Ave.*

9 *e-1*

DAVID CENCI

This dignified shop is a handsome setting for an expensive but outstanding selection of impeccably tailored classics, showcasing wonderful fabrics in everything from suits and sportswear to coats and formal wear. *801 Madison Ave. (near 67th St.), Upper East Side, 212/628–5910. Closed Sun. Subway: 68th St./Hunter College.*

9 *e-8*

EMPORIO ARMANI

Against a mellow Milanese backdrop (blond wood, stainless steel, pale-cream lampshades) in a Stanford White building, the oft-imitated but rarely equaled Italian master showcases his "mid" range: slightly less expensive, sportier, and more experimental than the Collezioni. If you're out to see what Gio has on his mind, this is the place to witness his ever-changing moods. They're generally arrayed around a basic theme—a concoction of Indian motifs, gray, corduroy, tweed, and red, each depending on the season—and take shape in classic separates, casual sweaters, trousers, ties, shoes, belts, accessories, and formal wear! This store is something of a touchstone; stroll by each season to take stock of menswear and to be entertained by the always-inventive and frequently modified window displays. *110 5th Ave. (at 16th St.), Chelsea, 212/727–3240. Subway: F to 14th St.*

9 *e-3*

FAÇONNABLE

A limber, sporty, Mediterranean mood dominates this unimposing two-story shop in the middle of Manhattan's poshest shopping strip. The clothes are simple, French interpretations of American classics: button-down check shirts, khakis, windbreakers, lightweight cotton sweaters, fun-in-the-sun accessories, colorful ties, and conservatively tailored suits and separates. Frenchmen can't get enough of this stuff; it combines the European flair for relaxed elegance with durable fabrics that can wear several hats. Perfect threads for a weekend jaunt to Sag Harbor, or a late weekday lunch at Balthazar. *689 5th Ave. (at 54th St.), Midtown, 212/319–0111. Subway: E, F to 5th Ave.*

9 *e-3*

GAP

Why, in New York City, shop at the Gap when you can go to a thousand other stores? Well, the clothes are comfortable, cheap, and no two items will ever clash. It's also convenient. They're probably building another one on your corner right now. *680 Fifth Ave. (at 54th St.), Midtown, 212/977–7023. Subway: 47th–50th St./Rockefeller Ctr.*

9 *e-3*

60 W. 34th St. (Herald Sq.), Garment District, 212/643–8960. Subway: 34th St./Herald Sq.

9 *d-6*

734 Lexington Ave. (at 59th St.), Midtown, 212/751–1543. Subway: 59th St./Lexington Ave.

9 *e-2*

1131–1149 3rd Ave. (between 66th and 67th Sts.), Upper East Side, 212/472–5559. Subway: 68th St./Hunter College; and other locations.

9 *d-3*

HARRISON JAMES

This brand-new menswear emporium stresses exquisite Italian tailoring and personal service. The store itself is remarkable—it's in a town house across the street from the MoMA sculpture garden, in a building whose first floor once served as Cary Grant's office. The spirit of Grant's debonair ease dominates this clubby store, not to mention its movie-star prices (think nothing of spending $1,000 on a sport coat, or

$400 on a pair of loafers). There are almost no salespeople; instead, customers are greeted in the store's lobby and assigned a "guide" who provides a tour of the shop, including a glimpse at the tailoring room and the cigar humidor. The philosophy is snooty, but it doesn't overwhelm the store's understanding that fine menswear should be comfortable and basically conservative. Also available are formal wear, custom shirtings, a bar, and a barber shop whose waiting area contains a pool table, on which customers can, as the management says, "pay off their bills" by wagering. *5 W. 54th St. (between 5th and 6th Aves.), Midtown, 212/541–6870. Subway: E, F to 5th Ave.*

9 *e-3*

HERMÈS

East 57th Street is home to some of the most exclusive boutiques this side of the Rive Gauche, but the French import that has made the biggest splash, particularly in the wake of the runaway bull market on Wall Street, is this longtime French saddle-maker and purveyor of ultrafine silk prints. A fashionable man will tell you that if you have $1,000 to spend on your whole ensemble, this is the place to buy that tie that you'll pass down to your grandson. The average price for a whimsical bridle-tack print? $120. Also on the block are Hermès suits, jackets, leather goods, and, of course, saddles. Don't forget to save the boxes! They're the best in retailing, and their signature color is now commonly known as "Hermès Orange." *11 E. 57th St. (between 5th and Madison Aves.), Midtown, 212/751–3181. Subway: E, F to 5th Ave.*

9 *d-8*

J. CREW

The best thing about the catalog was always the models, and they don't sell them at the store. Since its heyday 10 years ago, J. Crew has retrenched into the pale of modern preppiedom, not conservative enough to be fetishy, not flashy enough to be interesting. The stores are spare and lovely but so are lots of others. Go for the underwear, if it's on sale. *91 5th Ave. (between 16th and 17th Sts.), Chelsea, 212/255–4848, F to 14th St., N, R to 23rd St.*

10 *f-7*

99 Prince St. (between Mercer and Greene Sts.), SoHo, 212/966–2739. Subway: Prince St.

11 *e-4*

203 Front St. (South Street Seaport), Lower Manhattan, 212/385–3500. Subway: 2, 3 to Fulton St.

9 *e-5*

J. PRESS

It's been almost a hundred years since this store opened its doors in New Haven, Connecticut, ready to serve the basic sartorial needs of Yalies. In New York the stock has gone through precious few changes since the '60s—lapels and ties have gotten wider, maybe a few more belts have been added to the mix, but Press still delivers that natural-shoulder, hyperpreppy, button-down look for new generations determined to perpetuate Ivy League style (even if most people at the Ivies have moved on). If you've just gotten into Skull and Bones, this is where you go to buy your club tie. *7 E. 44th St. (near 5th Ave.), Midtown, 212/687–7642. Closed Sun. Subway: 42nd St./Grand Central.*

9 *e-4*

PAUL STUART

The mood here is natty, dashing, conservative but unstuffy, with an emphasis on variety where it counts; hence the tiny shoe section adjacent to the largest selection of good ties in the city (including more bows and knits than you've ever seen under a single glass display). Men who buy here spend huge amounts on few choice items, don't noodle with the basics, and know that this is the place to come for, bar none, the best fedora in the Big Apple. Sales do happen, but they seem to be advertised by ESP; those who benefit are those who drop in often. *10 E. 45th St. (near 5th Ave.), Midtown, 212/682–0320. Closed Sun. Subway: 42nd St./Grand Central.*

9 *e-1*

POLO/RALPH LAUREN/POLO SPORT

Ah, what a pompous paean to the vanished days of merrie olde England, all jammed, at the the flagship store on Madison Avenue, into the Rhinelander Mansion amid more mahogany and green baize than anyone should ever see in one place. (The new SoHo store achieves a certain *je ne sais quoi* country look.) Trimmings include dog prints, and plenty of them; images of blue-bloods on horseback in red hunting jackets; weathered leather; and scads of clean-cut, impeccably bronze employees, buzzing around attending to every imaginable (or imagined) need. What Bronx-born Lauren has done is out-WASP those WASPs whose casual, hale-and-hearty, outdoorsman style inspired his designs. Frugality, however, is not one of the things he has borrowed from the Old Newport crowd: Everything he sells is of obsessively high quality, maybe too high if you're not sure you need flannels designed for Arctic conditions or herringbone tweeds that weigh more than the average beagle. The khakis, signature polo shirts, shoes, sport coats, and other preppy staples are all here, but so is Lauren's new Purple Label line of English suits, something he's lately been passionately promoting after decades of showing up everywhere in jeans and a bomber jacket. *867 Madison Ave. (at 72nd St.), Upper East Side, 212/606–2100. Closed Sun. Subway: 68th St./Hunter College.*

11 *d-5*

379 W. Broadway (between Spring and Broome Sts.), SoHo, 212/625–1660. Subway: C, E to Spring St.

9 *d-4*

SAKS FIFTH AVENUE

Once perhaps the most fabled store in town, Saks has in recent years seen its thunder stolen by a host of competitors, everyone from Barneys to The Gap. However, for a clean, well-mannered menswear experience, and one that suits most fellas head-to-toe, Saks continues to sustain enormous snob appeal, if limited hipness. All of the usual suspects can be found on the 6th floor: Armani Collezioni, Calvin Klein, Versace Versus, Donna Karan. However, where Saks really shines is in the classic arena. Oxford Clothes, the nearly century-old Savile Row–style clothier, delivers that Prince of Wales look—snugly tailored conservative suits in dashing pinstripes and sturdy flannels—while across the aisle is Alan Flusser's shop, a Saks exclusive since Flusser's independent business went belly-up several years back; this remains one of the few places in town where you can buy Flusser's indispensable menswear guide. *611 5th Ave. (at 50th St.), Midtown, 212/940–2455. Subway: E, F to 5th Ave.*

9 *e-1*

YVES SAINT LAURENT RIVE GAUCHE FOR MEN

Saint Laurent's high-priced high fashion is worn by almost no one. Cowards. There are few other places in town to obtain a correctly cut, side-vented navy blazer, a Parisian standby. *859 Madison Ave. (between 70th and 71st Sts.), Upper East Side, 212/517–7400. Closed Sun. Subway: 68th St./Hunter College.*

contemporary

11 *e-4*

AGNÈS B. HOMME

Taking its cue from the early 1960s, this medium-size SoHo shop—bedecked with old French New Wave cinema posters and such baubles as postcards of *Psycho*'s Tony Perkins grinning in blue gingham and tweed—is perhaps the finest example anywhere of the Parisian take on American Rat Pack style. Suits, stacks of exquisite shirts, leather porkpie chapeaux (for that Dean Martin snap), dozens of ties no wider than 2 inches, leather car coats, striped boatsman T-shirts, and an assortment of witty accessories make Agnès B. Homme a must-stop for any cat infatuated with the Sands Hotel heyday of Old Blue Eyes or who simply wants to affect a chic Parisian style at its casual best. *79 Greene St. (at Spring St.), SoHo, 212/431–4339. Subway: 6 to Spring St.*

11 *e-4*

A.P.C.

This store resembles a cross between an American barn and a French farmhouse, yet the clothes are anything but country. Anything but cheap, either. The style tends to be nerdish urban slacker, drawing heavily on the aesthetic of thrift-store finds from the '70s: fuzzy wool sweaters, in colors such as aqua and avocado; narrow-wale corduroy jeans; velvet jackets with trousers to match, in chocolate; white shirts. All very Beck, circa 1996. It's not for everybody, but A.P.C. can generally be counted on for comfortable, unforced threads that mine current fringe trends in a high-quality manner (no one really wants to wear some moth-eaten mohair cardigan from Cheap Jack's, anyway). *131 Mercer St. (between Prince and Spring Sts.), SoHo, 212/966–9685. Subway: 6 to Spring St.; Prince St.*

11 *e-4*

A/X (ARMANI EXCHANGE)

Perhaps a bit more Euro than absolutely necessary (What's up with those enormous belt buckles? And really, who wears indigo denim besides Italian photojournalists?), but nevertheless a commendable distillation of the Milanese Master's easy, fluid, and in this case even colorful sportswear designs, meant to compete with The Gap and J. Crew. "A/X" is meant to recall the buy-everything U.S. Army "P/X" (Post Exchange) of the Gomer Pyle era; truth is, if you don't mind shelling out some heavy dollars for a shirt (say, $100), there's scant reason to shop anywhere else, so comprehensive is the A/X selection. The stuff—jeans, jackets, outerwear, T-shirts, and so on—is superbly made, beautifully textured and styled, and comfortable. Some of the sales are succulent. *568 Broadway (between Houston and Prince Sts.), SoHo, 212/431–6000. Subway: Prince St.; Broadway–Lafayette St.*

9 *e-2*

BARNEYS NEW YORK

Oh, how the mighty have fallen! With the close of Barneys' flagship store on 17th Street and the Pressman family's resolution of their battle with Japanese investors over the fate of the uptown palace (they've been bailed out by Hong Kong financier Dickson Poon), it's beginning to look as if this New York institution, started three generations ago as a discount menswear shop, is going to go the way of B. Altman. For the time being, however, this is the place to go for that quintessentially snotty Manhattan shopping experience. From the supple staples of Giorgio Armani and Calvin Klein to the vanguard fantasies of Helmut Lang, Paul Smith, and Dries van Noten—not to mention the sticker shock supplied by Hermès—the Madison Avenue store sells merchandise that's available in plenty of other places, but not in the über-stylish, forward gestalt that Barneys has built its reputation on. For a more egalitarian vibe, there's always the annual downtown warehouse sale, which finds Gotham's male population lined up for hours to snare deeply discounted suits, acres of shirts, yards of designer ties, and avant-garde items that just didn't move on the main floor, such as that Comme des Garçons linen jacket with seven pockets, marked down from

$1,200 to a tidy $600. Alterations are free. *660 Madison Ave. (at 61st St.), Upper East Side, 212/826–8900, Subway: 59th St./Lexington Ave.*

10 *d-7*

World Financial Center, 225 Liberty St., Lower Manhattan, 212/945–1600, Subway: World Trade Ctr.

11 *e-4*

BEAU BRUMMEL

This is shopping for the confused: The store's own line shares space with no-brainer professional standbys, such as Hugo Boss, but the whole affair exudes a dated, overly flashy vibe that looks more discount than upscale, despite the steep prices. *421 W. Broadway (between Prince and Spring Sts.), SoHo, 212/219–2666. Subway: C, E to Spring St.*

9 *e-2*

CALVIN KLEIN

The boutique-as–art gallery metaphor flourishes at this multifloor architectural promo for America's prime minimalist. You name it, CK's got it: sportswear, the drapey suits, the textured, monochrome ties, socks, and, of course, scads of that scanty underwear. The place is a real Madison Avenue scene on a Saturday afternoon in early spring or fall. *654 Madison Ave. (at 60th St.), Upper East Side, 212/292–9000. Subway: 59th St./Lexington Ave.*

9 *e-8*

CLUB MONACO

This mini-chain has caused a sensation with its sleek, trendy, reasonably priced sportswear. Known to some as the Gay Gap, it provides the same kind of no-brainer one stop shopping but in a sexier, more body-conscious, Prada knock-off way. Clingy sweaters, filmy shirts, bulky jeans, and skinny trousers are all the rage, if you've got the body for it. *160 Fifth Ave. (at 21st St.), 212/352–0936. Subway: Union Sq.*

7 *b-7*

2376 Broadway (at 87th St.), Upper West Side, 212/579–2587. Subway: 1, 9 to 86th St.

10 *f-3*

510 Broadway (at Spring St.), SoHo, 212/941–1511. Subway: Broadway/Lafayette.

9 *b-8*

COMME DES GARÇONS

Astoundingly expensive avant-garde designs (multifabric jackets, innovative textures, tricks with linings, funky shoes, $60 socks) from Japanese fashion radical Rei Kawakubo are displayed in a stunning white space in far west Chelsea. *520 W. 22nd St. (between 10th and 11th Aves.), Chelsea, 212/604–9200. Subway: C, E to 23rd St.*

7 *a-7*

FRANK STELLA

Stella offers super men's fashions, including silk shirts in solids and stripes along with the more common, 100%-cotton variety; sweaters; hundreds of ties; and accessories. *440 Columbus Ave. (at 81st St.), Upper West Side, 212/877–5566. Subway: 79th St.*

9 *d-4*

FRENCH CONNECTION

Okay, okay; the colors and styles aren't for everybody, and unless you're in entertainment or advertising, it might be tough to get away with some of the four-button Euro-casual suits and separates in which this pseudo-Gallic, slightly libertine version of Banana Republic specializes. They deliver big, though, on the inventory-clearing sales. *1270 6th Ave. (at 51st St.), Midtown, 212/262–6623. Subway: 47th–50th Sts./Rockefeller Ctr.*

11 *e-4*

435 W. Broadway (at Prince St.), SoHo, 212/219–1197. Subway: Prince St., Broadway–Lafayette St.

9 *e-2*

GIORGIO ARMANI/ EMPORIO ARMANI

Nearly across the street from his snazzier main boutique, Armani has opened a second store to sell his midprice Emporio line. While the older shop is a spiritual cousin of Calvin Klein's (white, open, airy), the Emporio resembles a pre–World War I Berlin department store. It's funky, but certainly not excessive, and it's hard to beat either location for high-quality, supremely reserved, and ever-so-inhabitable styles for everyone from lawyers to Indian chiefs with a thing for beige. *760 Madison Ave. (between 65th and 66th Sts.), Upper East Side, 212/988–9191. Subway: 68th St./Hunter College.*

9 *e-3*

Emporio, 601 Madison Ave. (between 57th and 58th Sts.), Midtown, 212/317–0800. Subway: 59th St./Lexington Ave.

11 *e-4*
LAUNDRY INDUSTRY
You have three color choices at this Amsterdam import: white, beige, and black—lots and lots of black. The clothes are nothing complicated, just reliable SoHo casual stuff with an eye toward body-consciousness that will carry the unflappable wearer from office to event to late-night bistro. *122 Spring St. (at Greene St.), SoHo, 212/343–2225. Subway: Spring St.*

9 *d-8*
OLD NAVY
From the people at the Gap, who brought you meaningless clothing, comes this deeper discount emporium, specializing in disposable clothing. Not much sells for more than $20, and nothing lasts for more than three washes. Secret bargains: belts, bathing suits. *610 Sixth Ave. (at 18th St.), Flatiron District, 212/645–0663. Subway: F to 14th St.*

10 *e-4*
503–511 Broadway (at Broome St.), SoHo, 212/226–0865. Subway: 6 to Spring St.

7
300 W. 125th St. (between 8th and St. Nicholas Aves.), Harlem, 212/531–1544. Subway: A, B, C, D to 125th St.

11 *e-8*
PAUL SMITH
Smith's ideas of menswear are a bit much for some. He adores pattern clash, is addicted to a slim, mod silhouette that hefty guys might not cotton to, and is excessively buffeted by the winds of change. Still, for top-flight duds, glibly designed accessories (the best watch, cufflink, and eyeglass styles going), supremely slick, wanna-be Italian suits, nifty ties, and shoes to die for—not to mention biannual seasonal sales (75% off during their final days)—Paul Smith continues to dazzle. Celebrity customers include David Hockney, which should reveal something about Smith's fearless attitude toward color. Not for the monochrome set. *108 5th Ave. (at 16th St.), Chelsea, 212/627–9770. Subway: F to 14th St.*

10 *e-3*
PHAT FARM
The boutique for hip-hop fashion, phat farm's house label offers baggy jeans, madras shirts, and colorful, sometimes bizarre T-shirts, in sizes ranging from large to xxl but meant to fit everyone. *129 Prince St. (between Wooster St. and West Broadway), SoHo, 212/533–7428, Subway: N, R to Prince St.*

9 *e-3*
PRADA
This very expensive, very Italian, very minimal boutique delivers the styles of the moment amid lime walls and chrome railings: slim, neo-mod suits in charcoal and black, chunky shoes, exquisite leathers, and no small measure of attitude. Absolutely the current It Store, the place to see and be seen—so much so that, at press time, Prada is opening a branch in SoHo. *45 E. 57th St. (between Madison and Park Aves.), Midtown, 212/308–2332. Closed Sun. Subway: E, F to 5th Ave.*

9 *e-3*
724 5th Ave. (between 57th and 56th Sts.), Midtown, 212/664–0010. Subway: N, R to 5th Ave.

9 *e-1*
841 Madison Ave. (at 70th St.), Upper East Side, 212/327–4200. Subway: 68th St./Hunter College.

10 *e-3*
PRADA SPORT
An odd mix of athletic, futuristic, and Euro-luxe characterizes Prada's Sport line. In the winter you'll find down parkas that look like space suits and hooded sweatshirts made of cashmere. Year round finds more standard upscale warm-up clothes and possibly the ugliest selection of shoes ever created. What do you get when you cross mules with sneakers? Flats for nurses, but that doesn't mean no one's wearing them. *116 Wooster St. (between Prince and Spring), SoHo, 212/925–2221. Subway: N, R to Prince St.*

11 *d-4*
SEAN
Amid the black-and-white boxes that litter SoHo is this warm little boutique that quietly yet gleefully out-Euros them all. It's the only U.S. store to carry the understated, carefully crafted clothes of

French designer Pierre Emile Lafaurie, and it quietly lays on its Continental hands with such gems as a corduroy "painter's jacket" (about $100) and multi-hued dress shirts. *132 Thompson St. (between Prince and Houston Sts.), SoHo, 212/598–5980. Subway: Prince St.*

10 a-3

224 Columbus Ave. (between 70th and 71st Sts.), Upper West Side, 212/769–1489. Subway: B, C to 72nd St.

10 e-2

TRANSIT
This boutique-size glorified sneaker store is cleverly designed to look like a subway station. Indeed it sells the sort of clothes that have the most street credibility. Designers such as Pelle Pelle, Enyce, and Fubu can be found here along with the usual urban faddish duds by Tommy Hilfiger and Ralph Lauren. *665 Broadway (at Bond St.), Greenwich Village, 212/358–8726. Subway: Broadway/Lafayette.*

11 e-5

ZARA
Like fellow newcomer Club Monaco, Zara specializes in cutting-edge Euro knockoffs with more of a dressy approach. Modern but not too-too trendy suits, sweaters, and separates can be found along with a lot of big-buckle, square-toe shoes. The discount does, however, show in the fabric. Shirts are paper thin and blazers tend to have a few loose threads. Still, if you can't afford Gucci for the office, it's about your only alternative. *580 Broadway (at Prince), SoHo, 212/343–1725. Subway: Broadway–Lafayette St.*

9 e-3

750 Lexington (at 59th. St.), Midtown East, 212/754–1120. Subway: 59th St./Lexington Ave.

9 d-7

101 Fifth Ave. (at 18th St.), Flatiron District, 212/741–0555. Subway: 14th St./Union Sq.

custom

9 e-3

ALFRED DUNHILL TAILORS OF LONDON
Dunhill supplies old-school British tailoring perfection in the form of custom men's suits and shirts (remarkably,

they'll come to you for a fitting) and off-the-peg imports. The facade is suitably imposing, as the wares are very luxurious and very expensive; secondary treats include sweaters, custom-made shoes, ties, scarves, leather goods, jewelry, writing instruments, fine gifts, and smokers' accessories. *450 Park Ave. (at 57th St.), Midtown, 212/753–9292. Subway: N, R to 5th Ave.*

9 e-1

846 Madison Ave. (at 69th St.), Upper East Side, 212/879–8711. Subway: 68th St./Hunter College.

9 e-4

CHIPP
Custom tailoring rules here. The high-quality, bespoke suits, plus ready-to-wear suits, jackets, and trousers, are very expensive. *11 E. 44th St. (between 5th and Madison Aves.), Suite 501, Midtown, 212/687–0850. Closed Sun.; also closed Sat. in summer. Subway: 42nd St./Grand Central.*

9 e-6

CHRIS-ARTO CUSTOM SHIRT COMPANY
Take your pick of nearly 500 natural fabrics in this Garment District shirt shop. The minimum order is six shirts; delivery takes four weeks. Other custom options are pajamas and boxers. *39 W. 32nd St. (between 5th and 6th Aves.), 6th floor, Garment District, 212/563–4455. Closed weekends. Subway: 34th St./Herald Sq.*

9 e-2

CUSTOM SHOP
These stores are clearinghouses for custom-made shirts. Shoppers can choose from over 300 cotton and cotton-blend fabrics and a variety of collar and cuff styles, as well as ready-to-wear. Delivery takes six weeks. *618 5th Ave. (at 50th St.), Midtown, 212/245–2499. Subway: E, F to 5th Ave.*

9 e-5

338 Madison Ave. (between 43rd and 44th Sts.), Midtown, 212/867–3650. Subway: 42nd St./Grand Central.

10 d-7

115 Broadway (between Cedar and Pine Sts.), Lower Manhattan, 212/267–8535. Subway: Rector St.

10 *e-7*
60 Wall St. (at Hanover St.), Lower Manhattan, 212/480–2954. Closed Sun. Subway: Wall St.

9 *e-1*
SULKA
Custom-made shirts and such trifles as silk pajamas are the order of the day at this perennial *GQ* favorite, which caters to both rich tastes and deep pockets. The off-the-peg selection features English-style suits, sport jackets, and slacks. *840 Madison Ave. (between 69th and 70th Sts.), Upper East Side, 212/452–1900. Subway: 68th St./Hunter College.*

9 *e-3*
430 Park Ave. (at 55th St.), Midtown, 212/980–5200. Subway: 59th St./Lexington Ave.

9 *e-4*
301 Park Ave. (at 50th St., in the Waldorf-Astoria), Midtown, 212/872–4592. Closed Sun. Subway: 51st St./Lexington–3rd Aves.

discount & off-price

9 *d-8*
BURLINGTON COAT FACTORY
Don't let the fluorescent strip lights drive you away. This store is bigger and less crowded than Century 21 and they have fitting rooms. Off-the-rack suits stretch for miles and are made by such dependable names as Perry Ellis and Hugo Boss, and, of course, they're all amazingly cheap. The casual section is less impressive but will occasionally yield up something fabulous. *707 6th Ave. (at 23rd St.), Flatiron District, 212/229–1300. Subway: F to 23rd St.*

10 *e-4*
45 Park Pl. (between Church St. and West Broadway), City Hall, 212/571–2630. Subway: City Hall/Brooklyn Bridge.

10 *e-6*
CENTURY 21
It's combat shopping, but where else are you going to score that Gaultier or Gigli suit at half price? They sell absolutely everything here, and they sell it cheap; but they don't have fitting rooms, so the idea is to grab, grab, grab and return later. The store's a favorite of the nearby Wall Street broker crowd, who hit the gigantic cut-rate department store's racks regularly to load up on Gene Meyer ties, underwear, socks, and

Ralph Lauren suits. There's also an enormous selection of dress shirts, and a bevy of shoes (including Bruno Magli) downstairs. *22 Cortlandt St. (between Broadway and Church St.; near the World Trade Center), Lower Manhattan, 212/227–9092. Subway: Cortlandt St./World Trade Ctr.*

9 *e-8*
DAFFY'S
Like Century 21, Daffy's is an endurance test, full of as much garbage as gold; it rewards the diligent shopper who visits often enough to recognize the dandy stuff. Recent gems have included Industria jackets and sportswear by Les Copains, a popular French purveyor of simple, slightly dressy casual duds including jackets, sweaters, and suits. Don't miss the oceans of ties and socks, not to mention suits and formal wear from countries you didn't know were in the rag trade. *111 5th Ave. (at 18th St.), Chelsea, 212/529–4477. Subway: F to 14th St., N, R to 23rd St.*

9 *e-5*
335 Madison Ave. (at 44th St.), Midtown, 212/557–4422. Subway: 42nd St./Grand Central.

9 *d-6*
1311 Broadway (at 34th St.), Garment District, 212/736–4477. Subway: 34th St./Herald Sq.

9 *d-7*
DAVE'S
The cheapest Levi's 501s in the city can be found here and every size is always in stock. Also workwear and leather from Carhartt, Schott, and Dickies and an exhaustive selection of work boots by Red Wing, Caterpillar, and Carolina. *779 Sixth Ave. (at 26th St.), Flatiron District, 212/989–6444. Subway F to 23rd St.*

9 *e-5*
DOLLAR BILL'S GENERAL STORE
This well-located, well-stocked, well-priced menswear store sells many designer names. Low frills, high savings. *32 E. 42nd St. (Between 5th and Madison Aves.), Midtown, 212/867–0212. Subway: 42nd St./Grand Central.*

10 *e-6*
GORSART
This no-frill Manhattan standby offers classic, natural-shoulder clothing. Prices

are low, and alterations are free. *9 Murray St. (between Broadway and Church St.), 2nd floor, Lower Manhattan, 212/962–0024. Closed Sun. Subway: 2, 3 to Park Pl.; N, R to Brooklyn Bridge/City Hall.*

9 *e-8*

MOE GINSBURG

Need a suit? Why not get four? This is the place to go if you've just landed an entry-level job at Merrill Lynch and need something to wear for the first week. Slicker than Brooks Brothers, Moe provides a shot at some flash (read: designer) clothing for less than you would pay at a fine department store. The suits are many, and the salespeople are low-pressure, honest fellas who deliver competent advice on fit and alterations. *162 5th Ave. (at 21st St.), 2nd to 5th floors, Flatiron District, 212/242–3482. Subway: F to 23rd St.*

9 *e-8*

ROTHMAN'S

Rothman's is a reliable source of quality men's clothing, though the overall sportswear look is stuck in the '80s, with lots of too-slick Italianate stuff upstairs. Belts and ties (some of the ugliest prints in town) are particularly lost in a vanished moment. A more businesslike demeanor reigns downstairs on the suit racks, which feature Perry Ellis, Alexander Julian, and Ralph Lauren as well as deep discounts on Hickey Freeman and Norman Hilton. *200 Park Ave. S (at 17th St.), Flatiron District, 212/777–7400. Closed Sun. Subway: 14th St./Union Sq.*

9 *e-4*

SAINT LAURIE, LTD.

The specialty here is well-tailored business suits in fine fabrics, supplemented by sport coats, overcoats, and slacks. The huge selection is discounted 30%. Alterations are free, and custom tailoring is available by appointment. *350 Park Ave. (between 51st and 52nd Sts.), Midtown, 212/317–8700. Closed Sun. Subway: 51st St./Lexington–3rd Aves.*

9 *e-3*

SYMS

This mondo-store offers three floors of off-price (30%–50%) men's apparel from shoes and socks to hats and coats to swimsuits and tuxes. Designers include Blass, Cerruti, Cardin, Hechter,

and After Six. The specialty? Shirts, and they leave the original labels on, an uncommon practice at the city's other discount centers. Avoid lunch hour here; it's madness. *400 Park Ave. (at 54th St.), Midtown, 212/317–8200. Subway: 51st St./Lexington–3rd Aves.*

10 *e-7*

42 Trinity Pl. (at Rector St.), Lower Manhattan, 212/797–1199. Subway: Rector St.

9 *d-8*

TODAY'S MAN

You'll have no trouble finding a suit here, even if the selection is sort of crummy. Today's Man is one of the superstores (along with Barnes & Noble and Bed, Bath, & Beyond) that led to the dazzling revival of a desolate stretch of 6th Avenue below 23rd Street, a turf once ruled by bike messengers. It aims to appeal to Everyman, a guy who might have any job or any budget, but who in any case dislikes shopping enough to cleave to the promise that he can yank out his Visa once a year and stock up for the next 12 months. The stock includes the full upscale Monty: easy, Italian threads alongside more traditional button-down styles as well as accessories, shoes, and underwear. *625 6th Ave. (at 18th St.), Chelsea, 212/924–0200. Subway: F to 14th St.*

9 *e-5*

529 5th Ave. (at 44th St.), Midtown, 212/557–3111. Subway: 42nd St./Grand Central.

resale, vintage, surplus

10 *e-6*

CHURCH STREET SURPLUS

New and used government-issue, civilian surplus, and vintage clothing fill this store and the overflowing bins on the street, making for a candy store of dusty bargains. *327 Church St. (between Canal and Lispenard Sts.), Lower Manhattan, 212/226–5280. Closed Sun. Subway: 1, 9, A, C, E to Canal St.*

11 *e-4*

UNIQUE CLOTHING WAREHOUSE

This is street-chic headquarters for war surplus, new and renewed; athletic wear; industrial uniforms; and colorfully dyed stuff, all fairly priced. *118A Greene St.*

(between Prince and Spring Sts.), SoHo, 212/431–8210. Subway: 6 to Spring St.

9 *e-8*

WEISS & MAHONEY

Here's an authentic army-navy surplus shop from the pre–cheap chic era (est. 1924). It bills itself as "peaceful" and delivers good buys on fatigues, pea coats, jumpsuits, sweaters, and leather flight jackets. *142 5th Ave. (at 19th St.), Chelsea, 212/675–1915. Subway: F, N, R to 23rd St.*

unusual sizes

9 *d-3*

ROCHESTER BIG & TALL

Yes, the large man can obtain a styling look in the Big Apple without having to slink into the tailoring nether-regions of the outer boroughs. This store, which stocks XL sizes from such formidable sources as Zegna, Canali, and Burberrys, plus shoes from Bally, has branches in both Midtown and Wall Street, both territories where giants stride the earth. And giants need sharp clothes. *1301 6th Ave. (at 52nd St.), Midtown, 212/247–7300. Subway: 47th–50th St./Rockefeller Ctr.*

10 *f-6*

67 Wall St. (at Pearl St.), Lower Manhattan, 212/952–8500. Subway: Wall St.

CLOTHING FOR MEN/SPECIALTY

formal wear

9 *e-4*

HARRISON FORMAL WEAR

Harrison can always be counted on for the latest styles, including After Six, Adolfo, Bill Blass, Yves Saint Laurent, and Lord West. The shop provides same-day service, along with free delivery and pickup. Sunday by appointment only. *560 5th Ave. (at 46th St.), 2nd floor, Midtown, 212/302–1742. Closed Sun. in summer. Subway: 42nd St./Grand Central.*

9 *e-3*

ZELLER TUXEDO

The penguin suits range from traditional to trendy at this Upper East Side shop. Makers include Ungaro, Ferragamo, Valentino, Bally, and Canali, and the selection includes formal accessories. Alterations are free with a purchase. *201 E. 56th St. (between 3rd and 2nd Aves.),*

2nd floor, Midtown, 212/355–0707. Closed Sun. Subway: 59th St./Lexington Ave.

hats

11 *a-1*

CHAMPION SHOES AND HATS

This wide variety of headgear includes Borsalino, Stetson, and Van Dyke's own brand, plus cleaning and blocking. *94 Greenwich Ave. (at W. 12th St.), West Village, 212/929–5696. Closed Sun.; also closed Sat. in summer. Subway: F, 1, 2, 3, 9 to 14th St.*

9 *e-5*

WORTH & WORTH LTD.

The complete hatter for men, Worth & Worth specializes in fedoras by Borsalino, Cavanagh, Stetson, and Christy's of London. Equally worthy are caps and walking hats in cashmere, shetland, viyella, and Harris tweed, as well as a variety of straw summer lids. There's even a catalog. *331 Madison Ave. (at 43rd St.), Midtown, 212/867–6058. Closed Sun. Subway: 42nd St./Grand Central.*

shirts

9 *e-2*

ADDISON ON MADISON

This small shop sells private-label, French-made cotton shirts and silk ties. *698 Madison Ave. (between 62nd and 63rd Sts.), Midtown, 212/308–2660. Closed Sun. Subway: 59th St./Lexington Ave.*

9 *e-3*

ASCOT CHANG

The only games at this prestigious address are the ready-to-wear and custom shirts from the renowned Hong Kong shirtmaker. The vast selection of glorious fabrics, along with 12 different collar styles, amounts to a guarantee that the shirt will, after multiple fittings, feel like you were born in it. Chang also sells made-to-measure suits, dressing gowns, PJs, and handcrafted umbrellas. *7 W. 57th St. (between 5th and 6th Aves.), Midtown, 212/759–3333. Closed Sun. Subway: E, F to 5th Ave.*

9 *e-2*

TURNBULL & ASSER

London's legendary haberdasher, T & A has supplied candy-stripe shirts to everyone from Dominick Dunne to media divas. *745 5th Ave. (at 58th St., in Bergdorf Goodman Men), Midtown, 212/753–7300. Subway: N, R to 5th Ave.*

10 f-7
VICTORY, THE SHIRT EXPERTS
Victory sells its own 100% cotton shirts, comparable in quality to the clubwear uptown. Ready-to-wear shirts range from sizes 14/32 to 18½/36, but if nothing fits, they'll make to measure. Also on sale are silk ties, "braces," and other accessories. *125 Maiden La. (between Water and Pearl Sts.), Lower Manhattan, 212/480–1366. Closed Sun.; also closed Sat. from Jan. to Sept. Subway: Wall St.*

shoes & boots

ATHLETE'S FOOT
See Sporting Goods & Clothing–Running, *below.*

9 e-3
BALLY OF SWITZERLAND
This is the place to come for high-quality, classic yet stylish shoes, all imported from Switzerland. *628 Madison Ave. (at 59th St.), Midtown, 212/751–9082. Subway: 59th St./Lexington Ave.*

9 e-5
347 Madison Ave. (at 44th St.), Midtown, 212/986–0872. Subway: 42nd St./Grand Central.

9 e-4
BOTTICELLI
This store's cachet has fallen somewhat since the return to tailoring and a trimmer cut in the mid-'90s, American men's newfound preference for English rather than Italian styles, and the general disdain for flash. But the shoes are as sleek and soft as ever. *522 5th Ave. (between 43rd and 44th Sts.), Midtown, 212/221–9075. Subway: 42nd St./Grand Central.*

9 e-4
CHURCH'S ENGLISH SHOES
Fast by Brooks Brothers, Paul Stuart, and J. Press, this is New York's best alternative to Weston and Cole-Haan for elegant, conservative footwear. Regular Joes can exploit the great sales. *428 Madison Ave. (at 49th St.), Midtown, 212/755–4313. Subway: 51st St./Lexington–3rd Aves.*

9 e-3
GUCCI
It's not just for shoes anymore, though you can still get the classic horsebit loafer in brown or black, a true barefoot-preppie standard. Lately, with the appointment of designer Tom Ford to run the label, Gucci has mined its '70s heyday, pillaging styles that run a gamut from slick to slicker. If you're beginning to crave gloss, and a tone of overt sexiness, you may want to chuck your Weejuns and head for this joint. *10 W. 57th St. (between 5th and 6th Aves.), Midtown, 212/826–2600. Subway: B, Q to 57th St.*

7 b-8
HARRY'S SHOES
At some point in the life of every New Yorker comes a pilgrimage to Harry's Shoes, shoe mecca of the Upper West Side. The shopping is full-contact, but the salespeople know their way around every style, from suede Hush Puppy loafers to rugged Timberland boots. They even print a catalog. *2299 Broadway (at 83rd St.), Upper West Side, 212/874–2035. Subway: 1, 9 to 86th St.*

9 e-1
J. M. WESTON
Exclusive bootmakers in Paris since 1865, this establishment makes the best penny loafer known to man or beast. Weston is renowned for styling and fit; 80% of each shoe is made by hand, and you can choose from among 60 styles in 24 sizes and five widths. *812 Madison (at 68th St.), Upper East Side, 212/535–2100. Subway: 68th St./Hunter College.*

9 e-8
KENNETH COLE
Cole provides a steady supply of fresh, never over-the-top, shoe styles to younger customers. Accoutrements include ties, leather goods, jackets, and socks. Those who care will notice that Cole also runs one of footwear's cleverer ad campaigns, and that the stores sponsor seasonal (predatory) sales. *95 5th Ave. (at 17th St.), Chelsea, 212/675–2550. Subway: F to 14th St.; N, R to 23rd St.*

9 5-e
107 E. 42nd St. (at Park Ave.), Midtown, 212/949–8079. Subway: 42nd St./Grand Central.

11 *e-4*

597 Broadway (between Houston and Prince Sts.), SoHo, 212/965–0283. Subway: Bleecker St./Broadway–Lafayette St.

7 *b-8*

353 Columbus Ave. (between 76th and 77th Sts.), Upper West Side, 212/873–2061. Subway: 79th St.

9 *d-4*

MCCREEDY & SCHREIBER

This longtime emporium has one of New York's best selections of boots (including Lucchese) and shoes for both casual and dress wear. Pick up Frye, Timberland, Cole-Haan, Sperry, Rockport, Sebago, Alden, Allen Edmonds, Dan Post, Justin, Tony Lama, and Larry Mehan at competitive prices. *37 W. 46th St. (between 5th and 6th Aves.), Midtown, 212/719–1552. Subway: B, D, F, Q to 42nd St.*

9 *e-2*

213 E. 59th St. (between 2nd and 3rd Aves.), Midtown, 212/759–9241. Subway: 59th St./Lexington Ave.

9 *d-3*

TO BOOT

The famed boot selection, including handmade exotic leathers, has been joined by men's casual, leisure, business, and formal footwear. *745 5th Ave. (at 58th St., in Bergdorf Goodman Men), Midtown, 212/339–3335. Subway: N, R to 5th Ave.*

9 *e-3*

TOD'S

Audrey Hepburn wore 'em; so did Steve McQueen. And they are way expensive, averaging around $400 for the coveted butter-soft driving loafer. Lately, this purveyor of premium casual footwear has captivated the Hamptons set, displacing Gucci and Belgian Shoes as the maker of choice for gents in jeans and khakis. Airs aside, however, these are absolutely fabulous shoes. *650 Madison Ave. (between 59th and 60th Sts.), Midtown, 212/644–5945. Closed Sun. Subway: N, R to 5th Ave.*

ties

Allen Street between Delancey and Houston streets on the Lower East Side has several necktie stores featuring nice, inexpensive ties.

7 *e-6*

SEIGO

Atop the haughty shopper's miracle row that is Madison Avenue resides this small, exquisite shop, literally stuffed with neckwear style. The only place with a more intriguing selection is Paul Stuart. The hook at Seigo is the marriage of East and West: the four-in-hands and bows are all classically English, the patterns borrow something from Italy, France, and the United States, but the printing process is the same one the Japanese use to create kimonos. The results, which begin around $50, are lovely. As if that weren't enough, the owners have divided the store in half, with one side devoted to more fragile, textured fabrics, the other to smoother, sturdier prints. *1248 Madison Ave. (at 90th St.), Upper East Side, 212/987–0191. Closed Sun. Subway: 4, 5, 6 to 86th St.*

9 *e-7*

TIECRAFTERS

A sort of tie hospital, Tiecrafters will remove even the most difficult stains. For fussy stylists, they'll also narrow, widen, and shorten ties. *252 W. 29th St. (between 7th and 8th Aves.), Murray Hill, 212/629–5800. Closed weekends. Subway: 1, 9 to 28th St.*

9 *e-3*

TIE RACK

There's something for just about every guy in these bevies of reasonably priced ties. *599 Lexington Ave. (between 52nd and 53rd Sts.), Midtown, 212/355–0656. Subway: 51st St./Lexington–3rd Aves.*

9 *e-5*

200 Park Ave. (at 45th St., in MetLife building), 212/697–0337. Subway: 42nd St./Grand Central.

10 *d-6*

World Trade Center, concourse level, Lower Manhattan, 212/432–7074. Subway: World Trade Ctr.

COINS

9 *d-4*

COIN DEALER, INC.

This shop in the Diamond District buys, appraises, and sells rare coins both domestic and foreign, and specializes in gold coins and coin jewelry. *15 W. 47th St. (between 5th and 6th Aves.),*

Midtown, 212/246–5025. Subway: B, D, F, Q to 50th St.

9 *f-3*

PAUL J. BOSCO

Bosco has America's most comprehensive stock of worldwide coins dated 1500–1900, and a top-notch selection of medals—from the Renaissance to Art Deco periods. *1050 2nd Ave. (at 55th St.), Midtown, 212/758–2646. Subway: 4, 5, 6, N, R to 59th St./Lexington Ave.*

9 *e-2*

SPINK AMERICA

A member of the Christie's group, Spink America deals and auctions rare coins, historical medals, and bank notes from antiquity to the present. *55 E. 59th St. (between Madison and Park Aves.), 15th floor, Midtown, 212/486–3660. Subway: 4, 5, 6, N, R to 59th St./Lexington Ave.*

9 *d-3*

STACK'S

America's oldest and largest coin dealer, Stack's deals in rare coins (U.S. and foreign) and sells ancient gold, silver, and copper coins as well. The house holds eight auctions a year. *123 W. 57th St. (between 6th and 7th Aves.), Midtown, 212/582–2580. Closed weekends. Subway: B, Q, N, R to 57th St.*

COMPUTERS & SOFTWARE

10 *e-6*

J&R MUSIC & COMPUTER WORLD

It's chaos in here, but J&R is staffed with savvy salespeople who are far more patient than you'd think, if you can only flag one down. You'll find all the major brands: Apple, AT&T, Brother, Compaq, Epson, HP, IBM, Intel, NEC, Panasonic, Sony, Texas Instruments, and more. *15 Park Row (between Ann & Beekman Sts.), Lower Manhattan, 212/238–9100. Subway: 4, 5, 6, to Brooklyn Bridge/City Hall.*

9 *d-7*

TEKSERVE

It's almost quaint, their nickname: "The Old Reliable Mac Service Shop." True, Mac sales are secondary to service and repair at this haven for Mac users, but these salespeople are some of the most knowledgeable in New York, and they're incredibly honest and friendly. Doubts? Check out the line in their hallway at 8:55 a.m. This writer once spilled a beer on her PowerBook, and Tekserve was entirely sympathetic—said a Diet Coke would have been worse. *155 W. 23rd St. (between 6th and 7th Aves.), 4th floor, Chelsea, 212/929–3645. Subway: 1, 9, F to 23rd St.*

COSTUME RENTAL

All of these companies rent costumes to both consumers and folks in the trade. Note that you will be allowed to take Polaroids when you try the costumes on, but may be charged a fee for each picture, as companies don't want their costumes to be copied. You may want to call ahead for the company's policy.

9 *d-8*

ABRACADABRA

Here's a huge inventory of costumes, with masks, magic, and makeup to top them off. *19 W. 21st St. (between 5th and 6th Aves.), Flatiron District, 212/627–5194. Subway: N, R to 23rd St.*

3 *c-4*

DODGER COSTUME CO.

Specializing in Broadway rentals, Dodger has thousands of costumes in very good condition and can also manufacture to your specifications. *21–07 41st Ave. (near 21st St.), Long Island City, Queens, 718/729–1010. Closed weekends. Subway: B, Q to 21st St./Queensbridge.*

9 *c-7*

ODD'S COSTUME RENTALS

This huge loft area is filled with costumes and associated props. *231 W. 29th St. (between 7th and 8th Aves.), Garment District, 212/268–6227. Closed weekends. Subway: 34th St./Penn Station.*

10 *d-1*

PARTY CITY

Perfect for last-minute Halloween ideas, this store carries wigs, masks, costumes, and party supplies, plus they'll deliver. *38 W. 14th St. (between 5th and 6th Aves.), Greenwich Village, 212/271–7310. Subway: 14th St./Union Sq.*

CRAFTS

10 f-1
CLAYWORKS POTTERY

Clayworks is a retail shop by day, and a studio in the evening, with classes in stoneware and earthenware. *332 E. 9th St. (between 1st and 2nd Aves.), East Village, 212/677–8311. Hours vary; call first. Subway: Astor Pl.; 1st Ave.*

9 e-2
THE WOMAN'S EXCHANGE

Sixty percent of each sale here goes to the consignor, who is generally a craftsperson in need. Wares include hand-smocked clothing for children, furniture, stationery, sweaters, toys, quilts, homemade jams, and chocolates. *149 E. 60th St. (between Lexington and 3rd Aves.), Upper East Side, 212/753–2330. Closed Sat. mid-June–Labor Day. Closed Sun. Subway: 59th St./Lexington Ave.*

DISCOUNT

These stores make it easy to go broke saving money. There's a heavy concentration of thrift shops from 75th to 85th streets between 2nd and 3rd avenues; all offer secondhand and some new merchandise of varying quality. Patience can yield bargains, and the proceeds do go to charity. Caveat emptor: not all shops with "thrift" in their names are charity stores.

10 e-6
CENTURY 21

These three chaotic floors of discounted merchandise include name-brand clothing, electronics, home furnishings, and more. *See also* Discount & Off-Price *in* Clothing for Women *and* Clothing for Men, *above. 22 Cortlandt St. (between Broadway and Church St.), Lower Manhattan, 212/227–9092. Closed Sun. Subway: Cortlandt St.; World Trade Ctr.*

10 g-4
DEMBITZER BROS.

Small and large appliances both sell for small prices here, but it's hectic, so you'd best know what you want. *5 Essex St. (at Canal St.), Lower East Side, 212/254–1310. Closed Sat. Subway: Delancey St.*

11 e-3
NATIONAL WHOLESALE LIQUIDATORS

You name it, it's here at a super-discounted price. These two floors are stuffed with home furnishings, electronics, clothing, cleaning supplies, storage bins and other plastic items, art supplies, and more. It's a bit of a mishmash, but savvy downtowners swear by it. *632 Broadway (between Houston and Bleecker Sts.), Greenwich Village, 212/979–2400. Subway: Bleecker St.; Broadway–Lafayette St.*

10 e-6
ODD JOB TRADING CORP.

Come here for closeouts of brand-name consumer goods. The best buys are in sports gear and small appliances. *10 Cortlandt St. (at Broadway), Lower Manhattan, 212/571–0959. Subway: Cortlandt St.; World Trade Ctr.*

9 d-6
390 5th Ave. (at 36th St.), Garment District, 212/239–3336. Subway: 34th St./Herald Sq.

9 d-6
149 W. 32nd St. (between 6th and 7th Aves.), Garment District, 212/564–7370. Subway: 34th St./Herald Sq.; other locations.

ELECTRONICS & AUDIO

10 g-4
ABC TRADING COMPANY

They stock most major brands of both household appliances and hi-fi audio/visual electronics. They will order what they don't have. Discounts are deep. *31 Canal St. (between Essex and Ludlow Sts.), Lower East Side, 212/228–5080. Closed Sat. Subway: F to E. Broadway.*

9 e-5
FORTY-SECOND STREET PHOTO

Despite the name, Forty-Second Street Photo has more electronic equipment than photography equipment: Their VCRs, computers, fax machines, phones, CD and cassette players, and so forth are offered at discount prices. *109 E. 42nd St. (between Park and Lexington Aves.), Midtown, 212/490–1994. Subway: 4,5,6, to 42nd St./Grand Central.*

9 d-6

378 5th Ave. (at 35th St.), Garment District, 212/594–6565. Subway: 34th St./Herald Sq.

9 d-4

HARVEY

Harvey has sold and installed fine audio and video systems since 1927. Current stock includes home-theater and stereo components from Adcom, McIntosh, Krell, Sony, Sharpvision, Meridian and other high-end brands. Harvey's second location is a boutique in the ABC home-furnishings megastore. *2 W. 45th St., Midtown, 212/575–5000. Subway: B, D, F, Q to 42nd St.*

9 e-8

ABC Carpet & Home, 888 Broadway (at 19th St.), Flatiron District, 212/473–3000. Subway: 14th St./Union Sq.; N, R to 23rd St.

10 e-6

J&R MUSIC & COMPUTER WORLD

J & R may well have the most complete selection of electronic products anywhere, which, happily, assures that all budgets can be accommodated. The sales staff is knowledgeable, prices are competitive, and crowds are here in force. Be patient; it's worth it in the end. *23 Park Row (between Ann and Beekman Sts.), Lower Manhattan, 212/238–9000 or 800/221–8180. Subway: Brooklyn Bridge/City Hall.*

9 d-8

RADIOSHACK

RadioShack carries mainly its own brand of consumer electronics, including stereos, telephones, and pagers, and has a handy stash of electrical converters for travel abroad. It's worth a look if you're not a label snob. *641A 6th Ave. (at 20th St.), Chelsea, 212/604–0695. Subway: F to 23rd St.*

9 e-5

287 Madison Ave. (at 41st St.), Midtown, 212/682–9309. Subway: 42nd St./Grand Central.

7 f-7

1477 3rd Ave. (at 84th St.), Upper East Side, 212/327–0979. Subway: 4, 5, 6 to 86th St.

7 b-4

2812 Broadway (at 108th St.), Upper West Side, 212/662–7332. Subway: 110th St./Cathedral Pkwy.

9 e-3

SONY PLAZA

Sony has cleverly designed a consumer-friendly atrium housing Sony Wonder Technology Lab (an interactive multimedia exhibit) and the Sony Style store, which offers only the latest Sony products. Staff take a "no-pressure" approach, so browsing is welcome and encouraged, but complimentary personal shopping is also available for those who wish to purchase but require expert advice. *550 Madison Ave. (between 55th and 56th Sts.), Midtown, 212/833–8830. Subway: F to 5th Ave.; N,R, 6 to 5th Ave.*

9 e-8

SOUND BY SINGER

Singer's sales and service get consistently high reviews from serious audio/videophiles, but the great sales staff will also work with tight budgets. *18 E. 6th St., Flatiron District, 212/924–8600. Subway: 14th St./Union Sq.*

9 d-5

SOUND CITY

Here you'll find all major brands of stereo, video, and photo equipment at very reasonable prices. Affable staff shares expert knowledge. Air conditioners and space heaters also are sold seasonally. *58 W. 45th St. (between 5th and 6th Aves.), Midtown, 212/575–0210. Subway: B, D, F, Q to 42nd St.*

10 e-4

UNCLE UNCLE ELECTRONICS

Head to Canal for these low prices on stereo equipment, TVs, and VCRs. You can try the stuff out in the sound room. *343 Canal St. (near Church St.), Lower Manhattan, 212/226–4010. Subway: A, C, E to Canal St.*

10 g-3

VICMARR AUDIO

Vicmarr is one of very few electronics stores that will give prices over the phone, indicating its uncommonly low-pressure sales approach. The store's well-organized shelves are packed with well-priced merchandise from brands such as JVC, Alpine, and Panasonic. *88*

Delancey St. (at Orchard St.), Lower East Side, 212/505–0380. Subway: Delancey St.

EYEWEAR

11 *d-5*

MORGENTHAL-FREDERICS EYEWEAR AND ACCESSORIES

In an environment based on Shaker design, designer and president Richard Morgenthal's creations have lured the likes of Puff Daddy, Jackie O, and Uma Thurman. In addition to Morgenthal's own line, which includes vintage-inspired frames in solid gold and platinum, precious stones, ebony, and teakwood (accessories range from men's nubuck wallets to a combination magnifier-letter opener to women's "boudoir pieces"), specs by Oliver Peoples, l.a. Eyeworks, and Yohji Yamamoto can be found here. *399 W. Broadway (at Spring St.), SoHo, 212/966–0099. Subway: C, E to Spring St.*

9 *e-1*

944 Madison Ave. (at 74th St.), Midtown, 212/744–9444. Subway: 68th St./Hunter College.

9 *e-2*

699 Madison Ave. (at 62nd St.), Midtown, 212/838–3090. Subway: 59th St./Lexington Ave.

9 *3-e*

754 5th Ave. (at 57th St. in Bergdorf Goodman), Midtown, 212/753–7300. Subway: 59th St./Lexington Ave.

9 *e-3*

ROBERT MARC OPTICIANS

Robert Marc is the only place in New York to find the exclusive lines of Lunor, Frédéric Beausoleil, and Kirei Titan, as well as the vintage line Retrospecs. *575 Madison Ave. (at 56th St.), Midtown, 212/319–2000. Subway: 59th St./Lexington Ave.*

9 *b-1*

190 Columbus Ave. (at 68th St.), Upper West Side, 212/799–4600. Subway: 66th St.; and other locations.

10 *f-2*

SELIMA OPTIQUE

For the coolest mid-price frames around, Selima Salaun's store is the place to go. In addition to her own line, she scours France for vintage, never-worn frames. Special orders and replications welcome. *84 E. 7th St. (between 1st and 2nd Aves.), Greenwich Village, 212/260–2495. Subway: Astor Pl.*

10 *e-4*

159 Wooster St. (at Broome St.), SoHo, 212/343–9490. Subway: Prince St.

FABRICS

Orchard Street south of Houston Street is New York's center for discounted fabric. Be prepared to pick through roll after roll; you'll find major manufacturers' overstock at about 40% off the retail price.

9 *c-5*

ART MAX FABRICS

The fashion fabrics include full lines of linens, English wool suitings, domestic and imported wools, cotton prints and solids, cashmere coatings, and silks. Bridal fabrics are a particular specialty. *250 W. 40th St. (between 7th and 8th Aves.), Garment District, 212/398–0755. Closed Sun. Subway: 42nd St./Times Sq.*

9 *c-5*

B & J FABRICS

Family-owned since 1940, B & J is three floors of fashion fabrics, many imported. *263 W. 40th St. (between 7th and 8th Aves.), Garment District, 212/354–8150. Closed Sun. Subway: 42nd St./Times Sq.*

9 *f-2*

BARANZELLI HOME

Designer silk, velvet, and brocades for draperies, upholstery, and slipcovers join Scalamandre closeouts and seconds in a shop popular with the trade as well as retail customers. *1127 2nd Ave. (between 59th and 60th Sts.), Midtown, 212/753–6511. Subway: 59th St./Lexington Ave.*

10 *g-3*

BECKENSTEIN HOME FABRICS

This store has a wide variety of well-priced fabrics. *4 W. 20th St. (near 5th Ave.), Flatiron District, 212/366–5142. Subway: 1, 9 to 18th St.*

10 *g-3*

BECKENSTEIN MEN'S FABRICS

Some say this is the finest men's-fabric store in the United States. The nation's custom tailors, top men's-clothing man-ufacturers, and a who's-who list of clients shop here for the finest quality in every type of men's fashion fabric. *133 Orchard St. (near Delancey St.), Lower East Side, 212/475–6666. Closed Sat. Subway: Delancey St.*

12 *f-5*

FABRIC ALTERNATIVE

Pick up high-quality home-decor fabrics at a discount, including Schumacher, Waverly, and Riverdale. They'll do the sewing, too. *78 7th Ave. (at Berkeley Pl.), Park Slope, Brooklyn, 718/857–5482. Subway: D, Q, F to 7th Ave.*

11 *h-5*

FABRIC WORLD

Fabric World offers a lovely line of fabrics at discount prices, with a bonus if you're renovating: they'll convert your chosen fabric into wallpaper. *283 Grand St. (near Eldridge St.), Lower East Side, 212/925–0412. Closed Sat. Subway: Grand St.*

7 *b-8*

LAURA ASHLEY

The finest purveyor of the English coun-try-house look, Laura Ashley offers gen-teel prints on natural cotton fabrics, with wallpapers and furnishings to match. *398 Columbus Ave. (at 79th St.), Upper West Side, 212/496–5110. Subway: 79th St.*

11 *e-6*

LONG ISLAND FABRICS

Selections include designer, upholstery, and some imported fabrics as well as a good selection of notions, all at fantas-tic savings. *406 Broadway (near Canal St.), Lower Manhattan, 212/431–9510. Subway: N, R to Canal St.*

9 *e-1*

PIERRE DEUX

Pierre Deux is the exclusive American outlet for hand-screened Souleiado print fabric from Provence; the store also has reproduction furniture and beautiful accessories. They custom-design window and bed treatments. *870 Madison Ave. (at 71st St.), Upper East Side, 212/570–9343. Subway: 68th St./Hunter College.*

FLOWERS & PLANTS

For the freshest flowers, go to the wholesale flower market on and around 28th Street between 6th and 7th avenues, where New York's florists buy their flowers. Wholesalers will often sell at retail if you're willing to pay cash.

9 *d-8*

BLOOM FLOWERS HOME GARDEN

Bloom Flowers does everything from weddings to private and corporate par-ties to individual arrangements and fresh cut flowers. There's also a small selection of home furnishings. *16 W. 21st St. (between 5th and 6th Aves.), Chelsea, 212/620–5666. Closed Sun. Subway: F to 23rd St.*

9 *b-7*

PRESTON BAILEY INC. ENTERTAINMENT & SET DESIGN

Preston Bailey has 15 years' experience designing floral arrangements for big events. Corporate clients include Tiffany & Co., Christie's, and Disney; weddings and large parties are a specialty. *147 W. 25th St. (between 6th and 7th Aves.), Chelsea, 212/691–6777. Open by appt. only. Subway: 1,9 to 23rd St.*

9 *e-2*

RENNY

This well-known floral designer doesn't kid around; clients include some serious society, and prices can reflect that. The handiwork is extraordinary. *505 Park Ave. (between 59th and 60th Sts.), Midtown, 212/288–7000. Closed Sun. Sept.–May, weekends July–Aug. Subway: 59th St./Lex-ington Ave.*

7 *e-8*

Carlyle Hotel, 35 E. 76th St. (at Madison Ave.), Upper East Side, 212/988–5588. Closed Sun. Sept.–May, weekends July–Aug. Subway: 77th St.

10 *b-1*

ROBERT ISABELL

Isabell is famous for decorating over-the-top society parties on big budgets. *410 W. 13th St. (near Washington St.), West Village, 212/645–7767. Subway: A, C, E to 14th St.*

9 *e-1*

RONALDO MAIA LTD.

These expensive and inventive floral creations come in natural cachepots or baskets and make elegant, simple centerpieces. The potpourri and candles are wonderful. *27 E. 67th St. (between 5th and Madison Aves.), Upper East Side, 212/288–1049. Subway: 68th St./Hunter College.*

11 *d-4*

SPRING ST. GARDEN

Order personalized floral arrangements, wreaths, garlands, or whatever strikes you. The small retail area includes plants, fresh cut flowers, and gardening objets. *186½ Spring St. (near Thompson St.), SoHo, 212/966–2015. Closed Sun. Subway: C, E to Spring St.*

7 *b-8*

SURROUNDINGS

These designers do arrangements for parties and events and also make up floral and gourmet food gift baskets. *224 W. 79th St. (between Broadway and Amsterdam Ave.), Upper West Side, 212/580–8982. Subway: 79th St.*

9 *e-8*

VICTOR'S GARDEN DISTRICT

The attentive staff designs stunning arrangements for all budgets, and the Midtown location makes this a convenient after-work stop for last-minute flower emergencies. *260 Madison Ave. (near 38th St.), Midtown, 212/532-9838. Subway: 42nd St./Grand Central.*

10 *c-1*

VSF

A-list clients hire this designer for English country–style weddings, special events, holiday decorations, or just the perfect flower arrangement. *204 W. 10th St. (near Bleecker St.), 212/206–7236. Closed Sun.; closed weekends in summer. Subway: Christopher St./Sheridan Sq.*

9 *f-3*

ZEZÉ

Known for its dramatic arrangements, Zezé specializes in exotic orchids. *398 E. 52nd St. (between 1st Ave. and the East River), Midtown, 212/753–7767. Closed weekends except holiday weekends. Subway: 51st St./Lexington–3rd Aves.*

FOOD & DRINK

bread and pastries

9 *b-4*

AMY'S BREAD

Choose from sourdough, semolina, rosemary, black olive, organic whole wheat, and rye breads, as well as specialty breads, sandwiches, and sweets. All breads are made with a natural starter, quality ingredients, and no preservatives; the most popular are sourdough and semolina with golden raisins and fennel. *672 9th Ave. (at 46th St.), Hell's Kitchen, 212/977–2670. Subway: 42nd St./8th Ave.*

10 *b-1*

75 9th Ave. (at 15th St.), Chelsea, 212/ 462–4338. Subway: A, C, E to 14th St.

11 *e-5*

BALTHAZAR BAKERY

Adjacent to the trendsetting restaurant of the same name, this is a Parisian-style patisserie with an amazing array of French-style breads. Try chocolate, rye, multigrain, olive, cranberry-raisin-pecan, potato-onion, and the signature *pain de seigle* of rye and wheat. You can also pick up tarts, sandwiches, salads, soups, and delicious coffee by the cup. *80 Spring St. (at Broadway), 212/965–1785. Subway: 6 to Spring St.*

9 *f-4*

BUTTERCUP BAKE SHOP

Opened by one of the original owners of the much loved Magnolia Bakery, the butter-yellow walls here house some of the most delectable desserts in midtown: scrumptious layer cakes, lick-your-fork-clean pies, and delicately iced cupcakes. The buttercream on the cakes here is habit forming, but worth every calorie. *973 2nd Ave. (between 51st and 52nd Sts.), Midtown East, 212/350–4144. Subway: E, F to Lexington Ave.*

9 *e-8*

THE CITY BAKERY

Beautiful tarts; an exceptional selection of cookies, brownies, desserts, and breads; and a tasty selection of lunchtime fare keeps City Bakery hopping. February is hot chocolate month when a different decadent variation is offered daily. *22 E. 17th St. (between 5th Ave. and Union Sq. W), Flatiron District, 212/366–1414. Subway: 14th St./Union Sq.*

7 f-8

CREATIVE CAKES

Here's the deal: you name a person, pet, building, car, or any other shape or design you fancy, and they create a "portrait-likeness" three-dimensional cake—buttercream outside, chocolate fudge inside. It's expensive, but delicious and most impressive. Order two weeks in advance. *400 E. 74th St. (between 1st and York Aves.), Upper East Side, 212/794–9811. Subway: 77th St.*

9 b-5

CUPCAKE CAFÉ

This funky store offers daintily decorated cupcakes and tantalizing cakes covered in sinfully rich buttercream icing. There are also pies, doughnuts, and muffins, as well as soups and sandwiches. *522 9th Ave. (at 39th St.), Hell's Kitchen, 212/465–1530. Subway: 42nd St./8th Ave.*

11 e-4

DEAN & DELUCA

The city's finest gourmet shop has a magnificent selection of breads, desserts, and pastries. The gingerbread makes a delicious energizer during a SoHo shopping trip. *560 Broadway (at Prince St.), SoHo, 212/431–1691 or 800/221–7714. Subway: Prince St.*

7 e-8

E.A.T.

The home of Eli's famous sourdough ficelles and raisin-nut bread also supplies bread to many of New York's restaurants. The terrific holiday gift baskets can be shipped anywhere. *1064 Madison Ave. (at 80th St.), Upper East Side, 212/772–0022. Subway: 77th St.*

9 e-2

ECCE PANIS

The aroma makes it difficult to pass this place by; and why should you? Ecce Panis serves glorious bread—light and dark sourdough, double-walnut, plain or rosemary neo-Tuscan, chocolate—as well as various focaccias, biscotti, cookies, brioches, and breakfast treats. *1120 3rd Ave. (at 65th St.), Upper East Side, 212/535–2099. Subway: 68th St./Hunter College.*

9 b-1

Columbus Ave. (at 73rd St.), Upper West Side, 212/362–7189. Subway: 72nd St.

10 d-1

6th Ave. (at 10th St.), West Village, 212/460–5616. Subway: W. 4th St./Washington Sq.

9 b-5

LITTLE PIE COMPANY

This gourmet bakery specializes in delicious all-American pies—just like Grandma used to make, only better. The ever-popular Sour Cream Apple Walnut Pie is legendary. *424 W. 43rd St., Hell's Kitchen, 212/736–4780. Subway: 42nd St./8th Ave.*

10 b-1

407 W. 14th St. (at 9th St.), Chelsea, 212/414–2324. Subway: A, C, E to 14th St.; L to 8th Ave.

11 a-1

MAGNOLIA BAKERY

Tucked away on a quiet West Village corner, Magnolia has a loyal following of sweet-tooth devotees who line up for the legendary layer cakes topped with delectable buttercream icing. There's also an array of cupcakes that will make you wax nostalgic for elementary school, plus pies, brownies, and cookies. *401 Bleecker St. (at W. 11th St.), West Village, 212/462–2572. Subway: Christopher St./Sheridan Sq.*

11 b-1

MOISHE'S HOMEMADE KOSHER BAKERY

Moishe's is one of New York's oldest and finest kosher Jewish bakeries, serving very special corn bread, egg challah, homemade bagels (some call them the only authentic bagels in the city), rugelach, and hamantaschen. *115 2nd Ave. (between 6th and 7th Sts.), East Village, 212/505–8555. Subway: 2nd Ave.*

11 h-3

181 E. Houston St. (near Orchard St.), Lower East Side, 212/472–9624. Subway: Delancey St.

11 c-4

ONCE UPON A TART

Ensconced in a century-old storefront with tin ceilings and exposed brick, the cleverly named bakery serves tantalizing muffins, scones, cookies, and gourmet sandwiches. But the tart's the thing—freshly baked in both sweet and savory varieties. Tuck into one in the quiet café section and escape from SoHo's shopping hordes. *135 Sullivan St. (between*

Prince and Houston Sts.), SoHo, 212/387–8869. Subway: Prince St.

7 f-8

ORWASHER'S
Certified kosher, Orwasher offers 35 varieties of handmade breads and rolls, baked on the premises in hearth ovens using no preservatives or additives. Specialties include Hungarian potato bread and Vienna twists; inventions include raisin pumpernickel and marble bread. Pick up cheeses, coffees, teas, and condiments while you're here. *308 E. 78th St. (between 2nd and 1st Aves.), Upper East Side, 212/288–6569. Subway: 77th St.*

10 b-1

PATISSERIE LANCIANI
These beautiful baked goods include a great Sacher torte, over which you can linger in the adjoining café. *414 W. 14th St. (between 9th and 10th Aves.), West Village, 212/989–1213. Subway: A, C, E to 14th St.*

9 e-5

PAYARD PATISSERIE
Chef Francois Payard creates some of the most exquisite French pastries in the city, turning out light-as-a-feather croissants as well as sinfully rich chocolate delights. Among the latter is the Louvre—hazelnut dacquoise and chocolate and hazelnut mousse encased in a dark chocolate shell. There's also amazing baguette and other French breads, fruit tarts, decadent cakes, and luscious truffles. Afternoon tea is a special treat. *1032 Lexington Ave. (between 73rd and 74th Sts.), Upper East Side, 212/717–5252. Subway: 77th St.*

9 c-5

POSEIDON CONFECTIONERY CO.
Serving the best in Greek pastries, Poseidon also offers spinach-and-cheese pies and stuffed vine leaves. *629 9th Ave. (at 44th St.), Hell's Kitchen, 212/757–6173. Subway: 42nd St./8th Ave.*

9 b-1

SOUTINE
A full-service neighborhood bakery, Soutine makes American and French-style bread, croissants, and brioche. Birthday cakes and holiday goodies are specialties, and the store will ship them any-where. *104 W. 70th St. (between Broadway and Columbus Ave.), Upper West Side, 212/496–1450. Subway: 72nd St.*

11 b-5

SULLIVAN ST. BAKERY
The crusty, chewy bread here is the stuff of food fantasies . . . but don't let it blind you to one of the greatest taste treats in the city: true Roman pizza. The golden, rectangular dough is served at room temperature and topped with simple ingredients such as fresh artichokes (only in spring); a combination of sea salt, rosemary, and extra-virgin olive oil (a pizza *bianca*); or fresh tomatoes. One taste and you're sure to be addicted. *73 Sullivan St. (near Broome St.), SoHo, 212/334–9435. Subway: A, C, E to Canal St.*

9 c-8

TAYLOR'S
Taylor's accompanies its sandwiches and salads with old-fashioned comfort food—huge fudge brownies, oversize muffins, and homey pies. *228 W. 18th St., Chelsea, 212/366–9081. Subway: A, C, E to 14th St.*

10 c-1

523 Hudson St. (near W. 10th St.), West Village, 212/645–8200. Subway: Christopher St./Sheridan Sq.

10 f-1

175 2nd Ave. (near 11th St.), East Village, 212/674–9501. Subway: Astor Pl.; 3rd Ave.

12 g-8

TWO LITTLE RED HENS BAKERY
The muffins, cakes, and pastries at this cozy nook a block off Prospect Park have inspired many a picnic. Bestsellers include the chocolate "crinkle" cookies, elegant cupcakes (the palette changes with the season), and raspberry–chocolate mousse cake. *1112 8th Ave. (near 12th St.), Park Slope, Brooklyn, 718/499–8108. Subway: F to 7th Ave.*

10 f-1

VENIERO'S PASTICCERIA
In business since 1894, Veniero's makes Italian sweets as tasty as they are beautiful, including cannoli, gelato, and marzipan. The café serves old-fashioned espresso and cappuccino. *342 E. 11th St. (between 1st and 2nd Aves.), East Village, 212/674–7264. Subway: 1st Ave.*

11 *d-4*

VESUVIO

White, whole-wheat, and seeded Italian breads are baked in coal-fired ovens in the basement, without sugar, fat, or preservatives. Just follow your nose. *160 Prince St. (near W. Broadway), 212/925–8248. Subway: Prince St.*

7 *e-7*

WILLIAM GREENBERG, JR., BAKERY

Greenberg is said to make the best brownies in the city, and whips up spectacular custom cakes. *1100 Madison Ave. (at 82nd St.), Upper East Side, 212/744–0304. Subway: 4, 5, 6 to 86th St.*

7 *b-8*

2187 Broadway (at 77th St.), Upper West Side, 212/580–7300. Subway: 79th St.

9 *e-6*

518 3rd Ave. (near 34th St.), Murray Hill, 212/686–3344. Subway: 33rd St.

11 *e-1*

60 E. 8th St. (near Broadway), East Village, 212/995–9184. Subway: 8th St.

11 *b-2*

ZITO & SONS

Zito's best seller is a delicious, crusty whole-wheat loaf, followed closely by a Sicilian loaf. Frank Sinatra used to have this stuff delivered fresh to the Waldorf. *259 Bleecker St. (near 7th Ave.), West Village, 212/929–6139. Subway: W. 4th St./Washington Sq.*

cheese

7 *f-8*

AGATA & VALENTINA

This Italian gourmet shop has an outstanding international selection of cheeses plus extremely attentive and friendly service. *1505 1st Ave. (at 78th St.), Upper East Side, 212/452–0690. Subway: 77th St.*

10 *d-1*

BALDUCCI'S

Balducci's is especially well known for Italian cheeses, but the cheese lover's selection is unbeatable all around. Pop in for a free sample. *424 6th Ave. (at 9th St.), Greenwich Village, 212/673–2600 or 800/BALDUCCI. Subway: F to 14th St.*

10 *g-3*

BEN'S CHEESE SHOP

Ben is renowned for his homemade farmer cheese, baked with vegetables, scallions, raisins, blueberries, strawberries, or pineapple. The homemade cream cheese is enhanced by chives, caviar, lox, or herbs and garlic. *181 E. Houston St. (near Orchard St.), Lower East Side, 212/254–8290. Closed Sat. Subway: 2nd Ave.*

9 *b-7*

CHEESE UNLIMITED

The name's no exaggeration: you'll find 400 varieties of cheese from the world over. *240 9th Ave. (at 24th St.), Chelsea, 212/691–1512. Subway: C, E to 23rd St.*

11 *e-4*

DEAN & DELUCA

Cheese from all over the world is (like everything else) beautifully displayed here, and the knowledgeable staff will help you explore unfamiliar varieties. Especially noteworthy is the selection of American artisanal cheeses. *560 Broadway (at Prince St.), SoHo, 212/431–1691 or 800/221–7714. Subway: Prince St.*

11 *f-5*

DI PALO'S DAIRY STORE

In the heart of Little Italy, Di Palo's offers fresh-ground Parmesan cheese, smoked mozzarella, and homemade ricotta-filled ravioli. *206 Grand St. (at Mott St.), 212/226–1033. Subway: Bowery.*

10 *f-1*

EAST VILLAGE CHEESE STORE

The prices in this neighborhood shop can't be beat (but beware of prices that seem too good to be true—they usually indicate an overripe product). People file in for the weekly specials (with a half-pound minimum purchase). Domestic and imported cheese are joined by cold cuts, pâtés, coffees, crackers, jams, and condiments. *34 3rd Ave. (at 9th St.), East Village, 212/477–2601. Subway: Astor Pl.*

7 *f-8*

ELI'S

The giant selection here includes an impressive selection of imported cheeses, including a delicious assortment of French goat cheese. *1411 3rd*

Ave. (at 80th St.), Upper East Side, 212/717–8100. Subway: 77th St.

7 b-8

FAIRWAY

Fairway has one of the best cheese selections in the city, assembled by one of the foremost experts in the field, Steve Jenkins, author of The Cheese Primer. Highlights include an extensive array of blue and goat cheeses. 2127 Broadway (at 75th St.), Upper West Side, 212/595–1888. Subway: 72nd St.

6 c-8

133rd St.(at West Side Hwy.), Harlem, 212/234–3883. Subway: 137th St./City College.

9 f-1

GRACE'S MARKETPLACE

The upscale clientele has its pick of many fine domestic and imported cheese. The staff is happy to fix you up with samples. 1237 3rd Ave. (at 71st St.), Upper East Side, 212/737–0600. Subway: 68th St./Hunter College.

9 f-2

IDEAL CHEESE

This top-rated cheese shop has more than 300 varieties of domestic and imported cheese, and adds pâtés to the mix. 1205 2nd Ave. (at 63rd St.), Upper East Side, 212/688–7579. Subway: 59th St./Lexington Ave.

9 e-8

LA MARCA CHEESE SHOP

Choose from a wide variety of cheeses cut to order, plus fresh-baked farmer cheese with various fruit fillings, and good croissants. 161 E. 22nd St. (between Lexington and 3rd Aves.), Gramercy, 212/673–7920. Subway: 6 to 23rd St.

11 b-3

MURRAY'S CHEESE SHOP

Cheese connoisseurs consider the selection at this village institution the best in the city. Expert help will assist you with the overwhelming task of selecting from the tantalizing display. 257 Bleecker St. (at Cornelia St.), West Village, 212/243–3289. Subway: W. 4th St./Washington Sq.

7 f-6

THE VINEGAR FACTORY

Owned by Eli Zabar, of E.A.T. fame, this gourmet grocery store carries a large array of domestic and imported cheeses. 431 E. 91st St. (between 1st and York Aves.), Upper East Side, 212/987–0885. Subway: 4, 5, 6 to 86th St.

chocolate & other candy

9 e-2

AU CHOCOLAT

Boxed, loose, solid, filled, domestic, European—it's all here, from such makers as Godiva, Perugina, Laderach, Lindt, Corne, Dalloyen, and Bloomie's own. Custom gift baskets are available. Bloomingdale's, 1000 3rd Ave. (at 59th St.), Midtown, 212/705–2953. Subway: 59th St./Lexington Ave.

10 f-1

BLACKHOUND

The elegant packages of chocolates and truffles in Shaker boxes make perfect gifts. Cookies, cakes, and pies are also available. 149 1st Ave. (at 9th St.), East Village, 212/979–9505 or 800/344–4417. Subway: Astor Pl.

7 f-7

ELK CANDY

Elk's specialty is delicious homemade marzipan, coated with chocolate or otherwise flavored. 240 E. 86th St. (between 2nd and 3rd Aves.), Upper East Side, 212/650–1177. Subway: 4, 5, 6 to 86th St.

10 e-6

GODIVA

Eighty years old and justly famous, these Belgians proffer elaborately boxed sweets for spontaneous consumption or carefully meditated gifts. 33 Maiden La. (near Nassau St.), Lower Manhattan, 212/809–8990. Subway: Broadway–Nassau St.

9 e-3

701 5th Ave. (near 54th St.), Midtown, 212/593–2845. Subway: E, F to 5th Ave.

9 e-1

793 Madison Ave. (near 67th St.), Upper East Side, 212/249–9444. Subway: 68th St./Hunter College.

9 c-1

245 Columbus Ave. (near 71st St.), Upper West Side, 212/787–5804. Subway: 72nd St.; other locations.

9 *e-1*

LA MAISON DU CHOCOLAT

Parisian chocolatier Robert Linxe whips up expensive, exquisitely flavored chocolate morsels filled with cinnamon, honey, mint, lemon, marzipan, kirsch, and more. Snap them up by the piece or the pound. *25 E. 73rd St. (near Madison Ave.), Upper East Side, 212/744–7117. Subway: 77th St.*

11 *b-2*

LI-LAC CHOCOLATES

These homemade chocolates include French mint patties, hazelnut truffles, almond bark, and highly edible, hand-molded milk, dark, and white Empire State Buildings and Statues of Liberty. The goods have been made on the premises since 1923. *120 Christopher St. (at Bleecker St.), West Village, 212/242–7374. Subway: Christopher St./Sheridan Sq.*

9 *d-6*

MACY'S MARKETPLACE

This place is a dream—or a nightmare, depending on how you look at it. You'll find every boxed chocolate on the market, plus loose samples from Michel Guerard, Godiva, Neuhaus, and Perugina. It all adds up to over 2,000 square ft of candy. *Macy's, 155 W. 34th St. (Herald Sq.), The Cellar (lower level), Garment District, 212/695–4400. Subway: 34th St./Herald Sq.*

9 *d-3*

MANON, LE CHOCOLATIER

Shopping on 5th tiring you out? Duck into Bergdorf and choose from over 30 varieties of high-quality chocolate to nibble on the spot or ship to a friend. *Bergdorf Goodman, 754 5th Ave. (at 57th St.), 7th floor, Midtown, 212/753–7300. Closed Sun. Subway: N, R to 5th Ave.*

7 *b-3*

MONDEL CHOCOLATES

This family business has produced an amazing array of naturally flavored chocolates with little fat for over 45 years—mint, orange, coffee, amaretto, and more. Beautiful boxes and baskets make presentation a snap. *2913 Broadway (at 114th St.), Morningside Heights, 212/864–2111. Subway: 116th St./Columbia University.*

9 *d-3*

NEUCHATEL CHOCOLATES

In business for five generations, Neuchatel has more than 60 different Swiss-European chocolates, truffles, and treats, with a specialty in champagne truffles. Other truffle options include Grand Marnier, espresso, and white chocolate. *Plaza Hotel, 5th Ave. and 59th St., Midtown, 212/751–7742. Subway: N, R to 5th Ave.*

9 *e-3*

PERUGINA

Pick up a box of chocolate Baci and lovely gift-packaged candies at the company's own store. *520 Madison Ave. (at 53rd St.), Midtown, 212/688–2490. Subway: 51st St./Lexington–3rd Aves.*

9 *e-3*

RICHART DESIGN ET CHOCOLAT

Resembling a gallery more than a chocolate shop, Richart presents edibles that are truly works of art. The signature Petits Richart Collection of miniature chocolates that resemble jewelry are embellished with modern abstract designs. All are made in France, flown in weekly, and made with the finest cocoa available. *7 E. 55th St., (near Fifth Ave.), Midtown, 212/371–9369. Closed Sun. Subway: N, R to 5th Ave.*

9 *e-2, d-4*

TEUSCHER CHOCOLATES OF SWITZERLAND

The ultimate Swiss-chocolate treats are flown in weekly from Switzerland. Try the delectable champagne truffles—happily, you can buy just one. *25 E. 61st St. (between 5th and Madison Aves.), Upper East Side, 212/751–8482. Subway: 59th St./Lexington Ave.*

9 *e-4*

620 5th Ave. (at 50th St.), Midtown, 212/246–4416. Subway: E, F to 5th Ave.

coffee & tea

Zabar's and Macy's Cellar have a variety of fresh and packaged teas and coffees. The two used to go head-to-head in their own little coffee price wars.

10 *e-1*

DANAL

In this charming café and gift shop are more than 32 teas (in bulk or gift-boxed): aromatics from France (try the four red-berries), classics from India and China, decaf varieties, herbal infusions, and more. Highlights include Taganda, an exclusive from Zimbabwe; packaged teas by G. Ford; and Barrow's unblended Darjeeling. The only coffee in stock is the high-quality Sumatra blend served in the café, also available in decaf. *90 E. 10th St. (between 3rd and 4th Aves.), East Village, 212/982–6930. Closed Mon. Subway: 8th St.; Astor Pl.*

9 *d-3*

FELISSIMO

The Japanese-owned boutique has a top-floor tea room, where you can sip tea between shopping spells or choose from over 50 varieties of loose tea to take home. *10 W. 56th St. (between 5th and 6th Aves.), Midtown, 212/247–5656. Closed Sun. Subway: N, R to 5th Ave.*

11 *b-2*

MCNULTY'S TEA & COFFEE COMPANY

Established in 1895, this well-known Village shop sells rare teas and more than 200 choice imported coffees, straight or custom-blended. Imported jams and jellies are tempting accompaniments. *109 Christopher St. (near Bleecker St.), 212/242–5351. Subway: Christopher St./Sheridan Sq.*

11 *d-1*

OREN'S DAILY ROAST

The widespread Oren's serves and scoops a wide selection of coffee from around the world. *31 Waverly Pl. (near University Pl.), Greenwich Village, 212/420–5958. Subway: 8th St.*

9 *e-6*

434 3rd Ave. (near 31st St.), Murray Hill, 212/779–1241. Subway: 33rd St.

9 *e-3*

33 E. 58th St. (near Madison Ave.), Midtown, 212/838–3345. Subway: N, R to 5th Ave.

7 *e-8*

1144 Lexington Ave. (near 79th St.), Upper East Side, 212/472–6830. Subway: 77th St.; other locations.

11 *c-3*

PORTO RICO IMPORTING CO.

Porto Rico has sold high-grade teas and coffees since 1907, and now roasts 50 different coffees each week. Options

include custom blends, Jamaican Blue Mountain, decaffeinated espresso, 120 kinds of tea, and every conceivable coffee and tea accessory at 30%–50% off the list price. *201 Bleecker St. (near 6th Ave.), Greenwich Village, 212/477–5421. Subway: W. 4th St./Washington Sq.*

11 *g-1*

40½ St. Mark's Pl. (between 1st and 2nd Aves.), East Village, 212/533–1982. Subway: Astor Pl.

9 *c-1*

SENSUOUS BEAN

The friendly folks who run this pretty shop will blend from a wide variety of coffees. *66 W. 70th St. (between Central Park W and Columbus Ave.), Upper West Side, 212/724–7725. Subway: 72nd St.*

11 *e-1*

STARBUCKS

Exported from Seattle, Starbucks has become the McDonald's of coffee—it seems you can hardly walk three blocks in this town without passing one, maybe two, of the cafés. But the coffee is good, and the now-classic café mix of coffee-based drinks, baked goods, and a small lunch menu is a reliable standby for many a city dweller. The Astor Place location is the liveliest in town, with performers on some nights and a hip village crowd that infuses the franchise with a bit of personality. *13–25 Astor Pl. (near 4th Ave.), East Village, 212/982–3563. Subway: Astor Pl.*

9 *c-3*

1656 Broadway (at 52nd St.), Theater District, 212/397–7124. Subway: 1, 9 to 50th St.

7 *e-8*

1290 3rd Ave. (at 74th St.), Upper East Side, 212/772–6903. Subway: 77th St.

7 *b-4*

2681 Broadway (at 102nd St.), Upper West Side, 212/280–1811; other locations.

9 *e-3*

TAKASHIMAYA

Fifth Avenue has the flagship American store for this 160-year-old Japanese company. The Tea Box, downstairs, serves lunch and afternoon tea and sells about 40 varieties of loose tea by the ounce. You'll find excellent, domestically grown black and herbal teas as well as green teas from Japan and a beautiful variety of teacups, teapots, and accessories. *693 5th Ave. (between 54th and*

55th Sts.), Midtown, 212/350–0100. Closed Sun. Subway: E, F to 5th Ave.

9 f-2

TIMOTHY'S COFFEES OF THE WORLD

This local chain sells passable coffee, cappuccino, iced tea, lemonade, baked goods, and fresh coffee by the pound. The stores are quite cozy, even if the mulled cider (in fall) is a bit of a sham. 1033 3rd Ave. (at 61st St.), Upper East Side, 212/755–6456. Subway: 59th St./Lexington Ave.

9 f-1

1296 1st Ave. (near 69th St.), Upper East Side, 212/794–7059. Subway: 68th St./Hunter College.

7 e-7

1188 Lexington Ave. (at 81st St.), Upper East Side, 212/879–0384. Subway: 77th St.; other locations.

ethnic foods

New York's food markets reflect the diversity of the city's population—unbeatable for variety, vitality, and, in most cases, authenticity.

12 b-4

ATLANTIC AVENUE (MIDDLE EASTERN)

Dodge the traffic for such Mediterranean delights as Turkish coffees, Lebanese pita breads, hummus, stuffed grape leaves, halvah, and baklava. Atlantic Ave. from Henry to Court Sts., bordering Brooklyn Heights. Subway: Borough Hall.

5 h-5

BELMONT (ITALIAN)

Belmont is still good for homemade pasta, pepperoni, bread, pastries, and espresso cafés. Arthur Ave. and E. 187th St., Bronx. Subway: 182nd–183rd Sts.

4 f-5

BENSONHURST (ITALIAN)

The shops teem with salamis, sausages, cheeses, prosciutto, and pizza rustica. 18th Ave. from 61st to 86th St., Brooklyn. Subway: 18th Ave.

10 f-4

CHINATOWN

Chinatown's main artery is Mott Street, but it takes the whole neighborhood to produce such a wealth of Chinese restaurants, tea parlors, bakeries, and gift shops. Bordered by Canal, Worth, and Mulberry Sts.; the Bowery; and Chatham Sq. Subway: 6, N, R, J, M, Z to Canal St.; Grand St.

9 c-5

HELL'S KITCHEN

Once predominantly Italian and Greek, stores with sidewalk stands have replaced the pushcarts of yore, and Hell's Kitchen is now a United Nations of food, with everything from apple pie to Ethiopian injera bread available for consumption. The 9th Avenue International Food Festival celebrates this rather cool diversity in May (see Events in Chapter 4). 9th Ave. from 37th to 49th St., Hell's Kitchen. Subway: 42nd St./8th Ave.

3 f-3

JACKSON HEIGHTS (INDIAN)

Shop for Indian spices, condiments, sweets, and saris and stop for a breathtaking meal at one of several unassuming Indian restaurants in this melting pot of a neighborhood. 74th St. from 37th to Roosevelt Aves., Queens. Subway: 7 to 74th St./Broadway.

7 e-3

LA MARQUETA

East Harlem has its own, muy aromatic Latin American market, with more than 250 stalls displaying exotic fruits and vegetables; grains, spices, hot sauces, smoked meats, and fish. Park Ave. from 110th to 116th St., East Harlem. Subway: 6 to 116th St. Subway: 6 to 116th St.

8 d-4

LITTLE ATHENS

Astoria houses one of the largest Greek communities outside Greece, so this is the place to explore Greek tavernas, coffeehouses (raffenion), restaurants, and churches to the tunes of bouzouki music, baklava, and thick, rich Greek coffee. Ditmars Blvd. from 31st to 38th Sts., Astoria, Queens. Subway: Ditmars Blvd./Astoria.

11 f-5

LITTLE ITALY

Little Italy has more or less dwindled away as an Italian residential neighborhood, but its restaurants, pastry and espresso cafés, and cheese and pasta shops live on. You won't find cannolis like these uptown. The Feast of San Gennaro packs the streets each fall (*see* Events *in* Chapter 4). *Mulberry St. between Houston and Canal Sts. Subway: 6, N, R, J, M, Z to Canal St.*

3 *c-7*

LOWER EAST SIDE

Okay, so it's becoming an extension of the East Village, but the Lower East Side retains a few vestiges of its Jewish era. Knishes, barreled schmaltz herring, pastrami, corned beef, pickles, and bagels share this neighborhood with the discount shops. *Roughly Houston–Canal Sts. from Bowery to the East River. Subway: Delancey St.; Grand St.*

10 *f-1*

UKRAINIAN AND POLISH AREA

Emerge from that dive bar and check out the East Village's first cultural legacy: wonderful pierogi, blintzes, kielbasa, headcheese, babka, and black bread. If you need an excuse, the Ukrainian Festival shows them all off every May (*see* Events *in* Chapter 4). *1st Ave. near 7th St. Subway: 2nd Ave.*

7 *f-7*

YORKVILLE

The German area has nearly disappeared, but a few restaurants still serve hearty, home-style foods and bock beer; a few Konditoreien serve exquisite pastries; and a few shops sell specialty foods. There's still a small Hungarian enclave within this district. *Lexington Ave. to York Ave., mainly on E. 86th St. Subway: 4, 5, 6 to 86th St.*

fish & seafood

10 *d-1*

BALDUCCI'S

Like most foods in this gourmet bastion, the seafood is high-quality and creatively selected. With advance notice, Balducci's can special order anything that swims. *424 6th Ave. (at 9th St.), West Village, 212/673–2600 or 800/BALDUCCI. Subway: W. 4th St./Washington Sq.*

9 *c-5*

CENTRAL FISH COMPANY

True, it's not centrally located, but the selection of fresh fish is enormous and prices are extremely reasonable. *527 9th Ave. (at 39th St.), Garment District, 212/279–2317. Subway: 42nd St./8th Ave.*

7 *f-8*

CITARELLA

Citarella's Upper West Side store was so successful that the owners opened up shop on the East Side, offering much more than just fish. The West Side shop has long been cherished for its amazing window displays of fresh seafood sculptures, and, of course, its superior selection of fresh fish. *2135 Broadway (at 75th St.), Upper West Side, 212/874–0383. Subway: 72nd St.*

7 *f-8*

1313 3rd Ave. (at 75th St.), Upper East Side, 212/452–2780. Subway: 77th St.

7 *b-6*

JAKE'S FISH MARKET

Everyone seems to love this shop for its fresh fish and savvy staff. Prices are high, but the quality and variety are beyond dispute. *2425 Broadway (at 89th St.), Upper West Side, 212/580–5253. Subway: 1, 9 to 86th St.*

10 *d-1*

JEFFERSON MARKET

This neighborhood West Village shop has a good selection of fresh fish and is particularly appreciated for its friendly staff and personal service. *450 6th Ave. (near W. 10th St.), Greenwich Village, 212/533–3377. Subway: F to 14th St.*

9 *f-1*

LEONARD'S

The exquisite selection includes smoked or poached salmon, caviar, crabmeat, and boiled lobster. Delivery is free. *1241 3rd Ave. (between 71st and 72nd Sts.), Upper East Side, 212/744–2600. Subway: 68th St./Hunter College.*

9 *f-4*

PISACANE

Here in U.N. territory is a good general selection of high-quality fish. *940 1st Ave. (between 51st and 52nd Sts.), Midtown, 212/355–1850. Subway: 51st St./Lexington–3rd Aves.*

7 *e-8*

ROSEDALE

You can't beat Rosedale for quality and selection, but you can definitely beat its prices. This shop is known for delicious soft-shell crabs and superior salmon. *1129 Lexington Ave. (at 78th St.), Upper East Side, 212/288–5013. Closed Sun. Subway: 77th St.*

gourmet foods

10 *d-1*

BALDUCCI'S

This New York institution is a foodie destination for natives and tourists alike. Inhale olives, vinegars, cheeses, pâtés, breads and pastries, chocolates, meats, desserts, and coffees. *424 6th Ave. (at 9th St.), West Village, 212/673–2600 or 800/BALDUCCI. Subway: W. 4th St./Washington Sq.*

9 *f-3*

CALL CUISINE

Don't feel like cooking? Choose from about 15 different gourmet dinners, each prepared daily. The retail shop clues you in to the ingredients. *1032 1st Ave. (between 56th and 57th Sts.), Midtown, 212/752–7070. Subway: 59th St./Lexington Ave.*

9 *e-2*

CAVIARTERIA

Eight varieties of fresh caviar and six varieties preserved are the raison d'être, but you can also buy foie gras and Scottish and Nova Scotia salmon. *29 E. 60th St. (near Madison Ave.), Upper East Side, 212/759–7410. Subway: 59th St./Lexington Ave.*

10 *c-1*

CHELSEA MARKET

This giant warehouse space on the edge of the meat-packing district is an exciting development for foodies in New York. More than a dozen independently operated shops coexist within the enormous space, from delicious Amy's Bread to freshly squeezed Juice Company juices, to decadent desserts at Sarabeth's, to aged prime rib at Frank's, to gourmet wholesale priced Italian goodies at Bon'Italia. *75 9th Ave. (between 15th and 16th Sts.), Chelsea. Subway: A, C, E to 14th St.*

11 *e-4*

DEAN & DELUCA

Who doesn't love this fabulous food emporium? A well-edited department in every food category means you'll find only the best of the best. The quality and beauty of the food are matched only by the quality and beauty of the clientele. To prepare your purchase in style, head to the back of the store, where great-looking kitchenware and cookbooks are temptingly displayed. *560 Broadway (at Prince St.), SoHo, 212/431–1691 or 800/221–7714. Subway: Prince St.*

7 *e-8*

E.A.T.

Ah, such lovely imports at such breath-taking prices! The handsome E.A.T. offers daily specials on its excellent assortment of pâtés, cheeses, coffees, and breads. The chocolate roulade cake is particularly magnificent. *1064 Madison Ave. (at 80th St.), Upper East Side, 212/772–0022. Subway: 77th St.*

7 *f-8*

ELI'S

This two-floor extravaganza of upscale gourmet treats is from the same food guru who brought us Zabar's, the Vinegar Factory, and E.A.T. Prices are quite high, but the selection of delicious prepared foods, extraordinary cheeses, and interesting produce keeps customers coming back. There's also a beautiful flower selection and a small, but well chosen array of cookbooks and kitchen implements. *1411 3rd Ave. (at 80th St.), Upper East Side, 212/717–8100. Subway: 77th St.*

11 *e-5*

GOURMET GARAGE

Known for such staples as fresh produce, pastas, breads, oils, and vinegars, Gourmet Garage sells a fine selection of quality goods at reasonable prices. *453 Broome St. (near Mercer St.), SoHo, 212/941–5850. Subway: 6 to Spring St.*

7 *b-5*

2571 Broadway (at 96th St.), Upper West Side, 212/663–0656. Subway: 1, 2, 3, 9 to 96th St.

9 *f-2*

301 E. 64th St. (at 2nd Ave.), Upper East Side, 212/535–6271. Subway: 68th St./Hunter College.

11 *b-2*

117 7th Ave. S (between Christopher and W. 10th Sts.), West Village, 212/699–5980. Subway: Christopher St./Sheridan Sq.

9 *f-1*

GRACE'S MARKETPLACE

This upscale store has a loyal neighborhood following and is always busy. Pick up fresh produce, pasta, oils and vinegars, fresh dairy products and cheeses, sliced meats, olives, baked goods, candy, desserts, fresh coffee, prepared foods, sandwiches and more. *1237 3rd Ave. (at 71st St.), Upper East Side, 212/737–0600. Subway: 68th St./Hunter College.*

9 *e-3*

MAISON GLASS

Maison Glass is a good general store for smoked Scottish and Nova Scotia salmon, Smithfield ham, foie gras, cheese, and canned and packaged gourmet food. *111 E. 58th St. (between Park and Lexington Aves.), Midtown, 212/755–3316. Subway: 59th St./Lexington Ave.*

10 *c-1*

MYERS OF KESWICK

It may be a stretch to call it "gourmet," but anglophiles will love this charming grocer. Knock yourself out with sausage rolls, kidney pies, pork pies, Scotch eggs, Stilton cheese, and Aberdeen kippers, along with packaged British cookies, candy, and other foods. Yes—they do have HobNobs! *634 Hudson St. (near Jane St.), West Village, 212/691–4194. Subway: A, C, E to 14th St.*

7 *f-6*

THE VINEGAR FACTORY

Eli Zabar, the founder of both Zabar's and E.A.T., has another big, bustling shop in a converted turn-of-the-20th-century vinegar factory. The great selection of everything from prepared foods to produce means you'll find whatever you need. The Factory sells Eli's famous bread for less than you'd pay at E.A.T. Bonus: there's free parking nearby. *431 E. 91st St. (between 1st and York Aves.), Upper East Side, 212/987–0885. Subway: 4, 5, 6 to 86th St.*

9 *d-3*

PETROSSIAN BOUTIQUE

Indulge in the world's finest caviar, and try the delicious buckwheat blinis, sturgeon, pâté, and prepared foods. Prices are not low. *182 E. 58th St. (between Lexington and 3rd Aves.), Midtown, 212/245–2217. Subway: N, R to 57th St.*

7 *e-8*

WILLIAM POLL

This Upper East Side caterer and store has undoubtedly made many a society dinner party. They're known for delicious hors d'oeuvres, thin sandwiches, prepared foods, spreads, and specialty items. *1051 Lexington Ave. (between 74th and 75th Sts.), Upper East Side, 212/288–0501. Closed Sun. Subway: 77th St.*

7 *b-8*

ZABAR'S

From its humble beginnings as a deli and cheese shop, Zabar's has become the king of New York's gourmet stores. Its mind-boggling array of cheeses, meats, smoked fish, coffees, teas, and prepared entrées has won the city over. Kitchenwares are discounted 20%–40% on the mezzanine. Go just for the sights, sounds, smells, and social life. *2245 Broadway (at 80th St.), Upper West Side, 212/787–2000. Subway: 79th St.*

health food

11 *c-7*

COMMODITIES NATURAL

With over 5,000 square ft to play with in its Tribeca store, this supermarket has 24 kinds of granola, 50 kinds of honey, 125 kinds of tea, 30 bins of grains, and tons of fresh organic produce. *117 Hudson St. (at N. Moore St.), Tribeca, 212/334–8330. Subway: Franklin St.*

10 *f-1*

165 1st Ave. (at 10th St.), East Village, 212/260–2600. Subway: 1st Ave.; Astor Pl.

10 *e-1*

HEALTHY PLEASURES

The feature presentations are an organic salad bar and a selection of healthy prepared foods. Other health- and environment-conscious products include vitamins, personal-care items, and cleaning products. *93 University Pl. (near 11th St.), Greenwich Village, 212/353–3663. Subway: 8th St./NYU.*

10 *c-1*

INTEGRAL YOGA NATURAL FOODS

Health-food enthusiasts flock here for the wide selection, including freshly made prepared foods. *229 W. 13th St. (between 7th and 8th Aves.), West Village, 212/243–2642. Subway: A, C, E to 14th St.; L to 8th Ave.*

10 d-1

LIFETHYME NATURAL MARKET

Appetizing even to junk food fans, this market offers organic produce, a juice and salad bar, a vegan bakery, and a wide selection of packaged all-natural products from soy ice cream to gluten-free pasta. *410 6th Ave. (between 8th and 9th Sts.), West Village, 212/420–9099. Subway: W. 4th St./Washington Sq.*

11 e-4

WHOLE FOODS

Whole Foods is a complete natural-food market, with specialties in produce, chicken, and fish. There's a large bulk department, many fresh herbs, and a selection of gourmet takeout meals. Natural cosmetics and vitamins complete your personal package nicely. *117 Prince St. (between Wooster and Greene Sts.), SoHo, 212/982–1000. Subway: Prince St.*

7 b-6

2421 Broadway (at 89th St.), Upper West Side, 212/874–4000. Subway: 1, 9 to 86th St.

herbs & spices

11 c-2

APHRODISIA

This inviting Villager has an interesting selection of herbs at reasonable prices. *264 Bleecker St. (near 6th Ave.), West Village, 212/989–6440. Subway: W. 4th St./Washington Sq.*

11 e-4

DEAN & DELUCA

Image is everything: Dean & DeLuca's immense variety of spices are, upon purchase, packaged in signature round tins. They look so spiffy in the kitchen that you may want to start collecting them. *560 Broadway (at Prince St.), SoHo, 212/431–1691 or 800/221–7714. Subway: Prince St.*

12 c-4

SAHADI IMPORTING CO.

This exotic market is well worth the trip for its great selection of spices and Middle Eastern food at excellent prices. Bulk purchases offer even more savings. *187–89 Atlantic Ave. (near Court St.), Brooklyn Heights, Brooklyn, 718/624–4550. Closed Sun. Subway: Borough Hall.*

meat & poultry

New York's meatpacking district is otherwise known as Washington Market, spanning 9th and 10th avenues from Gansevoort Street to West 14th Street. From here, wholesale meat distributors supply hotels and restaurants. Many of these outlets sell retail as well, providing a mighty colorful experience and incomparable selection and savings.

11 c-2

FAICCO'S PORK STORE

In business since the exact turn of the 20th century, Faicco's has become a New York institution, renowned for its delicious sausages. *260 Bleecker St. (near 6th Ave.), West Village, 212/243–1974. Subway: W. 4th St./Washington Sq.*

4 e-4

6511 11th Ave. (at 65th St.), Bay Ridge, Brooklyn, 718/236–0119. Closed Mon. Subway: Fort Hamilton Pkwy.

10 d-1

JEFFERSON MARKET

Jefferson's fans prefer it to neighboring Balducci's for meat. Don't hesitate to ask questions; the friendly staff is into customer service. *450 6th Ave. (near W. 10th St.), West Village, 212/533–3377. Subway: F to 14th St.*

11 h-1

KUROWYCKY MEATS

This family-run shop has been in business for nearly 40 years, preparing and purveying some of the city's finest smoked (on the premises) and cured meats. Look for baked hams, unusual sausages (including sausage with caraway seeds, or the spicy Ukrainian kielbasa). Top off your purchase with dark Lithuanian bread, homemade Polish mustard, and sauerkraut. *124 1st Ave. (near 7th St.), East Village, 212/477–0344. Subway: Astor Pl.*

9 e-7

LES HALLES

The popular French bistro (*see* French *in* Chapter 1) also has a highly regarded butcher shop for French cuts of meat. *411 Park Ave. S (between 28th and 29th Sts.), Murray Hill, 212/679–4111. Subway: 6 to 28th St.*

7 *e-7*

LOBEL'S

Many New Yorkers consider this to be the prime outlet for meat in the city. Although prices can be astronomically high, you definitely get what you pay for, and the service is knowledgeable and professional. *1096 Madison Ave. (between 82nd and 83rd Sts.), Upper East Side, 212/737–1373. Subway: 4, 5, 6 to 86th St.*

7 *b-5*

OPPENHEIMER PRIME MEATS

The butcher and owner of this old-fashioned shop carries a top selection of meats, game, and poultry. *2606 Broadway (at 99th St.), Upper West Side, 212/662–0246. Closed Sun. Subway: 1, 2, 3, 9 to 96th St.*

7 *g-7*

OTTOMANELLI BROS.

Catch prime cuts and fresh game in season. They'll deliver to nearby addresses. *1549 York Ave. (at 82nd St.), Upper East Side, 212/772–7900. Subway: 4, 5, 6 to 86th St.*

1 *b-8*

395 Amsterdam Ave. (at 79th St.), Upper West Side, 212/496–1049. Subway: 1, 9 to 79th.

7 *e-7*

SCHALLER & WEBBER

A holdout of the German Yorkville stores that used to line the streets here—the high-quality smoked meats, sausages, and hams will make you think you're back in the old country. *1654 2nd Ave. (between 85th and 86th Sts.), Upper East Side, 212/879–3047. Subway: 4, 5, 6 to 86th St.*

nuts & seeds

11 *c-8*

A. L. BAZZINI

Since 1886 Bazzini has served up dried fruit, nuts, coffees, candies, chocolates, gourmet cookies, specialty sandwiches and more. Try their famous pistachios and nut crunches. *339 Greenwich St. (at Jay St.), Tribeca, 212/334–1280. Closed Sun. Subway: Chambers St.*

7 *b-7*

BROADWAY NUT SHOPPE

The name is no joke: this store has Georgia pecans, black walnuts in season, pignoli nuts, Indian nuts, macadamias, cashews, almonds, pistachios, and filberts roasted on the premises. Add imported candies and dried fruit to your mix. *2246 Broadway (at 81st St.), Upper West Side, 212/874–5214. Subway: 79th St.*

12 *c-4*

SAHADI IMPORTING CO.

Purveyors of nuts and dried fruit since 1895, Sahadi has nearly 100 varieties between the two. *See Herbs & Spices, above. 187–89 Atlantic Ave. (near Court St.), Brooklyn Heights, Brooklyn, 718/624–4550. Closed Sun. Subway: Borough Hall.*

7 *f-7*

TREAT BOUTIQUE

Treat stocks candy, nuts, dried fruit, and assorted gourmet items, and makes fudge on the premises. *200 E. 86th St. (at Third Ave.), Upper East Side, 212/737–6619. Subway: 4, 5, 6 to 86th St.*

pasta

9 *c-4*

BRUNO RAVIOLI CO.

Pasta makers since 1905, Bruno supplies many restaurants and caterers with its fresh manicotti; tortellini; vegetable lasagna; egg fettuccine; and ravioli with sun-dried tomatoes, shiitake mushrooms, or pesto. Pick up a homemade sauce, too. *653 9th Ave. (near 45th St.), Hell's Kitchen, 212/246–8456. Subway: 42nd St./8th Ave.*

9 *c-8*

249 8th Ave. (near 22nd St.), Chelsea, 212/627–0767. Subway: C, E to 23rd St.

7 *b-8*

2204 Broadway (near 78th St.), Upper West Side, 212/580–8150. Subway: 79th St.

11 *f-5*

PIEMONTE HOMEMADE RAVIOLI COMPANY

In the heart of Little Italy, Piemonte makes a variety of fresh pastas daily, including gluten-free macaroni for those with an allergy. *190 Grand St. (near Mul-*

berry St.), 212/226–0475. Closed Mon.
Subway: 6, J, M, N, R, Z to Canal St.

---

11 *d-3*

RAFFETTO'S CORPORATION

This long-standing Village shop (est.
1906) cuts fresh pasta and egg or
spinach noodles to your specifications
as you watch. Every day brings new
batches of ravioli stuffed with cheese or
meat. Nobody does it better, or for less.
*144 W. Houston St. (near Sullivan St.),
West Village, 212/777–1261. Closed Sun.–
Mon. Subway: Houston St.*

---

11 *c-5*

THE RAVIOLI STORE INC.

Will you go for the all-out gourmet ravioli with wild mushrooms and white truffles in a saffron pasta or traditional with
fresh ricotta in a parsley flecked dough?
You won't go wrong with either one, or
with any of the dozens of other fresh
gourmet pastas cranked-out on the
premises. Oh, and ever wonder where
Dean & Deluca gets their pricey pasta?
Well look no farther (and pay a lot less).
*75 Sullivan St. (between Spring & Broome
Sts.), SoHo, 212/925–1737. Subway: A, C,
E to Canal St.*

---

produce

10 *d-1*

BALDUCCI'S

Balducci's is known for many things, but
everyone loves the place for its amazing
and delicious variety of fresh fruits and
vegetables. For custom baskets, call 212/
206–4600. *424 6th Ave. (at 9th St.), West
Village, 212/673–2600 or 800/BALDUCCI.
Subway: W. 4th St./Washington Sq.*

---

11 *e-4*

DEAN & DELUCA

It is, after all, the strikingly colorful array
of fresh produce that entices passers-by
into this gourmet nirvana. The stuff is
pricey, but people pay—for the pleasure
of shopping here. And note that at day's
end, the produce staff sometimes offers
the wares at steep discounts. Stylists
and still-life photographers sometimes
drop in, looking for the perfect fruit or
veggie for that day's shoot. *560 Broadway (at Prince St.), SoHo, 212/431–1691
or 800/221–7714. Subway: Prince St.*

---

7 *b-8*

FAIRWAY

Famous for good produce at low prices,
Fairway goes further by stocking an
unbelievable selection—every conceivable fruit and vegetable, from A to Z,
include seasonal specialties and baby
vegetables. Deliveries arrive daily, so
there's never an "off" day, though weekends can be unpleasantly hectic. *2127
Broadway (at 75th St.), Upper West Side,
212/595–1888. Subway: 72nd, 79th Sts.*

---

6 *c-8*

*133rd St. at West Side Hwy., Harlem, 212/
234–3883. Subway: 137th St./City College.*

---

11 *e-5*

GOURMET GARAGE

Fear not, family shoppers: here you'll
find fruit and vegetables both basic and
rarefied, to satisfy both the discerning
gourmand and the average Joe (or
child). Prices are generally reasonable,
but keep an eye on them. *453 Broome St.
(at Mercer St.), SoHo, 212/941–5850.
Subway: 6 to Spring St.*

---

7 *b-5*

*2571 Broadway (at 96th St.), Upper West
Side, 212/663–0656. Subway: 1, 2, 3, 9 to
96th St.*

---

9 *f-2*

*301 E. 64th St. (at 2nd Ave.), Upper East
Side, 212/535–6271. Subway: 68th
St./Hunter College.*

---

11 *b-2*

*117 7th Ave. S (between Christopher and
W. 10th Sts.), West Village, 212/699–5980.
Subway: Christopher St./Sheridan Sq.*

---

9 *f-1*

GRACE'S MARKETPLACE

The exotic selection of fresh produce
includes hard-to-find seasonal specialties from around the world, including
Kiwano and Pepino melons, loquats,
white Queen Anne cherries, and Cere-
moya fruit. Apricots, plums, peaches,
nectarines, and cherries are available
year-round. *1237 3rd Ave. (at 71st St.),
Upper East Side, 212/737–0600. Subway:
68th St./Hunter College.*

---

greenmarkets

New York's year-round greenmarkets
give the city a breath of fresh air, with
the help of area farmers. Produce is
often cheaper than at grocery stores and
gourmet shops; and it's sold by the

grower, so freshness is guaranteed. In addition to local seasonal fruits and vegetables, you'll find fresh-cut wildflowers, baked goods, cheeses, fresh milk, and apple cider in season. Ask around in your neighborhood; major squares throughout the five boroughs (such as Union Square) have the most abundant markets.

7 *e-7*

PARADISE MARKET

Indeed, it's Eden for fresh produce, with a wide selection of exotic yet (may we hope?) permissible fruits and vegetables. The prices, alas, are postlapsarian. *1100 Madison Ave. (at 83rd St.), Upper East Side, 212/737–0049. Subway: 4, 5, 6 to 86th St.*

7 *e-8*

1080 Lexington Ave. (at 76th St.), Upper East Side, 212/57–1190. Subway: 77th St.

7 *f-6*

THE VINEGAR FACTORY

Not surprisingly, they've got a wide selection of fresh fruits and veggies, including hard-to-find items. *431 E. 91st St. (between 1st and York Aves.), Upper East Side, 212/987–0885. Subway: 4, 5, 6 to 86th St.*

FRAMING

9 *d-8*

A. I. FRIEDMAN

More than 2,000 styles of ready-made wood, plexi, and metal frames go for 20% off the list price, and the staff will custom-frame as well. *44 W. 18th St. (between 5th and 6th Aves.), Chelsea, 212/243–9000. Subway: F to 14th St.*

7 *e-8*

A.P.F., INC.

This company's own factory makes a variety of custom frames, including museum-quality reproductions as well as contemporary styles. *172 E. 75th St. (between Lexington and 3rd Aves.), Upper East Side, 212/988–1090. Subway: 77th St.*

9 *f-2*

231 E. 60th St. (between 3rd and 2nd Aves.), Upper East Side, 212/223–0726. Subway: 59th St./Lexington Ave.

11 *e-5*

BARK FRAMEWORKS

Bark has specialized in archivally correct framing for over 20 years. The service doesn't come cheap, but it's worth it for fine works of art and photography that you want to last a lifetime. *270 Lafayette St. (at Prince St.), SoHo, 212/431–9080. Open by appt. only. Subway: 6 to Spring St.*

9 *c-8*

CHELSEA FRAMES

This shop concentrates on custom and archival framing of everything from posters to conservation pieces. The staff is helpful, turnaround is fast, and prices are reasonable. *207 8th Ave. (between 20th and 21st Sts.), Chelsea, 212/807–8957. Subway: C, E to 23rd St.*

7 *g-8*

HOUSE OF HEYDENRYK

Heydenryk has sold, repaired, and restored antique frames since 1935; the company now also sells reproduction frames, made by a staff of craftsmen who work above the showroom. Repros take four weeks. *417 E. 76th St. (between 1st and York Aves.), Upper East Side, 212/249–4903. Subway: 77th St.*

9 *e-2*

J. POCKER & SON

Expert framers since 1926, J. Pocker & Son provide custom work, including conservation, in a wide range of styles, from ornate, hand-carved gilt to plexi. They'll even pick up and deliver your piece. Drop into the gallery to browse prints and posters, including a selection of views of New York and English sporting scenes. *135 E. 63rd St. (between Lexington and Park Aves.), Upper East Side, 212/838–5488 or 800/782–8434. Subway: 59th St./Lexington Ave.*

4 *d-2*

YALE PICTURE FRAME & MOULDING CORP.

This estimable firm imports and manufactures picture frames; discounts over 400 moldings for custom-made frames by 25%; and offers over 20,000 ready-made frames. *770 5th Ave. (at 28th St.), Sunset Park, Brooklyn, 718/788–6200. Closed Sat.; Sun. by appt. only. Subway: 25th St.*

GARDEN ACCESSORIES

9 *e-1*

LEXINGTON GARDENS

Always brimming with interesting new items, Lexington Gardens features English country–style accessories and furniture for the home and garden, including fabulous dried-flower arrangements and topiaries. *1011 Lexington Ave. (at 73rd St.), Upper East Side, 212/861–4390. Closed Sun. Subway: 77th St.*

11 *d-5*

SMITH & HAWKEN

This popular SoHo outlet of the famous catalogue retailer contains everything you need to create a classic garden—from teakwood furniture to flower bulbs, gardening clogs to garden hoses. Apartment dwellers can choose from herbal hand creams, hand-thrown dishes, and terrariums. *394 W. Broadway (between Broome and Spring Sts.), SoHo, 212/925–1190. Subway: C, E to Spring St.*

7 *f-8*

TREILLAGE LTD.

This unusual and stylish mix of antique and reproduction garden furniture and accessories encompasses English terracotta pots and plants, gardening tools, watering cans, gloves, candles, home- and garden-design books, and interesting Christmas decorations in season. *418 E. 75th St. (between 1st and York Aves.), Upper East Side, 212/535–2288. Closed Sun.; closed Sat. in July and Aug. Subway: 77th St.*

GIFTS

10 *f-6*

BROOKSTONE

The famed New Hampshire purveyor of hard-to-find tools and gadgets displays a sample of every item it sells. Pick up a clipboard upon entering—it's your order form. *South Street Seaport, Schermerhorn Row, 18 Fulton St., Lower Manhattan, 212/344–8108. Subway: Fulton St.*

9 *d-4*

Rockefeller Center, 5th Ave. between 49th and 50th Sts., Midtown, 212/262–3237. Subway: 47th–50th Sts./Rockefeller Ctr.

9 *d-3*

20 W. 57th St. (between 5th and 6th Aves.), Midtown, 212/245–1405. Subway: B, Q to 57th St.

7 *e-8*

E.A.T. GIFTS

Here lie thousands of super-cute little gifts and favors for children's parties, many of which would make great stocking stuffers. *1062 Madison Ave. (at 80th St.), Upper East Side, 212/861–2544. Subway: 77th St.*

9 *d-3*

FELISSIMO

An oasis of quiet in mid-Midtown, the whole of Felissimo is configured according to feng shui, the Eastern art of placement, so you've got to feel harmonious. The first floor features gardening accessories; the second floor has clothing, accessories, and a beautiful bedroom area, with fine linens and bath products; the third floor covers the dining-room table; and once you've made it to the fourth floor, you can plop elegantly down in the Tea Room (see Food–Coffee & Tea, *above*). *10 W. 56th St. (between 5th and 6th Aves.), Midtown, 212/247–5656. Subway: N, R to 5th Ave.*

9 *e-3*

HAMMACHER SCHLEMMER

Established on the Bowery in 1848, Hammacher Schlemmer has been on 57th Street since 1926, filling its six floors with unique gadgets, conveniences, and indulgences for every room in the home; the car; the sauna; the yacht; or the private airplane. *147 E. 57th St. (between Lexington and 3rd Aves.), Midtown, 212/421–9000. Subway: 59th St./Lexington Ave.*

11 *e-4*

THE L.S. COLLECTION

A large selection of unique and stylish giftware including china, handblown crystal, glasses, and sterling. *494 Broome St. (between Wooster St. and W. Broadway), SoHo, 212/334–1194. Subway: C, E to Spring St.; Prince St.*

9 *d-3*

MOMA DESIGN STORE

The Museum of Modern Art's retail showroom sells modern furniture, home accessories, kitchenware, tools, desk accessories, jewelry, children's toys, and books, all with a nod toward good design. *44 W. 53rd St. (between 5th and 6th Aves.), Midtown, 212/708–9800. Subway: E, F to 5th Ave.*

`10` *c-1*

MXYPLYZYK

Don't even try to pronounce the name; just try to stop by this beautiful West Village store, a favorite of editors and stylists alike. Mxy focuses on high-style, but not high-price, home furnishings and gifts, including books, jewelry, and pet accessories. *125 Greenwich Ave. (between Jane and Horatio Sts.), West Village, 212/989–4300. Subway: 1, 9, C, E to 14th St.*

`11` *f-4*

POP SHOP

Yes, it's an entire store devoted to the designs of Keith Haring: T-shirts for the whole family, games, bags, and, of course, posters. Hours can be erratic; call first. *292 Lafayette St. (between Prince and Houston Sts.), SoHo, 212/219–2784. Subway: Broadway–Lafayette St.; Prince St.*

`9` *d-3*

THE SHARPER IMAGE

The gadget-filled catalog comes to life: Here are all those intriguing items you know you can live without but aren't sure you want to. Fall for a massage chair, a robot that serves hors d'oeuvres, a safari hat with a built-in fan, a talking scale . . . . *4 W. 57th St. (between 5th and 6th Aves.), Midtown, 212/265–2550. Subway: E, F to 5th Ave.*

`10` *f-7*

South Street Seaport, Pier 17, Lower Manhattan, 212/693–0477. Subway: Fulton St.

HOME FURNISHINGS

architectural artifacts

`11` *g-3*

IRREPLACEABLE ARTIFACTS

Head to the East Village for original, spectacular architectural ornamentation for interior and exterior use—stained glass, mantel pieces, fountains, wrought iron, paneling, and much, much more. *14 2nd Ave. (at Houston St.), East Village, 212/777–2900. Subway: 2nd Ave.*

`11` *f-4*

URBAN ARCHAEOLOGY

The name is literal: all of these gargoyles and other grand bygone architectural embellishments were saved from the wrecking ball. With a focus on New York City, this shop carries Americana from the 1880s to 1925, antique slot and arcade machines, and a celebrated collection of Art Deco interiors and exteriors. Displays spill outdoors. *285 Lafayette St. (between Prince and Houston Sts.), SoHo, 212/431–6969. Subway: Broadway–Lafayette St.*

`11` *d-7*

143 Franklin St. (between Varick and Hudson Sts.), Tribeca, 212/431–4646. Subway: Franklin St.

`9` *f-3*

239 E. 58th St. (between 2nd and 3rd Aves.), Midtown, 212/371–4646. Subway: 59th St./Lexington Ave.

bedroom & bath

`9` *e-8*

HASTING TILE & IL BAGNO

The whole store is a knockout, with bold designs for bathrooms and all the fittings, including artful designer tiles. They do kitchens, too. *230 Park Ave. S (at 19th St.), Gramercy, 212/674–9700. Subway: N, R, 6 to 23rd St.*

`11` *g-3*

IRREPLACEABLE ARTIFACTS

Mixed into this well-known stash of architectural miscellany is a collection of antique bathroom fixtures and accessories. *14 2nd Ave. (at Houston St.), East Village, 212/777–2900. Subway: 2nd Ave.*

`9` *f-2*

KRAFT HARDWARE

Kraft is an Upper East Side source for high-end fixtures and bath accessories. *306 E. 61st St. (between 2nd and 1st Aves.), Upper East Side, 212/838–2214. Subway: 59th St./Lexington Ave.*

`9` *e-8*

NEMO TILE

Finish off your bath project with these medicine cabinets, bath fixtures, porcelain and glass tiles, mosaics, and accessories. Nemo is a full-line distributor and importer of ceramic tile. *48 E. 21st St. (between Broadway and Park Ave.),*

Gramercy, 212/505–0009. Subway: N, R, 6 to 23rd St.

9 *e-3*

SHERLE WAGNER INTERNATIONAL

Here they are: the world's most elegant and expensive bathroom fixtures. *60 E. 57th St. (at Park Ave.), Midtown, 212/758–3300. Closed weekends. Subway: E, F to 5th Ave.*

9 *f-7*

SIMON'S HARDWARE

Simon's has everything for the bath, including an impressive line of tiles in marble, granite, stone, and slate. *421 3rd Ave. (between 29th and 30th Sts.), Murray Hill, 212/532–9220. Closed Sun. Subway: 6 to 28th St.*

9 *f-3*

WATERWORKS

This pair of shops carries classic, elegant, British-inspired bath fixtures plus a full line of tiles and stones. *237 E. 58th St., Midtown, 212/371–9266. Subway: 59th St./Lexington Ave.*

10 *e-4*

469 Broome St. (at Greene St.), SoHo, 212/966–0605. Subway: 6 to Spring St.; N, R to Canal St.

carpets & rugs

New York's rug district spans 30th–33rd streets between 5th and Madison avenues, where you'll find a particular concentration of Orientals and Persians. Bloomingdale's and Macy's also carry Oriental rugs.

9 *e-8*

ABC CARPET & HOME

Opened in 1897, this amazing emporium boasts two of the largest carpet showrooms anywhere. The holdings include Oriental, designer, area, scatter, rag rugs, and over 5,000 rolls of national brands plus (downstairs at no. 881), a large selection of remnants in a variety of fibers, colors, and sizes. You can arrange for immediate delivery and installation. *881 and 888 Broadway (at 19th St.), Flatiron District, 212/473–3000. Subway: 14th St./Union Sq.; N, R to 23rd St.*

11 *e-3*

A. BESHAR & CO.

Beshar has been selling handsome Oriental rugs, as well as cleaning and repairing them, since 1898. *611 Broadway (near Bleecker St.), Room 405, Greenwich Village, 212/529–7300. Subway: Bleecker St.*

9 *d-8*

ARONSON'S

This floor-covering supermarket meets all your flooring needs with carpet remnants, closeouts, or custom cuts; tile; and linoleum. *135 W. 17th St. (between 6th and 7th Aves.), Chelsea, 212/243–4993. Subway: F, 1, 2, 3, 9 to 14th St.*

7 *b-7*

CENTRAL CARPET

Come here first—Central Carpet is a great source for low-priced (they guarantee New York's lowest) antique, semi-antique, and new handmade Chinese, Persian, and Caucasian rugs. There's a large selection of Art Deco Chinese rugs and flat-weave Indian dhurries, as well as modern Belgian rugs—a total of more than 5,000 rugs on two floors. Prices range from $19 to $10,000. *426 Columbus Ave. (near 81st St.), Upper West Side, 212/787–8813. Subway: 79th St.*

10 *c-1*

81 8th Ave. (at 14th St.), Chelsea, 212/741–3700. Subway: A, C, E to 14th St.

9 *e-3*

EINSTEIN-MOOMJY

This oddly named carpet department store features new Orientals, broadlooms, and area rugs. *150 E. 58th St. (between Lexington and 3rd Aves.), Midtown, 212/758–0900. Subway: 59th St./Lexington Ave.*

11 *e-4*

MODERN AGE

Modern Age is New York City's only retail outlet for Christine Van Der Hurd rugs, with their uniquely beautiful contemporary designs. *102 Wooster St. (between Spring and Prince Sts.), SoHo, 212/966–0669. Subway: 6 to Spring St.; Prince St.*

7 *b-8*

RUG WAREHOUSE

For over 50 years this store has maintained a best-price guarantee on its Caucasians, Persians, Art Deco Chinese, dhurries, and kilims, both antique and modern. *220 W. 80th St. (between Broadway and Amsterdam Ave.), Upper West Side, 212/787–6665. Subway: 79th St.*

9 *e-8*

SAFAVIEH CARPETS

A reputable source for new and antique Oriental rugs, Safavieh will also buy, wash, appraise, and restore old rugs. *902 Broadway (between 20th and 21st Sts.), Flatiron District, 212/477–1234. Subway: N, R to 23rd St.*

9 *e-6*

153 Madison Ave. (at 32nd St.), Murray Hill, 212/683–8399. Subway: 33rd St.

9 *f-2*

238 E. 59th St./Lexington Ave., Midtown, 212/888–0626. Subway: 59th St./Lexington Ave.

ceramic tiles

9 *e-8*

ANN SACKS TILE & STONE

Ann Sacks will fit limestone, slate, terracotta, marble mosaics, handcrafted tile, and stone antiquities to your commercial or residential specifications. *5 E. 16th St. (near 5th Ave.), Gramercy, 212/463–8400. Subway: 14th St./Union Sq.*

9 *e-8*

ARTISTIC TILE

A wide range of beautiful tile is available, including tumbled stone mosaics in basketweave and fan patterns. *79 5th Ave. (at 16th St.), Union Sq., 212/727–9331. Subway: 14th St./Union Sq.*

9 *f-8*

COUNTRY FLOORS

This appealing shop specializes in fine hand-painted tiles, both antique and modern; most are imported from Italy, France, Holland, Peru, Finland, Spain, and Portugal. Sinks can be designed to match tiles. *315 E. 16th St. (between 1st and 2nd Aves.), Gramercy, 212/627–8300. Closed weekends. Subway: 14th St./Union Sq.*

9 *e-8*

HASTING TILE & IL BAGNO

See Bedroom & Bath, *above.*

9 *f-4*

IDEAL TILE

These importers of Italian ceramic tiles will provide expert installation or a do-it-yourself guide. *405 E. 51st St. (between 1st and 2nd Aves.), Midtown, 212/759–2339. Subway: 51st St./Lexington–3rd Aves.*

9 *e-8*

NEMO TILE

See Bedroom & Bath, *above.*

9 *e-6*

THE QUARRY

New York's largest stock of reasonably priced Spanish, Dutch, French, Portuguese, and Mexican tiles comes mainly in bright colors and patterns. The Quarry will install your choices or provide do-it-yourself guidance and supplies. Also on sale are bathroom and kitchen accessories and a complete line of wallpaper. *128 E. 32nd St. (between Park and Lexington Aves.), Murray Hill, 212/679–8889. Closed Sat. after 3 PM. Subway: 33rd St.*

china, glassware, porcelain, pottery, silver

You can buy fine china in any of the large department stores, and even finer china at Tiffany's and Cartier (see Jewelry–Contemporary, *below*). See also Antiques *and* Jewelry: Antique & Collectible.

9 *e-3*

ASPREY & CO., LTD.

This prestigious London firm is known for its exclusive silver patterns, both antique and modern, as well as crystal and china. Consider one of the luxurious gift items, such as a hand-bound book, rare first edition, or 18K-gold beard comb. *Trump Tower (725 5th Ave., at 56th St.), Midtown, 212/688–1811. Subway: N, R to 5th Ave.*

7 *b-7*

AVVENTURA

This wide selection of glassware and tablesettings contains china, serving pieces, and flatware. The stock is heavy on Italian manufacturers and hard-to-find pieces and tends to be of extremely high quality and unique design. Some distinctive Venetian jewelry is also on hand. *463 Amsterdam Ave. (near 83rd St.), Upper West Side, 212/769–2510. Close Sat. Subway: 1, 9 to 86th St.*

9 e-3

BACCARAT, INC.

Baccarat sells its own famed and expensive French crystal plus china by Limoges, Ceralene, and Raynaud; pewter by Etains du Manoir; and silver by Christofle and Puiforcat. *625 Madison Ave. (near 58th St.), Midtown, 212/826–4100. Subway: 59th St./Lexington Ave.*

9 e-3

CARDEL

Cast your eye on all major brands of high-end china, crystal, and silver in one location. This stuff makes great wedding gifts. *621 Madison Ave. (near 58th St.), Midtown, 212/753–8690. Closed Sun. Subway: 59th St./Lexington Ave.*

11 d-4

CERAMICA

Hand-painted ceramics and reproduction majolica are imported straight from Italy to this cheerful, charming, chock-full-of-china shop. New shipments arrive every three months. *59 Thompson St. (near Spring St.), SoHo, 212/941–1307. Closed Mon. Subway: C, E to Spring St.*

9 e-2

CHRISTOFLE

Here you'll find Christofle's full line of elegant sterling, silver-plate, and stainless tableware and home accessories in addition to crystal by Baccarat and St. Louis, china by Haviland and Ceralene, and private-label linens. *680 Madison Ave. (near 62nd St.), Upper East Side, 212/308–9390. Closed Sun. Subway: 59th St./Lexington Ave.*

10 g-4

EASTERN SILVER CO.

Eastern carries a large general selection of silver items and does repairs. *54 Canal St. (near Orchard St.), 2nd floor, Lower East Side, 212/226–5708. Closed Sat. Subway: E. Broadway.*

9 e-8

FISHS EDDY

These highly whimsical shops sell 1930s and '40s china and glassware that once belonged to corporations, restaurants, hotels, private clubs, and the government—making for some fascinating logos. Sugar bowls, creamers, and other vintage kitchen and dining accessories join the tableware, along with some modern kitchen overstocks and retro-looking pieces created just for this store. There are always some interesting collectibles here, and their prices are low; the shop is highly browsable. *889 Broadway (near 19th St.), Flatiron District, 212/420–9020. Subway: 14th St./Union Sq., N, R to 23rd St.*

7 b-8

2176 Broadway (at 76th St.), Upper West Side, 212/873–8819. Subway: 79th St.

9 e-3

FORTUNOFF

The impressive antique-silver department at the jewelry giant has American, Georgian, Russian, and Chinese silverware; tea services and various objets as well as contemporary flatware in sterling, plate, and stainless. *681 5th Ave. (near 54th St.), Midtown, 212/758–6660. Subway: E, F to 5th Ave.*

9 e-3

GALLERI ORREFORS
KOSTA BODA

Top-of-the-line Swedish crystal is on display here—Orrefors shows traditional vases and plates while Kosta Boda incorporates vibrant colors and funky designs. *58 E. 57th St. (between Madison and Park Aves.), Midtown, 212/752–1095. Subway: N, R to 5th Ave.*

9 e-2

HOYA CRYSTAL GALLERY

Here is the world's largest collection of this respected Japanese firm's art and functional pieces. Hoya is known for its low iron content, which results in glass with no discolorations or bubbles. Prices range from $30 to $30,000. *689 Madison Ave. (at 62nd St.), Upper East Side, 212/223–6335. Subway: 59th St./Lexington Ave.*

9 e-3

JAMES ROBINSON

For more than 70 years Robinson has purveyed fine 17th- to 19th-century English hallmark silver, rare porcelain dinner sets, and antique jewelry. The store is also known for its own hand-forged silver flatware. *480 Park Ave. (at 58th St.), Midtown, 212/752–6166. Closed Sun. Subway: 59th St./Lexington Ave.*

9 d-4

JEAN'S SILVERSMITHS

Jean's has the city's largest selection of discontinued silver patterns—over

900—plus new flat- and hollowware at winning prices. *16 W. 45th St. (between 5th and 6th Aves.), Midtown, 212/575–0723. Closed weekends. Subway: B, D, F Q to 42nd St.*

9 *e-2*

LALIQUE

Lalique's posh shop sells its own rightly famous, incredibly beautiful French crystal. *680 Madison Ave. (between 61st and 62nd Sts.), Upper East Side, 212/355–6550. Subway: 59th St./Lexington Ave.*

9 *e-1*

LA TERRINE

Concoct wonderful house presents or special accent pieces from the hand-painted Portuguese, Italian, and French ceramics in this neighborhood shop. Complementary table linens from Provence and India complete the international look. *1024 Lexington Ave. (at 73rd St.), Upper East Side, 212/988–6550. Closed Sun. Subway: 77th St.*

9 *e-1*

MACKENZIE-CHILDS LTD.

This is the flagship New York store for MacKenzie-Childs' whimsical line of hand-painted ceramics, glassware, and furniture. It is, shall we say, not the place to bargain-hunt. *824 Madison Ave. (near 69th St.), Upper East Side, 212/570–6050. Closed Sun. Subway: 68th St./Hunter College.*

10 *d-1*

MAD MONK

This shop is a longtime Village source for interesting handmade pottery and mirrors. *500 6th Ave. (near 13th St.), West Village, 212/242–6678. Subway: F to 14th St.*

9 *e-5*

MICHAEL C. FINA

This well-known store, a popular bridal registry choice, features an extensive stock of jewelry, sterling silver flatware, tea sets, giftware, clocks, and more. *545 5th Ave. (at 45th St.), Midtown, 212/557–2500. Subway: 42nd St./Grand Central.*

9 *e-2*

ROYAL COPENHAGEN PORCELAIN

Danish china and Orrefors and Kosta Boda crystal join Georg Jensen silver flatware and jewelry. *683 Madison Ave.*

(near 61st St.), Upper East Side, 212/759–6457. Subway: 59th St./Lexington Ave.

9 *e-1*

SARA

Sara focuses on imported Japanese ceramics of fine handcrafted quality. *953 Lexington Ave. (near 69th St.), Upper East Side, 212/772–3243. Closed Sun. Subway: 68th St./Hunter College.*

11 *d-4*

SIMON PEARCE

All of these simple and elegant hand-blown glasses, pitchers, candlesticks, and vases are made in Vermont. *120 Wooster St. (near Spring St.), SoHo, 212/334–2393. Subway: Spring St.*

9 *e-2*

500 Park Ave. (near 59th St.), Midtown, 212/421–8801. Subway: 59th St./Lexington Ave.

9 *e-3*

S. J. SHRUBSOLE

A trove of antique English and early American silver and jewelry, this is the best selection of silver in New York. *104 E. 57th St. (between Park and Lexington Aves.), Midtown, 212/753–8920. Subway: 59th St./Lexington Ave.*

9 *e-3*

STEUBEN GLASS

Steuben's showroom is like a museum, its pieces both beautiful and precious. Make time to browse both the unique glass sculptures and the functional pieces. *715 5th Ave. (at 56th St.), Midtown, 212/752–1441. Subway: N, R to 5th Ave.*

9 *e-1*

S. WYLER, INC.

Established in 1890, S. Wyler is the oldest silver dealer in the United States, with antique and modern silver, fine porcelain, and antiques. *941 Lexington Ave. (at 69th St.), Upper East Side, 212/879–9848. Closed Sun. Subway: 68th St./Hunter College.*

9 *e-3*

TIFFANY & CO.

The jeweler of renown sells its own china, crystal, and sterling tableware on the third floor, at surprisingly reasonable prices. *727 5th Ave. (at 57th St.), Mid-*

town, 212/755–8000. Closed Sun. Subway:
N, R to 5th Ave.

9 c-8
WILLIAMS-SONOMA
In addition to the famous cookware,
you'll find a stylish, well-priced selection
of china, pottery, wine glasses,
bistroware, flatware, and serving pieces.
As one fan put it, Williams-Sonoma
stores are not about cooking; they're
about lifestyle. Both camps are happy
here. 110 7th Ave. (near 17th St.), Chelsea,
212/633–2203. Subway: 1, 2, 3, 9 to 14th St.

9 e-2
20 E. 60th St. (near Madison Ave.), Upper
East Side, 212/980–5155. Subway: 59th
St./Lexington Ave.

9 f-1
1309 2nd Ave. (near 69th St.), Upper East
Side, 212/288–8408. Subway: 68th
St./Hunter College.

7 e-7
1175 Madison Ave. (near 86th St.), Upper
East Side, 212/289–6832. Subway: 4, 5, 6
to 86th St.

furniture & accessories
In addition to these specialist shops,
Bloomingdale's and Macy's have extensive collections of home furnishings,
mostly contemporary and traditional.
Bloomingdale's model rooms are always
well designed. You may not get the personal service you need, though, at these
retail behemoths.

9 e-8
ABC CARPET & HOME
The heartwarming ABC is a wonderful
source for antique furniture and acces-
sories as well as contemporary linens.
On the second floor you'll find Herman
Miller, vintage stainless steel, and tradi-
tional furniture. 888 Broadway (at 19th
St.), Flatiron District, 212/473–3000. Sub-
way: 14th St./Union Sq.; N, R to 23rd St.

11 d-4
AERO
Aero sells highly chic furniture of its
own design as well as vintage pieces. 132
Spring St. (near Wooster St.), SoHo, 212/

966–1500. Closed Sun. Subway: 6 to
Spring St.

11 c-1
AMALGAMATED HOME
Amalgamated comprises three small
stores all devoted to chic and sleek
home furnishings, with an emphasis on
funky, ultramodern designs and unusual
materials. Traditionalists may cringe,
but others find the mix fresh and pleasingly cutting-edge. 13, 19 Christopher St.
(between 6th Ave. and Gay St.), West Village, 212/255–4160, 212/691–8695. Subway: Christopher St./Sheridan Sq.

11 d-5
ANTHROPOLOGIE
Now a national chain, Anthropologie
features an interesting mix of both new
and antique home furnishings, including upholstered pieces, smaller decorative items, and bath and kitchen
accessories. There's also a great clothing department (see Clothing for
Women, above). Both the home and the
fashion selections are basic, but they're
very well edited, and prices are fairly reasonable for such a trendy shopping destination. 375 W. Broadway (at Broome
St.), SoHo, 212/343–7070. Subway: C, E
to Canal St.

10 e-1
85 5th Ave. (at 16th St.), Flatiron District,
212/627–5885. Subway: 14th St./Union Sq.

9 d-8
APARTMENT 48
The genius of this store is that it really
does look like an apartment, but almost
everything in it is for sale. In the living
room, you'll find furniture and books; in
the kitchen, a variety of kitchen utensils;
in the bath, everything from rubber
duckies to soap; and so on. It's probably
the most comfortable shopping experience in the city. 48 W. 17th St. (between
5th and 6th Aves.), Chelsea, 212/807–
1391. Subway: F to 14th St.; L to 6th Ave.

9 e-8
THE BOMBAY COMPANY
Butler's tray tables, Biedermeier con-
soles, tole lamps, Verona mirrors—the
Bombay Company sells an heirloom

look in home furnishings, accessories, and wall decor at good prices. Okay, so it isn't heirloom quality, but that's for your heirs to worry about. *900 Broadway (at 20th St.), Flatiron District, 212/420–1315. Subway: N, R to 23rd St.; and other locations.*

9 *e-2*

1062A 3rd Ave. (at 63rd St.), Upper East Side, 212/759–7217. Subway: 59th St./Lexington Ave.

9 *b-1*

2001 Broadway (at 68th St.), Upper West Side, 212/721–7701. Subway: 66th St./Lincoln Ctr.

9 *f-4*

BRANCUSI

Choose from a large selection of modern tables in glass, chrome, brass, stainless steel, and forged iron. *938 1st Ave. (near 51st St.), Midtown, 212/688–7980. Subway: 51st St./Lexington–3rd Aves.*

9 *e-3*

CASSINA USA

Cassina is the licensed representative for classic modern furniture, including pieces by Frank Lloyd Wright, Le Corbusier, Charles Rennie Macintosh, and Gerrit Rietveld. *155 E. 56th St. (between Lexington and 3rd Aves.), Midtown, 212/245–2121. Closed weekends. Subway: 59th St./Lexington Ave.*

9 *d-7*

CASTRO CONVERTIBLES

This chain has one of New York's largest selections of sofabeds, recliners, and wall units. *43 W. 23rd St. (between 5th and 6th Aves.), Chelsea, 212/255–7000. Subway: F to 23rd St.; other locations.*

9 *d-7*

CLASSIC SOFA

You'll find both sofas and chairs here available in a variety of custom fabrics and ready for delivery in just a few short weeks. *5 W. 22nd St. (between 5th and 6th Aves.), Chelsea, 212/620–0485. Subway: F to 23rd St.*

9 *e-2*

CRATE & BARREL

Crate & Barrel has become an all-American favorite for first-time furniture buyers, with a variety of styles in both traditional and modern silhouettes. You get good quality at a reasonable price.

Plus there's an entire floor of decorative accessories to complement your new furnishings. *650 Madison Ave. (at 59th St.), Midtown, 212/308–0011. Subway: 59th St./Lexington Ave.; N, R to 5th Ave.*

11 *a-2*

DETAILS

An eclectic array of bath and home furnishings to put a little zip into your home décor. Highlights of the well-edited selections include gorgeous glassware, lovely bath products, Walker totes and cosmetic bags, and trendy tabletop settings. *347 Bleecker St. (at W. 10th St.), West Village, 212/414–0039. Subway: Christopher St./Sheridan Sq.*

9 *b-1*

188 Columbus Ave. (between 68th and 69th Sts.), Upper West Side, 212/362–7344. Subway: 66th St./Lincoln Ctr.

9 *e-7*

DEVON SHOP

Formerly for decorators only, the Devon Shop now offers its beautiful custom-made, hand-carved traditional furniture, as well as all of its design services, to the public. *111 E. 27th St. (between Park and Lexington Aves.), Murray Hill, 212/686–1760. Subway: 6 to 28th St.*

11 *d-5*

DIALOGICA

This duo is known for brightly colored velvet upholstery pieces in bold designs. *484 Broome St. (near Wooster St.), SoHo, 212/966–1934. Subway: 6 to Spring St.*

7 *e-7*

1070 Madison Ave. (near 81st St.), Upper East Side, 212/737–7811. Subway: 77th St.

9 *f-1*

DOMAIN

Domain specializes in European-country oversized upholstery pieces, reproduction painted farm tables, and armoires. *1179 3rd Ave. (at 69th St.), Upper East Side, 212/639–1101. Subway: 68th St./Hunter College.*

9 *e-8*

938 Broadway (at 22nd St.), Flatiron District, 212/228–7450. Subway: N, R to 23rd St.

9 *d-8*

DOOR STORE

This local chain tends toward reasonably priced contemporary furniture, with some traditional looks mixed in. There's an extensive chair selection. It's a solid option for the first-time apartment-filler. *123 W. 17th St. (between 6th and 7th Aves.), Chelsea, 212/627–1515. Subway: F, 1, 2, 3, 9 to 14th St.*

9 *e-6*

1 Park Ave. (at 33rd St.), Murray Hill, 212/679–9700. Subway: 33rd St.

9 *e-3*

599 Lexington Ave. (at 53rd St.), Midtown, 212/832–7500. Subway: 51st St./Lexington–3rd Aves.

9 *f-1*

1201 3rd Ave. (at 70th St.), Upper East Side, 212/772–1110. Subway: 68th St./Hunter College.

10 *d-1*

GALILEO

This small but extremely stylish store is devoted to the home, packing its shelves with new and vintage ceramics, linens, lighting, and other trimmings, including furniture by Heywood Wakefield. *167½ 7th Ave. S (at 12th St.), West Village, 212/243–1629. Subway: Christopher St./Sheridan Sq.*

9 *e-8*

GOTHIC CABINET CRAFT

Gothic shops are sprouting up all over the place—and a good thing, too. The store sells both unpainted stock and custom-built furniture; one handy option is to pick an unfinished piece and have it finished in your choice of hue. They're fast and reliable, and the prices are great. *909 Broadway (between 20th and 21st Sts.), Flatiron District, 212/673–2270. Subway: N, R to 23rd St.*

10 *f-1*

104 3rd Ave. (at 13th St.), Greenwich Village, 212/420–9556. Subway: 14th St./Union Sq.

7 *f-7*

1655 2nd Ave. (at 86th St.), 212/288–2999. Subway: 4, 5, 6 to 86th St.; other locations.

11 *d-5*

JAMSON WHYTE

Imported from Singapore, Whyte showcases antiques, artifacts and home furnishings that either come from Asia or look like they might have. It's so well styled as to be slightly intimidating, but don't be; just look at the prices, which are extremely reasonable for SoHo. Whether you have $20 or $2,000 to spend, you'll find something here. *47 Wooster St. (at Broome St.), SoHo, 212/965–9405. Subway: A, C, E, N, R to Canal St.*

10 *c-1*

JENSEN-LEWIS

This low-key Chelsea store started out featuring the director's chair in every possible shape, height, and color—and personalized if desired. You'll now find a roomy display of contemporary furniture and accessories, and canvas by the yard, in 34 colors. *89 7th Ave. (at 15th St.), Chelsea, 212/929–4880. Subway: 1, 2, 3, 9 to 14th St.*

11 *e-4*

KNOLL

Modern office furniture is mixed with residential furniture and textiles. Construction is high-quality, and prices are stiff. *105 Wooster St. (near Prince St.), SoHo, 212/343–4000. Closed Sun. Subway: Prince St.*

9 *e-2*

LIGNE ROSET

Crafted in France, this modern furniture by top European designers is both understated and distinctive. *1090 3rd Ave. (near 64th St.), Upper East Side, 212/794–2903. Subway: 68th St./Hunter College.*

9 *c-8*

LOBEL

You'll want to buy everything at this "classical modern" collection of vintage furnishings, mostly from the 50s and 60s. The staff will help you choose from the pristine-condition furniture, and even hunt down special pieces if you desire. *207 W. 18th St. (at 7th Ave.), Chelsea, 212/242–9078. Subway: 18th St.*

9 *e-6*

MAURICE VILLENCY

High-quality contemporary furniture fills model rooms in this commodious Murray Hill store. *200 Madison Ave. (at 35th St.), Murray Hill, 212/725–4840. Subway: 33rd St.*

11 *e-4*

MODERN AGE

Come here for contemporary European furniture. *102 Wooster St. (near Prince*

St.), SoHo, 212/966–0669. Closed Sun. Subway: Prince St.

11 *e-4*

MOSS

Moss is heaven for anyone into very, very modern, European-designed furnishings and accessories. Think Alessi, Kartell, Starck . . . if it's new and cool, or not-so-new but classically modern, it's here. *146 Greene St. (between Prince and Houston Sts.), SoHo, 212/226–2190. Subway: Prince St.*

9 *e-3*

PALAZZETTI

Palazzetti has faithful reproductions of 20th-century classic furniture, including licensed copies of styles by Eames, Breuer, Le Corbusier, and Mies van der Rohe. *515 Madison Ave. (near 53rd St.), Midtown, 212/832–1199. Subway: 51st St./Lexington–3rd Aves.*

11 *e-4*

152 Wooster St. (near Prince St.), SoHo, 212/260–8815. Subway: Prince St.

11 *d-4*

PORTICO HOME

Simple French-country furniture is mixed with a good number of Shaker-inspired and cherry pieces. Prices can be quite steep, which isn't a surprise considering the neighborhood. *379 W. Broadway (near Spring St.), SoHo, 212/941–7800. Subway: C, E to Spring St.*

10 *e-3*

POTTERY BARN

Once known for it's large array of tableware, Pottery Barn has recreated itself into a home design store that pretty closely resembles Crate & Barrel. Wares now run the gamut from leather couches to armoires with a few lamps and picture frames thrown in for good measure. What you'll be hard pressed to find, however, are any sort of dishes. At the flagship store in SoHo, you'll find yourself surrounded by as many upwardly mobile Manhattanites as you will be at the trendy eateries that surround it. *600 Broadway (near Houston St.), SoHo, 212/505–6377. Subway: Broadway–Lafayette St.*

9 *b-2*

1965 Broadway (near 66th St.), Lincoln Center, 212/579–8477. Subway: 1, 9 to 66th St./Lincoln Ctr.

11 *f-4*

SALON MODERNE

These styles are either contemporary or '40s- and '50s-inspired, with a certain flair; most are new, but a few antiques are mixed in. *281 Lafayette St. (near Prince St.), SoHo, 212/219–3439. Subway: Prince St.; Broadway–Lafayette St.*

9 *e-8*

SEE LTD.

SEE, or Spatial Environmental Elements, sells the work of over 70 avant-garde designers of European and contemporary furniture, lamps, lighting, and accessories. *920 Broadway (near 21st St.), Flatiron District, 212/228–3600. Subway: N, R to 23rd St.*

11 *e-4*

SHABBY CHIC

The name says it all: this custom-slip-covered furniture has a homey, lived-in look that fits in as well in a SoHo loft as it does in a country home. Interesting throw pillows, linens, and period accessories follow through on the lovably scruffy theme. *93 Greene St. (between Spring and Prince Sts.), SoHo, 212/274–9842. Subway: 6 to Spring St.*

9 *e-1*

SLATKIN & COMPANY

This jewel box of a shop is owned by a decorator and features private-label traditional English-country–style accessories. *131 E. 70th St. (between Park and Lexington Aves.), Upper East Side, 212/794–1661. Closed Sun. Sept.–May, closed weekends July–Aug. Subway: 68th St./Hunter College.*

9 *c-8*

THOMASVILLE

Super-spacious furniture store, with a wide—if somewhat uninspired—selection of reasonably priced leather and wood furniture created to look like it was passed down for generations. *91 7th Ave. (at 16th St.), Chelsea, 212/924–7862. Subway: 18th St.*

11 *e-4*

TROY

Yes, there is a Troy, and he has great taste. Expensive taste. This store is an incredibly chic mixture of contemporary home furnishings and accessories, both new and antique, and the only retail source in the city for ICF furniture.

You're bound to fall in love with something here, so come in a generous mood. *138 Greene St. (between Prince and Houston Sts.), 212/941–4777. Subway: Broadway–Lafayette St.; Prince St.*

9 *e-2*

WILLIAM WAYNE & COMPANY

With a pair of shops on Lexington and an offshoot downtown, this store divides its stock between gardening wares and a traditional mix of home accessories, including well-chosen objets, lamps, furniture, and gifts. Monkeys are a favored motif. *846 Lexington Ave. (at 64th St.), Upper East Side, 212/737–8934. Subway: 68th St./Hunter College.*

9 *e-2*

850 Lexington Ave. (at 64th St.), Upper East Side, 212/288–9243. Subway: 68th St./Hunter College.

10 *e-1*

40 University Pl. (at 9th St.), Greenwich Village, 212/533–4711. Subway: 8th St.; Astor Pl.

9 *e-6*

WORKBENCH

This attractive American and European contemporary furniture is reasonably priced, and the sales are excellent. The overall look is somewhat minimal. *470 Park Ave. S (near 32nd St.), Murray Hill, 212/481–5454. Subway: 33rd St.*

11 *c-4*

161 6th Ave. (at Spring St.), SoHo, 212/675–7775. Subway: C, E to Spring St.; other locations.

9 *e-8*

XYZ TOTAL HOME

A treasure box filled with beautiful pieces chosen for their handsome elegance. Upscale home accessories include Indonesian wood pieces, antique reproductions, sterling silver picture frames, and elegant throw pillows. XYZ also offers accessory makeovers and personal styling for your entire home. *15 E. 18th St. (between 5th Ave. and Broadway), Flatiron District, 212/388–1942. Subway: 14th St./Union Sq.; N, R to 23rd St.*

11 *d-5*

ZONA

Best known for hip, handmade home accessories, Zona is now branching out into furniture as well. *97 Greene St. (between Prince and Spring Sts.), SoHo, 212/925–6750. Subway: Prince St.*

lamps & lighting

Department stores stock both modern and traditional lamps, and many neighborhood houseware and hardware stores carry inexpensive modern fixtures. The Bowery from Delancey to Grand Streets is the city's cash-and-carry district for discounted lamps and light fixtures; shop after shop offers what's new and modern or—in most cases—what's tacky and tasteless, all below list prices.

11 *e-5*

ARTEMIDE

Artemide's very modern line of Italian lighting—tabletop, floor, hanging, and wall-mounted—includes the now-classic Tizio desk lamp. *46 Greene St. (near Broome St.), SoHo, 212/925–1588. Subway: Spring St.; A, C, E, N, R to Canal St.*

9 *c-8*

BARRY OF CHELSEA

Here's an antique twist: Barry specializes in original American lighting from 1880 to 1940. *154 9th Ave. (near 19th St.), Chelsea, 212/242–2666. Closed Sun.–Mon. Subway: C, E to 23rd St.*

9 *e-8*

JUST BULBS

Just Bulbs is just that—nearly 3,000 light bulbs of every description, for every need. This shop is great for the hard-to-find. *938 Broadway (at 22nd St.), Flatiron District, 212/228–7820. Closed weekends. Subway: N, R to 23rd St.*

11 *g-5*

JUST SHADES

Look no further for that elusive dream shade: SoHo has New York's largest selection of lampshades. Every size and material is discounted 20%–30%. If you're still attached to the old girl, Just Shades can help you re-cover her. *21 Spring St. (at Elizabeth St.), 212/966–2757. Closed Wed. Subway: 6 to Spring St.*

9 *c-3*

LEE'S STUDIO

Lee specializes in designer lighting from such makers as Halo, Lightolier, Kovacs, Artemide, Flos, and from smaller firms.

There's a good selection of bulbs, and the studio will install, rent, and repair your lighting after helpful consultations. *1755 Broadway (at 56th St.), Midtown, 212/581–4400. Subway: 59th St./Columbus Circle.*

9 *f-2*

1069 3rd Ave. (at 63rd St.), Upper East Side, 212/371–1122. Subway: 59th St./Lexington Ave.

9 *c-8*
LIGHTFORMS
The mostly modern, groovy lighting by a variety of U.S. and foreign designers is accompanied by a full line of bulbs, shades, and dimmers. Repairs are made on-site. *168 8th Ave. (between 18th and 19th Sts.), Chelsea, 212/255–4664. Subway: C, E to 23rd St.*

7 *b-7*

509 Amsterdam Ave. (between 84th and 85th Sts.), Upper West Side, 212/875–0407. Subway: 1, 9 to 86th St.

11 *g-5*
LIGHTING BY GREGORY
An almost overwhelming shopping experience, this store carries everything a body needs in residential and stage lighting. Rentals are available. *158 Bowery (between Delancey and Broome Sts.), Lower East Side, 212/226–1276. Subway: Grand St.*

9 *f-2*
THE LIGHTING CENTER
The Lighting Center has a generous selection of domestic and imported lighting and a critical mass of bulbs. *111 2nd Ave. (at 59th St.), Midtown, 212/888–8383. Subway: 59th St./Lexington Ave.*

paint & wallpaper
Hardware stores carry basic paints and supplies; the extent of the stock depends mainly on the size of the shop. The stores below are specialists.

11 *c-4*
JANOVIC/PLAZA
This wholesale and retail paint-and-wallpaper center has 15,000 wallpaper patterns and will mix paint to match any one of them. Bath, fabric, and window departments keep your imagination whirring. The professional staff is

expert, and delivery is free. *161 6th Ave. (near Spring St.), SoHo, 212/627–1100. Subway: C, E to Spring St.*

9 *c-7*

213 7th Ave. (near 23rd St.), Chelsea, 212/243–2186. Subway: 1, 9 to 23rd St.

9 *e-1*

1150 3rd Ave. (at 67th St.), Upper East Side, 212/772–1400. Subway: 68th St./Hunter College.

9 *b-1*

159 W. 72nd St. (between Amsterdam and Columbus Aves.), Upper West Side, 212/595–2500. Subway: 72nd St.

wicker

11 *c-2*
BAZAAR
Vaguely chaotic in appearance, Bazaar is nonetheless a solid option for wicker (and other) furnishings at reasonable prices. There's also a full line of housewares, which accost you visually as you approach the store. *125 W. 3rd St. (between 6th Ave. and MacDougal St.), Greenwich Village, 212/673–4138. Subway: W. 4th St./Washington Sq.*

9 *f-7*
COCONUT COMPANY
High-style furniture and decorative objets for the home come in wicker and rattan—not to mention wood. Many of the pieces are from Bali and Indonesia. *129 Greene St. (between Houston and Prince Sts.), SoHo, 212/539–1940. Subway: Prince St.*

7 *e-6*
PAMELA SCURRY'S WICKER GARDEN
Pamela Scurry specializes in antique wicker furniture for both adults' and children's rooms. *1318–27 Madison Ave. (between 93rd and 94th Sts.), Upper East Side, 212/348–1166. Open by appt. only. Subway: 4, 5, 6 to 96th St.*

7 *e-7*
PIER 1 IMPORTS
Widely popular for its attractive and affordable furnishings, Pier 1 is a main source for contemporary wicker furniture and accessories. *1550 3rd Ave. (at 87th St.), Upper East Side, 212/987–1746. Subway: 4, 5, 6 to 86th St.*

10 *e-1*

71 5th Ave. (between 14th and 15th Sts.), Flatiron District, 212/206–1911. Subway: 14th St./Union Sq.

9 *e-5*

461 5th Ave. (at 40th St.), Midtown, 212/447–1610. Subway: B, D, F, Q to 42nd St.

HOUSEWARES & HARDWARE

The large department stores have good selections of kitchenware. Restaurant suppliers are clustered on the Bowery, near Cooper Square, and below Grand Street; travel here for good buys on practical, no-frills, professional cooking implements. Hardware buffs should wander over to the stretch of Canal Street from Lafayette to West Broadway.

9 *d-8*

BED, BATH & BEYOND

This Chelsea emporium has billions and billions of kitchen appliances, gadgets, and accessories, plus a good selection of linens, tabletop, and general home stuff. *620 6th Ave. (at 19th St.), Chelsea, 212/255–3550. Subway: F to 23rd St.*

9 *f-3*

BRIDGE KITCHENWARE

No-nonsense Bridge has best-quality professional equipment for the home at great prices: copperware (and retinning), earthenware, woodware, French porcelain baking supplies, restaurant-size stockpots, and more. Know what you want before you go—they have more than 40,000 items—but do go. Julia Child does. *214 E. 52nd St. (between 2nd and 3rd Aves.), Midtown, 212/688–4220. Subway: 51st St./Lexington–3rd Aves.*

11 *e-5*

BROADWAY PANHANDLER

This roomy and attractive SoHo store carries an extensive collection of top-notch gourmet cookware, cutlery, and gadgets at low prices. Check out the huge stock of bakeware; cake molds and decorating implements are a specialty. *477 Broome St. (between Wooster and Greene Sts.), SoHo, 212/966–3434. Subway: 6 to Spring St.*

9 *e-1*

GRACIOUS HOME

Anything and everything you can think of for the home: custom kitchens, appliances, wall coverings, bath accessories, brass hardware, lighting, tableware, paint, and all the rest. *1220 3rd Ave. (at 70th St.), Upper East Side, 212/517–6300. Subway: 68th St./Hunter College.*

9 *b-2*

1992 Broadway (at 67th St.), Upper West Side, 212/231–7800. Subway: 66th St./Lincoln Ctr.

9 *d-6*

HENRY WESTPFAL & CO.

This legendary cutlery shop will also sharpen your tired knives. *105 W. 30th St. (between 6th and 7th Aves.), Garment District, 212/563–5990. Subway: 34th St./Herald Sq.*

9 *e-5*

HOFFRITZ

The most impressive selection of cutlery and gadgetry in town. *Madison Ave. near 43rd St., Midtown, 212/697–7344. Subway: 42nd St./Grand Central.*

9 *c-3*

203 W. 57th St. (between 6th and 7th Aves.), Midtown, 212/757–3431. Subway: 59th St./Columbus Circle; other locations.

9 *c-8*

HOLD EVERYTHING

What a great idea! This division of Williams-Sonoma sells the means for you to store almost anything neatly and attractively. *104 7th Ave. (near 16th St.), Chelsea, 212/633–1674. Subway: 1, 2, 3, 9 to 14th St.*

9 *b-1*

2109 Broadway (at 73rd St.), Upper West Side, 212/579–7354. Subway: 1, 2, 3, 9 to 72nd St.

9 *c-3*

250 W. 57th St. (at 8th Ave.), Midtown West, 212/957–9313. Subway: 59th St./Columbus Circle.

9 *f-1*

1311 2nd Ave. (at 69th St.), Upper East Side, 212/535–9446. Subway: 68th St./Hunter College.

11 *a-2*

KITSCHEN

Here is the kitchenware our parents grew up with: Kitschen is chockablock with vintage (circa 1920–60) mixing bowls, cookie jars, pitchers, waffle irons, salt and pepper shakers, corn-on-the-cob plates, and other dedicated nostalgia, all displayed in color-coordinated tableaux. *380 Bleecker St. (at W. 10th St.), West Village, 212/727–0430. Subway: Christopher St./Sheridan Sq.*

9 *f-2*
KRAFT HARDWARE

With more than 12,000 square ft of basic hardware, Kraft is the largest store of its kind in Manhattan (*see* Home— Bedroom & Bath, *above*). *306 E. 61st St. (between 2nd and 1st Aves.), Upper East Side, 212/838–2214. Closed weekends. Subway: 59th St./Lexington Ave.*

9 *d-7*
LAMALLE KITCHENWARE

One of the city's best high-end kitchenware stores, LaMalle's got pots and pans by Sitram, Paderno, and Mauviel Copperware; knives by Wusthof and Dexter-Russell; baking supplies; and every imaginable gadget. *36 W. 25th St. (between 5th and 6th Aves.), 6th floor, Chelsea, 212/242–0750. Subway: F, N, R to 23rd St.*

11 *e-1*
LECHTER'S HOUSEWARES & GIFTS

The ubiquitous Lechter's has a conveniently large selection of basic kitchen, bath, and home items at very reasonable prices. Only the posh brands are missing. There's not much for the trousseau, but a lot for the teeny apartment. *55 E. 8th St. (between Broadway and University Pl.), Greenwich Village, 212/505–0576. Subway: 8th St.; Astor Pl.*

9 *c-3*
250 W. 57th St. (at Broadway), Midtown, 212/956–7290. Subway: 59th St./Columbus Circle.

9 *f-1*
1198 3rd Ave. (at 69th St.), Upper East Side, 212/744–1427. Subway: 68th St./Hunter College.

7 *b-8*
2151 Broadway (at 75th St.), Upper West Side, 212/580–1610. Subway: 1, 2, 3, 9 to 72nd St.; other locations.

9 *d-6*
MACY'S—THE CELLAR

A Shangri-La for cooks, Macy's beautifully stocked series of "shops" is dedicated to housewares. Wander through mazes of utensils and equipment for creative cookery. This floor always has a festive atmosphere. *155 W. 34th St. (Herald Sq.), Garment District, lower level, 212/695–4400. Subway: 34th St./Herald Sq.*

10 *b-1*
P. E. GUERIN

This importers and manufacturer of decorative hardware and bath accessories is actually the oldest American firm of its kind. *23 Jane St. (near Greenwich St.), West Village, 212/243–5270. Open by appt. only. Subway: 1, 2, 3, 9 to 14th St.*

9 *e-8*
RESTORATION HARDWARE

Everything at this store has a slick retro feel, from actual hardware—house numbers to shower heads—to leather couches, gardening supplies, and cool kitchen gadgetry. The best part? It's actually fun to shop here. There's tons of space and the funky array of wares won't break the bank. *935 Broadway (at 22nd St.), Flatiron District, 212/260–9479. Subway: N, R to 23rd St.*

9 *d-4*
RIO TRADING INTERNATIONAL

Rio Trading is an authorized dealer of Henckels, Swiss Army, Gerber, and Buck knives. *10 W. 46th St. (near Fifth Ave.), Midtown, 212/819–0304. Subway: B, D, F, Q to 42nd St.*

9 *e-7*
SIMON'S HARDWARE & BATH

This busy, highly regarded shop has ample decorative hardware plus tools and supplies. Trust them; they're problem-solvers. *421 3rd Ave. (near 30th St.), Murray Hill, 212/532–9220. Closed Sun. Subway: 6 to 28th St.*

9 *c-8*
WILLIAMS-SONOMA

The famed San Francisco kitchen-supply chain excels in providing attractive, sturdy wares, well-stocked stores, and a total understanding of the yuppie aesthetic. There's a culinary consultant on hand, and the occasional cooking demonstration. *110 7th Ave. (near 17th St.), Chelsea, 212/633–2203. Subway: 1, 9 to 18th St.*

9 *e-2*
20 E. 60th St. (near Madison Ave.), Upper East Side, 212/980–5155. Subway: 59th St./Lexington Ave.

9 f-1

1309 2nd Ave. (near 69th St.), Upper East Side, 212/288–8408. Subway: 68th St./Hunter College.

7 e-7

1175 Madison Ave. (near 86th St.), Upper East Side, 212/289–6832. Subway: 4, 5, 6 to 86th St.

7 b-8

ZABAR'S

The gourmet giant's housewares department on the mezzanine offers some of the lowest prices in town on top-of-the-line kitchen accessories and cookware. 2245 Broadway (near 80th St.), Upper West Side, 212/787–2000. Subway: 79th St.

JEWELRY

New York's wholesale and retail jewelry center, also known as the Diamond District, is West 47th Street between 5th and 6th avenues. Taken together, these stores offer a dazzling selection of gold, silver, and precious stones in antique, traditional, and modern designs. The proximity of shops and stalls makes comparison shopping easy, pleasant, and—since prices are not necessarily firm—eminently practical. See Historic Buildings & Areas in Chapter 4.

The large department stores have basic but attractive collections of gold and silver jewelry (see Silver, below).

antique & collectible items

9 e-2

A LA VIEILLE RUSSIE

Focuses here are authentic Fabergé jewelry and accessories and American and European period jewelry, especially Victorian pieces. 781 5th Ave. (at 59th St.), Midtown, 212/752–1727. Subway: N, R to 5th Ave.

9 e-3

ALICE KWARTLER

Kwartler has amassed one of the city's largest collections of cufflinks, supplemented by such Victorian items as lockets and cameos. Engraving is available. 123 E. 57th St., (between Lexington and Park Aves.), Midtown, 212/752–3590. Subway: 59th St./Lexington Ave.

9 e-3

ARES RARE

The time line here is very long: Ares has jewelry from antiquity through the 1940s, though the focus does fall in the 19th and early 20th centuries. The store will appraise any piece, and offers a selection of books on jewelry. 605 Madison Ave. (between 57th and 58th Sts.), 4th floor, Midtown, 212/352–2344. Subway: 59th St./Lexington Ave.

CAMILLA DIETZ BERGERON

Bergeron deals in period and estate jewelry from all over the world, including a good selection of cufflinks, from her Upper East Side apartment. 212/794–9100. Open by appt. only.

9 e-1

DECO DELUXE

Specializing in jewelry from the Art Deco period, Deco Deluxe also has a good selection of Bakelite. 993 Lexington Ave. (between 71st and 72nd Sts.), Upper East Side, 212/472–7222. Subway: 6 to 68th St./Hunter College.

10 e-1

DULLSVILLE

Bakelite, Bakelite, Bakelite, in all of its adornment forms. 143 E. 13th St. (between 3rd and 4th Aves.), East Village, 212/505–2505. Subway: 14th St./Union Sq.

7 e-8

EDITH WEBER & ASSOCIATES

Weber's eclectic collection of period jewelry includes pieces formerly owned by such luminaries as Andy Warhol, Queen Victoria, and even Napoléon. 994 Madison Ave. (at 77th St.), Upper East Side, 212/570–9668. Subway: 77th St.

10 e-1

FICHERA & PERKINS

We can't resist calling this a gem of a place; it has a fine variety of vintage pieces at prices to suit almost anyone's budget. 50 University Pl. (between 9th and 10th Sts.), Greenwich Village, 212/533–1430. Subway: 8th St./NYU.

9 e-1

FRED LEIGHTON, LTD.

Devoted exclusively to luxurious and rare antique and estate jewelry, Leighton emphasizes the 1920s, particularly extravagant Cartier pieces. Other chronological concentrations are the 1800s and the 1950s. *773 Madison Ave. (at 66th St.), Upper East Side, 212/288–1872. Subway: 68th St./Hunter College.*

ILENE CHAZENOF

The jewelry and objets that cram this loft near Union Square date from the late 19th to mid-20th centuries; range across the Victorian, Art Deco, Art Nouveau, Retro Moderne, and post WWII styles; and are priced very reasonably. Add to this Arts-and-Crafts jewelry, metalwork, and furniture, and 1950s Scandinavian and Italian glass. The proprietor is knowledgeable and lovely, and her services include research, shipping, appraisal, and rental. Prices range from $1–$5,000. *212/254–5564. Open by appt. only. Closed Sun.*

9 *e-3*

JAMES II GALLERIES

The bright and personable staff at James II will tell you all about their fine collection of English and Scottish 19th- and 20th-century jewelry, particularly their fine selection of cufflinks and 19th-century glass intaglio seals. Prices ranges from the 100s to the 10,000s of dollars. *11 E. 57th St. (between 5th and Madison Aves.), 4th floor, Midtown, 212/355–7040. Subway: N, R to 5th Ave.*

7 *e-8*

J. MAVEC & CO.

Mavec carries a wonderful selection of stick pins and other unique pieces from the 19th century, and hosts occasional exhibits of unusual items with an animal or garden theme. *946 Madison Ave. (between 74th and 75th Sts.), Upper East Side, 212/517–7665. Subway: 77th St.*

9 *e-2*

MACKLOWE GALLERY

Impressive and expensive, this jewelry hails mainly from the Art Deco, Georgian, Victorian, and Art Nouveau periods. Cartier, David Webb, Fouquet, and Van Cleef are among the many illustrious designers featured here. *667 Madison (between 60th and 61st Sts.), Upper East Side, 212/644–6400. Subway: 59th St./Lexington Ave.*

10 *e-1*

MULLEN & STACY

Mullen & Stacy is for the serious Bakelite collector, ready to pay serious prices. *17 E.16th St. (between 5th Ave. and Union Sq. W), Gramercy, 212/226–4240. Subway: N, R, 4, 5, 6, to 14th St./Union Sq.*

9 *e-1*

PRIMAVERA GALLERY

Elegant Primavera has a stellar collection of unusual antique and period pieces. *808 Madison Ave. (near 68th St.), Upper East Side, 212/288–1569. Subway: 68th St./Hunter College.*

7 *e-8*

SYLVIA PINES UNIQUITIES

Sylvia Pines has a truly exquisite (and indeed unique) array of antique and estate jewelry—from Victorian to Deco, with some Georgian pieces thrown in. Deco marquisite is a particular strength, and the collection of beaded and jeweled bags, bronzes, picture frames, and enameled boxes is spectacular. *1102 Lexington Ave. (near 77th St.), Upper East Side, 212/744–5141. Subway: 77th St.*

contemporary pieces

9 *d-3*

AARON FABER

Imaginative contemporary designs in gold join a fine collection of vintage wristwatches. Every eight weeks the gallery showcases a particular artist. Custom work, repairs, and restoration are available. *666 5th Ave. (entrance is at 53rd St. between 5th and 6th Aves.), Midtown, 212/586–8411. Subway: E, F to 5th Ave.*

11 *e-1*

BIJOUX

French-born Sophie Pujebet will customize any of her lovely sculptural gold and silver pieces. Many also have engraved floral and geometric designs. Look into custom wedding rings. *127 E. 7th St. (between 1st and 2nd Aves.), East Village, 212/777–1669. Subway: Astor Pl.; 2nd Ave.*

9 *e-3*

BUCCELLATI

Each piece from this renowned Milanese silver- and goldsmith is uniquely handcrafted, but Bucellati's golden weave designs are most extraordinary. Peruse finely created artisan pieces with precious stones and gold pieces, priced in the medium range (a relative term). *46 E. 57th St. (between 5th and Madison Aves.), Midtown, 212/308–2900. Subway: N, R to 5th Ave.*

9 *e-2*

BULGARI

Bulgari's contemporary Italian designs are marked by their stunning color combinations of large stones in unusual settings of 18k gold. *730 5th Ave. (at 57th St.), Midtown, 212/315–9000. Subway: N, R to 5th Ave.*

9 *e-2*

Pierre Hotel, 2 E. 61st St. (at 5th Ave.), Upper East Side, 212/486–0326. Subway: N, R to 5th Ave.

9 *e-3*

CARTIER

One of Cartier's main attractions is its shell: the store is in a beautiful former mansion traded to Cartier for two strands of Oriental pearls. Inside you'll find jewelry, silver, fine porcelain, picture frames, and all the other prestigious items that have become modern classics. *653 5th Ave. (at 52nd St.), Midtown, 212/753–0111. Subway: E, F to 5th Ave.*

9 *e-3*

Trump Tower (725 5th Ave., at 56th St.), Midtown, 212/308–0840. Subway: E, F to 5th Ave.

4 *d-4*

CLAY POT

Clay Pot's unique assortment of jewelry is comprised of work exclusively by American artisans. Handcrafted wedding rings are their specialty, and there are a variety of styles to choose from— from Victorian reproductions to sleek contemporary designs—at prices to suit any pocketbook. *162 7th Ave. (between 1st St. and Garfield Pl.), Park Slope, Brooklyn, 718/788–6564. Subway: D, Q to 7th Ave.*

9 *e-3*

FORTUNOFF

The self-appointed "Source" is four floors of contemporary and antique gold, silver, diamonds, watches, flatware, and pewter, all at very special prices. *681 5th Ave. (near 54th St.), Midtown, 212/758–6660. Subway: E, F to 5th Ave.*

9 *d-3*

HARRY WINSTON

Behind these lovely, locked doors are the largest, rarest, finest gems in the world. The wealthy don't just buy Harry Winston jewelry; they invest in it. Service is reputed to be the best in town. *718 5th Ave. (at 56th St.), Midtown, 212/245–2000. Subway: E, F to 5th Ave.*

9 *e-2*

JULIE ARTISANS' GALLERY

The owner of this Madison Avenue standby, Julie Schafler Dale, is the author of *Art to Wear*. Here in her gallery-store, she presents her artful collection of unique handmade jewelry by contemporary artisans, and also displays a fine collection of vintage pieces. *762 Madison Ave. (between 65th and 66th Sts.), Upper East Side, 212/717–5959. Subway: 68th St./Hunter College.*

9 *e-2*

MICHAEL DAWKINS

Dawkins specializes in sterling silver pieces, many of which have simple pearl and diamond accents. His line of men's jewelry is elegant, and women will also find many classically-influenced contemporary items that suit any style. Plus, the merchandise tends to be well priced. *33 E. 65th St. (between 5th and Madison Aves.), Upper East Side, 212/639–9822. Subway: 68th St./Hunter College.*

9 *e-1*

REINSTEIN/ROSS

Much of this handmade jewelry designed by Susan Reinstein has a medieval feel. In all of her finely wrought pieces, she uses 18-, 20-, or 22-k gold, often with cabochon stones. *29 E. 73rd St. (between 5th and Madison Aves.), Upper East Side, 212/772–1901. Subway: 77th St.*

11 *e-4*

122 Prince St. (between Greene and Wooster Sts.), SoHo, 212/226–4513. Subway: Prince St.

11 *d-5*

ROBERT LEE MORRIS

Each one made by Morris himself, these adornments—necklaces, bracelets, earrings, hair ornaments—are really works of art. He creates jewelry to suit almost any budget—here you'll find pieces with precious gems, diamonds, and cultured pearls, as well as less expensive pieces with gold overlay. *400 W. Broadway (between Broome and Spring Sts.), 212/431–9405. Subway: C, E to Spring St.*

11 *e-5*

TED MUEHLING

These special pieces are designed by Muehling and other artists, including Gabriella Kiss. Many of the ring designs will suit both men and women. Owning one is worth the investment. *47 Greene St. (between Grand and Broome Sts.), SoHo, 212/431–3825. Subway: A, C, E, N, R to Canal St.*

9 *e-3*

TIFFANY & CO.

Now over a century old, the beloved treasure house still makes an elegant ground zero for fine gold and silver jewelry, including the designs of Jean Schlumberger, Elsa Peretti, and Paloma Picasso; diamond engagement rings; famous-name watches; gems; crystal, china, and sterling; clocks; and stationery. The newest additions are Tiffany's own scarves and perfume. Don't be intimidated; there are some very reasonably priced items here. The windows are almost as famous as the interior—have a look at both. *727 5th Ave. (at 57th St.), Midtown, 212/755–8000. Subway: E, F, N, R to 5th Ave.*

9 *d-3*

VAN CLEEF & ARPELS

The name is synonymous with price and perfection. The Bergdorf Goodman setting is tiny, but it easily packs a king's ransom of diamonds, rubies, emeralds, pearls, and platinum. *744 5th Ave. (at 57th St.), Midtown, 212/644–9500. Subway: E, F, N, R to 5th Ave.*

costume

The large department stores and many boutiques have plenty of au courant costume jewelry.

1.1 *d-4*

AGATHA

Agatha's fun French jewelry encompasses everything from classic to kitsch, at good prices. Colorful earrings, bracelets, watches, and necklaces suit both young and mature tastes. *158 Spring St. (at W. Broadway), SoHo, 212/925–7701. Subway: C, E to Spring St.*

9 *d-4*

Rockefeller Center (Promenade, 5th Ave. between 49th and 50th Sts.), Midtown, 212/586–5890. Subway: E, F to 5th Ave., 47th–50th Sts./Rockefeller Ctr.

9 *e-1*

611 Madison Ave. (at 58th St.), Upper Midtown, 212/758–4301. Subway: N, R to 5th Ave.

10 *d-3*

ANDREA RENEE BOUTIQUE

Andrea Renee and her husband Vincent Pólino offer their own delicate, often whimsical adornments along with friendly service and gracious discounts at this cozy SoHo boutique. Designs run the gamut from retro to trendy. They have a loyal celebrity clientele, but that doesn't mean the prices are in the stars. *119 Sullivan St. (between Prince and Spring Sts.), SoHo, 212/343–2059. Subway: C, E to Spring St./Prince St.*

9 *e-1*

DIAMOND ESSENCE

All of these fantastic faux diamonds are set in 14k gold, and the faux pearls are attractive as well. Only you will know they're not real. *784 Madison Ave. (between 66th and 67th Sts.), Upper East Side, 212/472–2690. Subway: 68th St./Hunter College.*

9 *e-3*

ERWIN PEARL

This store is by no means just pearls, but it must be said that the big draw is the replica of Jackie O's famous triple-strand pearl necklace. You'll pay somewhat less than that piece fetched at auction. *677 5th Ave. (between 53rd and 54th Sts.), Midtown, 212/207–3820. Subway: E, F to 5th Ave.*

9 *e-3*

697 Madison Ave. (at 62nd St.), Upper East Side, 212/753–3155. Subway: 59th St./Lexington Ave.

9 *e-4*

GALE GRANT

Grant specializes in reproductions of such high-priced originals as Chanel and Tiffany. *485 Madison Ave. (between 51st and 52nd Sts.), Midtown, 212/752–3142. Subway: 51st St.; E, F to Lexington–3rd Aves.*

KITES

7 *e-7*

BIG CITY KITES

Your spirits will soar in this joyful venue, with 200 varieties of colorful kites for every level of expertise and aspiration. Accessories include kite-making supplies and air toys. Prices range from $2 to $200. *1210 Lexington Ave. (near 82nd St.), Upper East Side, 212/472–2623. Subway: 77th St.*

LEATHER GOODS & LUGGAGE

11 *h-4*

ALTMAN LUGGAGE

Come down east for luggage, trunks, and other leather goods from American Tourister, Travelpro, Andiamo, Delsey, Kenneth Cole, Briggs & Riley, Samsonite, and Halliburton. *135 Orchard St. (near Rivington St.), Lower East Side, 212/254–7275. Closed Sat. Subway: Delancey St.*

10 *e-1*

THE BAG HOUSE

Well placed in a university neighborhood, The Bag House has a huge selection of soft luggage: backpacks and duffels from such brands as Jansport, Manhattan Portage, Tumi, Gregory, Club USA, Le Sportsac, Kipling, EastPak, and Temba. The service isn't always as sweet as the selection. *797 Broadway (between 10th and 11th Sts.), Greenwich Village, 212/260–0940. Subway: 8th St.; Astor Pl.*

11 *h-5*

BRIDGE MERCHANDISE CORPORATION

This substantial store substantially discounts its substantial selection of leatherwear. *100 Orchard St. (between Delancey and Broome Sts.), Lower East Side, 212/674–6320. Closed Fri. and Sat. Subway: Delancey St.*

9 *e-3*

COACH

Coach legend holds that the founders were inspired by the sturdy yet supple leather of a baseball glove. Now handbags and accessories come in the classic glove-tanned leather plus some textured leathers, twill-and-leather, weather-resistant leather, and microfiber. You can go the classic route with the bucket bags, satchels, and clasped pocketbooks, or dabble in the more streamlined totes and zip purses. Each design series has a range of colors, some including the likes of cherry red or pale blue as well as warm browns and black. Over the past couple of years, they've increasingly

expanded into accessories, shoes, travel bags, and even furniture. *595 Madison Ave. (at 57th St.), Midtown, 212/754–0041. Subway: 59th St./Lexington Ave.*

9 *e-2*

710 Madison Ave. (at 63rd St.), Upper East Side, 212/319–1772. Subway: 59th St./Lexington Ave.

9 *e-5*

342 Madison Ave. (at 44th St.), Midtown, 212/599–4777. Subway: 42nd St./Grand Central.

10 *d-6*

The Mall at the World Trade Center (Church and Vesey Sts.), Lower Manhattan, 212/488–0080. Subway: World Trade Ctr.; other locations.

9 *e-5*

INNOVATION LUGGAGE

This chain has everything from the hardy to the hip, at not-bad prices. The sales staff is not always savvy about the merchandise, but Innovation's best when you've got a flight the next morning and have just discovered a tear in your favorite garment bag. *10 E. 34th St. (between 5th and Madison Aves.), Murray Hill, 212/685–4611. Subway: 33rd St.*

9 *f-5*

300 E. 42nd St. (at 2nd Ave.), Midtown, 212/599–2998. Subway: 42nd St./Grand Central.

9 *c-3*

1755 Broadway (at 57th St.), Midtown, 212/582–2044. Subway: 59th St./Columbus Circle; and other locations.

9 *f-3*

LEATHERCRAFT PROCESS

Since 1919 these specialists have been treating shearlings, sheepskins, suede, and leather. This address is a drop-off point; ask the folks at Meurice Cleaners to pass your garments along to Leathercraft. *245 E. 57th St. (between 3rd and 2nd Aves.), Midtown, 212/564–8980. Subway: 59th St./Lexington Ave.*

11 *b-2*

LEATHER MAN

An emporium for custom-fit leather jackets, pants, vests, tees, and briefs, many of which lean toward the homoerotic, is perfectly understandable on this block, only a few doors from the site of the Stonewall Riot and the beginnings of Gay Lib. Prices are moderately high, the quality first-rate. *111 Christopher St. (between Bleecker and Hudson Sts.), West Village, 212/243–5339. Subway: Christopher St./Sheridan Sq.*

7 *e-8*

LOUIS VUITTON

Vuitton's famous monogram adorns everything from wallets to steamer trunks. Besides the brown-on-brown LVs, there's the Epi leather line, with a striated texture and fun colors. *49 E. 57th St. (near Madison Ave.), Midtown, 212/371–6111. Subway: E, F to 5th Ave.*

10 *2-f*

TRASH & VAUDEVILLE

They've worked hard, here in the guts of Lou Reed and Ramones territory, to perfect the punk look in leather: jackets, boots, and accessories that will help you to pass as an East Village native. *4 St. Mark's Pl. (between 2nd and 3rd Aves.), East Village, 212/982–3590. Subway: Astor Pl.*

LINENS

Barneys New York, Bergdorf Goodman, Bloomingdale's, and Macy's all have fine linen departments; hit them up for discounts during the January and August white sales. Year-round bargains are available on the Lower East Side, specifically Grand Street from Allen to Forsyth Streets for first-quality seconds and discontinued designer lines. The Lower East Side shops are closed on Saturday; just remember that when they open again on Sunday, they fill with crowds.

general

9 *e-8*

ABC CARPET & HOME

This ever-exciting gallery of shops has a fine selection of imported and domestic bed and bath linens, as well as custom services. *888 Broadway (at 19th St.), Flatiron District, 212/677–6970. Subway: 14th St./Union Sq.; N, R to 23rd St.*

11 *d-4*

AD HOC SOFTWARES

Creative and intriguing, this selection of sheets, blankets, bath towels, kitchen towels, and table linens ranges from traditional to funky. It's always fun to see how they throw things together. *410 W.*

Broadway (at Spring St.), SoHo, 212/925–2652. Subway: C, E to Spring St.

9 *d-8*

BED, BATH, & BEYOND

This store is the size of an airplane hangar. Grab a shopping cart and fill it from the hundreds of options in discounted bedding. *620 6th Ave. (at 19th St.), Chelsea, 212/255–3550. Subway: F to 14th St.*

11 *h-5*

EZRA COHEN

Known far and wide for its splendid selection of discount merchandise, Cohen carries the latest in sheets from every brand plus famous-maker bedspreads. Down comforters come both ready- and custom-made. Cover your bed and soften your bathroom for 15%–30% off retail. *275 Grand St. (near Eldridge St.), Lower East Side, 212/431–9025 Closed Sat. Subway: Grand St.*

9 *e-1*

FRETTE

Frette makes Italian bed and table linens and lingerie of very fine quality. It's expensive, but still cheaper than Porthault (*see below*). *799 Madison Ave. (near 67th St.), Upper East Side, 212/988–5221. Closed Sun. Subway: 68th St./Hunter College.*

9 *e-1*

GRACIOUS HOME

If it's quality and good taste you want, Gracious Home has linens for every room in your house. The sizable stock of high-end bed linens includes makers such as Peter Reed, Designer's Guild, and Palais Royal; top them off with bed blankets, decorative throws, and baby bedding. Designer table linens for both everyday use and special occasions come in every price range. The folks over in bathroom linens make a point of stocking towels to match any bathroom color. The staff is knowledgeable and helpful. *1220 3rd Ave. (near 70th St.), Upper East Side, 212/517–6300. Subway: 68th St./Hunter College.*

11 *h-5*

HARRIS LEVY

It's hectic, but this Lower East Side experience is worth the trouble for 20%–40% discounts on name-brand bed linens, bathroom linens, and imported tablecloths. The second floor features custom- and ready-made curtains, bedspreads, dust ruffles, throw pillows, lamp shades, and draperies. *278 Grand St. (near Eldridge St.), Lower East Side, 212/226–3102. Closed Sat. Subway: Grand St.*

7 *f-7*
LAYTNER'S LINEN
Laytner's delivers high-quality designer linens for the bed, bath, and table. *237 E. 86th St. (between 2nd and 3rd Aves.), Upper East Side, 212/996–4439. Subway: 4, 5, 6 to 86th St.*

7 *b-7*
2270 Broadway (near 81st St.), Upper West Side, 212/724–0180. Subway: 79th St.

11 *5-e*
512 Broadway (between Spring and Broome Sts.), SoHo, 212/965–9382. Subway: N, R to Prince St.

9 *e-2*
LERON
Beautiful hand-sewn linens and lingerie can be matched here with Old World handmade lace and appliquées. Leron will custom-embroider table linens and towels to match any fabric. *750 Madison Ave. (near 65th St.), Upper East Side, 212/753–6300. Closed Sun. Sept.–May, closed weekends July–Aug. Subway: 68th St./Hunter College.*

9 *e-1*
POLO/RALPH LAUREN
Ascend to the fourth floor for a wide selection of bedding, including sheets, wool and cotton blankets, decorative comforters, down pillows, and duvets. The "White Label" bedding features an astonishing thread count of 350. Ample towels come in bath, hand, and beach sizes; table linens come in popular patterns. They will match department-store prices if you ask. *867 Madison Ave. (at 72nd St.), Upper East Side, 212/606–2100. Closed Sun. Subway: 68th St./Hunter College.*

9 *e-1*
PORTHAULT
Porthault makes the Rolls-Royce of sheets. The store's exclusive and extravagantly expensive line of 100%-cotton bed linens come in 600 prints in a variety of colors. You can also shop for table and bath linens, exquisite children's clothes, and gift items. *18 E. 69th St. (between 5th and Madison Aves.), Upper East Side, 212/688–1660. Subway: 68th St./Hunter College.*

11 *d-4*
PORTICO BED & BATH
A discerning eye creates this special mix of fine domestic and imported linens for the bed and bath. Portico also has a wide array of cast- and wrought-iron beds. The abundance of bath and body products makes shopping here a sensual experience. *139 Spring St. (at Wooster St.), SoHo, 212/941–7722. Subway: Spring St.*

9 *e-8*
903 Broadway (at 20th St.), Flatiron District, 212/328–4343. Subway: N, R to 23rd St.

7 *c-7*
450 Columbus Ave. (near 81st St.), Upper West Side, 212/579–9500. Subway: 79th St.

9 *e-1*
PRATESI
Pratesi has been manufacturing fine bed, bath, and table linens in Florence since the turn of the 20th century, as well as linens and clothing for infants. It's all mighty expensive. *829 Madison Ave. (at 69th St.), Upper East Side, 212/288–2315. Subway: 68th St./Hunter College.*

7 *e-7*
SCHWEITZER LINEN
An established purveyor of fine imported linens, Schweitzer specializes in sleeping pillows, custom-made to odd sizes in both down and poly. *1132 Madison Ave. (near 84th St.), Upper East Side, 212/249–8361. Subway: 4, 5, 6 to 86th St.*

7 *b-8*
457 Columbus Ave. (between 81st and 82nd Sts.), Upper West Side, 212/799–9642. Subway: B, C to 79th St.

pillows
Most department stores and home-furnishing stores carry decorative pillows.

9 *e-8*
ABC CARPET & HOME
This may be the largest selection of decorative and throw pillows in New York.

888 Broadway (at 19th St.), Flatiron District, 212/473–3000. Subway: 14th St./Union Sq.; N, R to 23rd St.

11 *c-1*

AMALGAMATED HOME

Amalgamated has a small selection of well-chosen, highly funky pillows in interesting materials. *9 Christopher St. (between Greenwich Ave. and Gay St.), West Village, 212/255–4160. Subway: W. 4th St./Washington Sq.*

9 *d-8*

BANANA REPUBLIC HOME

The new home collection in this popular clothing chain features many pillows as well as sheets, tabletop items, and other accessories. *128 5th Ave. (at 16th St.), Flatiron District, 212/366–4630. Subway: F to 14th St.*

9 *d-3*

BERGDORF GOODMAN

The seventh-floor home-furnishing department stocks classic high-end pillows. *754 5th Ave. (at 57th St.), Midtown, 212/753–7300. Subway: E, F, N, R to 5th Ave.*

11 *h-3*

ECONOMY FOAM & FUTON CENTER

Foam is cut to size and shape while you wait, or shredded by the pound for "piller filler." Fiberfill is another option. The Center also sells ready-made decorative and bed pillows, foam mattresses, designer sheets and spreads, and futons, all closing out at 30%–50% off retail. Accompaniments include custom covers, wall coverings, and upholstery fabric and vinyl. *173 E. Houston St. (at 1st Ave.), East Village, 212/473–4462. Closed Sat. Subway: 2nd Ave.*

11 *e-8*

IZ DESIGN

These chenille and velvet throw pillows are designed by Elizabeth Tapper. *92 Reade St. (near Broadway), Tribeca, 212/608–4223. Subway: Chambers St.*

7 *b-7*

LAYTNER'S LINEN & HOME

Laytner's has throw pillows ranging from classic to corduroy, damask to down. *237 E. 86th St. (between 2nd and 3rd Aves.), Upper East Side, 212/996–4439. Subway: 4, 5, 6 to 86th St.*

7 *b-7*

2270 Broadway (near 81st St.), Upper West Side, 212/724–0180. Subway: 79th St.

11 *5-e*

512 Broadway (between Spring and Broome Sts.), SoHo, 212/965–9382. Subway: N, R to Prince St.

11 *h-3*

PILLOW TALK

Head over to Ludlow Street for custom-made seat cushions, decorative pillows, and sleeping pillows in every shape and size; you pick the filling. *See also* Quilts & Duvets, *below. 174 Ludlow St. (near Houston St.), 212/477–1788. Closed Sat. Subway: 2nd Ave.*

9 *e-3*

PORTANTINA

This small shop carries a beautiful line of pillows in velvet, silk, and satin, all designed by Susan Unger. *895 Madison Ave. (at 55th St.), Upper East Side, 212/472–0636. Subway: 59th St./Lexington Ave.*

quilts & duvets

Most major department stores carry ready-made quilts with a variety of fillings and prices.

7 *e-6*

DOWN & QUILT SHOP

These folks will custom-design your bedroom. They've got plenty to work with: private-label down quilts and down pillows; downlike polyester fiberfill quilts and pillows (for customers with allergies); antique iron beds; hundreds of sheets and duvet covers; patchwork quilts; floor coverings; and probably whatever else you've dreamed up. *1225 Madison Ave. (near 88th St.), Upper East Side, 212/423–9358. Subway: 4, 5, 6 to 86th St.*

7 *c-7*

518 Columbus Ave. (near 85th St.), Upper West Side, 212/496–8980. Subway: 4, 5, 6 to 86th St.

11 *h-3*

I. ITZKOWITZ

Itzkowitz is the best quilt man in America, and, alas, the last of a breed. You pick the filling and the covering, and he'll make you a new quilt or refurbish your old one. Go for a custom-made sleeping pillow, too. *174 Ludlow St. (near*

Houston St.), Lower East Side, 212/477–
1788. Closed Sat. Subway: 2nd Ave.

10 *g-3*

J. SCHACHTER

This longtime Lower East Side source
has new digs from which to wow you
with their custom- and ready-made comforters and quilts. Choose a new filling,
design, and covering, or have your
favorite old patchwork quilt made into a
comforter. Schachter will also re-cover
and sterilize your down comforters and
pillows. Current domestic and imported
linens are 25%–40% off. *85 Ludlow St.
(near Delancey St.), Lower East Side, 212/
533–1150 or 800/468–6233. Closed Sat.
Subway: Delancey St.*

MAPS

9 *e-2*

ARGOSY BOOK STORE

Aficionados of antique maps will find a
haven at Argosy, which specializes in
maps from the 17th to the 19th centuries. Framing is available. Also a vintage book store, Argosy holds a strong
collection of map books as well. *116 E.
59th St. (between Park and Lexington
Aves.), 2nd floor, Midtown, 212/753–4455.
Subway: 59th St./Lexington Ave.*

11 *f-5*

DOWN EAST ENTERPRISES

This store deals primarily with books on
outdoor travel, so within its solid selection of maps are those of our National
Parks. *50 Spring St. (between Lafayette
and Mulberry Sts.), SoHo/Little Italy, 212/
925–2632. Subway: 6 to Spring St.*

9 *d-5*

HAGSTROM MAP AND
TRAVEL CENTER

Makers of the familiar yellow-and-green
city maps, Hagstrom specializes, of
course, in cartography, globes, and
atlases. *57 W. 43rd St. (between 5th and
6th Aves.), Midtown, 212/398–1222. Subway: B, D, F, Q to 42nd St.*

10 *f-7*

*125 Maiden La. (at Water St.), Lower
Manhattan, 212/785–5343. Subway: 2, 3 to
Wall St.*

9 *d-3*

RAND MCNALLY—THE MAP
AND TRAVEL STORE

A household name in travel aids, Rand
sells guidebooks, maps, travel literature,
luggage, gifts, and accessories in its
own, peaceful Midtown store. There's
even a children's section. *150 E. 52nd St.
(between Lexington and 3rd Aves.), Midtown, 212/758–7488. Subway: 51st St./Lex-
ington–3rd Aves.*

9 *c-5*

*555 7th Ave. (between 39th and 40th Sts.),
Midtown, 212/944–4477. Subway: 42nd
St./Times Sq.*

MEMORABILIA

9 *c-2*

BALLET COMPANY

Ballet memorabilia abounds here,
including rare programs, signed books,
autographs, and art. They also have a
strong collection of out-of-print dance
books. *1887 Broadway (near 63rd St.),
Upper West Side, 212/246–6893. Subway:
66th St./Lincoln Ctr.*

10 *c-1*

JERRY OHLINGER'S MOVIE
MATERIAL STORE

Ohlinger's has a large stock of still photos from films and TV shows, as well as
movie posters. *242 W. 14th St. (between
7th and 8th Aves.), Chelsea, 212/989–
0869. Subway: 1, 2, 3, 9, A, C, E to 14th St.*

9 *d-8*

MOVIE STAR NEWS

Another New York superlative: this store
claims to have the world's largest collections of movie-star photos, both originals and reissues. Check out the posters,
too. *134 W. 18th St. (between 6th and 7th
Aves.), Chelsea, 212/620–8160. Closed
Sun. Subway: F, 1, 2, 3, 9 to 14th St.*

11 *f-4*

NEW YORK FIREFIGHTER'S
FRIEND

Clothing, accessories, and toys celebrate
the fire-slayers of yore. *265 Lafayette St.
(between Spring and Prince Sts.), SoHo,
212/226–3142. Subway: Prince St.; 6 to
Spring St.*

9 *e-8*

RICHARD STODDARD PERFORMING ARTS BOOKS

Everything in this great selection of old, rare, and out-of-print books and ephemera relates to the performing arts. Vintage playbills, autographs, original costume and scene designs, photographs, and memorabilia keep the glamorous past alive. *18 E. 16th St. (between 5th and 6th Aves.), Room 305, Flatiron District, 212/645–9576. Closed Wed. and Sun. Subway: 14th St./ Union Sq.*

MINIATURES

7 *e-6*

DOLLHOUSE ANTICS, INC.

Head here for your next dollhouse and all of its miniature furnishings, including fine hand-painted pieces; accessories; and, of course, occupants. The store can provide electrification and (whoa) interior decoration. *1343 Madison Ave. (at 94th St.), Upper East Side, 212/876–2288. Subway: 4, 5, 6 to 96th St.*

7 *e-8*

TINY DOLL HOUSE

Tiny Doll House has everything conceivable, but in miniature. They can wire and wallpaper the house before you start tinkering—or after you're done. *1146 Lexington Ave. (between 79th and 80th Sts.), Upper East Side, 212/744–3719. Subway: 6 to 77th St.*

MUSIC & MUSICAL INSTRUMENTS

cds, tapes & vinyl

11 *d-2*

BLEECKER BOB'S GOLDEN OLDIES

Bleecker Bob specializes in New Wave music, independent labels, British imports, and rare and collectible vinyl. The hip staff knows what's up with today's music, and the hip opening hours last well beyond midnight. *118 W. 3rd St. (between 6th Ave. and MacDougal St.), West Village, 212/475–9677. Subway: W. 4th St./Washington Sq.*

11 *c-2*

BLEECKER STREET RECORDS

Billing itself as the world's largest oldies shop, this Village standby carries rock, blues, reggae, jazz, and soundtrack LPs, 45s, and CDs. *239 Bleecker St. (between 6th and 7th Aves.), West Village, 212/255–7899. Subway: W. 4th St./Washington Sq.*

7 *e-3*

CASA LATINA

This store carries CDs, records, and books on all varieties of Latin music, as well as instruments. *151 E. 116th St. (between Lexington and 3rd Aves.), 212/427–6062, East Harlem. Subway: 6 to 116th St.*

9 *c-4*

COLONY RECORDS

A Broadway institution, Colony carries the latest releases but specializes in hard-to-find items: rare and out-of-print LPs, cassettes, and CDs, as well as sheet music and books. *1619 Broadway (at 49th St.), 212/265–2050. Subway: N, R to 49th St.*

11 *c-2*

DISCORAMA

Choose from a large selection of discounted CDs; 12-inch dance records; cassettes; and videos. *186 W. 4th St. (between 6th and 7th Aves.), West Village, 212/206–8417. Subway: Christopher St./Sheridan Sq.*

11 *c-2*

Classical and clearance titles. *146 W. 4th St. (between 6th Ave. and MacDougal St.), Greenwich Village, 212/477–9410. Subway: W. 4th St./Washington Sq.*

9 *e-8*

Annex, *40 Union Sq. E (between 16th and 17th Sts.), Flatiron District, 212/260–8616. Subway: 14th St./Union Sq.*

9 *d-5*

DOWNSTAIRS RECORDS

Downstairs specializes in the hard-to-find and stocks a robust, well-organized selection of oldies, including doo-wop, R&B, and soul. There's even a phonograph on which to give things a whirl. *1026 6th Ave. (near 38th St.), Garment District, 212/354–4684. Subway: 34th St./Herald Sq.*

11 f-1

FINYL VINYL

This amply stocked and well-organized shop features the sounds of the '40s to the '70s—everything from Robert Johnson to Bootsy Collins. True to its name, the store stocks records only. 204 E. 6th St. (just off Cooper Sq.), East Village, 212/533–8007. Subway: 8th St.; Astor Pl.

10 e-1

FOOTLIGHT RECORDS

Footlight's an excellent East Village outpost for out-of-print and hard-to-find Broadway cast albums, movie soundtracks, big bands, jazz, and vocals from the 1940s–'60s. 113 E. 12th St. (between 3rd and 4th Aves.), East Village, 212/533–1572. Subway: 14th St./Union Sq.; 3rd Ave.

9 b-1

GRYPHON RECORD SHOP

Within its book shop on Broadway, Gryphon has amassed scores of thousands of jazz, rock, folk, and spoken-word recordings. Down on 72nd Street, they're selling rare and out-of-print LPs, mainly classical with some soundtracks, vocals, and jazz thrown in. Prices are reasonable, and they welcome "want" lists. 233 W. 72nd St. (between Amsterdam and West End Aves.), Upper West Side, 212/874–1588. Subway: 1, 2, 3, 9 to 72nd St.

7 b-7

2246 Broadway (between 80th and 81st Sts.), Upper West Side, 212/362–0706. Subway: 79th St.

9 d-6

HMV

With more than 300,000 recordings, this English chain is giving Tower a run for its money. It's well stocked in all areas. 57 W. 34th St. (at 6th Ave.), Garment District, 212/629–0900. Subway: 34th St./Herald Sq.

9 e-4

565 5th Ave. (at 46th St.), Midtown, 212/681–6700. Subway: B, D, F, Q to 42nd St., 47th–50th Sts./Rockefeller Ctr.

7 e-7

1280 Lexington Ave. (at 86th St.), Upper East Side, 212/348–0800. Subway: 4, 5, 6 to 86th St.

10 e-6

J&R MUSIC WORLD

J & R inspires faith by dividing its stock among different storefronts: classical CDs are at No. 33, jazz is at No. 25, and the rest is at No. 23. Selections are comprehensive, and, of course, you can also walk out with new equipment to play yours on (see Electronics, above). 23, 25, 33 Park Row (between Ann and Beekman Sts.), Lower Manhattan, 212/732–8600 (212/349–8400 for jazz, 212/349–0062 for classical). Subway: Brooklyn Bridge/City Hall.

9 c-8

JAZZ RECORD CENTER

Videos, books, and pretty much any jazz record you can think of draw hardcore aficionados. 236 W. 26th St. (between 7th and 8th Aves.), 8th floor, Chelsea, 212/675–4480. Subway: 1, 9 to 28th St.

11 c-2

MUSIC INN

Don't give up on that obscure international or ethnic title, on record, tape, or CD—while primarily a musical instrument store, Music Inn also carries foreign recordings, such as African music and English, Irish, and Celtic folk. 169 W. 4th St. (near 6th Ave.), West Village, 212/243–5715. Closed Sun.–Mon. Subway: W. 4th St./Washington Sq.

11 d-3

NOSTALGIA AND ALL THAT JAZZ

Recordings of jazz, movie soundtracks, and early radio broadcasts are surrounded by posters and movie stills. 217 Thompson St. (near Bleecker St.), Greenwich Village, 212/420–1940. Subway: Broadway–Lafayette St.

10 e-2

OTHER MUSIC

A stone's throw from Tower, this shop offers all the independent, eclectic and arcane selections the chains don't bother with. 15 E. 4th St. (between Broadway and Lafayette St.), East Village, 212/477–8150. Subway: Astor Pl.

11 c-1

SAM GOODY

Goody has a large and standard stock and offers excellent weekly sales on current recordings. Sales on specific labels pop up as well; check "Arts and Leisure" in Sunday's New York Times for detailed advertisements. 390 6th Ave. (between 8th St. and Waverly Pl.), West Village, 212/674–7131. Subway: W. 4th St./Washington Sq.

9 *f-5*

230 E. 42nd St. (between 2nd and 3rd Aves.), Midtown, 212/490–0568. Subway: 42nd St./Grand Central.

9 *f-2*

1011 3rd Ave. (at 60th St.), Upper East Side, 212/751–5809. Subway: 59th St./Lexington Ave.; other locations.

9 *b-1*

TOWER RECORDS AND VIDEO

Tower has more than 500,000 titles, but finding more obscure recordings can still be difficult. The selection includes the usual assortment of rock, r&b, jazz, world, show tunes, and so forth. The classical section uptown may be the best anywhere. Check out the downtown store's annex for bargains. 1961 Broadway (at 66th St.), Upper West Side, 212/799–2500. Subway: 66th St./Lincoln Ctr.

11 *e-2*

692 Broadway (at 4th St.), Greenwich Village, 212/505–1500. Subway: 8th St.

11 *c-3*

VINYLMANIA

This never-say-die shop has used records, collector's items, LPs, and 45s, with a specialty in the 12-inch dance record. CDs and cassettes are also available. 60 Carmine St. (between 6th and 7th Aves.), West Village, 212/924–7223. Subway: W. 4th St./Washington Sq.

9 *c-4*

VIRGIN MEGASTORE

The largest retail music and entertainment center in the world, Virgin stocks 1 million CDs in stock, including a 12,000-square-ft classical section. You feel rather like Jonah in the whale's belly. 1540 Broadway (near 45th St.), Theater District, 212/921–1020. Subway: 42nd St./Times Sq.

10 *e-1*

52 E. 14th St. (at Broadway), Union Square, 212/598–4666. Subway: 14th St./Union Sq.

music boxes

9 *c-2*

RITA FORD MUSIC BOXES

Rita Ford's is the best collection of working antique music boxes (circa 1830–1910) in the world, and it includes contemporary specimens, too. Some of the handcrafted carousels and other unique items are made expressly for this shop. The price range is wide, and the store restores and repairs as well. 19 E. 65th St. (between 5th and Madison Aves.), Upper East Side, 212/535–6717. Subway: 68th St./Hunter College.

musical instruments & sheet music

9 *d-3*

HAVIVI VIOLINS

These folks sell and appraise violins, cellos, violas, bows, strings, and accessories as well as repair all of the above. 881 7th Ave. (at 56th St.), Midtown, 212/265–5818. Closed weekends. Subway: N, R to 57th St.

9 *d-3*

JOSEPH PATELSON'S MUSIC HOUSE

Patelson's is one of those rare stores whose bag you're proud to carry. This quiet, wood-floor shop near Carnegie Hall is a musician's haven for classical and Broadway sheet music and scores, with an exhaustive, meticulously organized stock (both new and used), knowledgeable staff, and serious atmosphere. Your purchase is slipped into a delightfully unnecessary gray envelope adorned with Patelson's name dancing across a lute, and off you go to finger your cargo fondly before attempting to play it. 160 W. 56th St. (between 6th and 7th Aves.), Midtown, 212/582–5840. Subway: N, R, B, Q to 57th St.

11 *b-2*

MATT UMANOV GUITARS

Umanov has a fine selection of new and used guitars in a wide price range, and an excellent repair department. 273 Bleecker St. (near 7th Ave. S), West Village, 212/675–2157. Subway: W. 4th St./Washington Sq.

11 *c-2*

MUSIC INN

Come here for less-classical instruments, such as banjos, mandolins, dobros, dulcimers, sitars, balalaikas, ethnic flutes, tabla drums, zithers, and more. Guitars are a specialty; they're sold new and used, and expertly repaired. Browse ethnic art on the side. 169 W. 4th St. (near 6th Ave.), 212/243–5715. Closed Sun.–Mon. Subway: W. 4th St./Washington Sq.

9 *c-2*

THE MUSIC STORE

Formerly Brown's Music Company, this venue is a long-established source for both classical and popular sheet music (new and used), instruments, and accessories. *44 W. 62nd St. (between Broadway and Central Park W), Upper West Side, 212/541–6236. Subway: 59th St./Columbus Circle.*

9 *d-4*

SAM ASH

If you're coming here for the first time, prepare to be whisked back to your days with the high-school band. In business since 1924, Sam Ash is popular with professional musicians for its wide inventory, good prices, and savvy staff. The wares are divided between a cluster of shops and include wind instruments and supplies; electronic keyboards, guitars, and amplifiers; and drums. Some instruments can be rented. Sheet music, scores, and books on music give you something to play. *155, 160, 166 W. 48th St. (near Broadway), Theater District, 212/719–2299, 212/719–2625, or 212/719–5109. Subway: 47th–50th Sts./Rockefeller Ctr.*

9 *d-3*

STEINWAY & SONS

Steinway's longtime home, this elegant piano showroom is appropriately within whistling distance of Carnegie Hall. *109 W. 57th St. (between 6th and 7th Aves.), Midtown, 212/246–1100. Subway: B, Q to 57th St.*

NEEDLEWORK & KNITTING

9 *e-2*

ERICA WILSON NEEDLEWORKS

This store is a real resource for needle arts and supplies, including gear for knitting, embroidery, needlepoint, and crewel, and custom canvases. *717 Madison Ave. (near 63rd St.), 2nd floor, Upper East Side, 212/832–7290. Subway: 59th St./Lexington Ave.*

7 *b-7*

THE YARN COMPANY

Somebody's knitting on the Upper West Side; this shop has yarn, needles, patterns, buttons, needlepoint canvases, and kits. *2274 Broadway (near 82nd St.),*

Upper West Side, 212/787–7878. Closed Sun.–Mon. Subway: 79th St.

NEWSPAPERS & MAGAZINES

Street-corner newsstands are all over the city, most with such local essentials as *New York* and such national nonessentials as *People*. For indoor magazine browsing, try Barnes & Noble or Borders (*see* Books, *above*), neither of which seems to care if you hang out all day.

9 *f-4*

HOTALINGS NEWS AGENCY

With more than 200 out-of-town newspapers and 35 foreign-language newspapers, Hotaling's is like a down-market university library. The scale of the magazine selection isn't far behind, and they throw in state maps for good measure. *1516 Broadway (between 46th and 47th Sts., in the Times Square Visitors Center), Theater District, 212/840-1868. Subway: 42nd St./Times Sq.*

11 *e-1*

HUDSON NEWS COMPANY

Hudson News is all over town, but this branch has a gratifyingly huge selection of magazines, both domestic and foreign, inspiring uptowners to make special trips. The biggest bonus: There's room to turn around, making browsing extra-pleasant. *753 Broadway (at 8th St.), Greenwich Village, 212/674–6655. Subway: 8th St.*

9 *d-7*

JAY BEE MAGAZINES

Some of these back-dated magazines and periodicals go back as far as 1920—Jay Bee has more than 2 million lying around. (Isn't that a fire hazard?) The setting is cluttered, but the store is now fully computerized, making it a great source for research. *150 W. 28th St. (between 6th and 7th Aves.), 6th floor, 212/675–1600. Subway: 1, 9 to 28th St.*

9 *c-3*

UNIVERSAL NEWS & MAGAZINE

If they don't have it, it may not exist. Universal stocks more than 7,000 titles, including foreign newspapers and magazines. *977 8th Ave. (between 57th and 58th Sts.), Hell's Kitchen, 212/459–0932. Subway: N, R to 57th St.; 59th St./Columbus Circle.*

NOTIONS

Some large stores have small notions departments, but this city has a notions street: On West 38th Street between 5th and 6th avenues, there are 20 stores full of trimmings. Here are some of the best.

9 *d-5*

HYMAN HENDLER & SONS

It's filled to the brim with ribbons: satin, grosgrain, velvet, silk, you name it, in every color, size, and width. *67 W. 38th St., Garment District, 212/840–8393. Closed Sun. Subway: 34th St./Herald Sq.*

9 *d-5*

M & J TRIMMING

All you need supply is the idea. M & J has the trimmings for any day's fashion accessories: rhinestones, studs, feathers, cords, buttons, bindings, satin ribbons, lace, eyelets, embroidered trim, silk ropes, even large feather boas. A few doors up 6th Avenue, at No. 1014, the same folks sell home-decorating accessories. *1008 6th Ave. (near 37th St.), Garment District, 212/391–9072. Closed Sun. Subway: 34th St./Herald Sq.*

9 *d-5*

TINSEL TRADING COMPANY

Bring a pair of shades: this place specializes in metallic yarns, threads, lamés, gauzes, tassels, fringe, rosettes, buttons, antique ribbons, embroideries, and fabrics. There's much from the '20s and '30s. *47 W. 38th St., Garment District, 212/730–1030. Closed weekends. Subway: 34th St./Herald Sq.*

PHOTO EQUIPMENT

9 *c-6*

B & H PHOTO & ELECTRONICS

You may want to read up before you come: B & H stocks more than 200 camera styles from top manufacturers, as well as professional photo and video equipment. *420 9th Ave. (near 33rd St.), Hell's Kitchen, 212/444–6600. Closed Sat. Subway: 34th St./Penn Station.*

10 *d-1*

CAMERA DISCOUNT CENTER

These folks will meet or beat any advertised price with these discounts on name-brand cameras. They also repair. *45 7th Ave. (near 14th St.), Chelsea, 212/206–0077. Closed Sat. Subway: 1, 2, 3, 9 to 14th St.*

9 *e-5*

FORTY-SECOND STREET PHOTO

See Electronics, above.

10 *e-2*

TAMARKIN

They cater to serious amateurs and professionals and have vintage Leica, Contax, and Hasselblad cameras, among others, for collectors. *670 Broadway (between 3rd and Bond Sts.), Greenwich Village 212/677–8665. Subway: Houston St.*

9 *d-6*

WILLOUGHBY'S

This longtime top shop for cameras and audio carries a complete range of cameras, lighting, and darkroom equipment. There's also a secondhand department. *136 W. 32nd St. (between 6th and 7th Aves.), Garment District, 212/564–1600. Subway: 34th St./Penn Station.*

9 *e-6*

385 5th Ave. (at 36th St.), Midtown, 212/213-1515. Subway: 33rd St.

9 *e-5*

50 E. 42nd St. (near Madison Ave.), Midtown, 212/681–7844. Subway: 42nd St./Grand Central.

POSTCARDS

11 *c-3*

ARTFUL POSTERS LTD

Stands and stands of postcards spill onto the sidewalk in front of this tiny shop. Inside you'll find more cards, mostly photographic variety, plus a wide selection of photographic posters. Think New York City views, celebrities, and classic black-and-white photography. *194 Bleecker St. (between 6th Ave. and MacDougal St.), Greenwich Village, 212/473–1747. Subway: W. 4th St./Washington Sq.*

POSTERS

Most museum gift shops have some high-quality posters of art from their permanent collections, as well as banner posters from special exhibitions. *See also* Galleries–Prints & Original Posters in Chapter 4.

9 *e-3*

MOTION PICTURE ARTS GALLERY

Original movie posters take you from the silent era to the present, with the emphasis on older material, both American and European. Prices range from $20 to $10,000. *133 E. 58th St. (between Park and Lexington Aves.), 10th floor, Midtown, 212/223–1009. Closed Sat.–Mon. Subway: 59th St./Lexington Ave.*

9 *d-8*

POSTER AMERICA

These original American and European posters range from 1890 to 1960; you'll also find a few advertising graphics. The staff is friendly and knowledgeable, and will arrange custom framing. *138 W. 18th St. (between 6th and 7th Aves.), Chelsea, 212/206–0499. Closed Mon. Subway: F, 1, 2, 3, 9 to 14th St.*

7 *e-8*

REINHOLD-BROWN GALLERY

Expect fine posters of works by Klimt, Lautrec, Lissitzky, and more. *1100 Madison Ave. (between 82nd and 83rd Sts.), Upper East Side, 212/734–7999. Closed Sun.–Mon. Subway: 77th St.*

9 *c-4*

TRITON GALLERY

Triton has a huge inventory of posters featuring Broadway, Off-Broadway, and Off-Off-Broadway shows; West End productions; and dance. In much smaller form, they make nice note cards, also on sale. Custom framing is available. *323 W. 45th St. (between 8th and 9th Aves.), Theater District, 212/765–2472. Subway: A, C, E to 42nd St.*

SPORTING GOODS & CLOTHING

general

9 *e-3*

GYM SOURCE

The largest exercise-equipment dealer in the area, Gym Source has bikes, stair and weight machines, rowers, and treadmills for rent or sale. The helpful staff will assist you in designing a home or office gym. *40 E. 52nd St. (between Madison and Park Aves.), Midtown, 212/688–4222. Closed Sun. Subway: 6 to 51st St./E, F to Lexington–Park Aves.*

10 *e-5*

MODELL'S SPORTING GOODS

Family-run since 1889, Mo's has a variety of sporting goods and footwear, particularly team wear. *280 Broadway (near Chambers St.), Lower Manhattan, 212/962–6200. Subway: Chambers St.*

10 *e-6*

200 Broadway (near Fulton St.), Lower Manhattan, 212/964–4007. Subway: Fulton St.

9 *e-5*

51 E. 42nd St. (near Madison Ave.), Midtown, 212/661–4242. Subway: 42nd St./Grand Central.

6 *h-6*

2929 3rd Ave. (between 151st and 152nd Sts.), Bronx, 718/993–1844. Subway: 2, 5 to 3rd Ave.

9 *e-8*

PARAGON SPORTING GOODS

Almost 100 years old, Paragon has the city's most impressive collection of clothes and equipment for every imaginable sport. The deep stock contains down jackets, track shoes, and shorts; baseball, football, lacrosse, golf, and hockey equipment; skates, skis, and swimwear; and camping, fishing, and backpacking paraphernalia. Values can be excellent. *867 Broadway (at 18th St.), Flatiron District, 212/255–8036. Subway: 4, 5, 6, N, R to 14th St./Union Sq.*

9 *e-8*

PRINCETON SKI SHOP

Make tracks here for ski equipment and apparel and the ever-important custom boot-fitting. Other specialized departments cater to tennis, skateboarding, and in-line skating. *21 E. 22nd St. (near Broadway), Flatiron District, 212/228–4400. Subway: N, R to 23rd St.*

9 *d-6*

THE SPORTS AUTHORITY

Departments include tennis, golf, skiing, camping, footwear, apparel, and exercise. *401 7th Ave. (at 33rd St.), Garment District, 212/563–7195. Subway: 34th St./Penn Station.*

9 f-4

845 3rd Ave. (at 51st St.), Midtown, 212/ 355–9725. Subway: 51st St./Lexington–3rd Aves.

9 d-3

57 W. 57 St. (between Madison and Park Aves.), Midtown, 212/355–6430. Subway: E, F, N, R to 5th Ave.; B, Q to 57th St.

9 d-8

636 Ave. of the Americas (at 19th St.), Flatiron District, 212/929–8971. Subway: 1, 9 to 18th St./F to 23rd St.

boating

9 d-6

WEST MARINE

Head straight here for marine supplies at a discount; they've got all the necessities, from global positioning systems to foul-weather apparel. *12 W. 37th St. (between 5th and 6th Aves.), Garment District, 212/594–6065. Subway: 34th St./Herald Sq.*

camping & climbing

11 e-3

EMS—THE OUTDOOR SPECIALISTS

This familiar, ruggedly spiffy chain specializes in backpacking and climbing, and is also well stocked for downhill and cross-country skiing, tennis, and running. *611 Broadway (between Houston and Bleecker Sts.), Greenwich Village, 212/ 505–9860. Subway: B, D, F, Q to Broadway–Lafayette St., 6 to Bleecker St.*

9 c-2

20 W. 61st St. (between Broadway and West End Ave.), Upper West Side, 212/ 397–4860. Subway: A, B, C, D, 1, 9 to 59th St./Columbus Circle.

10 e-6

TENTS & TRAILS

Top-quality camping supplies are for sale or rent next to apparel and footwear for adults and children. Shipping is available. *21 Park Pl. (between Church St. and Broadway), Lower Manhattan, 212/ 227–1760. Subway: Park Pl.*

fishing tackle & supplies

9 c-7

CAPITOL FISHING TACKLE CO.

A fisherman's friend since 1897, Capitol Fishing Tackle can equip you for freshwater, saltwater, deep-sea, and big-game fishing, all at ample discounts. Fly-casting lessons are also available. *218 W. 23rd St. (between 7th and 8th Aves.), Chelsea, 212/929–6132. Closed Sun. Subway: 1, 9, C, E to 23rd St.*

9 e-3

HUNTING WORLD/ ANGLER'S WORLD

The Angler's World department has a fine selection of fly-fishing equipment. *16 E. 53rd St. (between 5th and Madison Aves.), Midtown, 212/755–3400. Subway: E, F to 5th Ave.*

9 e-4

ORVIS NEW YORK

Peruse a complete line of fly rods, reels, and accessories including vests, jackets, hip boots, and waders at the oldest rod-building company in the country. *355 Madison Ave. (at 45th St.), Midtown, 212/697–3133. Subway: 42nd St./Grand Central.*

9 e-7

URBAN ANGLER

True to the charming name, this Gramercy shop features fly-fishing rods, reels, and the attention of a caring specialist. Fly-fishing is Urban Angler's specialty, but those interested in spinning equipment will find their selection one of the best around. *118 E. 25th St. (between Park and Lexington Aves.), 3rd floor, Gramercy, 212/979–7600. Closed Sun. Subway: 6 to 23rd St.*

golf

9 e-4

AL LIEBER'S WORLD OF GOLF

Lieber has the latest in well-priced golf equipment. *147 E. 47th St. (between Lexington and 3rd Aves.), 2nd floor, Midtown, 212/755–9398. Subway: 51st St./Lexington–3rd Aves.*

9 *e-4*

RICHARD METZ GOLF STUDIO

Richard Metz sells the latest and best of golf equipment and supplies for both men and women. Expert instruction will help improve your stroke, which you can refine to precision in their special practice area. *425 Madison Ave. (near 49th St.), Midtown, 212/759–6940. Subway: 51st St./Lexington–3rd Aves.*

riding

9 *e-3*

HERMÈS

Though most New Yorkers associate Hermès with chic silk items (for the horsey set), the French firm has in fact made saddles and bridle equipment for over 150 years. *11 E. 57th St. (between 5th and Madison Aves.), Midtown, 212/751–3181. Subway: E, F to 5th Ave.*

9 *e-7*

MILLER HARNESS COMPANY

This informed source has everything for the horse and rider: equipment, clothing (including a large selection of Barber), and an extensive selection of boots. *117 E. 24th St. (between Park and Lexington Aves.), Gramercy, 212/673–1400. Closed Sun. Subway: 6 to 23rd St.*

running

11 *e-2*

ATHLETE'S FOOT

This national outfit offers an incredible selection of moderately priced athletic footwear—by Reebok, Nike, Adidas, New Balance, Avia, Converse, et al.—as well as related accessories and clothing. *2563 Broadway (at 96th St.), Upper West Side, 212/961–9556. Subway: 1, 2, 3, 9 to 96th St.*

9 *e-5*

390 5th Ave. (at 36th St.), Midtown, 212/947–6972. Subway: 34th St./Herald Sq.

9 *e-4*

41 E. 42nd St. (near Madison Ave.), Midtown, 212/867–4599. Subway: 42nd St./Grand Central.

9 *e-3*

NIKETOWN

In a high-tech setting inspired by sports arenas and old school gyms, this Midtown monster has five floors of

footwear, accessories, and apparel for tennis, golf, basketball, football, baseball, team sports (pro and college), running, and cross-training for men, women, boys, and girls. *6 E. 57th St. (between 5th and Madison Aves.), Midtown, 212/891–6453. Subway: E, F to 5th Ave.*

9 *e-1*

SUPER RUNNER'S SHOP

A complete running store, this chain has shoes, gear, and accessories from all the big names. Helpful service will find the styles that suit your needs. *1246 3rd Ave. (at 72nd St.), Upper East Side, 212/249–2133. Subway: 68th St./Hunter College.*

7 *b-8*

360 Amsterdam Ave. (at 77th St.), Upper West Side, 212/787–7665. Subway: 79th St.

7 *e-6*

1337 Lexington Ave. (at 89th St.), Upper East Side, 212/369–6010. Subway: 4, 5, 6 to 86th St.

skating

9 *a-7*

BLADES BOARD & SKATE

These folks sell, rent, and repair in-line, ice, and hockey skates; snowboards; and skateboards, and sell related clothing and accessories. They also arrange bus trips to Hunter Mountain every Thursday, Friday, and Sunday in ski season. For general information, call 888/55–BLADES. *Chelsea Piers (12th Ave. and 23rd St.), Chelsea, 212/336–6299. Subway: C, E to 23rd St.*

11 *e-3*

659 Broadway (near Bleecker St.), Greenwich Village, 212/477–7350. Subway: Broadway–Lafayette St., Bleecker St.

9 *b-1*

120 W. 72nd St. (between Broadway and Columbus Ave.), Upper West Side, 212/787–3911. Subway: 1, 2, 3, 9 to 72nd St.

9 *f-1*

1414 2nd Ave. (near 73rd St.), Upper East Side, 212/249–3178. Subway: 77th St.; other locations.

9 *c-3*

PECK & GOODIE SKATES

Some say Peck & Goodie is New York's finest skate shop. Family-owned since

1940, it's in any case the city's original in-line and roller skate dealer. In addition to an excellent selection of in-line skates, you'll find a complete line of figure, hockey, and speed skates and roller blades, as well as equipment. You also can bring your old stuff in for sharpening or repair. *917 8th Ave. (near 54th St.), Hell's Kitchen, 212/246–6123. Subway: C, E to 50th St.*

skiing

9 *e-1*

BOGNER

These are the people who revolutionized the ski slopes with stretch pants in the 1950s. Ski fashions and Bogner ready-to-wear are imported from Germany. *821 Madison Ave. (near 68th St.), Upper East Side, 212/472–0266. Subway: 68th St./Hunter College.*

9 *d-3*

SCANDINAVIAN SKI & SPORTS SHOP

This top city source for ski equipment fills three floors with it, and throws in brand-name ski wear to boot. They also sponsor a ski clinic known as "rep rap" in early November, and run one-day ski trips to Hunter Mountain December–March, for which they have rental equipment available. *40 W. 57th St. (between 5th and 6th Aves.), Midtown, 212/757–8524. Subway: B, Q to 57th St.*

tennis

9 *e-4*

MASON'S TENNIS MART

Shop for rackets, balls, bags, high-fashion European tennis wear, and, in season, ski wear. They'll restring your racket, as well. *56 E. 53rd St. (between Madison and Park Aves.), Midtown, 212/757–5374. Subway: 51st St./Lexington–3rd Aves.*

STATIONERY & OFFICE SUPPLIES

office supplies

9 *e-5*

AIRLINE STATIONERY COMPANY, INC.

Long-established and reputable, Airline is bound to have what you need. *284 Madison Ave. (at 40th St.), Midtown, 212/532–*

6525; 155 E. 44th St., Midtown, 212/532–9410. Subway: 42nd St./Grand Central.

9 *e-3*

KROLL STATIONERS, INC.

This fine stationery and office-supply store also sells computer supplies and office furniture and arranges fine printing and engraving. *145 E. 54th St. (between 3rd and Lexington Aves.), Midtown, 212/750–5300. Subway: 51st St./Lexington–3rd Aves.*

9 *c-6*

STAPLES

The office-supply megastore carries everything from paper clips to paper to printers to furniture. For a full list of locations, call 800/237–0413. *250 W. 34th St. (between 7th and 8th Aves.), Garment District, 212/629–3990. Subway: 34th St./Penn Station.*

9 *e-6*

16 E. 34th St. (between 5th and Madison Aves.), Murray Hill, 212/683–8003. Subway: 33rd St.

9 *d-5*

1075 6th Ave. (between 40th and 41st Sts.), Midtown, 212/944–6791. Subway: B, D, F, Q to 42nd St.

7 *e-7*

1280 Lexington Ave. (between 86th and 87th Sts.), Upper East Side, 212/426–6190. Subway: 4, 5, 6 to 86th St.; other locations.

pens and pencils

9 *d-4*

ARTHUR BROWN & BROS., INC.

Arthur Brown has one of the world's largest pen selections. Every brand you can name is here—including Mont Blanc, Cartier, Cross, and Waterman—in a wide variety of styles. The store also arranges repairs. *2 W. 46th St. (near 5th Ave.), Midtown, 212/575–5555. Subway: B, D, F, Q to 42nd St.*

9 *d-3*

AUTHORIZED SALES AND SERVICE

This shop sells and repairs electric shavers, fine cigarette lighters, and vintage and contemporary pens. *30 W. 57th St. (between 5th and 6th Aves.), 2nd floor, Midtown, 212/586–0947. Closed Sun. Subway: N, R to 5th Ave.; B, Q to 57th St.*

9 *e-8*

BERLINER PEN

Jeffrey Berliner is an true pen historian, and his shop reflects his taste in both the new and the old. Brands include Waterman, Mont Blanc, and Omas. *928 Broadway (near 22nd St.), Flatiron District, 212/614–3020. Closed weekends. Subway: N, R to 23rd St.*

10 *e-5*

FOUNTAIN PEN HOSPITAL

Collectors swear by this out-of-the-way shop, to the extent that its clientele extends worldwide. Bill Cosby is a regular. You'll find all major brands, limited editions, and collectible pens, and, true to the name, they'll fix what you already own if it's ailing. *10 Warren St. (across from City Hall), Lower Manhattan, 212/964–0580. Closed weekends. Subway: Chambers St.*

9 *e-3*

MONT BLANC BOUTIQUE

The famous pen maker has a whole store for its "snow-capped" creations. *595 Madison Ave. (between 57th and 58th Sts.), Midtown, 212/223–8888. Subway: N, R to 5th Ave.*

9 *e-3*

REBECCA MOSS

At this Midtown shop, they know their high-end writing instruments. *510 Madison Ave. (at 53rd St.), Midtown, 212/832–7671. Subway: 51st St./Lexington–3rd Aves.*

9 *d-8*

SAM FLAX, INC.

See Art Supplies, above.

stationery

Tiffany, Cartier, and the major department stores sell fine stationery. *See also* Art Supplies *and* Office Supplies, *above.*

9 *e-3*

DEMPSEY & CARROLL

These folks know their business having been at it since 1878. They create fine, hand-engraved stationery from more than 200 monogram styles. *110 E. 57th St. (between Park and Lexington Aves.), Midtown, 212/486–7508. Subway: 59th St./Lexington Ave.*

10 *f-1*

HUDSON ENVELOPE
JAM PAPER

This store is a terrific source for both basic and unusual-hue stationery; they have more than 150 colors in stock. Try the map stationery for overseas mail. *111 3rd Ave. (near 13th St.), East Village, 212/473–6666. Subway: 3rd Ave.*

9 *d-8*

611 6th Ave. (near 17th St.), Chelsea, 212/255–4593. Subway: F to 14th St. Closed weekends.

7 *e-8*

IL PAPIRO

Direct from Italy, this charmer carries delightful gifts and stationery, all made with hand-marbled Florentine papers: picture frames, desk accessories, decorative boxes, albums, and more. *1021 Lexington Ave. (between 73rd and 74th Sts.), Upper East Side, 212/288–9330. Subway: 77th St.*

9 *d-8*

IS

Super-sleek IS carries minimalist looking stationery—no superfluous design elements here—perfect for the hip modern letter writer. They also have pens, photo albums, and notebooks. *136 W. 17th St. (between 6th and 7th Aves.), Chelsea, 212/620–0300. Subway: 18th St.*

9 *e-1*

JAMIE OSTROW

Ostrow creates custom invitations, holiday greeting cards, and personalized stationery with a contemporary edge. *876 Madison Ave. (near 71st St.), Upper East Side, 212/734–8890. Closed Sun. Subway: 68th St./Hunter College.*

11 *d-6*

KATE SPADE PAPER

The hip handbag queen has turned her sights to charming paper products—day planners, address books, and calendars in Kate's signature fabrics. Also available are wrapping paper, stationery, and a range of other paper products. *59 Thompson St. (between Spring and Broome Sts.), SoHo, 212/965–8654. Subway: A, C, E to Canal St.*

11 *e-4*

KATE'S PAPERIE

Kate's is beloved for its handmade fine-art papers for artists, photographers, and mere mortals who just can't walk past them. The wonderfully spacious store is worth the trip to SoHo, with exquisite paper in all of its varieties: for writing, wrapping, and making collages or matting pictures. The gorgeous desk accessories are just as compelling, as are the handmade greeting cards and the diaries, photo albums, storage boxes—we could go on and on. There are also creative invitations for everything from backyard barbecues to black-tie weddings, and the Christmas-card selection is one of the finest in town. *561 Broadway (at Prince St.), SoHo, 212/941–9816. Subway: Prince St.*

9 *f-1*

1282 3rd Ave. (between 73rd and 74th Sts.), Upper East Side, 212/396–3670. Subway: 77th St.

10 *d-1*

8 W. 13th St. (near 5th Ave.), Greenwich Village, 212/633–0570. Subway: F to 14th St.

9 *e-2*

MRS. JOHN L. STRONG

The original stationer to the Duke and Duchess of Windsor, Mrs. Strong provides hand-engraved invitations, announcements, and social stationery on the company's own, 100%-cotton paper. Motifs are whimsical and interesting, and the matching envelopes are hand-lined. The boxed cards are also sold at Barneys (*see* Department Stores, *above*). *699 Madison Ave. (near 62nd St.), Upper East Side, 212/838–3775. Open by appt. only. Subway: 59th St./Lexington Ave.*

10 *c-2*

PAPIVORE

This tiny but delightful paperie carries vibrantly colored paper from Marie Papier Paris, as well as a small, expertly chosen selection of notebooks, photo albums, and desk accessories. *117 Perry St. (between Greenwich and Hudson Sts.), West Village, 212/627–6055. Subway: Christopher St./Sheridan Sq.*

9 *e-2*

PAPYRUS

Contemplate personalized stationery, wrapping paper, photo albums, cards, stickers, frames, address books, and the like. *852 Lexington Ave. (at 65th St.), Upper East Side, 212/717–0002. Subway: 68th St./Hunter College.*

9 *e-1*

107 E. 42nd St. (between Lexington and 5th Aves.), Midtown, 212/490–9894. Subway: 42nd St./Grand Central.

THEATRICAL ITEMS

See Books, Costume Rental, *and* Memorabilia.

9 *c-4*

ONE SHUBERT ALLEY

It's a tourist's dream, but natives may also find themselves charmed amid these posters, buttons, T-shirts, sweatshirts, theatrical-theme jewelry, duffel bags, and soundtracks to past and present Broadway and off-Broadway shows. *1 Shubert Alley (between 44th and 45th Sts., west of 7th Ave.), Theater District, 212/944–4133. Subway: 42nd St./Times Sq.*

TOBACCONISTS

9 *e-3*

ALFRED DUNHILL OF LONDON

The esteemed tobacconist produces custom-blended tobaccos, pipes, humidors, cigars, and gifts, including, of course, their own renowned and pricey lighters. *450 Park Ave. (near 57th St.), Midtown, 212/753–9292. Subway: 59th St./Lexington Ave.*

9 *e-4*

Saks Fifth Ave., 611 5th Ave. (at 50th St.), Midtown, 212/940–2243. Subway: E, F to 5th Ave.

10 *e-6*

BARCLAY-REX

The self-proclaimed "Blockbuster Video" of cigar shops, Barclay-Rex is also the city's oldest tobacconist. Mail order is available for anything from their array of hand-made pipes, cigars and cigarettes, and accessories including humidors and lighters. Pipe broken? They also repair. *7 Maiden La. (near Broadway), Lower Manhattan, 212/962–3355. Subway: 4, 5, A, C to Broadway/Nassau.*

9 *e-5*

70 E. 42nd St. (between Park and Madison Aves.), Midtown, 212/692–9680. Subway: 42nd St./Grand Central Station.

9 *d-4*

CONNOISSEUR PIPE SHOP

Established in 1917, the Connoisseur offers unique custom- and handmade pipes—including one-of-a-kind unstained, unvarnished, natural-finish pipes—and skillful pipe repairs. Fill them with hand-blended tobacco mixtures and choose from a full range of tobacco pouches, humidors, racks, and accessories. Prices range from $27.50 to $4,200. 1285 6th Ave. (between 51st and 52nd Sts.), concourse level, Midtown, 212/247–6054. Closed weekends. Subway: 47th–50th Sts./Rockefeller Ctr.

9 *e-3*

DAVIDOFF OF GENEVA

Davidoff sells fine tobaccos and a variety of smoking accessories. 535 Madison Ave. (near 54th St.), Midtown, 212/751–9060. Subway: 51st St./Lexington–3rd Aves.

9 *e-4*

J & R TOBACCO CORPORATION

The world's largest cigar store stocks over 2,800 different sizes, shapes, and colors, from nickel cigars to the rare and expensive. 11 E. 45th St. (between 5th and Madison Aves.), Midtown, 212/983–4160, closed Sun. Subway: 42nd St./Grand Central.

10 *f-7*

1 Wall St. Court (at the corner of Wall and Pearl Sts.), Lower Manhattan, 212/269–6000, Subway: Wall St.

9 *d-5*

NAT SHERMAN CIGARS

Choose from pipe tobacco, an imported selection of cigars in a walk-in humidor, and 30 blends of cigarette tobacco—wrapped in your choice of colored paper, with your name or company's name imprinted if you wish. Pipes and cigarette lighters are also in good supply. 500 5th Ave. (at 42nd St.), Midtown, 212/764–4175. Subway: B, D, Q, F to 5th Ave.

9 *c-8*

TOBACCO PRODUCTS

A long-standing family-run operation, Tobacco Products custom-blends cigars using tobaccos from Brazil, the Dominican Republic, Nicaragua, and Mexico and sells pipes and lighters. 133 8th Ave. (near 16th St.), Chelsea, 212/989–3900. Subway: A, C, E to 14th St.

TOYS & GAMES

collectibles

11 *c-3*

ALPHAVILLE

Check out vintage toys, posters, magic, TV memorabilia, comics, and games from the American past. 226 W. Houston St. (between Varick St. and 6th Ave.), West Village, 212/675–6850. Subway: Houston St.

7 *e-7*

BURLINGTON ANTIQUE TOYS

These miniature fighter planes, wooden boats, racing cars, and die-cast model cars are both new and collectible. There's a fine selection of tin soldiers (circa 1900–1960). Burlington Books, 1082 Madison Ave. (near 81st St.), downstairs, Upper East Side, 212/861–9708. Subway: 77th St.

11 *d-3*

CLASSIC TOYS

The mix is both new and antique, including military miniatures; a wonderful collection of old matchbox and other collectible cars; and zoo, farm, and prehistoric animals. 218 Sullivan St. (between Bleecker and W. 3rd Sts.), Greenwich Village, 212/674–4434. Subway: W. 4th St./Washington Sq.

9 *f-2*

DARROW'S FUN ANTIQUES

Founded in 1964 by Chick Darrow (see Antiques—Collectibles, above), this longtime mecca for nostalgia is now lovingly tended by Chick's son. The stock includes vintage windup toys, rare robots, tiny trucks and cars, vending machines, arcade games, carousel figures, character watches, and campaign buttons. 1101 1st Ave. (near 60th St.), Upper East Side, 212/838–0730. Closed Sun.–Mon. Subway: 59th St./Lexington Ave.

new

11 *h-1*

ALPHABETS

These fun stores sell small toys and novelty items for both children and adults. There's a good selection of Hello Kitty items (remember them?), kitschy T-shirts, cards, games, books, and gag gifts. It's a great stop for affordable last-minute gifts. *115 Ave. A (between 7th and 8th Sts.), East Village, 212/475–7250. Subway: Astor Pl.*

11 *a-1*

47 Greenwich Ave. (between Perry and Charles Sts.), West Village, 212/229–2966. Subway: Christopher St./Sheridan Sq.

7 *b-7*

2284 Broadway (between 82nd and 83rd Sts.), Upper West Side, 212/579–5702. Subway: 1, 9 to 86th St.

7 *b-6*

CHILDREN'S GENERAL STORE

Conveniently located at Playspace, this shop focuses on classic, wooden, and educational toys. *Playspace, 2473 Broadway (at 92nd St.), Upper West Side, 212/580–2723. Subway: 1, 2, 3, 9 to 96th St.*

9 *e-5*

Grand Central Station (Lexington Passage), Midtown, 212/682–0004. Subway: 42nd St./Grand Central Station.

10 *f-1*

DINOSAUR HILL

Dinosaur Hill specializes in hand-made toys from around the world, plus clothing for children ages 6 months–6 years. *306 E. 9th St. (between 2nd and 3rd Aves.), East Village, 212/473–5850. Subway: 8th St.; Astor Pl.*

11 *e-5*

ENCHANTED FOREST

This shop is SoHo's own wonderland, with an interior created by a professional set designer. It's a magical place, with books and toys that will appeal to adults as well as children. *85 Mercer St. (between Broome and Spring Sts.), SoHo, 212/925–6677. Subway: C, E to Spring St.*

9 *e-3*

F.A.O. SCHWARZ

It's a child's idea of heaven, a parent's idea of sensory overload. F.A.O. Schwarz has three floors absolutely packed with toys and tourists. The Madison Avenue entrance is the secret way to slip in during the busy holiday season, albeit through the Barbie Shop. Can't deal? Hire one of the store's personal shoppers. *767 5th Ave. (between 58th and 59th Sts.), Midtown, 212/644–9400. Subway: N, R to 5th Ave.*

10 *d-1*

GEPPETTO'S TOY BOX

This West Villager has become very popular. In addition to puppets, stuffed animals, books, and jack-in-the-boxes, they carry one the city's largest selections of Steiff, a full-line of Tucher Walthers wind-up toys, Thomas the Tank Engine train sets, and they are downtown's only merchant of Madame Alexander dolls. *161 7th Ave. S (between Waverly Pl. and Perry St.), West Village, 212/620–7511. Subway: Christopher St./Sheridan Sq.*

11 *d-8*

JUST JAKE

Voted the "Best Downtown Toy Store" in 1997 by *New York Press*, Just Jake's is full of such brainy toys as ant farms, books, and—well—small, quirky stuff. There's even a personal-shopping service. *40 Hudson St. (between Duane and Thomas Sts.), Tribeca, 212/267–1716. Subway: Chambers St.*

7 *e-8*

PENNY WHISTLE TOYS

This is the place to go for gifts to the artsy-craftsy child. In addition to such items as jewelry-making sets and model cars, Penny Whistle carries a large selection of jigsaw puzzles and dolls. *448 Madison Ave. (at 81st St.), Upper East Side, 212/873–9090. Subway: 77th St.*

9 *e-6*

1283 Madison Ave (at 91st St.), Upper East Side, 212/369–3868. Subway: 4, 5, 6 to 86th St.

9 *e-8*

TOYS "R" US

The holiday crowds and lines can be rough, but for the latest kid-fads in toys, games, bikes, and crafts—at decent discounts—you can't beat the world's largest toy store. *24–30 Union Sq. E (between 14th and 15th Sts.), Flatiron District, 212/674–8697. Subway: 14th St./Union Sq.*

9 d-6

1293 Broadway (at Herald Square, 34th St.), Garment District, 212/594–8697. Subway: 34th St./Herald Sq.

UMBRELLAS

Department stores and many handbag shops and boutiques carry umbrellas. If you forget yours on a rainy day, however, you're bound to find someone hawking $4 umbrellas on the next street corner. They're guaranteed to last—through that particular shower.

11 h-5
SALWEN

This friendly, well-established shop sells designer umbrellas at a discount. 45 Orchard St. (near Grand St.), Lower East Side, 212/226–1693. Closed Sat. Subway: Grand St.; Delancey St.

9 d-3
UNCLE SAM

Uncle Sam's been in business since 1866, and now stocks 50,000 umbrellas and 1,000 walking canes in every color, size, and description, including parasols and beach and garden umbrellas. The store performs expert, reasonably priced restorations and repairs, too. 161 W. 57th St. (between 6th and 7th Aves.), Midtown, 212/582–1976. Subway: B, Q, N, R to 57th St.

VIDEOS

BLOCKBUSTER VIDEO

The national video megachain has a store in virtually every neighborhood in Manhattan and many 'hoods in the neighboring boroughs. Most stores are open until midnight and handle both rentals and sales. Check the business listings in your White Pages for the location nearest you.

10 f-2
KIM'S VIDEO

Despite its reputation for crabby service, Kim's is staffed with movie buffs who are actually pretty helpful, and these two branches sell hard-to-find, out of print, cult, and foreign titles you probably won't see anywhere else. 6 St. Mark's Pl. (between 2nd and 3rd Aves.), 2nd floor, East Village, 212/505–0311. Subway: Astor Pl.

10 e-3

144 Bleecker St. (at LaGuardia Pl.), Greenwich Village, 212/260–1010. Subway: W. 4th St.

11 f-2
TOWER VIDEO

Never to be outdone, Tower has thousands of music and film video titles for rent or sale, and the Village and Upper West Side stores are open until midnight. 383 Lafayette St. (at 4th St.), East Village, 212/505–1166. Subway: Astor Pl., 8th St.

9 b-1

1961 Broadway (at 66th St.), Upper West Side, 212/799–2500. Subway: 66th St./Lincoln Ctr.

9 e-3

Trump Tower (sales only: 725 5th Ave., at 56th St.), Midtown, 212/838–8110. Subway: E, F to 5th Ave.

9 f-7
VIDEO STOP

A cut above the homogenized chains, this store has a knowledgeable staff and a good selection of videos for rent and for sale. 367 3rd Ave. (between 26th and 27th Sts.), 685–6199. Subway: 6 to 28th St.

WATCHES & CLOCKS

The large department stores stock a variety of watches in the inexpensive and moderate ranges, with the accent on fashion.

antique

9 d-3
AARON FABER

Faber carries a sizable selection of antique and vintage wristwatches from the turn of the 20th century to the 1960s, by such makers as Elgin, Hamilton, Patek Philippe, and Rolex. Within their smaller selection of contemporary timepieces, they feature a studio art line—one-of-a-kind watches created by contemporary artists. 666 5th Ave. (entrance is between 52nd and 53rd Sts.), Midtown, 212/586–8411. Subway: E, F to 5th Ave.

9 *e-1*

FANELLI ANTIQUE TIMEPIECES

This large selection of antique timepieces includes pocket- and wristwatches, wall clocks, shelf clocks, tall case clocks, and carriage clocks. The quality is high, and rare pieces abound. Prices range from $225 to $50,000. Expert appraisals and repairs are available. *790 Madison Ave. (between 66th and 67th Sts.), Upper East Side, 212/517–2300. Subway: 6 to 68th St./Hunter College.*

7 *e-8*

TIME WILL TELL

This shop is full of beautiful, one-of-a-kind classic timepieces from the 1920s to the present. Brands include Audemars Piguet, Cartier, Hamilton, Bulova, Rolex, Tiffany, and Patek Philippe; bands are made of alligator, ostrich, and lizard. Pocket-watch lovers, you have some choices here, too. Prices range from $300 to $40,000. Repairs are available. *962 Madison Ave. (near 75th St.), Upper East Side, 212/861–2663. Subway: 6 to 77th St.*

contemporary

9 *e-3*

CELLINI

Known as one of the best high-end watch shops in town, Cellini carries such exclusive brands as Frank Mueller, Breguet, and Cartier. *509 Madison Ave. (between 52nd and 53rd St.), Midtown, 212/888–0505. Subway: E, F, to 5th Ave.*

9 *e-4*

Waldorf-Astoria Hotel (Park Ave. and 50th St.), Midtown, 212/751–9824. Subway: 51st St./Lexington–3rd Aves.

9 *e-2*

EXCLUSIVELY BREITLING

It's an exclusive address for an exclusive line of superb Swiss watches, which start at about $900 and top out over $100,000. *740 Madison Ave. (between 64th and 65th Sts.), Upper East Side, 212/628–5678. Subway: 6 to 68th St./Hunter College.*

9 *e-3*

GEORGE PAUL JEWELERS

George Paul sells not watches, but a large selection of fine leather watchbands, including alligator, lizard, crocodile, pig, buffalo, snake, and bird. If they don't stock it, they'll make it to order. *1023 3rd Ave. (between 60th and 61st Sts.), Upper East Side, 212/308–0077. Closed Sun. Subway: 59th St./Lexington Ave.*

9 *d-5*

JOSEPH EDWARDS

The new and used watches include Omegas, Tags, Citizen, and Hamiltons. Repairs are done on-site. *500 5th Ave. (between 42nd and 43rd Sts.), Midtown, 800/833–1195. Subway: B, D, F, Q to 42nd St.*

9 *e-5*

323 Madison Ave. (between 42nd and 43rd Sts.), Midtown, 212/682–0383. Subway: 42nd St./Grand Central.

9 *d-3*

MOSTLY WATCHES

The small storefront hides a good selection of Omega, Swiss Army, and other watches, including both new and collectible Swatches. Repairs are done on-site. *200 W. 57th St. (between 7th Ave. and Broadway), Midtown, 212/265–7100. Subway: B, Q, N, R to 57th St.*

9 *d-4*

MOVADO

Movado is the home of the famous Museum Watch, as well as several other watch styles and a selection of jewelry. *610 5th Ave. (between 49th and 50th Sts.), Midtown, 212/218–7555. Subway: E, F to 5th Ave.*

9 *d-3*

SWATCH STORE

Each Swatch store is independently owned and operated, so selections may vary, but prices should be consistent for these high-design but well-priced cult icons. *5 E. 57th St. (between 5th and Madison Aves.), Midtown, 212/317–1100. Subway: E, F to 5th Ave.*

9 *b-1*

100 W. 72nd St. (at Columbus Ave.), Upper West Side, 212/595-9640. Subway: 1, 2, 3, 9 to 72nd St.

10 *e-3*

640 Broadway (at Bleecker St.), NoHo, 212/777–1002. Subway: 6 to Bleecker St.

`9` *e-3*

TOURNEAU

Tourneau specializes in handsome, elegant, and famous watches for the fashion-conscious. Choose from Rolex, Cartier, Piaget, Corum, Patek Philippe, Baume & Mercier, Vaucheron Constantin, and many more; they're expensive, but battery replacements are free for life. (Let's see, where's my calculator . . . .) There's also a fine selection of vintage watches. *500 Madison Ave. (at 52nd St.), Midtown, 212/758–6098. Subway: 51st St./Lexington–3rd Aves.*

`9` *e-3*

635 Madison Ave. (at 59th St.), Midtown, 212/758–6688. Subway: 59th St./Lexington Ave.

`9` *c-6*

200 W. 34th St. (near 7th Ave.), Garment District, 212/563–6880. Subway: 1, 2, 3, 9 to 34th St./Penn Station.

`10` *f-6*

VINCENT GERARD

Gerard carries a good selection of both low- and high-priced brands, such as Fossil, Tissot, Omega, and Longines. *Pier 17, South Street Seaport, Lower Manhattan, 212/732–6400. Subway: Fulton St.*

`9` *e-3*

WATCH WORLD

As the name suggests, this shop carries a wide variety of watches for children and adults. Brands include Guess, Citizen, Timex, Boy London, and such designer brands as Skagen and M & Co. *Trump Tower (725 5th Ave., at 56th St.), Midtown, 212/310–0115. Subway: E, F to 5th Ave.*

`11` *e-3*

649 Broadway (at Bleecker St.), Greenwich Village, 212/475–6090. Subway: 6 to Bleecker St.

`9` *e-4*

YAEGER WATCH OUTLET

Yaeger will meet or beat any price for a variety of name-brand watches, including Movado, Omega, Gruen, and Swiss Army. *578 5th Ave. (at 47th St.), Midtown, 212/819–0088. Subway: B, D, F, Q to 50th St./Rockefeller Plaza.*

WINES & SPIRITS

Prices can vary tremendously, so it's wise to shop around before splurging on that special Burgundy. Be wary of stores that post numerical wine ratings everywhere, often the sign of lazy or clueless service. Instead, ask questions, develop a relationship with trustworthy salespeople, and hit tastings where you can sample before you buy. And don't forget—city wine and liquor stores are closed on Sundays.

`9` *b-1*

ACKER MERRALL AND CONDIT

A grande dame of New York wine stores, Acker Merrall carries all the heavy hitters and has one of the city's largest selection of Australian wines. *160 W. 72nd St. (between Broadway and Columbus Ave.), Upper West Side, 212/787–1700. Subway: 72nd St.*

`11` *f-1*

ASTOR WINES & SPIRITS

The largest liquor store in New York State is a must for bargain-hunting oenophiles. The service needs some work. *12 Astor Pl. (at Lafayette St.), East Village, 212/674–7500. Subway: Astor Pl.*

`7` *e-7*

BEST CELLARS

With an eclectic group of white, red, dessert, and sparkling wines priced around $10 and helpful service, this store offers a welcome antidote to stuffy, overpriced wine purveyors. Stock up here for your next party. *1291 Lexington Avenue (between 86th and 87th Sts.), Upper East Side, 212/426–4200. Subway: 4, 5, 6 to 86th St.*

`10` *d-1*

CROSSROADS

It's cramped, and not always cheap, but they have wines you won't find anywhere else. *55 W. 14th St. (between 5th and 6th Aves.), Chelsea, 212/924–3060. Subway: F to 14th St.; L to 6th Ave.*

`9` *e-1*

GARNET WINES & LIQUORS

For selection and price, this is the best all-around wine store in town. *929 Lexington Ave. (between 68th and 69th Sts.), Upper East Side, 212/772–3211. Subway: 68th St./Hunter College.*

9 *e-5*

GRANDE HARVEST WINES

Don't expect bargains at this über-convenient store in Grand Central Terminal, just a good selection focusing on Italian and Californian wines and single malts. *33 Grand Central Terminal, across from Track 17, Midtown, 212/682–5855. Subway: 42nd St./Grand Central.*

9 *e-3*

MORRELL & COMPANY

This beautiful, well-run wine shop features a large collection of port and an excellent selection of California wines. Wine catering is available. *1 Rockefeller Plaza (between 5th and 6th Aves.), Midtown, 212/688–9370. Subway: 47–50 Sts/Rockefeller Ctr.*

9 *e-6*

PARK AVENUE LIQUORS

Overlook the disheveled appearance and incongruous name of this Madison Avenue shop, and you'll find savvy help and some good, lesser-known bottles. *292 Madison Ave. (between 40th and 41st Sts.), Midtown, 212/685–2442. Subway: 42nd St./Grand Central.*

9 *e-2*

SHERRY LEHMANN WINES & SPIRITS

One of the best liquor stores around, this elegant shop has a comprehensive stock and knowledgeable staff. *679 Madison Ave. (near 61st St.), Upper East Side, 212/838–7500. Subway: 59th St./Lexington Ave.*

9 *b-2*

67 WINE & SPIRIT MERCHANTS

Two floors of wine and spirits, plus a kitchen for visiting chefs and wine and food events. Wine club members get special discounts. *179 Columbus Ave. (between 67th and 68th Sts.), Upper West Side, 212/724–6767. Subway: 66th St./Lincoln Ctr.*

ZIPPERS

Most notions purveyors (*see* Notions, *above*) also carry zippers.

11 *h-6*

A. FEIBUSCH ZIPPERS

Feibusch has zippers in every length and every color, with thread to match. If they don't, they'll cut it to order. *27 Allen St. (between Hester and Canal St.), Lower East Side, 212/226–3964. Closed Sat. Subway: Canal St.*

chapter 3

PARKS, GARDENS, & SPORTS

I t may seem counterintuitive, but New York is and always has been a great place for sports. It all goes back to why the city sprang up here in the first place—lots of water, a strong rock foundation, forests, marshlands, and proximity to other areas of commercial interest. Over the years, New Yorkers have made the most of their natural environment and created their own exercise options indoors as well. Pick any block (well, almost any block), and what do you see walking down the street but gorgeous bodies, young and old. Then look at the facilities—the city with the biggest and best of everything is never willing to be outdone. Lured by the vast market potential and capital resources, sports outfitters will launch just about anything here, hence the endless cycle of fitness trends—roller basketball, a new trendy workout every month, even such seemingly rural pastimes as rock climbing and kayaking. It's hard to find a better combination of natural and man-made facilities—and if anyone tries to argue about that, you can just remind them that another popular New York exercise is kvetching.

parks

It's easy to get frustrated in a city where green signs that say PARK point you to a garage rather than a green space. But New York has its share of parks, large and small, teeming and tranquil—26,220 acres at last count. From the seemingly endless Pelham Bay Park and the Staten Island Greenbelt to midtown's vest-pocket delights, parks have saved the soul of many a harried New Yorker. One recent survey found that almost two-thirds of all New Yorkers visit a park more than once a week.

Landscape architects Frederick Law Olmsted and Calvert Vaux come up again and again in New York City—and American—park history, as they designed a number of the city's most impressive "natural" spaces and introduced concepts that now seem essential to our enjoyment of parks. They sought to enhance the natural topography of their sites, focusing on "turf, wood, and water," and they felt that different types of park users—such as walkers, horseback riders, and (then) carriage users—needed separate paths. Central Park, Prospect Park, and several other parks and parkways are some of Olmsted and Vaux's lasting gifts to New York. A survey of the city's natural history also includes Robert Moses, who held various city positions from the WPA era through the 1960s, including parks commissioner (he united what had been five independent agencies) and chair of the Triborough Bridge and Tunnel Authority. Though he's responsible for the creation and rehabilitation of some treasured parks, Moses eventually grew more interested in building highways than greenways, so he's also responsible for much of New York's isolating asphalt.

When visiting a park, use common sense: After dark, you're safer with other people. During the day, try not to interfere with activities, whether it's a ball game or a skater whizzing by. Motor vehicles are allowed on some park roads, so watch out for those, too.

PARK INFORMATION

The City of New York/Parks and Recreation, also known as the Parks Department or the Department of Parks and Recreation, is responsible for the vast majority of parks, beaches, malls, playgrounds, and woodlands within city limits. The department offers a number of phone information lines, provides permits for games and events in parks, and staffs Urban Park Ranger programs. Much of their work is handled by individual borough offices. The general **parks hot line,** for information and emergencies, is 800/201–PARK. For recorded information pertaining to **special events** in the city's parks, call 212/360–3456 or 888/NY–PARKS, which offers a fax-on-demand service. **Borough headquarters offices** have information about the parks in their respective boroughs and can help you locate sporting facilities near you: Bronx (718/430–1868), Brooklyn (718/965–8900), Manhattan (212/408–0100), Queens (718/520–5900), and Staten Island (718/390–8000).

The New York State Department of Parks, Recreation and Historic Preservation (518/474–0456) also manages some of the city's outdoor spaces, including Staten Island's Clay Pit Ponds Preserve (718/967–1976) and Manhattan's Riverbank State Park (212/694–3600). Gateway National Recreation Area, formed as the first urban national recreation area in 1972, consists of National Park Service parklands spread out over waterfront districts in Queens, Brooklyn, Staten Island, and New Jersey. Together, these spits of land form a natural gateway (get it?) to New York's great harbor. Among its treasures are a wildlife refuge, historic forts and airfields, and beaches. Headquarters are at Brooklyn's Floyd Bennett Field (718/338–3338).

PERMITS

For details about and permits for use of city ball fields, call or stop by the **Parks Department permit office** (16 W. 61st St., 6th floor, Manhattan, 212/408–0209). Other borough offices are: Bronx (718/430–1840), Brooklyn (718/965–8919), Queens (718/520–5933), and Staten Island (718/816–6529). There's nothing to stop you from using an open field, but if someone with a permit and field reservation shows up, you'll have to leave. For tennis permits, *see* Tennis, *below*.

URBAN PARK RANGERS

Trained in the history, landscape design, geology, wildlife, and botany of the city's parks, these uniformed officers guide tours and lead workshops to help visitors better understand and appreciate the parks. Topics include everything from horseshoe-crab mating habits to the buildings surrounding Central Park; all are free and fascinating. For program information call the appropriate number: Bronx (718/430–1832), Brooklyn (718/438–0100), Manhattan (212/427–4040), Queens (718/699–4204), and Staten Island (718/667–6042).

bronx

2 *d-4*

BRONX PARK

Laid out in the 1880s, this 718-acre park became the home of the city's zoo and botanical gardens in 1899 (*see* Botanical Gardens *and* Zoos, Aquariums, & Wildlife Preserves *below*). *Bronx Park E at Brady Ave., Bronxdale. Subway: Bronx Park E or E. 180th St.*

2 *c-6*

CROTONA PARK

Formerly the estate of the Bathgate family and known as Bathgate Woods, it was renamed after the ancient Greek city of Croton. The 128-acre park contains a bathhouse and pool dating back to the 1930s. *Fulton Ave. at E. 175th St., Claremont Village. Subway: 2, 5 to E. 174th St.*

2 *g-2*

PELHAM BAY PARK

This 2,117-acre park is one of the city's most versatile. It was named after Englishman Thomas Pell, who bought land in the area in 1654. Fish, egrets, frogs, raccoons, owls, fox, ospreys, and even seals share the land with New Yorkers. Habitats of the last group include tennis courts, baseball diamonds, a track, a playground, golf courses, and a stable. Some relics of the past include the Bartow-Pell Mansion (*see* Chapter 4). **Orchard Beach,** a crescent-shape Robert Moses creation, is one highlight (*see* Beaches, *below*). Southeast of here, **Rodman's Neck** is a meadow-and-scrub area where the NYPD practices shooting. The **Thomas Pell Wildlife Refuge and Sanctuary,** established in 1967, contains wetlands and woodlands. **Split Rock,** a massive glacier-split boulder, is where poet Anne Hutchinson died in 1643 at the hands of the Siwanoy Indians. **Hunter Island** is a coastal area full of tidal wetlands and the park's largest continuous forest. The 6-mi Siwanoy

---

OUTDOORS ONLINE

Many of the organizations and parks listed here tell their stories on the Web. Here are some URLs for rainy-day exploration.

Central Park
www.centralpark.org

City of New York Parks and Recreation
www.nycparks.org

New York Botanical Garden
www.nybg.org

New York Sports On Line
www.nynow.com/nysol/first.html

Prospect Park Alliance
www.prospectpark.org

Wildlife Conservation Society
www.wcs.org

Trail runs through the entire park. *Bruckner Blvd. and Middletown Rd., 718/430–1890. Pelham Bay Park Environmental Center (near Orchard Beach), 718/885–3466. Subway: Pelham Bay Park.*

2 b-2
VAN CORTLANDT PARK

Despite the intrusion of various parkways, this park's 1,000-plus acres of wetlands and woodlands are home to a remarkable variety of critters. The **Parade Ground** is the most popular area for people, featuring several fields and the **Van Cortlandt House** (*see* Chapter 4), the oldest building in the Bronx. The Van Cortlandt family burial, **Vault Hill,** has fine views from its perch 169 ft above sea level. **Tibbets Brook** flows through marshy areas into the 13-acre **Van Cortlandt Lake.** Hikers have plenty of options: the **John Kieran Nature Trail** runs alongside the lake, the **Aqueduct Trail** follows the route of the Croton Aqueduct, and the **Cass Gallagher Nature Trail** winds its way through the **Northwest Forest.** Summer brings New York Philharmonic concerts and many other events. *W. 242nd St. to city line, between Broadway and Jerome Ave., 718/430–1890. Subway: 242nd St./Van Cortlandt Park.*

brooklyn

4 d-6
DYKER BEACH PARK

This 217-acre park, adjacent to the Fort Hamilton Military Reservation, has beautiful views of Gravesend Bay and the Verrazano Narrows Bridge. Fine expanses of lawn, sea breezes, and good fishing make it a relaxing place to spend a few hours. *Shore Pkwy., east of the Verrazano Narrows Bridge, Fort Hamilton. Subway: B, M to 18th Ave.*

12 b-1
EMPIRE FULTON FERRY STATE PARK

New York City needs more parks like this one—a grassy area right on the waterfront. The views of Manhattan from between the Manhattan and Brooklyn bridges are spectacular, the breezes keep summer sunbathers cool, and the out-of-the-way location means it's terribly underappreciated. *Plymouth St. at Main St., Brooklyn Heights. Subway: York St.; High St./Brooklyn Bridge.*

12 e-2
FORT GREENE PARK

The site of Fort Putnam during the Revolutionary War and Fort Greene during the War of 1812, this 30-acre hill was turned into Brooklyn's first major park by Olmsted and Vaux in 1848. (Then called Washington Park, it was renamed in 1897.) Pretty paths meander up and down the park's hills, past tennis courts, playgrounds, and harbor views. In the center stands the Prison Ship Martyrs' Monument, designed in 1908 by architect Stanford White. *Myrtle to DeKalb Aves.; St. Edward to Washington Park Ave. Subway: Atlantic Ave.*

4 f-7
MARINE PARK

This 1,024-acre expanse borders Gateway National Recreation Area and includes several scenic coves as well as trails, fields, and a golf course. *Inlet between Gerritsen and Flatbush Aves., inland to Fillmore Ave., between Burnet and E. 32nd Sts.*

1 h-6
PROSPECT PARK

Olmsted and Vaux's ode to Brooklyn covers 526 acres, and its designers liked it better than Central Park. Though Brooklynites first planned to have their park designed around Flatbush Avenue by Egbert Viele, chief engineer of Central Park, the Civil War gave them time to reconsider. In an act that would surely be criticized today as a bureaucratic delay tactic, the park commissioners had Calvert Vaux reexamine the proposal. Vaux quickly realized that a highway bisecting a park would greatly detract from the greenery, and instead suggested a layout west of Flatbush Avenue. Starting in 1865, he and Olmsted designed the park's broad meadows, gardens, terraces, and landscaped walks.

Like many large city parks, this one has endless recreational possibilities. Joggers and people on wheels seem to circle the loop road endlessly, yet other paths through woods and fields are barely touched. Boats float around in summer near where skaters spin in winter. The playgrounds are alive with children's squeals, the fields with barbecues and ball games (including cricket matches). Prospect Park's roadways are closed to motor vehicles the same hours as Central Park's (*see* Manhattan, *below*).

The main entrance to the park is **Grand Army Plaza,** planned in the spirit of Paris's L'Etoile (a.k.a. Place Charles-de-Gaulle, home of the Arc de Triomphe). The neo-Roman Soldiers and Sailors Memorial Arch is a memorial to the Union Army (open to climbers mid-May–early July weekends and holidays 1–5). This grandiose structure and most of the other entrance gates were added after Olmsted and Vaux had finished their work, much to their chagrin. Just inside the park, along the footpath to the east of the roadway, **Endale Arch** beautifully frames your view of **Long Meadow,** whose crescent shape makes its 90 acres seem even bigger. Frisbee, volleyball, soccer, and lounging are popular on this luxurious expanse; it's also the site of summer Philharmonic concerts. Other concert venues are the **Bandshell** at 9th Street, which hosts "Celebrate Brooklyn" festivities of all kinds, and the **Music Pagoda,** designed to resemble a traditional Chinese gateway (just north of Lullwater, a kind of feeder to Prospect Lake). Between Long Meadow and Flatbush Avenue toward the northern end of the park, the **Vale of Cashmere** is a natural amphitheater and a refuge for small birds. The **Prospect Park Wildlife Center** (*see below*), **Lefferts Homestead Children's Museum** (*see* Chapter 4), and the restored 1912 **Carousel** (weekends and holidays noon–5, additional hours and days in summer) comprise the most child-friendly section of the park, right off Flatbush Avenue. Prospect Park Alliance offices are in Litchfield Villa (95 Prospect Park West, near 3rd Street). Woods, rocky hills, and a small stream distinguish the **Ravine,** the rugged central area, which was restored in 1998 and 1999 to its entrancing rustic state. The 60-acre **Prospect Lake** is the main body of water in the park; its water is delivered through a complicated plumbing and water-recycling system. Vaux's **Terrace Bridge,** added in 1890, gives a good view of the lake and Lullwater. You can rent boats from Kate's Corner at the Wollman Ice Skating Rink, which is at the northern end of the lake, and cruise past the breathtaking Italian-style **Boathouse** on Lullwater (unfortunately now closed to the public because of water damage to its terra-cotta facade), which stands practically in the shadow of the wonderfully gnarled **Camperdown Elm.** *Bordered by Flatbush Ave., Ocean Ave., Parkside Ave., Prospect Park SW, and Prospect Park W, 718/965–8999. Subway: Grand Army Plaza; D, Q to Prospect Park; F to 7th Ave.; 15th St./Prospect Park.*

manhattan

10 *e-8*

BATTERY PARK

Jutting out as if it were Manhattan's green toe, this verdant landfill is loaded with monuments and sculpture. Because it's at the junction of the Hudson and East rivers, it has a great view of New York Harbor: Governors Island, Brooklyn, the Verrazano Narrows Bridge, Staten Island, the Statue of Liberty, Ellis Island, and New Jersey. The park's name refers to a line of cannons once mounted here to defend the shoreline, which ran along what is currently State Street. Castle Clinton, first known as the West Battery, was erected offshore on a pile of rock for the War of 1812 (nary a shot was ever fired). Landfill later joined it to the mainland, and it has since served as an entertainment and concert facility (Castle Garden), a federal immigration center, and the New York City Aquarium. Robert Moses tried to knock it down after forcing the aquarium out in the early 1940s—claiming that its 8-ft-thick walls weren't stable—but he lost that battle (*see Zoos, Aquariums, & Wildlife Preserves, below*). Now slated for yet another renovation, Castle Clinton sits squarely in Battery Park and is home to the ticket booth for the Statue of Liberty and Ellis Island ferries. Greenery, sea breezes, and great vistas draw mainly bankers and brokers at noon on sunny days, but tourists come to catch the ferries no matter what the weather. *State St. and Battery Pl., Lower Manhattan. Subway: 1, 9 to South Ferry.*

10 *c-6*

BATTERY PARK ESPLANADE

This 1.2-mi linear park, running along the perimeter of Battery Park City, is one of the city's newest and best. Old-fashioned lampposts, shade trees, well-maintained lawns, and benches facing unimpeded Hudson River views make this an inviting spot. *Enter at West and Liberty Sts., Lower Manhattan. Battery Park City Parks Corporation, 212/267–9700. Subway: Cortlandt St.; World Trade Center.*

10 *e-8*

BOWLING GREEN

Rented out to local residents for the outrageous price of one peppercorn a year starting in 1733, this park was not fully available to everyone until 1850, but it's still the city's oldest extant public park. The British erected its simple iron fence in 1771 to protect a statue of George III, but on July 9, 1776 the statue was toppled. The fence still stands. *Broadway and Battery Pl., Lower Manhattan. Subway: Bowling Green.*

9 *d-5*

BRYANT PARK

In 1823, these 9 acres were set aside as a potters' field, but they became a public park (called Reservoir Square, after the drinking-water reservoir that lay where the library is now) in 1847. New York's version of London's Crystal Palace was erected here in 1853, but it burned down five years later. The land was renamed for poet and editor William Cullen Bryant in 1884. It degenerated into a good place to buy and sell drugs in the 1970s but, having been renovated and restored in the late 1980s, it now teems with well-dressed professionals who snatch up the lawn chairs for their brown-bag power lunches. Weekday and evening concerts, an outdoor movie festival (Monday night in summer), and daily chess and backgammon games help keep it hopping. *6th Ave. between 40th and 42nd Sts., behind New York Public Library Center for the Humanities, Midtown. Subway: B, D, F, Q to 42nd St.*

7 *g-7*

CARL SCHURZ PARK

During the American Revolution, a house on this promontory was used as a fortification by the Continental Army, then taken over as a British outpost. Later, in more peaceful times, the land became known as East End Park. It was renamed in 1911 to honor Carl Schurz, a prominent 19th-century German immigrant who had been a senator and secretary of the interior. A curved stone staircase leads up to John Finley Walk, lined with wrought-iron railings, which overlooks the East River. The view—of the Triborough, Hell's Gate, and Queensboro bridges; Wards, Randalls, and Roosevelt islands; and Astoria, Queens—is so tranquil that you'd never guess you're directly above the FDR Drive. Behind you, along the walk, are raised flower beds as well as some enclosed dog runs. Other popular hangouts are the hill at the north end (for sledding in winter and sunning in summer) and the playground. The city's first family—the mayor's—lives behind the high fence in **Gracie Mansion,** at the north end of the park. *East End Ave. to East River, between 84th and 90th Sts., Upper East Side. Subway: 4, 5, 6 to 86th St.*

1 *d-4*

CENTRAL PARK

America's premier urban park, this 843-acre oasis is 2½ mi long, ¾ mi wide, and smack in the middle of Manhattan. Every day, thousands of joggers, cyclists, skaters, and walkers make their daily jaunts about "the loop," the reservoir, and the rest of the park. Sunseekers crowd the grassy lawns in summer, and athletes of all stripes make use of the fields, trails, courts, and other facilities year-round. In fall, the foliage is magnificent and the air is crisp. Ice skaters come out for the rinks and frozen lakes in winter, while cross-country skiers and sledders hit the fields and trails. In spring, blooming flowers turn the park into a scented wonderland. Summer especially sees a crowded calendar of concerts, readings, and theater and opera performances. All told, some 20 million users take advantage of the park each year.

Although it appears to be nothing more than a swatch of rolling countryside excused from urban development, Central Park is an artificial landscape. After the city acquired the land for the park, it held a competition for the park's design. Park superintendent Frederick Law Olmsted and landscape architect Calvert Vaux beat the nearly three dozen other entries with their "Greensward Plan"— part formal, part pastoral, part picturesque, it skillfully blends man-made lakes and ponds, hills and dales, secluded glens, wide meadows, a bird sanctuary, bridle paths, and nature trails. Four transverse roads were designed to carry crosstown traffic beneath the park's hills and tunnels without disturbing those at play, and 40 bridges were conceived—each with a unique design and name—to give people easy access to various areas.

Construction was a monumental task. Entire communities were displaced, swamps were drained, millions of cubic yards of soil were removed, walls of schist were blasted, and hundreds of thousands of trees and shrubs were planted. Almost a century and a half later, we can see ongoing construction, restoration, and maintenance. In the mid-1990s alone, the Turtle Pond has been enlarged, the Great Lawn has been completely revamped, and entrance gates have been remodeled. The two-year restoration of the North Meadow's 28 acres is scheduled to wrap up in the spring of 2000. The landscape around the resevoir, including the jogging and bridle paths, is to be spruced up starting the following fall. And the 59th Street Pond will receive an 18-month, $4-million rennovation, also beginning in the fall.

Those who wish to stroll unharassed by traffic should bear in mind that the circular drive through the park is closed to auto traffic on weekdays 10 AM–3 PM (except the southeastern portion of the road, below 72nd Street, which remains open) and 7 PM–10 PM, and on weekends and holidays. Nonautomotive traffic on the road is often heavy and sometimes fast-moving, so always be careful when you're crossing the road, and stay toward the inside when you're walking. Tip: The first two digits of the number plate of each lamppost in the park indicate the nearest cross street.

For the classic old-fashioned indulgence, you can glide gently through the park on a horse-drawn carriage (operated by Chateau Stables, 212/246–0520, or Hansom Cabs). It's the perfect way to amuse visiting relatives from out of town. Just walk up to any carriage along Central Park South, especially near 5th Ave.; the rates, which are reasonable, should be posted on each one. Only on extremely hot days do the horses take a break.

Whole volumes have been filled by writers extolling Central Park and its landmarks. In the southeast corner, the **Pond,** dominated by Overlook Rock, is home to swans and ducks. Picturesque **Gapstow Bridge** gives you a good view of midtown and leads to **Wollman Rink,** a popular ice- and roller-skating rink. **The Dairy** (midpark at 64th St., 212/794–6564, closed Mon.) is to the north, with its pointed eaves, steeple, and high-pitched roof; once a working dairy, it's now the park information center. In what was planned as a Children's District is an antique-horse **Carousel;** the **zoo** (see Zoos, Aquariums, & Wildlife Preserves, below) is to

the east. The expansive field in the southern section of the park is **Sheep Meadow,** once frequented by sheep but now a favorite of picnickers and sunbathers. The sheep who did graze here lived in what is now **Tavern on the Green** (see Chapter 1). East of Sheep Meadow is the **Mall,** a formal promenade lined by elms and statues of literary figures in a section called the Literary Walk. At the north end of the Mall, across the 72nd Street transverse, are **Bethesda Terrace** and **Bethesda Fountain,** the latter built in 1863. Willows, rhododendrons, and cherry trees surround the magnificent staircase. If you continue west on 72nd Street you'll come to **Strawberry Fields,** 2½ landscaped acres that form an "International Peace Garden" in memory of John Lennon. Follow the water northwest from Bethesda Terrace and you'll cross **Bow Bridge** into **The Ramble,** a heavily wooded, wild 37-acre area laced with twisting, climbing paths. This is prime bird-watching territory. The neo-Victorian **Loeb Boathouse,** on the lake, has boats and bikes for rent and a waterside café. On the east side of the park at 74th Street is **Conservatory Water** (commonly known as the Sailboat Lake), a symmetrical stone basin where model yachts race Saturday morning near statues of the fanciful Hans Christian Andersen and *Alice in Wonderland.* Midpark at 79th Street, **Belvedere Castle** towers above the **Turtle Pond** and the outdoor **Delacorte Theater,** where the Public Theater stages plays in the summer. On the castle's ground floor, the **Henry Luce Nature Observatory** (212/772–0210, closed Mon.) has nature exhibits, children's workshops, and educational programs. To its west is the dark-wood **Swedish Chalet,** a marionette theater. Behind all this are the restored **Turtle Pond** and the **Great Lawn,** 13 acres of Kentucky bluegrass, ball fields, and courts. Between the Great Lawn and the Metropolitan Museum of Art, which encroaches on park territory, stands **Cleopatra's Needle,** an Egyptian obelisk given to the city in 1881. The **Jacqueline Kennedy Onassis Reservoir** (midpark, 85th–96th Sts.) is a 106-acre lake that is *not* used for drinking water—thus the ceaseless rumors that it might be drained. The path around it makes for great running. Further north, at 105th Street, the formal **Conservatory Garden** (see Botanical Gardens, below) presides over Fifth Avenue. **Harlem Meer** is another striking body of water—the adjacent **Charles A. Dana Discovery Center**

(212/860–1370, closed Mon.) runs many nature programs for families. *Bordered by Central Park W, 59th St., 5th Ave., and 110th St. General information 212/360–3444. Subway: 59th St./Columbus Circle; N, R to 5th Ave.; B, C to 72nd–110th Sts.*

10 *e-6*

CITY HALL PARK

Known in Colonial times as the Fields or the Common, this green spot has hosted hangings, riots, and demonstrations. Now as City Hall's front yard, it's full of concrete barricades and parked police cars. In 1999 it received a massive renovation that restored lampposts and a fountain from 1871, giving the site a 19th-century feel. Critics of the renovation have drawn attention to certain changes, like gate houses and high iron fences, that are designed to restrict access to City Hall, which overlooks the park. *Between Broadway, Park Row, and Chambers Sts., Lower Manhattan. Subway: Brooklyn Bridge/City Hall.*

3 *c-1*

EAST RIVER ESPLANADE

You have to stretch your imagination to call this a park, but any long stretch of water with pedestrian access bears mentioning. This one starts near the heliport at East 59th Street—to reach the promenade, take the funky pedestrian suspension bridge at 60th Street. The paved strip, lined by benches, patches of grass, and the occasional small tree, continues to a staircase at 80th Street. Up the steps is the lovely Carl Schurz Park (*see above*), and the esplanade continues past Gracie Mansion all the way to 125th Street. There's usually a crew of fishermen near 100th Street, but most other people on the path remain in motion. *East River from 59th St. to 125th St., Upper East Side/East Harlem. Subway: 6 to 59th St.–125th Sts.*

10 *h-2*

EAST RIVER PARK

This park is wider and greener than its newer cousin on the Hudson, but it doesn't draw half as many people. The facilities—tennis courts, a track, fields, a playground, basketball courts—aren't all in the best condition, but that's no reason to stay away. Plans have been laid to renovate the decrepit theater—the original home of the Public Theatre's "Shakespeare in the Park"—but so far nothing has happened. Keep your fin-

gers crossed. *East River Dr. between 14th and Delancey Sts., East Village/Lower East Side. Subway: Delancey St.*

5 *b-7*

FORT TRYON PARK

Named after New York's last English governor, William Tryon, Fort Tryon Park occupies the site of Fort Washington, the last holdout against the British invasion of Manhattan (it fell November 16, 1776). Capping a hill 250 ft above the river, these 66 acres of wooded hills and dales overlooking the Hudson were a gift to the city from the Rockefeller family. The beautiful flower gardens and terracing, and the view of the Palisades across the Hudson, make you feel miles away from the city. The **Cloisters** museum (*see* Chapter 4) is in the middle of the park. *Between Riverside Dr. and Broadway from 192nd to Dyckman Sts., Washington Heights. Subway: A to 190th St.*

9 *e-8*

GRAMERCY PARK

This tiny patch of land, originally swamp, is New York's only surviving private square. It was bought and drained by early real-estate developer Samuel B. Ruggles, who then created a park (in 1831) for the exclusive use of those who would buy the surrounding lots. Sixty-six of the city's fashionable elite did just that, and no less than golden keys were provided for them to penetrate the park's 8-ft-high fence. Although no longer golden, keys are still given to residents only. The rest of us can only gaze at the pristine park and the landmark 19th-century row houses that surround it; still, the pretty square is refreshing to look at. *Lexington Ave. between 20th and 21st Sts. Subway: 6, N, R to 23rd St.*

6 *d-3*

HIGH BRIDGE PARK

High Bridge, built as Aqueduct Bridge between 1837 and 1848 to carry upstate reservoir water to the city, is the oldest remaining bridge connecting Manhattan to the mainland. The landmark **Water Tower** on the Manhattan side was once in use. The forested terraces and rocky ledges here have good views across the Harlem River. *Between Harlem River Dr. and Edgecombe and Amsterdam Aves., from 155th to Dyckman Sts., Washington Heights. Subway: A, B to 155th St. or 163rd St.*

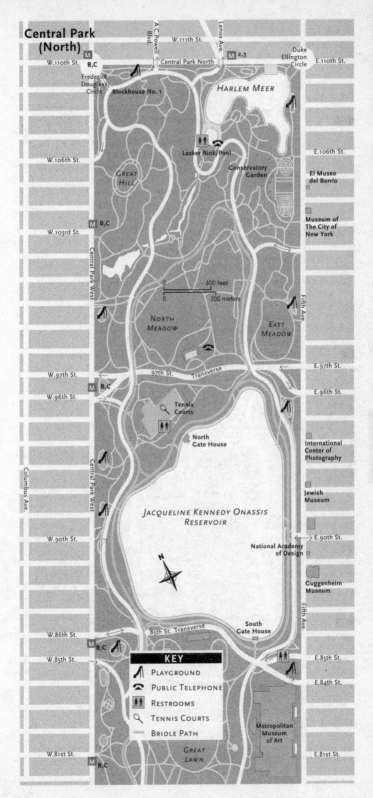

Central Park (North)

A.C. Powell Blvd.

Lenox Ave.

W.111th St.

M B,C

W.110th St.

Central Park North

M 2,3

Duke Ellington Circle

E.110th St.

Frederick Douglass Circle

Blockhouse No. 1

HARLEM MEER

W.106th St.

Lasker Rink/Pool

Conservatory Garden

E.106th St.

GREAT HILL

El Museo del Barrio

Museum of The City of New York

W.103rd St.

M B,C

Central Park West

0   600 feet
0   200 meters

NORTH MEADOW

EAST MEADOW

Fifth Ave.

W.97th St.

97th St. Transverse

E.97th St.

M B,C

W.96th St.

E.96th St.

Tennis Courts

North Gate House

International Center of Photography

Jewish Museum

JACQUELINE KENNEDY ONASSIS RESERVOIR

E.90th St.

W.90th St.

National Academy of Design

N

Guggenheim Museum

Columbus Ave.

Central Park West

Fifth Ave.

85th St. Transverse

South Gate House

W.86th St.

M B,C

E.85th St.

W.85th St.

E.84th St.

KEY

- Playground
- Public Telephone
- Restrooms
- Tennis Courts
- Bridle Path

Metropolitan Museum of Art

W.81st St.

M B,C

GREAT LAWN

E.81st St.

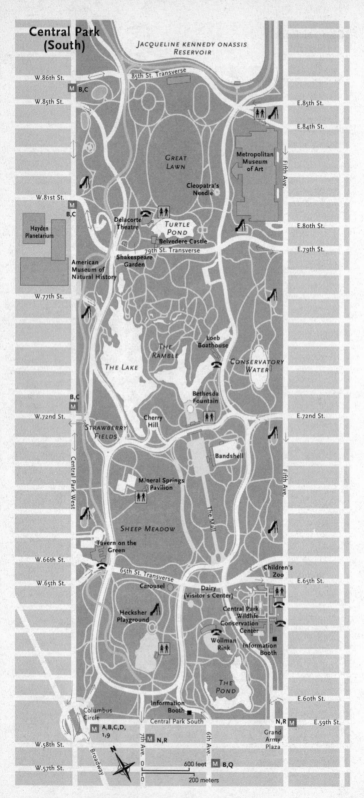

Central Park (South)

JACQUELINE KENNEDY ONASSIS Reservoir

W.86th St.

M B,C

W.85th St.

85th St. Transverse

E.85th St.

E.84th St.

GREAT LAWN

Metropolitan Museum of Art

Cleopatra's Needle

W.81st St.

M B,C

E.80th St.

Hayden Planetarium

Delacorte Theatre

TURTLE POND

Belvedere Castle

E.79th St.

79th St. Transverse

American Museum of Natural History

Shakespeare Garden

Fifth Ave.

W.77th St.

Loeb Boathouse

THE RAMBLE

CONSERVATORY WATER

THE LAKE

B,C

M

Bethesda Fountain

W.72nd St.

STRAWBERRY FIELDS

Cherry Hill

E.72nd St.

Bandshell

Central Park West

Mineral Springs Pavilion

SHEEP MEADOW

The Mall

Fifth Ave.

Tavern on the Green

W.66th St.

Children's Zoo

65th St. Transverse

E.65th St.

W.65th St.

Carousel

Dairy (Visitor's Center)

Hecksher Playground

Central Park Wildlife Conservation Center

Information Booth

Wollman Rink

THE POND

E.60th St.

Information Booth

Central Park South

M A,B,C,D, 1,9

Columbus Circle

E.59th St.

N,R M

W.58th St.

7th Ave.

N,R

6th Ave.

Grand Army Plaza

W.57th St.

Broadway

N

0   600 feet

M B,Q

0   200 meters

224

1 c-5

HUDSON RIVER PARK

Though plans involving design and funding for this park probably won't be settled until the park is completed years from now, we will someday have a waterfront walking, cycling, and blading path and more than 10 public piers stretching from 59th Street all the way down the West Side. The park is already a reality up to 14th Street, where bladers and Village people convening at all hours attest to how sorely New Yorkers need more waterfront space. The southern end of the park, now called **Nelson A. Rockefeller Park,** has expansive green lawns and the Lilliputian, cast-bronze "Real World" sculptures by artist Tom Otterness. (Youngsters love these; you can climb on them and play in the water that surrounds some of them.) Pier 25 at North Moore Street, has summertime activities for children, including fishing, games, and environmental education. Pier 84, at West 44th Street, has been undergoing emergency construction during 1998 and 1999 but it's still open to the public with activities organized by Floating the Apple (*see Boating, below*). Piers 45 (Christopher St.), 54 (13th St.), and 62 (W. 23rd St.) also allow public access. The Hudson River Park Trust, the group working to realize the park, sponsors activities such as outdoor movies, regattas, and even swims. *Battery Park to 59th St. along the Hudson River, 212/533–PARK for event information. Subway: 1, 9 to Canal–14th Sts.; A, C, E to 14th St.; L to 8th Ave.*

5 b-5

INWOOD HILL PARK

The Hudson and Harlem rivers meet at the tip of this unbelievably quiet, scenic park. Its 196 acres of hill-climbing woods are laced with hidden paths and contain Manhattan's only remaining natural forest. Its history is rich, too: Algonquin Indians once dwelled in caves on this site, and British and Hessian troops were quartered here during the American Revolution. *Dyckman St. to the Harlem River, from Seaman to Payson Aves., Inwood. Subway: A to Dyckman St./200th St. or 207th St./Inwood.*

7 h-7

LIGHTHOUSE PARK

This lovely green area has views you'd otherwise need a boat to admire. Manhattan's Upper East Side and Ward's Island, Queens's Long Island City and Astoria, as well as a few bridges, are all visible from water level. It's named for the 50-ft stone lighthouse, vintage 1872, that used to help sailors navigate the East River. *Northern tip of Roosevelt Island. Subway: B, Q to Roosevelt Island.*

9 e-7

MADISON SQUARE PARK

At various times in its history the area was a potter's field, the site of the city's first baseball games (1845), a luxurious residential area, and the location of the original Madison Square Garden. Now there are small flower plantings and several splendid sculptures here, including a statue of Alaska buyer William H. Seward. The park, which was renovated in 1999, is popular nowadays with office workers and dog owners. *23rd–26th Sts. between 5th and Madison Aves., Murray Hill. Subway: 6, N, R to 23rd St.*

7 d-2

MARCUS GARVEY PARK

As the city pushed northward, it didn't want Harlem to be without a park, so it built one around this 70-ft-high rocky eminence in the middle of Fifth Avenue. From the street on the park's southern side, you can see the three-tier, cast-iron fire tower (1856), the only remaining tower in a now-defunct citywide network. First called Mt. Morris Park, it was renamed in 1973 after Marcus Garvey, who led the back-to-Africa movement. It's not known for being safe. *120th–124th Sts. at 5th Ave, Harlem. Subway: 2, 3 to 125th St.*

7 b-2

MORNINGSIDE PARK

Sadly, this 1887 Olmsted and Vaux gem in Morningside Heights is another park that's just not safe. It follows the crest of the cliffs above Harlem, pressing up to the Columbia University campus. *110th–123rd Sts. from Morningside Dr. to Manhattan and Morningside Aves. Subway: B, C to 110th–125th Sts.*

9 d-3

PALEY PARK

A boon to midtown's weary, this memorial to former CBS executive Samuel Paley is remarkable not so much for its features but for its historical status as one of the first of New York's "vest-pocket parks" to be inserted into the concrete canyons. A recycling waterfall blocks out traffic noise, and feathery honey-locust trees provide shade. The snack bar opens in warm weather. *3 E. 53rd St., Midtown. Subway: E, F to 5th Ave.*

1. c-3
RIVERSIDE PARK
In the tradition of English landscaping, Frederick Law Olmsted met the challenge of this sloping terrain to provide a 300-acre playground along and above the Hudson River for Upper West Siders. Its various promenades make for usually uncrowded walking, especially beautiful in spring when crab apple and cherry trees are in bloom. The **79th Street Boat Basin,** home for those who live in its flotilla of houseboats, has a 110-slip public marina. The **Rotunda,** behind it, occupies a wonderful circular space punctuated by a fountain. The park holds several important monuments, including the **Soldiers' and Sailors' Memorial** and **Grant's Tomb** (*see* Chapter 4). The **Eleanor Roosevelt statue,** at the 72nd Street entrance, is the park's latest addition. *72nd–159th Sts. between Riverside Dr. and the Hudson River, Upper West Side. Subway: 1, 9 to 72nd St.–157th St.*

6. b-7
RIVERBANK STATE PARK
This unlikely 28-acre park opened in 1993 atop a sewage treatment plant. Elevated as high as 69 ft above the Hudson, it's not at all marred by its neighbor below, and its facilities—including indoor and outdoor pools, an outdoor track, a skating rink, numerous playing fields, and a playground—are state-of-the-art. Just being cooled by the breeze and admiring the view is rewarding, too. *Entrances: Riverside Dr. at 138th and 145th Sts., Harlem, 212/694–3600. Subway: 1, 9 to 137th St./City College or 145th St.*

7. b-3
ST. NICHOLAS PARK
Like Morningside Park, this thin green strip climbs a steep hill and backs up to a college—in this case, City College. Its designer, Frederick Law Olmsted, feared that its narrowness and difficult terrain would make it unsafe, and he was right. The playgrounds and courts that edge the park see a lot of use, but the interior is desolate and poorly maintained. If the National Park Service moves Hamilton Grange (*see* Chapter 4) here from its location just around the corner, per the

rumors, the park might get some needed help. *128th–141st Sts. between St. Nicholas Ave. and St. Nicholas Terr., Harlem. Subway: B, C to 135th St.*

10. f-1
STUYVESANT SQUARE
This historic square, now full of flower plantings, was once part of Peter Stuyvesant's farm but was ceded to the city in 1836 by his great-great-grandson. It comprised the core of fashionable New York in the late 19th century. *2nd Ave. from 15th St. to 17th St., Gramercy. Subway: 3rd Ave.*

10. g-2
TOMPKINS SQUARE PARK
Named after one-time New York State Governor Daniel P. Tompkins, this 16-acre park looks better than it has in years. The oldest park on the Lower East Side, its post-1960s troubles have included violent clashes between city officials and the park's permanent residents, and its reputation as a drug center. None of those who now use it for basketball, dog walking, relaxing, and other park activities seems to care. *7th–10th Sts. between Aves. A and B, East Village. Subway: Astor Pl.; 2nd Ave.*

10. e-1
UNION SQUARE
Though its name comes from its function as a transportation nexus, the square has been the site of many union protests, and several radical groups once had their headquarters nearby. At the time—in the late 19th century—the surrounding neighborhood was a commercial area, with fine shops such as Tiffany's, but by World War I it had turned shabby. The park was refurbished in the 1980s and now has a colorful **Greenmarket** at its western and northern edges every Monday, Wednesday, Friday, and Saturday. Manicured lawns and flower beds and numerous trendy restaurants around and even in the park prove that happy days are here again. *14th–17th Sts. between Broadway and Park Ave. S., Flatiron District. Subway: 14th St./Union Sq.*

9. g-5
UNITED NATIONS
Adjacent to the UN headquarters are lovely lawns and trees, full of energetic squirrels, and a small formal rose garden, all overlooking the East River. *Main*

public entrance, 1st Ave. at 46th St., Midtown. Open weekdays 9 AM–4:45 PM, weekends 9:15–4:45. Subway: 42nd St./Grand Central.

1 d-3

WARD'S AND RANDALL'S ISLANDS

Formerly separate pieces of land, these East River islands have been joined by landfill. Downing Stadium, on Randall's Island, hosts concerts and sporting events, including rugby games and track-and-field meets (see Sports Stadiums, below). Both islands have parklands and playing fields used by many community groups. Picnicking and fishing East Harlemites stream across the footbridge at 104th Street in good weather, but the islands remain uncrowded. The roads are good for running, skating, and biking. Junction of East and Harlem rivers. Enter via Triborough Bridge or footbridge from East River Esplanade, 104th St. Subway: 6 to 103rd St.

11 g-8

WASHINGTON MARKET PARK

This former vacant lot has been turned into a delightful 1½-acre park with a Victorian gazebo and an adventure playground. Greenwich St. between Chambers and Duane Sts., Tribeca. Subway: Chambers St.

11 d-2

WASHINGTON SQUARE PARK

Once a marshy area favored by duck hunters, then a potter's field, then the site of hanging gallows, this square became a public park in 1828 and a fashionable residential area shortly thereafter (Edith Wharton and Henry James lived in the row of Greek Revival houses on Washington Square North). At the park's center is its landmark arch, designed by Stanford White in 1892. Though it sometimes feels like NYU is trying to claim the park as its front yard, Washington Square is the emotional, if not geographical, heart of Greenwich Village. Park goers include playground-happy children, chess players, Frisbee throwers, skilled skaters, dog walkers, guitar strummers, folk singers, and magicians. W. 4th St.–Waverly Pl. (at the foot of 5th Ave.) between MacDougal St. and University Pl., Greenwich Village. Subway: W. 4th St./Washington Square.

queens

1 g-3

ALLEY POND PARK

Alley Pond was named after a row of 18th-century commercial buildings, including a gristmill and a general store. The buildings and the pond are long gone (the latter disappeared when the LIE was built), but the parkland retains the name—and its 655 acres of highlands, ponds, marshes, creeks, trees, and an amazing array of wildlife, including rabbits, muskrats, and opossums. Bisected by the LIE, it has meadowlands to the north and woodlands to the south. Pitobik Trail is a 2-mi walk through a former Mattinecock Indian camp, and Turtle Pond Trail takes you through dense vegetation past glacial kettles. The **Alley Pond Environmental Center** (228–06 Northern Blvd., 718/229–4000) has live animals, offers trail walks, and hosts lively children's programs on weekends (registration required). Grand Central Pkwy. at Winchester Blvd., Bayside.

3 d-2

ASTORIA PARK

This waterfront park, opened in 1913, provides great vistas of several bridges and the Manhattan skyline. Facilities

---

NATURE TRAILS

You don't have to leave the city to bushwhack, wade through marshes, or get lost on wooded paths. Here are some favorite hikes.

Greenbelt
28 mi of trails incl. a 13-mi circular trail and the 7-mi La Tourette Trail.

Inwood Hill Park
Short nature trails pass tree identifications and an Indian cave.

Jamaica Bay Wildlife Refuge
Nearly 3,000 acres are reserved for nature walks and bird-watching.

Pelham Bay Park
The Siwanoy Trail.

Van Cortlandt Park
Old Putnam Railroad Track, Aqueduct Trail, and Cass Gallagher Nature Trail.

Wave Hill Ctr for Environmental Studies
A 1½-mi marked trail.

include tennis courts and a large out-door pool. *Hoyt Ave.–Ditmars Blvd. between 19th St. and the East River. Subway: Ditmars Blvd./Astoria.*

1 *g-3*

CUNNINGHAM PARK

This large park, seemingly an endless array of fields, courts, and picnic grounds strung together, is all over the Queens outdoor-event calendar. In the summer it hosts the New York Philharmonic, opera, and jazz. *193rd–210th Sts. between Long Island Expressway and Grand Central Pkwy., Fresh Meadows. Subway: 179th St./Jamaica.*

3 *h-2*

FLUSHING MEADOWS–CORONA PARK

Queens's largest park (1,257 acres) has a Cinderella history: Originally a swamp, then a garbage dump, the area was the site of the 1939–40 World's Fair, the meeting ground of the nascent United Nations 1946–50, and the host of another World's Fair in 1964–65. Structures we now know as the **Queens Museum of Art, Shea Stadium,** the **United States Tennis Association (U.S.T.A.) National Tennis Center,** the **New York Hall of Science,** the **boathouse,** and the **World's Fair marina,** on Flushing Bay, are all remnants of the world's fairs, as is the steel **Unisphere,** the symbol of the later one. Smaller remnants from the fairs, such as salt shakers, ties, pins, programs, silverware, and general kitsch are on display in the Queens Museum (*see* Chapter 4) along with a history of the land. The park's wide range of activities means you're bound to find something to do. Families enjoy the **Queens Wildlife Center** and the **Playground for All Children** (718/699–8283), which was the first in the country to include facilities for both able and disabled children. Athletes have overwhelming options—tennis, golf, swimming, boating, bicycling, ice skating, and lots of playing fields. The **Theater-in-the-Park** (718/760–0064) hosts performances with particular appeal to immigrants from the surrounding neighborhoods. *Union Tpke. from 111th St. and Grand Central Pkwy. to the Van Wyck Extension, Flushing, 718/760–6565. Subway: 7 to 111th St. or Willets Point/Shea Stadium; Union Tpke./Kew Gardens.*

1 *f-5*

FOREST PARK

This 538-acre park is another Olmsted treasure. Its roads, trails, and dense forests are well traveled by hikers, bikers, and bird-watchers; other draws are a golf course, tennis courts, fields, a carousel, a model-airplane field, and a bandshell. *Union Ave. and Union Tpke. to Park La. S, between Park La. and Cypress Hill Cemetery, 718/235–0684. Subway: J, Z to Woodhaven Blvd.; Union Tpke./Kew Gardens.*

1 *g-6*

JAMAICA BAY WILDLIFE REFUGE

Though departing planes from JFK command aural attention, it's the smaller aviators that are worth noting here. These 9,155 acres of salt marshes, fresh and brackish ponds, and open bay attract hundreds of species of shorebirds and constitute a major stop on the Atlantic Flyway. It's most exciting in spring, when hundreds of thousands of birds are nesting—including the great egret, snowy egret, and glossy ibis—and during the fall migratory season. Now that Jamaica Bay is part of Gateway National Recreation Area, and cleaner thanks to pollution-control efforts, we can hope for even more avian action. There are over 5 mi of trails, and rangers guide tours regularly. *Broad Channel, 718/318–4340. Subway: Broad Channel.*

1 *f-3*

KISSENA PARK

A pretty landscape of hills, trees, and water, along with tennis courts and a golf course, are expected and appreciated at this 235-acre park. More unusual is a grove of exotic trees, many of them Asian imports, planted in the 19th century by Parsons Nursery. Long forgotten, the grove was rediscovered only in 1981. *Nature Center: Rose Ave. and Parsons Blvd., Kissena, 718/217–6034 Subway: Main St./Flushing.*

staten island

1 *a-4*

CLAY PIT PONDS STATE PARK PRESERVE

This 260-acre former clay mine is unique for its location at the terminal point for some northern and southern plant species, which live in its swamps, bogs, spring-fed streams, sandy barrens, wetlands, and woodlands along with numerous species of birds, reptiles, amphibians, and mammals. Birders, horseback riders, and hikers are welcome on trails during daylight hours, and the nature center leads weekend programs (advance registration required) year-round. An interesting novelty is the composting toilet, which you'll have to use if nature calls. *Entrance off Carlin St., Charleston, 718/967–1976. Nature center open Mon.–Sat. 9–5.*

4 *a-7*

CLOVE LAKES PARK

Bucolic pleasures at this popular and picturesque park, created by the damming of an ancient glacial valley, include a brook, waterfalls, a quartet of lakes, forests of oaks and beeches, and picnic grounds. The more active might enjoy ice skating, horseback riding, football, softball, jogging, and fishing. *Clove Rd. near Victory Blvd., Sunnyside, 718/390–8000.*

1 *b-3*

EVERGREEN PARK

Rare ferns and orchids grow in the 22½ acres of Staten Island's newest park. *Greaves St. between Dewey Ave. and Evergreen St., Great Kills.*

1 *d-8*

FORT WADSWORTH

First used during the Revolutionary War, this military installation was an active part of the harbor defense system up until the 1970s. Because of its location just off the Verrazano Narrows Bridge, it's tromped on by thousands of runners (and becomes the site of the world's longest urinal) at the start of the New York City Marathon. Now part of Gateway National Recreation Area and newly open to the public, the place has a 1½-mi self-guided trail around its fortifications. Other ranger-led tours can be reserved in advance. *Bay St. at Wadsworth Ave., Shore Acres, 718/354–4500. Open Sun.*

1 *b-2*

GREENBELT

One of New York's newer large parks (land acquisition began in 1964), Greenbelt is also one of the best. Designed by the last of the great glaciers, its nearly 2,000 contiguous acres comprise linked woodlands, meadows, ponds, wetlands, golf courses, and cemeteries, all form-

ing a green ring in the center of Staten Island. The rambling woods, teeming with plant and animal wildlife, are all the more remarkable given the developed lands—including the Fresh Kills landfill—that border them. The park protects five kinds of owls, shelters the most northerly example of the sweetbay magnolia tree, is home to more than 50 species of birds, and grows such rare wildflowers as blue cohosh and Virginia waterleaf. Hikers have 28 mi of trails to cover, so it's a good idea to carry a map (available at the main office). Urban Park Rangers lead hikes, bird walks, and other nature activities. *Office: 200 Nevada Ave., Egbertville, 718/667–2165. Office open weekdays 9–4.*

1 *b-2*

HIGH ROCK PARK IN THE GREENBELT

Bird-watching is especially good in this 86-acre section of peaceful woods. A visit to the environmental education center is on many schools' calendars, but it offers walks, talks, and exhibits to all. *200 Nevada Ave., Egbertville, 718/667–2165. Center open weekdays 9–4.*

1 *b-2*

LA TOURETTE PARK IN THE GREENBELT

This 511-acre park features a beautiful golf course and clubhouse—once the farmland and mansion of the La Tourette family—as well as wooded and uninterrupted wetland trails popular with cross-country skiers in winter. The best trail is Buck's Hollow. *Forest Hill and Richmond Hill Rds., Richmondtown.*

1 *c-2*

MILLER FIELD

Like Fort Wadsworth, this is a former military base (U.S. Army) that's now part of Gateway National Recreation Area, and tours sometimes focus on its military history (it has two post–World War I hangars). It's Staten Island's host for summer opera and Philharmonic concerts. *Between New Dorp and Elmtree Sts., New Dorp, 718/351–6970.*

1 *d-8*

VON BRIESEN PARK

A small but meticulously groomed city park, Von Briesen somehow doesn't attract many people. Its elevated, harbor-front location provides a stunning panorama of lower Manhattan, the

Upper and Lower New York bays, and Brooklyn. *Bay St. and Wadsworth Ave., Shore Acres.*

1 *a-2*

WILLIAM T. DAVIS WILDLIFE REFUGE

Named for noted Staten Island naturalist William Thompson Davis, these 802 acres of dry and wetland attract many birds rarely seen in this area, and the wide variety of habitats makes for an ideal sanctuary. *Travis Ave. off Richmond Ave., New Springville, 718/667–2165.*

1 *a-2*

WILLOWBROOK PARK IN THE GREENBELT

American soldiers called it the Great Swamp when they hid here during the Revolutionary War, but Willowbrook is now one of Staten Island's more popular parks. Picnic tables, a fishing lake, athletic fields, an archery range, horseshoe pitches, a playground, and a kite-flying area are spread throughout the 164 acres. *Victory Blvd. and Richmond Ave., New Springville, 718/698–2186.*

other green spaces

BEACHES

Manhattan lacks a sandswept beach, but that doesn't stop anyone from sunbathing—on rooftops ("tar beaches"), river piers ("splinter beaches"), and parks ("Manhattan Rivieras"). The other boroughs, however, are blessed with miles and miles of beaches, all easily accessible by bus, subway, or car. City beaches are officially open from Memorial Day weekend to Labor Day, sunrise to midnight, with swimming allowed when lifeguards are on duty (usually 10 AM–6 PM).

bronx

2 *g-2*

ORCHARD BEACH

For sun, sand, and salsa, this section of Pelham Bay Park is the place. A white-sand, crescent-shape beauty on the Long Island Sound, Orchard Beach was one of Robert Moses's pride and joys. It draws crowds, largely from the Bronx's Latino population. *Shore Rd. and City Island Rd., Eastchester, 718/885–2275. Drinking water, grills, picnic tables, phones, restrooms, showers, snack bar. Subway: Pelham Bay Park.*

brooklyn

4 *h-6*

BRIGHTON BEACH

Brighton Beach is actually the "beginning" of the beach that becomes Coney Island farther west. At this end you'll find locals: mothers with children, older retired folks, and Russians who have emigrated to this shore, commonly called "Odessa by the Sea." The boardwalk has little but benches, so bring your lunch or buy it on your way. *15th St. to Ocean Pkwy., Brighton. Drinking water, phones. Subway: Brighton Beach; Ocean Pkwy.*

4 *g-7*

CONEY ISLAND BEACH

Named for the rabbits that were once its main inhabitants (from the Dutch *Konijn Eiland*), Coney Island began its resort days in the 1830s, when elegant hotels drew the elite. Railroads were eventually built to connect it with other parts of Brooklyn, carting in people attracted to its increasing array of entertainment: horse races, sporting events, amusement parks, and, of course, beaches. The first roller coaster opened in 1884, and by 1904 there were three amusement parks. It's now a mere shadow of its early-20th-century self, but Coney Island still has a fine 2½-mi sandy beach and a 2-mi boardwalk with everything you'd expect to find at a beach resort (cotton candy, soft ice cream) plus a few unique extras—Nathan's hot dogs, bona fide freak shows, and a landmark roller coaster (the Cyclone). Hot summer days have brought as many as a million people to Coney Island at once, which at times makes it a bit difficult to find a place in the sun without stepping on someone else's blanket. *Ocean Pkwy. to 37th St., 718/946–1350. Drinking water, phones. Subway: Stillwell Ave./Coney Island.*

1 *f-8*

MANHATTAN BEACH

This small beach draws a young and energetic crowd and is a nice place for sunning and swimming. Adjacent to the beach is a park, with barbecue facilities as well as handball, tennis, and basketball. *Ocean Ave. between Oriental Blvd. and MacKenzie St., 718/946–1373. Drinking water, picnic tables, phones, restrooms, showers, snack bar. Subway: Brighton Beach.*

queens

1 g-7
JACOB RIIS PARK

Just over the Marine Parkway Bridge from Brooklyn, this mile-long stretch of Rockaway Beach was named for the Danish reformer-photographer and is part of the Gateway National Recreation Area. There is a concrete "boardwalk" for strolling and a wide, sandy beach. Sports facilities include softball fields and paddle-tennis courts. Though it draws crowds, the less central areas are usually peaceful enough. *Beach 149th–Beach 169th Sts., 718/318–4300. Drinking water, grills, picnic tables, phones, rest rooms, snack bar. Access: Flatbush Ave. to Marine Pkwy./Gil Hodges Memorial Bridge.*

1 h-7
ROCKAWAY BEACH

Nearly 10 mi of glorious sandy beach and 7½ mi of boardwalk fronting the Atlantic form the core of this recreational area, with surfable waves and relatively clean water adding to the appeal. Best of all, the A train can get you—and everyone else—here. Due to lifeguard shortages, beach erosion, and plover nestings, parts of the strand were closed in recent years; call ahead before reaching for your towel and Metrocard. *Beach 1st–Beach 149th Sts., 718/318–4000. Drinking water, picnic tables, phones, rest rooms, showers, snack bar. Subway: Rockaway Park/Beach 116 St.*

staten island

1 c-3
GREAT KILLS PARK

Built on landfill, with a major recent cleanup and renovations to the actual beach as well as public buildings, Great Kills offers surfable waves, a marina, fields, a public boat ramp, a model-airplane flying field, fishing, and trails. Migrating monarch butterflies stop here in late summer and fall. *Hylan Blvd. and Hopkins Ave., 718/987–6729. Drinking water, picnic tables, phones, rest rooms, showers, snack bar.*

4 d-8
MIDLAND AND SOUTH BEACH

Connected by the **Franklin D. Roosevelt Boardwalk,** which starts at Miller Field and continues for 7,500 ft, these two beaches are sandy and attractive. Midland is somewhat cleaner, though South Beach has been improved in recent years. You can fish off the boardwalk until 1 PM, except in summer. Even if you don't want to swim, you might enjoy the view of lower New York Bay. *From Miller Field to Fort Wadsworth, parallel to Fr. Capodanno Blvd., 718/987–0709 (Midland), 718/816–6804 (South). Drinking water, grills, picnic tables, phones, rest rooms, showers.*

1 b-4
WOLFE'S POND PARK

This 312-acre park has saltwater swimming and surfing, a large wooded area, a freshwater lake, and rustic picnic settings. *Holton–Cornelia Aves. on Raritan Bay, Prince's Bay, 718/984–8266. Changing rooms, drinking water, grills, picnic tables, phones, rest rooms, showers.*

long island

New York's Atlantic beaches don't stop at the city line, but extend out past Rockaway along Long Island all the way to The End (Montauk). Several are popular among New York City day-trippers. **Long Beach**—a unique community in that its street plan discourages cars—has a mile-long boardwalk. **Jones Beach,** built by Robert Moses, has beautiful bathhouses and teems with happy crowds, though it's big enough that if you're willing to walk, you can escape the densely packed bodies. **Robert Moses State Park,** on the westernmost tip of Fire Island, is also easy to reach from New York, but it draws more of a Long Island crowd. The Long Island Rail Road offers package day trips to all three beaches, and others, for under $15; call 718/217–LIRR.

BOTANICAL GARDENS

New York City's first botanical garden opened in 1801, covering 20 acres that is now Rockefeller Center; it was the first public garden in the country. Today, each borough has its own public botanical garden and many smaller horticultural delights as well.

bronx

2 c-4

NEW YORK BOTANICAL GARDEN

This 250-acre garden, founded in 1891, was patterned after the Royal Botanical Gardens at Kew, England. Every season is spectacular. The **Peggy Rockefeller Rose Garden** has 2,700 bushes of 230 different varieties; the **Arlow B. Stout Daylily Garden** glows in July; and there are also an herb garden, an azalea glen (spectacular in May), a pine grove, a rock garden full of Alpine plants (admission $1), trails through 40 acres of old-growth forest, and much more. The 11 interconnecting galleries of the **Enid A. Haupt Conservatory** (which closes an hour earlier than the garden grounds), including a striking Victorian glasshouse that reopened in 1997 following a major restoration, showcase plant life around the world and seasonal flower shows. A restored 1840 **Snuff Mill** overlooking the Bronx River and a stone cottage from the same year are other man-made treasures. Narrated tram tours (tickets $1) run every 30 minutes and can transport you across the immense grounds, while walks and self-guided tours focus on topics and areas of special interest. The 12-acre **Everett Children's Adventure Garden**, which opened in 1998, has a hedge maze, hands-on gardening, and other discovery activities, indoors and out. *Bronx Park at 200th St. and Southern Blvd., 718/817–8700, 718/817–8779 for directions. Admission: garden $3, conservatory $3.50, Garden Passport (all admissions and tram tour) $10. Free Wed., Sat. 10–noon. Open Apr.–Oct., Tues.–Sun. and Mon. holidays 10–6, Nov.–Mar. 10–4. Subway: Bedford Park Blvd.*

2 a-3

WAVE HILL

A nonprofit environmental center, these 28 acres overlook the Hudson and the Palisades from their Riverdale location. The former estate of conservation-minded financier George Perkins, rented at various times to Theodore Roosevelt, Mark Twain, and Arturo Toscanini, Wave Hill was donated to the city in 1960. With 18 acres of gardens, it has greenhouses (open limited hours) and exquisite herb, wildflower, and aquatic gardens. Directors of other public gardens come from all over the country to admire the plants and their unusual juxtapositions, which change from year to year. Family art projects, guided garden walks, an art museum, and concerts round out the possibilities. *Main entrance: 249th St. and Independence Ave., Riverdale, 718/549–3200. Admission: $4; free Nov. 16–Mar. 14. Open Tues.–Sun. 9–4:30, and until dusk on Wednesday during the summer. Metro-North: Harlem Line to Riverdale.*

brooklyn

4 e-1

BROOKLYN BOTANIC GARDEN

Founded in 1910 on the site of a city dump, Brooklyn's garden is just one-fifth the size of its Bronx cousin, but within its 52 acres are more than enough wonders to fill a day. Spring flowers include Japanese cherry trees along the **Cherry Esplanade,** magnolias in **Magnolia Plaza,** lilacs in the **Louisa Clark Spencer Lilac Collection,** and daffodils on **Daffodil Hill.** More than 5,000 varieties of roses bloom through the summer in the **Cranford Rose Garden.** The **Shakespeare Garden** contains 80 plants mentioned by the playwright in his works. Lots of giant carp and turtles call the **Japanese Hill-and-Pond Garden** home, and the lily pools are another unusual delight. Other green attractions include the **Fragrance Garden,** designed for the blind but a pleasure for all; an herb garden; a rock garden; and a garden planted only with flora from the metropolitan region. While most of the **Steinhardt Conservatory** follows the "Trail of Evolution," one room has dozens of bonsai plants. Free guided tours leave from the conservatory at 1 PM on weekends. *1000 Washington Ave. (at Carroll St.), Park Slope, 718/623–7200. Admission: $3, free Tues. Open Apr.–Sept., Tues.–Fri. 8–6, weekends and Mon. holidays 10–6; Oct.–Mar., Tues.–Fri. 8–4:30, weekends and holidays 10–4:30. Subway: Grand Army Plaza, Eastern Pkwy./Brooklyn Museum.*

manhattan

5 a-7

THE CLOISTERS GARDEN

Green-thumbed monks from the 15th century would be right at home with the 250 species of plants and flowers planted among the cloisters here. The Gothic **Trie Cloister** houses the 50 species identified in the museum's *Uni-*

corn Tapestries. Flowering bulbs are displayed year-round in the skylighted **St. Guilhem Cloister.** *Fort Tryon Park (see Parks, above). Subway: A to 190th St.*

7 *d-4*

CONSERVATORY GARDEN
Established in 1937, this formal, 6-acre garden is almost secretly ensconced in a forgotten corner of Central Park. Named for the elegant old greenhouses that stood here before the Depression, the garden is a lavishly landscaped conglomerate: an ornate and manicured French garden, a classic old Italian garden flanked by crab-apple allées, and a densely planted perennial garden. Opening onto the main lawn is the handsome wrought-iron Vanderbilt Gate, a popular spot for wedding portraits. *5th Ave. and 105th St., Central Park, 212/360–2766. Open daily 8 AM–dusk. Subway: 6 to 103rd St.*

11 *g-3*

LIZ CHRISTY MEMORIAL GARDEN
Planted in 1972 by the Green Guerrillas, this tiny but lush garden is an unlikely rest stop. Since its creation, hundreds of other community gardens have sprung up in vacant lots around the city. *Northeast corner of Houston St. and Bowery, East Village. Open May–Sept., daily noon–4. Subway: 2nd Ave.*

7 *c-8*

SHAKESPEARE GARDEN
This garden grew from seeds and cuttings of the same mulberry and hawthorn trees Shakespeare himself once tended. The lushly landscaped terraced hill provides a peaceful setting. *Central Park near W. 81st St., south of Delacorte Theater. Subway: B, C to 81st St.*

queens

1 *f-3*

QUEENS BOTANICAL GARDEN
Originally created for the 1939–40 World's Fair, held at Flushing Meadows, and later transplanted here, the garden is now 39 acres of specialized plantings. Stepping in here from Main Street feels like entering someone's backyard. Then, though, you see the bridal parties traipsing through to pose in the gazebo in the Wedding Garden. The best green attraction here is the rose garden, which has

1,440 bushes (as well as 13,000 tulips). Other treats include bird and bee gardens, a pine cove, and formal flower plantings along the center mall. *43–50 Main St., Flushing, 718/886–3800. Open Apr.–Oct., Tues.–Fri. 8–6, weekends 8–7; Nov.–Mar., Tues.–Sun. 8–4:30. Subway: Main St./Flushing.*

staten island

4 *a-6*

STATEN ISLAND BOTANICAL GARDEN
Visit the Snug Harbor Cultural Center and you can't help but stumble upon this garden, a newcomer to the outerborough botanical-garden scene (established 1977) and a trove of English perennials. Other highlights are a Chinese garden, a pond garden, special plants meant to attract butterflies, and a greenhouse that houses the Neil Vanderbilt Orchid Collection. *Richmondtown Terr. from Tysen St. to Kissel Ave., Snug Harbor, 718/273–8200. Open daily dawn–dusk.*

zoos, aquariums, & wildlife preserves

Haven't you heard? It's no longer politically correct to call them zoos— "wildlife conservation centers" more accurately describes their missions, and all but the Staten Island Zoo are run by the Wildlife Conservation Society (718/220–5100), headquartered at the Bronx Zoo. But no matter the name, these great centers of animal life draw millions of New Yorkers every year. Most were completely renovated in the late 1980s and early '90s to better serve both inhabitants and admirers.

bronx

2 *b-3*

BRONX ZOO/WILDLIFE CONSERVATION PARK
Who knew you could visit a baboon reserve, smell a skunk, watch sea lions laze around on a simulation of the rocky California coastline, and penetrate the world of animal nightlife, all in the Bronx? Opened in Bronx Park in 1899,

this 265-acre behemoth is the world's largest urban zoo. About 6,000 animals of 612 species live here, mainly in realistic habitats and often separated from you by no more than a moat—accommodations include Himalayan highlands (snow leopards, red pandas, and cranes), the rugged Patagonian coast (penguins, terns, and cormorants), and African plains (lions, gazelles, and zebras, among others). The Beaux Arts **Keith W. Johnson Zoo Center**'s elephants and tapirs; the **World of Reptiles'** crocs, snakes, and turtles; and separate giraffe, mouse, monkey, and aquatic bird houses are among the popular indoor exhibits. Bats, naked moles, rats and other nocturnal critters are fooled into thinking it's night—which means they're awake for you—in the **World of Darkness.** The **Congo Gorilla Forest** opened in 1999, and its 6-plus acres of African rain forest are home to 19 gorillas and 75 different species of wildlife. (The exhibit's $3 admission is donated to conservation efforts in Africa.) In season, you can perambulate via shuttle and skyfari through the entire zoo, take the **Bengali Express Monorail** through **Wild Asia**, or opt for a leisurely camel ride. Children are encouraged to act out their animal instincts, whether it's sitting in a nest, wearing a turtle shell, or outfoxing a fox at the **Children's Zoo** (Apr.–Oct., $2 adults; $1.50 children 2–12); they can also pet and feed domestic animals. *Fordham Rd. at Bronx River Pkwy., Bronx Park, 718/367–1010. Admission: Apr.–Oct. $7.75, Nov.–Jan. $6, Feb.–Mar. $4, free Wed. year-round. Open Apr.–Oct., weekdays 10–5, weekends 10–5:30; Nov.–Mar., daily 10–4:30. Subway: 2 to Pelham Pkwy.*

brooklyn

4 h-7

AQUARIUM FOR WILDLIFE CONSERVATION

The New York Aquarium was immensely popular at its Castle Clinton, Manhattan, location from its inception in 1896 until its closing (by Robert Moses) in 1941. After moving temporarily to the Bronx, the aquatic creatures found a new home in Coney Island in 1957. Inside this 14-acre complex you can hear beluga whales whistle and moan, look massive sharks in the eye, and drool over the walrus's 400-pound weekly ration of squid, smelt, and herring. All told, the aquarium has about 7,500 residents, including mammals (otters, dolphins, whales, seals), birds (penguins), reptiles (sea turtles), cartilaginous fish (sharks, rays, skate), bony fish (tarpon, eels, trout, cod, piranhas, puffers), and invertebrates (jellyfish, sea urchins, lobsters, mollusks), some of them lucky enough to live in beachside outdoor pools. Dolphins and sea lions perform in the 1,600-seat Aquatheater, and penguins, sharks, sea otters, seals, walruses, and other creatures don't mind if you watch them eat. Curious children can check out jellyfish, walk under a crashing wave, and touch crabs and sea urchins in the Discovery Cove. *W. 8th St. and Surf Ave., Coney Island, 718/265–FISH. Admission: $8.75. Open Memorial Day–Labor Day, weekdays 10–5, weekends and holidays 10–6; Labor Day–Memorial Day daily 10–5. Subway: W. 8th St./Aquarium.*

4 3-1

PROSPECT PARK WILDLIFE CENTER

This small zoo focuses on small animals, like prairie dogs, wallabies, baboons, and capybaras. "The World of Animals," "Animal Lifestyles," and "Animals in our Lives" exhibit areas help children learn by observing, mimicking, and touching. *450 Flatbush Ave., Prospect Park, 718/399–7339. Admission: $2.50. Open Apr.–Oct., weekdays 10–5, weekends and holidays 10–5:30; Nov.–Mar. daily 10–4:30. Subway: D, Q to Prospect Park.*

manhattan

9 d-2

CENTRAL PARK WILDLIFE CENTER

Much of New York's oldest zoo has been demolished (though several of the WPA-era buildings have been restored), and a more modern, more humane, 6-acre habitat has taken its place. Clustered around the central **Sea Lion Pool** are separate exhibits for each of the earth's major environments: the **Polar Circle** features a huge penguin tank and polar-bear ice floe; the open-air **Temperate Territory** is highlighted by a pit of chattering monkeys; and the **Tropic Zone** contains the flora and fauna of a miniature rain forest. The **Tisch Children's Zoo**, on the north side of Denesmouth Arch, reopened in fall 1997 after a complete reconstruction. In its Enchanted Forest, small animals such as rabbits, frogs, and free-flying birds are all at home; children learn to relate to their fellow creatures by hopping on lily pads, peering underwater through a fish's-eye lens, and fidgeting with other interactive amusements. *Entrance: 5th Ave. and 64th St., Central Park, 212/439–6500. Admission: $3.50. Open Apr.–Oct., weekdays 10–5, weekends and holidays 10:30–5:30; Nov.–Mar., daily 10–4:30. Subway: N, R to 5th Ave.*

queens

3 *h-2*

QUEENS WILDLIFE CENTER

About 340 animals of just over 50 American species live in this lightly populated, 11-acre zoo. Strolling through treetops amid free-flying birds in the aviary is a highlight. Outside, elk are at home on the range, speckled bears play in their pseudo-Adirondack territory, and sea lions swim off a faux Pacific Coast. You can paw domesticated plants and animals in the petting zoo. *53–51 111th St., Flushing Meadows–Corona Park, 718/271–1500. Admission: $2.50. Open Apr.–Oct., weekdays 10–5, weekends and holidays 10–5:30; Nov.–Mar. daily 10–4:30. Subway: 7 to 111th St.*

staten island

1 *c-8*

STATEN ISLAND ZOO

Operated by its own Staten Island Zoological Society, this small zoo (established 1936) is known for its reptiles, especially rattlesnakes, who slither through the **Serpentarium.** Shrimp and sharks jockey for position in the aquarium, otters goof around in an outdoor pool, and endangered South American plants and animals live in an indoor re-creation of a tropical forest. Leopards and baboons lurk in the theatrical **African Savannah at Twilight** exhibit. The feeding schedule isn't for the faint of heart—mealtimes for reptiles, sharks, piranha, and bats are scheduled for your visiting pleasure. If you're weak-kneed, you might find the domesticated farm animals at the outdoor children's center more enjoyable. *614 Broadway, Barrett Park, 718/442–3100. Admission: $3, free Wed. after 2. Open daily 10–4:45.*

sports & outdoor activities

With nearly 8 million people living within the city limits, New York could field a winning team in just about any sport. Organized amateur options range from casual leagues and clubs, where socializing is as important as the game, to extremely competitive teams with die-hard coaches. If you can't find exactly what you're looking for, ask your friends, check the Yellow Pages, or call the Parks Department (*see* Parks Information, *above*); it's got to be around here somewhere. Ongoing leagues abound, especially for such popular sports as basketball and softball; check with your employer, school, or local gym for information. Chelsea Piers (*see* Fitness Centers, Health Clubs, & Spa Services, *below*) and the Yorkville Sport Association (212/645–6488), for example, arrange many.

If your idea of a good workout is *watching* a great game, you're still in luck. New York's professional baseball, basketball, football, hockey, and soccer teams play in local stadiums, and these same arenas host a full calendar of various sporting events year-round.

BASEBALL

Many places in and around New York claim an important role in baseball's history, and the sport remains one of New York's favorite pastimes. You're either a Mets fan or a Yankees fan, period; and you'd better choose your friends carefully, because allegiances run deep. Since 1997 the Mets and the Yankees have played each other a few times a year during the regular season, and came closer than ever to a subway series in '99. The professional baseball season runs from early April through September, a few weeks longer if your team is lucky. Tickets are usually available both in advance and at the stadium on game day.

where to watch

6 *f-5*

NEW YORK YANKEES

Home games for this much beloved American League team are at **Yankee**

Stadium (*see* Sports Stadiums, *below*). The Bronx Bombers' petulant owner, George Steinbrenner, has threatened to pick up and move his boys into New Jersey—or, heaven forbid, Manhattan—but ever since they won the World Series in '96, '98, and again in '99, bigger crowds have been returning to the South Bronx. *718/293–6000.*

3 *h-1*
NEW YORK METS

It's not easy being a Mets fan these days, what with all the attention paid to the Yankees' taking the pennant and threatening to leave the city. Let them go! Still, the National League Mets have a large and spirited following. Home games are at **Shea Stadium** (*see* Sports Stadiums, *below*), in Flushing, Queens. *718/507–8499.*

where to play

There are hundreds of municipal baseball facilities in the city, but many of them are reserved by softball and baseball leagues. For details on permits, *see* Permits *under* Parks, *above*.

BASKETBALL

The regular men's professional season (NBA) runs in the winter, from November to April. Women (WNBA) have been slotted into the traditionally slow summer season, mid-June–August. In addition to teams listed below, **Madison Square Garden** (*see* Sports Stadiums, *below*) often hosts college games in winter.

where to watch

NEW JERSEY NETS

The up-and-coming Nets can be seen at the Continental Airlines Arena. *Meadowlands Sports Complex, East Rutherford, NJ, 201/935–3900.*

9 *c-6*
NEW YORK KNICKS

Latrell Sprewell and Co. play to intense sell-out crowds at Madison Square Garden. *7th Ave. between 31st and 33rd Sts., Midtown, 212/465–JUMP. Subway: 34th St./Penn Station.*

9 *c-6*
NEW YORK LIBERTY

They play halves instead of quarters and use a smaller ball than the men, but the Women's National Basketball Association (WNBA) is as full of fierce competition as the NBA, and it's been gaining popularity and respect since its 1997 inaugural season. Olympic champ Rebecca Lobo is the center for New York's team, which plays at Madison Square Garden. *7th Ave. between 31st and 33rd Sts., Midtown, 212/564–WNBA.*

where to play

Call the Parks Department (*see* Parks Information, *above*) for the basketball court nearest you—in some neighborhoods they're on almost every corner. Hoops on Manhattan's West 4th Street (at 6th Ave.) often have lively games with spectators. Other popular pickup locations in Manhattan are on West 76th Street (at Columbus Ave.), at Asphalt Green (90th St. at York Ave.), and at Riverbank State Park (*see* Parks, *above*).

BICYCLING

With all of its long, flat, paved stretches, New York City should be a biker's dream. Unfortunately, motor vehicle traffic, potholes, and pollution make it one big obstacle course. Still, there are some good recreational routes, especially in parks and along the waterfront, and biking is often the fastest and most convenient way to get around town. The Department of Transportation (Bicycle Program, 212/442–9890) and Department of City Planning (Bicycle Network Development Program, 212/442–4713) produce highly-detailed bicycle maps for each borough; in addition to showing recommended routes (greenways and paths as well as street routes), these pinpoint bike shops and explain cycling regulations. They are free and can be found at the Department of City Planning Bookstore (22 Reade St., 212/720–3300) and at bike shops around town. Even if you read up, though, navigating roads and figuring out how to access bridges can be challenging, so ride with someone who's experienced before setting out on your own.

Bicycles are considered vehicles, which means they have to stop at red lights, obey speed limits, stay off sidewalks (if the rider's over 13 years old), and ride in the direction of traffic. In city parks, riding off trails is not allowed. Children under 14 must wear helmets. Bikes are permitted on the subway and the Staten Island ferry without a permit, and most other regional mass transport allows them with a free or inexpensive permit; **Transportation Alternatives** (*see below*) can provide details. The city's bike clubs send out calendars to their members, who generally pay a modest annual fee, but welcome everyone on rides.

CENTURY ROAD CLUB ASSOCIATION

The CRCA has been around for more than 100 years and is for *serious* racers. The club holds Saturday races in Central Park and offers coaching, clinics, and a monthly newsletter. *212/222–8062.*

FAST AND FABULOUS CYCLING CLUB

This lesbian and gay outfit was formed when a group of tri-athletes began training for the Gay Games in 1994. It holds weekly rides in and out of the city for every level of rider. *212/567–7160.*

FIVE BOROUGH BICYCLE CLUB

The 5BBC has road and all-terrain bike (ATB) rides for all levels year-round, with many especially suited to cyclists not used to heavy mileage. Its parent organization, American Youth Hostels, is also the parent of **Bike New York,** which puts on an annual mass tour of the five boroughs in early May (*see* Sporting Events, *below*). *891 Amsterdam Ave. (at 103rd St.), 212/932–2300.*

NEW YORK CYCLE CLUB

This club has something for everybody. Rides are classified by average speed, and the calendar has trips for all cyclists from beginners to pace-line racers. One member describes it as the "most aggressively enthusiastic club in the city." Its annual Escape from New York century ride (110 mi, usually in late Sept. or early Oct.) is a nice, early-fall break. *212/828–5711.*

STATEN ISLAND BICYCLING ASSOCIATION

Staten Island and New Jersey are the usual focus for this group's day rides. They're categorized by level and include mountain-biking outings and additional weekly on-island spins on Wednesday and Saturday. *718/605–2453.*

TIME'S UP

Time's Up promotes environmental awareness through biking. Rides are generally just one or two hours, but offer unique glimpses of the city. The monthly Central Park Moonlight Ride, for example, travels the scenic paths. Other regular rides are the critical-mass attempt and historic tours. Though the club produces a free calendar every once in a while, you're better off calling for upcoming events. *212/802–8222.*

TRANSPORTATION ALTERNATIVES

The city's bicycle-and-pedestrian advocacy group gets its members discounts at several bike stores and can help you decrease the amount of pollution in your life. Its bimonthly newsletter, **"City Cyclist,"** available in bike stores throughout the city, lists rides and events of interest to cyclists. Every September, TA organizes a century (100-mi) ride within city boundaries. *115 W. 30th St., Suite 1207, 212/629–8080.*

bronx

Mosholu Parkway and **Pelham Parkway** are paralleled by scenic bike routes for miles and they connect the borough's two premier greenspaces, Van Cortland Park and Pelham Bay Park, where you'll find Orchard Beach and routes to City Island, an area that feels like coastal New England set to a salsa beat. The Bronx Chapter of Transportation Alternatives (718/653–2203; *see above*) leads tours throughout the borough.

brooklyn

The 3½-mi loop road in **Prospect Park** provides excellent cycling, especially when the park is closed to cars (*see* Parks, *above*). Beware a short strip on the eastern side of the park near the boathouse and skating rink—cars can access the parking lot at all times. The **Ocean Parkway** bike path, which turned 100 in 1995, starts just outside the southwest exit of Prospect Park and ends about 6 mi later, near Coney Island, where the boardwalk is open to cyclists before 10 AM. Along the parkway, you ride on elevated medians in the shade of trees. The **Shore Parkway Path** goes from Owl's Head Park, in Bay Ridge, under the Verrazano Narrows Bridge to Bay 8th in Bensonhurst, and picks up again off Emmons Avenue in Sheepshead Bay. From here you can connect to a path that runs parallel to **Flatbush Avenue** and brings you to Rockaway, or continue to Jamaica Bay.

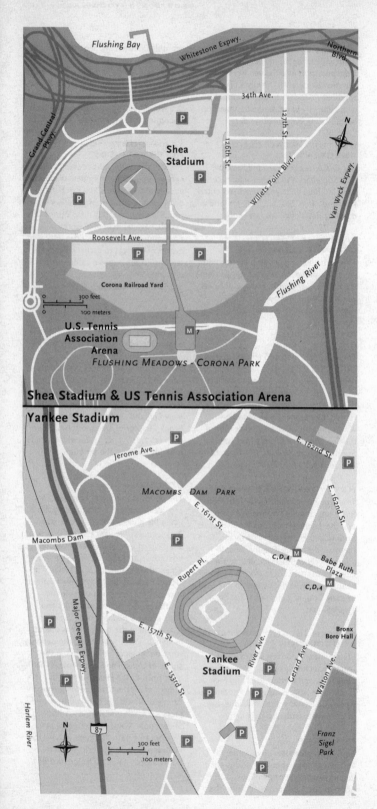

Shea Stadium & US Tennis Association Arena

Yankee Stadium

The Meadowlands

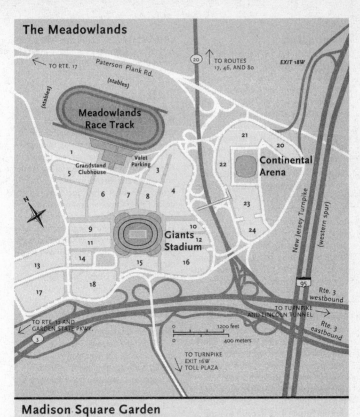

Madison Square Garden

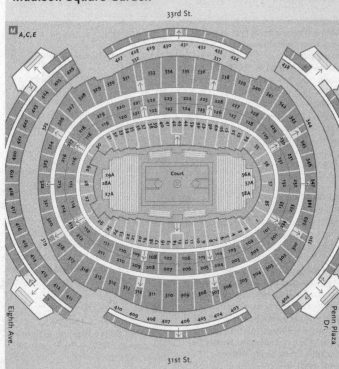

manhattan

The 6-mi loop road in **Central Park** probably logs the most cycler miles in the city, but it's often crowded (sometimes with cars, when they're allowed in, forcing bikers, bladers, and joggers to share a narrow lane) and requires adept navigation skills. Always beware other park users. Bike rentals are available at the boathouse (212/861–4137). Leaving Central Park, the **Broadway/St. Nicholas Avenue** bike lane brings you nearly to the **George Washington Bridge,** whose pedestrian crossway gives cyclists spectacular views up and down the Hudson and easy access to Palisades Interstate Park (River Road, left off the bridge and then left again, is a hilly favorite) and Route 9W in New Jersey. Lower Manhattan is surrounded by greenways—**Hudson River Park** from Battery Park to West 14th Street gets crowded with cruising bikers and skaters; the path along **East River Park** is much greener and less congested. Uptown, you can bike right along the water in the West Side's **Riverside Park** and from 61st Street up to 125th Street on the **East River Esplanade** between the F.D.R. Drive and the water's edge. From April to October a bridge at 103rd Street is open, leading to the calm expanse of Randall's Island.

The south outer roadway of the **Queensboro Bridge** is open to cyclists (except for a temporary closing during afternoon rush hour, when bikes must be carted in a free shuttle bus), and the north outer roadway opened full-time in the fall of 1999. The walkway on the **Williamsburg Bridge** has recently been renovated and cyclists and skaters split the spectacular elevated roadway/boardwalk on the **Brooklyn Bridge.** All of the Manhattan–Bronx bridges accommodate cyclists as well.

queens

Rockaway Peninsula is a long, flat strip crying out for your cruiser on either the road or the boardwalk; take the Marine Parkway Bridge from Brooklyn's Flatbush Avenue bike path. In **Forest Park,** near the Brooklyn border, take the main road for a gorgeous ride through the woods. **Flushing Meadows–Corona Park** has lakeside routes as well as plenty of pavement separating playing fields and attractions. The lack of hills makes it popular with families, and rentals are available by the tennis stadium (718/699–9598). The few miles of bike path

on the west edge of **Little Neck Bay, Fort Totten,** and **Little Bay Park** have great views of the Long Island Sound.

staten island

Staten Island's traffic often seems less threatening than that of other boroughs—which helps make up for the lack of separate bike paths on this park-filled island. For a relaxing and scenic ride, take the ferry and then follow Front and Edgewater streets to Fort Wadsworth, after which you can head down Father Capodanno Boulevard along several beaches on the eastern shore. The **Bayonne Bridge,** with its narrow pedestrian crossway separated from the main part of the bridge, makes for an exhilarating trip into New Jersey, where you'll find lovely Liberty State Park.

BILLIARDS

Trends come and go, but the city's pool halls are a recreational mainstay. The sport is no longer synonymous with smoky and vaguely sinister halls, but don't let that stop you from enjoying a game or two. Tables usually cost $10–$15 per hour, many halls have lounges and/or snack bars attached, and most operate around-the-clock.

7 b-8

AMSTERDAM BILLIARD CLUB

This upscale club, partly owned by comedian David Brenner, has 31 tables. The newer East Side location is equally well-equipped. *344 Amsterdam Ave. (at 77th St.), Upper West Side, 212/496–8180. Subway: 79th St.*

7 f-7

210 E. 86th St., Upper East Side, 212/570–4545. Subway: 4, 5, 6 to 86th St.

9 c-8

THE BILLIARD CLUB

High ceilings, velvet curtains, and pseudo-Victorian decor give this place class. The 33 tables help, too. *220 W. 19th St., Chelsea, 212/206–7665. Subway: C, E to 23rd St.*

9 d-8

CHELSEA BILLIARDS

Crowds fill the two floors, looking to play pool or snooker—there are 50 pool tables and 8 snooker tables. *54 W. 21st St., 212/989–0096. Subway: F to 23rd St.*

10 *e-1*

CORNER BILLIARDS
East Village yuppies congregate around the 28 tables. *85 4th Ave. (at 11th St.), Greenwich Village, Manhattan, 212/995-1314. Subway: 14th St./Union Sq.*

10 *e-1*

LE Q
These 30 tables are among the cheapest in town: $3 per person, per hour. *36 E. 12th St., East Village, 212/995-8512. Subway: 14th St./Union Sq.*

11 *f-3*

SOHO BILLIARDS
These 28 tables have a choice NoHo location for after-hours action. *298 Mulberry St. (at Houston St.), Greenwich Village, 212/925-3753. Subway: Bleecker St.; Broadway-Lafayette St.*

9 *a-4*

WEST SIDE BILLIARD AND TABLE TENNIS CLUB
Several Ping-Pong tables complement the pool offerings (12 tables) at this western outpost. *601 W. 50th St., Hell's Kitchen, 212/246-1060. Subway: C, E to 50th St.*

BIRD-WATCHING

Pigeons (rock pigeons, if you're in the know) may be the first species that comes to mind when you think about avian life in the city, but New York City's parks, marshes, and woodlands are home to thousands of species of birds, including Canada geese, Kentucky warblers, fork-tailed flycatchers, downy woodpeckers, barn owls, dark-eyed juncos, and glossy ibises. The city is also on the Atlantic Flyway, a major spring and fall migratory route; birds heading to or from as far away as the High Arctic pass through. May is the best season for bird-watching, since the songbirds are in their freshest colors; the fall migration is less concentrated and less colorful. As the local chapter of our nation's premier birding organization, the New York City Audubon Society (71 W. 23rd St., Room 606, 212/691-7483) can fill you in on area bird walks and help you with your watching. Rare Bird Alert (212/979-3070) has up-to-the-minute news on what's been seen where. In addition to the sources below, check with the Urban Park Rangers (*see* Parks, *above*) for information on walks.

bronx

2 *c-4*

NEW YORK BOTANICAL GARDEN
Many species of birds live on garden grounds year-round or stop by seasonally. Great horned owls are most likely found in the grove of evergreen trees, while ring-necked pheasants prefer the wetlands, daffodil hill, and the rose garden. There are bird walks every Saturday and Sunday at 12:30 and there's an annual bird count in late December. *Bronx Park at 200th St. and Southern Blvd., 718/817-8700, 718/817-8779 for directions. Admission: garden $3, conservatory $3.50, Garden Passport (all admissions and tram tour) $10; free Wed., Sat. 10-noon. Open Apr.-Oct., Tues.-Sun. and Mon. holidays 10-6; Nov.-Mar., Tues.-Sun. 10-4. Subway: Bedford Park Blvd.*

2 *g-2*

PELHAM BAY PARK
The saltwater marsh and lagoon have been known to attract bald eagles, ospreys, and great horned owls. *Bruckner Blvd. and Middletown Rd., 718/430-1890. Pelham Bay Park Environmental Center (near Orchard Beach), 718/885-3466. Subway: Pelham Bay Park.*

brooklyn

1 *f-7*

MARINE PARK
A springtime warbler watch is part of each year's birding highlights at the marsh. *Inlet between Gerritsen and Flatbush Aves., inland to Fillmore Ave., between Burnet and E. 32nd Sts.*

1 *h-6*

PROSPECT PARK
Birds similar to those in Central Park (*see below*) settle in Prospect Park's lakes and hills. The Rose Garden, Midwood, Prospect Lake, and Lookout Hill are good viewing spots. *Park bordered by Flatbush Ave., Ocean Ave., Parkside Ave., Prospect Park SW, and Prospect Park W, 718/965-8999. Subway: Grand Army Plaza; D, Q to Prospect Park; F to 15th St./Prospect Park.*

manhattan

1 d-4

CENTRAL PARK

The Pond near East 59th Street, the Reservoir, the Ravine, and especially the Ramble are prime birding areas. Species that nest in the park include cardinals, gray catbirds, and mallard ducks; among those that pass through (typically March–mid-May) are blue-gray gnatcatchers, brown creepers, orioles, and warblers. The **Henry Luce Nature Observatory,** at Belvedere Castle (212/772–0210), loans out the *Discovery Kit* to help mainly (but not exclusively) children learn about park wildlife. The **Dana Discovery Center** (212/860–1370) invites families to learn birding basics while exploring northern sections of the park with the Family Bird Watching Club, a free program that meets Saturday at 11 AM in spring. *Park bordered by Central Park W, 59th St., 5th Ave., and 110th St. General information 212/360–3444. Subway: 59th St./Columbus Circle; N, R to 5th Ave.; B, C to 72nd–110th Sts.; for Dana Discovery Center, 2, 3 to 110th St./Central Park North.*

queens

1 g-3

ALLEY POND PARK

Shorebirds and small birds live in abundance in Alley Pond's woodlands and wetlands. The active **Queens County Bird Club** (718/939–6224) meets at the environmental center on the third Wednesday of every month. The club welcomes new birders and arranges slide programs and weekly trips (though fewer in July and August). *Grand Central Pkwy. at Winchester Blvd., Bayside.*

1 g-6

JAMAICA BAY WILDLIFE REFUGE

Ten percent of the bird species known to live in the continental United States have been spotted here. It's a prime habitat for waterfowl and shelters migrating shorebirds and wading birds such as herons, plovers, and sandpipers. The visitor center (Broad Channel Island, 718/318–4340) has more details. *Broad Channel, 718/318–4340. Subway: Broad Channel.*

staten island

1 a-4

CLAY PIT PONDS STATE PARK PRESERVE

More than 40 species of birds breed in the preserve's fields, wetlands, barrens, and streams, and about 170 species live here. The visitor center has a checklist of birds you might see, and when you might see them. *Entrance off Carlin St., Charleston, 718/967–1976. Nature center open Mon.–Sat. 9–5.*

1 a-2

WILLIAM T. DAVIS WILDLIFE REFUGE

A variety of birds lives here due to the luxurious position between salt marshes and hardwood forests. It's an especially good place to sight hawks. *Travis Ave. off Richmond Ave., New Springville, 718/667–2165.*

1 b-4

WOLFE'S POND PARK

Duck, geese, herons, and cormorants are some of the waterbirds that like the mix of saltwater and freshwater here. *Holton to Cornelia Aves. on Raritan Bay, Prince's Bay, 718/984–8266.*

BOATING

Water, water, everywhere, but not as many boating options as we'd like (unless you own your own craft). Look for more operators as the city better utilizes its waterways. Most rental agents require identification and/or a deposit in addition to the hourly rental charge (usually $10–$20).

bronx

2 h-3

CITY ISLAND

From here you can row to your heart's content in Pelham Bay and the Long Island Sound. *Boat Livery, 663 City Island Ave., 718/885–1843. Subway: 6 to Pelham Bay Park, then BX29 bus to City Island Ave.*

2 g-2

PELHAM BAY PARK

This is the only regatta course in the city for both canoeing and rowing, but you have to bring your own boat. *Bruckner Blvd. and Middletown Rd. Hunter Island Lagoon: 718/430–1890. Subway: Pelham Bay Park.*

brooklyn

1 h-6

PROSPECT PARK

You and up to three friends can rent a pedal boat to tool around Prospect Lake and Lullwater. *Boat rentals: Kate's Corner (at the Wollman Center), off East Lake Dr. (near Flatbush Ave. and Empire Blvd.), 718/282–7789. Subway: D, Q to Prospect Park.*

manhattan

9 d-1

CENTRAL PARK

Row around the 18-acre lake under gorgeous arched bridges in fine view of some of Manhattan's most beautiful apartment buildings. *Enter park at 5th Ave. and 72nd St., Upper East Side, 212/517–2233. Subway: 77th St.*

11 b-7

DOWNTOWN BOATHOUSE

Free kayaking lessons on summer weekends, a boat launch for human-powered watercraft, and friendly, informative people make these spots inviting. *Hudson River Park, Pier 26, N. Moore St., Tribeca, Subway: Franklin St.; Pier 64, at 24th St., 212/385–8169. Subway: C, E to 23rd St.*

9 b-5

FLOATING THE APPLE

Comprised of maritime historians, boat-builders, and the interested public, this group is dedicated to keeping New York's small-craft history alive. From their boathouses on Pier 84 (W. 44th St.), Pier 40 (W. Houston St.), in Red Hook, Brooklyn, and in Hunts Point, in the Bronx, they have weekly public rows and sails on boats made by community groups, and they also organize reenactments of important boating events. *212/564–5412.*

9 a-8

MANHATTAN KAYAK COMPANY

Kayak owners can keep their equipment here, and newbies can learn paddling basics. Statue of Liberty and nighttime tours depart regularly. *Pier 63 (23rd St. and 12th Ave.), 212/924–1788. Subway: C, E to 23rd St.*

queens

3 h-2

FLUSHING MEADOWS– CORONA PARK

Rent rowboats on Meadow Lake. *Park: Union Tpke. from 111th St. and Grand Central Pkwy. to the Van Wyck Extension, Flushing, 718/699–9596. Subway: 7 to 111th St. or Willets Point/Shea Stadium; Union Tpke./Kew Gardens.*

BOCCIE

New York has about 100 boccie courts; here are a few choice options.

7 f-1

CULLIVER PARK

There are eight courts near the East River at 125th St. *East Harlem. Subway: 4, 5, 6 to 125th St.*

9 g-5

EAST RIVER DRIVE AT 42ND STREET

There are two courts here, near the UN building. *Midtown. Subway: 42nd St./Grand Central.*

10 h-2

EAST RIVER PARK

Like most facilities in this neglected park, the three boccie courts are underutilized but perfectly good. *East River Dr. between 14th and Delancey Sts., East Village/Lower East Side. Subway: Delancey St.*

11 g-3

HOUSTON STREET AND 1ST AVENUE

This playground has five courts. *East Village. Subway: 2nd Ave.*

BOWLING

For a few decades, bowling just *wasn't* cool in most circles; but thanks to the retro-chic craze of the '90s, bowling is back in style. It must be the fab shoes and glow-in-the-dark lanes. Call before you go to make sure a league isn't camped out on your lane.

bronx

2 f-4

FIESTA LANES

Open bowling times in these 28 lanes are mainly during the day. *2826 Westchester Ave. (near Middletown Rd.), Pelham Bay, 718/824–2600. Subway: Middletown Rd.*

brooklyn

4 d-3

MELODY LANES

Bumper bowling (with guard rails on the gutters) is usually available for children at this 28-lane facility. *461 37th St., Sunset Park, 718/499–3848. Subway: 36th St.*

manhattan

9 a-8

AMF CHELSEA PIERS BOWL

If it wasn't big (40 lanes) and new (Manhattan's first new lanes in decades) and state-of-the-art, it wouldn't be at Chelsea Piers. *Chelsea Piers (23rd St. and 12th Ave.), between Piers 59 and 60, 212/835–2695. Subway: C, E to 23rd St.*

10 e-1

BOWLMOR LANES

This lively, old-time bowling center has 42 lanes on two floors. Monday night the lights go out and a DJ spins. But just about every day of the week Bowlmor stays busy with a downtown crowd until the wee hours. *110 University Pl. (between 12th and 13th Sts.), Greenwich Village, 212/255–8188. Subway: 14th St./Union Sq.*

9 c-5

LEISURE TIME BOWLING AND RECREATION

Bowling in the Port Authority? It makes sense when you think about it, given the central location and vaguely festive surroundings. Complete with a bar and billiards, this modern center has 30 lanes. *Port Authority Bus Terminal, 2nd level, Theater District, 212/268–6909. Subway: 42nd St./Port Authority.*

queens

3 h-3

HOLLYWOOD LANES

This underground, 30-lane facility is the finest in Queens. *99–23 Queens Blvd. (at*

67th Ave.), Rego Park, 718/896–2121. Subway: 67th Ave.

2 h-8

WHITESTONE LANES

Can't sleep? These 48 lanes are open 24 hours a day, 7 days a week. *30–05 Whitestone Expressway (at Linden Pl.), Flushing, 718/353–6300. Subway: Main St./Flushing.*

BOXING

Major boxing events are held monthly at **Madison Square Garden** (*see* Sports Stadiums, *below*). Many health clubs offer "Boxercise," a noncontact exercise involving boxing drills, gloves, and punching bags. The gyms listed here have bona fide rings.

brooklyn

12 b-1

GLEASON'S GYM

Gleason's *is* boxing in New York. Since 1937 it's trained more than 100 world champions, including Muhammad Ali. You can spar (partners supplied, lessons available) or just watch, and women are welcome and encouraged. *75 Front St. (at Main St.), Brooklyn Heights, 718/797–2872. Subway: York St.; High St./Brooklyn Bridge.*

manhattan

9 a-8

CHELSEA PIERS

This waterside complex offers a boxing program that includes first-time training and an equipment circuit. Nonmembers have to pay the steep day-pass fee to access the ring, which is in the Sports Center. *Sports Center, Chelsea Piers (23rd St. and 12th Ave.), Pier 60, 212/336–6000. Subway: C, E to 23rd St.*

10 6-e

HEAVY HANDS CHURCH STREET BOXING GYM

Its lack of glitz allows it to focus on quality personalized training. *25 Park Pl., Lower Manhattan, 212/571–1333. Closed Sun. Subway: Park Pl.*

CRICKET

Pitching wickets is especially popular among West Indian immigrants. The

World Cricket League (914/827–3222) and the **Commonwealth Cricket League** (718/601–6704) have information on events.

bronx

 g-5

FERRY POINT PARK

There are three pitches here, in the shadow of the Whitestone Bridge. *Schley Ave. at Emerson Ave.*

2 b-2

VAN CORTLANDT PARK

There are 10 pitches at the Parade Ground, at approximately 243rd Street. Columbia University's cricket club plays home games here. *Park: W. 242nd St. to city line, between Broadway and Jerome Ave., 718/430–1890. Subway: 242nd St./Van Cortlandt Park.*

brooklyn

1 f-6

CANARSIE BEACH PARK

There are four cricket pitches here; one pair at Seaview Avenue and 108th Street and another at Seaview Avenue and 88th Street. *Park: Seaview Ave, Paerdegat Basin.*

1 f-7

MARINE PARK

There are four cricket pitches at 33rd and Stuart streets. *Inlet between Gerritsen and Flatbush Aves., inland to Fillmore Ave., between Burnet and E. 32nd Sts.*

queens

3 h-2

FLUSHING MEADOWS–CORONA PARK

This park has six pitches. *Union Tpke. from 111th St. and Grand Central Pkwy. to the Van Wyck Extension, Flushing, 718/760–6565. Subway: 7 to 111th St.*

staten island

 b-1

WALKER PARK

This park has one cricket pitch, the oldest in the city. *Delafield Pl. and Bard Ave., Livingston.*

CROQUET

You need a permit to play on the croquet grounds in Central Park; call 212/360–8133 for information. You can also show up at 6 PM on Tuesday in the summer for a free clinic for prospective members, hosted by **New York Croquet Club** (212/369–7949).

9 d-1

CENTRAL PARK

Just north of Sheep Meadow is the city's lovely croquet ground, where players in bright white and flat shoes wield mallets. The season runs from April to early November. *Enter park at Central Park W. and 72nd St., Upper West Side, Manhattan. General information 212/360–3444. Subway: B, C to 72nd St.*

CROSS-COUNTRY SKIING

After a heavy snow, cross-country skiers emerge from their apartments and take to the streets in that brief period before the fluff becomes trampled and brown. Bridle paths and fields tend to remain fresh longer. The **Scandinavian Ski Shop** (40 W. 57th St., Manhattan, 212/757–8524) rents equipment. For park locations, *see* Parks, *above*.

bronx

VAN CORTLANDT PARK

The vast terrain, when it's smooth, makes for lovely skiing. *W. 242nd St. to city line, between Broadway and Jerome Ave., 718/430–1890. Subway: 242nd St./Van Cortlandt Park.*

brooklyn

4 c-4

OWL'S HEAD PARK

The views of the harbor just after a snowfall are otherworldly. The skiing is good here if you're comfortable on rolling hills. *Colonial Rd. at 68th St., Bay Ridge. Subway: Bay Ridge Ave.*

1 h-6

PROSPECT PARK

Long Meadow and Nethermead are good for beginners, though most everyone will enjoy them. *Park bordered by Flatbush Ave., Ocean Ave., Parkside Ave., Prospect Park SW, and Prospect Park W, 718/965–8999. Subway: Grand Army*

Plaza; D, Q to Prospect Park; F to 7th Ave.; 15th St./Prospect Park.

manhattan

9 *c-9*

CENTRAL PARK

The Sheep Meadow, the Great Lawn, and North Meadow are big and relatively flat, but you'll need to get there early for the best conditions. The bridle paths and pedestrian walkways are also lovely trails. *Enter the park at Central Park W and 72nd St. or 85th St. General information 212/360–3444. Subway: B, C to 72nd St. or 81st St.*

queens

1 *g-3*

ALLEY POND PARK

The old Vanderbilt Highway provides good, gladed skiing for miles. The wetlands trail is another option.

3 *h-2*

FLUSHING MEADOWS– CORONA PARK

The bike paths and walkways throughout the park provide plenty of routes. *Union Tpke. from 111th St. and Grand Central Pkwy. to the Van Wyck Extension, Flushing, 718/699–4209. Subway: 7 to 111th St. or Willets Point/Shea Stadium; Union Tpke./Kew Gardens.*

staten island

1 *b-2*

HIGH ROCK PARK

The small hills and quick turns on the nature trails are best for experienced skiers. *Richmond Pkwy. and Moravian Cemetary at Rockland Ave.*

FENCING

Fencing can be recreational, competitive, or theatrical. Aficionados claim it's addictive.

9 *c-8*

BLADE FENCING

Private lessons are by appointment. *245 W. 29th St., Chelsea, 212/244–3090. Subway: C, E to 23rd St.*

9 *b-1*

FENCERS CLUB, INC.

Founded in 1883, this nonprofit organization is America's oldest fencing club. It teaches men and women of all levels and all ages, sometimes for free. The pickup area is open nightly. *119 W. 25th St., Chelsea, 212/807–6947. Subway: C, E to 23rd St.*

9 *d-8*

METROPOLIS FENCING CENTER

Group lessons provide a supportive atmosphere for novices. *45 W. 21st St., Chelsea, 212/463–8044. Subway: F to 23rd St.*

FISHING

You need a New York State freshwater-fishing license (ages 16–70) to freshwater-fish in the city; get an application from tackle stores or the **Department of Environmental Conservation** (718/482–4999). Saltwater fishing requires only a line and reel, though if you drive to a spot in the Gateway National Recreation Area, you'll need a parking permit (Breezy Point, Queens, 718/318–4300; Jamaica Bay, Brooklyn, 718/338–3799; Staten Island, 718/351–6970).

Fishers line the many waterways of New York City, from the East River Esplanade on Manhattan's Upper East Side to the Marine Parkway Bridge between Brooklyn and Queens. For some, fishing is a social event—secure your pole, kick back, and turn up the music. For others, it's a solitary, man-vs.-nature affair.

New York City Trout Unlimited (212/439–4741), dedicated to preserving cold-water fisheries, publishes a bimonthly newsletter, "The Urban Fisherman" (available through membership or at tackle stores), and sponsors events such as fly-casting in parks.

bronx

2 *h-3*

CITY ISLAND

Rent a skiff and head out into the sound for flounder and blackfish. Try Jack's Bait and Tackle (551 City Island Ave., 718/885–2042), Rosenberger's Boat Livery (663 City Island Ave., 718/885–1843), or any other outfitter that looks suitably salty. Fishing boats, including the *Riptide III*

(718/885–0236) and *New Daybreak II* (718/409–9765), generally set out for day trips. *Subway: 6 to Pelham Bay Park, then BX29 bus to City Island Ave.*

2 *g-2*
PELHAM BAY PARK
Cast for black bass, flounder, catfish, bullheads, and fluke from Orchard Beach and Hunter's and Twins islands. *Park: Bruckner Blvd. and Middletown Rd., 718/430–1890. Environmental Center (near Orchard Beach), 718/885–3466. Subway: Pelham Bay Park.*

2 *b-2*
VAN CORTLANDT PARK
The catfish and bullheads are biting in the Bronx's largest freshwater lake. *W. 242 St. east of Broadway, 718/430–1890. Subway: 242nd St./Van Cortlandt Park.*

brooklyn

1 *h-6*
PROSPECT LAKE
Fish in designated areas—you might catch catfish and carp. *Prospect Park, bordered by Flatbush Ave., Ocean Ave., Parkside Ave., Prospect Park SW, and Prospect Park W, 718/965–8999. Subway: D, Q to Prospect Park; F to 15th St./Prospect Park.*

1 *f-8*
SHEEPSHEAD BAY
Fishing boats line the piers along Emmons Avenue, crying out for you to join them in search of fluke, bluefish, striped bass, sea bass, and blackfish, among others. Many boats head to Mudhole, a prime fishing ground, between 6 AM and 8 AM for all-day trips or at 8 AM and 1 PM for half-day outings. Options include the *Dorothy B. VIII* (Pier 6, 718/646–4057) and *Blue Sea* (Pier 8, 718/332–9148). Check with Stella Maris Bait and Tackle (2702 Emmons Ave., 718/646–9754) for more information. *Subway: Sheepshead Bay.*

manhattan

7 *d-4*
CENTRAL PARK
The lake has carp, catfish, and bullheads. You can also use free bamboo poles and bait from the **Dana Discovery Center** to angle (catch and release) in the Harlem Meer, which is stocked with

bluegills, bass, shiners, and catfish. No permit is required. This site is popular with families. *Dana Discovery Center, Harlem Meer (near 110th St. and 5th Ave.), 212/860–1370. Program runs July–Aug.; closed Mon.*

HUDSON RIVER PARK
Organizers supply bait and tackle for youngsters to catch and release in the Hudson. *Various piers, probably including 25 (N. Moore St.), 62 (W. 23rd St.), and 84 (W. 44th St.), 212/533–7275 for more information and locations.*

queens

1 *h-6*
ROCKAWAY
Catch bass, flounder, and porgies in the Atlantic saltwater off Breezy Point. There's freshwater fishing at Beach Channel Drive and Beach 32 Street. *Subway: Beach 36 St./Edgemere.*

staten island

1 *b-4*
WOLFE'S POND
There's freshwater fishing year-round and saltwater fishing October–May. *Wolfe's Pond Park: Holton to Cornelia Aves. on Raritan Bay, Prince's Bay, 718/984–8266.*

FLYING

You'll need a single- or multi-engine license to fly a plane in the New York City area.

3 *e-4*
ACADEMICS OF FLIGHT
A ground school and flying lessons (at Republic Airport, Farmingdale, Long Island) will get your feet off the ground. *43–49 45th St., Sunnyside, Queens, 718/937–5716. Subway: 46th St./Bliss St.*

FOOTBALL

The pro-football season extends from early September through December. All local games take place at New Jersey's **Giants Stadium** (*see* Sports Stadiums, *below*). Tickets are extremely difficult, if not impossible, to come by, though you might luck out at the stadium just before a game if the visiting team hasn't used up its share. Arena football, a chaotic game resembling a cross between indoor soccer and football, is played April–July.

where to watch

NEW JERSEY RED DOGS

New Jersey's arena football team had a losing season in 1999 (6–8), but recently acquired top-rated wide receiver and defensive back Barry Wagner so hopes are on the rise for 2000. *Continental Airlines Arena, Meadowlands Sports Complex, East Rutherford, NJ (see Sports Stadiums, below), 201/507–8900.*

NEW YORK GIANTS

The Giants played at the New York Polo Grounds, Yankee Stadium, and Shea Stadium before settling into their New Jersey home in 1976. Their recent seasons have been disappointing, but that didn't make tickets any easier to come by: all are sold through season subscriptions. *Meadowlands Sports Complex, East Rutherford, NJ, 201/935–8222.*

NEW YORK JETS

Longtime owner Leon Hess died in 1999 and the terms of his will called for the sale of the team. As of press time the purchaser hadn't been named, but this uncertainty is unlikely to affect coach Bill Parcells, who in 1998 lead the team to within one game of the Super Bowl. *Giants Stadium, Meadowlands Sports Complex, East Rutherford, NJ, 516/560–8200.*

where to play

There are about two dozen municipal football/soccer fields in New York City; call the Parks Department (*see Parks Information, above*) for a permit and a field near you.

GOLF

Manhattanites may find this hard to picture, but there are 13 public golf courses in the outer boroughs, and most are in good condition. Call the individual course to reserve your tee time. Fees are usually just under $20 for city residents (depending on tee time), slightly higher on weekends, and reservations and cart rentals cost about $2 extra. Golf season runs from mid-March through October or November.

bronx

2 *b-2*

MOSHOLU GOLF COURSE

The nine holes on this 3,119-yard course include many challenging shots. *Van Cortlandt Park, Jerome Ave. and 213rd St., 718/655–9164. Subway: 242nd St./Van Cortlandt Park.*

2 *g-2*

PELHAM GOLF COURSE

There are two scenic 18-hole courses here—the 6,281-yard **Split Rock,** one of the city's most challenging (USGA rating 70.3), and the 6,405-yard **Pelham** course. The former is hilly, with many trees (once convenient for disposing of Mafia kill), while the latter is flatter and open. *Pelham Bay Park, 870 Shore Rd., 718/885–1258. Subway: Pelham Bay Park.*

2 *b-2*

VAN CORTLANDT GOLF COURSE

Opened in 1895, this is the oldest public golf course in the country. Its 18 holes include two longer than 600 yards, for 6,102 yards total. *Van Cortlandt Park, Bailey Ave., 718/543–4595. Subway: 242nd St./Van Cortlandt Park.*

brooklyn

4 *d-6*

DYKER BEACH PARK

The wide fairways on this long (6,548 yards), busy course are tough but forgiving. *7th Ave. and 86th St., Bay Ridge, 718/836–9722. Subway: R to 86th St.*

1 *f-7*

MARINE PARK

Its 6,866 yards make this Robert Trent Jones–designed course the longest in the city, and its seaside location means it's flat and breezy. *2880 Flatbush Ave. (between Ave. U and Belt Pkwy.), Flatlands, 718/338–7113.*

queens

1 *g-3*

CLEARVIEW

One of the most heavily trafficked courses in the country, if not the world, Clearview is straight, flat, and good for beginners. The championship course is 6,473 yards. *202–12 Willets Point Blvd., Bayside, 718/229–2570.*

In case you want to see the world.

At American Express, we're here to make your journey a smooth one. So we have over 1,700 travel service locations in over 130 countries ready to help. What else would you expect from the world's largest travel agency?

do more

Travel

Call 1 800 AXP-3429 or visit
www.americanexpress.com/travel

In case you want to be welcomed there.

We're here to see that you're always welcomed at

establishments everywhere. That's why millions

of people carry the American Express® Card – for

peace of mind, confidence, and security, around

the world or just around the corner.

do more

In case you're running low.

We're here to help with more than 190,000 Express Cash locations around the world. In order to enroll, just call American Express at 1 800 CASH-NOW before you start your vacation.

do more

Express Cash

And in case you'd rather be safe than sorry.

We're here with American Express® Travelers Cheques.

They're the safe way to carry money on your vacation,

because if they're ever lost or stolen you can get a refund,

practically anywhere or anytime. To find the nearest

place to buy Travelers Cheques, call 1 800 495-1153.

Another way we help you do more.

do more

Travelers Cheques

DOUGLASTON PARK
The 6,500-yard layout is rolling, with small greens and narrow fairways. *6320 Marathon Pkwy. and Commonwealth Blvd., Douglaston, 718/224–6566. Long Island Rail Road: Port Washington line to Douglaston.*

1 *f-5*
FOREST PARK
This course is 6,300 challenging yards in aptly named Woodhaven. *1 Forest Park Dr. S, Woodhaven, 718/296–0999. Subway: J, Z to Woodhaven Blvd.*

1 *f-3*
KISSENA PARK
The fairways are well-used and close together at this relatively short, hilly course. *164–15 Booth Memorial Ave., 718/939-4594. Subway: Main St./Flushing.*

staten island

1 *b-2*
LA TOURETTE GOLF COURSE
The fairways are long and varied at this scenic and challenging (par 72) course. *1001 Richmond Hill Rd., 718/351–1889.*

4 *a-7*
SILVER LAKE
At this pretty, 6,050-yard course, hills and tight fairways challenge golfers, of whom there are usually many. *915 Victory Blvd. (near Forest Ave.), 718/447–5686.*

1 *a-3*
SOUTH SHORE
Formerly part of a country club, this 6,366-yard course is still very well maintained, with lots of trees. *Huguenot Ave. and Rally St., 718/984–0101.*

HANDBALL

Handball is usually played on a four-walled court. There are over 2,000 such municipal facilities throughout the boroughs, many of them at playgrounds. Call your local Parks office (*see Parks Information, above*) for one near you.

HOCKEY

The professional hockey season runs from October through April.

where to watch

NEW JERSEY DEVILS
New Jersey's tough and generally losing team surprised everyone by winning the Stanley Cup in 1995. *Continental Airlines Arena, Meadowlands Sports Complex, East Rutherford, NJ, (see Sports Stadiums, below), 201/935–3900.*

9 *c-6*
NEW YORK RANGERS
The beloved Mark Messier left after the 1996–97 season and the legendary Wayne Gretsky hung up his jersey in 1999, but even these changes probably won't subdue the team's fanatical fans. *Madison Square Garden (see Sports Stadiums, below), 212/465–6741.*

NEW YORK ISLANDERS
Of our three local teams, you'll have the easiest time getting tickets for this one—unless they ever play half as well as they did in the 1980s. *Nassau Veterans Memorial Coliseum, 1255 Hempstead Tpke., Uniondale, NY, 516/794–4100.*

where to play

7 *d-4*
LASKER RINK
You can drop in on games on weekends during the skating season; bring your own equipment. *Central Park at 106th St., 212/534–7639. Subway: B, C to 103rd St.*

HORSE RACING

A day at the races can be exciting and very lucrative. Just don't bet more than you can afford to lose.

1 *g-5*
AQUEDUCT
Thoroughbreds have been racing at Aqueduct, the only racetrack in the city, since 1894. Its season runs from October to early May, Wednesday–Sunday. *Rockaway Blvd. and 110th St., Ozone Park, Queens, 718/641–4700. Subway: Aqueduct/North Conduit Ave.*

1 *g-3*
BELMONT PARK
Thoroughbred races move here from Aqueduct in mid-May, continue through June, and then pick up again from early September through October (Wed.–Sun.). Belmont Stakes, held in June, is the third event in horse racing's Triple

Crown. The so-called Breakfast at Belmont—trackside breakfast and then a tram tour—can be fun (weekends and holidays 7 AM–9:30 AM). *Hempstead Tpke. and Plainfield Ave., Elmont, NY, 516/488–6000 or 718/641–4700. Long Island Rail Road: Hempstead Line to Belmont.*

MEADOWLANDS RACETRACK

Trotters and pacers race January through mid-August; the flat-track season is Labor Day through December. *Meadowlands Sports Complex, East Rutherford, NJ, 201/935–8500.*

YONKERS RACEWAY

There's harness racing every evening except Wednesday and Sunday year-round. *Yonkers Ave., Yonkers, NY, 718/562–9500 or 914/968–4200. For bus information, call Westchester Bee Lines at 914/682–2020.*

HORSEBACK RIDING

It's always startling to see jodhpur-wearing riders trotting their way through city parks or down the street, but they have plenty of trails at their disposal. Manhattan's Central Park has 4½ mi of horse trails, including one around the reservoir (one level down from the jogging path). Though stables are usually busy, especially on weekends, the limited number of horses available means that your route won't be too congested.

bronx

2 g-2

PELHAM BIT STABLE

You can rent horses and Western saddles to ride on trails in Pelham Bay Park, or you can take lessons in an outdoor ring. Small children might enjoy the pony rides. *Pelham Bay Park, 9 Shore Rd., 718/885–9723. Subway: Pelham Bay Park.*

2 a-3

RIVERDALE EQUESTRIAN CENTRE

This "centre" for learning and competing was created by two former Olympians, who renovated, expanded, and generally improved the Van Cortlandt Riding Academy. Facilities include an Olympic-size indoor arena (100 ft by 200 ft) and outdoor rings, and the trails in Van Cortlandt Park. There are pony rides for children daily. *Broadway and W.*

254th St., 718/548–4848. Subway: 242nd St./Van Cortlandt Park.

brooklyn

4 e-2

KENSINGTON STABLES

These horses are convenient to easy rides through Prospect Park. *51 Caton Pl. (between E. State St. and Coney Island Ave.), Kensington, 718/972–4588. Subway: Fort Hamilton Pkwy.*

1 f-6

JAMAICA BAY RIDING ACADEMY

Choose between deserted wooded trails and sandy beaches as you explore the 300 acres open to you, or take a lesson on the indoor ring. *7000 Shore Pkwy., 718/531–8949. Subway: Rockaway Pkwy.*

manhattan

7 b-6

CLAREMONT RIDING ACADEMY

A National Historic Site, this academy has been in its Upper West Side location since it opened in 1892. Claremont has an indoor ring and prides itself on its teaching, but this is also the place to rent a horse for a ride through Central Park. *175 W. 89th St., Upper West Side, 212/724–5100. Subway: 1, 9 to 86th St.*

queens

1 f-4

LYNNE'S RIDING ACADEMY

This low-key place has an indoor ring, guided trail riding through Forest Park, and lessons. *88–03 70th Rd., Forest Hills, 718/261–7679. Subway: 71st–Continental Aves./Forest Hills.*

staten island

1 a-4

EQUUS STABLES

Children's lessons are the specialty, but adults are welcome, too. Everything is done in rings; there are no trail horses. *2498 Veterans Rd. W, 718/948–9515.*

HORSESHOES

New York has hundreds of horseshoe pitches throughout the boroughs; all you need are horseshoes. Call the Parks Department (*see* Parks Information, *above*) for the pitch nearest you.

ICE SKATING

Skating is allowed on park lakes and ponds in all boroughs when we have a "hard freeze," but you shouldn't count on this happening even once in any given year. The Department of Parks and Recreation operates a number of rinks that get very crowded at predictable times; the season is November–April. Private rinks also fill up, but some have longer or year-round seasons. All rinks rent skates.

where to skate

All of these rinks rent skates—leaving you with no excuse not to give them a whirl.

brooklyn

4 f-2
KATE WOLLMAN MEMORIAL RINK

This popular outdoor rink is surrounded by Prospect Park's trees and offers both open skating and closed figure-skating practice sessions. It's open daily in season, and you can rent skates. *East Dr. (near Lincoln Rd. and Parkside Ave.), Prospect Park, 718/287–6431. Subway: Prospect Park.*

manhattan

7 e-8
ICE STUDIO

Just 35 ft by 55 ft, this tiny indoor rink (open year-round) is fun for children. *1034 Lexington Ave. (at 74th St.), 2nd floor, Upper East Side, 212/535–0304. Closed Aug. Subway: 77th St.*

7 d-4
LASKER RINK

These large outdoor rinks are cheaper and less crowded than Wollman. Instead of skyscrapers, they have woodsy views. *Central Park at 106th St., 212/534–7639. Subway: B, C to 103rd St.*

6 c-6
RIVERBANK STATE PARK

This covered outdoor rink is popular with families. *Riverside Dr. at 145th St., Harlem, 212/694–3642. Subway: 1, 9 to 145th St.*

9 d-4
ROCKEFELLER CENTER

This small, very busy, private outdoor rink is the classic place to skate in New York. Just watching from above is very entertaining—seasoned locals and giddy tourists scuttle around together. With late-night skating under the famous Christmas tree in December, it's festive and romantic. *Rockefeller Plaza (5th Ave. at 50th St.), Midtown, 212/332–7654. Open Oct.–Apr. Subway: 47th–50th Sts./Rockefeller Center; E, F to 5th Ave.*

9 a-8
SKY RINK

The entire Chelsea Piers Complex got started because its developer needed a place for his daughter to skate. Several years later, we have two private, Olympic-size indoor rinks—one for events and the other for general skating—with lessons, hockey leagues, and special events galore. The views from the top of the pier are amazing but sometimes disorienting—when the sun is beating down and sails are flapping on the Hudson, for example. *Chelsea Piers (23rd St. and 12th Ave.), Pier 61, 212/336–6100. Rink open 24 hrs year-round; call for open skating hours. Subway: C, E to 23rd St.*

9 d-2
WOLLMAN RINK

Nestled within trees nestled within skyscrapers, Wollman has a picture-perfect urban setting. Even when its crowded, and it usually is, people are having the time of their lives. There's late-night skating to popular music on weekend evenings. *Central Park, East Dr. near 63rd St., 212/396–1010. Subway: N, R to 5th Ave.*

queens

1 f-3
WORLD'S FAIR ICE RINK

This indoor rink gets crowded; the critical mass can be intimidating. *Flushing Meadows–Corona Park, New York City Bldg., Long Island Expressway and Grand Central Pkwy., 718/271–1996. Closed Mon., Tues., Thurs. Subway: Willets Point/Shea Stadium.*

staten island

4 a-7

STATEN ISLAND WAR MEMORIAL RINK

These two enclosed outdoor rinks are the best places to skate on Staten Island. *Clove Lakes Park, Victory Blvd. at Clove Rd., 718/720–1010.*

INLINE SKATING

In just a decade, inline skating has gone from barely existing to hooking nearly 2 million New Yorkers. Such phenomenal popularity attests to how well-suited this sport/transportation/way of life is to city streets—and city dwellers. Convenience, speed, and simplicity are among the draws: all you need are skates and padding (a helmet and wrist guards are highly recommended, and the former is required for children 14 and under), which can fit even in the tiniest apartment, and the most important skill to master is stopping. Need we mention that it's also a great workout?

For suggested routes beyond those listed here, *see* Bicycling, *above.* For lessons, *see* Roller Skating, *below.*

While skaters are allowed on sidewalks and on streets, neither is a good place for beginners, and sidewalks are really best left to pedestrians. When using your skates to get somewhere, remember to bring shoes—most buildings don't allow you to wear wheels inside. If you're new to blades, practice stopping on a deserted strip of pavement until you're good enough to be around other people. The **Central Park Skate Patrol** (212/439–1234) holds free stopping clinics in Central Park (at both 72nd Street entrances, from April through October, 12:30–5:30 weekends) and in-depth classes.

Central Park—specifically the block-long stretch of Loop Road south of the West 67th Street entrance—is the heart of city skating. Hang out here to watch people navigate the cone slalom course (weekends) on one leg and backwards faster than most ever dream of moving. The less-traveled Cherry Hill, the Mall, and the "dead road" parallel to the Mall are good for practicing. The lower portion of the Loop Road is skate central, but only slightly more so than the rest of the park. Wollman Rink (*see* Roller Skating, *below*) is good for tinier laps. Other popular skating grounds in Manhattan are the north section of **Union Square Park** (when it's not a Greenmarket), the waterfront esplanade from **Battery Park** to **Hudson River Park,** and **Riverside Park.** Aggressive skaters do tricks at what's known at the **Brooklyn Banks,** the sloped asphalt directly under the Manhattan side of the Brooklyn Bridge. Vert ramps, half pipes, quarter pipes, rails, and other amenities specifically for skating are at the skate parks at **Chelsea Piers** (23rd St. and 12th Ave., 212/336–6200) and **Riverside Park** (Riverside Dr. and 108th St., 212/408–0264). Both charge admission.

Two skating institutions are the **Tuesday Night Skate** and Wednesday's **Blade Night Out.** Wednesday's adventure, which meets at Union Square around 8 PM (times vary; 212/505–9985), covers a leisurely but exhilarating (and not always incident-free) few miles in Manhattan, drawing up to 200 people. The Tuesday Night Skate, which is currently run by the Empire Skate Club (*see below*), requires more endurance. It leaves at 8 from Blades Board and Skate (120 W. 72nd St.). For information, call 774–1774. **Time's Up** (*see* Bicycling, *above*) events also accommodate skaters.

EMPIRE SKATE CLUB

Founded in 1997 because New York skating needed at least some semblance of organization, Empire Skate runs recreational skating trips and skate-centric social events, including the Tuesday Night Skate (*see above*) and the leisurely Thursday Evening Roll through a car-free Central Park. *212/774–1774.*

JUGGLING

If you don't think keeping several objects in motion at once is a sport, just try it. Jugglers perform often outside South Street Seaport.

where to play

11 b-3

CARMINE STREET IRREGULARS

The time to stop by is Thursday from 7:30 PM to 10 PM, when well-practiced jugglers, entertainers, and beginners go at it. Drop in with a few things to juggle and someone will help you get started. *Carmine Street Gym, Clarkson St. and 7th Ave. S, West Village, 212/242–5228. Subway: Houston St.*

LAWN BOWLING

Brought to us by the Dutch, lawn bowling was probably the first sport played in New York City, dating back to 1626—at Bowling Green. You'll need a seasonal permit to bowl on a municipal green; inquire with the Parks Department (see Parks Information, above).

where to play

9 d-1

NEW YORK LAWN BOWLING CLUB

You must be a member to use the bowling green in Central Park, north of the Sheep Meadow (67th St. near West Dr.). Lawn bowlers and croquet players share the greens and clubhouse. 212/650–9218. Subway: B, C to 72nd St.

MARTIAL ARTS

The martial arts are an Eastern mix of physical training and philosophy for self-defense and mental discipline. Varieties include jiu-jitsu, judo, karate, iaido, and tai chi ch'uan. Consult the Yellow Pages for an exhaustive listing of outlets.

brooklyn

4 d-1

BROOKLYN WOMEN'S MARTIAL ARTS

This all-women center has many loyal students and volunteers. Beginners' courses in self-defense, karate, and tai chi start at least once every three months. 421 5th Ave. (between 7th and 8th Sts.), 2nd floor, Park Slope, 718/788–1775. Subway: 4th Ave./9th St.

manhattan

9 d-5

TAI CHI CH'UAN CENTER OF NEW YORK

Participants and observers are welcome at this small studio for tai chi and nei kung. 125 W. 43rd St. Theater District, 212/221–6110. Subway: 42nd St./Times Sq.

9 d-7

WORLD SEIDO KARATE ORGANIZATION

A traditional karate school, World Seido was founded by 9th-degree black belt Kaicho Tadashi Nakamura. Men, women, and children are welcome to observe or participate in classes, which run all day long and are excellent. The karate training can provide conditioning and teach skills useful for self-defense. 61 W. 23rd St., Chelsea, 212/924–0511. Subway: F to 23rd St.

MINIATURE GOLF

brooklyn

1 f-7

GATEWAY SPORTS CENTER

Right on Rockaway Inlet, this 18-hole, rough-terrain course and 100-tee driving range offer peaceful putting. 3200 Flatbush Ave. (opposite Floyd Bennett Field), Flatlands, 718/253–6816.

manhattan

11 a-8

PIER 25

This outdoor course is open seasonally. The 18 holes are your typical miniature course, but the river breeze and views make it special. Pier 25 (near Reade St.), Tribeca, 212/732–7467. Subway: Chambers St.

7 h-2

RANDALL'S ISLAND GOLF AND FAMILY ENTERTAINMENT CENTER

There are two 18-hole minigolf courses and a driving range at this off-the-beaten-track site. A shuttle bus runs on the hour 3–7 during the week and from 10–6 on weekends. The charge is $8 round-trip. Randall's Island Golf Center, 212/427–5689. Shuttle bus leaves from 3rd Ave. and 86th St., Upper East Side.

queens

1 g-3

GOLDEN BEAR GOLF CENTER

These two 18-hole courses are opposite the salt marshes of the Alley Pond Environmental Center. They have your basic greens, holes, and bumps, though the masters course is more challenging. Alley Pond Park, Douglaston, 718/225–9187.

PADDLEBALL

Paddleball requires one wall and very little expense, which is one reason for its popularity, especially among agile young men. There are over 400 paddleball courts in the city—including **Coney Island,** Brooklyn; **Orchard Beach,** Bronx; and **Central Park,** Manhattan. Call the parks hot line in your borough for the nearest court. The National Paddleball Association organizes tournaments and instruction.

RACQUETBALL

Easier than tennis or squash to learn, racquetball requires more skill than force. Most clubs charge a guest fee in addition to an hourly court fee for non-members; many don't allow them at all.

brooklyn

12 b-2

EASTERN ATHLETIC CLUBS
The five courts host lessons and leagues in addition to regular games. Nonmembers pay a guest fee ($20), but the court fee during off-peak periods is only $6 per hour (peak is $16). *43 Clark St., Brooklyn Heights, 718/625–0500. Subway: Clark St.*

manhattan

9 d-3

CLUB LA RAQUETTE
Nonmembers pay a guest fee ($15 weekdays) on top of the court fee; there are two racquetball courts. *Hotel Le Parker Meridien, 119 W. 56th St., Midtown, 212/245–1144. Subway: 57th St.*

11 b-3

PRINTING HOUSE FITNESS AND RACQUET
The racquetball court at this full-service fitness club is for members only. *421 Hudson St. (at Leroy St.), West Village, 212/243–7600. Subway: Franklin St.*

queens

3 e-3

BQE RACQUETBALL CLUB
Guests pay a guest fee on top of the court fee to play here, but it's a very nice facility. There are seven courts. *26–50 Brooklyn–Queens Expressway W, Woodside, 718/726–4343. Subway: Northern Blvd.*

staten island

1 a-3

NEW YORK SPORTS CLUB
These four racquetball courts are only open to members. *300 W. Service Rd., 718/698–4500.*

ROCK CLIMBING

It's you against the rock (or the wall) in this sport, and it's quite popular in the city, mainly because of the combination of strength, flexibility, coordination, and endurance that it develops. Several new walls have opened recently, all requiring that you take a lesson or pass a belay test (in which you hold the rope while your partner climbs) before you can climb or spot, and they'll rent you equipment if you don't have your own. Routes are changed regularly (by moving the holds around) to keep the climbing interesting.

9 a-7

CHELSEA PIERS
There are two walls here, one 30 ft high (primarily for children and nonmembers; in the field house) and the other 46 ft high (in the Sports Center). With 10,000 square ft total, the latter has endless challenging routes. There's a bouldering wall, too, for ropeless climbing. *Field House (between Piers 61 and 62), Chelsea Piers (23rd St. and 12th Ave.), 212/336–6500. Sports Center, Pier 60, Chelsea Piers, 212/336–6000. Subway: C, E to 23rd St.*

9 c-2

EXTRAVERTICAL CLIMBING CENTER
This wall ranges from 30 ft to 50 ft high, and since it's in the public, open-air Harmony Atrium, it's a fun place to watch. There's also a climbing store, where you can rent or buy equipment. ExtraVertical offers membership packages, but its prices for day passes (New York Sports Club members get discounts one day a week) are reasonable. *61 W. 62nd St., Upper West Side, 212/586–5718. Subway: 59th St./Columbus Circle.*

9 b-2

WEST 59TH STREET RECREATION CENTER
The first indoor wall in Manhattan, this one has a fiercely loyal clientele despite the opening of several more sophisticated climbing centers. Bring your own equipment. Climbing membership is separate from general rec-center mem-

bership, but the year-round and day-use fees are reasonable. *533 W. 59th St., Midtown, 212/974–2250. Open weekdays 5 PM–10 PM, Sat. noon–5. Subway: 59th St./Columbus Circle.*

MANHATTAN PLAZA HEALTH CLUB

Another pioneer on the climbing scene, the 20-ft indoor wall is run by instructors with extensive outdoor experience. Use of the wall is included in club membership, but nonmembers will have to pay for a club guest pass ($25) as well as a day pass for the wall ($10). *450 W. 43rd St., Hell's Kitchen, 212/563–7001. Subway: 42nd St./Port Authority.*

ROLLER SKATING

Watch the feet of all the skaters whizzing by on park roads and you'll see a small number of traditional roller skates, but since the advent of inline skating, the more traditional wheels are most popular for dancing. As with inline skating, the five boroughs offer endless outdoor opportunities for skaters confident enough to hit the streets. Parks and rinks are preferred by many, though, for obvious reasons. For more tips, *see* Inline Skating, *above.*

LEZLY SKATE SCHOOL

A few skating lessons with Lezly's skating specialists (indoor and outdoor, traditional and inline) will stop your ankles from wobbling in no time. Roller-dancing is taught, too. This is also the home of the **Central Park Dance Skaters Association,** whose members you'll find disco dancing in a giant loop on the defunct park road south of 72nd Street on weekend afternoons. *212/777–3232.*

9 *b-8*

ROXY

Manhattan's only indoor rink usually serves as a concert venue, but on Wednesday (when it opens to skaters) it becomes a roller disco, drawing a crowd that remembers when disco was the new thing. *515 W. 18th St., Chelsea, 212/645–5156. Subway: A, C, E to 14th St.*

9 *d-2*

WOLLMAN RINK

When the ice thaws, this wonderfully situated rink is turned over to the wheeled crowd. *Central Park, East Dr. near 63rd St., 212/396–1010. Subway: N, R to 5th Ave.*

RUGBY

The **New York Rugby Club** fields both men's and women's sides. In addition to training and games during the league seasons (spring and fall), the club schedules drinking practice around televised rugby events—or for no reason. New members are always welcome; call 212/988–9201 for more information.

3 *c-1*

RANDALLS ISLAND

Playing fields are to the right of the ramp off the Triborough Bridge; there are games most Saturday mornings in spring and fall.

RUNNING & JOGGING

The **Jacqueline Kennedy Onassis Reservoir** in Central Park is a beautiful, 1.6-mi gravel path that most Manhattan runners have circled more times than they'd care to count. Waterfront paths and trails through the larger parks in all five boroughs are all well traveled by runners. **Prospect Park** and **Central Park** both have popular running lanes around their loop roads. Manhattan's **East River Esplanade,** about 4 mi round-trip from Carl Schurz Park to 125th Street, is prettiest at sunrise, though you should probably run with someone at that hour. Watch the sunset from **Riverside Park** while running between 72nd and 116th streets, also about 4 mi round-trip. There are cross-country courses in the Bronx's **Van Cortlandt Park** (6 mi), Brooklyn's **Marine Park** (0.8 mi) and **Alley Pond Park** (1.5 mi), Queens's **Forest Park** (2.5 mi), and Staten Island's **Clove Lakes Park** (3.3 mi). The general rule for figuring mileage in Manhattan is 20 short blocks to a mile. Call the Parks office in your borough for the municipal running track nearest you, and for other distance-running ideas *see* Bicycling *and* Inline Skating, *above.*

NEW YORK HASH HOUSE HARRIERS

They call themselves drinkers with a running problem, but they actually organize fun scavenger *runs* throughout New York. If you successfully follow the trail, you end up in a bar with a cold drink. *212/427–4692.*

NEW YORK ROAD RUNNERS CLUB

Best known for the New York City Marathon (early Nov.) and the New Year's Eve fun run, this is the largest runner's club in the world. It offers a full range of classes, clinics, group runs, races, and even merchandise for everyone from beginning runners to elite champions. Members get substantial discounts and a subscription to *Running News*. The **Achilles Track Club** (42 W. 38th St., 4th floor, 212/354–0300) has programs for physically challenged runners. *9 E. 89th St., Upper East Side, Manhattan, 212/860–4455. Subway: 4, 5, 6 to 86th St.*

SAILING

New York City was the national center for sailing in the 19th century, and the New York Yacht Club is still very influential nationwide. The city's nautical heritage is most pronounced on City Island, whose shingled waterfront shacks, briny air, and salty characters seem more New England than Bronx; some people here still build sails or boats for a living. Experienced sailors should be able to help crew a boat off the island during the summer-long Wednesday-night race series (City Island Yacht Club, 718/885–2487). In a recent epiphany, Manhattanites realized what they were missing, and there are now several sailing options in New York Harbor as well.

9 *a-8*

CHELSEA SAILING SCHOOL

Basic sailing, navigation, and seamanship are taught from Chelsea Piers' Hudson River marina. Alumni may join the Chelsea Sailing Club. *Chelsea Piers (23rd St. and 12th Ave.), Pier 59, 212/627-SAIL. Subway: C, E to 23rd St.*

10 *d-7*

MANHATTAN SAILING SCHOOL

The Manhattan Sailing School teaches sailing at all skill levels on J-24 boats in New York Harbor; you can also rent or charter boats. The school was founded in 1991 by the Manhattan Yacht Club, which had just reintroduced recreational sailing to Manhattan in 1987 after the sport's absence for more than half a century. You can join the Yacht Club once you complete Basic Sailing. *World Financial Center, 393 South End Ave.,* *Lower Manhattan, 212/786–0400. Subway: Cortlandt St./World Trade Center.*

10 *d-7*

NORTH COVE SAILING SCHOOL

An affiliate of the American Sailing Association and a neighbor of the larger Manhattan Sailing School, North Cove also teaches you to sail on J-24s. Experienced sailors can skipper or crew on boats from the fleet. *World Financial Center, 393 South End Ave., Lower Manhattan, 800/532–5552. Subway: Cortlandt St./World Trade Center.*

SCUBA DIVING

You never know what you might find off the coast—reefs, wrecks, subs, or garbage. Most scuba certification is either through **NAUI** (National Association of Underwater Instructors, 800/553–6284) or **PADI** (Professional Association of Diving Instructors, 800/729–7234), and both organizations can direct you to local programs. Classes include pool instruction and an open dive, which some people choose to complete while on vacation (your teacher should help you arrange this). Fees can vary from about $170 up to $400, and class sessions can last anywhere from one intensive week to a few months.

brooklyn

1 *f-8*

PROFESSIONAL DIVING SERVICES

Master Instructor and Captain Bill Reddan takes certified divers out on evenings and weekends on the *Jeanne II* to explore wrecks such as the *Algol* (80–120 ft) and the *Arundo* (125 ft). Call for a schedule and to make reservations. *Pier 5, Sheepshead Bay, 718/332–9574. Subway: Sheepshead Bay.*

manhattan

9 *e-1*

AQUA-LUNG SCHOOL OF NEW YORK

Using the pool at Hunter College, Fran Gaar, the first female master instructor in the country, and her instructors will prepare you for PADI or NAUI certification. Each student's record is kept individually, meaning you can show up for sessions whenever it's convenient. All equipment is provided. *Hunter College: Lexington Ave. at 68th St., Upper East Side, 212/582–2800. Subway: 68th St./Hunter College.*

9 *b-5*
PAN AQUA DIVING
Pan Aqua teaches certification courses at seven Manhattan locations, including the 92nd St. YM-YWHA, West Side YMCA, Vanderbilt YMCA, and Manhattan Plaza Health Club. Based at Manhattan Plaza, Pan Aqua also offers free scuba trials, rentals, and repairs. *460 W. 43rd St., Hell's Kitchen, 212/736–DIVE. Subway: 42nd St./Port Authority.*

queens

3 *h-3*
NEW YORK SCUBA
This center has everything—instruction, sales, rentals, and occasional weekend trips along the Eastern seaboard. In addition to a 10-day PADI certification program, you can take an evening-long refresher course. *95-58 Queens Blvd. (near 63rd Dr.), Rego Park, 718/897–2885. Subway: 63rd Dr./Rego Park.*

SOCCER

Professional soccer was extremely popular in New York when Pelé played for the Cosmos in the 1970s, but the league died in the 1980s and many people forgot about it—until the United States hosted the World Cup in 1994. Will "football" ever catch on in this country?

where to watch
METROSTARS
New York's local Major League soccer team, born in 1996, hasn't realized its potential yet. The season is late March–September. *Giants Stadium, Meadowlands Sports Complex, East Rutherford, NJ, 201/935–3900.*

where to play
You need a permit to reserve any of the park soccer fields; call the appropriate parks office for information and locations. At many fields you'll have to bring your own net.

SOFTBALL

New York has more than 600 baseball diamonds, heavily used by softball players. Many companies form softball teams and compete in leagues. If you're not part of a league, you'll need a permit; call your borough's parks office for fields near you.

SPORTING EVENTS

New Yorkers of all stripes come out for these sports and outdoor annuals.

ADVIL MINI MARATHON
Thousands of women race, jog, and walk the 10K course through Central Park, forming the world's largest race for women only. Runners start at the park's West Drive, near 66th Street, and finish at Tavern on the Green. *New York Road Runners Club, 212/860–4455. Early June.*

BELMONT STAKES
This prestigious track hosts the final race in the Triple Crown. *Belmont Park, Hempstead Tpke. and Plainfield Ave., Belmont, NY, 516/488–6000 or 718/641–4700. Long Island Rail Road: Hempstead Line to Belmont. June.*

BIKE NEW YORK
Bike New York is to cyclists what the New York Marathon is to runners. At last count, about 30,000 people have been turning out for this five-borough, 42-mi tour. It's all car-free, from the starting line in Battery Park to the long stretch on the Belt Parkway to the finish over the Verazzano Narrows Bridge (which doesn't otherwise allow bikes). A free ferry brings cyclists back to Manhattan. *212/932–BIKE. Early May.*

CHERRY BLOSSOM FESTIVAL
The Brooklyn Botanic Garden celebrates its cherry trees during Sakura Matsuri, a Japanese-theme festival that usually includes music and dance, Japanese-crafts demonstrations, special tours, and a tea ceremony in honor of the lush blooms. The trees form one of Mother Nature's most spectacular limited engagements. *718/622–4433. Early May.*

COREL W.T.A. CHASE CHAMPIONSHIPS
Closing an 11-month schedule of tennis tournaments, this is the biggest

women's sports event in the world. *Madison Square Garden (see Sports Stadiums, below), 212/465–6000. November.*

EARTH DAY

Celebrations usually include numerous outdoor events. Check with the Parks Department and with Transportation Alternatives (*see Biking, above*), which traditionally sponsors a pollution-free ride. *Apr. 22.*

MANHATTAN ISLAND MARATHON SWIM AND WATER FESTIVAL

Individuals and relay team members, covered in Vaseline and shot through with immunizations, swim 28½ mi counterclockwise around Manhattan. In celebration of the race, Battery Park hosts a daylong Water Festival. *212/873–8311. July.*

MAYOR'S CUP

Schooners and classic yachts compete in New York Harbor in this race, organized by the South Street Seaport Museum. *212/748–8786. Late Sept.*

MILLROSE GAMES

These track-and-field championships are Madison Square Garden's oldest continuous sports event, and the longest-running invitational meet in the country. The prestigious Wanamaker Mile race is a highlight. *Madison Square Garden (see Sports Stadiums, below), 212/465–6000. February.*

NEW YORK MARATHON

Nearly 30,000 runners (about one-third of them New Yorkers) gulp Gatorade and wave at the cheering crowds on this five-borough foot race. Elite champions lead the pack; most of the runners are just looking to have a good time and to make it to the finish line in Central Park. *New York Road Runners Club, 212/860–4455. Early November.*

RUNNER'S WORLD/ASICS MIDNIGHT RUN

Thousands of costumed runners ring in the New Year with fireworks and a 5K midnight run through Central Park. *New York Road Runners Club, 212/860–4455. New Year's Eve.*

U.S. OPEN TENNIS TOURNAMENT

Celebrities always appear in the stands, and the boxes in Arthur Ashe Stadium are to die for, but the real excitement is the Grand Slam tennis. With a stadium ticket you can also catch matches in outlying courts and in the grandstand, where bleacher seating is first-come, first served. *U.S.T.A. National Tennis Center, Flushing Meadows–Corona Park, 800/524–8440. Late August–early September. Subway: Willets Point/Shea Stadium.*

SPORTS STADIUMS

CONTINENTAL AIRLINES ARENA

Formerly the Brendon Byrne Arena, this 20,000-seater has its hands full with the ferocious fans of the New Jersey Nets (basketball); New Jersey Devils (hockey); and, more recently, Mad Dogs (arena football). *Meadowlands Sports Complex, East Rutherford, NJ, 201/935–3900.*

7 *h-2*

DOWNING STADIUM

Pelé played for the New York Cosmos soccer team here in the 1970s, but now it's as likely to host a concert as a sporting event. *Randalls Island, 212/860–1828. Subway: 4, 5, 6 to 125th St.*

GIANTS STADIUM

It's rumored that Jimmy Hoffa rests in peace under the Astroturf trod by New York's two football teams (the Jets and the Giants), the MetroStars (soccer), and legions of concertgoers. The stadium seats almost 78,000. *Meadowlands Sports Complex, East Rutherford, NJ, 201/935–3900.*

9 *c-6*

MADISON SQUARE GARDEN

There's never a dull moment in midtown's 20,000-seat showcase. The New York Knicks and the New York Liberty shoot hoops, and the New York Rangers slam pucks. Many up-and-coming college athletes, track stars, boxers, wrestlers, and figure skaters find themselves here at some point. *7th Ave. between 31st and 33rd Sts., Midtown, Manhattan, 212/465–6741. Tours daily.*

NASSAU VETERANS MEMORIAL COLISEUM

Built in 1972, the New York Islanders' 16,000-seat home is showing its age. *1255 Hempstead Tpke., Uniondale, NY, 516/794–9300.*

3 *h-1*

SHEA STADIUM

New York Mets ball games are always fun at this 55,777-seat stadium—the fans drown out the noise from nearby La Guardia Airport. *126th St. and Roosevelt Ave., Flushing, Queens, 718/507–8499.*

3 *h-1*

U.S.T.A. NATIONAL TENNIS CENTER

The host of the U.S. Open lets the rest of us play most of the year (*see Tennis, below*). *Flushing Meadows–Corona Park, Flushing, Queens, 718/760–6200.*

6 *f-5*

YANKEE STADIUM

The 57,545-seat 1923 "House That Ruth Built" has watched its boys win 24 World Championships. Steinbrenner's not moving them anywhere. *161st St. and River Ave., Bronx, 718/293–6000. Subway: 161st St./Yankee Stadium.*

SQUASH

Squash is available at many private gyms. Court fees vary with supply and demand.

brooklyn

12 *b-2*

EASTERN ATHLETIC CLUBS

The Brooklyn Heights branch has two squash courts. Nonmembers pay a guest fee. *43 Clark St., Brooklyn Heights, 718/625–0500. Subway: Clark St.*

manhattan

9 *e-6*

ATHLETIC COMPLEX

Before this place became a complete fitness center it was strictly racquet sports; now there's just one squash court left. Nonmembers are permitted for a fee. *3 Park Ave. (entrance on 34th St.), Murray Hill, 212/686–1085. Subway: 33rd St.*

9 *d-3*

CLUB LA RAQUETTE

There is one squash court. Nonmembers pay a guest fee on top of the court fee. *Hotel Le Parker Meridien, 119 W. 56th St., Midtown, 212/245–1144. Subway: 57th St.*

10 *e-8*

NEW YORK HEALTH & RACQUET CLUB

This racquet-sports specialist club has courts at two locations. Nonmembers pay an extremely steep visitor's fee. *39 Whitehall St., Lower Manhattan, 212/269–9800. Subway: Whitehall St./South Ferry.*

9 *e-4*

20 E. 50th St., Midtown, 212/593–1500. Subway: E, F to 5th Ave.

9 *c-2*

NEW YORK SPORTS CLUB

Take your pick of locations. *61 W. 62nd St., Upper West Side, 212/265–0995. Subway: 59th St./Columbus Circle.*

9 *d-6*

404 5th Ave. (between 36th and 37th Sts.), Midtown, 212/594–3120. Subway: 34th St./Herald Square.

7 *e-7*

151 E. 86th St., Upper East Side, 212/860–8630. Subway: 4, 5, 6 to 86th St.

12 *c-4*

110 Boerum Pl., Cobble Hill, Brooklyn, 718/643–4400. Subway: F, G to Bergen St.

11 *b-3*

PRINTING HOUSE FITNESS AND RACQUET

This full-service, members-only fitness club has six squash courts. *421 Hudson St. (at Leroy St.), West Village, 212/243–7600. Subway: Houston St.*

9 *c-2*

WEST SIDE YMCA

The two courts here are for members only. *5 W. 63rd St., Upper West Side, 212/787–4400. Subway: 59th St./Columbus Circle.*

SWIMMING

More than 30 city-run outdoor pools are open from the 4th of July weekend through Labor Day, and they're free— just bring a bathing suit, towel, and lock. Hours are usually 11–7, with an hour's break in midafternoon. The Aquatics Division of the Department of Parks and Recreation (718/699–4219) has information about pools, lessons, and lap swimming. Despite a few highly publicized incidents regarding sexual harassment at public pools, they're generally a safe (if crowded) diversion. Use common sense—city pools probably aren't the best place to model your new Brazilian bikini, for example, and even with life-guards on duty, you shouldn't swim alone. (*See* Beaches, *above,* for more out-door swimming.) Indoor pools are open year-round, with the exception of those at public-recreation centers that also have outdoor pools. For more municipal pools, check the government listings pages of the phone book under Parks and Recreation—Swimming Pools.

bronx

5 *f-3*

APEX

The beautiful 50-meter, 8-lane indoor pool at Lehman College's athletic center allows anyone to be a member for a rea-sonable yearly fee. *Lehman College, 250 Bedford Park Blvd. W, Jerome Park, 718/ 960–1117. Subway: Bedford Park Blvd./Lehman College.*

5 *h-8*

CROTONA POOL

This outdoor pool is very large, but it still gets crowded. *E. 175th St. and Fulton Ave., Morrisania, 718/822–4440. Subway: C, D to 174th–175th Sts.*

2 *c-8*

ST. MARY'S RECREATION CENTER

The rec center has an indoor pool. *St. Ann's Ave. and E. 145th St., 718/402–5157. Subway: E. 143rd St./St. Mary's St.*

2 *b-3*

VAN CORTLANDT POOL

Van Cortlandt's outdoor pool is bigger than most. *W. 244th St. east of Broadway, 718/548–2415. Subway: 242nd St./Van Cortlandt Park.*

brooklyn

1 *f-5*

BROWNSVILLE PLAYGROUND RECREATION CENTER

For $10 a year you can swim as a mem-ber in this 75-ft indoor pool. *1555 Linden Blvd. (at Christopher Ave.), 718/345–2706. Subway: L to New Lots Ave.*

1 *d-6*

RED HOOK POOL

This outdoor pool is Brooklyn's largest. *Bay and Henry Sts., 718/722–3211. Sub-way: Smith–9th Sts.*

1 *e-6*

ST. JOHN'S RECREATION CENTER

There's a 75-ft indoor pool at this public rec center. *1251 Prospect Pl. (between Troy and Schenectady Aves.), Crown Heights, 718/771–2787. Subway: 3, 4 to Utica Ave.*

4 *d-3*

SUNSET PARK POOL

This outdoor neighborhood pool is large and popular. *7th Ave. and 43rd St., 718/ 965–6578. Subway: 45th St.*

manhattan

7 *g-6*

ASPHALT GREEN AQUACENTER

This indoor sea—oops, pool—is state-of-the-art, with a movable bottom and bulkheads that can divide it into man-ageable subsections. It's Olympic-size—50 meters long—and nonmembers can swim at certain hours for a fee. *1750 York Ave. (at 91st St.), Upper East Side, 212/369–8890. Subway: 4, 5, 6 to 86th St.*

9 *g-8*

ASSER LEVY RECREATION CENTER

This public rec center used to be a bath-house, and its indoor pool is small but beautiful—natural light, high ceiling. There's a larger outdoor pool, too; the indoor one closes when the other is open. *E. 23rd St. and Asser Levy Pl. (between 1st Ave. and FDR Dr.), Gramercy, 212/447–2020. Subway: 6 to 23rd St.*

11 *b-3*

CARMINE RECREATION CENTER

The indoor pool closes when the out-door one opens. Both are no-frills but in good condition. *7th Ave. S at Clarkson St., West Village, 212/242–5228. Subway: Houston St.; W. 4th St.*

9 *f-3*

EAST 54TH ST. RECREATION CENTER

There's a small indoor pool here. *348 E. 54th St., Midtown, 212/397–3154. Subway: 6 to 51st St. or E, F to 53rd/Lexington Ave.*

7 *g-8*

JOHN JAY PARK POOL

Parks Commissioner Stern does his morning laps here. The park has a nice view from its perch above the East River. *E. 77th St. and Cherokee Pl. (near York Ave.), Upper East Side, 212/794–6566. Subway: 77th St.*

7 *c-4*

LASKER POOL

This is Manhattan's largest outdoor pool. *Central Park at 106th St., Morningside Heights, 212/534–7639.*

9 *b-5*

MANHATTAN PLAZA HEALTH CLUB

The 75-ft lap pool at this private club is a big draw, especially on bright summer days when the atrium roof opens. Nonmembers are welcome, for a fee. *482 W. 43rd St., Hell's Kitchen, 212/563–7001. Subway: 42nd St./Port Authority.*

6 *c-6*

RIVERBANK STATE PARK

This indoor lap pool is one of the cheapest nonmunicipal options ($3); there's also an outdoor pool in summer. *Riverside Dr. at 145th St., Harlem, 212/694–3600. Subway: 145th St.*

9 *f-4*

VANDERBILT YMCA

There are two pools here: a 75-ft shallow lap pool and a smaller pool with a deep end for lessons and classes. Nonmembers are welcome for a guest fee. *224 E. 47th St., Midtown, 212/756–9600. Subway: 51st St.*

9 *b-2*

WEST 59TH STREET RECREATION CENTER

This 60-ft indoor lap pool is underutilized. *533 W. 59th St., Midtown, 212/974–2250. Subway: 59th St./Columbus Circle.*

9 *c-2*

WEST SIDE YMCA

As at the Vanderbilt YMCA, there are two pools here. The one meant for laps has a beautiful tile ceiling. *5 W. 63rd St., Upper West Side, 212/787–4400. Subway: 59th St./Columbus Circle.*

queens

8 *b-5*

ASTORIA PARK POOL

The 1936 Olympic trials were held in this large outdoor pool near the East River. *19th St. and 23rd Dr., Astoria, 718/626–8620. Subway: Ditmars Blvd./Astoria.*

1 *g-4*

ROY WILKINS RECREATION CENTER

There's an indoor pool at this St. Albans rec center. *177th St. and Baisley Blvd., 718/276–8686.*

staten island

1 *a-1*

FABER PARK POOL

This outdoor pool is a good size. *2175 Richmond Terr at Faber St., Port Richmond, 718/816–5259.*

4 *b-5*

LYONS POOL

Though the outdoor pool is fairly large and in good condition, it's not in the best neighborhood. *Victory Blvd. east of Bay St., Tompkinsville, 718/816–9571.*

1 *a-4*

TOTTENVILLE POOL

This standard-size outdoor pool is on the country club–inspired south shore. *Hylan Blvd. and Joline Ave., Tottenville, 718/356–8242*

1 *b-1*

WEST BRIGHTON POOL

This is a standard-size outdoor pool. *Broadway and Henderson Ave., West Brighton, 718/816–5019.*

TENNIS

Staten Islander Mary Outerbridge introduced Americans to tennis in the 19th century, and New Yorkers have expressed their love for the sport ever since. To play on a municipal court (Apr.–Nov.), you'll need a permit. In Manhattan they're available at the Parks Department's headquarters at the Arsenal (830 5th Ave., at 64th St.) and from Paragon Sporting Goods (867 Broadway, at 18th St., 212/255–8026). Permits are $50 for the year; single-play passes are also available. Reservations, which are useful at some courts, cost extra, and many facilities have lockers for a charge as well. For complete information about permits, and for numbers to call in other boroughs, listen to the long recording at 212/360–8133.

where to watch

See **U.S. Open Tennis Tournament** and **Corel W.T.A. Chase Championships** in Sporting Events, *above*.

where to play

All of these courts are city-owned unless otherwise noted. For an exhaustive list, call your borough's Parks office.

bronx

2 *d-4*
BRONX PARK
There are six courts here. *Bronx Park E and Brady Ave., Bronxdale.*

2 *c-6*
CROTONA PARK
These 20 hard courts are the among best in the Bronx. *E. 173rd St. and Crotona Ave., Morrisania. Subway: C, D to 174th–175th Sts.*

6 *f-4*
MULLALY PARK
There are 16 good courts here. *164th St. and Jerome Ave., Highbridge. Subway: 164th St.*

2 *g-2*
PELHAM BAY PARK
This park has 10 courts. *Bruckner Blvd. and Middletown Rd., Pelham Bay. Subway: Pelham Bay Park.*

2 *b-2*
VAN CORTLANDT PARK
There are eight clay courts here. *W. 241st St. and Broadway, Riverdale. Subway: 242nd St./Van Cortlandt Park.*

5 *g-1*
WILLIAMSBRIDGE OVAL
This area has eight hard courts. *E. 208th St. and Bainbridge Ave., Norwood. Subway: 205th St.*

brooklyn

4 *g-6*
BROOKLYN RACQUET CLUB
There are 11 clay courts under a bubble here. This private facility opens early and doesn't close until the wee hours; courts are available for an hourly fee. *2781 Shell Rd. (near Ave. Z and McDonald Ave.), Brighton Beach, 718/769–5167. Subway: Avenue Z.*

12 *e-2*
FORT GREENE PARK
This park has six hard courts. *DeKalb and S. Portland Aves. Subway: Atlantic Ave.*

4 *g-7*
KAISER PLAYGROUND
There are 12 hard courts here. *Neptune Ave. and W. 25th St., Coney Island. Subway: Stillwell Ave./Coney Island.*

4 *d-4*
LEIF ERICSON PARK
There are nine hard courts here. *8th Ave. and 66th St., Bay Ridge. Subway: 8th Ave.*

1 *f-8*
MANHATTAN BEACH
This small beach has six hard courts that aren't too busy. *Oriental Blvd. and Mackenzie St. Subway: Brighton Beach.*

1 *f-7*
MARINE PARK
There are 15 hard courts here. *Inlet between Gerritsen and Flatbush Aves., inland to Fillmore Ave., between Burnet and E. 32nd Sts.*

4 *f-2*
PROSPECT PARK PARADE GROUND
There are 10 clay courts here. *Coney Island Ave. and Parkside Ave., Prospect Park S. Subway: Fort Hamilton Pkwy.*

manhattan

7 *d-5*
CENTRAL PARK TENNIS CENTER
Reservations are a good idea at these busy city courts. In addition to four hard courts and 26 Har-Tru courts, the center offers professional instruction, tournaments, and locker rooms. *Park*

bordered by Central Park W, 110th St., 5th Ave., and 59th St. Courts midpark (enter at W. 96th St.), 212/280–0205. Subway: B, C to 96th St.

9 *d-6*

CROSSTOWN TENNIS

Take note: On hot summer days, these four indoor courts are air-conditioned. They're available for an hourly fee. *14 W. 31st St., Garment District, 212/947–5780. Subway: 34th St./Herald Square.*

10 *h-2*

EAST RIVER PARK

These 12 courts are in good shape but are not busy—perhaps because they're a little too close to the cacophonous East River Drive. *East River Dr. between 14th and Delancey Sts., East Village/Lower East Side. Subway: Delancey St.*

6 *e-6*

FRED JOHNSON MEMORIAL PARK

They turn the lights on at night for these eight hard courts. *Adam Clayton Powell, Jr., Blvd. At 151st St., Harlem. Subway: 148th St./Lenox Terminal.*

5 *b-5*

INWOOD HILL PARK

These nine courts aren't too busy except on weekends. *W. 207th St. at Seaman Ave. Subway: 207th St./Inwood.*

9 *b-5*

MANHATTAN PLAZA RACQUET CLUB

The five rooftop courts are covered by a bubble in the winter, open-air (with great views) in the summer, and light after dark. They're open to nonmembers by appointment; fees vary, so call ahead. *450 W. 43rd St., Hell's Kitchen, 212/594–0554. Subway: 42nd St./Port Authority.*

9 *c-7*

MIDTOWN TENNIS CLUB

The eight Har-Tru courts—all under a bubble in winter and half bubbled (and air-conditioned) in summer—charge an hourly fee for nonmembers. *341 8th Ave. (at 27th St.), Garment District, 212/989–8572. Subway: C, E to 23rd St.*

1 *d-3*

RANDALL'S ISLAND

These 11 outdoor courts are covered by a bubble during the winter. *Randall's Island.*

7 *a-5*

RIVERSIDE PARK

There are 10 clay courts at 96th Street and 10 hard courts at 119th Street. *Enter park at Riverside Dr. and 96th St. or 115th St., Upper West Side. Subway: 1, 2, 3, 9 to 96th St.; 116th St./Columbia University.*

9 *g-2*

SUTTON EAST TENNIS CLUB

From October to April there's a bubble under the Queensboro Bridge, with eight clay courts inside available for a steep fee. *488 E. 60th St., Upper East Side, 212/751–3452. Subway: 59th St.*

9 *e-5*

TENNIS CLUB AT GRAND CENTRAL

This club has the city's oldest and most uniquely located indoor courts, but the hourly fees top a whopping $100. *15 Vanderbilt Ave., 3rd floor, Midtown, 212/687–3841. Subway: 42nd St./Grand Central.*

queens

1 *g-3*

ALLEY POND PARK

In winter these 16 municipal courts are covered by a bubble to become the private **Alley Pond Tennis Club** (718/468–1239). *Grand Central Pkwy. and Winchester Blvd., Bayside.*

3 *d-2*

ASTORIA PARK

There are 14 courts here under the Triborough Bridge. *21st St. and Hoyt Ave., Astoria. Subway: Astoria Blvd./Hoyt Ave.*

1 *g-3*

CUNNINGHAM PARK

This park has 20 hard courts. *Union Tpke. and 193rd St., Holliswood.*

3 *c-4*

FILA SPORTS CLUB

You can take a shuttle bus from Manhattan to this large private tennis club. The 20 courts are outdoors in the summer, indoors in the winter. *44–02 Vernon Blvd. (at 44th Ave.), Long Island City, 718/784–0600. Shuttle from Sutton Theatre, 3rd Ave. and 57th St., Midtown. Subway: 21st St./Queensbridge.*

3 h-1

FLUSHING FIELDS

In the shadow of the U.S.T.A. Center, these eight courts are kept in excellent shape and are accordingly busy. *Flushing Meadows–Corona Park, Flushing. Subway: Willets Point/Shea Stadium.*

1 f-5

FOREST PARK

This park has 14 courts—seven hard and seven clay. *Park La. S and 89th St., Woodhaven. Subway: 85th St./Forest Pkwy.*

1 f-3

KISSENA PARK

This quiet section of the park has eight clay courts and four hard courts. *Rose Ave. and Parsons Blvd., Kissena. Subway: Main St./Flushing.*

3 h-2

U.S.T.A. NATIONAL TENNIS CENTER

Considering the great playing that takes place on these courts, the hourly fees are pretty reasonable, generally topping out at $25. There are 22 courts, some of them indoors and lighted. *Flushing Meadows–Corona Park, 718/760–6200. Subway: Willets Point/Shea Stadium.*

staten island

1 b-1

SILVER LAKE PARK

These four courts have an idyllic locale, but they've seen better days. *Hart Blvd. and Revere St., Brighton Heights.*

1 b-1

WALKER PARK

There are six hard courts here. *Bard Ave. and Delafield Pl., Livingston.*

VOLLEYBALL

There are more than 330 volleyball courts in New York City; young 9-to-5ers spike hard after work. Call your borough's Parks office (*see* Parks Information, *above*) for the one nearest you.

BIG CITY VOLLEYBALL LEAGUE

Show up for the four-hour Friday Night Club ($12) to spike and socialize. Call for locations, which depend on your level of play. *212/288–4240.*

NEW YORK URBAN PROFESSIONALS

It sounds like a yuppie group, and it is, but they have games open to all ($10) on Friday night. Locations vary depending on level. *212/877–3614.*

11 b-7

PIER 25

There's an outdoor sand volleyball court right on the Hudson, on so-called Manhattan Beach Inc. A group can rent the entire court for an hourly fee; individuals can play for a daily rate. *N. Moore St. and 12th Ave., Tribeca, 212/732–7467. Subway: Chambers St.*

WRESTLING

Madison Square Garden (*see* Sports Stadiums, *above*) has championship, professional, and exhibition wrestling matches one weekend a month. For information, call 212/465–6741.

YOGA

A system of exercises for mental and physical well-being, yoga techniques teach breathing, postures, movement, and meditation. Most gyms around town offer some kind of yoga program, but you usually have to be a member to take the classes.

brooklyn

12 f-6

CENTRAL PARK SLOPE YOGA CENTER

Hatha, Astanga, Vinyasa, and Jivamukti yoga are all offered at this laid-back center, which opened in 1999. *792 Union St., Park Slope, 718/789–2288. Subway: D, Q to 7th Ave.*

12 g-7

PARK SLOPE YOGA CENTER

The inner body is the focus at this center, which teaches Kundalini yoga. Kundalini is a dynamic blend of breathing, movement, and flexibility. Classes are $10 each, with quantity discounts. *473 13th St. (between 8th Ave. and Prospect Park W), Park Slope, 718/832–1559. Subway: 15th St./Prospect Park.*

manhattan

10 c-1

INTEGRAL YOGA INSTITUTE

This is New York's best-known yoga institute, with Hatha classes, including ones for prenatal and postpartum needs, Spanish speakers, and HIV-positive students, at all levels but not all prices—each costs under $12. *227 W. 13th St., West Village, 212/929–0586. Subway: A, C, E to 14th St.; L to 8th Ave.*

9 b-1

200 W. 72nd St., Upper West Side, 212/721–4000. Subway: 1, 2, 3, 9 to 72nd St.

9 d-7

IYENGAR YOGA INSTITUTE

The Iyengar method is rooted in Hatha yoga and focuses heavily on postures and alignments. The postures are adapted to the needs of the students and while the classes are not overly athletic, they are not static either. This institute offers a free introductory class once a month and others at different levels for under $20 per class. *27 W. 24th St., Suite 800, Chelsea, 212/691–9642. Subway: F to 23rd St.*

9 f-3

JIVAMUKTI YOGA CENTER

The Taj Mahal of Manhattan yoga centers, this glamorous facility boasts meditation rooms, loads of classes, and the occasional celebrity fashion show. *404 Lafayette St., 3rd floor, Greenwich Village, 212/353–0214. Subway: 6 to Astor Pl.*

11 f-2

KUNDALINI YOGA CENTER

As at the Park Slope Yoga Center (see Brooklyn, *above*), here they teach the Kundalini method, the "Yoga of Awareness." Call for schedule and class location. *419 Lafayette St., 5th floor, Greenwich Village, 212/475–0212. Subway: Astor Pl.*

9 c-7

SIVANANDA YOGA VEDANTA CENTER

One of the oldest and busiest yoga centers in Manhattan, Sivananda teaches Hatha yoga and follows the practice of stilling the body to still the mind. It has classes for all ages and all levels. Both 1- and 1½-hour classes are under $10, with member discounts, and the first class is free. *243 W. 24th St., Chelsea, 212/255–4560. Subway: C, E to 23rd St.*

9 e-8

YOGA ASANA CENTER

This establishment, which opened in 1999, is on the second floor of a walk-up building and it is spare and peaceful. It is run by Yogi Dharma Mittra and offers children's yoga, as well as more advanced classes. The drop in price is $15 and there are discounts for monthly purchases. *297 3rd Ave. (between 22nd and 23rd Sts.), Flatiron District, 212/889–8160/ Subway: N, R to 23rd St.*

9 e-3

YOGA ZONE

The teaching method is called ISHTAR (Integral Science of Hatha and Tantra Arts), and the studios are elegant. Classes are $15. *160 E. 56th St., Midtown, 212/935–9642. Subway: 59th St./Lexington Ave.*

9 e-8

38 5th Ave. (between 18th and 19th Sts.), Flatiron District, 212/647–9642. Subway: N, R to 23rd St.

fitness centers, health clubs, & spa services

With striking views, plush locker rooms, state-of-the-art equipment, and spa services at so many private gyms, you'd think people just showed up to relax. But no matter how much time gym members might spend networking, flexing in the mirror, or adjusting their spandex, they do go to the gym to work out. And only a city with such a fitness-obsessed populace could support such a variety of options. Don't take the decision of which gym to join lightly—you're choosing an identity. You're also probably forking over an arm and a leg initiation fee plus a chunk of your salary in monthly dues. Look for corporate discounts, join-with-a-friend specials, and sales, and ask if any fees can be waived or reduced.

Many of the more exclusive clubs are so intent on keeping the riffraff out that only members and prospective members are allowed past the front desk. These institutions are designated "Members Only" below. Those that allow members to bring guests are designated "Member Guests Only." Others charge visitors fees for classes or one-day use of all facilities; often these fees are discounted or waived if a member brings you. All clubs have people to show you around personally if you profess an interest in membership.

PUBLIC HEALTH CLUBS

City-operated rec centers are unbelievable bargains. For just $10–$25 per year you have everything you'd expect from a health club—pools, basketball, weights, training equipment, machines, and even classes. The schedules aren't as packed as those at private clubs, but neither are the locker rooms. Manhattan locations include the magnificent, former public-bath building **Asser Levy** (see Swimming, above), **Carmine Street** (see Swimming, above), **East 54th Street** (1st Ave. and 54th St., 212/397–3154), and **West 59th Street** (10th Ave. and 59th St., 212/397–3159). All told, there are more than 30 centers throughout the five boroughs. For more information call the Parks Department (see Parks, above).

PRIVATE HEALTH CLUBS

9 c-8

AMERICAN FITNESS CENTER
This club is heavy on strength training, cardio equipment, and personal training, but it has a full schedule of aerobic and conditioning classes. Non-members can use the facilities after paying a $15 fee. *128 8th Ave. (at 16th St.), Chelsea, 212/627–0065. Subway: A, C, E to 14th St.; L to 8th Ave.*

7 g-6

ASPHALT GREEN
A unique public-private partnership turned an old asphalt plant into this fitness and arts complex. The 50-meter pool blows everything else in the city out of the water, but don't underestimate the rest of the place—weights and weight training overlooking the East River, aerobic and conditioning classes such as Guts and Butts, an eye-catching AstroTurf field, and numerous community programs and programs for people with disabilities. *555 E. 90th St., Upper East Side, 212/369–8890. Subway: 4, 5, 6 to 86th St.*

9 e-3

BALLY TOTAL FITNESS
Inexpensive and convenient locations (in the city and across the country) are the pluses; waits for machines and limited class offerings and amenities are the minuses. For a full list of locations, call 800/846–0256. *45 E. 55th St., Midtown, 212/688–6630. Subway: E, F to 5th Ave.*

7 e-7

144–146 E. 86th St., Upper East Side, 212/722–7371. Subway: 4, 5, 6 to 86th St.

10 e-6

641 6th Ave. (between 19th and 20th Sts.), Chelsea, 212/645–4565. Subway: F to 23rd St.

9 f-2

THE SPORTS CLUB/LA
The same folks who run the Reebok club (see below) bring a West Coast state of mind (and style) to the world of fitness for pay. The club, which is scheduled to open in early 2000, will measure 140,000 square ft and will include a rock-climbing wall, two NBA-size basketball courts, and a 4,000 square-ft rooftop "Terrace Body Mind Solarium" (translation: an outdoor yoga studio where classes are held in fair weather). *330 E. 61st St., Upper East Side, 212/355–5100. Member guests only. Subway: 59th St./Lexington Ave.*

9 a-7

BASKETBALL CITY
With six full-size hardwood courts, electronic scoreboards, and computer-arranged pickup games, there's no denying the focus here. But Basketball City also has volleyball courts, a complete fitness center, and good locker rooms. *Chelsea Piers, Pier 63 (23rd St. and 12th Ave.), Chelsea, 212/924–4040. Member guests only. Subway: C, E to 23rd St.*

9 a-7

CHELSEA PIERS SPORTS CENTER
Imagine passing endless rows of top-of-the-line weight machines, cardio equipment, and free weights; fitness studios with every imaginable class; a boxing ring; basketball/volleyball courts; and then a 46-ft climbing wall, and then seeing it all again on your way back to a six-lane, 25-yard pool, and you're probably out of breath already. Now imagine seeing all that as you run around an *indoor* ¼-mi track, and you have some idea of

what the Sports Center is like. The pool is at the end of the pier above the Hudson and has deck-to-ceiling glass windows on three sides, just in case you didn't notice the view. Add a sundeck and appropriately luxurious locker rooms and you don't feel so bad about the $1,600 a year (or $36/day) it takes to be here. *Chelsea Piers (23rd St. and 12th Ave.), Pier 60, Chelsea, 212/336–6000. Subway: C, E to 23rd St.*

9 *f-3*

CRUNCH

A failed actor put his creative talents to good use in building this empire of fitness clubs and associated paraphernalia. The classes are loud, in-your-face, and sometimes unexpected—African Dancing, Thighs and Gossip, Fat Blaster. The machines are abundant, but locker-room amenities are not. The Second Avenue location has a small climbing wall. A $22 guest fee gets non-members in the door for the day. *1109 2nd Ave. (at 59th St.), Upper East Side, 212/758–3434; for other locations, 212/620–7867. Subway: 59th St./Lexington Ave.*

11 *f-1*

404 Lafayette St. (at Astor Pl.), Greenwich Village, 212/614–0120. Subway: Astor Pl.

7 *e-7*

DAVID BARTON

Individual training, cardio equipment, and cushy couches, rather than extensive classes, are what draw people to this eponymous, bodybuilder-owned gym. *30 E. 85th St., Upper East Side, 212/517–7577. Members only. Subway: 4, 5, 6 to 86th St.*

11 *e-3*

623 Broadway (between Houston and Bleecker Sts.), Greenwich Village, 212/420–0507. Subway: Bleecker St., Broadway–Lafayette St.

10 *d-1*

522 6th Ave. (at 15th St.), Chelsea, 212/727–0004. Subway: F to 14th St.

12 *b-2*

EASTERN ATHLETIC CLUBS

These spacious Brooklyn centers have full programs of classes and numerous sports offerings, including swimming, martial arts, racquet sports, and dance. A day pass costs $20. *43 Clark St., Brooklyn Heights, 718/625–0500. Subway: Clark St.*

12 *g-5*

17 Eastern Pkwy. (between Plaza and Underhill Sts.), Park Slope, Brooklyn, 718/789–4600. Subway: Grand Army Plaza.

7 *b-8*

EQUINOX

All three of your selves—physical, mental, and spiritual—will be challenged here, with East-meets-West and martial arts–based classes taught by instructors who have become local celebrities. As you'd expect for the premium you pay to belong, equipment is up-to-date, plentiful, and in good working order. *344 Amsterdam Ave. (at 76th St.), Upper West Side, 212/721–4200. Subway: 79th St.; other locations. Members only.*

9 *b-5*

MANHATTAN PLAZA HEALTH CLUB

One of the few independent clubs in town, this Hell's Kitchen standout stays one step ahead of its bigger competitors without being outrageously expensive or intimidating. It has everything you expect in a complete health club—25-yard lap pool, quality equipment, and a full schedule of classes including the latest trends (spinning, PowerBoards). Then there are the extras—the pool's retractable roof; the outdoor sundeck; the climbing wall that opened years before people had heard of such a thing; the tennis club's rooftop courts. *482 W. 43rd St., Hell's Kitchen, 212/563–7001. Members only. Subway: 42nd St./Port Authority*

10 *e-8*

NEW YORK HEALTH AND RACQUET CLUB

As the name suggests, this club is best for tennis and racquetball, but for people into those games it's a way of life—you get access to the club's party yacht, Westchester beach club, and social calendar. Its many locations offer plenty of courts, machines, and classes. Though visitors are allowed, the $50 fee is unwelcoming. *39 Whitehall St., Lower Manhattan, 212/269–9800; call for other locations. Subway: Whitehall St./South Ferry.*

9 *c-2*

NEW YORK SPORTS CLUB

The omnipresence award goes to NYSC—chances are you're within a few blocks of one now. They also win the high-strung–yuppie award: 9-to-5ers pack the clubs after work for reservations-only classes, willing to wait anxiously to burn their calories on equipment that's gathering dust the rest of the day. That said, it's worth mentioning that the equipment is kept up-to-date, the classes incorporate the latest trends, and thousands of people swear by this gym. Day passes go for $25 here. *61 W. 62nd St., Upper West Side, 212/265–0995; for other locations call 800/796–6972. Subway: 59th St./Columbus Circle.*

10 *e-7*

30 Wall St., Lower Manhattan, 212/482–4800. Subway: Wall St.

9 *d-6*

50 W. 34th St., Garment District, 212/868–0820. Subway: 34th St./Herald Square.

11 *b-3*

PRINTING HOUSE FITNESS AND RACQUET CLUB

With great West Side views, plenty of space, and diverse offerings, this is another down-to-earth independent option, and it draws some West Village celebs. Racquetball and squash courts are available, as is a classes-only membership. *421 Hudson St. (at Leroy St.), West Village, 212/243–7600. Members only. Subway: Houston St.*

9 *b-1*

REEBOK SPORTS CLUB NEW YORK

The line between theme park and what this purports to be is a thin one. The facilities are awesome—25-yard lap pool, ⅙-mi track, full-size basketball courts with stands, 45-ft climbing wall, every machine you can think of. The classes, in 2,500-square-ft studios, also run the full range. The initiation fee is more than $1,000, after which the monthly rate is still no bargain. *160 Columbus Ave. (at 67th St.), Upper West Side, 212/362–6800. Members only. Subway: 66th St./Lincoln Center.*

11 *e-3*

WORLD GYM

For pumping iron and an outrageous number of classes 24 hours a day, this is your place. *232 Mercer St. (between Bleecker and W. 3rd Sts.), Greenwich Village, 212/780–7407. Subway: W. 4th St./Washington Square.*

9 *b-2*

1926 Broadway (between 64th and 65th Sts.), Upper West Side, 212/874–0942. Subway: 66th St./Lincoln Center.

9 *f-4*

YMCA

If you feel out-glitzed, out-priced, and old-fashioned at the city's other fitness emporiums, do yourself a favor and visit the Y. Built as veritable community centers, city Ys do a fine job of keeping you fit and making you feel good about the world. Make no assumptions about the offerings—equipment is in good shape, classes are challenging, locker rooms are clean, and pools are excellent. You might not end up ahead of this week's fitness trend, but you'll stay in shape. *Vanderbilt Y, 224 E. 47th St., Midtown, 212/756–9600; call for other locations. Subway: 51st St./Lexington–3rd Aves.*

7 *e-6*

92ND STREET YM-YWHA

Best known for its cultural programming, the 92nd Street Y deserves recognition for its fitness facilities, too. Classes here cover everything from yoga to spinning to line dancing, for all age groups; facilities include a 25-yard pool, racquetball courts, and a 5,000-square-ft, fully stocked "cardio court," with machines that keep your heart in motion. *1395 Lexington Ave. (at 92nd St.), Upper East Side, 212/415–5729. Subway: 6 to 96th St.*

9 *e-3*

YWCA

This predominantly female center is another down-to-earth deal. It has a pool, a good array of machines, and an unusually large selection of self-improvement classes. *610 Lexington Ave. (at 53rd St.), Midtown, 212/735–9753. Subway: 51st St./Lexington–3rd Aves.*

DAY SPAS

New York is a city with something for everyone, and spa services are no exception. With enough time, and money, experts will slough your skin with sugar, wrap you in seaweed, submerge you in mud, encase you in wax, rub you with stones—and basically find a way to pamper you with any material they can get their hands on. The results are usually heavenly, but be warned—if it sounds too good to be true, it probably is.

9 *e-3*

AVON CENTRE

This is not your mother's Avon. Gone are the days of apricot lipstick and door-to-door sales. In their place is this slick spa that sports a waiting room as large as a hotel lobby and top-notch treatment rooms. Massages are delightful, facials are first class, and eyebrow guru Eliza is the best in the city—as you'll begin to discover when you try to get an appointment. Brad Johns, the king of blonde, is slated to take over the hair salon. *Trump Tower, 725 5th Ave. (at 57th St.), 5th floor, Midtown, 212/310–6305. Subway: N, R to 5th Ave.*

9 *e-4*

AWAY SPA
Your reward for traversing the frenetic lobby of the W Hotel is the quiet and elegant atmosphere of this New Age–style spa. Come with an open mind and try such unique treatments as color hydrotherapy, aura imaging, and the Javanese Lulur—a Far East treatment where you'll be massaged with rice, turmeric, and yogurt and leave feeling sensuously smooth. There's also a full menu of more traditional skin and body treatments. *W Hotel, 541 Lexington Ave. (at 49th St.), Midtown, 212/407–2970. Subway: 51st St./Lexington–3rd Aves.*

11 *e-4*

BLISS SPA
Possibly the first spa that's as trendy as a nightclub—wasn't that Uma?—Bliss is so popular it can often take months to get an appointment here. What awaits when you finally make it in? Wine and cheese in the lounge area, oxygen facials, dreamy pedicures, and first-rate massage. *568 Broadway (at Prince St.), 212/219–8970. Subway: Broadway–Lafayette St.; Prince St.*

9 *e-3*

19 E. 57th St. (between 5th and Madison Aves.), 3rd floor, Midtown, 212/219–9870. Subway: 57th St.

9 *d-3*

CHRISTINA & CARMEN
This Romanian mother-and-daughter team uses traditional techniques in their deep pore-cleansing facials, body-sloughing with paraffin, and stress-relieving shiatsu massage. *128 Central Park S (between 6th and 7th Aves.), Midtown, 212/757–5811. Subway: B, Q, N, R to 57th St.*

9 *e-3*

CHRISTINE VALMY
Renowned skin-care expert Christine Valmy helped American women discover skin care. Using Swiss fresh-cell therapy, she gives both men and women two-hour facials and offers post-plastic surgery care, makeup, and foot massage. A special pretheater package includes facial, manicure, shampoo, and blow-dry. Weekdays you can opt for a lower-price facial by a supervised student at the Valmy School for Aestheticians (212/581–1520 for appt.). *767 5th Ave. (at 58th St.), Midtown, 212/752–0303. Subway: N, R to 5th Ave.*

9 *d-3*

101 W. 57th St. (between 6th and 7th Aves.), Midtown, 212/581–9488. Subway: B, Q to 57th St.

9 *d-3*

DIANE YOUNG
Come here for holistic skin care in a beautiful setting. Young offers facials, treatments, herbal aromatherapy, expert nutritional advice, makeup lessons, manicures, pedicures, Swedish massage, waxing, and electrolysis (with disposable needles). *38 E. 57th St., Midtown (near Madison Ave.), 212/753–1200. Subway: N, R to 5th Ave.*

9 *d-3*

DORIT BAXTER
Facials, body scrubs and treatments, and a full-service salon are wrapped up in a convenient Midtown location. *47 W. 57th. St. (between 5th and 6th Ave.), Midtown, 212/371–4542. Subway: B, Q to 57th St.*

9 *e-1*

ELENA POCIU
Romanian-born Pociu runs a full-service skin-care salon, specializing in facials. Her masks are made on the premises. *23 E. 67th St. (near Madison Ave.), Upper East Side, 212/717–5543. Subway: 68th St./Hunter College.*

9 *e-3*

ELIZABETH ARDEN/THE SALON
Just knock on the red door for head-to-toenail pampering in this Midtown minispa. Expert facials and free makeup applications are among the many highlights. Treat yourself or a loved one to a Miracle Morning or a Main Chance Day:

You get a spell in the sauna followed by massage, haircut and styling, facial, manicure and pedicure, eyebrow shaping, and makeup. *691 5th Ave. (near 54th St.), 212/486–7900. Subway: E, F to 5th Ave.*

11 *d-4*

ERBE

A favorite with SoHo denizens, Erbe offers both facials and massages as well as an amazing line of Italian herb- and flower-based skin products. *196 Prince St. (near MacDougal St.), SoHo, 212/ 966–1445. Subway: Prince St.*

9 *f-3*

ESTEE LAUDER

Reward yourself after a hard day of shopping at this spa nestled in the heart of Bloomingdale's. Facials are a specialty here, and are an exceptionally good value for the level of expertise and amount of attention involved. Other top choices include a jet lag treatment, sunless tanning, massage, and pedicure. *1000 3rd Ave. (at 59th St.), 212/705–2318. Subway: 59th St./Lexington Ave.*

9 *e-3*

FREDERIC FEKKAI BEAUTÉ DE PROVENCE

The top floors of celebrity stylist Fekkai's Provençal-style townhouse serve as a home to upscale body and facial services ranging from European facials to sunless tanning treatments. *15 E. 57th St. (near Madison Ave.), Midtown, 212/ 753–9500. Subway: E, F, N, R to 5th Ave.*

9 *e-3*

GEORGETTE KLINGER SKIN CARE

Klinger's famously expert skin treatments include surface peeling, deep-pore cleansing, and scalp care for both women and men. Take advantage of the new full-day, full-body "Intensive Curriculum," also for both sexes. The only drawback is a hard sell of the product line. *501 Madison Ave. (near 52nd St.), Midtown, 212/838–3200. Subway: 51st St./Lexington–3rd Aves.*

7 *e-8*

978 Madison Ave. (near 77th St.), Upper East Side, 212/744–6900. Subway: 77th St.

9 *e-3*

JANET SARTIN

Come in for a consultation and get a product-and-treatment prescription from a world-famous skin expert—Sartin herself charges $400 for a 90-minute pore-cleansing facial. The staff is well trained, and the clientele is high on the social registry. *480 Park Ave. (near 58th St.), Midtown, 212/751–5858. Subway: 59th St./Lexington Ave.*

9 *e-3*

LIA SCHORR SKIN CARE

Every client's skin is analyzed prior to treatment, resulting in sensible care, especially for sensitive and acne-plagued skin. The restorative Day of Beauty includes a facial, body massage, manicure, pedicure, makeup, and snack. Men are welcome, too. *686 Lexington Ave. (near 57th St.), Midtown, 212/486–9670. Subway: 59th St./Lexington Ave.*

9 *f-3*

MARIO BADESCU SKIN CARE

Sadly, Mario is gone, but his expert analyses and natural-formula skin products for women and men still have a loyal following. Other options include manicures, pedicures, massage, waxing, and electrolysis. *320 E. 52nd St. (between 2nd and 3rd Aves.), Midtown, 212/758–1065. Subway: 51st St./Lexington–3rd Aves.*

11 *d-7*

MILLEFLEURS

Patterned after an Egyptian temple, Millefleurs offers herbal wraps, scrubs, massages, facials, reflexology, acupuncture, and even colonics in an incredible setting complete with waterfalls. *6 Varick St. (at Franklin St.), Tribeca, 212/966–3656. Subway: Franklin St.*

9 *a-7*

ORIGINS FEEL-GOOD SPA

Reward yourself after a hard Chelsea Piers workout at this somewhat cramped spa where massage, reflexology, facials, acupressure, and body treatments are administered using the popular line of Origins products. *The Sports Center, Pier 60, Chelsea Piers (12th Ave. and 23rd St.), Chelsea, 212/336–6780. Subway: C, E to 23rd St.*

9 *d-3*

PENINSULA SPA

Tucked in the Peninsula Hotel, this truly deluxe facility provides all the expected treatments plus a full gym, a salon, and an incredible outdoor pool by which to take in the equally incredible view. Facials here are some of the best in the city. *700 5th Ave. (at 55th St.), 21st floor, Midtown, 212/903–3910. Subway: N, R to 5th Ave.*

9 *e-2*

PETER COPPOLA SALON

A solid hour of old-fashioned pampering, using hypo-allergenic Italian products, cleans your skin without the usual squeezing. *746 Madison Ave. (between 64th and 65th Sts.), Upper East Side, 212/988–9404. Subway: 68th St./Hunter College.*

11 *e-5*

SOHO SANCTUARY

An oasis of tranquillity in a hectic city, this women-only spa combines traditional facials and massages with New Age music, meditation, and yoga to such a positive effect that you'll feel light-years away from the tension that sent you there. The super-spacious locker area includes a soothing eucalyptus steam room. *119 Mercer St. (between Prince and Spring Sts.), SoHo, 212/334-5550. Subway: Prince St.*

11 *c-7*

ULA SKIN CARE SALON

In a discreet Tribeca location, Ula offers nine different facials and seven different body treatments plus waxing, electrolysis, manicures, and pedicures in a highly relaxing setting. *22 Harrison St. (between Hudson and Greenwich Sts.), 212/343–2376. Subway: Franklin St.*

11 *c-3*

YANA HERBAL BEAUTY SALON

Fans of Yana's have raved about her relaxing herbal facials for years. A little-known fact is that Yana also waxes, using the ancient Middle Eastern technique that involves sugar instead of wax. *270 6th Ave. (between Houston and Bleecker Sts.), West Village, 212/254–6200. Subway: W. 4th St./Washington Sq.*

MASSAGE

In addition to the names listed below, almost all day spas in the city offer massage services. *See above* for more information.

9 *d-8*

CARAPAN

Decorated to look and feel like New Mexico, Carapan specializes in Swedish massage but offers seven other kinds, as well as facials, craniosacral therapy, and other healing measures. It's a treasure. *5 W. 16th St. (between 5th and 6th Aves.), Chelsea, 212/633–6220. Subway: F to 14th St.*

7 *b-8*

CYNTHIA CRISP

A licensed massage therapist, Cynthia Crisp is trained in everything from acupuncture to lymph drainage to Mongolian bone massage. Her fans include Donna Karan and Lou Reed. *127 W. 79th St. (between Amsterdam and Columbus Aves.), Upper West Side, 212/228–0900. Subway: 79th St.*

9 *d-7*

OHASHI INSTITUTE

This spa offers Ohashi Shiatsu, a form of traditional bodywork created by Japanese healer Ohashi. The environment is low-key; clients lie on soft mats surrounded by Japanese paper screens *12 W. 27th St. (between 5th and 6th Aves.), Chelsea, 212/684–4190. Subway: N, R to 28th St.; F to 23rd St.*

10 *d-1*

STONE SPA

If you come here with an open mind, you're sure to leave with a relaxed body. At the beginning of a massage, smooth stones from the Salt River in Arizona are heated through and placed at strategic points on the body. The heat radiates from the stones as skilled masseurs knead your stress away. *104 W. 14th St. (at 6th Ave.), Chelsea, 212/741–8881. Subway: F to 14th St.*

9 *e-2*

THE STRESS LESS STEP

This no-nonsense massage center— note the "Talking Discouraged" signs— offers Swedish, shiatsu, and reflexology. Celebrities drop in from the Regency Hotel, across the street. *48 E. 61st St. (near Madison Ave.), Upper East Side, 212/826–6222. Subway: 59th St./Lexington Ave.*

chapter 4

PLACES TO EXPLORE

galleries, gargoyles, museums, and more

New York is one of those cities that beguiles you into thinking you've seen it all, then reveals itself anew again and again. In fact, one of the greatest pleasures of exploring the city is to discover, or to rediscover, the charms to be found virtually everywhere, whether the discovery is an entire neighborhood or an old mansion or a monumental skyscraper. Often, these discoveries are subtle. Walking through Grand Central Station for the hundredth time, for instance, you may suddenly be overwhelmed by the amazing elegance and efficiency of this public space. Of course, New York is often anything but subtle, and you may well succumb to the spells of even its brashest landmarks—even the most sophisticated native might thrill at the view from the top of the Empire State Building. The lesson? Take time to enjoy the fabled sidewalks of New York in all their richness—and, of course, look up every once in a while, too.

where to go

ARCHITECTURE

Nothing evokes New York City more dramatically than its skyline, an ever-evolving mountain range of steel, glass, and concrete. Here are the city's most significant achievements in urban architecture—the buildings that taken in sum constitute the world's most famous skyline but should be admired individually, too. Each site is introduced with the name of its architect and the year the project was completed.

9 b-1

ANSONIA HOTEL

(Paul E.M. Duboy, 1904) An exuberant architectural masterpiece, complete with turrets, a mansard roof, and filigreed-iron balconies, the Upper West Side's Ansonia Hotel was inspired by turn-of-the-20th-century Beaux-Arts buildings in Paris. The luxury doesn't stop on the outside; the apartments inside are soundproof, and once attracted such musical stars as Enrico Caruso, Igor Stravinsky, Lily Pons, and Arturo Toscanini as longtime residents. *2109 Broadway (between 73rd and 74th Sts.), Upper West Side. Subway: 1, 2, 3, 9 to 72nd St.*

10 d-7

BATTERY PARK CITY

(Master plan by Cooper, Eckstut Assoc., 1979; individual buildings by various architects) Not since Rockefeller Center has New York undertaken such an ambitious physical project. Battery Park City was a mere gleam in urban planners' eyes until the 1980s, and though it's largely complete, parts of it are still under construction. Built on a 92-acre stretch of landfill along the Hudson River at Manhattan's southern tip, this city within a city combines high-rise office and residential towers with open space, outdoor sculpture, and a delightful, riverside public esplanande. Its stone, ceramic, glass, and bronze buildings—in shapes recalling the '30s—are a spectacular addition to the downtown skyline. The most impressive of these, the four-tower World Financial Center (Cesar Pelli, 1988) has 6 million square ft of office space and 220,000 square ft of shops and restaurants. Its centerpiece, the Winter Garden, a towering glass pavilion–cum–urban greenhouse, houses 16 palm trees (New York's first) under its 120-ft vaulted roof and overlooks a 3-acre river plaza and yacht marina. Nearby, a little commuter ferry shuttles workers to and from New Jersey. *Hudson River from Battery Pl. to Vesey St., Lower Manhattan. Subway: Cortlandt St./World Trade Center.*

9 d-4

CBS BUILDING

(Eero Saarinen & Associates, 1965) Best known for his sleek, minimalist designs, Saarinen applied Modernism only once to a skyscraper—and you can observe the results right here. Framed in concrete and covered with dark granite, the pet name of this 38-story high-rise is Black Rock. *51 W. 52nd St. (at 6th Ave.), Midtown. Subway: 47th–50th St./Rockefeller Center.*

9 e-5

CHANIN BUILDING

(Sloan & Robertson, 1929) Like the nearby Chrysler Building (*see below*), the Chanin Building is one of the masterpieces of Art Deco. Most notable are its stylized ornamentation and intricate detail, ranging from the terra-cotta bas-relief and bronze frieze on the lower facade to the bronze grills and "jeweled" clocks in the lobby. *122 E. 42nd St. (at Lexington Ave.), Midtown. Subway: 42nd St./Grand Central.*

10 e-7
CHASE MANHATTAN BANK TOWER & PLAZA

(Skidmore, Owings & Merrill, 1960) In front of this 65-story tower, lower Manhattan's first boxy, aluminum-and-glass high-rise, is a plaza that contains a circular sculpture garden designed by famed sculptor Isamu Noguchi (*see* Isamu Noguchi Garden Museum in Art Museums, *below*) and a whimsical, 25-ton papier-mâché-like sculpture by Jean Dubuffet, "Group of Four Trees." *1 Chase Manhattan Plaza (between Nassau & William Sts., below Liberty St.), Lower Manhattan. Subway: Wall St.*

9 e-5
CHRYSLER BUILDING

(William Van Alen, 1930) Particularly at dusk, when the setting sun makes the building's gleaming Art Deco spire practically glow, the Chrysler Building is perhaps the most pleasing of New York's many skyscrapers. The Chrysler was one of the first skyscrapers to be faced with stainless steel—including the gargoyles, which were modeled after car-hood ornaments. At 1,048 ft, it was the tallest building in the world until the Empire State Building was completed only a few months later. *405 Lexington Ave. (at 42nd St.), Midtown. Subway: 42nd St./Grand Central.*

9 e-4
CITICORP CENTER

(Hugh Stubbins & Associates, 1977) With its uniquely angled silhouette and greenish-silver satin veneer, the Citicorp Center is among the most eye-catching forms in the Midtown skyline. At street level it appears to stand on monster stilts, and its sunlit, three-level atrium—one of the city's most successful—is a modern agora of shops and pedestrian activity. The building's jauntily slanted top was meant to be practical: It was intended for a solar-energy collector that was never installed. (*See* St. Peter's Church at the Citicorp Center in Churches & Synagogues, *below*.) *Lexington Ave. between 53rd and 54th Sts., Mid-town. Subway: 51st St./Lexington–3rd Aves.*

9 f-5
DAILY NEWS BUILDING

(Howells & Hood, 1930) Although the *News* moved out in 1995, this building's inspiring Art Deco ornamentation, commissioned by Joseph Patterson, the founder of the nation's first tabloid newspaper, remains. After admiring the striped brickwork and the entrance relief depicting light dawning on the urban populace (an obvious reference to the enlightening power of the press), check out the lobby, which houses a huge, revolving globe (12 ft in diameter) and a floor that resembles a gigantic compass. *220 E. 42nd St. (between 2nd and 3rd Aves.), Midtown. Subway: 42nd St./Grand Central.*

9 d-6
EMPIRE STATE BUILDING

(Shreve, Lamb & Harmon, 1931) Although at 1,454 ft it's no longer the world's tallest building (it currently ranks seventh), the Empire State Building remains the world's most glamorous skyscrapers—the defining structure of the New York City skyline and the symbol of Manhattan. Its enormity (the steel frame alone weighs 60,000 tons) is belied by the delicacy and balance of its design; the needlelike spire and dramatic setbacks create a sense of height and majesty that when viewed for the first time (or even the thousandth) has sent many a heart aflutter with excitement. Illumination heightens the romance: blazing white light at nighttime and in holiday colors for special occasions: red and white for Valentine's Day, orange and yellow for Halloween, and blue and white when the Yankees win big. *350 5th Ave. (at 34th St.), Garment District. Subway: 34th St./Herald Sq.* For admission to the observatory, *see* Viewpoints, *below*.

10 e-7
EQUITABLE BUILDING

(Ernest R. Graham, 1915) An unrelenting mass, the 909-ft-high, 40-story Equitable Building swallowed up so much airspace from such a small plot of land (less than an acre) that it inspired the nation's first zoning laws in 1916. *120 Broadway (at Cedar St.), Lower Manhattan. Subway: Wall St.*

9 *e-8*

FLATIRON BUILDING

(D. H. Burnham & Co., 1902) Thanks to its alluring triangular shape (conceived to fit its triangular plot between 5th Ave., Broadway, and 23rd St.), this 286-ft-tall example of early "modern" architecture was New York's first true skyscraper and most famous building in the early 1900s, the subject of as many picture postcards as the Empire State Building and World Trade Center are today. The city's tallest building until 1908, the Flatiron was built with a revolutionary steel frame covered by a limestone and terracotta skin designed in the Italian Renaissance style. Due to blustery winds that kicked up at the building's busy front corner on the south side of Madison Square, policemen were assigned to chase away loafers who stopped to gaze at the upturned skirts of women, thus originating the phrase "23 skidoo." To see the Flatiron in all its splendor, take a walk down 5th Avenue from the north side of Madison Square. *175 5th Ave. (at 23rd St.), Flatiron District. Subway: N, R to 23rd St.*

9 *f-5*

FORD FOUNDATION BUILDING

(Kevin Roche, John Dinkeloo & Associates, 1967) Home to one of the largest philanthropic organizations in the world, the Ford Foundation Building is best known for its glass-wall, 130-ft-high atrium. Filled with trees, shrubs, a still-water pool, and all manner of greenery, this enclosed garden is a real respite from the crush around Grand Central Terminal. *320 E. 43rd St. (between 1st and 2nd Aves.), Midtown. Open weekdays 9–5. Subway: 42nd St./Grand Central.*

9 *e-5*

GRAND CENTRAL TERMINAL

(Warren & Wetmore, Reed & Stem, 1913; Beyer Blinder Belle, restoration plan 1998) This massive Beaux-Arts pile boasts the grandest interior space anywhere in New York, and an incredible four-year renovation (completed 1998) has rendered it all the more appealing. Crossed by more than 500,000 commuters every weekday, its massive main concourse (200 ft long, 120 ft wide, and 12 stories high) maintains a humane scale. Its vaulted ceiling is an enchanting piece of theater that displays a restored map of the night sky with starry constellations shining with fiber-optic light. A new marble staircase (like its twin across the concourse, modeled after the Garnier stair at the Paris Opera and included in the original terminal plans but never before built, has been seamlessly installed onto the concourse's east end, while gold- and nickel-plated chandeliers gleam once more in the passageways. With the recent renovation's doubling the original shop space (much of which had been abandoned by merchants), Grand Central has once again become a place where you might go not just to catch the train but to have dinner or simply stroll. And the outside isn't bad, either; Grand Central's southern facade, with three 60-ft-high arched windows overlooking Park Avenue, is topped by a soaring statue of Mercury, Hercules, and Minerva and a giant clock. Although it's hard to imagine now, Grand Central was on the verge of destruction in the 1960s, when the station's owners planned to build an office tower there—despite its landmark status. In the ensuing fracas, the city's Landmarks Commission defended Grand Central all the way to the U.S. Supreme Court, and in 1978, they won, affirming the city's tough landmark laws and setting a precedent for preserving New York's thousands of other historic buildings. *Vanderbilt Ave. and 42nd St., Midtown. Tours of Grand Central are given by the Municipal Art Society (212/935–3960) on Wed. at 12:30; meet at the information booth on the main concourse. Subway: 42nd St./Grand Central.*

9 *d-5*

GRACE BUILDING

(Skidmore, Owings & Merrill, 1974) This swooping glass behemoth across from Bryant Park has been derided as "flashy" and "flamboyant" yet is strangely appealing. The building's facade curves from a broad base to a slender top, accommodating public spaces on the lower floors and creating the overall effect of a ski jump. *41 W. 42nd St. (between 5th and 6th Aves.), Midtown. Subway: B, D, F, Q to 42nd St.*

7 *e-6*

GUGGENHEIM MUSEUM

(Frank Lloyd Wright, 1959) The Guggenheim is one of only two buildings in Manhattan designed by Frank Lloyd Wright (the other is a Mercedes-Benz showroom at Park Avenue and 56th Street), and is often visited as much for its architecture as for the art inside. The white exterior resembles an inverted cone; the much-vaunted interior houses a six-story rotunda under a skylit glass dome and a ¼-mi-long spiraling ramp leads down past exhibitions of modern art. The 10-story tower annex, opened in 1992 to provide much-needed extra gallery space, was designed by Gwathmey, Siegel & Assoc. based on Wright's original conception for the museum (see Art Museums, below). 1071 5th Ave. (at 89th St.), Upper East Side. Subway: 4, 5, 6 to 86th St.

11 e-6

HAUGHWOUT BUILDING

(J. P. Gaynor, 1857) With each window framed by Corinthian columns and rounded arches, this five-story, Palladio-inspired building is considered one of the best examples of cast-iron architecture in the world. It was equipped with the world's first elevator, designed by Elisha Graves Otis, who went on to found an elevator empire and make high-rises (and the modern skyscraper) practical possibilities. See SoHo Cast-Iron Historic District, below. 488–492 Broadway (at Broome St.), SoHo. Subway: N, R to Canal St.; 6 to Spring St.

9 e-3

IBM BUILDING

(Edward Larrabee Barnes, 1982) The 57th Street entrance to this sleek, green-granite-and-glass, prism-shape tower is set back under 40 cantilevered floors. Inside, a huge, glass atrium, filled with bamboo trees, is a tranquil public plaza for sitting. 590 Madison Ave. (at 57th St.), Midtown. Subway: E, F, N, R to 5th Ave.

9 a-6

JACOB K. JAVITS CONVENTION CENTER

(I. M. Pei & Partners, 1986) New York's mecca for conventions and trade shows occupies 1.8 million square ft of floor space on a 22-acre site and is built almost entirely of glass, drawing its inspiration from 19th-century "glass houses" designed to showcase exotic botanical exhibits. Little wonder that, with a dark green, crystalline-glass exterior made up of 16,100 glass panes, the convention center is sometimes called the Crystal Palace. 11th and 12th Aves. from 34th to 39th Sts, Hell's Kitchen. Subway: 34th St./Penn Station.

9 f-4

LESCAZE HOUSE

(William Lescaze, 1934) Designed by pioneering architect William Lescaze as his home and office, this town house—with its glass-block and ribboned windows—is considered the first Modern-style building in the city. 211 E. 48th St. (between 2nd and 3rd Aves.), Midtown. Subway: 51st St./Lexington–3rd Aves.

9 e-4

LEVER HOUSE

(Gordon Bunshaft of Skidmore, Owings & Merrill, 1952) One of the first metal-and-glass skyscrapers, this slim, blue-green tower stands on a one-story horizontal slab supported by chrome columns. Made for the soap-and-detergent empire Lever Brothers, it was designed to exude an aura of cleanliness. Its completion was considered an architectural watershed, leaving older skyscraper designs behind in favor of the increasingly sleek and commercial International Style. 390 Park Ave. (between 53rd and 54th Sts.), Midtown. Subway: 51st St./Lexington–3rd Aves.

9 b-2

LINCOLN CENTER FOR THE PERFORMING ARTS

(Various architects, 1962–68) Although Lincoln Center is unsurpassed for artistic variety and integrity, its architectural whole is greater than the sum of its parts. The center's buildings, all classical imitations decked out in the same cream-color travertine, include Avery Fisher Hall (Max Abramovitz, 1962, redesign Johnson/Burgee 1976), the New York State Theater (Philip Johnson, 1964), the Metropolitan Opera House (Wallace Harrison, 1966), the Juilliard School of Music (Pietro Bellushci, 1968), and the Vivian Beaumont Theater (Eero Saarinen, 1965). Although the list of architects reads like a Who's Who of Modernism, none of the buildings is terribly impressive on its own. Still, there is something tremendously freeing about the open spaces and plazas here at the foot of the Upper West Side. The public art is also notable: murals by Marc Chagall inside the Met, a Henry Moore sculpture in the reflecting pool, and two white marble sculptures by Elie Nadelman in the foyer of the New York State Theater. Columbus and Amsterdam Aves. from 62nd to 66th Sts., Upper West Side. Subway: 66th St./Lincoln Center.

9 f-4

THE LIPSTICK BUILDING

(Philip Johnson for John Burgee Architects, 1986) Architecture buffs love this rose-color office tower, a truly unique design by Philip Johnson, the founder of American Modernism. Elliptical in shape, the smooth, 34-story exterior has no corners, making it a dramatic departure from the rectangular megaboxes that dominate the rest of Midtown. "Effect before everything" was Johnson's personal motto. The building's resemblance to a tube of lipstick is augmented by two setbacks in its midsection. *885 3rd Ave. (between 53rd and 54th Sts.), Midtown. Subway: 51st St/Lexington–3rd Aves.*

9 c-5

MCGRAW-HILL BUILDING

(Raymond Hood, Godley & Fouilhoux, 1931) Sometimes said to look like a jukebox, this Art Moderne–cum–International Style high-rise is considered a masterpiece of design. Covered in sea-green terra-cotta, it has Art Deco details at street level and Carrera glass in the lobby. *330 W. 42nd St. (between 8th and 9th Aves.), Midtown. Subway: 47th–50th Sts./Rockefeller Center.*

9 e-1

PAUL MELLON HOUSE

(Mazza & Seccia, 1965) Snug alongside Italianate brownstones and neo-Georgian mansions on one of the city's most beautiful residential blocks, this light-as-air postwar town house is characterized by the experts as "French provincial." *125 E. 70th St. (between Park and Lexington Aves.), Upper East Side. Subway: 68th St./Hunter College.*

9 e-4

METROPOLITAN LIFE BUILDING (FORMERLY PAN AM BUILDING)

(Emery Roth & Sons, Pietro Belluschi, and Walther Gropius, 1963) Plunked down in the middle of Park Avenue, hovering over Grand Central Station, the 808-ft-tall Pan Am Building was reviled as an outsize concrete-clad monstrosity when it was built in the 1960s. With 2.4 million square ft of office space, it was the largest office building in Manhattan, and it destroyed a cherished vista down Park Avenue. One architecture critic even called it "toxic." Since the 1960s, however, it's become such an integral part of the city's skyline that people were upset when the name on the top of the building was changed from Pan Am to MetLife in the early '90s. *200 Park Ave. (at 46th St.), Midtown. Subway: 42nd St./Grand Central.*

9 d-5

NEW YORK PUBLIC LIBRARY

(Carrère & Hastings, 1911) Flanked by its two famous stone lions, the NYPL's Humanities and Social Sciences Library is considered, along with Grand Central Terminal, one of New York's most magnificent Beaux-Arts buildings. The beauty of its broad, plazalike stairway and column exterior is matched by the interior, particularly the grand stairways of the lobby and the princely third-floor main reading room. Renovated in 1999, the reading room consists of two connected halls stretching for 297 ft and is lined with row after row of long wooden tables, brass reading lamps, and 15 massive arched windows. Its ceiling rises 52 ft above the floor and is painted with an ethereal sky-and-cloud mural: Completely lost before the renovation and recreated with the help of old lantern slides, it is said to be inspired by the Italian artists Tiepolo and Tintoretto. Even if you never crack a book, the library is, more than ever, worth a visit; it is one of New York City's most sumptuous public spaces. *(See Libraries, below.) 5th Ave. and 42nd St., Midtown. Open Mon. and Thurs.–Sat. 10–6, Tues.–Wed. 11–7:30. Subway: B, D, F, Q to 42nd St.*

9 d-5

NEW YORK YACHT CLUB

(Warren & Wetmore, 1899) Built on land donated by yacht-club member J. P. Morgan, this Beaux Arts structure is famous for its three decorative bay windows fashioned after the sterns of 18th-century sailing ships. The fanciful limestone facade is adorned with carvings of dolphins and waves. *37 W. 44th St. (between 5th and 6th Aves.), Midtown. Subway: B, D, F, Q to 42nd St.*

9 f-3

919 THIRD AVENUE

(Skidmore, Owings, & Merrill, 1970). What's most interesting about this brown-glass office structure is the little, redbrick 1890 building that seems to stand as its sentry box—P. J. Clarke's Tavern, famed watering hole and holdout against Tishman Realty. Have a peek at the mahogony and stained glass inside the bar—you might recognize it as the film set from the 1945 Best Picture-winner *The Lost Weekend*. (*See* American Casual *in* Chapter 1.) *919 3rd Ave. (between 55th and 56th Sts.), Midtown. Subway: 4, 5, 6 to 59th St.*

10 *e-7*

140 BROADWAY

(Skidmore, Owings & Merrill, 1967) A more successful version of Skidmore, Owings & Merrill's earlier Chase Manhattan Bank Tower & Plaza, this sleek, elegant glass skyscraper rises 52 orderly stories above an attractive travertine plaza—home to Isamu Noguchi's delicately balanced red sculpture "Cube." When the building was completed, architecture critic Ada Louise Huxtable wrote, "Sometimes we do it right." *140 Broadway (at Cedar St.), Lower Manhattan. Subway: Wall St.*

9 *f-5*

ONE & TWO UNITED NATIONS PLAZA

(Kevin Roche, John Dinkeloo & Associates One: 1976; Two: 1984) This elegant pair of 500-ft-tall aquamarine, glass-and-aluminum towers holds offices and the Regal U.N. Plaza Hotel (*see* Very Expensive Lodgings *in* Chapter 6). The attractive, reflective glass in which the buildings are clad reflects the surrounding buildings and passing clouds. Cool, green-and-white marble makes the towers' shared lobby one of the most attractive in the city. *1st Ave. and 44th St., Midtown. Subway: 42nd St./Grand Central.*

9 *g-4*

RIVER HOUSE

(Bottomly, Wagner & White, 1931) Then and now, a classic residential building for the very rich, the 26-story River House boasts a gated entrance for cars and a cobbled circular driveway. When the house was first built, residents had their own private yacht mooring, but alas, it was displaced by the construction of the FDR Drive in the 1940s. *435 E. 52nd St. (at Sutton Pl.), Midtown. Subway: 51st St./Lexington–3rd Aves.*

9 *d-4*

ROCKEFELLER CENTER

(Various architects, dir. by Raymond Hood, mostly 1931–40) A miniature Art Deco city in the heart of Manhattan, 22-acre Rockefeller Center encompasses 19 limestone buildings soaring above cleverly connected, people-friendly plazas. The Channel Gardens, with their rock pools, topiary, and colorful flower beds, lead from 5th Avenue between 49th and 50th Streets past shops to the sunken Lower Plaza, which transforms itself into an open-air café in warmer months and an ice rink in winter. Towering above the plaza is the 850-ft G.E. Building (formerly the RCA Building), which in addition to being home to NBC Studios is famous for its sleek, black-granite Deco lobby and the super-swank, just-renovated Rainbow Room on the 65th floor. In front of the G.E. Building is a gilt statue of Prometheus, which watches over the lighting of the Rockefeller Center Christmas tree every year in early December. A block farther north on 5th Avenue, you'll find an enormous statue of Atlas supporting the world—ever a symbol of Manhattan's power and scale—before the International Building (*see* Atlas and Prometheus in Statues & Public Art, *below*; and Radio City Music Hall *in* Historic Buildings & Areas, *below*). *5th and 6th Aves. from 48th to 51st Sts., Midtown. Subway: 47th–50th Sts., Rockefeller Center.*

9 *e-4*

SEAGRAM BUILDING

(Ludwig Mies van der Rohe and Philip Johnson, Kahn & Jacobs, 1958) An austere tribute to modernity by Mies van der Rohe, this sleek, bronze-color skyscraper and its plaza and fountains—all highly innovative at the time of construction—create a pleasing geometry. Although this International Style skyscraper inspired many less-successful imitations, *Times* architecture critic Paul Goldberger still calls the Seagram "one of the great buildings of the [20th] century." The interior, much of which was designed by Philip Johnson, also features exquisite, minimalist detail. Tours of the building start in the lobby every Tuesday at 3. *375 Park Ave. (between 52nd and 53rd Sts.), 212/572–7404 for tours. Midtown. Subway: 51st St./Lexington–3rd Aves.*

10 *e-8*

17 STATE STREET

(Emery Roth & Sons, 1988) A sleek, wedge-shape, reflective-glass tower following the arc of State Street, this late-model International Style building has a twist: a high-tech glass-enclosed lobby 25 ft up. *17 State St., Lower Manhattan. Subway: Bowling Green; South Ferry.*

11 *e-5*

SINGER BUILDING

The SoHo Singer is sometimes known as the Little Singer Building to distinguish it from the beautiful Singer Tower, also designed by Ernest Flagg but demolished 30 years ago to make way for the hulking One Liberty Plaza in the financial district. The Little Singer is unique in its use of decorative terracotta paneling, recessed plate glass, and filigreed iron. Above 11 stories of balconies, the facade culminates in a graceful iron arch. *561 Broadway (between Spring and Prince Sts.). Subway: Prince St.; 6 to Spring St.*

9 *d-4*

666 5TH AVENUE

(Carson & Lundin, 1957) This embossed-aluminum skyscraper, just north of Rockefeller Center, is most notable for the Isamu Noguchi waterfall in its arcade and the sculpted Noguchi ceiling in its lobby. *666 5th Ave. (between 52nd and 53rd Sts.), Midtown. Subway: E, F to 5th Ave.*

10 *e-3*

SOHO CAST-IRON HISTORIC DISTRICT

One of the city's most vibrant areas, full of art galleries and upscale shops, SoHo is also home to the world's largest concentration of cast-iron architecture. In the mid-19th century, commercial builders successfully duplicated elaborate, carved masonry by buying prefabricated facades made from cast iron. Though made from molds, the results were anything but dull; SoHo is filled with five- and six-story commercial buildings that look like Italian palazzos, featuring Corinthian columns, multiple tiers of arched windows, and elaborate French Empire pediments. SoHo's Haughwout Building (*see above*) is generally considered the finest example of cast-iron architecture in the world. Tribeca and the Village have some cast-iron gems as well. For more information, call Friends of Cast-Iron Architecture at 212/886–3742. *Canal and Houston Sts. from W. Broadway to Crosby St. Subway: Prince St.; Spring St.; A, C, E, N, R to Canal St.*

9 *e-3*

SONY BUILDING

(Johnson & Burgee, 1984) Formerly the headquarters of AT&T, this monumental corporate statement is considered the first postmodern skyscraper. Its 36 stories of rose-color granite climb 660 ft (the equivalent of 60 stories) and are topped by a much-ballyhooed "Chippendale" pediment. Archways worthy of Imperial Rome lead to a six-story arcade with public seating and an elevator that whisks you to the Sony Wonder Technology Lab (*see Science Museums, below*). *550 Madison Ave. (at 56th St.), Midtown. Subway: E, F, N, R to 5th Ave.*

9 *g-8*

STUYVESANT TOWN

(Irwin Clavan and Gilmore Clarke, 1947) A densely populated apartment complex built by the Metropolitan Life Insurance Company for returning World War II servicemen, Stuy Town is essentially a gargantuan housing project, now home to more than 8,000 families. But it's one that works. Though the multiple redbrick towers are essentially identical, the decades-old trees, benches, and curving paths ease the sense of anonymity. *1st Ave. and FDR Dr. from 14th to 20th Sts., Gramercy. Subway: 1st Ave.*

9 *d-4*

TIME-LIFE BUILDING

(Harrison & Abramovitz, 1960) The construction of the Time-Life Building, next to Rockefeller Center, led to a corporate building boom along Avenue of the Americas. The sleek but banal slab of limestone, aluminum, and glass is now but one many such office high rises along this stretch, including the Exxon (at 1251), McGraw-Hill (1221), and Celanese (1211) buildings. *1271 6th Ave. (at 50th St), Midtown. Subway: 47th–50th Sts./Rockefeller Center.*

9 *e-3*

TRUMP TOWER

(Swanke, Hayden, Connell & Partners, 1983) A 68-story, bronze-glass megastructure named for the headline-grabbing developer Donald Trump, Trump Tower is most famed for the prices of its condos (90% cost over $1 million) and for its huge, glitzy atrium of peach-color marble—chosen because it flatters certain complexions. Manhattan's first vertical shopping mall, the public atrium comes complete with a five-story waterwall that, depending on your mood, is either glorious or just plain silly. *725 5th Ave. (at 56th St.), Midtown. Subway: E, F, N, R to 5th Ave.*

9 *f-5*

TUDOR CITY

(Fred F. French Co., 1925–28; head architect, H. Douglas Ives) Built in the 1920s to attract middle-income residents, this private "city" centers around 12 buildings containing 3,000 apartments. Situated on a bluff above 1st Avenue, Tudor City now affords great views of the United Nations and the East River. Interestingly, some of the facades facing in this direction did not originally have windows at all—since they overlooked what were then riverside slaughterhouses and glue factories. *1st and 2nd Aves. from 40th to 43rd Sts., Midtown. Subway: 42nd St./Grand Central.*

9 *f-4*

UNITED NATIONS HEADQUARTERS

(International Committee of Architects, Wallace K. Harrison, chairman, 1947–53) This complex became the U.N.'s permanent headquarters in 1952. The tall, slim, green-glass Secretariat Building; the much smaller, domed General Assembly Building; and the Dag Hammarskjold Library (Harrison, Abramovitz & Harris, 1963) form the current complex, before which the flags of its member nations fly in alphabetical order when the General Assembly is in session. Built on 17 acres, the U.N. was profoundly influenced in design by Le Corbusier's "towers in open space" philosophy. Although the buildings may look a bit dated today, their windswept park and plaza remain visionary: They are embellished with a beautiful riverside promenade, a garden with 1,400 rosebushes, views of open sky (rare in Manhattan), and sculptures donated by member nations. *1st Ave. from 42nd to 48th Sts. (enter at 46th St.), Midtown, 212/963–7713. Tours ($7.50) leave approximately every 30 min., Mar.–Dec. daily 9:15–4:45; Jan.–Feb. weekdays 9:15–4:45. Subway: 42nd St./Grand Central.*

10 *e-6*

WOOLWORTH BUILDING

(Cass Gilbert, 1913) One of New York's most dramatic commercial buildings, this neo-Gothic tower rises 792 ft and, clad in terra-cotta, is the jewel of the downtown skyline. Fittingly dubbed a "cathedral of commerce," it was the world's tallest building until 1930. Don't miss the ornate lobby: Carved figures on the ceiling represent the architect holding a model of the building and F. W. Woolworth himself, counting nickels and dimes. (He paid $13 million in cash to have the place built.) *233 Broadway (between Park Pl. and Barclay St.), Lower Manhattan. Subway: Park Pl.; Cortlandt St./World Trade Center.*

10 *d-6*

WORLD FINANCIAL CENTER

See Battery Park City, *above.*

10 *d-6*

WORLD TRADE CENTER

(Minoru Yamasaki & Associates and Emery Roth & Sons, 1962–77) Dreamed up by the Port Authority of New York and New Jersey to replace an aging neighborhood of electronics shops and other low-rent businesses, the World Trade Center consists of seven commercial buildings containing a staggering 12 million square ft of office space. With more than 50,000 workers pouring into the complex every day, the WTC not only transformed the city's already famous skyline; it redefined all of lower Manhattan. The stainless-steel "Twin Towers" are the city's tallest buildings—1,368 ft and 110 stories high, they loom over a vast open plaza. The 1993 terrorist bombing of one of the center's parking garages killed six people, caused extensive damage, and made this New York icon seem momentarily vulnerable; but since then, repairs have been made, security has been tightened, and the wheels of commerce have kept turning. (*See* Viewpoints, *below.*) *Bordered by West, Vesey, Church, and Liberty Sts., Lower Manhattan. Subway: Cortlandt St./World Trade Center.*

ART GALLERIES

A word of advice: if you make an art gallery trek during the summer, please note that many galleries keep limited summer hours and galleries that do stay open tend to present smaller-scale shows and group shows. It's a good idea to call for summer hours before you make the trip.

uptown galleries

These exclusive, white-glove spaces, catering largely to serious collectors and often emphasizing furniture and prints over paintings, are located primarily on and off Madison Avenue from 57th to 86th Street.

9 *e-3*

ACA GALLERIES

This standout Midtown gallery shows both contemporary art and 19th-century American works from its impressive collection. *41 E. 57th St. (near Madiosn Ave.), Midtown, 212/644–8300. Closed Sun.–Mon. Subway: E, F, N, R to 5th Ave.*

7 *e-8*

ACQUAVELLA GALLERIES, INC.

Acquavalla's Impressionist and post-Impressionist holdings include Monet, Matisse, Picasso, Miró, and Pissarro. Downstairs you'll find post–World War II and contemporary paintings by such artists as Guston, Gottlieb, Lichtenstein, and Pollock. *18 E. 79th St. (between 5th and Madison Aves.), Upper East Side, 212/734–6300. Closed Sun. Subway: 77th St.*

9 *e-3*

ANDRE EMMERICH GALLERY

Painters represented include Al Held, Hans Hofmann, Morris Louis, David Hockney, and Helen Frankenthaler; sculptors include Anthony Caro, Beverly Pepper, and Anne Truitt. *41 E. 57th St. (between Park and Madison Aves.), Midtown, 212/752–0124. Closed Sun.–Mon., also closed July–Aug. except by appointment. Subway: E, F, N, R to 5th Ave.*

9 *d-3*

BABCOCK GALLERIES

Established in 1852, this old-line gallery specializes in art of the 19th and 20th centuries, but also has plenty of contemporary paintings, drawings, and sculpture. *724 5th Ave. (between 56th and 57th Sts.), Midtown, 212/535–9355. Closed Sun.–Mon. Subway: E, F, N, R to 5th Ave.*

9 *e-1*

BERRY–HILL GALLERIES, INC.

American painting and sculpture from the 19th and 20th centuries, plus 19th century China Trade paintings, are the order of the day. *11 E. 70th St. (between 5th and Madison Aves.), Upper East Side, 212/744–2300. Closed Sun. Subway: 68th St./Hunter College.*

9 *d-3*

BREWSTER ARTS LTD.

Brewster specializes in 20th-century European and Latin American masters and is one of the world's largest dealers in Miró and Chagall. The gallery serves as exclusive representative for Branko Bahunek and Leonora Carrington, and publishes Francisco Zuñiga. *41 W. 57th St. (between 5th and 6th Aves.), Midtown, 212/980–1975. Closed Sun. Subway: B, Q to 57th St.*

9 *e-2*

BRUTON GALLERY

Just the place to go if you have a spare pedestal: Bruton offers French and European sculpture of the 19th and 20th centuries by Joseph Bernard, Antoine Bourdekke, Stephen Buxin, Jean Carton, Paul Cornet, Aristide Maillol, Auguste Rodin, and others. *40 E. 61st St. (between Madison and Park Aves.), Upper East Side, 212/980–1640. By appointment only. Subway: 4, 5, 6 to 59th St.; B, N, Q, R to Lexington Ave.*

7 *e-8*

CDS

CDS is one of Manhattan's more formidable galleries for the lions of mid-20th-century abstraction. If Motherwell and de Kooning are your thing, put this space high on your list. *76 E. 79th St. (between Madison and Park Aves.), Upper East Side, 212/772–9555. Closed Sun.–Mon. Subway: 77th St.*

7 *e-8*

CLAUDE BERNARD GALLERY

Claude Bernard showcases 19th- and 20th-century South American, American, and European artists including Fernando Botero, Balthus, Jim Dine, Jean Dubuffet, Ferdinand Leger, Miró, Picasso, and Toledo. *900 Park Ave. (at 79th St.), Upper East Side, 212/988–2050. Closed Sun.–Mon. Subway: 77th St.*

9 *e-2*

DAVIS & LANGDALE CO.

Dignified 18th-, 19th-, and 20th-century American and English paintings, watercolors, and drawings hang at this gallery, which caters to the Ralph Lauren/Prince of Wales look. Contemporary means traditional here, with American work by such artists as Lennart Anderson, Aaron Shikler, Albert York, and Harry Roseman. *231 E. 60th St. (between*

3rd and 2nd Aves.), Upper East Side, 212/838–0333. Closed Sun.–Mon. Subway: 59th St.

7 e-8
THE ELKON GALLERY
Twentieth-century masters are the focus here: paintings, drawings, and sculpture from Balthus, Botero, Dubuffet, Ernst, Leger, Magritte, Matisse, Miró, and Picasso. 18 E. 81st St. (between 5th and Madison Aves.), Upper East Side, 212/535–3940. Closed Sun.–Mon. Subway: 77th St.

9 d-3
FISCHBACH GALLERY
Fischbach is a showcase for 20th-century American paintings and drawings—very eclectic, very New York. 24 W. 57th St. (between 5th and 6th Aves.), Midtown, 212/759–2345. Closed Sun.–Mon.; weekends July–Aug. Subway: B, Q to 57th St.

9 e-3
FORUM GALLERY
Forum features contemporary American figurative paintings and sculpture. 745 5th Ave. (between 57th and 58th Sts.), Midtown, 212/355–4545. Closed Sun.–Mon. Subway: E, F, N, R to 5th Ave.

9 d-3
GALERIE LELONG
The focus here is on contemporary American and European sculpture, drawings, and paintings. 20 W. 57th St. (between 5th and 6th Aves.), Midtown 212/315–0470. Closed Sun.–Mon. Subway: B, Q to 57th St.

9 d-3
GALERIE ST. ETIENNE
This private dealer specializes in 19th- and 20th-century Austrian and German expressionism, 19th- and 20th-century folk art, and Grandma Moses. 24 W. 57th St. (between 5th and 6th Aves.), Midtown, 212/245–6734. Closed Sun.–Mon. Subway: B, Q to 57th St.

9 d-3
GARTH CLARK
Clark's is a niche gallery specializing in high-quality sculpture and crafts from around the world. The pieces are exquisite and the patrons armored with wealth. 24 W. 57th St. (between 5th and 6th Aves.), Midtown, 212/246–2205. Closed Sun.–Mon. Subway: B, Q to 57th St.

9 d-3
HAMMER GALLERIES
Got it in your head to check out sports painter LeRoy Neiman's fundamentally mediocre work? Head for Hammer. If it's prints you seek, try Hammer Graphics, on the third of this emporium's many floors. 33 W. 57th St. (between 5th and 6th Aves.), Midtown, 212/644–4400. Closed Sun. Subway: B, Q to 57th St.

7 e-1
HIRSCHL & ADLER GALLERIES
Top-quality 18th-, 19th-, and 20th-century American painting, sculpture, drawing, and folk art rest here, and they're the kind of works that would send critic Robert Hughes scurrying for a thesaurus. Also on offer are European Impressionist and modern painting and drawing, as well as the patron saint of bird painting, John J. Audubon. Mary Cassatt, Frederick Church, John Singleton Copley, Childe Hassam, Homer, Hopper, Matisse, O'Keeffe, Picasso, and Renoir flesh out the reserves. 21 E. 70th St. (at Madison Ave.), Upper East Side, 212/535–8810. Closed Sun.–Mon. Subway: 68th St./Hunter College.

7 e-1
HIRSCHL & ADLER MODERN
Hirschl & Adler's 20th-century gallery shows both American and European art. 21 E. 70th St. (at Madison Ave.), Upper East Side, 212/535–8810. Closed Sun.–Mon. Subway: 68th St./Hunter College.

9 e-3
JAMES GOODMAN GALLERY
A haven for 20th-century American and European paintings, drawings, watercolors, and sculpture, Goodman's roster includes Botero, Calder, de Kooning, Dubuffet, Giacometti, Leger, Lichtenstein, Matisse, Miró, Henry Moore, and Rauschenberg. 41 E. 57th St. (at Madison Ave.), Midtown, 212/593–3737. Closed Sun.; closed Mon. except by appointment. Subway: E, F, N, R to 5th Ave.

9 e-1
JANE KAHAN
Kahan nearly always has a stunning roster of greats—everyone from Arp to Calder, from Delaunay to Picasso. 922 Madison Ave. (at 73rd St.), Upper East Side, 212/744–1490. Closed Sun.–Mon. Subway: 77th St.

9 *e-3*

JOAN WASHBURN GALLERIES

American abstract art of the 1930s and '40s is mixed here with folk art and contemporary paintings, sculpture, and drawings. *20 W. 57th St. (between 5th and 6th Aves.), Midtown, 212/397–6780. Closed Sun.–Mon. Subway: E, F, N, R to 5th Ave.*

7 *e-3*

KENNEDY GALLERIES

American paintings, sculpture, and graphics of the 18th, 19th, and 20th centuries share space with European fine prints. *730 5th Ave. (at 57th St.), Midtown, 212/541–9600. Closed Sun.–Mon. Subway: B, Q to 57th St.*

9 *e-1*

KNOEDLER & CO.

One of Manhattan's top-flight galleries, Knoedler is a must-stop for those in search of contemporary European and American paintings and sculpture. *19 E. 70th St. (between 5th and Madison Aves.), Upper East Side, 212/794–0550. Closed Sun. Subway: 68th St./Hunter College.*

9 *e-3*

KRAUSHAAR GALLERIES

The vibe here is distinctly unflamboyant: paintings, drawings, and sculpture by 20th-century American artists such as Peggy Bacon, William Glackens, Leon Goldin, Elsie Manville, Ben Frank Moss, and John Sloan. *724 5th Ave. (at 57th St.), Midtown, 212/307–5730. Closed Sun.–Mon. Subway: E, F, N, R to 5th Ave.*

7 *e-8*

LEO CASTELLI GALLERY

The grand old man of the sixties avant-garde passed away in the summer of 1999, but his gallery lives on, if somewhat tenuously, through new director Amy Poll-Schell and the continued representation of heavy hitters who include Rauschenburg, Johns, Nauman, and Oldenberg. *59 E. 79th St. (between Madison and Park Aves.), Upper East Side, 212/249–4470. Closed Sun.–Mon. Subway: 77th St.*

7 *e-8*

LEONARD HUTTON GALLERIES

Here German Expressionists and Russian avant-garde art reign supreme. *41 E. 57th St. (at Madison Ave.), Midtown, 212/751–7373. Closed Sun.–Mon; closed Aug. except by appointment. Subway: 77th St.*

9 *d-3*

MARLBOROUGH GALLERY

Along with Knoedler, Robert Miller, and Gagosian, Marlborough is one of the most important stops on any uptown gallery tour. The focus is on 20th-century and contemporary paintings, sculpture, photographs, and graphics; artists represented include Frank Auerbach, Francis Bacon, Fernando Botero, Red Grooms, Barbara Hepworth, Alex Katz, Antonio Lopez Garcia, Henry Moore, Larry Rivers, and Rufino Tamayo. *40 W. 57th St. (between 5th and 6th Aves.), Midtown, 212/541–4900. Closed Sun. Subway: B, Q to 57th St.*

9 *e-3*

McKEE GALLERY

McKee exhibits contemporary paintings, drawings, sculpture, and prints. *745 5th Ave. (between 57th and 58th Sts.), Midtown, 212/688–5951. Closed Sun.–Mon. Subway: E, F, N, R to 5th Ave.*

9 *e-3*

NOHRA HAIME GALLERY

Contemporary Latin American, American, and European art are the main courses at this standby. *41 E. 57th St. (at Madison Ave.), Midtown, 212/888–3550. Closed Sun. Subway: E, F, N, R to 5th Ave.*

9 *e-3*

PACE/WILDENSTEIN/ MACGILL

The mighty Pace, a corporate art empire ruled by superdealer Arne Glimcher, is so big, so vast, and such a part of the art world that nothing as trivial as the '87 stock crash could even dent its business. After the merger with Wildenstein, one of New York's older and most venerable dealer clans, Glimcher's reach extended even farther. Pace/Wildenstein, on the 2nd floor, exhibits paintings and sculpture; Pace/Wildenstein/ MacGill, on the 9th floor, shows photography. Some of the heavyweights represented are Rothko, Nevelson, Mangold, and Steinberg. (For Pace Primitive, *see* Eastern Art, *below;* for Pace Master Prints and Pace Prints, *see* Prints, *below.*) *32 E. 57th St. (between 5th and Madison Aves.), Midtown, 212/421–3292. Closed Sun. Subway: B, Q to 57th St.*

7 *e-8*

SALANDER O'REILLY GALLERIES

One of uptown's more significant galleries, Salander O'Reilly represents 19th to 20th century American modernist paintings, primarily from the Ashcan, precisionist, and New York schools, as well as contemporary and 19th-century European painters and antique European and American frames. *20 E. 79th St. (between 5th and Madison Aves.), Upper East Side, 212/879–6606. Closed Sun. Subway: 77th St.*

9 *d-3*

SCHMIDT BINGHAM GALLERY

The focus here is contemporary American realism. *41 E. 57th St. (at Madison Ave.), Midtown, 212/888–1122. Closed Sun. Subway: B, Q to 57th St.*

7 *e-8*

SOLOMON & CO. FINE ART

Solomon's roster of 20th-century American and European painters and sculptors includes Avery, Calder, de Kooning, Dubuffet, Hoffman, Pollock, and Stella. *959 Madison Ave. (at 75th St.), Upper East Side, 212/737–8200. Closed Sun. Subway: 77th St.*

7 *e-8*

SOUFER

Post-Impressionist and European paintings of the 1920s–1940s are this gallery's forte, but there's also a cluster of German Expressionist works. *1015 Madison Ave. (between 78th and 79th Sts.), Upper East Side, 212/628–3225. Closed Sun.–Mon. Subway: 77th St.*

9 *d-3*

TATISTCHEFF & COMPANY

Tatistcheff showcases contemporary American painting and works on paper. *50 W. 57th St. (between 5th and 6th Aves.), Midtown, 212/664–0907. Closed Sun.–Mon. Subway: B, Q to 57th St.*

9 *d-3*

TIBOR DE NAGY GALLERY

One of the city's prime purveyors of good taste with a forward eye, de Nagy eschews trends and high-concept, specializing instead in figurative masters of the 20th century. *724 5th Ave. (between 56th and 57th Sts.), Midtown, 212/262–5050. Closed Sun.–Mon. Subway: B, Q to 57th St.*

7 *e-8*

UBU GALLERY

This fresh new space engages art that deviates from the tried-and-true. Shows focus on unusual practices—photomontage, for instance—as well as the funkier products of surrealist and Eastern European art. *16 E. 78th St. (between 5th and Madison Aves.), Upper East Side, 212/794–4444. Closed Sun.–Mon. Subway: 77th St.*

9 *d-3*

VIRIDIAN GALLERY

Viridian specializes in contemporary art, painting, sculpture, and graphics. *24 W. 57th St. (between 5th and 6th Aves.), Midtown, 212/245–2882. Closed Sun.–Mon. Subway: B, Q to 57th St.*

9 *e-3*

WALLY FINDLAY

Findlay offers Impressionist, post-Impressionist, and contemporary art of the French school, all with mass appeal. *14 E. 60th St. (between 5th and Madison Aves), Midtown, 212/421–5390. Closed Sun. Subway: E, F, N, R to 5th Ave.*

9 *d-3*

ZABRISKIE GALLERY

Early-20th-century American painting, sculpture, and drawing, along with contemporary, large-scale sculpture and photography, have built this gallery a loyal following. *724 5th Ave. (at 56th St.), Midtown, 212/307–7430. Closed Sun.–Mon. Subway: E, F, N, R to 5th Ave.*

soho galleries

With each ensuing season, SoHo becomes more about commerce and less about art. Chic shops continue to proliferate, and openings at many galleries are so carefully choreographed by PR firms that they've turned into photo-ops for the fashion editors, rock stars, and restaurateurs who attend, as opposed to celebrations of the pictures on the walls. Even so, SoHo remains, well, SoHo—the former warehouse district that artists colonized in the late 1970s remains the neighborhood where art trends, as opposed to century-old art works, trace their roots. The fact is, SoHo has a long way to go before losing any real credibility in the art world, and you can ignore the glitz while paying attention to the real business of a vibrant artistic community in the midst of making and selling culture.

Some tips for serious gallery visiting: Avoid galleries that put art in the windows; stick to more earnest looking places, often those that inhabit upper floors. Another option is to head down toward Canal Street, where the more serious spaces have set up shop far from the madding crowds. For a glimpse of the way all of SoHo looked before it's reincarnation in the 1970s, seek out Crosby Street, just east of Broadway. A trot down the street's cobblestones is like boarding a time machine, particularly since it terminates to the north at the foot of the only building in New York designed by turn-of-the-20th-century architect Louis Sullivan.

11 *b-4*

A.C.E. GALLERY

This major-league space recently hosted a section of the Guggenheim SoHo's massive Robert Rauschenberg retrospective. It's more serious, perhaps, than some of the other players, but not quite avant-garde—a superb example of the middle ground. *275 Hudson St. (at Spring St.), West Village, 212/255–5599. Closed Mon. and Tues. Subway: A, C to Spring St.; 1, 9 to Canal St.*

11 *b-5*

AC PROJECT ROOM

It's just what it sounds like: an experimental space devoted to newer forms of expression (i.e., not painting)—video, performance, and installation. *15 Renwick St. (west of Hudson St., between Canal and Spring Sts.), 212/219–8275. Closed Sun.–Mon. Subway: C, E to Spring St.; 1, 9 to Canal St.*

11 *d-5*

A.I.R. GALLERY

A.I.R. is a cooperative gallery for women artists. Special events include talks (say, women artists in history) and seminars on the biz of art. *40 Wooster St. (between Broome and Grand Sts.), 212/966–0799. Closed Sun.–Mon. Subway: A, C, E, N, R to Canal St.*

11 *d-5*

AMERICAN FINE ARTS

Gallerist Colin de Land has an eye for the decadent and controversial. Work like Garry Gross's Brooke Shields kiddy porn photos sit alongside more conceptual, sometimes confusing, pieces for a thought-provoking mix. *22 Wooster St. (between Grand and Canal Sts.), 212/941–0401. Closed Sun. and Mon. Subway: C, E to Spring St.*

11 *d-5*

BASILICO FINE ARTS

Basilico is one of those terrific little galleries below Spring Street that remain must-sees, even for a casual surveyor of the state of the SoHo scene. On display are photography, group work, installations, and some painting. *26 Wooster St. (at Grand St.), 212/966–1831. Closed Sun.–Mon. Subway: A, C, E, N, R to Canal St.*

11 *f-6*

BRONWYN KEENAN

One of Manhattan's newer gallerists, Keenan features edgy, younger artists on their way up, working in a variety of mediums. The space is trendy, but intimate—a nice way of saying that it's very small. *3 Crosby St. (at Howard St.), 212/431–5083. Closed Sun.–Mon. Subway: N, R, 6 to Canal St.*

11 *d-5*

BROOKE ALEXANDER

Having weathered the art-market storms of the late 1980s and early '90s, Alexander continues to show the cream, if not the cutting edge, of the contemporary scene, along with prints. *59 Wooster St. (at Broome St.), 212/925–4338. Closed Sun.–Mon. Subway: A, C, E, N, R to Canal St.*

11 *e-4*

CHARLES COWLES

Cowles focuses on contemporary paintings, photography, and sculpture. *420 W. Broadway (between Prince and Spring Sts.), 212/925–3500. Closed Sun.–Mon. Subway: C, E to Spring St.*

11 *e-5*

DAVID ZWIRNER

Zwirner is another far-SoHo gallery that's snatching the bright young things up. In this case, the star is installationist Jason Rhoades, whose postmodern gatherings of brightly colored junk and everyday objects, arranged into Rube Goldbergesque clusters that fill entire spaces, have made him a favorite of the *Parkett*-magazine crowd. *43 Greene St. (between Grand and Broome Sts.), 212/ 966–9074. Closed Sun. and Mon. Subway: A, C, E, N, R to Canal St.*

11 *e-5*

DEITCH PROJECTS
This avant-garde, sometimes downright weird gallery shows a variety of work, from contemporary painting to installation to long-term performance pieces. *76 Grand St. (between Wooster and Greene Sts.), 212/343–7300. Closed Sun.– Mon. Subway: N, R to Canal St.*

11 *d-6*

THE DRAWING CENTER
This far-SoHo stalwart refuses to bow to caprice, preferring instead to mount idiosyncratic shows—a group of artists with similar styles, say—or simply focus on the Center's ostensible purpose, drawing. Perhaps the most celebrated show of the past few years was one on the history of tattooing. Rising big-timers, such as Kara Walker, have exhibited large-scale works in the impressive quarters. *35 Wooster St. (between Grand and Broome Sts.), 212/219—2166. Closed Sun.–Mon. Subway: A, C, E, N, R to Canal St.*

11 *e-4*

EDWARD THORP
Contemporary American painting and sculpture get top billing here. *103 Prince St. (between Greene and Mercer Sts.), 212/431–6880. Closed Sun.–Mon. Subway: N, R to Prince St.*

11 *d-6*

FRIEDRICH PETZEL
Petzel is a SoHo veteran, considered by many to be in the same league with Gagosian and the other movers and shakers of the 1980s. At the turn of the century he still has his ear to the ground with debut artists like Richard Phillips. *26 Wooster (between Grand and Canal Sts.), 212/334–9466. Closed Sun.–Mon. Subway: C, E to Spring St.*

11 *d-3*

GAGOSIAN
Well, what can you say? Twenty years ago the guy was selling posters on the beach

in Venice, California. Now, with Arne Glimcher of Pace, he competes for the "Biggest Dealer" title on both coasts. Larry Gagosian's roster, featuring Schnabel, Salle, and Serra, might be starting to look a little too go-go art-star, but he continues to add new talent, including Ivory Coast painter Ouattara. Unlike his uptown temple, Gagosian's downtown space is spare—more like a garage than a gallery—which suits it to Serra's enormous iron curves and blocks, Damien Hirst's bisected livestock, and Annette Messager's creepy, gallery-filling installations of yarn, photos, and stuffed varmints. While Pace is the scene for openings that require socialites and bankers, Gagosian is the place to spot David Geffen, rock stars, matinee idols, and the fashion tribe. *136 Wooster St. (between Prince and Houston Sts.), 212/ 228–2828. Closed Sun.–Mon. Subway: Prince St.; Broadway–Lafayette St.*

11 *e-5*

HELLER GALLERY
Contemporary glass sculpture gets its due. *71 Greene St. (between Broome and Spring Sts.), 212/966–5948. Closed Mon. Subway: 6 to Spring St.*

11 *d-6*

JACK TILTON
Live nudes, even live pigs might be found at Tilton's cutting-edge space, which favors off-the-wall performance and video installations. *49 Greene St. (at Broome St.), 212/941–1775. Closed Sun.– Mon. Subway: Broadway–Lafayette St.*

11 *e-5*

JOHN MCENROE
The former tennis champion is trying to make the shift to a more buttoned-up profession, with some success; he's put together some superb little shows since opening a few years ago. *41 Greene St. (between Grand and Broome Sts.), 212/ 219–0395. Closed Sept.–May, Sun.–Mon.; June–Aug., weekends. Subway: A, C, E, N, R to Canal St.*

11 *e-4*

JUNE KELLY
June Kelly's taste is solid, with a focus on a multicultural roster. *591 Broadway (between Prince and Houston Sts.), 212/ 226–1660. Closed Sun.–Mon. Subway: Prince St.; Broadway–Lafayette St.*

11 e-4

KENT GALLERY

This tidy, two-level space is squeezed between SoHo and Little Italy, in a sliver of neighborhood just shy of the mythical NoHo in flavor. Kent shows mainly "smart" work, from such artists as Vivienne Koorland and Richard Artschwager. It's not a rock-the-world gallery, but it can be relied on show after show to mount lively, intelligent work that steers clear of obvious trends. *67 Prince St. (between Broadway and Lafayette Sts.), 212/966–4500. Closed Sun.–Mon. Subway: Prince St.; Broadway–Lafayette St.*

11 d-5

LOUIS K. MEISEL

Photorealist art by Audrey Flack, Charles Bell, Hilo Chen and the like covers the walls at this reliable space. *141 Prince St. (between Wooster St. and W. Broadway), 212/677–1340. Closed Sun.–Mon. Subway: Prince St.*

11 d-4

NANCY HOFFMAN

Hoffman shows good contemporary art, including works by Carolyn Brady, Don Eddy, Juan Gonzalez, Joseph Raffael, Rafael Ferrer, Howard Buchwald, John Okulick, and Alan Siegel. *429 W. Broadway (between Spring and Prince Sts.), 212/966–6676. Closed Sun.–Mon. Subway: C, E to Spring St.*

11 d-5

PAUL KASMIN

This lively, contemporary space keeps an eye on traditional mediums, mainly painting and drawing. *74 Grand St. (at Wooster St.), 212/219–3219. Closed Sun.–Mon. Subway: A, C, E, N, R to Canal St.*

11 d-4

PETER BLUM

Blum's continues to indulge in its ongoing passion for intelligent contemporary painting. *99 Wooster St. (between Prince and Spring Sts.), 212/343–0441. Closed Sun.–Mon. Subway: Prince St.*

11 e-4

PHYLLIS KIND GALLERY

Kind specializes in contemporary American, Soviet, and European art, as well as 20th-century American and European art brut. *136 Greene St. (between Prince and Houston Sts.), 212/925–1200. Closed Sun.–Mon.; closed Aug. except by appointment. Subway: Prince St.; Broadway–Lafayette St.*

11 e-4

PLEIADES GALLERY

Figurative, abstract, and experimental art have their way here. *591 Broadway (between Prince and Houston Sts.), 212/274–8825. Closed Sun.–Mon. Subway: Prince St.; Broadway–Lafayette St.*

11 e-5

P.P.O.W.

Contemporary international artists have the spotlight here. *476 Broome St. (between Greene and Wooster Sts.), 212/941–8642. Closed Sun.–Mon. Subway: A, C, E, N, R to Canal St.*

11 d-4

PRINCE ST. GALLERY

This gallery shows contemporary expressionist and representational paintings, sculpture, and drawings; nothing anyone is going to be talking about in café society, but reliabe. *121 Wooster St. (between Spring and Prince Sts.), 212/226–9402. Closed Sun.–Mon. Subway: Prince St.; 6 to Spring St.*

11 e-6

RONALD FELDMAN FINE ARTS

Feldman has long been renowned as one of SoHo's prime tastemakers, not because he shows the big shots, but because he shows truly significant work by the likes of Ida Applebroog. As at Kent, Basilico, and Fredrich Petzel, scarcely a false note is struck here, so dive in if the rest of the long march through Art Land has been getting you down. *31 Mercer St. (between Grand and Canal Sts.), 212/226–3232. Closed Sun.; closed Mon., July, and Aug. except by appointment. Subway: N, R to Canal St.*

11 e-5

SEAN KELLY

Sean Kelly's stable includes such luminaries as Julie Roberts, Cathy de Monchaux, Lorna Simpson, and Ann Hamilton. Detect a theme? This is one of New York's most important spaces for women artists. *43 Mercer St. (between Grand and Broome Sts.), 212/343–2405. Closed Sun.–Mon. Subway: N, R to Canal St.*

11 *d-5*

SPENCER BROWNSTONE

Another of those terribly contemporary spaces, Spencer Brownstone specializes in installation, which has lately displaced painting and sculpture as young artists' métier of choice. *39 Wooster St. (between Broome and Grand Sts.), 212/ 334–3455. Closed Sun.–Mon. Subway: A, C, E, N, R to Canal St.*

11 *e-4*

SPERONE WESTWATER

Westwater's bent is European and American contemporary art. *142 Greene St. (between Prince and Houston Sts.), 212/431–3685. Closed Sun.–Mon. Subway: Prince St.; Broadway–Lafayette St.*

11 *f-5*

THREAD WAXING SPACE

So called because it used to be a thread factory, this exceptional space features installation and performance art. It's a slightly more austere alternative to Exit Art (*see Alternative Exhibition Spaces, below*). *476 Broadway (between Grand and Broome Sts.), 212/966–9520. Closed Sun.–Mon. Subway: N, R to Canal St.; 6 to Spring St.*

11 *d-4*

TONY SHAFRAZI GALLERY

This huge space is presided over by an '80s style megadealer who, after he defaced Picasso's Guernica by spray-painting an obscure slogan on the canvas, went on to show graffiti artists such as Kenny Scharf and Jean-Michel Basquiat. *119 Wooster St. (between Spring and Prince Sts.), 212/274–9300. Closed Sun.–Mon. Subway: Prince St.; 6 to Spring St.*

11 *d-4*

VORPAL SOHO

Vorpal SoHo can claim the world's largest collection of M. C. Escher prints; other holdings include contemporary paintings, sculpture, and prints. *459 W. Broadway (between Prince and Houston Sts.), 212/777–3939. Closed Sun.–Mon. Subway: Prince St.; C, E to Spring St.*

11 *d-4*

WARD NASSE GALLERY

This cooperative gallery displays all mediums. *178 Prince St. (between Thompson and Sullivan Sts.), 212/925–6951. Closed Sun.–Mon. Subway: C, E to Spring St.*

west chelsea galleries

Never have so many traveled to so barren a landscape to make so few feel so hip so quickly. Critics claim that West Chelsea, a cluster of enormous galleries—many hewn from former taxi garages—west of 10th Avenue between 22nd and 26th Sts., is the scene that ended before it began. When many of SoHo's heaviest hitters moved up here in the mid-90's, they lent the area instant credibility, but the gentrification that has slowly sapped much of downtown's energy over the past two decades has infected the new hot spot at a shocking rate. Just a quick glance at the fashion-plate mobs trekking here from across town to chic shops and clubs reveals how slick the whole enterprise has become. Time will only tell if an infusion of cash and bold industrial architecture can sustain an artistic community already overrun by capitalism at its flashiest.

To reach this glossy frontier, take the 1, 9, A, C, or E trains to 23rd St. stations.

9 *b-7*

ANDREA ROSEN

Another SoHo migrator, Rosen has moved to wide open spaces up north, no doubt to have more room for her wacky installations, surveillance cameras, and Sean Landers comic strips. *525 W. 24th St. (between 10th and 11th Aves.), 212/627–6000. Closed Sun.–Mon.*

9 *b-8*

ANNINA NOSEI

Life springs eternal for the gallerist who gave the late Jean-Michel Basquiat a basement in which to crank out paintings, and signed on as his first dealer. Now in West Chelsea, Nosei continues to champion new painting. *530 W. 22nd St. (between 10th and 11th Aves.), 212/ 741–8695. Closed Sun.–Mon.*

9 *b-7*

BARBARA GLADSTONE GALLERY

Gladstone has on her commendable roster one of the most important artists currently working, Russian conceptualist Ilya Kabakov. *515 W. 24th St. (between 10th and 11th Aves.), 212/206–9300. Closed Sun. and Mon.*

9 b-8

BONAKDAR JANCOU GALLERY

Yet another Sohoite to break camp and move up north, Bonakdar excels in group shows of sculpture, painting, and drawings. *521 W. 21st (between 10th and 11th Aves.), 212/414–4144, Closed Sun.–Mon.*

9 b-8

CLEMENTINE

This small, smartly managed space has mounted a dozen fine exhibits of painting and photography since opening in late 1996. A gallery specialty is the two-person show, with each artist getting one side of the space. *526 W. 21st St. (between 10th and 11th Aves.), 212/255–1105. Closed Sun.–Mon.*

9 b-8

GAVIN BROWN'S ENTERPRISE

Always having to be different, Brown inaugurated the meat packing district into what's already become the next real-estate feeding frenzy. Check out the latest European art sensation before going around the corner to one of the new shops that will help you dress like the latest Eurotrash rich kid. *436 W. 15th St. (between 9th and 10th Aves.), 212/627–5258. Closed Sun.–Mon.*

9 b-7

GREENE NAFTALI

Of West Chelsea's smaller galleries, this one gets the most ink, for its zany contemporary-art installations. *526 W. 26th St. (between 10th and 11th Aves.), 212/463–7770. Closed Sun.–Mon.*

9 b-8

JOHN WEBER GALLERY

Weber shows European and contemporary artists, with an emphasis on minimalist and conceptual art. *529 W. 20th St. (between 10th and 11th Aves.), 212/691–5711. Closed Sun.–Mon.*

9 b-8

KIM FOSTER

Foster has relocated from the fringe of Soho to the thick of Chelsea and still retains her edgy roster of twentysomething conceptualists. *529 W. 20th (between 10th and 11th Aves.), 212/966–9024. Closed Sun.–Mon.*

9 b-7

LUHRING AUGUSTINE GALLERY

Luhring takes advantage of a huge new space to stage elaborate group shows of every medium imaginable. *531 W. 24th St. (between 10th and 11th Aves.), 212/206–9100. Closed Sun.–Mon.*

9 b-7

MATTHEW MARKS

Same telephone number, two vast and formidable spaces only two blocks apart. Marks was the first major gallerist to make the move west, and he can really be credited with setting the architectural tone for the area: big. His 24th Street space could shelter a blimp. He has cutting-edge taste, as well as the savvy to show older artists. The latter include arch-abstractionist Ellsworth Kelly, whose massive orange-and-blue curves and circles look right at home in Marks's white caverns. *523 W. 24th St. (between 10th and 11th Aves.), 212/243–0047. Closed Sun.–Mon.*

9 b-8

522 W. 22nd St., between 10th and 11th Aves., Chelsea.

9 b-8

MAX PROTECH

Like most Chelsea galleries, Protech shows all things contemporary, including photo, sculpture, painting, and ceramics. An added specialty is a large collection of architectural drawings spanning the whole of the 20th century and including original drafting from the hands of Frank Lloyd Wright. *511 W. 22nd St. (between 10th and 11th Aves.), 212/633–6999. Closed Sun.–Mon.*

9 b-7

METRO PICTURES

Formerly on the northern edge of SoHo, Metro Pictures joined the exodus and opened a huge and spectacular space out west. Major artists represented include photographer Cindy Sherman and painter Carroll Dunham. *519 W. 24th St. (between 10th and 11th Aves.), 212/337–0070. Closed Sun.–Mon.*

9 b-8

PAT HEARN

Hearn emerged from the style wars of the 1980s such a beloved figure that her bout with liver cancer galvanized the support of the entire art world, which established the Pat Hearn Fund so the gallerist could get a liver transplant (her insurance wouldn't pay) and continue to show incisive contemporary work. *530 W. 22nd St. (between 10th and 11th Aves.), 212/727–7366. Closed Sun.–Mon.*

9 *b-8*
PAULA COOPER
Gagosian's former neighbor in SoHo gave it all up for the desolate West Side, but photographer and bête noire Andres Serrano has followed her; so at the very least, those in search of an illicit burst of porno-religious imagery will flock to the openings. With any luck her pioneering spirit will be rewarded, and she'll trump the big boys in the end. *534 W. 21st St. (between 10th and 11th Aves.), 212/255–1105. Closed Sun.–Mon.*

9 *b-7*
SONNABEND GALLERY
They needed a backhoe to pull the roots out of one of the most respected galleries in SoHo and transplant it to new digs. If anything signals Chelsea's coming-of-age, it's the arrival of Illeana Sonnabend and her impeccable roster of contemporary photographers and established 1960s masters. *532–536 W. 22nd St. (between 10th and 11th Aves.), 212-966–6160. Closed Sun.–Mon.*

9 *b-8*
303
This medium-size, street-level space has defined itself with medium-size shows by up-and-coming photographers and installationists. *525 W. 22nd St. (between 10th and 11th Aves.), 212/255–1121. Closed Sun.–Mon.*

9 *b-7*
WESSEL & O'CONNOR
This interesting new space specializes in photography, sculpture, and installation. *242 W. 26th St., 212/242–8811. Closed Sun.–Mon.*

williamsburg galleries
In the late '80s, Williamsburg, Brooklyn, was already being touted as the new bohemia. Since then it has come into its own as a community where working artists, some established, some still up-and-coming, live and create. A handful of scrappy, tough galleries have sprouted up to show their work, and some have had astonishing success.

Williamsburg is still an ethnic enclave of working-class Poles and Puerto Ricans. The East River provides a natural barrier to the glamour hordes, and while some of the twentysomething slacker kids who live here may have attitude problems of their own, they by no means define the neighborhood.

"Funky" is a relatively mild way to describe the architecture and atmosphere of Williamsburg, and its galleries, too. Some gallery spaces are converted garages, some are lofts, some are people's living rooms. At times youthful enthusiasm overtakes good sense in regard to the quality of the work shown. But as the scene has been allowed to mature organically, it's become more and more interesting for the casual observer. The Williamsburg scene, though it's struggling, is definitely here to stay. Its galleries may disappoint from time to time, but one gets the feeling that it's definitely a place to watch.

Many of the galleries here are open only on weekends and Mondays. Take the L Train to Bedford Avenue to be in the thick of it or the J to Marcy Avenue to get to spaces on the south side of the 'hood.

3 *d-6*
BINGO HALL
Owner Dennis Farrell has used red and white paint to fashion a little jewel box of a gallery out of an old garage. Opened in March of 1999, this space focuses on paintings by local artists. *212 Berry St. (between Metropolitan Ave. and N. 3rd St.), 718/599–0844. Open Fri.–Sun.*

3 *d-6*
EYEWASH
This loft space, half a block from the L train, shows paintings and sculpture by local and European artists. *143 N. 7th St. (between Bedford and Driggs Aves.), 718/387–2714. Open weekends, by appt. only in July.*

3 *d-6*
MOMENTA ART
Dedicated to the exposure of emerging artists, Momenta is a non-profit gallery run by two working artists, Eric Heist and Laura Parnes. A big part of the mission here is to provide a venue for the sort of conceptual art passed over by other galleries due to lack of saleability.

Happenings and large installations can be found along with almost any other form of artistic expression, including film screenings and readings. Momenta is also an excellent first stop in the neighborhood, as the directors produce a newsletter listing their own exhibits as well as work showing at other area spaces. *72 Berry St. (between N. 10th and N. 11th Sts.), 718/218–8058. Open Sat.–Mon., closed July–Aug.*

3 *d-6*

PIEROGI 2000

Despite its goofy name, Pierogi is actually the longest-running (since September '94) and most commercially viable of all the Williamsburg galleries. Founder and director Joe Amrhein credits his longevity to showing good work, and the space has an aura of businesslike credibility that makes it a cornerstone of the scene. A major innovation is the gallery's flat file, in which which each artist gets a drawer space to fill with paintings, photos, lithographs, and whatever other work they have available for sale. *177 N. 9th St. (between Bedford and Driggs Aves.), 718/599–2144. Open Sat.–Mon.*

3 *d-7*

WILLIAMSBURG ART AND HISTORICAL CENTER

Opened in November 1996 by painter, curator, and all-around neighborhood cheerleader Yuko Nii, The Art and Historical Center acts as a gallery, coffee shop, school, performance space, and community center for Williamsburg's ragged but up-and-coming south side. All of this is housed in the stunning former Kings County Savings Bank, a Victorian landmark erected in 1876 and one of the many architectural hints of the area's past glories. Nii's vision brings together local and international artists while building a sense of community—and publicity—that will keep Williamsburg connected to the larger artistic community and flourishing within it. *135 Broadway (at Bedford Ave.), 718/486–7372. Open weekends, call for dates of special programs.*

eastern art

7 *e-6*

ART OF THE PAST

The collection features art from Nepal, Tibet, and India. *1242 Madison Ave. (at 89th St.), Upper East Side, 212/860–7070. Closed Sun. Subway: 4, 5, 6 to 86th St.*

7 *e-8*

E & J FRANKEL LTD

E & J Frankel specializes in Oriental art from China (porcelain and jade from the Shang Dynasty through the 1840s) and Japan (screen paintings and furnishings from all periods). *1040 Madison Ave. (at 79th St.), Upper East Side, 212/879–5733. Closed Sun. Subway: 77th St.*

11 *e-4*

JACQUES CARCANAGUES

Carcanagues features ethnographic items from Afghanistan, Central America, Guatemala, India, Thailand, Indonesia, Japan, Korea, the Philippines, and more. *106 Spring St. (at Mercer St.), SoHo, 212/925–8110. Subway: Prince St.; 6 to Spring St.*

7 *e-7*

MERTON SIMPSON GALLERY

Most of this art is from Africa, but Oceanic and Native American works are mixed in. *1063 Madison Ave. (at 81st St.), Upper East Side, 212/988–6290. Closed Sun.–Mon. Subway: 77th St.*

9 *e-3*

PACE PRIMITIVE

This branch of the Pace tree features antique African masks and sculpture and Himalayan masks. *32 E. 57th St. (between Madison and Park Aves.), Midtown, 212/421–3688. Closed Sun.–Mon. Subway: B, Q to 57th St.*

9 *e-3*

RALPH M. CHAIT GALLERIES, INC.

Chait shows top-quality Chinese art, including export silver; porcelain; and pottery from the Neolithic period to 1800. *12 E. 56th St. (between 5th and Madison Aves.), Midtown, 212/758–0937. Closed Sun. Subway: E, F, N, R to 5th Ave.*

9 *e-3*

RONIN GALLERY

Ronin has a large selection of 17th- to 20th-century Japanese woodblock prints, as well as netsuke. *605 Madison Ave. (between 57th and 58th Sts.), Midtown, 212/688–0188. Closed Sun. Subway: 59th St.*

prints & original posters

9 d-3

ASSOCIATED AMERICAN ARTISTS (A.A.A.)

America's largest print dealer has prints from the 16th–20th centuries and original etchings, lithographs, woodcuts, and serigraphs from the 15th–20th centuries. *20 W. 57th St. (between 5th and 6th Aves.), Midtown, 212/399–5510. Closed Sun.–Mon.; also closed June–Aug., weekends. Subway: B, Q to 57th St.*

11 d-5

BROOKE ALEXANDER EDITIONS

These contemporary prints, multiples, and illustrated books come from such heavyweights as Richard Artschwager, Richard Bosman, Jasper Johns, Claes Oldenburg, and Andy Warhol. *59 Wooster St. (at Broome St.), SoHo, 212/925–2070. Closed Sun.–Mon. Subway: A, C, E, N, R to Canal St.*

7 e-8

DAVID TUNICK, INC.

Tunick carries fine old masters, modern prints, and drawings by such masters as Rembrandt, Dürer, Tiepolo, Brueghel, and Canaletto; 19th-century prints by Bonnard, Goya, Cézanne, Degas, Delacroix, Gericault, Manet, Toulouse-Lautrec, and Pissarro; and 20th-century works by Picasso, Matisse, Braque, Whistler, Bellows, and Villon. *46 E. 65th St. (between Madison and Park Aves.), Upper East Side, 212/570–0090. Closed weekends; appointment advised. Subway: 77th St.*

9 e-3

FITCH-FEBVREL GALLERY

Fitch-Febvrel specializes in fine prints and drawings from the 19th and 20th centuries. *5 E. 57th St. (between 5th and Madison Aves.), Midtown, 212/688–8522. Closed Sun.–Mon.; closed Aug. except by appointment. Subway: E, F, N, R to 5th Ave.*

9 e-3

JANE KAHAN GALLERY

Kahan has a large collection of Chagall prints, as well as works by Appel, Calder, Delaunay, Dubuffet, Francis, Lichtenstein, Matisse, Matta, Miró, Picasso, Pissarro, and Stella. *922 Madison Ave. (at 73rd St.), Upper East Side, 212/744–1490. Closed Sun. Subway: 77th St.*

7 e-7

JAPAN GALLERY

Here the focus is Japanese woodblock prints from the 18th century to the present. *1210 Lexington Ave. (at 82nd St.), Upper East Side, 212/288–2241. Closed Sun.–Mon. Subway: 4, 5, 6 to 86th St.*

9 d-2

MARGO FEIDEN GALLERIES

Feiden has a thorough collection of Al Hirschfield's drawings, watercolors, lithographs, and etchings. *699 Madison Ave. (between 62nd and 63rd Sts.), Upper East Side, 212/223–4230. Subway: 68th St./Hunter College.*

11 e-4

MULTIPLE IMPRESSIONS, LTD.

These contemporary American and European original graphics come from such artists as Kozo, Andre Masson, Johnny Friedlaender, Harold Altman, Elizabeth Schippert, and Mikio Watanabe. The gallery mounts several solo shows annually. *128 Spring St. (at Greene St.), SoHo, 212/925–1313. Subway: A, C, E to Spring St.*

9 f-7

OLD PRINT SHOP

This is the place to retreat for original prints of Audubon, Currier & Ives, 18th-century maps, and nauticalia, as well as some American paintings. *150 Lexington Ave. (between 29th and 30th Sts.), Murray Hill, 212/683–3950. Closed Sun.–Mon.; June–Aug., closed weekends. Subway: 6 to 28th St.*

9 e-3

PACE MASTER PRINTS

This substantial collection includes 15th-to 20th-century master prints and drawings by Canaletto, Dürer, Goya, Kandinsky, Matisse, Miró, Picasso, Piranesi, Rembrandt, Tiepolo, Toulouse-Lautrec, and Whistler. It's probably the finest print annex (of a major gallery) in town. *32 E. 57th St. (between Madison and Park Aves.), Midtown, 212/421–3688. Closed Sun.–Mon. Subway: B, Q to 57th St.*

9 e-3

PACE PRINTS

Stop off on Pace's third floor for contemporary prints and multiples. *32 E. 57th St. (between Madison and Park*

Aves.), Midtown, 212/421–3237. Closed Sun.–Mon.; summer, closed weekends. Subway: B, Q to 57th St.

9 *b-7*

ROBERT MILLER

Miller shows both contemporary American art and 19th- and 20th-century photography by such greats as Berenice Abbott, Diane Arbus, Jean-Michel Basquiat, Walker Evans, Man Ray, Robert Mapplethorpe, David McDermott, Peter McGough, Alice Neel, and Bruce Weber. *524 W 26th St. (between 10th and 11th Aves.), Chelsea, 212/980–5454. Closed Sun.–Mon.; closed Aug. except by appointment. Subway: C, E to 23rd St.*

alternative exhibition spaces

These spaces draw devoted art junkies with the very newest of the new, and sometimes the very strangest of the strange. In contrast to the scenes at SoHo or West Chelsea openings—and, frankly, about as far from Midtown and the Upper East Side as you can get—fashion and money are not the key concepts here. The sites can be difficult to find and the intrepid visitors a bit shaggy, but many art world veterans figure that these galleries and "complexes" are gestational holds for the future of American art.

11 *e-4*

EXIT ART/ THE FIRST WORLD

This large SoHo space is atypical in that it encourages hanging out—in the gift shop or the café—rather than quick visits. The shows, mounted by freelance curators as well as staff, tend to focus on social concerns, so the place has a late '60s–early '90s feel that counters the cash chase currently raging elsewhere. Recent installations have included a clever show of artists invited to live and work in the space for a few weeks. *548 Broadway (between Spring and Prince Sts.), SoHo, 212/966–7745. Closed Mon. Subway: Prince St.*

9 *b-8*

THE KITCHEN

Boasting a huge, bleacher-surrounded performance space and high-tech video projection equipment, The Kitchen is

the place to see experimental film and video. It's also the place to see performance artist/sex worker Annie Sprinkle do her thing (she makes Karen Finley look tame). Occasionally someone might be cooking pancakes, then laminating them, in the lobby. *512 W. 19th St. (between 10th and 11th Aves.), Chelsea, 212/255–5793, call or stop in for calendar of events. Subway: C, E to 23rd St.*

3 *d-3*

P.S. 1 CONTEMPORARY ART CENTER

See Art Museums, *below.*

ART MUSEUMS

Some landmark buildings and mansions have their own art collections and period furnishings; *see* Historic Buildings & Areas, *below.*

6 *b-5*

AMERICAN ACADEMY OF ARTS & LETTERS

Although the Academy is not usually open to the public, its doors are thrown open for two annual exhibitions, featuring the work of American sculptors, painters, architects, composers, and authors. For more on the Academy's attractive Italian Renaissance surroundings, *see* Audubon Terrace Historic District *in* Historic Buildings & Areas, *below. 633 W. 155th St. (Audubon Terrace Museum Complex), Washington Heights, 212/368–5900. Call for exhibit schedules and hours. Subway: 1 or 9 to 157th St.*

9 *d-4*

AMERICAN CRAFT MUSEUM

Right across the street from the Museum of Modern Art, the American Craft Museum raises crafts—often taken for granted—to the level of high art. The museum's changing exhibits feature quilts, handblown glass, pottery, basketry, woodwork, and hand-woven textiles. Classes, workshops, and lectures bring expert craftspeople to New York and give novices a chance to weave, mold, carve, and create. *40 W. 53rd St. (between 5th and 6th Aves.), Midtown, 212/956–6047. Admission: $5, free Thurs. evenings; $2.50 students and seniors, free children under 12. Open Tues., Wed., and Fri.–Sun. 10–6, Thurs. 10–8. Subway: E, F to 5th Ave.*

9 *e-1*

AMERICAS SOCIETY

In a 1911 mansion designed by the renowned architectural firm McKim, Mead, & White that once housed the Soviet Union's mission to the U.N. (1948–1963), the Americas Society attempts to inform U.S. citizens about what's going on in the rest of the Western Hemisphere. To help fulfill this mission, their small art gallery mounts three to four exhibits a year from Latin America, the Caribbean, and Canada, covering everything from pre-Columbian art to contemporary painting, sculpture, photography, and the decorative arts. *680 Park Ave. (at 68th St.), Upper East Side, 212/249–8950. Suggested contribution: $3. Open Tues.–Sun. 11–6. Subway: 68th St./Hunter College.*

9 *e-1*

ASIA SOCIETY

A nonprofit educational organization, the Asia Society regularly sponsors lectures, films, dance, and musical programs in addition to its art exhibits, which have included Japanese painting, Korean ceramics, South Asian stone and bronze sculpture, and artworks from China, Nepal, India, Pakistan, and Afghanistan. *725 Park Ave. (at 70th St.), Upper East Side, 212/288–6400. Admission: $4 adults; $2 students and seniors; free Thurs. 6–8. Open Tues., Wed. and Fri.–Sat. 11–6, Thurs. 11–8, Sun. noon–5. Subway: 68th St./Hunter College.*

6 *f-4*

BRONX MUSEUM OF THE ARTS

In a former synagogue on the Grand Concourse—a Bronx boulevard lined with Art Deco and Art Moderne apartment buildings—the permanent collection contains 20th-century works on paper by African, African-American, Latin, Latin American, South Asian, and Asian-American artists. Rotating exhibits in the museum's newly renovated galleries feature contemporary works by international artists and often focus on the cultural and social history of the Bronx. *1040 Grand Concourse (at 165th St.), Bronx, 718/681–6000. Suggested donation: $3 adults, $2 students and seniors, free children under 12. Open Wed. 3–9, Thurs. and Fri. 10–5, weekends noon–6. Subway: C, D to 167th St.*

12 *b-2*

BROOKLYN BRIDGE ANCHORAGE

The two massive stone towers that support the Brooklyn Bridge are actually hollow, and inside the interior of the Brooklyn tower is a cool, cavernous gallery that hosts contemporary art, fashion, and design exhibits every summer. *Cadman Plaza W and Old Fulton St., Brooklyn, 212/206–6674, ext. 251 (Manhattan office). Call for information on hours and exhibits. Subway: Clark St.*

4 *e-1*

BROOKLYN MUSEUM OF ART

With approximately 1½ million pieces, the Brooklyn Museum is housed in a massive, regal building designed by McKim, Mead & White in 1893 and ranks as the second-largest art museum in New York City—and one that's hip quotient is on the rise. Its temporary exhibits are often among the city's best (and as "Sensation," a showing of work by young British artists, proved, most adventurous) and several of its permanent exhibits are world-renowned. Most notable are the Egyptian Art Collection, with its hieroglyphic-covered sarcophagi; the American Painting and Sculpture Galleries, with works by Georgia O'Keeffe, Mark Rothko, Winslow Homer, Gilbert Stuart, and John Singer Sargent; and the outdoor Sculpture Garden, with 19th-century architectural ornaments, including fragments of the original Pennsylvania Station. *200 Eastern Pkwy. (at Washington Ave.), Brooklyn, 718/638–5000. Suggested contribution: $4 adults, $2 students, $1.50 seniors, free children under 12. Open Wed.–Fri. 10–5, weekends 11–6. On "First Saturdays" each month, the museum is open until 11 at night, with free admission from 5–11, gallery tours, popular films, and a dance band playing in the lobby. Subway: Eastern Pkwy./Brooklyn Museum.*

9 *e-2*

CHINA INSTITUTE GALLERY

Housed in a redbrick mansion flanked by two stone lions, the China Institute's gallery features two exhibits of traditional and contemporary Chinese art each year. *125 E. 65th St. (between Park and Lexington Aves.), Upper East Side, 212/744–8181. Suggested contribution: $5. Open Mon. and Wed.–Sat. 10–5, Tues. 10–8, Sun. 1–5. Subway: 68th St./Hunter College.*

5 *b-7*

THE CLOISTERS

One of New York's artistic and spiritual treasures, the Cloisters is situated high on a hill in Upper Manhattan's wooded Ft. Tryon Park, overlooking the Hudson River. The castlelike structure, a branch of the Metropolitan Museum of Art, incorporates parts of five different cloisters from medieval monasteries, including a Romanesque chapel and a 12th-century Spanish apse; the collection of European medieval artwork includes the famed Unicorn Tapestries from the 15th and 16th centuries. Outside, three enchanting gardens shelter more than 250 species of plants similar to those grown during the Middle Ages, including herbs and medicinals. *Ft. Tryon Park (Riverside Dr. and Broadway from 192nd to Dyckman Sts.), Inwood, 212/923–3700. Suggested contribution: $10 adults, students and seniors $5, children under 12 free. Open Mar.–Oct., Tues.–Sun. 9:30–5:15; Nov.–Feb., Tues.–Sun. 9:30–4:45. Subway: 190th St.*

7 *e-6*

COOPER-HEWITT NATIONAL DESIGN MUSEUM

Beautifully restored, this 64-room 5th Avenue mansion—built by industrialist Andrew Carnegie in 1901—is now home to the Smithsonian Institution's design and decorative arts collections. With more than 250,000 objects spanning 3,000 years of design history, the museum's holdings include ceramics, textiles, drawings, prints, glass, furniture, metalwork, book papers, woodwork, wall coverings, embroidery, and lace. The major exhibitions are typically both fun and creative, ranging from the history of water fountains to Walt Disney's impact on the American landscape. In summer, exhibitions often filter out into the Arthur Ross Terrace and Garden, a flower-filled, tree-shaded haven. *2 E. 91st St. (at 5th Ave.), Upper East Side, 212/849–8400. Admission: $5 adults, $3 students and seniors, free Tues. 5–9. Open Tues. 10–9, Wed.–Sat. 10–5, Sun. noon–5. Subway: 4, 5, 6 to 86th St.*

9 *e-4*

DAHESH MUSEUM

While the Whitney, MOMA, and Guggenheim vie for the latest contemporary artworks, the Dahesh revels in tradition. Opened in 1995 with the collection of late Lebanese art-collector Salim Moussa Achi (a.k.a. Dr. Dahesh), this free Midtown museum is devoted to 19th-century European "academic" art, most notably works by Bouguereau and Gérôme, who taught an entire generation of artists, including the Impressionists. Shows are clever and highly informative, often reintroducing works by artists once famed, now forgotten. *601 5th Ave. (between 48th and 49th Sts.), Midtown, 212/759–0606. Open Tues.–Sat. 11–6. Subway: E, F to 5th Ave.*

9 *b-8*

DIA CENTER FOR THE ARTS

Surrounded by the ultra-trendy West Chelsea gallery scene, the Dia is a showplace and laboratory for contemporary artists, with three floors of galleries, a roof garden with permanent installations by Dan Graham, a bookstore, lectures, readings, and live performances. *548 W. 22nd St. (between 10th and 11th Aves.), Chelsea, 212/989–5566. Admission: $6 adults, $4 students and seniors. Open Wed.–Sun. noon–6. Subway: C or E to 23rd St.*

9 *c-4*

THE EQUITABLE GALLERY

This free, eclectic museum in the lobby of the Equitable Building in Midtown has changing exhibits on everything from folk to fine art. Past exhibits have highlighted Colonial American furniture, Haitian sculpture and painting, and the stateside photography of Henri Cartier-Bresson. *787 7th Ave. (at 51st St.), Midtown, 212/554–4818 (call for information on current exhibitions). Open weekdays 11–6, Sat. noon–5. Subway: 49th St.; 1, 9 to 50th St.*

9 *e-1*

FRICK COLLECTION

Don't miss this tranquil jewel. Coke-and-steel baron Henry Clay Frick's former mansion (built in 1914) houses masterpieces of 14th- to 19th-century European painting, including pieces by Rembrandt, Vermeer, Gainsborough, Turner, Titian, Goya, and El Greco; exquisite 18th-century French and Italian Renaissance furniture; Oriental porcelain; and Limoges enamel. The intimate interior is wonderfully illuminated by overhead skylights, and there's a lovely garden court with a splashing fountain. *1 E. 70th St. (at 5th Ave.), Upper East*

Side, 212/288–0700. Admission: $7 adults, $5 seniors and students, no children under 10. Open Tues.–Sat. 10–6, Sun. 1–6. Subway: 68th St./Hunter College.

7 *e-7*

GOETHE HOUSE NEW YORK

Smack in the middle of Museum Mile, in a 1907 Beaux-Arts town house, Goethe House showcases German art, film, and culture. The gallery features changing exhibits of contemporary German art. *1014 5th Ave. (between 82nd and 83rd Sts.), Upper East Side, 212/439–8700. Open Tues. and Thurs. 10–7, Wed. and Fri. 10–5, Sat. noon–5. Subway: 4, 5, 6 to 86th St.*

10 *e-2*

GREY ART GALLERY

New York University's main building contains a welcoming street-level space with changing exhibitions, usually devoted to contemporary art. *100 Washington Sq. E (between Washington and Waverly Pls.), Greenwich Village, 212/998–6780. Admission: $2.50 suggested donation. Tues. and Thurs.–Fri. 11–6, Wed. 11–8., Sat. 11–5. Subway: 8th St.*

7 *e-6*

SOLOMON R. GUGGENHEIM MUSEUM

Frank Lloyd Wright's building (*see Architecture, above*) provides a unique setting for modern art and jam-packed openings for the Guggenheim's powerhouse exhibitions. Holdings of the Thannhauser Collection, a permanent display of 19th- and 20th-century Impressionist, post-Impressionist, and early modern masterpieces, include a renowned Kandinsky collection, Paul Klees, Picassos, Chagalls, and a newly aquired series of Maplethorpes. Jazz performances are held on summer weekends in the Frank Lloyd Wright Rotunda. The warmer months are also a pleasant time to hang out on the LeFrak Sculpture Terrace, where you can examine the museum's oversize minimalist pieces and take in the view of Central Park. *1071 5th Ave. (at 89th St.), Upper East Side, 212/423–3500. Admission: $12 adults, $7 students and seniors, free children under 12; pay what you wish Fri. 6–8. Open Sun.–Wed. 9–6, Fri. and Sat. 9–8. Subway: 4, 5, 6 to 86th St.*

11 *e-4*

GUGGENHEIM MUSEUM SOHO

Perhaps best known for its enormous museum shop, the Guggenheim's downtown space focuses primarily on multimedia installations, such as video art by Nam June Paik, work by Jenny Holzer, and Andy Warhol's *Last Supper.* The art is flattered by this landmark building, the lofty interiors of which were redesigned by architect Arata Isozaki. *575 Broadway (at Prince St.), SoHo, 212/423–3500. Admission: free. Open Thurs.–Mon. 11–6. Subway: Prince St.; Broadway–Lafayette St.*

6 *b-5*

HISPANIC SOCIETY OF AMERICA

Because it's off-the-beaten path, the Hispanic Society only draws about 20,000 visitors per year—but here's the secret: it has what's considered the best collection of Spanish art outside of the Prado. And because its neighboring institutions in the Audubon Terrace district keep moving out (the Museum of the American Indian and the National Geographic Society are both former tenants), the Hispanic Society's been able to purchase extra gallery space. On display are paintings, sculptures, manuscripts, and decorative artworks from prehistoric times to the present (from Spain, Portugal, Latin America, and the Philippines), including pieces by Goya, El Greco, and Velazquez. For more on the handsome surroundings, *see* Audubon Terrace Historic District *in* Historic Buildings & Areas, *below. Broadway and 155th St. (Audubon Terrace Museum Complex), Morningside Heights, 212/926–2234. Admission: free (donations accepted). Open Tues.–Sat. 10–4:30, Sun. 1–4. Subway: 157th St.; 155th St.*

7 *e-6*

INTERNATIONAL CENTER OF PHOTOGRAPHY (ICP)

ICP, founded in 1974 in a lovely Georgian-revival mansion, is devoted exclusively to photography as a fine art and a medium of communication. The permanent collection contains works by important 20th-century photographers including Robert Capa, W. Eugene Smith, Henri Cartier-Bresson, Yousuf Karsh, Man Ray, Lee Miller, Gordon Parks, Roman Vishniac, and Ernst Haas.

Temporary exhibitions focus on individual photographers and themes. *1130 5th Ave. (at 94th St.), Upper East Side, 212/860–1777. Admission: $6 adults, $4 students and seniors, $1 children under 12; pay what you wish Fri. 5–8. Open Tues.–Thurs 10–5, Fri. 10–8, weekends 10–6. Subway: 4, 5, 6 to 96th St.*

9 *d-5*

ICP MIDTOWN

A branch of the original, ICP Midtown presents several photography shows annually, including selections from the extensive permanent collection. *1133 6th Ave. (at 43rd St.), Midtown, 212/768–4682. $6 adults, $4 students and seniors, $1 children under 12; pay what you wish Fri. 5–8. Open Tues.–Thurs. 10–5, Fri. 10–8, weekends 10–6. Subway: B, D, F, Q to 42nd St.*

8 *a-6*

ISAMU NOGUCHI GARDEN MUSEUM

A large, open-air garden and two floors of gallery space hold over 250 pieces by the renowned Japanese-American sculptor Isamu Noguchi. Originally a photo-engraving plant, the building was converted by Noguchi himself, and now houses his sculptures (in stone, bronze, wood, clay, and steel), models, drawings, and even stage sets for dances by Martha Graham. *Vernon Boulevard at 33rd Rd., Long Island City, Queens, 718/721–1932. Suggested contribution: $4 adults, $2 students and seniors. Open Apr.–Oct., Wed.–Fri. 10–5, weekends 11–6. Weekend shuttle bus service leaves from Park Ave. and 70th St. 11:30–3:30 every hour on the half-hour; $5. Subway: N to Broadway.*

1 *b-2*

JACQUES MARCHAIS MUSEUM OF TIBETAN ART

This replica of a Tibetan mountain temple houses a major collection of Tibetan and other Asian art, including bronzes, paintings, scrolls, and ritual objects. Surrounded by lovely gardens, it's the perfect spot for a day of contemplation. *338 Lighthouse Ave. (off Richmond Rd.), Staten Island, 718/987–3500. Admission: $3. Open Apr.–Nov., Wed.–Sun. 1–5; shorter hrs winter. Take S74 bus from Staten Island Ferry terminal to Lighthouse Ave. and walk ¼ mi up Lighthouse Hill.*

9 *f-4*

JAPAN SOCIETY GALLERY

This spare and serene space displays ancient as well as contemporary Japanese art and sponsors films, performances, and lectures. *333 E. 47th St. (between 1st and 2nd Aves.), Midtown, 212/832–1155. Suggested contribution: $5. Open Tues.–Sun. 11–6. Subway: 51st. St./Lexington–3rd Aves.*

7 *e-6*

THE JEWISH MUSEUM

Housed in a Gothic-style mansion (1908) facing Central Park, the Jewish Museum is one of the largest and most beautiful collections of Judaica in the country. Ceremonial objects, paintings, prints, drawings, sculpture, manuscripts, photographs, videos, and antiquities trace the development of Jewish culture over the past 4,000 years. Special exhibitions—on such subjects as German modernism and Sigmund Freud—are often among the city's most heavily attended. *1109 5th Ave. (at 92nd St.), Upper East Side, 212/423–3230. Admission: $8 adults, $5.50 students and seniors, free children under 12; pay what you wish Tues. 5–8. Open Sun., Mon., Wed., and Thurs. 11–5:45, Tues. 11–8. Subway: 4, 5, 6 to 96th St.*

7 *d-7*

METROPOLITAN MUSEUM OF ART

The Met is the largest museum in the Western Hemisphere, with 1.6 million square ft of gallery space and a permanent collection of more than 2 million works of art. Covering 5,000 years of cultural history, the Met is so enormous it's hard to know where to begin. You might want to start in the spectacularly renovated galleries for classical art, which contain Greek and Roman statuary, perfectly preserved Grecian urns, and rare Roman wall paintings excavated from the lava of Mt. Vesuvius. The renowned Egyptian collection centers around the Temple of Dendur, an entire Roman-period temple transported to the museum from Egypt and housed in its own, specially built atrium. A stunning collection of European paintings includes 30 by Monet, 17 by Cézanne, 7 by Vermeer (more than any other museum in the world), and works by Gauguin, Van Gogh, Degas, El Greco, Rembrandt, and Rubens. Monumental Chinese Buddhas, Ming Dynasty furniture, and the re-creation of a Ming scholar's garden are highlights of the Asian galleries. Three floors of 20th-century art, centering on Picasso's portrait of Gertrude Stein, make up the Lila Acheson Wallace Wing. The American Wing contains 25 period rooms, and paintings by Thomas Cole and Winslow Homer. The arms and armor collection holds more than 14,000 weapons and a cavernous hall of knights in helmets and chain mail, mounted on their steeds and ready for jousting. Moral of the story: don't try to pop in for a quick peek. *5th Ave. at 82nd St., Upper East Side, 212/535–7710. Suggested contribution: $10 adults, $5 students and seniors, free children under 12. Open Sun. and Tues.–Thurs. 9:30–5:15, Fri. and Sat. 9:30–8:45. For sculpture garden, see Viewpoints, below. Subway: 4, 5, 6 to 86th St.*

9 *e-4*

MUNICIPAL ART SOCIETY URBAN CENTER GALLERIES

The Municipal Art Society is dedicated to the idea of cities as aesthetic places and its free exhibits have focused on everything from 3-D re-creations of department-store window displays to architectural renderings of a better New York. *457 Madison Ave. (at 51st St.), Midtown, 212/935–3960. Open Mon.–Wed., Fri., and Sat. 11–5. Subway: 51st St./Lex.–3rd Aves.*

7 *e-4*

EL MUSEO DEL BARRIO

The art and culture of Latin America speak here through artifacts, photographs, and paintings. The permanent collection of 8,000 objects contains numerous pre-Columbian artifacts and is particularly strong on Puerto Rican art, featuring numerous Puerto Rican santos. Every year, the museum puts up a major exhibition of contemporary Latino artists. *1230 5th Ave. (at 104th St.), East Harlem, 212/831–7272. Suggested contribution: $4 adults, $2 students and seniors, free children under 13. Open Wed.–Sun. 11–5. Subway: 6 to 103rd St.*

9 *b-2*

MUSEUM OF AMERICAN FOLK ART

Like the American Craft Museum (*see above*), the Museum of American Folk Art brings crafts, pastimes, and commercial work by traditional American artisans to a new level. Changing exhibitions feature folk paintings, textiles (especially quilts), and sculpture (often in the form of weather vanes) from Colonial times to the present. *2 Lincoln Sq. (Columbus Ave. between 65th and 66th Sts.), Upper West Side, 212/595–9533. Admission: free (donations accepted). Open Tues.–Sun. 11:30–7:30. Subway: 66th St./Lincoln Center.*

9 *e-2*

MUSEUM OF AMERICAN ILLUSTRATION

This specialized museum was founded in 1901 to "promote and stimulate interest in the art of illustration, past, present, and future." The Society of Illustrators assembles highly eclectic monthly exhibitions, focusing on everything from *New Yorker* cartoons and Norman Rockwell paintings to pictures from *Mad* magazine and children's books. *128 E. 63rd St. (between Park and Lex. Aves.), Upper East Side, 212/838–2560. Open Tues. 10–8, Wed.–Fri. 10–5, Sat. noon–4. Subway: 4, 5, or 6 to 59th St.; B, N, Q, R to Lexington Ave.*

11 *e-4*

MUSEUM FOR AFRICAN ART

Celebrating the art of an entire continent in one small space is a tall order, but the Museum for African Art manages to do it, and with panache. Exhibits range from ceremonial masks to contemporary painting. The unique interior, with galleries connected by a spiral staircase, was designed by Maya Lin, best known for her design of the Vietnam Veterans Memorial in Washington, D.C. *593 Broadway (between Houston and Prince Sts.), SoHo, 212/966–1313. Admission: $5 adults, $2.50 students, seniors, and children. Open Tues.–Fri. 10:30–5:30, weekends noon–6. Subway: Prince St.; Broadway–Lafayette St.*

9 *d-4*

MUSEUM OF MODERN ART (MOMA)

MOMA is the greatest repository of modern art in the world, its six stories brandishing such works as Van Gogh's *Starry Night*, Monet's *Water Lilies*, Matisse's *Dance*, Picasso's *Les Demoiselles d'Avignon*, and Warhol's *Marilyn Monroe*. Altogether, there are more than 100,000 works on display, including paintings and sculpture; architecture and design; drawings; prints and illustrated books; photography; and film and video. The first museum to recognize film as an art form, MOMA has documented the development of motion pictures for nearly 50 years and still screens six films daily in its two theaters. The museum's sculpture garden (designed by Philip Johnson), around which the galleries are built, remains one of New York's most treasured spaces and contains works by Rodin, Matisse, and Moore; in the summer it is the setting for a classical concert series. The museum shop has unusually fine art books, design objects, and gifts. What's more, MOMA is determined to remain modern and is starting the 21st century with a bang: A major expansion and redesign (slated for completion in 2004) will double the exhibition space, adding large skylit galleries, a new theater, and an education and research complex. (Construction will cause periodic gallery closures.) *11 W. 53rd St. (between 5th and 6th Aves.), Midtown, 212/708–9400. Admission: $9.50 adults, $6.50 students and seniors, free children under 16; pay what you wish Fri. 4:30– 8:15. Open Sat.–Tues., Thurs. 10:30–5:45, Fri. 10:30–8:15. Subway: E, F to 5th Ave.*

7 *e-6*

NATIONAL ACADEMY OF DESIGN

Founded in 1825 as a drawing society and school, the academy is devoted to America's artistic and architectural heritage. The extensive collection of 19th- and 20th-century paintings, prints, drawings, photography, and sculpture includes works by Mary Cassatt, Winslow Homer, Frank Lloyd Wright, I.M. Pei, and Robert Rauschenberg—all of whom were members of the academy. *1083 5th Ave. (at 89th St.), Upper East Side, 212/369–4880. Admission: $8 adults, $4.50 students and seniors, free children under 12. Open Wed., Thurs., and weekends noon–5, Fri. 10–6. Subway: 4, 5, 6 to 86th St.*

11 *e-4*

NEW MUSEUM OF CONTEMPORARY ART

Founded in 1977, this avant-garde center for art and ideas focuses exclusively on art by living artists, most of them emerging or experimental. A new, recently completed design spotlights international artists and includes a subterranean "project space"—free to the public—with a hip bookstore that hosts readings, performance art, and film and

video screenings. *583 Broadway (between Prince and Houston Sts.), SoHo, 212/219– 1222. Admission: $5 adults, $3 artists, students, and seniors, free under age 18; free Thurs. 6–8. Open Wed. and Sun. noon–6, Thurs.–Sat. noon–8. Subway: Prince St.; Broadway–Lafayette St.*

4 *a-6*

NEWHOUSE CENTER FOR CONTEMPORARY ART

In the historic main hall at the Snug Harbor Cultural Center (see Historic Buildings & Areas, *below*), the Newhouse Center's three galleries feature thought-provoking exhibitions by contemporary artists. *1000 Richmond Terr., Staten Island, 718/448–2500. Admission: $2 suggested donation. Open Wed.–Sun. noon–5. From the Staten Island Ferry terminal, take the S40 bus to Snug Harbor Cultural Center.*

7 *a-4*

NICHOLAS ROERICH MUSEUM

In an Upper West Side 1898 town house, this eccentric little museum's permanent collection focuses exclusively on the work of the Russian artist Nicholas Roerich, who came to New York in the 1920s and quickly developed an ardent following. The museum centers on Roerich's vast paintings of the Himalayas. The museum also hosts a chamber-music series and poetry readings. *319 W. 107th St. (between Broadway and Riverside Dr.), Upper West Side, 212/ 864–7752. Admission: free (donations accepted). Open Tues.–Sun. 2–5. Subway: 110th St./Cathedral Pkwy.*

9 *e-6*

PIERPONT MORGAN LIBRARY

See Libraries, *below*.

3 *d-4*

P.S. 1 CONTEMPORARY ART CENTER

A former public school, this wonderful old Romanesque building has vast galleries (reopened with enormous hoopla after extensive renovations in 1997) and an enormous outdoor space for showing contemporary art. The emphasis at this seminal space is on an ever-changing cast of innovative new artists, plus old hands at the experimental game. There's also live music, films, performances, and sometimes even a D.J.

with dancing. It's well worth the trip to Long Island City, a mere hop, skip, and a jump across the East River. P.S. 1 recently merged with the Museum of Modern Art (*see above*), giving P.S. 1— which has no permanent collection— access to MOMA's vast holdings. *22–25 Jackson Ave. (at 46th Ave.), Long Island City, Queens, 718/784–2084. Suggested admission: $5 adults, $2 students and seniors. Open Wed.–Sun. noon–6. Subway: E, F to 23rd St./Ely Ave.*

3 *h-2*

QUEENS MUSEUM OF ART

On the site of two famous World Fairs, the Queens Museum features painting and sculpture exhibitions from the classical to the avant-garde, often with an emphasis on New York City's own art history and ethnic heritage. On permanent view is Panorama, a detailed (9,000-square-ft) scale model of New York City's five boroughs that includes nearly every brownstone and skyscraper; it's fascinating and updated frequently. *New York City Building (opposite the Unisphere), Flushing Meadows–Corona Park, Flushing, Queens, 718/592–9700. Suggested admission: $4 adults, $2 students and seniors, free children under 5. Open Wed.–Fri. 10–5, weekends noon–5. Subway: Willets Pt./Shea Stadium.*

7 *d-1*

STUDIO MUSEUM IN HARLEM

This distingushed museum is devoted to the study, documentation, collection, promotion, and exhibition of painting, sculpture, and photography by African-Americans. Major exhibits feature both established and emerging black artists. There are also frequent concerts and lectures, as well as a lovely sculpture garden and a hip museum shop. *144 W. 125th St. (between Lenox and 7th Aves.), Harlem, 212/864–4500. Admission: $5 adults, $3 students and seniors, $1 children under 12; free first Sat. of each month. Open Wed.–Fri. 10–5, weekends 1–6. Subway: 2, 3 to 125th St.*

10 *f-1*

UKRAINIAN MUSEUM

This small East Village museum celebrates the culture and history of Ukrainian people, a small community of whom have settled in the neighborhood. Folk art and costumes, fine arts, documentary photography, letters and manuscripts, and hundreds of brilliantly colored Easter eggs are on display. A major expansion is in the works. *203 2nd Ave. (between 12th and 13th Sts.), East Village, 212/228–0110. Admission: $3 adults, $2 seniors and students. Open Wed.–Sun. 1–5. Subway: Astor Pl.; 3rd Ave.; 1st Ave.*

7 *e-8*

WHITNEY MUSEUM OF AMERICAN ART

Founded in 1930 in the studio of artist Gertrude Vanderbilt Whitney, who wanted to highlight the work of living American artists, the Whitney now occupies a striking modern building (it's an upside-down ziggurat) designed by the Bauhaus architect Marcel Breuer. Inside the cubist structure are five floors of modern works, including Georgia O'Keeffe's *White Calico Flower*, sculptor Alexander Calder's playful *Circus*, and Edward Hopper's haunting *Early Sunday Morning*. Special exhibits focus on major 20th-century artists, including photographers, filmmakers, and video artists; and every odd year the Whitney hosts its controversial Biennial, featuring the best (or the worst, depending on your point of view) new works of living American artists. *945 Madison Ave. (at 75th St.), Upper East Side, 212/570–3676. Admission: $12.50 adults, $10.50 students and seniors, free children under 12; pay what you wish on the first Thurs. of each month 6–8. Open Tues., Wed. and Fri.–Sun. 11–6, Thurs. 1–8. Subway: 77th St.*

9 *e-5*

WHITNEY MUSEUM OF AMERICAN ART AT PHILIP MORRIS

A wonderful retreat from Grand Central Terminal's maddening crowds, the Whitney's free Midtown branch in the Philip Morris building features a 42-ft-high sculpture court with outstanding examples of 20th-century sculpture—and an espresso bar. In the adjacent gallery, five shows annually cover all aspects of American art. *120 Park Ave. (at 42nd St.), Midtown, 917/663–2550. Sculpture court Mon.–Sat. 7:30–9:30, Sun. 11–7; gallery Mon.–Wed. and Fri. 11–6, Thurs. 11–7:30. Subway: 42nd St./Grand Central.*

BRIDGES

New York has 65 bridges, connecting its boroughs and islands to each other and to the world beyond. Here are some of the most impressive.

10 g-6

BROOKLYN BRIDGE

(John A., Washington, and Emily Roebling, 1867–83) A triumph of Victorian engineering, this graceful 1,595-ft-long suspension bridge was the world's longest when it opened in 1883. Spanning the East River, it connected Manhattan island to the then-independent city of Brooklyn, and instantly became one of the city's most enduring symbols. Alas, the bridge's construction was fraught with peril. Designer John A. Roebling was killed in a construction accident while the bridge was being built; his son, Washington, took over the project and was himself permanently crippled in another accident. With the help of his wife, Emily, Washington nonetheless saw the bridge's construction through to completion. Today, a walkway across the bridge affords unparalleled views of the East River and the downtown skyline (*see* Viewpoints, *below*), as well as a unique look at the bridge's Gothic stone towers and arching steel cables. *City Hall Park, Manhattan, to Cadman Plaza, Brooklyn. Subway: Brooklyn Bridge/City Hall; High St./Brooklyn Bridge.*

6 a-2

GEORGE WASHINGTON BRIDGE

(O. H. Ammann, engineer, and Cass Gilbert, architect, 1931) New York City's only bridge to New Jersey, the GWB is one pure, 3,500-ft line across the Hudson River. A suspension bridge made entirely of exposed steel, the GWB was originally going to have its towers sheathed in concrete, but that plan was scrapped to save money. Most of the bridge's fans don't seem to mind its raw structure; according to architecture critic Paul Goldberger, the bridge "leaps over space in a way that still causes the heart to skip a beat." A walkway and bikeway on the upper deck provide stunning views of the Hudson and the New Jersey Palisades. *Hudson River and 178th St. to Fort Lee, N.J. Subway: 175th St.; 181st St.*

10 g-5

MANHATTAN BRIDGE

(O.F. Nichols and Gustav Lindenthal, 1905) A 1,470-ft-long suspension bridge of exposed steel, the Manhattan Bridge spans the East River just north of the Brooklyn Bridge and carries cars, trucks, and several subway lines between Manhattan and Brooklyn. Inspired by the Porte St. Denis in Paris and the Bernini Colonnade in Rome, its Manhattan entrance is adorned by a regal arch and colonnade by Carrère and Hastings (1905). *Canal St. and Bowery (Manhattan) to Flatbush Ave. Extension (Brooklyn). Subway: Grand St.; E. Broadway.*

9 g-3

QUEENSBORO BRIDGE

(Gustav Lindenthal, engineer; Palmer & Hornbostel, architects, 1909) An ornate, cantilevered mass of exposed steel, the 1,182-ft-long Queensboro Bridge spans the East River, connecting Queens to Manhattan and offering fantastic views of the Midtown skyline. In *The Great Gatsby*, F. Scott Fitzgerald writes, on driving into Manhattan: "The city seen from the Queensboro Bridge is always the city seen for the first time, in its wild promise of all the mystery and the beauty in the world"; his observation still holds true. *E. 59th St. (Manhattan) to Queens Plaza. Subway: 4, 5, 6 to 59th St.*

7 g-1

TRIBOROUGH BRIDGE

(O. H. Ammann, engineer; Aymar Embury II, architect; 1936) The Triborough was considered the ultimate congestion-buster when it opened to auto traffic in 1936. A series of four interconnecting bridges, it crosses the East River, Harlem River, and Bronx Kills, joining Manhattan, the Bronx, and Queens—with 1 million cars passing through every day. Lewis Mumford called the view from the Triborough's walkway "one of the most dazzling urban views in the world." *Subway: 4, 5, 6 to 125th St.*

4 d-7

VERRAZANO-NARROWS BRIDGE

(O. H. Ammann, 1964) At 4,260 ft long, the beautiful Verrazano is the world's second-longest suspension bridge, surpassed only by the Humber Bridge in England. Named for Giovanni da Verrazano, the first European to sight New York Harbor (in 1524), it spans the mouth of the harbor to link Brooklyn and Staten Island. The bridge inspired a development boom on Staten Island; before its construction, Staten Island was accessible from the other boroughs only by ferry. *Ft. Hamilton at 92nd St.,*

Bay Ridge (Brooklyn) to Lily Pond Rd., Fort Wadsworth (Staten Island). Subway: 95th St./Ft. Hamilton.

3 *d-7*

WILLIAMSBURG BRIDGE

(Leffert L. Buck, 1903) When it was first completed, this 1,600-ft steel suspension bridge snatched the title of "World's Longest" from the Brooklyn Bridge and had a profound effect on the city's makeup, offering Lower East Side immigrants easy access to a new promised land: Brooklyn. But time and tides have not been kind to this structure; in 1988 the bridge was found to be deteriorating so seriously that it was temporarily closed. An ongoing repair project is bringing the bridge back up to speed, and the plans include a new walkway and bikeway. *Delancey and Clinton Sts. (Manhattan) to Washington Plaza (Brooklyn). Subway: Delancey St.; Marcy Ave.*

CHILDREN'S MUSEUMS

3 *f-8*

BROOKLYN CHILDREN'S MUSEUM

The world's oldest museum designed specifically for children was founded in 1899 and, designed for children ages 2–14, is full of tunnels to crawl through, animals to pet, stories to read, and plants to water. *145 Brooklyn Ave. (at St. Mark's Ave.), Crown Heights, Brooklyn, 718/735–4432. Suggested contribution: $3. Open July–Aug., Mon., Wed., and Thurs. noon–5, Fri. noon–6:30, weekends 10–5; Sept.–June, Wed.–Fri. 2–5, weekends 10–5. Subway: A to Kingston–Throop Aves.; 3 to Kingston Ave.; 2 to President St.*

7 *b-7*

CHILDREN'S MUSEUM OF MANHATTAN

In this wonderful five-story building, children ages 1–10 can climb, crawl, paint, make collages, try on costumes, and even film their own newscasts. Every day, there are art workshops, storytelling sessions, science programs, and drama workshops. *212 W. 83rd St., Upper West Side, 212/721–1234. Admission: $6. Open mid-June–Aug., Tues.–Sun. 10–5; Sept.–mid-June, Wed.–Sun. 10–5. Subway: 1, 9 to 86th St.*

10 *e-4*

CHILDREN'S MUSEUM OF THE ARTS

For youngsters ages 10 months to 10 years, this bi-level art space has a "ball pond," where children can play with brightly colored physio-balls; an "actor's studio" complete with costumes and musical instruments where young divas put on shows; a computer art station; and daily art activities that get children painting, sculpting, and making collages. *182 Lafayette St. between Broome and Grand Sts., SoHo, 212/274–0986. Admission: $5. Open Wed. noon–7, Thurs.–Sun. noon–5. Subway: 6 to Spring St.*

4 *a-6*

STATEN ISLAND CHILDREN'S MUSEUM

This award-winning museum assembles changing exhibits that have focused on bugs, international cooking, the mysteries of water, costuming for film and theater, and the five senses. There are also special events and craft workshops on weekends. *Snug Harbor Cultural Center, 1000 Richmond Terr., Staten Island, 718/273–2060. Admission: $4. Open Tues.–Sun. noon–5.*

CHURCHES & SYNAGOGUES

New York City has more than 2,250 churches and 600 synagogues. Here are some of the most historic and architecturally interesting. We list phone numbers for those that welcome sightseers when services are not in session.

6 *e-8*

ABYSSINIAN BAPTIST CHURCH

Abyssinian's congregation was originally founded in the early 1800s by African-Americans who were unwilling to accept segregation at the Baptist church they attended in downtown Manhattan. Under the direction of minister Adam Clayton Powell, Sr., this Gothic-style church was erected as the congregation's permanent home in 1923. Powell's son and successor, Adam Clayton Powell, Jr., went on to become the nation's first black congressman. Stop in on Sunday to hear a fiery sermon delivered by the present activist minister Calvin O. Butts and the church's gospel choir. *132 Odell Clark Pl. (formerly 138th St.) between Adam Clayton Powell and*

Malcolm X. Blvds., Harlem. 212/862–7474. Subway: 2 or 3 to 135th St.

10 g-3

ANSCHE CHESED
(OLD CONGREGATION)

(Alexander Saeltzer, 1849) Despite its designation as a city landmark, New York's oldest surviving synagogue, and at one time its largest, is in a state of woeful disrepair. The Lower East Side's well-remembered Jewish community has largely dispersed, and the Ansche Chesed congregation has long since moved uptown. Brooding, Gothic-revival architecture gives this abandoned building a ghostly air. *172–176 Norfolk St. (between Stanton and E. Houston Sts.), Lower East Side. Subway: 2nd Ave.*

10 h-4

BIALYSTOKER SYNAGOGUE

A Federal-style stone building erected in 1826, this synagogue, like many others in the city, was originally a Protestant church. In 1908, reflecting the massive influx of Eastern European Jews into New York City and the Lower East Side in particular, it was turned into a synagogue and became the home of a congregation originally founded in Bialystok, Poland. *7–13 Bialystoker Pl. (at Grand St.), Lower East Side. Subway: Delancey St.*

4 b-5

BRIGHTON HEIGHTS
REFORMED CHURCH

A lovely, white wood-framed building dating from 1864, this Dutch Reformed Protestant church is crowned with a tall spire that's visible from incoming Staten Island ferries. *320 St. Mark's Pl. (at Fort Pl.), St. George, Staten Island.*

9 e-8

BROTHERHOOD
SYNAGOGUE (FRIENDS'
MEETING HOUSE)

Built in 1859 alongside Gramercy Park, this landmark house of worship was long the Friends' Meeting House, one of two original Quaker meeting houses in Manhattan. Simple in design and built from brownstone, it was lovingly renovated and turned into a synagogue in 1975. *28 Gramercy Park S (between Irving Pl. and 3rd Ave.), Gramercy. Subway: N, R, 6 to 23rd St.*

7 b-3

CATHEDRAL CHURCH OF
ST. JOHN THE DIVINE
(EPISCOPAL)

Construction of the cathedral in Morningside Heights began on St. John's Day, December 27, 1892, and continued until 1941, when it was halted—still unfinished—by World War II. Work resumed in 1979 and is still going on in the medieval manner, each stone handcut. Two football fields (601 ft) long and 14 stories high, this massive, architecturally eclectic structure will be the world's largest Gothic cathedral when complete. The church hosts several special events each year, including concerts and an enormous Halloween bash; the high point is the blessing of the animals, in honor of St. Francis (October), when the cathedral's bronze doors are opened to circus elephants and pet tarantulas *(see* Events, *below). Amsterdam Ave. at 112th St., 212/316–7540. Open Mon.–Sat. 8–6, Sun. 8–8. Cathedral tours, $3, depart Tues.–Sat. 11, Sun. 1. Special "vertical" tours, $10, (for which you must reserve in advance; 212/932–7347) take visitors on a 12-story climb into the cathedral's neo-Gothic towers on the 1st and 3rd Sat. of month, noon and 2. Subway: 110th St./Cathedral Pkwy.*

9 e-3

CENTRAL SYNAGOGUE
(REFORM)

(Henry Fernbach) Founded in 1872, this Moorish Revival edifice—crowned by two fanciful onion-shape domes and now surrounded by high-rises—is the oldest synagogue in the city in continuous use. Its Eternal Light, kindled in 1872 and replaced by an electric bulb in 1946, continues to burn. *Lexington Ave. and 55th St., Midtown. Subway: 51st St./Lexington–3rd Aves.*

2 a-3

CHRIST CHURCH
(EPISCOPAL)

(R.M. Upjohn, 1866) This landmarked 19th-century stone church in Riverdale—an affluent and disarmingly picturesque community of hilly, winding streets in the southwest Bronx—was designed to look like a medieval English parish church. Well-known members of its congregation have included baseball player Lou Gehrig and Mayor Fiorello La Guardia. *5030 Riverdale Ave. at 252nd St. and the Henry Hudson Parkway, Riverdale, Bronx. Subway: 1, 9 to 231st St.*

10 e-1

CHURCH OF THE ASCENSION (EPISCOPAL)

(Richard Upjohn, 1841; interior remodeled by McKim, Mead & White, 1889) In the heart of Greenwich Village, New York's first Gothic Revival church features a beautiful altar mural, *The Ascension,* and illuminated stained-glass windows, both by John La Farge, who was rivaled only by Louis Comfort Tiffany as the foremost stained-glass artist of the 19th-century. There's also a marble altar sculpture by Augustus Saint-Gaudens. *36–38 5th Ave. (at 10th St.), 212/254–8620. Usually open weekdays noon–2. Subway: 8th St.*

6 b-5

CHURCH OF THE INTERCESSION COMPLEX (EPISCOPAL)

(Bertram Goodhue for Cram, Goodhue & Ferguson, 1914) Beautifully situated in rural Trinity Cemetery (*see Graveyards, below*), the local parish of this large, English Gothic–style country church was founded in 1846. Once the farm of famed artist and ornithologist John J. Audubon, the complex is also home to an impressive parish house, cloister, and vicarage. *Broadway at 155th St., Washington Heights, 212/283–6200. Subway: 157th St.*

1 b-2

CHURCH OF ST. ANDREW (EPISCOPAL)

(William H. Mersereau, 1872) As if transplanted from New England, or even old England, this fieldstone parish church and its ramshackle graveyard sit on a picturesque green hillock near Staten Island's Historic Richmondtown. *4 Arthur Kill Rd. (at Old Mill Rd.), Richmondtown, Staten Island.*

7 e-7

CHURCH OF ST. IGNATIUS LOYOLA (ROMAN CATHOLIC)

(Ditmas & Schickel, 1898) This Beaux-Arts limestone landmark on Park Avenue was modeled on Jesuit churches in Rome. The main altar is dedicated to St. Ignatius Loyola, founder of the Jesuits, and the church is built upon an earlier house of worship (never completed) dedicated to St. Laurence O'Toole, a popular saint with the city's 19th-century Irish immigrants. *See Concerts in Churches in Chapter 5.) 980 Park Ave. (at 84th St.), Upper East Side. Subway: 4, 5, 6 to 86th St.*

9 d-4

CHURCH OF ST. MARY THE VIRGIN (EPISCOPAL) COMPLEX

Now surrounded by the theater district (TKTS is just around the corner), this 1895 French Gothic–style church is accompanied by a brick clergy house, a chapel, a rectory, and a mission house. The church is believed to be the first built on a steel frame à la the modern-day skyscraper. *133–145 W. 46th St. (between 6th and 7th Aves.). Subway: 42nd St./Times Sq.*

9 e-2

CHURCH OF ST. VINCENT FERRER (ROMAN CATHOLIC, DOMINICAN ORDER)

(Bertram Goodhue, 1918) Set inside a large Midtown church complex, Goodhue's Gothic-inspired church of granite with limestone carvings features a magnificent rose window. Nearby is the Victorian Gothic Old Priory of the Dominican Fathers (William Schickel, 1881), the Holy Name Society Building, and the St. Vincent Ferrer School. *869 Lexington Ave. (at 66th St.), Upper East Side. Subway: 68th St./Hunter College.*

7 b-7

CONGREGATION B'NAI JESHURUN

(Henry B. Herts & Walter Schneider, 1918) An exotic Byzantine edifice with a high, Romanesque entryway, this conservative Upper West Side synagogue has an extremely active congregation. *257 W. 88th St. (between Broadway and West End Ave.), Upper West Side. Subway: 1, 9 to 86th St.*

10 g-3

CONGREGATION CHASAM SOFER

Built in 1853 and now one of the many abandoned relics of the Lower East Side, Chasam Sofer is the city's second-oldest standing synagogue, after Anshe Chesed, two blocks west. *810 Clinton St. (between Stanton and Houston Sts.), Lower East Side. Subway: 2nd Ave.*

10 f-4

ELDRIDGE STREET SYNAGOGUE

(Herter Brothers, 1887) The most luxurious of the hundreds of synagogues that once thrived on the Lower East Side, this Orthodox temple is lined with keyhole-shape arches and has an enormous

Gothic-wheel window in its center. Although the main sanctuary was abandoned in the 1950s, it is currently being restored by the Eldridge Street Project, which also offers tours of the synagogue focusing on Jewish-American history and the history of the Lower East Side. Services, weddings, and bar mitzvahs are still held downstairs. *12 Eldridge St. (between Canal and Division Sts.), Lower East Side, 212/219–0888. Tours Tues. and Thurs. at 11:30 and 2:30, Sun. hourly 11–4; admission $4, $2.50 children, students, and seniors. Subway: Grand St.; E. Broadway.*

9 *c-1*

CONGREGATION SHEARITH ISRAEL (ORTHODOX)

(Brunner & Tryon, 1897) The fifth home of North America's oldest Jewish congregation (founded in 1654), this Sephardic (of Spanish and Portuguese origin) synagogue contains religious articles from three centuries. The adjoining "Little Synagogue" is a Georgian-style replica of the congregation's first synagogue. For the synagogue's annual fair, *see* Events, *below*; for its three associated burial grounds, *see* Graveyards & Cemeteries, *below*. *99 Central Park W (at 70th St.), Upper West Side. Subway: B, C to 72nd St.*

9 *e-2*

5TH AVENUE SYNAGOGUE

(Percival Goodman, 1959) Opposite Central Park, this modern limestone temple is adorned with stained-glass windows that are best appreciated after dark, when the interior lights come on. *5 E. 62nd St., Upper East Side. Subway: N, R to 5th Ave.*

10 *e-1*

FIRST PRESBYTERIAN CHURCH

(Joseph C. Wells, 1846; south transept McKim, Mead, & White, 1893) Near the Church of the Ascension (*see above*) and just a few years younger, this Gothic Revival church features a square tower and elaborately carved turrets; its grounds are surrounded by a lovely fence of wood and cast iron. *48 5th Ave. (between 11th and 12th Sts.), Greenwich Village. Subway: 8th St.; F to 14th St.*

2 *g-8*

FIRST REFORMED CHURCH OF COLLEGE POINT

This 1872 country church is a New York City rarity, built of wood and dressed with ornate details in the style of the well-known 19th-century architect Charles Eastlake. *14th Ave. at 119th St., College Point, Queens.*

10 *f-3*

FIRST WARSAW CONGREGATION

Built in 1903, this synagogue originally housed the Congregation Adath Jeshurun of Jassy, Romania, and then the First Warsaw Congregation. Vacant and vandalized, it's now another Lower East Side ghost, but its ornate facade survives as a reminder of another era. *5860 Rivington St. (between Eldridge and Allen Sts.), Lower East Side. Subway: 2nd Ave.*

4 *f-2*

FLATBUSH DUTCH REFORMED CHURCH

Built 1793–98 with an elegant clock tower and steeple, this Federal-style church still has its original bell, imported from Holland; it tolled the death of President Washington in 1799 and still rings each year on the anniversary of his demise. Behind the church is an old cemetery, with graves going back to the 1600s. *890 Flatbush Ave. (at Church Ave.), Brooklyn. Subway: Church Ave.*

4 *h-3*

FLATLANDS DUTCH REFORMED CHURCH

This Georgian Federal church, with white-clapboard siding and a tall steeple, dates from 1848, and its congregation, which had several previous church buildings on the same site, dates from 1654, when this part of Brooklyn was still farmland and many of its residents still spoke Dutch. Many graves in an adjacent cemetery are from the 17th century. *3931 Kings Highway (between Flatbush Ave. and E. 40th St.), Brooklyn. Subway: 2, 5 to Flatbush Ave./Brooklyn College (from station, walk 1 mi down Flatbush Ave.).*

1 *f-3*

FRIENDS' MEETING HOUSE

This plain, wood-shingle building with cast-iron door hinges and latches is the oldest house of worship in New York City, and one of the oldest in the United States. It has been in continuous use since 1694, except for a period during the American Revolution when the occupying British used it successively as a prison, storehouse, and hospital. The two wooden doors in the rear were originally separate entrances for men and women. The Friends (popularly known as the Quakers) were pioneers in asserting the right of religious freedom; the meeting house was built following the trial and acquittal of John Bowne after he was arrested for "illegal worship and assembly." (*See* Bowne House *in* Historic Buildings & Areas, *below*.) *137–16 Northern Blvd. (between Main and Union Sts.), Flushing, Queens, 718/358–9636. Subway: 7 to Main St./Flushing.*

10 *f-1*

FRIENDS' MEETING HOUSE & SEMINARY

(Charles T. Bunting, 1860) These simple but elegant buildings of redbrick and brownstone embody the no-frills Quaker style. *221 E. 15th St. and Rutherford Pl., Gramercy. Subway: 14th St./Union Sq.*

10 *e-1*

GRACE CHURCH & RECTORY (EPISCOPAL)

(James Renwick, Jr., 1846) One of the most magnificent examples of Gothic Revival architecture in the nation, Grace Church was designed by James Renwick—later celebrated for his masterpiece, St. Patrick's Cathedral. The church's ornate marble tower, surmounted by a tall spire, is among Lower Manhattan's most picturesque sights. Countless society couples have wed here over the years, but one particular union—that of P. T. Barnum's little trouper, Tom Thumb, in 1863—particularly scandalized the congregation. *800 Broadway (at 10th St.), Greenwich Village. Subway: 8th St.*

1 *g-4*

GRACE EPISCOPAL CHURCH

(Dudley Field, 1862) The third church to be built on this site, this rugged Gothic Revival building serves a congregation that first assembled in 1702. Statesman and four-time U.S. senator Rufus King is buried in the charming churchyard, which dates from 1734. (*See* King Manor Museum in Historic Buildings & Areas, *below*.) *155–03 Jamaica Ave. (between 155th St. and Parsons Blvd.), Jamaica, Queens. Subway: Jamaica Center.*

12 *b-4*

GRACE CHURCH, BROOKLYN HEIGHTS (EPISCOPAL)

(Richard Upjohn, 1848) This neo-Gothic brownstone church in the heart of historic Brooklyn Heights features three

stained-glass Tiffany windows. The church is particularly popular for its outdoor entrance court, where benches are shaded by an old elm. (*See* Grace Court Alley in Historic Buildings & Areas, *below*.) *254 Hicks St. (at Grace Ct.), Brooklyn Heights. Subway: Borough Hall; Court St.*

10 *e-6*

JOHN STREET UNITED METHODIST CHURCH

(William Hurry) Now dwarfed by Wall Street high-rises, this Georgian-style brownstone is the home of America's oldest Methodist congregation. Built in 1841, it was already the third church on this site; the first was built in 1768. The church and a small museum are open Monday, Wednesday, and Friday noon–4. *44 John St. (between Nassau and William Sts.), Lower Manhattan, 212/ 269–0014. Subway: Fulton St.*

10 *d-2*

JUDSON MEMORIAL BAPTIST CHURCH

(McKim, Mead & White, 1892) Best known for its 10-story campanile, this church is considered one of architect Stanford White's most significant buildings. Designed in the Italian Renaissance style of yellow brick and limestone, it's adorned with 12 stained-glass windows by John LaFarge, intricate terra-cotta ornamentation, and a marble relief by Augustus Saint-Gaudens. Since the 1960s, the church has supported an avant-garde arts program, which showcases modern dance. *55 Washington Sq. S (between Thompson and Sullivan Sts.), Greenwich Village. Subway: W. 4th St./Washington Sq.*

9 *e-7*

THE LITTLE CHURCH AROUND THE CORNER (CHURCH OF THE TRANSFIGURATION) (EPISCOPAL)

Founded in 1849, this Gothic Revival complex is set back from the street in a well-landscaped garden. Here's how it got its nickname: In 1870, the minister at another local church refused to perform funeral services for the actor George Holland, and suggested that Holland's friends try "the little church around the corner." The name stuck, and the church's popularity with theater folks is now a tradition. The stained-glass windows by John LaFarge are dedicated to actors; one depicts the

19th-century superstar Edwin Booth in his most celebrated role, Hamlet. *1 E. 29th St., Murray Hill. 212/684-6770. Free tours are offered Sun. after the 11 AM service. Subway: N, R, 6 to 28th St.*

9 *e-7*

MARBLE COLLEGIATE CHURCH (DUTCH REFORMED)

(S. A. Warner, 1854) This Gothic Revival church in Murray Hill gets its name from the Tuckahoe marble in which it is clad. Its congregation traces its roots back to the city's very first church, which was founded by the Reformed Protestant Dutch Congregation organized by the Dutch governor Peter Minuit, in 1628. Dr. Norman Vincent Peale (*The Power of Positive Thinking*) was the pastor here from 1932 to 1984, and his inspiring sermons were known for drawing thousands of listeners every Sunday. *1 W. 29th St. (at 5th Ave.). Subway: N, R, 6 to 28th St.*

10 *f-5*

MARINERS' TEMPLE (BAPTIST)

(Isaac Lucas, 1842) The AIA [American Institute of Architects] *Guide to New York City* refers to this building as a "temple to Athena"; indeed, the two Ionic columns at the church's entrance make this Greek Revival structure look like a shrine. The church was originally built to lift the spirits—and morals—of the many lonely sailors who passed through the city during the 19th century. *3 Henry St. (at Oliver St.), Chinatown. Subway: Brooklyn Bridge/City Hall.*

7 *f-5*

MOSQUE OF NEW YORK

(Main Building: Skidmore, Owings, & Merrill; Minaret: Swanke, Hayden, Connell, Ltd, 1991) A new focal point for New York's Muslims and a new landmark on the uptown skyline, this granite-and-glass pile, topped with a copper dome and a thin gold crescent, is the first building in New York City to be built as a mosque. The cornerstone of the 130-ft minaret was laid by the Emir of Kuwait in 1988. *Islamic Cultural Center of New York, 1711 3rd Ave. (at 96th St.), Upper East Side, 212/722–5234. Subway: 4, 5, 6 to 96th St.*

1 *f-6*

NEW LOTS REFORMED DUTCH CHURCH

Built in 1824, this one-story, white, wooden church with simple, Gothic-style windows and a short tower, stands virtually unaltered. Records show that the Dutch farmers of New Lots built it for $35. *630 New Lots Ave. (at Schenck Ave.), East New York, Brooklyn. Subway: 3 to Van Siclen Ave.*

4 *f-5*

NEW UTRECHT REFORMED CHURCH

The fieldstone for this 1828 Georgian Gothic edifice came from the original 1699 church that stood on the same site. The windows are made of Victorian milk glass. *18th Ave. between 83rd and 84th Sts., Bensonhurst, Brooklyn. Subway: B to 18th Ave.*

11 *f-4*

OLD ST. PATRICK'S CATHEDRAL (ROMAN CATHOLIC)

(Joseph Mangin, 1815) New York's original Roman Catholic cathedral, Old St. Patrick's was replaced by the uptown St. Patrick's in 1879, after a disastrous fire in 1866. Although the building was restored in 1868, the cathedral was "demoted" to a parish church. Note the high walls surrounding the churchyard, designed to protect the cathedral from the anti-Catholic mobs who once threatened to burn the place down. (*See Graveyards, below.*) *260–264 Mulberry St. (between Prince and Houston Sts.), SoHo. Subway: Broadway–Lafayette St.; Prince St.*

12 *b-3*

OUR LADY OF LEBANON ROMAN CATHOLIC CHURCH

(Richard Upjohn, 1846) A Romanesque Revival by the architect of Manhattan's famous Trinity Church, this was the Congregational Church of the Pilgrims until 1934; it is said that a fragment of Plymouth Rock projects from one of its walls. Sadly, the church's original steeple has been removed, but two interesting post-Upjohn touches are the west and south doors, which were salvaged from the ocean liner *Normandie* after it was scuttled in the Hudson River in 1942. Look for the panel picturing an ocean liner. *113 Remsen St. (at Henry St.), Brooklyn Heights. Subway: Borough Hall; Court St.*

12 *b-2*

PLYMOUTH CHURCH OF THE PILGRIMS

(Joseph C. Wells, 1849) The abolitionist minister Henry Ward Beecher delivered fiery sermons in this simple church from 1847 to 1887, preaching against slavery and for women's rights. Along with a fine statue of Beecher in the garden, the church's hall has stained-glass windows by Louis Comfort Tiffany. Inside, a plaque on Pew 89 points out that Abraham Lincoln once worshipped here. *75 Hicks St. (at Orange St.), Brooklyn Heights, 718/624–4743. Tours Sun. 12:15 or by appointment. Subway: Clark St.*

3 *g-3*

REFORMED DUTCH CHURCH OF NEWTOWN

Topped with an elegant cupola, this white-clapboard church from 1831 is one of the oldest wooden churches in the city. *85–15 Broadway (at Corona Ave.), Elmhurst, Queens. Subway: R to Grand Ave.*

2 *a-3*

RIVERDALE PRESBYTERIAN CHURCH AND MANSE

(James Renwick, Jr., 1863) A Gothic Revival by master church-builder James Renwick, this charming stone church in Riverdale is very much in the style of the English parish church, surrounded by trees. *4765 Henry Hudson Pkwy. W (at 249th St.), Bronx. Subway: 242nd St./Van Cortlandt Park.*

7 *a-2*

RIVERSIDE CHURCH (INTERDENOMINATIONAL)

(Allen & Collens and Henry C. Pelton, 1930) Modeled after Chartres Cathedral, this impressive Gothic-style church is prominently sited above the Hudson River, right next to Riverside Park. Rising 21 stories (392 ft), the tower offers an astonishing view of the river (*see Viewpoints, below*) and houses a 74-bell carillon, the largest in the world. The church's interracial, interdenominational congregation sponsors numerous community, cultural, and political programs. *Riverside Dr. and 120th St., Morningside Heights, 212/870–6700. Open Mon.–Sat. 9–5, Sun. noon–4. Live carillon concerts can be heard throughout the immediate neighborhood on Sun. at 12:30 and 3. Subway: 116 St./Columbia University; 1, 9 to 125th St.*

11 *g-8*

ROMAN CATHOLIC CHURCH OF THE TRANSFIGURATION

This unpretentious Gothic-Georgian blend, built from locally quarried Manhattan schist, was built in 1801 by English Lutherans. Sold to an Irish-Catholic congregation in the 1850s, it has served a succession of immigrants, first predominantly Irish, then Italian, and now Chinese. These days the church is distinguished by its trilingualism: Each Sunday mass is said in Cantonese, Mandarin, and English. *29 Mott St. (at Pell St.), Chinatown. Subway: J, M, Z to Canal St.*

12 *b-3*

ST. ANN & THE HOLY TRINITY

(Minard Lafever, 1847) The 60 stained-glass windows at this neo-Gothic brownstone church are the first ever made in the United States, and they are undergoing care at the St. Ann's Center for Restoration and the Arts. The church also has its own performing arts center, "Arts at St. Ann's," which stages musical performances and occasionally films. *157 Montague St. (at Clinton St.), Brooklyn Heights, 718/858–2424. Open weekdays 10–1. Subway: Borough Hall; Court St.*

12 *c-4*

ST. ANN'S CHURCH (EPISCOPAL)

(James Renwick, Jr., 1869) Here, Renwick—of St. Patrick's Cathedral and Manhattan's Grace Church—gave Brooklyn its only example of the Venetian Gothic, characterized primarily by a facade of varying colors and textures of stone. *Clinton St. (at Livingston St.), Brooklyn Heights. Subway: Borough Hall; Court St.*

2 *c-8*

ST. ANN'S CHURCH (EPISCOPAL)

Gouverneur Morris, Jr., built this fieldstone church on his estate for family worship. Consecrated in 1841, it's the earliest surviving church in the Bronx. The cemetery and crypts contain many members of the Morris family—after which the Bronx neighborhood Morrisania was named. Among the family's most prominent members was Gouverneur Morris, Sr., who helped draft the U.S. Constitution. *295 St. Ann's Ave. (between 139th and 141st Sts.), Bronx. Subway: 6 to Brook Ave.*

10 h-4
ST. AUGUSTINE'S CHAPEL (EPISCOPAL)

A landmark Georgian-Gothic building dating from 1828, this Lower East Side fieldstone church was originally All Saints' Free Church—"free" meaning that you didn't have to pay to worship. *290 Henry St. (between Montgomery and Jackson Sts.), Lower East Side. Subway: E. Broadway.*

12 f-5
ST. AUGUSTINE'S ROMAN CATHOLIC CHURCH

(Parfitt Brothers, 1897) Among the elegantly preserved brownstones on Park Slope's 6th Avenue is this monumental church, with its tall bell-tower, intricate sculptural detail (including carved owls on the exterior), and splendid stained-glass windows. Architects consider it one of Brooklyn's finest churches. *116 6th Ave. (between Park and Sterling Pls.), Park Slope, Brooklyn. Subway: Bergen St.; 7th Ave.*

9 e-4
ST. BARTHOLOMEW'S CHURCH (EPISCOPAL)

(Bertram Grosvenor Goodhue, 1919) Time and again, historic preservationists have saved this Byzantine-domed Park Avenue landmark from becoming one of the skyscrapers that surround it. The church's impressive triple-arch entry (McKim, Mead & White, 1902) was actually moved here from the congregation's former building on Madison Avenue. Classical concerts—choral music, early music, and organ recitals on the church's 12,422-pipe organ—are given throughout the year. *Park Ave. at 50th St., Midtown. 212/378-0200. Open daily 8–6. Subway: 51st St./Lexington–3rd Aves.*

9 b-4
ST. CLEMENT'S CHURCH (EPISCOPAL)

(Edward D. Lindsey, 1870) This picturesque parish church was originally known as Faith Chapel West Presbyterian. Perhaps reflecting its proximity to the theater district, the church regularly hosts performances in its sanctuary and parish house. *423 W. 46th St. (between 9th and 10th Aves.), Hell's Kitchen, 212/246–7277 (ext. 32 for information on upcoming performances.). Subway: A, C, E to 42nd St.*

9 f-8
ST. GEORGE'S EPISCOPAL CHURCH

(Blesch & Eidlitz, 1856) A Romanesque brownstone known as "Morgan's church" after one of its most famous parishioners, financier J. P. Morgan, this beautiful complex features rounded exterior arches and, inside, lovely stained-glass windows. *Rutherford Pl. and 16th St. (off Stuyvesant Sq.), Gramercy. Subway: 14th St./Union Sq.*

11 g-2
ST. GEORGE'S UKRAINIAN CATHOLIC CHURCH

(Apollinaire Osadca, 1977) Topped by an impressive dome and graced with three brightly colored religious murals on its facade, this is the new religious centerpiece of an old Ukrainian neighborhood. It's also the focal point of the annual Ukrainian Festival (see Events, below). *30 E. 7th St. (between 2nd and 3rd Aves.), East Village. Subway: Astor Pl.; 2nd Ave.*

10 f-5
ST. JAMES CHURCH (ROMAN CATHOLIC)

Founded by Irish immigrants in 1837, the city's second-oldest Roman Catholic Church is a stately building with a brownstone facade and two Doric columns. Al Smith, former governor of New York and renowned political reformer, was an altar boy here when this was still a predominantly Irish neighborhood. *32 James St. (between St. James Pl. and Madison St.), Chinatown. Subway: Brooklyn Bridge/City Hall.*

7 f-8
ST. JEAN BAPTISTE CHURCH (ROMAN CATHOLIC)

(Nicholas Serracino, 1913) A single patron, Thomas Fortune Ryan, paid for the construction of this two-tower, domed building after he could not find a seat one Sunday in the crowded little church that stood here earlier. The original congregation was French-Canadian. *184 E. 76th St. (between Lexington and 3rd Aves.), Upper East Side. Subway: 77th St.*

9 c-7
ST. JOHN THE BAPTIST ROMAN CATHOLIC CHURCH

(Napoleon Le Brun, 1872) A brownstone church with one spire, this exquisite building near Penn Station has a lovely, white-marble interior. *210 W. 30th St. (between 7th and 8th Aves.), Garment District. Subway: 1 or 9 to 28th St.*

4 c-7
ST. JOHN'S EPISCOPAL CHURCH

(Arthur D. Gilman, 1871) Ferry magnate Cornelius Vanderbilt was baptized in this high-steeple Gothic Revival church of rose-color granite. *1331 Bay St. (at New Lane), Rosebank, Staten Island, 718/447–1605.*

12 g-5
ST. JOHN'S PROTESTANT EPISCOPAL CHURCH

(Edward T. Potter, 1869) This Park Slope intersection boasts a wonderful trio of Gothic Revival churches. The oldest is St. John's, which resembles an English country church. Memorial Presbyterian (Pugin & Walter, 1883) is a brownstone church with a tall octagonal spire and stained-glass Tiffany windows. Grace United Methodist Church (Parfitt Brothers, 1882) completes the trio with variegated brownstone facade. Standing on this corner, you begin to understand why Brooklyn once was nicknamed "the city of churches." *St. John's Place and 7th Ave., Park Slope, Brooklyn. Subway: D, Q to 7th Ave.*

11 c-2
ST. JOSEPH'S ROMAN CATHOLIC CHURCH

(John Doran, 1834) Just west of Washington Square Park on bustling 6th Avenue is Manhattan's oldest surviving Roman Catholic church, the exterior of which was renovated in 1998. In keeping with its Greek Revival style it is topped with a simple triangular pediment, and its entryway is supported by two massive columns. *365 6th Ave. (at Washington Pl.), Greenwich Village. Subway: W. 4th St./Washington Sq.*

11 a-3
ST. LUKE-IN-THE-FIELDS CHURCH (EPISCOPAL)

(James N. Wells, 1822) To this church's early parishioners, today's West Village was the sticks; hence their name for what was then a charming country parish, an annex of Trinity Church, downtown. A fire devastated the building in 1981, but it was successfully restored in 1986. A peaceful little garden (open to the public) preserves some of the church's original country spirit. *487 Hudson St. (between Grove and Christopher Sts.), West Village, 212/924–0562. Grounds open weekdays 7–7, Sat. 7–6, Sun. 7–3. Subway: Christopher St./Sheridan Sq.*

10 f-1
ST. MARK'S CHURCH IN-THE-BOWERY (EPISCOPAL)

Originally a stark Georgian structure (1799), St. Mark's served as the first parish in Manhattan that was independent of Trinity Church, farther downtown. The Greek Revival steeple, an East Village landmark, was completed in 1828; the cast-iron Italianate portico was added in 1854. Beautifully restored following a devastating fire in 1978, St. Mark's stands on the site of Dutch governor Peter Stuyvesant's family chapel. Stuyvesant is buried in the churchyard (*see Haunted Places, below*).

Even in its early days, St. Mark's was considered progressive, and historically it has been a haven for the arts as well as for the spirit. Ballerina Isadora Duncan once danced here, and poets Edna St. Vincent Millay and Robert Frost read their works; today, Danspace and the Poetry Project stage performances and readings. (*See St. Mark's Historic District in* Historic Buildings & Areas, *below.*) *2nd Ave. and 10th St., East Village, 212/674–6377. Subway: Astor Pl.; 3rd Ave.*

9 e-4
ST. PATRICK'S CATHEDRAL (ROMAN CATHOLIC)

(James Renwick, Jr., 1858–79) The most famous church in New York City, St. Patrick's Cathedral is also one of the most architecturally significant churches in the nation. Designed by the famed 19th-century church architect James Renwick (and considered his masterpiece), the marble Gothic Revival edifice is based on Germany's Cologne Cathedral and took 21 years to build. The tallest structures in the area when first erected, the cathedral's two 330-ft-high towers are now dwarfed by Midtown's skyscrapers. St. Patrick's is the seat of the Archdiocese of New York. *5th Ave. and 50th St., Midtown, 212/753–2261. Open daily 7 AM–8:45 PM; free tours June–Sept., Tues. and Thurs. 1:30. Subway: E, F to 5th Ave.*

7 b-2

ST. PAUL'S CHAPEL (INTERDENOMINATIONAL)

(Howells & Stokes, 1907) Considered one of Columbia University's finest buildings, this wonderful brick, terra-cotta, and limestone chapel has 24 windows in its Byzantine-style dome, decorated with the coats-of-arms of old New York families associated with city and university history. *Columbia University, Amsterdam Ave. (between 116th and 117th Sts.), Morningside Heights, 212/854–6625. When classes are in session, the chapel is open daily from 10 AM–11PM. Otherwise, call for chapel hours. Subway: 116th St./Columbia University.*

10 e-6

ST. PAUL'S CHAPEL (EPISCOPAL)

(Archibald Thomas McBean, 1764–66; tower, steeple, porch by James CromMelin Lawrence, 1794) This Georgian-style church, with its distinctive brownstone spire, is Manhattan's oldest surviving building. Early worshippers included George Washington (his pew can be found in the north aisle); New York's first governor, George Clinton; the Marquis de Lafayette; and General Cornwallis. The oak interior was designed primarily by architect Pierre L'Enfant, who later laid out the city plan for Washington, D.C. The chapel is fronted by a peaceful 18th-century cemetery, a unique bit of open space in the pit of Manhattan's bustling financial district (*see Graveyards & Cemeteries, below*). *Broadway and Fulton St., Lower Manhattan, 212/602–0800; for information on free lunchtime concerts, call 212/602–0747. Subway: Fulton St.*

9 c-8

ST. PETER'S CHURCH (EPISCOPAL)

(James W. Smith, 1836–38) Based on designs by Clement Clarke Moore, this fieldstone church in Chelsea was one of the first of the English-style Gothic Revival churches that became so popular in New York in the years to follow. *346 W. 20th St. (between 8th and 9th Aves.), Chelsea. Subway: C, E to 23rd St.*

2 e-5

ST. PETER'S CHURCH (EPISCOPAL)

(Leopold Eidlitz, 1855) This picturesque Gothic Revival church serves the community of Westchester Square. The gravestones in the adjacent cemetery go back to the 1700s. *2500 Westchester Ave. (near St. Peter's Ave.), Bronx. Subway: 6 to Westchester Sq./E. Tremont Ave.*

9 e-3

ST. PETER'S CHURCH (LUTHERAN)

(Hugh Stubbins & Associates, 1977) When the original St. Peter's Church was torn down to make way for Citicorp Center (*see Architecture, above*), this ultramodern church—complete with a chapel by artist Louise Nevelson—went up on the same site, nesting in the skyscraper's shadow. In the modern spirit, "jazz vespers" are held at 5 every Sunday afternoon. *Lexington Ave. at 54th St., Midtown, 212/935–2200. Subway: 51st St./Lexington–3rd Aves.*

10 e-6

ST. PETER'S CHURCH (ROMAN CATHOLIC)

(John R. Haggerty and Thomas Thomas, 1838) An impressive Greek Revival building made of smooth blocks of granite, St. Peter's, like Trinity and St. Paul's, is a piece of early New York history that survives amid the glass-and-steel pillars of Wall Street. Its first incarnation, built on this site in 1786, was the city's second Catholic church. *22 Barclay St. (at Church St.), Lower Manhattan. Subway: Park Pl.*

9 e-7

ST. STEPHEN'S CHURCH (ROMAN CATHOLIC)

(James Renwick, Jr., 1854) A brownstone Romanesque Revival in Murray Hill, this church has a large cast-iron interior that features a mural by Constantino Brumidi. *149 E. 28th St. (between Lexington and 3rd Aves.), Murray Hill. Subway: 6 to 28th St.*

10 g-4

ST. TERESA'S ROMAN CATHOLIC CHURCH

Built in 1841 in the then-popular Gothic Revival style, this was originally the First Presbyterian Church of New York. Converted into a Catholic church in 1863 to serve the Lower East Side's growing Irish population, today it conducts services in English, Spanish, and Chinese, reflecting the area's current ethnic makeup. *141 Henry St. (at Rutgers St.), Lower East Side. Subway: East Broadway.*

9 *d-4*

ST. THOMAS CHURCH 5TH AVENUE (EPISCOPAL)

(Cram, Goodhue & Ferguson, 1914) Just two blocks north of St. Patrick's Cathedral, this richly detailed French Gothic church gives its more-famous 5th Avenue counterpart a run for its money in terms of aesthetics. Architects consider St. Thomas the more beautiful of the two; "St. Patrick's seems to want to be off in a tiny village somewhere," says *New York Times* architecture critic Paul Goldberger, while "St. Thomas was made to be on a Manhattan street and nowhere else." The elaborate interior is gloriously detailed, and the carvings on the "Bride's Door" include both a love knot and a dollar sign—the stonemason's comment on the institution of matrimony. St. Thomas's church music program is the best in the city, most notably because of its internationally renowned men's and boys' choir. *1 W. 53rd St., Midtown, 212/757–7013; call for tour schedule. Open 8–6:30. Subway: E, F to 5th Ave.*

10 *g-5*

SEA AND LAND CHURCH

A Georgian Federal church with Gothic windows—and one of four downtown churches of this period made from locally quarried Manhattan schist—this Lower East Side landmark was originally built in 1817 as the Northern Reformed Church. In 1865 it became the Sea and Land Church, dedicated to serving the city's seafaring population. It's now the First Chinese Presbyterian Church. *61 Henry St. (at Market St.), Lower East Side. Subway: East Broadway.*

9 *d-7*

SERBIAN ORTHODOX CATHEDRAL OF ST. SAVA

(Richard Upjohn, 1855) Originally Trinity Chapel, part of downtown's Trinity Parish, this brownstone church was transferred to the Serbian Orthodox Church in 1943. The neighboring parish house, designed by J. Wrey Mould in the Victorian Gothic style in 1860, stands in contrast to the church's Gothic heaviness. *15 W. 25th St. (at Broadway), Chelsea. Subway: F, N, or R to 23rd St.*

9 *e-2*

TEMPLE EMANUEL (REFORM)

(Robert D. Kohn, Charles Butler, and Clarence Stein, 1929) Built in the Byzantine-Romanesque style and covered with mosaics, this fashionable Upper East Side synagogue seats 2,500, making it the largest Reform temple in the nation. A free museum displays 250 artifacts from the congregation's history and Jewish life. *1 E. 65th St. (at 5th Ave.), Upper East Side, 212/744–1400. Museum open Sun.–Thurs. 10–4:30, Fri. 10–4, Sat. 1–4:30. Subway: N, R to 5th Ave.*

10 *e-7*

TRINITY CHURCH (EPISCOPAL)

(Richard Upjohn, 1846) Founded by royal charter during the reign of England's King William III in 1697, Trinity Church was the city's first Episcopal congregation. The first church built on this site was destroyed by fire during the Revolutionary War; Upjohn's Gothic Revival edifice is the third, and remains one of New York's best-known landmarks. Its 280-ft spire made it New York's tallest building for the second half of the 19th century, and it is still sometimes credited as the city's first skyscraper—author Judith Dupré calls Trinity an "ecclesiastical exclamation point in Wall Street's sea of corporate towers." The adjacent 2½-acre cemetery is also a landmark, and a quiet green oasis in summertime (*see* Graveyards & Cemeteries, *below*). The church hosts a popular lunchtime concert series. *Broadway and Wall St., Lower Manhattan, 212/602–0800. Subway: Wall St.*

graveyards & cemeteries

Of some 90 known New York burial grounds from the 18th and early 19th centuries, only a few remain. Note, too, that a serious search for graveyards should take you off Manhattan Island—after 1830 one needed a special permit for burial south of Canal Street, and after 1852, burial in Manhattan was prohibited altogether. Indeed, the city's most entrancing final resting places are Woodlawn Cemetery, in the Bronx, and Green-Wood Cemetery, in Brooklyn.

10 *e-5*

AFRICAN BURIAL GROUND

In 1991, construction workers discovered that the area they were excavating, just two blocks north of City Hall, held the unmarked graves of thousands of 17th- and 18th-century African-Americans. Now designated a National Historic Landmark, this long-forgotten burial ground honors some of the city's earliest residents and serves as a reminder that slavery was legal in New York City from 1626 to 1827. *Just off Duane St. near Federal Plaza, Lower Manhattan. Subway: Chambers St.; Brooklyn Bridge/City Hall.*

10 *f-5*

FIRST SHEARITH ISRAEL GRAVEYARD

Dating from its members' arrival from Brazil in 1654, the Congregation Beth Shearith is the oldest Jewish congregation in America. Tucked into present-day Chinatown, this small graveyard is the earliest surviving burial ground of these Sephardic Jews. The graveyard was consecrated in 1656, and the oldest remaining gravestone is dated 1683; the newest dates from 1828. An English translation on one of the tombstones reads:

Here lies buried
The unmarried man Walter J. Judah
Old in wisdom, tender in years

St. James Pl. (between Oliver and James Sts.) Lower Manhattan. Subway: E. Broadway; Brooklyn Bridge/City Hall.

4 *d-2*

GREEN-WOOD CEMETERY

(Grounds: Henry Pierrepont, 1840; Gates: Richard Upjohn, 1861–75) Breaking with the traditional forms of interment—churchyards, family plots, and compact enclosures—ingenious Brooklyn planner Henry Pierrepont laid out Green-Wood's 478 rolling acres to create a cemetery full of hills, ponds, lakes, and meandering drives. Encompassing Brooklyn's highest point, 216 ft above sea level, the cemetery's natural setting is unsurpassed, and when it first opened in 1840 it was as much a public park as a burial ground. Magnificent Gothic Revival mausoleums and monuments decorate many of the 500,000 graves, and the list of those interred reads like a Who's Who of the 19th century, including artists Nathaniel Currier,

James Merrit Ives, and Louis Comfort Tiffany; Governor De Witt Clinton; William Marcy "Boss" Tweed; piano manufacturer Henry Engelhard Steinway; newspaper king Horace Greeley; abolitionist minister Henry Ward Beecher; and inventors Samuel F. B. Morse (telegraph), Peter Cooper (steam locomotive), and Elias Howe (sewing machine). Green-Wood still operates as a full-service, nonsectarian, nonprofit cemetery; composer/conductor Leonard Bernstein was laid to rest here in 1990. For information on two-hour walking tours on Sunday in spring and fall, call 718/469–5277. *Main Gate: 5th Ave. and 25th St., Sunset Park, Brooklyn, 718/768–7300. Open daily 8–4. Subway: 25th St.*

8 *d-2*

LAWRENCE FAMILY GRAVEYARD

The distinguished Lawrence family, relatives of George Washington, first settled in Queens in 1664. Their private burial ground spans an incredible 272 years of family history, with the earliest of 89 graves dated 1703 and the last dated 1975. *20th Rd. and 35th St., Steinway, Queens. Subway: N to Ditmars Blvd.*

1 *g-3*

LAWRENCE MEMORIAL PARK

A second Lawrence-family graveyard, first used in 1832, contains the remains of a New York City mayor, Cornelius W. Lawrence, and a Native American named Moccasin, who was given the first name Lawrence and buried with the family. *216th St. and 42nd Ave., Bayside, Queens.*

1 *b-2*

MORAVIAN CEMETERY

Best known as the site of a million-dollar mausoleum (1866) designed by Richard Morris Hunt and landscaped by Frederick Law Olmsted for railroad tycoon Cornelius Vanderbilt and his family, the Moravian Cemetery covers 80 green, terraced acres, with the earliest grave dating back to 1740. *Richmond Rd. at Otis Ave. (between Todt Hill Rd. and Altamont), New Dorp, Staten Island, 718/351–0136. Open daily 8–4. From Staten Island Ferry terminal, take the train to the Grant City stop and walk north on Lincoln Ave.*

11 *g-3*

NEW YORK CITY MARBLE CEMETERY

The markers and headstones in this private East Village cemetery (opened in 1832) can be viewed from the sidewalk through a handsome iron fence. Shipping merchant Preserved Fish (his real name) and James Henry Roosevelt (the founder of Roosevelt Hospital) are among those buried here. *52–74 E. 2nd St., East Village. Subway: 2nd Ave.*

11 *g-3*

NEW YORK MARBLE CEMETERY

Opened in the East Village in 1830, this was Manhattan's first nonsecterian graveyard and offered prominent New Yorkers an opportunity for burial in what was then a fashionable area. Among the 156 New Yorkers buried below ground in Tuckahoe marble vaults are members of the Scribner, Hoyt, Varick, and Beekman families. Instead of headstones, tablets on the brick wall serve as the only markers. The cemetery is closed to the public, but is visible from its gates. *Entrance on 2nd Ave. between 2nd and 3rd Sts., East Village. Subway: 2nd Ave.*

4 *g-5*

OLD GRAVESEND CEMETERY

Founded in 1643, this burial ground served the people of Gravesend, one of six original 17th-century towns in Brooklyn. While the other towns were Dutch, Gravesend was founded by English anabaptists fleeing religious persecution in New England. Their leader was a woman, Lady Deborah Moody, and though her grave is no longer marked, it lies here somewhere among the aging gravestones. *Gravesend Neck Rd. between McDonald Ave. and Van Sicklen St., Gravesend, Brooklyn. Subway: F or N to Avenue U.*

11 *f-4*

OLD ST. PATRICK'S CEMETERY

On a quiet street in Little Italy next to Old St. Patrick's Cathedral, a 9-ft brick wall hides most of this churchyard from view. The crypt beneath the church holds the remains of two of New York's early bishops, as well as some of the country's first Irish-Catholic settlers. (The high wall and underground burials were a prudent response to anti-Catholic vandalism and,

occasionally, violence.) The earliest graves date from 1804. The remains of Pierre Toussaint (1766–1863) were exhumed in the early 1990s and sent to the Vatican, a step toward possible canonization of the former slave famous for his acts of charity. (*See* Old St. Patrick's Cathedral *in* Churches & Synagogues, *above.*) *Mulberry St. (between Prince and Houston Sts.), SoHo. Subway: Broadway–Lafayette St.; Prince St.*

2 *d-5*

OLD WEST FARMS SOLDIER CEMETERY

Forty veterans of the War of 1812, the Civil War, the Spanish-American War, and World War I are buried in this small landmarked cemetery built in 1815. *Bryant Ave. and 180th St., Bronx. Subway: 2, 5 to East 180th St.*

10 *f-1*

ST. MARK'S IN-THE-BOWERY EAST & WEST YARDS

The former site of Peter Stuyvesant's country chapel, this peaceful graveyard has been covered over by cobblestones, but some memorial tablets and markers are still visible. Stuyvesant himself is buried in a crypt beneath the church. The East Yard is now a children's play area. (*See* St. Mark's Church in-the-Bowery *in* Churches & Synagogues, *above.*) *2nd Ave. and 10th St., East Village. Subway: Astor Pl.; 3rd Ave.*

10 *e-6*

ST. PAUL'S CHURCHYARD

Dating from the mid- to late-18th century, St. Paul's churchyard, with its tumble of blackened headstones, offers a pleasant, albeit somber, spot to reflect upon the city's past in the shadow of modern life: the World Trade Center towers above—and the contrast is powerful. (*See* St. Paul's Chapel *in* Churches & Synagogues, *above.*) *Broadway and Fulton St., Lower Manhattan. Subway: Fulton St.*

10 *d-1*

SECOND SHEARITH ISRAEL GRAVEYARD

Active from 1805 until 1829, the original burial ground was reduced and made triangular by the laying out of West 11th Street, making this the smallest surviving graveyard in Manhattan. The displaced graves were moved to the congregation's third cemetery, on West 21st Street. *72–76 W. 11th St., Greenwich Village. Subway: 8th St.; F to 14th St.*

1 *a-3*

SLEIGHT FAMILY GRAVEYARD

Also known as the Rossville or Blazing Star Burial Ground, this was originally a family plot and later served the entire village of Rossville. The graveyard was in use from 1750 to 1850; many of Staten Island's early settlers are buried here. *Arthur Kill Rd. at Rossville Ave., Rossville, Staten Island.*

9 *d-8*

THIRD SHEARITH ISRAEL GRAVEYARD

The northernmost burial ground of the Congregation Shearith Israel, this picturesque little graveyard, used 1829–51, is now surrounded by buildings. *W. 21st St. between 6th and 7th Aves., Chelsea. Subway: F, 1, 9 to 23rd St.*

6 *c-5*

TRINITY CEMETERY

Once part of the farm belonging to artist and naturalist John James Audubon, who is buried here, Trinity Cemetery became the rural burial place for Wall Street's Trinity Church in 1842. In an uncrowded area of Upper Manhattan next to the Church of the Intercession, rural peace still prevails on these grounds, which climb from the Hudson River up to Amsterdam Avenue. Among those buried here are John Jacob Astor; Eliza Brown Jumel, once owner of the Morris Jumel Mansion; and Clement Clarke Moore, author of "A Visit from St. Nicholas." (*See* Church of the Intercession *in* Churches & Synagogues, *above.*) *153rd–155th Sts. (between Riverside Dr. and Amsterdam Ave.), Washington Heights., 212/368–1600. Open daily 9–4:30. Subway: 157th St.; 155th St.*

10 *e-7*

TRINITY CHURCH GRAVEYARD

The oldest stone in this 2½-acre graveyard is dated 1681, predating the church and making it Manhattan's earliest burial ground. Here beneath the trees are Alexander Hamilton; Robert Fulton, the inventor of the steamboat; William Bradford, the editor of New York City's first newspaper; and Captain James Lawrence, the War of 1812 hero who

exhorted, "Don't give up the ship!" Also of note is the Martyr's Monument, honoring the rebel soldiers who died imprisoned at the old sugar house on nearby Liberty Street during the American Revolution. At the north end of the cemetery, a faded stone reads "Hark from tombs a doleful sound / Mine ears attend the cry / Ye living men come view the ground / Where you must shortly lie." (*See* Trinity Church *in* Churches & Synagogues, *above.*) *Broadway and Wall St., Lower Manhattan, 212/602–0872. Open weekdays 7–3:45, Sat. 8–4, Sun. 7–4. Subway: Wall St.*

1 *b-2*

VAN PELT–REZEAU CEMETERY

A homestead burial plot containing five generations of the Van Pelt–Rezeau families, this private cemetery (begun circa 1780) is on the grounds of Historic Richmondtown. (*See* Historic Richmondtown *in* Historic Buildings & Areas, *below.*) *Tysen Court, Historic Richmondtown, Staten Island. From Staten Island Ferry, take Bus S74.*

2 *c-2*

WOODLAWN CEMETERY

Along with Green-Wood Cemetery in Brooklyn, Woodlawn Cemetery is one of the most ornate and star-studded burial grounds in the world. First opened in 1863, it is filled with elaborate tombs, some of them replicas of European chapels and Egyptian burial sites. Among the resting luminaries are Mayor Fiorello LaGuardia, F. W. Woolworth, R. H. Macy, J. C. Penney, Jay Gould, Henry H. Westinghouse, Joseph Pulitzer, Elizabeth Cady Stanton, Herman Melville, Damon Runyon, Duke Ellington, and Miles Davis. Maps are available at the cemetery office, and guided tours are offered in spring and fall. *Entrances on Jerome Ave. north of Bainbridge Ave., 233rd St., and Webster Ave., Woodlawn, Bronx, 718/920–0500. Open daily 9–4:30. Subway: 4 to Woodlawn; 2 to 233rd St.*

HISTORIC BUILDINGS & AREAS

New York City's architecture and layout are deeply layered in history, ranging from the days of Dutch rule over Nieuw Amsterdam and the American Revolution to horse-drawn carriages of the gaslit era and the waves of European immigrants who transformed the city's neighborhoods.

The Metropolitan Historic Structures Association is a coalition of 70 small history museums, including historic houses, religious sites, military sites, and historical societies. Call the association for information on historic sites throughout the five boroughs or for workshops on preserving historic buildings and their interiors. 212/473–6045.

bronx

1 e-1

BARTOW-PELL MANSION

A Greek Revival country house built circa 1836, this old mansion is filled with period furnishings and surrounded by sunken gardens. 895 Shore Rd., Pelham Bay Park, 718/885–1461. Admission: $2.50 adults, $1.25 students and seniors. Open Sept.–July, Wed. and weekends noon–4. Call for directions.

1 f-1

CITY ISLAND

A narrow, 230-acre island with a salty, New England flavor, City Island is just off the Bronx shore, attached to the mainland by a single narrow bridge. You'll find weathered bungalows, Victorian houses, boatyards, seafood restaurants, and sea breezes. 6 to Pelham Bay Park, then BX29 bus to City Island Ave.

1 d-2

LORILLARD SNUFF MILL

Built on the Bronx River in 1840 by the Lorillard tobacco family, this fieldstone building was orginally a mill used to grind snuff. It's currently found on the edge of a shady, green woodland at the New York Botanical Garden. New York Botanical Garden (see Botanical Gardens in Chapter 3), Bronx Park. Subway: Bedford Park Blvd.

5 f-4

POE COTTAGE

Built in 1812, this little cottage was the home of Edgar Allan Poe and his consumptive young wife, Virginia, from 1846 to 1849. Here, Poe wrote such haunting works as "Annabelle Lee" and "The Bells." Administered by the Bronx Historical Society. 2640 Grand Concourse (at E. Kingsbridge Rd.), Fordham, 718/881–8900. Admission: $2. Open mid.-Jan.–mid.-Dec. Sat. 10–4, Sun. 1–5. Subway: C, D to Kingsbridge Rd.

5 g-1

VALENTINE-VARIAN HOUSE (BRONX COUNTY HISTORICAL SOCIETY MUSEUM)

Dating from 1758, this pre-Revolution fieldstone farmhouse now serves as a museum of local history. 3266 Bainbridge Ave. (between Van Cortlandt Ave. and 208th St.), Norwood, 718/881–8900. Admission: $2, free children under 12. Open Sat. 10–4, Sun. 1–5. Subway: D to 205th St.

1 d-1

VAN CORTLANDT MANSION

Built in 1748, this Georgian-style, fieldstone manor house was Washington's headquarters at various times during the American Revolution. The interior houses a wealth of Colonial artifacts and furnishings. Van Cortlandt Park (Broadway north of 242nd St.), Riverdale, 718/543–3344. Admission: $2, $1.50 seniors and students, free children under 12. Open Tues.–Fri. 10–3, weekends 11–4. Subway: 242nd St./Van Cortlandt Park.

brooklyn

4 f-2

ALBEMARLE-KENMORE TERRACES HISTORIC DISTRICT

In the heart of Flatbush, behind the Flatbush Dutch Reformed Church (see Churches & Synagogues, above), these two attractive dead-end streets are lined with landmark Georgian Revival row houses and Arts and Crafts Revival cottages built 1916–20. South of Church Ave. and east of 21st St. between Flatbush and Ocean Aves. Subway: Church Ave.

1 d-6

BROOKLYN HEIGHTS

Called Ihpetonga (high, sandy bank) by the Canarsie Indians, Brooklyn Heights sits high on a bluff above the East River. Its airy location attracted 19th-century financiers to build their mansions here—they could take the Fulton Ferry to their jobs on Wall Street—and today, its 50 blocks of incredibly rich 19th-century architecture are among the best-preserved in the city. Almost every block has some kind of architectural gem; try wandering down Columbia Heights,

Pierrepont Street, Joralemon Street, and Willow Place in particular. Save time at the end of your stroll for the Brooklyn Heights Promenade, with its breathtaking vista of the downtown-Manhattan skyline (*see* Viewpoints, *below*). *Bordered roughly by the East River (the Promenade), Atlantic Ave., Cadman Plaza W, and the Brooklyn Bridge. Subway: Borough Hall; Court St.; Clark St.; High St./Brooklyn Bridge.*

12 *b-4*

GRACE COURT ALLEY

A charming mews, this was once the stable alley for mansions on neighboring Remsen and Joralemon streets. Today, those stables and brownstone carriage houses are luxury homes. *East of Hicks St. (between Joralemon and Remsen Sts.), Brooklyn Heights. Subway: Borough Hall; Court St.*

12 *h-5*

GRAND ARMY PLAZA

(Frederick Law Olmsted and Calvert Vaux, 1870) Grand is indeed the word for this Park Slope plaza, designed in the spirit of L'Etoile (a.k.a. Place Charles-de-Gaulle) in Paris. At its center is the 80-ft-tall Soldiers and Sailors Memorial Arch (1892), reminiscent of the Arc de Triomphe, with enormous bronze sculptures honoring the Union Army's efforts in the Civil War. The Plaza is a fitting entry to Brooklyn's beloved Prospect Park (*see* Parks *in* Chapter 3). *Intersection of Flatbush Ave., Prospect Park W, Eastern Pkwy., and Vanderbilt Ave. Subway: Grand Army Plaza; D, Q to 7th Ave.*

12 *c-4*

JENNIE JEROME HOUSE

Tucked away in Cobble Hill, this old Greek Revival was the birthplace of Jennie Jerome on January 9, 1854. While Jerome Avenue in the Bronx is named after her father, financier Leonard Jerome, Jennie herself became better known for marrying a British lord and becoming the mother of Winston Churchill. *197 Amity St. (between Clinton and Court Sts.). Subway: F to Bergen St.*

4 *f-1*

LEFFERTS HOMESTEAD

A Dutch Colonial farmhouse built in 1783 on Flatbush Avenue, the Lefferts

Homestead was moved to its current Prospect Park location in 1918. Today it's a historic museum geared toward children, with reproductions of period furnishings. Next door is a painstakingly restored 1912 carousel that operates on weekends. *Prospect Park, Flatbush Ave. at Empire Blvd., 718/965–6505. Open Thur.–Fri. 1–4, weekends 1–5. Subway: Prospect Park.*

12 *h-7*

LITCHFIELD VILLA

(Alexander Jackson Davis, 1857) A romantic Italianate pile built for railroad baron Edwin C. Litchfield, the villa was once the heart of a vast estate that took in virtually all of present-day Park Slope. It now serves as the Department of Parks and Recreation's Brooklyn headquarters. *Prospect Park, Prospect Park W between 4th and 5th Sts., Park Slope. Subway: Grand Army Plaza; F to 7th Ave.*

12 *b-2*

MIDDAGH STREET

One of the first streets laid out in Brooklyn Heights (circa 1817), Middagh Street retains some of its oldest houses, many made from wood. Take particular note of No. 24 (1824), a gambrel-roof Federal house—one of the finest in the city. *Between northern ends of Willow and Hicks Sts., Brooklyn Heights. Subway: Clark St.; High St./Brooklyn Bridge.*

12 *b-3*

MONTAGUE TERRACE

This delightful stretch of English-style row houses was built in 1886 and has been wonderfully preserved. In the 1930s, novelist Thomas Wolfe lived at No. 5, where he wrote *You Can't Go Home Again*. *Montague Terr. (between Remsen and Montague Sts.), Brooklyn Heights. Subway: Borough Hall; Court St.*

12 *f-6*

OLD STONE HOUSE (VECHTE-CORTELYOU HOUSE)

A 1935 reproduction of a house built in 1699 at this site, the Old Stone House is a center for historic walks and activities focusing on Brooklyn's role in the Revolutionary War. Some of the most heated fighting of the Battle of Long Island in 1776 took place nearby. *3rd St. and 5th Ave., Park Slope. Subway: F to 4th Ave.*

4 *e-1*

PARK SLOPE HISTORIC DISTRICT

Covering more than 30 blocks, this beautiful, tree-lined residential area contains 1,900 structures of architectural interest, including some of the finest Queen Anne and Romanesque Revival homes in the nation. Don't miss the dazzling 1880s and '90s gems on Montgomery Place and Carroll Street just below Prospect Park, or the palazzolike Montauk Club, at Lincoln Place and 8th Avenue, with its friezes depicting the history of the Montauk Indians. Prospect Park itself, designed by Frederick Law Olmsted and Calvert Vaux (the same pair who designed Central Park) is a triumph of landscape design; Olmsted and Vaux openly preferred it to Central Park. (*See* Parks *in* Chapter 3.) *Prospect Park W to as far as 6th Ave. from Grand Army Plaza to Bartel Pritchard Sq. (15th St.). Subway: Grand Army Plaza; D, Q to 7th Ave.; F to 7th Ave.*

1 *f-7*

SHEEPSHEAD BAY

A small but active fishing port, Sheepshead Bay is best known for its fleet of "party boats," which whisk anglers to secret fishing holes out in the ocean. This salty old neighborhood is also known for its seafood restaurants, the preeminent of which— Lundy's—reopened a few years ago with much fanfare. *Emmons Ave. from Knapp St. to Shore Ave. Subway: Sheepshead Bay.*

4 *h-3*

VAN NUYSE HOUSE (COE HOUSE)

When the Dutch first settled New York, the southern part of Brooklyn was prime farmland. Parts of this landmark Dutch house date back to 1744, when it was part of Joost and Elizabeth Van Nuyse's 85-acre farm. *1128 E. 34th St. (between Flatbush Ave. and Ave. J). Subway: 2, 5 to Flatbush Ave.*

4 *g-3*

VAN NUYSE–MAGAW HOUSE

A Dutch Colonial house from around 1800, this gambrel-roof structure was transported to its present site in 1916 to ensure permanent preservation. *1041 E. 22nd St. (between Aves. I and J), Midwood. Subway: D to Ave. J.*

4 *h-4*

WYCKOFF-BENNETT HOUSE

Built around 1766, complete with little dormers and a six-column porch, this house is considered Brooklyn's finest example of Dutch Colonial architecture. Two glass windowpanes are etched with the name and rank of two Hessian soldiers quartered here during the Revolution. *1669 E. 22nd St. (at Kings Hwy.). Subway: D to Kings Highway.*

manhattan

9 *f-2*

ABIGAIL ADAMS SMITH MUSEUM

Built in 1799, this elegant, Federal-style stone carriage house was converted into a country resort (the Mt. Vernon Hotel) in 1826 and a residence in 1833. Restored by the Colonial Dames of America, it is one of the few 18th-century historic structures left on Manhattan. Open to the public, its nine period rooms are decorated in the style of the old hotel, with Federal and Empire-style furniture. In summer, period music is performed in a charming Colonial-style garden adjoining the house. *421 E. 61st St. between 1st Ave. and York Ave., Upper East Side, 212/838–6878. Open Sept.–May, Tues.–Sun. 11–4; June and July, Tues. 11–9, Wed.–Sun. 11–4. Admission: $3 adults, $2 students and seniors, free children under 12. Subway: 4, 5, 6 to 59th St.*

9 *d-2*

THE ARSENAL

(Martin E. Thompson, 1848) Predating the completion of Central Park itself by 10 years, this brick fortress was originally built to house the state's cache of artillery and ammunition. Troops were then quartered here during the Civil War. Over the years, the Arsenal has served variously as a police station and the original home of the American Museum of Natural History; today it houses the main offices of the city's Department of Parks and Recreation. *Central Park, 5th Ave. and 64th St., Upper East Side. Subway: 68th St./Hunter College.*

6 *b-5*

AUDUBON TERRACE HISTORIC DISTRICT

Originally part of the estate belonging to artist and naturalist John James Audubon, Audubon Terrace was turned into a cultural center in 1908 by philanthropist Archer M. Huntington and his cousin, architect Charles Pratt Huntington. Several cultural institutions, all designed in the Italian Renaissance style, surround a small plaza; they include the American Numismatic Society, with a collection of coins dating from ancient times to the present; the Hispanic Society of America; and the American Academy of Arts & Letters. (*See Art Museums, above.*) *Broadway between 155th and 156th Sts., Washington Heights. Subway: 157th St.; 155th St.*

9 *g-4*

BEEKMAN PLACE

A retreat from Manhattan's chaos, this charming and exclusive two-block street on a bluff overlooking the East River is one of New York's almost-hidden treasures. Town-house residents have included Irving Berlin, Ethel Barrymore, and the Rockefellers. *East of (and parallel*

to) 1st Ave., from 49th to 51st Sts. Subway: 51st St./Lexington–3rd Aves.

11 *f-3*

BOUWERIE LANE THEATRE

(Henry Englebert, 1874) Originally the Bond Street Savings Bank, and later the German Exchange Bank (catering to the neighborhood's many German immigrants), this unusual cast-iron building is in the French Second Empire style, with paired Corinthian and Ionic columns running up the facade. It's currently an off-off-Broadway playhouse and the home of the well-respected Jean Cocteau Repertory Company. *330 Bowery (at 2nd St.), East Village, 212/677–0060. Subway: Astor Pl.; 2nd Ave.*

9 *d-3*

CARNEGIE HALL

(William B. Tuthill, 1891) Built by steel magnate–cum–philanthropist Andrew

---

HAUNTED PLACES

The spirits of disgruntled (and dead) New Yorkers are believed to hang out in several locales around the city.

The Dakota (upper west side)
The Dakota, with the severe miasma of a mad French marquis's torture castle, was the setting for Roman Polanski's Rosemary's Baby, and John Lennon was murdered just outside in 1980. (See Historic Buildings & Areas.)

Jane Street, between Washington and Hudson Streets (West Village)
Here wanders the ghost of founding father Alexander Hamilton, no doubt restless after his death in a duel with Vice President Aaron Burr. Hamilton most commonly makes his presence known by flicking lights and flushing toilets; according to Jane Street residents, he's fascinated by modern technology.

Old Merchant's House (East Village)
Once owned by the wealthy merchant Seabury Tredwell, this house is said to be haunted by a lovely young woman in 19th-century dress. She is assumed to be Tredwell's daughter, Gertrude, who became a solitary recluse following a romance thwarted by her father.

St. Mark's Church In-the-Bowery (East Village)
Seventeenth-century Dutch governor Peter Stuyvesant once owned this land, and he's buried under the church's garden. Worshippers have occasionally been disturbed by a strange tapping, which the psychically attuned have identified as the sound of the old governor angrily approaching on his peg leg. (See Churches & Synagogues.)

Washington Square (Greenwich Village)
This former potter's field is estimated to have housed the graves of some 20,000 impoverished souls and executed convicts. An old elm tree that still stands in the park's northwest corner was once known as the "Hanging Elm"; public hangings took place here until 1819.

The White Horse Tavern (West Village)
"Do not go gentle into that good night," wrote the poet Dylan Thomas—and he didn't. Thomas died at this Greenwich Village hangout in 1953 after downing close to 20 shots of scotch. Regulars say that his ghost still drops in late at night, sitting at an unobtrusive corner table and scribbling.

Carnegie, this world-famous music hall opened in 1891 with a concert conducted by Tchaikovsky. Since then it has seen the likes of Leonard Bernstein, Isaac Stern, Yo-Yo Ma, the Beatles, and countless other stars. Hour-long tours are full of history and backstage anecdotes. And the free Rose Museum just around the corner (881 7th Avenue) holds memorabilia from Carnegie Hall's illustrious past, including photos of Maria Callas, Benny Goodman's clarinet, and a baton used by Arturo Toscanini. (*See* Concert Halls *in* Chapter 5.) *154 W. 57th St. (at 7th Ave.), Midtown. 212/247-7800. Tours mid-Sept.–June, Mon., Tues., Thurs., Fri. at 11:30, 2, and 3. Museum open mid-Sept.–mid-July daily except Wed. 11–4:30. Tours, $6. Subway: 57th St.; 7th Ave.*

10 *e-8*

CASTLE CLINTON NATIONAL MONUMENT

(John McComb, Jr., 1807–11) This circular brownstone fortress in Battery Park was first built as a defense for New York Harbor, in preparation for the War of 1812. Originally sited on an island 200 ft from shore, it was eventually connected to Lower Manhattan by landfill. The U.S. government gave the old fort to the city in 1823 and it successively became Castle Garden, an enormously popular concert hall where impresario P. T. Barnum presented "Swedish nightingale" Jenny Lind in 1850; the Emigrant Landing Depot, 1855–90, where 8 million of New York's immigrants were processed before the opening of Ellis Island; and then, until 1941, the city's first aquarium. Today Castle Clinton houses a small museum, as well as the ticket office for ferries to the Statue of Liberty and Ellis Island. (*See* Parks *in* Chapter 3.) *Battery Park (State St. and Battery Pl.) Lower Manhattan, 212/344-7220. Daily 8:30–5. Free. Subway: Bowling Green.*

10 *e-7*

CHAMBER OF COMMERCE OF THE STATE OF NEW YORK

(James B. Baker, 1901) An ornate Beaux-Arts landmark deep in the heart of the financial district, this homage to trade features white-marble Ionic columns and a mansard roof. *65 Liberty St. (at Liberty Pl.), Lower Manhattan. Subway: Cortlandt St./World Trade Center.*

11 *c-5*

CHARLTON-KING-VANDAM HISTORIC DISTRICT

Below Houston Street on the far west side is the city's largest concentration of Federal-style row houses (characterized by redbrick, high stoops, narrow dormers, and leaded-glass windows). Now surrounded by large commercial buildings, this area belonged originally to Aaron Burr and later to John Jacob Astor. Walking down these streets is like stumbling upon the turn of the 19th century. *9–43 and 20–42 Charlton St.; 1–49 and 16–54 King St.; 9–29 Vandam St.; 43–51 MacDougal St., West Village. Subway: Houston St.*

9 *b-8*

CHELSEA HISTORIC DISTRICT

Composed mainly of land from the estate of Clement Clark Moore, an influential 19th-century clergyman and the author of "A Visit from St. Nicholas" (better known as "T'was the Night Before Christmas"), Chelsea was developed on Moore's plan between 1825 and 1860. Among the lovely buildings here are Greek Revival row houses (the best of which are on West 20th Street's "Cushman Row," named for Moore's friend Don Alonzo Cushman, dry-goods merchant); 1890s apartment buildings; St. Peter's Episcopal Church (*see* Churches & Synagogues, *above*); and the block-long, high-fenced General Theological Seminary, which has a redbrick-and-brownstone campus accessible to the public from 175 9th Avenue. *8th–10th Aves. from 20th to 22th Sts. Subway: A, C, E to 23rd St.*

9 *c-8*

CHELSEA HOTEL

(Hubert, Pirsson & Co., 1884) Constructed of redbrick with intricate wrought-iron balconies, this 12-story literary landmark began life as a cooperative apartment house in the late 19th century. In 1905 it became a hotel catering to long-term tenants and attracted many famous authors, artists, and musicians, including Thomas Wolfe, Dylan Thomas, O. Henry, Mark Twain, Vladimir Nabokov, Tennesee Williams, Arthur Miller, and William S. Burroughs. The list even includes punk-rock star Sid Vicious, who stabbed his girlfriend Nancy Spungen to death here. (*See* Moderately Priced Lodgings *in* Chapter

6.) *222 W. 23rd St. between 7th and 8th Aves. Subway: A, C, E, 1, 9 to 23rd St.*

10 *f-4*

CHINATOWN

Traditionally contained within Canal, Worth, and Mulberry streets; the Bowery; and Chatham Square, Chinatown has recently expanded on all sides due to an influx of new immigrants and capital, primarily from Hong Kong. A feast for the senses—full of tea and rice shops, Asian vegetable stands, and Chinese apothecaries—this bustling enclave has been the heart of New York's Chinese immigrant community since the mid-1800s., Chinatown's residents originally hailed mainly from the province of Canton but today are highly diverse, a fact reflected in the multiple dialects spoken, the seven different Chinese newspapers, and cuisine ranging from Hunan and Szechuan to Mandarin, Shanghai, and Southeast Asian. For restaurant selections, *see* Chinese *in* Chapter 1. *Subway: Grand St.; N, R, 6, J, M, Z to Canal St.*

10 *e-6*

CITY HALL

(Mangin and McComb, 1802–1811) A surprisingly diminutive building, City Hall has been the seat of city government since 1811. Its architecture is Federal, enriched by French Renaissance detailing. The interior is striking: The main entrance opens into a dome rotunda with a graceful twin stairway that curves upward to second-floor rooms containing original 19th-century furnishings and portraits. Because security is tight, however, it is not always possible to get a peek inside. *City Hall Park, Broadway and Park Row. Subway: Brooklyn Bridge/City Hall.*

10 *g-5*

WILLIAM CLARK HOUSE

A superb, four-story Federal structure built in 1824, this house was built for grocer William Clark and his wife, Rosamond, and still has its original fanlit entrance and window lintels. *51 Market St. (between Monroe and Madison Sts.), Lower East Side. Subway: E. Broadway.*

11 *f-2*

COLONNADE ROW (LA GRANGE TERRACE)

(Attributed to Alexander Jackson Davis, 1833) Across from Joseph Papp's Public Theater are four survivors of nine original Greek Revival town houses that were the most coveted addresses in New York in their day. For a few years in the 1830s and '40s, these now-dilapidated marble buildings, lined by a patrician row of Corinthian columns, housed New York's elite—John Jacob Astor, Cornelius Vanderbilt, and Warren Delano (FDR's grandpa)—before the millionaires moved en masse to spanking-new 5th Avenue mansions. *428–434 Lafayette St. (between Astor Pl. and E. 4th St.), East Village. Subway: Astor Pl.*

10 *f-2*

COOPER UNION

(Frederick A. Peterson, 1859) An enormous, Italianate brownstone with high-arch windows, this is the oldest building in America framed with steel beams. The beams—actually railroad rails—were provided by the college's benefactor, the 19th-century inventor and steel magnate Peter Cooper (whose statue dominates neighboring Cooper Square), who founded the school to provide free technical education to the working class. Cooper Union remains a tuition-free private college to this day—one of the city's best for architecture, design, and engineering. In 1860, Abraham Lincoln delivered his famous "Right Makes Right" speech here, which catapulted him into the White House. *7th St. between 4th Ave. and Bowery, East Village. Subway: Astor Pl.*

9 *c-1*

THE DAKOTA

(Henry J. Hardenbergh, 1884) Built by Singer Sewing Machine heir Edward Clark amid rundown farms and shanties, New York's first luxury apartment house was initially criticized for being as remote as the "Dakotas in Indian territory." Though it's difficult to imagine now, the Dakota's severe triangular turrets loomed alone, like a provincial castle, when it first went up on the edge of Central Park. In the end, of course, the Dakota became a prestigious address and served as a sort of grand cornerstone for the Upper West Side. Lauren Bacall, Boris Karloff, Rudolf Nureyev, Leonard Bernstein, Rosemary Clooney, and Gilda Radner all called the Dakota home, as did John Lennon, who was murdered outside by a "fan" on December 8, 1980. (*See* Haunted Places, *above.*) *1 W. 72 St., Upper West Side. Subway: B, C, to 72nd St.*

9 *d-4*

DIAMOND & JEWELRY WAY

This is really the only street in America that comes close to being paved with gold. Eighty percent of all the diamonds in the country are bought and sold here, mainly by Hasidic Jews, who can sometimes be seen walking around with gem-packed briefcases handcuffed to their arms. Before World War II, the diamond district was on the Lower East Side, but, following the money, it eventually moved uptown. Lined with slightly retro jewelry stores, West 47th Street crackles with activity on weekdays. *W. 47th St. between 5th and 6th Aves., Midtown. Subway 47th–50th Sts./Rockefeller Center; E, F to 5th Ave.*

5 *b-6*

DYCKMAN FARMHOUSE MUSUEM

This gambrel-roof fieldstone building is the only 18th-century Dutch farmhouse still standing in Manhattan. Built in 1785, it was restored and furnished with Dutch and English Colonial antiques and now serves as a museum of Dutch New York. *4881 Broadway (at W. 204th St.), Inwood, 212/304–9422. Open Tues.–Sun. 11–4. Subway: 207th St./Inwood.*

3 *c-6*

EAST VILLAGE

For a short time in the 1820s and 1830s, the East Village was aristocratic; later in the century, it housed a large German community; at the turn of the century, it was an extension of the Lower East Side, packed with Eastern Europeans; and in the 1960s, hippies and flower children put the area on the wider cultural map. Architecture and business reflecting all of these eras remain in this multi-ethnic neighborhood; in fact, it's the human fauna that give the neighorhood it's greatest appeal: fresh-faced NYU students with tattoos, gay lovers, aging Hells Angels, and former Mayor Ed Koch can often be found dining harmoniously at local restaurants that serve everything from kielbasa to lamb curry. *Houston–14th Sts., from 4th Ave./Bowery to East River. Subway: Astor Pl.; Bleecker St.; 1st Ave.; 2nd Ave.; 3rd Ave.*

1 *c-6*

ELLIS ISLAND NATIONAL MONUMENT

(Boring & Tilton, 1898; restored 1990) Ellis Island was the first glimpse of America for more than 17 million European immigrants, from 1892 to 1954. Long abandoned, its buildings underwent an extraordinary restoration in the 1980s, and reopened in 1990 as the Ellis Island Immigration Museum—now one of the city's busiest tourist attractions. Through the magnificent Victorian Great Hall; the enormous Registry Hall; the Baggage Room; and the Ticket Office, visitors can retrace the steps of their immigrant forebears. The major exhibits—including historic photographs, documentary films, and audio tapes of immigrants' reminiscences—are poignant reminders of many Americans' roots. It's estimated that more than 40% of U.S. citizens have ancestors who passed through here. The island's Wall of Honor, overlooking the Statue of Liberty, is inscribed with the names of more than 400,000 immigrants. *Ferries to Ellis Island depart from Battery Park, Lower Manhattan. Ferry information: 212/269–5755. Admission: $7 adults, $6 seniors, $3 children 3–17. Departures: Daily every 20 mins 8:30–4:30. Subway: South Ferry.*

10 *d-1*

ENGLISH TERRACE ROW

(James Renwick, Jr., 1856–58) When the Dutch settled New Amsterdam, they brought their architectural styles with them, and one of the most enduring was the "stoop," a high stairway leading up to the front door. The stoop has become a fixture on New York brownstones and row houses, serving as a playground for children and a front porch for adults. These elegant homes on West 10th Street, however, were modeled on the English style—they were the first houses in the city without stoops, and their front doors are a mere two steps up from the sidewalk. *20–38 W. 10th St. (between 5th and 6th Aves.), Greenwich Village. Subway: 8th St.; West 4th St./Washington Sq.*

10 *e-7*

FEDERAL HALL NATIONAL MEMORIAL

(Town & Davis, 1842) Just up the street from the New York Stock Exchange, this imposing Greek Revival building occupies one of the most historic sites in the city. Originally the site of New York's second city hall, Federal Hall later served as the nation's capital, in which the Bill of Rights was adopted and George Washington took his presidential oath in 1789. The present building served as a customs house from 1842 to 1862, and then as the U.S. subtreasury until 1920. Now a National Historic Site, with a statue of George Washington on the very spot where he took the oath of office, Federal Hall houses artifacts from Colonial and early Federal New York, including Washington's inaugural suit. Free brochures outline self-guided walking tours through Lower Manhattan. *26 Wall St. (at Nassau St.), Lower Manhattan, 212/825–6888. Admission: Free. Open weekdays 9–5. Subway: Wall St.*

10 *e-7*

FEDERAL RESERVE BANK

A block-long, 14-story neo-Renaissance behemoth built of stone and iron in 1924, the Federal Reserve Bank in Lower Manhattan houses the largest stockpile of gold in the world—about $140 billion worth. One-hour tours of the Fed provide an overview of the bank's operations, an explanation of its role in the economy, a look at currency processing, and a visit to the gold vault, where you can salivate over bars of solid gold. Tour reservations must be made at least one week in advance. *33 Liberty St. (near William St.), Lower Manhattan, 212/720–6130. Admission: Free. Tours depart weekdays on the half hour 9:30–2:30. Subway: Fulton St.; Wall St.*

7 *e-2*

FIRE WATCHTOWER

Built in 1856 on the rocky high ground of what was once called Mt. Morris Park, this is the last remaining fire tower in the city. A landmark cast-iron structure with a spiral iron staircase and octagonal lookout, it became obsolete when fire-alarm boxes were invented in 1883. *Marcus Garvey Park, Madison Ave. and 121st St., East Harlem. Subway: 4, 5, 6 to 125th St.*

10 *f-6*

FULTON FISH MARKET

Opened in 1823, the fish originally wholesaled here along South Street were delivered by schooner. And though the market is still located on the East River, these days the fish arrive in refrigerated trucks. More than 200 species—from swordfish to sea urchin roe—are sold by hundreds of fishmongers, making this the largest fish market in the nation. Early birds who want to see the catch should get up early or stay up late; the

action starts around 3 AM and is over by 8 AM. Tours, $10, through the stalls are given by the South Street Seaport Museum (212/748–8590) from May to October, first and third Thursday of the month at 6 AM; reserve in advance. *Fulton and South Sts., Lower Manhattan. Subway: Fulton St.*

9 *c-6*

GENERAL POST OFFICE

(McKim, Mead & White, 1913) Topping off an imposing row of enormous Corinthian columns and a two-block-long staircase, the letter carrier's famous motto is carved in stone: "Neither snow, nor rain, nor heat, nor gloom of night stays these couriers from the swift completion of their appointed rounds." This monumental post office is open 24 hours, 365 days a year, making it the site of an annual midnight frenzy on April 15th. Despite the sonorous credo, the building is slated to retire as a U.S. post office and become the new home of Amtrak's passenger trains, now harbored just across 8th Avenue in Penn Station. *8th Ave. from 31st to 33rd Sts., Garment District. Subway: 34th St./Penn Station.*

1 *d-6*

GOVERNOR'S ISLAND

Sitting squarely at the mouth of the East River, this island was reputedly purchased by the Dutch governor of New Netherland from the Native Americans in 1637 for a bunch of trinkets. When the British arrived, they co-opted the island for the use of Colonial governors; their circa-1708 Governor's House is one of the city's only surviving Georgian buildings. From the 1790s on, the island was used mainly as a military fortification; the 1811 Castle William—a 40-ft-high circular fort with walls 8 ft thick—housed Rebel P.O.W.s during the Civil War. In 1966 the U.S. Coast Guard moved in, but in the late 1990s, they decided to give up the island. Now this former military base has become a political football, with community groups lobbying for it to become an offshore public park and developers hoping to turn it into a luxury housing development.

7 *g-7*

GRACIE MANSION

A Federal country villa built in 1799 by wealthy merchant Archibald Gracie, Gracie Mansion has served as the residence for New York's mayors since 1942. *East End Ave. and 88th St., Upper East Side. Tour reservations: 212/570–4751. Admission: $4. Tours of the public rooms, the garden, and the private quarters (except the mayor's bedroom) are given mid-Mar.–mid-Nov. on Wed. at 10, 11, 1, and 2 and are arranged by appointment only. Subway: 4, 5, 6 to 86th St.*

7 *a-2*

GENERAL GRANT NATIONAL MEMORIAL (GRANT'S TOMB)
(John H. Duncan, 1897) Civil War general and U.S. President Ulysses S. Grant and his wife, Julia Dent Grant, are entombed in this colossal white-granite mausoleum—made from 8,000 tons of stone. *Riverside Dr. and 122nd St., Morningside Heights, 212/666–1640. Open daily 9–5. Subway: 116th St./Columbia University; 1, 9 to 125th St.*

3 *b-6*

GREENWICH VILLAGE
The largest designated historic district in New York City, Greenwich Village was a semirural retreat for the well-to-do during the early 19th century. It has since become a haven for students, artists, immigrants, and bohemians. Its winding streets (laid out before Manhattan adopted its orderly street grid pattern) offer a wealth of architectural treasures, charming bistros, coffee houses, and trendy boutiques. The best way to experience the Village is simply to meander. *Houston–14th Sts., from roughly University Pl. to the Hudson River. Subway: West 4th St./Washington Square, Christopher St./Sheridan Square, 8th St./NYU, 14th St.*

11 *a-3*

GROVE COURT
Built in 1854 as laborers' quarters, this charming secluded mews in Greenwich Village was then known as Mixed Ale Alley for its residents' affinity for pooling beverages. The surrounding row houses on Grove Street—brick-and-clapboard Federal and Greek Revival—date from the early 1800s. *10–12 Grove St. (between Bedford and Hudson Sts.), West Village. Subway: Christopher St./Sheridan Sq.*

6 *c-7*

HAMILTON GRANGE NATIONAL MONUMENT
Just north of City College, in Hamilton Heights, is founding father Alexander

Hamilton's country retreat, designed by John McComb, Jr., and built in 1801. It's one of the few Federal frame houses still standing in Manhattan, and is now a National Historic Site administered by the National Park Service. *287 Convent Ave. (near W. 141st St.), 212/283–5154. Admission: Free. Open Fri.–Sun. 9–5. Subway: 137th St./City College.*

3 *b-1*

HARLEM
A thriving 17th- and 18th-century farming community, Harlem took off as a fashionable address in the 1880s, with brownstones, high-class apartments, and polo on horseback at the original Polo Grounds. In the decades that followed, Harlem housed succeeding waves of immigrants, first German and Irish, then Jewish and Italian; but by 1910, it was well on its way to becoming the largest black community in America. In the Roaring '20s, nightclubs and dance halls like the Cotton Club and the Savoy Ballroom showcased Duke Ellington, Louis Armstrong, and Cab Calloway, and artists and writers, such as Langston Hughes, helped round out the fabulous Harlem Renaissance. The good times ended with the Depression, however, and by the 1960s most of the neighborhood's more affluent residents had moved away, and Harlem was deeply troubled by poverty. Today, as Harlem is being revitalized by black professionals and young families who are pumping new life into the community, there are still many burned-out buildings and vacant lots. But there are also vestiges of Harlem's proud past—elegant row houses, fine commercial structures, and historic churches. Be sure to visit the landmarked Apollo Theater which has showcased such singers as Billie Holiday, Ella Fitzgerald, and Aretha Franklin (*see* Concert Halls *in* Chap. 5) and features a "Wall of Fame" in the lobby. *Broadway to the Harlem River from 125th to 155 Sts. Subway: 125th St., 135th St., 145th St., 148th St., 155th St. (The Apollo Theater is located at 253 W. 125th St. between 7th and 8th Aves. 212/531–5300. Tours are given daily; call for reservations and admission fees.)*

7 *e-2*

HARLEM COURTHOUSE
(Thom & Wilson, 1893) A richly decorated brick-and-stone courthouse with gables and a four-face clock, the Harlem

Courthouse is now a landmark. *170 E. 121st St. (at Sylvan Pl.), East Harlem. Subway: 4, 5, 6 to 125th St.*

11 b-3
ISAACS-HENDRICKS HOUSE
Built in 1799, Isaacs-Hendricks House is the oldest surviving house in Greenwich Village. Though some alterations have been made, the side and rear retain restored versions of the original Federal clapboard structure. The "Narrowest House" (*see below*) is next door. *77 Bedford St. (at Commerce St.), West Village. Subway: Christopher St./Sheridan Sq.*

10 d-1
JEFFERSON MARKET LIBRARY
(Vaux & Withers, 1877; renovated interiors: Giorgio Cavaglieri, 1967) Originally a courthouse built on the site of an old market, this extraordinary building and its fanciful clock tower are a veritable celebration of the Victorian Gothic. Threatened with destruction in the 1960s, the building was saved by a determined band of Greenwich Village residents and is now a branch of the New York Public Library. *425 6th Ave. (at 10th St.), West Village, 212/243–4334. Subway: W. 4th St./Washington Sq.*

9 d-8
LADIES' MILE HISTORIC DISTRICT
At the heart of the Gilded Age, the Ladies' Mile was the 5th Avenue of its day—a shopping district traversed by mostly female, mostly elegant, turn-of-the-20th-century shoppers. Once populated by well-known department stores, such as the original Macy's and Lord & Taylor, the Ladies' Mile was (and is) lined with imposing, block-long buildings—grandiose emporiums designed to impress shoppers both inside and out. A surprising number of these wonderful old buildings still have their original cast-iron and otherwise decorative facades; others have been restored as modern "superstores" such as Bed, Bath, & Beyond, Today's Man, Barnes & Noble, and Old Navy. The retail recolonization of the late 1990s has re-established this area as one of the city's most popular shopping districts. *6th Ave. and Broadway from 14th to 23rd Sts., Chelsea. Subway: N, R to 8th St., 14th St., 23rd St.*

11 f-5
LITTLE ITALY
First settled between 1880 and 1924, New York's old Italian community is shrinking as Chinatown expands, but visitors still clog the narrow streets in search of hearty Neapolitan fare, cappuccino, and cannoli at the area's many cafés. Mulberry Street remains the main drag, and becomes a proud, pedestrian-only fairground during the 10-day Feast of San Gennaro (*see September in Events, below*). *Canal–Houston Sts. from Lafayette St. to Bowery. Subway: 6 to Spring St.; Bowery.*

6 a-2
LITTLE RED LIGHTHOUSE (JEFFREY'S HOOK LIGHT)
Tucked under the George Washington Bridge is this 40-ft-tall namesake from the beloved children's story "The Little Red Lighthouse and the Great Gray Bridge." Originally constructed in 1880, and once a critical warning signal that kept Hudson River barges from dashing themselves against the rocky shore, the lighthouse is now a landmark, occasionally brought to life in tours given by the New York City Parks Department (800/201–7275). *Ft. Washington Park off 178th St., Washington Heights. Subway: 175th St.*

3 c-7
LOWER EAST SIDE
Historically the absorption center for New York's floods of Jewish immigrants in the 1880s and 1890s, the Lower East Side was at one time the world's largest Jewish community. Today the pushcarts are gone, and many of the synagogues stand abandoned. Lately, however, the neighborhood is being revitalized, and it's become the latest off-the-beaten-path Manhattan neighborhood to be trendified, with a slew of new low-key bars and clubs. For a closer look at the area's immigrant history, take one of the fascinating tours presented by the Lower East Side Tenement Museum (*see History Museums, below*). *Roughly Houston–Canal Sts. from Bowery to East River. Subway: Delancey St., Essex St., Grand St.*

11 d-2
MACDOUGAL ALLEY
A charming little dead-end street in Greenwich Village, McDougal Alley is lined with tiny houses, originally built as stables in the 19th century. *Off MacDou-*

gal St. between Washington Sq. N and 8th St., Greenwich Village. Subway: West 4th St./Washington Sq.; 8th St. Map note: on Map 11, Washington Square North is marked as Waverly.

10 e-7

MERCHANTS' EXCHANGE

(Isaiah Rogers, 1836–42; remodeled by McKim, Mead & White, 1907) This massive building with two colonnades (one Ionic and the other Corinthian) originally had only one floor, serving first as a merchants' exchange and later as the U.S Customs House (1863–99). The second set of columns and the second story were added in 1907, when the building was turned into a bank. 55 Wall St. (between William and Hanover Sts.), Lower Manhattan. Subway: Wall St.

10 d-1

MILLIGAN PLACE/ PATCHIN PLACE

The houses on these two secluded Greenwich Village culs-de-sac were originally built in 1848–49 as boarding-houses for the Basque employees of a nearby hotel. Later many famous writers lived on Patchin Place, including Theodore Dreiser and e. e. cummings. Off 6th Ave. (west side) between 10th and 11th Sts.; off W. 10th St. (north side) between Greenwich and 6th Aves. Subway: West 4th St./Washington Sq.; F to 14th St.

11 g-8

EDWARD MOONEY HOUSE

Chinatown's Georgian Mooney House is thought to be Manhattan's oldest surviving row house. Restored in 1971, it was built between the British evacuation (1785) and Washington's inauguration (1789) by merchant Edward Mooney, known in his day as a breeder of championship racehorses. 18 Bowery (at Pell St.), Chinatown. Subway: J, M, Z to Canal St.

6 c-4

MORRIS-JUMEL MANSION

This pre-Revolution Georgian mansion, built in 1765 in the Palladian style (remodeled 1810), is the oldest surviving private dwelling on Manhattan. Originally the "summer villa" of British officer Roger Morris's family, it later served famously as General George Washington's headquarters in 1776. Bought in 1810 by the wealthy French merchant Stephen Jumel, it was occu-pied by his widow, Eliza Bowen (who married Aaron Burr in 1833) until 1865. (See Haunted Places, above.) The mansion contains nine rooms with magnificent Georgian, Federal, and French Empire furnishings, silver, and china, a Colonial kitchen, and has a lovely herb and rose garden. While you're here, stop by Sylvan Terrace, a completely restored cobblestone street between Jumel Terrace and St. Nicholas Avenue which is lined with rare wooden row houses dating from 1882. 1765 Jumel Terr. (near the intersection of Edgecombe Ave. and 160th St.), Washington Heights, 212/923–8008. Admission: $3 adults, $2 students and seniors, free children under 12. Open Wed.–Sun. 10–4. Subway: 163rd St./Amsterdam Ave.

10 e-5

MUNICIPAL BUILDING

(McKim, Mead & White, 1914) Straddling Chambers Street, the Beaux-Arts Municipal Building is an almost imperial civic skyscraper. The building looks like a wedding cake and is topped with a 10-story turreted central tower at whose pinnacle stands "Civic Fame," a 25-ft-high gilt statue. Inside the building is a jumble of city offices; each year thousands of couples get married in a civil chapel on the second floor. Centre St. at Chambers St. Subway: Chambers St.

11 b-3

"NARROWEST HOUSE"

Only 9½ ft wide, the "narrowest house" occupies what was once a carriageway. Built in 1873, it has the honor of snuggling up to the oldest residence in Greenwich Village, the Isaacs-Hendricks House next door. Poet Edna St. Vincent Millay lived here in 1923. 75½ Bedford St. (between Morton and Commerce Sts.), West Village. Subway: Christopher St./Sheridan Sq.

10 e-7

NEW YORK STOCK EXCHANGE

In front of what is now 60 Wall Street, 24 brokers met under a buttonwood tree in 1792 and agreed on some rules of business, thereby creating the New York Stock Exchange. The Exchange's current digs are in a neoclassical building with an august Corinthian entrance that dates from 1901. The largest securities exchange in the world, the "Big Board" can handle the transfer of a trillion shares of stock per day. The visitor's center has a self-guided tour, interactive video displays, helpful docents, and a view of the chaotic 50-ft-high trading floor where brokers go about their frenetic business. *20 Broad St. (between Wall St. and Exchange Pl.), 212/656–5165. Free tickets distributed beginning at 8:45 AM; come before 11 AM to assure entrance. Open weekdays 9–4:30. Subway: 2, 3, 4, 5 to Wall St.*

11 *f-2*
OLD MERCHANT'S HOUSE
(Attributed to Minard Lafever, 1832) This completely intact, four-story Greek Revival house became the property of Seabury Tredwell, a wealthy merchant and hardware importer, in 1835. It retains most of its original fittings and furniture, as well as clothing belonging to Tredwell's daughter Gertrude, who lived here until her death in 1933 at the age of 93. Restored and open to the public, the house is particularly appealing during the Christmas season, when it's decorated in the style of a 19th-century holiday party. *29 E. 4th St. (between Lafayette St. and the Bowery), East Village, 212/777–1089. Admission: $5 adults, $3 students and seniors, free children under 12. Open Sun.–Thurs. 1–4. Subway: Astor Pl.; Bleecker St.*

10 *e-5*
OLD NEW YORK COUNTY COURTHOUSE
(John Kellum, 1872) This stately Italianate edifice is better known as the Tweed Courthouse. Built during political boss William Tweed's iron reign over city government, its construction dragged on for nine years at a then-unheard-of cost of $8–$12 million, most of which lined the pockets of Boss Tweed and his cronies. *52 Chambers St. (between Broadway and Centre St., behind City Hall), Lower Manhattan. Subway: Chambers St.*

10 *d-1*
PATCHIN PLACE
See Milligan Place/Patchin Place, *above.*

10 *f-6*
PEARL STREET
Now in the financial district, this street formed the shoreline of the East River in Dutch Colonial times, and was named

for the mother-of-pearl oyster shells scattered along the beach. *Lower Manhattan. Subway: 2, 3, 4, 5 to Wall St.*

9 *e-8*
PLAYERS CLUB
Built in 1845, the Players Club was remodeled by Stanford White in 1888, when actor Edwin Booth turned it into a private club for members of the "theatrical profession." Peek through the bars of adjacent Gramercy Park to see a statue depicting Booth playing Hamlet (*see* Statues & Public Art, *below*). *16 Gramercy Park S (between Irving Pl. and Park Ave. S). Subway: 6 to 23rd St.*

9 *d-3*
THE PLAZA HOTEL
(Henry J. Hardenbergh, 1907) This 18-story French Renaissance building by the same architect who designed the Dakota is more than an architectural landmark. Its exuberant style; its fortuitous location on spacious Grand Army Plaza, across from Central Park; and its legendary past make it a sentimental favorite. Ernest Hemingway supposedly recommended to F. Scott Fitzgerald that when he died, he should leave his liver to Princeton but his heart to the Plaza. (*See* Expensive Lodgings *in* Chapter 6.) *5th Ave. and Central Park S, Midtown, 212/759–3000. Subway: N, R to 5th Ave.*

11 *f-6*
POLICE HEADQUARTERS
(Hoppin & Koen, 1909) A baroque beauty with an impressive dome, this was the city's main police station when future President Teddy Roosevelt was New York City's police chief. The police moved out in 1973, and this lovely old building became a luxury coop residence in the booming '80s. *240 Centre St. (between Broome and Grand Sts.), Little Italy. Subway: 6 to Spring St.; J, M, Z to Canal St.*

9 *g-8*
PUBLIC BATHS, CITY OF NEW YORK
(Arnold W. Brunner and William Martin Aiken, 1906) Public baths worthy of ancient Rome, these relics are now incorporated into the municipal swimming pool at the Asser Levy Recreation Center. *E. 23rd St. near FDR Dr., Gramercy. Subway: 6 to 23rd St.*

11 f-2
PUBLIC THEATER
(Alexander Saeltzer, 1849; additions by Griffith Thomas, 1859, and Thomas Sent, 1881; renovation by Giorgio Cavaglieri, 1967) Designed in the style of an Italian palazzo, the Public Theatre was originally the Astor Library, New York's first free public library. Today, after a 1967 interior renovation, it houses the creative legacy of theater impresario Joseph Papp: the old reading rooms became auditoriums, which function as five different theaters. *Hair* and *A Chorus Line* both premiered here. *425 Lafayette St. (near Astor Pl.), East Village, 212/260–2400. Subway: Astor Pl.; 8th St.*

11 f-4
PUCK BUILDING
(Albert Wagner, 1886–1993) This giant, redbrick Romanesque Revival was home to the satirical weekly *Puck* from 1887 to 1916, and eventually housed the world's largest concentration of lithographers and printers. Today, it holds gallery and studio space and the Manhattan campus of the Pratt Institute. Two gold-leaf statues of Puck continue to gaze whimsically at passersby. *295–307 Lafayette St. (at Houston St.), SoHo. Subway: Bleecker St.; Broadway–Lafayette St.*

9 d-4
RADIO CITY MUSIC HALL
(Edward Durrell Stone and Donald Deskey) The opulent interior of this 1932 Art Deco theater—seating 6,200—was designed on a grand scale. Two-ton chandeliers were hung from a 60-ft ceiling in the foyer, astonishing Depression-era patrons who came here to see movies accompanied by live acts, such as the famed Rockettes chorus line. One-hour tours of the theater are given daily. *(See Concert Halls in Chapter 5.) 1260 6th Ave. (at 50th St.), Midtown. 212/632–47th–50th Sts./Rockefeller Center.*

10 f-1
RENWICK TRIANGLE
Attributed to James Renwick, Jr., the architect of both St. Patrick's Cathedral and Grace Church (downtown), these 1861 brick row houses form a handsome historic enclave in the bustling East Village. *112–128 E. 10th St. and 2335 Stuyvesant St. (between 2nd and 3rd Aves.), East Village. Subway: Astor Pl.*

7 a-4
RIVERSIDE DRIVE—WEST 105TH STREET HISTORIC DISTRICT
Limestone Beaux-Arts houses built between 1899 and 1902 form a tiny enclave beside Riverside Park. *Riverside Dr. between 105th and 106th Sts., Upper West Side. Subway: 1, 9 to 103rd St.*

9 h-2
ROOSEVELT ISLAND
Known as Blackwell's Island in the early 1700s when it was owned and farmed by Robert Blackwell and as Welfare Island in the mid-1800s when it came to house the city's poor and chronically ill, this 2-mi long strip of land in the middle of the East River became a "self-sufficient" residential complex in the 1970s. Burnt-out traces of the old institutions peek out from the edges of this otherwise clean-lined environment, and north-south promenades offer impressive river views. Getting to Roosevelt Island is a delight: opened in 1976, the Roosevelt Island tramway is the only aerial commuter tram in the United States. From the tram plaza at 2nd Avenue and 60th Street, the 25-person cabin rises 250 ft in the air above the East River and glides to a stop on the island in four minutes. *East River, roughly parallel to 50th–86th Sts. 212/832–4543. Subway: Roosevelt Island.*

9 e-2
SARA DELANO ROOSEVELT MEMORIAL HOUSE
(Charles A. Platt, 1907–08) Mrs. Roosevelt commissioned Platt to build twin town houses, one for her son Franklin and his future wife, Eleanor, and one for herself. FDR lived here until he became governor of New York, in 1928; his mother lived at No. 47 until her death in 1941. *47–49 E. 65th St. between Madison and Park Aves., Upper East Side. Subway: 68th St./Hunter College; N, R to 5th Ave.*

11 b-4
ST. LUKE'S PLACE
This handsome block of 1850s brick and brownstone row houses in Greenwich Village has billeted many famous residents. New York mayor Jimmy Walker (elected in 1926) lived in No. 6, poet Marianne Moore lived in No. 14, and novelist Theodore Dreiser wrote *An American Tragedy* in No. 16. *Between Hudson St. and 7th Ave. S. Subway: 1, 9 to Houston St.*

6 *d-7*

ST. NICHOLAS HISTORIC DISTRICT ("STRIVERS ROW")

In 1891, builder David H. King commissioned several leading architects of the day—James Brown Lord, Bruce Price and Clarence S. Luce; and McKim, Mead & White—and the results were the King Model Houses, a harmonious grouping of row houses and apartments. Originally built for well-to-do white residents, they were purchased by aspiring African-American professionals in the '20s and '30s and acquired the collective nickname "Strivers Row" as Harlem evolved into a black community. *Adam Clayton Powell–Frederick Douglass Blvds. from 138th to 139th Sts., Harlem. Subway: C to 135th St.*

10 *f-1*

ST. MARK'S HISTORIC DISTRICT

This historic East Village oasis contains three of Manhattan's earliest Federal buildings: St. Mark's Church in-the-Bowery (1799), the Stuyvesant-Fish House (1804), and 44 Stuyvesant Street (1795), all traceable back to Dutch governor Peter Stuyvesant, on whose farmland the district rests. Stuyvesant Street, the only true east-west street in Manhattan, was the driveway to the governor's mansion. *E. 10th and Stuyvesant Sts. between 2nd and 3rd Aves. Subway: Astor Pl.*

10 *f-2*

ST. MARK'S PLACE

In the 1960s, the 1830s Greek Revival row houses lining these blocks went psychedelic and formed the main street of the hippie phenomenon. Later, St. Mark's became a haven for punk rockers, and though a few punks remain, the counterculture has largely given way to tourism. Jewelry stands, T-shirt stalls, ethnic restaurants, and body piercers now line the East Village's gritty main drag. *Between 3rd Ave. and Tompkins Sq. Park, East Village. Subway: Astor Pl.*

10 *f-7*

SCHERMERHORN ROW

Dating from the early 19th century, these 12 peak-roof Georgian Federal and Greek Revival buildings were originally warehouses and countinghouses serving New York's then-bustling seaport. Now landmarks, they have been carefully restored as part of the South Street Seaport Museum's efforts to evoke the area's rich history (*see* History Museums, *below*). *2–18 Fulton, 91–92 South, 159–171 John, and 189–195 Front Sts., Lower Manhattan. Subway: Fulton St.*

9 *e-2*

SEVENTH REGIMENT ARMORY

(Charles W. Clinton, 1879) A Victorian incarnation of a medieval fortress, the vast armory houses a great drill hall (187 ft by 290 ft) and a Veterans' Room and library decorated under the direction of Louis Comfort Tiffany. Every January, this behemoth fills with the renowned Winter Antiques Show (*see* Events, *below*). *643 Park Ave. (between 66th and 67th Sts.), Upper East Side, 212/744–2968 (curator's office). Tours by appointment. Subway: 68th St./Hunter College.*

9 *c-5*

SHUBERT ALLEY

Now just a glitzy shortcut in the theater district, this private alley was the commercial domain of brothers J. J., Lee, and Sam Shubert, theater impresarios, in the early 1900s. Actors and chorus girls thronged to Shubert Alley whenever new shows were being cast. *Between 44th–45th Sts., west of 7th Ave. Subway: 42nd St./Times Sq.*

9 *f-6*

SNIFFEN COURT HISTORIC DISTRICT

In Murray Hill, New York's smallest designated historic district is a charming 19th-century mews of 10 Romanesque Revival brick carriage houses. Built as stables in the 1860s, they were converted to residences in the 1920s. *150–158 E. 36th St. (between Lexington and 3rd Aves.), Murray Hill. Subway: 33rd St.*

10 *e-3*

SOHO

An acronym meaning south of Houston Street, SoHo is bounded by West Broadway and Canal and Lafayette streets. Filled with galleries, trendy boutiques, shops, restaurants, and artists' lofts, this wonderfully with-it neighborhood is also a splendid treasure trove of 19th-century cast-iron architecture (*see* Cast-Iron Historic District *in* Architecture, *above*). *Subway: Prince St.; 1, 6, 9 to Spring St.*

11 *f-1*

STUYVESANT-FISH HOUSE

Dating from 1804, this brick Federal house in the East Village was built by the Dutch governor Peter Stuyvesant's great-grandson as a wedding gift for his daughter Elizabeth and her husband, *Nicholas Fish. 21 Stuyvesant St. (at 9th St., between 2nd and 3rd Aves.), East Village. Subway: Astor Pl.*

10 *e-5*

SURROGATE'S COURT/ HALL OF RECORDS

(John R. Thomas, Horgan & Slattery, 1899–1907) The Surrogate's Court forms a delightful and impressive civic monument opposite City Hall Park. With marble walls, a vaulted ceiling, and encircling corridors, its central hall is one of the finest Beaux-Arts rooms this side of the Paris Opera House. *31 Chambers St. (at Centre St.), Lower Manhattan. Subway: Chambers St.*

9 *g-3*

SUTTON PLACE

Overlooking the East River, Sutton Place is a quiet and prestigious enclave of luxury apartments and lavish town houses with private gardens. The address is synonymous with status; affluence; and, in the case of former resident Greta Garbo, mystery. *1 block east of 1st Ave., from 53rd to 59th Sts., Upper East Side. Subway: 4, 5, 6 to 59th St.*

9 *e-8*

THEODORE ROOSEVELT BIRTHPLACE NATIONAL HISTORIC SITE

Theodore Roosevelt, the 26th President and the only U.S. president from New York City, was born on this site in 1858. The original 1848 brownstone was demolished in 1916, but this Gothic Revival replica was constructed in 1923. Now administered by the National Park Service, Roosevelt's restored boyhood home has a fascinating collection of Teddyana in five Victorian period rooms. *28 E. 20th St. (between Broadway and Park Ave. S), Gramercy, 212/260–1616. Admission: $2. Open Wed.–Sun. 9–5. House tours on the hour. Subway: N, R, 6 to 23rd St.*

9 *c-5*

TIMES SQUARE

Named for the Times Tower—which no longer houses the *New York Times*, but still "drops the ball" on hordes of revelers every New Year's Eve—Times Square has long been synonymous with Broadway shows, bright lights, and seedy doings. In a somewhat surprising recent turn, however, a redevelopment scheme has almost completely sanitized Times Square. The neon lights remain, but the porn businesses, which long occupied abandoned theaters on 42nd Street, have been booted out, and 42nd Street is filling with gleaming megastores, each visually louder than the last. Although tourists seem to like it, many New Yorkers smell Disneyland in this unlikely metamorphosis. Once just crass, Times Square is now crassly commercial. *42nd–47th Sts. at Broadway and 7th Ave. Subway: Times Square.*

11 *e-2*

TRIANGLE FIRE PLAQUE

Just east of Washington Square is a plaque commemorating a tragic fire in the building that once housed the Triangle Shirtwaist Company. On March 25, 1911, fire broke out on the upper floors of this sweatshop, and within a single hour 146 young women were killed, many of them leaping in flames to their deaths on the streets below. The building was equipped with fire escapes and was supposed to be fireproof, but supervisors had locked the workers into their workrooms. A state investigation following the fire led to new labor laws and improved safety conditions for factory workers. *Washington Pl. and Greene St., Greenwich Village. Subway: 8th St.; Astor Pl.*

10 *d-5*

TRIBECA

Tribeca translates as the Triangle Below Canal. Once a 19th-century wholesaling district (there are still some aging signs advertising fresh dairy products), Tribeca is one of the city's many fashionably transformed neighborhoods and is still very much in flux. The surprisingly attractive old warehouses—many clad in cast iron and patterned brick—have been turned into artists' lofts, luxury condos, and offices. Reflecting this influx, Tribeca also houses some of the city's trendiest and priciest restaurants, including Nobu, Chanterelle, and the Tribeca Grill, co-owned by actor Robert Deniro. *Broadway–West St. from Chambers St. to Canal St. Subway: Franklin St.; Chambers St.; 1, 9 to Canal St.*

9 *e-1*

UNION CLUB

(Delano & Aldrich, 1932) This lime-stone-and-granite behemoth with a mansard roof houses the oldest private club in New York. (The club, which is more than twice as old as the building, was formed in 1836.) *101 E. 69th St. (at Park Ave.), Upper East Side. Subway: 68th St./Hunter College.*

10 *e-7*

U.S. CUSTOMS HOUSE

(Cass Gilbert, 1907) A monumental Beaux-Arts building with 44 Corinthian columns, the Customs House is now home to the George Gustav Heye Center of the National Museum of the American Indian (*see* History Museums, *below*). Since the building was originally used to collect import taxes on foreign goods shipped into the Port of New York, its architectural theme is "world trade": Four massive limestone sculptures embedded in the facade represent Asia, the Americas, Europe, and Africa, while 12 smaller ones arrayed above represent the world's "greatest trading nations." The huge oval rotunda has 1937 WPA murals by Reginald Marsh. *1 Bowling Green (Broadway and Whitehall St.), Lower Manhattan. Subway: Bowling Green.*

9 *e-4*

VILLARD HOUSES

(McKim, Mead & White, 1882–85) Surrounding a peaceful courtyard, this cluster of Italian Renaissance–style brownstones was modeled on Rome's Palazzo della Cancelleria. Built by newspaper owner and railroad entrepreneur Henry Villard, they have served variously as the home of the Catholic Archdiocese of New York and Random House Publishing Co. Today they comprise the landmark section of the New York Palace Hotel (*see* Very Expensive Lodgings *in* Chapter 6), containing its opulent public rooms and the hot Le Cirque 2000 (*see* French *in* Chapter 1). *451–457 Madison Ave. (between 50th and 51st Sts.), Midtown. Subway: 51st St./Lexington–3rd Aves.*

10 *e-7*

WALL STREET

In 1653 this was the northern frontier of the city, fortified against attack by a Dutch wall of thick wooden planks. The wall was completely dismantled by the English in 1699, but the name stuck, and The Street is now synonymous with the downtown financial district and the world of high finance in general. *Broadway to William St., Lower Manhattan. Subway: Wall St.*

11 *d-2*

WASHINGTON MEWS

Lined with converted stables, this 19th-century Greenwich Village mews once housed the carriage horses of fashionable Washington Square area residents. *University Pl.to 5th Ave., (between 8th St. and Washington Sq. N), Greenwich Village. Subway: 8th St.*

11 *d-2*

WASHINGTON SQUARE NORTH

(Town & Davis, ca. 1831) Immortalized in Henry James's *Washington Square*, "the Row" housed New York's most prominent citizens when it was first built. No. 8 was the mayor's official residence. Lovingly preserved, these stylish Greek Revival row houses are an affecting reminder of Old New York. *1–13 and 21–26 Washington Sq. N (between 5th Ave. and MacDougal St.), Greenwich Village. Subway: W. 4th St./Washington Sq.*

7 *f-7*

YORKVILLE

A remote hamlet known as Klein Deutschland (little Germany) in the 19th century, Yorkville has also been a haven for immigrants from Austria, Hungary, and Czechoslovakia. *Lexington–York Aves. from 75th to 88th Sts., Upper East Side. Subway: 77th St.; 4, 5, 6 to 86th St.*

queens

1 *f-3*

BOWNE HOUSE

The oldest building in Queens and the former home of Quaker John Bowne, this 1661 Colonial residence was a clandestine meeting place for the then-forbidden Society of Friends (Quakers). Bowne's arrest and subsequent acquittal by Dutch authorities set a precedent for freedom of worship in the New World. (*See* Friends Meeting House *in* Churches & Synagogues, *above*.) *37–01 Bowne St. (between 37th and 38th Aves.), Flushing, 718/359–0528. Guided tours Tues., Sat., Sun. between 2:30 and 4:30; tours for larger groups other days by* appointment. *Subway: 7 to Main St./Flushing.*

1 f-4
FOREST HILLS GARDENS
(Frederick Law Olmsted, Jr., landscape architect; Grosvenor Atterbury, architect; 1908–1917) When you're feeling assaulted by concrete and wondering why New York can't be a more livable city, try taking a walk through Forest Hills Gardens in Queens. What's most interesting here is the layout: The gardens were planned as a "garden community," and their pleasantly winding streets are complemented by quaint wood-and-brick homes, a "town green," trim English-style hedges, and leafy trees. The neighborhood's architectural style defies precise classification, but it evokes a romantic European village. *Between Union Tpke. and Burns St., Forest Hills, Queens. Subway: 71st–Continental Aves./Forest Hills.*

3 d-4
HUNTER'S POINT HISTORIC DISTRICT
Dating from the 1870s, this block of middle-income row houses is excellently preserved. *45th Ave. (between 21st and 23rd Sts.), Long Island City. Subway: 7 to 45th Rd.*

1 g-4
KING MANOR MUSEUM
The home of Rufus King—member of the Continental Congress, U.S. senator, and unsuccessful candidate for president—this gambrel-roof farmhouse dates back to 1750. It's now a history museum with a nine-room interior restored and decorated in period furniture. *King Park, Jamaica Ave. between 150th and 153rd Sts., Jamaica, 718/206–0545. Admission: $2, $1 children. Open weekends noon–4. Subway: Jamaica Center.*

3 h-1
KINGSLAND HOMESTEAD
Home to the Queens Historical Society, this farmhouse, built in 1774 by a wealthy Quaker farmer, is an interesting mix of Dutch and English architectural traditions. Moved from its original location on 155th Street, it now houses period rooms and changing exhibits. *Weeping Beech Park, 143–34 37th Ave. (at Parsons Blvd.), Flushing, 718/939–0647. Admission: $2, $1 seniors and children.*

Open Tues., Sat., and Sun. 2:30–4:30. Subway: 7 to Main St./Flushing.

8 f-2
LENT HOMESTEAD
Well preserved since its construction in 1729, this simple, Dutch Colonial farmhouse retains its original stonework and overhanging, wood-shingle roof. *78–03 19th Rd. (at 78th St.), Astoria.*

staten island

4 c-6
ALICE AUSTEN HOUSE (CLEAR COMFORT)
Probably built between 1700 and 1750, this Dutch-style cottage was the home of Alice Austen, a pioneering photographer, from 1866 to 1952. Austen's legacy: 3,000 glass-plate negatives of photos taken 1880–1930. View prints from those plates among Victorian furnishings at the house-cum-museum. *2 Hylan Blvd., Rosebank, 718/816–4506. Suggested contribution: $2. Open Thurs.–Sun. noon–5. From Staten Island Ferry, take bus S51.*

1 a-4
CONFERENCE HOUSE (BILLOPP HOUSE)
Built by British naval captain Christopher Billopp circa 1675, this manor house is renowned as the site of the only attempted peace conference during the American Revolution. On September 11, 1776, rebels Ben Franklin, John Adams, and Edward Rutledge met with British Admiral Lord Howe and refused to negotiate a cease-fire unless the Colonies were granted complete independence. *7455 Hylan Blvd., Tottenville, 718/984–2086. Admission: $2 adults, $1 seniors and children. Open Fri.–Sun. 1–4.*

1 b-1
GARDINER TYLER RESIDENCE
A grand mansion across from St. Peter's Cemetery, this 1835 house was the home of President John Tyler's widow, Julia Gardiner Tyler, from 1868 to 1874. *27 Tyler St. (at Clove Rd. and Broadway), West Brighton.*

4 c-7
GARIBALDI-MEUCCI MUSEUM
Housed in an old farmhouse, this quirky museum is full of letters and pho-

tographs from the life of Italian patriot Giuseppe Garibaldi, who lived in this house during a respite from his freedom fighting in 1850–51. The collection also documents Antonio Meucci's claim that he invented the telephone before Alexander Graham Bell did. *420 Tompkins Ave. (just north of Hylan Blvd.), Rosebank, 718/442–1608. Open Tues.–Sun. 1–5. From Staten Island Ferry, take bus S78 or S52 to Chestnut and Tompkins Aves.*

1 *b-3*

POILLON HOUSE

Frederick Law Olmsted, the co-designer of Central Park, lived in this 1720 house in his youth, and made extensive changes to the place in 1848. *4515 Hylan Blvd. (between Hales Ave. and Woods of Arden Rd.), Annadale.*

1 *b-2*

HISTORIC RICHMONDTOWN

Known as Cocclestown when it was founded in 1685 by Dutch, French Walloon, and English settlers, present-day Richmondtown is the site of approximately 26 buildings of major historical interest, 1690–1890. Highlights include the Voorlezer's House (1695), the oldest known elementary-school building in the United States, and the Stephens General Store & House, a reconstructed 19th-century store. In summer, costumed interpreters and craftspeople, such as a tinsmith, basketmaker, and shoemaker, recreate a 19th-century village; on Labor Day weekend the County Fair takes over; and at the end of December, folks convene for candlelight tours and holiday revels. From January to April, there are tavern concerts in a period tavern lit by candles and heated by a woodburning stove. *441 Clarke Ave. (at Arthur Kill and Richmond Rds.), Richmondtown, 718/351–1611. Admission: $4 adults, $2.50 seniors and children 6–18. Open Wed.–Sun. 1–5 with extended hours in July and Aug. From Staten Island Ferry, take Bus S74.*

4 *a-6*

SNUG HARBOR
CULTURAL CENTER

Sailor's Snug Harbor originally consisted of five magnificent Greek Revival buildings built in the 1830s and '40s as a home for "aged, decrepit and worn-out sailors." In all, there are now 28 buildings on 83 acres of park, and they serve as a performing- and visual-arts facility offering art exhibits, theater, recitals, concerts, and outdoor sculpture in a landmark maritime setting. Components include the Staten Island Botanical Garden (*see* Botanical Gardens *in* Chapter 3), the Newhouse Center for Contemporary Art (*see* Art Museums, *above*), and the Staten Island Children's Museum (*see* Children's Museums, *above*). *1000 Richmond Terr. (from Tysen St. to Kissel Avenue), Livingston, 718/448–2500. Grounds open daily 8 AM–dusk. In summer, tours depart from the main gate weekends at 2. From Staten Island Ferry Terminal take Bus S40.*

4 *b-5*

STATEN ISLAND
BOROUGH HALL

(Carrère & Hastings, 1906) Just above the ferry landing in St. George, Staten Island's seat of government, with its slender clock tower, was designed in the style of a French château. *Richmond Terr. at Borough Pl.*

HISTORY
MUSEUMS

Some landmark buildings and mansions have their own collections and period furnishings; *see* Historic Buildings & Areas, *above*, and Libraries, *below*.

8 *d-7*

AMERICAN MUSEUM
OF THE MOVING IMAGE

Adjacent to the Kaufman-Astoria Studios, this unique museum is devoted to the art, technology, and history of the film and television industries. It contains a state-of-the-art, 190-seat theater, a 60-seat screening room, and 25,000 square ft of exhibit space. In addition to the Zoetrope—a giant spinning disk on which the first primitive movies were shown—and costumes worn by Marilyn Monroe, Marlene Dietrich, Robin Williams, and Jerry Seinfeld, hundreds of classic films are "displayed" annually. Live demonstrations on computer animation and film editing are given every weekend. *35th Ave. (between 36th and 37th Sts.), Astoria, Queens, 718/784–0077. Admission: $8.50 adults, $5.50 seniors 65 and over and college students, $4.50 students 5–18, free children under 5 (screenings included in daytime admissions; $8 evenings, $4 seniors). Open Tues.–Fri. noon–5, weekends 11–6. Subway: Steinway St.*

6 *b-5*

AMERICAN NUMISMATIC SOCIETY

Founded in 1858 and devoted to the study of coins and currency, the Numismatic Society has two public galleries, displaying examples of "the root of all evil" from as far back as ancient Rome. *Audubon Terr. Museum Complex, Broadway and 155th St., Washington Heights, 212/234–3130. Open Tues.–Sat. 9–4:30, Sun. 1–4. Subway: 157th St.*

12 *b-3*

BROOKLYN HISTORICAL SOCIETY

The gallery here, which typically features Brooklyn Dodgers baseball bats and trick mirrors from Coney Island alongside exhibits on the borough's history, is closed for a major renovation. It's scheduled to re-open in spring 2001 with a larger space, re-vamped library, and Brooklyn-centric gift store. *128 Pierrepont St., Brooklyn Heights, 718/624–0890. Call for information on the gallery's new hours, and fees. Subway: Borough Hall.*

9 *d-3*

CARNEGIE HALL MUSEUM (ROSE MUSEUM)

See Carnegie Hall *in* Historic Buildings & Areas, *above.*

4 *h-7*

CONEY ISLAND MUSEUM

In the same building as the Coney Island Sideshow, just a block away from the boardwalk, this museum documents the history of this beachside amusement park from the late 19th century to the present. On display are original horses from the old steeplechase, a wicker rolling chair in which older folks were pushed down the boardwalk for 75 cents an hour, and banners and photos from old sideshow acts. Performances and lectures on the history of Coney Island are staged on weekend nights. *1208 Surf Ave. (at 12th St.), Brooklyn, 718/372–5159. Admission: 99¢. Open year-round weekends noon–6. Subway: West 8th St./N.Y. Aquarium.*

1 *c-6*

ELLIS ISLAND IMMIGRATION MUSEUM

See Historic Buildings & Areas, *above.*

10 *d-1*

FORBES MAGAZINE GALLERIES

This minimuseum in the Village displays the Forbes family's idiosyncratic collections, including 10,000 toy soldiers, more than 500 toy boats, jeweled Fabergé eggs made for the last two Russian czars, and a wealth of historic American manuscripts and presidential papers, including letters from Abraham Lincoln. Children tend to like the toy soldiers, while their parents may appreciate the adjacent picture gallery, with changing exhibitions. *62 5th Ave. (at 12th St.), 212/206–5548. Open Tues., Wed., Fri., and Sat. 10–4. Subway: 8th St.; F to 14th St.*

10 *e-7*

FRAUNCES TAVERN MUSEUM

This museum commemorates the site of the original tavern of Samuel Fraunces, where George Washington bade farewell to his officers in 1783 after having forced the redcoats from New York. Founded in 1907 in five reconstructed Federal buildings, the museum interprets the history and culture of Colonial America through Revolutionary War artifacts and Colonial-period rooms, decorative arts, flags, prints, and paintings. Call for a current schedule of exhibits, lectures, performances, and workshops for children. *54 Pearl St. (at Broad St.), Lower Manhattan, 212/425–1778. Admission: $2.50 adults, $1 students and seniors, free children under 6. Open weekdays 10–4:45, weekends noon–4. Subway: Whitehall St., South Ferry.*

10 *e-7*

GEORGE GUSTAV HEYE CENTER OF THE NATIONAL MUSEUM OF THE AMERICAN INDIAN

With access to more than 1 million artifacts, this is the world's largest and best collection of ethnology and archaeology on the Native Americans of North, South, and Central America and the West Indies. Run by the Smithsonian Institution, the museum is rich in sound and video recordings of Native Americans explaining the significance of exhibits, which range from Navajo weaving to pre-Columbian sculpture. Live dance performances and craft demonstrations by master craftspeople, such as totem-pole carvers, bring the exhibits to life. (*See* U.S. Customs House *in* Historic Buildings & Areas, *above.*) *1 Bowl-*

ing Green (at Broadway and Whitehall St.), Lower Manhattan, 212/668–6624. Admission: free. Open Sun.–Wed., Fri.– Sat. 10–5, Thurs. 10–8. Subway: Bowling Green.

1 *b-2*

HISTORIC RICHMONDTOWN

See Historic Buildings & Areas, *above.*

1 *f-4*

LOUIS ARMSTRONG HOUSE AND ARCHIVES

While Satchmo's former home at 34–56 107th Street in Corona, Queens, is being transformed into a museum (it's expected to open in late summer 2001), his personal effects—including 5,000 photographs, 650 homemade audio-tapes, and five gold-plate trumpets—are on display at the Louis Armstrong Archives at Queens College. *Rosenthal Library, Rm. 332, Queens College, 65–30 Kissena Blvd., Flushing, Queens, 718/997–3670. Open weekdays 10–5; hours, however, may vary, so call before visiting. Subway: Main St./Flushing.*

11 *h-5*

LOWER EAST SIDE TENEMENT MUSEUM

This restored 1863 tenement building is a poignant tribute to the immigrants who lived on New York's Lower East Side during the 19th and early 20th centuries. You'll be guided through apartments furnished as they were by those who actually lived here: the Gumpertzes, a German Jewish family from the 1870s; the Rogarshevskys, Eastern Europeans from the 1910s; the Confinos, Sephardic Jews from Turkey who lived here in the 1910s; and the Baldizzis, a Sicilian Catholic family from the 1930s. Reservations for apartment tours are best made in advance. *90 Orchard St. (at Broome St.), 212/431–0233. Admission: $8, $6 students and seniors. Open Tues.–Fri. 1–4, weekends 11–4:30. Subway: Delancey St.; Essex St.; Grand St.*

9 *c-7*

MUSEUM AT THE FASHION INSTITUTE OF TECHNOLOGY

Deep in the garment district, F.I.T. is home to a substantial museum space documenting the history of fashion both high and low. The textile collection holds more than 3 million indexed swatches,

alongside ½ million costumes and accessories from the 18th century to the present. Past shows have addressed topics ranging from the history of automobile upholstery to haute couture of the past five decades. *7th Ave. and 27th St., Garment District, 212/217–5800. Admission: free. Open Tues.–Fri. noon–8, Sat. 10–5. Subway: 1, 9 to 28th St.*

10 *e-7*

MUSEUM OF AMERICAN FINANCIAL HISTORY

This four-room museum displays artifacts from Wall Street, including a vintage ticker-tape machine, and special exhibits on the history of finance and famous tycoons. *28 Broadway (between Beaver St. and Exchange Pl.), Lower Manhattan, 212/908–4519. Suggested admission: $2. Open Tues.–Sat. 10–4. Subway: Rector St.; 4, 5 to Wall St.*

11 *f-7*

MUSEUM OF CHINESE IN THE AMERICAS

In the heart of Manhattan's blossoming Chinatown, these exhibits document the vibrant history and culture of Chinese immigrants in New York, San Francisco, Canada, and Latin America. (*See* Walking Tours, *below*). *70 Mulberry St. (at Bayard St.), 2nd floor, Chinatown, 212/619–4785. Admission: $3, $1 students and seniors, free children under 12. Open Tues.–Sat. noon–5. Subway: 6, J, M, Z to Canal St.*

10 *d-8*

MUSEUM OF JEWISH HERITAGE—A LIVING MEMORIAL TO THE HOLOCAUST

Opened in 1997 in a star-of-David-shape building designed by Kevin Roche, this three-floor museum is devoted to preserving the memory of the Holocaust and the history of Jewish culture through photographs, artifacts, and videotaped oral histories. Permanent exhibits include "The War Against the Jews" documenting the rise of Nazism, the Holocaust, and World War II; and "Jewish Life a Century Ago." *18 1st Pl. (at Battery Pl.), Battery Park City, Lower Manhattan, 212/968–1800; Admission: $7 adults, $5 students and seniors, free children under 5. Open Sun.–Wed. 9–5, Thurs. 9–8, Fri. and eve of Jewish holidays 9–2. Subway: South Ferry; Bowling Green.*

9 *d-4*

MUSEUM OF TELEVISION AND RADIO

If you harbor secret addictions to reruns of "Mary Tyler Moore" and "I Dream of Jeannie," this is the place for you. With 75,000 radio and TV programs preserved forever in its permanent collection, the museum encourages visitors to select their favorite shows and watch them at one of the personal consoles. Try the Beatles on the "Ed Sullivan Show," the pilot episode of "Charlie's Angels," or the original radio broadcast of Orson Welles's "War of the Worlds." There are 96 television consoles, a 200-seat theater, a 96-seat theater, two 45-seat screening rooms, and a listening room for radio programs. Special screenings aired throughout the day in the various theaters bring rare programs—complete with vintage commercials—back to light. *25 W. 52nd St. (between 5th and 6th Aves.), Midtown, 212/621–6800. Suggested admission: $6, $4 seniors and students, $3 children under 13. Open Tues., Wed., and Fri.–Sun. noon–6, Thurs. noon–8. Subway: E, F to 5th Ave.; 47th–50th Sts./Rockefeller Center.*

7 *e-4*

MUSEUM OF THE CITY OF NEW YORK

The amazing life and history of New York City—from the Native Americans and early Dutch settlers through the present day—is chronicled in this massive Georgian mansion via costumes, furniture, paintings, artifacts, oral histories, dollhouses, and toys. Special exhibits feature such topics as the Harlem Renaissance, the Astor Place Riot, and Tin Pan Alley. (*See,* Walking Tours, *below*). *1220 5th Ave. (at 103rd St.), Upper East Side, 212/534–1672. Admission: $5 adults; $4 students, seniors, and children; $10 families. Open Wed.–Sat. 10–5, Sun. noon–5. Subway: 6 to 103rd St.*

9 *e-3*

NEWSEUM/NY

Opened in 1997, Newseum/NY, a branch of Newseum in Washington, D.C., presents changing exhibits on news and photojournalism, focusing on First Amendment issues and how news is made. Displays are accompanied by documentary films, lectures, and roundtable discussions with newsmakers and newsbreakers. *580 Madison Ave.*

(between 56th and 57th Sts.), Midtown, 212/317–7596. Admission: free. Open Mon.–Sat. 10–5:30. Subway: 59th St.; N, R to 5th Ave.

11 *b-5*

NEW YORK CITY FIRE MUSEUM

Examine hand-pulled and horse-drawn firefighting apparatus, uniforms, and sliding poles at this restored 1904 firehouse, which chronicles the efforts of New York's Bravest from the 18th century to the present. *278 Spring St. (between Hudson and Varick Sts.), West Village, 212/691–1303. Suggested admission: $4, $2 seniors, $1 children under 12. Open Tues.–Sun. 10–4. Subway: C, E to Spring St.*

10 *e-7*

NEW YORK CITY POLICE MUSEUM

In brand new digs in the Cunard Building on Bowling Green, this large collection features cop paraphernalia from the Dutch era to the present, including guns, ammo, handcuffs, billy clubs, and uniforms. *25 Broadway (at Morris St.), Lower Manhattan, 212/301–4440. Open daily 10–6. Subway: Bowling Green.*

7 *c-8*

NEW-YORK HISTORICAL SOCIETY

Founded in 1804, this is the oldest museum in the city. Changing exhibits are culled from the society's elegant collection of paintings, prints, folk art, and vintage toys, and cover everything from the history of Central Park to the lights of Times Square. The society houses a major research library of 600,000 volumes; an impressive collection of 18th-century New York newspapers; and more than a million maps, prints, photos, lithographs, and architectural drawings—including the original watercolors for John James Audubon's *Birds of America*. One of the latest additions is the new installation of 40,000 of the museum's most-treasured objects in the new Henry Luce III Center on the museum's fourth floor—including George Washington's inaugural chair, the largest U.S. collection of Tiffany lamps, and paintings by Hudson River School artists Thomas Cole and Frederic Church. Also on permanent display is "Kid City," a re-creation of a turn-of-the-20th-century New York City street corner. *2 W. 77th St., Upper West Side, 212/*

873–3400. Suggested admission: $5, $3 students and seniors, free children under 12. Open Tues.–Sun. 11–5. Subway: B, C to 81st St.

12 *c-4*

NEW YORK TRANSIT MUSEUM

Appropriately located underground, in an authentic 1938 subway station, the Transit Museum contains full-size classic subway cars dating back to 1903, including wooden cars with rattan seating. It's great for children, who can climb all over the seats and pretend they're driving without anyone looking askance. Volunteers dressed as subway conductors give impromptu tours. There are also vintage turnstiles, station signs, trolley models, and well-researched temporary exhibits on the history of the subway system. *Boerum Pl. and Schermerhorn St., Downtown Brooklyn, 718/243–3060; Admission: $3, $1.50 seniors and children under 17. Open Tues.–Fri. 10–4, weekends noon–5. Subway: Borough Hall.*

10 *e-7*

SKYSCRAPER MUSEUM

If you like big buildings, drop by this little museum to see exhibits on high-rises from around the world. In 2001, the Skyscraper Museum will be relocating to permanent digs in a brand-new skyscraper in Battery Park City—also to be the home of the new Ritz-Carlton Hotel. *16 Wall St. (at Nassau St.), Lower Manhattan, 212/766–1324. Suggested admission: $2, free students and seniors. Open Tues.–Sat. noon–6. Subway: Broad St., Wall. St.*

10 *f-7*

SOUTH STREET SEAPORT MUSEUM

Filling 11 square seaport blocks on the East River, this "museum without walls" features cobblestone streets, historic sailing ships, 18th- and 19th-century architecture, an old print shop, a boat-building center, and a children's crafts center with hands-on displays illuminating the history of seafaring. If you're feeling salty, book passage on the *Pioneer*, a 102-ft schooner built in 1885, and be sure to visit the other ships docked at Pier 16 as well, including the *Peking*, the second-largest sailing ship in the world; the lightship *Ambrose*; and the full-rigged *Wavertree*. Call for details on

classes, special exhibitions, and events. *Visitors' center: 12 Fulton St. (at South St.), Lower Manhattan, 212/748–8600. Admission: $6, 5 seniors, $4 students, $3 children under 12. Open Apr. 1–Sept. 30, Sun.–Wed. 10–6, Thurs. 10–8, Fri.–Sat. 10–6; Oct. 1–Mar. 31, Sun.–Mon., Wed.–Sat. 10–5. Subway: Fulton St.; Broadway–Nassau St.*

4 *c-2*

WATERFRONT MUSEUM

In a historic wooden barge on the Brooklyn waterfront, this makeshift museum presents changing art exhibits and maritime artifacts from New York Harbor. The adjacent pier offers stunning harbor views stretching from the Verrazano Bridge to the Statue of Liberty. Call for information about museum tours, special events, circus performances, and concerts. *290 Conover St., Red Hook Garden Pier, Brooklyn, 718/624–4719. Admission: free (donations accepted). Museum open for special events and by appointment only; pier open daily, 24 hours. Subway: Borough Hall, then Bus B61 toward Red Hook.*

6 *c-1*

YESHIVA UNIVERSITY MUSEUM

Changing exhibits of paintings, photographs, ceremonial objects, and architectural models of synagogues around the world reflect the Jewish historical and cultural experience. *2520 Amsterdam Ave. (at 185th St.), Washington Heights, 212/960–5390. Admission: $3 adults, $2 students and seniors. Open Tues.–Thurs. 10:30–5, Sun. noon–6. Subway: 181st St.*

LIBRARIES

If nothing else, New Yorkers are certified readers. We love books, authors, stories . . . the whole literary idea. The five boroughs have close to 200 public libraries between them, which, in addition to loaning books, sponsor more than 500 free programs monthly, including film screenings, discussions with well-known and emerging authors, and storytelling hours for children. These are the city's most significant public and private collections; if you're conducting research in art, design, or history, tap the city's museums as well—many open their specialized collections to the public.

9 *c-2*

AMERICAN BIBLE SOCIETY ARCHIVES

Outside the Vatican, this is the largest Bible collection in the world, with nearly 50,000 scriptural items in 2,000 languages and dialects. Appointments can be made to tour the library, which contains leaves of a first-edition Gutenberg Bible; Helen Keller's braille Bible; and a Kai Feng Fu Torah scroll from China. A public gallery holds exhibits on various forms of scriptural and sacred art. *1865 Broadway (at 61st St.), Upper West Side, 212/408–1200. Gallery: open Mon.–Wed. and Fri. 10–6, Thurs. 10–7, Sat. 10–5. Library: by appointment. Subway: 59th st./Columbus Circle.*

12 *g-5*

BROOKLYN PUBLIC LIBRARY (CENTRAL LIBRARY)

An art moderne building erected in 1941 next to the Grand Army Plaza entrance to Prospect Park, Brooklyn's central library is a grand affair. A recent renovation opened up the library's long, wonderfully curving interior spaces, and the exterior, with its golden doorways, gilt bas-reliefs, and uplifting carved maxims, is as glorious as ever. Brooklyn's independent, 58-branch library system, a holdover from the days when Brooklyn was a separate city, is headquartered here. In addition to the heavily trafficked circulating areas, periodical and microfilm rooms, and a Web-linked computer lab, the library's research facilities include the Brooklyn Collection, which contains tens of thousands of black-and-white historical photographs and the photo file from the *Brooklyn Eagle*, the newspaper for which poet and Brooklynite Walt Whitman wrote. *Grand Army Plaza (see Historic Buildings & Areas, above), Park Slope, 718/230–2100. Open Mon.–Thurs. 9–8, Fri., and Sat. 9–6; Sun. 1–5. Subway: Grand Army Plaza.*

9 *d-5*

NEW YORK PUBLIC LIBRARY

A national historic landmark covering two city blocks, the New York Public Library first opened its doors—guarded always by the famous stone lions—on May 24, 1911 *(see Architecture, above)*. Today the library is one of the greatest research institutions in the world, with 6 million books, 12 million manuscripts, and 2.8 million pictures. Among the more unusual items in the research collection are magician Harry Houdini's personal library; a selection of 19th- and 20th-century restaurant menus; and the original stuffed animals on which A.A. Milne based his Winnie-the-Pooh stories. The library's beautiful Main Reading Room (completely renovated in 1999) is now functional as well as inspiring: light flows in through new UV-light filtering panes (the original glass had been blacked out since World War II!) and the old hand-carved wooden tables have been wired to the Web and electrical outlets, making them Computer Age friendly. It's the perfect blend of old meets new. The library regularly mounts full-scale exhibits on such lettered topics as American novelists, early English Bibles, New York City history, and typography. *5th Ave. and 42nd St., Midtown, 212/930–0830 Current gallery exhibits: 212/869–8089. Open Mon. and Thurs.–Sat. 10–6, Tues.–Wed. 11–7:30; call for hrs for special collections. Tours Mon.–Sat. 11 and 2. Subway: B, D, F, Q to 42nd St.*

9 *e-6*

PIERPONT MORGAN LIBRARY

(McKim, Mead & White, 1906) Housed in an austere, Italian Renaissance–style palazzo, the library was originally built for the collections of Wall Street baron J. Pierpont (J. P.) Morgan (1837–1913). The opulent interior is rich not only in furnishings and paintings, but in medieval and Renaissance illuminated manuscripts, old-master drawings and prints, rare books, and autographed literary and musical manuscripts. Among countless historic documents in the collection are three Guttenberg bibles, the only known manuscript fragment of Milton's *Paradise Lost*, and letters penned by Jane Austen and Thomas Jefferson. Augmented in recent years by the acquisition of the adjacent 45-room brownstone mansion—once the residence of J. P. Morgan, Jr.—the library now includes a graceful, glass-enclosed garden court, in which lunch and tea are served. Changing exhibits of works on paper bring visitors into intimate contact with great authors and artists. *Madison Ave. and 36th St., Murray Hill, 212/685–0008. Suggested donation: $7 adults, $5 seniors and students, free children under 12. Open Tues.–Thurs. 10:30–5, Fri. 10:30–8, Sat. 10:30–6, Sun. noon–6. Subway: 33rd St.*

9 b-2

NEW YORK PUBLIC LIBRARY FOR THE PERFORMING ARTS

While couch potatoes are gazing their way through the Museum of Television and Radio, the ear-trained should scrutinize this wonderful library's musical scores, videotapes of great ballets, and recordings of famous opera performances. Because the library's Lincoln Center facility is undergoing a two-year renovation (scheduled for completion in February 2001), circulating and research materials are being housed in temporary locations; call for hours and locations. *40 Lincoln Center Plaza (Broadway and 64th St., just north of the Metropolitan Opera), Upper West Side, 212/870–1600. Subway: 66th St.*

9 e-6

NEW YORK PUBLIC LIBRARY SCIENCE, INDUSTRY, AND BUSINESS LIBRARY

This state-of-the-art research facility, opened in 1996, houses the NYPL's science, technology, and business materials. A bank of TVs tuned to business news stations and an electronic ticker tape with the latest stock prices set the library's high-tech tone. But the real draw are the scientific, business, and government databases on the library's Web-linked computers. *188 Madison Ave. (at 34th St.), Murray Hill, 212/592–7000. Open: Mon. 10–6, Tues. 11–8, Wed. 11–7, Thurs. 11–8, Fri. 10–6, Sat. noon-6. Subway: 33rd St.*

6 e-8

SCHOMBURG CENTER FOR RESEARCH IN BLACK CULTURE

A branch of the New York Public Library, this internationally renowned cultural facility in the heart of Harlem began with Arthur Schomburg's personal collection of black literature and history. Now the largest collection of its kind in the world, the library has 20,000 microfilm reels of news clippings, over 1,000 rare books, 30,000 photographs, 15,000 hours of taped oral history, 10,000 records, and 3,000 videotapes and films. In addition to its research facilities, the library has exhibits on African and African-American art and history and hosts lectures and performances in the American Negro Theatre and Langston Hughes Auditorium. *515 Malcolm X Blvd. (at 135th St.), Harlem, 212/*

491–2200. Open Mon.–Wed. noon–8, Thurs.–Sat. 10–6; exhibit also open Sun. 1–5. Subway: 2, 3 to 135th St.

9 d-8

YIVO INSTITUTE FOR JEWISH RESEARCH

Established in 1925 in Vilna, Lithuania, this academic-research center for Eastern European Jewry and Jewish culture contains more than 22 million archival documents, 100,000 photographs, and 300,000 books. *22 W. 17th St. between 5th and 6th Aves., Chelsea, 212/246–6080. Open Mon.–Thurs. 9:30–5:30. Subway: N or R to 23rd St.*

SCIENCE MUSEUMS

7 c-8

AMERICAN MUSEUM OF NATURAL HISTORY

With 30 million artifacts and specimens, more than 800 staff members, and 42 exhibition halls, the largest museum of natural history in the world has slowly but surely been remaking itself. Alongside halls of Victorian-era dioramas depicting stuffed lions, gorillas, and zebras posed in front of hand-painted backgrounds, there are a dozen new, high-tech halls filled with the latest exhibits on everything from giant squid to dinosaurs—currently the museum's biggest draw. Three spectacular new dinosaur halls on the fourth floor—the Hall of Saurischian Dinosaurs, the Hall of Ornithischian Dinosaurs, and the Hall of Vertebrate Origins—use real fossils and dinosaur skeletons to explain the latest theories on how T. rex and velociraptors might have looked, lived, and behaved. But dinosaurs are just the beginning: Don't miss the Hall of Biodiversity and its life-size recreation of the Dzanga-Sangha Rainforest; the Hall of Fossil Mammals, with interactive video monitors on virtually every exhibit; the Hall of Meteorites, featuring the 4-billion-year-old Ahnighito, the largest meteorite ever retrieved from the Earth's surface; the Hall of Human Biology and Evolution, with dioramas tracing human origins back to such early examples of the species as Lucy; or, the new Hall of Planet Earth, which explains the geological origins of Earth (with the help of 100 giant rocks) and links the museum to the spectacularly rebuilt Hayden Planetarium (*see, below*). IMAX films exploring the natural world are shown daily on the museum's colossal screen, and there's even a "dinner theater" on Friday and Saturday nights that includes cocktails (beneath the museum's beloved 94-ft-long replica of a blue whale in the "Ocean Life Cafe") and an IMAX double-feature. *Central Park W and 79th St., Upper West Side, 212/769–5100. Admission: $8 adults, $6 seniors and students, $4.50 children. Open Sun.–Thurs. 10–5:45, Fri. and Sat. 10–8:45. Subway: 81st St.*

7 *c-8*

HAYDEN PLANETARIUM
Completely revamped and technologically updated, the planetarium reopened in early 2000. Now part of the American Museum of Natural History's new Rose Center for Earth and Space, the planetarium is housed inside a six-story-high, glass-walled sphere, with exhibits tracking 15 billion years of the universe's evolution. An ultra-modern Sky Theater transports visitors from galaxy to galaxy, showing scenes that otherwise can only be seen by traveling in outer space. *Central Park W and 81st. St., Upper West Side, 212/769–5100. Admission: $19.50 adults, $11 children 3–12, free children under 3. Open Sun.–Thurs. 10–5:45, Fri. and Sat. 10–8:45. Subway: 81st St.*

9 *a-5*

INTREPID SEA-AIR-SPACE MUSEUM
Formerly the U.S.S. *Intrepid*, this 900-ft aircraft carrier docked in the Hudson River is now a floating museum dedicated to air, naval, and space technology—some of it formerly top secret. On deck is an envelope-pushing array of air- and spacecraft, including the A-12 Blackbird spy plane, lunar landing modules, helicopters, and seaplanes. Docked alongside, and ready for boarding, are the *Growler*, a strategic-missile submarine; the destroyer *Edson*; and other battle-scarred naval veterans. Children will enjoy exploring the *Intrepid*'s skinny hallways and winding staircases and (for an extra $5) flying a simulated F-18 fighter-jet mission off the flight deck. *Hudson River, Pier 86 (12th Ave. and 46th St.), Hell's Kitchen, 212/245–0072. Admission: $10 adults; $7.50 seniors, veterans, U.S. reservists, college students, and students 12–17; $5 children 6–11; $1 children 2–5; and free active-duty U.S. military personnel. Open May–Sept., weekdays 10–5,* weekends 10–6; Oct.–Apr., Wed.–Sun. 10–5. Subway: A, C, E to 42nd St.*

1 *c-6*

LIBERTY SCIENCE CENTER
Just across the Hudson River in Liberty State Park, New Jersey, the high-tech Liberty Science Center is the New York area's largest science museum for children. Its three theme floors cover Environment, Health, and Invention. Highlights include the insect zoo, the 100-ft touch tunnel, the 700-pound geodesic globe, IMAX movies, and 3-D laser shows. Special exhibits well-staffed with volunteers get children involved with everything from robots to raptors. *Liberty State Park, 251 Philip St., Jersey City, NJ, 201/200–1000. Admission: $9.50, $8.50 students, $7.50 seniors and children 2–12. Open Apr.–Aug., daily 9:30–5:30; Sept.–Mar., Tues.–Sun. 9:30–5:30. Call for directions by ferry or train.*

3 *h-2*

NEW YORK HALL OF SCIENCE
An easy ride on the No. 7 train from Manhattan, the New York Hall of Science is ranked as one of the nation's top 10 science museums. Children and other budding researchers are invited to explore 160 hands-on exhibits on subjects ranging from lasers to microbes. Preschoolers can make crafts at the Discovery Center; older children will enjoy the museum's insanely popular outdoor science playground. *111th St. and 48th Ave., Flushing Meadows–Corona Park, Queens; 718/699–0005. Admission: $7.50; $5 children and seniors; free children under 3; Sept.–May. free Thurs. and Fri. 2–5. Open Sept.–May, Mon.–Wed. 9:30–2, Thurs.–Sun. 9:30–5.; Jun.–Aug., Mon. 9:30–2, Tues.–Sun 9:30–5. Subway: 7 to 111th St.*

9 *e-3*

SONY WONDER TECHNOLOGY LAB
In the postmodern Sony Building (*see* Architecture, *above*), a free, four-floor science and technology exhibit (sponsored by guess who? Sony!) lets children log onto computers, play sound engineer, watch high-definition TV, and learn about video-game design. *550 Madison Ave. (at 56th St.), Midtown, 212/833–8100. Open Tues., Wed., Fri., and Sat. 10–6; Thurs. 10–8, Sun. noon–6. Subway: 4, 5, 6 to 59th St.; N, R to 5th Ave.*

1 *b-1*

STATEN ISLAND INSTITUTE OF ART & SCIENCE

Founded in 1881 and just a block up the hill from the Staten Island Ferry terminal, the Staten Island Institute celebrates art, science, and history. The high point is the remarkable natural-history collection, with specimens covering anthropology to zoology. *75 Stuyvesant Pl., St. George, Staten Island, 718/727–1135. Suggested contribution: $2.50 adults, $1.50 children.*

STATUES & PUBLIC ART

From 19th-century memorials cast in bronze to 21st-century installations crafted from used hubcaps, outdoor artworks give the city's streets and parks some unexpected twists—and occasionally offer a history lesson.

10 *e-2*

ALAMO

(Bernard Rosenthal, 1967) One of the city's first abstract outdoor sculptures, this enormous black, all-steel cube—sited in the middle of an East Village traffic island—was originally intended to be a temporary installation. The cube's popularity proved overwhelming, however, and it's now a neighborhood fixture. Although *Alamo* doesn't look movable, the sculpture actually turns. You—and a couple of friends—can set the off-kilter cube in motion by leaning a shoulder against it and applying a little muscle. *Astor Pl. and Lafayette St., East Village. Subway: Astor Place.*

7 *d-8*

ALICE IN WONDERLAND

(Jose de Creeft, 1959) One of Central Park's most beloved statues, bronze Alice—based on the popular drawings by Tenniel for the book *Alice in Wonderland*—is climbed and crawled upon by local youngsters. *Central Park, Sailboat Lake (near E. 74th St.). Subway: 77th St.*

7 *b-3*

ALMA MATER

(Daniel Chester French, 1903) Atop the broad, sweeping staircase of Columbia's Low Library and overlooking the university's main plaza, this 8-ft-tall seated lady in bronze has presided over hundreds of graduation ceremonies—and,

in the 1960s, riots. On sunny days, it's nice to have a seat beside her, sip your coffee, and enjoy a bite—along with the view. *Low Library, Columbia University, east of Broadway and 116th St., Morningside Heights. Subway: 116th St./Columbia University.*

7 *d-8*

HANS CHRISTIAN ANDERSEN

(Georg John Lober, 1956) A gift to the city from Danish and American schoolchildren, bronze *Hans* provides the perfect setting for reading his fairy tales. (The Central Park Conservancy sponsors readings on weekends.) Sculptural sidekick the *Ugly Duckling* was stolen in 1974, but it was soon recovered and returned to its creator's side. *Central Park, Sailboat Lake (near E. 74th St.). Subway: 77th St.*

9 *d-1*

ANGEL OF THE WATERS (BETHESDA FOUNTAIN)

(Emma Stebbins, 1868) Central Park's centerpiece and the focal point of one of the prettiest spots in the city, Bethesda Fountain was named for the biblical pool in Jerusalem, which was said to have been given healing powers by an angel. Fittingly, a bronze angel rises from the splashing fountain and is waited upon by cherubs representing Temperance, Purity, Health, and Peace. Behind them, rowboats and the occasional gondola drift by on the Lake. *Central Park, Bethesda Terr. (near 72nd St. Transverse). Subway: B, C to 72nd St.*

9 *d-4*

ATLAS

(Lee Lawrie, 1937) A 15-ft-tall bronze statue on a 9-ft-high granite pedestal, *Atlas*—terminally persistent in bearing the world on his shoulders—is the defining figure of Midtown's Rockefeller Center. Interestingly, the statue was picketed when originally installed because Atlas reputedly bore a resemblance to Benito Mussolini. *International Bldg., Rockefeller Center, 5th Ave. between 50th and 51st Sts. Subway: E, F to 5th Ave.; 47th–50th Sts./Rockefeller Center.*

9 *d-2*

BALTO

(Frederick George Richard Roth, 1925) Adoring schoolchildren supposedly helped finance this bronze statue commemorating Balto, a real-life sled dog who led a team of huskies carrying medicine through a blizzard to Nome, Alaska, during a 1925 diphtheria epidemic. Note the shiny patches where children have petted his snout and sat on his back. *Central Park near E. 66th St. Subway: N, R to 5th Ave.; 68th St./Hunter College.*

12 *c-3*

HENRY WARD BEECHER

(John Quincy Adams Ward, 1891) This fine bronze of the abolitionist minister was cast by an abolitionist sculptor, one of the most prolific creators of public art in his day. A few blocks away is Beecher's former pulpit, Plymouth Church of the Pilgrims (*see* Churches & Synagogues, *above*), where his stirring oratory helped foster the anti-slavery movement in the years before the Civil War. *Fulton St. at Court St., Brooklyn Heights. Subway: Borough Hall.*

9 *d-3*

SIMON BOLIVAR

(Sally James Farnham, 1921) One of the many enormous bronze statues fronting Central Park to the south, this one has the South American liberator on horseback atop a polished-granite pedestal. *6th Ave. and Central Park S. Subway: B, Q, N, R to 57th St.*

9 *e-8*

EDWIN BOOTH AS HAMLET

(Edmond T. Quinn, 1918) Booth was America's leading Shakespearean actor in his day. He lived at 16 Gramercy Park South from 1888 until his death in 1906. (*See* Players Club *in* Historic Buildings & Areas, *above*, and Gramercy Park *in* Chapter 3.) *Gramercy Park. Subway: 6 to 23rd St.*

9 *d-5*

WILLIAM CULLEN BRYANT

(Herbert Adams, 1911) A bronze statue of the famed 19th-century poet and journalist sits fittingly in the now-hip Midtown park that bears his name. *Bryant Park, 6th Ave. and 42nd St., Midtown. Subway: B, D, F, Q to 42nd St.*

1 *f-4*

CIVIC VIRTUE

(Frederick William MacMonnies, 1922) Once the most prominent sculpture in City Hall Park, this nearly nude male figure carved from a single block of marble appears to tred carelessly upon writhing figures of women in similar dishabille. It's not clear if citizens were more bothered by the nudity or by the idea that virtue meant crushing women with bare feet, but the muscular statue was protested and banished to Queens in 1941. *Queens Blvd. and Union Tpke., Forest Hills, Queens. Subway: E, F to Union Tpke./Kew Gardens.*

7 *d-8*

CLEOPATRA'S NEEDLE

Located behind the Metropolitan Museum of Art, this hieroglyphic-covered obelisk was a gift from Egypt in 1880. It is believed to date from the year 1600 BC. *Central Park near E. 80th St. Subway: 77th St.*

9 *c-4*

GEORGE M. COHAN

(Georg John Lober, 1959) Cast in bronze, the famed song-and-dance man now gives his regards to Broadway come rain or shine. Pay him a visit next time you're stuck in a queue at the TKTS booth. *Broadway and 46th St., Theater District. Subway: 42nd St./Times Sq.; 49th St.*

9 *c-3*

COLUMBUS MONUMENT

(Gaetano Russo, 1892) Now isolated in a traffic island in busy Columbus Circle, this white marble statue (perched on a 26-ft-high, 700-ton granite column) was erected on the 400th anniversary of Columbus's first voyage to the New World. *Columbus Circle (Broadway and 59th St.), Upper West Side. Subway: 59th St./Columbus Circle.*

9 *d-2*

DELACORTE MUSICAL CLOCK

(Andrea Spadini, 1965) Almost as popular as the zoo's live residents, these bronze denizens do an hourly dance to the tune of one of 32 nursery songs. *Central Park Zoo, near 5th Ave. and 64th St. Subway: N, R to 5th Ave.; 68th St./Hunter College.*

10 *e-7*

ABRAHAM DE PEYSTER

(George Edwin Bissell, 1896) This bronze statue of prosperous colonial merchant Abraham de Peyster replaced an ill-fated model of King George III. George was pulled down by an angry Colonial mob following the signing of the Declaration of Independence, and was then melted down to make bullets. *Bowling Green (Broadway at Whitehall St.), Lower Manhattan. Subway: Bowling Green.*

9 *c-4*

FATHER DUFFY MEMORIAL

(Charles Keck, 1937) Cast in bronze atop a polished granite base and cross, Father Duffy was a figure straight out of Damon Runyon. Duffy, whose parish was honky-tonk Times Square in the 1920s, was chaplain to the Fighting 69th in World War I. *Duffy Sq. (Broadway between 46th and 47th Sts.), Theater District. Subway: 49th St.; 42nd St./Times Sq.*

9 *c-1*

EAGLES AND PREY

(Kristin Fratin, 1850) This is one of Central Park's earliest sculptures. *Central Park northwest of the Mall. Subway: B, C to 72nd St.*

9 *c-1*

THE FALCONER

(George B. Simonds, 1871) This bronze statue rises a graceful 10 ft. above Central Park. *72nd St. Transverse. Subway: B, C to 72nd St.*

7 *a-5*

FIREMEN'S MEMORIAL

(Attilio Piccirilli, 1912) The representations of Duty and Courage pay tribute to New York's Bravest, and the bronze plaque is a tribute to their horses, which once pulled the apparatus for the city's Fire Department. *Riverside Dr. and 100th St., Upper West Side. Subway: 1, 9 to 103rd St.*

10 *e-6*

BENJAMIN FRANKLIN

(Ernst Plassmann, 1872) Here the founding father holds a copy of the newspaper he edited, the *Pennsylvania Gazette*. *Park Row at Nassau and Spruce Sts., Lower Manhattan. Subway: Brooklyn Bridge/City Hall.*

9 *d-3*

DORIS C. FREEDMAN PLAZA

Old meets new. Not far from such New York landmarks as the Plaza Hotel,

Saint-Gaudin's monument to General Sherman, and the Pulitzer Fountain (*see below*), the southeast corner of Central Park has become a showcase for outdoor sculpture by contemporary artists. The Public Art Fund curates rotating exhibits here of oversize works by the likes of Keith Haring and Tom Otterness. *5th Ave. and 60th St., Midtown. 212/980–4575. Subway: N or R to 5th Ave.*

9 *d-2*

FRIEDSAM MEMORIAL CAROUSEL

You might not think that merry-go-rounds class as art or sculpture, but Central Park's carousel—originally built in 1903 and operated at a Coney Island amusement park (it was moved to the park in 1952)—is considered a fabulous example of turn-of-the-20th-century folk art. And, hey, it's interactive, too. While the organ plays, you can ride the colorful hand-carved wooden horsies for $1. *Central Park at Center Dr. and the 65th St. transverse, 212/879–0244. Apr.–Oct., weekdays 10–6, weekends 10–6:30; Nov.–Mar., weekends 10–4:30, weather permitting. Subway: 66th Street/Lincoln Center.*

10 *e-1*

MOHANDAS GANDHI

(Kantilal B. Patel, 1986) The famous Indian nationalist is memorialized in Union Square. *Union Sq. (Broadway and 14th St.), Flatiron District. Subway: 14th St./Union Sq.*

9 *f-4*

GOOD DEFEATS EVIL

(Zurab Tsereteli, 1990) The dragon that St. George is spearing was made of slices of what were once Soviet SS-20 and American Pershing ballistic missiles, chopped up in accordance with the 1988 treaty eliminating intermediate-range missiles. The statue was a gift from the Soviet government. *United Nations (1st Ave. between 42nd and 48th Sts.), Midtown. Subway: 42nd St./Grand Central.*

10 *e-6*

HORACE GREELEY

(John Quincy Adams Ward, 1916) Seated in an armchair, this bronze figure of Greeley holds a copy of the *New York Tribune*—fair enough, since he owned it. *City Hall Park (Broadway and Park Row), Lower Manhattan. Subway: Brooklyn Bridge/City Hall.*

Finally, a travel companion that doesn't snore on the plane or eat all your peanuts.

When traveling, your MCI WorldCom℠ Card is the best way to keep in touch. Our operators speak your language, so they'll be able to connect you back home—no matter where your travels take you. Plus, your MCI WorldCom Card is easy to use, and even earns you frequent flyer miles* every time you use it. When you add in our great rates, you get something even more valuable: peace-of-mind. So go ahead. Travel the world. MCI WorldCom just brought it a whole lot closer.

You can even sign up today at www.mci.com/worldphone or ask your operator to make a collect call to 1-410-314-2938.

EASY TO CALL WORLDWIDE

1 Dial 1-800-888-8000.
2 Dial or give the operator your MCI WorldCom Card number.
3 Dial or give the number you're calling.

EARN FREQUENT FLYER MILES

American Airlines®
A'Advantage®

Continental Airlines
OnePass

▲ **Delta Air Lines**
SkyMiles®

HAWAIIANMILES
HAWAIIAN AIRLINES

MIDWEST EXPRESS AIRLINES
PROGRAM PARTNER

SOUTHWEST AIRLINES®
RAPIDREWARDS
A SYMBOL OF FREEDOM®

◢ MILEAGE PLUS®
United Airlines

U·S AIRWAYS
DIVIDEND MILES

*You will earn flight credits in the Southwest Airlines Rapid Rewards Program. All airline names and logos are proprietary marks of the respective airlines. All airline program rules and conditions apply.

Distinctive guides packed with up-to-date expert
advice and smart choices for every type of traveler.

Fodor's. For the world of ways you travel.

`10` e-6

NATHAN HALE

(Frederick MacMonnies, 1890) This imagined bronze portrait of Hale depicts a very real hero, who was executed by the British as a spy in 1776. *City Hall Park (see above).*

`7` d-7

ALEXANDER HAMILTON

(Carl Conrads, 1880) This granite statue of the famed Federalist was presented to the city by Hamilton's son John C. Hamilton. *Central Park, East Dr. near 83rd St. Subway: 4, 5, 6 to 86th St.*

`11` d-2

ALEXANDER LYMAN HOLLEY

(John Quincy Adams Ward, 1889) Holley was an American inventor; his bronze likeness is considered one of this prolific sculptor's best public works. *Washington Sq. Park, (at foot of 5th Ave.), Greenwich Village. Subway: 8th St.; West 4th St./Washington Sq.*

`5` b-3

HUDSON MEMORIAL COLUMN

(Walter Cook, 1909) This 100-ft-high column was commissioned to commemorate the 300th anniversary of Hudson's discovery of the river down below. It's topped with a 16-ft-high bronze statue of Hudson himself (Karl Gruppe and Karl Bitter, 1938). *Henry Hudson Memorial Park at Kappock Ave. and Independence Pkwy., Bronx. Subway: 1, 9 to 225th St.*

`9` c-1

INDIAN HUNTER

(John Quincy Adams Ward, 1866) Initially cast in plaster, this realistic bronze group grew out of sketches made during a visit to the American West. It was Central Park's first statue by an American sculptor, and it led to countless commissions for the prolific Ward. *Central Park northwest of the Mall. Subway: B, C to 72nd St.*

`7` a-6

JOAN OF ARC

(Anna Vaughn Hyatt Huntington, 1915) This bronze statue on a granite pedestal contains stone fragments from the tower where Joan was imprisoned in Rouen, and from Rheims Cathedral. It was the city's first public work to be erected to honor a woman and the first

by a woman sculptor. *Riverside Dr. and 93rd St., Upper West Side. Subway: 1, 2, 3, 9 to 96th St.*

`10` e-1

LAFAYETTE

(Frederic-Auguste Bartholdi, 1876) Quoting the Marquis de Lafayette, the inscription for the statue—by the same French sculptor who gave New York the Statue of Liberty (*see below*)—reads: "As soon as I heard of American independence my heart was enlisted." *Union Sq. (Broadway and 14th St.), Flatiron District. Subway: 14th St./Union Sq.*

`4` f-2

ABRAHAM LINCOLN

(Henry Kirke Brown, 1869) Located in Brooklyn's Prospect Park, this statue is said to be the first of Lincoln cast after his assassination. Yet history has not been kind to it. Lincoln's right hand points to a manuscript that is now, alas, missing. And the nearby Kate Wollman Memorial Rink—a 20th-century addition to the park—has directed pedestrian and skating traffic toward Lincoln's back. For the sake of both art and history, Honest Abe deserves better treatment. *Concert Grove, Prospect Park, Brooklyn. Subway: D, Q to Prospect Park.*

`9` d-5

LIONS

(Edward Clark Potter, 1911) The closest thing New York has to a mascot, these stone lions are a matched pair. Dubbed Patience and Fortitude by Mayor Fiorello LaGuardia, they are dear to the hearts of New Yorkers and look especially smart at Christmastime, when they are bedecked with red-trimmed wreaths. *New York Public Library, 5th Ave. and 41st St., Midtown. Subway: B, D, F, Q to 42nd St.*

`9` c-3

MAINE MONUMENT

(Attilio Piccirilli, 1913) A Beaux-Arts memorial of gleaming gilt-bronze equestrian figures atop an imposing limestone pedestal, this dramatic work—guarding the southwest entrance to Central Park—commemorates those who perished on the battleship *Maine* in 1898. *Columbus Circle (Broadway and 59th St.), Midtown. Subway: 59th St./Columbus Circle.*

4 e-1

MANHATTAN & BROOKLYN

(Daniel Chester French, 1916) This symbolic representation of the two boroughs originally stood at the Brooklyn end of the Manhattan Bridge. It now graces the entryway to a world-class museum. *Brooklyn Museum of Art, 200 Eastern Pkwy. (at Washington Ave.), Park Slope, Brooklyn. Subway: Eastern Pkwy./Brooklyn Museum.*

9 d-1

MOTHER GOOSE

(Frederick G. R. Roth, 1938) This 8-ft granite embodiment of the feathered matriarch stands on the site of the old Central Park Casino. *Central Park, East Dr. near 72nd St. Subway: 68th St./Hunter College.*

10 f-8

NEW YORK VIETNAM VETERANS MEMORIAL

(Pete Wormser, William Fellows) Unveiled on May 6, 1985, 10 years after the war ended, New York's Vietnam Veterans Memorial is a translucent wall of glass blocks, 14 ft high and 70 ft long, inscribed with excerpts of letters to and from those who served. Only some of those commemorated here came home. Visitors leave candles, notes, and flowers on the granite shelves. *Vietnam Veterans Plaza, 55 Water St. (near Broad St.), Lower Manhattan. Subway: Whitehall St./South Ferry.*

9 e-2

107TH INFANTRY

(Karl M. Illava, 1927) An alumnus of the 107th in World War I, the sculptor includes himself in this bronze depiction of valiant doughboys. *5th Ave. and 67th St., Upper East Side. Subway: 68th St./Hunter College.*

9 f-4

PEACE

(Antun Augustincic, 1954) This heroic bronze statue was presented to the U.N. by the government of Yugoslavia. *United Nations Gardens, near 1st Ave. and 46th St., Midtown. Subway: 42nd St./Grand Central.*

12 e-2

PRISON SHIP MARTYRS' MONUMENT

(McKim, Mead & White, 1908) The world's tallest Doric column—148 ft, 8 inches—is a memorial to the American patriots who died on British prison ships anchored in New York Harbor during the Revolution. *Ft. Greene Park, Brooklyn. Subway: Atlantic Ave.*

9 d-4

PROMETHEUS

(Paul Manship, 1934) Cast in bronze and finished in gold leaf, the fire thief is set in a flashing fountain-pool overseeing ice-skaters in winter and alfresco diners in summer. *Lower Plaza, Rockefeller Center, 5th–6th Aves. between 50th and 51st Sts., Midtown. Subway: 47th–50th Sts., Rockefeller Center.*

9 d-3

PULITZER FOUNTAIN

(Carrère & Hastings; sculptor: Karl Bitter, 1916) This fountain became a legendary icon of the Roaring '20s once F. Scott and Zelda Fitzgerald went wading in it. Originally built of limestone, it eventually deteriorated to the point of crumbling, and was virtually rebuilt in more-durable granite. The goddess Pomona was given a new patina. *Grand Army Plaza (5th Ave. between 58th and 59th Sts.), Midtown. Subway: N, R to 5th Ave.*

10 c-6

THE REAL WORLD

(Tom Otterness, 1992) In this whimsical bronze sculpture garden in Hudson River Park, lilliputian bronze figures frolic along a trail of oversize pennies, playfully poking fun at the money-making activities in the nearby World Financial Center. *North end of Hudson River Park, near Chambers Sts., TriBeCa. Subway: Chambers St.*

9 a-1

ELEANOR ROOSEVELT

(Penelope Jencks, 1996) Unless you count fictional characters like Alice in Wonderland (*see above*), there aren't many statues commemorating women in the Big Apple. It's fitting, though, that the first monument commissioned to depict an American woman in a New York City park should be of former first lady Eleanor Roosevelt (1884–1962)—both a women's rights advocate and a longtime New Yorker. Mrs. Roosevelt gave many of her years to public service, most notably as U.N. Human Rights Commissioner during her tenure as U.S. delegate to the United Nations, and this statue is a suitable tribute. Gracing the southern entrance to Riverside Park, the 8-ft-high bronze is posed deep in thought. *Riverside Park (at W. 72nd St. and Riverside Dr.), Upper West Side. Subway: 1, 2, 3, 9 to 72nd St.*

7 *c-8*

THEODORE ROOSEVELT MEMORIAL

(James Earle Fraser, 1940) Ride 'em, Teddy! At 16 ft tall, this bronze group—with president Theodore Roosevelt astride a sinewy steed—is one of the largest and best equestrian statues in the world. *American Museum of Natural History, Central Park W and 79th St., Upper West Side. Subway: B, C to 81st St.*

4 *e-1*

SCULPTURE GARDEN

The Brooklyn Museum's outdoor garden displays architectural sculpture and ornamentation salvaged from demolition sites around the city—most notably the original Penn Station. *Brooklyn Museum of Art, 200 Eastern Pkwy. (at Washington Ave.), Park Slope, Brooklyn. Subway: Eastern Pkwy./Brooklyn Museum.*

9 *c-2*

SEVENTH REGIMENT MEMORIAL

(John Quincy Adams Ward, 1873) The 58 members of this New York State regiment who died in the Civil War are memorialized here. *Central Park, West Dr. near 67th St. Subway: B, C to 72nd St.*

9 *e-7*

WILLIAM H. SEWARD

(Randolph Rogers, 1876) Truth or fiction? Word on the street is that the sculptor set Secretary of State Seward's head on President Lincoln's body—for which he already had molds from another project in Philadelphia. *Madison Sq. Park (5th–Madison Aves., 23rd–26th Sts.), Murray Hill. Subway: 6, N, R to 23rd St.*

9 *d-3*

SHERMAN MONUMENT

(Augustus Saint-Gaudens, 1903) A graceful equestrian group depicting William Tecumseh Sherman on horseback preceded by an all-powerful angel, this bronze tribute to the Civil War general is one of several monuments towering over the southern edge of Central Park. It was one of the last works created by Saint-Gaudens, who in the latter decades of the 1800s set the stage for works that blended sculpture and landscape architecture. *Grand Army Plaza, 5th Ave. and 59th St., Midtown. Subway: N, R to 5th Ave.*

3 *d-3*

SOCRATES SCULPTURE PARK

Once a local dump site, this 4.2-acre park was reclaimed by local artists in the 1980s as a venue for outdoor sculpture. Now officially a city park, it displays huge installation works, with the Manhattan skyline and East River as backdrops. *Vernon Blvd. at Broadway, Long Island City, Queens. 718/956–1819. Daily 10 AM–sunset. Subway: N to Broadway.*

7 *a-6*

SOLDIERS' AND SAILORS' MEMORIAL

(Paul E.M. Duboy) Built in 1902 to commemorate the Civil War dead, this 96-ft white marble column along Riverside Park was fashioned after Athens's monument to Lysicrates. *Riverside Dr. and 89th St., Upper West Side. Subway: 1, 9 to 86th St.*

4 *e-1*

SOLDIERS' AND SAILORS' MEMORIAL ARCH

(John H. Duncan, 1892) Designed after the Arc de Triomphe in Paris as a monument to Civil War veterans, this 80-ft-high, 80-ft-wide limestone arch dominates a busy traffic circle next to Brooklyn's Prospect Park, creating one of the city's grandest streetscapes. A fantastic bronze sculpture of a four-horse chariot (symbolizing victory) by Frederick MacMonnies adorns the top. Occasionally on weekends, Prospect Park's Urban Park Rangers open the interior stairways to the public, and the views from the roof are marvelous. *Grand Army Plaza at the intersection of Propect Park W, Eastern Pkwy., and Flatbush and Vanderbilt Aves., Park Slope, Brooklyn. 718/965–8999. Subway: Grand Army Plaza.*

1 *c-6*

STATUE OF LIBERTY NATIONAL MONUMENT

Probably the most famous statue in the world, *Liberty Enlightening the World* was sculpted by Frederic-Auguste Bartholdi and presented to the United States as a gift from France in 1886. Since then she has since become a near-universal symbol of freedom, standing a proud 152 ft high on top of an 89-ft pedestal (executed by Richard Morris Hunt) on an island in New York Harbor. Gustav Eiffel designed the statue's iron skeleton, through which visitors can climb spiral stairs to reach the statue's crown (*see Viewpoints, below*). In anticipation of her centennial, Liberty underwent a long-overdue restoration in the mid-'80s and emerged with great fanfare on July 4, 1986, more beautiful and awe-inspiring than ever. *Liberty Island, New York Harbor, off Lower Manhattan. Ferry tickets: Castle Clinton, Battery Park, 212/269–5755. Admission: $7 adults, $6 seniors, $3 children under 17. Boats leave for the island daily 8:30–4:30, every 20 minutes. For statue information, call the National Parks Service, 212/363–3200. Subway: South Ferry.*

7 *d-8*

STILL HUNT

(Edward Kemeys, 1883) Perched on one of the park's natural outcroppings, this crouched bronze panther is so realistic that you may feel the cat has snuck up on you. *Central Park, East Dr. near 76th St. Subway: 77th St.*

7 *a-4*

STRAUS MEMORIAL

(Henry Augustus Lukeman, 1915) Although women were offered space in the *Titanic*'s lifeboats, Ida Straus chose to stay with her husband, Isador, and both perished on the doomed ocean liner's maiden voyage. The philanthropist couple had lived near this memorial. *Broadway and 106th St., Upper West Side. Subway: 1, 9 to 103rd St.*

10 *f-1*

PETER STUYVESANT

(Gertrude Vanderbilt Whitney, 1941) This life-size bronze was cast by the founder of the Whitney Museum. Standing on what was once part of his farm, it depicts New York's last Dutch governor, the peg-legged Peter Stuyvesant, buried at nearby St. Mark's Church in-the-Bowery (*see Churches & Synagogues and Haunted Places, above*). *Stuyvesant Sq. (1st to 3rd Aves., between 15th and 17th Sts.), East Village. Subway: 3rd Ave.; 14th St./Union Sq.*

SUBWAY STATION ART

As part of the ongoing capital improvement program for the subway system, historic subway mosaics and ceramics are being restored and many new works commissioned. One of the most nicely restored stations is the East Village's Astor Place, which is decorated with ceramic tiles of beavers (symbolizing how the wealthy Astor family made their fortune in the 19th-century fur trade). One of the most impressive new works, found in the Houston Street station on the "1" line, is a series of highly detailed, colorful glass mosaic "windows" (Deborah Brown, 1994). Featuring undersea creatures, such as sea turtles, the mosaics suggest what might be glimpsed if the subway traveled underwater instead of underground.

9 *g-4*

SWORDS INTO PLOWSHARES

(Evgeniy Vuchetich, 1958) This dramatic, 9-ft-tall bronze was a gift from the U.S.S.R. *United Nations Gardens, near 1st Ave. and 46th St., Midtown. Subway: 42nd St./Grand Central.*

7 *d-8*

TEMPEST

(Milton Hebald, 1966) Depicting Shakespeare's Prospero, the *Tempest* monument is dedicated to Joseph Papp, the theatrical guru who brought free Shakespeare to the park. This statue violated an 1876 law prohibiting commemorative statues until five years after the subject's death, but no one complained and Papp continued to work his magic on New York theater for 25 years after it was erected. *Central Park, near Delacorte Theater (enter at W. 81st St.). Subway: B, C to 72nd St. or 81st St.*

7 *d-5*

ALBERT BERTIL THORVALSDEN, SELF-PORTRAIT

(Donated by Denmark, 1894) Cast from the marble original, this self-portrait by the great neoclassical sculptor was donated by the Danish in recognition of Thorvalsden's influence on early American sculpture. *Central Park near E. 96th St. Subway: 6 to 96th St.*

3 *h-2*

UNISPHERE

(Peter Muller-Munk, 1964) Made for the 1964–1965 World's Fair in Flushing Meadows-Corona Park, the truly massive Unisphere is a 140-ft-high, 380-ton steel globe of the Earth. Its gleaming frame—famously adorning the back entrance to the U.S.T.A. Tennis Center and pictured in countless TV commercials—shows latitude and longitude lines and the seven continents. *Flushing Meadows–Corona Park, Queens, near 54th Ave. Subway: Shea Stadium.*

7 *d-4*

UNTERMEYER FOUNTAIN (DANCING GIRLS)

(Walter Schott, 1947) These beautifully sculpted, spirited maidens from Untermeyer's Yonkers estate are among the showpieces of Central Park's only European-style garden. (*See* Botanical Gardens *in* Chapter 3.) *Central Park, Conservatory Gardens, 5th Ave. and 104th St., Upper East Side. Subway: 6 to 103rd St.*

9 *b-1*

GIUSEPPI VERDI

(Pasquale Civiletti, 1906) Made of Carrara marble, this statue in triangular Verdi Square commemorates the great 19th-century composer. It's flanked by figures from Verdi's operas *Aida, Otello, and Falstaff. Verdi Sq., Broadway and 73rd St., Upper West Side. Subway: 1, 2, 3, 9 to 72nd St.*

10 *e-8*

GIOVANNI DA VERRAZANO

(Ettore Ximenes, 1909) Italian-Americans erected this monument to honor the captain of the ship that first sighted New York Harbor in 1524. *Battery Park, Battery Pl., and State St., Lower Manhattan. Subway: Bowling Green; South Ferry.*

10 *e-1*

GEORGE WASHINGTON

(Henry Kirke Brown, with John Quincy Adams Ward, 1856) Washington on horseback marches beautifully into battle, in bronze. One of the oldest public sculptures surviving in the city, Washington and his horse were commissioned by Yankee merchants when the South first threatened to secede from the Union. *Union Sq. (Broadway and 14th St.), Flatiron District. Subway: 14th St./Union Sq.*

10 *e-7*

GEORGE WASHINGTON

(John Quincy Adams Ward, 1883) Occupying the site where Washington was inaugurated in 1789 as the first president of the United States, the statue is said to contain a stone (in its pedestal) from the spot where Washington stood. *Steps of Federal Hall, Wall and Broad Sts., Lower Manhattan. Subway: Wall St.*

11 *d-2*

WASHINGTON ARCH

(McKim, Mead & White, 1892) First erected in wood in 1889 for the centennial of Washington's inauguration, this marble arch was designed by famed New York architect Stanford White. The statues, *Washington at War* (1916) and *Washington at Peace* (1917), were added later; bodybuilder Charles Atlas is said to have modeled for the civilian version of Washington. *Washington Sq. Park (at foot of 5th Ave.), Greenwich Village. Subway: 8th St.; West 4th St./Washington Square.*

9 *c-1*

DANIEL WEBSTER

(Thomas Ball, 1876) The famed American statesman and orator is here adorned with his own memorable maxim "Liberty and union, now and forever, one and inseparable." *Central Park, West Dr. near 72nd St., Upper West Side. Subway: B, C to 72nd St.*

VIEWPOINTS

One of the best ways to acquaint yourself with New York City's famous skyline is to join it in the clouds.

10 *g-6*

BROOKLYN BRIDGE

No bridge in the world had an elevated promenade when John Roebling conceived one for his bridge in 1869 (*see* Bridges, *above*). Dedicated exclusively to pedestrians (and now bicycles and Rollerbladers), the boardwalk was designed to allow uninterrupted views in every direction. When the Great East River Bridge (as it was then called) was opened, in 1883, 150,300 pedestrians paid a penny each to walk the mile across it. The walk is free now, and the view considerably different, but the experience is no less magnificent. Don't miss this trek, even if you only go to the first tower; if you do cross to Brooklyn, wander over to the Brooklyn Heights Promenade (see below) for another famous view. *City Hall Park, Manhattan, to Cadman Plaza W, Brooklyn. Subway: Brooklyn Bridge/City Hall; High St./Brooklyn Bridge.*

12 *a-3*

BROOKLYN HEIGHTS PROMENADE

Strolling, sitting on a classic park bench, and watching the sunset on this riverbank esplanade are divine, backed by an incomparable, bird's-eye view of the Manhattan skyline. (*See Historic Buildings & Areas, above.*) *1 block west of Columbia Heights from Remsen to Orange Sts. Subway: Clark St.*

9 *d-6*

EMPIRE STATE BUILDING

At 102 stories (1,250 ft), it's now only the seventh-tallest building in the world, but it's still the most elegant aerie. The observation deck—outdoors on the 86th floor—has 360-degree views, with 80-mi visibility on clear days. The views of the city's incomparable architecture, toy-size taxis jockeying on the streets below, and—at night—New York's twinkling lights never fail to take one's breath away. For a different kind of view, stop off on the second floor and take the New York Skyride, a big-screen "thrill ride" that simulates a flight over New York City. (*See Architecture, above*). *350 5th Ave. (at 34th St.), 212/736–3100. Observatory admission: $6 adults; $3 seniors and children under 12; free children under 5. Open daily 9:30 AM–midnight; last elevator leaves at 11:30 PM. New York Skyride, 212/279–9777. Admission $11.50 adults and teens, $8.50 seniors and children under 12. Open 10 AM–10 PM. Subway: 34th St./Herald Sq.*

7 *e-7*

METROPOLITAN MUSEUM OF ART ROOFTOP SCULPTURE GARDEN (THE IRIS AND B. GERALD CANTOR ROOF GARDEN)

Topping off the Lila Acheson Wallace wing, the Met's rooftop sculpture garden overlooks Central Park, with Midtown and the Upper West Side as beautiful backdrops. Come at twilight and watch the city's lights slowly and glamorously emerge as the sky darkens. (*See Art Museums, above.*) *5th Ave. and 82nd St., Upper East Side. Sculpture Garden open May–Oct., weather permitting. Subway: 4, 5, 6 to 86th St.*

7 *a-2*

RIVERSIDE CHURCH

The church's observation platform affords a lovely, unobstructed view of the Hudson River, New Jersey Palisades, and George Washington Bridge from 392 ft. (*See Churches & Synagogues, above.*) *Riverside Dr. at 120th St., Upper West Side, 212/870–6700. Admission: $2 adults, $1 seniors and students. Open Tues.–Sat. 11–4, Sun. 12:15–4. Subway: 116th St./Columbia Univ.*

10 *f-7*

SOUTH STREET SEAPORT, PIER 17

This shopping and dining pier juts 500 yards into the East River, offering superb views of the Brooklyn Bridge and the harbor. Sunset is the best time to visit; head to the far end of the pier, where you can sit right on the river on the upper or lower promenade. (*See History Museums, above, and Malls in Chapter 2.*) *Fulton St. and East River, Lower Manhattan. Subway: 2, 3 to Fulton St.; Broadway–Nassau St.*

10 *e-8*

STATEN ISLAND FERRY

See Boat Tours, *below.*

1 *c-6*

STATUE OF LIBERTY NATIONAL MONUMENT

The 20-minute boat ride to resplendent Lady Liberty (*see Statues & Public Art, above*) provides lovely vistas of New York Harbor. Once you're there, the view from Liberty's crown is unforgettable— just be prepared for a 1- to 1½-hour wait to ascend. *New York Harbor, off Lower Manhattan. Ferry tickets: Castle Clinton, Battery Park, 212/269–5755. Admission: $7 adults, $6 seniors, $3 children under 17. Boats leave for the island daily 8:30–4:30, every 20 minutes. Subway: South Ferry.*

10 *d-6*

WORLD TRADE CENTER, OBSERVATION DECK

At 1,377 ft tall, the World Trade Center's Twin Towers are New York's tallest buildings; the "Top of the World" observation deck on the 107th floor of the south tower is ¼-mi high, and its Rooftop Observatory, located a few floors up, is the world's highest open-air viewing platform. Day or night the view is literally breathtaking (*see* Architecture, *above*). On the 107th floor of the north tower, the Windows on the World restaurant affords the most luscious excuse for lingering over the twinkling lights (*see* Continental *in* Chapter 1). *South Tower (No. 2), Lower Manhattan, 212/323–2340. Admission: $12.50 adults, $10.75 students with valid I.D., $9.50 seniors, $6.25 children 6–12, free children under 6. Open Sept.–May, daily 9:30–9:30; June and Aug., daily 9:30 AM–11:30 PM. Subway: Cortlandt St./World Trade Center.*

guided tours

AIR TOURS

9 *a-7*

LIBERTY HELICOPTER

Fasten your seat belt and choose from different flights overlooking sights from the Statue of Liberty and Brooklyn Bridge to Midtown's skyscrapers. These pilot-narrated tours range from the 4½ minute "Lady Liberty" to the 15-minute "Great Adventure," which includes views of all five boroughs. Get a whole new angle on life. *Heliport: 12th Ave. and 30th St. on the Hudson River, Garment District, 212/465–8905. Open daily 9–9 (weather permitting). Subway: 34th St./Penn Station.*

BOAT TOURS

10 *f-7*

THE BEAST

Reaching speeds up to 45 m.p.h., this speedboat takes you on a wild 30-minute ride around the harbor. *Pier 16 (Fulton and South Sts.), South Street Seaport, 212/563–3200. Season: May–Oct. Subway: Fulton St.*

9 *a-5*

CIRCLE LINE CRUISES

Manhattan is an island, after all, and this 35-mi, three-hour cruise circumnavigates it, offering odd views and a funny and informative commentary. The cruise also offers a much appreciated chance to put your feet up and relax while seeing the sights. For a more romantic ride,

try the 8 PM "Harbor Lights" cruise from the same location. *Pier 83 (12th Ave. and 42nd St.), Hell's Kitchen, 212/563–3200. Subway: A, C, E to 42nd St.*

1 *c-6*

ELLIS ISLAND NATIONAL MONUMENT

See Historic Buildings & Areas, *above.*

10 *d-6*

PETREL

Sail New York Harbor on the same spectacular 70-ft yawl that JFK sailed as President; just take care to reserve two days in advance. Cruises last one–two hours. *North Cove Yacht Harbor (in front of the World Financial Center, south of Vesey St.), Battery Park City, 212/825–1976. Subway: Cortlandt St.*

10 *f-7*

PIONEER

Take a two-hour sail on a 102-ft twin-mast schooner built in 1885. *Pier 16, South Street Seaport (Fulton and South Sts.), Lower Manhattan, 212/748–8600. Sails May–Sept. Subway: Fulton St.*

10 *f-7*

SEAPORT MUSIC CRUISES

When it's warm, two-hour evening cruises feature live jazz, blues, and funk, as well as DJ'ed dance parties. *Pier 16, South Street Seaport (Fulton and South Sts.), Lower Manhattan, 212/630–8888. Sails May–Sept. Subway: Fulton St.*

10 *e-8*

STATEN ISLAND FERRY

This 25-minute boat ride crosses Upper New York Bay and offers wonderfully panoramic views—and it's absolutely free. *Whitehall St. at State St., Lower Manhattan; foot of Bay Street, St. George, Staten Island, 718/727–2508. Departures: usually every 30 min, otherwise every 20 min. during rush hour, and every hour after 12:30 AM and in the morning on weekends. Subway: South Ferry, Bowling Green, and Whitehall St.*

1 *c-6*

STATUE OF LIBERTY NATIONAL MONUMENT

See Viewpoints, *above.*

9 *d-1*

VENETIAN GONDOLA

What to do with that breathless summer evening? Try gliding the waters of Central Park Lake in an authentic Venetian gondola—the 37½-ft *Daughter of Venice*—expertly navigated by a traditionally attired gondolier. It's expensive, but it's pure magic. The gondola can hold up to six people. *Loeb Boathouse, Central Park, near E. 74th St., 212/517–3623. Available May–Sept., nightly 5–10. Subway: 77th St.*

9 *a-5*

WORLD YACHT CRUISES

These luxury restaurant yachts offer three-hour, four-course dinner and dancing cruises around the tip of Manhattan. You'll need to reserve in advance. *Pier 81 (12th Ave. and 41st St.), Hell's Kitchen, 212/630–8100. Subway: A, C, E to 42nd St.*

BUS TOURS

Rise just a bit above it all—physically, anyway—in a comfortable, air-conditioned bus. Commentaries are given en route.

9 *c-5*

GRAY LINE NEW YORK

Great for tourists, Gray Line offers more than 20 bus tours of New York City, ranging from quick, two-hour trips to all-day excursions. A popular option is the double-decker "Hop on, hop off" bus, which shuttles visitors to major sights around town and allows them to linger at each one as long as they like. *Port Authority Bus Terminal, North Wing, 8th Ave. and 42nd St., Hell's Kitchen, 212/397–2600. Subway: A, C, E to 42nd St.*

9 *c-5*

HARLEM SPIRITUALS

This outfit offers four-hour Sunday gospel trips to Harlem, as well as bus tours of Brooklyn and the Bronx. *690 8th Ave.(at 43rd St.), Theater District, 212/757–0425. Subway: A, C, E to 42nd St.*

9 *b-5*

KRAMER'S REALITY TOUR

Although "Seinfeld" addicts now can only get their fix from daily re-runs, the real-life Kramer is still putting on a good show. The irascible Cosmo Kramer is based on real-life New Yorker, Kenny

Kramer, who, lacking no commercial spirit, started his own tour company to take visitors past the show's New York sites. You'll visit the real-life Soup Nazi, and, of course Tom's Restaurant, where Jerry, Elaine, and George vent their respective spleens. Tours only on weekends. Reserve in advance. *Pulse Theater, 432 W. 42nd St. (between 9th and 10th Aves.), Hell's Kitchen, 212/268–5525. Subway: A, C, E to 42nd St.*

9 *b-2*

METROPOLITAN OPERA BACKSTAGE

Opera singers love this six-tier, 3,800-seat auditorium—and so does the Metropolitan Opera Guild. Their tours offer a fascinating backstage look at the often bustling scenery and costume shops, auditorium, stage area, and rehearsal facilities. They don't promise Pavarotti, but you never know. Reserve in advance. *Lincoln Center Plaza (Broadway at 64th St.), Upper West Side, 212/769–7020. Tours depart Oct.–June, weekdays 3:45, Sat. 10 AM. Subway: 66th St./Lincoln Center.*

9 *d-4*

NBC STUDIO TOUR

NBC has hung its hat in the GE Building for over 50 years. Daily hour-long tours let visitors onto the sets of "Saturday Night Live," "The Today Show," "Late Night with Conan O'Brien," and "The Rosie O'Donnell Show." *30 Rockefeller Plaza (50th St. between 5th and 6th Aves.), Midtown, 212/664–7174. Tours 9:30–4:30. Subway: 47th–50th Sts./Rockefeller Center.*

9 *d-6*

NEW YORK DOUBLEDECKER TOURS

These authentic London double-decker buses make a loop, stopping every half-hour at different tourist sites. Passengers board and re-board at their leisure. The downtown loop covers the Empire State Building, Greenwich Village, Chinatown, the World Trade Center, the South Street Seaport, and the Statue of Liberty. The uptown loop hits Central Park, the Metropolitan Museum, the Cathedral of St. John the Divine, and more. *Empire State Building (350 5th Ave., at 34th St.), Garment District, 212/967–6008. Subway: 34th St./Herald Sq.*

10 g-3

SCHAPIRO'S WINERY

Napa Valley it's not, but Schapiro's, founded in 1899, is Manhattan's only working winery. Its motto (no joke): "The wine you can cut with a knife." Tour the wine cellars, see the presses, and taste the wine. *126 Rivington St. (at Essex St.), Lower East Side, 212/674–4404. Tours depart hourly Sun. 11–4. Subway: Delancey St.*

WALKING TOURS

ADVENTURE ON A SHOESTRING

This group's motto is "Exploring the world within our reach, within our means." Jaunts include historic walking tours of Chinatown, Hell's Kitchen, "elegant" Gramercy Park, and "haunted" Greenwich Village. What makes this outfit unique is the price: $5 per person, the same price they charged when they started up in 1963. *212/265–2663.*

BIG APPLE GREETER

Who says New York isn't welcoming? Friendly New Yorkers show the ins and out of their city on two- to four-hour jaunts on foot and via public tansport through neighborhoods of your choice in all five boroughs. And it's free. *212/ 669–8159.*

BIG ONION WALKING TOURS

Focusing on urban history and the city's multiethnic neighborhoods, Big Onion—founded in 1990 by a group of Columbia University graduate students—leads two-hour walking tours in Manhattan Thurs.–Sun. One of the most popular is "The Multiethnic Eating Tour," on which you can sample the Lower East Side's mozzarella, pickles, and dim sum. *212/439–1090.*

BROOKLYN CENTER FOR THE URBAN ENVIRONMENT

These unique walking tours traverse Brooklyn's lesser-known neighborhoods and occasionally include boat rides on such unlikely waterways as the Gowanus Canal, focusing always on the borough's unique history, culture, and ecology. *718/ 788–8500.*

9 e-5

GRAND TOUR

This free Grand Central neighborhood tour, sponsored by the Grand Central Partnership, focuses on the area's architecture and history. The walk includes Grand Central Terminal and its environs: the Art Deco interiors of the Chanin and Chrysler buildings, the Helmsley Building, and more. *Midtown, 212/818–1777.*

HERITAGE TRAILS

Explore 400 years of history from Colonial New York to the present day. In addition to several guided tours of Lower Manhattan, heritage trails gives away free maps of downtown marked with self-guided trails. *212/269–1500.*

JOYCE GOLD HISTORY TOURS OF NEW YORK

Historian and author Joyce Gold's enthusiastic and highly informative tours cover over 20 different New York City neighborhoods, from the financial district to Harlem. *212/242–5762.*

9 d-6

MIRACLE TOUR OF 34TH STREET

The 34th Street Partnership offers free weekly walking tours of the architecture and history of this endlessly colorful street and its surroundings. *Garment District, 212/818–1777.*

MUNICIPAL ART SOCIETY

New York's premier preservationist group leads several walking tours each week, examining current happenings in city architecture and neighborhoods in light of their social history. *212/935–3960 or 212/439–1049.*

MUSEUM OF THE CITY OF NEW YORK

For over 30 years the museum has sponsored leisurely explorations of New York neighborhoods, highlighting architectural and social history. *212/534–1672.*

NEW YORK CITY CULTURAL WALKING TOURS

Longtime guide Alfred Pommer escorts folks around every Sunday at 2 to such theme 'hoods as Millionaire's Mile and Little Italy. He also organizes private tours for groups and individuals from a menu of over 25 different walks, ranging from "Gargoyles in Manhattan" to an Irish-heritage tour. *212/979–2388.*

92ND STREET Y

The Y organizes fascinating treks through neighborhoods of historic, social, artistic, and architectural importance throughout the five boroughs. *212/996–1100.*

RADICAL WALKING TOURS

If you're into movements and causes, revolutionary thinking, or the anarchic ideal, Radical Walking Tours are for you. They cast a different light on the history of New York and the figures who have tried to rouse its rabble, from Thomas Paine to Ethel and Julius Rosenberg. *718/492–0069.*

STREET SMARTS NEW YORK

Street Smarts sponsors several excursions through downtown Manhattan each weekend, ranging from daytime tours of the Ladies' Mile Historic District to evening rambles through "Ghostly Greenwich Village." *212/969–8262.*

URBAN PARK RANGERS, NEW YORK CITY DEPARTMENT OF PARKS

Park rangers conduct several free walking tours in parks throughout the city each weekend. Topics include birdwatching, tree identification, general ecology, history, and geology. *800/201–PARK.*

events

New Yorkers may be cynical, but they turn out for parties in droves. It's hard to imagine this town without, say, the Feast of San Gennaro, the New York City Marathon, or the Halloween Parade. NYC & Company (212/484–1222, weekdays 9–5) has exact dates and times for many of the annual events listed below, and its Web site (www.nycvisit. com) has yet more information on free activities, vacation ideas, transportation, restaurants, hotels, and airports. Browsing the Web is much better than lingering on the phone, and the site has an invaluable directory of URLs for organizations across the city. All of these events are free unless otherwise indicated.

JANUARY

LEGAL HOLIDAYS
New Year's Day Jan. 1.

Martin Luther King Day 3rd Mon.

10 *f-1*
POETRY PROJECT

Ring in the first day of the new year! Performances at the annual New Year's Benefit for the resident Poetry Project at this landmark church range from the traditionally modern to the East Village avant-garde. More than 100 poets, dancers, and musicians pop into the spotlight. *St. Mark's Church In-the-Bowery, 2nd Ave. at 10th St., East Village, 212/674–0910. Jan. 1, 2 PM–midnight.*

9 *a-6*
NATIONAL BOAT SHOW

New York's 10-day boat show is just the thing to float your spirits during a gray spell in early January. Check out the latest in pleasure craft (power boats and sailboats) and equipment, and dream of the Caribbean. *Jacob K. Javits Convention Center, 11th Ave. at 35th St., Hell's Kitchen, 212/216–2000. Early Jan.*

9 *e-2*
WINTER ANTIQUES SHOW

The grande dame of New York antiques shows has been around for more than 40 years. Dealers large and small converge from all over the country to show off their furniture, collectibles, clothing, and memorabilia at this 10-day extravaganza. *7th Regiment Armory, Park Ave. at 67th St., Upper East Side, 212/255–0020. Mid-Jan.–early Feb.*

10 *f-5*
CHINESE NEW YEAR

This two-week celebration is launched with a barrage of fireworks and a colorful paper-dragon dance through the narrow streets of Chinatown. Local restaurants put on extravagant banquets, making this a feast in more ways than one, and the price of flowering quince branches goes up all over the city. *212/484–1222. Mid-Jan.–late Feb.*

11 *f-4*
OUTSIDER ART FAIR

This long weekend is a wild ride through the major artworks and practitioners of what's become known as outsider art, sometimes called naive art or art of the self-taught. If you like folk art, stop in and be amazed at this oft-misunderstood genre. Just vow beforehand not to blurt, "My three-year-old could do that!" It's not true. *Puck Bldg., 295 Lafayette St. (at Houston St.), SoHo, 212/777–5218. Late Jan.*

FEBRUARY

In honor of Abraham Lincoln's and George Washington's birthdays, New York's major departments stores traditionally hold big sales in mid- to late February. Keep your eyes peeled for dates and details in the daily newspapers.

LEGAL HOLIDAYS
Lincoln's Birthday Feb. 12 (New York State holiday).

Presidents' Day 3rd Mon.

BLACK HISTORY MONTH
February is devoted to a celebration of black American history and culture. Check newspapers and magazines for events.

`9` *c-6*

WESTMINSTER KENNEL CLUB DOG SHOW
For two days in early February, it's a dog's life at Madison Square Garden. This show of shows draws nearly 3,000 dogs and their humans from every state of the union to join paws and hands in competition. *Madison Sq. Garden, 4 Penn Plaza (7th Ave. between 31st and 33rd Sts.), Garment District, 800/455–3647. Early Feb.*

`9` *d-6*

EMPIRE STATE BUILDING RUN-UP
Forget cinder tracks: This course starts in the Art Deco lobby and ends on the 86th-floor observation deck. The Run-Up is a New York Road Runners Club invitational, so contact them in advance if you've decided that gravity is no object. *Empire State Bldg., 350 5th Ave. (at 34th St.), Garment District. New York Road Runners Club, 212/860–4455. Late Feb.*

MARCH

`3` *b-3*

MODEL YACHT RACES
Every Saturday in the milder months, beautifully crafted radio-controlled boats buzz around Central Park's Conservatory Water, also known as the Sailboat Lake. *Central Park, entrance at 5th Ave. at 74th St., Upper East Side. Mid-Mar.–mid-Nov., Sat. 10–2 (rain date Sun.).*

`9` *d-5*

ST. PATRICK'S DAY PARADE
New York's first parade in honor of St. Patrick took place in 1762, and the tradition has yet to gather a speck of dust. It's a boisterous affair (a little too much so), with traditional music that sticks in your brain for days and a sea of "Kiss Me—I'm Irish" buttons. Don't stop at a measly button, though; 'tis a fine day for wearin' the green. Views are excellent all along the route. *5th Ave., from 44th St. to 86th St, 212/484–1222. Mar. 17 around 11:30.*

`10` *d-6*

VERNAL EQUINOX
What are you doing for Vernal Equinox? Celebrate the very moment of spring's arrival by attempting to balance an egg on one end. The ritual is an ancient Chinese folk (yolk?) tradition, supposed to bring good luck for the coming year. Eggs are free. For details call performance artist Donna Henes, who initiated this annual event in 1976. *World Trade Center Plaza (Church, Liberty, and Vesey Sts.), Lower Manhattan, 718/857–2247. Mar. 20 or 21.*

`9` *c-6*

RINGLING BROS. AND BARNUM & BAILEY CIRCUS
Forget Groundhog Day: You know winter has ended when this world-famous, three-ring circus arrives, filling the subways and sidewalks with giddy children and their parents, clutching cotton candy and spewing popcorn. Just before opening night the Animal Walk takes the show's four-legged stars along 34th Street from their train at Penn Station to the Garden; it happens around midnight and is well worth the sleep deprivation. *Madison Sq. Garden, 4 Penn Plaza (7th Ave. between 31st and 33rd Sts.), Garment District, 212/465–6741. Late Mar.–early Apr.*

EASTER WEEKEND

3 b-3

EASTER EGG ROLL

Children ages 4–11 scramble to this traditional Central Park event. Don't worry; the eggs are wooden. Refreshments, prizes, and entertainment add activity to the charming sight of a sea of Easter bonnets. *212/360–3456. Day before Easter 9–2.*

9 d-4

EASTER LILIES DISPLAY

Rockefeller Center's Easter feast of blooms is always dazzling. *Channel Gardens, Rockefeller Center, 5th Ave. between 49th and 50th Sts.*

9 d-5

EASTER PARADE

New York's traditional Easter procession is a showcase of springtime finery—especially millinery—rather than a real parade. The excitement centers around St. Patrick's Cathedral, at 51st Street. *5th Ave. from 44th to 57th Sts., 11–2:30. Easter Sun.*

9 d-6

EASTER SUNRISE SERVICE

Reverend Frank Rafter, who began this tradition in 1973, leads a special, high-rise, sunrise Easter service at 6. Most churches don't have these views—you're in the Empire State Building observatory, on the 86th floor. Reserve in advance; space is limited. *Empire State Bldg., 350 5th Ave. (at 34th St.), Garment District, 718/849–3580. Easter Sun.*

9 d-6

MACY'S SPRING FLOWER SHOW

The week before Easter, Macy's sets its Broadway windows abloom, and arranges lush displays throughout the main floor. Step inside the emporium for a better whiff, and to hear talks by floral and interior designers. *Macy's Herald Sq., Broadway at 34th St., Garment District. Palm Sun.–Easter Sun.*

10 f-1

UKRAINIAN EASTER EGG EXHIBIT

The Ukrainian Museum rolls out the heavy cultural artillery in mid-February and keeps it out until summer, with a display of more than 400 *pysanky*—colorful Ukrainian Easter eggs. Egg-decorating workshops run through Easter; call for details. *Ukrainian Museum, 203 2nd Ave. (between 12th and 13th Sts.), East Village, 212/228–0110. Admission: $3 adults, $2 seniors and students. Wed.–Sun., 1–5.*

APRIL

It's time for the Mets and the Yankees to play ball (the Dodgers haven't returned from L.A. yet, but no true Brooklynite has given up hope), and for Coney Island Amusement Park to dust itself off. (*See* Sports & Outdoor Activities *in* Chapter 3.)

BIKE NEW YORK/FIVE BORO BIKE TOUR

See Sporting Events *in* Chapter 3.

9 d-2

BROADWAY SHOW SOFTBALL LEAGUE

Is that Norma Desmond on the diamond? Two great American institutions merge when New York's theater people form a 20-team softball league. Generally, one Broadway show plays another—cast, crew, and all. *Heckscher Field, Central Park, near E. 62nd St. Mid-April–July, Thurs. noon–5:30 (weather permitting).*

4 e-1

CHERRY BLOSSOM FESTIVAL

See Sporting Events *in* Chapter 3.

9 e-2

NEW YORK ANTIQUARIAN BOOK FAIR

First editions, manuscripts, autographs, atlases, drawings, prints, maps—it's book-lovers' heaven at the Armory. Wear your tweed blazer and carry your leather checkbook: Prices range from $25 to more than $25,000. *7th Regiment Armory, Park Ave. at 67th St., Upper East Side, 212/944–8291. Mid-Apr.*

MAY

Check the April listings for ongoing events.

LEGAL HOLIDAY

Memorial Day Last Mon.

PARADES

Armed Forces Day Parade

Bronx Day Parade

Salute to Israel Parade

NYC & Company's Norwegian Constitution Day Parade

For exact dates and routes, call 212/484–1222 or visit Web site at www.nycvisit.com.

STREET ENTERTAINERS

Out of hibernation at last, New York's street performers—accordionists, mimes, jugglers, magicians—reappear with the daffodils in May. Street theater tends to spring up where the crowds are. Here are some of the best "stages."

Battery Park & Wall Street. *Weekdays at noon.*

Central Park, The Mall (near E. 72nd St.). *Mon.–Sun.*

5th Avenue Artists and performers gather from Rockefeller Center (49th–50th Sts.) to Central Park (59th St.), especially around Grand Army Plaza (59th St.), in front of the Plaza Hotel. *Mon.–Sun. noon–5.*

Greenwich Village Washington Sq. Park. *Mon.–Sun.*

New York Public Library 5th Ave. at 42nd St. *Weekdays at noon.*

Theater District Intermission (matinee and evening performances).

GREENMARKETS

Starved for pastoral touches, New Yorkers support more than 30 greenmarkets around the city. Farm-fresh produce and baked goods arrive in neighborhood parks and plazas courtesy of farmers, dairymen, butchers, and bakers from upstate, New Jersey, and Pennsylvania. Union Square Park's year-round greenmarket is the biggest and busiest (open year-round, Mon., Wed., Fri., Sat. 8–7; 212/477–3220); most greenmarkets are open May–December.

HISTORIC HOUSE TOURS

Private houses in several historic neighborhoods open their doors to the public in May. The Park Slope Civic Council sponsors an annual tour of 10 historic Brooklyn homes on the third Sunday (daytime 718/832–8227); the Brooklyn Heights Association offers a self-guided afternoon tour of five historic homes and private gardens, often including the sanctuary of the landmark Plymouth Church of the Pilgrims, usually on the second Saturday (718/858–9193). The Village Community School sponsors a tour of six Manhattan homes to benefit its school fund (212/691–5146).

STREET FAIRS

Street fairs and block parties have become traditional summer fare in New York, featuring music, games, food, and wares—often for the benefit of neighborhood and block beautification projects. Some street fairs have become epic events, but even the tiniest block parties make for fine people-watching and usually draw friendly folks. For each weekend's fairs and festivals, check the "Weekend" section of Friday's *New York Times* and watch for notices on billboards and lampposts.

9 *C-1*

ADVIL MINI MARATHON

See Sporting Events *in Chapter 3.*

12 *g-5*

WELCOME BACK TO BROOKLYN FESTIVAL

You can go home again, at least on the second Sunday in May. Street games, local-history exhibits, Junior's cheesecake, and Nathan's hot dogs educate tourists from Peoria, Pakistan, and Manhattan and confirm the locals' suspicions that they really do live in the coolest borough. *Eastern Pkwy., Grand Army Plaza (north end of Prospect Park) to Brooklyn Museum, Park Slope, 718/855–7882. Noon–5. 2nd Sun. in May.*

9 *C-2*

SEPHARDIC FAIR

Congregation Shearith Israel (The Spanish and Portuguese Synagogue) is the landmark home of America's oldest Orthodox Jewish congregation. Watch artists making prayer shawls and crafting jewelry, potters vending wine cups, and scribes penning marriage contracts, and nibble Sephardic delicacies. *Congre-*

gation Shearith Israel, Central Park West at 67th St., Upper West Side, 212/873–0300. One Sunday in mid-May, 10–5.

9 *b-5*

9TH AVENUE INTERNATIONAL FOOD FESTIVAL

A mile-long annual gustatory celebration of New York's ethnic diversity greets wanderers in Hell's Kitchen on the third weekend in May. Try kebabs and kimchi, chow mein and gazpacho, tempura and falafel, ravioli and bratwurst . . . it's all topped off with crafts and entertainment. *9th Ave., 37th–57th Sts.,11–7, 212/581–7217. 3rd weekend in May*

10 *f-2*

UKRAINIAN FESTIVAL

Old-country music accompanies pierogi, polkas, *pysanky* (colored eggs), and dancing in the heart of the East Village Ukrainian community. *E. 7th St. between 2nd Ave. and Bowery. 3rd weekend in May.*

11 *d-2*

WASHINGTON SQUARE OUTDOOR ART EXHIBIT

For over half a century, Memorial Day has turned the Washington Square area into an open-air arts-and-crafts gallery, bringing some 600 exhibitors to lower 5th Avenue, Washington Square Park, and the surrounding streets. The action continues for three weekends, from noon to sundown. *Greenwich Village, 212/982–6255. Late May–mid-June.*

3 *b-3*

STORYTELLING HOUR

If this town could talk, the stories it would tell—well, maybe not these stories. Come hear wonderful children's tales read aloud at the Hans Christian Andersen statue, near Central Park's Sailboat Lake—an appropriate and charming site for storytelling. Selections are geared toward ages 3–7. *Central Park, entrance at 5th Ave. and 74th St., 212/360–3456. Late May–Sept., Sat. 11–noon.*

YOU GOTTA HAVE PARK!

A variety of park-related festivities—races, concerts, games—celebrates our greenest patches and remind us why we've managed to live here for so many years. *212/360–3456.*

JUNE

Check the April and May listings for ongoing summer events.

PARADES

Puerto Rican Day Parade: Take a salsa lesson before joining New York's hottest parade. *212/484–1222.*

9 *d-1*

SUMMERSTAGE IN CENTRAL PARK

Talk about a crowd-pleaser: Summer-Stage offers free weekday-evening and weekend-afternoon blues, Latin, pop, African, and country music; dance; opera; and readings. You can often enjoy the sounds without stopping by in earnest. Recent performers have included Morrissey and the one and only James Brown. *Central Park (enter at 72nd St.), 212/360–2777. June–Aug.*

10 *g-4*

LOWER EAST SIDE JEWISH FESTIVAL

Yiddish is now mixed with Spanish and Chinese in these parts, but once a year the neighborhood's Old World kicks up its heels. Baked goods, kosher food, books, and entertainment fill East Broadway from Rutgers to Montgomery Streets. So go—would it kill you to have a good time? *1 Sun. in late May or early June.*

1 *h-3*

BELMONT STAKES

This is New York's Thoroughbred of horse races, and the final jewel in the Triple Crown. *Belmont Park Racetrack, Hempstead Tpke. and Plainfield Ave., Belmont, Long Island, 718/641–4700. Early June.*

11 *d-4*

FEAST OF ST. ANTHONY OF PADUA

The music, games of chance, and kids' rides at this classic street festival beg you to inhale and ingest the glorious Italian food. *Sullivan St. between W. Houston and Spring Sts., SoHo, 212/777–2755. Early June.*

3 *b-3*

MUSEUM MILE FESTIVAL

One evening in mid-June, 10 of New York's cultural treasure chests open their doors free of charge. Upper 5th

Avenue is closed to traffic, and musicians, clowns, and jugglers entertain strollers. *5th Ave. from 82nd to 104th Sts. 2nd or 3rd Tues. in June, 6–9.*

TEXACO NEW YORK JAZZ FESTIVAL

In 1997, Texaco climbed on board as primary sponsor of this decade-old festival, which began life as "What Is Jazz?", an alternative to the JVC Jazz Festival. If you need an excuse to give up your day job, the festival already sponsors 350 performances at clubs and public spaces around town. Exhaustion will most likely be the end of you, but it's not a bad closing riff. *The Knitting Factory (74 Leonard St., Tribeca) is a main venue. 212/219–3006. 2 wks in mid-June.*

9 *b-2*

AMERICAN CRAFTS FESTIVAL

Some 400 skilled artisans display their crafts at Lincoln Center on June weekends. Support the arts and carry something home: leather, jewelry, blown and stained glass, quilts, baskets, furniture, and toys are all for sale. *Lincoln Center Plaza, Broadway at 64th St., Upper West Side, Mid- to late June, noon–9.*

9 *d-5*

BRYANT PARK SUMMER FILM FESTIVAL

Monday nights in summer are classic-movie nights in the nearly bucolic Bryant Park, behind the New York Public Library. This hugely popular (read: get there early) outdoor series runs throughout the summer and becomes more of a scene each year. Dash from work around 5 to claim a spot on the lawn, spread out your blanket and snacks, and get comfortable—films start at sundown. You can check the Web for the screening schedule—newyork.citysearch.com is a particularly good resource. *Bryant Park, 6th Ave. between 40th and 42nd Sts., Midtown. Mid-June–late Aug.*

12 *h-7*

CELEBRATE BROOKLYN PERFORMING ARTS FESTIVAL

From mid-June to late August, a delectable potpourri of music—pop, jazz, rock, classical, klezmer, African, Latin, Caribbean—comes to Prospect Park, along with dance, film, and more. Take

advantage! *Prospect Park Band Shell, Prospect Park W at 9th St., Park Slope, Brooklyn, 718/855–7882, ext. 52. Mid-June–late Aug.*

7 *d-8*

SHAKESPEARE IN THE PARK

Central Park's outdoor Delacorte Theater hosts one of New York's most blazingly popular summer traditions. Joseph Papp's Public Theater stages two major productions here each year, most featuring at least one star performer from the big or small screen. The program does depart from Shakespeare, but only to celebrate another masterpiece, such as Leonard Bernstein's *On the Town*. The whole affair is free, so while the play might later come indoors if it's a smash (as *The Tempest* did, with Patrick Stewart), you won't get the same bang for your buck. Tickets are distributed the day of the performance, two per person, at the Public Theater (425 Lafayette St., East Village, 1–3) and the Delacorte (beginning at 1)—line up early and bring some Mad Libs. (Call for information on ticket distrubution in the outer boroughs on selected days.) *Central Park, Delacorte Theater (enter at E. or W. 81st St.), 212/861–PAPP or 212/539–8750. Mid-June–late Aug., Tues.–Sun. at 8.*

THE MET IN THE PARKS

This summer, have some Puccini with your tortillas and brie. Free outdoor performances by the Metropolitan Opera Company start at 8 PM in rotating city parks (*see below*). The acoustics are better elsewhere, and you might want to bring some bug spray, but the atmosphere and the price are unbeatable. *212/362–6000. Mid-June–July.*

Bronx Van Cortlandt Park

Brooklyn Prospect Park; Marine Park

Manhattan Central Park.

Queens Cunningham Park.

Staten Island Snug Harbor; Miller Field; Great Kills Park

JVC JAZZ FESTIVAL NEW YORK

This much-loved summer festival brings giants of jazz and new faces alike to Carnegie Hall, Lincoln Center, the Beacon Theater, Bryant Park, and other theaters and clubs about town. Check newspapers for performers and schedules. Tickets are available through Ticketmaster. *212/501–1390. Late June.*

4 *g-7*

MERMAID PARADE

The Mermaid Parade is a pagan tribute to Coney Island, once the parade capital of the world. This weird and wild affair begins at Brooklyn's Surf Avenue and West 10th Street, right in front of that proto–roller coaster, the Cyclone. Break out your sequins and blond wig, and become a mermaid for the day (you'll fit right in)—or dress as King Neptune. If you're weak on maritime history, build a float, don flippers and goggles, and be Liza Minnelli. Whatever. *718/372–5159. 1st Sat. after summer solstice at 2.*

9 *b-2*

MIDSUMMER NIGHT SWING

It's amazing to see: on balmy summer evenings, New York's highest-brow plaza becomes an enormous, old-fashioned dance hall. Top big bands provide swing, jump, salsa, merengue, mambo, Dixieland, R&B, calypso, and disco, and zillions of people of all ages fill both the checkerboard dance floor (for a fee) and the periphery (no charge). *Dance lessons 6:30–7:30. Lincoln Center Plaza, Broadway at 64th St., Upper West Side, 212/875–5766. Late June–late July, Tues.–Sat. at 8:15.*

INDEPENDENCE DAY WEEKEND

10 *e-8*

GREAT 4TH OF JULY FESTIVAL

Manhattan's oldest quarter celebrates the nation's birthday with arts, crafts, ethnic food, live entertainment, and a parade from Bowling Green to City Hall. *Water St. from Battery Park–John St., 212/484–1222. July 4, 11–7.*

9 *f-6*

MACY'S FIREWORKS DISPLAY

The nation's largest display of pyrotechnical wizardry is launched from barges in the East River. The best viewing points are FDR Drive from 14th to 41st Sts. (access via 23rd, 34th, and 48th Sts.) and the Brooklyn Heights Promenade. The FDR Drive is closed to traffic,

but you'll want to get there early, as police sometimes restrict even pedestrian traffic. *July 4, 9:15.*

10 *f-7*

SOUTH STREET SEAPORT INDEPENDENCE WEEKEND

The Seaport is awash in celebrations and jammed with visitors and residents alike for the entire weekend. Concerts, street performers, and other special events make for excellent people-watching. *South Street Seaport, Lower Manhattan.*

JULY

Check the April, May, and June listings for ongoing summer events.

LEGAL HOLIDAY

Independence Day July 4 *(see above for listings).*

9 *d-3*

SUMMERGARDEN

Enjoy 20th-century classical music in the Museum of Modern Art's popular sculpture garden. Performers are graduate students and alumni of the Juilliard School. *Museum of Modern Art, 11 W. 53rd St., Midtown, 212/708–9400. Early July–mid-Aug., Fri. at 6, Sat. at 8:30.*

NEW YORK PHILHARMONIC PARK CONCERTS

Bronx Van Cortlandt Park

Brooklyn Prospect Park

Manhattan Central Park

Queens Cunningham Park

Staten Island Miller Field

Each summer the New York Philharmonic Orchestra performs a light program under the stars, and caps each concert with fireworks. Bring a picnic. *212/875–5709. Mid-July–early Aug.*

11 *d-2*

WASHINGTON SQUARE MUSIC FESTIVAL

Washington Square Park gets even louder in midsummer, when one of the city's oldest open-air concert series kicks in. *Washington Sq. Park (5th Ave. at Waverly Pl.), Greenwich Village, 212/431–1088. Mid-July–mid-Aug., Tues. at 8.*

AUGUST

Check the April, May, June, and July listings for ongoing summer events.

9 *b-2*

LINCOLN CENTER OUT-OF-DOORS

Lincoln Plaza devotes itself to a four-week open-air bonanza of music, dance, and theater. *Lincoln Center Plaza, Broadway at 64th St., Upper West Side, 212/875–5108. Aug.*

9 *b-2*

MOSTLY MOZART FESTIVAL

This world-renowned August concert series is just what it sounds like: a generous helping of Mozart, with dashes of other masters for good measure. The Mostly Mozart Festival Orchestra holds forth, and various solo performers illuminate chamber works in recitals. Free outdoor afternoon concerts are followed by casual evening concerts at reasonable prices. *Avery Fisher Hall, 10 Lincoln Center Plaza (Broadway at 64th St.), Upper West Side, 212/875–5103. Aug.*

1 *d-3*

HARLEM WEEK

Fortunately for all, the largest black and Hispanic festival in the world actually runs for about two weeks. Indoor and outdoor activities for every age celebrate the community's past, present, and future. Try to catch a feature at the Black Film Festival, and don't rush through the Taste of Harlem Food Festival. *Early to mid-Aug.*

3 *c-7*

NEW YORK INTERNATIONAL FRINGE FESTIVAL

In this event modeled on the Edinburgh Festival, emerging theater companies and performing artists take over two dozen performance spaces on the Lower East Side for the last two weeks of August. Make the trip—summer's winding down, and this is what the Lower East Side does best. *212/420–8877. Last 2 wks of Aug.*

9 *d-6*

TAP-O-MANIA

Be a part of Broadway's—okay, 34th Street's—longest tapping chorus line, and try to outdo yourselves: The Guinness Book of World Records puts the biggest one at 6,676 dancers. *Macy's Herald Sq., Broadway at 34th St., Garment District, 3rd Sun. in Aug. Registration at 8.*

3 *h-2*

U.S. OPEN

See Sporting Events *in* Chapter 3.

SEPTEMBER

The New York Philharmonic, the New York City and Metropolitan operas, and Broadway launch their new seasons, and the pace of the city quickens—especially on the first day of crisp fall weather.

LEGAL HOLIDAY

Labor Day 1st Mon.

PARADES

Labor Day Parade 1st Mon.

Steuben Day (German) Parade.

LABOR DAY WEEKEND

For many New Yorkers, the nation's unofficial end of summer marks the last chance for a beach-escape weekend. As a result, you'll hardly suffer for hanging around the city; a pleasant lull descends. The city is peaceful and almost quiet, providing great opportunities to visit otherwise jam-packed venues. Just the thought of going out for bagels and not standing in line should make your bowl of corn flakes that much more savory.

11 *d-2*

WASHINGTON SQUARE OUTDOOR ART EXHIBIT

Like its Memorial Day cousin (*see above*), this fair turns Washington Square Park and its environs into an alfresco art gallery. *Greenwich Village, 212/982–6255. 1st weekend in early Sept., noon–6.*

4 *e-1*

WEST INDIAN AMERICAN DAY PARADE

Labor Day weekend brings out the largest parade in New York City—no mean distinction. Modeled after the harvest carnival of Trinidad and Tobago, this Caribbean revel has been observed in New York since the 1940s, when it sprang up in Harlem. The festivities begin with a Friday-evening salsa, reggae, and calypso extravaganza at the

Brooklyn Museum (admission), and end on Monday afternoon with a gigantic, Mardi Gras–style parade of floats, elaborately costumed dancers, stilt-walkers, and West Indian food and music. *Eastern Pkwy. from Utica Ave. to Brooklyn Museum, Brooklyn, 212/484–1222. Labor Day weekend.*

9 b-2
AUTUMN CRAFTS FESTIVAL
More than 400 craftspeople show up and sell their unique and comforting wares to world-weary New Yorkers. Think you've seen it all? Drop by for the sheep-shearing demonstration. *Lincoln Center Plaza, Broadway at 64th St., Upper West Side. Two weeks, early to mid-Sept.*

10 f-4
FEAST OF SAN GENNARO
The oldest, grandest, largest, and most crowded festa of them all, in honor of the patron saint of Naples, begins with the "Triumphal March" from Verdi's *Aida* and continues for 11 days of eating and shenanigans. *Mulberry St. from Canal to Houston Sts., Little Italy, 212/484–1222. Mid- to late Sept., 11 AM–11:30 PM.*

9 d-4
NEW YORK IS BOOK COUNTRY
This midtown stretch of 5th Avenue contains—oops, used to contain—the country's largest concentration of bookstores, so on this Indian Summer day the street is filled with kiosks representing publishers of all stripes. Preview forthcoming books, meet authors, admire beautiful book jackets, chat with George Plimpton at the *Paris Review* booth, and enjoy live entertainment and bookbinding demonstrations. Bring the kids. *5th Ave. from 48th to 57th Sts., 212/207–7242. 3rd Sun. in Sept., 11–5.*

12 d-4
ATLANTIC ANTIC
This 12-block-long festival celebrates downtown Brooklyn, and there is much to celebrate. Food, entertainment, antiques, and a parade (at 11:30) beckon all toward the Williamsburg Clock Tower. *Atlantic Ave. from Flatbush to Furman St., Downtown Brooklyn, 212/484–1222. One Sun. in late Sept., 10–6.*

9 e-2
FALL ANTIQUES SHOW
Over 75 dealers converge from all over the U.S. for this relaxed yet refined affair, the foremost American-antiques show in the country and a bonanza for collectors of Americana. The Museum of American Folk Art benefits. *7th Regiment Armory, Park Ave. at 67th St., Upper East Side, 212/777–5218. 4 days in late Sept.*

7 e-7
FIFTH AVENUE MILE
The world's fastest runners crash New York's most exclusive strip, and thousands cheer them on—brief, but exhilarating. *5th Ave. from 62nd to 82nd Sts., Upper East Side, 212/860–4455. One Sat. in late Sept.*

9 b-2
NEW YORK FILM FESTIVAL
Founded in 1963, New York's exceptional international film festival is an autumn tradition for cinephiles. Afternoon and evening screenings provide plenty of temptations, and advance tickets make them real events. *Alice Tully Hall, Broadway at 65th St., Upper West Side, 212/875–5050. 2 wks, late Sept.–early Oct.*

OCTOBER

The New York Rangers and New York Knicks snap into public action at Madison Square Garden. (*See* Sporting Events *in* Chapter 3.)

LEGAL HOLIDAY
Columbus Day 2nd Mon.

PARADES
Columbus Day Parade

Hispanic Day Parade

Pulaski Day Parade

7 b-3
FEAST OF ST. FRANCIS
Obedience school too pricey? Ask for divine intervention at this wonderful service, otherwise known as the Blessing of the Animals. Most of the blessed are garden-variety cats and dogs, but you never know; often an elephant shows up. *Cathedral Church of St. John the Divine, 1047 Amsterdam Ave. (at 112th*

St.), *Upper West Side, 212/316–7540. 1st Sun. in Oct., mass at 11, blessings 1–5.*

9 *b-2*

BIG APPLE CIRCUS

No one is more than 50 ft from the action at this heated little big top in Lincoln Center's Damrosch Park. From late October through early January, this new New York tradition tips its hat to the classical American circus with simplicity, charm, and magic in one ring. Advance tickets are available. *Damrosch Park, Lincoln Center, Columbus Ave. at 63rd St., Upper West Side, 212/268–2500. Late Oct.–early Jan., generally Tues.–Sun., matinee and evening shows.*

7 *b-3*

HALLOWEEN EXTRAVAGANZA AND PROCESSION OF GHOULS

The massive Cathedral Church of St. John the Divine lends gothic cachet to these creepy goings-on: a silent movie is accompanied by organ music, and a procession of giant puppets brings on spiders, skeletons, ghouls, and spooks. *Cathedral Church of St. John the Divine, 1047 Amsterdam Ave. (at 112th St.), Upper West Side, 212/662–2133. Oct. 31 at 7 and 10.*

3 *b-6*

VILLAGE HALLOWEEN PARADE

What started as a handful of weirdos in the streets now draws 50,000 yahoos of all ages and persuasions. This anything-goes annual procession features some bizarre but brilliant costumes and exuberant live music. Join the march or just watch the massive spectacle from the sidelines. *6th Ave. from Spring to 23rd Sts., SoHo/W. Village/Chelsea. 914/758–5519. Oct. 31st, sundown (about 7)–about 10.*

NOVEMBER

LEGAL HOLIDAYS

Veteran's Day Nov. 11.

Thanksgiving Day 4th Thurs.

9 *a-4*

TRIPLE PIER EXPO

This semi-annual collectibles and antiques extravaganza (also held in March) is not for the faint of heart, even if the faint of heart love antiques. Wear comfortable shoes and be prepared for a feast of Art Deco furniture, 19th-century decorative arts, American quilts, memorabilia, silver, prints, jewelry, dolls, and much more. The price range is pleasingly broad. *Passenger Ship Terminals, Piers 88, 90, 92, 12th Ave. from 48th to 55th Sts., Hell's Kitchen, 212/255–0020. 1st two weekends in Nov.*

9 *d-4*

RADIO CITY CHRISTMAS SPECTACULAR

The famed Christmas Spectacular at the famed music hall features the famed Rockettes. A quieter tradition within the show is the Nativity Pageant, with live donkeys, camels, and sheep. Buy tickets in advance. *Radio City Music Hall, 1260 6th Ave. (at 50th St.), Midtown, 212/247–4777. Mid-Nov.–early Jan.*

9 *d-5*

LORD & TAYLOR'S CHRISTMAS WINDOWS

Early in the season the mannequins disappear, and lavish, animated holiday scenes fill this classic store's 5th Avenue windows. The line moves quickly, but the best viewing is after 9 PM, when the shoppers have cleared out. *Lord & Taylor, 424 5th Ave. (at 39th St.), Midtown, 212/391–3344. Tues. before Thanksgiving–Jan. 1.*

9 *d-6*

MACY'S THANKSGIVING DAY PARADE

You watched it on TV growing up; now break away from the set and watch the real thing. Macy's Thanksgiving Day parade moves south from Central Park West and 77th Street to Columbus Circle, then down Broadway to the float-reviewing stand at Macy's Herald Square (Broadway and 34th St.). The biggest stars are the gigantic balloons, which are inflated the night before the parade to antic effect (77th and 81st Sts. between Central Park West and Columbus Ave., 6–wee hours). Dress warmly, and take your position by 8. *212/695–4400. Thanksgiving Day, 9–noon.*

9 *d-6*

MACY'S SANTA CLAUS ADVENTURE AT MACYLAND

St. Nick is in residence—and in demand—at Macy's from the day after Thanksgiving until Christmas Eve, greeting and posing with children of all ages.

So who's stuck managing the elves? The Mrs.? There is a 20-minute holiday marionette show every hour 10:30–4:30. *Macy's Herald Sq., Broadway at 34th St., Garment District, 212/695–4400. Fri. after Thanksgiving-Dec. 24.*

9 *b-2*

THE NUTCRACKER

The Nutcracker is the most popular ballet in the world, and who better than the New York City Ballet to perform it? The company is ably assisted by children from the School of American Ballet. This magical show is very much a holiday tradition in New York, so buy tickets well in advance. *New York State Theater, Lincoln Center, Broadway and 64th St., Upper West Side, 212/870–5590. Late Nov.–early Jan.*

NEW YORK CITY MARATHON
See Sporting Events *in* Chapter 3.

DECEMBER

New York's holiday pleasures are sweet but not cloying. It's bloody difficult to remain unmoved by the strings of lights, classic store windows, concerts, and general hullabaloo. Feel like Handel's *Messiah*? You'll have to choose from a dozen different performances—each week. (*See* November, *above*, for ongoing holiday festivities.)

LEGAL HOLIDAY
Christmas Day Dec. 25.

9 *e-3*

CHANUKAH CELEBRATIONS

A 32-ft-tall menorah at Grand Army Plaza (5th Ave. and 59th St.) makes for a grand candle-lighting ceremony each night at sundown during the 8-day Festival of Lights. The 92nd St. Y (395 Lexington Ave., at 92nd St., 212/996–1100) holds a family celebration, geared toward ages 4–12, at which the gang can make holiday crafts, sing along to holiday music, hear an expert storyteller, and nibble refreshments (usually the Sun. before Chanukah).

7 *e-7*

METROPOLITAN MUSEUM OF ART CHRISTMAS TREE

Folks come from far and wide to see the Met's stunning tree in the solemn Medieval Sculpture Hall. The 30-ft

Baroque wonder is decorated with 18th-century cherubs and angels and accompanied by an elaborate Neapolitan nativity scene. *Metropolitan Museum of Art, 5th Ave. at 82nd St., Upper East Side, 212/879–5500. Dec.–early Jan.*

9 *e-2*

MIRACLE ON MADISON AVENUE

Madison Avenue's slickest shopping stretch is closed to traffic on the first Sunday in December for an afternoon of (civilized?) holiday shopping, with participating stores donating 20 percent of every sale to children's charities. Festive heated tents keep the wee ones warm as they enjoy the strolling musicians and the hot cider and cookies. *Madison Ave. from 55th to 79th Sts., 212/988–4001. Noon–5. 1st Sun. in Dec.*

9 *e-3*

CAROUSEL AND HOLIDAY DISPLAY

An animated carousel and colorful decorations will delight kids of all ages. Tantrum-prevention tip: Kids may look at, but may not ride, the carousel, so you may want to call a conference before taking Junior to see this gorgeous machine. *Lever House, 390 Park Ave. (at 53rd St.), lobby, Midtown, 212/688–6000. Early Dec.–Jan. 2.*

9 *d-4*

TREE-LIGHTING CEREMONY

Perhaps New York's most famous holiday tradition, the Rockefeller Center tree-lighting began in 1933 and has only picked up steam since. All at once, on the first Tuesday in December, the 20,000 lights on Rockefeller Center's mammoth Christmas tree come into view, accompanied by cheers, carols, and, of course, figure skating down below. It's a magical sight—if you can see it, which is unlikely, as thundering hordes of people pack several of the plaza's surrounding blocks. *Rockefeller Plaza, 5th Ave. between 49th and 50th Sts., 212/632–3975. Early evening, 1st Tues in Dec.*

1 *b-2*

CHRISTMAS IN RICHMONDTOWN

Restored buildings are decorated for Christmas in period (18th- and 19th-century) fashion and open to the public. Costumed guides explain local history, parlor games and popcorn stringing keep the kids occupied, and homemade food and gifts make a dent in your shopping list. *Historic Richmondtown, 441 Clarke Ave. (near Arthur Kill Rd.), Staten Island, 718/351–1611. Admission to Historic Richmondtown. 1st or 2nd Sun. in Dec., 10–4.*

9 *b-2*
MESSIAH SING-IN
Led by 21 different conductors and punctuated by four soloists, the chorus for this *Messiah* consists of everyone else who shows up—a good three thousand. Handel never sounded so good. Make your big break from the shower to Lincoln Center; bring the score or buy one in the lobby from the National Choral Council. *Avery Fisher Hall, Lincoln Center, Broadway at 64th St., Upper West Side, 212/333–5333. Admission. 1 evening several days before Christmas at 8.*

6 *c-5*
"'TWAS THE NIGHT BEFORE CHRISTMAS"
In a charmingly esoteric tradition that dates from 1911, a procession of carolers lays a wreath on Clement Clarke Moore's grave in Trinity Cemetery and reads his beloved poem "A Visit from St. Nicholas." *Church of the Intercession, Broadway at 155th St., Washington Heights, 212/283–6200. Sun. before Christmas at 4.*

KWANZAA
Kwanzaa is a seven-day African-American cultural festival (Dec. 26–Jan. 1) celebrating the traditional first fruit of the harvest. Events are citywide; check newspapers for details.

7 *c-8*
KWANZAA AT THE AMERICAN MUSEUM OF NATURAL HISTORY
Music and dance help augment the re-creation of an African marketplace, complete with African-style gifts for sale. *American Museum of Natural History, Central Park West at 79th St., Upper West Side, 212/769–5000. Admission to museum. Late Dec.*

NEW YEAR'S EVE

FIREWORKS
Fireworks greet the New Year at midnight in Central Park. Catch the best views at Bethesda Fountain, 72nd St.; Tavern-on-the Green, Central Park West and 67th St.; Central Park West and 96th St.; and 5th Ave. at 90th St. Fireworks also light up Brooklyn's Prospect Park; in Park Slope's Grand Army Plaza, the show is tastefully accompanied by music, hot cider, and cookies; festivities begin at 11:30 PM. If it's just too cold to stand around until midnight, watch the 'works at South Street Seaport at 11:30 PM.

9 *d-6*
EMPIRE STATE BUILDING
It's a grand place to be at midnight—even if you're not sleepless in Seattle. The last ticket is sold at 11:25 PM. *Empire State Bldg., 350 5th Ave. (at 34th St.), Garment District. Admission.*

9 *e-5*
FIRST NIGHT
Sponsored by the Grand Central Partnership, New York's First Night is a wonderful new tradition, begun in 1991. It's a family-oriented alternative to high-priced, high-octane celebrations, though most revelers are in fact adults. Choose from more than 40 events—ice-skating, concerts, storytelling, circus arts, dance, and more—in places like the MetLife Building, the Winter Garden at the World Financial Center, and Grand Central Terminal. A First Night button buys you admission to all events; children 3 and under get in free. *Grand Central Terminal and environs, Park Ave. and 42nd St., 212/883–2476. Dec. 31 noon–1 AM.*

9 *c-2*
MIDNIGHT RUN
Beginning and ending at Tavern-on-the-Green, some 3,000 men and women take a chilly but relatively short run around Central Park. Lose the sweats: many run in evening dress, others in costume. Prizes go to the fastest and best-dressed, and every runner gets champagne and a T-shirt. *Tavern-on-the-Green, Central Park West and 67th St., 212/860–4455. Registration fee. Jan. 1, midnight.*

7 *b-3*

NEW YEAR'S EVE CONCERT FOR PEACE

Leonard Bernstein used to conduct this stirring, 2-hour program at St. John the Divine. Like the cathedral itself, the music still soars. Doors open at 6 PM, a fact you should heed if you want a seat. *Cathedral Church of St. John the Divine, 1047 Amsterdam Ave. (at 112th St.), Upper West Side, 212/662–2133. Dec. 31 at 7:30; doors open at 6.*

9 *c-5*

TIMES SQUARE

There are people who spend every New Year's Eve in Times Square; this is not necessary. But there's nothing quite like Times Square on December 31. Ever since 1907 (well—minus a few electric-apple years in the '80s and the Waterford crystal ball for the new millennium), a 6-ft, illuminated, wrought-iron ball has welcomed the new year by moving slowly down a flagpole atop the Times Tower, now the One Times Square Building. The descent takes the last 59 seconds of the old year, and at midnight the ball is illuminated at the pole's base. Hardy revelers start to gather in the square in the afternoon; the rest of the country watches the event on TV. *Times Sq., Broadway and 42nd St., Theater District, 212/484–1222.*

day trips out of town

If hauling yourself efficiently out of the city seems as nerve-wracking as staying in it, Metro-North and the Long Island Rail Road (*see Public Transportation in* Chapter 7) offer package day trips to a variety of intriguing destinations, such as Long Island wineries and various historic homes. The tours are escorted and include all admission fees.

ATLANTIC CITY, NJ

If you're itchy for a little action, catch a bus down to Atlantic City, where casinos line the seaside boardwalk. Try your hand at craps, the slots, roulette, and table after table of blackjack. If your luck turns sour, there's still the saltwater taffy and ocean breezes. Gray Line's (212/397–2600) one-day bus trips from Port Authority make transport a snap.

BAYARD CUTTING ARBORETUM

An easy jaunt from the city, this 690-acre arboretum is just a ten-minute walk from the train station. Spread out along the lazy Connetquot River, the arboretum is best known for its stands of pines, native woods and bogs, meandering paths, and carefully laid rows of rhododendrons and azaleas. *Oakdale, NY, 516/581–1002. Open Tues.–Sun. 10 AM–sunset. Long Island Rail Road: Montauk Line to Great River.*

BOSCOBEL RESTORATION

A grand Federal-style mansion surrounded by formal gardens and lawns and overlooking the Hudson River, Boscobel (from bosco bello, "beautiful woods") was built in 1808 by Morris Dyckman. You can tour both the grounds and the interior, with its canopy beds, elaborate woodwork, and wonderful collection of 19th-century furniture, including some pieces by the famous New York cabinetmaker Duncan Phyfe. Special events include nature walks, lectures on horticulture, concerts, and storytelling hours. *Rte. 9D (8 mi north of Bear Mtn. Bridge), Garrison-on-Hudson, NY, 914/265–3638. Open Apr.–Oct., Mon. and Wed.–Sun. 9:30–5; Nov., Dec., and Mar., Mon. and Wed.–Sun. 10–3:15. Metro-North: Hudson Line to Cold Spring.*

LYNDHURST

An 1838 Gothic Revival mansion designed by Alexander Jackson Davis for Gen. William Paulding, an early New York City mayor, Lyndhurst was later purchased by railroad tycoon Jay Gould in 1870. Perched above the Hudson River and surrounded by 67 acres of lush grounds, the house itself—often referred to as "the castle"—is characterized by grandiose rooms and holds period furnishings and paintings. *635 S. Broadway, Tarrytown, NY, 914/631–4481. Open mid-Apr.–Oct., Tues.–Sun. 10–5; Nov.–mid-Apr., weekends, 10–4. Metro-North: Hudson Line to Tarrytown.*

HISTORIC HUDSON VALLEY

These three Hudson River Valley mansions, ranging in age from pre-Revolutionary to Federal, can be toured with guides dressed in period costumes. All three estates are designated as National Historic Landmarks; visits are free, and you're welcome to bring a picnic.

PHILIPSBURG MANOR

Once owned by Frederick Philips, a Dutch carpenter who rose to become the richest man in the colony, this working farm dates from the early 1700s, when it was run by African slaves. Now restored, Philipsburg features a stone manor house, a water-powered grist mill and mill pond, and a barn filled with farm animals. Guides in Colonial dress demonstrate spinning and weaving. *Rte. 9, Sleepy Hollow, NY (2 mi north of Tappan Zee Bridge), 914/631–3992. Open Mar., weekends 10–4; Apr.–Dec., Wed.–Mon. 10–5; Nov.–Dec., Wed.–Mon. 10–4. Metro-North: Hudson Line to Tarrytown.*

SUNNYSIDE

Covering 20 acres is the picturesque estate of Washington Irving, author of the classic American stories "The Legend of Sleepy Hollow" and "Rip Van Winkle." Purchased in 1835, Irving's charming cottage, topped by a Spanish-style tower, is filled with his furnishings and memorabilia, including more than 3,000 books. On the surrounding grounds, garden plantings and walkways follow a plan devised by Irving himself. *W. Sunnyside Ln. (off Rte 9; 1 mi south of Tappan Zee Bridge), Tarrytown, NY, 914/591–8763. Open Mar., weekends 10–4; Apr.–Oct., Wed.–Mon. 10–5; Nov.–Dec., Wed.–Mon. 10–4. Metro-North: Hudson Line to Tarrytown.*

VAN CORTLANDT MANOR

The centerpiece of this Revolutionary War estate is an 18th-century brick manor house filled with Georgian and Federal period furniture and paintings; also on the grounds is a restored 18th-century tavern. Frequent demonstrations of open-hearth cooking, brickmaking, and blacksmithing appeal to all five senses; and in summer, the staff cooks Colonial-style dinners according to 18th-century recipe books. *S. Riverside Ave. (off Rte. 9, Croton Pt. Ave. exit), Croton-on-Hudson, NY, 914/271–8981. Apr.–Oct., Wed.–Mon.; Nov.–Dec., weekends 10–4. Metro-North: Hudson Line to Croton-Harmon.*

OLD WESTBURY GARDENS

Several hundred acres of formal English gardens surround a beautifully furnished, Georgian-style country house, once the property of millionaire John S. Phipps. Each weekend brings concerts, hay rides, walking tours, art exhibits, and other activities. *71 Old Westbury Rd., Old Westbury, NY, 516/333–0048. Open Apr.–Oct., Wed.–Mon. 10–5; longer hrs summer. Long Island Rail Road: Port Jefferson Line to Westbury.*

PLANTING FIELDS ARBORETUM STATE HISTORIC PARK

This 409-acre country estate comprises extensive European-style gardens, greenhouses, woodlands, and Coe Hall, a 65-room Tudor-style mansion. *Planting Fields Rd., Upper Brookville, Long Island, 516/922–9201. Gardens open daily 9–5. Long Island Rail Road: Oyster Bay Line to Locust Valley or Oyster Bay.*

SAG HARBOR, LONG ISLAND

For a charming getaway, try this 19th-century whaling center on Long Island's South Fork. Along with historic houses and chic boutiques and cafés, there's an old cemetery, a Customs House dating from 1793, and a Whaling Museum (516/725–0770).

VANDERBILT MANSION

Designed by McKim, Mead & White, this sumptuous 1898 Italian Renaissance manor was the home of Frederick Vanderbilt, the commodore's son. Inside you'll find opulent furnishings and paintings from the 16th to 18th centuries. *Rte. 9, Hyde Park, NY, 914/229–9115. Open daily 9–5. Metro-North: Hudson Line to Poughkeepsie.*

chapter 5

ARTS, ENTERTAINMENT, & NIGHTLIFE

New York has always been an epicenter for the arts, but today the scene really is more dynamic and vigorous than ever. Purveyors and producers compete frantically for the patronage of increasingly savvy and voracious audiences. Who has not been admonished about the long lines for The Lion King or free Shakespeare in the Park tickets; the all-night queues of audience hopefuls for The Rosie O'Donnell Show; or the distraught crowds outside the Metropolitan Opera House moments before curtain time, offering incoming ticket holders a small fortune to see Tristan und Isolde? These fans know precisely what they want, and pleasing them has become a real challenge—not least because of enormous production costs.

In each of the arts, there is a palpable sense of rising standards. As the Times Square renaissance continues with no end in sight, Broadway's theaters are booked solid with productions that seem more rewarding every season, both financially and (many agree) artistically. The Metropolitan Opera and its magnificent orchestra have not been this consistently exciting in decades. Similarly, Kurt Masur has returned the New York Philharmonic to its top form; the art-gallery scene is flourishing in new Chelsea venues; and film lovers swarm to the Film Forum to catch movies they aren't likely to see on the big screen anywhere else in the world.

arts

tickets

You can buy advance tickets to most arts presentations at full price by mail, in person at the box office, or by phone (with a credit card). You can also buy tickets on-line; Ticketweb (www.ticketweb.com) and Culturefinder (www.culturefinder.com) are both good sites. Buying tickets directly from the theater by mail (using a certified check or money order) is the charmingly old-fashioned way, but you may end up in old-fashioned seats under the overhang in the side-rear orchestra—at $75 a pop. Your best bet for choice seats is to go to the box office well in advance of your preferred date; box-office personnel usually know the theater and its current production very well, and if they're in a good mood, they'll help you nab the best of what's available. Of course, this process can be inconvenient, so Telecharge (212/239–6200) and TicketMaster (212/307–7171) will describe seat locations upon request. Newspaper and magazine listings for each show will tell you which service to use. The catch is that you pay a surcharge of up to $7 when you order tickets by phone. If you call well in advance of the performance, your tickets can be mailed to you; otherwise they'll be held at the box office until just before curtain time. If you need to pick up held tickets to a very popular show, be sure to arrive at the theater in plenty of time and bring your credit card. Less-expensive tickets to off- and off-off-Broadway shows (no less exciting than the biggies) may be similarly obtained through a joint box office called Ticket Central (416 W. 42nd St, 212/279–4200; open daily 1 PM to 8 PM).

The following two discount ticket booths sell half-price or ¾-price tickets (for cash or traveler's checks only) for same-day Broadway and off-Broadway shows, as well as some music and dance performances. Be prepared to stand in line after checking the board for available shows and performances, and be sure to have alternate selections; shows inevitably sell out as you wait your turn. Be prepared for the $2.50 service charge. TKTS makes a dizzying two transactions per minute, but you'll still have to queue outdoors here, so remember your umbrella if necessary. Tickets for Saturday matinees can be purchased only on Friday; tickets for Sunday matinees can be bought only on Saturday. The World Trade Center outpost is open Monday–Friday from 11 to 5:30 and Saturday from 11 to 3:30. TKTS in Times Square is open Monday–Saturday from 3 to 8; Wednesday and Saturday from 10 to 2; and Sunday from 11 to 7.

If you can afford to lose, wait until just before curtain time (half an hour or less), when some shows release unclaimed or unsold tickets; lines are much shorter at that point.

9 *C-4*

TDF TIMES SQUARE THEATER CENTER (TKTS)
Broadway at 47th St., Theater District, 212/221–0013. Subway: 49th St.; Times Sq./42nd St. Open for same-day evening performances Mon.–Sat. 3–8 PM; for matinee performances Wed. and Sat. 10–2; for Sun. matinee and evening performances 11–7.

3 *b-8*

TDF LOWER MANHATTAN THEATER CENTER
2 World Trade Center, Mezzanine, Lower Manhattan. Subway: Cortlandt St./World Trade Center. Open for same-day evening performances weekdays 11–5:30; Sat. 11–3:30. Matinee and Sun. performances: sold one day before performance.

NEW YORK CITY ONSTAGE
Here's a phone number well worth memorizing: 212/768–1818. Courtesy of the Theater Development Fund (TDF), this touch-tone menu gives you an impressive and accurate array of recorded information, in English or Spanish, on theater, dance, and music events; performance cancellations; and arts events in all five boroughs, including subway directions.

STUBS AND PLAYBILL ONLINE
The glossy pamphlet *Stubs* gives detailed seating plans for all of New York's Broadway theaters and major off-Broadway theaters, stadiums, and concert halls. You can pick it up for $9.95 at many newsstands and bookstores. On-line, check out *Playbill*'s Web site at www.Playbill.com, where you'll find a wealth of resources: links to seating charts for all Broadway theaters and quite a few others, including those on London's West End; access to Telecharge services; feature articles on Broadway and off-Broadway happenings; dozens of daily news items; listings for American regional theaters; and links to a dizzying 650 other theater-oriented sites.

CONCERT HALLS

9 *b-2*

ALICE TULLY HALL
Many have declared the acoustics in this medium-size auditorium the fairest of them all, including a great many international soloists. The Chamber Music Society of Lincoln Center performs here, and the New York Film Festival takes over in late September. *1941 Broadway (at 65th St.), Upper West Side, 212/875–5050. Subway: 66th St./Lincoln Center.*

7 *b-1*

APOLLO THEATER
Ever since it opened in 1913, this legendary Harlem high point has been everything from a burlesque hall to a showcase for the ongoing Wednesday Amateur Nights. Ella Fitzgerald, Duke Ellington, Billie Holiday, Count Basie, Bill Cosby, and Aretha Franklin are only a few of those who have lit the place up. *253 W. 125th St., Harlem, 212/749–5838. Subway: A, B, C, D to 125th St.*

9 *b-2*

AVERY FISHER HALL
Well-worn as the home of the New York Philharmonic from September to June, this austere modern hall also hosts the beloved Mostly Mozart festival in summer and all sorts of other special events, from superstar recitals to the annual American Film Institute salutes. *Lincoln Center Plaza (Broadway at 64th St.), Upper West Side, 212/875–5030. Subway: 66th St./Lincoln Center.*

1 *a-1*

BARGEMUSIC LTD.
Against the incomparable skyline of lower Manhattan and the Brooklyn Bridge, Bargemusic presents chamber music year-round on an enclosed former coffee barge. The attractive performance space is paneled in cherry and backed by a glass wall onto the view. *Fulton Ferry Landing, Brooklyn Heights, Brooklyn, 718/624–4061. Subway: High St. (Fulton exit); Clark St.*

7 *b-8*

BEACON THEATER
This huge theater has a wildly diverse history, but it currently tends to present pop and rock concerts. *2124 Broadway (near 74th St.), Upper West Side, 212/496–7070. Subway: 1, 2, 3, 9 to 72nd St.*

1 *e-3*

BROOKLYN ACADEMY OF MUSIC (BAM)
Home to the Brooklyn Philharmonic, BAM also presents important, often innovative operatic and theatrical perfor-

mances, as well as experimental and established dance companies (see Dance, below). *30 Lafayette Ave. (at Flatbush Ave.), Downtown Brooklyn, 718/636–4100. Subway: Atlantic Ave.; Pacific St.; BAM Bus to and from Manhattan.*

9 *c-3*

CARNEGIE HALL/WEILL RECITAL HALL

Carnegie Hall's acoustics are as legendary as the musicians who have benefited from them over the last 100 years. Orchestras sound their very best here, but so do solo pianists; something about the place inspires all kinds of performers to outdo themselves. The hall still looks fresh from its total renovation in 1986. Intimate Weill Recital Hall is wonderfully unpretentious, with clean acoustics and a no-nonsense atmosphere. *154 W. 57th St., Midtown, 212/247–7800. Subway: N, R to 57th St.*

7 *e-7*

GRACE RAINEY ROGERS AUDITORIUM

The Met presents classical music, mostly chamber, in the glorious surroundings of one of the world's greatest art museums. Concerts run from early October to late May, with a concurrent lecture series. *Metropolitan Museum of Art, 1000 5th Ave. (at 82nd St.), Upper East Side, 212/570–3949. Subway: 4, 5, 6 to 86th St.*

9 *b-8*

THE KITCHEN

This diminutive space is currently the epicenter of performance art—but it highlights dance, video, and music as well. *512 W. 19th St., Chelsea, 212/255–5793. Subway: C, E to 23rd St.*

9 *c-6*

MADISON SQUARE GARDEN

Where else can 20,000 people see Barbra Streisand, Phish, or the New York Knicks? The Garden complex includes the 5,600-seat Paramount Theater, where megamusical versions of *A Christmas Carol* and *The Wizard of Oz* make annual appearances. *7th Ave. at 31st–33rd Sts., Midtown, 212/465–6741. Subway: 34th St.*

9 *b-1*

MERKIN CONCERT HALL

This relative newcomer to the concert-hall pantheon gained rapid prestige with its ambitious programming: the smallish auditorium is almost entirely devoted to 20th-century chamber music. *Abraham Goodman House, 129 W. 67th St. (at Broadway), Upper West Side, 212/362–8719. Subway: 66th St./Lincoln Center.*

9 *d-4*

RADIO CITY MUSIC HALL

Still breathtaking after all these years, Radio City's just-fully-renovated 6,000-seat auditorium features two-ton chandeliers, a 60-ft-high Art Deco lobby and foyer, and some of the glitziest acts ever concocted. The resident Rockettes still kick higher than any chorus line, and their Christmas and Easter performances will curl your toes. Pop stars from Bette Midler to k.d. lang to Tony Bennett also pack the house. *1260 Ave. of the Americas (at 50th St.), Midtown, 212/247–4777. Subway: 47th–50th Sts./Rockefeller Center.*

7 *b-6*

SYMPHONY SPACE

Formerly a movie theater, this enormous auditorium now functions as a life-size multimedia venue. Symphony Space boasts the most varied programs in town—all-day readings of *Ulysses*, zither recitals, gospel, Gershwin—and the friendly flavor of its neighborhood. *2737 Broadway (at 95th St.), Upper West Side, 212/864–5400. Subway: 1, 2, 3, 9 to 96th St.*

7 *e-6*

TISCH CENTER FOR THE ARTS

The Tisch Center at the 92nd Street Y offers an endless, fascinating, and fairly affordable array of readings, lectures, and concerts—classical, pop, and jazz. Most series take a breather in summer, but the jazz plays on. *92nd Street Y, 1395 Lexington Ave. (at 92nd St.), Yorkville, 212/996–1100. Subway: 4, 5, 6 to 86th St.; 6 to 96th St.*

9 *d-5*

TOWN HALL

This low-key historic beauty quietly hosts an eclectic mix of chamber music, staged readings, stand-up comedy, high-end cabaret acts, and pop. *123 W. 43rd St., Theater District, 212/840–2824. Subway: Times Sq./42nd St.*

CONCERTS IN CHURCHES

Churches play a quiet but crucial role in New York's classical scene, allowing both amateur and professional performers to find their own audiences. See Saturday's *New York Times* for additional venues and specific programs.

7 *b-3*

CATHEDRAL CHURCH OF ST. JOHN THE DIVINE

Huge, dark, and majestic, to say the least, St. John's has the acoustics and atmosphere to make any musical event a stirring experience. *1047 Amsterdam Ave. (at 112th St.), Morningside Heights, 212/316–7449. Subway: 110th St./Cathedral Pkwy.*

7 *e-7*

CHURCH OF ST. IGNATIUS LOYOLA

The acclaimed "Sacred Music in a Sacred Space" concert series uses this lush Italianate setting to showcase the church's own professional choir and fabulous organ as well as to host visiting artists. Solemn mass, every Sunday at 11 AM, features Gregorian chant and a new musical program each week. *980 Park Ave. (at 84th St.), Upper East Side, 212/288–3588. Subway: 4, 5, 6 to 86th St.*

10 *e-1*

GRACE CHURCH

Further downtown, this magnificent church sponsors frequent concerts and recitals, usually in early evening. *802 Broadway (at 10th St.), Greenwich Village, 212/254–2000. Subway: 8th St.; 14th St./Union Sq.*

12 *b-3*

ST. ANN'S AND THE HOLY TRINITY CHURCH

This National Historic Landmark in Brooklyn Heights holds sixty of the very first stained-glass windows ever made in America. Since 1980, the church has also featured a performing arts center which hosts a wide variety of quality musical events, including jazz, blues, world music, experimental opera, and musical theater. Performances are held March–May and October–December. *157 Montague St. (at Clinton St), Brooklyn Heights, Brooklyn, 718/858–2424. Tues.–Sat., noon–6. Subway: Borough Hall, Court St.*

9 *e-4*

ST. BARTHOLOMEW'S CHURCH

This Byzantine-style church has been making and sponsoring great music for 100 years. *109 E. 50th St., Midtown, 212/378–0200. Subway: 51st St./Lexington Ave.*

9 *e-3*

ST. PETER'S CHURCH AT CITICORP CENTER

Stop by on your lunch hour (or just peer through the street-level windows) for midday jazz or an organ recital on this innovative stage, or check out the unique Jazz Vespers on Sunday. Weekend evenings see choral action. *619 Lexington Ave. (at 54th St.), Midtown, 212/935–2200. Subway: 51st St./Lexington Ave.*

9 *d-3*

ST. THOMAS CHURCH

New York's most famous men-and-boys choir works magic in this soaring Episcopal space. *1 W. 53rd St., Midtown, 212/757–7013. Subway: E, F to 5th Ave.*

9 *e-2*

TEMPLE EMANU-EL

The world's largest Reform synagogue offers regular recitals, organ and otherwise. *1 E. 65th St., Upper East Side, 212/744–1400. Subway: 6 to 68th St.*

DANCE

Ballet and modern dance flourish year-round in New York. Check the *New Yorker*, *New York* magazine, the *New York Times*, and *Time Out* for current programs. Before you let anyone sound the death knell for New York dance—a noise some fans made when the Joffrey Ballet moved to Chicago in 1995—let 'em know that over 150 dance companies are alive and well in this town, not counting the steady flow of world-famous troupes that leap through every year. You have more than one performance option almost any night of the year.

1 *e-3*

BROOKLYN ACADEMY OF MUSIC (BAM)

Every fall, BAM's three-month Next Wave Festival features cutting-edge dance groups from the United States and abroad. Classical dance companies perform in the spring. *30 Lafayette Ave. (at Flatbush Ave.), Downtown Brooklyn,*

718/636–4100. *Subway: Atlantic Ave.; Pacific St.; BAM Bus to and from Manhattan.*

9 *d-3*
CITY CENTER
This busy ballet and modern dance theater hosts the Paul Taylor Dance Company and the Alvin Ailey American Dance Theater on a regular basis. It's also New York's most popular stop with touring international companies. *131 W. 55th St., Midtown, 212/581–1212. Subway: N, R to 57th St.*

9 *c-8*
DANCE THEATER WORKSHOP (DTW)
DTW is one of the country's most ambitious and successful laboratories for modern dance and performance art. *Bessie Schoenberg Theater, 219 W. 19th St., 2nd floor, Chelsea, 212/924–0077. Subway: C, E to 23rd St.*

10 *f-1*
DANSPACE PROJECT
This hallowed space, once graced by Isadora Duncan and Martha Graham, presents some of the most adventurous dance of the moment. *St. Mark's Church In-the-Bowery, 2nd Ave. at 10th St., East Village, 212/674–8194. Subway: Astor Pl.; 2nd Ave.*

9 *c-8*
THE JOYCE THEATER
A fine, highly eclectic modern-dance venue, the Joyce is the permanent home of the Feld Ballets/NY and features several other modern companies, including Pilobolus, Lar Lubovitch Dance Company, and Ballet Hispanico. It's medium-size and unusually comfortable. *175 8th Ave. (at 18th St.), Chelsea, 212/242–0800. Subway: A, C, E to 14th St.*

9 *b-2*
METROPOLITAN OPERA HOUSE
The renowned American Ballet Theater presents a new season each year from April to June. In summer the hopping Lincoln Center Festival features visiting national ballet companies, including the Royal Ballet. *Lincoln Center Plaza (Broadway at 64th St.), Upper West Side, 212/362–6000. Subway: 66th St./Lincoln Center.*

9 *b-2*
NEW YORK STATE THEATER
The famed New York City Ballet holds court April–June and November–February. From Thanksgiving through the New Year, the company stages its legendary production of George Balanchine's *Nutcracker (see Events in Chapter 4). Lincoln Center Plaza (Broadway at 64th St.), Upper West Side, 212/870–5570. Subway: 66th St./Lincoln Center.*

10 *f-1*
P.S. 122
Very obviously a tumble-down public school, this fascinating and idiomatic experimental dance/performance space operates year-round. *150 1st Ave. (at 9th St.), East Village, 212/477–5288. Subway: Astor Pl.; 2nd Ave.*

9 *d-7*
GRAMERCY ARTS THEATER
Gramercy Arts Theater's Repertorio Español is best known as the frequent host of Spanish choreographer Pilar Rioja, who recently celebrated her 25th anniversary at this space. *138 E. 27th St., Gramercy, 212/889–2850. Subway: 28th St.*

9 *e-1*
SYLVIA AND DANNY KAYE PLAYHOUSE
A frequent host to upwardly mobile dance companies, this space is notable for its comfortably small audience capacity, paired with a stage that accommodates good-size productions. *Hunter College, 68th St. between Park and Lexington Aves., Upper East Side, 212/772–4448. Subway: 68th St./Hunter College.*

7 *b-6*
SYMPHONY SPACE
Watch this space for varied and electrifying ethnic dance. *2537 Broadway (at 95th St.), Upper West Side, 212/864–5400. Subway: 1, 2, 3, 9 to 96th St.*

11 *c-8*
TRIBECA PERFORMING ARTS CENTER
Catch fine international dance troupes at this versatile space with two theaters, one intimate, the other more substantial. Tickets are an encouraging $7–$20. *199 Chambers St. (between Greenwich Ave. and West Side Hwy.), Tribeca, 212/346–8500. Subway: Chambers St.*

FREE ENTERTAINMENT

Call 212/360–1333 daily for a list of the day's free events in city parks, and check Events (*see* Chapter 4) for special annual happenings, especially summer festivals.

MOVIE THEATERS WORTH NOTING

Due mainly to the invention of the VCR, most of the fabled movie-repertory houses of the 1960s and '70s are gone now (the 80 St. Mark's, the Elgin, the Regency, the Thalia). Their absence makes the independent theaters listed here that much more valuable (and popular)—their programming supports not only the work of indy filmmakers but also keeps repertory fare alive, including films unavailable on video. Meanwhile, first-run movie theaters have proliferated wildly throughout Manhattan, with multiscreen complexes sprouting in every neighborhood, most owned by Sony, Loews, Clearview, or City Cinemas. Alas, while the theaters are more numerous, the screens have often shrunk, and ticket prices have skyrocketed. For current listings, check any daily newspaper, the *New Yorker, New York* magazine, or *Time Out* (particularly good on art-house listings).

8 *c-5*

AMERICAN MUSEUM OF THE MOVING IMAGE
36–01 35th Ave. (at 36th St.), Astoria, Queens, 718/784–0077. Subway: Steinway St.

1 *e-3*

BAM ROSE CINEMAS
30 Lafayette Ave. (at Flatbush Ave.), Downtown Brooklyn, 718/623–2270. Subway: Atlantic Ave., Pacific St.

10 *e-1*

CINEMA VILLAGE
E. 12th St. between 5th Ave. and University Pl., Greenwich Village, 212/924–3363. Subway: 14th St./Union Sq.

10 *c-3*

FILM FORUM
209 W. Houston St. (between 6th Ave. and Varick St.), West Village, 212/727–8110. Subway: Houston St.

9 *d-3*

MUSEUM OF MODERN ART
11 W. 53rd St., Midtown, 212/708–9480. Subway: E, F to 5th Ave.

9 *d-3*

MUSEUM OF TELEVISION AND RADIO
25 W. 52nd St., Midtown, 212/621–6600. Subway: E, F to 5th Ave.

9 *b-2*

WALTER READE THEATER/FILM SOCIETY OF LINCOLN CENTER
165 W. 65th St. (at Broadway), Upper West Side, 212/875–5600. Subway: 66th St./Lincoln Center.

OPERA

11 *f-2*

AMATO OPERA
Since 1947 this tiny theater has provided a unique showcase for some thrilling singing. Where else can you see and hear 50 (usually young) singers on a 20-ft stage, performing Verdi's *Falstaff* with real passion? Repertory standards are performed on varying weekends from September through June. *319 Bowery (at 2nd St.), East Village, 212/228–8200. Subway: Bleecker St./Broadway–Lafayette St.*

1 *e-3*

BROOKLYN ACADEMY OF MUSIC (BAM)
BAM has hosted several of the most important operatic premieres of the last decade (including the brilliant *Nixon in China*), and several august companies, including the Welsh National Opera, have performed brilliantly here. *30 Lafayette Ave. (at Flatbush Ave.), Downtown Brooklyn, 718/636–4100. Subway: Atlantic Ave.; Pacific St.; BAM Bus to and from Manhattan.*

9 *b-2*

METROPOLITAN OPERA COMPANY
Tickets are pricey, to say the least, but most agree that the Met is the finest opera company in the country—the finest in the world, on some nights. The company's hefty season runs from September to April. *Metropolitan Opera House, Lincoln Center Plaza (Broadway and 64th St.), Upper West Side, 212/362–6000. Subway: 66th St./Lincoln Center.*

9 b-2

NEW YORK CITY OPERA

This courageous and remarkable company performs standards (*Carmen, Traviata*); Broadway musicals with operatic aspirations (*Street Scene, A Little Night Music*); and, best of all, new works (*Malcolm X, The Times of Harvey Milk*) and unforgivably neglected masterpieces (*The Cunning Little Vixen, The Makropulos Case*). Ticket prices are decidedly more welcoming than those across the plaza. The season runs from September to November and from March to April. *New York State Theater, Lincoln Center Plaza (Broadway at 64th St.), Upper West Side, 212/870–5570. Subway: 66th St./Lincoln Center.*

9 c-3

OPERA ORCHESTRA OF NEW YORK

Under the intrepid guidance of Eve Queler, OONY performs concert versions of (usually) rarely performed works by major composers, often featuring star soloists and always furnishing libretti for the audience (the lights are kept up). *Carnegie Hall* (see *Concert Halls*, above).

TELEVISION SHOWS

Getting free tickets to television tapings is a lot trickier than it used to be. Most shows require a postcard—with your name, address, phone number, and the number of tickets requested—at least a month in advance. But standby (same-day) tickets are usually available to those willing to spend several hours standing in line.

9 d-4

LATE NIGHT WITH CONAN O'BRIEN

Same-day standby tickets are available after 10 AM at the NBC Page Desk in the lobby of 30 Rockefeller Plaza—but you're better off writing well in advance. *NBC Tickets, Late Night with Conan O'Brien, 30 Rockefeller Plaza, New York, NY 10112. Information: 212/664–3056. Subway: 47th–50th Sts./Rockefeller Center.*

9 c-3

THE LATE SHOW WITH DAVID LETTERMAN

Standby tickets are distributed by phone on the day of taping. To grab a pair, call 212/247–6497 at 11 AM. You're better off writing in advance. All audience members must be over 16. *Late Show Tickets, 1697 Broadway, New York, NY 10019. Information: 212/975–1003. Subway: 50th St.*

9 c-1

LIVE WITH REGIS AND KATHY LEE

You need to be over 18 to attend this one live. Standby tickets go on sale weekdays at 8 AM at the ABC headquarters; line up at the corner of 67th Street and Columbus Avenue. Otherwise, write a full year in advance. *Live Tickets, Ansonia Station, Box 777, New York, NY 10023-0777. Information: 212/456–3537. Subway: 66th St./Lincoln Center.*

9 d-4

THE ROSIE O'DONNELL SHOW

Highly coveted standby tickets (one per person) are distributed by lottery Monday–Thursday at 7:30 AM, at the 49th Street entrance to 30 Rockefeller Plaza. There is currently a 9- to 12-month wait for tickets requested by postcard; if you can plan ahead, write *during April, May, or June*. Only two tickets are allotted per postcard, and children under five are not permitted. Call 212/506–3288 for all sorts of information on Rosie's show, including recipes, internships, and how to apply for a guest appearance. *ABC Studios, Rosie O'Donnell Show, 30 Rockefeller Plaza, Suite 800E, New York, NY 10112. Subway: 47th–50th Sts./Rockefeller Center.*

9 d-4

SATURDAY NIGHT LIVE

Standby tickets go on sale at 9:15 AM, at the 49th Street entrance to 30 Rockefeller Plaza. Advance tickets for performances and dress rehearsals are available by lottery; postcards are accepted during August only. You must be over 16. *NBC Tickets, Saturday Night Live, 30 Rockefeller Plaza, New York, NY 10112. Information: 212/664–4000. Subway: 47th–50th Sts./Rockefeller Center.*

9 c-3

WNET (CHANNEL 13)

There are no regular tapings with a live audience, but the network offers periodic tours. *356 W. 58th St., Midtown, 212/560–2000. Subway: 59th St./Columbus Circle.*

THEATERS & THEATER COMPANIES

Until fairly recently, "theater" in New York City meant "Broadway." Today, off-Broadway drama is just as vital and important as the blockbuster musicals. More than a few current Tony Award–winning megahits can claim to have originated off-Broadway, where ticket prices are usually about half of those on the well-traveled Great White Way. An off-off-Broadway experience may involve sitting on a folding chair in a church basement or at the back of a coffeehouse, but many feel that the true pulse of American theater beats most steadily in these settings, where actors often work for free, runs are limited, and admission amounts to little more than a donation.

For current theater information, call New York City Onstage (see Tickets, below), or consult the New Yorker, New York magazine, the New York Times (especially Friday's "Weekend" and Sunday's "Arts and Leisure" sections), or Time Out. For off- and off-off-Broadway, Time Out is best.

Note that few Broadway box offices accept phone calls; Telecharge and TicketMaster field the thousands of calls for Broadway shows. The phone numbers below will lead you to the appropriate ticket vendor.

broadway

9 c-4

AMBASSADOR THEATER
219 W. 49th St., 212/239–6200. Subway: 49th St.; 50th St.

9 c-4

BROOKS ATKINSON THEATER
256 W. 47th St., 212/719–4098. Subway: 49th St.; 50th St.

9 d-4

BELASCO THEATER
111 W. 44th St. (at 6th Ave.), 212/239–6200. Subway: B, D, F, Q to 42nd St.

9 c-4

BOOTH THEATER
222 W. 45th St., 212/239–6200. Subway: 42nd St.

9 c-4

BROADHURST THEATER
235 W. 44th St., Theater District, 212/239–6200. Subway: 42nd St.

9 c-3

BROADWAY THEATER
1681 Broadway (at 53rd St.), 212/239–6200. Subway: 50th St.; 7th Ave.

9 c-4

CIRCLE IN THE SQUARE
235 W. 50th St., Theater District, 212/239–6200. Subway: 50th St.

9 d-4

CORT THEATER
138 W. 48th St., Theater District, 212/239–6200. Subway: 49th St.; 50th St.

9 c-4

CRITERION CENTER
1514 Broadway (at 45th St.), 212/764–7902. Subway: Times Sq./42nd St.

9 c-4

ETHEL BARRYMORE THEATER
243 W. 47th St., Theater District, 212/239–6200. Subway: 49th St.; 50th St.

9 c-4

EUGENE O'NEILL THEATRE
230 W. 49th St., Theater District, 212/246–0220. Subway: 49th St.; 50th St.

9 c-5

FORD CENTER FOR THE PERFORMING ARTS
214 W. 42nd St., Theater District, 212/307–4100. Subway: 42nd St.

9 c-4

GERSHWIN THEATER
222 W. 51st St., Theater District, 212/307–4100. Subway: 50th St.

9 c-4

GOLDEN THEATER
252 W. 45th St., Theater District, 212/239–6200. Subway: 42nd St.

9 c-4

HELEN HAYES THEATRE
240 W. 44th St., Theater District, 212/307–4100. Subway: 42nd St.

9 c-4

IMPERIAL THEATER
249 W. 45th St., Theater District, 212/239–6200. Subway: 42nd St.

9 c-4

LONGACRE THEATER
220 W. 48th St., Theater District, 212/239–6200. Subway: 49th St.; 50th St.

9 c-4

LUNT-FONTANNE THEATRE
205 W. 46th St., Theater District, 212/307–4100. Subway: 42nd St.

9 c-4

LYCEUM THEATER
149 W. 45th St., Theater District, 212/239–6200. Subway: B, D, F, Q to 42nd St.

9 c-4

MAJESTIC THEATER
247 W. 44th St., Theater District, 212/239–6200. Subway: 42nd St.

9 c-4

MARQUIS THEATER
211 W. 45th St., Theater District, 212/307–4100. Subway: Times Sq./42nd St.

9 c-4

MARTIN BECK THEATER
302 W. 45th St., Midtown, 212/246–6363. Subway: Port Authority/42nd St.

9 c-4

MINSKOFF THEATER
200 W. 45th St., Theater District, 212/307–4100. Subway: Times Sq./42nd St.

9 c-4

MUSIC BOX THEATER
239 W. 45th St., Theater District, 212/239–6200. Subway: 42nd St.

9 c-5

NEDERLANDER THEATER
208 W. 41st St., Theater District, 212/307–4100. Subway: 42nd St.

9 c-3

NEIL SIMON THEATRE
250 W. 52nd St., Theater District, 212/757–8646. Subway: 50th St.

9 c-5

NEW AMSTERDAM THEATER
214 W. 42nd St., Theater District, 212/307–4100. Subway: 42nd St.

9 c-4

PALACE THEATER
1564 Broadway (at 47th St.), Theater District, 212/307–4100. Subway: 49th St.; 50th St.

9 c-4

PLYMOUTH THEATER
236 W. 45th St., Theater District, 212/239–6200. Subway: 42nd St.

9 c-4

RICHARD RODGERS THEATRE
226 W. 46th St., Theater District, 212/221–1211. Subway: 42nd St.

9 c-4

ROUNDABOUT THEATER COMPANY
1530 Broadway (at 45th St.), Theater District, 212/869–8400. Subway: Times Sq./42nd St.

9 c-4

ROYALE THEATRE
242 W. 45th St., Theater District, 212/239–6200. Subway: 42nd St.

9 c-4

ST. JAMES THEATRE
246 W. 44th St., Theater District, 212/239–6200. Subway: 42nd St.

9 c-4

SHUBERT THEATER
225 W. 44th St., Theater District, 212/239–6200. Subway: 42nd St.

9 c-3

VIRGINIA THEATRE
245 W. 52nd St., Theater District, 212/239–6200. Subway: 50th St.

9 b-2

VIVIAN BEAUMONT THEATER
Lincoln Center, 150 W. 65th St., Upper West Side, 212/239–6200. Subway: 66th St./Lincoln Center.

9 *c-4*

WALTER KERR THEATER
219 W. 48th St., Theater District, 212/239–6200. Subway: 49th St.; 50th St.

9 *c-4*

WINTER GARDEN THEATER
1634 Broadway (at 50th St.), Theater District, 212/239–6200. Subway: 50th St.

off broadway

11 *b-2*

ACTORS' PLAYHOUSE
100 7th Ave. S (between Bleecker and Christopher Sts.), West Village, 212/239–6200. Subway: Christopher St./Sheridan Sq.

9 *c-7*

AMERICAN JEWISH THEATER
307 W. 26th St., Chelsea, 212/633–9797. Subway: C, E to 23rd St.

9 *d-4*

AMERICAN PLACE THEATER
111 W. 46th St., Theater District, 212/840–3074. Subway: B, D, F, Q to 42nd St.

11 *e-2*

ASTOR PLACE THEATER
434 Lafayette St., East Village, 212/254–4370. Subway: Astor Pl.; 8th St.

9 *d-8*

ATLANTIC THEATER COMPANY
33 W. 20th St., Chelsea, 212/645–1242. Subway: F to 23rd St.

11 *f-2*

BOUWERIE LANE THEATER
330 Bowery (at 2nd St.), East Village, 212/677–0060. Subway: Bleecker St./Broadway–Lafayette St.

10 *d-1*

CENTURY THEATER CENTER
111 E. 15th St., Gramercy, 212/239–6200. Subway: 14th St./Union Sq.

11 *a-1*

CHERRY LANE THEATER
38 Commerce St. (between Bedford and Barrow Sts.; off 7th Ave. S), West Village, 212/989–2020. Subway: Christopher St./Sheridan Sq.

9 *d-3*

CITY CENTER, I & II
131 W. 55th St., Midtown, 212/581–1212. Subway: B, Q to 57th St.

10 *e-1*

CSC REPERTORY
136 E. 13th St., East Village, 212/677–4210. Subway: 14th St./Union Sq.

10 *e-1*

DARYL ROTH THEATRE
20 Union Sq. E (at 15th St.), Gramercy, 212/239–6200. Subway: 14th St./Union Sq.

9 *b-5*

DOUGLAS FAIRBANKS THEATER
432 W. 42nd St., Hell's Kitchen, 212/239–6200. Subway: Port Authority/42nd St.

9 *c-4*

DUFFY THEATER
1553 Broadway (at 46th St.), Theater District, 212/695–3401. Subway: Times Sq./42nd St.

9 *a-3*

ENSEMBLE STUDIO THEATER
549 W. 52nd St., Hell's Kitchen, 212/247–3405. Subway: 50th St.

9 *b-4*

47TH STREET THEATER
307 W. 47th St., Midtown, 212/239–6200. Subway: 49th St.; 50th St.

9 *b-5*

HAROLD CLURMAN THEATER
412 W. 42nd St., Hell's Kitchen, 212/594–2826. Subway: Port Authority/42nd St.

9 *b-7*

HUDSON GUILD THEATER
441 W. 26th St., Chelsea, 212/760–9810. Subway: C, E to 23rd St.

9 *b-5*

INTAR THEATER
420 W. 42nd St., Hell's Kitchen, 212/279–4200. Subway: Port Authority/42nd St.

9 *a-3*

IRISH ARTS CENTER
553 W. 52nd St., Hell's Kitchen, 212/757–3318. Subway: 50th St.

9 *d-8*

IRISH REPERTORY THEATER
132 W. 22nd St., Chelsea, 212/727–2737.
Subway: F to 23rd St.

7 *e-6*

JEWISH REPERTORY THEATER
316 E. 91st St., Yorkville, 212/831–2000.
Subway: 4, 5, 6 to 86th St.

9 *b-5*

JOHN HOUSEMAN THEATER
450 42nd St., Hell's Kitchen, 212/967–9077. Subway: Port Authority/42nd St.

11 *f-2*

JOSEPH PAPP PUBLIC THEATER
425 Lafayette St. (near Astor Pl.), East Village, 212/598–7150. Subway: Astor Pl.; 8th St.

11 *g-2*

LA MAMA E.T.C.
74A E. 4th St. (between Bowery and 2nd Ave.), East Village, 212/475–7710. Subway: 2nd Ave.; Astor Pl.; Bleecker St./Broadway–Lafayette St.

9 *d-4*

LAMBS THEATER
130 W. 44th St., Theater District, 212/239–6200. Subway: B, D, F, Q to 42nd St.

9 *c-4*

LAURA PELS THEATER
1530 Broadway (at 45th St.), Theater District, 212/869–8400. Subway: Times Sq./42nd St.

11 *a-2*

LUCILLE LORTEL THEATER
121 Christopher St. (between Bleecker and Hudson Sts.), West Village, 212/239–6200. Subway: Christopher St./Sheridan Sq.

12 *d-3*

MAJESTIC THEATER
651 Fulton St. (2 blocks west of the Brooklyn Academy of Music), Downtown Brooklyn, 718/636–4100. Subway: Atlantic Ave.; Pacific St.

9 *d-3*

MANHATTAN THEATER CLUB
131 W. 55th St., Midtown, 212/581–1212.
Subway: 57th St.

11 *c-2*

MINETTA LANE THEATER
18 Minetta La. (between Bleecker and W. 3rd Sts.; off 6th Ave.), Greenwich Village, 212/420–8000. Subway: W. 4th St.

9 *b-2*

MITZI E. NEWHOUSE THEATER
Lincoln Center, 150 W. 65th St., Upper West Side, 212/239–6200. Subway: 66th St./Lincoln Center.

9 *b-3*

NEGRO ENSEMBLE COMPANY
424 W. 55th St., Hell's Kitchen, 212/246–8545. Subway: 57th St.

11 *g-2*

NEW YORK THEATER WORKSHOP
79 E. 4th St. (between Bowery and 2nd Ave.), East Village, 212/460–5475. Subway: 2nd Ave.; Bleecker St./Broadway–Lafayette St.

11 *e-4*

OHIO THEATER
66 Wooster St. (between Broome and Spring Sts.), SoHo, 212/966–2509. Subway: Spring St.

11 *g-1*

ORPHEUM THEATER
126 2nd Ave. (at 8th St.), East Village, 212/307–4100. Subway: 2nd Ave.

9 *b-4*

PAN ASIAN REPERTORY THEATER
423 W. 46th St., Hell's Kitchen, 212/245–2660. Subway: Port Authority/42nd St.

11 *g-1*

PEARL THEATER COMPANY
80 St. Mark's Pl. (between 2nd and 3rd Aves.), East Village, 212/598–9802. Subway: Astor Pl.; 8th St.

11 *d-2*

PLAYERS THEATER
115 MacDougal St. (at Minetta La., between Bleecker and W. 4th Sts.), Greenwich Village, 212/254–5076. Subway: W. 4th St.

7 *f-6*

PLAYHOUSE 91
316 E. 91st St., Yorkville, 212/207–4100. Subway: 4, 5, 6 to 86th St.

9 *b-5*

PLAYWRIGHTS HORIZONS MAIN STAGE
416 W. 42nd St., Hell's Kitchen, 212/279–4200. Subway: Port Authority/42nd St.

9 *c-4*

PRIMARY STAGES
345 W. 45th St., Midtown, 212/333–4052. Subway: Port Authority/42nd St.

7 *b-8*

PROMENADE THEATER
2162 Broadway (at 76th St.), Upper West Side, 212/239–6200. Subway: 1, 2, 3, 9 to 72nd St.

9 *d-7*

REPERTORIO ESPAÑOL
138 E. 27th St. (between Park and Lexington Aves.), Gramercy, 212/889–2850. Subway: 28th St.

9 *b-5*

SAMUEL BECKETT THEATER
410 W. 42nd St., Hell's Kitchen, 212/594–2826. Subway: Port Authority/42nd St.

11 *a-3*

ST. JOHN'S CHURCH
81 Christopher St. (between Bleecker St. and 7th Ave.), West Village, 212/239–6200. Subway: Christopher St./Sheridan Sq.

9 *c-4*

ST. LUKE'S CHURCH
308 W. 46th St., Midtown 212/239–6200. Subway: Port Authority/42nd St.

7 *b-8*

SECOND STAGE
2162 Broadway (at 76th St.), Upper West Side, 212/239–6200. Subway: 1, 2, 3, 9 to 72nd St.

11 *b-4*

SOHO PLAYHOUSE
15 Vandam St. (between 6th Ave. and Varick St.), SoHo, 212/691–1555. Subway: Spring St.

9 *c-3*

STARDUST THEATER
1650 Broadway (at 51st St.), Theater District, 212/239–6200. Subway: 49th St.; 50th St.

11 *d-3*

SULLIVAN STREET PLAYHOUSE
The world's longest-running musical, *The Fantasticks*, is now in its 37th year here. *181 Sullivan St. (between Houston and Bleecker Sts.), Greenwich Village, 212/674–3838. Subway: Bleecker St./Broadway–Lafayette St.*

11 *c-1*

THEATER OFF PARK
224 Waverly Pl. (between 11th and Perry Sts.; west of 7th Ave.), West Village, 212/627–2556. Subway: A, C, E to 14th St..

10 *d-1*

THE 13TH STREET THEATER
50 W. 13th St., Greenwich Village, 212/627–2556. Subway: A, C, E to 14th St.

9 *f-8*

UNION SQUARE THEATER
100 E. 17th St., Gramercy, 212/307–4100. Subway: 14th St./Union Sq.

10 *f-1*

VARIETY ARTS
110 3rd Ave. (between 13th and 14th Sts.), East Village, 212/239–6200. Subway: 14th St./Union Sq.

9 *c-4*

VILLAGE GATE
240 W. 52nd St., Theater District, 212/307–5252. Subway: 50th St.

10 *e-1*

VINEYARD THEATER
108 E. 15th St., Gramercy, 212/353–3366. Subway: 14th St./Union Sq.

10 *b-2*

WESTBETH THEATER CENTER
151 Bank St. (between Hudson St. and 12th Ave.), West Village, 212/741–0391. Subway: A, C, E to 14th St.

9 *b-5*

WESTSIDE ARTS THEATER
407 W. 43rd St., Hell's Kitchen, 212/239–6200. Subway: Port Authority/42nd St.

9 *b-7*

WPA THEATER
519 W. 23rd St., Chelsea, 212/206–0523. Subway: C, E to 23rd St.

9 *e-3*

YORK THEATER COMPANY
St. Peter's Church at Citicorp Center, 619 Lexington Ave. (at 54th St.), Midtown, 212/935–5820. Subway: 51st St./Lexington Ave.

nightlife

New York's nightlife has been shaken up in the past few years, as Mayor Rudy Giuliani's crackdown on "quality-of-life" issues has grown to include nightspots that disturb their neighbors. Peter Gatien (owner of the Limelight and Tunnel clubs) was arrested for profiting from drug dealing at his venues, and Limelight closed for while he was on trial. He was cleared and Limelight has since reopened, but it's a bit tamer than before. Drug raids, strict ID checks, and security guards have become a common feature of large clubs such as the Tunnel, putting everyone on edge. On the positive side, swing dancing continues to be a popular activity, with live bands playing almost every night of the week. There also seem to be more and more lounges and bars open, especially downtown. The Lower East Side probably has more bars now than in a generation. The seamy, gritty meatpacking district, north of the West Village, has also become a hot new nightspot area. If you're looking for the velvet-rope crowd, SoHo continues to be a sure bet. But the best news of all is that the cigar-bar trend has waned.

All nightspots stop serving alcohol at 4 AM, but die-hards keep grooving in dance clubs until long after the sun rises.

BARS

7 *e-8*

AMERICAN TRASH
Bikers, slackers, and yuppies mix well at this divey bar with a pool table and a good jukebox. *1471 1st Ave. (between 76th and 77th Sts.), Upper East Side, 212/988–9008. Subway: 77th St.*

11 *f-2*

B BAR
Although it's been replaced as *the* place to be seen, B Bar still has a cool vibe and a huge and wonderful outdoor patio. *358 Bowery (at 4th St.), East Village, 212/475–2220. Subway: Astor Pl.*

10 *d-1*

BAR SIX
Beautiful people and not a lot of attitude distinguish this hip spot. During the summer they open the French doors and you can take in the breeze. *502 6th Ave. (between 12th and 13th Sts.), Greenwich Village, 212/691–1363. Subway: F to 14th St., L to 6th Ave.*

10 *f-1*

BEAUTY BAR
Get a happy-hour manicure at this kitschy space with an old-time beauty-parlor vibe but an East Village clientele. *231 E. 14th St., East Village, 212/539–1389. Subway: 14th St./Union Sq.*

11 *g-2*

BOILER ROOM
A relaxed, dark gay bar with cheap drinks, a pool table, and an '80s-theme jukebox, this hot spot attracts Village dudes rather than Chelsea muscle boys. Girls take over one Sunday a month. *86 E. 4th St., East Village, 212/254–7536. Subway: Astor Pl.*

12 *d-4*

BROOKLYN INN
You'll find a killer jukebox, a pool table, an elaborate mahogany bar, and great bartenders—but no television—at this stalwart pub. The crowd is a friendly lot in their mid-twenties to mid-thirties. *138 Bergen St. (at Hoyt St.), Boerum Hill, Brooklyn, no phone. Subway: F, G to Bergen St.*

11 f-3
CHEZ ES SAADA
Follow the rose-petal strewn stairwell of this neo-Moroccan supper club to the catacomb-like lounge, recline on a hassock, and order a house cocktail. "Place of happiness" is the loose translation of the French-Arabic name, and it's hard not to be content in this setting that evokes the post-war Tangier of Paul Bowles. *42 E. 1st St., East Village, 212/ 777–5671. Subway: 2nd Ave.*

9 c-8
CIEL ROUGE
The room is red and smoky, and the cocktails are creative. A chanteuse takes over the piano on Tuesday night and coos Piaf-like songs—you'll think you've touched down on the Left Bank. During the summer you can breathe easier in the garden. *176 7th Ave., Chelsea, 212/ 929–5542. Subway: 1, 9 to 23rd St.*

9 f-4
CONNOLLY'S
This midtown Irish tavern is the current home of Black 47 (*see Paddy Reilly's Music Bar, below*). When the Celtic rockers aren't on tour, they're entertaining here on Saturday night. *14 E. 47th St. (near 5th Ave.), Midtown, 212/867–3767. Subway: B, D, F, Q to 42nd St.*

10 c-1
CORNER BISTRO
For more than 30 years this cozy, down-to-earth spot has been serving cold beer, mixed drinks, and the best hamburgers in town. Sometimes there's nothing better at 3 in the morning. Cash only. *331 W. 4th St. (at Jane St.), West Village, 212/242– 9502. Subway: A, C, E to 14th St., L to 8th Ave.*

11 g-1
DECIBEL SAKE BAR
The sign outside warns, "no sushi, no karaoke." The menu inside offers more than 40 kinds of sake. The crowd is young and hip and it's easy to loose the better part of the night here. *210 E. 9th St., East Village, 212/979–2733. Subway: Astor Pl.*

10 f-4
DOUBLE HAPPINESS
A subterranean lounge that opened in 1999, Double Happiness draws a hip crowd. Try the green tea martini and you

won't regret it. If you arrive early enough you can secure the so-called kissing room, a small, out-of-the-way banquette-lined space that has glass in the ceiling leading to the sidewalk above. *173 Mott St. (at Broome St.), Chinatown, 212/941–1282. Subway: Grand St.*

12 f-4
FREDDY'S
From the sidewalk it looks like a scary old-man's dive, but step in to this corner bar and you'll find a speakeasy-like back room with live music, film programs, and a hip, laid-back clientele. *485 Dean St. (at 6th Ave.), Prospect Heights, Brooklyn, 718/622–7035. Subway: 2, 3 to Bergen St.*

3 d-6
GALAPAGOS
Neighborhood hipsters flocked to this converted factory space when it opened in 1998. Since then the curious from across the East River have joined them, drawn by the reflecting pool, candlelight, experimental DJs, and by Ocularis, the popular Sunday night independent-film series. *70 N. 6th St. (between Wythe and Kent Aves.), Williamsburg, Brooklyn, 718/782–5188. Subway: L to Bedford Ave.*

12 f-6
GREAT LAKES
An outboard motor hangs from the ceiling and maps of Lake Michigan decorate the walls of this low-key lounge. It's frequented by Park Slope residents who prefer a night on a local barstool to one on the subway into Manhattan. *284 5th Ave. (at 1st St.), Park Slope, Brooklyn, 718/ 499–3710. Subway: F, N, R, to 4th Ave.*

11 b-3
HENRIETTA HUDSON
The best lesbian bar in town, this pick-up joint with two huge rooms and a pool table attracts all types of women. Some nights feature comedy or live music. *438 Hudson St. (off Morton St.), West Village, 212/924–3347. Subway: Houston St.*

10 b-1
HOGS & HEIFERS
Drew Barrymore and Julia Roberts have added their bras to the moose-head collection, and Harrison Ford and JFK, Jr. once stopped in. Why? They needed a break from the slick-n-trendy in spots

where one is *expected* to hang out. This is a pseudo-redneck dive, plain and simple. Leave your politically correct friends at the door, order a domestic beer, and dance on the bar. *859 Washington St. (at 13th St.), West Village, 212/929–0655. Subway: A, C, E to 14th St., L to 8th Ave.*

11 g-2

K.G.B.

This second-story bar with red walls and Soviet-era posters isn't a fake theme bar. The room actually was once the Ukrain-

---

HOTEL BARS

The city's hotel bars are among the most relaxing and refined places in town for a drink. And they can be a wonderfully deserted (and elegant) place to wind up a date.

Algonquin Hotel (59 W. 44th St.)
An old haunt of New Yorker writers, this gem lives on with a charmingly Victorian lobby.

King Cole Bar, St. Regis (2 E. 55th St.)
The cigar smoking can be overwhelming, but this spot with the famous Maxfield Parrish mural is where the Bloody Mary was invented.

The Mark (25 E. 77th St.)
Settle into one of the refined couches or arm chairs in this small salon and wait for the waiter to fill your request.

Oak Bar, Plaza Hotel (5th Ave. and 58th St.)
With dark wood walls and a convivial, monied, atmosphere, this is a great place to warm up after a winter's afternoon in Central Park.

The Paramount (235 W. 46th St.)
Head upstairs upon entering and tell them you might order a snack so you can sit at one of the tables overlooking the Philippe Starck lobby.

Soho Grand (310 W. Broadway)
A casual yet refined resting stop during a day of gallery hopping.

Whaler Bar, Jolly Madison Towers (22 E. 38th St.)
You wouldn't believe this obscure, almost always empty bar existed if you didn't see its grand piano, ship models, fireplace, and couches for yourself.

---

ian Communist Party headquarters, and before that it was a speakeasy. Today the K.G.B. attracts a literary crowd. *85 E. 4th St. (between 2nd and 3rd Aves.), East Village, 212/505–3360. Subway: 2nd Ave.*

10 g-3

LANSKY LOUNGE

A former speakeasy and haunt of gangster Myer Lansky, this spot was an instant hit when it opened a few years back. Girls in high heels and guys hoping to meet them love traipsing through an alley to down steeply priced cocktails. It's all part of the adventure. Closed Friday. *104 Norfolk St. (between Delancey and Rivington Sts.), Lower East Side, 212/677–9489. Subway: Delancey St.*

LAST EXIT

In a neighborhood full of sports bars and divey holes-in-the-wall, this popular spot—a chic retro-lounge straight out of the East Village—stands alone. The crowd is mostly local, from Brooklyn Heights yuppies to Cobble Hill writers. *136 Atlantic Ave. (between Henry and Clinton Sts), Cobble Hill, Brooklyn, 718/222–9198. Subway: N, R, 2, 3, 4, 5 to Borough Hall or F to Bergen St.*

11 d-6

LUCKY STRIKE

The grand daddy of hip SoHo bistros, this nightspot still draws the monied Euro crowd. The DJ-driven scene at the bar can get uncomfortably crowded, but Lucky Strike is hard to beat when it comes to finding a good meal after a night out, at say 2:45 AM. *59 Grand St. (between W. Broadway and Wooster St.), SoHo, 212/941–0479. Subway: Canal St.*

11 f-6

MARECHIARO TAVERN

Also known as Tony's, this Little Italy watering hole is a real throwback, in manners as well as atmosphere. It draws a strange mix of locals, literary types, and Silicon Alley entrepeneurs. *176 Mulberry St. (between Broome and Grand Sts.), Little Italy, no phone. Subway: 6 to Spring St.*

11 f-3

MARION'S CONTINENTAL LOUNGE

The tiny bar at the front of this dimly-lit restaurant serves up the best Martini in town. *354 Bowery (between Great Jones and W. 4th Sts.), East Village, 212/475–7621. Subway: Astor Pl.*

11 *g-2*

MCSORLEY'S OLD ALE HOUSE

Established in 1854, McSorley's is one of New York's oldest watering holes. The epitome of a saloon, it's dark, cramped, and dusty around the edges, but the old Irish barkeeps serve McSorley's own excellent dark and pale brews. *15 E. 7th St. (between 2nd and 3rd Aves.), East Village, 212/726-7600. Subway: Astor Pl.*

10 *g-3*

MEOW MIX

This East Village nightspot draws a solid lesbian crowd. The women are young, and they fill the leopard-skin chairs prepared to drink. *269 E. Houston St. (between Aves. A and B), East Village, 212/254–0688. Subway: 2nd Ave.*

9 *e-6*

MORGAN'S BAR

This dark subterranean space oozes coolness; it's popular with models, record-company executives, and those who just look like them. Thursday evenings during the summer, it fills up with young professionals bound for the Hamptons. Call ahead to reserve a table. *237 Madison Ave. (between 37th and 38th Sts.), Midtown, 212/726–7600. Subway: 33rd St.*

9 *e-8*

OLD TOWN BAR AND RESTAURANT

The name is accurate: this classic, wood-paneled, New York bar has been around since 1892 and still serves a great burger. *45 E. 18th St. (between Broadway and Park Ave. S), Gramercy, 212/529–6732. Subway: 14th St./Union Sq.*

11 *h-4*

ORCHARD

Look for the small glowing terrarium in the front window of this narrow lounge; there's little else to distinguish it. Inside you'll find a good-looking crowd and great DJs. *200 Orchard St. (between Houston and Stanton Sts.), Lower East Side, 212/673–5350. Subway: 2nd Ave.*

9 *f-7*

PADDY REILLY'S MUSIC BAR

This Irish hole-in-the-wall launched the rocking-roots band Black 47 (see Con-

nolly's, *above*). Another up-and-coming Celtic rock outfit, The Prodigals, plays Saturday night. Live music is frequent, including a regular Irish jam session on Thursday night. Grab a Guinness and pogo with the crowd. *519 2nd Ave. (between 28th and 29th Sts.), Gramercy, 212/686–1210. Subway: 28th St.*

11 *f-4*

PEN TOP BAR AND TERRACE

Come summertime, if you're earning the big bucks, there's no better place for an after-work drink. This bar has outdoor seating 23 stories high; you'll have an eye-level view of the moon rising between the sky scrapers. *Peninsula Hotel, 700 Fifth Ave. (at 55th St.), Midtown, 212/903–3097. Subway: E, F to Fifth Ave.*

11 *f-4*

PRAVDA

The martinis are divine at this trendy but friendly Russian-theme lounge with a tiny upstairs bar. If yours is an obscure brand of vodka, this is the place to track it down: There are more than 70 brands behind the bar. The street entrance is difficult to find; look for stairs going down. Tip: Brush up on your Russian before you venture into the loo. *281 Lafayette St. (between Prince and Houston Sts.), East Village, 212/226–4696. Subway: Houston St.*

9 *d-4*

THE ROYALTON

The lobby of this Phillipe Starck–designed hotel is a cool place to keep an eye on the parade of celebrities and guests dining at 44. Everything, including the entrance to the hotel (look for the curved silver railings) is hidden. The intimate Vodka Bar is to your right as you enter from the street. Dress: sleek. *44 W. 44th St., Midtown, 212/768–5000 or 212/869–4400. Subway: 42nd St./Grand Central.*

7 *b-8*

SHARK BAR

Anyone who wants to eat at this fantastic Southern restaurant has to make it through the slick but friendly yuppie crowd at the bar. *307 Amsterdam Ave. (between 73rd and 74th Sts.), Upper West Side, 212/874–8500. Subway: 72nd St.*

11 *e-4*

SOHO KITCHEN AND BAR

Bartenders behind this big, paper-clip–shape bar can pour from an enormous selection of beers and wines by the glass or the flight—for example, a tasting of three South American reds. Those not into SoHo's black-clothing-only vibe will fit in just fine here. *103 Greene St. (between Spring and Prince Sts.), SoHo, 212/925–1866. Subway: Spring or Prince St.*

11 *e-4*

SPY

If you can get past the velvet rope, settle into a plush couch and enjoy the baroque parlor setting and pretty people. Opened in 1995, Spy was a setter of the lounge trend and it somehow has maintained its hot status. *101 Greene St. (between Spring and Prince Sts.), SoHo. 212/343–9000. Subway: Spring or Prince St.*

11 *b-1*

STONEWALL

This unpretentious gay bar, the site of the Stonewall riot, attracts a mix of tourists and neighborhood regulars. *53 Christopher St. (between 7th Ave. S and Waverly Pl.), West Village, 212/463–0950. Subway: Christopher St.*

10 *f-1*

TELEPHONE BAR

Red English telephone booths decorate the entrance and a handsome, thirty-something crowd lines the bar at this publike restaurant. *149 2nd Ave. (between 10th and 11th Sts.), East Village, 212/529–5000. Subway: Astor Pl.*

10 *f-1*

TENTH STREET LOUNGE

Since this sleek lounge opened in 1992, its cavernous space (formerly an ambulance garage) has been packed with handsome patrons, who look even better in glow of the tapers on the cinder block walls. *212 E. 10th St. (between 1st and 2nd Aves.), East Village, 212/473–5252. Subway: Astor Pl.*

11 *f-3*

TEMPLE BAR

Look for the painted iguana skeleton (there's no sign) and walk past the slim bar to the back, where, in near-total darkness, you can lounge on a plush banquette surrounded by velvet drapes. *332 Lafayette St. (at Bleecker St.), East Village, 212/925–4242. Subway: Houston St.*

9 *d-3*

21 CLUB

Long a haunt for power suits toasting their latest M&A, the bar in this dark bastion is staid and discreet, and attracts more than its share of recognizable faces. (*See* Continental *in* Chapter 1.) *21 W. 52nd St., Midtown, 212/582–7200. Subway: 50th St.; 47–50th Sts./Rockefeller Center.*

9 *d-5*

THE VIEW LOUNGE

This large, bilevel, slowly revolving lounge has a phenomenal view of the city. You might concede the prices are worth it when you sink into a banquette and notice how serene the city looks from the 48th floor. *Marriott Marquis, 1700 Broadway (at 44th St.), 48th floor, Theater District. 212/398–1900. Subway: 42nd St./Times Sq.*

9 *g-7*

WATER CLUB

You'll feel like you're in a private club in Darien, but you're actually on a docked barge on the East River. On one side is a polished wood bar accented by floral arrangements and framed prints; on the other is the lovely dining room, with New York's version of a water view. But if you hit the weather and the timing's right (call ahead), you can slouch in a director's chair at the open-deck bar upstairs. *500 E. 30th St., Murray Hill, 212/683–3333. Subway: 28th St.*

12 *b-4*

WATERFRONT ALE HOUSE

Come here for more beers-on-tap than you can taste in a single night, free popcorn, and decent grub from the kitchen. *155 Atlantic Ave. (between Henry and Clinton Sts), Cobble Hill, Brooklyn, 718/522–3794. Subway: N, R, 2, 3, 4, 5 to Borough Hall or F to Bergen St.*

BLUES

10 *c-1*

CHICAGO BLUES

This club has become an institution, with open jam nights about once a week, and a regular roster of top-notch blues stars. *73 8th Ave. (between 12th and 13th Sts.), West Village, 212/924–9755. Subway: A, C, E to 14th St., L to 8th Ave.*

10 *f-6*

SEAPORT LIBERTY CRUISES
Every Wednesday in the summer, these boats with live blues bands circle Manhattan. *Pier 16, South Street Seaport, Lower Manhattan, 888/322–2583. Subway: Fulton St.*

11 *c-2*

TERRA BLUES
Smokin' local blues bands as well as traveling names take the stage here in New York's blues district. *149 Bleecker St. (between Thompson St. and LaGuardia Pl.), Greenwich Village, 212/777–7776. Subway: Bleecker St./Broadway–Lafayette St.*

CABARET

7 *d-8*

CAFE CARLYLE
See Piano Bars, *below.*

9 *c-4*

DON'T TELL MAMA
Catch singers, comedians, and female impersonators in the long-running backroom cabaret. Extroverts will be tempted by the open mike at the piano bar up front. *343 W. 46th St., Theater District, 212/757–0788. Subway: 42nd St./Times Sq.*

9 *b-5*

DOWNSTAIRS AT THE WEST BANK CAFE
Below a restaurant across from Theater Row, this club makes the most of its surroundings, serving up plays, cabaret, and musical revues. *407 W. 42nd St., Theater District, 212/695–6909. Subway: 42nd St./Times Sq.*

11 *b-1*

THE DUPLEX
Opened in 1951, this gay, campy cabaret claims to be New York's oldest. Upstairs you might find a singer, comedian, or rock band (or, on open-mike night, folks who fancy themselves any of the above); downstairs, a piano bar. *61 Christopher St. (at 7th Ave.), West Village, 212/255–5438. Subway: Christopher St.*

11 *b-2*

55 GROVE STREET
Above Rose's bar, this landmark cabaret offers a piano bar, singers, celebrity impersonators, and sketch comedy. *55 Grove St. (between Bleecker St. and 7th Ave. S.), West Village, 212/366–5438. Subway: Christopher St.*

9 *b-5*

FIREBIRD CAFE
A mosaic of Klimt's *Kiss* on this intimate space's red walls is a good indication of the sophisticated music and cuisine on the bill; caviar and vodka are the choice accompaniment here. *356 W. 46th St., Theater District, 212/586–0244. Subway: 42nd St./Times Sq.*

11 *h-3*

JOE'S PUB
The Public Theatre's "pub" is the poshest one in town, with red-velvet walls chosen by legendary nightclub impresario Serge Becker. Among other sirens, the hybrid exclusive nightclub and cabaret space has hosted down-to-earth diva Ute Lemper. *425 Lafayette St. (between Astor Pl and W. 4th St.), East Village, 212/539-8770. Subway: Bleecker St./Broadway–Lafayette St.*

11 *h-3*

LUCKY CHENG'S
Lucky Cheng's is more a restaurant (serving Asian fare) than a cabaret, but you will see Asian drag queens cavorting with Jersey bridesmaids on a stage near the bar. Costumed queens also strut their stuff to taped music in front of the cellar's goldfish pond. *24 1st Ave. (between 1st and 2nd Sts.), East Village, 212/473–0516. Subway: 2nd Ave.*

9 *d-5*

OAK ROOM
Gifted song stylists such as Andrea Marcovicci draw crowds at this sophisticated, long and narrow club-cum-watering hole. One of the great classic cabarets, the Oak Room is formal (jacket and tie for men) and offers pre-theater dining; diners get better tables. *Algonquin Hotel, 59 W. 44th St., Midtown, 212/840–6800. Subway: 42nd St./Grand Central.*

COMEDY

10 *d-3*

BOSTON COMEDY CLUB
This club gets its name because of its owner's fondness for the city on the Charles River. It's often packed with

NYU students. Be kind if you drop in on Monday, open-mike night. *82 W. 3rd St. (between Thompson and Sullivan Sts.), Greenwich Village, 212/477–1000. Subway: W. 4th St.*

9 *c-4*

CAROLINE'S

This high-gloss stand-up club features established names as well as those on the brink; Joy Behar, Sandra Bernhard, and Gilbert Gottfried have appeared. Head downstairs when you arrive; the entrance to the show area is to the right of the bar. *1626 Broadway (between 49th and 50th Sts.), Midtown, 212/757–4100. Subway: 50th St.*

9 *f-2*

CHICAGO CITY LIMITS

This improv troupe has been doing what they describe as "comedy without a net" for almost 20 years. They're big on audience participation. *1105 1st Ave. (between 58th and 59th Sts.), Upper East Side, 212/888–5233. Subway: 59th St./Lexington Ave.*

11 *c-3*

THE COMEDY CELLAR

Beneath the Olive Tree Café, this long-standing, tightly packed club has had consistently good bills for nearly 20 years and shows no sign of slowing down; it's open nightly until 2:30 AM. *117 MacDougal St. (between Bleecker and W. 3rd Sts.), Greenwich Village, 212/254–3480. Subway: W. 4th St.*

7 *f-8*

COMIC STRIP

This classic comedy showcase is packed, yet it feels like a corner bar. Eddie Murphy got some of his first laughs here. *1568 2nd Ave. (between 81st and 82nd Sts.), Upper East Side, 212/861–9386. Subway: 77th St.*

9 *f-2*

DANGERFIELD'S

Comedian Rodney Dangerfield owns this club, an important stand-up showcase since 1969. *1118 1st Ave. (between 61st and 62nd Sts.), Upper East Side, 212/593–1650. Subway: 59th St./Lexington Ave.*

9 *d-8*

GOTHAM COMEDY CLUB

This relative newcomer shoots for the upscale crowd. It's in a landmark building and is decorated with mahogany furnishings and a turn-of-the-century chandelier. Headliners have included Chris Rock and David Brenner. Once a month the club presents a Latino comedy show. *34 W. 22nd St., Chelsea, 212/367–9000. Subway: 34th St.*

9 *c-6*

ORIGINAL IMPROV

Lots of now-famous comedians, including Richard Pryor and Bette Midler, got their first laughs with this troupe, which left its longtime home in the Garment District for these Restaurant Row digs in 1999. *Danny's Skylight Room, 346 W. 46th St. 212/475–6147. Subway: 34th St.*

7 *a-8*

STAND-UP NEW YORK

If you're on the West Side and need some comic relief, make tracks to this club—the stage gets some recognizable faces. *236 W. 78th St., Upper West Side, 212/595–0850. Subway: 79th St.*

9 *c-8*

THE UPRIGHT CITIZENS BRIGADE THEATRE

Sketch comedy, improv, and even classes are available at this venue which was recently opened by the UCB. *161 W. 22nd St., Chelsea, 212/366–9176. Subway: F to 23rd St.*

DANCE CLUBS

9 *b-3*

COPACABANA NEW YORK

A well-dressed (by club law) Latino crowd comes to salsa to a live orchestra at this legendary club on Tuesday, Friday, and Saturday. *617 W. 57th St., Midtown, 212/582–2672. Subway: 57th St.*

10 *d-1*

KEY CLUB

If you just want to dance and perhaps make some new Eurofriends, the Key Club is the place. It has a strong sound system and a sizable dance floor. *76 E. 13th St., East Village, 212/388–1060. Subway: 14th St./Union Sq.*

9 *b-3*

LE BAR BAT

Yes, there are fake bats and a Halloween feel at this flashy monster on Theme Restaurant Row, but don't expect to find Goths. There's no

Bauhaus; just upbeat, danceable tunes to sing along to. *11 W. 57th St., Midtown, 212/307–7228. Subway: 57th St.*

9 *d-8*

LIMELIGHT

After a law-enforcement-induced hiatus, this club reopened its doors in 1999. The girls dancing in cages are gone, replaced by such respectability-seeking decor as an art gallery, but you still never know what amusement you'll find in the dark corners of this labyrinthine space in a former church. *660 6th Ave. (between 20th and 21st Sts.), Chelsea, 212/807–7850. Subway: F to 23rd St.*

10 *b-1*

MOTHER

This small, mostly gay club in the meat-packing district hosts the legendary Tuesday-night party Jackie 60, at which flamboyance rules. The theme changes each week; call ahead and dress appropriately. Saturday night's cyber-themed Click & Drag party is popular, but you might not make it past the door without thigh-high silver platform boots and some S&M gear. The DJ spins mainly industrial and hard house, and there are performances late in the evening. Fridays draw lipstick lesbians to the Clit Club party. *432 W. 14th St. (at Washington St.), West Village, 212/366–5680. Subway: A, C, E to 14th St., L to 8th Ave.*

9 *c-8*

OHM

One of the city's newest dance halls, this sleek club draws hordes of twenty-something professionals who come to free themselves with house and techno music. *16 W. 22nd St., Chelsea, 212/229–2000. Subway: F to 23rd St.*

11 *e-2*

POLLY ESTHER'S

The walls of this club (really more like a bar) make it look like a suburban teenage bedroom, circa 1977: Posters and pinups of Charlie's Angels, Cheryl Tiegs, Leif Garrett, and Shaun Cassidy cover every inch. Young yups make new friends as they catch disco fever on the small dance floor. *186 W. 4th St., Greenwich Village, 212/924–5707. Subway: W. 4th St.*

11 *h-1*

PYRAMID

This quintessential East Village club relives the '80s—in all of its New Wave

glory—with "1984" on Friday. Other nights you'll find kitsch art shows, avant-garde theme parties, and a highly unpredictable assortment of live performances. *101 Ave. A (between 8th and 9th Sts.), East Village, 212/473–7184. Subway: Astor Pl.*

9 *c-3*

ROSELAND

They're serious about ballroom dancing here. It's no longer 10 cents a dance, but this enormous space still recalls another time. Dancing happens Thursday (with a DJ) and Sunday (with an orchestra *and* a DJ). The average age of the patrons nose-dives the rest of the week, when bands such as the Foo Fighters and GWAR fill the space with distinctly modern music. *239 W. 52nd St., Midtown, 212/247–0200. Subway: 50th St.*

9 *b-8*

ROXY

Roxy's 5,000-square-ft dance floor turns into a chaotic, pulsating roller disco on Wednesday and a multiborough dance club Friday and Saturday. *515 W. 18th St., Chelsea, 212/645–5156. Subway: 14th St.*

11 *c-4*

S.O.B.'S

The name stands for Sounds of Brazil. The decor is tropical, and a joyful carnival atmosphere prevails year-round. Regional Brazilian food is served, and there's live, spirited Brazilian, Caribbean, African, and Latin music and dancing on the small dance floor. *200 Varick St. (at W. Houston St.), West Village, 212/243–4940. Subway: Houston St.*

9 *a-7*

TUNNEL

This laser-lit megaclub has about a million rooms, with about a million DJs spinning about a million types of music. Be prepared for the unisex bathroom, with its own bar and lounge. *220 12th Ave. (at 27th St.), Chelsea, 212/695–4682. Subway: C, E to 23rd St.*

9 *a-7*

TWILO

Some of Europe's finest DJs spin all night long at this mega club that's popular with everyone from gay muscle boys to straight arrows. *530 W. 27th St. (at 12th Ave.), Chelsea, 212/268–1600. Subway: C, E to 23rd St.*

10 *d-4*

VINYL

One of the high temples of dance, this intimate alchohol-free club regularly features top name international DJs, and hosts the popular Body & Soul party on Sunday afternoons. *6 Hubert St. (between Hudson and Greenwich Sts.), Tribeca, 212/343–1379. Subway: 1, 9 to Franklin St.*

10 *e-1*

WEBSTER HALL

A fave with NYU students and the bridge and tunnel crowd, Webster Hall has four floors, five eras of music, trapeze artists, and occasionally live bands. *125 E. 11th St., East Village, 212/353–1600. Subway: 14th St. or Astor Pl.*

DINING & DANCING

9 *c-6*

RED BLAZER HIDEAWAY

On average the crowd is in the Social Security–drawing age, but there are often younger folks—on dates or with bachelorette parties—enjoying their chance to learn a step or two from the seniors. *32 W. 37th St., Theater District, 212/947–6428. Subway: 42nd St./Times Sq.*

9 *c-4*

SUPPER CLUB

This is exactly what a supper club should look like: a true ballroom, two levels to explore, and plush banquettes to hide away in. A full orchestra plays big-band swing on Friday and Saturday nights. During the rest of the week, touring alternative and rock-and-roll bands take the stage. *240 W. 47th St., Theater District, 212/921–1940. Subway: 42nd St./Times Sq.*

JAZZ

10 *c-2*

ARTHUR'S TAVERN

Dixieland jazz is nearly always on tap at this ancient venue, which was once one of Charlie Parker's regular hangouts. There's rarely a cover charge. *57 Grove St., West Village, 212/675–6879. Subway: Christopher St.*

9 *b-5*

BIRDLAND

Originally Charlie Parker's place on 57th Street, this club was one of the centers of jazz's golden age, with everyone up to Miles Davis and the Bird himself taking the stage. From 5 PM to midnight you'll find up-and-coming groups and well-known performers, plus dinner. *315 W. 44th St., Theater District, 212/581–3080. Subway: 42nd St./Times Sq.*

11 *c-2*

BLUE NOTE

This large jazz club presents respected jazz, Latin, and blues artists. Ticket prices dive on Monday, when record labels promote their artists' new releases. *131 W. 3rd St. (between 6th Ave. and MacDougal St.), Greenwich Village, 212/475–8592. Subway: W. 4th St.*

10 *c-1*

CAJUN

This landlocked Chelsea restaurant with a riverboat feel dishes New Orleans–style jazz alongside Cajun-Creole grub. Live music from the likes of former Louis Armstrong clarinetist Joe Muranyi makes you feel like you've ducked in off Bourbon Street. Dixieland is the fare every night save Wednesday, when modern swing takes over. *129 8th Ave. (between 14th and 15th Sts.), Chelsea, 212/691–6174. Subway: A, C, E to 14th St., L to 8th Ave.*

9 *b-2*

IRIDIUM

This subterranean space, beneath the Dali-esque Merlot Bar and Grill, routinely features some of the finest names in jazz. *48 W. 63rd St., Upper West Side, 212/582–2121. Subway: Lincoln Center.*

9 *e-7*

JAZZ STANDARD

A relative newcomer to the jazz scene, this restaurant is coolly decorated and brightly furnished. It serves up top talent each week. *116 E. 27th St., Flatiron District, 212/576–2232. Subway: 28th St.*

11 *d-7*

KNITTING FACTORY

This downtown venue has become an institution. The bar is laid-back, and the three performance spaces often showcase avant-garde jazz artists, as well as rock acts and some electronica. *74 Leonard St. (between Broadway and*

Church St.), Tribeca, 212/219–3055. Subway: Franklin St.

7 *d-1*

LENOX LOUNGE

Uptown is the place for smoking jazz in an equally smoky ambience. Mickey Bass, a former bassist for Art Blakey's Jazz Messengers, takes care of the booking, so quality is assured. *288 Lenox Ave. (between 124th and 125th Sts.), Harlem, 212/722–9566. Subway: Lenox Ave.*

11 *b-2*

SMALL'S

If you're hankering for a jazz jam at 5 AM, head to this pocket-size club, where sessions run from 10 PM to 8 AM. The look is exposed brick and low lighting. They don't serve liquor, but you can bring your own. The cover charge is only $10. *183 W. 10th St. (at 7th Ave.), West Village, 212/929–7565. Subway: Christopher St.*

11 *b-2*

SWEET BASIL

Sweet Basil is a little ritzier than most dark jazz spots. It's a popular eatery and bar with mainstream jazz in comfortable, brick-and-wood surroundings. There are three shows nightly and a Sunday brunch. *88 7th Ave. S (between Grove and Bleecker Sts.), West Village, 212/242–1785. Subway: Christopher St.*

10 *g-3*

TONIC

Much in the way the Knitting Factory (*see above*) provided a home for experimental music in the eighties, this former kosher winery on the Lower East Side is now *the* place for avant-garde jazz and other unusual sounds. *107 Norfolk St. (between Delancey and Rivington Sts.), Lower East Side, 212/358–7503. Subway: Delancey St.*

10 *c-1*

VILLAGE VANGUARD

Since 1935 this renowned New York jazz institution has featured all the greats—Monk, Coltrane, Charles Mingus, Gordon, Marsalis, and so on. It's a quintessential, noisy, smoky, no-frills, Greenwich Village basement club. Get there early if you want a good seat. *178 7th Ave. S (between 11th and Perry Sts.), West Village, 212/255–4037. Subway: A, C, E to 14th St., L to 8th Ave.*

10 *d-3*

ZINC BAR

This petite subterranean spot features Brazilian jazz on the weekends and the bebop guitarist Ron Affif most Monday nights. During the rest of the week you'll find a variety of swinging performers. *90 W. Houston St., Greenwich Village, 212/477–8337. Subway: Bleecker St./Broadway–Lafayette St.*

NIGHTCLUBS

9 *f-2*

DECADE

This smart dance club draws a fortyish crowd—hence, perhaps, the tame music. There's a serious pick-up scene at the bar and, of course, a cigar lounge. The decor is spare and funky, and the food is passable. *1117 1st Ave. (between 58th and 59th Sts.), Midtown, 212/835–5979. Subway: 59th St./Lexington Ave.*

10 *d-6*

GREATEST BAR ON EARTH

Extraordinary views and DJ Lucien's '60s lounge repertoire draws an unusual mix of suits and retro-clad downtowners to this tourist attraction. The Strato Lounge party is on Wednesday; other nights, DJs and live bands play swing, funk, and blues. You won't get past the elevator if you wear sneakers. *1 World Trade Center, 107th floor, Lower Manhattan, 212/524–7000. Subway: World Trade Center.*

11 *c-2*

LIFE

Wednesday night is Lust for Life, a guy punk night. Other nights, drag queens, Europoseurs, and SoHo types groove to house at this glamorous club in the heart of the Village. *158 Bleecker St. (at Thompson St.), Greenwich Village, 212/420–1999. Subway: W. 4th St.*

10 *c-1*

NELL'S

It's *intime* with all the trappings of a time past—overstuffed seating, subdued lighting, wood paneling, gilt mirrors, and quiet places to drink, dine, and talk. Downstairs you can dance to house, reggae, hip-hop, or whatever the DJ decrees. *246 W. 14th St., Chelsea, 212/675–1567. Subway: A, C, E to 14th St., L to 8th Ave.*

9 *e-4*

ONE51

The latest celebrity hang-out, this bilevel supper club was teeming with the likes of Sean "Puffy" Combs, Jennifer Lopez, Milla Javovich, and Michael Douglas shortly after opening in the fall of 1999. If you can get in you'll find a domed dance floor (topped by a graffiti version of Matisse's *The Dance*), a Technicolor light show, and, from time to time, live bands. *151 E. 50th St. (between Lexington and 3rd Aves.), Midtown, 212/753–1144. Subway: 51st St.*

PIANO BARS

Of the cabarets listed above, Don't Tell Mama, Duplex, and the Oak Room have piano bars as well.

7 *e-7*

BRANDY'S PIANO BAR

This small, convivial neighborhood spot is packed with smiling people. There's piano entertainment nightly and sometimes other fare as well, such as folk or swing. *235 E. 84th St., Upper East Side, 212/650–1944. Subway: 4, 5, 6 to 86th St.*

7 *d-8*

CAFÉ CARLYLE AND BEMELMANS BAR

The unpretentiously elegant Café Carlyle is a must, especially when witty, urbane entertainer Bobby Short is in residence (September–December and April–June); he's as New York as Gershwin. The rest of the year you might find Barbara Cook or Eartha Kitt purring by the piano. The dining is intimate, especially if you're on a comfy banquette. You can dine at the bar for a fraction of the price. Next door, sophisticated Bemelmans Bar is perfect for a cocktail or cognac, with murals by the author of the *Madeline* books as a backdrop. *Carlyle Hotel, 35 E. 76th St. (enter through main hotel or at 981 Madison Ave.), Upper East Side, 212/744–1600. Subway: 77th St.*

9 *d-2*

CAFÉ PIERRE

The piano in this classy venue plays nightly to a dressy (jacket required), upscale international crowd. *2 E. 61st St., Upper East Side, 212/838–8000. Subway: 59th St./Lexington Ave.*

9 *g-4*

TOP OF THE TOWER

This seductive, 26th-floor, penthouse cocktail lounge is filled with romantic duos gazing at one another and the twinkling city lights. The atmosphere is elegant and subdued. There's piano music every night save Monday. *Beekman Tower, 3 Mitchell Pl. (off 1st Ave./49th St.), Midtown, 212/355–7300. Subway: 51st St.*

POP/ROCK

10 *g-3*

ARLENE GROCERY

Shane Doyle closed down his much-loved Sin-e Cafe in the East Village, and converted an old bodega into perhaps the best spot to catch an up-and-coming rock band. The grocery is small, friendly, and always free. *95 Stanton St. (between Ludlow and Orchard Sts.), Lower East Side, 212/358–1633. Subway: 2nd Ave.*

11 *c-2*

THE BITTER END

Once upon a time Bob Dylan, Lisa Loeb, and Warren Zevon played The Bitter End, a Village standby for middle-of-the-road rock, fusion, folk, and blues. Moral: You never know which of this week's unknowns will be accepting a Grammy a few years hence. *147 Bleecker St. (between Thompson St. and LaGuardia Pl.), Greenwich Village, 212/673–7030. Subway: W. 4th St.*

11 *e-2*

BOTTOM LINE

A warm and intimate space built mainly of wood, this granddaddy of clubs has showcased such budding talents as Stevie Wonder and Bruce Springsteen. David Johansen, a.k.a. Buster Poindexter, regularly tries out new projects here; other recent headliners include Mathew Sweet and Willie Nelson. When there's a crowd, patrons are packed like sardines at long, thin tables; but most don't mind, as there's not a bad seat in the house, and, remarkably, smoking is not allowed. *15 W. 4th St., Greenwich Village, 212/228–7880. Subway: W. 4th St.*

10 *g-3*

BOWERY BALLROOM

The folks who own the Mercury Lounge (see below) opened this sparkling mid-size venue a few years ago. It is one of the best places to see bands before they start selling out arenas. *6 Delancey St., Lower East Side, 212/533–2111. Subway: Delancey St.*

10 *g-1*
BROWNIES
This hole-in-the-wall has been a fixture on the guitar-rock circuit since it opened some 10 years ago. An upgraded sound system and a solid booking policy keeps Brownies among the best places to find the best new music. The cover is usually cheap and the music loud. *169 Ave. A (between 10th and 11th Sts.), East Village, 212/420–8392. Subway: 2nd Ave.*

11 *f-3*
CBGB AND OMFUG/CB'S 313 GALLERY
Punk was born at CB's, a long, dark tunnel of a club featuring bands with inventive names like Shirley Temple of Doom and Reuben Kincaid (hey—who had heard of Blondie or the Ramones in 1976?). Next door, 313 attracts a quieter crowd with mostly acoustic music. *313– 315 Bowery (between 1st and 2nd Sts.), East Village, 212/982–4052 (CBGB), 212/677– 0455 (CB's 313 Gallery). Subway: Bleecker St./Broadway–Lafayette St.; Astor Pl.*

10 *e-2*
FEZ
Below Time Cafe you'll find this swank neo-Moroccan hideaway. The music is eclectic, anything from folk to rock to the weekly Mingus Big Band, but it is uniformly good. *380 Lafayette St., (at Great Jones St.), East Village, 212/533– 7000. Subway: Astor Pl.*

10 *e-1*
IRVING PLAZA
The perfect size for general-admission live music, Irving Plaza serves up everything from Macy Gray and Bob Mould to Southside Johnny and the Asbury

Jukes. There's a small balcony with a bar and an even smaller lounge. *17 Irving Pl. (at E. 15th St.), Gramercy, 212/777–1224. Subway: 14th St./Union Sq.*

11 *d-7*
KNITTING FACTORY
See Jazz, *above.*

10 *g-3*
TONIC
See Jazz, *above.*

10 *g-3:*
MERCURY LOUNGE
A former tombstone display parlor hosts two to five bands a night, rocking away on an above-average sound system. There are only two rooms here, a bar in the front and the cozy space in the back where the bands perform. *217 E. Houston St., East Village, 212/260–4700. Subway: 2nd Ave.*

11 *c-3*
ROCK 'N' ROLL CAFÉ
Nostalgic for the Doors, Led Zep, Hendrix, or Clapton? Choose a night and the appropriate sleeveless concert T, and rock out to a cover band. *149 Bleecker St., Greenwich Village, 212/677–7630. Subway: W. 4th St.*

11 *c-7*
WETLANDS
Throw on your tie-dye and get down-to-earth at this ode to the '60s—VW bus and everything—with an environmental-'90s bent. The live music, often psychedelic and often danceable, ranges from reggae and grass-roots rock to bluegrass and folk. Dave Matthews and Hootie and the Blowfish used to play this small space, known as the Sweatlands when it's packed. *161 Hudson St. (at Laight St.), Tribeca, 212/966–4225. Subway: Canal St.*

chapter 6

HOTELS

If you haven't checked the prices of New York City hotels lately, prepare for a rude awakening—it is truly difficult to find decent rooms for less than $200, and most cost twice that. What will a romantic splurge run you these days? Premium hotels such as the Four Seasons and the St. Regis charge over $550 for standard rooms.

On a more reassuring note, you rarely have to pay the full "rack rate," or standard room cost that hotels print in their brochures and quote over the phone. Hotels almost always offer corporate rates, seasonal specials, and weekend deals that typically include such extras as complimentary meals, drinks, or tickets to events. Ask about specials when booking; ask your travel agent for brochures; and look for advertisements on-line or in travel magazines or the Sunday travel section of the New York Times. Of course, booking any all-inclusive package, for a weekend or longer, will also reduce the hotel rate.

In general, Manhattan hotels make up for their small rooms and lack of parking with amenities befitting a cosmopolitan crowd: sophisticated restaurants, top-flight service, fine fitness facilities, and in-room extras such as phones with voice mail and data ports. Unless otherwise noted, hotels in this book have air-conditioning and designated no-smoking rooms and/or floors.

The majority of Manhattan's hotels are in Midtown and the Theater District—convenient locations for out-of-town visitors who want to be in the heart of it all. The more residential Upper East Side is home to many of the city's small, deluxe boutique hotels, such as the Carlyle and the Mark. Gramercy Park, Murray Hill, and Chelsea are other choice neighborhoods with plenty of hotel options in most price ranges. Farther downtown, the choices are limited.

PRICE CATEGORIES

Very Expensive	over $400
Expensive	$275–$400
Moderately Priced	$175–$275
Budget	under $175

*All prices are for a standard double room, excluding 13¼% city and state taxes plus an occupancy charge of $2 per room, per night.

VERY EXPENSIVE

7 e-8

THE CARLYLE

It's tough to decide where to spend your time in this Madison Avenue landmark: Should you stay in your Mark Hampton–designed guest room, admiring the fine antique furniture and artfully framed Audubons and botanicals? Or should you venture downstairs to the cozy little Bemelmans Bar, with murals by Ludwig Bemelmans, illustrator of the beloved *Madeline* books? Either way, you're sure to enjoy the swanky yet refined ambience of this Manhattan classic. *35 E. 76th St., 10021, Upper East Side, 212/744–1600 or 800/227–5737, fax 212/717–4682. 145 rooms, 45 suites. Restaurant, bar, café, in-room faxes, in-room data ports, kitchenettes, room service, spa, parking (fee). AE, DC, MC, V. Subway: 77th St.*

9 e-3

THE DRAKE

Part of the Swissôtel chain, the Drake is a model of Swiss-style efficiency; witness the extensive business center, where guests have access to three workstations, each with its own private desk, telephone, and computer. The spanking-new rooms have an art deco look, and all have oversize desks and overstuffed chairs and sofas. The Drake Bar is a convivial meeting place, with Swiss specialties and some good Swiss wines. *440 Park Ave. (between 56th and 57th Sts.), 10022, Midtown, 212/421–0900 or 800/372–5369, fax 212/371–4190. 385 rooms, 110 suites. Restaurant, bar, in-room faxes, in-room data ports, room service, spa, baby-sitting, parking (fee). AE, D, DC, MC, V. Subway: 59th St.*

9 d-3

ESSEX HOUSE, A WESTIN HOTEL

The lobby here is an Art Deco masterpiece fit for Fred and Ginger—and the restaurant, Les Célebrités, is one of New

York's finest. Guest rooms and suites, some with Louis XIV–style furnishings and others with English Chippendale, are comfortable and classic enough to make you want to move in. Many have dazzling views of Central Park, which is right across the street. Service is excellent. *160 Central Park S., 10019, Midtown, 212/247–0300 or 800/645–5687, fax 212/315–1839. 520 rooms, 77 suites. 2 restaurants, bar, in-room faxes, in-room data ports, room service, in-room VCRs, spa, baby-sitting, parking (fee). AE, D, DC, MC, V. Subway: N, R, B, Q to 57th St.*

9 *e-3*
FOUR SEASONS
Everything about this I.M. Pei–designed hotel is epic: the spired, limestone-clad structure itself; the giant guest rooms (average size is 600 square ft, and all have 10-ft-high ceilings); and, of course, the prices. Even if you can't stay here, step inside just to see the marvelous Grand Foyer, with French-limestone pillars, marble, onyx, and acre upon acre of blond wood. Guest rooms are soundproof (a rarity in New York), and all have walk-in closets paneled with English sycamore. *57 E. 57th St., 10022, Midtown, 212/758–5700 or 800/332–3442, fax 212/758–5711. 310 rooms, 60 suites. Restaurant, bar, in-room data ports, room service, spa, piano, baby-sitting, car rental, parking (fee). AE, DC, MC, V. Subway: 59th St.*

9 *e-2*
THE LOWELL
Like Noël Coward, you may be tempted to check in long-term at this pied-à-terre–style landmark on a tree-lined street between Madison and Park avenues. Guest rooms, more than half of which are suites, have all the comforts of home—kitchenettes (or mini-bars), stocked bookshelves, and even umbrellas; 33 of the suites have working fireplaces, and 10 have private terraces. A gym suite has its own fitness center, and a garden suite has two beautifully planted terraces. The Pembroke Room serves a fine high tea, and the Post House is renowned for its steaks. *28 E. 63rd St., 10021, Upper East Side, 212/838–1400 or 800/221–4444, fax 212/319–4230. 21 rooms, 44 suites. Restaurant, breakfast room, in-room faxes, in-room data ports, kitchenettes, room service, in-room VCRs, massage, health club, baby-sitting, parking (fee). AE, D, DC, MC, V. Subway: 59th St.*

7 *e-8*
THE MARK
Along with its neighbor, the Carlyle, the Mark is widely considered the classiest small hotel in New York. On a tree-lined street just steps from Central Park, it's a bastion of serenity; the cool, Biedermeier-furnished, marble lobby is truly one of the New York's most charming small spaces. Guest rooms are luxurious and soothing, with cream-color walls, museum-quality prints, plump armchairs, fresh flowers, and Frette bed linens. *25 E. 77th St., 10021, Upper East Side, 212/744–4300 or 800/843–6275, fax 212/744–2749. 120 rooms, 60 suites. Restaurant, bar, in-room faxes, in-room data ports, kitchenettes, room service, in-room VCRs, massage, health club, baby-sitting, parking (fee). AE, D, DC, MC, V. Subway: 77th St.*

9 *c-4*
MARRIOTT MARQUIS
This theater-district behemoth has nearly 2,000 rooms, plus a slew of restaurants (including a revolving restaurant and lounge on the 46th floor), shops, ballrooms, and even a Broadway theater. It's a favorite with tour groups and conventioneers. Guest rooms are generic but clean and functional; some have nice city views. *1535 Broadway (at 45th St.), 10036, Theater District, 212/398–1900 or 800/843–4898, fax 212/704–8966. 1,911 rooms, 95 suites. 3 restaurants, 3 bars, café, coffee shop, in-room data ports, room service, beauty salon, massage, health club, theater, baby-sitting, parking (fee). AE, D, DC, MC, V. Subway: 42nd St./Times Sq.*

9 *d-4*
THE MICHELANGELO
A touch of Italian luxury in midtown Manhattan, the esteemed Michelangelo welcomes you with multihue marble and quasi-Veronese oil paintings. All guest rooms have marble foyers, sitting areas, king-size beds, marble bathrooms with bidets and 55-gallon bathtubs. Complimentary cappuccino and pastries are served each morning in the lobby lounge. *152 W. 51st St., 10019, Midtown, 212/765–1900 or 800/237–0990, fax 212/581–7618. 123 rooms, 55 suites. Restaurant, bar, in-room faxes, in-room data ports, room service, exercise room, baby-sitting, parking (fee). AE, DC, MC, V. Subway: 7th Ave.; 50th St.; 47th–50th Sts./Rockefeller Center.*

10 d-6

NEW YORK MARRIOTT WORLD TRADE CENTER

This giant hotel between the World Trade Center's twin towers is one of the few places to get a room downtown. The skylit lobby has a contemporary green-granite and marble entrance, a grand curved staircase, and a fountain. Rooms are sleek, modern, and spacious by Manhattan standards. The 22nd-floor health club has phenomenal views of Lower Manhattan. *3 World Trade Center (between Liberty and Vesey Sts.), 10048, Lower Manhattan, 212/938–9100 or 800/550–2344, fax 212/321–2107. 788 rooms, 29 suites. Restaurant, bar, in-room data ports, room service, indoor pool, health club, travel services, car rental, parking (fee). AE, D, DC, MC, V. Subway: World Trade Center.*

9 e-4

NEW YORK PALACE

The New York Palace remains one of Manhattan's most inviting deluxe hotels to combine Old World flavor with modern pleasures. The guest rooms have an Empire flavor, with bold colors and dark woods, though some of the more luxurious rooms and suites in the Tower (Floors 41–55) have an art deco look, with oversized furniture and polished blond-wood headboards. The health club has top-of-the-line equipment and an awesome view of St. Patrick's Cathedral. Behind the hotel, the landmark 1882 Villard House, known for its Tiffany glass-work and frescoed murals, houses the ultrachic, five-star restaurant Le Cirque 2000, an outrageous, futuristic riot of color (*see French in* Chapter 1). For more modest meals, there's a lobby-lounge restaurant with an olive bar and an afternoon "tapas" tea service with a Mediterranean twist. *455 Madison Ave. (between 50th and 51st Sts.), 10022, Midtown, 212/888–7000 or 800/697–2522, fax 212/303–6000. 800 rooms, 100 suites. 2 restaurants, 2 bars, in-room faxes, in-room data ports, room service, spa, health club, baby-sitting, parking (fee). AE, D, DC, MC, V. Subway: 51st St./Lexington–3rd Aves.*

9 e-3

OMNI BERKSHIRE PLACE

Watch Siamese fighting fish swim in little bowls as you relax in front of the fireplace in the two-story atrium lounge—or just retire to one of the 375-square-ft guest rooms. The bedside comfort controls and fax machines are nice additions to the contemporary, Asian-influenced decor. *21 E. 52nd St., 10022, Midtown, 212/753–5800 or 800/843–6664, fax 212/754–5020. 396 rooms, 44 suites. Restaurant, bar, in-room faxes, in-room data ports, room service, massage, health club, parking (fee). AE, D, DC, MC, V. Subway: E, F to 5th Ave.*

9 d-3

LE PARKER MERIDIEN

The atrium of this French-owned and -operated hotel strikes an exotic, eclectic note, with two-story arched mirrors, a mosaic ceiling, palm trees, and Doric columns. Equally dramatic are the glass-enclosed rooftop swimming pool (where it's fashionable to dine poolside), the rooftop outdoor track, and the enormous Club Raquette health club, with racquetball and squash courts. Rooms have an elegant neoclassical motif. *118 W. 57th St., 10019, Midtown, 212/245–5000 or 800/543–4300, fax 212/708–7477. 449 rooms, 249 suites. Restaurant, bar, in-room faxes, in-room data ports, in-room safes, minibars, room service, indoor pool, spa, health club, racquetball, squash, nightclub, baby-sitting, parking (fee). AE, D, DC, MC, V. Subway: 57th St.*

9 e-3

THE PENINSULA

The marble, Art Nouveau lobby of this opulent landmark recalls a grander era, when bell captains wore sailor suits and afternoon tea was on everyone's schedule. Many of the rooms have sweeping views down Fifth Avenue, and the new sumptuous marble bathrooms in all guest rooms feature separate shower stalls. Don't miss the glass-enclosed, trilevel health club and spa, with an indoor, rooftop swimming pool where you can gaze down at Midtown between laps. *700 5th Ave. (at 55th St.), 10019, Midtown, 212/247–2200 or 800/262–9467, fax 212/903–3943. 200 rooms, 42 suites. 2 restaurants, bar, lounge, in-room faxes, in-room data ports, room service, indoor pool, beauty salon, spa, health club, baby-sitting, parking (fee). AE, D, DC, MC, V. Subway: E, F to 5th Ave.*

9 e-2

THE PIERRE

Since the 1930s, the Pierre has occupied its Fifth Avenue post with all the grandeur of a French château. The public areas drip with chandeliers, handmade carpets, and Corinthian columns.

The king-size guest rooms are resplendent with traditional chintz fabrics and dark-wood furniture; spacious bathrooms have Art Nouveau fixtures. Service is predictably first-rate—the Pierre is a Four Seasons hotel. *2 E. 61st St., 10021, Upper East Side, 212/838–8000 or 800/332–3442, fax 212/758–1615. 149 rooms, 54 suites. Restaurant, bar, in-room faxes, in-room data ports, room service, beauty salon, massage, health club, babysitting, parking (fee). AE, D, DC, MC, V. Subway: N, R to 5th Ave.*

⑨ *e-2*

THE PLAZA

Ernest Hemingway is said to have advised F. Scott Fitzgerald to bequeath his liver to Princeton but his heart to the Plaza. Enjoy brunch at the fin-de-siècle Palm Court or a drink at the clubby Oak Bar, where horse-drawn carriages clip-clop past the windows. Though the guest rooms are small for such a luxury hotel, their high ceilings and lavish decor (including crystal chandeliers) give you a taste of real New York glamour. The public spaces do show the effects of high traffic. *5th Ave. at 59th St., 10019, Midtown, 212/759–3000 or 800/759–3000, 212/546–5324. 670 rooms, 135 suites. 4 restaurants, 2 bars, in-room faxes, in-room data ports, room service, massage, exercise room, baby-sitting, parking (fee). AE, D, DC, MC, V. Subway: N, R to 5th Ave.*

⑨ *e-2*

PLAZA ATHÉNÉE

Step into this 16-story bastion of Louis XIV elegance on a quiet Upper East Side street and you may think you've landed in Paris. Rooms are extremely elegant, with French Directoire–style mahogany furniture and hand-painted silk drapery and bedspreads. The European-trained staff delivers polished service to a cosmopolitan clientele. *37 E. 64th St., 10021, Upper East Side, 212/734–9100 or 800/447–8800, fax 212/772–0958. 117 rooms, 36 suites. Restaurant, bar, in-room data ports, room service, massage, exercise room, baby-sitting, parking (fee). AE, D, DC, MC, V. Subway: 68th St./Hunter College.*

⑨ *f-5*

REGAL U.N. PLAZA HOTEL

Beginning on the 28th floor of each of two sleek skyscraper towers, this dazzling 13-story hotel attracts an international, diplomatic set thanks to its location just a well-aimed stone's throw

from the United Nations. Guest rooms are simple but tasteful, with breathtaking river views. There's a pool on the 27th floor, also with superb views, and a health club with indoor tennis courts. *1 United Nations Plaza (44th St. between 1st and 2nd Aves.), 10017, Midtown, 212/758–1234 or 800/223–1234, fax 212/702–5051. 393 rooms, 33 suites. Restaurant, bar, in-room faxes, in-room data ports, room service, pool, massage, tennis court, health club, baby-sitting, parking (fee). AE, D, DC, MC, V. Subway: 42nd St./Grand Central.*

⑨ *e-2*

THE REGENCY

The Regency is a truly regal hotel, from the elegant lobby with its gilded antiques and massive chandelier to the posh Park Avenue location. The restaurant, 540 Park, has long been known as *the* place for power breakfasts, but more

---

OF BATHTUBS AND BIDETS

If you live in New York, chances are your bathroom is about the size of your closet. This is where luxury hotels come in.

Four Seasons (Very Expensive)
The enormous tubs fill in 60 seconds.

The Mansfield (Expensive)
High-style, black-marble bathrooms.

The Michelangelo (Very Expensive)
Bidets and 55-gallon tubs.

Morgans (Expensive)
Crystal shower doors and poured-granite floors.

Omni Berkshire Place (Very Expensive)
Loos in the suites have TVS and CD players.

The Paramount (Moderately Priced)
Conical steel sinks designed by Philippe Starck.

The Pierre (Very Expensive)
Gleaming white marble with red and black trim; luxurious lighted mirrors.

Roger Williams (Expensive)
Doorless, recessed showers with cedar-grill floors.

Trump International Hotel and Towers (Very Expensive)
Bath salts and loofahs are on the house.

---

inviting is the Library, a cozy, wood-paneled lounge full of bookcases and comfortable seating arrangements—here drinks and light meals are served all day long. The traditional guest rooms have celadon carpets and salmon-color silk bedspreads. *540 Park Ave. (at 61st St.), 10021, Upper East Side, 212/759–4100 or 800/235–6397. 288 rooms, 74 suites. Restaurants, bar, lobby lounge, in-room faxes, in-room data ports, room service, beauty salon, massage, exercise room, baby-sitting, parking (fee). AE, D, DC, MC, V. Subway: 59th St.*

9 *C-4*

RENAISSANCE

In the heart of Times Square, the Renaissance is one of the Theater District's classier hotels, and business travelers make up a good part of the clientele. The third-floor lobby has an elegant, Art Deco style, and guest rooms are warm and inviting, with dark cherry wood and a black-and-tan color scheme. *2 Times Sq. (7th Ave. between 47th and 48th Sts.), 10036, Theater District, 212/765–7676 or 800/628–5222, fax 212/765–1962. 283 rooms, 22 suites. Restaurant, bar, in-room data ports, room service, in-room VCRs, massage, exercise room, baby-sitting, parking (fee). AE, D, DC, MC, V. Subway: 49th St.; 50th St.*

9 *d-3*

RIHGA ROYAL

The Rihga Royal has 50 floors of contemporary suites, some with bay windows and French doors. The location suits many business travelers and celebrities, as do the fax machines in every room. The Pinnacle Suites (on the top floors) have CD players, cellular phones, and "miniature business center" machines that print and copy. *151 W. 54th St., 10019, Midtown, 212/307–5000 or 800/937–5454, fax 212/765–6530. 500 suites. Restaurant, bar, in-room faxes, in-room data ports, room service, in-room VCRs, massage, exercise room, baby-sitting, parking (fee). AE, D, DC, MC, V. Subway: 7th Ave; 57th St..*

9 *d-5*

THE ROYALTON

Created by Ian Schrager and the late Steve Rubell, designed with minimalist chicness by Philippe Starck, this hotel can't help but attract those whose eyes like to flutter from beautiful person to more beautiful person. Fashion and media folk gather to drink martinis in the cooler-than-cool lobby. The showpiece of each spartan guest room is a low-lying, custom-made bed with a down comforter and Italian sheets; there are also window banquettes and fireplaces. *44 W. 44th St., Theater District, 10036, 212/869–4400 or 800/635–9013, fax 212/575–0012. 140 rooms, 28 suites. Restaurant, bar, in-room data ports, in-room VCRs, room service, massage, exercise room, baby-sitting, parking (fee). AE, DC, MC, V. Subway: B, D, F, Q to 42nd St.*

9 *e-3*

ST. REGIS

Built in 1904 by John Jacob Astor for those who could afford "the best of everything," this Fifth Avenue Beaux-Arts landmark was bought by Sheraton in the early 1990s and restored to its original splendor. Highlights are the Astor Court tea lounge, with its trompe-l'oeil cloud ceiling; the King Cole Bar, with its famous Maxfield Parrish mural; and the celebrated restaurant Lespinasse (*see* French *in* Chapter 1). The opulent guest rooms have butler service, crystal chandeliers, silk wall coverings, and Louis XV–style furnishings. *2 E. 55th St., 10022, Midtown, 212/753–4500 or 800/759–7550, fax 212/787–3447. 221 rooms, 92 suites. Restaurant, bar, in-room faxes, in-room data ports, room service, beauty salon, massage, sauna, health club, massage, baby-sitting, parking (fee). AE, D, DC, MC, V. Subway: E, F to 5th Ave.*

9 *C-2*

TRUMP INTERNATIONAL HOTEL AND TOWERS

Donald Trump's showy namesake hotel caters to business travelers with money to burn. The rooms and suites are more like contemporary apartments than hotel rooms; all have Sony sound systems, a selection of coffee-table books for guests to browse through, and minitelescopes for discreet spying on the action in Central Park. The restaurant, Jean Georges, is one of the city's finest (*see* French *in* Chapter 1), and Lincoln Center is close by. *1 Central Park W. (at 59th St.), 10023, Midtown, 212/299–1000, fax 212/299–1150. 86 rooms, 82 suites. Restaurant, bar, café, in-room faxes, in-room data ports, in-room VCRs, kitchenettes, indoor pool, spa, baby-sitting, parking (fee). AE, D, DC, MC, V. Subway: 59th St./Columbus Circle.*

EXPENSIVE LODGINGS

9 e-4

W NEW YORK

This boutique business hotel has made quite a splash. The fuss has more to do with its restaurant Heartbeat and bars Whiskey Blue and Oasis than its small rooms, but the rooms do feature Internet TV, complimentary Aveeda products, and great views. For hobnobbing with the media elite, this is the place to be. An in-house spa and fitness center provide ample ways to unwind. *541 Lexington Ave. (at 50th St.), 10022, Midtown, 212–755–1200, fax 212–319–8344. 722 rooms. Restaurant, 2 bars, in-room faxes, in-room data ports, minibars, spa, fitness center. AE, D, DC, MC, V. Subway 6 to 51st St.*

9 e-4

WALDORF-ASTORIA

A New York institution, the Waldorf has attracted every president since Hoover and a handful of luminous longtime residents, including the late Frank Sinatra. The magnificent Art Deco lobby, with its original murals and mosaics, is a meeting place for the rich and powerful. Guest rooms, each individually decorated, are all traditional and elegant; Astoria-level rooms have the added advantages of great views, fax machines, and access to the Astoria lounge, where a lovely, free afternoon tea is served. *301 Park Ave. (at 50th St.), 10022, Midtown, 212/355–3000 or 800/925–3673, fax 212/872–7272. 1,176 rooms, 276 suites. 4 restaurants, 2 bars, in-room data ports, room service, massage, health club, baby-sitting, parking (fee). AE, D, DC, MC, V. Subway: 51st St./Lexington–3rd Aves.*

9 e-1

THE WESTBURY

British formality meets congeniality at the Forte Hotel chain's New York outpost. Leather banquettes look out on Madison Avenue at the clubby Polo Bar and Restaurant. Rooms and suites have a lived-in, English-country look, with floral chintz, Oriental rugs, and mahogany furnishings. *15 E. 69th St., 10021, Upper East Side, 212/535–2000 or 800/321–1569, fax 212/535–5058. 143 rooms, 85 suites. Restaurant, bar, in-room faxes, in-room data ports, room service, massage, exercise room, baby-sitting, parking (fee). AE, D, DC, MC, V. Subway: 68th St./Hunter College.*

9 d-5

THE ALGONQUIN

Once the meeting place of the famed Round Table of wits and critics, the Algonquin has attracted literary and theatrical types since it opened in 1902. In the clubby, oak-paneled lobby, overstuffed sofas and easy chairs encourage lolling over cocktails and conversation or afternoon tea. Victorian fixtures and furnishings give the comfortable guest rooms a traditional look; some specialty suites dedicated to Dorothy Parker and her contemporaries. *59 W. 44th St., 10036, Midtown, 212/840–6800 or 800/548–0345, fax 212/944–1618. 142 rooms, 23 suites. 2 restaurants, bar, in-room data ports, room service, cabaret, parking (fee). AE, D, DC, MC, V. Subway: B, D, F, Q to 42nd St.*

9 e-4

THE BENJAMIN

Formerly the Hotel Beverly, the Executive Suite Hotel Benjamin is a true blend of Old World style and modern amenities. A recent renovation both underscored the original design of famed architect Emery Roth and added high-tech communications. All suites offer executive desks, ergonomic chairs, 2-line phones with voicemail, data ports, and a separate line for a combination fax/printer/copier. *125 E. 50th St., 10022, Midtown, 212/753–2700 or 800/637–8483, fax 212/715–2525. 130 suites. Restaurant, bar, in-room data ports, room service, fitness center, spa, parking (fee). AE, DC, MC, V. Subway: 51st St./Lexington–3rd Aves.*

9 d-3

CENTRAL PARK SOUTH INTER-CONTINENTAL

The hotel formerly known as the Ritz-Carlton is still the ultimate in luxury, with its prime Central Park South address, polished service, and tasteful decor. Fine art fills the public rooms, and guest rooms are little masterpieces, with rich brocades, polished woods, and marble bathrooms. Some rooms have breathtaking views of the park. *112 Central Park S., 10019, Midtown, 212/757–1900 or 800/937–8461, fax 212/757–9620. 192 rooms, 16 suites. Restaurant, bar, in-room data ports, room service, massage, health club, baby-sitting, parking (fee). AE, D, DC, MC, V. Subway: N, R, B, Q to 57th St.*

9 e-5

DORAL PARK AVENUE

An amusingly eclectic look sets the Doral Park Avenue apart from the other nearby Doral hotels (it's under separate management). The lobby showcases a giant painting of an ancient Greek city, but its seriousness is offset by palm trees and Art Deco details. Guest rooms are decorated in a similarly playful style. For $10, guests can work out at the nearby Doral Fitness Center. *70 Park Ave. (at 38th St.), 10016, Murray Hill, 212/687–7050 or 800/ 223–6725, fax 212/973–2497. 188 rooms, 6 suites. Restaurant, bar, in-room data ports, room service, massage, baby-sitting, parking (fee). AE, D, DC, MC, V. Subway: 42nd St./Grand Central.*

9 e-3

THE FITZPATRICK

Just south of Bloomingdale's, the Irish-owned Fitzpatrick is one of the friendliest hotels around. The mostly Irish staff loves to chat with the guests—especially with the occasional celebrities. Rooms are spacious and cheerful, with emerald-green carpets and traditional furnishings. The publike bar at the heart of the hotel is as welcoming as any in Dublin. Guests have free access to the Excelsior Athletic Club, next door. *687 Lexington Ave. (at 57th St.), 10022, Midtown, 212/355–0100 or 800/367–7701, fax 212/355–1371. 42 rooms, 50 suites. Restaurant, bar, in-room data ports, room service, massage, parking (fee). AE, D, DC, MC, V. Subway: 59th St.*

9 e-3

HOTEL ELYSÉE

There are only 99 guest rooms here, which means guests receive personalized service and attention. Big, comfortable chairs and couches in the Club Room invite guests to linger over coffee anytime, plus there's free wine and hors d'oeuvres on weeknights and complimentary breakfast in the morning. Other perks include free passes to the nearby New York Sports Club and easy access to the famed Monkey Bar, a trendy place for drinks and dinner. A few of the beautifully decorated guest rooms have terraces at no extra charge; request one far in advance. *60 E. 54th St., 10022, Midtown, 212/753–1066 or 800/535–9733, fax 212/ 980–9278. 87 rooms, 12 suites. Bar, restaurant, in-room data ports, in-room VCRs, room service, massage, parking (fee). AE, DC, MC, V. Subway: E, F to 5th Ave.*

9 d-5

THE MANSFIELD

In a 1904 Stanford White building where well-heeled bachelors once lodged, this small hotel is Victorian and clublike. Guest rooms have stylish, black-marble bathrooms, ebony-stained floors and doors, dark-wood venetian blinds, and sleigh beds. There are nightly piano and harp recitals in the intimate concert salon, where complimentary breakfast and after-theater dessert are served. And can you believe there's even free parking? *12 W. 44th St., 10036, Midtown, 212/ 944–6050 or 800/255–5167, fax 212/764– 4477. 123 rooms, 25 suites. In-room VCRs, room service, free parking. AE, MC, V. Subway: 42nd St./Times Sq.*

11 e-5

MERCER HOTEL

It's SoHo industrial all the way here. So minimalist is the sprawling 100-seat lobby with its vintage book library and casual bar, that you may not even realize it's a hotel until you notice the unmarked reception desk toward the back wall. Guest rooms are enormous, with long entryways, high ceilings, and walk-in closets. No chintz or framed Monet prints here—instead, dark African woods and high-tech light fixtures make a subtle statement. But the bathrooms steal the show with their decadent two-person tubs, some of them surrounded by mirrors. *99 Prince St., at Mercer St., 10012, Soho, 212/966–6060, fax 212/965–3838. 67 rooms, 8 suites. Restaurant, 2 bars, in-room data ports, room service, in-room VCRs. AE, D, DC, MC, V.*

9 e-6

MILLENIUM HILTON

The class act of downtown, this sleek black monolith is across the street from the World Trade Center. The modern, beige-and-wood rooms have contoured built-in desks and night tables; almost all have expansive views of landmark buildings and both the Hudson and the East rivers. The health club has an Olympic-size pool with windows that look out on St. Paul's Church. Live piano music adds sparkle to the smart lobby lounge. *55 Church St., 10007, Lower Manhattan, 212/693–2001 or 800/ 752–0014, fax 212/571–2317. 458 rooms, 103 suites. 2 restaurants, bar, in-room data ports, room service, indoor pool, massage, health club, baby-sitting, parking (fee).*

AE, D, DC, MC, V. Subway: Cortlandt St./World Trade Ctr; Chambers St.

❾ d-5
MILLENNIUM BROADWAY
The lobby is sleek and dramatic, with black marble floors; rich African-mahogany walls; enormous, outrageously stylized paintings of fleshy, classical figures; and striking flower arrangements. Rooms, too, have a sleek, modern look: leather and suede are the materials of choice; appliances are high-tech chrome; and everything is black, brown, and gray. 145 W. 44th St., 10036, Theater District, 212/768–4400 or 800/622–5569, fax 212/768–0847. 617 rooms, 10 rooms. Restaurant, bar, in-room data ports, room service, massage, exercise room, baby-sitting, parking (fee). AE, D, DC, MC, V. Subway: 42nd St./Times Sq.

❾ e-6
MORGANS
The first hotel created by Ian Schrager and the late Steve Rubell is a magnet for celebrities (there's no sign outside). A minimalist, high-tech look prevails in the stunning rooms, with low-lying, futonlike beds and 27-inch Sony TVS on wheels; the tiny bathrooms have crystal shower doors, steel surgical sinks, and poured-granite floors. Asia de Cuba, the scene-making restaurant, is booked solid by the young and the trendy—the same crowd that frequents the cavelike, candlelit Morgans Bar downstairs. 237 Madison Ave. (between 37th and 38th Sts.), 10016, Murray Hill, 212/686–0300 or 800/334–3408, fax 212/779–8352. 113 rooms, 26 suites. Restaurant, 2 bars, breakfast room, in-room data ports, room service, baby-sitting, parking (fee). AE, D, DC, MC, V. Subway: 42nd St./Grand Central.

❾ d-3
NEW YORK HILTON AND TOWERS
New York City's largest hotel and the epicenter of the city's hotel-based conventions, the Hilton has myriad business facilities, eating establishments, and shops, all designed for convenience. The sprawling, brassy lobby is more businesslike than beautiful but always buzzing. Considering the size of this property, guest rooms are surprisingly well maintained, and all have coffeemakers, hair dryers, and ironing boards. Those in the towers have dazzling views. 1335 6th Ave. (at 54th St.), 10019, Mid-town, 212/586–7000 or 800/445–8667, fax 212/261–5902. 2,041 rooms, 20 suites. 2 restaurants, café, sports bar, in-room data ports, room service, barbershop, beauty salon, hot tub, massage, health club, baby-sitting, parking (fee). AE, D, DC, MC, V. Subway: 47th–50th Sts./Rockefeller Ctr.

❾ e-4
PLAZA FIFTY
This Manhattan East suite hotel has a distinctly businesslike atmosphere—witness the granite-wall lobby, with its mirrors, stainless steel, and leather furniture—but it's also supremely comfortable. In addition to suites, there are large standard rooms, each with a microwave, refrigerator, and coffeemaker. All quarters have a clean, modern look that makes them very livable—an excellent home away from home. A restaurant next door provides room service 5 PM–10:30 PM. 155 E. 50th St., 10022, Midtown, 212/751–5710 or 800/637–8483, fax 212/753–1468. 74 rooms, 138 suites. In-room data ports, exercise room, parking (fee). AE, D, DC, MC, V. Subway: 51st St./Lexington–3rd Aves.

❾ e-6
THE ROGER WILLIAMS
This circa-1920s building sits ideally between Midtown and Downtown. The minimalist rooms are extremely stylish, with custom-made blond-birch furnishings and dramatic downlighting, and each comes with a 27-inch Sony TV, VCR, and CD player (guests have access to complimentary VCR and CD libraries). The bathrooms are artworks unto themselves, with chrome surgical sinks and recessed showers with cedar-grill floors. Don't miss the complimentary Continental breakfast and nightly dessert buffets on the mezzanine. 131 Madison Ave. (at 31st St.), 10016, Murray Hill, 212/448–7000, fax 212/448–7007. 183 rooms, 1 suite. Breakfast room, in-room data ports, in-room VCRs, free parking. Subway: 6 to 33rd St.

❾ e-4
ROOSEVELT HOTEL
Though it's huge and somewhat impersonal, the Roosevelt puts visitors in the thick of things—it's in a shopping arcade near Grand Central Station. There's a constant buzz in the grand marble lobby with Corinthian columns, which, alas, makes a much better impression than the slightly sterile guest

rooms. All of the latter have the same decor: dark-wood reproduction furniture, loud floral bedspreads, and framed botanical prints. *45 E. 45th St., 10017, Midtown, 212/661–9600 or 800/223–1870, fax 212/687–5064. 1,040 rooms, 50 suites. Restaurant, bar, breakfast room, in-room data ports, room service, massage, baby-sitting, parking (fee). AE, D, DC, MC, V. Subway: 42nd St./Grand Central.*

9 *e-2*

SHERRY-NETHERLAND

This Fifth Avenue grande dame is actually a cooperative-apartment complex, with a 3-to-1 ratio of permanent residents to guests. As a result, in-room amenities are somewhat hit-or-miss, depending on the whims of the individual owners; but all of the suites are utterly luxurious, with separate living and dining areas, pantries, decorative fireplaces, fine antiques, and marble baths. The dastardly expensive Harry Cipriani (*see* Italian *in* Chapter 1) provides room service; a liter of water costs about $20, no joke. *781 5th Ave. (at 59th St.), 10022, Midtown, 212/355–2800, fax 212/319–4306. 40 rooms, 35 suites. Restaurant, bar, in-room faxes, in-room VCRs, room service, barbershop, beauty salon, exercise room, parking (fee). AE, D, DC, MC, V. Subway: N, R to 5th Ave.*

9 *d-3*

THE SHOREHAM

Almost everything here is metal or metal-color—even the headboards are made of perforated steel and lit from behind. Cedar-lined closets and in-room VCRs and CD players add to the high-tech amenities. There are plenty of freebies here, including Continental breakfast, a nightly dessert buffet, and 24-hour cappuccino and espresso that's good enough for coffee snobs. *33 W. 55th St., 10019, Midtown, 212/247–6700, fax 212/765–9741. 47 rooms, 37 suites. Breakfast room, in-room data ports, in-room VCRs, massage, baby-sitting, parking (fee). AE, DC, MC, V. Subway: E, F to 5th Ave.*

10 *d-4*

SOHO GRAND

SoHo's first hotel is a remarkable amalgam of 19th-century SoHo–style architecture. A translucent, bottle-glass staircase with cast-iron embellishments leads to the second-floor lobby and its oversize furniture. Rooms have an industrial look: custom-designed draft-

ing tables serve as desks, and the night-stands mimic sculptors' desks. The Canal House restaurant serves remarkably creative renditions of American comfort food—macaroni-and-cheese is a trademark dish. The hotel is owned by Hartz Mountain, the pet-food company, so dogs get extra-special treatment here. *310 W. Broadway (between Grand and Canal Sts.), 10013, SoHo, 212/965–3000 or 800/965–3000, fax 212/965–3244. 365 rooms, 4 suites. Restaurant, bar, in-room data ports, room service, massage, exercise room, baby-sitting, parking (fee). Pets allowed. AE, D, DC, MC, V. Subway: A, C, E, N, R to Canal St.*

9 *e-5*

W NEW YORK—THE COURT

Like its sister hotel, the W Tuscany, The W Court is located in the peaceful residential neighborhood of Murray Hill, and offers spacious rooms decorated in soothing colors. Guest rooms feature an oversize desk, down-and-feather upholstered chaise lounge, and pillow-top mattresses as well as the latest technology, including ultra-fast Internet access. The W Court offers more activity than the W Tuscany, but choose either one and enjoy the facilities of both, which include a state-of-the-art health club and spacious meeting room. *130 E. 39th St., 10016, Murray Hill, 212/685–1100 or 800/223–6725, fax 212/779–0148. 199 rooms, 47 suites. Restaurant, bar, room service, massage, spa, baby-sitting, parking (fee). AE, DC, MC, V. Subway: 42nd St./Grand Central.*

9 *e-5*

W NEW YORK— THE TUSCANY

The W Tuscany is similar its sister hotel, the W Court, but it offers a more private "club" atmosphere. Rooms are state-of-the-art, both in terms of comfort and technology. And when you stay at the W Tuscany, you can use the facilities of the W Court. *120 E. 39th St., 10016, Murray Hill, 212/686–1600 or 800/223–6725, fax 212/779–0148. 122 rooms, 11 suites. Café, bar, room service, massage, spa, baby-sitting, parking (fee). AE, DC, MC, V. Subway: 42nd St./Grand Central.*

9 *d-3*

THE WARWICK

The Warwick has a loyal following, thanks to its prime Midtown location and its sophisticated, but not stuffy, ambience. The Beatles stayed here when they first came to the United States, to appear on the Ed Sullivan Show. The elegant, marble-floor lobby is flanked by the convivial Warwick Bar and Ciao Europa Italian restaurant. Rooms are tastefully decorated, with soft pastel color schemes, mahogany armoires, and nice marble bathrooms. William Randolph Hearst, who built the place in 1927, would be proud. *65 W. 54th St., 10019, Midtown, 212/247–2700 or 800/223–4099, fax 212/957–8915. 352 rooms, 75 suites. Restaurant, bar, room service, parking (fee). AE, DC, MC, V. Subway: E, F to 5th Ave.; B, Q to 57th St.*

MODERATELY PRICED LODGINGS

9 *c-3*

AMERITANIA

This busy crash pad just off Broadway has raised its standards (and its prices) and is now one of the area's trendiest hotels. Settle into one of the oversize chairs in the cavernous, terrazzo-floored lobby and size up the young, hip crowd, many of whom choose the Ameritania for its proximity to the Letterman Show's Ed Sullivan Theater. Black-metal furniture dominates the bedrooms, which have small, black-marble bathrooms. Bar 54 stays open until 2 AM. *1701 Broadway (at 54th St.), 10019, Theater District, 212/247–5000 or 800/922–0330, fax 212/247–3316. 195 rooms, 12 suites. Restaurant, bar, exercise room. AE, D, DC, MC, V. Subway: 7th Ave.*

9 *e-2*

BARBIZON HOTEL

A women's residence club from 1927 to 1981, the Barbizon was home at various times to Grace Kelly, Joan Crawford, and Liza Minelli. The chic lobby has a beautiful, marble-and-limestone floor and luxurious gilt chairs with mohair upholstery. The shell-pink or celadon rooms are more modest but thoroughly pleasant, with eclectic accents such as zigzag wrought-iron floor lamps. The on-site health club has an Olympic-size pool. *140 E. 63rd St., 10021, Upper East Side, 212/838–5700 or 800/223–5652, fax 212/888–4271. 310 rooms, 13 suites. Breakfast room, in-room data ports, room service, indoor pool, spa, health club, baby-sitting, parking (fee). AE, D, DC, MC, V. Subway: 59th St.*

9 *d-6*

BEST WESTERN MANHATTAN

Rooms come in three different styles—"Fifth Avenue" (ritzy), "Central Park" (lots of florals), and "SoHo" (bold colors)—and all have coffeemakers. Guests have access to a tiny exercise room. Just south of the Empire State Building, this heavily Korean neighborhood is lively, with lots of cheap shops and restaurants. *17 W. 32nd St., 10001, Garment District, 212/736–1600 or 800/567–7720, fax 212/695–1813. 136 rooms, 40 suites. Restaurant, bar, exercise room, parking (fee). Subway: 34th St./Herald Sq.*

10 *f-6*

BEST WESTERN SEAPORT INN

This thoroughly pleasant, restored 19th-century building is one block from the waterfront, close to South Street Seaport and the Financial Center. A cross between a Colonial sea captain's house and a chain hotel, this place is thoroughly inviting, with a cozy, librarylike lobby and a friendly staff. Rooms are standard chain-motel fare, and a few have whirlpool tubs and outdoor terraces with views of the Brooklyn Bridge. *33 Peck Slip (at Front St.), 10038, Lower Manhattan, 212/766–6600 or 800/468–3569, fax 212/766–6615. 72 rooms. In-room VCRs. AE, D, DC, MC, V. Subway: 2, 3 to Fulton St.*

9 *c-7*

CHELSEA HOTEL

You may well be inspired by your muse at the landmark Chelsea Hotel, home at various times to Sarah Bernhardt, Arthur Miller, Thomas Wolfe, Dylan Thomas, Robert Mapplethorpe, Christo, and Willem de Kooning. You may not get away with leaving art as payment for your room, though, as some of these residents have—there's a gallery of their work in the lobby. Rooms are a mixed bag: some are high-style, while others look straight out of the '70s and dumpy. *222 W. 23rd St., 10011, Chelsea, phone and fax 212/243–3700. 330 rooms, 310 with bath. Kitchenettes. AE, MC, V. Subway: C, E to 23rd St.*

9 *d-6*

COMFORT INN MURRAY HILL

Comfort is what you get here: all of the spacious rooms are equipped with big, comfy sofabeds for extra guests, and some have refrigerators and microwaves. On top of that, you get complimentary Continental breakfast and a quiet but convenient location. The lobby is surprisingly elegant, with atmospheric lighting, fresh flowers, and a classical motif set off by Corinthian columns and tall, Greek-style vases in mirrored recesses. *42 W. 35th St., 10001, Garment District, 212/947–0200, fax 212/594–3047. 131 rooms. AE, D, DC, MC, V. Subway: 34th St./Herald Sq.*

7 *b-7*

THE EXCELSIOR

Directly across from the American Museum of Natural History, on a block full of fine, prewar doorman buildings, the Excelsior is an old-time hotel with an old-time feel. The lobby's inlaid-gold ceiling recalls grander days, and the down-home coffee shop serves breakfast all day. An extensive refurbishing has given the rooms a much-needed pick-me-up; they now have warm, earth-tone color schemes and traditional furnishings. *45 W. 81st St., 10024, Upper West Side, 212/362–9200 or 800/368–4575, fax 212/721–2994. 130 rooms, 60 suites. Coffee shop. AE, MC, V. Subway: 81st St.*

7 *e-7*

THE FRANKLIN

The Upper East Side's hippest, funkiest hotel has a pint-size lobby furnished with black granite, brushed steel, and cherry wood. The tiny rooms have custom-built steel furniture, gauzy white canopies over the beds, and cedar closets; bathrooms have steel-bowl sinks. Guests are invited to borrow CDs and videotapes for free (all rooms have CD players and VCRs). To add to the excellent value, there's a generous complimentary breakfast (including homemade granola) and a nightly dessert buffet, and—hold onto your seat—parking is free! *164 E. 87th St., 10128, Upper East Side, 212/369–1000 or 800/428–5252, fax 212/369–8000. 47 rooms. Breakfast room, in-room VCRs, free parking. AE, MC, V. Subway: 4, 5, 6 to 86th St.*

9 *e-8*

GRAMERCY PARK HOTEL

One of Manhattan's greenest, quietest, most delightful parks is locked to anyone who doesn't live right on its periphery—but you hold the key as long as you're a guest at this aged, Queen Anne–style hotel. Guest rooms are a little the worse for wear, with worn furniture and old-fashioned bathrooms; but

the charming locale makes up for these flaws. *2 Lexington Ave. (at 21st St.), 10010, Gramercy, 212/475–4320 or 800/221–4083, fax 212/505–0535. 543 rooms, 157 suites. Restaurant, bar, beauty salon. AE, D, DC, MC, V. Subway: 6 to 23rd St.*

9 *d-3*

HELMSLEY WINDSOR

The cozy, wood-paneled, red-carpeted lobby tells you that the Helmsley Windsor delivers comfort as well as value. Rooms are spacious and pleasant enough; most have framed photos of Old New York. Continental breakfast is complimentary. *100 W. 58th St., 10019, Midtown, 212/265–2100 or 800/221–4982, fax 212/315–0371. 229 rooms, 15 suites. Breakfast room, parking (fee). AE, D, DC, MC, V. Subway: B, Q to 57th St.*

10 *e-4*

HOLIDAY INN DOWNTOWN

The excellent dim sum at Pacifica restaurant is reason enough to stay at this downtown hotel, a favorite with Chinese business travelers. Rooms and suites are sleek and modern, with pastel walls and carpets, black-frame furniture, and framed watercolors with an Asian motif. This is a great location for anyone who wants to be near Chinatown and Little Italy as well as SoHo and the Financial District. *138 Lafayette St. (between Canal and Howard Sts.), 10013, Chinatown, 212/966–8898 or 800/465–4329, fax 212/966–3933. 213 rooms, 12 suites. Restaurant, bar, room service, parking (fee). AE, D, DC, MC, V. Subway: 6, N, R, J, M, Z to Canal St.*

7 *b-8*

HOTEL BEACON

A true home away from home, each Beacon suite has a kitchenette with coffeemaker, full-size refrigerator, and stove—all for only $40 more than a standard room. What's more, the hotel is near Central Park, Lincoln Center, and scores of gourmet food stores such as Zabar's, so you can make good use of all those appliances. *2130 Broadway (at 75th St.), 10023, Upper West Side, 212/787–1100 or 800/572–4969, fax 212/724–0839. 110 rooms, 100 suites. Kitchenettes, refrigerators, business services, meeting room, parking (fee). AE, D, DC, MC, V. Subway: 1, 2, 3, 9 to 72nd St.*

9 *e-4*

HOTEL INTER-CONTINENTAL

Not to be confused with the more upscale Central Park Inter-Continental, this member of the Inter-Continental chain does have the advantage of occupying a 1930s building whose grand, marble lobby still has its original ornate skylight and gilded crown moldings. Rooms are predictably traditional, with framed neoclassical prints and glass-top coffee tables; the only surprise is the brass-eagle doorbells mounted on the outside of each door—they're remnants of the building's former life as the Barclay Hotel. *111 E. 48th St., 10017, Midtown, 212/755–5900 or 800/327–0200, fax 212/644–0079. 601 rooms, 82 suites. Bar, restaurant, in-room data ports, massage, sauna, health club, baby-sitting, parking (fee). AE, D, DC, MC, V. Subway: 51st St./Lexington–3rd Aves.; 42nd St./Grand Central.*

9 *e-4*

HOTEL LEXINGTON

The Lexington attracts many tour groups because of its central location. There's usually lots of activity in the two-level lobby, which is elegantly appointed with a marble floor and rosewood pillars. Rooms are somewhat small, but all have nice marble bathrooms. On-site restaurants are Raffles coffee shop, and Sung Dynasty Chinese restaurant. *511 Lexington Ave. (at 48th St.), 10017, Midtown, 212/755–4400 or 800/448–4471, fax 212/751–4091. 688 rooms, 12 suites. 2 restaurants, 2 bars, coffee shop, in-room data ports, room service, exercise room, nightclub. AE, D, DC, MC, V. Subway: 42nd St./Grand Central.*

9 *d-4*

HOTEL REMINGTON

The ornate awning outside hints at what you'll find in the lobby: faux-marble walls with mirror paneling, a ceiling painted gold to look like gilding, and glass chandeliers. Rooms are endearingly retro, with pink-shag carpeting and white-wood furniture—though at press time a complete renovation was in the works. Bathrooms are spacious, but many have only a shower stall (no tub). *129 W. 46th St., 10036, Theater District, 212/221–2600 or 800/755–3194, fax 212/764–7481. 85 rooms. Airport shuttle. AE, DC, MC, V. Subway: 47th–50th Sts./Rockefeller Center.*

9 *e-6*

HOTEL WALES

The modestly priced Wales is a true find in the tony Carnegie Hill area. Built in 1901, it still has a turn-of-the-20th-century mood; there's even a "Pied Piper" parlor decorated with vintage children's illustrations (this is where the generous complimentary breakfast and nightly dessert buffets are served). Guest rooms are small and show signs of wear and tear, but they do have fine oak woodwork, and all are equipped with CD players. Most of the suites face Madison Avenue. *1295 Madison Ave. (between 92nd and 93rd Sts.), 10128, Upper East Side, 212/876–6000 or 800/528–5252, fax 212/860–7000. 87 rooms, 30 suites. Breakfast room, in-room VCRs, parking (fee). AE, MC, V. Subway: 6 to 96th St.*

9 *c-6*

HOWARD JOHNSON ON 34TH STREET

Once the dumpy Penn Plaza Hotel, this Midtown HoJo is now a decent business hotel. Though the tiny rooms are depressingly sterile, with jade-green and brown color schemes and tired-looking bathrooms (some have peeling plaster), it's a great location. Avoid the rooms facing 7th Avenue unless you don't mind street noise. *215 W. 34th St., 10001, Garment District, 212/947–5050 or 800/446–4656, fax 212/268–4829. 111 rooms. Subway: 34th St./Penn Station.*

9 *e-5*

JOLLY MADISON TOWERS

Part of the Italian Jolly Hotel chain, this is a great little bargain in Murray Hill. Rooms are cheerful and well kept, and bathrooms have separate glass shower stalls. The colorful restaurant, Cinque Terre, serves good Northern Italian cuisine. *22 E. 38th St., 10016, Murray Hill, 212/802–0600 or 800/225–4340, fax 212/447–0747. 245 rooms, 6 suites. Restaurant, bar, massage, sauna. AE, DC, MC, V. Subway: 33th St.*

9 *e-4*

LOEWS NEW YORK HOTEL

This is a large, lively, reasonably priced hotel with an always-bustling lobby-lounge restaurant, a shopping arcade, and on-site parking. Prices drop substantially during low-occupancy periods; even suites are under $250. *569 Lexington Ave. (at 51st St.), 10022, Midtown, 212/752–7000 or 800/836–6471, fax 212/*

752–3817. 722 rooms, 40 suites. Restaurant, in-room data ports, room service, barbershop, beauty salon, health club, parking (fee). AE, D, DC, MC, V. Subway: 51st St./Lexington–3rd Aves.

9 c-2

THE MAYFLOWER

You'll feel at home the moment you enter the wood-paneled lobby of this friendly hotel on Central Park West, where a basket of apples and complimentary coffee and cookies are offered all day long. Rooms are large and comfortable, with thick carpeting, fruit-and-flower drapes, dark-wood Colonial-style furniture, and walk-in closets. Some have park views, and most have walk-in pantries with refrigerators and sinks. 15 Central Park W. (between 61st and 62nd Sts.), 10023, Upper West Side, 212/265–0060 or 800/223–4164, fax 212/265–2026. 117 rooms, 160 suites. Restaurant, bar, in-room data ports, room service, exercise room, parking (fee). AE, DC, MC, V. Subway: 59th St./Columbus Circle.

10 f-3

OFF SOHO SUITES HOTEL

Though the Bowery is not a pretty neighborhood, it's part of the trendy Lower East Side and convenient to Chinatown, Little Italy, and SoHo. The two- and four-person suites here have fully equipped kitchens and are clean and functional, if totally generic. 11 Rivington St. (between Chrystie St. and Bowery), 10002, Lower East Side, 212/979–9808 or 800/633–7646, fax 212/979–9801. 40 suites, 28 with bath. Kitchenettes. AE, MC, V. Subway: 2nd Ave.

7 b-8

ON THE AVE

In the heart of the Upper West Side, this newcomer offers state-of-the art entertainment and communications. Rooms feature center air "floating" beds, and passes to the nearby Equinox Fitness club are available, as well as discount parking. 2178 Broadway (at 77th St.), 10024, Upper West Side, 212/362–1100, 800/509–7598, fax 212/787–9521. 250 rooms. AE, D, DC, MC, V. Subway: 79th St.

9 c-4

THE PARAMOUNT

The dramatic, multilevel lobby is a creation of Ian Schrager and Philippe Starck, also responsible for Morgans and the Royalton. The young and the hip come here in droves; it's fashionable and fun. The postage stamp–size rooms have modern, angular furniture and beds with frame headboards, several of them bearing a print of Vermeer's The Lacemaker; bathrooms have bizarre conical sinks. 235 W. 46th St., 10036, Theater District, 212/764–5500 or 800/225–7474, fax 212/575–4892. 590 rooms, 10 suites. 2 restaurants, bar, café, in-room data ports, room service, in-room VCRs, exercise room, nursery. AE, D, DC, MC, V. Subway: 42nd St./Times Sq.

9 c-2

RADISSON EMPIRE HOTEL

This is one of the few hotel bargains near Lincoln Center, and it's thoroughly pleasant to boot. The lobby is modified English-country style, complete with warm wood furniture and a hanging tapestry. Rooms are small but perfectly adequate, with textured teal carpets and dark-wood furnishings. 44 W. 63rd St., 10023, Upper West Side, 212/265–7400 or 800/333–3333, fax 212/244–3382. 355 rooms, 20 suites. Restaurant, bar, in-room data ports, minibars, in-room VCRs, parking (fee). AE, D, DC, MC, V. Subway: 59th St./Columbus Circle.

9 e-4

THE ROGER SMITH

Here's a boutique hotel for art lovers, or for anyone who appreciates bold color schemes and unconventional combinations. Take the lobby, which might well be a very civilized nightclub—crimson carpet, splashy paintings, bronze busts here and there. All bedrooms are individually decorated, some with slightly outlandish touches such as ivy-trellis wallpaper. This is a very friendly place; you may even meet Roger Smith himself, as he owns the art gallery next door. 501 Lexington Ave. (between 47th and 48th Sts.), 10017, Midtown, 212/755–1400 or 800/445–0277, fax 212/758–4061. 134 rooms. Restaurant, bar, room service, parking (fee). AE, D, DC, MC, V. Subway: 51st St./Lexington–3rd Aves.; 42nd St./Grand Central.

9 d-4

QUALITY HOTEL AND SUITES MIDTOWN

Housed in a prewar building, this hotel has more unique touches than the usual Quality franchise. Witness the slightly bizarre lobby, with its long, narrow corridor and loud, photorealist paintings.

Rooms, on the other hand, have the sanitized look of a chain hotel, with teal carpeting, blond-wood furniture, and spacious, serviceable bathrooms. You're near theaters, Rockefeller Center, and a cluster of Brazilian restaurants. *59 W. 46th St., 10036, Midtown, 212/719–2300 or 800/228–5151, fax 212/768–3477. 193 rooms, 21 suites. In-room data ports, barbershop, beauty salon. AE, D, DC, MC, V. Subway: 47th–50th Sts./Rockefeller Center.*

9 *e-7*

QUALITY HOTEL EAST SIDE

Patriotic types will appreciate the American-eagle wallpaper at this Murray Hill newcomer, originally called the Americana. Rooms are reasonably priced and come with such extras as hair dryers and ironing boards with irons; shared-bath rooms also have sinks. Checkered curtains and prints of American quilts add to the Yankee theme. *161 Lexington Ave. (at 30th St.), 10016, Murray Hill, 212/532–2255, fax 212/790–2758. 79 rooms. In-room data ports, exercise room. Subway: 6 to 28th St.*

9 *e-4*

SAN CARLOS

There's nothing remarkable about this small hotel, conveniently located near Fifth Avenue attractions—just friendly service and clean, modern accommodations. Every room has a kitchenette, walk-in closet, and two phones. Continental breakfast is complimentary. *150 E. 50th St., 10022, Midtown, 212/755–1800 or 800/722–2012, fax 212/688–9778. 70 rooms, 85 suites. Breakfast room, kitchenettes. AE, DC, MC, V. Subway: 51st St./Lexington–3rd Aves.*

9 *d-3*

THE WELLINGTON

The Wellington's traditionally decorated rooms are surprisingly tasteful for such a well-priced hotel, with dark-wood furniture, high-quality fabrics in soft color schemes, and nicely framed prints. The lobby is constantly crammed with tourists and feels hectic, but that's part of this old-timer's charm. Carnegie Hall is a stone's throw away. *871 7th Ave. (at 55th St.), 10019, Theater District, 212/247–3900 or 800/652–1212, fax 212/581–1719. 550 rooms, 150 suites. Restaurant, bar, coffee shop, beauty salon, parking (fee). AE, DC, MC, V. Subway: N, R to 57th St.*

9 *d-3*

THE WYNDHAM

Anyone who appreciates fine art and whimsical colors will love the Wyndham, whose lobby is a cross between a museum gallery and the comfortable salon of an art collector. The spacious, individually decorated guest rooms all have the feel of a summer house with a breezy rococo motif: light powder-blue, peach, or yellow fabric wall-coverings, flowers everywhere, and, of course, fine art. Closets are enormous. It's hard to find a better deal anywhere in Manhattan, let alone in such a prime location, right across from Central Park. *42 W. 58th St., 10019, Midtown, 212/753–3500 or 800/257–1111, fax 212/754–5638. 142 rooms, 70 suites. Restaurant, bar. AE, DC, MC, V. Subway: 59th St./Columbus Circle.*

BUDGET LODGINGS

9 *d-7*

ARLINGTON HOTEL

Signs are in both English and Chinese at this Chelsea hotel, a favorite of Chinese businesspeople on their way to import/export wholesale showrooms in the area. Rooms are spacious, with generic decor. There's a gift shop in the lobby, and American breakfast in the hotel's pleasant restaurant is included. The Flatiron district's Madison Park and trendy restaurants are just around the corner. *18 W. 25th St., 10010, Chelsea, 212/645–3990, fax 212/633–8952. 96 rooms. AE, D, MC, V. Subway: F to 23rd St.*

9 *c-4*

BROADWAY INN BED & BREAKFAST

Though it isn't the kind of bed-and-breakfast where you linger over omelettes in the garden, the Broadway Inn is every bit as friendly and comfortable. Continental breakfast is served in the brick-wall lobby, where stocked bookshelves and photos of Old New York create a homey mood. Theater hounds can fall quickly into bed after their Broadway show. *264 W. 46th St., 10036, Theater District, 212/997–9200 or 800/826–6300, fax 212/768–2807. 22 rooms, 11 suites. Breakfast room. AE, D, DC, MC, V. Subway: 42nd St./Times Sq.*

9 *e-7*

CARLTON ARMS

Though the rooms here are phoneless, TV-less, lack air conditioning, almost free of furniture, and sometimes bathless, they score a perfect 10 when it comes to character. Over the years the managers have commissioned artists to cover every wall, ceiling, and other surface with murals, some of them with outrageous themes. The Cow Spot Room (3C), for example, has a Holstein motif of cow-spotted rugs, bedspreads, and walls; while the Versailles Room (5A) is a symphony of trompe l'oeil trellises and classical urns. Only in New York. *160 E. 25th St., 10010, Gramercy, 212/684–8337. 54 rooms, 20 with bath. MC, V. Subway: N, R to 28th St.*

9 *d-8*

CHELSEA INN

Perhaps the best budget find in downtown Manhattan, this quaint old brownstone is just a few blocks from Union Square. The in-room cooking facilities (some have full kitchenettes; others have just a refrigerator and sink) make it a favorite of young travelers. Most rooms share a bath and are inviting with dark-wood furniture, country-style quilts, and big TVs. *46 W. 17th St., 10011, Chelsea, 212/645–8989, fax 212/645–1903. 27 rooms, 3 with bath. AE, D, MC, V. Subway: 14th St./Union Sq.; F to 14th St.*

9 *d-7*

GERSHWIN HOTEL

There's always a lot going on at this young, arty mecca for foreign budget travelers—summer rooftop barbecues, gallery openings, and socializing in the giant, art-filled lobby. Rooms are all painted in custard yellow and kelly green and are somewhat crumbly in places, with no air-conditioning. Dormitories have four or eight beds and a remarkable rate of $22 a person. The hotel occupies a 13-story Greek Revival building. *7 E. 27th St., 10016, Murray Hill, 212/545–8000, fax 212/684–5546. 120 rooms, 15 dorm rooms. Restaurant, bar. MC, V. Subway: 6, N, R to 28th St.*

9 *e-3*

HABITAT HOTEL

Habitat has small yet comfortable and modern guest rooms with a distinct European feel. By summer 2000 the roof deck will offer breakfast and great views of the heart of Midtown. Until then Continental breakfast is served in the lobby. Rooms have cable TV, and Internet hookup. Bloomingdales, Tiffany, Bergdorf Goodman and Bendels are around the corner. *130 E. 57th St., 10022, Midtown, 212/753–8841, 800/255–0482, fax 212–829–9605. 350 rooms, 30 with bath. Restaurant, bar. AE, MC, V. Subway: 59th St.*

9 *d-6*

HERALD SQUARE HOTEL

Housed in the former *Life* building, the Herald Square pays homage to its predecessor with framed vintage magazine covers in the hallways. The rooms are basic, with TVs, phones with voice mail, and in-room safes; what really stands out here is the service, which is remarkably attentive for such an inexpensive hotel. *19 W. 31st St., 10001, Garment District, 212/279–4017 or 800/727–1888, fax 212/643–9208. 127 rooms. AE, D, MC, V. Subway: 34th St./Herald Sq.*

9 *c-4*

HOTEL EDISON

Fans of Al Pacino may recall Sophia's, the Edison's restaurant, from the loan-shark murder scene in *The Godfather*. The hotel is a hit with tour groups, with its reasonable prices and on-site facilities. The pink-plaster coffee shop is a great place to spy on show-biz types. *228 W. 47th St., 10036, Theater District, 212/840–5000 or 800/637–7070, fax 212/596–6850. 1,000 rooms. Restaurant, bar, coffee shop, beauty salon, airport shuttle. AE, D, DC, MC, V. Subway: 50th St.*

9 *f-8*

HOTEL 17

Madonna and David Bowie were among the first to frequent this trendy, dirt-cheap, Euro-style hotel. Most rooms are small and share a bath, but you come here for image, not luxury. The location, right off beautiful Stuyvesant Square, puts you in walking distance of Park Avenue South's many great restaurants. *225 E. 17th St., 10003, Gramercy, 212/475–2845, fax 212/677–8178. 200 rooms, 12 with bath. No credit cards. Subway: 14th St./Union Sq.*

10 *d-1*

LARCHMONT HOTEL

On this residential, West Village street, the Larchmont looks more like a charming brownstone home than a hotel. Rooms have a safari theme, with rattan furniture, ceiling fans, and framed animal or botanical prints. Bathrooms are shared, but kept clean, and every bedroom has a private sink. The staff is extra-friendly, and the rates include Continental breakfast. *27 W. 11th St., 10011, West Village, 212/989–9333, fax 212/989–9496. 55 rooms. Breakfast room, kitchen. AE, D, DC, MC, V. Subway: W. 4th St./Washington Sq.*

7 *b-8*

THE MILBURN

You may think you've entered King Ludwig's pied-à-terre when you step inside the lobby, which is full of heraldic doodads and gilt. The spacious rooms are more low-key, albeit slightly chaotic (witness the clashing color schemes in some)—but all have kitchenettes. Lincoln Center, Central Park, and Zabar's are nearby. *242 W. 76th St., 10023, Upper West Side, 212/362–1006 or 800/833–9622, fax 212/721–5476. 50 rooms, 50 suites. Kitchenettes, coin laundry. AE, DC, MC, V. Subway: 1, 2, 3, 9 to 72nd St.*

9 *c-1*

OLCOTT HOTEL

This semiresidential hotel occupies a fine, prewar building, with easy access to Central Park and the Museum of Natural History. There are daily and weekly rates for both comfortable studios (each with cooking pantry) and suites (with kitchenette). The lobby is large and inviting, with ornate gilded elevators and Corinthian columns. *27 W. 72nd St., 10023, Upper West Side, 212/877–4200, fax 212/580–0511. 150 rooms, 100 suites. Restaurant, bar, kitchenettes, parking (fee). MC, V. Subway: B, C to 72nd St.*

9 *d-3*

PARK SAVOY

Save money on a room here and spend it on a concert at Carnegie Hall or brunch at the Plaza—both a few blocks away. Rooms have rock-hard beds, no direct-dial phones, and while there are TVs, there's no cable. Nevertheless, the room's are colorful and sunny. The staff is friendly, and there's lots of repeat business. *158 W. 58th St., 10019, Midtown, 212/245–5755, fax 212/765–0668. 96 rooms. Restaurant, bar. AE, MC, V. Subway: 57th St.*

9 *f-4*

PICKWICK ARMS HOTEL

A convenient location, a rooftop garden, and views of the Manhattan skyline (from some rooms) are among the advantages at this bargain favorite. What's more, the café spreads out an irresistible Middle Eastern buffet at lunchtime on weekdays for less than $7. Drawbacks: the rooms are tiny, and the furniture is nothing special. *230 E. 51st St., 10022, Midtown, 212/355–0300 or 800/742–5945, fax 212/755–5029. 350 rooms, 175 with bath. Café, airport shuttle. AE, DC, MC, V. Subway: 51st St./Lexington–3rd Aves.*

9 *d-4*

PORTLAND SQUARE HOTEL

Built in 1904 as the Rio Hotel, this friendly little place was once the home of James Cagney and a few of his Radio City Rockette acquaintances. Prices are good value as you get phones with voice mail, in-room safes, a laundry room, and even a small exercise room. Rooms in the east wing have bigger bathrooms. *132 W. 47th St., 10036, Theater District, 212/382–0600 or 800/388–8988, fax 212/382–0684. 142 rooms, 112 with bath. Exercise room. AE, MC, V. Subway: 49th St.*

7 *a-8*

RIVERSIDE TOWER

Rooms above the sixth floor have sweeping views of Riverside Park, the mighty Hudson River, and the New Jersey skyline. They're small, dark, and occasionally smoke-singed, but the location is good, and the price is right. European backpackers come in droves. *80 Riverside Dr. (at 80th St.), 10024, Upper West Side, 212/877–5200 or 800/724–3136, fax 212/873–1400. 120 rooms, 116 with bath. AE, D, DC, MC, V. Subway: 79th St.*

9 *d-6*

STANFORD HOTEL

Near Macy's and the Manhattan Mall, the Stanford attracts a Latin American and Japanese clientele. Rooms are tidy, and all are equipped with TVs and refrigerators. There's karaoke in the cocktail bar. *43 W. 32nd St., 10001, Garment District, 212/563–1500, fax 212/629–0043. 130 rooms. Bar. Subway: 34th St./Herald Sq.*

9 *b-5*

TRAVEL INN

Though it's on a desolate block near the Port Authority Bus Terminal, the Travel Inn is worthwhile for its generous amenities and low price. The spanking-new rooms—all with reproduction furniture, green carpets, and blue-tile bathrooms—occupy four wings that center around a lovely outdoor swimming pool surrounded by greenery and colorful plants. You also get free parking and a helpful travel-services desk. *515 W. 42nd St., 10036, Hell's Kitchen, 212/695–7171 or 800/869–4630, fax 212/967–5025. 160 rooms. Deli, room service, pool, travel services, free parking. AE, D, DC, MC, V. Subway: 42nd St./Port Authority.*

9 *c-4*

WASHINGTON JEFFERSON HOTEL

The tiny rooms here have pink walls, but each comes with cable TV, and some have mini-refrigerators. Though the hotel is on a somewhat lonely side street, away from the Broadway action, it's still convenient to the shows. Prices are rock-bottom. *318 W. 51st St., 10019, Midtown, 212/246–7550, fax 212/246–7622. 260 rooms, 130 with bath. AE, MC, V. Subway: 50th St.*

10 *d-2*

WASHINGTON SQUARE HOTEL

This is *the* place to stay in the Village: It's quaint and historic (built in 1902), with a European-style lobby full of wrought iron and gleaming brass; it's convenient, especially for night owls (the Blue Note jazz club is just around the corner); and, more to the point, it's one of the only hotels in the area. Free breakfast is served at the little restaurant, C3, on the premises. There's even a tiny exercise room. Rooms are simple but well maintained; some don't have a window, so request one that does. *103 Waverly Pl. (at MacDougal St.), 10011, West Village, 212/777–9515 or 800/222–0418, fax 212/979–8373. 165 rooms. Restaurant, bar, exercise room. AE, MC, V. Subway: W. 4th St./Washington Sq.*

9 *b-3*

WESTPARK HOTEL

If you don't mind retro decor—pink or emerald-green shag carpeting, velour-covered seats, and mustard-yellow bathroom tiles—opt for this small hotel right off Columbus Circle, across from a major subway station that makes exploring the city a breeze. The management is friendly. *308 W. 58th St., 10019, Midtown, 212/246–6440 or 800/228–1122, fax 212/246–3131. 90 rooms, 9 suites. AE, D, DC, MC, V. Subway: 59th St./Columbus Circle.*

9 *d-6*

THE WOLCOTT

Beyond the gilded lobby lie unremarkable but functional guest rooms. All have phones with voice mail, color TVs, and some have mini-refrigerators. You're just three blocks south of the Empire State Building, and have easy access to Macy's and Madison Square Garden. *4 W. 31st St., 10001, Garment District, 212/268–2900, fax 212/563–0096. 200 rooms, 190 with bath. AE, MC, V. Subway: 34th St./Herald Sq.*

HOSTELS & YMCAS

Independent hostels and those affiliated with Hostelling International (HI) are similar in price and style: they almost always have private rooms as well as dorms that sleep 4–12 people. The three private hostels in Harlem charge $14–$16 per dorm bed, while Midtown properties generally cost $20 or more. Very few hostels have air conditioning. Many hostels have an unadvertised policy of accepting foreigners only; those listed below accept Americans but require identification for check-in. Hostelers would be wise to carry a passport.

Another budget option is to stay in one of Manhattan's handful of YMCAs, where double rooms generally range from about $60 to $90. Though most YMCAs have bare-bones rooms and few facilities, they compensate by offering guests free use of their extensive gym facilities.

9 *d-4*

BIG APPLE HOSTEL

In the heart of Times Square, the Big Apple has brisk service, bathrooms that sparkle, and a big outdoor patio where you can sip free coffee with an international crowd. There are four-person dorms and a handful of private doubles. *119 W. 45th St., 10036, Midtown, 212/302–2603, fax 212/302–2605. 106 beds. Kitchen, coin laundry. MC, V. Subway: 42nd St./Times Sq.*

6 *d-6*

BLUE RABBIT INTERNATIONAL HOUSE

In Harlem's affluent Sugar Hill, this hostel is just two blocks from St. Nick's Pub, one of Manhattan's best jazz clubs. Coed and women-only dorm-style rooms sleep four–eight, and there are also a few giant doubles. There's no air-conditioning, but fans are provided. You can survey the street scene from a rooftop terrace. Note: a passport is required for check-in. *730 St. Nicholas Ave. (between 145th and 146th Sts.), 10031, Harlem, 212/491–3892 or 800/610–2030, fax 212/283–0108. 25 beds. Kitchen. No credit cards. Subway: A, B, C, D to 145th St.*

9 *c-8*

CHELSEA INTERNATIONAL HOSTEL

The free pizza party every Wednesday night draws a boisterous young crowd. The four-person dorm rooms are somewhat cramped, and only some have air conditioning, but they're half the price of the private doubles. A common room has a TV. A passport is required for check-in, even for Americans. *251 W. 20th St., 10011, Chelsea, 212/647–0010, fax 212/727–7289. 310 beds. Kitchen, coin laundry. AE, MC, V. Subway: 1, 9, C, E to 23rd St.*

7 *e-6*

DE HIRSCH RESIDENCE AT THE 92ND STREET YM-YWHA

Right off Museum Mile in posh Carnegie Hill, the De Hirsch Residence is an excellent bargain: Every floor has its own kitchen, laundry, and shared bath, and you have free use of the excellent fitness facilities. The Y also sponsors many cultural and social events. There's a three-night minimum stay; reserve as far in advance as possible. *1395 Lexington Ave. (at 92nd St.), 10128, Upper East Side, 212/415–5650 or 800/858–4692, fax 212/415–5578. 350 beds. Health club, pool, coin laundry. Subway: 4, 5, 6 to 86th St.*

7 *b-4*

HOSTELLING INTERNATIONAL–NEW YORK

Nineteenth-century architect Richard Morris Hunt designed this building, now home to the largest youth hostel in North America. Besides its sheer size, the main draws here are a garden and outdoor terrace and an excellent neighborhood location. There are about 100 4- to 12-person dorms, as well as some private rooms (with bath) that accommodate up to four people; these cost $75. Those with a Hostelling International card get a $3 discount. *891 Amsterdam Ave. (at 103rd St.), 10025, Upper West Side, 212/932–2300, fax 212/932–2574. 540 beds. Kitchen, coin laundry. MC, V. Subway: 1, 9 to 103rd St.*

6 *c-6*

SUGAR HILL INTERNATIONAL HOUSE

Like the Blue Rabbit International House (it has the same owners), this Harlem hostel is clean, comfortable, and friendly, with easy subway access and a sunny back garden. There are three four- to eight-bed dorms (some coed, some women-only) and one private double. Reserve in advance, check in before 9 PM, and remember your passport—it's required for check-in. *722 St. Nicholas Ave. (at 146th St.), 10031, Harlem, 212/926–7030, fax 212/283–0108. 20 beds. Kitchen. No credit cards. Subway: A, B, C, D to 145th St.*

7 *d-2*

UPTOWN HOSTEL

This beautiful Harlem brownstone is a real find thanks to Giselle, the hard-working Canadian owner who loves to debunk visitors' preconceptions about Harlem. (It's the friendliest neighborhood she's ever lived in, she says.) There are 30 coed dorms (four–six beds) and two private doubles. *239 Lenox Ave./Malcolm X Blvd. (at 122nd St.), 10027, Harlem, 212/666–0559. 30 beds. Kitchen. No credit cards. Subway: 2, 3 to 125th St.*

9 *c-7*

YMCA–MCBURNEY

Despite the uninviting entrance—with a security guard and a glassed-in reception window—the McBurney is a good deal. Rooms are small but decent, and guests have free use of the gym. Beware, though: there are only two large bathrooms for all 270 rooms. A $40 deposit is required to secure your reservation, unless you arrive before 6 PM. *206 W. 24th St., 10011, Chelsea, 212/741–9226, fax 212/741–8724. 270 rooms, none with bath. Health club. Subway: 1, 9, C, E to 23rd St.*

9 *f-4*

YMCA–VANDERBILT

Tiny rooms with linoleum floors and shared bathrooms are a small price to pay for such a prime location and great fitness perks: guests have free use of the pools, cardiovascular equipment, and Nautilus machines. *224 E. 47th St., 10017, Midtown, 212/756–9600, fax 212/752–0210. 377 rooms, none with bath. MC, V. 2 pools, health club, airport shuttle. Subway: 51st St./Lexington–3rd Aves.*

9 *c-2*

YMCA—WEST SIDE

A few blocks from Lincoln Center, this Y has extensive fitness facilities, including a pool, indoor track, and squash courts. You must be at least 18 years old to stay here; reservations (credit card required) are best made two weeks in advance. *5 W. 63rd St., 10023, Upper West Side, 212/787–4400, fax 212/875–1334. 550 rooms, 100 with bath. Cafeteria, pool, sauna, health club, squash, coin laundry, airport shuttle. AE, MC, V. Subway: 59th St./Columbus Circle.*

HOTELS NEAR THE AIRPORTS

3 *f-1*

LA GUARDIA MARRIOTT AIRPORT HOTEL

A quarter of a mile from the airport and—barring traffic—about 20 minutes from Manhattan, this hotel is out of the direct line of most flights. The airport shuttle is free. *102–05 Ditmars Blvd., East Elmhurst, Queens, 11369, 718/565–8900 or 800/882–1043, fax 718/899–0764. 432 rooms, 4 suites. Restaurant, sports bar, in-room data ports, room service, indoor pool, health club, airport shuttle, parking (fee). AE, D, DC, MC, V. Moderately priced.*

1 *b-7*

NEWARK AIRPORT MARRIOTT

The Marriott is right on airport premises and provides free 24-hour shuttle service to all terminals, as well as free parking. In light traffic it's only 30 minutes from Manhattan. *Newark International Airport, Newark, NJ 07114, 201/623–0006 or 800/228–9290, fax 201/623–7618. 584 rooms, 6 suites. 2 restaurants, bar, room service, indoor-outdoor pool, health club, airport shuttle, free parking. AE, D, DC, MC, V. Moderately priced.*

B&B RESERVATION SERVICES

If you're looking for a more personal (and significantly cheaper) overnight experience in a more residential neighborhood than most hotels can offer, try one of the hundreds of bed-and-breakfasts throughout the city, especially in Brooklyn. Beware, however, that although you often pay less than $100, the accommodations, amenities, service, and privacy may fall short of what you get in hotels; and, despite the B&B name, you often don't get breakfast. Ask your B&B reservation agency for the details on your property before checking in.

B&Bs booked through a service may be either hosted (you're the guest in someone's quarters) or unhosted (you have full use of someone's vacated apartment, including kitchen privileges). Needless to say, the latter option is the more expensive. Most B&B services represent both kinds. Make reservations as far in advance as possible; refunds (minus a $25 service charge) are possible up to 10 days before arrival.

All Around the Town (150 5th Ave., Suite 711, New York, NY 10011, 212/675–5600, fax 212/675–6366).

Bed-and-Breakfast in Manhattan (Box 533, New York, NY 10150, 212/472–2528, fax 212/988–9818).

Bed-and-Breakfast Network of New York (134 W. 32nd St., Suite 602, New York, NY 10001, 212/645–8134 or 800/900–8134).

City Lights Bed-and-Breakfast (Box 20355, Cherokee Station, New York, NY 10021, 212/737–7049, fax 212/535–2755).

Manhattan Home Stays (Box 20684, Cherokee Station, New York, NY 10021, 212/737–3868, fax 212/265–3561).

New World Bed and Breakfast (150 5th Ave., Suite 711, New York, NY 10011, 212/675–5600; 800/443–3800 in the U.S., fax 212/675–6366).

New York Habitat (307 7th Ave., Suite 306, New York, NY 10001, 212/647–9365, fax 212/627–1416).

Urban Ventures (38 W. 32nd St., Suite 1412, New York, NY 10001, 212/594–5650, fax 212/947–9320).

chapter 7

CITY SOURCES

getting a handle on the city

basics of city life

APARTMENT LOCATOR SERVICES

If you want to live here, you'll have to pay the price. And, while nothing short of a revolution is likely to lower NYC rents any time soon, you can circumvent the web of real-estate brokers by using an apartment locator service, which for less than a broker's fee can help you find a home, a roommate, or both. Most companies issue you a password to browse their listings on the web, although many will also send you an E-mail or fax when apartments that meet your criteria become available.

Apartment Fone Over 500 sublet and long-term rental and sale listings updated weekly; an automated menu allows you shop by neighborhood, price-range, size, etc.; it's $10 to list an apartment and free for apartment hunters (212/278–3663).

The Apartment Store If your definition of living in New York includes Brooklyn and Queens, this one's for you. The average client finds an apartment in just over a week. $79.99 for 30-day subscription, includes credit check (212/545–1996; www.apartmentstores.com).

Apartment Source Promises new daily listings; you can do your credit check online (fee). Open 9–7 daily; $120 for 2 months (212/343–8155; www.apartmentsource.com).

Roommate Finders Drop in to the oldest New York City agency between noon and 7 PM weekdays or call their phone banks until 6 PM to find your match. They keep a turkey file on serious roommate rejects, so the seedy, thieving, and unreliable stay away. $300 for 1-year (250 W. 57th St., Suite 1629, at Broadway, Midtown, 212/489–6862; www.roommatefinders.com).

BANKS

Commercial banks are generally open weekdays from 9 AM to 4 PM and closed weekends and holidays. A few savings institutions are also open Friday evening and Saturday morning.

Amalgamated Bank of New York (212/255–6200).

Apple Savings Bank (212/472–4545).

Chase Manhattan (212/935–9935).

Citibank (212/627–3999).

Republic National Bank of New York (800/737–8254).

DRIVING

Because owning, driving, and parking your own car is such a hassle here, most New Yorkers relish the role of perpetual passenger. In fact, only in New York City is it *not* a shameful thing to not know how to drive. (Just over 3 million New Yorkers have a license.) Go with the masses on this one—save your driver's license for weekend duty, and line up with fellow city dwellers at rental car agencies on Friday afternoon to escape the city. If you want to pony up the money and years off your life to own and drive a car here, you'll have little sympathy from others when whining about the exorbitant cost of storage or dearth of streetside parking spots (*see* Parking, *below*). Drivers in NYC are to observe a 30 mph (48 km/h) speed limit, and make no right turns at red lights unless a sign is posted permitting it but has anyone ever seen such a sign?

licenses

It turns out that the folks at the DMV don't want to see you any more than you want to see them. Amazingly clear instructions about how to get and renew a New York State license, the driver's test manual, and forms for car and plates registration hover in cyberspace on the DMV website, so you won't have to wait in line. And, if you have a New York State driver's license or ID, and your address hasn't changed, you can renew your license online (about $28).

To get a license, you'll have to pay a visit to one of the DMV offices. You'll need a valid license from another state (which you must surrender in exchange for your New York State one) or at least two pieces of valid ID, one specifying your date of birth, and another with your signature—assuming, that is, that you're at least 16 years old, with decent eyesight and a Social Security Number. Some types of ID are not acceptable, so make sure your ID is one they'll recognize before you go. It's $44 for a new passenger-car license if you re exactly 16, and less ($38–$41) if you aren't.

To register your car and get plates, you can download the MV-82: Vehicle Registration/Title Application forms in advance from the DMV website, but you must go in person with the following: proof of ownership; an original New York State Insurance Identification Card (FS-20), in the same name as the registration application; acceptable proof of identity and age; proof of sales tax payment or purchase price; and your checkbook. Registration fees are determined by the weight of your car ($86–$112), plus you'll pay a plate fee ($5.50), title fee ($5), and a passenger-vehicle-use tax ($30).

DEPARTMENT OF MOTOR VEHICLES

Just like snowflakes, no two DMV offices are alike, as each has its own hours of operation study them carefully before setting out. Even the centralized phone number, the DMV Call Center, has its own hours of operation. If you want custom plates, you can call direct, seven days a week, and get a friendly, helpful person to take your order.

Custom Plates (Daily ; 800/364–7528).

DMV Albany To renew or replace your license by mail (Regular mail: License Production Bureau, Box 2688, ESP, Albany, NY 12220-0668; express-mail service: NYS DMV License Production Bureau Room 223, 6 Empire State Plaza, Albany, NY 12228).

DMV Call Center Information about DMVs in the five boroughs (Open Mon.–Wed., Fri. 7:30–4:30; Thurs. 7:30–5:30; 212/645–5550 or 718/966–6155).

Harlem Office–NYSDMV (Mon.–Wed., Fri. 8:30–4; Thurs. 10–6; 2110 Adam Clayton Powell, Jr. Blvd., at 126th St., 10027).

Herald Square Office (Weekdays 8:30–4; 1293–1311 Broadway, 8th floor, between W. 33rd and W. 34th Sts., 10001).

Manhattan License X-Press Office Only handles license and registration renewals and duplicates, and surrendered license plates (Mon.–Wed. 8–5:30, Thurs. 8–7; closed Fri.; 300 W. 34th St., at 9th Ave., 10001).

New York Office–NYSDMV (Weekdays 8:30–4; 141–155 Worth St., at Center St., 10013).

TRAFFIC

It's always rush hour in New York. Just assume there's traffic wherever you're headed, particularly if it's over a bridge into Manhattan in the morning or out of Manhattan in the afternoon. Leave it to the professionals with helicopters to tell you where there isn't any traffic and tune in to a radio station that has frequent traffic reports (see Radio Stations, *below*).

GAS STATIONS

Gas stations are most plentiful in SoHo and toward the island's outer rims, particularly in Hell's Kitchen and at various points on the West Side Highway. They're easy to stumble upon in the other four boroughs.

downtown

Amoco (Broadway at Houston St., Greenwich Village, 212/473–5924).

Gulf (FDR Dr. at 23rd St., Stuyvesant Town, 212/686–4546).

Mobil (E. Broadway at Pike St., Lower East Side, 212/966–0571; 6th Ave. at Spring St., SoHo, 212/925–6126).

uptown

Merit (7th Ave. at 145th St., Harlem, 212/283–9354).

Mobil (11th Ave. at 51st St., Hell's Kitchen, 212/582–9269).

Shell (Amsterdam Ave. at 181st St., Washington Heights, 212/928–3100).

GEOGRAPHY

New York City's five boroughs—the Bronx, Brooklyn, Manhattan, Queens, and Staten Island—are linked by a series of bridges, tunnels, and ferries. Although residents most likely spend the bulk of their time in Manhattan, an island only 13.4 mi long and 2.3 mi wide (at its widest). The island's grid layout makes getting around easy. Avenues run north and south, with 5th Avenue dividing the east and west sides—the lower the house address on a street, whether it's east or west, the closer it is to 5th Avenue. Broadway, a former wagon trail, is the grand exception to the rule—it cuts diagonally through Manhattan from the Upper

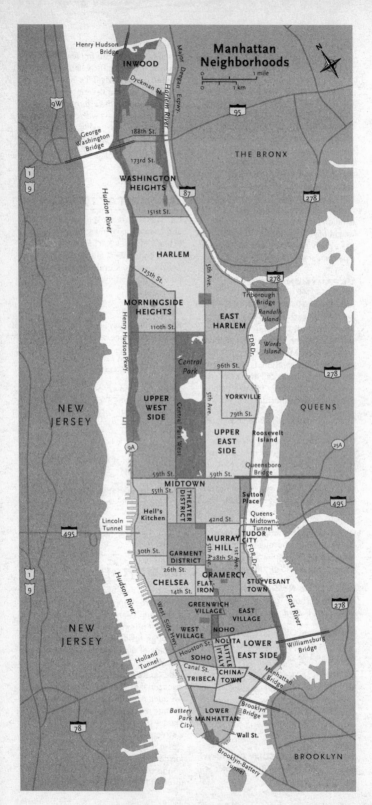

Manhattan
Neighborhoods

1 mile

1 km

HENRY HUDSON BRIDGE

INWOOD

Dyckman St.

Major Deegan Expwy.

Harlem River Dr.

188th St.

173rd St.

WASHINGTON HEIGHTS

151st St.

HARLEM

125th St.

MORNINGSIDE HEIGHTS

110th St.

Central Park

5th Ave.

Central Park West

UPPER WEST SIDE

EAST HARLEM

Triborough Bridge

Randalls Island

Wards Island

96th St.

YORKVILLE

79th St.

UPPER EAST SIDE

Roosevelt Island

59th St.

59th St.

Queensboro Bridge

MIDTOWN

55th St.

THEATER DISTRICT

Hell's Kitchen

Sutton Place

Queens-Midtown Tunnel

42nd St.

MURRAY HILL

TUDOR CITY

Lincoln Tunnel

30th St.

GARMENT DISTRICT

26th St.

CHELSEA

14th St.

FLAT-IRON

GRAMERCY

STUYVESANT TOWN

GREENWICH VILLAGE

EAST VILLAGE

WEST VILLAGE

NOHO

NOLITA

LOWER EAST SIDE

Houston St.

SOHO

LITTLE ITALY

Canal St.

TRIBECA

CHINA-TOWN

Williamsburg Bridge

Manhattan Bridge

Battery Park City

LOWER MANHATTAN

Brooklyn Bridge

Wall St.

Brooklyn-Battery Tunnel

Henry Hudson Pkwy.

Hudson River

West Side Hwy.

Holland Tunnel

East River

FDR Dr.

5th Ave.

1st Ave.

THE BRONX

NEW JERSEY

NEW JERSEY

QUEENS

BROOKLYN

George Washington Bridge

Hudson River

Henry Hudson Bridge

9W

1 9

95

87

278

278

278

25A

495

495

1 9

78

N

418

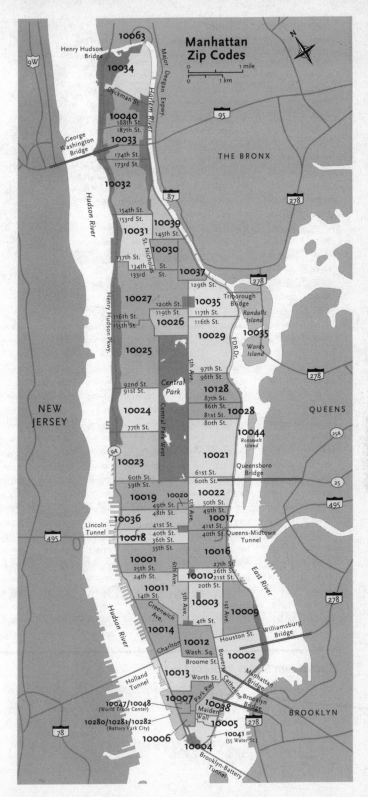

Manhattan Zip Codes

0 ____ 1 mile
0 ____ 1 km

NEW JERSEY

THE BRONX

QUEENS

BROOKLYN

10063
10034
Henry Hudson Bridge
Dyckman St.
Harlem River
Major Deegan Expwy.

10040
188th St.
187th St.
10033
George Washington Bridge
174th St.
173rd St.

10032
Hudson River
Henry Hudson Pkwy.

154th St.
153rd St.
10031
10039
145th St.
St. Nicholas
10030
137th St.
134th St.
133rd
St. St.
10037
129th St.

10027
120th St.
119th St.
10035
117th St.
116th St.
10026
Triborough Bridge
Randalls Island

116th St.
115th St.

10025
10029
5th Ave.
FDR Dr.
10035
Wards Island

97th St.
96th St.
Central Park
92nd St.
91st St.
10128
87th St.
86th St.
10024
81st St.
10028
Central Park West
77th St.
80th St.

10044
Roosevelt Island

10023
Queensboro Bridge
61st St.
6th St.
60th St.
59th St.
10021

10019
10020
10022
50th St.
49th St.
5th Ave.
Lincoln Tunnel
49th St.
48th St.
10036
41st St.
10017
41st St.
Queens-Midtown Tunnel
10018
40th St.
36th St.
40th St.
35th St.
10016

10001
27th St.
26th St.
25th St.
24th St.
10010
21st St.
20th St.
10011
14th St.
6th Ave.
5th Ave.
1st Ave.
10003
Greenwich Ave.
4th St.
10009

10014
Houston St.
Williamsburg Bridge
Charlton
10012
Wash. Sq.
Broome St.
Bowery
10002
10013
Worth St.
Catherine
Manhattan Bridge

Holland Tunnel
10007
Park Row
Brooklyn Bridge
10047/10048
(World Trade Center)
10038
Maiden
Wall
10280/10281/10282
(Battery Park City)
10005
10006
10041
(55 Water St.)
10004
Brooklyn-Battery Tunnel

East River
Hudson River

9W
9A
87
95
278
278
278
278
278
495
495
78
25A
25

N

419

Avenue Address Finder

Streets	West End Ave.	Broadway	Amsterdam Ave.	Columbus Ave.	Central Park West
94–96	700–737	2520–2554	702–733	701–740	350–360
92–94	660–699	2476–2519	656–701	661–700	322–336
90–92	620–659	2440–2475	620–655	621–660	300–320
88–90	578–619	2401–2439	580–619	581–620	279–295
86–88	540–577	2361–2400	540–579	541–580	262–275
84–86	500–539	2321–2360	500–539	501–540	241–257
82–84	460–499	2281–2320	460–499	461–500	212–239
80–82	420–459	2241–2280	420–459	421–460	211 American Museum of Natural History
78–80	380–419	2201–2240	380–419	381–420	
76–78	340–379	2161–2200	340–379	341–380	
74–76	300–339	2121–2160	300–339	301–340	145–160
72–74	262–299	2081–2114	261–299	261–300	121–135
70–72	221–261	2040–2079	221–260	221–260	101–115
68–70	176–220	1999–2030	181–220	181–220	80–99
66–68	122–175	1961–1998	140–180	141–180	65–79
64–66	74–121	1920–1960	100–139	101–140	50–55
62–64	44–73	Lincoln Center	60–99	61–100	25–33
60–62	20–43	1841–1880	20–59	21–60	15
58–60	2–19	Columbus Circle	1–19	2–20	Columbus Circle

	11th Ave.	Broadway	10th Ave.	9th Ave.	8th Ave.	7th Ave.	6th Ave.
56–58	823–854	1752–1791	852–889	864–907	946–992	888–921	1381–1419
54–56	775–822	1710–1751	812–851	824–863	908–945	842–887	1341–1377
52–54	741–774	1674–1709	772–811	782–823	870–907	798–841	1301–1330
50–52	701–740	1634–1673	737–770	742–781	830–869	761–797	1261–1297
48–50	665–700	1596–1633	686–735	702–741	791–829	720–760	1221–1260
46–48	625–664	1551–1595	654–685	662–701	735–790	701–719	1180–1217
44–46	589–624	1514–1550	614–653	622–661	701–734	Times Square	1141–1178
42–44	553–588	1472–1513	576–613	582–621	661–700		1100–1140
40–42	503–552	1440–1471	538–575	Port Authority	620–660	560–598	1061–1097
38–40	480–502	1400–1439	502–537		570–619	522–559	1020–1060
36–38	431–471	1352–1399	466–501	468–501	520–569	482–521	981–1019
34–36	405–430	Macy's	430–465	432–467	480–519	442–481	Herald Square
32–34	360–404	1260–1282	380–429	412–431	442–479	Penn Station	
30–32	319–359	1220–1279	341–379	Post Office	403–441	362–399	855–892
28–30	282–318	1178–1219	314–340	314–351	362–402	322–361	815–844
26–28	242–281	1135–1177	288–313	262–313	321–361	282–321	775–814
24–26	202–241	1100–1134	239–287	230–261	281–320	244–281	733–774
22–24	162–201	940–1099	210–238	198–229	236–280	210–243	696–732
20–22	120–161	902–939	162–209	167–197	198–235	170–209	656–695
18–20	82–119	873–901	130–161	128–166	162–197	134–169	613–655
16–18	54–81	860–872	92–129	92–127	126–161	100–133	574–612
14–16	26–53	Union Square	58–91	91–44	80–125	64–99	573–530

Crosstown Street Address Finder

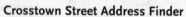

West End Ave. ← 200 ← Amsterdam Ave. ← 100 ← Columbus Ave. ← 1 ← Central Park W.

NOTE: Odd number addresses are on the north side, even numbers are on the south side.

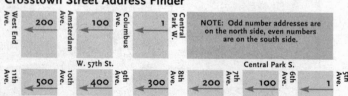

W. 57th St.: 11th Ave. ← 500 ← 10th Ave. ← 400 ← 9th Ave. ← 300 ← 8th Ave. ← 200 ← 7th Ave. ← 100 ← 6th Ave. ← 1 ← 5th Ave.

Central Park S.

5th Ave.	Madison Ave.	Park Ave.	Lexington Ave.	3rd Ave.	2nd Ave.	1st Ave.	Streets
1130–1148	1340–1379	1199–1236	1449–1486	1678–1709	1817–1868	1817–1855	94–96
1109–1125	1295–1335	1160–1192	1400–1444	1644–1677	1766–1808	1780–1811	92–94
1090–1107	1254–1294	1120–1155	1361–1396	1601–1643	1736–1763	1740–1779	90–92
1070–1089	1220–1250	1080–1114	1311–1355	1568–1602	1700–1739	1701–1735	88–90
1050–1069	1178–1221	1044–1076	1280–1301	1530–1566	1660–1698	1652–1689	86–88
1030–1048	1130–1171	1000–1035	1248–1278	1490–1529	1624–1659	1618–1651	84–86
1010–1028	1090–1128	960–993	1210–1248	1450–1489	1584–1623	1578–1617	82–84
990–1009	1058–1088	916–959	1164–1209	1410–1449	1538–1583	1540–1577	80–82
970–989	1012–1046	878–911	1120–1161	1374–1409	1498–1537	1495–1539	78–80
950–969	974–1006	840–877	1080–1116	1330–1373	1456–1497	1462–1494	76–78
930–947	940–970	799–830	1036–1071	1290–1329	1420–1454	1429–1460	74–76
910–929	896–939	760–791	1004–1032	1250–1289	1389–1417	1344–1384	72–74
895–907	856–872	720–755	962–993	1210–1249	1328–1363	1306–1343	70–72
870–885	813–850	680–715	926–961	1166–1208	1296–1327	1266–1300	68–70
850–860	772–811	640–679	900–922	1130–1165	1260–1295	1222–1260	66–68
830–849	733–771	600–639	841–886	1084–1129	1222–1259	1168–1221	64–66
810–828	690–727	560–599	803–842	1050–1083	1180–1221	1130–1167	62–64
790–807	654–680	520–559	770–802	1010–1049	1140–1197	1102–1129	60–62
755–789	621–649	476–519	722–759	972–1009	Queensborough Bridge		58–60
720–754	572–611	434–475	677–721	942–968	1066–1101	1026–1063	56–58
680–719	532–568	408–430	636–665	894–933	1028–1062	985–1021	54–56
656–679	500–531	360–399	596–629	856–893	984–1027	945–984	52–54
626–655	452–488	320–350	556–593	818–855	944–983	889–944	50–52
600–625	412–444	280–300	518–555	776–817	902–943	860–888	48–50
562–599	377–400	240–277	476–515	741–775	862–891	827	46–48
530–561	346–375	Met Life (200)	441–475	702–735	824–860	785	United Nations 44–46
500–529	316–345	Grand Central	395–435	660–701	793–823		42–44
460–499	284–315		354–394	622–659	746–773	Tudor City	40–42
424–459	250–283	68–99	314–353	578–621	707–747	666–701	38–40
392–423	218–249	40–67	284–311	542–577	666–700	Midtown Tunnel	36–38
352–391	188–217	5–35	240–283	508–541	622–659	599–626	34–36
320–351	152–184	1–4	196–239	470–507	585–621	556–598	32–34
284–319	118–150	444–470	160–195	432–469	543–581	Kips Bay	30–32
250–283	79–117	404–431	120–159	394–431	500–541	NYU Hosp.	28–30
213–249	50–78	364–403	81–119	358–393	462–499	446–478	26–28
201–212	11–37	323–361	40–77	321–355	422–461	411–445	24–26
172–200	1–7	286–322	9–39	282–318	382–421	390–410	22–24
154–170		251–285	1–8	244–281	344–381	315–389	20–22
109–153		221–250	70–78	206–243	310–343	310–314	18–20
85–127		184–220	40–69	166–205	301–309	280–309	16–18
69–108		Union Square	2–30	126–165	230–240	240–279	14–16

(Park Ave. / Park Ave. S. / Lexington Ave. / Irving Pl. run vertically between columns)

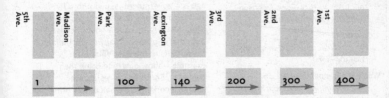

5th Ave.   Madison Ave.   Park Ave.   Lexington Ave.   3rd Ave.   2nd Ave.   1st Ave.

1 →   100 →   140 →   200 →   300 →   400 →

West Side to Lower Manhattan and the Financial District. As it intersects other avenues on its way, Broadway creates Columbus Circle (at 59th St.), Times Square (at 42nd St.), Herald Square (at 34th St.), Madison Square (at 23rd St.), and Union Square (at 14th St.). Streets in Manhattan run east and west and ascend in numerical order going north. As a general rule, traffic is one-way going east on even-number streets, one-way going west on odd-number streets.

Most of Manhattan's downtown areas—those below 14th Street on the west and 1st Street on the east—were settled before the grid system and follow no particular pattern. These are among the city's oldest districts and include Greenwich Village, SoHo, Tribeca, Chinatown, and the financial district. New Yorkers and visitors alike should remember that asking directions in an unfamiliar part of town will not get them killed; most New Yorkers are happy to give directions, and will then go quickly on their way. Try it.

ESSENTIAL NUMBERS

Once you've decided what to do, give one of New York's entertainment hot lines a call for comprehensive listings and schedules.

Central Park Information Line
Recorded information covering all park sites, as well as sports and recreation programs and specials events (212/360–3444).

Citywide Special Events
A recorded listing of upcoming events on city properties (212/360–3456).

Department of Parks and Recreation
A staffed hot line for information and emergencies. For details on specific parks and for Parks Department headquarters in individual boroughs, see Parks in Chapter 3 (800/201–PARK).

Film
212 or 718/777–FILM.

Greenmarket Information
Market dates for the city's 26 locations (212/477–3220).

Jazz
212/866–3616.

Library Branch Information
212/340–0849.

Sportsphone
For scores and statistics (212/976–1313 or 212/976–2525; charge applies).

Theater
For details on this hot line—New York City Onstage—see Tickets in Chapter 5 (212/768–1818).

Ticketron
For schedules and ticket information (212/307–7171).

Weather Channel Connection
95¢ per minute from a touch-tone phone (900/932–8437).

HOLIDAYS

New York's banks, post offices, schools, offices, and most businesses close on these days. (*See* Events *in* Chapter 4 for holiday festivities.)

New Year's Day (January 1).

Martin Luther King Day (3rd Monday in January).

Presidents' Day (3rd Monday in February).

Memorial Day (last Monday in May).

Independence Day (July 4th).

Labor Day (1st Monday in September).

Columbus Day (2nd Monday in October).

Election Day (1st Tuesday in November).

Veterans' Day (November 11th).

Thanksgiving (4th Thursday in November.)

Christmas (December 25th).

LIQUOR LAWS

You must be 21 years old to purchase alcohol in New York State. Your proof of age is a government-issued photo ID, such as a driver's license or a passport. Most restaurants have a liquor license, but smaller places—many of the Indian restaurants in the East Village, for example—allow diners to bring their own beer. Some BYOB restaurants charge a corking fee when diners bring their own wine.

NO SMOKING

In 1988, New York City passed one of the toughest antismoking laws in the country: It is illegal to puff in hotel lobbies, banks, public rest rooms, and taxis and at playgrounds, sports stadiums, and race tracks. Smoking has also been restricted in restaurants seating more than 35 people, in retail stores, and in schools.

PARKING

rules and enforcement

Street parking in Manhattan, if you can find it, is subject to a variety of restrictions. Metered street parking lasts from 20 minutes to an hour. Be sure to read the signs carefully, since to understand New York's parking rules you have to have scored 800 on the logic section of your GRE or be Stephen Hawkings—and once you figure them out, you'll have to move your car periodically to allow for street cleaning. There is no "grace period" for an expired or absent parking permit. And unless it's one of the city's 30 legal or religious holidays, strict alternate-side-of-the-street rules are probably in effect; call 718/ or 212/225–5368 or listen to a news radio station in the morning (see Radio Stations, below).

(Simply put, alternate-side-of-the-street rules are a class of their own. Signs typically read "No Parking 8 AM–11 AM Tuesday and Thursday or Monday, Wednesday, and Friday": these are for street cleaning. Signs that restrict parking for a longer period of time, for instance from 8 AM–6 PM, are to improve traffic flow and are still in effect when alternate-side-of-street rules are suspended. Got it?)

If you stray from the rules, your car may be ticketed, vandalized with a fluorescent sticker that never entirely scrapes off, locked in place with a "boot," or towed away (if illegally parked); all can be expensive and a tremendous hassle.

Parking Violations Operations Pay your tickets by phone (credit card only) or mail; include your plate number, state of registration, and the ticket number(s) on the front of your payment (PVO, New York City Department of Finance, Box 2127, Peck Slip Station, New York, NY 10272-2127, 877/769–2729).

Towed Vehicle Information Want to know where your car is and how much money you'll need to get it back? (212/ 869–2929, 718/422–7800, 212/869– 2929, or 212/971–0770).

parking lots

There are hundreds of private parking facilities in Manhattan, with costs varying by location, day, and time. Be sure to check the closing time, or you might lose your car for the night. Read the fine print on the price list, too; taxes and "special" conditions can make parking even more expensive than you expect. Even better, fix a price with the attendant before you park. These short-term parking facilities have long hours and reasonable prices.

DOWNTOWN
756 Parking Corp. (756 Washington St., near 12th St.).

MIDTOWN
Edison Park Fast (1120 Ave. of the Americas; entrances on 43rd and 44th Sts.).

Rapid 63 Street Corp. (411 W. 55th St., between 9th and 10th Aves.).

Real Pro Parking Corp. (330 E. 39th St., at 1st Ave.).

River Edge Sutton Garden Garage (425 E. 54th St., at Sutton Pl.).

UPPER EAST SIDE
200 East 61st Street Garage Corp. (200 E. 61st St., at 3rd Ave.).

Waterview (10 East End Ave., at 80th St.).

UPPER WEST SIDE
Edison Park Fast (214 W. 80th St., between Amsterdam and West End Aves.).

Hudson West Garage (101 W. 90th St., at Columbus Ave.).

PERSONAL SECURITY

Common sense must dictate where you go and when you go there—anywhere in the world. New York has enjoyed a reduction in violent crime of late, but of course it's always better to travel with a companion late at night, and to know where you are and where you're going. It may be even more important to *look* like you know where you are and where you're going. Secure your wallet or purse—wallets are better off in a front pocket than a back pocket. Don't flaunt cash or jewelry. On a crowded subway or bus, keep your bag zipped and in front of you, where you can see it.

PUBLIC TRANSPORTATION

New York's mass-transit system is extensive and efficient. Subways offer speed and economy but minimal comfort and capricious schedules. Buses offer a view in exchange for a slower pace. Taxis can be expensive in rush-hour traffic jams and elusive during rainstorms, but a blessing when your feet hurt, or when you've got too many parcels. Many cabs are air-conditioned; you can bet that a cab with its windows rolled up in summer is cool. Flag one of these down—no sweat.

Information, including bus and train detours, and directions to any destination by subway or bus are available 24 hours daily from the Travel Information Bureau (718/330–1234), a courteous, knowledgeable bunch. The bureau staffs booths at Grand Central Terminal weekdays 8–8 and weekends 9–5, and at 370 Jay St. (downstairs lobby), Brooklyn Heights, weekdays 9–5.

metrocard

With an eye toward dragging New York's subways and buses into the modern age, the Metropolitan Transit Authority (MTA) introduced the MetroCard in 1997, to quiet applause. Did they think New Yorkers didn't know of all the other cities that had been using a tokenless subway pass for a decade? Available in stores, newsstands, and at in-station booths and vending machines, the MetroCard answered New Yorkers' other transit prayer in 1998 with a discount for frequent riders. Regular riders are now divided into two MetroCard camps: those who go with the unlimited-ride card and those who choose pay-per-ride.

With the 7-day or 30-day unlimited-ride MetroCard, you get unlimited rides for a fixed price of $17 and $63, respectively. (A 30-day Express Bus Plus pass gives you unlimited rides on express buses, local buses, and subways for $120.) If you ride more than 12 times a week, but can't shell out the big bucks for the 30-day card (or fear you might lose it), the

7-day MetroCard is the one to get. With pay-per-ride cards, you get 11 rides for the price of 10 if you put $15 on your MetroCard. Invest $30, and you'll get two free rides, and so on; and the system prorates cents toward your next free ride if you put an odd amount on your card—as long as the amount is over $15. If you have visitors, you might want to get them a Fun Pass ($4), good for unlimited travel from the day of purchase through 3 AM the following day—oddly, it's sold in stores, at newsstands, and underground vending machines, but not in station booths.

The MetroCard discounts and free bus-to-subway and subway-to-bus transfers (good for two hours) have caused the near extinction of the beloved token. In fact, many new MetroCard turnstiles at unstaffed station entrances no longer accept tokens, leaving would-be passengers in the lurch. The MTA's dawdling remedy has been to add MetroCard vending machines at the busiest stations, with the goal of adding at least one to every station by summer 2000. This improvement should make subway-booth lines shorter—especially on Monday morning, when everyone's MetroCard seems to expires.

bus

Bus fare is $1.50. Reduced fare for senior citizens and travelers with disabilities is 75¢, except during rush hour, when the full fare applies. You need exact change, a subway token, or a MetroCard to ride the bus—no bills, pennies, or Susan B. Anthony dollars. Bus stops are marked with signs showing the route numbers of buses that stop there, approximate schedules, and route maps. North–south (uptown–downtown) buses usually stop every two to three blocks; east–west (crosstown) buses usually stop on every block. Many bus stops have glass-enclosed shelters. Route maps for the bus system are available at most subway stations or (sometimes) from bus drivers.

Board and deposit your fare (or insert your card) in the machine at the front of the bus; exit in the rear. Smoking is not allowed, nor are animals, with the exceptions of pets in carrying cases and seeing-eye dogs. Most buses run 24 hours daily, though less frequently during off-peak hours and days.

If you don't have a MetroCard (*above*) but want to transfer from an uptown or downtown bus to a crosstown bus, or vice versa, ask the driver for a transfer slip upon boarding; they're still free.

COMMUTER BUS
MTA Long Island Bus (516/766–6722).

George Washington Bridge Bus Terminal (Broadway at 178th St., Washington Heights, 212/564–1114).

LONG-DISTANCE BUSES
Adirondack, Pine Hill, and New York Trailways Service in New York State (800/858–8555).

Bonanza Bus Lines Service to Connecticut, Massachusetts, Rhode Island (800/556–3815).

Capital Trailways Service to Pennsylvania (800/444–2877 or 800/333–8444).

Greyhound United States and Canada (800/231–2222).

New Jersey Transit (NJTransit) (973/762–5100).

Peter Pan Trailways Serving northeast United States (800/343–9999).

Port Authority Bus Terminal The NYC hub for long-distance bus travel (42nd St. and 8th Ave., Theater District, 212/564–8484).

ferry
There is, in fact, such a thing as a free ride. The Staten Island Ferry's 50¢ fare was abolished in July 1997. The ride from South Street Seaport to Staten Island has wonderful views of the Statue of Liberty and Ellis Island, not to mention the Manhattan skyline. Did we mention it's free? Call 718/815–2628 for schedules.

subway
Subway fare is $1.50. Reduced fare for senior citizens and travelers with disabilities is 75¢, except during rush hour, when the full fare applies. (For a reduced-fare application, call 718/243–4999). You need a MetroCard or token to access the subway platform. If you'll be riding the subway often, buy a MetroCard to save time and money (*see above*). Free subway maps and information are available at every subway booth.

Smoking is not allowed in either stations or trains, and incorrigible smokers, like turnstile-hoppers, will most likely be fined by the sometimes plain-clothes transit police. Animals are not allowed on trains, with the exceptions of pets in carrying cases and seeing-eye dogs. The MTA's public service signs also ask riders to refrain from leaving newspapers behind, putting your bag on the seat beside you, and eating and drinking in stations and on trains—all of which are far less egregious than grooming (i.e.: clipping fingernails) en route.

The subways run 24 hours daily, though schedules are reduced during off-peak hours and days, and routes can be scrambled at night when maintenance and construction takes place. In the event of a stalled train or other unpleasant service interruption brought to your attention by an incomprehensible MTA announcement, you should always be aware of alternate subway lines or bus routes that will get you to your destination. Or, you can call the MTA Service Status Hotline (718/243–7777) for information on subway lines that are slow or stopped due to an "incident" of some kind.

taxi
Taxicabs are readily available in New York City, except during peak rush hours and, of course, rain. Simply walk to the curb (ideally at a street corner) and extend your arm. Licensed taxis are always yellow. You can tell if a cab is available by checking its rooftop light; if the center panel is lit and the side panels dark, the cab is available. It takes a trained eye to spot an available cab from a distance. That said, if others are waiting to hail a cab on your block, no matter how incompetent they appear, it's polite to let them do so before you—going a smidgen downstream to get one is considered an unscrupulous tactic.

Base fare for a cab ride is $2.30, then 30¢ for each additional ⅕ of a mi and 20¢ for each minute in stopped traffic. Pay only what's on the meter (there is a 50¢ surcharge from 8 PM to 6 AM) plus a 15%–20% gratuity. Make sure the driver remembers to start the meter. According to the rules, drivers must take you anywhere you want to go within the five boroughs, Nassau or Westchester counties, or Newark International Airport, though in practice you may find drivers who aren't interested in leaving Manhattan (or who need directions when doing so). For more information or to report a problem, call the New York City Taxi and Limousine Commission (212/221–8294).

rail

Trains leave the city from **Grand Central Station** (Lexington Ave. at 42nd St.) and **Pennsylvania (Penn) Station** (33rd St. at 7th Ave.).

COMMUTER

Long Island Rail Road (LIRR) departs from Penn Station; Atlantic Avenue, Brooklyn; and Jamaica, Queens (718/217–5477).

Metro-North trains for service to lower New York State and Connecticut leave from Grand Central Station (212/532–4900; outside New York City 800/638–7646).

New Jersey Transit (NJTransit), Penn Station (973/762–5100 or 800/626–7433).

PATH serves New Jersey from various points in the city, including the World Trade Center, 34th Street/Herald Square, and 14th Street at 6th Avenue (800/234–7284).

SEPTA picks up where NJTransit leaves off, in Trenton, to form the New Yorker's cheapest ride to Philadelphia (215/580–7800).

LONG-DISTANCE

Amtrak trains leave from Penn Station (800/USA–RAIL [800/872–7245].

PUBLICATIONS

New York is the publishing capital of the world, and many of its residents have a lot of commuting time to kill. Put the two together and you have an enormous reading public. All of these newspapers and magazines list goings-on, but each has a different angle. Pick them up at any newsstand and choose a favorite.

daily news

Subtitled "New York's Hometown Newspaper," the *Daily News* has a broader editorial range, with hearty metro and entertainment coverage, than its tabloid sibling, the *Post*—once you turn the grisly front page. Gossip columnists Rush & Molloy have a faithful following.

new york magazine

New York made its name being ultra-cool—is it now pursuing the mainstream? Cover stories range from fashion to politics to food to social trends. It's strong on the arts, although generally pretty skimpy. Weekly (Mon.).

new york observer

Easily spotted for its salmon-color paper, the *Observer* is New York's college newspaper for grown-ups. Gleefully trumpeting industry gossip on politics, publishing, and entertainment, it has many a closet addict. The focus shifts to the Hamptons in summer. Weekly (Wed.).

new york post

Owned by journalistic heavy hand Rupert Murdoch, the *Post* screams right-angle dish every day of the week, particularly on business and celebrity figures.

new york press

This downtown, Gen-X rag has aggressively targeted the *Village Voice*'s readership, but it's even more irreverent and can be just a little scary. Event listings are solid. Weekly (Tues.).

new york times

The *Times* still leads the national pack, though recent innovations aimed at widening its audience have stirred predictable debate. The Friday edition is the city's best source for weekend highbrow arts events, although with Janet Maslin's scepter being passed to Stephen Holden and new-Timers A. O. Scott and Elvis Mitchell, it's too soon to tell what will become of the film reviews. Daily; expanded edition Sunday.

new yorker

New York's most literate and literary source is for culture vultures. Longtime readers love to grouse that it's gone downhill in recent years, but they still can't live without it. The famous fact-checking department means that event listings are thorough and reliable, covering everything from classical recitals to nightly gigs at CBGB's. Weekly (Mon.).

paper

Paper will meet the needs of your inner club kid and reveal what the fashionistas are doing—oh, yes, and wearing. Listings for gay-friendly events, alternative music clubs, and new sites for shopping are particularly good, and columns favor the flavor of local scenesters such as Joey Arias. Monthly.

timeout new york

Modeled on its London predecessor, this magazine calls itself "The Obsessive Guide to Impulsive Entertainment" and lives up to the claim. The tone is young and cheeky, but fans of all ages appreciate the trendy restaurant reviews and virtually exhaustive event listings. Weekly (Wed.).

village voice

Culturally and politically lefty, the *Voice* is a great (and free) source for nightlife and music news and the last word on apartment listings—though the most eager apartment hunters visit *villagevoice.com* daily at 1 PM for the newest listings. Weekly (Wed.).

RADIO STATIONS

am
570 WMCA Religion
660 WFAN Sports
710 WOR Talk/news
740 WGSM News/talk/nostalgia
770 WABC Talk/news
820 WNYC News/talk
880 WCBS News
930 WPAT Adult contemporary
970 WWDJ Christian music
1010 WINS News
1100 WHLI Oldies
1130 WBBR News
1190 WLIB Talk/Caribbean
1230 WFAS Westchester news
1240 WGBB News/talk
1330 WWRV Ethnic
1370 WALK Adult contemporary
1380 WKDM Spanish

1440 WNYG Music
1460 WVOX Talk/nostalgia
1480 WZRC Korean
1560 WQEW Pop standards
1580 WLIM Big band/talk
1600 WWRL Gospel/talk

fm
88.1 WCWP C. W. Post University
88.3 WBGO Varied, jazz
88.7 WRHU Hofstra University
89.1 WNYU New York University
89.5 WSOU Seton Hall University
89.9 WKCR Columbia University
90.1 WUSB SUNY/Stony Brook
90.3 WHCR C.C.N.Y.
90.7 WFUV Fordham University
91.1 WFMU Varied
91.5 WNYE Community services
92.3 WXRK Alternative/progressive rock
93.1 WPAT Easy listening
93.5 WRTN Big band/standards
93.9 WNYC Classical/NPR
94.3 WMJC Light contemporary
95.5 WPLJ Top 40
96.3 WQXR Classical
97.1 WQHT Top 40/urban
97.5 WALK Adult contemporary
98.3 WKJY Adult contemporary
98.7 WRKS Urban contemporary
99.5 WBAI Varied
100.3 WHTZ Top 40
100.7 WHUD Light contemporary
101.1 WCBS Oldies
101.7 WBAZ Light contemporary
101.9 WQCD Contemporary jazz
102.3 WBAB Rock

102.7 WNEW Rock

103.5 WKTU Dance/freestyle

103.9 WFAS Adult contemporary

104.3 WAXQ Rock

105.1 WMXV Adult contemporary

105.9 WNWK Multi-ethnic

106.1 WBLI Adult contemporary

106.7 WLTW Light contemporary

107.1 WYNY Adult contemporary

107.5 WBLS Urban contemporary

RECYCLING

Sanitation Action Center The Department of Sanitation answers questions related to pick-up schedule, bulk disposal, leaf collection, etc. (weekends 7–4; 24-hr automated service 212/219–8090).

TAX & TIP

sales tax and beyond

You expect a lot from New York—and the city expects a lot from you in the form of sales tax and endless gratuities. Sales tax in the city is 8¼% and applies to all purchases not considered necessities. Guess what? That covers most store purchases and all restaurant meals.

tipping

Giving 'til it hurts? Fortunately gratuities are easy to figure, especially at restaurants: double the tax and round up a bit to bring the server's tip close to 20%. (Or think $2 for every $10 spent.) In elegant venues, give 5% to the captain and remember to give wine stewards about $5 per bottle of wine ordered. The coat-check clerk should receive $1 per coat. Cab drivers, hair stylists, your massage therapist, and the like should be tipped at least 15%.

The total room tax at hotels is a hefty 13¼%, plus an occupancy charge of $2 per room, per night. Leave the hotel maid about $1 for each night of your stay; the bellhop should get about $2.

TELEVISION

major broadcasters

Channel 2—WCBS

Channel 4—WNBC

Channel 5—WNYW (Fox)

Channel 7—WABC

Channel 9—WWOR (WB)

Channel 11—WPIX

Channel 13—WNET (PBS)

VOLUNTEERING

organizations

NYCares Matches you with New York City programs of all kinds, from one-time and seasonal opportunities to long-term placements that require training (116 E. 16th St., between Union Sq. E and Irving Pl., 6th floor, Gramercy, 212/228–5000; www.nycares.org).

VOTER REGISTRATION

As long as you ve been a resident of NYC for 30 days prior to an election in which you wish to vote, you can show up at the polls—that is, if you re a U.S. citizen over 18, not in jail or on parole for a felony, and not registered to vote elsewhere. First you'll have to register in one of three ways: call 212/VOTE–NYC (212/868–3692) for a postage-paid registration form or to request a form by fax; visit *www.vote.nyc.ny.us* for a registration form (in .pdf format) or to request one be sent to you; or register in person 9–5 at one of the five borough offices.

Bronx (1780 Grand Concourse, at 175th St., Bronx, NY 10457, 718/299–9017).

Brooklyn (345 Adams St., at Willoughby St., Brooklyn, NY 11201, 718/330–2250).

Manhattan (200 Varick St., at W. Houston St., West Village, New York, NY 10014, 212/886–3800).

Queens (42–16 West St., at Jackson Ave., Long Island City, NY 11101, 718/392–8989).

Staten Island (1 Edgewater Plaza, at Sylva La., Staten Island, NY 10304, 718/876–0079).

WEATHER

New York has four distinct seasons, each lending the city its own character. Spring and fall bring moderate temperatures, although the backlash of coastal hurricanes can be felt more and more in fall, with deluges canceling flights and messing up transportation; the mercury in summer averages 75°F (23°C) with fairly high humidity; and winter temperatures often hover near 32°F (0°C). But remember that indoor temperatures are often the opposite of those outside— chilly in summer due to air-conditioning and toasty in winter due to central heating. Things are further complicated if you ride the subway: Subterranean stations are subtropical in summer. Dress for comfort, preferably in removable layers. In winter, snow and slush can turn sidewalks and corner crosswalks into treacherous courses and hazardous pools, so think seriously about sturdy boots. Remember to enjoy the view; the city is gorgeous under a blanket of snow, however fleeting.

resources for challenges & crises

BABYSITTING SERVICES

See also Best Domestic *in* House Cleaning Agencies, *below.*

The Babysitters Guild Licensed and bonded, this organization's in business for over 50 years and is recommended by major hotels. The staff, all 25 or older, speaks a total of 16 languages. Same-day service. Office open daily 9–9; sitters available 24 hours (212/682–0227).

CATERING

Gourmet food shops such as Zabar s, Balducci s, Dean & Deluca, and Gourmet Garage happily assemble all manner of prepared foods in small and large orders for your event, as do city standbys such as Ess-a-Bagel and Katz's Deli. *See* Chapter 1 *and* Food & Drink *in* Chapter 2.

Glorious Food Plan on perfection from this veteran city caterer. Classic French and international cuisines (212/628–2320).

Simple Fare American regional cuisine. Prepares what the name suggests, with flair: breakfast pantry, salads, sandwiches, pasta, hors d'oeuvres, and desserts (212/691–4570).

Taste From corporate events to private parties. Versatile: American regional, Mediterranean, and Asian-influenced menus. Children's parties, too (212/255–8571).

CHILD CRISIS

Child Abuse Hotline (800/422–4453).

New York State Child Abuse and Neglect Prevention Information Line (800/342–7472).

24-hour Child Abuse and Maltreatment Register (800/342–3720).

CITY GOVERNMENT

complaints

Mayor's Action Center Handles complaints about city agencies; records your opinion for the Mayor; provides information on social service programs and housing; provides tax numbers; handles concerns related to parks, streets, and recycling; in English and Spanish; weekdays 9–5 (61 Chambers St., Lower Manhattan, 212/788–9600).

New York City No To Bias Hotline Handles reports of racial, ethnic, religious, or sexual bias (212/662–2427).

Civilian Complaint Review Board Handles complaints about police conduct (212/442–8833).

COAST GUARD

General information (212/668–7000).

Emergency search and rescue (212/668–7936).

CONSUMER PROTECTION

Attorney General's Consumer Help Line (800/771–7755).

Better Business Bureau (212/533–6200).

Department of Consumer Affairs Hotline (212/487–4444).

COUNSELING & REFERRALS

aids advice and services

Advanced Counseling and Testing Service Board-certified counselors; FDA-approved test; results in 15 minutes (212/246–0800).

AIDS Hot Line New York City Department of Health; 24-hour counseling and referrals (212/825–5448 or 212/447–8200; national 800/342–2437).

Gay Men's Health Crisis A leader in HIV/AIDS advocacy and education, providing a range of emotional support services, from crisis intervention and assigning a buddy to financial and nutritional counseling (119 W. 24th St., between 6th and 7th Aves., Chelsea, 212/807–6655 or 800/AIDS–NYC [800/243–7692).

alcohol treatment and support

Alcoholics Anonymous Hotline Support system for alcoholics who want to stop drinking; information and referrals to New York City area meetings; Monday–Thursday 9 AM–2 AM, Friday–Sunday 24 hours (212/647–1680; business office 212/870–3400).

crime victims

Crime Victims Board of New York State Financial aid and reimbursement of out-of-pocket medical expenses for crime victims (270 Broadway, at Church St., Lower Manhattan, 212/417–5160. Weekdays 9–5).

Crime Victims Hot Line 24-hour bilingual counseling and referral (212/577–7777).

domestic violence

Domestic Violence Hotline Shelter referrals available (800/942–6906 or 800/621–HOPE).

Violence Intervention Program Bilingual Hotline (212/360–5090).

drug abuse treatment

Daytop Village Rehabilitation facilities to help addicts with drug and drug-related problems. Weekdays 9–5 (54 W. 40th St., between 5th and 6th Aves., Garment District, 212/354–6000. 24-hour hot line: 800/232–9867).

Narcotics Anonymous Referral to meetings and drug-addiction related service organizations; crisis counseling (Daily 8 AM–2 AM, 212/929–6262).

New York State Division of Substance Abuse Services 24-hour referral to treatment programs, clinics, and hospitals (800/522–5353).

Phoenix House Foundation The city's largest drug-free residential rehabilitation program for teens and adults, with five facilities. Encourages responsibility, self-reliance, and trust (164 W. 74th St., between Amsterdam and Columbus Aves., Upper West Side, 212/787–3000. Open 24 hrs.).

families and housing

Citizens Advice Bureau Information, referral, and problem-solving center for housing, welfare, Medicaid, and immigration, and social services; weekdays 9–3:30 (178 Bennett Ave., at Broadway, Inwood, 212/923–2599; 2070 Grand Concourse, near Burnside Ave., Bronx, 718/731–3117).

Homeless Hotline Round-the-clock Department of Homeless Services emergency hot line provides shelter referral and Medicaid and food-stamps information for homeless residents of the New York area (including Long Island and Westchester counties) (800/994–6494).

Public Assistance/NYC Emergency Shelter (212/513–8849).

Salvation Army Social Services for Children Information and referral for family problems, foster homes, senior-citizen residence problems, adoption, and alcohol and drug rehabilitation. Two social workers on duty weekdays 8:30–4. Thirty-three centers throughout the city; summer camps; and a general hospital in Flushing, Queens (Emergency 212/505–4327; business 212/337–7200).

United Neighborhood Houses Information and referral for family and individual counseling; day care; nurseries; and senior-citizen programs; weekdays 8–5 (212/967–0322).

mental health information & referral

Lifenet The city's largest 24-hour crisis, information, and referral service for emotional and substance-abuse problems (800/LIFENET [800/543–3638]).

Mental Health Counseling Hot Line State-certified therapists available for information and referral. Don't be put off by the answering machine—someone always calls back (212/734–5876).

National Mental Health Association The New York chapter offers referrals and information (Weekdays 9–5, 800/969–6642).

new york city human resources administration

Provides public assistance in many areas; call for a referral to the appropriate division; weekdays 9–5 (212/274–5400 or 718/291–1900).

Child Services Foster care, adoption, day care, Head Start.

Crisis Intervention Unit Emergency housing, food, and clothing.

Family and Adult Services Home care, foster care for adults, protective services.

General Social Services Referral, interceding unit, outreach center.

Medicaid/Medicare Medical-insurance benefits.

Office of Income Support Child support from absent parents.

psychotherapy

New York Psychotherapy Collective Staffed by psychotherapists (877/REFER–NY [877/733–3769]).

rape victim advocacy

New York Police Department Rape Hot Line Female detectives assist in filing a police report and can make counseling referral; 24 hours a day (212/267–7273).

Rape Crisis Program St. Vincent's 24-hour medical care and advocacy; counseling 9–5 (212/604–8068).

Rape Intervention Program St. Luke's–Roosevelt Hospital; crisis counseling for survivors of childhood or adult abuse and violence (411 W. 114th St., Room 6D, Harlem, 212/523–4728).

Sexual Abuse Treatment and Training Institute Long-term support; services for adult survivors of childhood abuse (212/366–1490).

women's health

Women's Healthline Trained nurses available for reproductive information and referrals to low-cost or sliding-scale clinics; English and Spanish; weekdays 8 AM–6 PM (212/230–1111).

DOCTOR & DENTIST REFERRALS

Dental Referral Service National service based in Southern California (800/511–8663).

Physician Referral Service of Beth Israel Medical Center (212/420–2000).

EMERGENCIES

ambulance

In an emergency, dial 911 and a city ambulance will arrive free of charge. The patient will be taken to one of the city's 13 municipal hospitals, based on location and hospital specialty.

If the patient prefers a specific, nonpublic hospital, Keefe and Keefe provides 24-hour ambulance service to all five boroughs, for a fee (212/988–8800).

hospital emergency rooms

Beekman Downtown Hospital Mobile intensive care, two paramedic units (weekdays, 9–5), Basic EMT unit (24 hours, 7 days), coronary intensive care (170 William St., between Beekman and Spruce Sts., Lower Manhattan, 212/312–5070).

Bellevue Hospital Center Intensive-care units: coronary, surgical trauma, pediatric, psychiatric, neurosurgical, and alcohol detoxification (462 1st Ave., at 27th St., Gramercy, 212/562–4347, pediatrics 212/562–3025).

Beth Israel Medical Center Coronary care, neonatal intensive care, alcohol and drug detoxification (1st Ave. at 16th St., Gramercy, 212/420–2840).

Cabrini Medical Center Coronary care, trauma intensive care, alcohol detoxification and drug-overdose units, psychiatric facility (227 E. 19th St., between 2nd and 3rd Aves., Gramercy, 212/995–6000).

Columbia Presbyterian Medical Center Intensive-care units: metabolic, neurosurgical, pediatric (622 W. 168th St., at Ft. Washington Ave., Washington Heights, Main: 212/305–2500. Emergency, adult: 212/305–2255. Emergency, pediatric: 212/305–6628).

Harlem Hospital Coronary care; neonatal and respiratory critical care; alcohol and drug detoxification. Crisis intervention center for rape victims and battered wives and children (506 Lenox Ave., at 135th St., Harlem, 212/939–1000).

Lenox Hill Hospital Coronary and neonatal intensive care (100 E. 77th St., between Park and Lexington Aves., Upper East Side, 212/434–3030).

Manhattan Eye, Ear and Throat Hospital Ear, eye, nose, and throat emergencies (210 E. 64th St., between 2nd and 3rd Aves., Upper East Side, 212/838–9200).

Mount Sinai Hospital Coronary, trauma, and medical intensive care; dental emergencies; emergency pharmacy until midnight (5th Ave. at 101st St., East Harlem, 212/241–7171).

New York Eye and Ear Infirmary 24-hour emergency service for eye, ear, nose, or throat problems (310 E. 14th St., at 3rd Ave., East Village, 212/979–4000).

New York Hospital–Cornell Medical Center 24-hour paramedic unit; burn, coronary, neurological, and neonatal intensive care; high-risk infant-transport unit and treatment (525 E. 68th St., at York Ave., Upper East Side, 212/746–5454).

New York University Medical Center Coronary care (550 1st Ave., at 33rd St., Murray Hill, 212/263–5550).

St. Clare's Hospital and Health Center Coronary, medical, and surgical intensive care (415 W. 51st St., between 9th and 10th Aves., Hell's Kitchen, 212/586–1500).

St. Luke's Hospital Center Coronary, trauma, and neonatal intensive care; alcohol detoxification; rape-intervention team; 24-hour psychiatric emergency room (1111 Amsterdam Ave., at 114th St., Harlem, 212/523–3335).

St. Luke's–Roosevelt Hospital Coronary, surgical, and neonatal intensive-care units; alcohol detoxification (1000 10th Ave., at 59th St., Upper West Side, 212/523–6800).

St. Vincent's Hospital and Medical Center of New York Coronary, spinal-cord trauma, and psychiatric intensive care; alcohol detoxification; AIDS center; rape crisis program (153 W. 11th St., between 6th and 7th Aves., West Village, 212/604–7998, 212/602–8000).

poison control center

Poison Hot Line (212/340–4494 or 212/764–7667 [POISONS]).

suicide prevention

Help Line (212/532–2400).

Lifenet The city's largest 24-hour crisis, information, and referral service for emotional and substance-abuse problems (800/LIFENET [800/543–3638].

The Samaritans 24-hour hot line (212/673–3000).

Suicide Prevention Hot Line 24-hour hot line (800/543–3638; 7:30 PM–midnight 718/389–9608).

FAMILY PLANNING

Family Planning Information Service (212/677–3040).

Planned Parenthood (212/541–7800. Daily 8:30–5. 24-hour clinic locator 800/230–7526).

Women's Healthline Trained nurses available for reproductive information and referrals to low-cost or sliding-scale clinics; English and Spanish; weekdays 8 AM–6 PM (212/230–1111).

GAY & LESBIAN CONCERNS

Anti-Violence Project A crime-victims agency for the gay, lesbian, and transgender community; counseling, hot line, and legal advocacy services; volunteer opportunities (240 W. 35th St., Suite 200, between 8th and 9th Aves., Garment District, 212/807–6761).

Gay and Lesbian Anti-Violence Project 24-hour hot line arranges counseling, domestic-violence support groups, court and police accompaniment and monitoring, assistance in obtaining court-ordered protection, and legal services, all free (212/807–0197).

Lesbian and Gay Community Services Center Counseling, therapy, education, library and museum, and resources for couples considering children (1 Little W. 12th St., between 9th Ave. and Hudson St., 212/620–7310. Daily 9 AM–11 PM).

roommate referral services
See also Apartment Locator Services, above.

Gay Roommate Information Network (212/627–4242).

Rainbow Roommates (212/627–8612).

HOMEWORK HELP HOT LINE

Dial-A-Teacher The United Federation of Teachers staffs this service to help children answer difficult homework questions (212/777–3380. Mon.–Thurs. 4 –7 during academic year).

HOUSE CLEANING AGENCIES

Best Domestic In addition to general house cleaning, this citywide agency provides maid service, butlers, nannies, baby nurses, housekeepers, husband-and-wife teams, chefs and cooks, chauffeurs, majordomos, personal assistants, and office cleaners. Licensed, bonded, and insured, the company claims to reject about 85% of its candidates for employment (tougher than some Ivy League schools). 24 hours' notice is preferred (212/685–0351).

Green Clean General housecleaning in Manhattan, Brooklyn, and parts of Queens using nontoxic and environmentally friendly products. Call a week in advance; 10 days in advance for large jobs (212/216–9109).

LANDLORD/ TENANT ASSISTANCE

Metropolitan Council on Housing This advocacy group advises tenants in rent-controlled and rent-stabilized apartments on their rights and helps organize tenants (212/693–0550 Mon., Wed., Fri. 1:30–5. Walk-in location: 102

Fulton St., at William St., Room 302, Lower Manhattan. Open Wed. 4–7).

Rent InfoLine: Division of Housing and Community Renewal City offices assist both tenants and owners of rent-controlled and rent-stabilized apartments with legal advice on subletting, rent control, etc. (Information, weekdays 9–5: 718/739–6400; www.dhcr.state.ny.us. Walk-in offices: 25 Beaver St., at Broad St., Lower Manhattan, 212/480–6229 or 212/680–6227).

(163 W. 125th St., between Lenox Ave. and Adam Clayton Powell Jr. Blvd., 5th floor, Harlem, 212/961–8930).

(55 Hanson Pl., Room 702, between S. Elliot and Ft. Greene Pls., Ft. Greene, Brooklyn, 718/722–4778).

(92–31 Union Hall St., at Gertz Plaza, Jamaica, Queens, 718/739–6400).

(1 Fordham Plaza, between Webster and Washington Aves., Bronx, 718/563–5678. Walk-in hours: 9–4:45).

LEGAL SERVICES

Legal Aid Society (General information 212/577–3300).

Legal Referral Services Association of the Bar (In English, 212/626–7373; in Spanish, 212/626–7374).

LOST & FOUND

at airlines & airports
JFK International Airport Found property will be held by the airline on which you traveled. If loss occurred on airport grounds or at the International Arrivals Building, call 718/244–4225.

La Guardia Airport (Port Authority Police, 718/533–3988). Also call the airline on which you traveled.

Newark International Airport (201/961–6230). Also call the airline on which you traveled.

on other transportation
New York City Buses Brooklyn, Queens, Staten Island (718/625–6200); Bronx, Manhattan (212/690–9638).

New York City Subways (718/625–6200).

Port Authority Bus Terminal (212/435–7000).

Railroads Pennsylvania (Penn) Station (718/990–8384); Grand Central Terminal (212/340–2555).

Taxicabs Items left in taxis should be turned in to the police station closest to your destination. To report a loss, call the Taxi and Limousine Commission (212/302–8294).

lost animals

If your pet goes astray, post notices in the area of the pet's home and most recent whereabouts. Include a description and/or photo of your pet with your phone number only. Call all local veterinarians to check if your pet has been brought in, and inquire about posting notices at their offices. Report the missing animal to the ASPCA (424 E. 92nd St., 212/876–7700).

lost credit cards

American Express/Optima (800/528–4800).

Chase (800/632–3300).

Citibank (800/843–0777).

Diners Club/Carte Blanche (800/234–6377).

Discover (800/347–2683).

MasterCard (800/307–7309).

Visa (800/847–2911).

ONLINE SERVICES

These four ISP (internet service provider) giants will sign you up via phone or on their websites. Expect to pay about $19.95 a month for unlimited service.

America Online (800/827–0035; www.aol.com).

Big Planet (800/487–5100 or 800/487–5200; www.bigplanet.com).

Earthlink (800/EARTHLINK [800/327–8454; www.earthlink.com/join).

Movielink 777–FILM (777–3456). Online, www.777film.com is one-stop shopping for movie locations, times, previews, and tickets. The phone number works from any New York City area code.

NYC & Company Visit www.nycvisit.com for an invaluable directory of Web addresses for New York organizations of every stripe.

New York Public Library Although good for lots of inquiries, www.nypl.org has terrific New York City history information.

The New York Times On America Online, enter keyword *times* for news or events listings; on the Web, read the *Times* at www.nytimes.com.

The Village Voice The best searchable housing listings and comprehensive entertainment and events listings at www.villagevoice.com.

PETS

adoptions

ASPCA The national HQ of "America's first humane society" no longer kills unwanted animals. For an adoption fee of about $50, your new companion will be spayed or neutered and given the proper shots (424 E. 92nd St., between 1st and York Aves., Upper East Side, 212/876–7700).

Bide-a-Wee Very sweet mutts for dog lovers; domestic shorthairs for the feline-inclined. Adoption fee: $30–$50 (410 E. 38th St., at 1st Ave., Murray Hill, 212/532–4455).

North Shore Animal League Recommended by animal lovers region-wide. No adoption fee (25 Davis Ave., Port Washington, NY, 516/883–7575. Long Island Rail Road: Port Washington).

grooming

Finishing Touches by Stephanie Dental care and therapeutic baths, in addition to basic grooming (414 E. 58th St., between 1st Ave. and Sutton Pl., Upper East Side, 212/753–8234).

Furry Paws professional grooming with natural products—no sedatives. Evening hours for the busy pooch. Three locations (120 E. 34th St., between Park and Lexington Aves., Murray Hill, 212/725–1970; 141 Amsterdam, at W. 66th St., Upper West Side, 212/724–9321; 1039 2nd Ave., between 54th and 55th, Midtown, 212/813–1388.)

Private Grooming by Terrie Vitolo A veteran groomer who makes house calls (718/388–1442).

training

American Dog Trainers Network resource and referral hot line (212/727–7257).

ASPCA Group training classes, two months long, range from Puppy Kindergarten to Therapy Training (212/876–7700).

Center for Applied Animal Behavior and Canine Training, Inc. Consulting and treatment of behavior, mainly for dogs. By appointment (212/544–8797).

Dr. Ellen Lindell Specializes in kittens and cats with behavioral problems, but will work with Fido, too. Phone consultations and house calls (914/473–7406).

veterinarian referrals

Animal Emergency: Animal Medical Center 24 hours (Bobst Hospital, 510 E. 62nd St., between York Ave. and FDR Dr., Upper East Side, 212/838–8100).

Veterinary Clinics of America prescription pet food and emergency service 8 AM–11 PM daily (212/988–1000).

Veterinary Medical Association of NYC (212/246–0057).

PHARMACIES OPEN 24 HOURS

Duane Reade (224 W. 57th St., at Broadway, Midtown, 212/541–9708; 2465 Broadway, at 91st St., Upper West Side, 212/799–3172; 1279 3rd Ave., at 74th St., Upper East Side, 212/744–2668; 378 6th Ave., at Waverly Pl., Greenwich Village, 212/674–5357).

Genovese Free delivery (1229 2nd Ave., at 68th St., Upper East Side, 212/772–0104).

Rite Aid (282 8th Ave., between 26th and 27th Sts., Chelsea, 212/727–3854 or 800/RITEAID [800/748–3243 for other locations).

POLICE

Emergency Dial 911.

Non-emergency police services including reporting a burglary or auto theft, general information, and the location and phone number of the precinct nearest you (in all five boroughs), available 24 hours daily. (212/374–5000).

POSTAL SERVICES

Post offices are open weekdays 10–5 or 10–6. Many branches are open for a few hours on Saturday as well.

J. A. Farley General Post Office The city's main post office is open 24 hours daily, as is their infoline for that zip code you've gotta have at 3 AM or for the address of the post office nearest you (8th Ave., at 33rd St., 800/725–2161).

SENIOR CITIZEN SERVICES

Legal Aid Society (212/577–3300).

Legal Service for the Elderly Poor Part of the citywide agency Legal Services for New York City, LSEP provides free support for those elderly living below the poverty line (212/391–0120; for referral in all boroughs, 212/431–7200).

New York City Department for the Aging Extensive resources, including referrals to Meals on Wheels, at-home health care providers, etc. (212/442–1000).

Senior Action Line A part of the mayor's office, this information, referral, and advocacy program for senior citizens is staffed by volunteers (212/788–7504).

TELEVISION— CABLE COMPANIES

Call yours for service, repairs, and general information.

Manhattan North Time Warner of New York (212/567–3833).

Manhattan South Time Warner of New York (212/674–9100).

Bronx, Brooklyn Cablevision (718/617–3500).

Brooklyn Time Warner of New York (718/358–0900).

Queens Time Warner of New York (718/358–0900).

Staten Island Staten Island Cable (718/816–8686).

UTILITIES

gas and electric

Brooklyn Union Serves Queens (up to Jackson Heights), Staten Island, and Brooklyn (718/643–4050).

ConEdison Gas and electricity throughout the city, except Brooklyn, Staten

Island, and part of Queens, where Brooklyn Union provides gas service (212/338–3000. Gas leaks or emergencies, 212/683–8830. Electric and steam emergencies, 212/683–0862).

telephone

Bell Atlantic (Customer service, 212/890–1550; 24-hr account information, 800/698–3545).

water

City of New York Dept. of Environmental Protection (Customer service, 718/595–7000; 24-hr help: 718/337–4357).

ZONING AND PLANNING

Department of City Planning Bookstore sells maps and publications; office dispenses zoning information and schedules of upcoming meetings (22 Reade St., between Broadway and Centre St., Lower Manhattan, 212/720–3300; Brooklyn 718/643–7550; Queens 718/392–0656; Staten Island 718/727–8453).

Historic Landmarks Preservation Center (310 Madison Ave., at 42nd St., Midtown, 212/983–1197).

learning

ACTING SCHOOLS

Actors Connection Audition Seminars attended by agents and casting directors; a popular vehicle for audition experience (630 9th Ave., between 44th and 45th Sts., Hell's Kitchen, 212/977–6666).

The Actors Studio Inc. One of the most exclusive workshops for professional actors; over 50 years of experience (432 W. 44th St., 9th and 10th Aves., Hell's Kitchen, 212/757–0870).

American Academy of Dramatic Arts Acting, speech, voice, movement, mime (120 Madison Ave., between 30th and 31st Sts., Murray Hill, 212/686–9244).

Atlantic Theater Company Acting School Teaches the practical aesthetic technique developed by David Mamet and William H. Macy, founding members who drop by to teach periodically. Full-time two-year conservatory program; part-time programs for beginners and pros. Intensive summer program in Vermont (453 W. 16th St., at 10th Ave., Chelsea, 212/691–5919).

Creative Acting Company Beginner through pro. Scene study, monologue, commercials, sitcoms, more; some classes taught by casting directors. New sketch-comedy and improv group. Thursday is agent night: all the biggies, from ICM to William Morris (122 W. 26th St., between 6th and 7th Aves., Chelsea, 212/352–2103).

Herbert Berghof Studio All subjects, all levels. Founded by Uta Hagen and Herbert Berghof (120 Bank St., between Greenwich and Washington Sts., West Village, 212/675–2370).

Lee Strasberg Theater Institute, Inc. Pacino and DeNiro studied here. Founded by creative genius Lee Strasberg (115 E. 15th St., between Union Sq. E and Irving Pl., Gramercy, 212/533–5500).

ART SCHOOLS

Art Students' League Founded in 1875. Drawing, painting, sculpture (215 W. 57th St., 2nd floor, between Broadway and 7th Aves., Midtown, 212/247–4510).

Greenwich House Pottery Wheel-throwing, hand-building, glazes, and more, including children's classes (16 Jones St., between Bleecker and W. 4th Sts., West Village, 212/242–4106).

International Center of Photography (ICP) Seminars, workshops, special lectures, and classes in black-and-white photography, color printing, and digital media (1130 5th Ave., at 94th St., Upper East Side, 212/860–1777).

New York Studio School Full-time studio programs and weekly figure-drawing classes (8 W. 8th St., between 5th and MacDougal Sts., Greenwich Village, 212/673–6466).

Manhattan Graphics Center Not-for-profit printmaking workshop run by artists. Inexpensive courses in etching, lithography, silkscreen, and more. Fully equipped darkroom. $35 membership fee (481 Washington St., between Canal and Spring Sts., West Village, 212/219–8783).

Parsons School of Design Printmaking, book design, sculpture, computer and digital design, interior design and architecture, fashion textile design, floral design, and more, at all levels (2 W. 13th St., between 5th and 6th Aves., Greenwich Village, 212/229–8900).

School of Visual Arts (SVA) Drawing, painting, animation, computer art, graphic design, interior design, illustration, photography, film and video (209 E. 23rd St., at 2nd Ave., Gramercy, 212/592–2000).

COMPUTER TRAINING SCHOOLS

New York MacUsers' Group (NYMUG) A licensed training center for Adobe, Quark, and Claris applications, and Excel. Troubleshooting and other courses are offered as well. All are super-current (such as how to use new models and operating systems) and taught by professionals (1290 6th Ave., between 51st and 52nd Sts., 39th floor, Midtown, 212/906–1037).

Pratt Advance computer applications programs, including Autodesk, Macromedia, Kinetix; electronic publishing, programming, software update training, computer competency, computer design (fashion, graphics, etc.), and myriad art classes (200 Willoughby Ave., at St. James Pl., Downtown Brooklyn, 718/636–3453; 295 Lafayette St., between Houston and Jersey Sts., Lower East Side, 212/641–6000).

See also The New School for Social Research *and* New York University *in* continuing education, *below*.

CONTINUING EDUCATION

New York University NYU's School of Continuing Education offers more than 2,000 credit and non-credit courses around the city, for both business and pleasure, and a Virtual College of on-line courses (212/998–7080).

The New School for Social Research Guitar study, foreign languages, business and career, film, music, writing, theater, dance, HTML, and culinary arts in a cool, sociable atmosphere or via distance learning ("attend" classes on your computer). Year-round (66 W. 12th St., between 5th and 6th Aves., Greenwich Village, 212/229–5620).

92nd St. Y Language, literature, dance, music, arts, crafts, cooking, Jewish education (1395 Lexington Ave., at 92nd St., Upper East Side, 212/996–1100).

COOKING SCHOOLS AND WINE WORKSHOPS

Peter Kumps New York Cooking School The city's most popular culinary-arts program. Hundreds of courses, including kids in the kitchen, a well-attended knife-skills workshop, and wine workshops of all kinds. All levels (50 W. 23rd St., between 5th and 6th Aves., Flatiron District, 800/522–4610; 307 E. 92nd St., at 2nd Ave, Upper East Side, 800/522–4610).

The New School for Social Research Culinary arts classes, including pastry, wine, global cuisine classes, culinary walking tours, and restaurant management. Year-round (66 W. 12th St., between 5th and 6th Aves., Greenwich Village, 212/229–5620).

DANCE

Broadway Dance Center This high-energy, five-floor dance hub offers jazz, ballet, tap, modern, hip-hop, African, flamenco, aerobics, and more. All levels, including children's classes (221 W. 57th St., between 7th Ave. and Broadway, Midtown, 212/582–9304).

Dance Space Inc. Most dancers come here for the Lynn Simonson jazz-technique and modern classes, but you can also study ballet, Capoeira, yoga, and more, at several levels, although the mood is quite studious (451 Broadway, between Grand and Howard Sts., 2nd floor, SoHo, 212/625–8369).

DanceSport All levels of mambo, salsa, tango, swing, waltz, hustle, quickstep, and other Latin and ballroom classes in a bustling and sociable atmosphere, or in a private lesson (1845 Broadway, between 60th and 61st Sts., Upper West Side, 212/307–1111).

Sandra Cameron Dance Center Affordable social ballroom, swing and lindy, and salsa and tango lessons; private or group lessons (20 Cooper Sq., at E. 5th St., Greenwich Village, 212/674–0505).

LANGUAGE SCHOOLS

Berlitz Language Center Immersion courses for individuals and groups—in all spoken languages (40 W. 51st St., at Rockefeller Plaza, Midtown, 212/765–1000; 61 Broadway, near Exchange Pl., 212/425–3866).

The New School for Social Research Sixteen levels, including Japanese, Greek (Classical and Modern), Brazilian Portuguese, Chinese (Mandarin), Sign Language, and Russian. Accredited classes, such as "Italian for Italian speakers" and business-language courses (66 W. 12th St., between 5th and 6th Aves., Greenwich Village, 212/229–5620).

New York University NYU's School of Continuing Education offers a large variety (Arabic to Vietnamese) of credit and non-credit foreign-language, ESL, and translation classes, some of which are available through The Virtual College of on-line courses (212/998–7080).

french
Alliance Française/French Institute French at all levels (22 E. 60th St., at Madison Ave., Upper East Side, 212/355–6100).

german
The German House, NYU All levels plus business, conversation, and reading. "Meet the Authors" program: read 'em, meet 'em, discuss their work. Wunderbar (42 Washington Mews, between 5th Ave. and University Pl., Greenwich Village, 212/998–8660).

italian
Parliamo Italiano Language School Italian at all levels, in a lovely town house (132 E. 65th St., at Lexington Ave., Upper East Side, 212/744–4793).

japanese
Toyota Language Center The Japan Society has 12 levels of Japanese classes, including English classes for Japanese speakers, and cultural and business-related courses (333 E. 47th St., between 1st and 2nd Aves., Midtown, 212/715–1256).

russian
Russian Institute for Language and Culture Russian at all levels (134 W. 32nd St., between 6th and 7th Aves., Garment District, 212/244–5700).

spanish
Instituto Cervantes Spanish at all levels, and weekend immersion courses (122 E. 42nd St., at Lexington Ave., Suite 807, Theater District, 212/689–4232, ext. 6).

MUSIC SCHOOLS

Greenwich House Music School Instrumental and vocal classes and workshops; preschool program in music and art. Free concerts and recitals of students' work (46 Barrow St., near 7th Ave. S, West Village, 212/242–4770).

Juilliard School Evening Division Regular faculty teach music, dance, and drama. The most popular course seems to be piano lessons, but offerings extend to music criticism, studies of individual composers, and a wonderful class on overcoming performance anxiety (60 Lincoln Center Plaza, Broadway at 65th St., Upper West Side, 212/799–5040).

New York Singing Teachers Association Evaluation (all levels), referral, master classes (212/579–2461).

Third Street Music School Settlement Founded 1894. Private and group instruction for all ages (233 E. 11th St., between 2nd and 3rd Aves., East Village, 212/777–3240).

vacation & travel information

AIRLINES

The Central Airlines Ticket Office This satellite office handles ticketing for all major airlines (125 Park Ave., between 41st and 42nd Sts., Midtown, 212/986–0888).

Aer Lingus (800/IRISHAIR [800/474–7424]).

AeroMexico (800/237–6639).

Air Canada (800/776-3000).

Air Europa (800/238–7672).

Air France (800/237–2747).

Air India (212/751–6200).

Air Jamaica (800/523–5585).

Alitalia Air Lines (800/223–5730).

America West Airlines (800/235–9292).

American Airlines (800/433–7300).

Austrian Airlines (800/843–0002).

Avianca Airlines (800/284–2622).

British Airways (800/247–9297).

British West Indian Airlines (800/538–2942).

China Airlines (800/227–5118).

Continental Airlines (800/525–0280; international flights 800/231–0856).

Czech Airlines (212/765–6022).

Delta Airlines (800/221–1212; international flights 800/241–4141).

Egyptair (212/315–0900).

El Al Israel Airlines (800/223–6700).

Finnair (800/950–5000).

Iberia Airlines (800/772–4642).

IcelandAir (800/223–5500).

Japan Airlines (800/525–3663).

KLM/Northwest Airlines (800/225–2525 or 800/374–7747).

Lufthansa Airlines (800/645–3880).

Mexicana Airlines (800/531–7921).

Midway Airlines (800/446–4392).

Northwest/KLM Airlines (800/225–2525 or 800/447–4747).

Pan American World Airways (800/359–7262).

Qantas Airlines (800/227–4500).

Royal Air Maroc (212/750–6071 or 800/344–6726).

Sabena Belgian World Airlines (800/955–2000).

Scandinavian Airlines (800/221–2350).

Singapore Airlines (800/742–3333).

South African Airways (800/722–9675).

Swissair (800/221–4750).

TAP Air Portugal (800/221–7370).

Tower Air (800/34–TOWER [800/348–6937]).

Trans World Airlines (TWA) (800/221–2000).

United Airlines (800/241–6522).

USAir (800/428–4322).

Varig Brazilian Airlines (800/468–2744).

Virgin Atlantic (800/862–8621).

AIRPORTS

John F. Kennedy (JFK) International Airport Driving directions, ground transportation information, airport conditions, parking information; staffed 7 AM–11 PM, plus 24-hour automated service (Howard Beach, Queens, 718/244–4444).

La Guardia Airport (LGA) Driving directions, transportation information, airport conditions, baggage storage, foreign currency exchange information (Jackson Heights, Queens, 718/533–3400).

Newark International Airport (EWR) Driving directions and transportation information (Newark, NJ, 973/961–6000 or 888/EWR–INFO [888/397–4636]).

getting there by public transportation

For general information on transportation to New York's three major airports—JFK, La Guardia, and Newark—call the Port Authority of New York and New Jersey weekdays 8–6 (800/247–7433).

BY SUBWAY & BUS

The subway is the most economical way to reach the airports, but it can be slow given the length of the journey. That said, during rush hour the subway can beat cabs and car services by passing traffic altogether, particularly to JFK and La Guardia.

To reach JFK, take the Far Rockaway–bound A train (not the Lefferts Blvd. train) to the Howard Beach–JFK Airport station, then board the free, 24-hour airport shuttle bus (every 10 min 5 AM–midnight, every 30 min other times).

To return from JFK, reverse the above directions or take the Q3 bus from JFK's

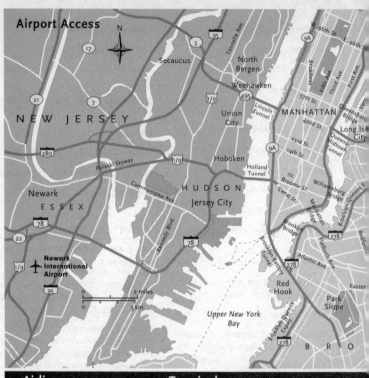

Airport Access

Airlines	Terminals		
	JFK	**LA GUARDIA**	**NEWARK**
Aer Lingus ☎ 212/557–1110	4E		A, B
Aeroflot ☎ 212/332–1050	3		
Aerolineas Argentinas ☎ 800/333–0276	4E		
AeroMexico ☎ 800/237–6639	2		B
Air Afrique ☎ 800/237–2747	4W		
Air Aruba ☎ 800/882–7822			B
Air Canada ☎ 800/776–3000		CTB-A	C
Air China ☎ 212/371–9898	3		
Air France ☎ 800/237–2747	4W		B
Air India ☎ 212/751–6200	4W		
Air Jamaica ☎ 800/523–5585	4W		B
Air Nova ☎ 800/776–3000			C
Air Ontario ☎ 800/776–3000			C
Alitalia ☎ 800/223–5730	4W		B, C
ALIA-Royal Jordanian ☎ 212/949–0050	4E		
All Nippon Airways ☎ 800/235–9262	3		
America West ☎ 800/235–9292	2	CTB-A	C
American ☎ 800/433–7300	8, 9	CTB-D	A
American Eagle ☎ 800/433–7300	9		
American Trans Air ☎ 800/435–9282	2		
Asiana Airlines ☎ 800/227–4262	4E		
Austrian Airlines ☎ 800/843–0002	3		
Avianca ☎ 800/284–2622	3		B
Balkan Bulgarian ☎ 800/796–5706	4E		
Biman Bangladesh ☎ 888/702–4626	4W		
British Airways ☎ 800/247–9297	7		B
Business Express ☎ 800/345–3400			B
BWIA ☎ 800/538–2942	8		
Canadian Airlines ☎ 800/426–7000	9	CTB-D	
Carnival ☎ 800/437–2110	4E	CTB-C	B
Cathay Pacific ☎ 800/233–2742	3		
China Airlines ☎ 800/227–5118	3		
Colgan Air ☎ 800/272–5488		CTB-B	A

440

Airlines | Terminals (cont.)

Airlines	JFK	LA GUARDIA	NEWARK
Continental ☎ 800/525–0280		CTB-A	C
Continental Express ☎ 800/525–0280	2	CTB-A	C
Czech Airlines ☎ 212/765–6022			B
Delta International ☎ 800/241–1414	3	Delta	B
Delta Domestic ☎ 800/221–1212	3	Delta	B
Delta Shuttle ☎ 212/239–0700		MAT	
Ecuatoriana ☎ 800/328–2367	3		
Egypt Air ☎ 212/315–0900	4W		
El-Al ☎ 800/223–6700	4W		B
EVA Airways ☎ 800/695–1188	4E		B
Finnair ☎ 212/499–9026	2		
Ghana Airways ☎ 800/404–4262	4W		
Guyana ☎ 718/657–7474	4E		
Iberia ☎ 800/772–4642	4E		
Icelandair ☎ 800/223–5500	4E		
Japan Air Lines ☎ 800/525–3663	4E		
KIWI ☎ 800/538–5494			A
KLM ☎ 212/759–3600; 800/374–7747	4E		B
Korean ☎ 800/438–5000	4W		B
Kuwait ☎ 212/308–5454	4E		
Lacsa Airlines ☎ 800/225–2272	7		
Lan Chile ☎ 800/488–0070	8		
LOT Polish ☎ 800/223–0593	8		B
LTU ☎ 800/888–0200	4E		
Lufthansa ☎ 800/645–3880	4E		
Malev Hungarian ☎ 212/757–6446	3		B
Mexicana Airlines ☎ 800/531–7921	4W	CTB-D	
Midway Airlines ☎ 800/446–4392		CTB-C	A
Midwest Express ☎ 800/452–2022			B
North American ☎ 718/656–3289	5	Delta	
Northwest International ☎ 800/447–4747	4E	Delta	B
Northwest Domestic ☎ 800/225–2525	4E	Delta	B
Northwest Airlink ☎ 800/225–2525	4E		B

JFK International Airport

Terminal 9
Terminal 8
Terminal 7
Terminal 6
Terminal 5
Terminal 1 ☆
Terminal 2
Terminal 3
Terminal 4W Gates 23–35
Terminal 4E Gates 9–22
Tower Air Terminal
Lot 1
Lot 2
Lot 3
Lot 4
Parking Garage
Rooftop Parking
International Arrivals Building (IAB)
CAR RENTAL RETURN AT FEDERAL CIRCLE
678
Van Wyck Expwy
150 th St. JFK Expressway
N
☆ under construction

0   600 feet
0   200 meters

Airlines	Terminals (cont.)		
	JFK	LA GUARDIA	NEWARK
Olympic ☎ 212/838–3600	4E		
Pakistan ☎ 212/370–9158	4W		
Pan Am ☎ 800/359–7262	4E		
Philippine Airlines ☎ 800/435–9725			B
Precision Airlink ☎ 888/635–5293		Delta	
Qantas ☎ 800/227–4500	4		
Royal Air Maroc ☎ 212/750–6071	4E		
SAS ☎ 800/221–2350	7		C
Sabena ☎ 800/955–2000	3		
SAETA ☎ 212/302–0004	7		
Singapore Airlines ☎ 800/742–3333	3		
South African Airways ☎ 212/826–0995	8		
Sun Country ☎ 800/359–5786	6		
Sun Jet ☎ 800/478–6538			A
Swissair ☎ 800/221–4750	3		B
Tarom-Romanian ☎ 212/687–6013	3		
TACA International ☎ 800/535–8780	2		
TAP Air Portugal ☎ 800/221–7370	3		B
Tower Air ☎ 718/553-8500	Tower		
TransBrasil ☎ 800/872–3153	4W		
TWA ☎ 212/290–2141; 201/643–3339	5, 6	CTB-B	A
Turkish Airlines ☎ 212/339–9650			B
TW Express	5		A
☎ 212/290–2141;201/643–3339	7		A
United ☎ 800/241–6522	7	CTB-C	A
United Express ☎ 800/241–6522	7	CTB-C	A
US Airways ☎ 800/428–4322	7	US Airways	A
US Airways Express ☎ 800/428–4322		US Airways	
US Airways Shuttle ☎ 800/428–4322	4W	US Airways Shuttle	
Uzbekistan Airways ☎ 212/489–3954	2		
Varig ☎ 212/682–3100	4W		
VASP ☎ 718/955–0540	2		B
Virgin Atlantic ☎ 800/862–8621			

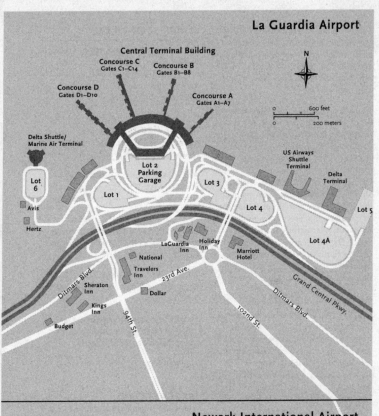

La Guardia Airport

Central Terminal Building

Concourse C
Gates C1–C14

Concourse B
Gates B1–B8

Concourse D
Gates D1–D10

Concourse A
Gates A1–A7

N

0   600 feet
0   200 meters

Delta Shuttle/
Marine Air Terminal

US Airways
Shuttle
Terminal

Delta
Terminal

Lot
6

Lot 2
Parking
Garage

Lot 3

Lot 4

Lot 5

Lot 1

Lot 4A

Avis

Hertz

LaGuardia
Inn

Holiday
Inn

Marriott
Hotel

National

Travelers
Inn

23rd Ave.

Grand Central Pkwy.

Ditmars Blvd.

Sheraton
Inn

Dollar

Ditmars Blvd.

Kings
Inn

94th St.

102nd St.

Budget

Newark International Airport

McClellan St.

TO TRENTON &
SHORE POINTS

1/9

81 TO NJ TURNPIKE
EXIT 13A

1/9

TO NEWARK

78

TO NEW YORK
(via Holland Tunnel)

Long-Term
Lot D

Rental Car
Return

Long-Term
Lot E

To
Long-Term
Lot 4,
Medical Clinic

A1
Gates 10–19

Marriott
Hotel

C3
Gates 120, 121

Terminal A

Hourly
Lot

Daily
Lot A

Daily
Lot C

Hourly
Lot

C2
Gates 100–115

A2
Gates 20–28

Daily
Lot B

A3
Gates 30–39

Hourly
Lot

Terminal C

C1
Gates 70–99

B3
Gates 60–68

B2
Gates
50–58

B1
Gates
40–48

Terminal B
International Arrivals

Main Terminal to the 179th Street subway station in Queens, where you can pick up the F or R train to Manhattan and Brooklyn. Buses run every 15 minutes until midnight, then every 30 minutes until 1:30 AM.

To reach La Guardia from Manhattan or Brooklyn, take the E, F, G, R, or 7 train to the 74th Street/Roosevelt Avenue (or 82nd Street/Roosevelt Avenue) subway station in Jackson Heights, Queens, then the Triboro Coach Lines Q33 bus to La Guardia's Main Terminal. The bus shuttles between Roosevelt Avenue and the airport every 12 minutes during the day and evening, every 40 minutes after midnight. Alternatively, the Triboro Coach Q47 bus leaves La Guardia's Marine Terminal every 20 minutes between 5:20 AM and 12:45 AM for the Roosevelt Avenue station.

BY AIRPORT SHUTTLE

Gray Line Air Shuttle Operates door-to-door minibuses to all three airports from Manhattan hotels between 23rd and 63rd streets and Port Authority, 5 AM–11 PM. Fare to JFK or Newark is $19 to the airport, $14 from the airport, or $24 round-trip; to La Guardia $16, from La Guardia $13, or $26 round-trip (212/757–6840; www.greyline.com).

New York Airport Service Express Bus Serves JFK ($13) and La Guardia ($10) from Grand Central, Port Authority, and Penn Station, every 30 minutes from 7 AM–10 PM and has transfers between the airports ($11) (718/706–9658).

Olympia Trails Airport Express Serves Newark Airport from Penn Station, Port Authority Bus Terminal, Midtown hotels, Grand Central Terminal, and 1 World Trade Center (West St., Lower Manhattan). Buses depart every 20 minutes or so in both directions. Fare is $10 one-way. Call for schedule (212/964–6233).

New Jersey Transit Airlink Leaves every 20 minutes from 6:15 AM to 2 AM for Penn Station in Newark, where you can catch the PATH Trains (800/234–7284). Airlink bus fare is $4 and exact change is required (973/762–5100).

See also car and limousine services, *below.*

CAR RENTAL

Do yourself a favor and rent in Brooklyn or New Jersey: Rates are often much more reasonable, and you'll skip the 45-minute lines and the traffic on the drive out and back in.

major agencies

Alamo (Reservations 800/327–9633; Newark Airport 973/733–2205).

Avis (Reservations: 800/831–2847 or 800/331–1212; JFK 718/244–5400; La Guardia 718/507–3600; Newark Airport 973/961–4300).

Budget (Reservations: 800/527–0700 or 212/807–8700; JFK 718/565–6010; La Guardia 718/639–6400).

Enterprise (Reservations: 800/736–8222; JFK 718/659–1200; La Guardia 718/457–2900).

Hertz (Reservations: 800/654–3131; JFK 718/656–7600; La Guardia 718/478–5300; Newark 973/621–2000).

National (800/227–7368).

local agencies

AAMCAR (Manhattan and Bronx locations, 212/222–8500).

New York Rent-A-Car (Mahattan and Queens locations, 212/799–1100).

Speedy Rent-A-Car (Brooklyn, Queens, and Jersey City locations, 718/783–0800).

Vogel's Eurocars (Yonkers, 914/968–8200).

CAR AND LIMOUSINE SERVICES

Carey Lincolns, Cadillacs, stretch limos, and chauffeurs available 24 hours. Hourly rates (212/599–1122; worldwide 800/336–4646).

Carmel Car and Limousine Service Point-to-point service and hourly arrangements (212/666–6666).

Eastern Car Service Point-to-point service in the five boroughs and Long Island (718/499–6227).

Fugazy Limousine Ltd. Limousines and sedans with courteous, uniformed chauffeurs serving all five boroughs, Westchester, and parts of Pennsylvania 24 hours daily (212/661–0100).

Legends Car and Limousine Service For service to, from, and around Brooklyn. 24 hours daily (718/788–1234 or 718/788–2346).

Smith Limousine Located in Manhattan, Smith has Cadillacs and Lincoln limos, stretches, and sedans, plus vintage cars for special occasions. Big date? Ask for the 1948 Cadillac limousine in dark blue. Cars available 24 hours daily (212/247–0711).

Tel-Aviv Car and Limousine Service Point-to-point service in the five boroughs (212/777–7777).

CURRENCY EXCHANGE

If you're going abroad, you may want to buy some foreign currency here before you leave. You can buy and sell currency at the Manhattan branches of several national banks, or at the old standby Thomas Cook (*see below*). Chase (800/287–4054) sells foreign currency at most of its Manhattan branches, and buys currency at all branches if the buyer has two forms of I.D. You can pay for foreign currency in cash, debit your Chase account, or flash a Visa or MasterCard; if you charge it, the amount will be treated as a cash advance. Most exchanges are handled on the spot, but you may have to come back the next day for exotic currencies or very large amounts.

Most banks sell traveler's checks, which you can buy in U.S. dollars or in any of several foreign currencies. Traveler's checks are issued by American Express, MasterCard, or Visa and are accepted worldwide. Banks and nearly all stores in New York accept traveler's checks, though they may want to see a photo I.D. first.

american express travel services

American Express Travel Service Offices buy and sell foreign currency, buy and sell American Express traveler's checks (and buy other brands for a higher fee), issue refunds for lost checks, and provide all standard cardmember services. You can buy foreign currency with cash or, if you're a cardmember, with a personal check—just bring your AmEx card. If you lose your AmEx traveler's checks, call 800/221–7282.

thomas cook currency services

Busy with other preparations? Thomas Cook can FedEx your foreign currency, traveler's checks, or foreign drafts right to your home. For general information and branch hours, call 800/287–7362 weekdays 8:30 AM–9 PM. The JFK office is open daily. If you lose your Thomas Cook traveler's checks, call 800/223–7373.

EMBASSIES & CONSULATES

British Consulate General (845 3rd Ave., between 51st and 52nd Sts., Midtown, 212/745–0200).

Chinese Consulate of the People's Republic of China (520 12th Ave., at 43rd St., Midtown, 212/330–7400).

Dominican Republic's Consulate General (1 Times Sq. Plaza, at Broadway, Midtown, 212/768–2480).

French Embassy (972 5th Ave., at 78th St., Upper East Side, 212/439–1400).

German Consulate General (460 Park Ave., at 57th St., Midtown, 212/610–9700).

Irish Consulate General (345 Park Ave., at 51st St., Midtown, 212/319–2555).

Italian Consulate General (54 E. 69th St., between Park and Madison Aves., Upper East Side, 212/737–9100).

Japanese Consulate General (299 Park Ave., at 48th St., Midtown, 212/371–8222).

Portuguese Consulate General (630 5th Ave., at 50th St., Midtown, 212/765–2980).

Spanish Consulate General (150 E. 58th St., between 3rd and Lexington Aves., Upper East Side, 212/355–4090).

INOCULATIONS, VACCINATIONS & TRAVEL HEALTH

Center for Disease Control's International Travel Line Knows which countries require which vaccines (404/332–4565).

International Health Care Service
Staffed by specialists in infectious disease, the IHCS is devoted exclusively to the medical needs of international travelers, providing worldwide health information, immunizations, and post-travel tests and treatment. The fee varies, but it's always a worthwhile investment if you're traveling to a developing nation. Make an appointment four to five weeks before departure (New York Hospital–Cornell Medical Center, 440 E. 69th St., Upper East Side, 212/746–1601. Mon.–Thurs. 4–8 PM by appointment).

Kennedy International Medical Office Building Vaccinations and inoculations for a fee (198 S. Cargo Road and 150th St., Howard Beach, Queens, 718/656–5344. Daily 8 AM–10 PM; 24 hrs for emergencies. No personal checks).

U.S. Department of State Overseas Citizen Services Automated travel-warning and emergency information by country (202/647–5225).

PASSPORTS

You can apply for a passport at any of New York's Passport Acceptance Agencies: designated post offices, county clerks' offices, and, in a pinch, the New York Passport Agency. Call the (800/275–8777) for the passport-accepting post office nearest you, as some city branches, such as Ansonia (212/362–7486), Main (800/725–2161), and others have offices open weekdays 10 AM–4 PM. During peak travel periods—spring and summer—apply for a first-time passport three months before your trip. All passport information, including printable applications and a locator of the passport agency nearest you, is handily available on the U.S. Postal Service website www.usps.gov.

Passport *renewal* is handled most easily through the mail. Renewal forms are available at many post offices (or on the postal service website; *see above*) and can be submitted by mail or at any passport acceptance agency.

If you're short on time and/or don't have Internet access, you can obtain passport information and forms by phone, for a fee. Call the National Passport Information Center at 900/225–5674 (35¢ per min) or, with a major credit card, 888/362–8668 ($4.95). In a grave emergency after hours (such as the death of a rela-

tive abroad), call the passport duty officer at the U.S. State Department in Washington (202/647–4000).

A new U.S. passport costs $65 ($40 for those under 18); a renewal costs $55. If you need an emergency passport for travel within 10 days, you'll pay an additional $30 fee for "expedited processing"; bring your plane ticket with you to the office.

County Clerk's Office The secret is out: there are no lines here. Come on down, for passports at least three weeks before departure (New York County Courthouse, 60 Centre St., at Pearl St., lower level, Lower Manhattan, 212/374–8361. Weekdays 9–2 except holidays. Bronx County Courthouse, 718/590–3643. Brooklyn Supreme Court, 718/643–5897. Queens County Courthouse, 718/520–3700. Richmond [Staten Island] County Court, 718/390–5386).

New York Passport Agency This office issues emergency passports for travel within two weeks. You must have an appointment, but you're still bound to spend most of the day waiting. First-timers must bring proof of U.S. citizenship, photo I.D. (or I.D. with description), and passport photos (376 Hudson St., between W. Houston and King Sts., West Village, 212/206–3500. Weekdays 7:30–3 except holidays).

Passport Plus This private document service is for travelers with more money than time. It can get you a passport in as little as one day and arrange visas to all countries, as well as snap your pictures on-site (20 E. 49th St., between Madison and 5th Aves., Midtown, 212/759–5540.)

passport photo agencies
Passports require two identical recent photos, each 2 inches square. These can be taken by any photographer; see the application for exact specifications.

TOURIST INFORMATION

nyc & company
The helpful, multilingual staff answers questions and provides printed guides and maps in six languages; tickets to TV shows; discount coupons for theater tickets; and a list of the city's

current hotel rates, weekend packages, major attractions, and seasonal events (810 7th Ave., between 51st and 52nd Sts., Theater District, 212/484–1222 for general inquiries, 800/692–8474 for brochures. Subway: 42nd St./Times Sq.)

new york state department of economic development/division of tourism

There is no office in New York City, but the state office has information on city tour packages and on vacations and recreation statewide. These folks are the geniuses behind the "I Love New York" campaign (800/225–5697).

tourist information carts and kiosks

In late 1997, the Grand Central Partnership (a sort of civic Good Samaritans' group) installed a prototype of an unstaffed information kiosk near Grand Central Terminal and loaded it up with maps and helpful brochures on attractions throughout the city. Seasonal outdoor carts are now sprinkled throughout the area (near Vanderbilt Ave. and 42nd St.), staffed by friendly, knowledgeable, multilingual New Yorkers. There's a kiosk in Grand Central Terminal's Main Concourse, the 34th Street Partnership runs a kiosk on the concourse level at Penn Station (33rd St. and 7th Ave.), and seasonal carts troll the streets surrounding the station. There's even a cart at the Empire State Building (5th Ave. at 34th St.).

TRAVELER'S AID

Crime Victims Hot Line 24-hour bilingual counseling and referral (212/577–7777).

Traveler's Aid Service Nationwide service helps crime victims, stranded travelers, and wayward children and works closely with the police; staffed Monday–Thursday 10–7, Friday 10–6, Saturday 11–6, Sunday noon–6 (International Arrivals Bldg., JFK Airport, 718/656–4870).

VISA INFORMATION & TRAVEL ADVISORIES

Call the embassy or consulate (*see above*) of the country you plan to visit for up-to-date information on visa requirements, travel advisories, and service strikes. For travel advisories on specific countries, call the U.S. State Department at (202/647–5225).

Ask Immigration Answers questions on immigration—citizenship, visas, relatives abroad, and more (800/375–5283).

U.S. Customs Service Refers you to the appropriate authority on importation of goods (800/697–3662).

DIRECTORIES

restaurants by neighborhood

ARTHUR AVENUE, THE BRONX

Dominick's (Italian), 49

ASTORIA, QUEENS

Christo's Hasapo-Taverna (Greek), 43
Elia's Corner (Greek), 43
Karyitis (Greek), 43
Uncle Georges (Greek), 44

BRIGHTON BEACH, BROOKLYN

Rasputin (Russian), 68

BROOKLYN HEIGHTS

Grimaldi's (Pizza), 65–66
La Bouillabaisse (French), 37
Noodle Pudding (Italian), 53
Queen (Italian), 55

CARROLL GARDENS, BROOKLYN

Patois (French), 41

CHELSEA

Bottino (Italian), 47
Bright Food Shop (Eclectic), 31
Cafeteria (American Casual), 11
Chelsea Bistro and Bar (French), 36
Chelsea Commons (American Casual), 11–12
Chelsea Lobster Company (Seafood), 69
Cola's (Italian), 48–49
El Cid (Spanish), 72
Empire Diner (American Casual), 12–13
Francisco's Centro Vasco (Spanish), 73
Frank's (Steak), 74
James (Thai), 77
Le Gamin (café), 19
Le Madri (Italian), 52
Lot 61 (Eclectic), 31
Merchants NY (Eclectic), 32
Negril (Caribbean), 20
Old Homestead Restaurant (Steak), 74
Pastis (French), 41
Petit Abeille (Belgian), 17
Red Cat (Contemporary), 26

Ristorante da Umberto (Italian), 55
Rocking Horse Café (Tex/Mex), 76
Royal Siam (Thai), 77
Siena (Italian), 55–56
Tonic (Contemporary), 26–27
Wild Lily Tea Room (Tea), 76

CHINATOWN

Bo Ky (Vietnamese), 78
Chinatown Ice Cream Factory (Café), 18
Jing Fong (Chinese), 21
Joe's Shanghai (Chinese), 21
Lin's Dumpling House (Chinese), 21
Mandarin Court (Chinese), 21
Nha Trang (Vietnamese), 79
Ny Noodle Town (Chinese), 21
Pongsri Thai (Thai), 77
Sweet-N-Tart (Chinese), 22
Tai Hong Lau (Chinese), 22
Viet-nam (Vietnamese), 79
Yumee Noodle (Chinese), 22

CITY ISLAND, BRONX

Lobster Box (Seafood), 70

CORONA, QUEENS

Green Field Churrascaria (Brazilian), 17

DOWNTOWN BROOKLYN

Junior's (American Casual), 13

EAST VILLAGE

Acme Bar & Grill (Southern), 71–72
Astor Restaurant and Lounge (French), 33
Bambou (Caribbean), 20
B–Bar (American Casual), 10
Benny's Burritos (Tex/Mex), 76
Briam (Greek), 43
Coup (Contemporary), 23–24
Cucina di Pesce (Italian), 49
Danal (Tea), 75–76
Dok Suni (Korean), 59
First (American), 4
Five Points (American), 4
Great Jones Cafe (American Casual), 13
Hasaki (Japanese), 56

Il Buco (Mediterranean), 62
Il Cantinori (Italian), 51
Indochine (Vietnamese), 79
Lucien (French), 40
Moustache (Middle Eastern), 64–65
O.G. (Oriental Grill) (Pan–Asian), 65
Roettelle A. G. (Swiss), 75
Sala (Spanish), 73
Second Avenue Kosher Delicatessen (Delicatessen), 29–30
Serafina Fabulous Grill (Pizza), 67
Sharaku (Japanese), 58
Sin Sin (American), 9
Takahachi (Japanese), 58
Veniero's (Café), 20
Veselka (Eastern European), 30

ELMHURST, QUEENS

Jai-Ya Thai (Thai), 76–77
Pings (Chinese), 22

FLATIRON

Alva (American), 3
Blue Water Grill (Seafood), 69
Bolo (Spanish), 72
Coffee Shop (Brazilian), 17
Follonico (Italian), 50
La Pizza Fresca (Pizza), 66
L'Express (French), 39–40
Mesa Grill (American), 6–7
Metronome (Mediterranean), 62
Patria (Latin), 61
Periyali (Greek), 44
Republic (Pan–Asian), 65
Union Square Cafe (American), 9
Zen Palate (Vegetarian and Macrobiotic Food), 78

FLUSHING, QUEENS

Kum Gang San (Korean), 59–60
Penang (Malaysian), 61

GARMENT DISTRICT

Biricchino (Italian), 47
Hangawi (Korean and Vegetarian and Macrobiotic Food), 59, 78
New York Kom Tang Soot Bul House (Korean), 60
Skylight Diner (American Casual), 15
Tir Na Nóg (Irish), 46

GRAMERCY

Campagna (Italian), 48
Candela (American), 3
Galaxy Global Eatery (Eclectic), 31
Gramercy Tavern (American), 5
Novita (Italian), 53
Pete's Tavern (American Casual), 14
Union Pacific, 33
Verbena (American), 9
Yama (Japanese), 59

GREENWICH VILLAGE

Alaia (Contemporary), 23
Arturo's Pizzeria (Pizza), 65
Babbo (Italian), 46
Baluchi's (Indian), 44
Bar Pitti (Italian), 47
Bar Six (French), 34
Belgo (Belgian), 16
Bond St (Japanese), 56
Bussola Bar and Grill (Italian), 48
Caffè Dante (Café), 18
Clementine (American), 4
Da Silvano (Italian), 49
EJ's Luncheonette (American Casual), 12
Gotham Bar & Grill (American), 5
Grand Ticino (Italian), 50–51
Il Mulino (Italian), 51
Japonica (Japanese), 57
L Ray (Latin), 61
Le Gamin (Café), 19
Lupa (Italian), 52
Piadina (Italian), 54
Pop (Contemporary), 26
Restaurant Boughalem (French), 42
Rice 'N' Beans, 17–18
Riodizio (Brazilian), 18
Cafe Spice (Indian), 45
Tea & Sympathy (Tea), 76
Temple Bar (American Casual), 15
Yama (Japanese), 59
Ye Waverly Inn (American), 10

GREENPOINT, BROOKLYN

Amarin Cafe (Thai), 76
Lomzynianka (Polish), 67

HARLEM

Charles' Southern Style Kitchen (Soul), 71
Copeland's (Soul), 71
Patsy's Pizza (Pizza), 66
Sylvia's (Soul), 71

HELL'S KITCHEN

Azuri Café (Middle Eastern), 64
Chimichurri Grill (Argentine), 16
Market Café (American Casual), 13–14
Meskerem (Ethiopian), 33
Pietrasanta (Italian), 54
Rachel's American Bistro (American), 8
Revolution (Eclectic), 32
Rice 'N' Beans (Brazilian), 17–18
Route 66 Café (American Casual), 14
Soul Café (Soul), 71
Zen Palate (Vegetarian and Macrobiotic Food), 78

JACKSON HEIGHTS, QUEENS

Jackson Diner (Indian), 45

LITTLE ITALY

Benito II (Italian), 47
Ferrara (Café), 19
Lombardi's (Pizza), 66
Puglia (Italian), 54–55

LONG ISLAND CITY, QUEENS

Manducati's (Italian), 52
Water's Edge (American), 10

LOWER EAST SIDE

Baby Jupiter (Contemporary), 23
Café Habana (Latin), 61
El Sombrero (Mexican), 63
Katz's Delicatessen (Delicatessen), 29
Ratner's Dairy Restaurant (Kosher), 60
Sammy's Roumanian (Eastern European), 30
Torch (American), 9

LOWER MANHATTAN

American Park at the Battery (Contemporary), 23
Bayard's (French), 34
Bridge Cafe (American), 3
Gemelli (Italian), 50
The Grill Room (American), 5
Hudson River Club (American), 5
Mangia (Eclectic), 31
Wall Street Kitchen & Bar (American), 10
Wild Blue (American), 10
Windows on the World (Continental), 29

MIDTOWN

Aquavit (Scandinavian), 68–69
Atlas (Eclectic), 30
Beacon (American), 3
Beijing Duck House (Chinese), 20
Ben Benson's (Steak), 73
Bice (Italian), 47
Billy's (American Casual), 11
Bistro Latino (Latin), 60
Bombay Palace (Indian), 45
Bouterin (French), 35
Box Tree (French), 35
Broadway Diner (American Casual), 11
Brooklyn Diner USA (American Casual), 11
Bryant Park Grill (Contemporary), 23
Bull & Bear (Steak), 73
Cafe Europa (Café), 18
Carnegie Delicatessen (Delicatessen), 29
Caviar Russe (Russian), 67–68
Chin Chin (Chinese), 20
China Grill (Contemporary), 23
Christer's (Scandinavian), 69
Columbus Bakery (Café), 18
Delegates' Dining Room (Eclectic), 31
Deniz a la Turk (Turkish), 77
Dock's Oyster Bar & Seafood Grill (Seafood), 69
Estiatorio Milos (Mediterranean), 43
Four Seasons (Continental), 28
Harry Cipriani (Italian), 51
Hatsuhana (Japanese), 57
Il Toscanaccio (Italian), 51
Inagiku (Japanese), 57
Jack's Fifth (American), 6
Jean Georges (French), 36–37
Judson Grill (Contemporary), 24
Kaplan's at the Delmonico (Delicatessen), 29
La Caravelle (French), 37
La Côte Basque (French), 38
La Grenouille (French), 38
Le Bernardin (French), 38
Le Cirque 2000 (French), 38–39
Le Marais (Kosher), 60
Lespinasse (French), 39
Lutèce (French), 40
Mangia (Eclectic), 31

shops by neighborhood

index